International Entrepreneurship

The International Library of Entrepreneurship

Series Editor: David B. Audretsch
Max Planck Institute of Economics, Jena, Germany
and Ameritech Chair of Economic Development
Indiana University, USA

Wherever possible, the articles in these volumes have been reproduced as originally published using facsimile reproduction, inclusive of footnotes and pagination to facilitate ease of reference.

For a list of all Edward Elgar published titles visit our site on the World Wide Web at
www.e-elgar.com

International
Entrepreneurship

Edited by

Benjamin M. Oviatt

Professor of Managerial Sciences
and Director, Herman J. Russell, Sr. International Center for
Entrepreneurship, Robinson College of Business
Georgia State University, USA

and

Patricia Phillips McDougall

Associate Dean – Faculty and Research
and William L. Haeberle Professor of Entrepreneurship, Kelley School of
Business
Indiana University, Bloomington, USA

THE INTERNATIONAL LIBRARY OF ENTREPRENEURSHIP

An Elgar Reference Collection
Cheltenham, UK • Northampton, MA, USA

© Benjamin M. Oviatt and Patricia Phillips McDougall 2007. For copyright of individual articles, please refer to the Acknowledgements.

Published by
Edward Elgar Publishing Limited
Glensanda House
Montpellier Parade
Cheltenham
Glos GL50 1UA
UK

Edward Elgar Publishing, Inc.
William Pratt House
9 Dewey Court
Northampton
Massachusetts 01060
USA

A catalogue record for this book is available from the British Library.

Library of Congress Control Number: 2006937963

ISBN: 978 1 84542 729 0

Printed and bound in Great Britain by MPG Books Ltd, Bodmin, Cornwall

Contents

Acknowledgements

The editors and publishers wish to thank the authors and the following publishers who have kindly given permission for the use of copyright material.

Academy of Management (NY) and Copyright Clearance Center for articles: Shaker A. Zahra, R. Duane Ireland and Michael A. Hitt (2000), 'International Expansion by New Venture Firms: International Diversity, Mode of Market Entry, Technological Learning, and Performance', *Academy of Management Journal*, **43** (5), October, 925–50; Lowell W. Busenitz, Carolina Gómez and Jennifer W. Spencer (2000), 'Country Institutional Profiles: Unlocking Entrepreneurial Phenomena', *Academy of Management Journal*, **43** (5), October, 994–1003; Rodney C. Shrader, Benjamin M. Oviatt and Patricia Phillips McDougall (2000), 'How New Ventures Exploit Trade-Offs Among International Risk Factors: Lessons for the Accelerated Internationalization of the 21st Century', *Academy of Management Journal*, **43** (6), December, 1227–47.

American Marketing Association for articles: Oliver Burgel and Gordon C. Murray (2000), 'The International Market Entry Choices of Start-Up Companies in High-Technology Industries', *Journal of International Marketing*, **8** (2), 33–62; Øystein Moen and Per Servais (2002), 'Born Global or Gradual Global? Examining the Export Behavior of Small and Medium-Sized Enterprises', *Journal of International Marketing*, **10** (3), 49–72.

Blackwell Publishing Ltd for excerpt and article: Shaker A. Zahra and Gerard George (2002), 'International Entrepreneurship: The Current Status of the Field and Future Research Agenda', in Michael A. Hitt, R. Duane Ireland, S. Michael Camp and Donald L. Sexton (eds), *Strategic Entrepreneurship: Creating a New Mindset*, Chapter Twelve, 255–88; Benjamin M. Oviatt and Patricia P. McDougall (2005), 'Defining International Entrepreneurship and Modeling the Speed of Internationalization', *Entrepreneurship Theory and Practice*, **29** (5), September, 537–53.

Elsevier for articles: Patricia Phillips McDougall, Scott Shane and Benjamin M. Oviatt (1994), 'Explaining the Formation of International New Ventures: The Limits of Theories from International Business Research', *Journal of Business Venturing*, **9**, 469–87; Nicole Coviello and Hugh Munro (1997), 'Network Relationships and the Internationalisation Process of Small Software Firms', *International Business Review*, **6** (4), 361–86; Tage Koed Madsen and Per Servais (1997), 'The Internationalization of Born Globals: An Evolutionary Process?', *International Business Review*, **6** (6), 561–83; Stephen L. Mueller and Anisya S. Thomas (2001), 'Culture and Entrepreneurial Potential: A Nine Country Study of Locus of Control and Innovativeness', *Journal of Business Venturing*, **16** (1), January, 51–75; Walter Kuemmerle (2002), 'Home Base and Knowledge Management in International Ventures', *Journal of*

Business Venturing, **17**, 99–122; Garry D. Bruton and David Ahlstrom (2003), 'An Institutional View of China's Venture Capital Industry: Explaining the Differences between China and the West', *Journal of Business Venturing*, **18**, 233–59; Branko Bucar, Miroslav Glas and Robert D. Hisrich (2003), 'Ethics and Entrepreneurs: An International Comparative Study', *Journal of Business Venturing*, **18**, 261–81; Michael J. Leiblein and Jeffrey J. Reuer (2004), 'Building a Foreign Sales Base: The Roles of Capabilities and Alliances for Entrepreneurial Firms', *Journal of Business Venturing*, **19**, 285–307; Nicole E. Coviello and Marian V. Jones (2004), 'Methodological Issues in International Entrepreneurship Research', *Journal of Business Venturing*, **19**, 485–508; Harry J. Sapienza, Dirk De Clercq and William R. Sandberg (2005), 'Antecedents of International and Domestic Learning Effort', *Journal of Business Venturing*, **20**, 437–57; Jane W. Lu and Paul W. Beamish (2006), 'Partnering Strategies and Performance of SMEs' International Joint Ventures', *Journal of Business Venturing*, **21**, 461–86.

Palgrave Macmillan for articles: Benjamin M. Oviatt and Patricia Phillips McDougall (1994), 'Toward a Theory of International New Ventures', *Journal of International Business Studies*, **25** (1), First Quarter, 45–64; Rebecca Reuber and Eileen Fischer (1997), 'The Influence of the Management Team's International Experience on the Internationalization Behaviors of SMEs', *Journal of International Business Studies*, **28** (4), 807–25; Gary A. Knight and S. Tamar Cavusgil (2004), 'Innovation, Organizational Capabilities, and the Born-Global Firm', *Journal of International Business Studies*, **35** (2), March, 124–41; Marian V. Jones and Nicole E. Coviello (2005), 'Internationalisation: Conceptualising an Entrepreneurial Process of Behaviour in Time', *Journal of International Business Studies*, **36** (3), May, 284–303; Ted Baker, Eric Gedajlovic and Michael Lubatkin (2005), 'A Framework for Comparing Entrepreneurship Processes Across Nations', *Journal of International Business Studies*, **36** (5), September, 492–504.

Springer Science and Business Media for articles: Jan Johanson and Jan-Erik Vahlne (2003), 'Business Relationship Learning and Commitment in the Internationalization Process', *Journal of International Entrepreneurship*, **1** (1), March, 83–101; Richard W. Wright and Léo-Paul Dana (2003), 'Changing Paradigms of International Entrepreneurship Strategy', *Journal of International Entrepreneurship*, **1** (1), March, 135–52; Jim Bell, Rod McNaughton, Stephen Young and Dave Crick (2003), 'Towards an Integrative Model of Small Firm Internationalisation', *Journal of International Entrepreneurship*, **1** (4), December, 339–62; Mike Wright, Andy Lockett, Sarika Pruthi, Sophie Manigart, Harry Sapienza, Philippe Desbrieres and Ulrich Hommel (2004), 'Venture Capital Investors, Capital Markets, Valuation and Information: US, Europe and Asia', *Journal of International Entrepreneurship*, **2**, 305–26; André van Stel, Martin Carree and Roy Thurik (2005), 'The Effect of Entrepreneurial Activity on National Economic Growth', *Small Business Economics*, **24** (3), April, 311–21; Zoltán J. Ács and Attila Varga (2005), 'Entrepreneurship, Agglomeration and Technological Change', *Small Business Economics*, **24** (3), April, 323–34.

John Wiley and Sons Limited for articles: Jane W. Lu and Paul W. Beamish (2001), 'The Internationalization and Performance of SMEs', *Strategic Management Journal*, **22** (6–7), June–July, 565–86; Mason A. Carpenter, Timothy G. Pollock and Myleen M. Leary (2003), 'Testing a Model of Reasoned Risk-Taking: Governance, the Experience of Principals and

Agents, and Global Strategy in High-Technology IPO Firms', *Strategic Management Journal*, **24** (9), September, 803–20.

Every effort has been made to trace all the copyright holders but if any have been inadvertently overlooked the publishers will be pleased to make the necessary arrangement at the first opportunity.

In addition the publishers wish to thank the Library at the University of Warwick, UK, and the Library of Indiana University at Bloomington, USA, for their assistance in obtaining these articles.

Introduction

Benjamin M. Oviatt and Patricia P. McDougall

We have been conducting research and writing about international entrepreneurship now for more than a decade. Over that time many scholars have found the topic of significant interest. Through their efforts, scholarship in the arena of international entrepreneurship is becoming increasingly well developed and sophisticated, and new research questions are emerging. Therefore, this seems like an auspicious time to assemble some of the important scholarly contributions in international entrepreneurship into a single collection. Such a collection may be used by scholars who are interested but new to the field, by doctoral students who need an overview of the field, and by experienced scholars in the field who can use a central repository of sources. We also hope this volume will be used to identify established ideas so that current and future scholars can focus on developing new knowledge instead of exploring what is actually already a well-traveled path.

We have endeavored to identify articles for this collection from a variety of high-quality academic journals that cover the variety of topics usually included in international entrepreneurship. In addition, we have tried to include a varied group of authors from several locations and universities so that many points of view are represented. Inevitably, however, our biases for certain topics and points of view influenced us to choose articles that others would not and to not include some articles that others would. However, we believe readers will find a valuable variety in our collection. We hope that the academic community interested in international entrepreneurship finds this volume to be a valuable contribution.

In this introduction we want to briefly outline our subject and to briefly highlight the topics and the articles included in this collection. International entrepreneurship has been defined in several ways. Over time the definition has changed and different people use different definitions, as readers will see in the articles that follow. In the sixth article in the 'Concepts and Models' section, readers will find a full explanation of why we currently define international entrepreneurship as:

> the discovery, enactment, evaluation, and exploitation of opportunities – across national borders – to create future goods and services.

> The phrase 'across national borders' is highlighted above because it has particular meaning in this context. Actors (organizations, groups, or individuals) who discover, enact, evaluate, or exploit opportunities to create future goods or services and who *cross national borders* to do so are internationally entrepreneurial actors. Scholars who study those actors, how they act, and the effects of their actions are studying international entrepreneurship. So too are scholars who compare domestic entrepreneurial systems, cultures, and behaviors *across national borders*. Thus, there are two branches to the study of international entrepreneurship, one focusing on the cross-national-border *behavior* of entrepreneurial actors and another focusing on the cross-national-border *comparison* of entrepreneurs, their behaviors, and the circumstances in which they are embedded. (Oviatt and McDougall, 2005)

We have included 31 articles in this volume organized by eight broad topics that fall within the definition we provided above. Although some articles could fit into more than one of the broad topics, we have grouped the articles in ways we believe make sense to readers and aid in their research. Readers interested in the important area of corporate entrepreneurship in an international context are asked to consult the first volume of Edward Elgar's International Library of Entrepreneurship: Zahra, S. (Ed.), 2005. *Corporate Entrepreneurship*, Cheltenham UK and Northampton, MA, USA: Edward Elgar.

Our volume begins by highlighting essential Concepts and Models (Part I) that are important in understanding the whole area of international entrepreneurship. That topic is followed by New Ventures (Part II), a subject that initiated scholarly interest in international entrepreneurship. Knowledge and Learning (Part III) represents an important approach in understanding many aspects of our subject. Top Management Teams (Part IV) have been an important area of inquiry in understanding how and why firms go international. Alliances and Networks (Part V) are pathways by which entrepreneurs take their firms international and by which all entrepreneurial firms grow. Many firms are helped to overcome some of the risks of internationalizing by Venture Capital (Part VI) and, of course, venture capitalists differ significantly from country to country. Comparisons of entrepreneurs and the cultures in which they are embedded are the foci of Country Comparisons (Part VII). And finally, two articles that depend on data developed by the Global Entrepreneurship Monitor (GEM) highlight differences in Economic Growth (Part VIII) among countries with different entrepreneurial traditions. Within these eight topics, the articles appear in alphabetical order, by the family name of the first author.

Part I   Concepts and Models

In the first article, Bell, McNaughton, Young, and Crick (Chapter 1, this volume) consider the research they have conducted on small firms that internationalize. They describe three types: the 'traditional firm' that internationalizes slowly and only in reaction to forces impinging upon them; the 'born global' that is proactive in its internationalization; and the 'born-again global' firm that after a long period of domestic operation internationalizes rapidly. A complex and interesting model is presented that explains the behaviors of each of these internationalization types.

In the first of two articles in this section by Coviello and Jones (Chapters 2 and 3), the authors review the empirical methods of 55 international entrepreneurship studies. The authors conclude that scholars need to improve their sampling techniques, to find better ways of comparing studies across national samples, and to include greater consideration of the issue of time. In addition to offering excellent suggestions for many methodological improvements, they also call for the integration of positivist and interpretive methods.

In their second article, Jones and Coviello reconsider much of the literature on the internationalization of entrepreneurial firms and discuss multiple theoretical models at varying levels of analysis. Heeding their own advice from the previous article, they use time as a central organizing concept.

Madsen and Servais (Chapter 4), in a widely cited article, provide a sophisticated and nuanced comparison of various models of internationalization and the empirical findings about born-global firms. Their work leads them to focus on the antecedents that may explain variance in the speed of firm internationalization and to several interesting propositions worth testing.

Our most frequently cited article appears next (Oviatt and McDougall, Chapter 5) and describes a theoretical framework that we believe explains the existence of international new ventures. It also describes different types of international new ventures that vary according to the number of countries entered and the number of value chain activities involved in the internationalization.

Our most recent article appears next (Chapter 6) and explains the reasoning behind the definition of international entrepreneurship that is quoted above. It also provides a model of how various forces affect the speed of firm internationalization.

In an article in the first issue of the new *Journal of International Entrepreneurship* two pioneers in the field, Richard Wright and Léo-Paul Dana (Chapter 7), bring our attention to broad changes going on in the world that affect international entrepreneurship. They highlight the weakening of the nation-state and the power of the lone corporation no matter what its size. They point to trends toward a 'multipolar distribution of power and control' that leads all entities toward cooperative action and toward an increasingly important international role for small and new ventures.

The final article in this section of the book by Zahra and George (Chapter 8) is a comprehensive review of the literature on how entrepreneurial firms internationalize. Alternative definitions are considered, many concepts are explored in detail, and a new model is depicted. The implications for research are clear.

Part II   New Ventures

Given that new venture internationalization initiated scholarly interest in international entrepreneurship more than 15 years ago, it is not surprising that it also represents one of the most widely studied aspects of the field. With the exception of one article, we have chosen to focus on relatively recent work.

In the first article, Burgel and Murray (Chapter 9) focus on technology-based start-ups. They examine the foreign entry mode decisions of a sample of UK firms. They compare the organizational capability perspective, transaction cost theory, and stage theory and conclude that an organizational capability perspective offers a better explanation of the entry decisions in these types of firms.

Knight and Cavusgil (Chapter 10), two of the earliest authors studying born-global firms, use a case study approach, followed by a survey-based study to validate findings, in analyzing key orientations and strategies that lead to international success. Their interesting study reveals that youth and lack of experience, as well as limited financial, human, and tangible resources, need not be major impediments to large-scale internationalization and global success in new ventures.

While their sample is small and medium-sized firms, we included the Lu and Beamish (Chapter 11) article in this section on new ventures because the work has strongly influenced and closely parallels the new venture internationalization literature. Focusing on performance, the authors explore the differential impacts of exporting, foreign direct investment, and alliances. They find that building alliances with partners who possess local knowledge is an effective strategy for overcoming the deficiencies small and medium-sized enterprises face in resources and capabilities as they expand into international markets. Their results provide a foundation for their later study that is included in our section on Alliances and Networks (Part V).

Our article (Chapter 12), which we co-authored with Scott Shane, presents one of the early challenges to existing international business theories. Citing specific examples from case studies, the article argues that monopolistic advantage theory, product cycle theory, stage theory of internationalization, oligopolistic reaction theory, and internalization theory cannot explain the formation process of international new ventures. It is further argued that traditional international business theories focus too much on the firm level and largely ignore the individual and small group level of analysis (i.e., the entrepreneur and his/her network).

Utilizing a sample from three different countries, Moen and Servais (Chapter 13) compare the internationalization of born-global firms with those who pursue internationalization through a gradual process. They find that the future export involvement of a firm is to a large extent influenced by its behavior shortly after establishment. Such a finding underlines the importance of new ventures seeking to compete in the international arena in their infancy.

Our final article (Chapter 14), one that we co-authored with Rodney Shrader, takes the unlikely stance that entrepreneurs manage risk. While some may argue that entrepreneurs pursue business opportunities without regard to risk, our empirical study reveals that entrepreneurs manage the risks of accelerated internationalization by exploiting simultaneous trade-offs among foreign revenue exposure, country risk, and entry mode commitment in each country they enter.

Part III   Knowledge and Learning

The first of the three articles in this section is one of Kuemmerle's (Chapter 15) from his stream of research on knowledge management. Using a framework that distinguishes two types of cross-border knowledge flows – knowledge flows that augment the venture's home base and knowledge flows that exploit their home base – Kuemmerle develops a set of propositions for international ventures.

Building on their earlier work related to learning, Sapienza, De Clercq, and Sandberg (Chapter 16) combine learning theory with the attention-based view to examine how a firm's degree of internationalization, age at international entry, and entrepreneurial orientation is associated with its engagement in foreign and domestic learning activities.

The award winning article by Zahra, Ireland, and Hitt (Chapter 17) is interesting both for its complex findings and its resourceful methodological approach. Using diverse data sources, their study examines the effects of international expansion on a firm's technological learning and the effects of this learning on its financial performance.

Part IV   Top Management Teams

Carpenter, Pollock, and Leary (Chapter 18) find the surprising result that technology-based firms that have had an initial public offering of equity are less likely to build extensive international sales when they are backed by a venture capitalist. However, risk-seeking in international markets is strongest with an internationally seasoned board and top management team at the helm. The authors' development of a theoretical framework of reasoned risk-taking and their excellent discussion of future research opportunities suggest rich research possibilities for scholars interested in this area of inquiry.

The article by Reuber and Fischer (Chapter 19) has influenced much of the most recent work on top management teams in entrepreneurial firms. This article presents a strong case for the importance of international experience in the top management team of those firms seeking to expand into the international marketplace.

Part V   Alliances and Networks

We identified four articles in what we believe will be an increasingly important topic in international entrepreneurship. The first article is from Coviello and Munro (Chapter 20) who were two of the earliest international entrepreneurship scholars exploring networks. They present a conceptual framework of the small firm internationalization process integrating the stage model and network perspectives.

In what they term as a response to researchers who suggest that the incremental models of internationalization are no longer valid in the current world of global competition and accelerating technological development, Johanson and Vahlne (Chapter 21) outline a network model of the internationalization process of the firm. Their model combines the experiential learning–commitment interplay as the driving mechanism from the old process models with a similar experiential learning-commitment mechanism that focuses on business network relationships. In their new and more complex model, firms use the learning from relationships as a platform for entering new country markets.

Leiblein and Reuer (Chapter 22) examine the effects of international collaborative linkages and technological capabilities on building a foreign sales base. The article also makes some interesting observations on differences between entrepreneurial and established firms and cautions entrepreneurial firms engaged in international collaborations to be sensitive to potential adverse selection and moral hazard problems when attempting to exchange technological capabilities for market access.

Employing a sample of 1,117 international joint ventures established in 43 countries by 614 Japanese small and medium-sized enterprises, Lu and Beamish (Chapter 23) examine the performance implications of international joint venture partners and size-based resources. Their findings offer pros and cons to the entrepreneurial firm considering engaging in international joint ventures.

Part VI   Venture Capital

While the Bruton and Ahlstrom (Chapter 24) article is included in our Venture Capital section, it could just as easily have been included in the Country Comparisons section. Based on interviews with 36 venture capitalists in 24 venture capital firms investing in China, their article compares China's institutional environment with that of the West.

Wright, Lockett, Pruthi, Manigart, Sapienza, Desbrieres, and Hommel (Chapter 25) study the information used to make decisions by venture capital investors in a wide variety of countries and cultures on three continents. The authors show significant and systematic differences among countries in the use by venture capitalists of discounted cash flow, price–earnings ratios, liquidation values, information from the financial press, and interviews with entrepreneurs and venture employees.

Part VII   Country Comparisons

The first article in this section, by Baker, Gedajlovic, and Lubatkin (Chapter 26), identifies social factors, such as a society's division of labor, the nature of opportunity costs, and resource availability, that differ among nations and determine how entrepreneurial opportunities are discovered, evaluated, and exploited around the world.

Bucar, Glas, and Hisrich (Chapter 27) delve into the under-researched topic of ethics among entrepreneurs. Drawing from integrative social contract theory, the authors develop a conceptual framework for examining cross-cultural differences in ethical attitudes of entrepreneurs.

Another effective tool for studying entrepreneurs in multiple countries is found in the Busenitz, Gómez, and Spencer (Chapter 28) article. They develop and validate a country institutional profile measure consisting of regulatory, cognitive, and normative dimensions for the domain of entrepreneurship.

Focusing specifically on internal locus of control and innovativeness, Mueller and Thomas (Chapter 29) ask whether entrepreneurial traits vary systematically across cultures and if so, why. They test their hypotheses on a sample of over 1,800 survey responses from university students in nine countries.

Part VIII   Economic Growth

The last section of this volume is devoted to two articles focusing on the economic importance of entrepreneurial activities. Both articles are drawn from a special issue of *Small Business Economics* that is dedicated to research using data collected as part of the GEM. GEM is a collaborative research initiative in which more than 40 countries have participated. The internationally harmonized data provides a rich database for examining entrepreneurial activity across countries.

The Ács and Varga (Chapter 30) article draws upon economic geography and entrepreneurship to develop an empirical model that uses both knowledge spillovers (measured using patent application data) and entrepreneurial activity in an endogenous model within a Romer-based growth framework. GEM data on entrepreneurial activity from seven industrial sectors in nine different countries is used to measure entrepreneurial activity in each particular economy. Their findings from their nine-country study are consistent with the growing body of literature supporting the positive role of entrepreneurship activity and agglomeration in knowledge spillovers and ultimately economic growth.

The final article by van Stel, Carree, and Thurik (Chapter 31) investigates the effect of entrepreneurial activity on economic growth at the country level. Analyzing data from 36 different countries the authors find that entrepreneurial activity affects economic growth, but that the effect is dependent upon the level of per capita income. For relatively richer countries, the effect was positive; however, for relatively poorer countries, the effect was negative. These results are striking and merit additional research. The authors provide a rich discussion of how entrepreneurship may play a different role in countries in different stages of economic development.

References

Oviatt, B.M. and McDougall, P.P. (2005), 'Defining international entrepreneurship and modeling the speed of internationalization', *Entrepreneurship Theory and Practice*, **29**: 537–53.

Part I
Concepts and Models

[1]

 Journal of International Entrepreneurship 1, 339–362, 2003
© 2003 Kluwer Academic Publishers. Manufactured in The Netherlands.

Towards an Integrative Model of Small Firm Internationalisation

JIM BELL*   jd.bell@ulst.ac.uk
University of Ulster, Northern Ireland

ROD McNAUGHTON
University of Waterloo, Canada

STEPHEN YOUNG
University of Strathclyde, Scotland

DAVE CRICK
University of Central England

Abstract. Firm internationalisation has long been regarded as an incremental process, wherein firms gravitate towards 'psychologically close' markets and increase commitment to international markets in a gradual, step-wise, manner through a series of evolutionary 'stages'. However, much of the recent literature provides clear evidence of rapid and dedicated internationalisation by 'born global firms'. Typically, these are smaller entrepreneurial firms that internationalise from inception, or start to shortly thereafter. Their main source of competitive advantage is often related to a more sophisticated knowledge base. In addition, the authors have found evidence of firms supporting this 'born global' pattern of behaviour but also evidence of firms that suddenly internationalise after a long period of focusing on the domestic market. These 'born-again' globals appear to be influenced by critical events that provide them with additional human or financial resources, such as changes in ownership/management, being taken over by another company with international networks, or themselves acquiring such a firm. Based upon the extant literature and our own research, we propose an integrative model that recognises the existence of different internationalisation 'pathways'. We then explore differences in behaviour due to the firm's internationalisation trajectory and discuss the strategic and public policy implications.

Keywords: integrative model small firm internationalisation

Introduction

The emergence of a new stream of literature on 'born global' firms in the early 1990s presents a significant challenge to public policy in support of internationalisation. These smaller entrepreneurial firms tend to adopt a global focus from the outset and embark on rapid and dedicated internationalisation (McKinsey and Co., 1993). Their evolution has been influenced by an inexorable trend towards globalisation and the pervasive impact of new technologies (Knight and Cavusgil, 1996). In

*Corresponding author. Jim Bell, School of International Business, University of Ulster Magee College, Londonderry, BT48 7JL, Northern Ireland. Tel.: 00 44 2871 375336; Fax: 00 44 2871 375323.

addition, these firms often possess a knowledge-based competitive advantage that enables them to offer value-added products and services (McKinsey and Co., 1993). Evidence from the literature concerning differences in the patterns, pace, and intensity of internationalisation of 'born global' firms *vis-à-vis* their more traditional counterparts, suggests that researchers need to re-conceptualise their views on the internationalisation process of smaller firms.

More recently, a study by Bell et al. (2001) identifies 'born-again' global firms that have internationalised rapidly after a long period during which they focused on the domestic market. These firms also fail to conform to the conventional 'stage' theories of small firm internationalisation. Following a review of the extant literature and a summary of the results of this research, the present contribution proposes an integrative model of small firm internationalisation. This normative model seeks to integrate the diverse 'pathways' that smaller firms may take during the internationalisation process. Thereafter, the differences in motivation and behaviour of firms pursuing alternative internationalisation trajectories are explored and the implications for firm's strategies and for public policy in support of small firm internationalisation are discussed.

Review and synthesis of the literature

Most of the extant models posit that firms gradually internationalise in an incremental manner through a series of evolutionary 'stages'. As they do so, they commit greater resources to overseas markets gradually and tend to target countries that are increasingly 'psychically' distant. An underlying assumption of all these models is that firms are well established in the domestic market before venturing abroad. (For comprehensive reviews of the literature see Leonidou and Katsikeas, 1996; Ellis and Pecotich, 1998.)

Criticisms that such conceptualisations wrongly assume step-wise progression and forward motion, pay insufficient attention to industry, company, or people contexts and are generally 'much too deterministic' emanated as long ago as the late 1970s (Buckley et al., 1979; Cannon and Willis, 1981; Reid, 1983; Rosson, 1984; Turnbull, 1987). Buckley et al. (1979) argued that firms do not necessarily adopt consistent organisational approaches to internationalisation. Turnbull (1987) also found little empirical support for incremental internationalisation as firms often omitted stages in the process.

More recently, Andersen's (1993) conceptual critique focused on the weak theoretical underpinning of most process models and the lack of congruence between theory and practice. He concluded that the ability of such models to delineate boundaries between stages, or adequately explain the processes that lead to movement between them, was rather limited.

Despite criticisms of these process models, there is empirical evidence that many firms have internationalised in incremental stages and that others continue to do so. Moreover, such approaches are, arguably, still popular among traditional

INTEGRATIVE MODEL OF SMALL FIRM INTERNATIONALISATION 341

firms gravitating outwards from large economies. Nevertheless, various emerging streams of research in the 1990s have served to seriously challenge 'stage' process models.

Firstly, many researchers have focused on network theory and internationalisation (Sharma and Johanson, 1987; Johanson and Mattsson, 1988; Axelsson and Johanson, 1992; Johanson and Vahlne, 1992; Benito and Welch, 1994; Vatne, 1995). The latter offers a model that nicely summarises the relationship between such networks and SME internationalisation. Therein, internationalisation is seen as an entrepreneurial process that is embedded in an institutional and social web which supports the firm in terms of access to information, human capital, finance, and so on.

However, incremental and network perspectives are not necessarily mutually exclusive. Based upon comprehensive case studies of four software firms, Coviello and Munro (1997) conclude that:

> ... Our understanding of the internationalisation process for small firms, at least small software firms, can be enhanced by integrating the models of incremental internationalisation with the network perspective.

Secondly, research into 'born global' firms (McKinsey and Co., 1993; Knight and Cavusgil, 1996), 'international new ventures' (McDougall et al., 1994; Oviatt and McDougall, 1994), and 'committed internationalists' (Bonaccorsi, 1992; Brush, 1992; Jolly et al., 1992) demonstrates early and rapid international expansion by smaller technology-intensive firms. (See also the more recent work of Jones, 1999; Autio et al., 2000; Crick and Jones, 2000; Eriksson et al., 2000, 2001; Harveston, 2000; Kedia, 2000; Yip et al., 2000; Yli-Renko et al., 2001.) Many of these 'born global' and 'knowledge-intensive' firms are formed by active entrepreneurs, often due to a significant breakthrough in process or technology, and their offerings commonly involve substantial value adding (McKinsey and Co., 1993). A common characteristic is that management adopts a global focus from the outset and embarks on rapid and dedicated internationalisation. This internationalisation behaviour is commonplace among firms that target small, highly specialised global 'niches'.

Enquiries conducted among smaller 'knowledge-intensive' firms also find that many ignore the home market altogether and target 'lead' markets, or enter domestic and international markets concurrently (see, e.g. Coviello, 1994; Bell, 1995; Boter and Holmquist, 1996; Coviello and Munro, 1997; Madsen and Servais, 1997). According to Bell (1995), if these firms are already established in the home market, they tend to follow domestic clients' abroad, regardless of the 'psychic proximity' of the market, a pattern that is also observable among more traditional firms. Evidence of inter-firm relationships supports network theories and such behaviour is particularly prevalent among firms operating in small open economies and in emerging nations, where domestic demand may be limited. (See Coviello and McAuley, 1999; for an excellent review and synthesis of sixteen contemporary empirical studies on internationalisation and the smaller firm.)

Thirdly, the literature on the globalisation of services (see Knight, 1999, for a comprehensive review) argues that service firms tend to internationalise in a 'different' way than their manufacturing counterparts (Erramilli and Rao, 1991, 1994; Chadee and Mattsson, 1998). Thus, the explanatory power of 'stage' theories for service sector firms is questionable. Moreover, the robustness of process models may be diminishing as boundaries between 'product' and 'service' offerings become increasingly blurred and as manufacturing firms incorporate a higher service component.

Fourthly, there is also evidence in the literature that firm internationalisation may be precipitated by particular 'episodes' that lead to rapid international expansion or de-internationalisation (Oesterle, 1997). On the other hand, specific events may encourage firms to focus on domestic markets. Accordingly, firms may subsequently experience 'epochs' of internationalisation, followed by periods of consolidation or retrenchment. These critical incidents may be triggered by forces that impact on the internationalisation strategies of domestic and overseas clients, or other network partners, as well as those that directly influence the focal firm (Bell et al., 1998). Thus, some firms may pursue 'sporadic' internationalisation trajectories that are different from both the traditional 'incremental' and 'born global' pathways.

Finally, recognition that firm internationalisation may be affected by multiple influences over time (Melin, 1992), has led to a reawakening of interest in contingency approaches first articulated by Reid (1983). In recent years various authors have developed contingency frameworks in the international business and exporting fields (Woodcock et al., 1994; Yeoh and Jeong, 1995; Kumar and Subramaniam, 1997). The latter, in justifying a contingency approach, argue that the existing literature has not devoted much attention to evaluating market selection and mode of entry as interdependent decisions. One might go further and suggest that the range of the firms' internationalisation decisions, incorporating product decisions, market choice, and entry modes, are made in a holistic way (a notion initially presented by Luostarinen, 1979).

Allied to these contingency approaches may be the resource-based perspective. Its basic premise is that it is the firm's ability to generate and build or leverage resources and competencies that is the key to competitive advantage and organisational survival (Wernerfelt, 1984; Barney, 1991; Grant, 1991). Small internationalising firms will respond differently in their efforts to overcome resource/competence deficiencies in areas such as finance and human resources. Such responses will also be 'contingent' on the levels of resources the firm has at its disposal (Reid, 1983; Woodcock et al., 1994; Yeoh and Jeong, 1995).

Research focus and approach

In recent years the authors have conducted a series of small firm internationalisation studies in several UK regions (England, Northern Ireland, and Scotland), Australia, and New Zealand. As previously reported (Bell et al., 1998, 2001), these enquiries adopted an exploratory, qualitative, case study approach and involved in total 50 in-depth semi-structured interviews with Chief Executive Officers (CEOs) or export managers of small-to-medium sized internationalising firms. Judgement samples, in which ten 'knowledge-intensive' and 'traditional' firms were equally represented at each location, were constructed using directories of SMEs known to have an international involvement (such as, databases provided by Scottish Enterprise, Northern Ireland Local Enterprise Development Unit, Dunedin City Council, and the Victoria Chamber of Commerce). In addition, other published information (press reports, trade association listings, etc.) and the researchers' preexisting knowledge of firms were used in sample selection.

The overall objective of these investigations was to gain a deeper understanding of the internationalisation processes of SMEs. In particular, the original aim was to explore and seek to explain any variations in the patterns, pace, and processes of internationalisation between 'traditional' and knowledge-intensive 'born global' firms. Data were collected and analysed utilising a template specifically designed for the purpose of obtaining deep and rich qualitative insights into the phenomenon under investigation. This instrument contained a number of structured questions designed to gather data for classification purposes (firm size, age, export experience, export ratio, first export market/s, current market/s, etc.). In addition, a series of open-ended questions were used to probe the strategic directions of firms and underlying reasons for key internationalisation decisions.

A qualitative approach was employed to systematically analyse open-ended questions and identify variations in patterns of response between 'knowledge-intensive' and 'traditional' groups. This involved a thematic analysis, conducted manually, that explored a number of pertinent issues including:

- the factors that motivated firms to internationalise
- firms internationalisation objectives
- the patterns and pace of internationalisation
- market entry and distribution strategies
- strategic approaches to international marketing
- methods of financing international expansion.

Firms were drawn from a variety of industries including electrical and mechanical engineering, food and beverage, information communications technology, printing and textiles. All were current exporters, employed less that 250 staff (over 90% had less than 100 employees) and were independent operations indigenous to the location. A demographic profile of the firms is shown in Table 1.

Findings

Results from the UK studies have been reported previously (Bell et al., 1998). In summary, they revealed some significant differences in the patterns and pace of internationalisation between knowledge-intensive and traditional firms. The former firms adopted much more proactive and structured approaches to internationalisation and

Table 1.   Demographic profile of firms.

Firm characteristics	% ($n = 50$)
Age of firm	
Less than 10 years	20
10–20 years	56
More than 20 years	24
Size of firm (turnover)	
Up to £1 m	16
£1.0 m–£1.9 m	26
£2.0 m–£4.9 m	44
More than £5.0 m	14
International experience	
Less than 5 years	24
5–10 years	44
More than 10 years	32
Export initiation	
Less than 2 years after start-up	20
2–5 years after start-up	24
5–10 years after start-up	20
Over 10 years after start-up	36
Export ratio (% of turnover)	
Less than 20%	26
20–49%	34
50–69%	24
Over 70%	16
Industry sector	
Clothing and textiles	14
Engineering	26
Food and Drink	20
Electronics & ICT	24
Printing	6
Other (giftware, furniture)	10

were more flexible in relation to their choice of entry modes. They also internationalised more rapidly, many from inception or shortly thereafter, following the Oviatt and McDougall (1994) 'born global' classification. In some cases, domestic and international expansion occurred concurrently. In others international involvement preceded domestic expansion or the home market was ignored altogether as firms targeted 'lead' markets. In contrast, traditional firms tended to adopt a more *ad hoc*, reactive and opportunistic approach to internationalisation. This was likely to occur in an incremental manner over a longer period of time, with firms often focusing on 'psychically' and/or geographically 'close' markets. Evidence also emerged that; while knowledge-intensive firms tended to focus on 'lead' markets (such as the USA, Europe, or Japan), many of the traditional firms targeted 'lag' markets that were technologically less sophisticated.

These findings were corroborated by the results from the Australian and New Zealand sample, with the exception that, due to their location, these firms considered Asia-Pacific markets as geographically and/or psychically proximate. Taken together, they support the main themes emerging from the recent literature on knowledge-intensive firms and 'international new ventures' (see e.g. Boter and Holmquist, 1996; Coviello and McAuley, 1999; Jones, 1999; Crick and Jones, 2000; Ericksson et al., 2000, 2001; Shrader et al., 2000). However, they also provide evidence of incremental approaches to internationalisation among traditional firms that support more conventional views on the subject.

During the course of these enquiries, evidence also emerged that a number of long-established 'traditional' firms, 16 in all, had suddenly internationalised, having previously shown little or no enthusiasm for the task. In virtually every case, their dramatic change in strategic focus was precipitated by a 'critical' incident, or through a combination of several 'incidents' occurring around the same time. (For a detailed discussion of these episodes, together with supporting case studies, see Bell et al., 2001). Especially noteworthy was that these 'episodes' were common to a number of the firms in the different countries under investigation. These findings support Oesterle's (1997) arguments on 'epochs' of internationalisation and we decided to re-classify this group of firms as 'born-again' globals.

Further exploration revealed that the most common 'episode' was a change in ownership and/or management that typically occurred in a number of ways. Firstly, through a management buyout (MBO), of which there were at least six examples (over 10% of cases). Secondly, where the focal firm was taken over by another (four cases). Thirdly, where a firm had actually ceased trading or was in receivership and was acquired either by the existing management, or a third party (three cases). Perhaps a more apposite term for the latter is 're-born' or 'resurrected' global firms as, like Lazarus, they had literally returned from the dead. In each of these cases the change in ownership and/or management introduced new decision-makers with a greater international orientation. This was often accompanied by an infusion of additional finance and access networks in overseas markets. Another quite frequently occurring event was where an existing domestic customer had suddenly internationalised and the firm had 'followed' the client into new markets (six cases). Allied to this, were several cases where a new client already operating internationally had entered the home market. Finally, there was evidence that increasing adoption of information communication technologies (ICT) was influencing the internationalisation behaviour of these firms. Though not 'episodic' in nature, embracing such technologies can facilitate these 'born-again' firms to embark on an 'epoch' of internationalisation.

The main differences in the internationalisation motivation and behaviour of 'traditional', 'born global', and 'born-again global' firms emerging from the extant literature and our own enquiries are summarised in Table 2. As can be seen, clear differences in motivation are manifest. 'Traditional' firms tend to be much more reactive, firms are 'pushed' into international markets by adverse domestic market conditions, unsolicited orders or enquiries, or the need to generate revenues to

Table 2. Differences in internationalisation behaviour.

	'Traditional'	'Born global' firms	'Born-again' global firms
Motivation	Reactive Adverse home market Unsolicited/enquiries orders 'Reluctant' management Cost of new production Processes force export initiation	Proactive Global 'niche' markets 'Committed' management International from inception Active search	Reactive Response to a 'critical' incident (MBO, take-over, acquisition, etc.)
Objectives	Firm survival/growth Increasing sales volume Gaining market share Extending product life-cycle	Competitive advantage 'First-mover' advantage 'Locking-in' customers Rapid penetration of global 'niches' or segments Protecting and exploiting proprietary knowledge	Exploit new networks and resources gained from critical incident
Expansion patterns	Incremental Domestic expansion first Focus on 'psychic' markets 'Low-tech'/less sophisticated markets targeted Limited evidence of networks	Concurrent Near-simultaneous domestic and export expansion (exporting may precede domestic market activity) Focus on 'lead' markes Some evidence of client 'followership' Strong evidence of networks	'Epoch' of domestic market orientation, followed by rapid internationalisation. Focus on 'parent' company's networks and overseas markets Strong evidence of client 'followership'
Pace	Gradual Slow internationalisation (small number of markets) Single market at a time Adaptation of existing offering	Rapid Speedy internationalisation (large number of markets) Many markets at once Global product development	Late/rapid No international focus then rapid internationalisation Several markets at once Adaptation/NPD

Method of distribution/ entry modes	Conventional Use of agents/distributors or wholesalers Direct to customers	Flexible and networks Use of agents or distributors Also evidence of integration with client's channels, use of licensing, joint ventures, overseas production, etc.	Networks Existing channel/s of new 'parent', partner/s or client/s
International strategies	Ad-hoc and opportunistic Evidence of continued reactive behaviour to new opportunities Atomistic expansion, unrelated new customers/markets	Structured Evidence of planned approach to international expansion Expansion of global networks	Reactive in response to 'critical' incident but more structured thereafter Expansion of newly acquired networks
Financing	'Boot-strap' into new markets	Self-financed via rapid growth Venture capital, Initial public offerings (IPO)	Capital injection by 'parent' Refinancing after MBO

finance future product or process improvements and management is more reluctant to internationalise. The 'born global' firms have more committed management, pursue global 'niches' from the outset and are generally more proactive. The 'born-again' global firms' sudden change of focus from a domestic to an international orientation is triggered by an infusion of new human and/or financial resources, access to new networks in overseas markets, acquisition of new product/market knowledge, or some other critical incident.

Firms' international objectives are also markedly different. For 'traditional' firms the main goals appear to be survival by increasing sales volume, greater market share, or extending product life cycles. The 'born global' firms seek to gain 'first mover' advantage and achieve rapid penetration of global 'niches' or segments. They attempt to protect and exploit proprietary knowledge and 'lock-in' clients. Often, the pace of technological innovation leads to very short life cycles and narrow windows of commercial opportunity. For 'born-again globals' the main objective appears to be to exploit new networks and resources gained as a result of particular 'critical episodes'.

In these circumstances, the patterns and pace of internationalisation vary considerably. 'Traditional' firms tend to focus on the domestic market first, expand incrementally, gravitate to 'psychically close' markets, and/or target less developed markets. They often internationalise one market at a time and concentrate on a small number of key markets, adapting existing offerings to the needs of each new market. Among 'born global' firms, domestic and international expansion tends to be concurrent and internationalisation may even precede domestic market activities. Firms are also likely to be influenced by global industry trends, enter many 'lead' markets simultaneously, undertake global product development and not be overly influenced by 'psychic' proximity. However, as Jain (1996) observes, the need to maintain strong intellectual property rights can impose certain restrictions on their expansion patterns, particularly to markets where protection of patents can be a problem. Among 'born-again global' firms an epoch of domestic market orientation is replaced by one of rapid and dedicated internationalisation.

Among 'born global' and 'born-again global' firms there is stronger evidence of export or domestic client followership and of the importance of networking with suppliers and other channel-partners. In terms of channel selection, 'traditional' firms tend to adopt fairly conventional approaches such as agents or distributors. In addition to these methods, 'born global' and 'born-again global' firms are more likely to integrate into client's existing channels (e.g. by adopting customers dealer networks or value added retailers, or in the case of the latter, new networks provided by the acquiring or acquired partners). Both categories are also more likely to set up licensing agreements or enter alliances with (new) clients and/or suppliers.

Finally, there is also evidence that 'traditional' firms continue to be *more ad hoc*, reactive and opportunistic, whereas 'born global' firms generally adopt much more structured approaches to internationalisation. In the case of 'born-again' global firms, strategies tend to be much more systematic once the decision to internationalise has eventually been triggered by a critical incident. All of these differences are incorporated in the integrative model of small firm internationalisation that is proposed and discussed hereafter.

An integrative model of small firm internationalisation

The normative model proposed in Figure 1 is based on the extant internationalisation literature, incorporates recent empirical enquiry into the processes of 'born global' firms and includes our own observations on the 'born-again global' phenomenon (McKinsey and Co., 1993; Knight and Cavusgil, 1996). A number of pertinent observations should be made regarding this conceptualisation. Firstly, the three main trajectories shown in the model are intended to indicate stereotypical internationalisation patterns rather than rigid 'pathways'. In practice, the actual trajectories of firms will be highly individualistic, situation specific, and unique. Secondly, we posit that the knowledge base of the firm is a source of competitive advantage that influences both the patterns and pace of internationalisation. Thus, firms with highly sophisticated knowledge bases are likely to internationalise much more rapidly than are those with more basic capabilities.

In the proposed model firms can be classified as 'traditional', 'born global', and 'born-again global'. 'Traditional' firms are those that follow an incremental approach to internationalisation, becoming established in their domestic markets before initiating international activities (and often entering markets with increasing 'psychic' distance). Among 'traditional' firms, the knowledge-based element of offerings need not necessarily be high, although some quite sophisticated processes may be involved. Typically however, neither products nor processes are particularly advanced.

'Born global' firms may be further classified as either 'knowledge-intensive' or 'knowledge-based' firms. Firms in both of these categories can be defined as those 'having a high added value of scientific knowledge embedded in both product and process. . . . Often, this knowledge is also required in sales and marketing functions' (Coviello, 1994). The essential difference between them is that 'knowledge-based' firms exist because of the emergence of new technologies (such as ICT, biotechnology, etc.). They will either have developed proprietary knowledge or acquired knowledge, without which they would not exist (e.g. software developers, Internet providers, or firms offering other distance independent services). In contrast, 'knowledge-intensive firms' may use knowledge to develop new offerings, improve productivity, introduce new methods of production, and/or improve service delivery but are not inherently knowledge-based. The use of computer aided design (CAD), computer aided manufacturing (CAM), and high-tech fabrics in the clothing industry is a case in point. Similar developments have also occurred in the printing industry as a result of electronic publishing technologies.

'Knowledge-based' firms are likely to internationalise very rapidly. However, it is postulated that the pace of internationalisation of 'knowledge-intensive' firms is likely to be determined by whether they are technological 'innovators' or 'adopters'.

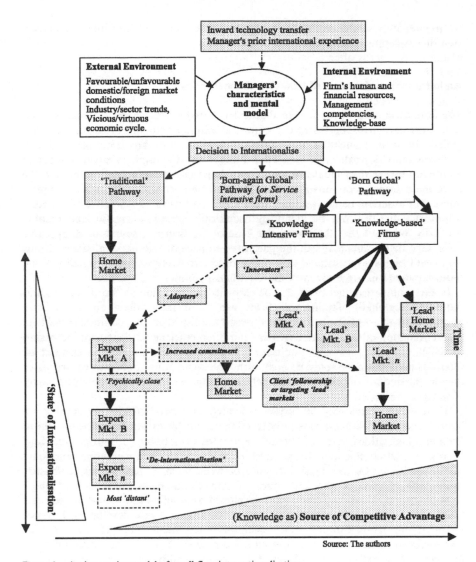

Figure 1.   An integrative model of small firm internationalisation.

The former are more likely to internationalise at a faster pace than the latter, however, in smaller open economies limited domestic market opportunities may also be a driver. Nevertheless, in all cases, the knowledge base can be regarded as a core competence and a source of competitive advantage (Autio et al., 2000; Ericksson et al., 2000; McNaughton, 2001).

INTEGRATIVE MODEL OF SMALL FIRM INTERNATIONALISATION   351

In respect to service-intensive firms, particularly those that involve franchising and/or retailing operations, successful commercialisation of the business concept in the home market is often a prerequisite to any international involvement (McIntyre and Huszagh, 1995; Björkman and Kock, 1997). Thus a firm may spend a longer period of time designing, testing, and developing the service offering for domestic consumption, before initiating rapid international expansion. In this context, the lag between start up and internationalisation can be explained by the need to gain the requisite market knowledge in order to culturally adapt service offerings and marketing strategies for foreign consumers (Knight, 1999; Lovelock, 1999).

'Born-again global' manufacturing firms tend to emanate from traditional industries rather than high technology sectors. However, their knowledge intensity may increase due to improvements in product and/or process technology in their particular industry, or due to new product and/or market intelligence acquired as a result of the critical incident. In some cases, this new knowledge will be acquired through a take over of another firm. Gaining greater knowledge of products, processes, or markets may increase the pace of internationalisation. The term 'born-again' is increasingly also being applied to firms that have changed or modified their traditional business formats in order to internationalise via the Internet. Thus the adaptation of product and/or market innovation, or the adoption of new information technologies may also be 'drivers' of internationalisation.

The model acknowledges views articulated in the contemporary literature on knowledge intensity as a major source of international competitive advantage (Coviello and McAuley, 1999; Jones, 1999; Autio et al., 2000; Yli-Renko et al., 2001). This knowledge intensity may stem from greater proprietary knowledge in terms of product or service offerings, new design, development and production processes, technological innovations, or the adoption of e-business solutions (Brock, 2000). It may also be influenced by greater knowledge of global industry sector and of 'niche' markets for offerings. In these circumstances, the pace of internationalisation will be rapid as firms seek to exploit narrow windows and gain first mover advantage (McNaughton, 2001). Conversely, lower knowledge intensity of products, processes, sectors or markets is likely to lead to more gradual internationalisation.

Secondly, the model recognises that the small firm internationalisation process is neither linear nor unidirectional (Turnbull, 1987; Bell, 1995). The use of the term 'state of internationalisation' (rather than 'stage') in the model is intended to reflect the potential for forward and backward momentum. This 'state' is contingent upon prevailing external environment conditions, the availability or absence of human and financial resources within the firm, other internal considerations and arguably of greatest importance, the key decision-makers' mental model and global mindset (Berry, 1998). Accordingly, firms may experience 'epochs' of internationalisation, followed by periods of consolidation or retrenchment, or they may be involved in 'episodes' that lead to rapid international expansion or de-internationalisation (Oesterle, 1997). Equally, specific events may encourage firms to focus on the home market. These 'episodes' or 'epochs' may be triggered by forces that impact on the internationalisation strategies of domestic or overseas customers and other network partners, as well as those that directly influence the focal firm.

Thirdly, given that 'no single theory appears to have sufficient explanatory power on its own' (Coviello and McAuley, 1999), the proposed model incorporates dimensions of extant incremental 'stage' theories and network perspectives. It also recognises the explanatory value of contingency approaches and allied resource-based theories. By integrating elements of each of these conceptualisations, the intention is to seek to provide a coherent perspective of small firm internationalisation.

Finally, the main thrust of the proposed model is to focus on strategic rather than operational issues. Thus, it does not focus explicitly on the development of marketing activities in specific overseas markets. However, it is intended to provide a basis for the development of prescriptive models that will contribute to managerial decision-making and address issues relating to the financing of international operations. Furthermore, the model offers useful perspectives on policy formulation and implementation in support of small firm internationalisation, given that the nature and level of firms' support needs are likely to vary considerably depending on the different internationalisation 'pathways' or trajectories.

Managerial, public policy, and research implications

Managerial implications

The different internationalisation trajectories identified in the model offer some useful insights into firm's internationalisation strategies, in particular, the means of financing of international operations. Firms pursuing the traditional 'pathway' are likely to 'bootstrap' into international markets using revenues generated from the domestic market and/or from the initial excursion into export markets and any support they may be able to obtain from government sources to finance subsequent international activities and expansion. Clearly, an unsatisfactory outcome at any stage may delay the internationalisation process, or indeed, result in subsequent de-internationalisation. Moreover, the lack of capital to finance such activities may often lead to a slower, and perhaps a less optimal, pace of internationalisation, with firms being unable to exploit all of the export opportunities presented to them.

Firms pursuing the 'born global' trajectory will face quite different problems. Here the firm's strategy is likely to be to gain first-mover advantage by internationalising rapidly into key 'lead' markets. This will require substantial up-front financing and involve significant product and market development costs. If they successfully penetrate a large 'lead' market (which might include the home market) they may have sufficient revenues to expand rapidly into other markets, otherwise, they may need to seek venture capital or secure *mezzanine* financing. Indeed a strategy, from the outset may be to make the firm sufficiently attractive to be taken over by a larger domestic or international player. This not only provides the firm with the resource

INTEGRATIVE MODEL OF SMALL FIRM INTERNATIONALISATION 353

base it requires for internationalisation, but often makes a rather nice contribution to the founder's pension plan, or provides them with the capital to set up a new venture!

The financial considerations involved in pursuing a 'born global' strategy are especially critical in circumstances where long research and development lead-times and/or product approval processes are involved prior to commercialisation. For example, in pharmaceutical or biotechnology sectors, the time scale for new product development may be 3–5 years or longer, during which time costs are being incurred without a supporting revenue stream. Such issues clearly require much greater research enquiry and public-policy attention.

Once they have eventually opted to pursue an internationalisation strategy, firms pursuing the 'born-again global' pathway may be in a better position to finance rapid international expansion. This may be due to having established a good revenue stream from a more robust domestic market position. Alternatively, they may have gained a substantial infusion of human and financial resources, proprietary knowledge, or international marketing expertise following an acquisition, as a result of having been taken over, or due to another critical incident. In the case of MBOs, the strategies pursued by the new owners or management team (and/or the influence of non-executive directors on strategy) may lead to rapid internationalisation in order to make the firm a more attractive take over proposition. However, in circumstances where 'a born-again global' strategy is pursued because of difficulties in the domestic market, or when substantial investment in an acquisition has been required, the financial issues may have more in common with the 'traditional' trajectory.

This 'born-again' trajectory is also more likely to be adopted by service-intensive firms in retailing, leisure, and hospitality, because of a tendency towards direct and more costly modes of investment, or for franchisers who need to develop and 'prove' the business concept in the domestic market before expanding internationally. Regardless of whether service offerings are targeted at business-to-business or to consumer markets, rapid internationalisation is unlikely to take place until the concept and the quality of service delivery are proven in the home market and can be culturally adapted (Grönroos, 1999; Samiee, 1999; Stauss and Mang, 1999).

Clearly, the choice of internationalisation 'pathway' will also influence other dimensions of firms' business strategies and the resources they must acquire or leverage to successfully pursue their objectives. For example, the management of human resources will vary according to internationalisation trajectory, with incremental firms investing in human capital as and when financial circumstances permit and when these resources are needed. For 'born global' firms, recruitment of key members of the management team will almost certainly be a prerequisite and having the necessary spectrum of skills are in place from the outset is paramount to ensure the success of the strategy (Elkjaer, 2000; Ranft and Lord, 2000). As already indicated firms pursuing a 'born-again' pathway may do so because they have acquired additional human capital.

354   BELL ET AL.

Implications for public policy in support of firm internationalisation

Evidence of different internationalisation trajectories also has profound implications
for public policy support for SMEs, given that the focus of many national Export
Promotion Organisation (EPO) strategies is on supporting this sector. Seringhaus
and Botschen (1990) conclude that the specific goals of EPOs are:

1. 'to develop a broad awareness of export opportunities and to stimulate interest
   among the business community;
2. to assist firms in the planning and preparation for export market involvement;
3. to assist firms in acquiring the needed expertise and know-how to successfully
   enter and develop export markets;
4. to support foreign market activity tangibly through organisational help and cost-
   sharing programmes'.

Seringhaus (1986) argues that these goals hold particular relevance to under-
resourced SMEs, whose significant economic, social, and international contributions
are increasingly recognised by public policy makers and researchers alike
(UNCTAD/ITC, 1986, 1988: EIM/ENSR, 1993; US SBA, 1993; Czinkota, 1994;
Acs et al., 1997; OECD, 1997). However, an extensive literature on export assistance
has generally been highly critical of EPO support for smaller firms. Serious concerns
have been raised regarding the utility of export market information and the efficacy,
timeliness and value of services (Pointon, 1978; Buckley, 1983; Cavusgil, 1983;
Bannock and Partners, 1987; Howard and Herremans, 1988). Typically, awareness
of EPO offerings and satisfaction with provisions among smaller firms are also
found to be very low (Kaynak and Stevenson, 1982; Albaum, 1983; Walters, 1983;
Denis and Depelteau, 1985; Kedia and Chhokar, 1986).

The scope and nature of direct and indirect export assistance is comprehensively
discussed by Diamantopoulos et al. (1993), who contend that EPO offerings in
different countries are generally very similar (see Figure 2). Evidence from the
literature (Bowen, 1986; Seringhaus, 1987; Elvey, 1990; Seringhaus and Rosson,
1990; Camino, 1991; Rosson and Seringhaus, 1991), also suggests that most national
EPO provisions are geared towards offering support and assistance to firms pursuing
the 'traditional' incremental pathway. This focus places great emphasis on the pre-
export phase and in particular on stimulating export initiation, where considerable
EPO resources are employed in providing standardised information on foreign
markets. Although such an emphasis is consistent with the prevailing views on
internationalisation during the 1980s, it is debatable if it is of any real value to 'born
global' firms, or indeed to rapidly internationalizing 'born-again globals'. These
firms are highly motivated to internationalise and recognise the benefits of doing so.
Further attempts to stimulate export activity are akin to preaching to the converted
and an inefficient use of scarce EPO resources.

INTEGRATIVE MODEL OF SMALL FIRM INTERNATIONALISATION 355

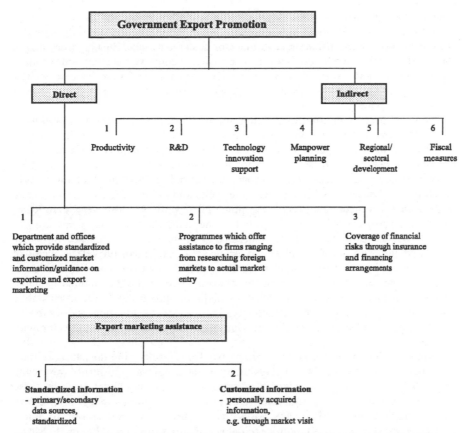

Figure 2. The scope of government export promotion. (Source: Understanding the Role of Export Marketing Assistance: Empirical Evidence and Research Needs, Diamantopoulos et al., 1993)

Secondly, the provision of standardised export market information is not of particular benefit to 'born global' firms that target narrow global 'niches'. They are more likely to have better market knowledge than their 'traditional' counterparts, or find it relatively easier to obtain (Bell, 1997). As players in knowledge-based sectors, they are also more likely to have better access to the shared 'intellectual capital' embedded in the global industry. For example, a developer of banking software will not find it hard to identify a small number of banks operating in any given market. Moreover, with the globalisation of this sector, it is highly likely that the banks will have known affiliates or subsidiaries in other countries that may also adopt the solution. Similarly, an obvious distribution channel for software packages that are designed for an IBM platform, for example, may well be the IBM world wide dealer network. Hence, pre-existing relationships between hardware and software firms may obviate the need for an extensive agent/distributor search. In this context, relationships with the local subsidiary or dealer network may provide valuable contacts with overseas affiliates, customers, or dealer networks. Finally, according to Bell (1997), knowledge-based firms have a greater facility with the new information technologies, such as the world wide web (www) and demonstrate a greater propensity to use them to obtain knowledge of competitors offerings and export market intelligence.

The rapid pace of internationalisation among 'born global' firms also presents a major challenge to EPOs, not only in terms of providing assistance in a timely manner, but also in respect to the nature of the support provided. Such firms may not only be developing new products for multiple markets, but also entering these markets concurrently. Such activities incur substantial up-front product and market development costs. In addition, shorter life cycles and more complex offerings make these high-risk ventures, although the potential rewards are also very significant. Moreover, narrower 'windows' in global 'niche' markets mean that firms are less likely to be able to use the revenues generated in one international market to finance expansion into another. Clearly any assistance that EPOs can provide in terms of defraying market research, and research and development costs is welcome. However, such assistance as is presently available is probably too limited to make a significant impact. Furthermore, greater collaboration between EPOs, other public bodies involved in supporting technological innovation and academia is desirable to enable firms to develop more cohesive international product/market development strategies.

Another major support need for 'born global' firms results from the nature of their offerings. As Coviello (1994) observes many of these have a significant 'knowledge embedded ... that is also required in sales and marketing functions'. In these circumstances, levels of pre- and after-sales services required in support of offerings will be high. Whether these are provided in-house or contracted-out to intermediaries, the skills required in order to deliver quality support will be costly. Moreover, more frequent visits to a greater number of markets will be required to maintain and develop good relationships with clients and/or channel partners. While support for attending trade fairs or participation in outward missions may facilitate occasional contact with overseas partners, few support mechanisms exist to assist 'born global' firms to develop their international networks effectively and systematically.

In respect to 'born-again' global firms, the precipitated shift in market focus may lead to similar support requirements to those of born globals. Arguably, their financial situation may be stronger due to an influx of additional capital, or critical incidents may have provided access to new global networks, technologies, markets, or greater management expertise. Nevertheless, they too will have some very specific support needs due to the pace at which they will be seeking to internationalise, particularly in respect to new product development for multiple international markets. In the case of internationalising service firms, once the concept has been 'proven', substantial human, financial, and management resources will be required to identify appropriate international channel partners or franchisees.

From the preceding discussion it is clear that public policy for SME internationalisation requires a fundamental reconsideration to better address the support needs of 'born global' and 'born-again global' firms. In summary:

- The value of stimulation programmes for firms that are committed to internationalisation is doubtful. EPOs should re-deploy their scarce resources in other areas.
- The provision of generalised export market information is of limited value. EPOs should seek to become repositories of 'hard' market intelligence. Acting as www portals, they should also screen other useful secondary sources and direct firms to them.
- The pace of internationalisation among 'born global' and 'born-again global' firms demands a fast response from EPOs and greater levels of assistance for concurrent entry into multiple international markets. Greater collaboration is also required with other agencies in support of innovation, and research and development. Creating an environment conducive to encouraging the availability of venture capital is also an important priority.
- Greater support is required for 'born global' and 'born-again global' firms in respect to developing international network relationships. At the same time, EPOs should help firms capitalise on any opportunities to access these networks from within the domestic market.

Clearly, many EPOs have sought to address earlier criticisms in the literature regarding the general nature of provisions and most now accept the need to provide appropriate support for 'born global' firms. Nevertheless, many still need to adopt more holistic approaches to supporting SMEs that recognise that firm internationalisation is much broader in scope than merely exporting goods or services as it often include inward as well as outward strategies (for a good discussion of these issues, see Fletcher, 2001). Secondly, greater acknowledgement that internationalisation may result from contacts in the domestic market is important and assistance in developing such networks is clearly desirable. Thirdly, that as internationalisation may involve a wider spectrum of activities including acquisitions or sell outs, mergers, joint ventures, or alliances and other strategies, guidance and support for these activities is crucial. Fourthly, that the support needs of firms pursuing different internationalisation trajectories or 'pathways' will be significantly different and must therefore be addressed in a much more targeted manner. Finally, it is evident that acquisition of additional resources is vitally important to the internationalisation process. In these circumstances, the remits of EPOs could be usefully extended beyond providing export information to include facilitation to assist internationalising SMEs to identify, leverage, and harness additional human, financial, and knowledge resources.

Research implications

The proposed integrative small firm internationalisation model highlights differences in processes, patterns, and pace among 'traditional', 'born global', and 'born-gain global' firms. It also seeks to incorporate aspects of process and network theories in order to offer a broader viewpoint on SME internationalisation. Elements of contingency approaches and resource-based theory are incorporated, particularly in the 'born-again' pathway. In attempting to integrate these diverse, yet complementary, perspectives, this contribution support previous calls for more holistic approaches to research in the field. As Coviello and McAuley (1999) observe 'conceptually, future research should integrate the extant views of internationalisation, recognising that no single view may be appropriate'.

It is also the authors' intention to seek to move the small firm internationalisation research agenda forward to enable enquiry to focus on specific and important issues in the area. In particular, much greater enquiry is required into ways in which internationalizing SMEs can leverage additional external financing, acquire and exploit knowledge, improve their stock of human capital, and enhance their networking capabilities. Acknowledging the existence of multiple internationalisation 'pathways' will facilitate such research. It will also assist policy formulation in support of SME internationalisation and the development of much more targeted export assistance programmes.

Conclusion

While the internationalisation process of individual firms is situation specific and unique, the present study identifies a number of stereotypical 'pathways' that firms may follow. In each of these trajectories differences in motivation, objectives, and knowledge intensity impact on the patterns and pace of internationalisation and influence the strategic approaches adopted by firms. Based upon the empirical findings, an integrative model of small firm internationalisation is proposed and managerial, public policy, and research implications are discussed.

References

Acs, Z.J., R. Morck, M. Shaver, and B. Yeung, 1997, 'The Internationalization of Small and Medium-Sized Enterprises: A Policy Perspective', *Small Business Economics* **9**, 7–20.

Albaum, G., 1983, 'Effectiveness of Government Export Assistance for U.S. Smaller-Sized Manufacturers: Some Further Evidence', *International Marketing Review* **1** (1), 68–75.

Andersen, O. and L.S. Kheam, 1998, 'Resource-Based Theory and International Growth Strategies: An Exploratory Study', *International Business Review* **7**, 163–184.

Andersen, O., 1993, 'On the Internationalization Process of Firms: A Critical Analysis', *Journal of International Business Studies*, Second Quarter, 209–231.

Autio, E., H.J. Sapienza, and J.G. Almieda, 2000, 'Effects of Age at Entry, Knowledge Intensity, and Imitability on International Growth', *Academy of Management Journal* **43** (5), 909–924.

Axelsson, B. and J. Johanson, 1992, 'Foreign Market Entry—The Textbook vs. The Network View', in B. Axelsson and G. Easton (eds.), *Industrial Networks: A New View of Reality*, London: Routledge, pp. 218–234.

Bannock, G. and Partners, 1987, 'Into Active Exporting', *BOTB Occasional Papers, HMSO. Dd 8934782 J0229NJ*, London.

Barney, J., 1991, 'Firm Resources and Sustained Competitive Advantage', *Journal of Management* **17**, 99–120.

Bell, J., R. McNaughton, and S. Young, 2001, ' "Born-Again Global" Firms: An Extension to the "Born Global" Phenomenon', *Journal of International Management* **7** (3), 1–17.

Bell, J., S. Young, and D. Crick, 1998, 'A Holistic Perspective on Small Firm Internationalization and Growth', in C.C. Millar and C.J. Choi (eds.), *International Business and Emerging Markets* vol. 1, pp. 9–29.

Bell, J., 1997, 'A Comparative Study of Export Problems of Small Computer Software Exporters in Finland, Ireland and Norway', *International Business Review* **6** (2), 1–20.

Bell, J., 1995, 'The Internationalization of Small Computer Software Firms—A Further Challenge to 'Stage' Theories', *European Journal of Marketing* **29** (8), 60–75.

Benito, G.R.G. and L.S. Welch, 1994, 'Foreign Market Servicing: Beyond Choice of Entry Mode', *Journal of International Marketing* **2** (2), 7–27.

Berry, M., 1998, 'Strategic Planning in Small High Tech Firms', *Long Range Planning* **31** (3), 455–466.

Björkman, I. and S. Kock, 1997, 'Inward International Activities of Service Firms-Illustrated by Three Cases From the Tourism Industry', *International Journal of Service Industry Management* **8** (5), 363–376.

Bonaccorsi, A., 1992, 'On the Relationship Between Firm Size and Export Intensity', *Journal of International Business Studies* **4** (4), 605–635.

Boter, H. and C. Holmquist, 1996, 'Industry Characteristics and Internationalization Processes in Small Firms', *Journal of Business Venturing* **11** (6), 471–487.

Bowen, D., 1986, 'A World Guide to Export Services', *Business*, June, 55–62.

Brock, J.K-U., 2000, 'Virtual Globals—Marketspace and the Internationalisation of Small Technology-Based Firms', *Unpublished Doctoral Dissertation*, Scotland: University of Strathclyde.

Brush, G.G., 1992, 'Factors Motivating Small Firms to Internationalize: The Effects of Firm Age', *Unpublished Doctoral Dissertation*, USA: Boston University.

Buckley, P.J., 1983, 'Government-Industry Relations in Exporting: Lessons from the United Kingdom' in M.R. Czinkota (ed.), *Export Promotion, the Public and Private Sector Interaction*, New York: Praeger, pp. 89–109.

Buckley, P., D. Newbould, and J. Thurwell, 1979, 'Going International—The Foreign Direct Investment Decisions of Smaller UK Firms', *EIBA Proceedings*, Uppsala, pp. 72–87.

Camino, D., 1991, 'Export Promotion in Spain and other EEC Countries: Systems and Performance', in F.H.R. Seringhaus and P.J. Rosson (eds.), *Export Development and Promotion: The Role of Public Organisations*, Boston: Kluwer Academic Publishers, pp. 119–144.

Cannon, T. and M. Willis, 1981, 'The Smaller Firm in International Trade', *European Small Business Journal* **1** (3), 45–55.

Cavusgil, S.T., 1983, 'Public Policy Implications of Research on the Export Behaviour of Firms', *Akron Business and Economic Review* **14** (3), 16–22.

Chadee, D. and J. Mattsson, 1998, 'Do Service and Merchandise Exporters Behave and Perform Differently?', *European Journal of Marketing* **32** (9/10), 830–842.

Coviello, N.E. and A. McAuley, 1999, 'Internationalization and the Smaller Firm: A Review of Contemporary Empirical Research', *Management International Review* **39** (3), 223–256.

Coviello, N.E. and H. Munro, 1997, 'Network Relationships and the Internationalization Process of Small Software Firms', *International Business Review* **6** (4), 361–386.

Coviello, N.E., 1994, 'Internationalizing the Entrepreneurial High Technology, Knowledge-Intensive Firm', *Unpublished Ph.D. Dissertation*, New Zealand: University of Auckland.

Crick, D. and M. Jones, 2000, 'Small High Technology Firms and International High Technology Markets', *Journal of International Marketing* **8** (2), 63–85.

Czinkota, M.R., 1994, 'A National Export Assistance Policy for New and Growing Businesses', *Journal of International Marketing* **2** (1), 91–101.

Denis, J.E. and D. Depelteau, 1985, 'Market Knowledge Diversification and Export Expansion', *Journal of International Business Studies* **16** (3), 77–89.

Diamantopoulos, A., B.B. Schlegelmilch, and K.Y. Katy Tse, 1993, 'Understanding the Role of Export Marketing Assistance: Empirical Evidence and Research Needs', *European Journal of Marketing* 27, 5–18.

EIM/ENSR, 1993, '*European Observatory for SME's: First Annual Report*', *Economisch Instituut vor het Midden-en Kleinbedrijf*, Holland: Zoetermeer.

Elkjaer, B., 2000, 'Learning and Getting to Know, the Case of Knowledge Workers', *Human Resource Development International* 3 (3), 343–359.

Ellis, P.D. and A. Pecotich, 1998, 'Export Marketing: Historical Development and Theoretical Integration', in G. Ogunmokun and R. Gabbay (eds.), *Contemporary Issues in International Business*, Western Australia: Academic Press International, pp. 1–40.

Elvey, L.A., 1990, 'Export Promotion and Assistance: A Comparative Analysis', in S.T. Cavusgil and M.R. Czinkota (eds.), *International Perspectives on Trade Promotion*, Westport, CT: Quorum Books, pp. 133–148.

Ericsson, K.J., A. Majkgård, and D.D. Sharma, 2001, 'Time and Experience in the Internationalization Process', *Zeitschrift Für Betreibwirtschaft*, http://www.zfb-online.de/.

Ericsson, K., J. Johanson, A. Majkgård, and D.D. Sharma, 2000, 'Effects of Variation on Knowledge Accumulation in the Internationalization Process', *International Studies of Management and Organisation* 30 (1), 26–44.

Erramilli, M.K. and C.P. Rao, 1994, 'Service Firm's International Entry Mode Choice: A Modified Transaction-Cost Analysis Approach', *Journal of Marketing* 57, 19–38.

Erramilli, M.K. and C.P. Rao, 1991, 'The Experience Factor in Foreign Market Entry Behaviour of Service Firms', *Journal of International Business Studies* Fall, 479–501.

Fletcher, R., 2001, 'A Holistic Approach to Internationalisation', *International Business Review* 10 (1), 25–49.

Grant R.M., 1991, 'The Resource-Based Theory of Competitive Advantage: Implications for Strategy Formulation', *California Management Review* Spring, 114–135.

Grönroos, C., 1999, 'Internationalization Strategies for Services', *Journal of Services Marketing* 13 (4/5), 290–297.

Harveston, P.D., 2000, 'Internationalization of Born Global and Gradual Globalizing Firms', *Unpublished Doctoral Dissertation*, University of Memphis, Memphis, Tenn.

Howard, D.G. and I.M. Herremans, 1988, 'Sources of Assistance for Small Business Exporters: Advice from Successful Firms', *Journal of Small Business Management* 26 (3), 48–54.

Jain, S., 1996, 'Problems in International Protection of Intellectual Property', *Journal of International Marketing* 4 (1), 9–32.

Johanson, J. and L.-G. Mattsson, 1988, 'Internationalization in Industrial Systems—A Network Approach', in N. Hood and J-E. Vahlne (eds.), *Strategies in Global Competition*, London: Croom Helm, pp. 287–314.

Johanson, J. and J-E. Vahlne, 1992, 'Management of Foreign Market Entry', *Scandinavian International Business Review* 1 (3), 9–27.

Jolly, V., M. Alahuhta, and J. Jeannet, 1992, 'Challenging the Incumbents: How High Technology Start-ups Compete Globally', *Journal of Strategic Change* 1, 71–82.

Jones, M.V., 1999, 'The Internationalisation of Small UK High Technology Based Firms', *Journal of International Marketing* 7 (4), 15–41.

Julien, P.-A., A. Joyal, L. Deshaies, and V. Ramangalahy, 1997, 'A Typology of Strategic Export Behaviour Among Small and Medium-Sized Exporting Businesses. A Case Study', *International Small Business Journal* 15 (2), 33–49.

Kaynak, E. and L. Stevenson, 1982, 'Export Orientation of Nova Scotia Manufacturers', in M.R. Czinkota and G. Tesar (eds.), *Export Management*, New York: Praeger, pp. 132–145.

Kedia, B.L. and J.S. Chhokar, 1986, 'An Empirical Investigation of Export Promotion Programs', *Columbia Journal of World Business*, Winter, 13–20.

Kedia, B.L., 2000, 'Internationalization of Born Global and Gradual Globalizing Firms: The Impact of Firm Strategy, Technology Intensity, and International Entrepreneurial Orientation', *Paper Presented at AOM Annual Meetings*, Academy of Management, Toronto, Canada, August 4–9.

Knight, G. and Cavusgil, S. Tamer, 1996, 'The Born Global Firm: A Challenge to Traditional Internationalization Theory', *Advances in International Marketing* **8**, Jai Press, 11–26.

Knight, G., 1999, 'International Services Marketing: Review of Research, 1980–1998', *Journal of Services Marketing* **13** (4/5), 347–360.

Kumar, V. and V. Subramaniam, 1997. 'A Contingency Framework For the Mode of Entry Decision', *Journal of World Business* **32** (1), 53–72.

Leonidou, L.C. and C.S. Katsikeas, 1996, 'The Export Development Process: An Integrative Review of Empirical Models', *Journal of International Business Studies* **27** (3), 517–551.

Lindqvist, M., 1988, 'Internationalization of Small Technology Based Firms: Three Illustrative Case Studies on Swedish Firms', *Stockholm School of Economicsm, Research Paper 88/15*.

Lovelock, C.H., 1999, 'Developing Marketing Strategies for Transnational Service Operations', *Journal of Services Marketing* **13** (4/5), 278–295.

Luostarinen, R.K., 1979, *The Internationalization of the Firm*, Helsinki: Acta Academic Oeconomicae Helsingiensis.

Madsen, T. and P. Servais, 1997, 'The Internationalization of Born Globals: An Evolutionary Process?' *International Business Review* **6** (6), 561–583.

McAuley, A., 1992, 'The Perceived Usefulness of Export Information Sources', *European Journal of Marketing* **27** (10), 52–64.

McIntyre, F. and S. Huszagh, 1995, 'Internationalization of Franchise Systems', *Journal of International Marketing* **3** (4), 39–56.

McDougall, P.P., S. Shane, and B.M. Oviatt, 1994, 'Explaining the Formation of International New Ventures: The Limits of Theories From International Business Research', *Journal of Business Venturing* **9**, 469–487.

McKinsey and Co., 1993, *Emerging Exporters: Australia's High Value-Added Manufacturing Exporters* Melbourne: Australian Manufacturing Council.

McNaughton, R., 2001, 'The Export Mode Decision-Making Process in Small Knowledge-Intensive Firms', *Marketing Intelligence and Planning* **19** (1), 12–20.

Melin, L., 1992, 'Internationalization as a Strategy Process', *Strategic Management Journal* **13**, 99–118.

Oesterle, M-J., 1997, 'Time Span Until Internationalization: Foreign Market Entry as a Built-In Mechanism of Innovation', *Management International Review* **37** (2), 125–149.

OECD, 1997, *Globalization and Small and Medium Enterprises*, Organisation for Co-operation and Development, Paris.

Oviatt, B.M. and P.P. McDougall, 1994, 'Toward a Theory of International New Ventures', *Journal of International Business Studies* **25** (1), 45–64.

Pointon, T., 1978, 'Measuring the Gains from Government Export Promotion', *European Journal of Marketing* **12** (6), 451–462.

Ranft, A.L. and M.D. Lord, 2000, 'Acquiring New Knowledge: The Role of Retaining Human Capital in Acquisitions of High-Tech Firms', *The Journal of High Technology Management Research* **11** (2), 295–319.

Reid, S.D., 1983, 'Firm Internationalization, Transaction Costs and Strategic Choice', *International Marketing Review* **1** (2), 45–55.

Rosson, P.J. and Seringhaus, F.H.R., 1991, 'Export Promotion and Public Organisations: Present and Future Research' in F.H.R. Seringhaus and P.J. Rosson (eds.), *Export Development and Promotion: The Role of Public Organisations*, Boston, MA: Kluwer, pp. 319–339.

Rosson, P.J., 1984, 'Success Factors in Manufacturer-Overseas Distributor Relationships in International Marketing', in Kaynak, E. (ed.), *International Marketing Management* New York: Praeger, pp. 91–107.

Samiee, S., 1999, 'The Internationalization of Services: Tends, Obstacles and Issues', *Journal of Services Marketing* **13** (4/5), 319–336.

Seringhaus, F.H.R., 1986, 'The Impact of Government Export Marketing Assistance', *International Marketing Review* **3** (2), 55–65.

Seringhaus, F.H.R., 1987, 'Export Promotion: The Role and Impact of Government Services', *Irish Marketing Review* **2**, 106–116.

Seringhaus, F.H.R. and G. Botschen, 1990, 'Cross National Comparison of the Export Promotion Services and their Usage by Canadian and Austrian Companies', *Proceedings of the 19th European Marketing Academy Conference*, 1563–1582.

Seringhaus, F.H.R. and P.J. Rosson, 1990, *Government Export Promotion: A Global Perspective*, London: Routledge, p. 295.

Seringhaus, F.H.R. and P.J. Rosson, 1991, 'Export Promotion and Public Organisations: The State of the Art', in F.H.R. Seringhaus and P.J. Rosson (eds.), *Export Development and Promotion: The Role of Public Organisations*, Boston, MA: Kluwer Academic Publishers, pp. 3–18.

Sharma, D.D. and J. Johanson, 1987, 'Technical Consultancy in Internationalization', *International Marketing Review*, Winter, 20–29.

Shrader, R.C., B.M. Oviatt, and P.P. McDougall, 2000, 'How New Ventures Exploit Trade-Offs Among International Risk Factors: Lessons for the Accelerated Internationalization of the 21st Century', *Academy of Management Journal* **43** (6): 1227–1247.

Stauss, B. and P. Mang, 1999, 'Culture Shocks' in Inter-Cultural Service Encounters', *Journal of Services Marketing* **13** (4/5), 329–346.

Turnbull, P.W., 1987, 'A Challenge to the Stages Theory of the Internationalization Process', in P.J. Rosson and S.D. Reid (eds.), *Managing Export Entry and Expansion*, New York: Praeger, pp. 21–40.

UNCTAD/ITC, 1986, *Selected Export Promotion Organisations: Structures, Functions and Activities*, International Trade Centre UNCTAD/GATT, Geneva.

UNCTAD/ITC, 1988, *Profile of Trade Promotion Organisations*, International Trade Centre UNCTAD/GATT, Geneva.

US SBA, 1993, 'The Wide World of International Trade', *Small Business Success* **6**, 30–42.

Vatne, E., 1995, 'Local Resource Mobilization and Internationalization Strategies in Small and Medium Sized Enterprises', *Environment and Planning A* **27**, 63–80.

Walters, P.G.P., 1983, 'Export Information Sources—A Study of their Usage and Utility', *International Marketing Review* **1** (2), 34–43.

Wernerfelt, B., 1984, 'A Resource-Based View of the Firm', *Strategic Management Journal* **5**, 171–180.

Woodcock, P.C., P.W. Beamish, and S. Makino, 1994, 'Ownership-Based Entry Mode Strategies and International Performance', *Journal of International Business Studies* **25** (2), 253–273.

Yeoh, P.-L. and I. Jeong, 1995, 'Contingency Relationships Between Entrepreneurship, Export Channel Structure and Environment', *European Journal of Marketing* **29** (8), 95–115.

Yip, G.S., J.G. Biscarri, and J.A. Monti, 2000, 'The Role of the Internationalization Process in the Performance of Newly Internationalizing Firms', *Journal of International Marketing* **8** (3), 10–35.

Yli-Renko, H., E. Autio, and H. Sapienza, 2001, 'Social Capital, Knowledge Acquisition, and Knowledge Exploitation in Young Technology-Based Firms', *Strategic Management Journal* **22** (6–7), 587–613.

[2]

ELSEVIER   Journal of Business Venturing 19 (2004) 485–508

JOURNAL
of BUSINESS
VENTURING

Methodological issues in international entrepreneurship research ☆

Nicole E. Coviello[a,*], Marian V. Jones[b,1]

[a]*Department of Marketing, University of Auckland, Private Bag 92019, Auckland, New Zealand*
[b]*Department of Business and Management, University of Glasgow, Gilbert Scott Building (5th floor),
Western Quadrangle, University Avenue, Glasgow, Scotland G12 8QQ, UK*

Received 1 June 2002; received in revised form 1 April 2003; accepted 1 June 2003

Abstract

Empirical research in the emerging field of international entrepreneurship (IE) is assessed to provide insight as to the 'state of the art' of IE methodologies. Fifty-five articles were systematically analyzed focusing on time frame and research context, sample characteristics, data collection/analysis procedures, and equivalence issues. Results indicate both strengths and weaknesses in IE methods. The authors present implications for developing a unifying methodological direction in the field and the evolution of a truly multidisciplinary approach. They also outline the need for dynamic research designs that integrate positivist with interpretivist methodologies and incorporate time as a key dimension. Finally, they discuss the need for better IE sampling frames and call for more effort in establishing and reporting equivalence in cross-national studies.
© 2003 Elsevier Inc. All rights reserved.

Keywords: International entrepreneurship; Research; Methodological issues

---

☆ A previous version of this paper was presented at the 2002 Small Business and Enterprise Development Conference, Nottingham, UK.
 * Corresponding author. Tel.: +64-9-373-7599x87213.
 E-mail addresses: n.coviello@auckland.ac.nz (N.E. Coviello), m.v.jones@mgt.gla.ac.uk (M.V. Jones).
 [1] Tel.: +44-141-330-3316.

486   *N.E. Coviello, M.V. Jones / Journal of Business Venturing 19 (2004) 485–508*

1. Executive Summary

As defined by McDougall and Oviatt (2000, p. 903), international entrepreneurship (IE) is: "...a combination of innovative, proactive and risk-seeking behavior that crosses national borders and is intended to create value in organizations...the study of IE includes research on such behavior and research comparing domestic entrepreneurial behavior in multiple countries."

This paper reviews and assesses fifty-five empirical studies within the emerging field of IE, providing insight as to the 'state of the art' of IE methodologies. The articles were systematically analyzed focusing on research context and time frame, sample characteristics, data collection/analysis procedures, and equivalence issues.

The results indicate that in terms of context, IE research has a rich international perspective with cross-national collaboration evident in research teams. To date, IE studies have generated a definable pool of manufacturing and high-technology studies for comparative examination. The extant literature also reflects efforts to integrate the international and entrepreneurship fields and has expanded beyond an SME focus. At the same time, IE research is characterized by static, cross-sectional studies, and a lack of service sector research and/or comparative research within and across sectors. Studies tend to favor either the international or entrepreneurship side of the theoretical interface, and the extant research is characterized by inconsistent use of measures and definitions of key variables such as firm size and age. As regards sample characteristics, IE studies focus on relevant micro level units of analysis by collecting readily obtainable data. Typically, they also have carefully selected samples with high response rates, and the views of the lead decision maker pertaining to IE issues are captured. However, by focusing on obtainable data, 'important' yet harder to obtain data are generally lacking (e.g., research on complex entrepreneurial internationalization behaviors over time). The emphasis on judgement-based or purposive sampling also means that results are difficult to generalize, and IE research lacks the rich perspective provided by multiple informants involved with various entrepreneurial processes.

In terms of data collection and analysis, the IE literature has applied a range of methods with a relatively high level of sophistication and rigor. At the same time, studies tend to focus on aggregate level survey data or sector-specific qualitative data. As a result, complex processes are not captured, unless at a very narrow level. The review also shows that IE research falls short in ensuring sample, instrument, and data collection equivalence across countries. This could reflect a lack of reporting on equivalence or a lack of attention to this issue from the outset of research investigations. This is a major concern given IE research, by definition, may involve cross-national studies.

Based on these findings, the authors suggest that while a 'single' methodological direction is inappropriate to IE research, it is important to develop a commonly understood IE vocabulary that allows for comparison between studies. This would contribute to a unifying methodological direction. Researchers also need to increase cross-disciplinary collaboration to resolve the imbalance in knowledge contribution between the fields of international business and entrepreneurship. Methodologically, the authors suggest that IE would benefit from a process of research or series of complementary studies rather than static, isolated pieces of work. This reflects Patton's (2002) view of the holistic perspective in the sense of 'understanding the whole process.' Such an approach would encompass multiple data sources, applying both coarse-grained methods that result in generalizable, statistically significant data and fine-grained methods that capture the nuance, context, and rich understanding of the phenomena in question. This would also allow for collection of both 'obtainable' and 'important' data.

It is also hoped that future developments of the IE field will be marked by a growth in the number of studies utilizing and developing longitudinal methodologies. This is important since the dimension of time has been stressed as fundamental to isolating key developments in studies of internationalization (Buckley and Chapman, 1996; Andersen, 1997) and to studies of entrepreneurial behavior and other processes (Chandler and Lyon, 2001). Finally, a fundamental challenge for IE research is that firms with international activity need to be properly identified, yet there is a lack of quality sampling frames available. To some extent, this contributes to the preponderance of judgement and purposive sampling, and an apparent reluctance to document the sampling design and procedure. However, as significant effort is required to capture and list entrepreneurial firms, the authors suggest a more pragmatic approach would be to accept the use of judgement sampling, provided sampling criteria are well and consistently specified and the data are assessed for validity and reliability.

2. Introduction

This work is positioned at the intersection of the international business and entrepreneurship research paths; an intersection described by McDougall and Oviatt (2000) as the emerging field of IE. IE research is increasingly visible, yet McDougall and Oviatt (2000) argue that work in the area lacks a unifying and clear methodological direction. Thus, the primary objectives of this paper are to (1) review and assess the methodological aspects of the emerging IE literature, (2) offer insight as to the 'state of the art' of IE methods, and (3) discuss the implications for future development of the field.

3. Method

This review is focused on empirical literature representing McDougall and Oviatt's (2000, p. 903) definition of IE as "...a combination of innovative, proactive and risk-seeking behavior that crosses national borders and is intended to create value in organizations...the study of IE includes research on such behavior and research comparing domestic entrepreneurial behavior in multiple countries."

At a general level, studies eligible for review were those explicitly integrating theory and concepts from both 'international business' and 'entrepreneurship.' At a more specific level, some studies were specifically positioned to the international new venture literature or focused on entrepreneurial behavior across borders. Other investigations compared entrepreneurship across countries and cultures. The studies could be conducted at the individual, firm, group, or organization levels (as per McDougall and Oviatt, 2000) and were not restricted to small or new ventures. Furthermore, each study needed to include sufficient information regarding its methodology to allow for a thorough review and assessment.

Articles excluded from the review included those with a focus on 'international SMEs' rather than IE per se (i.e., while they studied small- and medium-sized firms, entrepreneurship issues or theory were not integrated or addressed). While we acknowledge the role played by the SME internationalization literature in establishing the IE field, the focus of this review, for sake of parsimony, is on those studies directly and explicitly integrating the fields of entrepreneurship and international business. Examples of the international SME work excluded from the review include that of Haug (1991), Erramilli and D'Souza (1993), Bell (1995), Korhonen et al. (1996), Roberts and Senturia (1996), Coviello and Munro (1997), Barringer and Greening (1998), Holmlund and Kock (1998), O'Farrell et al. (1998), Liesch and Knight (1999), Prasad (1999), Lautanen (2000), Chen and Martin (2001), de Chiara and Minguzzi (2002), Lamb and Liesch (2002), and Nakos and Brouthers (2002). For similar reasons, studies focused on SME exporting were excluded (e.g., Beamish et al., 1993; Bijmolt and Zwart, 1994; Burpitt and Rondinelli, 2000), as were studies comparing internationalization by firm size (e.g., Bonaccorsi, 1992; Calof, 1993, 1994; Moen, 2000).

The given IE research is also defined to include internationally comparative studies of entrepreneurial behavior; research focused on domestic entrepreneurship in a single foreign country was excluded (e.g., Lyles et al., 1996; Kuznetsov and McDonald, 2000; Ardichvili, 2001; Bliss and Garratt, 2001; Etemad and Salmasi, 2001; Ahlstrom and Bruton, 2002; Bruton and Rubanki, 2002). Similarly, cross-cultural assessments of entrepreneurial orientation measures were excluded (Knight, 1997; Busenitz et al., 2000; Kreiser et al., 2002). This is because all three studies focus on scale development or validation rather than behavioral research.

Beyond these studies, we identified a number of investigations of general interest to IE researchers but with an emphasis other than IE per se. For example, Larson (1991), Hara and Kanai (1994), and Lipparini and Sobrero (1994) emphasize network relationships or strategic alliances rather than IE. Zahra et al. (1997) focus on environmental influences in the general context of new ventures, while Barkema and Vermeulen (1998) emphasize the relationship between learning and the acquisition versus start-up decision in foreign markets. Also, Madhok and Osegowitsch (2000) study the international diffusion of technology using the dynamic capabilities perspective. Given the parameters of this review, all these studies were excluded from the review process. Finally, non-empirical papers including Madsen and Servais (1997), Zacharakis (1997), and Tiessen (1997) were not part of the review.

To identify relevant IE articles, we conducted a keyword search on ProQuest/ABI Inform encompassing 1988–2002. Keywords included 'international new ventures,' 'IE,' 'INV(s),' 'Oviatt,' 'McDougall,' 'global startups,' 'born globals,' 'international,' and 'entrepreneurship.' To ensure thorough coverage, we also conducted a manual review of three general sources. First, we reviewed the 1996–2002 volumes of the *Journal of Business Venturing* and *Entrepreneurship Theory and Practice*, acknowledged as the leading entrepreneurship journals (Romano and Ratanatunga, 1997; Chandler and Lyon, 2001). Second, we reviewed the *Journal of International Business Studies*, *Management International Review*, *Academy of Management Journal*, and *Strategic Management Journal*. These are generally considered to be the leading peer-reviewed journals in international business and management/strategy.

Third, we identified and reviewed articles from the McGill Conferences on IE published in special issues of the *Journal of International Management, Journal of International Marketing, Small Business Economics, Journal of Euro-Marketing,* and *Global Focus.* Finally, we identified other articles through additional electronic searches and manual cross referencing. Research published in edited books and conference proceedings was excluded as not all these sources are widely accessible and/or peer reviewed.

3.1. Process of review

Once an article was identified, it was assessed for eligibility using the criteria previously outlined. This resulted in fifty-five articles. Each was examined using content analysis, guided by a rating form based on similar reviews by Leonidou and Katsikeas (1996), Coviello and McAuley (1999), Chandler and Lyon (2001), and Zahra and George (2002). The focus of our review was on the methodology employed. This was assessed in relation to four categories:

1. Time frame and context issues: fieldwork time frame, geographic focus, industry scope, firm size, and firm age;
2. Sample issues: unit of analysis, sampling design, sample criteria, sample size, and key informant;
3. Data collection and analysis issues: approach to data collection and analytical approach;
4. Cross-national equivalence issues: sample equivalence, instrument equivalence and data analysis equivalence.

4. Results

As summarized in Table 1, the early empirical literature pertaining to IE began with McDougall's foundation study in 1989, followed by Kolvereid et al. (1993). More studies emerged in 1995/1996, including those published in a special issue of *Entrepreneurship Theory and Practice.* IE research continued to be somewhat sporadic until 1999, when the first publications from the inaugural McGill IE conference appeared in the *Journal of International Marketing.* 2000 was a banner year for the field with 17 articles, 10 of which were found in special issues of the *Academy of Management Journal* and *Journal of International Marketing.* In 2002, IE articles appeared in a variety of journals although that year, a special issue on culture and entrepreneurship in *Entrepreneurship Theory and Practice* contributed the most articles to the field. Overall, the IE literature is most common in the leading entrepreneurship journals (*Journal of Business Venturing* and *Entrepreneurship Theory and Practice*) and in special issues.

Turning to the studies in question, this review assessed the fifty-five articles summarized in Appendix 1 that (1) examined entrepreneurial behavior crossing international boundaries ($n = 39$) and (2) compared domestic entrepreneurial behavior in different countries ($n = 16$). These two groups of studies reflect the core aspects of McDougall and Oviatt's (2000)

490   N.E. Coviello, M.V. Jones / Journal of Business Venturing 19 (2004) 485–508

Table 1
Summary of IE articles by source and year

Year	Entrepreneurship		Strategy		International[a]	McGill special issues		Small Business Economics	Global Focus	Journal of International Management	Other	
	Journal of Business Venturing	Entrepreneurship Theory and Practice	Academy of Mgmt Journal	Strategic Mgmt Journal	Journal of International Business Studies	Journal of International Marketing	Journal of Euro-Marketing	Small Business Economics	Global Focus	Journal of International Management	Other	TOT
2002	1	5			1	1					3	10
2001	1		1	1	1			1		3	1	9
2000	2	1	5				1				2	17
1999						5						6
1998	1					3			2		1	2
1997	1	1									1	4
1996	1	2			1							3
1995											2	2
1994												
1993											1	1
1992												
1991												
1990												
1989	1											1
TOTAL	8	10	6	1	3	9	1	1	2	3	10	55

[a] Management International Review was not included in this summary table as no relevant articles were identified for the review.

definition of IE. Using the four previously defined assessment categories, the key patterns relating to IE methodology will now be presented.

4.1. Time frame/context issues

4.1.1. Fieldwork time frame

Only 5 of the 55 studies reviewed are longitudinal. Twenty-six are based on cross-sectional/single-year data. The other twenty-four studies are assumed to be cross-sectional based on how the data are collected and presented (although no dates are given). This pattern supports the observations made by Zahra and George (2002) regarding IE research and Chandler and Lyon (2001) regarding entrepreneurship studies. The bulk of IE research is therefore static, does not incorporate time-dependent variables (or time), and would have difficulty in revealing process over time rather than behavior at a given point in time.

4.1.2. Geographic focus

The IE literature is rich in geographic coverage at two levels: (1) the range of countries studied and (2) the researchers involved. At a country level, most IE studies focus on firms or entrepreneurs in single countries such as the United States (12), United Kingdom (6), and Canada (5). Similar investigations (10) are found in countries such as Nigeria, Slovenia, Portugal, Finland, and New Zealand. This single-country focus might suggest a certain amount of ethnocentrism in the field. However, three studies use either the United States or United Kingdom as a base from which to study different cultures within those countries, and seven studies compare two or three countries. Twelve studies incorporate 4–15 countries. This development of multicountry investigations is a pattern different from that identified by Zahra and George's (2002) review of IE research, which found only a few non-U.S. samples and a preponderance of single-country studies. It also varies from Coviello and McAuley's (1999) conclusions regarding SME internationalization studies given they also found a lack of multicountry studies. Overall, this is a positive trend for the IE field.

At the researcher level, the IE literature seems to reflect the globalization of business research noted by Wright and Ricks (1994), as studies are authored by scholars around the world. Although the fact that 31 studies involve U.S.-based authors might suggest American dominance of the field, only 18 of these are by 'Americans only' (in terms of university affiliation). An important point therefore is that the remaining 13 studies with U.S. authors involve cross-national collaboration. There are also 6 other examples of cross-national collaboration involving teams from different countries, 10 studies with UK authors only, and eight studies with research teams from countries such as Canada, Norway, and Sweden.

4.1.3. Industry scope/coverage

Fifteen studies focus on entrepreneurs or potential entrepreneurs as the unit of analysis, and thus an industry/sector focus is not specified. Of those remaining, 28 investigate manufacturers. Only one study examines service firms, three look at both goods and services, and one study defines its sectors as 'knowledge intensive' versus 'traditional,' but it is unclear if these are manufacturing firms. Seven studies fail to specify the sector of interest. This overall emphasis on manufacturing firms is also observed by Zahra and George (2002) and is found in the general international business literature (Leonidou and Katsikeas, 1996). This suggests that other settings (e.g., service firms) and comparative studies need examination.

In terms of technology, 22 studies focus their examination on high-technology firms. This emphasis is perhaps not surprising given the trends in both the international and entrepreneurship literatures, and it has generated a pool of high-technology studies available for comparison. A number of studies also focus on low-technology firms (9 studies) or a mix of low- and high-technology firms (8 studies). The remaining studies either fail to indicate technology level or this was irrelevant to the research. Interestingly, while Zahra and George (2002) suggest that the concentration of research on high-technology samples limits the ability to generalize to other industries, our review shows some diversity in the field. However, we agree with Zahra and George's (2002) call for investigations beyond high-technology samples.

4.1.4. Firm size

Two measures are most commonly used to capture firm size. The first is number of employees (40 studies), and the second is sales level (25 studies). Often, both measures are used. In addition to reporting sales and/or employee levels, 14 studies also measure firm size using percent of sales in export markets. Just over half the studies (29) have an SME focus of fewer than 200 employees. Furthermore, most of these studies examine firms with less than 100 employees. In contrast, six studies examine very large organizations while five studies use firms with the number of employees ranging from small to large. The remainder either fail to specify firm size or it is irrelevant to the study (e.g., studies on potential entrepreneurs).

4.1.5. Firm age

For the studies reporting venture age, there is a reasonable amount of diversity. For example, eight studies examine firms averaging less than 6 years of age, six studies look at 7- to 10-year-old firms, seven investigate 11- to 12-year-old firms, and six examine firms older than 20 years. This is perhaps reflective of the developing nature of the field as researchers struggle to establish commonly used criteria for firm choice based on venture age. Increasingly, it appears that 6 years is the cut-off used to define an international new venture.

4.2. Sample issues

4.2.1. Unit of analysis

The identifiable pattern shows the primary unit of analysis to be 'the firm' (32 studies) followed by 'the entrepreneur' (11 studies). In addition, four studies examine 'potential' entrepreneurs and five examine both the firm and entrepreneur. Single studies focus their analysis on (e.g.) business links or a combined industry/firm/individual level. Overall, the patterns regarding unit of analysis reflect those identified in the entrepreneurship literature by Chandler and Lyon (2001) and Davidsson and Wiklund (2001) in that IE research is dominated by micro level analysis. Similarly, the emphasis on the firm level reflects the pattern noted by Leonidou and Katsikeas (1996) in their review of the export development

N.E. Coviello, M.V. Jones / Journal of Business Venturing 19 (2004) 485–508   493

literature. One might also conclude, similar to Davidsson and Wiklund (2001), that IE researchers have focused on collecting 'obtainable' rather than 'important' data. As such, IE research on complex networks, clusters, or behavioral processes over time is relatively rare.

4.2.2. Sampling design

This issue is generally poorly addressed in the IE literature in that articles provide only limited discussion regarding the decision to (1) use a probability versus non-probability sample and (2) the specific procedures associated with such designs. Thirty-nine studies selected their sample/sites in a purposive and judgement-based manner, and these studies are non-probability in nature. Twelve studies use random selection, and four did not provide enough information to analyze this issue. The dominance of judgement-based samples is perhaps a cause for concern in that the results are less able to be generalized. Indeed, Zahra and George (2002) call for more representative samples in IE research. At the same time, the judgement-sample studies reviewed here all had high response rates and participation levels and as such might be expected to have good quality, albeit sample-specific, results.

4.2.3. Sample criteria

Explicit criteria for sample selection are found in fifty-two studies and are summarized in Table 2. Of these, 13 studies specify only one criterion, but the remainder include two criteria (11 studies), three criteria (8 studies), four criteria (12 studies), five criteria (7 studies), and even seven criteria (1 study). The most common criteria clearly reflect firm characteristics and are as follows: (1) firm size, (2) firm age, and (3) sector. The inclusion of explicit selection criteria is useful to the IE field in that research equivalence can be assessed across studies. As discussed by VanderWerf and Brush (1989) in the context of entrepreneurship, this helps achieve empirical progress in an undefined field. However, further formalization of

Table 2
Common criteria for IE sample selection

Criterion	Count	Percent of firms[a]
Firm size	21	38
Firm age	18	33
Sector	16	29
Serving export markets	12	22
Technology level (e.g., high, low)	10	18
Private or independent firm	10	18
Indigenous firm	7	13
Potential entrepreneurs	5	9
Founder managed	5	9
Access to respondents	4	7
Revenue level	4	7
New or start-up firm	3	5
IPO within a specified time frame	3	5
Other	20	36

[a] Percentages sum to greater than 100 as most studies use multiple criteria.

494   *N.E. Coviello, M.V. Jones / Journal of Business Venturing 19 (2004) 485–508*

criteria for both firm and entrepreneur-level research would be helpful. For example, in the studies where firm size is included as a criterion for sample selection, 'size' is specified using different measures (e.g., number of employees vs. sales revenue), and there is a range of categories within measures. That is, smaller firms can be less than 50 employees, less than 100 employees, less than 200 employees, or less than 500 employees. The same occurs for firm age. Thus, on one hand, we see fairly tightly defined sampling criteria, but on the other, inconsistency within these criteria. Generalization of findings and pooling of data is thus hampered.

4.2.4. Sample size

Again, this issue is discussed inconsistently in the IE literature, both in terms of targeted sample size and response rates. At a broad level, if the study applies case research or personal interviews, the general pattern suggests that 3–30 firms are studied. Surveys reported on 30–3600 responses, with half receiving less than 200 usable responses. IE research is therefore not generally characterized as using large samples in spite of the criticism of small sample studies found in the entrepreneurship, export, and IE literatures (e.g., Zahra and George, 2002). Leonidou and Katsikeas (1996, p. 531) also imply that case studies of (e.g.) four firms make 'cautious interpretation of findings necessary' and go on to say that "...a serious methodological flaw inherent in this type of small sample research is the sparse distribution of the overall sample of firms." However, our view follows Smith et al. (1989) by arguing that if the research problem necessitates rich deep information, then a small set of case studies are appropriate providing that generalizability is not assumed. Similarly, if high-quality survey data are obtainable from a smaller sample drawn using well-developed selection criteria, meaningful findings can still result.

4.2.5. Key informant

Beyond the small number of studies using student samples or archival data, the key informant in firm level studies is usually the president/VP/managing director (21) or founder/owner/manager (16). These individuals may actually be one and the same but are specified differently across studies. Regardless, most studies acknowledge the importance of accessing the informant who retains institutional history and influence as regards IE. In contrast, the international/export literature suggests a broader perspective is more relevant (e.g., Leonidou and Katsikeas, 1996), turning to the wider management team or other parties such as clients, suppliers, or venture capital investors. This breadth is generally lacking in the IE literature as only seven studies used multiple respondents, and only three studies compared respondent views (e.g., entrepreneur vs. investor or entrepreneur vs. executive).

4.3. Data collection and analysis issues

4.3.1. Data collection

There is evidence of a wide range of approaches to data collection, although IE studies are dominated by surveys. These include mail surveys (24 studies), self-administered surveys (6), and combined mail/telephone or mail/personal interview surveys (4). IE researchers also

N.E. Coviello, M.V. Jones / Journal of Business Venturing 19 (2004) 485–508   495

analyze annual reports/IPO prospectives (4 studies) and databases (1 study). Less than a quarter of studies employ qualitative techniques, such as personal interviews (6 studies) or case research (5 studies). Thus, the quantitative approach dominates, mirroring the SME internationalization literature reviewed by Coviello and McAuley (1999).

IE research also tends to be mono method, relying on either quantitative, aggregate-level data, or qualitative context-specific data. Only five studies integrate qualitative and quantitative approaches (Glas et al., 1999; Knight, 2000, 2001; Fillis, 2002; Yli-Renko et al., 2002). Even then, they apply a simple two-step approach, e.g., a discussion of database patterns followed by case studies or interviews followed by a survey. Furthermore, Knight (2000, 2001) and Yli-Renko et al. (2002) report only their survey results, again highlighting the quantitative emphasis.

4.3.2. Analytical approach

If IE research is survey based, the dominant analytical approach involves some form of regression (22 studies), followed by M/ANOVA (9), general descriptive statistics (7 studies), correlation analysis (6 studies), *t* tests (5 studies), factor analysis (4 studies), structural equation modeling (2 studies), cluster analysis (2 studies), and discriminant analysis (1 study). Overall, the analytic approaches are relatively sophisticated (in comparison with using only simple univariate or descriptive statistics) and mirror the patterns identified by both Chandler and Lyon (2001) in the entrepreneurship literature and Leonidou and Katsikeas (1996) in the export literature. This emphasis probably reflects the fact that 34 of the studies involve hypothesis testing and model validation.

For the qualitative IE studies, the general emphasis is on pattern identification/matching and explanation building. They also apply qualitative profiling, event, network, and critical incident analysis, and one is based on grounded theory. These analytic approaches seem appropriate to their research problems and demonstrate innovative methods in an effort to capture the complex processes under investigation (e.g., the event and network analyses).

4.4. Equivalence issues

Critical issues in cross-cultural research relate to establishing equivalence at a number of levels. This review focuses on sample equivalence, instrument equivalence, and data collection equivalence in the context of the 22 IE studies involving multiple countries or cultures.

4.4.1. Sample equivalence

A wide range of nations are studied in the 22 studies; however, only 13 studies identify specific criteria for country/culture selection. Typically, countries are chosen to ensure variance in values across different cultures and a desire for sample heterogeneity (nine studies). Other studies chose the cultures in question because they had a history of successful entrepreneurship (one study), were an interesting or relevant comparator for (e.g.) cultural and national differences (two studies), or provided a broad representation across developing and developed countries (one study). Nine studies fail to explain why the specific countries/

cultures were of interest. This is of some concern given the need for careful culture selection as discussed by Adler (1983) and Nasif et al. (1991).

4.4.2. Instrument equivalence

Green and White (1976) note that researchers have two options in developing their instruments and measures. They can follow an emic (culturally specific) approach or one that is etic (culturally universal), with instruments that are culture-free and, by virtue of formal equivalence, able to be applied across countries. Only 11 of the 22 cross-national IE studies discuss the extent to which their instrument is culture-free or culture-bound. Perhaps more importantly, while three of these studies assess the sensitivity of their instrument and conclude it to be etic in nature, the remaining eight studies seem to simply assume their instrument is culture-free. Various tests for instrument reliability and validity are found in 13 studies, one deems the issue to be irrelevant due to the theory-building nature of the research, and eight cross-cultural studies fail to discuss scale or instrument quality at all.

For those investigations requiring language adaptation and assurance of equivalence of meaning (Adler, 1983; Cavusgil and Das, 1997), 12 studies outline a process of forward/back translation, and one study notes that translation help was used where necessary. Five studies do not discuss how language issues or equivalence in meaning were addressed across countries. Again, in spite of the importance of ensuring instrument equivalence in cross-national investigations, IE research is weak in this area.

4.4.3. Data collection equivalence

The challenge of international data collection is to achieve an equivalent, not identical, process in terms of setting, instructions, timing, and response (Adler, 1983; Nasif et al., 1991). Cavusgil and Das (1997) also note that data collection is impacted by characteristics of the researcher (e.g., their perceived status, authority). Of the 22 studies, only nine try to ensure equivalence in terms of data collection setting, and three studies specifically note the settings to be very different across countries. Ten studies do not discuss the issue. Similarly, only six studies outline procedural details pertaining to instrument administration/interview protocol, and only two of the twenty-two studies comment on equivalence in timing of data collection or the role of the researcher. Thus, data collection equivalence is a final area of concern in IE research.

4.5. Summary

The results indicate that in terms of time frame and context, IE research has a strong international perspective generated by cross-national research teams. To date, IE studies have generated a rich pool of manufacturing and high-technology studies for comparative examination. The extant literature also reflects efforts to integrate the international and entrepreneurship fields and has expanded beyond an SME focus. At the same time, IE research is characterized by static cross-sectional studies and a lack of service sector and/or comparative research within and across sectors. Studies tend to favor either the international or entrepreneurship side of the theoretical interface, and the extant research is characterized by the use of inconsistent definitions and measures of key variables such as firm size and age.

As regards sample characteristics, IE studies focus on relevant micro level units of analysis by collecting readily obtainable data. Typically, they also have carefully selected samples with high response rates, and the views of the primary or lead decision maker as regards IE issues are captured. However, efforts to collect and understand important yet hard to obtain data are generally lacking. The emphasis on judgement-based or purposive sampling means that results are difficult to generalize, and IE research lacks the rich perspective offered by studying multiple parties involved with various entrepreneurial processes.

In terms of data collection and analysis, the IE literature has applied a range of methods with a relatively high level of sophistication and rigor. At the same time, studies tend to focus on aggregate level survey data or sector-specific qualitative data. As a result, complex processes are not captured, unless at a very narrow level. The review also shows that IE research falls short in terms of trying to ensure sample, instrument, and data collection equivalence across countries. This could reflect a lack of reporting on equivalence or a lack of attention to this issue from the outset of research investigations. This is a major concern given that IE research, by definition, may involve cross-national studies.

5. Implications for IE research

A number of implications emerge for IE researchers. We begin with issues that are relatively strategic in nature, including a discussion of the need for a unifying methodological direction, a multidisciplinary approach, pluralism in research design, and accommodation of the complexity of time in IE research. The paper concludes with operational implications regarding sampling design, data collection, and cross-national equivalence issues.

5.1. A unifying and clear methodological direction

At a macro level, the diversity of approaches found in the IE literature suggests that a unifying and clear methodological direction is currently remote. This begs the question as to what precisely is meant by a 'unifying methodological direction'? Furthermore, if such a direction could be clearly defined, would it in fact be a good thing for the development of a new field of study? Some might argue not, citing SME internationalization as an example of a field dominated by survey studies of export behavior and performance (i.e., a unifying direction that has emerged at the expense of other aspects of internationalization). Importantly too, the field of IE is probably too complex and broad in scope to be accommodated by any one model or any one investigation.

Perhaps more relevant to the question is the need for definitional rigor in order to make useful comparisons between studies (McDougall and Oviatt, 2000). This implies that IE researchers need to actively develop a commonly understood vocabulary that will, over time, contribute to the development of robust and comparable methodologies. Issues requiring definitional rigor include firm size and age, industry scope, unit of analysis, type of key

498   *N.E. Coviello, M.V. Jones / Journal of Business Venturing 19 (2004) 485–508*

informant, and sampling criteria. Advances in this area would provide useful guidance to the field. Furthermore, Buckley and Chapman (1996, p. 244) suggest that direction for a field of research might be found in "...developing a set of core concepts which are analytically rigorous and tractable, yet remain flexible." To accomplish this, it is necessary to integrate core concepts from entrepreneurship and international business theory into a flexible yet tractable conceptual model. Definitional rigor in the construction of studies and the reporting of results could then enable separate investigations to fit together like puzzle pieces.

One example of integration draws on Brazeal and Herbert's (1999) rudimentary model of the entrepreneurial process based on how the core concepts of innovation, change, and creativity result in entrepreneurial events. Such a model bears some resemblance to the classic stage and innovation models of internationalization wherein an endogenous or exogenous trigger (change) leads to the adoption of an entry mode in a selected country (innovation). Experiential knowledge and organizational learning also occur, which, coupled with further triggers (creativity), lead to the adoption of more risky and committed modes in psychologically distant countries (internationalization events).

This example suggests that by integrating entrepreneurship and internationalization models, it is possible to develop constructs and measures that are robust, validated, reliable, and clearly positioned within the domain of IE. The unifying effect of a flexible conceptual model, together with definitional rigor and consistency in the use of measures and constructs, would also enable IE researchers to pursue the three possibilities of comparative research as outlined by Buckley et al. (1988). That is (1) historical comparison, i.e., the situation relative to a different point in time; (2) spatial comparison, i.e., the situation relative to a different locational, national, cultural, or regional point; and (3) counter-factual comparison, i.e., the situation as it might have been but for an event, action, or occurrence.

5.2. A multidisciplinary approach

The call for multidisciplinary research has been voiced in international business (Buckley and Chapman, 1996), in studies of internationalization of the smaller firm (Coviello and McAuley, 1999), and now in IE (McDougall and Oviatt, 2000). One of the challenges facing IE researchers in the early stages of this developing field, however, is the need to have a significant level of substantive knowledge in both the international business and entrepreneurship literatures. At the present time, researchers tend to specialize in one discipline or the other, with the result that studies are well constructed and theory based in one field, yet perhaps deficient in the other. Cavusgil and Das (1997) identify a similar pattern in cross-cultural studies where researcher knowledge tends to be specific to his or her own culture. Again, in order to resolve the imbalance in knowledge contribution from different disciplines, collaboration between the international and entrepreneurship fields is sensible.

5.3. Combining positivist and interpretivist methods within a dynamic research design

The bulk of IE research captures data in a logical positivist manner, emphasizing inferential statistics, hypothesis testing, and so on. Overall, the aim of the positivist approach

N.E. Coviello, M.V. Jones / Journal of Business Venturing 19 (2004) 485–508 499

is generally to record, measure, and predict reality through sets of predetermined variables and constructs. This emphasis in the IE literature perhaps reflects a perceived need to provide 'significant' empirical evidence in order to justify research in a new field. Notably, IE studies adopting a more interpretivist approach are few in number. For example, ethnographic or phenomenological research on behavioral processes in international networks is rare. This represents a weakness in a field of study that by definition is concerned with behavior as well as value-creating processes (McDougall and Oviatt, 2000). A fuller understanding of such processes might best be gained through a reconciliation of positivist and interpretivist methodologies.

Such integration is discussed by Miles and Huberman (1994) who argue that a 'realist' approach to investigating social phenomena is possible. This involves accounting for events rather than simply documenting their sequence. That is "...we look for an individual or social process, a mechanism, a structure at the core of events that can be captured to provide a causal description of the forces at work" (Miles and Huberman, 1994, p. 4). This approach may represent a means for IE researchers to reconcile the need for interpretative insight with positivist measurement.

Researchers could also take a social constructivist approach that involves the construction of knowledge about reality and not the construction of reality itself (Shadish, 1995). Following this approach, knowledge construction takes place in the mind of the researcher or observer; hence, the different views of reality proffered by researchers from different disciplinary perspectives such as those contributing to the IE field.

Applying these approaches to an example of IE research, one of the foundation literatures contributing to IE is that on internationalization. This has been extensively examined from a logical positivist perspective, and to a certain extent in parallel, from the interpretivist perspective. One is predominantly static in its approach, the other longitudinal or at least evolutionary. A useful direction for methodological design in the IE field would be to bring these parallel fields together in order to view internationalization more holistically. That is, as an entrepreneurial activity including both the economic and social dimensions, which coexist within any organization and which evolve and change over time. If IE researchers interested in internationalization then view IE as the human, behavioral, individual, or social element that influences or drives internationalization events in an emergent rather than predetermined sequence, research designs need to identify flexible core concepts from the fields of entrepreneurship and international business and use these to build a general dynamic conceptual model of IE. They should then identify internationalization evidence and deconstruct it to its bare components and then reconstruct knowledge about reality from different complementary disciplinary perspectives. Finally, research designs should allow for collection of factual evidence on the reality of internationalization in order to construct patterns of entrepreneurial behavior. This suggests a need for a process of research or a series of complementary studies and multistage studies rather than static isolated pieces of work. A four-stage process of conceptual design, accommodating both positivist and interpretivist methods, might therefore include the following iterative stages: (1) construction, (2) deconstruction, (3) reconstruction, and (4) generalization.

500   *N.E. Coviello, M.V. Jones / Journal of Business Venturing 19 (2004) 485–508*

In this process, construction involves establishing the current relevant set of theories, frameworks, and approaches used to research, examine, and interpret internationalization (Cavusgil and Das, 1997; Brazeal and Herbert, 1999). From that body of knowledge, researchers could identify commonly recognized elements that represent the evidence that internationalization has occurred or is occurring. Deconstruction then involves unraveling the evidence of internationalization in an interdisciplinary fashion into events and sequences that, as far as possible, represent the reality of the process under study (Buckley and Chapman, 1996; Jones, 1999). Reconstruction then ascribes meaning to events and sequences through the investigation of social, economic, and contingent influences on significant events in the life or history of the firm. Approaches might include native categories (Buckley and Chapman, 1997; Harris, 2000), entrepreneurial stories, and time-based secondary data on exogenous events (Stewart et al., 1995). Finally, generalization involves searching for common patterns in the fabric of events and sequences experienced by each firm (Shadish, 1995).

This type of conceptual design is starting to emerge in IE research in that it purports to take an encompassing or holistic view of internationalization. It includes a range of complementary theories or alternatively, includes all forms of cross-border business activity, all value chain activities, or all aspects of a firm's business growth and development processes. Patton (2002) explains the holistic perspective in the sense of understanding the whole process. This, he suggests, involves the adoption of a systems perspective and has become increasingly important in "...dealing with and understanding real world complexities, viewing things as whole entities, embedded in context and still larger wholes" (Patton, 2002, p. 120).

Adoption of the systems perspective implies that the IE field could also benefit from using multiple data sources, an argument similar to that offered by Chandler and Lyon (2001) following their review of entrepreneurship methods. A unified methodological approach for IE research might therefore incorporate Harrigan's (1983, p. 400) call for 'hybrid methodologies,' whereby research methods are characterized by "...multiple sites, multiple data sources, and intricate sample designs." Such an approach encompasses both coarse-grained methods that result in generalizable, statistically significant data and also fine-grained methods that capture nuance, context, and rich understanding of the phenomena in question.

5.4. Reconciling static and longitudinal methodologies to accommodate the dimension of time

This review revealed only five longitudinal studies, with the others being static snapshot pictures of the situation at a point in time. To some extent, the dearth of longitudinal empirical work likely reflects the costs and difficulties associated with research on entrepreneurial processes; processes that evolve over considerable periods of time. It may also reflect the supposed incompatibility of interpretivist research with that which is more positivist. Given that IE research designs tend to be static (thus unable to capture certain dynamic processes) and positivist in nature, we argue that IE research could benefit from a more pluralistic approach to methodological application, recognizing that the positivist and interpretivist paradigms can be combined to better capture entrepreneurial behavior and processes over time.

The very few studies utilizing a longitudinal research design are also disappointing since the dimension of time has been identified as fundamental to isolating key developments in studies of internationalization (Buckley and Chapman, 1996; Andersen, 1997) and to studies of entrepreneurial behavior and other processes (Chandler and Lyon, 2001). Similarly, longitudinal data would allow IE researchers to address causal relationships in entrepreneurial internationalization behavior. There is also a need to better accommodate time as a measurable construct, and it is important to reconstruct IE as time-based behaviors or processes. Thus, it is hoped that future developments of the IE field will be marked by a growth in the number of studies developing and utilizing longitudinal methodologies.

5.5. Sampling design and data collection

The availability and use of sampling frames are issues not often discussed in IE methodological explanations but present a number of challenges for scholars in the field for a variety of reasons. For example, IE studies often examine multiple forms of mode of entry (as opposed to the export-only approach), and this precludes the use of export directories that bias the results towards export-driven internationalization (Jones, 1999). Furthermore, an OECD (1997) study on the globalization of SMEs in 18 countries found that the availability of sampling frames was a problem for researchers in at least 11 participating countries. The advent of mobile telephony and Internet communication excludes some enterprises even from telephone directories. Various privacy acts, together with the emergence of list brokering as a lucrative industry, may also place convenient and relevant sampling frames beyond the reach of parsimonious research. Finally, very small and start-up firms may be elusive and short lived and may never appear on any formal list (Yli-Renko et al., 2002).

Thus, a fundamental challenge for IE research is that significant effort is required to identify and catalogue firms with international activity. To some extent, this likely contributes to the preponderance of judgement and purposive sampling, as well as the apparent reluctance to document sampling design and procedure. Perhaps a more pragmatic approach is to accept the use of judgement samples, provided the sampling criteria are well and consistently specified and the data are assessed for validity and reliability.

5.6. Cross-national comparisons and replication studies

Finally, the richness of geographic coverage in IE studies and the multinationality of authors suggest that the field offers considerable potential for cross-national comparison and replication. The multinationality of authors also contributes to the development of a multi-cultural understanding of IE. As Nasif et al. (1991) and Cavusgil and Das (1997) caution, however, cross-national equivalence needs to be established at several levels in the research design and implementation process and fully reported in published research. If serious effort is not made to establish equivalence in sampling, instrumentation, and data collection procedures, IE research will be undermined as a whole. Beyond the areas of equivalence assessed in this paper, IE researchers should also address conceptual equivalence in the model or framework used and equivalence in data analysis. Results also need to be interpreted with appropriate cultural knowledge and insight. As noted by Tan (2002), research-comparing countries will need to be careful to distinguish between cultural and national effects on IE behavior.

6. Conclusion

As the field defined as IE begins to coalesce, our objectives were to review and assess the methodological aspects of the IE literature in order to offer insight as to the 'state of the art' of IE methods and discuss the implications for future development of the field. By providing a systematic and thorough review of empirical research defined to fall within McDougall and Oviatt's (2000) widely used definition of IE, we conclude that the field is rich in many dimensions, and in a relatively short period of time, an identifiable niche of IE research has been created. At the same time, we recommend that for the field to progress, IE researchers need to address their methodological decisions with greater coherency and thoroughness. This involves striving for more rigor and minimizing the tendency toward methodological simplicity.

Researchers should also construct their investigations with a sense of pluralism and an appreciation of the various methodological approaches that might best capture the dynamic processes characterizing IE.

Appendix A. List of IE articles reviewed (alphabetically categorized by topic)

Entrepreneurial behavior crossing international boundaries		Comparisons of entrepreneurial behavior in different countries
Andersson (2000)	Litvak (1990)	Begley and Tan (2001)
Autio et al. (2000)	Lu and Beamish (2001)	Chrisman et al. (2002)
Bell et al. (2001)	Manolova et al. (2002)	Holt (1997)
Bloodgood et al. (1996)	McAuley (1999)	Hornsby et al. (1999)
Boter and Holmquist (1996)	McDougall (1989)	Iyer and Shapiro (1999)
Burgel and Murray (2000)	McNaughton (2000)	Kirby et al. (1996)[a]
Coviello and Munro (1995)	Moen and Servais (2002)	Kolvereid et al. (1993)
Crick et al. (2001)	Preece et al. (1998)	Lussier and Pfeifer (2000)
Crick and Jones (2000)	Reuber and Fischer (1997)	Marino et al. (2002)
Fillis (2002)	Reuber and Fischer (2002)	Mitchell et al. (2000)
Fontes and Coombs (1997)	Rhee (2002)[a]	Mitchell et al. (2002)
Francis and Collins-Dodd (2000)	Shrader et al. (2000)	Morse et al. (1999)
Glas et al. (1999)	Shrader (2001)	Mueller and Thomas (2000)
Harveston et al. (2000)	Vatne (1995)	Murray (1996)
Ibeh and Young (2001)	Westhead et al. (2001)	Steensma et al. (2000)
Jolly et al. (1992)[a]	Yeoh (2000)	Tan (2002)
Jones (1999)	Yli-Renko et al. (2002)	Thomas and Mueller (2000)
Jones (2001)	Zahra et al. (1997)	

Appendix A (*continued*)

Entrepreneurial behavior crossing international boundaries	Comparisons of entrepreneurial behavior in different countries
Karagozoglu and Lindell (1998)	Zahra and Garvis (2000)
Knight (2000)	Zahra et al. (2000)
Knight (2001)	
Kuemmerle (2002)	

[a] These four articles (Jolly et al., 1992; Litvak, 1990; Kirby et al., 1996; Rhee, 2002) failed to provide sufficient information to assess the research method and were therefore excluded from the review. The final sample therefore includes 55 articles.

References

Adler, N.J., 1983. A typology of management studies involving culture. J. Int. Bus. Stud. 14 (2), 29–47.

Ahlstrom, D., Bruton, G.D., 2002. An institutional perspective on the role of culture in shaping strategic actions by technology-focused entrepreneurial firms in China. Entrep. Theory Pract. 26 (4), 53–69.

Andersen, O., 1997. Internationalisation and market entry mode: a review of theories and conceptual frameworks. Manag. Int. Rev. 37 (2), 7–42.

Andersson, S., 2000. The internationalization of the firm from an entrepreneurial perspective. Int. Stud. Manage. Organ. 30 (1), 63–92.

Ardichvili, A., 2001. Leadership styles of Russian entrepreneurs and managers. J. Dev. Entrep. 6 (2), 169–187.

Autio, E., Sapienza, H.J., Almeida, J.G., 2000. Effects of age at entry, knowledge intensity and imitability on international growth. Acad. Manage. J. 43 (5), 909–924.

Barkema, H.G., Vermeulen, F., 1998. International expansion through start-up or acquisition: a learning perspective. Acad. Manage. J. 41 (1), 7–26.

Barringer, B.R., Greening, D.W., 1998. Small business growth through geographic expansion: a comparative case study. J. Bus. Venturing 13 (6), 467–492.

Beamish, P.W., Craig, R., McLellan, K., 1993. The performance characteristics of Canadian vs. UK exporters in small and medium sized firms. Manag. Int. Rev. 33 (2), 121–137.

Begley, T.M., Tan, W.-L., 2001. The socio-cultural environment for entrepreneurship: a comparison between East Asian and Anglo-Saxon countries. J. Int. Bus. Stud. 32 (3), 537–553.

Bell, J., 1995. The internationalization of small computer software firms. Eur. J. Mark. 29 (8), 60–75.

Bell, J., McNaughton, R., Young, S., 2001. 'Born-again global' firms: an extension to the 'born global' phenomenon. J. Internat. Manag. 7 (3), 173–189.

Bijmolt, T.H.A., Zwart, P.W., 1994. The impact of internal factors on the export success of Dutch small and medium-sized firms. J. Small Bus. Manage. 32 (2), 48–59.

Bliss, R.T., Garratt, N., 2001. Supporting women entrepreneurs in transitioning economies. J. Small Bus. Manage. 39 (4), 336–344.

Bloodgood, J.M., Sapienza, H.J., Almeida, J.G., 1996. The internationalization of new high-potential US ventures: antecedents and outcomes. Entrep. Theory Pract. 20 (4), 61–76.

Bonaccorsi, A., 1992. On the relationship between firm size and export intensity. J. Int. Bus. Stud. 23 (4), 605–635.

Boter, H., Holmquist, C., 1996. Industry characteristics and internationalization processes in small firms. J. Bus. Venturing 11 (6), 471–487.

Brazeal, D.V., Herbert, T.T., 1999. The genesis of entrepreneurship. Entrep. Theory Pract. 23 (3), 29–45.

Bruton, G.D., Rubanki, Y., 2002. Resources of the firm, Russian high-technology startups, and firm growth. J. Bus. Venturing 17 (6), 553–576.

Buckley, P.J., Chapman, M., 1996. Theory and method in international business research. Int. Bus. Rev. 5 (3), 233–245.

Buckley, P.J., Chapman, M., 1997. The use of native categories in management research. Br. J. Manage. 8 (6), 283–299.

Buckley, P.J., Pass, C.L., Prescott, K., 1988. Measures of international competitiveness: a critical survey. J. Mark. Manag. 4 (2), 175–200.

Burgel, O., Murray, G.C., 2000. The international market entry choices of start-up companies in high technology industries. J. Int. Mark. 8 (2), 33–62.

Burpitt, W.J., Rondinelli, D.A., 2000. Small firms' motivations for exporting: to earn and learn? J. Small Bus. Manage. 38 (4), 1–14.

Busenitz, L.W., Gomez, C., Spencer, J.W., 2000. Country institutional profiles: unlocking entrepreneurial phenomena. Acad. Manage. J. 43 (5), 994–1003.

Calof, J.L., 1993. The impact of size on internationalization. J. Small Bus. Manage. 31 (4), 60–69.

Calof, J.L., 1994. The relationship between firm size and export behavior revisited. J. Int. Bus. Stud. 25 (2), 367–388.

Cavusgil, S.T., Das, A., 1997. Methodological issues in empirical cross-cultural research: a survey of the management literature and a framework. Manag. Int. Rev. 37 (1), 71–96.

Chandler, G.N., Lyon, D., 2001. Issues of design and construct measurement in entrepreneurship research: the past decade. Entrep. Theory Pract. 25 (4), 101–113.

Chen, R., Martin, M.J., 2001. Foreign expansion of small firms: the impact of domestic alternatives and prior foreign business involvement. J. Bus. Venturing 16 (6), 557–574.

Chrisman, J.J., Chua, J.H., Steier, L.P., 2002. The influence of national culture and family involvement on entrepreneurial perceptions and performance at the state level. Entrep. Theory Pract. 26 (4), 113–130.

Coviello, N.E., McAuley, A., 1999. Internationalization and the smaller firm: a review of contemporary empirical research. Manag. Int. Rev. 39 (3), 223–256.

Coviello, N.E., Munro, H.J., 1995. Growing the entrepreneurial firm: networking for international market development. Eur. J. Mark. 29 (7), 49–61.

Coviello, N.E., Munro, H.J., 1997. Network relationships and the internationalization process of small software firms. Int. Bus. Rev. 6 (4), 361–386.

Crick, D., Jones, M.V., 2000. Small high-technology firms and international high-technology markets. J. Int. Mark. 8 (2), 63–85.

Crick, D., Chaudhry, S., Batstone, S., 2001. An investigation into the overseas expansion of small Asian-owned UK firms. Small Bus. Econ. 16 (2), 75–94.

Davidsson, P., Wiklund, J., 2001. Levels of analysis in entrepreneurship research: current research practice and suggestions for the future. Entrep. Theory Pract. 25 (4), 81–99.

de Chiara, A., Minguzzi, A., 2002. Success factors in SMEs internationalization processes: an Italian investigation. J. Small Bus. Manage. 40 (2), 144–153.

Erramilli, M.K., D'Souza, D.E., 1993. Venturing into foreign markets: the case of the small service firm. Entrep. Theory Pract. 17 (4), 29–41.

Etemad, H., Salmasi, K.S., 2001. The rugged entrepreneurs of Iran's small-scale mining. Small Bus. Econ. 16 (2), 125–139.

Fillis, I., 2002. The internationalization process of the craft microenterprise. J. Dev. Entrep. 7 (1), 25–43.

Fontes, M., Coombs, R., 1997. The coincidence of technology and market objectives in the internationalization of new technology-based firms. Int. Small Bus. J. 15 (4), 14–35.

Francis, J., Collins-Dodd, C., 2000. The impact of firms' export orientation on the export performance of high-tech small and medium-sized enterprises. J. Int. Mark. 8 (3), 84–103.

Glas, M., Hisrich, R.D., Vahcic, A., Antoncic, B., 1999. The internationalization of SMEs in transition economies: evidence from Slovenia. Glob. Focus 11 (4), 107–124.

Green, R.T., White, P.D., 1976. Methodological considerations in cross-national consumer research. J. Int. Bus. Stud. 7 (2), 81–87.

Hara, G., Kanai, T., 1994. Entrepreneurial networks across oceans to promote international strategic alliances for small businesses. J. Bus. Venturing 9 (6), 489–507.

Harrigan, K.R., 1983. Research methodologies for contingency approaches to business strategy. Acad. Manage. Rev. 8 (3), 398–405.

Harris, S., 2000. Reconciling positive and interpretative international management research: a native category approach. Int. Bus. Rev. 9 (5), 755–770.

Harveston, P.D., Kedia, B.L., David, P.S., 2000. Internationalization of born global and gradual globalizing firms: the impact of the manager. Adv. Compet. Res. 8 (1), 92–99.

Haug, P., 1991. Survey evidence on the international operations of high technology firms. Manag. Int. Rev. 31 (1), 63–77.

Holmlund, M., Kock, S., 1998. Relationships and the internationalization of Finnish small and medium-sized companies. Int. Small Bus. J. 16 (4), 46–63.

Holt, D.H., 1997. A comparative study of values among Chinese and US entrepreneurs: pragmatic convergence between cultures. J. Bus. Venturing 12 (6), 483–505.

Hornsby, J.S., Kuratko, D.F., Montagno, R.V., 1999. Perception of internal factors for corporate entrepreneurship: a comparison of Canadian and US managers. Entrep. Theory Pract. 24 (2), 9–24.

Ibeh, K.I.N., Young, , 2001. Exporting as an entrepreneurial act: an empirical study of Nigerian firm. Eur. J. Mark. 35 (5/6), 566–586.

Iyer, G.R., Shapiro, J.M., 1999. Ethic entrepreneurial and marketing systems: implications for the global economy. J. Int. Mark. 7 (4), 83–110.

Jolly, V.K., Alahuta, M., Jeannet, J.-P., 1992. Challenging the incumbents: how high technology start-ups compete globally. J. Strateg. Change 1, 71–82.

Jones, M.V., 1999. The internationalization of small high technology firms. J. Int. Mark. 7 (4), 15–41.

Jones, M.V., 2001. First steps in internationalisation: concepts and evidence from a sample of small high technology firms. J. Internat. Manag. 7 (3), 191–210.

Karagozoglu, N., Lindell, M., 1998. Internationalization of small and medium-sized technology-based firms: an exploratory study. J. Small Bus. Manage. 36 (1), 44–59.

Kirby, D.A., Jones-Evans, D., Futo, P., Kwiatkowski, S., Schwalbach, J., 1996. Technical consultancy in Hungary, Poland and the UK: a comparative study of an emerging form of entrepreneurship. Entrep. Theory Pract. 20 (4), 9–23.

Knight, G., 1997. Cross-cultural reliability and validity of a scale to measure firm entrepreneurial orientation. J. Bus. Venturing 12 (3), 213–225.

Knight, G., 2000. Entrepreneurship and marketing strategy: the SME under globalization. J. Int. Mark. 8 (2), 12–32.

Knight, G.A., 2001. Entrepreneurship and strategy in the international SME. J. Internat. Manag. 7 (3), 155–171.

Kolvereid, L., Shane, S., Westhead, P., 1993. Is it equally difficult for female entrepreneurs to start businesses in all countries? J. Small Bus. Manage. 31 (4), 42–51.

Korhonen, H., Luostarinen, R., Welch, L.S., 1996. Internationalization of SMEs: inward–outward patterns and government policy. Manag. Int. Rev. 36 (4), 315–329.

Kreiser, P.M., Marino, L.D., Weaver, K.M., 2002. Assessing the psychometric properties of the entrepreneurial orientation scale: a multi-country analysis. Entrep. Theory Pract. 26 (4), 71–94.

Kuemmerle, W., 2002. Home base and knowledge management in international ventures. J. Bus. Venturing 17 (2), 99–122.

Kuznetsov, A., McDonald, F., 2000. Entrepreneurial qualities: a case from Russia. J. Small Bus. Manage. 38 (1), 108–114.

Lamb, P.W., Liesch, P.W., 2002. The internationalization process of the smaller firm: re-framing the relationships between market commitment, knowledge and involvement. Manag. Int. Rev. 42 (1), 7–26.

Larson, A., 1991. Partner networks: leveraging external ties to improve empirical performance. J. Bus. Venturing 6 (3), 173–188.

Lautanen, T., 2000. Modeling small firms decisions to export—evidence from manufacturing firms in Finland. Small Bus. Econ. 14 (2), 107–124.

Leonidou, L.C., Katsikeas, C.S., 1996. The export development process: an integrative review of empirical models. J. Int. Bus. Stud. 27 (3), 517–551.

Liesch, P.W., Knight, G., 1999. Information internalization and hurdle rates in small and medium enterprise internationalization. J. Int. Bus. Stud. 30 (2), 383–394.

Lipparini, A., Sobrero, M., 1994. The glue and the pieces: entrepreneurship and innovation in small networks. J. Bus. Venturing 9 (2), 125–140.

Litvak, I., 1990. Instant international: strategic reality for small high technology firms in Canada. Multinatl. Bus. 2, 1–12.

Lu, J.W., Beamish, P.W., 2001. The internationalization and performance of SMEs. Strateg. Manage. J. 22 (6/7), 565–586.

Lussier, R.N., Pfeifer, S., 2000. A comparison of business success versus failure variables between US and Central Eastern Europe Croatian entrepreneurs. Entrep. Theory Pract. 24 (2), 59–67.

Lyles, M.A., Carter, N.M., Baird, I.S., 1996. New ventures in Hungary: the impact of US partners. Manag. Int. Rev. 36 (4), 355–370.

Madhok, A., Osegowitsch, T., 2000. The international biotechnology industry: a dynamic capabilities perspective. J. Int. Bus. Stud. 31 (2), 325–335.

Madsen, T.K., Servais, P., 1997. The internationalization of born globals: an evolutionary process? Int. Bus. Rev. 6 (6), 561–583.

Manolova, T.S., Brush, C.G., Edelman, L.F., Greene, P.G., 2002. Internationalization of small firms: personal factors revisited. Int. Small Bus. J. 20 (1), 9–31.

Marino, L., Strandholm, K., Steensma, H.K., Weaver, K.M., 2002. The moderating effect of national culture on the relationships between entrepreneurial orientation and strategic alliance portfolio extensiveness. Entrep. Theory Pract. 26 (4), 145–163.

McAuley, A., 1999. Entrepreneurial instant exporters in the Scottish arts and crafts sector. J. Int. Mark. 7 (4), 67–82.

McDougall, P.P., 1989. International vs. domestic entrepreneurship: new venture strategic behavior and industry structure. J. Bus. Venturing 4 (6), 387–400.

McDougall, P.P., Oviatt, B.M., 2000. International entrepreneurship: the intersection of two research paths. Acad. Manage. J. 43 (5), 902–906.

McNaughton, R.B., 2000. Determinants of time-span to foreign market entry. J. Euro-mark. 9 (2), 99–112.

Miles, M.B., Huberman, A.M., 1994. Qualitative Data Analysis: An Expanded Sourcebook, 2nd ed. Sage, London.

Mitchell, R.K., Smith, B., Seawright, K.W., Morse, E.A., 2000. Cross-cultural cognitions and the venture creation decision. Acad. Manage. J. 43 (5), 974–993.

Mitchell, R.K., Smith, J.B., Morse, E.A., Seawright, K.W., Peredo, A.M., McKenzie, B., 2002. Are entrepreneurial cognitions universal? Assessing entrepreneurial cognitions across cultures. Entrep. Theory Pract. 26 (4), 9–32.

Moen, Ø., 2000. SMEs and international marketing: investigating the differences in export strategy between firms of different size. J. Glob. Mark. 13 (4), 7–28.

Moen, Ø., Servais, P., 2002. Born global or gradual global? Examining the export behaviour of small and medium-sized enterprises. J. Int. Mark. 10 (3), 49–72.

Morse, E.A., Mitchell, R.K., Smith, B., Seawright, K.W., 1999. Cultural values and venture cognitions on the Pacific Rim. Glob. Focus 11 (4), 135–153.

Mueller, S.L., Thomas, A.S., 2000. Culture and entrepreneurial potential: a nine-country study of locus of control and innovativeness. J. Bus. Venturing 16 (1), 51–75.

Murray, G., 1996. A synthesis of six exploratory, European case studies of successfully exited, venture capital-financed, new technology-based firms. Entrep. Theory Pract. 20 (4), 41–60.

Nakos, G., Brouthers, K.D., 2002. Entry mode choice of SMEs in Central and Eastern Europe. Entrep. Theory Pract. 27 (1), 47–63.

Nasif, E.G., Hamad, A.D., Ebrahimi, B., Thibodeaux, M.S., 1991. Methodological problems in cross-cultural research: an updated review. Manag. Int. Rev. 31 (1), 79–91.

OECD, 1997. Globalisation and Small and Medium Enterprises. OECD, Paris.

O'Farrell, P.N., Wood, P.A., Zheng, J., 1998. Internationalisation by business service SMEs: an inter-industry analysis. Int. Small Bus. J. 16 (2), 13–33.

Patton, M.Q., 2002. Qualitative Research and Evaluation Methods, 3rd ed. Sage, London.

Prasad, S.B., 1999. The globalization of smaller firms: field notes on processes. Small Bus. Econ. 13 (1), 1–7.

Preece, S.B., Miles, G., Baetz, M.C., 1998. Explaining the international intensity and global diversity of early-stage technology based firms. J. Bus. Venturing 14 (3), 259–281.

Reuber, A.R., Fischer, E., 1997. The influence of the management team's international experience on internationalization behavior. J. Int. Bus. Stud. 28 (4), 807–825.

Reuber, A.R., Fischer, E., 2002. Foreign sales and small firm growth: the moderating role of the management team. Entrep. Theory Pract. 27 (1), 29–45.

Rhee, J.H., 2002. An exploratory examination of propensity and performance in new venture internationalization. New Engl. J. Entrep. 5 (1), 51–66.

Roberts, E.B., Sentura, T.A., 1996. Globalizing the emerging high technology company. Ind. Mark. Manage. 25 (6), 491–506.

Romano, C., Ratanatunga, J., 1997. A 'citation classics' analysis of articles in contemporary small enterprise research. J. Bus. Venturing 12 (3), 197–212.

Shadish, W.R., 1995. Philosophy of science and quantitative-qualitative debates: thirteen common errors. Eval. Program Plann. 18 (1), 63–75.

Shrader, R., 2001. Collaboration and performance in foreign markets: the case of young high-technology manufacturing firms. Acad. Manage. J. 44 (1), 45–60.

Shrader, R.C., Oviatt, B.M., McDougall, P.P., 2000. How new ventures exploit trade-offs among international risk factors: lessons for the accelerated internationalization of the 21st century. Acad. Manage. J. 43 (6), 1227–1247.

Smith, K.G., Gannon, M.J., Sapienza, H.J., 1989. Selecting methodologies for entrepreneurial research: trade-offs and guidelines. Entrep. Theory Pract. 14 (1), 39–49.

Steensma, H., Marino, L., Weaver, M., Dickson, P.H., 2000. The influence of national culture on the formation of technology alliances by entrepreneurial firms. Acad. Manage. J. 43 (5), 951–973.

Stewart, A., Learned, K.E., Mandel, S.W., Kristin, M., 1995. Using field research on firm-level entrepreneurship: a coda. Entrep. Theory Pract. 19 (3), 175–184.

Tan, J., 2002. Culture, nation and entrepreneurial strategic orientations: implications for an emerging economy. Entrep. Theory Pract. 26 (4), 95–111.

Thomas, A.S., Mueller, S.L., 2000. A case for comparative entrepreneurship: assessing the relevance of culture. J. Int. Bus. Stud. 31 (2), 287–301.

Tiessen, J.H., 1997. Individualism, collectivism and entrepreneurship: a framework for international comparative research. J. Bus. Venturing 12 (5), 367–384.

VanderWerf, P.A., Brush, C., 1989. Achieving progress in an undefined field. Entrep. Theory Pract. 14 (2), 45–58.

Vatne, E., 1995. Local resource mobilization and internationalization strategies in small and medium-sized enterprises. Environ. Plan. 27 (1), 63–80.

Westhead, P., Wright, M., Ucbasaran, D., 2001. The internationalisation of new and small firms: a resource-based view. J. Bus. Venturing 16 (4), 333–358.

Wright, R.W., Ricks, D.A., 1994. Trends in international business research: twenty-five years later. J. Int. Bus. Stud. 25 (4), 687–701.

Yeoh, P.-L., 2000. Information acquisition activities: a study of global start-up exporting companies. J. Int. Mark. 8 (3), 36–60.

Yli-Renko, H., Autio, E., Tontti, V., 2002. Social capital, knowledge, and the international growth of technology-based new firms. Int. Bus. Rev. 11, 279–304.

Zacharakis, A.L., 1997. Entrepreneurial entry into foreign markets: a transaction cost perspective. Entrep. Theory Pract. 21 (3), 23–39.

Zahra, S.A., Garvis, D.M., 2000. International corporate entrepreneurship and firm performance: the moderating effect of international environmental hostility. J. Bus. Venturing 15 (5/6), 469–492.

Zahra, S., George, G., 2002. International entrepreneurship: the current status of the field and future research agenda. In: Hitt, M., Ireland, D., Sexton, D., Camp, M. (Eds.), Strategic Entrepreneurship: Creating an Integrated Mindset. Blackwell Publishers, Malden, MA, pp. 255–288.

Zahra, S.A., Neubaum, D.O., Huse, M., 1997. The effect of the environment on export performance among telecommunications new ventures. Entrep. Theory Pract. 22 (1), 25–46.

Zahra, S.A., Ireland, R.D., Hitt, M.A., 2000. International expansion by new venture firms: international diversity, mode of market entry, technological learning, and performance. Acad. Manage. J. 43 (5), 925–950.

[3]

Journal of International Business Studies (2005) 36, 284–303
© 2005 Palgrave Macmillan Ltd   All rights reserved 0047-2506 $30 00
www.jibs.net

Internationalisation: conceptualising an entrepreneurial process of behaviour in time

Marian V Jones[1] and
Nicole E Coviello[2]

[1] School of Business and Management, University of Glasgow, Glasgow, Scotland; [2] Department of Marketing, University of Auckland, Auckland, New Zealand

Correspondence:
Dr Nicole E Coviello, Professor of Marketing and International Entrepreneurship, Department of Marketing, University of Auckland, Private Bag 92019, Auckland, New Zealand.
Tel: +64 9 373 7599;
Fax: +64 9 373 7444;
E-mail: n.coviello@auckland.ac.nz

Abstract
This paper presents a three-stage process of conceptual development in response to the call for a unifying direction for research in the emergent field of international entrepreneurship. Drawing on classic approaches to internationalisation, and importing insight from entrepreneurship as a separate and distinct field of study, the paper develops three potential models of internationalisation as a time-based process of entrepreneurial behaviour. The models evolve from the simple through general to precise levels of conceptualisation. Research implications are discussed.
Journal of International Business Studies (2005) 36, 284–303.
doi.10.1057/palgrave.jibs.8400138

Keywords: international entrepreneurship; entrepreneurship; internationalisation; time; international new venture; born global; innovation

Introduction
In his comments on the international business research agenda, Buckley (2002) challenged researchers to think of their future work in terms of the past achievements of the discipline. One such achievement noted by Buckley (2002, 365) is the body of work concerned with 'understanding and predicting the development of the internationalisation of firms'. Indeed, there have been multiple efforts to explain internationalisation, the most recent relating to firms generally referred to as 'born globals' (Rennie, 1993) or 'international new ventures' (Oviatt and McDougall, 1994). A decade ago, the internationalisation of such firms was not readily explained by extant theory, but was characterised as a rapid process of international expansion from firm inception, using a range of market entry modes in multiple markets. Such behaviour was described as entrepreneurial, and led McDougall and Oviatt (2000) to identify 'international entrepreneurship' as an emergent field of study positioned at the intersection of the international business and entrepreneurship disciplines.

As defined by McDougall and Oviatt (2000, 903), international entrepreneurship is '...a combination of innovative, proactive and risk-seeking behaviour that crosses national borders and is intended to create value in organisations'. Important in this definition is explicit integration of the generally accepted understanding of internationalisation as a firm-level activity that crosses international borders (Wright and Ricks, 1994), with the characteristics of an entrepreneurial orientation as defined by Covin and

Received: 8 September 2003
Revised: 13 October 2004
Accepted: 18 October 2004
Online publication date: 3 February 2005

Slevin (1989): innovative, proactive and risk-seeking behaviour. Furthermore, McDougall and Oviatt's (2000) definition goes beyond the international new venture to incorporate the behaviour of larger, more established firms.

Although internationalisation research is well developed, research specific to international entrepreneurship may require an element of paradigmatic shift and a fresh research lens in order to understand how international firms develop competitive advantage through entrepreneurial behaviour, and how entrepreneurial firms can operate internationally. Unfortunately, McDougall and Oviatt (2000) raise the concern that international entrepreneurship research lacks a unifying and clear theoretical direction. In response to this concern, we follow Buckley's (2002) advice and suggest that, to move forward with international entrepreneurship research, it is appropriate to build on past achievements of international business researchers by importing concepts from the field of entrepreneurship. In doing so, we are able to reconceptualise internationalisation as an entrepreneurial process of behaviour. The general objectives of this paper are therefore to:

(1) identify core concepts common to internationalisation and entrepreneurship research;
(2) use those concepts as points of integration between the fields;
(3) develop integrative conceptual models relevant to the emergent field of international entrepreneurship in order to provide a sound basis for empirical examination; and
(4) discuss implications for research in the field.

The challenge of conceptual integration

As research on international entrepreneurship emerges, McDougall and Oviatt (2000) suggest the need for increased rigour in construct development, and for sophistication in the assertion of construct validity and reliability. In a different vein, Buckley and Chapman (1996, 244) suggest that another solution for an emerging field of research might lie in the development of '...a set of core concepts which are analytically rigorous and tractable, yet remain flexible', where core concepts refer to suitably grounded notions about the phenomena under study. These ideas seem to pull in opposite directions, in that the former calls for more attention to fine detail and specifically defined constructs and measures, and the latter for a holistic perspective with broad explanation.

This creates a tension between the need for 'precise' models and those more 'general' in nature. This tension is compounded by the fact that international entrepreneurship researchers might focus variously on macro or micro levels and units of analysis, and different aspects of the phenomenon such as internationalisation or cross-national comparison of cross-border activities and so on.

One of the problems in conceptualising any complex phenomenon is in trying to find a balance between very precise causal models that tend to be narrow in their focus, and broader universal models that offer general description but are challenging to operationalise. According to Weick (1999), the development of theoretical explanations and conceptual models that are simultaneously simple, general and precise is not impossible. It is, however, likely to be challenging. We argue that to minimise the need for trade-offs in attempting to conceptualise phenomena, what seems to be required is a *balanced* process of conceptual development. Such a process might commence by identifying the basic or simple concepts that provide parameters for the phenomenon under study. These concepts could then be applied to a general, holistic conceptualisation within which the major constructs are embedded—constructs from which the antecedent and consequent variables are drawn and incorporated into precise contingency models that form the basis for empirical validation. We believe that the evolution of a series of related models progressing through stages of conceptual development from the simple to the general to the precise may contribute to unification in thinking for international entrepreneurship researchers, and, more specifically, may provide a foundation for researchers interested in internationalisation as a process of entrepreneurial behaviour.

Focusing on this notion of entrepreneurial internationalisation behaviour, which we see as a firm-level manifestation of international entrepreneurship, we articulate a process of conceptualisation that draws on Weick (1999). Commencing with an overview of classic approaches to internationalisation and entrepreneurship, we present, as a first level, two *simple models* reflecting (1) the entrepreneurial process and (2) the internationalisation process. We then identify core concepts from these simple models and integrate them with enduring constructs drawn from the international and entrepreneurship literatures. This leads to the second level of conceptual development in the form of a *general model* that represents entrepreneurial internationalisation as a time-based behavioural process. The central dimensions and constructs of the general model can then be used at the third level of conceptualisation to develop and operationalise precise causal models. As an illustration of the last step, we develop one example of a *precise model* and outline a number of other possibilities for research at that level.

Moving through an integrative process of conceptual development, beginning with the abstract and simple to the general, and finally, precise models, reflects Patton's argument (2002, 120) for '...understanding the whole process' and '...understanding real world complexities, viewing things as whole entities, embedded in context and still larger wholes'. In taking this approach, we follow Buckley's (2002) advice to inform and build on the strengths of existing internationalisation theory by importing entrepreneurship theory. To this end, we begin with a brief review of insights from the extant internationalisation and entrepreneurship literatures.

Insights from the internationalisation and entrepreneurship literatures

A considerable number of theories from international business research have been used in the literature to describe and explain aspects of internationalisation. These various theories have been extensively critiqued elsewhere (e.g. Andersen 1993, 1997; Oviatt and McDougall, 1994; Coviello and McAuley, 1999; Jones, 1999); however, certain observations are relevant to our process of conceptual development. For example, the internalisation/transaction cost and resource-based approaches tend to emphasise rational and strategic decision-making criteria such as costs, investment, risk and control. They assume that foreign market entry decisions consist of discrete alternatives, and occur at specific and identified points in time. In contrast, the network/resource-dependency and organisation-learning approaches to internationalisation emphasise a process of internationalisation that takes place, or has taken place over a period of time – that is, a relationship- and learning-based process that may result in gradual internationalisation on the one hand, or a more discontinuous process consisting of specific events on the other. Finally, export development approaches, while describing a process of internationalisation through incremental stages of innovation for the firm, are concerned more with the predetermined stages that

a firm might have reached, than with its process of getting there.

Drawing these views together, the internalisation/transaction cost, resource-based and export development approaches have tended to focus on factors influencing internationalisation. In contrast, the network and organisational learning approaches have been more concerned with identifying and describing the behavioural processes underlying internationalisation. Most recently, what has been described as the international new venture approaches have emerged (Dana *et al.*, 1999; Arenius, 2002). Such approaches tend to be hybrid combinations of their aforementioned predecessors, and have attempted to explain early or rapid internationalisation and the born-global phenomenon. Their emphasis is on internationalisation as firm-level behaviour and a process of development, but they also accommodate the idea that certain conditions, that is, firm and environmental factors, must be necessary and sufficient to explain internationalisation (Oviatt and McDougall, 1994). Thus, recent developments in the literature reflect an apparent convergence in theory, suggesting that a contemporary understanding of internationalisation is informed by integrating multiple theoretical perspectives in a manner that is both pluralistic and holistic. This suggests that the internationalisation literature is moving towards a unifying theoretical framework. If, however, we are interested in understanding and explaining 'entrepreneurial' internationalisation behaviour, conceptual models need to be sufficiently flexible to accommodate the range of conditions that might influence and lend explanation to a firm's internationalisation decisions, actions and dynamic processes. This requires a greater understanding of entrepreneurial behaviour, and we thus turn to the entrepreneurship literature to help inform our understanding of internationalisation.

As noted by Dana *et al.* (1999) in their review of the theoretical foundations of international entrepreneurship, as well as Shane and Venkataraman (2000) and Ucbasaran *et al.* (2001) in their assessment of entrepreneurship research, the field of entrepreneurship is characterised by a plethora of theoretical contributions from diverse disciplines. This diversity is perhaps even more evident than in the internationalisation literature, and indeed, Shane and Venkataraman (2000) express concern that a unique and unifying conceptual framework is lacking in entrepreneurship. Nevertheless, identifiable themes of entrepreneurship research can be identified. More importantly, they show considerable theoretical convergence with developments in the field of internationalisation.

For example, the classic entrepreneurship literature considers the role of the entrepreneur in economic theory, specifically in terms of transaction cost economics, internalisation decisions, theories of the firm and firm growth, and theories of innovation. This parallels studies in internationalisation conducted from the internalisation/transaction cost perspective and the export development approach. Similarly, the entrepreneur's characteristics or traits and his/her role in identifying, accessing and leveraging resources in the pursuit of opportunity creation and innovation are relevant to the body of internationalisation research that discusses human and social capital in the context of resource-based theory, the organisation learning approach and the emerging research on international new ventures.

Related to the above, recent developments in the international business literature have turned to the phenomenon of social and industrial networks in internationalisation, and, similarly, entrepreneurship research has emphasised the role of the entrepreneur as a participant and manager of social systems and networks. Particular interest has been paid to examining entrepreneurship (at both the individual and firm level) as a process of behaviour manifest in entrepreneurial events, and exhibiting entrepreneurial orientations. This mirrors the internationalisation literature in terms of developments in the organisational learning and export development approaches, and network/resource dependency theory. Finally, like research in the internationalisation field, especially that pertaining to international new ventures, much of the entrepreneurship literature has focused on determining the necessary and sufficient conditions that explain decisions and actions pertaining to the start-up, growth and development of an enterprise, or the creation of value.

Overall, it appears that the intersection of research at the internationalisation/entrepreneurship interface is a logical one in that its emergence reflects complementary theoretical interests and empirical developments in both fields. What is evident in each area of research is that entrepreneurship and internationalisation are generally accepted as entailing processes, and, specifically, the behavioural processes associated with the creation of value by assembling a unique package of resources to exploit an opportunity (Morris *et al.*, 2001; Johanson and Vahlne, 2003). Process too is implicit in McDougall and Oviatt's (2000) definition of international entrepreneurship, which, following Covin and Slevin (1991), describes internationalisation as a composite of behaviour, innovation, proactivity, risk-seeking and value creation. Thus, we have the common foundational element of *behavioural process* from which an integrative conceptualisation can be developed.

Behaviour, as we shall discuss later in the paper, can be determined from the decisions and actions that occur in response to certain conditions at specific points in time, and which constitute the necessary and sufficient conditions that support theoretical explanation. The time at which, and over which, such actions occur provides the link between static and dynamic explanations, and between events and processes. Viewing entrepreneurial internationalisation behaviour through a temporal lens presents further opportunity to accommodate multiple theoretical explanations within the same, flexible conceptual models. Therefore, *time* becomes another important foundational element in our conceptualisation process.

From this base, we can now proceed through several levels of conceptual development in which core concepts pertaining to the entrepreneurial internationalisation process can be identified and unbundled into more finely detailed constructs. Ultimately, these constructs can then be transformed into precise variables and measures relevant for empirical validation and analysis. To elucidate core concepts common to the internationalisation and entrepreneurship literatures, we turn to the first level of conceptual development adapted from Weick (1999): simple models.

Simple models of the entrepreneurial and internationalisation processes
Internationalisation entails entry into new country markets. It may therefore be described as a process of innovation (Andersen, 1993; Casson, 2000). International new ventures have, in particular, been described as especially innovative in their internationalisation (Oviatt and McDougall, 1994; Knight and Cavusgil, 2004). Innovation is also central to the field of entrepreneurship (Schumpeter, 1934; Shane and Venkataraman, 2000). Therefore, we begin our conceptual development with the simple model of the entrepreneurial process offered by Brazeal and Herbert (1999). This model integrates distinct concepts from the

entrepreneurship literature (innovation, change and creativity), and, as seen in Figure 1, describes how they result in entrepreneurial events. In the model, environmental change, which may be internal or external to the firm, elicits a cyclical process of response (human volition) that results in innovation (innovation 1). This is classically defined as the successful implementation of creative ideas and, as such, is an outcome of a creative or innovative process (innovation 2). The entrepreneurial event involves the separation of the innovation from its predecessor (if any), and its separate exploitation (Brazeal and Herbert, 1999). Of note, this simple model has the potential to include both event- and outcome-driven approaches in process-focused research, and may be developed to accommodate a variance approach as described by Van de Ven and Engleman (2004).

Figure 1 represents entrepreneurship as *proactive behaviour* that results in *innovation* as a process, and as an outcome that implicitly has the potential to *create value* through separate exploitation. It also accommodates the process of *change*, which stimulates the process of innovation from which incremental or radical innovation outcomes emerge as entrepreneurial events. Thus, development may be

evolutionary or discontinuous. The model parallels the behavioural process described in McDougall and Oviatt's (2000) definition of international entrepreneurship, but while the level of abstraction it presents has the ability to describe the entrepreneurial process within internationalisation, it makes no specific reference to that phenomenon.

Drawing on Johanson and Vahlne's (2003) observation of similarities between the entrepreneurship and internationalisation processes, and using the Brazeal and Herbert (1999) model as a base, a simple model of the internationalisation process can also be developed (Figure 2). In this model, an internal or external environmental change leads to the adoption of an entry mode in a selected country. As considered in some explanations of the international expansion of the firm, this reflects innovation (Andersen, 1993; Knight and Cavusgil, 2004). From that outcome innovation, a cyclical innovation process involving experiential knowledge and organisational learning occurs. Coupled with further change (resource commitment), this may lead to the adoption of more risky and committed modes in psychologically distant countries (decision/action). Similar to Brazeal and Herbert's (1999) definition of the entrepreneurial

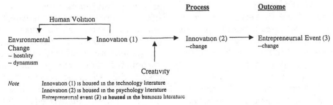

Figure 1 A simple model of the entrepreneurial process (Brazeal and Herbert, 1999: 32).

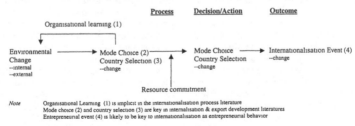

Figure 2 A simple model of the internationalisation process (the authors).

event, internationalisation events occur when they are exploited separately from their predecessors. Following Van de Ven and Engleman (2004), we see internationalisation events as the most valid representation of what occurs in the development and change process that is internationalisation. Further support is indicated in Zander's (1994) call for an evolutionary theory of the multinational firm in which he stresses that 'certain events' influence the long-term evolution of the firm.

Returning again to the terms identified in McDougall and Oviatt's (2000) definition, Figure 2 describes an internationalisation process that is *behavioural*; is potentially risk-seeking, depending on the radicalness of *innovation processes* and *outcomes* (in terms of entry mode and country); and which potentially *creates value* for the organisation through separate exploitation of the internationalisation event. This model also accommodates *change* as a result of environmental triggers and as part of an adaptation process in response to organisational learning following the adoption of new forms of business in new countries. Furthermore, it accommodates the occurrence of revolutionary or serendipitous events which may alter the firm's development path, and may be important in accounting for early or sudden internationalisation and the emergence of opportunities such as cross-border acquisitions (Zander, 1994).

Common to both simple models is an evolutionary and potentially discontinuous process determined by innovation, and influenced by environmental change and human volition, action or decision. Figure 1 views human volition and creativity as a cyclical process culminating in innovations marked by the evidence of a recognisable entrepreneurial event. Figure 2 views organisational learning and resource commitment in a similar way, that is, as cyclical processes culminating in mode and country decisions and actions, marked by the evidence of an internationalisation event.

Both models are process-based and describe a rudimentary sequence of behaviour that is inherently linear. However, the level of abstraction at which they operate provides no means to distinguish the specific influences of the environment, the firm or the entrepreneur. What they do offer is a number of shared core concepts. These include *innovation, change*, a *cyclical process of behaviour* and culmination in a specific *value-adding event*. Critically, the concept of *time* is implicit in both simple models, although not explicitly indicated. The concepts shared between these two models form the first level of conceptual thinking. They also provide the basis for the development of a general model of entrepreneurial internationalisation, that is, the second level of conceptual development.

Developing a general model of entrepreneurial internationalisation

Developing primary dimensions and constructs for a general model

In their discussion on levels of theory complexity, Ofori-Dankwa and Julian (2001) suggest that there are two dimensions to a phenomenon that may serve as building blocks between levels of conceptual abstraction: 'concept depth' and 'concept width'. By way of example, they cite Hock's (1999) dimensions of memory and language as the building blocks for his work on social diversity and social complexity. Following Ofori-Dankwa and Julian (2001), we argue, on the basis of our earlier discussion on theoretical development relating to international entrepreneurship, that the primary dimensions of entrepreneurial internationalisation are: (1) *time*, against which all processes can be described; and (2) *behaviour*, manifested as an accumulation of actions or events in relation to time. If these primary dimensions are then integrated with the core concepts identified from the two simple models, six basic components relevant to a general model of entrepreneurial internationalisation behaviour emerge. These are value-added events that manifest as (1) internationalisation behaviour influenced by (2) the entrepreneur and (3) the firm as moderated by (4) the external environment. The behavioural process is characterised by innovation and change, and consists of actions and decisions that determine the international development and (5) performance of the firm. The entire process is seen as fluid and potentially iterative as a result of learning from behaviour and performance. Finally, entrepreneurial internationalisation occurs within, and is characterised by, aspects of (6) time.

By positioning *time* and *behaviour* as concept width and concept depth, respectively, we have the potential to view the phenomenon of entrepreneurial internationalisation through both temporal and behavioural lenses. Both dimensions are now explained, followed by a discussion of the other four constructs relevant to the general model.

The primary dimension of time

Interestingly, although time is implicit in behavioural research in both internationalisation and entrepreneurship (Johanson and Vahlne, 1977, 1990; Brazeal and Herbert, 1999), it is seldom positioned as a primary conceptual dimension to which explicit behaviour may be tagged and understood (Ancona *et al.*, 2001). Furthermore, in their review of methodological issues in international entrepreneurship research, Coviello and Jones (2004) highlight a dearth of literature capturing the time-based dynamics of various behaviours and processes pertinent to entrepreneurial internationalisation. Time is, however, fundamental to internationalisation research in that each firm has a history composed of internationalisation events occurring at specific points in time. For example, establishing a new type of cross-border relationship is a landmark in the firm's chronology of internationalisation, as is the establishment of a relationship in a new country, or the cessation of a previously established connection. As described by Kutschker *et al.* (1997), successful internationalisation also requires that time be actively managed in terms of order, timing and speed of the process.

We argue that incorporating time as a primary conceptual dimension is essential to understanding entrepreneurial internationalisation. This reflects Stevenson and Harmeling's (1990, 10) view that: 'contingency theory conclusions are not only a function of industry and environment, but must also be a function of time and timing.' Also, we believe that entrepreneurship is essentially a behavioural process, and behaviour is represented as an accumulation of actions over time (Covin and Slevin, 1991). The firm itself and internationalisation behaviour are also functions of time, subject to its passing and influence on the wider environment.

As discussed by Harvey *et al.* (2000), time is composed of a number of elements in organisational research. Applying their arguments to entrepreneurial internationalisation, for example, time can be taken as a simple means of categorisation. *Chronological time* is fundamental, as it is the same for all firms, and it is likely that firms established in a particular era will differ in their behaviour either collectively (compared with firms established in previous eras), or individually (based on micro-level

influences). Thus, time-based patterns may emerge. For these reasons, it is important to peg the firm's international activities against a relevant historical backdrop, thus providing a *reference time* (Jones, 1999, 2001; Autio *et al.*, 2000).

At a descriptive level, internationalisation is a process, and therefore, by definition, internationalisation behaviour takes place over time, manifest in a *time sequence* in which events occur (Luostarinen *et al.*, 1994; Jones, 2001). Also, firms are founded at specific dates in time, and internationalisation activities occur over discernible *time periods* within a dynamic environment, with various activities differing in their *duration* (Reuber and Fischer, 1999; Westhead *et al.*, 2001).

At an interpretative level, the firm's internationalisation activities may be more or less concentrated at a specific reference time or over a time period (Jones, 1999, 2001), and therefore the notion of *time intensity* has relevance. Hurmerinta-Peltomäki (2003) also suggests that time has a *cyclical* dimension, with no fixed direction in that it can roll back to some objective and historical reference. Likewise, learning from past internationalisation experiences may feed forward into present and future internationalisation decisions and actions.

Time is also a key element that distinguishes studies focused on international new ventures (INVs) from studies of SME internationalisation. At a general level, studies of INVs have focused on the early stages of internationalisation in terms of chronology. At a more specific level, INVs are distinguished from other SMEs in terms of: (1) the time taken to commence international activity (Reuber and Fischer, 1997; McNaughton, 2000); and (2) the speed or rate at which internationalisation develops (Coviello and Munro, 1997; Jones, 1999). As noted by Autio *et al.* (2000), however, these characteristics have not been fully examined in the literature. This suggests that a general model of entrepreneurial internationalisation behaviour might also incorporate the *gap time* between the establishment of different forms of international activity, thereby accommodating a measure of the *rate* of internationalisation, that is, the speed of international development over time.

Overall, by including the conceptual dimension of time in the general model, we support Andersen (1993, 1997), Zander (1994), Zahra *et al.* (2000) and Coviello and Jones (2004) in their suggestions that research on internationalisation should explicitly incorporate the role and influence of time.

The primary dimension of behaviour

Covin and Slevin (1991, 7) argue that behaviour is the '...central and essential element in the entrepreneurial process,' and that an organisation's actions (or behaviour) are what make it entrepreneurial. In the context of the general model, the question arising from Covin and Slevin's discussion is the extent to which such behaviour can be identified, and, following from this, whether or not entrepreneurial internationalisation behaviour manifests itself in ways that can be measured. As noted by Covin and Slevin (1991, 8), however:

.behavior is, by definition, overt and demonstrable. Knowing the behavioral manifestations of entrepreneurship, we can reliably, verifiably, and objectively measure the entrepreneurial level of the firm.

By inference, this paper argues that by understanding the behavioural evidence of internationalisation, we should be able to reliably measure the entrepreneurial internationalisation of firms based on analysis of their patterns of behaviour.

Like entrepreneurial behaviour, internationalisation behaviour is overt and demonstrable, and manifest in recognisable ways. Indeed, the evidence of internationalisation behaviour is readily identifiable in measures used in the traditional internationalisation literature. Perhaps the most frequently used measures include modes of cross-border activity (foreign market entry modes), the countries of involvement and time-related dimensions (reported variously and somewhat loosely as, for example, stages of development or steps in a process). Andersen (1993, 1997) argues that country selection and entry mode choice are the key strategic decisions in relation to a firm's internationalisation, and suggests that what differentiates internationalisation from other growth processes is the transference of goods, services or resources across national borders. Interestingly, however, goods, services and resources tend to be treated as explanatory variables in the literature in that they are used to explain differences in internationalisation patterns, rather than as evidence that the process has taken place. For example, Ekeledo and Sivakumar (1998) propose that entry-mode choice and variations in these choices will be influenced by the nature of the firm's product offer (distinguished as goods, hard services or soft services). Furthermore, rapid internationalisation has repeatedly been found to occur among high-technology firms, and those seeking to augment their resource base through collaborative activity

(Coviello and Munro, 1995, 1997; Boter and Holmquist, 1996).

Therefore, although the range of goods, services and resources transferred may indicate whether a firm's internationalisation is concentrated in a specific line of business or represents a more comprehensive range of business interests, we view the primary evidence of internationalisation behaviour to be:

(1) the mode of transference (cross-border business modes);
(2) the place of transference (country); and
(3) the time at which it occurs.

In support of using these three characteristics as evidence of internationalisation behaviour, they are observable or at least able to be recorded. As Andersen (1997) indicates, this will increase the robustness of any predictions made. The following section discusses how the first two characteristics potentially indicate evidence of internationalisation behaviour, with time discussed in the previous section.

The *mode of transference*, that is, the cross-border business activity commonly referred to as foreign market entry modes, has been well documented in the internationalisation literature. Formal cross-border modes include the conventional outward entry modes of exporting, licensing and foreign direct investment (see Young *et al.* (1989) for a comprehensive discussion). Other studies have also included inward and cooperative modes (Luostarinen *et al.*, 1994; Jones, 1999), as well as service firm entry modes (Erramilli, 1989; Ekeledo and Sivakumar, 1998).

At a deeper level, the literature also discusses foreign market entry modes in terms of levels of risk and resource commitment (Hill *et al.*, 1990), levels of fixed and variable cost and return on investment (Luostarinen, 1980; Buckley and Casson, 1985), levels of involvement and organisational commitment (Johanson and Vahlne, 1977; Welch and Luostarinen, 1988), degree of control (Anderson and Gatignon, 1986) and locus of control (Luostarinen, 1980; Young *et al.*, 1989). Importantly, these studies imply naturally occurring hierarchies of modes, as discussed by Pan and Tse (2000). Hence this literature supports the assumptions of the conventional incremental pattern of internationalisation, which suggests that, over time, international activity evolves through a taxonomy of modes ordered by increasing risk, cost, commitment, control, return on investment and so on, as the firm's size, experience and knowledge grow.

However, rather than place modes into predetermined ranks or assumptions of order, we suggest that it is more appropriate to incorporate known measures of cross-border business modes to determine representative composite measures of cross-border activity undertaken by a firm, in relation to time – for example, a composite of the range of modes and range of countries established at a particular internationalisation event, or between events. Such composite measures also provide a useful proxy of the innovativeness of each mode or modes. That is, the extent to which an internationalisation event is a radical innovation from any predecessor, as illustrated in the simple model shown in Figure 2, if taken to a level of detail that incorporates levels of risk, cost, control and commitment. We argue that the firm's cross-border business modes are important because they provide evidence that value-creating activity has taken place (McDougall and Oviatt, 2000), the point of time it was established and the country with which the business occurs. Furthermore, discrete measures of entry modes can be used to construct indicators of the extent of internationalisation behaviour such as, for example, functional diversity (range of mode choice) and functional time intensity (range of modes in relation to time).

Turning to the place or *country of transference* as evidence of internationalisation behaviour, the choice of country has generally been described in terms of psychic and economic distance (Johanson and Wiedersheim-Paul, 1975; Luostarinen, 1980), geographic distance (Carlson, 1974) and cultural distance from the internationalising firm (Kogut and Singh, 1988; Benito and Gripsrud, 1992). Together, these measures reflect the notion of 'country distance'. Country distance is indicative of the extent and reach of the firm's internationalisation activities, and can be used to indicate country diversity and the intensity of a firm's internationalisation activities. Thus, country distance can provide a proxy measure for the radicalness of internationalisation events from any predecessors.

Positioning time and behaviour in the general model

The two primary dimensions of time and behaviour underpin the general model of entrepreneurial internationalisation presented in Figure 3. This model depicts entrepreneurial internationalisation

as it might be experienced by any firm, in any industry, under any circumstance, and thus is context free. It further develops the simple model (Figure 2) by making explicit the composition of internationalisation events. With the incorporation of time as a measurable dimension against which internationalisation may be examined, it also overcomes the inherent linearity of the simple model.

The dimension of time is illustrated as a continuous flow by means of the widely recognised notion of a time-line, illustrated in the general model as an all-embracing arrow pointing from left to right. Diagrammatically, two dimensions of time are illustrated: chronological time shown as a continuous horizontal timeline, and reference time indicated as points on the time-line at which events associated with the firm's internationalisation occur. Distance between different time points measures the duration of an activity or process.

Firms are founded at specific reference points in time, which may or may not coincide with the commencement of internationalisation behaviour. Thus, internationalisation behaviour is mapped as its evidence occurs in relation to time, illustrated in the general model as a floating box situated over a portion of the time-line, and to some extent in parallel with aspects of the entrepreneurial process and the firm. In addition to the key dimensions, therefore, the other constructs of the model include the entrepreneur, the firm and firm performance. As discussed in the next section, all operate with the external environment, and are influenced by the cyclical effect of time and forces of change.

Each establishment of a new business mode is evidence of innovation in internationalisation behaviour, as is the establishment of an existing business mode in a country new to the firm. These are illustrated in Figure 3 as events at specific reference points in time, and as processes that occur for specific durations of time. Examples of modes might include the setting up of an export arrangement (ex), licensing out technology to a foreign partner (lo) or setting up a production subsidiary off-shore (ps). Further, the country in which the event occurs is illustrated vertically as occurring at a specified country distance from the firm's domestic base. Together with each type of cross-border event, this indicates whether the innovation is radical or incremental. Internationalisation may therefore be captured as patterns of behaviour, formed by an accumulation of evidence manifest as events at specific reference points in time. Following

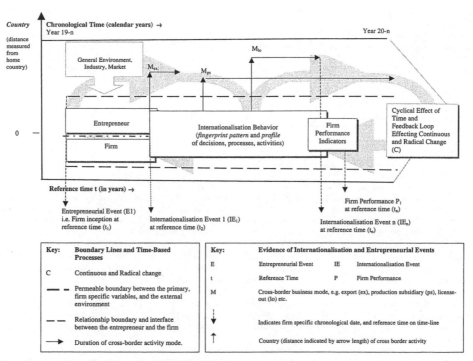

Figure 3   A general model of the entrepreneurial internationalisation process.

Kutschker *et al.* (1997), we describe this manifestation of evidence as a fingerprint pattern of internationalisation – that is, a static impression indicated by evidence at a specific point in time.

We define the *fingerprint pattern* in the general model as a composite of the number and range of cross-border business modes established by the firm, and the number and distance of countries with which those modes were established, at a specific point in time. Changes in the composition of business modes and countries over a period of time are described in the general model as dynamic *profiles* of the firm's internationalisation behaviour. Our purpose and definition differs from Kutschker *et al.* (1997), in that we emphasise mode and country diversity as indicative of entrepreneurial internationalisation behaviour patterns, whereas the latter authors emphasise integration between business activities (modes and countries) as indicative of the configuration of the firm's international expansion path. In common with Kutschker *et al.*

(1997), we distinguish static 'fingerprint patterns' from dynamic 'profiles' or processes.

The purpose of the general model is therefore not to predict which mode will be established when, or where, but to characterise firms according to their unique patterns and profiles of internationalisation. Of note, the extant literature contains examples of attempts to profile aspects of internationalisation behaviour (e.g. Oviatt and McDougall, 1994; Reuber and Fischer, 1997; Zahra *et al.*, 2000); however, these efforts focus on a few variables at specific points in time (such as the study date), and are often embedded in performance indicators – that is, as measures of the result of the behaviour, rather than as a profile of the behaviour itself. The usefulness of profiling behaviour, however, is profound, in that it 'explains why firms differ in their internationalisation profile (e.g. entry mode chosen, number of foreign markets served) at a specific time *t*' (Andersen, 1997, 30). It also describes the international evolution of the firm, and thus provides a developmental foundation for an evolutionary theory of multinational enterprise (Zander, 1994).

Drawing on Jones (1999), we propose that such patterns and profiles may be described in relation to the composition of modes and countries at any reference time or over a given time period, the rate at which new events occur, the sequence in which they occur, the intensity of activity over time, and whether events occur early or late in the time period or are equally distributed. Further depth in understanding may emerge from analysis of the gap time between events, their duration and cyclical time effects, all of which underpin the processes of innovation and learning.

Interaction of the dimensions of time and internationalisation behaviour in the general model specifically indicates:

- an entrepreneurial event (E) consisting of the establishment of the firm at a specific reference point in time (t);
- an internationalisation event (IE) measured from any reference point in time at which the firm establishes, or ceases a new cross-national business mode (M), or enters a country new to it (country distance);
- a fingerprint pattern at a specific reference point in time that reflects an accumulation of evidence of internationalisation behaviour as manifest in the business modes established and the countries to which transfer is made; and
- a dynamic profile of streams of events (internationalisation evidence) that reflects change and developments in the firm's internationalisation behaviour.

Following from this, entrepreneurial internationalisation behaviour is influenced by, and in turn influences, some important constructs. These are outlined in the next section.

Positioning contextual constructs in the general model

To this point, our emphasis has been on describing the two process dimensions – time and internationalisation behaviour – that are central to the general model of entrepreneurial internationalisation. There are, however, a number of other contextual elements that are likely to act as antecedent, moderating and outcome variables in relation to behaviour and time. As discussed in the international business literature (Calof and Beamish, 1995;

Ekeledo and Sivakumar, 1998), the entrepreneurship literature (Covin and Slevin, 1989; Chandler and Hanks, 1994; Lumpkin and Dess, 1996; Greene and Brown, 1997), and the emerging international entrepreneurship literature (Oviatt and McDougall, 1994; Bloodgood et al., 1996; Madsen and Servais, 1997; Reuber and Fischer, 1997; Yli-Renko et al., 2002), these generally include firm performance, the external environment, the firm or internal environment and the manager or management team.

As regards the manager/management team, it is worth noting that although Covin and Slevin (1991, 8) acknowledge: '...individual level behaviour on the part of the entrepreneur may affect an organisation's actions, and in many cases, the two will be synonymous,' their widely used behavioural model of entrepreneurship focuses on the firm level (of larger firms) rather than that of the individual entrepreneur. However, Madsen and Servais (1997) argue that the entrepreneur is a key antecedent of a born-global, with Shrader et al. (2000, 1244) concluding that, in the context of international new ventures, the '...locus of relevant foreign-market knowledge may be more with the entrepreneur or the entrepreneurial team than the organisational decision-making system.' Similar conclusions have been drawn by Ibeh (2003) and Kundu and Katz (2003). Extending this argument further, Kuemmerle (2002) posits that the entrepreneur may choose to establish the international new venture at a location where his/her resources and knowledge can best be allocated and managed, and from where knowledge may be augmented and exploited towards international growth.

Therefore, in developing the general model to ultimately provide a foundation for more precise contingency models across firm size, we argue that key constructs to include alongside the primary process dimensions of time and internationalisation behaviour are performance, the firm, the environment and, specifically, the entrepreneur. This follows Chrisman et al. (1999), who argue that the entrepreneur's personality, skills and values will affect their behaviours and decisions. In turn, the key decisions, strategies and management practices of the entrepreneur will shape the performance of the venture (Cooper et al., 1994). Thus, the firm has an entrepreneurial influence that serves to combine capabilities, competences and resources (Eisenhardt and Martin, 2000) as part of the strategic and tactical activity of the organisation. This includes specific decisions, processes and actions that result in or contribute to internationalisation. However, the relationship between the entrepreneur and the firm differs between firms, and changes over time. This is represented in Figure 3 as a variable relationship boundary (signified by a broken line). The individual entrepreneur and firm-level entrepreneurial behaviour are expected to influence internationalisation behaviour, both together and separately.

The relationship between the entrepreneur, the firm and the external environment is viewed from a systems perspective and assumes continuous input, process, output and feedback activity over time, whereby the external environment acts as a moderator on internationalisation behaviour (Kast and Rosenzweig, 1974). Figure 3 therefore shows the boundary between the entrepreneur, the firm and the external environment as permeable (signified by a heavy broken line), thus accommodating continuous interaction with, and response to, the outside world. External associations such as formal cross-border entry modes are seen here as part of that interaction (as indicated on two dimensions: time and country distance). The view taken is that the entrepreneur and firm consciously, or by osmosis, draw in and draw on knowledge and resources from external associations, while making a similar contribution outwards. In a similar manner, the entrepreneur and firm learn from their organisation's performance, leading to knowledge creation, the foundation of new organisational competences, innovation processes and outcomes (Zahra *et al.*, 1999).

Interaction of the entrepreneur, the firm and the external environment with the dimensions of time and internationalisation behaviour in the general model specifically indicates:

- a dynamic process of innovation in which internationalisation behaviour is indicative of the *entrepreneur's and firm's response* to a continuous process of change (*C*) in the composition of internal and external factors in relation to time, to learning, and to experiential knowledge.

To identify relevant variables underlying the four constructs added to the general model, we draw on the international business, entrepreneurship and international entrepreneurship literatures. As summarised in Table 1, firm-specific internationalisation behaviour is potentially influenced by the entrepreneur's unique combination of philosophic views, social capital and human capital.

The integration of literature summarised in Table 1 also suggests that, at the firm level, likely influences are the firm's structure, its resource base (both tangible and intangible), the nature of the firm's product offer and its entrepreneurial orientation. Of note, while some consider internationalisation behaviour as an entrepreneurial strategy *per se* (Lumpkin and Dess, 1996; Lu and Beamish, 2001), and others find that strategic actions influence internationalisation behaviour (McDougall, 1989; Calof and Beamish, 1995; Bloodgood *et al.*, 1996), strategy is not accommodated as a specific variable in the general model. Rather, we follow Chell (2001) in arguing that strategy should be inferred *post hoc* from the emergent patterns and dynamic profiles of internationalisation behaviour. Therefore, the model implicitly indicates:

- a dynamic process of innovation in which internationalisation behaviour is indicative of a *firm's strategic response* to a continuous process of change (*C*) in the composition of internal and external factors in relation to time, to learning and to experiential knowledge.

Turning to the environment, the international business and entrepreneurship literatures are particularly rich in their discussion of this construct as a driver of change. Focusing on the most prevalent and comprehensive factors discussed across both fields, the general model incorporates a range of potential influences from Table 1. The first set focuses on market characteristics, the second set on competitive factors, and the third set on industry characteristics.

Finally, as noted by Cooper (1993, 244), measuring firm performance is a challenge, and '...diversity among entrepreneurial firms should be kept in mind.' The general model suggests that the firm's fingerprint pattern and profile of internationalisation behaviour at a point in time and over time will directly influence firm performance in terms of both financial and non-financial measures (see Table 1). Importantly, any such measures also need to allow for examination of both larger public firms and smaller private firms. Furthermore, the general model allows for the firm's performance in terms of learning to influence the firm and entrepreneur over time through cyclical feedback, and thus moderate the firm's ongoing internationalisation behaviour. Therefore, the general model specifically indicates:

- firm performance indicators (*P*) that show the effect of internationalisation behaviour at any given point in time, or changes in performance over any period in time.

Table 1   Contextual constructs relevant to the general model of entrepreneurial internationalisation

Variable	Meaning	Source examples
The entrepreneur		
Philosophic view	The value placed by the entrepreneur on internationalisation. Also, their perceptions and attitudes regarding internationalisation risk, cost, profit, potential and complexity.	Cavusgil (1984); Covin and Slevin (1991); Calof and Beamish (1995); Leonidou et al (1998); Preece et al. (1998)
Social capital	The entrepreneur's proprietary network relationships such as communication/social networks, informal contacts.	Birley (1985); Jarillo (1989); Coviello and Munro (1995, 1997); Ellis (2000); Yli-Renko et al. (2002)
Human capital	The entrepreneur's innovativeness, tolerance for ambiguity/flexibility, commitment, need for achievement. Also, their general perception of risk and risk tolerance, entrepreneurial and management competence, international experience, education and language proficiency.	Johanson and Vahlne (1977, 1990); Chandler and Hanks (1994); Cooper et al. (1994); McDougall et al. (1994); Bloodgood et al. (1996); Lumpkin and Dess (1996); Reuber and Fischer (1997); Leonidou et al. (1998); Westhead et al. (2001); Kuemmerle (2002)
The firm		
Structure	The firm's level of formalisation, centralisation and process coordination; organic vs mechanistic.	Covin and Slevin (1991); Jolly et al. (1992); McDougall et al. (1994); Lumpkin and Dess (1996); Oviatt and McDougall (1997)
Resources	The firm's financial, physical and technology resources (tangible), as well as human and organisational/relational/network resources (intangible).	Chandler and Hanks (1994); Calof and Beamish (1995); Coviello and Munro (1995, 1997); Greene and Brown (1997); Eisenhardt and Martin (2000); Yli-Renko et al. (2001); Kuemmerle (2002)
Product offer	The product's degree of inseparability (e.g. goods vs hard services vs soft services).	Erramilli (1989); Ekeledo and Sivakumar (1998)
Entrepreneurial orientation	The firm's strategic posture in terms of innovativeness, risk-taking and being proactive, as well as competitive aggressiveness and autonomy.	Miller (1983); Covin and Slevin (1989); Yeoh and Jeong (1995); Lumpkin and Dess (1996); Kuemmerle (2002); Ibeh (2003); Knight and Cavusgil (2004)
The environment		
Market characteristics	The market's size, potential and degree of internationalisation (both domestic and foreign).	Johanson and Mattsson (1988); Calof and Beamish (1995); Madsen and Servais (1997); Oviatt and McDougall (1997); Ekeledo and Sivakumar (1998)
Industry characteristics	The industry's degree of internationalisation, knowledge intensity and technological intensity.	Johanson and Mattsson (1988); Aaby and Slater (1989); Oviatt and McDougall (1994, 1997); Coviello and Munro (1997); Madsen and Servais (1997); Reuber and Fischer (1997); Zahra et al. (2000); Bell et al. (2003)
Environmental characteristics	The competitive environment's dynamism, hostility and intensity.	McDougall (1989); Covin and Slevin (1991); Chandler and Hanks (1994); Becherer and Maurer (1997); Zahra et al. (1997); Ekeledo and Sivakumar (1998)
Performance		
Financial measures	Growth and profitability (absolute levels, relative to competition and/or relative to expectations).	Covin and Slevin (1990); Brush and Vanderwerf (1992); Bloodgood et al. (1996); Wiklund (1999); Zahra et al. (2000)
Non-financial measures	Learning, experiential knowledge creation.	Johanson and Vahlne (1977); Covin and Slevin (1989, 1990); Zahra et al. (1999); Autio et al. (2000)

Summary and premises of the general model

The general model of entrepreneurial internationalisation behaviour (Figure 3) positions the potential variables influencing internationalisation within the primary dimensions of time and behaviour. Therefore, it can accommodate an array of relationships combining various entrepreneurial and firm factors, environmental factors and performance factors. It also builds on the five core concepts common to the simple models. Thus, it depicts a *process of cyclical behaviour* involving the entrepreneur and firm, and moderated by the external environment within which the firm operates. As a specific example, *environmental change* may trigger change in internationalisation behaviour (Zander, 1994). This behaviour is demonstrated by a firm's composite pattern of international activities over time.

The evidence of internationalisation occurs as *value-creating events*—that is, behaviour manifest at points in time (as events), in locations (countries), consisting of cross-border business modes established between the firm and organisations/individuals in foreign countries. The *time* dimension is key, and marks the distinction between decisions emerging from process, and processes triggered by decisions or streams of actions. It also marks complementarity between static economic-based explanations at points in time (e.g. internalisation/transaction cost- and resource-based approaches), and more dynamic evolutionary behavioural explanation of processes, over periods of time (e.g. the network dependency or organisation learning approaches).

Innovation in the form of cross-border activity may commence or cease at any time, leading to a complex pattern of change in internationalisation decisions, processes and activities. The relative permeability of a firm's boundaries may be indicated by the ways in which it seeks out, establishes and manages its points of contact, and the ways in which these are used to augment the firm's resource and knowledge base. It is likely that firms with more boundary permeability will internationalise more rapidly and more successfully than those with boundaries that are relatively less permeable, that is, firms that are less responsive to change.

Overall, different fingerprints of internationalisation behaviour indicate differences between firms, and, as internationalisation behaviour evolves over time, firm performance will impact on future behaviour through an iterative process of organisational learning. This results in a dynamic profile of internationalisation behaviour for each firm (Jones, 1999), and therefore provides a basis by which firms may be grouped and compared. Importantly, the general model reflects internationalisation as a long-term entrepreneurial behavioural phenomenon unique to the experiences of individual firms, and thus avoids prescribing steps or stages in a pre-ordained view of international expansion. As with the simple model, the general model allows for event- and outcome-driven approaches to be applied in process-focused research. With the inclusion of entrepreneurial, firm, environmental and performance factors, it may be further developed for use in variance approaches (Van de Ven and Engleman, 2004). This is demonstrated in the third and final level of conceptualisation, where precise models are discussed.

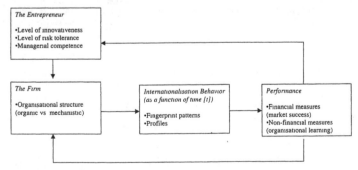

Figure 4   Example of a precise model for empirical examination.

Developing precise models

Following from the general model's holistic description of internationalisation as an entrepreneurial process of behaviour over time, it is now possible to develop context-specific models useful for focused empirical investigation of a narrow, more manageable set of constructs. This reflects the variance approach noted previously. As an illustration of this third level of the conceptual development process, we present one example of a precise model (see Figure 4). In developing this model, we select a specific set of constructs from the general model and Table 1. Here, the context is defined to be international new ventures (INVs). For this example, we have chosen four variables: the entrepreneur, organisational structure, internationalisation behaviour, and performance. Focusing on these variables allows researchers to examine a small 'piece of the puzzle' that is entrepreneurial internationalisation.

Central to Figure 4 is the INV's internationalisation behaviour, captured as both a fingerprint pattern and a profile over time. As previously noted in the general model, the fingerprint of internationalisation behaviour includes functional diversity (mode choice) and country diversity (geographic, economic and cultural distance), in relation to time. The firm's fingerprint therefore provides a measure of the firm's international involvement at a given point in time, and can be profiled and interpreted over specified time periods, particularly in terms of assessing (e.g.) the INV's rate, intensity and/or duration of internationalisation and related events.

As antecedents to internationalisation behaviour, we follow the arguments of Cooper et al. (1994) and Chrisman et al. (1999) from the entrepreneurship literature, and argue that, in the INV, the entrepreneur will be the driving influence on the firm's structure. In turn, firm structure will shape the firm's internationalisation behaviour and, ultimately, firm performance. This view also reflects the arguments of Madsen and Servais (1997) and Shrader et al. (2000), which place the entrepreneur as the key antecedent of an INV.

Looking at these variables in greater detail, we draw from Table 1 and suggest that, in the context of this example, the entrepreneur's levels of innovativeness and risk tolerance will influence his/her firm's organisational structure (drawing on Lumpkin and Dess, 1996), as will their managerial competence (Chandler and Hanks, 1994). For example, we suggest that while the entrepreneur is typically assumed to drive his/her firm in a

centralised manner and with strong leadership, s/he is also likely to create an organisation structure that allows for innovativeness, risk-taking and creativity. Thus, the characteristics of the entrepreneur in an INV will impact on the firm's level of organicity.

In turn, the extent to which a firm is organic *vs* mechanistic in structure will impact on firm behaviour. In the context of internationalisation, this relates to (e.g.) the rate, gap time and time intensity of internationalisation. Also, the degree of conventionality reflected in organisation structure is likely to be associated with the place and mode of transference (i.e. market choice and mode of entry), and the degree to which the internationalisation event represents a radical innovation for the firm.

Finally, differences in internationalisation behaviour will impact on performance, in terms of both market success and organisation learning, that is, the 'process of assimilating new knowledge into the organisation's knowledge base' (Autio et al., 2000, 911). This learning is arguably based on experiential knowledge generated through internationalisation behaviour. However, rather than position learning as an intermediate variable between internationalisation behaviour and performance, as done by Zahra et al. (2000), we argue that there exists a learning loop providing experience- and performance-based knowledge into the decision process, at the level both of the entrepreneur and of the firm, cyclically over time (Athanassiou and Nigh, 2000; Hurmerinta-Peltomäki, 2003).

Overall, this particular example of a precise model is specific to the context of a certain type of firm: the INV. Beyond the primary process dimensions of time and internationalisation behaviour, it comprises a select set of variables drawn from the list outlined in Table 1. A second (and related) precise model might also incorporate environmental hostility and dynamism in a moderating-effects test. Alternatively, if a researcher was interested in understanding how the international new venture compares with more established firms, firm-level measures such as organisational resources and entrepreneurial orientation might be introduced as antecedents to internationalisation behaviour, with firms assessed at various stages of the life cycle (e.g. start-up, early internationalisation, late internationalisation). If entrepreneur-level characteristics were included, interesting interaction-effects or independent-effects models could also be tested. Yet another example of a precise model might assess completely different aspects of the key constructs from Table 1, such as relationships between the firm's network resources and its internationalisation behaviour. More specifically, research could examine the extent to which network structure and internationalisation behaviour are self-reinforcing—that is, how network structure influences internationalisation, and vice versa, over time. Given that much of the extant network research has focused on technology-based firms (e.g. software or 'hard service' organisations), this analysis could compare firms with different product offers (e.g. goods *vs* hard services *vs* soft services) or firms from industries with different degrees of knowledge and/or technological intensity.

These illustrative examples provide some sense of the range of time-based entrepreneurial internationalisation research that is possible. As precise models examining component parts of the general model evolve, a holistic understanding of entrepreneurial internationalisation behaviour will emerge, informing both the international business and entrepreneurship literatures.

Discussion

This paper presents a three-level process of conceptual development. The first level entailed the identification of two simple models of entrepreneurship and internationalisation as behavioural processes, and the identification of core concepts common to both fields. Second, the shared concepts were used in the development of a general model of entrepreneurial internationalisation composed of two primary process dimensions (time and behaviour), and four key constructs (the entrepreneur, firm, environment and performance). To illustrate how the general model provides a basis for development of precise, context-specific contingency models, we detailed one example of such a model as the third level of conceptual development, and highlighted a number of other possibilities for precise models.

Our general premise is that to develop a unifying direction for international entrepreneurship researchers interested in internationalisation, it is essential to first understand the basic commonalities of the international and entrepreneurship literatures. Then, rather than moving immediately to precise models, an evolutionary process of conceptual development is more helpful, moving from the simple to the general to the precise. This approach also reflects the idea that multi-theoretical perspectives are useful in understanding complex social phenomena such as entrepreneurial

internationalisation behaviour. Our conceptualisation is sufficiently flexible to accommodate the necessary and sufficient conditions that influence and lend explanation to a firm's decisions and actions, and also the dynamic processes of entrepreneurial internationalisation behaviour over time. Consequently, it also lays a foundational framework for the development of an evolutionary theory of multinational firms.

Importantly, our arguments provide foundation for the development of an entrepreneurial theory of internationalisation, where entrepreneurship and internationalisation are seen as interdependent processes. Specifically, we also establish internationalisation as a firm-level entrepreneurial behaviour manifested by events and outcomes in relation to time. This is accomplished through our three levels of conceptual development, whereby the internationalisation literature is informed by concepts and ideas imported from the complementary field of entrepreneurship. We also incorporate a temporal focus, arguing that entrepreneurial internationalisation is both time based and time dependent. Thus we delineate the dimension of time as critical to internationalisation research. Similarly, we highlight the notion of the cyclical effect of time in respect of how the environment, firm and entrepreneur interact and learn to impact on internationalisation behaviour. Emphasis is also placed on defining internationalisation behaviour *per se*, where it is proposed to be a phenomenon determined by and manifest in measurable evidence represented as a firm's fingerprint pattern and profile. The discussion also distinguishes between behaviour and strategy in that the general model explicitly delineates the former and suggests that the latter may be determined *post hoc* from interpretation of internationalisation behaviour patterns and profiles.

We also suggest that entrepreneurial internationalisation is linked, directly and cyclically, to various aspects of firm performance, and our arguments distinguish between evidence of internationalisation behaviour (fingerprints and profiles) and the outcome of that behaviour, that is, firm performance. Critically, our view accounts for the competences and resources specific to the entrepreneur, and encourages future investigation of the entrepreneur's influence along with those of the firm and environment. Finally, the discussion regarding precise models illustrates how international entrepreneurship researchers can draw from the general model to then focus on narrow or precise models in order to understand specific aspects of entrepreneurial internationalisation behaviour over time. Such precise models can be used for the development and testing of individual hypotheses, allowing researchers to focus on fine detail and specifically defined constructs and measures. Importantly, these constructs and measures can be grounded in the definitions derived from the core concepts underpinning the integrative process of conceptual development presented here. Thus, the recommendations of both McDougall and Oviatt (2000) and Buckley and Chapman (1996) can be implemented.

Limitations and research implications

In moving forward with international entrepreneurship research, we acknowledge a number of limitations with the outcomes of our conceptual development. First, we chose the concepts of *process* and *time* as the initial foundations for our integration of the international and entrepreneurship literatures and our assessment of the simple models. Although we believe this is most relevant, we recognise that other bases for integration might exist. These should be drawn from further evaluation of the classic contributions from each field. Second, the general model is purposefully broad and integrative. It is therefore composed of multiple general constructs. We suggest that, beyond the primary dimensions of time and internationalisation behaviour, the likely antecedent, outcome and moderating variables are summarised in Table 1. However, we also recognise that there is scope for additional work to refine the composition of these variables, and ensure that measures are operationally defined in a manner appropriate to international entrepreneurship research.

Finally, testing the general model in its entirety within a single research study presents a daunting and prohibitive task. Indeed, it is not our intent to offer the general model as one that is testable. Rather, we have positioned the general model within the overall process of conceptual development as, essentially, a means to an end—that is, as a basis for use by international entrepreneurship researchers in developing narrower and more precise, context-focused models for empirical investigation. We feel there is clear opportunity for developing a range of precise models that fall within the umbrella of the general model. This is not, however, to suggest that the extant literature does not contribute to our understanding of entrepreneurial internationalisation. Rather, it provides a critical base from which to move forward with time-based research. As a simple example, the recent work of Ibeh (2003) examines individual, firm and industry influences on the decision to create an export venture in small firms. These are, of course, variables encompassed by the general model, but, as yet, Ibeh's (2003) work does not account for decisions or behaviour over time. Replication of this work by, for example, tracking Ibeh's sample firms will provide one step to understanding the dynamics of internationalisation antecedents, behaviour and outcomes.

Ideally, we suggest that future research might not only examine component parts of the general model, but also treat such parts as pieces of an emerging puzzle whereby adding one piece at a time reveals the nature of the larger process in question. However, as discussed in Coviello and Jones (2004), effort is needed to ensure that consistent definitions and measures are used across studies in order to truly advance an integrated understanding of entrepreneurial internationalisation behaviour. Additional work is required to develop a commonly accepted and rigorous set of definitions for the field.

Acknowledgements

We thank Michael Mayer, Ben Oviatt, two JIBS reviewers and Arie Lewin, *JIBS* Editor-in-Chief, for their comments on this work. We are also grateful to conference participants at the Third Biennial McGill Conference on International Entrepreneurship and the 2002 Conference of the Australia–New Zealand International Business Academy.

References

Aaby, N.E. and Slater, S.F. (1989) 'Management influences on export performance: a review of the empirical literature 1978–1988', *International Marketing Review* 6(4): 7–26.

Ancona, D.G., Goodman, P.S., Lawrence, B.S. and Tushman, M.L. (2001) 'Time: a new research lens', *Academy of Management Review* 26(4): 645–664.

Andersen, O. (1993) 'On the internationalization process of firms: a critical analysis', *Journal of International Business Studies* 24(2): 33–46.

Andersen, O. (1997) 'Internationalization and market entry mode: a review of theories and conceptual frameworks', *Management International Review* 37(2): 7–42.

Anderson, E. and Gatignon, H. (1986) 'Modes of foreign entry: a transaction cost analysis and proposition', *Journal of International Business Studies* 17(3): 1–26.

Arenius, P.M. (2002) *Creation of Firm-Level Social Capital, Its Exploitation, and the Process of Early Internationalization*, Helsinki University of Technology: Helsinki.

Athanassiou, N. and Nigh, D. (2000) 'Internationalization, tacit knowledge and the top management teams of MNCs', *Journal of International Business Studies* 31(3): 471–487.

Autio, E., Sapienza, H.J. and Almeida, J.G. (2000) 'Effects of age at entry, knowledge intensity and imitability on international growth', *Academy of Management Journal* 43(5): 909–924.

Becherer, R.C. and Maurer, J.G. (1997) 'The moderating effect of environmental variables on the entrepreneurial and marketing orientation of entrepreneur-led firms', *Entrepreneurship Theory and Practice* 22(1): 47–58.

Bell, J., McNaughton, R., Young, S. and Crick, D. (2003) 'Towards an integrative model of small firm internationalisation', *Journal of International Entrepreneurship* 1(4): 339–362.

Benito, G.R.G. and Gripsrud, G. (1992) 'The Expansion of foreign direct investments: discrete rational location choices or a cultural learning process? *Journal of International Business Studies* 23(3): 461–476.

Birley, S. (1985) 'The role of networks in the entrepreneurial process', *Journal of Business Venturing* 1: 107–117.

Bloodgood, J.M., Sapienza, H.J. and Almeida, J.G. (1996) 'The Internationalization of new high-potential US ventures: antecedents and outcomes', *Entrepreneurship Theory and Practice* 20(4): 61–76.

Boter, H. and Holmquist, C. (1996) 'Industry characteristics and internationalization processes in small firms', *Journal of Business Venturing* 11: 471–487.

Brazeal, D.V. and Herbert, T.T. (1999) 'The genesis of entrepreneurship', *Entrepreneurship Theory and Practice* 23(3): 29–45.

Brush, C.G. and Vanderwerf, P.A. (1992) 'A comparison of methods and sources for obtaining estimates of new venture performance', *Journal of Business Venturing* 7(2): 157–170.

Buckley, P.J. (2002) 'Is the international business research agenda running out of steam? *Journal of International Business Studies* 33(2): 365–374.

Buckley, P.J. and Casson, M. (1985) *The Economic Theory of the Multinational Enterprise*, Macmillan: London.

Buckley, P.J. and Chapman, M. (1996) 'Theory and method in international business research', *International Business Review* 5(3): 233–245.

Calof, J.C. and Beamish, P. (1995) 'Adapting to foreign markets: explaining internationalization', *International Business Review* 4(2): 115–131.

Carlson, S. (1974) 'International transmission of information and the business firm', *The Annals of the American Academy of Political and Social Science* 412: 55–63.

Casson, M. (2000) *The Economics of International Business*, Edward Elgar: Cheltenham.

Cavusgil, S.T. (1984) 'Differences among exporting firms based on their degree of internationalization', *Journal of Business Research* 12: 195–208.

Chandler, G.N. and Hanks, S.H. (1994) 'Founder competence, the environment, and venture performance', *Entrepreneurship Theory and Practice* 18(3): 77–89.

Chell, E. (2001) *Entrepreneurship: Globalisation, Innovation and Development*, Thomson Learning: London.

Chrisman, J.J., Bauerschmidt, A. and Hofer, C.W. (1999) 'The determinants of new venture performance', *Entrepreneurship Theory and Practice* 22(1): 5–29.

Cooper, A.C. (1993) 'Challenges in predicting new firm performance', *Journal of Business Venturing* 8(3): 241–253.

Cooper, A.C., Gimeno-Gascon, F.J. and Woo, C.Y. (1994) 'Initial human and financial capital predictors of new venture performance', *Journal of Business Venturing* 9(5): 371–395.

Coviello, N.E. and Jones, M.V. (2004) 'Methodological issues in international entrepreneurship research', *Journal of Business Venturing* 19(4): 485–508.

Coviello, N.E. and McAuley, A. (1999) 'Internationalisation and the smaller firm: a review of contemporary empirical research', *Management International Review* 39(3): 223–256.

Coviello, N.E. and Munro, H.J. (1995) 'Growing the entrepreneurial firm: networking for international market development', *European Journal of Marketing* 29(7): 49–61.

Coviello, N.E and Munro, H.J (1997) 'Network relationships and the internationalisation process of small software firms', *International Business Review* 6(4): 361–386.

Covin, J.G. and Slevin, D.P. (1989) 'Strategic management of small firms in hostile and benign environments', *Strategic Management Journal* 10(1): 75–87.

Covin, J.G. and Slevin, D.P. (1990) 'New venture strategic posture, structure and performance: an industry life cycle analysis', *Journal of Business Venturing* 5(2): 123–135.

Covin, J.G. and Slevin, D.P. (1991) 'A conceptual model of entrepreneurship as firm behavior', *Entrepreneurship Theory and Practice* 16(1): 7–25.

Dana, L.P., Etemad, H. and Wright, R.W. (1999) 'Theoretical Foundations of International Entrepreneurship', in R.W. Wright (ed.) *Research in Global Strategic Management*, vol. 7. JAI Press: Stamford, CT, pp. 3–22.

Eisenhardt, K.M. and Martin, J.A. (2000) 'Dynamic capabilities: what are they? *Strategic Management Journal* 21: 1105–1121.

Ekeledo, I. and Sivakumar, K. (1998) 'Foreign market entry mode choice of service firms: a contingency perspective', *Journal of the Academy of Marketing Science* 26(4): 274–292.

Ellis, P. (2000) 'Social ties and foreign market entry', *Journal of International Business Studies* 31(3): 443–469.

Erramilli, M.K. (1989) 'Entry mode choice in service industries', *International Marketing Review* 7(5): 50–62.

Greene, P.G. and Brown, T.E. (1997) 'Resource needs and the dynamic capitalism typology', *Journal of Business Venturing* 12(3): 161–173.

Harvey, M., Griffith, D. and Novicevic, M. (2000) 'Development of timescapes to effectively manage global interorganizational relational communications', *European Management Journal* 18(6): 646–662.

Hill, C.W.L., Hwang, P. and Kim, W.C. (1990) 'Global strategy and multinationals' entry mode choice', *Journal of International Business Studies* 23(1): 29–54.

Hock, D. (1999) *Birth of the Chaordic Age*, Berett-Koehler: San Francisco.

Hurmerinta-Peltomäki, L. (2003) 'Time and internationalisation: theoretical challenges set by rapid internationalisation', *Journal of International Entrepreneurship* 1(2): 217–236.

Ibeh, K. (2003) 'Toward a contingency framework of export entrepreneurship: conceptualizations and empirical evidence', *Small Business Economics* 20(1): 49–68.

Jarillo, J.C. (1989) 'Entrepreneurship and growth: the strategic use of external resources', *Journal of Business Venturing* 4: 133–147.

Johanson, J. and Mattsson, L.-G. (1988) 'Internationalisation in Industrial Systems: A Network Approach', in P.J. Buckley and P. Ghauri (eds.) *The Internationalization of the Firm: A Reader*, Academic Press: London, pp. 303–321.

Johanson, J. and Vahlne, J.-E. (1977) 'The internationalization process of the firm: a model of knowledge development and increasing foreign commitment', *Journal of International Business Studies* 8: 23–32.

Johanson, J. and Vahlne, J.-E. (1990) 'The mechanism of internationalisation', *International Marketing Review* 7(4): 11–24.

Johanson, J. and Vahlne, J.-E. (2003) 'Business relationship learning and commitment in the internationalisation process', *Journal of International Entrepreneurship* 1(1): 83–101.

Johanson, J. and Wiedersheim-Paul, F. (1975) 'The internationalisation of the firm: four Swedish case studies', *Journal of Management Studies* 12(3): 305–322.

Jolly, V.K., Alahuta, M. and Jeannet, J.-P. (1992) 'Challenging the incumbents: how high technology start-ups compete globally', *Journal of Strategic Change* 1: 71–82.

Jones, M.V. (1999) 'The internationalization of small high technology firms', *Journal of International Marketing* 7(4): 15–41.

Jones, M.V. (2001) 'First steps in internationalisation: concepts and evidence from a sample of small high technology firms', *Journal of International Management* 7(3): 191–210.

Kast, F.E. and Rosenzweig, J.E. (1974) *Organization and Management: A Systems Approach*, McGraw-Hill: London.

Knight, G.A. and Cavusgil, S.T. (2004) 'Innovation, organizational capabilities, and the born-global firm', *Journal of International Business Studies* 35(2): 124–141.

Kogut, B. and Singh, H. (1988) 'The effect of national culture on the choice of entry mode', *Journal of International Business Studies* 19(3): 411–432.

Kuemmerle, W. (2002) 'Home base and knowledge management in international ventures', *Journal of Business Venturing* 17: 99–122.

Kundu, S.K. and Katz, J.H. (2003) 'Born international SMEs: bi-level impacts of resources and intentions', *Small Business Economics* 20(1): 25–49.

Kutschker, M., Baurle, I. and Schmid, S. (1997) 'International evolution, international episodes, and international epochs: implications for managing internationalization', *Management International Review* 37(Special Issue 2): 101–124.

Leonidou, L.C., Katsikeas, C.S. and Piercy, N.F. (1998) 'Identifying managerial influences on exporting: past research and future directions', *Journal of International Marketing* 6(2): 74–102.

Lu, J.W. and Beamish, P.W. (2001) 'The internationalization and performance of SMEs', *Strategic Management Journal* 22(6/7): 565–586.

Lumpkin, G.T. and Dess, G.G. (1996) 'Clarifying the entrepreneurial orientation construct and linking it to performance', *Academy of Management Review* 21(1): 135–172.

Luostarinen, R. (1980) *The Internationalization of the Firm*, Helsinki School of Economics: Helsinki.

Luostarinen, R., Korhonen, H., Jokinen, J. and Pelkonen, T. (1994) *Globalisation and SME*, Ministry of Trade and Industry: Helsinki.

Madsen, T.K. and Servais, P. (1997) 'The Internationalization of born globals: an evolutionary process? *International Business Review* 6(6): 561–583.

McDougall, P.P. (1989) 'International vs domestic entrepreneurship: new venture strategic behavior and industry structure', *Journal of Business Venturing* 4: 387–400.

McDougall, P.P. and Oviatt, B.M. (2000) 'International entrepreneurship: the intersection of two research paths', *Academy of Management Journal* 43(5): 902–906.

McDougall, P.P., Shane, S and Oviatt, B.M. (1994) 'Explaining the formation of international new ventures: the limits of theories from international business research', *Journal of Business Venturing* 9: 469–487.

McNaughton, R.B. (2000) 'Determinants of time-span to foreign market entry', *Journal of Euromarketing* 9(2): 99–112.

Miller, D. (1983) 'The correlates of entrepreneurship in three types of firms', *Management Science* 29: 770–791.

Morris, M.H., Kuratko, D.F. and Schindehutte, M. (2001) 'Towards integration: understanding entrepreneurship through frameworks', *Entrepreneurship and Innovation* 2(1): 35–49.

Ofori-Dankwa, J. and Julian, S.D. (2001) 'Complexifying organizational theory: illustrations using time research', *Academy of Management Review* 26(3): 415–430.

Oviatt, B.M. and McDougall, P.P. (1994) 'Toward a theory of international new ventures', *Journal of International Business Studies* 25(1): 45–64.

Oviatt, B.M. and McDougall, P.P. (1997) 'Challenges for internationalization process theory: the case of international new ventures', *Management International Review* 37(2): 85–99.

Pan, Y. and Tse, D. (2000) 'The hierarchical model of market entry modes', *Journal of International Business Studies* 31(4): 535–554.

Patton, M.Q. (2002) *Qualitative Research and Evaluation Methods*, Sage: London.

Preece, S.B., Miles, G. and Baetz, M.C. (1998) 'Explaining the international intensity and global diversity of early-stage technology based firms', *Journal of Business Venturing* 14: 259–281.

Rennie, M.W. (1993) 'Global competitiveness: born global', *The McKinsey Quarterly* 4: 45–52.

Reuber, A.R. and Fischer, E. (1997) 'The influence of the management team's international experience on internationalization behavior', *Journal of International Business Studies* 28(4): 807–825.

Reuber, A.R. and Fischer, E. (1999) 'Understanding the consequences of founder's experience', *Journal of Small Business Management* 37(2): 30–45.

Schumpeter, J. (1934) *The Theory of Economic Development*, Cambridge University Press: Cambridge.

Shane, S. and Venkataraman, S. (2000) 'The promise of entrepreneurship as a field of research', *Academy of Management Review* 25(1): 217–226.

Shrader, R.C., Oviatt, B.M. and McDougall, P.P. (2000) 'How new ventures exploit trade-offs among international risk factors: lessons for the accelerated internationalization of the 21st century', *Academy of Management Journal* 43(6): 1227–1247.

Stevenson, H.H. and Harmeling, S. (1990) 'Entrepreneurial management's need for a more 'chaotic' theory', *Journal of Business Venturing* 5(1): 1–14.

Ucbasaran, D., Westhead, P. and Wright, M. (2001) 'The focus of entrepreneurial research: context, process and issues', *Entrepreneurship Theory and Practice* 25(4): 57–80.

Van de Ven, A.H. and Engleman, R.M. (2004) 'Event- and outcome-driven explanations of entrepreneurship', *Journal of Business Venturing* 19(3): 343–358.

Weick, K.E. (1999) 'Theory construction as disciplined reflexivity: tradeoffs in the 90s', *Academy of Management Review* 24(4): 787–806.

Welch, L.S. and Luostarinen, R. (1988) 'Internationalization: evolution of a concept', *Journal of General Management* 14(2): 34–55.

Westhead, P., Wright, M. and Ucbasaran, D. (2001) 'The internationalisation of new and small firms: a resource-based view', *Journal of Business Venturing* 16: 333–358.

Wiklund, J. (1999) 'The sustainability of the entrepreneurial orientation-performance relationship', *Entrepreneurship Theory and Practice* 24(1): 37–48.

Wright, R.W. and Ricks, D.A. (1994) 'Trends in international business research: twenty five years later', *Journal of International Business Studies* 25(4): 687–701.

Yeoh, P.-L. and Jeong, I. (1995) 'Contingency relationships between export, channel structure and environment: a proposed conceptual model of export performance', *European Journal of Marketing* 29(8): 95–115.

Yli-Renko, H., Autio, E. and Sapienza, H.J. (2001) 'Social capital, knowledge acquisition, and knowledge exploitation in young technology-based firms', *Strategic Management Journal* 22(6/7): 587–613.

Yli-Renko, H., Autio, E and Tontti, V. (2002) 'Social capital, knowledge and the international growth of technology-based new firms', *International Business Review* 11: 279–304.

Young, S., Hammill, J., Wheeler, C. and Davies, J.R. (1989) *International Market Entry and Development: Strategies and Management*, Harvester Wheatsheaf: Hemel Hempstead.

Zahra, S.A., Ireland, R.D. and Hitt, M.A. (2000) 'International expansion by new venture firms: international diversity, mode of market entry, technological learning, and performance', *Academy of Management Journal* **43**(5): 925–950.

Zahra, S.A., Neubaum, D.O. and Huse, M. (1997) 'The effect of the environment on export performance among telecommunications new ventures', *Entrepreneurship Theory and Practice* **22**(1): 25–46.

Zahra, S.A., Nielsen, A.P. and Bogner, W.C. (1999) 'Corporate entrepreneurs knowledge, and competence development', *Entrepreneurship Theory and Practice* **23**(3): 169–189.

Zander, I. (1994) *The Tortoise Evolution of the Multinational Corporation: Foreign Technological Activity in Swedish Multinational Firms 1890–1990*, Institute of International Business, Stockholm School of Economics: Stockholm.

About the authors

Marian V Jones is senior lecturer in international strategy and Director of the Doctoral Research Programme in the School of Business and Management at the University of Glasgow, Scotland, UK. Her research focuses on international entrepreneurship, internationalisation, innovation and competitiveness. She has published widely on small firm internationalisation, and is co-editor of the *Journal of International Entrepreneurship*.

Nicole Coviello is Professor of Marketing and International Entrepreneurship at the University of Auckland, New Zealand. Her research interests focus on international entrepreneurship, network dynamics and contemporary marketing practices. She sits on numerous editorial boards across the fields of marketing, international business and entrepreneurship.

Accepted by Arie Lewin, Editor in Chief, 18 October 2004 This paper has been with the author for two revisions

[4]

Pergamon

PII: S0969–5931(97)00032–2

International Business Review Vol. 6, No. 6, pp. 561–583, 1997
© 1997 Elsevier Science Ltd All rights reserved
Printed in Great Britain
0969-5931/97 $17 00 + 0.00

The Internationalization of Born Globals: an Evolutionary Process?

Tage Koed Madsen and Per Servais
Odense University, Department of Marketing, Campusvej 55, DK-5230 Odense M, Denmark

Abstract—Recently, the phenomenon of Born Globals has been highlighted in many articles concerning the internationalization processes of firms. Such firms adopt an international or even global approach right from their birth or very shortly thereafter. Some authors consider this phenomenon as being in strong opposition to the traditional models of internationalization. This is, of course, true if one considers the manifestations of these models, namely the so-called stages model, according to which the firm should internationalize like "rings in the water", i.e. in a slow and gradual manner with respect to geographical markets, market entry mode and product policy. This article contributes to the field in three ways: it summarizes the empirical evidence reported about Born Globals; it interprets the phenomenon at a deeper theoretical level and offers a new conceptionalization of the research issue; and it generates propositions about the antecedents of as well as the necessary and sufficient conditions for the rise of the phenomenon. In doing so, the conclusion is that Born Globals grow in a way which may be in accordance with evolutionary thinking. © 1997 Elsevier Science Ltd. All rights reserved

Key Words—Born Global, Internationalization, Evolutionary Process

Introduction

For two decades internationalization processes of firms has been the topic of much research in the field of international marketing. Two quite similar streams of research have emerged in Europe and the in the US. In a recent review article Andersen (1993) labels these original models "The Uppsala Internationalization Model (U-M)" (see, for example, Johanson and Wieder-sheim-Paul, 1975; Johanson and Vahlne, 1977) and "The Innovation-Related Internationalization Models (I-M)" (see, for example, Bilkey and Tesar, 1977; Cavusgil, 1980). Both streams of research contend that firms become international in a slow and incremental manner which may be due to lack of knowledge about foreign markets, high risk aversion, high perceived uncertainty, or similar factors. The U-M sees internationalization processes as involving time consuming organizational learning processes; the I-M tends to analyse the process as an innovative course of action and hence a question of adoption of new ways of doing business.

Still, both streams of research conceptualize the manifest internationalization process as an incremental process involving a varying number of stages. This type of conceptualization has been widely used as the basis for much empirical research around the world. In many instances the empirical data have supported the notion that firms often internationalize like "rings in the water", trying to gain market knowledge gradually, and hence reduce uncertainty and

562

International
Business
Review
6,6

risk over time for each country market. However, many researchers have accused the stages models for being too deterministic and of limited value (see, for example, Reid, 1983; Turnbull, 1987). After a more theoretical evaluation Andersen (1993) concludes that their theoretical boundaries, explanatory power, and operationalization need to be researched much more thoroughly in a longitudinal setting.

Recently, even more convincing evidence of the limitations of the manifest stages models has appeared in the literature. Research has identified an increasing number of firms which certainly do not follow the traditional stages pattern in their internationalization process. In contrast, they aim at international markets or maybe even the global market right from their birth. Such companies have been named Born Globals (Rennie, 1993; Knight and Cavusgil, 1996), Global Start-ups (Oviatt and McDougall, 1994), High Technology Start-ups (Jolly *et al.*, 1992), and International New Ventures (McDougall *et al.*, 1994). Here we adopt the name Born Globals.

This article explores some of the main characteristics reported about Born Globals; empirical support for the phenomenon is established by reviewing the findings of studies reported in the literature. These findings are related to the original internationalization model developed by the researchers in Uppsala as well as to evolutionary economic thinking and the network approach to international activities. It is demonstrated that the Born Globals phenomenon can partly be understood and analysed by existing theories and descriptions of internationalization processes in firms. It is argued, though, that evolutionary economics as well as the network approach offer some promising additional insights into the phenomenon. The conceptionalization of the phenomenon offered in this article has not explicitly appeared in previous writings about Born Globals. So, according to the arguments below it is not necessary to look for completely new theories in order to understand and further research Born Globals.

Finally, case studies reported about Born Globals in different countries are compared in order to explore situation specific differences in antecedents as well as necessary and sufficient conditions for the emergence and expansion of Born Globals. The article concludes with the generation of propositions about Born Globals and a discussion of future research topics.

Born Globals: Some Findings
McDougall *et al.* (1994) as well as Knight and Cavusgil (1996) refer to a number of empirical studies which appear to contradict the stages theory of internationalization. In a similar vein Welch and Luostarinen (1988) focus upon small English, Australian and Swedish firms that skipped different stages and who unexpectedly fast had foreign direct investments. Ganitsky (1989) investigated a sample of 18 Israeli exporters, who served foreign markets right from their inception. Brush (1992) found in a nationwide study of small US manufacturers that 13% of the sample had started international activities during the first year of operations. In an Australian study McKinsey and Co.

(1993) identified many Born Globals whose management viewed the world as its marketplace right from the birth of the company. Holstein (1992) reports similar findings among small US firms.

Inter-nationalization of Born Globals

Knight and Cavusgil (1996) even show that studies from the late 1970s have documented examples of internationalization patterns similar to such Born Globals in different countries (for example, Buckley *et al.*, 1979; Roux, 1979; Garnier, 1982). So, abundant empirical evidence can be found, showing that not all firms internationalize according to the stages models. Below, we review the most recent studies which have explicitly positioned their findings as opposed to traditional internationalization models.

Oviatt and McDougall (1994) focus on newly started firms and they define an International New Venture (INV) as a business organization that, from inception, seeks to derive significant competitive advantage from the use of resources from and the sale of outputs in multiple countries (p. 49). In contrast to traditional organizations that develop gradually from domestic firms to multinational enterprises, the INV starts out with a proactive international strategy—even though it starts with only one or a few employees/entrepreneurs.

In their study of 24INVs McDougall *et al.* (1994) found that none of them followed the incremental stages of internationalization. This lead them to conclude that the stages models fail to provide an appropriate explanation for why such firms operate on international markets rather than just on their home markets. Concerning the governance structure of activities, McDougall *et al.* (1994) claim that there are key differences between established firms and start-up firms, due to the amount and source of resources. The latter type of firms will only have few resources left over for expensive investments in for example distribution channels; therefore, in comparison with established firms, the entrepreneur must rely more on hybrid structures for controlling the sales and marketing activities (e.g. close personal relationships, joint ventures).

This is in accordance with the findings of Bell (1995) in his study of small computer software firms. In the study he argues that the U-M did not adequately reflect the underlying factors of the internationalization processes in these firms. He found that the process was strongly influenced by domestic and foreign client followership, the targeting of niche markets and industry specific consideration rather then the psychic distance to export markets. He also found very little support for the notion that the firms progress systematically from exporting to other market entry modes, even though he found an increasing commitment to exporting among the responding firms. Finally, not all firms established themselves with domestic sales before starting foreign sales; this could be due to prior experiences of the entrepreneur or to the fact that exports were often initiated when searching suppliers abroad.

In contrast to Oviatt and McDougall (1994), McKinsey and Co. (1993) focuses on already established firms, especially small- and medium-sized enterprises. In a research project conducted for the Australian Manufacturing

564

International
Business
Review
6,6

Council covering 310 firms, McKinsey splits the emerging exporters into two categories. The first one consists of more traditional domestic-based firms accounting for approximately 75% of the total sample. Firms in this category typically build a strong domestic base before exporting. On average they have been in business for 27 years when they first export and they reap 15–20% of sales in foreign markets. The second category is labeled Born Globals; they export 75% of their total sales, starting after less than two years of operation. They generally produce leading edge technology products with significant international niche markets, such as scientific instruments or machine tools. Rennie (1993) describes them as competing on quality and value created through innovative technology and product design. The mainstream Born Global of this study is very close to its customers, flexible and able to adapt its products to quickly changing needs and wants.

The latter findings are somewhat in contrast to Jolly *et al.* (1992), who conclude that "High Technology Start-ups" must choose a business area with homogeneous customers and mimimal adaptation in the marketing mix. The argument is that these small firms cannot take a multidomestic approach like large firms, simply because they do not have the sufficient scale in operations worldwide. They are vulnerable because they are dependent on a single product which they have to commercialize in lead markets first, no matter where such markets are situated geographically. The reason is that such markets are the key to broad and rapid market access which is important because the fixed costs in these firms is relatively high. Since this is the key factor influencing the choice of the initial market, the importance of psychic distance as market selection criteria is reduced. Often these firms govern their sales and marketing activities through a specialized network in which they seek partners who complement their own competences; this is necessary because of their limited resources.

Recent research carried out in the Nordic countries (Lindmark *et al.*, 1994) also demonstrates the existence of Born Globals. Based on the study of 328 exporters from Finland, Norway, Sweden, and Denmark it is concluded that the firms' domestic market no longer seems to be as important a "learning place" as earlier studies demonstrated. A high proportion of the exporters started their international activities just after the birth of the firm. About 20% of them did so within one year after their inception; two years later the percentage had risen to roughly 50. The Danish data reveal that the firms born within the last 10–15 years start exporting faster than older firms. Results from another empirical study in Denmark (Industri- og Handelsstyrelsen, 1992) show similar conclusions, and in a longitudinal study (over the years 1985–1993) of 948 newly established firms in Denmark, Christensen and Jacobsen (1996) report that a rising number of these firms started exporting within the first years of existence. They conclude that different firms have different routes to internationalization "...based on differences in established contacts and knowledge acquired prior to the initiated new business..." (p. 7). Market knowledge, personal networking of the entrepreneur, or international contacts and experience transmitted from former occupation, relations, and education are examples of such international skills obtained prior the birth of the firm.

As we have seen, findings in studies of Born Globals are sometimes in accordance with each other—but in other instances they are conflicting. There is general agreement about the fast and immediate pattern of internationalization and growth, and also to some extent about the type of governance structure used (mainly a hybrid form). Yet, there are disparate opinions about other characteristics of the situation of the Born Globals (as we have seen this is true, e.g. concerning the degree of customerization of products and closeness to customers in general). The reason for these discrepancies may be traced back to the fact that the phenomenon "Born Globals" is still very new and not well defined as a research area; therefore the samples of the individual studies are quite different and not fully comparable. In addition, most studies are purely descriptive without a well developed theoretical frame of reference.

Driving Forces and Theoretical Approaches
An important question concerns the drivers of the new picture of internationalization processes of firms. Why does this happen? An answer to this question also tells us something about the future diffusion of the phenomenon. Based on the literature (in general and as mentioned above) the rise of Born Globals may be attributed to at least three important factors: (1) new market conditions, (2) technological developments in the areas of production, transportation and communication, and finally (3) more elaborate capabilities of people, including the founder/entrepreneur who starts the Born Global firm. All three factors are, however, interrelated.

On the surface the rise of Born Globals may be explained by changing market conditions which many industries have been exposed to during the recent decades. One changing condition often mentioned is the increasing specialization and hence the number of niche markets seen; as a consequence we should see more firms producing very specific parts and components which they have to sell in the international marketplace, simply because domestic demand is too small—even in large countries. Entrepreneurs in high tech markets may have to sell their innovative product worldwide. The other side of the coin is the fact that many industries are characterized by global sourcing activities and also of networks across borders. The consequence is that innovative products very quickly can spread to country markets all over the world—also because the needs and wants of buyers become more homogeneous. Hence, the internationalization process of subcontractors may be quite diverse and different from the stages model (Andersen *et al.*, 1995). In other words the new market conditions pull the firms into many markets very fast. Finally, also financial markets have become international which means that an entrepreneur in any country may seek financial sources all over the world.

These new market characteristics have not emerged by themselves, though. They have to a high degree been caused by some basic changes in technology.

566

International
Business
Review
6,6

New production process technology has implied that small-scale operations may also be economically sound; therefore specialization, customization and niche production are more viable alternatives in today's markets. Transportation of people and goods has become much more frequent, reliable and even cheaper than ever before; this means that cost barriers for an international approach have been removed. This is also a result of developments in the area of communication; world markets have become more accessible (even for small firms) at low cost by the use of fax machines, e-mail, etc. "Day-to-day business" (e.g. sales and service operations) can often be carried out in many countries from the same desk. In the same vein, information about international markets may be collected, analysed and interpreted from the very same desk.

A final precondition for the changing market conditions and hence the rise of Born Globals is the increased ability of human resources to exploit the possibilities of the technological changes on the international markets. Basically the increased capabilities in this area are due to the fact that a dramatically increasing number of people have gained international experience during the last couple of decades. As an illustration, different programmes in the European Union exchange around 50,000 students every year. They go to other countries in order to complete 6–12 months of their study. Clearly, such mobility across nations, languages and cultures creates a much higher number of potential employees with a competence to communicate with, understand and operate in foreign cultures. Such capabilities are clearly a prerequisite for exploiting the opportunities offered by new production, communication, and transportation technology. Another effect of increased mobility and education across borders is that markets become more homogeneous (preferences and behaviour become less local). Therefore, the human resource side is certainly one of the driving forces behind the phenomenon of Born Globals. Especially the past experience and present competences or ambitions of the founder of the Born Global firm should be taken much more into consideration. We will return to the latter issue in subsequent sections.

In conclusion, it must be expected that the phenomenon of Born Globals will become more widespread in the future. Probably the driving forces mentioned will be even stronger in the years to come—and therefore more industries and firms can be expected to be affected.

As of now, a "missing link" in the research about Born Globals is the following question: Which theoretical framework should be applied in order to understand and explain the phenomenon? As it is the case for many new research areas the point of departure when studying the phenomenon has so far mainly been empirical.

However, McDougall *et al.* (1994) attempt to interpret the phenomenon in the light of some of the most generally accepted theories in the area of international business. They conclude that although one of the purposes of monopolistic advantage theory is to explain why firms choose to compete internationally rather than just in their home markets, this approach does not

567

provide an appropriate explanation of Born Globals/INVs (p. 474); the reason is that Born Globals make foreign investments before developing monopolistic advantages on the domestic market. For similar reasons McDougall *et al.* reject the International Product Life Cycle theory (Vernon, 1966). Oligopolistic reaction theory cannot explain the initial decision to invest in foreign markets either because often the Born Global/INV is the first firm in an industry to invest internationally.

Internalization theory claims that MNEs exist because of market imperfections; the firm may earn higher economic rents by internalizing transactions rather than having arm's-length transactions across borders. The study by McDougall *et al.* (1994) indicates that the Born Globals/INVs not always choose the lowest cost mode of operation for each activity the firm performs. It is reported that many of the firms rely heavily on strategic alliances in competing internationally. McDougall *et al.* (1994) conclude that the internalization theory fails to provide an appropriate explanation for INVs, since cost reduction is not the key issue for them; furthermore, internalization theory has its focus on the firm level rather than on the entrepreneurs and their social network which should be seen as very important when researching Born Globals/INVs (p. 478).

McDougall *et al.* (1994) argue that the founders of INVs are more concerned with the possibilities of combining resources from different national markets because of the competences they have developed from their earlier activities, so international entrepreneurs are able to avoid domestic path dependence by establishing ventures which already from the beginning have routines for managing a multicultural workforce, for coordinating resources located in different nations and for targeting customers in several geographic places simultaneously. In a similar vein Bell (1995) notes that the network approach to internationalization seems to have some merit. This is underlined by the following statement: "Evidence of client followership and indications that some firms initiated exporting because of contacts with foreign suppliers do offer a plausible explanation as to how and why software firms with such networks internationalized" (p. 72).

In order to fully understand this phenomenon we have to examine the background of the founders. In the case of Born Globals we may assume that background of the decision maker (founder) has a large influence on the internationalization path followed. Factors like education, experience from living abroad, experience from other internationally oriented jobs, etc. mould the mind of the founder and decrease the psychic distances to specific product markets significantly.

The implication is that from the inception of the firm the founder may not see national borders as an obstacle, but rather sees international markets as open, waiting to be exploited. Hence it is not necessarily so that the firm initially has to be engaged in a network which is primarily domestic. From the first stated argument it may very well follow, that previous experience and knowledge of the founder extends the network across national borders opening possibilities for new business ventures. In fact, the case of Born Global may be

568

International
Business
Review
6,6

similar to the situation of the "Late Starter" or the "International Among Others" (Johanson and Mattsson, 1988) (see Table 1). In the latter situation both the environment and the firm is highly internationalized. We will return to these issues in the next section.

Hence, we conclude this section by pointing out that comprehensive theoretical explanations of the phenomenon of Born Globals are still lacking. It has been demonstrated empirically that Born Globals do not internationalize in accordance with the stages models. Some important external driving forces for the phenomenon have been discussed. Furthermore, we agree with some authors in pointing out that the background and characteristics of the founder probably has a large influence on the commencement and development of Born Globals. In the next sections we will explore the phenomenon theoretically and we will argue that evolutionary economic thinking as well as the network approach to internationalization (and even the original thinking behind the stages models) can contribute to the understanding and perhaps give some adequate explanations of the rise of the Born Global phenomenon.

Links to the Original Uppsala Internationalization Model

There is no doubt that the studies of different Born Globals demonstrate the limited validity of the manifestations of the original internationalization models, i.e. the stage models and the idea that firms slowly grow more and more international like "rings in the water" with respect to their product, geographical markets served and entry mode. A falsification of the surface manifestations is, however, not necessarily the same thing as a falsification of the reasoning behind the traditional models. In this section we will explore a little more in detail, whether some of the underlying theoretical arguments of the stages model are still valid—even for Born Globals.

To explain the slow and incremental character of internationalization processes of firms, Johanson and Vahlne (1977) formulated a model in which the firm is assumed to strive for growth and long term profit, but at the same time attempts to keep risk taking at a low level. Interpreting the studies of Born Globals, we find that these basic asssumptions are still valid—even for Born Globals. Furthermore, the firm is assumed to lack the routines to solve new problems in relation to internationalization because of relatively high perceived market uncertainty; according to the behavioural theory of the firm it will then search for local optima in the area of the problem. However, Born

	Low degree of internationalization of the market	High degree of internationalization of the market
Low degree of internationalization of the firm	The Early Starter	The Late Starter
High degree of internationalization of the firm	The Lonely International	The International Among Others

Table 1. Internationalization Situations (Johanson and Mattsson, 1988, p. 298)

Global firms' perception of uncertainty with regard to international markets is typically lower because the founder and other employees have gained international experience prior to the start-up.

**Inter-
nationalization
of Born Globals**

In order to explain the path of the internationalization process itself, Johanson and Vahlne (1990) developed a dynamic theoretical model in which they make the distinction between state and change aspects of internationalization variables. In the model they argue that the present state of the firm is an important factor in explaining future changes and subsequent stages. The state aspects are represented by the firm's "market commitment" to the foreign markets and the "market knowledge" about foreign markets and operations. The change aspects are seen as "commitment decisions" and "current business activities".

The concept of market commitment is assumed to be composed of two factors; first, the amount of resources committed, e.g. the size of investments in the market (marketing, organization, personnel, etc.), and secondly, the difficulty of finding an alternative use for the resources and transferring them to alternative usage (degree of specificity). Market knowledge is seen as information about markets and operations which is somehow stored and reasonably retrievable in the minds of individuals inside the firm, in computer memories or in written reports. International activities require both general knowledge about market operations and market specific knowledge. The latter is assumed to be gained primarily through experience with the foreign markets, whereas knowledge of operations can better be transferred from one market to another. Knowledge may be objective or experiential in nature, but experiential knowledge is seen as the most crucial type for international activities.

Johanson and Vahlne (1977) postulate that current business activities are the prime source of experiential knowledge for the firm. Commitment decisions depend very much on experience since they are a response to perceived uncertainty and opportunities on the the market. Decisions to commit further resources to specific foreign operations will more often be taken if experiential market knowledge increases. This implies that additional market commitment as a rule will be made in small incremental steps because it takes time to gain experiential knowledge about foreign markets.

For a Born Global firm, the degree of country specificity of market knowledge is probably lower because of the driving forces mentioned in the third section. Furthermore, the founder of a Born Global may have prior experiential knowledge about the international marketplace in his particular industry. This implies that decision about additional market commitments do not necessarily have to be slow and incremental in such a firm. Based on the reasoning of the original (dynamic) state and change model one may explain the manifest internationalization process of some Born Globals as follows: since the founder of the Born Global has a high market knowledge built up through years of business activities in the industry, then the Born Global firm can easily take commitment decisions concerning international markets. Furthermore, market commitment may be relatively low because the country

570

International
Business
Review
6,6

specificity of market knowledge is relatively low and international sales and marketing channels are already in place.

In conclusion, we argue that many basic assumptions and the dynamic processes (state and change aspects) underlying the internationalization processes of Born Globals are not necessarily different from what is outlined in the original U-M referred to above. However, the founder characteristics and market conditions are different which is the reason why the manifestation of the internationalization processes of Born Globals must be deviating from the "rings in the water" model found to be a valid description of internationalization processes of firms in many empirical studies.

Whereas Johanson and Vahlne (1977) are preoccupied with the conditions for export and the development process, Wiedersheim-Paul *et al.* (1978) focus on the even more fundamental process before the initial exporting stage; they formulate a model of factors affecting the pre-export activities of the firm. In doing so, they conclude that these activities are important in explaining the start of an internationalization process. This is a very interesting perspective to discuss in relation to Born Globals.

In addition to the more traditional factors such as; decision maker characteristics and product line, they stress the importance of the history/ environment of the firm. Concerning the latter subject Wiedersheim-Paul *et al.* (1978) underline the importance of contact patterns that allow an efficient exchange of information, creating possibilities for transmission of ideas from other firms. They state that: "These contacts are likely to change the attitudes and mental maps of the decision-makers" (p. 56). In the same vein, Welch and Wiedersheim-Paul (1980) argue that pre-export "preparation" of the firm is important, because it requires managerial time for activities such as sales promotion abroad, visits and other means of gathering relevant information. They accentuate that the investment of managerial time in carrying out the pre-export activities is particularly important to smaller firms, because they have fewer resources to allocate to such uncertain and risky activities.

There is no doubt that this pre-export behaviour model is very relevant when studying Born Globals. The model underlines the importance of researching the interrelationships between the decision maker (in this case, the entrepreneur), the firm's environment and the firm itself. Clearly, as we have seen in the earlier sections this article, the attitudes and mental maps of the entrepreneur probably have a high explanatory power when trying to understand the internationalization patterns of such firms. In the study of Welch and Wiedersheim-Paul (1980) we even see an early indication of the Born Global phenomenon; firms established after the Second World War and having successful export activities had started export faster than firms established before the war. A similar pattern is documented in the McKinsey and Co. (1993) study referred to earlier.

So, we do contend that even the theoretical reasoning behind the original stages model, including the pre-export behaviour, has some merit when trying to understand the internationalization pattern of Born Globals. However, the manifestations of the stages model (internationalization like "rings in the water" with regard to product, geographical markets and entry mode) is not an adequate framework for modelling the manifest routes to internationalization of Born Globals. For the latter reason one should reject the manifest original models which many "Born Global authors" do, but for the former reason the conceptualizations behind the original models may be kept in mind when trying to understand why Born Globals take the route which has been empirically evidenced.

Links to Other Approaches and Theories

Johanson and Mattsson (1988) attempt to relate the internationalization process of firms to the notion of industrial networks. Instead of regarding the internationalization as a process between a firm and a somewhat anonymous market, they stress the relationships between independent firms forming the network. Due to an informal division of labour among the involved firms, each firm will become dependent of external resources to the extent to which it builds exchange relationships to other firms in the network. Such relationships often take time and effort to establish and develop; especially in long term relationships mutual trust and knowledge implies a high degree of commitment and interconnectedness by different types of bonds.

In relation to the internationalization processes of firms we interpret the network approach so, that the original Uppsala Internationalization Model has to take into account the network approach and that concepts like commitment, knowledge, current activities have to be studied inside the firm itself but also in connection with its cooperation with other firms. This means that each firm cannot be analysed separately, but that its state and change aspects must be understood in an interorganizational setting. Furthermore, networks might not only be confined to a country, but may extend beyond borders. Differences are seen between countries and products regarding the international extension, coordination and integration of networks. Accordingly, the degree of internationalization of the actual network has strong implications for the internationalization process of the particular firm. Such a process becomes much more individual, depending on the networks established in the industry as well as the position of the firm in the industry network.

Internationalization can involve that the firm develops business relationships in networks in other countries in three different ways; through the establishment of relationships in country networks that are new to the firm; through the development of relationships in those networks which are known to the firm; and through connecting/integrating networks in different countries by using the existing relationships of the firm as bridges to other networks. According to Johanson and Mattsson (1988), the firm's development is to a large extent dependent on its position in a network and it can use its markets assets (position) in its further development. The internationalization characteristics of both the firm and of the market influences this process (Johanson and Mattsson, 1988, p. 297). The firm's

572

International
Business
Review
6,6

market assets will have a different structure if the firm is highly internationalized than if it is not. In addition, the market assets of other firms in a network might have a different structure, depending on the degree of internationalization of the market, which is defined as the extent, intensity and degree of integration of relationships across borders in the industry in general. The degree of internationalization of the firm encompasses the extent, intensity and degree of integration of its positions with foreign partners.

Based on these assumptions Johanson and Mattsson (1988) establish the following model. Below we discuss how and why Born Globals fit into this model.

There is no doubt that the stages models are most valid when depicting the process of an Early Starter firm. Networks are local or national with only very few (if any) relationships crossing borders; this means that customer preferences and behaviour may be quite different across broders and the same is true for business customs. For the firm wanting to internationalize, perceived uncertainty is high and market specific knowledge is low. It is difficult to "buy" market knowledge because nobody has real international experience; therefore experiential learning becomes critical, and hence the slow and incremental internationalization pattern is relevant and probably also economically sound.

Late Starters have a much different situation because networks across borders are already well established. Having a position in such networks is a kind of a prerequisite for being active in the marketplace—perhaps most strongest on the lead markets in which all suppliers want to be present and strong players. In highly internationalized markets firms are often "pulled" into foreign markets through their position in a national net. In a study of Danish firms' investments in Turkey (Bodur and Madsen, 1993) evidence of such firms was found. For some very small Danish firms one of the first internatinal activities was a foreign direct investment in Turkey which is a quite distant market in terms of geography and culture. One of these firm had been "pulled" to Turkey in the first place because it was a subcontractor for a large Danish company.

In a review of subcontractors' internationalization processes, Andersen *et al.* (1995) report similar notions. Subcontractors often internationalize in a non-conventional manner because they follow domestic customers or because they cooperate with foreign system suppliers. Another route which may easily be similar to the pattern revealed for Born Globals is seen for subcontractors which internationalize through integration in the supply chain of a multinational company. In any case, the internationalization process of the individual firm cannot be seen in isolation; it can only be analysed by understanding the environmental conditions as well as the actual relationships of the firm in question. It is necessary to understand the whole value system (or network) in which the firm is active.

Johanson and Mattsson (1988) point out that internationalization processes of firms will be much faster in internationalized market conditions, among other things because the need for coordination and integration across borders is high. Since relevant partners/distributors will often be occupied on neighbouring markets, firms do not necessarily follow a "rings in the water" approach to market selection. In the same vein their "establishment chain" needs not follow the traditional picture because strategic alliances, joint venture, etc. are much more prevalent; firms seek partners with supplementary skills and resources. In other words, internationalization processes of firms will be much more individual and situation specific in internationalized markets.

Clearly, the situation of Late Starters and International Among Others is very much similar to the situation of a Born Global. We therefore argue that a network approach to internationalization processes offers a valuable approach when analysing such firms. Furthermore, the network approach stresses that the present activities and decisions of firms must be highly dependent on the particular firm's past experience and activities. Hence, also Born Globals may be seen as "locked" according to their history.

A deeper theoretical explanation of such "path dependencies" of Born Globals may be found in the evolutionary approach to the study of dynamic changes. The Born Global firm acts in an environment, but also in an internal context which is much different from that of an Early Starter. The uncertainty and learning aspect is not related to knowledge about geographical markets, but more to new production processes, specialization patterns, exchange patterns, etc. Their organizational routines are not depending very much on any local or national broders—and therefore they do not fit into the manifestation of the stages model. They probably do have a set of regular and predictable ways of doing things, though. And they do have routines, decision rules and capabilities which may be considered as the "genes" of the organization. Instead of being tied to geographical markets, these genes may be tied to certain specialized, value-adding processes which the firm solves in that particular, internationalized industry.

Interpreted in the light of these theoretical concepts, the Born Global phenomenon does not represent any revolutionary pattern of internationalization; also Born Globals may behave according to a evolutionary framework. However, when studying a Born Global firm, the time perspective should be extended beyond its birth. Probably, many of its "genes" have roots back to firms and networks in which its founder(s) and top mangers gained industry experience. Basically, in many instances it may be doubtful whether a Born Global can be considered a new company. In a legal sence the company may be new, but were its skills and capabilities not often born and matured prior to its legal birth?

Taking such an evolutionary approach to the study of Born Globals makes it more clear that even they possibly develop and grow in an evolutionary manner. Therefore, the theoretical understanding of evolutionary processes is highly relevant for Born Globals as well as for the firm which internationalizes like "rings in the water". Only the manifestations of their evolutionary processes are very different. Their "domestic" market is maybe

574

International
Business
Review
6,6

not geographical, but perhaps certain problem solving capabilities in a global industry. Evolution like "rings in the water", therefore, does not have the local market as its centre but certain problem solving routines originally possessed by the founder/entrepreneur, but later rooted in the organization as such. Research focusing on such issues is highly relevant in order to gain a better understanding of the Born Global phenomenon.

Additional empirical work is necessary to enrich our present insight into the phenomenon. The final part of the article is dedicated to the formulation of propositions that are relevant to investigate thoroughly; also general future research directions are discussed.

Theoretically and Empirically Derived Propositions
The theoretical analysis carried out above give rise to the formulation of many relevant propositions. To enrich the theoretical insight, case studies of Born Globals were searched for in the literature. Nine relevant studies were chosen to illustrate the phenomenon; the actual choice of cases was governed by the desire to maximize heterogeneity because the purpose is to generate propositions of relevance for the phenomenon as such (exploratory research phase). The nine cases describe Born Globals originting from the US, Australia, Denmark, Switzerland, Sweden, Italy, and France; they are summarized in Table 2.

These cases, along with the theoretical considerations, form the basis for formulation of propositions to be examined in future research. The propositions focus upon questions such as: What are the antecedents of Born Globals? What are the necessary conditions for their emergence? What are the sufficient conditions for their birth and expansion? What is the impact of the national settings? Does the industry setting matter (e.g. high tech vs low tech)?

As demonstrated theoretically and illustrated in some of the cases in Table 2, it is important to explore the history of Born Globals, even beyond their birth. Such firms may be started by genuine entrepreneurs or by very experienced persons with or without a strong product. Often, these persons have extensive international experience (including a personal network) and do not perceive their native country as the nucleus of their lives. International experience is a necessary condition for their international expansion, but it also creates the motivation and ambition to become Born Global, among other thing because it changes the perception of distance to other countries. The combination of a strong entrepreneur and a strong product is illustrated in Table 2 by the high tech firms whose product is firmly rooted in the technological capabilities of the founder(s) while others (e.g. trading companies) are examples of Born Globals driven exclusively by a strong entrepreneur who might have chosen many different products. These observations lead to the first proposition which is concerned with the roots of a Born Global.

McKinsey and Co. (1993)	Jolly *et al.* (1992)	Madsen and Servais (1996)
Invetech consults on business and technology strategy and was founded in 1987. Five years later the export contributed with more than 20% of the total sales. Invetech manufactures a range of specialized laboratory instruments. The successful marketing of these products has relied on linkages with the Swiss multinational Leica. Invetech markets its products worldwide through the partnership with Leica.	Logitech, a Swiss-based producer of desktop aids for PCs, was founded in 1982. Seven years later, more than 70% of the total sales originated from sales outside Europe. Moreover, it manufactures and engineers its products in the US, the Far East and in Europe. The firm was founded by a Swiss citizen and an Italian citizen who met while studying at Stanford University. Later on, a third person joined the group after a career in Olivetti and IBM. Physically, the firm was located both in Switzerland and Palo Alto in the US, but the main part of R&D was soon moved to Silicon Valley. Manufacturing was initially done on both locations, but when volume increased a new facility was set up in Taiwan.	Aaby Brakes was founded in 1990 by Mr Carlsen. The firm produces and sells hydraulic brake discs primarily for the windmill industry, but also for the mining industry and the crane industry. Nearly 60% of the total sales in 1995 originated from exporting. Aaby has managed to double the sales each year since its inception. The founder merely had a sales background and the export breakthrough was made through a takeover of a Swedish firm that had very good contacts on the German market. Aaby seeks to reach the market through a net of distributors in Europe, the US and Asia. Today, four sales directors with a technical background are responsible for the Polish market, the German market, the Asian market and the overseas market.
Cochlear originates from the University of Melbourne; research about implants for profoundly deaf was commerzialized. Exports represents 95% of the total sales, a figure that has been increasing 25% the last five years. The firm has strong links with hospitals around the world and in collaborative research in Switzerland, Germany and the US.	Technophone was founded in 1984 in the UK; it manufactures and markets hand-portable telephones with a substantial export share in 1989. It now has manufacturing plants in Europe and the Far East and sales to these regions and the US. The founder was a Swede who previously had work for Ericsson in France and the UK. When the liberalization of the telecommunication industry began he decided to exploit the possibilities in the UK as being the lead market.	ESX was founded in 1992; it produces and sells screw dies, a niche product of which ESX produces 60,000–70,000 units per year. Export now represents 80% of the total sales, exporting to 12 different countries. The founder, a business economist, was internationally oriented right from the inception. He attends different trade fairs around the world each year and since screw dies are simple products and easy to copy, a low price is essential for survival and the firm seeks to develop new products on a regular base. The most important export markets are the US, France, Germany and Japan.

Table 2.
Born Global Cases

576

International
Business
Review
6,6

McKinsey and Co. (1993)	Jolly *et al.* (1992)	Madsen and Servais (1996)
Precision Valve produces valves and plastic packaging products that are very innovative. The export share has risen to 25% of the total sales within five years. The firm believes that innovation and close customer and supplier involvement is critical to their export success. The product range differs from one market to another, especially in Southeast Asia.	Lasa Industries are established in both Europe and the US and produces systems for application software; it is heavily dependent on access to resources on a global scale. Four of the founders were US citizens; one was Swiss and one French. The operational HQ was placed in the US together with the R&D department, the marketing function was placed in France and finance in Switzerland but production was set up in Scotland due to attractive regional grants and the availability of suitable workforce.	MK electronics was founded in 1984. The founder, Mr Petersen, was head of the electronic development department in a local subsidiary of a MNC. When the MNC decided to externalize this function, Mr Petersen took the opportunity to start-up a firm that could carry out the tasks of developing of production of electronic control circuits. A few years later MK electronics took over a small Danish producer of automats. Due to the long and close relationships with local subunits relations was established with Electrolux and this again lead to a substantial export to Sweden and Germany.

Table 2.
Continued

P1. The antecedent of a Born Global is one or several strong entrepreneur(s) with strong international experience, and perhaps in addition a strong product.

According to theoretical arguments, it should be expected that the phenomenon Born Globals is more widespread in markets which are highly internationalized as understood by Johanson and Mattsson (1988). This is due to the fact that many Born Globals need to source resources from firms with complementary competences which is much easier in markets with established cross national networks at the firm level as well as the personal level. This may be the case for R&D as well as production resources, but it is even more prevalent for sales and marketing capabilities which is also demonstrated by many cases in Table 2. A radical proposition would be that internationalized markets are a necessary condition for Born Globals; we have, however, chosen a more weak proposition:

P2. The extension of the phenomenon Born Globals is positively associated with the degree of internationalization of the market.

Theoretical arguments indicate that one of the driving forces for Born Globals is changes in production technologies and better access to/lower costs in transportation as well as communication. Hence, the core competence of a Born Global must be expected to be narrow and focused to a higher extent than is the case for other exporting firms. Moreover, the competence may be linked to standardized production or physical products (e.g. Logitech, Technophone), but it may also rest in a deep knowledge about heterogeneous customer preferences and an ability to adapt to these preferences (e.g. Aaby Brakes, Precision Valve). In any case, the capabilities of a Born Global must be expected to be more cultivated and clear-cut than those of traditional exporters, so:

P3. In comparison with other exporting firms, Born Globals are more specialized and niche oriented with products that are either more custom-made or more standardized.

As demonstrated earlier, Born Globals do not choose geographical markets according to physical or psychic distance; this is in contrast to traditional internationalization patterns like "rings in the water". This is true for their sourcing, production, and sales/marketing activities. The cases of Logitech and Lasa clearly demonstrate that the location of sourcing and production facilities are highly influenced by the nationality of the founder as well as cost and R&D considerations. The geographical focus of sales and marketing activities are directed by lead customers (Cochlear), contacts already established by the founder (MK Elektronics), or options available because of client followership or through relationships to external partners (Invetech). A difference among Born Globals may be expected: High tech Born Globals may direct their sales and marketing activities to lead markets because they need rapid access to lead customers as well as edge technology; Born Globals who are trading companies, service firms or subcontractors may more often choose foreign markets because they follow their present customers. A general proposition about geographical decisions could be formulated like this:

P4. The geographical location of activities in Born Globals is determined by the past experience of founders and partners as well as economic and capability or customer-related factors—directly or in interaction.

The reliance on sourcing options from firms with complementary competences is probably a more common picture in Born Global companies than in other exporting firms because the internal competence and routines in such a firm are insufficient to achieve the desired development. Sourcing may happen by employing persons with specialized skills (from competitors of from related industries), or it may happen in different forms of collaboration with hybrid governance structures, especially in the distribution channels. This picture may be explained by more scarce resources in Born Globals (financial as well as human), but a higher degree of internationalization of the market is a facilitating factor contributing to the explanation. Finally, the international experience of the founder means that a Born Global is better able to take advantage of the increased international experience and intercultural

578

International
Business
Review
6,6

competence among people in general; they are not afraid of employing or collaborating with people who have a different background. Summing up, the mode of operation of a Born Global could be expected to be the following:

> P5. In comparison with other exporting firms, Born Globals more often rely on supplementary competences sourced from other firms; in their distribution channels they more often rely on hybrid structures (close relationships, network partners, joint ventures, etc.).

In order to survive and earn economic rents it is necessary for a Born Global to be at the edge of the development in their particular market or competence niche. Therefore, they have to be innovative (e.g. Precision Valve, ESX). They must be able to reap advantages from the new communication technologies such as fax, database marketing, and internet. Otherwise they will not be able to maintain effective contact with the huge number of firms in the network in which they operate, including their own, sometimes dispersed organization (e.g. Logitech, Lasa). Since Born Globals often operate on very internationalized markets, they have to think globally when deciding about their activities; they have to incorporate considerations about other foreign markets when they take decision about one particular foreign market. So, in summary:

> P6. The growth of a Born Global is positively associated with high innovative skills, including an ability to access effective R&D as well as distributions channels, often in partnerships with close collaboration in international relationships that involve frequent, intense, and integrated efforts across nations.

Finally, we consider the impact of the national setting. Comparing the cases in Table 2, it is possible to infer some interesting hypotheses. First of all, it is striking, that all American examples are high tech firms; this may be due the fact that such cases have deliberately been chosen. It may, however, also mirror that the US market is very large—and hence that only very high tech companies are pushed into the international marketplace right after their birth. In contrast, some more low tech Danish and Australian firms (with smaller domestic markets) have aimed at many foreign markets. Another reason form such a picture may be that the population of small nations such as Denmark are much more internationally oriented and have higher language profiencies than their US counterparts; in the same vein Australia has many immigrants which may also increase the propensity to become Born Global. The latter issue is in accordance with McDougall et al. (1994) who report that ethnic background has an impact.

> P7. Firms in nations with small domestic markets have a higher propensity to become Born Globals than firms in nations with large domestic markets. Therefore, Born Globals from small nations may rely on many different products whereas Born Globals from large nations may be limited to high

tech industries. Also, nations with a high number of immigrants may have a higher proportion of Born Globals.

Clearly, these are not the only propositions that could be formulated in the process of improving our research about Born Globals. They do represent, though, a good starting point for future reseach efforts because they cover the basic aspects about the antecedents, birth, and growth of Born Globals which can be identified through theoretical reasoning as well as present empirical studies.

Future Research Directions
In conclusion, we observe that different studies of firms' internationalization processes seem to identify various results, but that three main manifest categories of internationalization processes can be identified: (a) the traditional exporters, who's internationalization pattern to a large degree can be described and explained by traditional stages models of internationalization, (b) firms that leapfrog some stages, e.g. Late Starters that have only domestic sales for many years, but then suddenly invest in a distant foreign market, and (c) the Born Global firms. The progress and development of the categories (b) and (c) cannot fully be understood by traditional theories, but we have shown that a network approach and an evolutionary economic approach may be promising theoretical avenues to persue in order to better understand their internationalization processes.

In the future researchers should first of all attempt to reach a generally accepted definition of the phenomenon to be studied. As we have seen, the same phenomenon has been given many different names, of which we have adopted the name Born Global in this article. In order to compare studies it is important to know whether the unit of analysis is defined as being firms showing similar internationalization processes or as firms with similar characteristics such as high technology, size, etc. So far, we see a mixture of these approaches in the literature.

Since Born Globals are contrasted with other manifest internationalization patterns, we propose to define the phenomenon along the lines suggested by Oviatt and McDougall (1994), i.e. as firms that seek to derive significant advantages from the use of resources from or the sale of outputs to multiple countries/continents right form their legal birth. In accordance with the theoretical concepts outlined in this article we suggest that the analysis of Born Globals include a time perspective which goes beyond their legal birth; we also suggest that their relationships and joint cooperation/competences with collaborating firms should be analysed.

Secondly, the case studies carried out by Madsen and Servais (1996) of some very small Danish Born Globals seem to indicate that the patterns revealed in such companies are very diverse, depending to a very high degree on the background of the founder/entrepreneur. Perhaps it would be a good idea to separate the analysis of internationalization processes of such very small firms from processes of larger firms. It may be difficult to generalize

580

International
Business
Review
6,6

patterns and recommendations across both groups of firms because the impact of the founder (the completely individual aspects) will decrease as the size of the firm increases (more "professional" decision makers).

Thirdly, it seems that Born Globals may come from many industries and market very diverse product lines. The phenomenon is not limited to high technology industries, as it has sometimes been indicated in previous literature. Also specialized assortments of low technology products adapted to homogeneous niche segments in many countries may be the base for Born Globals—even trading companies may be Born Globals. Furthermore, it seems that a high diversity is also present in the competitive advantages on which Born Globals build their business. To some extent such patterns may be industry specific. Even among high technology firms differences are clear: Some sell standardized products through quite conventional channels while others customize their offer through highly specialized networks.

The three considerations mentioned above are all concerned with the unit of analysis and possible "segmentation" of the phenomenon. We want to conclude the article by suggesting, that further studies should be more theory driven than the previous ones reported. We have argued that some of the basic assumptions and processes pointed to in the original internationalization models are probably valid for Born Globals as well. However, the world has changed dramatically since the manifestation of these models were formulated in the 70s. Therefore the manifest stages approach is much less valid today. We have argued that the network approach to internationalization processes as well as the evolutionary economics approach do have some merit when attempting to understand the internationalization patterns of Born Globals. The international extension and integration of relationships in cross-national industry networks does have a strong impact on the internationalization processes of individual firms in the industry.

The seven propositions formulated in the previous section is a good starting point for further scientific inquiry since they reflect the theoretical as well as empirical aspects highlighted above.

When analysing small Born Globals it is necessary, though, to draw upon the literature on entrepreneurship as well. In any case, there seems to be a need for integration of the research streams in the areas of internationalization processes and entrepreneurship. Based on the findings and arguments set forth in this article we propose the research model in Fig. 1 as a framework for further research into the phenomenon of Born Globals.

The model proposed is only a framework which has to be "filled in" theoretically. As stated, the theoretical conceptualizations for empirical research could be drawn from the network and evolutionary approaches as well as from theories of entrepreneurship. McDougall *et al.* (1994) concluded that the history of the founder had a large influence on the appearance of International New Ventures. Secondly, the ambition level and the general motivation of the founder might be very influential in trying to understand the specific development pattern of a Born Global. We have argued that also the

581

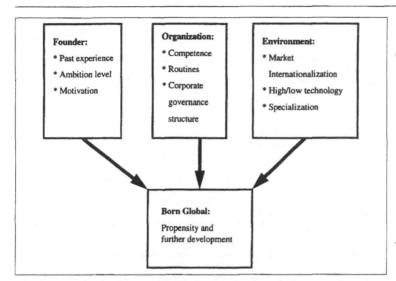

Inter-
nationalization
of Born Globals

Figure 1.
A Research Model of
"Born Globals"

past experience and history of the firm (competences, routines, etc.) have to be included in a study of Born Globals. By studying the history of the founder as well as the firm one might reveal clues in relation to possible interconnectedness with other firms. The same applies to the corporate governance structure, for example the composition of the board members and their backgrounds and networks. The nature of the product line and competences in general may indicate whether the offer of the firm might be marketed internationally. This should be seen in connection with the level of technology, specialization, and market internationalization.

For many Born Globals it is a special challenge that they often have to choose hybrid forms of governance structures in their export channels. An interesting research question is certainly to analyse how even small firms may make effektive use of strategic alliances and networking activities on a worldwide scale. Clearly. this is not an easy task—and hence it is a very important managerial issue.

We propose that theoretical aspects as outlined be considered explicitly in future research on Born Globals. More descriptive research could help clarify some of the issues. As for now, it is probably still too early to build more normative models of managerial relevance, although this should of course be one of the ultimate goals of the research in the area.

References
Andersen, O. (1993) On the internationalization process of firms—a critical analysis. *Journal of International Business Studies* 24(2), 203–209.

582

International
Business
Review
6,6

Andersen, P. H., Blenker, P. and Christensen, P. R. (1995) Generic routes to subcontractors' internationalization. Paper presented at the RENT IX Conference on Entrepreneurship and SMEs in Milano, Italy, November.

Bell, J. (1995) The internationalization of small computer software firms. *European Journal of Marketing* **29**(8), 60–75.

Bilkey, W. J. and Tesar, G. (1977) Attempted integration of the literature; the export behavior of firms. *Journal of International Business Studies* **Spring/Summer**, 33–46.

Bodur, M. and Madsen, T. K. (1993) Danish foreign investment in Turkey. *European Business Review* **5**, 28–43.

Brush, C. G. (1992) Factors motivating small companies to internationalize: the effect of firm age. Unpublished dissertation. Boston University, Boston.

Buckley, P., Newbould, G. D. and Thruwell, J. (1979) Going international—the foreign direct investment behaviour of smaller UK Firms. In *Recent Research on the Internationalization of Business*, eds L.-G. Mattsson and F. Wiedersheim-Paul. Uppsala, Sweden.

Cavusgil, S. T. (1980) On the internationalization process of firms. *European Research* **November**, 273–281.

Christensen, P. R. and Jacobsen, L. (1996) The role of export in new business formation. Paper presented to RENT X, Brussels.

Ganitsky, J. (1989) Strategies for innate and adoptive exporters. *International Marketing Review* **6**(5), 50–65.

Garnier, G. (1982) Comparative export behavior of small Canadian firms in the printing and electrical industries. In *Export Management*, eds M. R. Czinkota and G. Tesar. Praeger, New York.

Hedlund, G. and Kverneland, A. (1985) Are strategies for foreign markets changing?. *International Studies of Management and Organization* **15**(2), 41–59.

Holstein, W. J. (1992) Little companies, big exports. *Newsweek* **3261**, 70–72.

Industri- og Handelsstyrelsen (1992) Nye virksomheder og iværksættere i tal—1985/89. Industri- og Handelsstyrelsen, Copenhagen.

Johanson, J. and Mattsson, L.-G. (1988) Internationalization in industrial systems—a network approach. In *Strategies for Global Competition*, ed. N. Hood. Croom Helm, London.

Johanson, J. and Vahlne, J.-E. (1977) The internationalization process of the firm. *Journal of International Business Studies* **8**, 23–32.

Johanson, J. and Vahlne, J.-E. (1990) The mechanism of internationalization. *International Marketing Review* **7**(4), 11–24.

Johanson, J. and Wiedersheim-Paul, F. (1975) The internationalization of the firm—four Swedish cases. *Journal of Management Studies* **12**, 305–322.

Jolly, V. K., Alahuhta, M. and Jeannet, J.-P. (1992) Challenging the incumbents: how high technology start-ups compete globally. *Journal of Strategic Change* **1**, 71–82.

Knight, G. and Cavusgil, S. T. (1996) The Born Global firm: a challenge to traditional internationalization theory. *Advances of International Marketing*. JAI Press, forthcoming.

Lindmark, L., Christensen, P. R., Eskelinen, H., Forsström, B., Sørensen, O. J. and Vatn, E. (1994) Småföretagens internationalisering—en jämförende studie. *Nord REFO*, Vol. 7. Denmark.

Madsen, T. K. and Servais, P. (1996) Six case studies of Danish Born Globals. Unpublished reports, Odense University.

McDougall, P. P., Shane, S. and Oviatt, B. M. (1994) Explaining the formation of international new ventures. *Journal of Business Venturing* **9**, 469–487.

McKinsey and Co. (1993) *Emerging Exporters*. Australian Manufacturing Council, Melbourne.

Oviatt, B. M. and McDougall, P. P. (1994) Toward a theory of international new ventures. *Journal of International Business Studies* **24**, 45–64.

Reid, S. D. (1983) Firm internationalization transaction costs and strategic choice. *International Marketing Review* **1**(2), 45–56.

Rennie, M. W. (1993) Born Global. *McKinsey Quarterly* **4**, 45–52.

Roux, E. (1979) The export behavior of small and medium size French firms. In *Proceedings of the Annual Meeting in EIBA*, eds L.-G. Mattsson and F. Wiedersheim-Paul. Uppsala, Sweden.

583

Turnbull, P. (1987) A challenge to the stages theory of the internationalization process. In *Managing Export Entry and Expansion—Concepts and Practice*, eds P. J. Rosson and S. Reid. Praeger, New York.

Vernon, R. (1966) International investment and international trade in the product cycle. *Quarterly Journal of Economics* **80**, 190–207.

Welch, L. and Luostarinen, R. (1988) Internationalization—evolution of a concept. *Journal of General Management* **14**(2), 34–55.

Welch, L. and Wiedersheim-Paul, F. (1980) Initial exports—a marketing failure?. *Journal of Management Studies* **October**, 333–345.

Wiedersheim-Paul, F., Welch, L. and Olson. H. C. (1978) Pre-export activity—the first step in internationalization. *Journal of International Business Studies* **9**, 47–58.

Inter-
nationalization
of Born Globals

Received November 1996
Revised January 1997

[5]

TOWARD A THEORY OF INTERNATIONAL NEW VENTURES

Benjamin M. Oviatt*
Georgia State University

Patricia Phillips McDougall**
Georgia Institute of Technology

Abstract. The formation of organizations that are international from inception—international new ventures—is an increasingly important phenomenon that is incongruent with traditionally expected characteristics of multinational enterprises. A framework is presented that explains the phenomenon by integrating international business, entrepreneurship, and strategic management theory. That framework describes four necessary and sufficient elements for the existence of international new ventures: (1) organizational formation through internalization of some transactions, (2) strong reliance on alternative governance structures to access resources, (3) establishment of foreign location advantages, and (4) control over unique resources.

INTRODUCTION

The study of the multinational enterprise (MNE) has focused on large, mature corporations. Historically, many MNEs developed from large, mature, domestic firms [Chandler 1986], and they commanded attention because they wielded significant economic power, especially after World War II [Buckley & Casson 1976; Dunning 1981; Hennart 1982]. However, recent technological innovation and the presence of increasing numbers of people with international business experience have established new foundations for

*Benjamin M. Oviatt is Assistant Professor of Management at Georgia State University. He received his Ph.D. in strategic management from the University of South Carolina. His research focuses on strategic management, organizational turnaround, and international new ventures.

**Patricia Phillips McDougall is Associate Professor of Strategic Management at Georgia Institute of Technology. She received her Ph.D. in strategic management from the University of South Carolina. Her research focuses primarily on new and young firms, with a special emphasis on strategies and internationalization.

This article was awarded first prize in the 1993 *Competition for the Best Paper on Entrepreneurship and Innovation* sponsored by New York University's Center for Entrepreneurial Studies. The authors gratefully acknowledge financial support for this research from the Bernard B. & Eugenia A. Ramsey Chair of Private Enterprise at Georgia State University and from the Society of International Business Fellows, based in Atlanta, Georgia.

Received: June 1992; Revised: December 1992, April & August 1993; Accepted: August 1993.

MNEs. An internationally experienced person who can attract a moderate amount of capital can conduct business anywhere in the time it takes to press the buttons of a telephone, and, when required, he or she can travel virtually anywhere on the globe in no more than a day. Such facile use of low-cost communication technology and transportation means that the ability to discover and take advantage of business opportunities in multiple countries is not the preserve of large, mature corporations. New ventures with limited resources may also compete successfully in the international arena.

Since the late 1980s, the popular business press has been reporting, as a new and growing phenomenon, the establishment of new ventures that are international from inception [Brokaw 1990; *The Economist* 1992, 1993b; Gupta 1989; Mamis 1989]. These start-ups often raise capital, manufacture, and sell products on several continents, particularly in advanced technology industries where many established competitors are already global.

LASA Industries, Inc., which sold an unusually efficient microprocessor prototyping technology, is representative of these international new ventures formed within the past decade. As detailed by Jolly, Alahuhta and Jeannet [1992], LASA's strategy was international in multiple respects. Its founders were American, Swiss, and French. Its funding was European. The operational headquarters and R&D were located in the United States, while marketing was managed from France and finance from Switzerland. Manufacturing was centered in Scotland to take advantage of attractive regional grants, and initial sales were in France and the United States.

IXI Limited, a British venture that became a leading supplier of desktop windowing computer software for UNIX operating systems, violated the usual expectation that firms begin with sales in their home country and later sell to foreign countries. Ray Anderson, the venture's founder and chairman, had previously worked for a British computer company that failed. Through Anderson's work in that company's Boston and Canadian operations he became aware of the needs of the North American market. While discussing the failure of his former company Anderson said,

> ... it did not succeed because we tried to sell the product by starting up in England and then selling in the U.S., and by that time it was too late. We should have developed our products first of all for the U.S. market and then sold it back into England. [Anderson 1992]

When Anderson started IXI, his stated strategy was to target the United States first, Japan second, and then move back into the United Kingdom. Funding for the venture was from the United Kingdom, Germany, Austria and Japan. Foreign subsidiaries were set up in the United States and Japan. Only after establishing itself in both those countries did IXI turn its attention to its home country, and then to mainland Europe. In an interview four years after the product's introduction, Anderson estimated 60% of IXI's revenues came from the United States, 20% from the United Kingdom, 10% from Japan, and 10% from other countries.

Actually, international new ventures have existed for centuries. The famous East India Company was chartered in London in 1600 [Wilkins 1970]. In early 19th century America, the unprecedented value of cotton exports gave birth to specialized cotton traders [Chandler 1977]. The Ford Motor Company also seems to have been an international new venture at its founding in 1903 [Wilkins & Hill 1964]. However, the focus of interest has been on MNEs that developed over time from large, mature, integrated enterprises [Chandler 1986], and we believe that has obscured the existence of international new ventures.

As a result, scholars of organization science have ignored international new ventures until very recently. Figure 1 depicts our sense of the domain of scholarly literature on organizations. A substantial body of research has been published on established firms, both domestic and international, and on domestic new ventures. However, there is much less work in the quadrant of international new ventures. Entrepreneurship research on international issues has largely concerned itself with (1) the impact of public policies on small-firm exporting (e.g., Rossman [1984]), (2) entrepreneurs and entrepreneurial activities in various countries (e.g., Ohe, Honjo, Oliva, Considine & MacMillan [1991]; Westhead [1990]), and (3) comparisons between small-firm exporters and non-exporters (e.g., Kedia & Chhokar [1985]).

The age of an organization when it internationalizes has been considered infrequently. Vozikis and Mescon [1985] did show that exporters that were start-ups reported more problems with export operations than did mature small exporters. More often, reports of new ventures that were international at or near inception have been regarded as exceptional (e.g., Welch & Loustarinen [1988]). In addition, the age of small exporters has frequently been viewed as an unimportant demographic characteristic (e.g., Malekzadeh & Nahavandi [1985], or a side issue (e.g., Cooper & Kleinschmidt [1985]).

However, since 1989, reports based on case studies of international new ventures have begun to appear from scholars of entrepreneurship. Some have shown that such ventures form because internationally experienced and alert entrepreneurs are able to link resources from multiple countries to meet the demand of markets that are inherently international [Coviello & Munro 1992; Hoy, Pivoda & Mackrle 1992; McDougall & Oviatt 1991; Oviatt, McDougall, Simon & Shrader 1994; Ray 1989]. Other case studies have shown that the success of international new ventures seems to depend on having an international vision of the firm from inception, an innovative product or service marketed through a strong network, and a tightly managed organization focused on international sales growth [Ganitsky 1989; Jolly et al. 1992; McDougall, Shane & Oviatt 1994].

Collectively, these case studies indicate that international new ventures are an important phenomenon. They have identified the formation of international new ventures in more than ten countries in all parts of the world, suggesting that global forces may be promoting their development. In addition, the

FIGURE 1
The Domain of Academic Literature on Organizations[1]

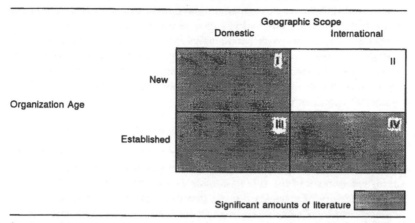

[1]adapted from the presentation of Candida Brush in McDougall, Oviatt & Brush [1991]

studies show that interest in the topic is recent and has emerged independently and nearly simultaneously from several groups of scholars. Finally, while many of the ventures studied were in high-tech businesses, services and even aquaculture were represented, suggesting that international new ventures may appear in a wide range of industries.

Additional indicators of the emergence of international new ventures have also appeared. Brush's [1992] study of small, internationalized, U.S. manufacturers found 17 firms—13% of her random nationwide sample—were internationalized during their first year of operation. Ernst and Young's survey of 303 firms in the North American electronics industry [Burrill & Almassy 1993] showed that in 1987 53% of the firms in the industry were operating domestically. In 1992, only 17% were domestic, and by 1997 only 9% were expected to be. A third of the firms surveyed were still in development with less than $5 million in revenue.

The fact that the business press believes the emerging phenomenon of international new ventures is important and that some academics working independently around the world have described similar organizations indicate a need for systematic research on these infrequently studied new ventures. However, the overall purpose of this paper is not to add to the growing descriptions of particular international new ventures. Rather, it is to define and describe the phenomenon and to present a framework explaining how international new ventures fit within the theory of the MNE. We hope that a well-delineated, theoretical framework will unify, stimulate and guide research in the area.

The next section provides a formal definition of international new ventures. Following that, certain problems are considered regarding the application of standard MNE concepts to international new ventures. Next, a theoretical framework explaining international new ventures is presented. It integrates accepted MNE theory with recent developments in entrepreneurship and strategic management research. Finally, four types of international new ventures are described in terms of our international new venture framework, the number of value chain activities they coordinate [Porter 1985], and the number of countries in which they operate.

A DEFINITION OF INTERNATIONAL NEW VENTURES

We define an *international new venture as a business organization that, from inception, seeks to derive significant competitive advantage from the use of resources and the sale of outputs in multiple countries*. The distinguishing feature of these start-ups is that their origins are international, as demonstrated by observable and significant commitments of resources (e.g., material, people, financing, time) in more than one nation. The focus here is on the age of firms when they become international, not on their size. In contrast to organizations that evolve gradually from domestic firms to MNEs, these new ventures begin with a proactive international strategy. However, they do not necessarily own foreign assets; in other words, foreign direct investment is not a requirement. Strategic alliances may be arranged for the use of foreign resources such as manufacturing capacity or marketing. Thus, consistent with Buckley and Casson's [1976] definition of the multinational enterprise, the definition of the international new venture is concerned with value added, not assets owned [Casson 1982].

The fact that international new ventures are international from inception implies that some decision must inevitably be made about when inception occurs. Much has been written in the entrepreneurship literature concerning the point at which a new venture is considered to exist as an organization (e.g., Katz & Gartner [1988]). However, Vesper argued that there can be no ultimate resolution, because the emergence of a venture is "spread over time in which its existence becomes progressively more established" [1990, p. 97]. Thus, empirical studies of international new ventures must resolve a definitional ambiguity. We believe researchers should rely on observable resource commitments to establish a point of venture inception. For new ventures that have no sales because their product or service is under development, there must be a demonstrated commitment to sell the output in multiple countries upon completion of development.

PROBLEMS IN THE APPLICATION OF MNE THEORY TO INTERNATIONAL NEW VENTURES

Stage theories of the MNE and the common emphasis on organizational scale as an important competitive advantage in the international arena are inappropriate explanations of multinational business activity for new ventures that are instantly international.

The Stage Theory of MNE Evolution

MNEs are believed by many people to evolve only after a period of domestic maturation and home market saturation [Caves 1982; Porter 1990]. Empirical researchers have in the past found that large, mature MNEs and small exporters go through distinct stages in the development of their international business. They begin perhaps with an unsolicited foreign order, proceed sometimes through exporting and the development of an international division, and occasionally advance to the establishment of a fully integrated, global enterprise [Aharoni 1966; Bilkey & Tesar 1977; Czinkota & Johnston 1981; Stopford & Wells 1972].

This staged development of firm internationalization is described as an incremental, risk-averse and reluctant adjustment to changes in a firm or its environment [Johanson & Vahlne 1977, 1990]. The process preserves routines that bind organizational coalitions, and recognizes the difficulty of gaining knowledge about foreign markets. Differences in language and culture and, in the past, the slow speed of communication and transportation channels between countries have inhibited the gathering of information about foreign markets and have increased the perceived risks of foreign operation.

With a logical explanatory theory and repeated empirical confirmation, stage models of MNE development have been transformed from descriptive models, and "were soon applied prescriptively by consultants, academics, and managers alike" [Bartlett & Ghoshal 1991, p. 31]. In addition, Caves indicated that international firms must experience an extended evolutionary process when he directly contrasted MNEs with "newly organized firms" [1982, p. 96]. However, recent studies have found contradictions. For example, Welch and Loustarinen [1988] discussed reports of small English firms, Australian start-ups, and established Swedish firms that skipped important stages and were involved with unexpected speed in direct foreign investments. In addition, Sullivan and Bauerschmidt [1990] found that a firm's stage of international involvement was an unexpectedly poor predictor of European managers' knowledge and beliefs. Finally, Turnbull [1987] presents a strong conceptual and empirical criticism of the stages theory of internationalization.

Johanson and Vahlne [1990] dismissed these concerns as merely indicative of the need for adjustment to their model of firm internationalization. We believe, however, that the emergence of international new ventures presents a unique challenge to stage theory. It purportedly best applies to the early stages of internationalization with only three exceptions [Johanson & Vahlne 1990]. First, firms with large resources are expected to take large steps toward internationalization. Second, when foreign market conditions are stable and homogeneous, learning about them is easier. Third, when firms have considerable experience with markets that are similar to a newly targeted foreign market, previous experience may be generalizable to the new arena. Yet none of the exceptions seem to apply to international new ventures. Resources are constrained by their young age and usually by small size. Their markets are among the most volatile (indeed, several of the international new ventures we have studied appear to contribute to industry volatility). Finally, new ventures, by definition, have little or no experience in any market. Therefore, according to Johanson and Vahlne's [1990] own standards, stage theory needs more than a minor adjustment.

Scale and the MNE

In addition to the belief that firms must go through stages of evolution before venturing into foreign lands, large size is often thought to be a requirement for multinationality. The first modern MNEs evolved in the 1880s and 1890s and were large, mature, integrated companies [Chandler 1986]. They and their descendants have reaped substantial economies of scale in R&D, production, marketing, and other areas. An additional advantage of large, vertically integrated or diversified MNEs has been their ability to efficiently manage international communication and transportation and the exchange of production and market information among many countries [Stopford & Wells 1972]. In addition, their market power in oligopolistic industries has been highlighted as a source of MNE advantage [Dunning 1981; Glickman & Woodward 1989; Porter 1990].

Yet, if large size were a requirement for multinationality, international new ventures would seldom form because they are almost always small organizations. One key to understanding how they can exist is to recognize that large size may be both a cause and an effect of multinational competitive advantage. In some industries, such as pharmaceuticals, the sales volume generated by multinational operation makes feasible a large-scale R&D effort. In turn, R&D produces differentiated products, such as patented drugs, that provide competitive advantages over purely domestic firms in many countries. Thus, despite the fact that size is the main firm-specific variable that has explained multinationality [Glickman & Woodward 1989], large MNE size may be a concomitant, not a cause, of other more elemental sources of competitive advantage [Casson 1987; Caves 1982]. Those more elemental sources of advantage make international new ventures possible.

THE CHANGING INTERNATIONAL ENVIRONMENT

Although large size continues to be an important source of advantage for some MNEs, changing economic, technological, and social conditions have in recent years highlighted additional sources. Dramatic increases in the speed, quality, and efficiency of international communication and transportation have reduced the transaction costs of multinational interchange [Porter 1990]. Furthermore, the increasing homogenization of many markets in distant countries has made the conduct of international business easier to understand for everyone [Hedlund & Kverneland 1985]. The upshot is that increasing numbers of business executives and entrepreneurs have been exposed to international business. International financing opportunities are increasingly available [Patricof 1989; Valeriano 1991]. And human capital is more internationally mobile [Johnston 1991; Reich 1991].

With such conditions, markets now link countries more efficiently than in the past, and the hierarchies of large, established firms no longer have the competitive advantage they once enjoyed in international communication and trade [*The Economist* 1993a]. Internationally sustainable advantage is increasingly recognized to depend on the possession of unique assets [Barney 1991; Caves 1982; Hamel & Prahalad 1990; Stalk, Evans & Shulman 1992].

A priori, valuable unique assets should permit organizations with more constrained resources, such as new ventures, to enter the international arena. In addition, improved international communication and transportation along with the homogenization of markets in many countries should, a priori, simplify and shorten the process of firm internationalization. Thus, firms may skip stages of international development that have been observed in the past, or internationalization may not occur in stages at all.

We believe that is precisely what has been observed recently by a number of business journalists and business academicians—firms not following the theories of incremental firm internationalization. However, that does not mean that established theories are wrong; they still apply to some firms and industries. Yet it does mean that the established theories are less applicable in an expanding number of situations where technology, specific industry environments, and firm capabilities have changed as we have described.

NECESSARY AND SUFFICIENT ELEMENTS FOR SUSTAINABLE INTERNATIONAL NEW VENTURES

With many markets internationalizing, fewer new ventures can escape confrontations with foreign competition, and more entrepreneurs are adopting a multinational viewpoint [Drucker 1991; Ohmae 1990; Porter 1986, 1990]. Thus, the stage theory of firm internationalization is increasingly incongruent with recent developments, and large scale has become only one among many ways to compete internationally. As a result, a new framework is needed to lead both theoretical development and empirical investigation toward greater understanding of international new ventures.

The foundation of the theoretical framework that we propose is traditional in its reliance on transaction cost analysis, market imperfections, and the international internalization of essential transactions to explain the existence of the MNE. However, the framework also incorporates recently developed ideas from entrepreneurship scholars about how ventures gain influence over vital resources without owning them and from strategic management scholars about how competitive advantage is developed and sustained. Together, all these elements describe the international new venture as a special kind of MNE.

Essentially, the theoretical framework is an elaboration of Figure 1 (shown earlier), which classifies four types of organizations by age and geographic scope. Figure 2 depicts the framework. The boxes show sets of economic transactions that are of particular interest in this paper. The arrows represent elements that distinguish a subset from a larger set of transactions.

The framework begins with the box at the upper left, which is the set of all types of *Economic Transactions*. Four necessary and sufficient elements, which are enumerated within the large arrows, progressively distinguish subsets of transactions. "Element 1: Internalization of Some Transactions" distinguishes transactions that take place in *Organizations* from those that are governed by markets. From the set of all *Organizations*, strong reliance on "Element 2: Alternative Governance Structures" separates the subset of transactions associated with *New Ventures* from those in established firms. Next, "Element 3: Foreign Location Advantage" distinguishes the subset of transactions constituting *International New Ventures* from those that constitute domestic new ventures. Finally, "Element 4: Unique Resources" differentiates the subset of *Sustainable International New Ventures* from those likely to be short-lived. The dashed concentric boxes highlight the fact that the interior boxes depict the progressively more narrow subsets, and the shading shows the path of our narrowing interests. The effects of the four elements are fully described in the sections below.

Element 1: Internalization of Some Transactions

The internalization element is most basic and is clearly part of traditional MNE theory. Organizations form where economic transactions are inefficiently governed by market prices [Coase 1937; Williamson 1985]; in other words, where market imperfections exist. It is the defining element of all organizations, whether new or established, domestic or multinational. When the transaction costs of constructing and executing a contract and monitoring the performance of the contracting parties are at their lowest in an organization, its hierarchical authority (not market prices or a hybrid contract) will be the governance mechanism chosen, and the transaction is said to have been internalized within an organization [Buckley & Casson 1976; Dunning 1981, 1988].

It should be noted that the internalization element of MNE theory is often used to explain foreign direct investment; that is, ownership of assets located in foreign countries. Indeed, Hymer's [1960] seminal work on the internalization of international transactions was among the first theoretical presentations to distinguish between passive portfolio investment and foreign direct investment, and it focused on explaining the latter. Nevertheless, *ownership* of foreign assets is not a defining characteristic of either MNEs or international

FIGURE 2
Necessary and Sufficient Elements
for Sustainable International New Ventures

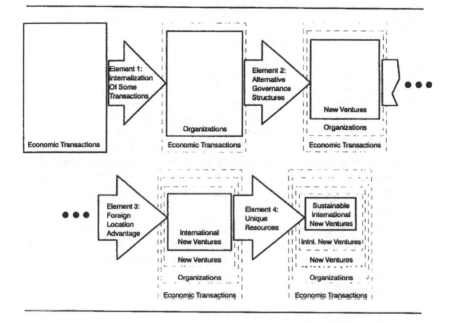

new ventures [Casson 1982]. Of course, an organization must own some assets, else it will have nothing of value to exchange in an economic transaction.

Element 2: Alternative Governance Structures

Poverty of resources and power may not be a defining characteristic of the new venture, but it is a nearly universal association [Stinchcombe 1965; Vesper 1990]. Thus, new ventures commonly lack sufficient resources to control many assets through ownership. The result is that new ventures tend to internalize, or own, a smaller percentage of the resources essential to their survival than do mature organizations. Entrepreneurs must rely on alternative modes of controlling many vital assets [Vesper 1990], and that fact distinguishes new ventures from other organizations.

Williamson [1991] noted that under conditions of moderate asset specificity and low to moderate disturbance frequency, hybrid structures, such as licensing, and franchising, are often useful alternatives to both internal control and market control over the exchange of resources. Hybrid partners share complementary assets to their mutual benefit. However, due to the potential for opportunism, as evidenced by the elaborate contracts that usually structure the relationships between the parties and the frequent reports of hybrid failure [Kanter 1989; Porter & Fuller 1986], new ventures risk expropriation by their hybrid partners of the valuable assets that they do own [Teece 1987]. Large Japanese firms, for example, have sometimes appeared to form predatory alliances with American high-technology start-ups.

An even more powerful resource-conserving alternative to internalization for new ventures is the network structure [Aldrich & Zimmer 1986; Larson 1992]. Networks depend on the social (i.e., informal) control of behavior through trust and moral obligation, not formal contracts. Cooperation dominates opportunism because business and personal reputations are at stake that may greatly affect economic rent in and beyond a spot transaction. Larson's [1992] rich description of the gains in resources and knowledge of four entrepreneurial organizations in seven intimate network alliances is impressive. Yet risks were also clear. Two of the seven relationships failed after many years of successful operation, leaving both partners with weaknesses. Nevertheless, even after failure, proprietary knowledge was protected and trust was maintained.

In summary, a major feature that distinguishes new ventures from established organizations is the minimal use of internalization and the greater use of alternative transaction governance structures. Due to their poverty of resources and power, new ventures may even use such structures when the risk of asset expropriation by hybrid partners is high.

Element 3: Foreign Location Advantage

The location advantage element of the framework distinguishes international from domestic organizations. Essentially, firms are international because they find advantage in transferring some moveable resources (e.g., raw material, knowledge, intermediate products) across a national border to be combined with an immobile, or less mobile, resource or opportunity (e.g., raw material, a market) [Dunning 1988].

However, a firm conducting transactions in a foreign country has certain disadvantages vis-à-vis indigenous firms, such as governmentally instituted barriers to trade and an incomplete understanding of laws, language, and business practices in foreign countries. As noted earlier, MNEs have often relied on the advantages of scale to overcome such obstacles. But international new ventures must usually rely on other resources.

Private knowledge is the most obvious alternative, and it has some interesting properties [Buckley & Casson 1976; Caves 1982; Rugman 1982]. The property that provides location advantage for modern MNEs, including international new ventures, is the great mobility of knowledge once it is produced. With modern communication infrastructures, valuable knowledge can be reproduced and can travel literally with the speed of light at minimal marginal cost. For example, software often requires years of development, but once written, it may be copied and used ad infinitum with insignificant additional costs. Knowledge can then be combined with less mobile resources in multiple countries (e.g., factories where the software is needed). Thus, private knowledge may create differentiation or cost advantages for MNEs and international new ventures that overcome the advantages of indigenous firms in many countries simultaneously.

That appears to be why knowledge-intensive industries have been globalizing at such a rapid pace [Reich 1991], and why a new venture with valuable knowledge is propelled to instant rather than evolutionary internationalization. When a firm introduces valuable innovative goods or services it signals at least the existence, if not the essence, of its special knowledge to outsiders.

Competitors, therefore, will try to uncover the secret or to produce equifinal alternative knowledge, and the recent increased efficiency of international markets speeds the whole competitive process. New ventures confronted with such circumstances must be international from inception or be at a disadvantage to other organizations that are international already. Thus, the prevalence of international new ventures is predicted to accompany the increasing efficiency of international markets.

Element 4: Unique Resources

The first three elements define the necessary conditions for the existence of an international new venture: Internalization of some transactions, extensive use of alternative transaction governance structures, and some advantage over indigenous firms in foreign locations. However, these are not sufficient conditions for sustainable competitive advantage.

Sustainable competitive advantage for any firm requires that its resources be unique [Barney 1991]. Unfortunately, for the knowledge-based international new venture, knowledge is at least to some degree a public good. Its easy dissemination threatens a firm's rent-earning opportunity because knowledge may not remain unique for long. Thus, the ability to reproduce and move knowledge at nearly zero marginal cost, is a simultaneously beneficial (as noted in Element 3) and troublesome property. The international new venture must limit the use of its knowledge by outsiders in many countries for it to have commercial value. In general, the use of such knowledge may be limited by four conditions.

First, if knowledge can be kept proprietary by direct means, such as patents, copyrights, or trade secrets, then the possessor of internalized valuable and rare knowledge may be able to prevent imitation and slow the development of substitutes. Yet patents and copyrights are ignored in some countries. Even where they are respected, release of patented knowledge into a market may advance competitors' production of alternative or even improved technology. Thus, knowledge that has potential commercial value is often best protected with secrecy.

Imperfect imitability is the second condition that may keep expropriable knowledge proprietary [Barney 1991; Schoemaker 1990]. A unique organizational history, socially complex knowledge, and ambiguous causal relationships between knowledge and the competitive advantage it provides may all prevent imitation by competitors. New ventures often claim their unique management style and organizational culture provide advantages, perhaps because they embody all three characteristics of imperfect imitability. However, it should be noted that these same characteristics that block competitors' imitations may constrain the spread of such intangible assets as management style into multiple national cultures within the same organization. Yet where it can be accomplished, the inimitability of an international new venture is further reinforced.

Licensing is the third way outside use of a venture's knowledge may be limited. When knowledge is expected to retain its value for a lengthy period, a limit pricing strategy (i.e., low license fees) may be used to discourage competitors or to influence the rate and direction of knowledge dissemination. When demand is strong for expropriable knowledge, but its valuable life is believed to be short (e.g., some personal computer innovations), high fees may be used to extract maximum rents over a short period.

The fact that new ventures frequently use network governance structures (as discussed under Element 2) is the fourth condition that may limit the expropriation of venture knowledge. Although alliances with complementary organizations, such as manufacturers and downstream channels, risk expropriation [Teece 1987], the network structure itself tends to control the risk. The relationships inherent in a network can have high personal and economic value because network members usually share rents and the relationships contrast so starkly with the usual background of economic opportunism [Larson 1992]. Thus, venture network members are at least somewhat inhibited from usurping the venture's knowledge. For such relationships to exist in new ventures that cross national borders, logic suggests that founding teams must usually include internationally experienced business persons of various national origins.

TYPES OF INTERNATIONAL NEW VENTURES

The previous section described basic elements for all sustainable international new ventures, but the published papers that describe actual cases indicate that these elements manifest themselves in a variety of ways. Some ventures actively coordinate the transformation of resources from many parts of the world into outputs that are sold wherever they are most highly valued [McDougall & Oviatt 1991]. Other international new ventures are primarily exporters that add value by moving outputs from where they are to locations where they are needed [Ray 1989]. In the sections that follow, different types of international new ventures will be identified, some published examples will be considered briefly, and the variety of ways that the necessary and sufficient elements are manifested will be described.

Figure 3 shows that different types of international new ventures may be distinguished by the number of value chain activities that are coordinated and by the number of countries entered. The figure identifies particular types of firms at the extremes of the two continua, but mixed types certainly appear in between, and over time new ventures may change type by coordinating additional or fewer activities and by operating in additional or fewer countries. Although the figure uses Porter's [1985] value chain and is similar to Porter's [1986] depiction of international strategy for established MNEs, Figure 3 focuses on international new ventures only. In addition, the horizontal dimension of Figure 3 simply concerns the number of countries in which any value chain activities occur. Porter's diagram focuses on the degree of dispersion among activities when sales are assumed to be in many countries.

New International Market Makers (Figure 3, quadrants i and ii)

New International Market Makers are an age-old type of firm. Importers and exporters profit by moving goods from nations where they are to nations where they are demanded. The most important value chain activities and, therefore, the ones most likely to be internalized are the systems and knowledge of inbound and outbound logistics. Transactions involving other activities tend to be governed by alternative structures. Direct investment in any country is typically kept at a minimum. The location advantage of such new ventures lies in their ability to discover imbalances of resources between countries and in creating markets where none existed. Sustained competitive advantage depends on (1) unusual abilities to spot and act on (sometimes by charging high fees) emerging opportunities before increased competition reduces profits in markets they had previously established, (2) knowledge of markets and suppliers, and (3) the ability to attract and maintain a loyal network of business associates. New International Market Makers may be either Export/Import Start-ups or Multinational Traders. Export/Import Start-ups focus on serving a few nations with which the entrepreneur is familiar. Multinational Traders serve an array of countries and are constantly scanning for trading opportunities where their networks are established or where they can quickly be set up.

Geographically Focused Start-ups (Figure 3, quadrant iii)

Geographically Focused Start-ups derive advantages by serving well the specialized needs of a particular region of the world through the use of foreign resources. They differ from the Multinational Trader in that they are geographically restricted to the location of the specialized need, and more than just the activities of inbound and outbound logistics are coordinated. They differ from the Export/Import Start-up only in the latter respect. In other words, competitive advantage is found in the coordination of multiple value chain activities, such as technological development, human resources, and production. Successful coordination may be inimitable because it is

FIGURE 3
Types of International New Ventures

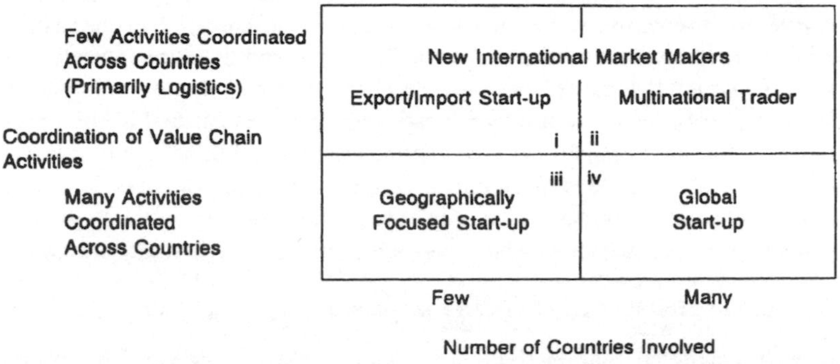

	Few	Many
Few Activities Coordinated Across Countries (Primarily Logistics)	New International Market Makers — Export/Import Start-up (i)	Multinational Trader (ii)
Many Activities Coordinated Across Countries	Geographically Focused Start-up (iii)	Global Start-up (iv)

Coordination of Value Chain Activities

Number of Countries Involved

socially complex or involves tacit knowledge. That advantage may be further protected by a close and exclusive network of alliances in the geographical area served.

For example, in recent years, numerous entrepreneurs have established firms to profit from the transfer of Western management and economic know-how to formerly communist countries. *Profit* magazine was formed by two former editors of *Soldier of Fortune* magazine who were familiar with Eastern Europe [McDougall & Oviatt 1991]. It published practical advice for Eastern European entrepreneurs, and it was written by or about successful entrepreneurs in the United States who came from Eastern Europe. The first issue of the magazine was printed in the Czech Republic with English and Czech translations on facing pages and was distributed by a Czech entrepreneur who shared the profits. Additional versions were planned for other European countries emerging from centrally planned to market-driven economies. However, there was no strategy to move beyond that geographic region because their competitive advantage was in their unique knowledge of the Eastern European culture and their ability to establish a network there.

Global Start-ups (Figure 3, quadrant iv)

The phrase ''Global Start-up'' is used because it is a common term of trade [Mamis 1989]. It is the most radical manifestation of the international new venture because it derives significant competitive advantage from extensive coordination among multiple organizational activities, the locations of which are geographically unlimited. Such firms not only respond to globalizing markets, but also proactively act on opportunities to acquire resources and sell outputs wherever in the world they have the greatest value.

Global Start-ups may be the most difficult international new ventures to develop because they require skills at both geographic and activity coordination. However, once successfully established, they appear to have the most sustainable competitive advantages due to a combination of historically unique, causally ambiguous, and socially complex inimitability with close network alliances in multiple countries. One global start-up we studied identified its "proprietary network" as its essential competitive advantage.

Another example was Momenta Corporation of Mountain View, California [Bhide 1991; McDougall & Oviatt 1991], a start-up in the emerging pen-based computer market. Its founders were from Cuba, Iran, Tanzania, and the United States. From its beginning in 1989, the founders wanted the venture to be global in its acquisition of inputs and in its target market. A global market would permit rapid growth and was believed to be necessary because potential competitors were global. Input acquisition was global because all the highest value (i.e., high quality to cost ratio) factors of production were not to be found in any single country. Thus, software design was conducted in the United States, hardware design in Germany, manufacturing in the Pacific Rim, and funding was received from Taiwan, Singapore, Europe, and the United States.

CONCLUSION

This article has identified, defined and described the emerging phenomenon of international new ventures, and has shown that some current theories of the MNE do not explain it well. Most important, it has integrated the traditional MNE concepts of internalization and location advantage with recent entrepreneurship research on alternative governance structures and with developments in strategic management on the requirements for sustainable competitive advantage. The result is a rich yet parsimonious theoretical framework that explains the existence of international new ventures, and appears useful in describing their distinct types.

Our framework describes sustainable international new ventures as controlling assets, especially unique knowledge, that create value in more than one country. Their internationality occurs at inception largely because competitive forces preclude a successful domestic focus. Their emphasis on controlling rather than owning assets is due to resource scarcity that is common among new organizations.

The framework indicates that empirical investigators interested in international new ventures will find larger sample sizes in industries where international competition for unique knowledge is a dominant characteristic. The framework also identifies ways of protecting rents derived from such knowledge (i.e., direct patent protection, uncertain imitability, license fees, and network alliances), but empirical research is needed to understand the differential success of these mechanisms more completely.

This article is partially a response to Casson's [1985] call to include the role of the entrepreneur in explaining the dynamics of the MNE. The defensive role of network formation and, thus, the importance of social interaction by entrepreneurs is highlighted. Although networks certainly provide vital information, their function as a defense against the expropriation of tenuously defended valuable and rare knowledge needs more attention. How unusual are the intimate alliances that Larson [1992] describes, and what social and economic processes and conditions promote network building across national borders? Although entrepreneurship scholars have examined some of these issues within various countries (e.g., Aldrich, Birley, Dubini, Greve, Johannisson, Reese & Sakano [1991]), we are unaware of investigations that explicitly include a sample of international new ventures.

Considering a wider arena, it may be recognized that our emphasis on the importance of alternative governance structures for new ventures is consistent with the advice of some scholars that all organizations may find advantages in outsourcing [Quinn, Doorley & Paquette 1990] and impartitioning [Barreyre 1988]. The primary advantages are (1) increased concentration of limited resources on the primary internal sources of competitive advantage and (2) the cost, quality and flexibility benefits that may be derived from using outside experts to supply all peripheral resources. However, the risks of dissipating competitive advantages, losing opportunities for learning, and becoming a "hollow corporation" are significant [Teece 1987]. The existence of international new ventures that must outsource many inputs provides a natural laboratory from which to gain insight into the results of this trade-off.

REFERENCES

Aharoni, Yair. 1966. *The foreign investment decision process*. Boston: Division of Research, Graduate School of Business Administration, Harvard University.

Aldrich, Howard & Catherine Zimmer. 1986. Entrepreneurship through social networks. In Donald L. Sexton & Raymond W. Smilor, editors, *The art and science of entrepreneurship*. Cambridge, MA: Ballinger.

Aldrich, Howard E., Sue Birley, Paola Dubini, Arent Greve, Bengt Johannisson, Pat R. Reese & Tomoaki Sakano. 1991. The generic entrepreneur? Insights from a multinational research project. Paper presented at the Babson Entrepreneurship Research Conference, Pittsburgh.

Anderson, Ray. 1992. Personal interview, June 23.

Barney, Jay. 1991. Firm resources and sustained competitive advantage. *Journal of Management*, 17: 99-120.

Barreyre, P. Y. 1988. The concept of 'impartition' policies: A different approach to vertical integration strategies. *Strategic Management Journal*, 9: 507-20.

Bartlett, Christopher A. & Sumantra Ghoshal. 1991. *Managing across borders*. Boston: Harvard Business School Press.

Bhide, Amar. 1991. Momenta Corporation (A) and (B). Case numbers N9-392-013 and N9-392-014. Boston: Harvard Business School, Harvard College.

Bilkey, Warren J. & George Tesar. 1977. The export behavior of smaller sized Wisconsin manufacturing firms. *Journal of International Business Studies*, 3(Spring/Summer): 93-98.

Brokaw, Leslie. 1990. Foreign affairs. *Inc.*, November: 92-104.

Brush, Candida G. 1992. *Factors motivating small companies to internationalize: The effect of firm age*. Unpublished dissertation. Boston University.

Buckley, Peter J. & Mark Casson. 1976. *The future of the multinational enterprise.* New York: Holmes & Meier.

Burrill, G. Steven & Stephen E. Almassy. 1993. *Electronics '93 the new global reality: Ernst & Young's fourth annual report on the electronics industry.* San Francisco: Ernst & Young.

Casson, Mark. 1982. Transaction costs and the theory of the multinational enterprise. In Alan M. Rugman, editor, *New theories of the multinational enterprise.* New York: St. Martin's Press.

_____. 1987. *The firm and the market.* Cambridge, MA: The MIT Press.

_____. 1985. Entrepreneurship and the dynamics of foreign direct investment. In Peter J. Buckley & Mark Casson, *The economic theory of the multinational enterprise.* New York: St. Martin's Press.

Caves, Richard E. 1982. *Multinational enterprise and economic analysis.* Cambridge, MA: Cambridge University Press.

Chandler, Alfred D., Jr. 1977. *The visible hand.* Cambridge, MA: The Belknap Press.

_____. 1986. The evolution of modern global competition. In Michael E. Porter, editor, *Competition in global industries,* 405-48. Boston: Harvard Business School Press.

Coase, Ronald H. 1937. The nature of the firm. *Economica N. S.,* 4: 386-405.

Cooper, Robert G. & Elko J. Kleinschmidt. 1985. The impact of export strategy on export sales performance. *Journal of International Business Studies,* 15: 37-55.

Coviello, Nicole & Hugh Munro. 1992. Internationalizing the entrepreneurial technology-intensive firm: Growth through linkage development. Paper presented at the Babson Entrepreneurship Research Conference, INSEAD, France.

Czinkota, Michael R. & Wesley J. Johnston. 1981. Segmenting U.S. firms for export development. *Journal of Business Research,* 9: 353-65.

Drucker, Peter F. 1991 (second edition). The changed world economy. In Heidi Vernon-Wortzel & Lawrence H. Wortzel, editors, *Global strategic management.* New York: Wiley.

Dunning, John H. 1981. *International production and the multinational enterprise.* London: George Allen & Unwin.

_____. 1988. The eclectic paradigm of international production: A restatement and some possible extensions. *Journal of International Business Studies,* 19: 1-31.

The Economist. 1992. Go west, young firm. May 9: 88-89.

_____. 1993a. The fall of big business. April 17: 13-14.

_____. 1993b. America's little fellows surge ahead. July 3: 59-60.

Ganitsky, Joseph. 1989. Strategies for innate and adoptive exporters: Lessons from Israel's case. *International Marketing Review,* 6(5): 50-65.

Glickman, Norman J. & Douglas P. Woodward. 1989. *The new competitors.* New York: Basic Books.

Gupta, Udayan. 1989. Small firms aren't waiting to grow up to go global. *The Wall Street Journal,* December 5: B2.

Hamel, Gary & C. K. Prahalad. 1990. The core competence of the corporation. *Harvard Business Review,* 68(3): 79-91.

Hedlund, Gunnar & Adne Kverneland. 1985. Are strategies for foreign markets changing? The case of Swedish investment in Japan. *International Studies of Management and Organization,* 15(2): 41-59.

Hennart, Jean-Francois. 1982. *A theory of multinational enterprise.* Ann Arbor: The University of Michigan Press.

Hoy, Frank, Miroslav Pivoda & Svatopluk Mackrle. 1992. A virus theory of organizational transformation. Paper presented at Babson Entrepreneurship Research Conference, INSEAD, Fountainebleau, France.

Hymer, Stephen H. 1960. *The international operations of national firms: A study of direct foreign investment.* Cambridge, MA: The MIT Press (published in 1976).

Johanson, Jan & Jan-Erik Vahlne. 1977. The internationalization process of the firm—A model of knowledge development and increasing foreign market commitment. *Journal of International Business Studies,* 8(1): 23-32.

_____. 1990. The mechanism of internationalization. *International Marketing Review,* 7(4): 11-24.

Johnston, William B. 1991. Global work force 2000: The new world labor market. *Harvard Business Review*, 69(2): 115-127.

Jolly, Vijay K., Matti Alahuhta & Jean-Pierre Jeannet. 1992. Challenging the incumbents: How high technology start-ups compete globally. *Journal of Strategic Change*, 1: 71-82.

Kanter, Rosabeth M. 1989. Becoming PALs: Pooling, allying, and linking across companies. *Academy of Management Executive*, 3: 183-93.

Katz, Jerome & William B. Gartner. 1988. Properties of emerging organizations. *Academy of Management Review*, 13: 429-41.

Kedia, Ben L. & Jagdeep Chhokar. 1985. The impact of managerial attitudes on export behavior. *American Journal of Small Business*, Fall: 7-17.

Larson, Andrea. 1992. Network dyads in entrepreneurial settings: A study of the governance of exchange relationships. *Administrative Science Quarterly*, 37: 76-104.

Malekzadeh, Ali R. & Afsaneh Nahavandi. 1985. Small business exporting: Misconceptions are abundant. *American Journal of Small Business*, 9(4): 7-14.

Mamis, Robert A. 1989. Global start-up. *Inc.*, August: 38-47.

McDougall, Patricia P. & Benjamin M. Oviatt. 1991. Global start-ups: New ventures without geographic limits. *The Entrepreneurship Forum*, Winter: 1-5.

_____ & Candida Brush. 1991. A symposium on global start-ups: Entrepreneurial firms that are born international. Presentation at the annual Academy of Management meeting, August, Miami.

McDougall, Patricia P., Scott Shane & Benjamin M. Oviatt. 1994. Explaining the formation of international new ventures: The limits of theories from international business research. *Journal of Business Venturing*, forthcoming.

Ohe, Takeru, Shuji Honjo, Mark Oliva & Ian C. MacMillan. 1991. Entrepreneurs in Japan and Silicon Valley: A study of perceived differences. *Journal of Business Venturing*, 6: 135-44.

Ohmae, Kenichi. 1990. *The borderless world*. New York: HarperBusiness.

Oviatt, Benjamin M., Patricia P. McDougall, Mark Simon & Rodney C. Shrader. 1994. Heartware International Corporation: A medical equipment company ''born international.'' *Entrepreneurship Theory and Practice*, forthcoming.

Patricof, Alan. 1989. The internationalization of venture capital. *Journal of Business Venturing*, 4: 227-30.

Porter, Michael E. 1985. *Competitive advantage*. New York: The Free Press.

_____. 1986. Competition in global industries: A conceptual framework. In Michael E. Porter, editor, *Competition in global industries*. Boston: Harvard Business School Press.

_____. 1990. *The competitive advantage of nations*. New York: The Free Press.

_____ & Mark B. Fuller. 1986. Coalitions and global strategy. In Michael E. Porter, editor, *Competition in global industries*. Boston: Harvard Business School Press.

Quinn, James B., Thomas L. Doorley & Penny C. Paquette. 1990. Technology in services: Rethinking strategic focus. *Sloan Management Review*,

Ray, Dennis M. 1989. Entrepreneurial companies 'born' international: Four case studies. Paper presented at Babson Entrepreneurship Research Conference on Entrepreneurship, St. Louis.

Reich, Robert B. 1991. *The work of nations*. New York: Alfred A. Knopf.

Rossman, Marlene L. 1984. Export trading company legislation: U.S. response to Japanese foreign market penetration. *Journal of Small Business Management*, October: 62-66.

Rugman, Alan M. 1982. Internalization and non-equity forms of international involvement. In Alan M. Rugman, editor, *New theories of the multinational enterprise*. New York: St. Martin's Press.

Schoemaker, Paul J.H. 1990. Strategy, complexity, and economic rent. *Management Science*, 10: 1178-92.

Stalk, George, Philip Evans & Lawrence E. Shulman. 1992. Competing on capabilities: The new rules of corporate strategy. *Harvard Business Review*, 70(2): 57-69.

Stinchcombe, Arthur L. 1965. Social structure and organizations. In James G. March, editor, *Handbook of organizations*, 142-93. Chicago: Rand McNally.

Stopford, John M. & Louis T. Wells. 1972. *Managing the multinational enterprise.* New York: Basic Books.

Sullivan, Daniel & Alan Bauerschmidt. 1990. Incremental internationalization: A test of Johanson and Vahlne's thesis. *Management International Review*, 30(1): 19-30.

Teece, David J. 1987. Profiting from technological innovation: Implications for integration, collaboration, licensing, and public policy. In David J. Teece, editor, *The competitive challenge.* Cambridge, MA: Ballinger.

Turnbull, P. W. 1987. A challenge to the stages theory of the internationalization process. In Philip J. Rosson & Stanley D. Reid, editors, *Managing export entry and expansion.* New York: Praeger.

Valeriano, Lourdes L. 1991. Other Asians follow Japanese as investors in U.S. firms. *Wall Street Journal*, January 7: B2.

Vesper, Karl H. 1990 (revised edition). *New venture strategies.* Englewood Cliffs, NJ: Prentice Hall.

Vozikis, George S. & Timothy S. Mescon. 1985. Small exporters and stages of development: An empirical study. *American Journal of Small Business*, 9: 49-64.

Welch, Lawrence S. & Reijo Loustarinen. 1988. Internationalization: Evolution of a concept. *Journal of General Management*, 14(2): 34-55.

Westhead, Paul. 1990. A typology of new manufacturing firm founders in Wales: Performance measures and public policy implications. *Journal of Business Venturing*, 5: 103-22.

Wilkins, Mira. 1970. *The emergence of multinational enterprise.* Cambridge, MA: Harvard University Press.

_____ & F. E. Hill. 1964. *American business abroad: Ford on six continents.* Detroit: Wayne State University Press.

Williamson, Oliver E. 1991. Comparative economic organization: The analysis of discrete structural alternatives. *Administrative Science Quarterly*, 36: 269-96.

_____. 1985. *The economic institutions of capitalism.* New York: The Free Press.

[6]

1042-2587
Copyright 2005 by
Baylor University

Defining International Entrepreneurship and Modeling the Speed of Internationalization

Benjamin M. Oviatt
Patricia P. McDougall

This article provides a reformulated definition of international entrepreneurship. Consistent with the new definition, a model is presented of how the speed of entrepreneurial internationalization is influenced by various forces. The model begins with an entrepreneurial opportunity and depicts the enabling forces of technology, the motivating forces of competition, the mediating perceptions of entrepreneurs, and the moderating forces of knowledge and networks that collectively determine the speed of internationalization.

According to Zahra and George (2002) the term "international entrepreneurship" first appeared in a short article by Morrow (1988). It highlighted recent technological advances and cultural awareness that appeared to open previously untapped foreign markets to new ventures. Soon after that, McDougall's (1989) empirical study comparing domestic and international new ventures paved the way for academic study in international entrepreneurship. Building on popular business press interest in rapid internationalization (e.g., Brokaw, 1990; Gupta, 1989; Mamis, 1989; *The Economist*, 1992, 1993), Oviatt and McDougall (1994) provided a theoretical base for the study of international new ventures, which they defined as business organizations "that, from inception, [seek] to derive significant competitive advantage from the use of resources and the sale of outputs in multiple countries" (p. 49). Thus, international entrepreneurship began with an interest in new ventures.

As additional studies were conducted and articles published, interest in the arena increased, and the field of international entrepreneurship broadened from its early studies of new venture internationalization. For example, insightful studies of differing national entrepreneurial cultures (McGrath & MacMillan, 1992; Thomas & Mueller, 2000), alliances, and cooperative strategies (Li & Atuahene-Gima, 2001; Steensma, Marino,

Please send correspondence to: Benjamin M. Oviatt, Department of Managerial Sciences, P.O. Box 4014, College of Business Administration, Georgia State University, Atlanta, GA 30302-4014; tel.: (404) 651-3021; fax: (404) 651-2896; email: BenOviatt@gsu.edu, and to Patricia P. McDougall, Kelley School of Business, Indiana University, 1309 E. Tenth Street, Bloomington, IN 47405-1701; tel.: (812) 855-7873; email: mcdougal@indiana.edu.
Submitted to *Entrepreneurship Theory & Practice* April 2005. Many thanks to Stephanie Fernhaber for helpful comments on drafts of the article.

Weaver, & Dickson, 2000), small and medium sized company internationalization (Lu & Beamish, 2001), top management teams (Reuber & Fischer, 1997), entry modes (Zacharakis, 1997), cognition (Mitchell, Smith, Seawright, & Morse, 2000), country profiles (Busenitz, Gomez, & Spencer, 2000), corporate entrepreneurship (Birkinshaw, 1997), exporting (Bilkey & Tesar, 1977), knowledge management (Kuemmerle, 2002), venture financing (Roure, Keeley, & Keller, 1992), and technological learning (Zahra, Ireland, & Hitt, 2000) have all helped move the field forward.

Reflective of the multidisciplinary nature of both entrepreneurship and international business, researchers have drawn upon theories and frameworks from international business, entrepreneurship, anthropology, economics, psychology, finance, marketing, and sociology. It is clear that the domain of international entrepreneurship is rich in opportunity. Because the field is broad, there are many interesting research questions to be explored, and many existing theories may be beneficially employed. Opportunities for both multidisciplinary and multicountry collaboration are clear.

The importance of the field has also been signaled by the appearance of special issues and forums on international entrepreneurship in various journals, such as *Entrepreneurship Theory & Practice* in 1996 and *Academy of Management Journal* in 2000. *Journal of Business Venturing* regularly publishes articles in the area. The *Journal of International Business Studies* has established an editorial area for international entrepreneurship, and the *Journal of International Entrepreneurship* was recently launched. Both the Kauffman Foundation and the Strategic Management Society have sponsored edited volumes that included reviews of international entrepreneurship literature and research issues (McDougall & Oviatt, 1997; Zahra & George, 2002). In 2004, an edited handbook of the field was published (Dana, 2004). Academic meetings focused on international entrepreneurship are held on multiple continents, and doctoral student consortia on the topic have emerged. In summary, academic interest in international entrepreneurship is strong.

Our research, however, indicates that the definition of international entrepreneurship should be updated so it is consistent with a recent emphasis on opportunity recognition in the broader discipline of entrepreneurship. Thus, this article presents a new definition.

An important topic within international entrepreneurship is the international new venture, and explaining its accelerated internationalization is an important focus of research (Hurmerinta-Peltomäki, 2004). However, no model of the forces influencing the speed of internationalization exists. Therefore, this article presents one. The model is consistent with the revised definition of international entrepreneurship that we provide. It describes four types of influential forces, and it is intended to guide empirical research concerning the speed of entrepreneurial internationalization.

Definitions of International Entrepreneurship

International business scholars Wright and Ricks (1994) highlighted international entrepreneurship as a newly emerging research arena, and it became clear that arena included: (1) comparisons of entrepreneurial behavior in multiple countries and cultures, as well as (2) organization behavior that extends across national borders and is entrepreneurial. While these foci have remained over time, the definition of "international entrepreneurship" has moved from a very broad one, which avoided prematurely proscribing important nascent interests (Giamartino, McDougall, & Bird, 1993), to excluding nonprofit and government organizations to be consistent with the commonly accepted definition of "international business" (McDougall & Oviatt, 1997). However, to be consistent with the interests of entrepreneurship scholars in such issues as social entrepreneurship, that exclusion was eliminated:

> International entrepreneurship is a combination of innovative, proactive, and risk-seeking behavior that crosses national borders and is intended to create value in organizations. (McDougall & Oviatt, 2000)

Individual, group, and organizational levels of behavior and academic study are included. Thus, international entrepreneurship has evolved from a focus on new ventures to include corporate entrepreneurship (Birkinshaw, 1997; Zahra et al., 2000; Zahra & George, 2002).

The definition of entrepreneurship, however, is a matter of continuing debate and evolution. The idea that entrepreneurship is a combination of innovative, proactive, and risk-seeking behavior finds its origins in strategic management literature (e.g., Covin & Slevin, 1989; Miller, 1983), but those are not the only entrepreneurial dimensions that scholars have identified. Lumpkin and Dess (1996) highlighted a variety of "entrepreneurial orientation" dimensions and distinguished them from the definition of entrepreneurship itself, which they equated with new entry, or the act of launching a new venture.

Venkataraman (1997) and Shane and Venkataraman (2000) maintain, however, that the creation of new organizations, while possible, is not a defining condition (cf., Gartner, 1988). Business opportunities may be sold to others, for example. Thus, they define the study of entrepreneurship as the:

> examination of how, by whom, and with what effects opportunities to create future goods and services are discovered, evaluated, and exploited. (Shane & Venkataraman, 2000, p. 218)

The authors emphasize that entrepreneurship has two parts: (1) opportunities; and (2) individuals who strive to take advantage of them. We agree with these observations. Increasingly, entrepreneurship is viewed as focusing on opportunities that may be bought and sold, or they may form the foundation of new organizations. Such a focus leads us away from an emphasis on entrepreneurial orientations, which McDougall and Oviatt (2000) relied upon for their definition of international entrepreneurship. That change has the advantage of obviating the debate over how many dimensions of entrepreneurial orientation are important for definitional purposes (Lumpkin & Dess, 1996).

As with all definitions, however, Shane and Venkataraman's (2000) definition has been criticized. Some scholars dislike their definition because it depicts opportunities as "objective phenomena" that do not require subjective creation among people influenced by their social milieu (Baker, Gedajlovic, & Lubatkin, 2003). However, we believe the issue is resolved by noting that opportunities may be enacted (Weick, 1995) as well as discovered. That is, people act and then interpret what their actions have created, and sometimes those creations are economic opportunities. Shane (2000), for example, described how eight new venture opportunities were created from different applications of a single technology. The patented technology, called three-dimensional printing, deposited multiple layers of material in a complex manner to produce a component. The proposed applications varied from creating architectural models to manufacturing pharmaceuticals. By the time Shane's article was written, four entrepreneurial efforts resulting from those applications had failed and four companies survived. The inventors of the technology did not discover any of the eight applications, and while the entrepreneurs may have discovered the technology, it was their idiosyncratic interpretations of its capabilities that appeared to create the opportunity. While Shane (2000) terms it a process of discovery, it seems very much like what Weick (1995) describes as a process of enactment.

Thus, with an adjustment to include enactment, we believe adopting a new definition of international entrepreneurship that relies to a large extent on Shane and Venkataraman's (2000) definition of entrepreneurship is appropriate at this time. Our definition: (1) focuses on opportunities, (2) permits but does not require the formation of new organizations, (3) allows for corporate entrepreneurship, (4) renders unnecessary a debate over how many dimensions entrepreneurial orientations include; and (5) highlights entrepreneurial activity across national borders. While definitional changes should be made only with care, we believe the current potential for improvement warrants a change. Therefore:

> International entrepreneurship is the discovery, enactment, evaluation, and exploitation of opportunities—across national borders—to create future goods and services.

The phrase "across national borders" is highlighted above because it has particular meaning in this context. Actors (organizations, groups, or individuals) who discover, enact, evaluate, or exploit opportunities to create future goods or services and who *cross national borders* to do so are internationally entrepreneurial actors. Scholars who study those actors, how they act, and the effects of their actions are studying international entrepreneurship. So, too, are scholars who compare domestic entrepreneurial systems, cultures, and behavior *across national borders*. Thus, there are two branches to the study of international entrepreneurship, one focusing on the cross-national-border *behavior* of entrepreneurial actors, and another focusing on the cross-national-border *comparison* of entrepreneurs, their behavior, and the circumstances in which they are imbedded. The comparison branch is included because it has always been a part of the study of international entrepreneurship from the first special issue on the topic to appear in an academic journal (Hisrich, Honig-Haftel, McDougall, & Oviatt, 1996) to the most recent comprehensive handbook on international entrepreneurship (Dana, 2004). However, to provide focus and to keep this article to a journal-length manuscript, from this point we confine our attention to the study of cross-national-border entrepreneurial behavior.

A Model of Internationalization Speed

Given our definition, the study of cross-border entrepreneurial behavior focuses on how actors discover, enact, evaluate, and exploit opportunities to create future goods and services. Several models inform our understanding of how the process works. Based on their studies of Swedish manufacturing firms, Johanson and Vahlne (1977, 1990) showed the initial internationalization activities of many firms were targeted to psychically close markets and used the less committed modes of entry, such as exporting. They explained that international actors learn and increase their foreign market knowledge over time primarily through experience, and only then do they start or increase their foreign market commitments and later expand to more psychically distant markets. Their Uppsala Model explains how foreign market risks are managed by acquiring tacit knowledge about foreign markets and incrementally changing their commitments to those markets. However, the Uppsala Model is focused on traditional cross-border behavior, not on accelerated internationalization or on entrepreneurial behavior.

Other models highlight how technological advances in transportation, communication, and computers permit entrepreneurial actors to form new ventures that internationalize rapidly (Knight & Cavusgil, 1996; Oviatt & McDougall, 1999). Started by individuals or small groups of entrepreneurs, international new ventures are said to own certain valuable assets, to use alliances and network structures to control a relatively large percentage of vital assets, and to have a unique resource that provides a sustainable advantage that is transferable to a foreign location (McDougall, Shane, & Oviatt, 1994; Oviatt & McDougall, 1994).

Environmental influences, industry conditions, and the thinking of entrepreneurial actors themselves are believed to be prime factors determining the speed of international involvement. Some scholars see all these influences as mediated by the perceptions and decision making of the entrepreneurial actors (Oviatt, Shrader, & McDougall, 2004). Others see organizational factors, including characteristics of the entrepreneurial actors, directly influencing international entrepreneurial behavior, while being moderated by environmental and strategic factors (Zahra & George, 2002).

It is important to resolve the form of these relationships among the environment, industry conditions, and entrepreneurial actors to achieve a better understanding of how international opportunities are discovered, enacted, evaluated, and exploited in an accelerated manner. There may be a performance advantage in rapid internationalization (Autio, Sapienza, & Almeida, 2000). That is, the earlier in its history that a firm internationalizes, the faster it seems to grow. Thus, it is fundamental to explain why some entrepreneurial behavior crosses national borders with greater speed than others. We propose a model in which mediating, moderating, and other forms of influence determine the speed of entrepreneurial internationalization.

Figure 1 depicts a model of influences on the speed of entrepreneurial internationalization. As shown, there are three vital aspects to such speed. First, there is the time between the discovery or enactment of an opportunity and its first foreign market entry. Second, is the speed with which country scope is increased. That is, how rapidly do entries into foreign markets accumulate and how rapidly are countries entered that are psychically distant from the entrepreneur's home country? Third, is the speed of international commitment. That is, how quickly does the percentage of foreign revenue increase? Obviously, our model focuses on foreign outputs, not foreign inputs.

Figure 1

A Model of Forces Influencing Internationalization Speed

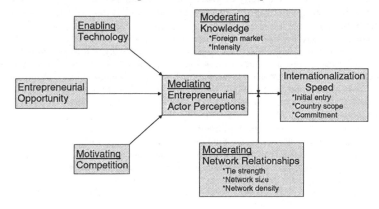

The process of entrepreneurial internationalization in our model begins, as shown in Figure 1, with a potential entrepreneurial opportunity. For example, a medical journal publishes an article on how broken bones may be healed faster. We will simply assume here that an entrepreneurial actor somehow discovers or enacts such an opportunity because our focus is not on the nature of the discovery or enactment, but on the speed with which that opportunity is internationalized. Most important, our model shows that the speed of entrepreneurial internationalization is determined by four types of forces: (1) enabling, (2) motivating, (3) mediating, and (4) moderating.

The first, or the *enabling* force, makes accelerated internationalization feasible (Oviatt & McDougall, 1999). Faster and more efficient transportation among multiple foreign countries has brought down costs for foreign trade and investment. Airline transportation prices have declined over a very long period, enabling more people to travel longer distances rapidly at historically lower costs. The containerization of freight has reduced costs and increased speed in the movement of goods among all countries. In 1970, it cost $10,268 to transport a container via ship from Los Angeles to Hong Kong, but by 1999 that cost had dropped to a mere $1,900 (in 1999 dollars) (Kuemmerle, 2005). Improvements and cost reductions in digital technology have also been dramatic over a long period. Computers, faxes, and wireless technologies have made high quality and rapid communication feasible in every country in the world. For example, knowledge of the new bone-healing process mentioned above may be communicated to many countries simultaneously over the Internet. Experienced physicians may quickly and inexpensively travel to many countries in order to provide instruction about the complex process, and any required chemicals can be shipped by UPS within two days to any country. Therefore, transportation, communication, and digital technology appear to be the foundation enabling rapid internationalization of such an entrepreneurial opportunity.

The second general force influencing the speed of internationalization is the *motivating* force of competition. Whereas technology enables faster internationalization, competitors encourage or even force it upon entrepreneurs. Many entrepreneurs have been motivated to take preemptive advantage of technological opportunities in foreign countries because they feared competitors would respond quickly to a new product introduction and prevent them from eventually going international if they initially competed only in their home country (McDougall et al., 1994; Oviatt & McDougall, 1995). Even with a patent on the new bone-healing process, an entrepreneurial actor might recognize competing processes could appear unless the actor quickly established his or her process as a standard in many countries. In other words, technology makes accelerated internationalization feasible, while the presence of competitors or potential competitors motivates or strongly encourages it.

The entrepreneurial actor is the third, the *mediating*, force. The person or group that discovers or enacts an opportunity is central to the dynamics of international exploitation. Through the lens of their personal characteristics (e.g., years of international business experience) and psychological traits (e.g., risk-taking propensity), entrepreneurs observe and interpret the potential of the opportunity, the potential of communication, transportation, and computer technology to enable internationalization, and the degree of threat from competitors (Oviatt, Shrader, & McDougall, 2004). These influences on perceptions clarify or cloud the entrepreneur's decision making. Therefore, accelerated or retarded international entrepreneurial behavior cannot be explained through some objective measure of technology and competition, but only by understanding how the opportunity, the enabling forces, and the motivating forces are interpreted, or mediated, by the entrepreneurial actor.

There are two types of *moderating* forces that influence the speed of internationalization. After an entrepreneurial actor discovers or enacts an opportunity and interprets the enabling and the motivating forces, then the *knowledge-intensity* of the opportunity combined with the know-how already available to the entrepreneurial actor, plus the characteristics of the entrepreneur's *international network* largely determine internationalization speed. Therefore, we view these as two types of moderating forces.

Bell, McNaughton, Young, and Crick (2003) propose that differences in the novelty, complexity, and sophistication of knowledge used in a firm explain the speed of internationalization. Three types of firms may be observed that differ in their reliance on knowledge and subsequent speed of internationalization. Traditional firms adapting well-understood technologies to new foreign markets usually internationalize incrementally. The principal entrepreneurial act is apparently the exploitation of an old concept in a new location. The Uppsala Model may best apply to these kinds of firms. Knowledge-intensive firms, a second type of firm in the model, use complex knowledge to design a new product, an improved production method, or more efficient service delivery. These firms internationalize faster because they usually hold a competitive advantage that can be exploited in multiple countries. Finally, there is the knowledge-based firm, the existence of which is totally dependent on some novel complex knowledge. For example, a knowledge-based firm might exist if the bone-healing process mentioned above involved some manipulation of human genes and was patented by a new venture. This type of firm is likely to have the most accelerated internationalization because it has a unique sustainable advantage that may be in demand in a number of countries. The characteristics of such firms are further described by Oviatt and McDougall (1994). In summary, knowledge-type may influence how quickly an entrepreneurial opportunity is exploited. Furthermore, we propose it is an influence that occurs largely after, albeit perhaps shortly after, an opportunity is perceived and interpreted by an entrepreneurial actor.

Johanson and Vahlne, the principal authors of the Uppsala Model, recently concluded that:

> we have a situation where old models of internationalization processes are still applied quite fruitfully at the same time as a number of studies have suggested that there is a need for new and network-based models of internationalization. We think it might be worthwhile to reconcile and even integrate the two approaches. (2003, p. 84)

They provide an outline of a proposed integration that uses the interplay of experiential, or tacit, learning and resource commitment in organizations as its driving mechanism. These are, of course, concepts from the traditional Uppsala Model, but they combine them with a new focus on network relationships involving customers and suppliers. They hypothesize that firms learn and benefit from such relationships and, therefore, make increasing commitments to them. Those relationships, in turn, sometimes lead them to enter foreign markets, at times incrementally and at times quite rapidly. Using a network perspective, Johanson and Vahlne (2003) propose that the establishment and development of foreign customer and supplier relationships determine much about the nature of international entry and expansion. We believe cross-national-border networks, along with knowledge-type, moderate the speed with which international entrepreneurial opportunities are exploited.

Because the moderating influences of knowledge-intensity and networks are more complex and have received less attention than the other forces highlighted above, we believe they are fundamental issues worthy of more exploration here. Thus, the remainder of the article focuses on the effects of networks and knowledge-intensity.

Network Influences

Networking is a powerful tool for the entrepreneur (Dubini & Aldrich, 1991), and network analysis has been a powerful framework for international entrepreneurship researchers (Bell, 1995; Coviello & Munro, 1995, 1997; Oviatt & McDougall, 1994).

Focusing on the personal and extended networks of the entrepreneur and his/her management team, several studies challenging traditional models of internationalization have drawn upon network theory. For example, a comparative study of export behavior among entrepreneurial software firms in Finland, Ireland, and Norway led Bell (1995) to conclude that the network approach was a better explanation of the internationalization process of these firms. McDougall et al. (1994) explained that networks helped founders of international new ventures, or born-globals, to identify international business opportunities, and those networks appeared to have more influence on the founders' country choices than did their psychic distance. Oviatt and McDougall (1995) identified strong international business networks as one of the seven most important characteristics of successful global start-ups. Servias and Rasmussen (2000) found that networks were important to the majority of the Danish firms in their study, although Rasmussen, Madsen, and Evangelista's (2001) case studies of five Danish and Australian born-globals did not find support for the importance of the founder's network. Finally, much of Coviello and Munro's international entrepreneurship research has used network theory to examine international market development and marketing-related activities within international markets. Based on the findings of their study of the internationalization processes of New Zealand software firms, Coviello and Munro (1995) noted:

> Our understanding of the internationalization processes of entrepreneurial firms is enriched when we expand the analysis beyond the individual firm's actions and address the impact of a firm's role and position within a network of relationships. From this perspective, foreign market selection and entry initiatives emanate from opportunities created through network contacts, rather than solely from the strategic decisions of managers in the firm. . . . it is not surprising that the observed patterns of international market growth for entrepreneurial high-technology firms differ from the processes of the larger manufacturing firms outlined in the literature. Their relatively rapid and dispersed involvement in foreign markets creates the impression of being random and somewhat irrational, when in fact the span of activities can be linked to opportunities emerging from a network of relationships. (p. 58)

In summary, networks help entrepreneurs identify international opportunities, establish credibility, and often lead to strategic alliances and other cooperative strategies.

Our model in Figure 1 depicts network relationships as a moderating influence on the speed of internationalization. After an entrepreneurial actor discovers or enacts an opportunity and perceives the technologies that enable internationalization and the competitors that motivate it, the entrepreneur uses established network links that cross national borders to explore where and how quickly the opportunity can be exploited in foreign locations. We believe there are three key aspects of such networks that moderate the speed of internationalization: (1) the strength of network ties, (2) the size of the network; and (3) overall density of the network.

In formal network analysis, the actors are called nodes and the links between them are called ties. Aldrich (1999) identified two types of ties. Strong ties between nodes, or actors, are durable and involve emotional investment, trust, reliability, and a desire to negotiate about differences in order to preserve the tie. Entrepreneurs are most dependent upon strong ties at start-up, and because strong ties require considerable investment and maintenance, their number for any individual entrepreneur rarely exceeds 20, and is more often in the range of 5 to 10. Because of their small number and the investment required, we believe strong ties are not the most important type for internationalization.

Weak ties are. They are relationships with customers, suppliers, and others that are friendly and business-like. Weak ties are far more numerous than strong ties because they require less investment. Their number can grow relatively quickly, and they are important because they are often vital sources of information and know-how. Especially important are weak ties with brokers. Brokers are nodes in a network, or actors, who are tied to nodes that are not tied themselves. In other words, brokers establish ties between actors who, without the broker, have no link to each other. Thus brokers enable indirect ties. In international business, brokers often provide links across national borders between actors who want to conduct international business with each other. For example, suppose a Swiss consultant handles the sale to a French buyer of equipment produced by an Italian manufacturer. The consultant is, therefore, in the role of a broker establishing an indirect tie between the Italian manufacturer and the French buyer.

In our model (Figure 1), entrepreneurial actors with an opportunity (enabled by technology and motivated by competition) and with an existing broker or brokers who can help tie them indirectly to other actors in a foreign country have the ability to engage in international business very soon after discovering or enacting the opportunity. Of course, it is also possible that the entrepreneurial actor has existing direct ties to other actors across national borders that do not rely on the indirect ties that brokers provide. In either case, we believe the existence of cross-border weak direct or indirect (i.e., brokered) ties can positively and significantly moderate the speed of venture internationalization. If an entrepreneur already has such ties when he or she discovers or enacts an opportunity, the initial foreign entry may occur with unusual speed. If the ties are yet to be established, internationalization is likely to be slowed.

Following from the above logic, the more direct or indirect cross border weak ties that an entrepreneurial actor has established, the greater the potential country scope of internationalization and the greater possible speed for increasing that scope. Thus, the size of an entrepreneurial actor's network is the second key aspect (after tie strength) that will moderate the speed of internationalization. As depicted in Figure 1, larger entrepreneurial networks are associated with faster venture internationalization and more rapid increases in country scope. Furthermore, with a large network in place, a relatively large portion of venture revenue comes rapidly from foreign sources, and the venture, therefore, has more rapid commitment to internationalization.

The third and final key moderating aspect of entrepreneurial networks is density. While sparse networks are especially good at gathering new information, dense networks are useful when trust and reciprocity are vital. Actors are said to have sparse networks when the nodes to which they are tied are, for the most part, not tied to each other. For example, if a German new venture has a link to two businesses in the United States, but those businesses have no ties to each other, then the network of the German venture is less dense than it would be if the two U.S. businesses were directly linked in some way. Sparse networks are believed to produce new information better than dense networks because the sparse networks link disparate nodes while the dense networks link nodes through redundant ties. For example, if the two U.S. businesses mentioned above sell to distinctively different product markets and have no ties to each other except their individual links to our German venture, the German venture has a chance to learn information about both markets. Alternatively, if the two U.S. firms sell to each other in addition to those distinctive product markets, then the German venture has redundant links through which it may get information about both U.S. firms and the markets that they serve. In summary, the redundant links of a dense network are believed to be inefficient at producing unique information. Sparse networks are believed to be more efficient.

The redundant links of dense networks, however, have the advantage that there are more links and, therefore, more interaction among all the actors in the network. Thus, monitoring of behavior is more efficiently accomplished and reputations are more quickly communicated to all actors in the network. Business behavior regarded as illegitimate in a dense network is quickly detected, widely known, and punished. Thus, trust is stronger in a dense network than in a sparse one because there are penalties for opportunistic behavior. Indeed, dense networks can be seen as a partial substitute for strong ties across national borders. Density engenders trust among network actors linked by weak ties, but the trust is established by the monitoring potential in a dense network rather than by the emotional investment present in strong ties. Since successful international business operations are dependent upon reliable interaction among actors in multiple foreign countries, dense cross-border networks provide relatively efficient support for internationalization. Entrepreneurial actors who have already established such networks can internationalize rapidly.

Knowledge Influences

The knowledge block in our model refers to both market knowledge and the intensity of knowledge in the product or service offering. As highlighted by our model, knowledge moderates the speed at which perceived opportunity is exploited internationally.

Knowledge was at the core of the process models of internationalization developed by Johanson and Vahlne (1977) and their Uppsala colleagues. Building on the behavioral view of the firm, they viewed the lack of foreign market knowledge as an impediment to international expansion as firms tended to confine their operations to the geographical vicinity of their existing knowledge. Thus, firms remained domestic until they were pushed or pulled internationally by an event such as an unsolicited export order. Even after moving into a foreign market, the speed of their internationalization was slow as internationalization occurred through a process of incremental stages. The firm progressed to further stages of internationalization as it accumulated foreign market knowledge. As noted by Autio et al. (2000), knowledge has also played an important role in the new venture theory of internationalization, with knowledge and vision being the keys to aggressive international opportunity seeking.

The need to acquire foreign market knowledge and the importance of organizational learning for entering or expanding in the international marketplace has been recognized by numerous scholars (e.g., Andersen, 1993; Barkema & Vermeulen, 1998; Erramilli, 1991; Inkpen & Beamish, 1997; Lord & Ranft, 2000; Luo, 1997; Zahra et al., 2000). The development of much of the growing body of research on knowledge management is closely related to learning theory. Organizational learning is defined by Autio et al. as "the process of assimilating new knowledge into the organization's knowledge base" (2000, p. 911), and Huber notes "an organization learns if any of its units acquires knowledge that it recognizes as potentially useful to the organization" (1991, p. 89). The development of knowledge depends on the firm's absorptive capacity, which is "largely a function of the firm's level of prior related knowledge" (Cohen & Levinthal, 1990, p. 128). The management of knowledge is particularly challenging in cross-national settings where different cultures, corporate governance systems, time zones, and languages are involved (Kuemmerle, 2002).

A firm's ability to learn about a new host country moderates the speed at which the venture internationalizes to exploit an entrepreneurial opportunity. For entrepreneurial firms competing in international markets, the learning process is critical in helping firms overcome their liabilities of foreignness (Hymer, 1976; Inkpen & Beamish, 1997; Zaheer, 1995), as much of this liability relates to the foreign firm's lack of local market knowledge (Lord & Ranft, 2000). Learning about a new host country is not a smooth and seamless process that is homogeneous across firms (Lord & Ranft, 2000), and the difficultly of its acquisition may serve to increase its benefits (Andersen, 1993). The importance of prior knowledge and learning is well illustrated in the case studies of international new ventures (Kuemmerle, 2002; McDougall et al., 1994; Simões & Dominguinhos, 2001).

When considering the ability of a firm to attain and assimilate new knowledge pertinent to internationalization, it is critical to keep in mind the firm's stock of existing knowledge. In contrast to multinational firms, knowledge in the entrepreneurial firm tends to be more individualized to the founder or entrepreneurial team. Firms in which the founder or entrepreneurial team had lived abroad or had prior work experience in international markets have exhibited speedier entry and/or commitment to internationalization (Almeida & Bloodgood, 1996; Bloodgood, Sapienza, & Almeida, 1996; Reuber & Fischer, 1997; Shrader, Oviatt, & McDougall, 2000). Thus, entrepreneurial firms led by founders or management teams who have a greater wealth of personal international knowledge are more likely to exploit entrepreneurial opportunities earlier. Their greater absorptive capacity makes these firms able to readily accumulate additional foreign knowledge, which reduces the uncertainty of operating abroad and increases their likelihood of entering additional countries and increasing their commitment to internationalization (Autio et al., 2000).

One of the most compelling international entrepreneurship studies using learning theory is that of Autio et al. (2000) in which the authors introduce the concept of "learning advantages of newness." Using panel data from the Finnish electronics industry, they concluded:

> as firms get older, they develop learning impediments that hamper their ability to successfully grow in new environments and that the relative flexibility of newer firms allows them to rapidly learn the competencies necessary to pursue continued growth in foreign markets. (2000, p. 919)

The learning advantages of newness represent a counterpoint to the widely accepted concept that there is a "liability of newness" for young organizations (Stinchcombe, 1965). While the concept of learning advantages of newness could apply to all entrepreneurial firms, it is particularly valuable for studying entrepreneurial firms that are seeking accelerated internationalization. The learning advantages of newness deserve additional empirical testing and conceptual development so that both the advantages and liabilities of young firms can be understood and compared.

The second dimension of knowledge in our model relates to the use of knowledge as a key source of competitive advantage for the entrepreneurial firm competing internationally. Oviatt and McDougall's (1994) new venture internationalization theory identified knowledge as a unique resource and one of four necessary and sufficient elements in their model of sustainable international new ventures. Knowledge intensity has been identified as a key source of international competitive advantage by several international entrepreneurship scholars (e.g., Autio et al., 2000; Bell et al., 2003; Coviello & McAuley, 1999; Jones, 1999). In his internationalization studies McNaughton (2001, 2003) found that knowledge-intense firms served a broader scope of international markets and had a more rapid pace of internationalization as they sought to exploit narrow windows of opportunity and to gain first mover advantage.

In their study on the learning advantages of newness Autio et al. (2000) detailed two reasons for what they term the "amplifying" effects of knowledge intensity on internationalization:

> First, firms focusing on knowledge creation and exploitation as the source of advantage are more likely to develop learning skills useful for adaptation and successful growth in new environments than are firms more dependent on tangible resources. . . . Second, because knowledge, explicit knowledge in particular, is a mobile resource, it provides a flexible platform for international expansion. Knowledge is inherently mobile in that it can be combined with fixed assets, such as distribution channels or manufacturing resource, in foreign markets at relatively low costs (Liebeskind, 1996; McDougall et al., 1994); thus, knowledge-intensive firms can exploit international growth opportunities more flexibly through such combinations than can firms dependent on fixed assets alone. Thus, knowledge-intensive firms are less constrained by distance or national boundaries. (2000, p. 913)

Results of their study showed that the more knowledge-intensive a firm, the more rapidly the firm grew in international sales, thus increasing its speed of commitment to internationalization.

As international entrepreneurship researchers continue to explore the role of the entrepreneurial actor in the relationship between entrepreneurial opportunity and the speed of internationalization, knowledge offers great promise as a moderating influence. Foreign market knowledge and the knowledge intensity of the firm are key variables that merit additional exploration.

Conclusion

The field of international entrepreneurship is rich with possibility and opportunity, and the full extent of its scope is undefined (Acs, Dana, & Jones, 2003). As the field moves from infancy to what appears will be a high level of growth, there are many interesting research questions that will surely be asked and investigated. We expect the revised definition we have provided in this article will help guide researchers to those questions. We hope that more scholars will focus on explaining the observed differences in the speed with which entrepreneurial opportunities are taken international. We believe our model will aid in finding those explanations.

As we reviewed research for this article, it was noteworthy to us that the authors of the majority of the multiauthored articles were either exclusively international business scholars or entrepreneurship scholars. Articles that have authors from both disciplines are unusual. International entrepreneurship researchers have embraced the notion of multi-country research teams and excellent examples of scholarly work have resulted—we believe disciplinary diversity would be just as beneficial. As the role of the entrepreneur is increasingly being explored in international business journals and the internationalization of the entrepreneurial firm appears in traditional entrepreneurship journals, we encourage the formation of research teams composed of entrepreneurship and international business scholars. Too often, international entrepreneurship articles appearing in entrepreneurship journals demonstrate a lack of knowledge of international business theories and research. Likewise, international entrepreneurship articles appearing in international business journals demonstrate a need for greater understanding of the scholarly work in entrepreneurship. Although both entrepreneurship and international business are multidisciplinary, there appears to have been limited collaboration in research between entrepreneurship and international business scholars. The increased comingling of entrepreneurship and international business scholars that is evident at research conferences is encouraging. As entrepreneurship scholars extend their networks to include international business scholars, and vice versa, we hope that collaborative research projects will be launched that consider some of the influences highlighted in this article.

REFERENCES

Acs, Z., Dana, L.-P., & Jones, M. (2003). Toward new horizons: The internationalization of entrepreneurship. *Journal of International Entrepreneurship, 1*, 5–12.

Aldrich, H. (1999). *Organizations evolving*. London: Sage Publications.

Almeida, J.G. & Bloodgood, J.M. (1996). Internationalization of new ventures: Implications of the value-chain. In P.D. Reynolds et al. (Eds), *Frontiers of entrepreneurship research* (pp. 211–225). Babson Park, MA: Center for Entrepreneurial Studies, Babson College.

Andersen, O. (1993). On the internationalization process of firms: A critical analysis. *Journal of International Business Studies, 24*, 209–231.

Autio, E., Sapienza, H.J., & Almeida, J.G. (2000). Effects of age at entry, knowledge intensity, and imitability on international growth. *Academy of Management Journal, 43*, 909–924.

Baker, T., Gedajlovic, E., & Lubatkin, M. (2003). The global entrepreneurship mosaic: A framework for fitting the piece together. Unpublished Manuscript.

Barkema, H.G. & Vermeulen, F. (1998). International expansion through start-up or acquisition: A learning perspective. *Academy of Management Journal, 41*, 7–26.

Bell, J. (1995). The internationalisation of small computer software firms—a further challenge to "stage" theories. *European Journal of Marketing, 29*(8), 60–75.

Bell, J., McNaughton, J., Young, R., & Crick, D. (2003). Towards an integrative model of small firm internationalisation. *Journal of International Entrepreneurship, 1*, 339–362.

Bilkey, W.J. & Tesar, G. (1977). The export behavior of smaller-sized Wisconsin manufacturing firms. *Journal of International Business Studies, 8*, 93–98.

Birkinshaw, J. (1997). Entrepreneurship in multinational corporations: The characteristics of subsidiary initiatives. *Strategic Management Journal, 18*, 207–229.

Bloodgood, J., Sapienza, H.J., & Almeida, J.G. (1996). The internationalization of new high-potential U.S. ventures: Antecedents and outcomes. *Entrepreneurship: Theory and Practice, 20*, 61–76.

Brokaw, L. (1990, November). Foreign affairs. *Inc.*, 92–104.

Busenitz, L.W., Gomez, C., & Spencer, J.W. (2000). Country institutional profiles: Unlocking entrepreneurial phenomena. *Academy of Management Journal, 43*(5), 994–1003.

Cohen, W.M. & Levinthal, D.A. (1990). Absorptive capacity: A new perspective on learning and innovation. *Administrative Science Quarterly, 35*, 128–152.

Coviello, N.E. & McAuley, A. (1999). Internationalization and the smaller firm: A review of contemporary empirical research. *Management International Review, 39*, 223–256.

Coviello, N.E. & Munro, H.J. (1995). Growing the entrepreneurial firm: Networking for international market development. *European Journal of Marketing, 29,* 49–61.

Coviello, N.E. & Munro, H.J. (1997). Network relationships and the internationalisation process of small software firms. *International Business Review, 6,* 361–386.

Covin, J.G. & Slevin, D.P. (1989). Strategic management of small firms in hostile and benign environments. *Strategic Management Journal, 10,* 75–87.

Dana, L.-P. (2004). *Handbook of research on international entrepreneurship.* Cheltenham, UK: Edward Elgar.

Dubini, P. & Aldrich, H. (1991). Personal and extended networks are central to the entrepreneurial process. *Journal of Business Venturing, 6,* 305–313.

Erramilli, M.K. (1991). The experience factor in foreign market entry behavior of service firms. *Journal of International Business Studies, 22,* 479–501.

Gartner, W.B. (1988). Who is an entrepreneur? is the wrong question. *American Journal of Small Business, 12,* 11–32.

Giamartino, G.A., McDougall, P.P., & Bird, B.J. (1993). International entrepreneurship: The state of the field. *Entrepreneurship: Theory and Practice, 18,* 37–41.

Gupta, U. (1989, December 5). Small firms aren't waiting to grow up to go global. *The Wall Street Journal,* p. B2.

Hisrich, R.D., Honig-Haftel, S., McDougall, P.P., & Oviatt, B.M. (1996). International entrepreneurship: Past, present, and future. *Entrepreneurship: Theory and Practice, Summer,* 5–7.

Huber, G.P. (1991). Organizational learning: An examination of the contributing processes and the literatures. *Organization Science, 2,* 88–115.

Hurmerinta-Peltomäki, L. (2004). Conceptual and methodological underpinnings in the study of rapid internationalizers. In M.V. Jones & P. Dimitratos (Eds), *Emerging paradigms in international entrepreneurship* (pp. 64–88). Cheltenham, UK: Edward Elgar.

Hymer, S.H. (1976). *The international operations of national firms.* Cambridge, MA: MIT Press.

Inkpen, A.C. & Beamish, P.W. (1997). Knowledge bargaining power and the instability of international joint ventures. *Academy of Management Review, 22,* 177–202.

Johanson, J. & Vahlne, J.-E. (1977). The internationalization process of the firm: A model of knowledge development and increasing foreign market commitment. *Journal of International Business Studies, 4,* 20–29.

Johanson, J. & Vahlne, J.-E. (1990). The mechanism of internationalization. *International Marketing Review, 7,* 11–24.

Johanson, J. & Vahlne, J.-E. (2003). Business relationship learning and commitment in the internationalization process. *Journal of International Entrepreneurship, 1,* 83–101.

Jones, M.V. (1999). The internationalization of small UK high technology based firms. *Journal of International Marketing, 7,* 15–41.

Knight, G.G. & Cavusgil, S.T. (1996). The born global firm: A challenge to traditional internationalization theory. *Advances in International Marketing, 8,* 11–26.

Kuemmerle, W. (2002). Home base and knowledge management in international ventures. *Journal of Business Venturing, 17,* 99–122.

Kuemmerle, W. (2005). The entrepreneur's path to global expansion. *MIT Sloan Management Review, 46*, 42–49.

Li, H. & Atuahene-Gima, K. (2001). Product innovation strategy and the performance of new technology ventures in China. *Academy of Management Journal, 44*, 1123–1134.

Liebeskind, J.P. (1996). Knowledge, strategy, and the theory of the firm. *Strategic Management Journal, 17*, 93–107.

Lord, M.D. & Ranft, A.L. (2000). Organizational learning about new international markets: Exploring the internal transfer of local market knowledge. *Journal of International Business Studies, 31*, 573–589.

Lu, J.W. & Beamish, P.W. (2001). The internationalization and performance of SMEs. *Strategic Management Journal, 22*, 565–586.

Lumpkin, G. & Dess, G. (1996). Clarifying the entrepreneurial orientation construct and linking it to performance. *Academy of Management Review, 21*, 135–172.

Luo, Y. (1997). Partner selection and venturing success: The case of joint ventures with firms in the People's Republic of China. *Organizational Science, 8*, 648–662.

Mamis, R.A. (1989, August). Global start-up. *Inc.*, 38–47.

McDougall, P.P. (1989). International versus domestic entrepreneurship: New venture strategic behavior and industry structure. *Journal of Business Venturing, 4*, 387–399.

McDougall, P.P. & Oviatt, B.M. (1997). International entrepreneurship literature in the 1990s and directions for future research. In D.L. Sexton & R.W. Smilor (Eds), *Entrepreneurship 2000* (pp. 291–320). Chicago: Upstart Publishing.

McDougall, P.P. & Oviatt, B.M. (2000). International entrepreneurship: The intersection of two research paths. *Academy of Management Journal, 43*, 902–908.

McDougall, P.P., Shane, S., & Oviatt, B.M. (1994). Explaining the formation of international new ventures: The limits of theories from international business research. *Journal of Business Venturing, 9*, 469–487.

McGrath, R.G. & MacMillan, I.C. (1992). More like each other than anyone else? A cross-cultural study of entrepreneurial perceptions. *Journal of Business Venturing, 7*, 419–429.

McNaughton, R.B. (2001). The export mode decision-making process in small knowledge-intensive firms. *Market Intelligence and Planning, 19*, 12–20.

McNaughton, R.B. (2003). The number of export markets that a firm serves: Process models versus the born-global phenomenon. *Journal of International Entrepreneurship, 1*, 297–311.

Miller, D. (1983). The correlates of entrepreneurship in three types of firms. *Management Science, 29*, 770–791.

Mitchell, R.K., Smith, B., Seawright, K., & Morse, E.A. (2000). Cross-cultural cognitions and venture creation decision. *Academy of Management Journal, 43*, 974–993.

Morrow, J.F. (1988). International entrepreneurship: A new growth opportunity. *New Management, 3*, 59–61.

Oviatt, B.M. & McDougall, P.P. (1994). Toward a theory of international new ventures. *Journal of International Business Studies, 25*(1), 45–64.

Oviatt, B.M. & McDougall, P.P. (1995). Global start-ups: Entrepreneurs on a worldwide stage. *Academy of Management Executive, 9*, 30–43.

Oviatt, B.M. & McDougall, P.P. (1999). A framework for understanding accelerated international entrepreneurship. In R. Wright (Ed.), *Research in global strategic management* (pp. 23–40). Stamford, CT: JAI Press.

Oviatt, B.M., Shrader, R.C., & McDougall, P.P. (2004). The internationalization of new ventures: A risk management model. In M.A. Hitt & J.L.C. Cheng (Eds), *Theories of the multinational enterprise: Diversity, complexity, and relevance. Advances in international management* (Vol. 16, pp. 165–185). Amsterdam: Elsevier.

Rasmussen, E.S., Madsen, T.K., & Evangelista, F. (2001). The founding of the born global company in Denmark and Australia: Sensemaking and networking. *Asia Pacific Journal of Marketing and Logistics, 13,* 75–107.

Reuber, A.R. & Fischer, E. (1997). The influence of the management team's international experience on the internationalization behavior of SMEs. *Journal of International Business Studies, 28*(4), 807–825.

Roure, J.B., Keeley, R., & Keller, T. (1992). Venture capital strategies in Europe and the U.S. Adapting to the 1990's. In N.C. Churchill et al. (Eds), *Frontiers of Entrepreneurship Research* (pp. 345–359). Babson Park, MA: Babson College.

Servias, P. & Rasmussen, E.S. (2000). *Different types of international new ventures.* Paper presented at the Academy of International Business Annual Meeting, Phoenix, AZ.

Shane, S. (2000). Prior knowledge and the discovery of entrepreneurial opportunities. *Organizational Science, 11,* 448–469.

Shane, S. & Venkataraman, S. (2000). The promise of entrepreneurship as a field of research. *Academy of Management Review, 25,* 217–226.

Shrader, R.C., Oviatt, B.M., & McDougall, P.P. (2000). How new ventures exploit trade-offs among international risk factors: Lessons for the accelerated internationalization of the 21st century. *Academy of Management Journal, 43,* 1227–1248.

Simões, V.C. & Dominguinhos, P.M. (2001). *Portuguese born globals: An exploratory study.* Paper presented at the 27th EIBA Conference, Paris, France.

Steensma, K., Marino, L., Weaver, M., & Dickson, P. (2000). The influence of national culture in the formation of technology alliances by entrepreneurial firms. *Academy of Management Journal, 43,* 951–973.

Stinchcombe, A.L. (1965). Social structure and organizations. In J.G. March (Ed.), *Handbook of organizations* (pp. 142–193). Chicago: Rand McNally.

The Economist. (1992, May 9). Go West, young firm. 88–89.

The Economist. (1993, July 3). America's little fellows surge ahead. 59–60.

Thomas, A.S. & Mueller, S.L. (2000). A case for comparative entrepreneurship: Assessing the relevance of culture. *Journal of International Business Studies, 31,* 287–301.

Venkataraman, S. (1997). The distinctive domain of entrepreneurship research. In J.A. Katz (Ed.), *Advances in entrepreneurship, firm emergence and growth* (Vol. 3, pp. 119–138). Greenwich, CT: JAI Press.

Weick, K.E. (1995). *Sensemaking in organizations.* Thousand Oaks, CA: Sage Publications.

Wright, R.W. & Ricks, D.A. (1994). Trends in international business research: Twenty-five years later. *Journal of International Business Studies, 25,* 687–701.

Zacharakis, A.L. (1997). Entrepreneurial entry into foreign markets: A transaction cost perspective. *Entrepreneurship Theory and Practice, 21,* 23–39.

Zaheer, S. (1995). Overcoming the liability of foreignness. *Academy of Management Journal, 38,* 341–363.

Zahra, S.A. & George, G. (2002). International entrepreneurship: The current status of the field and future research agenda. In M.A. Hitt, R.D. Ireland, S.M. Camp, & D.L. Sexton (Eds), *Strategic entrepreneurship: Creating a new mindset* (pp. 255–288). Oxford, UK: Blackwell Publishers.

Zahra, S.A., Ireland, R.D., & Hitt, M.A. (2000). International expansion by new venture firms: International diversity, mode of market entry, technological learning and performance. *Academy of Management Journal, 43*, 925–950.

[7]

Journal of International Entrepreneurship 1, 135–152, 2003
© 2003 Kluwer Academic Publishers. Manufactured in The Netherlands.

Changing Paradigms of International Entrepreneurship Strategy

RICHARD W. WRIGHT
University of Richmond, Robins School of Business, Richmond, UA 23173 USA

LÉO-PAUL DANA
University of Canterbury, Private Bag 4800, Christchurch, New Zealand

Abstract. This article identifies sweeping transformations taking place in the contemporary international business environment, and discusses their impact on international entrepreneurship. We focus on two overarching trends: (1) the demise of the nation-state as the relevant unit around which international business activity is organised and conducted; and (2) the demise of the stand-alone firm, with a hierarchic distribution of power and control, as the principal unit of business competition. We then discuss an alternate approach to internationalisation: one that involves a multi-polar distribution of power and control. Traditional approaches to internationalisation focus on the hierarchic centralised firm, with a uni-polar distribution of power and control. We suggest that the world is moving towards multi-polar networks of firms, involved in what we term symbiotic management: each entity benefits from working together within a multi-polar network. This includes large corporations as well as small and medium-sized enterprises (SMEs). As corporations out-source to specialised firms—increasingly SMEs—power and control are dispersed among independently owned firms that are cooperating voluntarily for increased efficiency and profit. The new paradigm moves from a focus on the firm, towards a focus on relationships within multi-polar networks. We conclude by illustrating how this emerging competitive paradigm may impact on the strategic management of small firms, with examples from a real-world company.

Keywords: International entrepreneurship, strategy, internationalization, paradigms, networks, competition.

Introduction

The global business environment is changing dramatically. Traditionally competition in international markets was the realm of large companies, while smaller businesses remained local or regional in scope. However, the removal of government-imposed barriers that segregated and protected domestic markets, and recent technological advances in manufacturing, transportation and telecommunications, allow even the smallest firms access to customers, suppliers, and collaborators around the world. Small companies and/or entrepreneurial enterprises—both domestically and internationally—are increasingly fuelling economic growth and innovation. These trends are transforming management strategies, public policies, and the daily lives of people around the world.

Globalisation is impacting dramatically on the opportunities and challenges facing business firms. Two changes, in particular, are revolutionising the management policies and competitive strategies of large and small firms alike. One is the demise of the nation-state as the primary macroeconomic player, or the principal unit around which international economic activity is organised and conducted. The other is the demise of the stand-alone firm as the primary microeconomic player, or the basic unit of competition. We will discuss each of these transformations and then illustrate their impact, with reference to real-world examples.

Demise of the nation-state as the primary macroeconomic player

For centuries, the nation-state was the basic unit around which international economic activity was planned, organised, and conducted, regardless of the origin of firms. Even business activities that appear highly "international," such as traditional foreign direct investment (FDI), have been moulded strongly by the boundaries of nation-states. The *multi-domestic* model of FDI, for example, which has typified foreign investment by European multinationals such as Ericsson, Nestlé, Philips, and Unilever, manages highly autonomous subsidiaries, each conforming to local or national environments. The so-called *international* model, characteristic of the foreign involvement of many American multinationals such as Procter & Gamble, is a more ethnocentric arrangement, in which products and technology are generated mainly by the parent company, but with national subsidiaries in each major (national) market to produce the parent's products for that market. Many Japanese firms, including Komatsu, Matsushita, Sony, and Toyota, have followed a more *global* approach. In this model, production may be centralised—often at home—to achieve large production runs of standardised products, but the parent firm still retains a highly national orientation, in its structure and control. Traditional practice and traditional theories thus conform to the prevailing paradigm of the times, reflecting a macroeconomic environment in which international economic activity is moulded and constrained largely by the power of individual nation-states.

The trend towards supra-national powers

The traditional models of business involvement, in which business activity is organised largely around the segmentation of factor and product markets into distinct nation-states, is giving way to a new paradigm in which the firm—regardless of where the parent company happens to be based—will obtain various elements of value added from wherever in the world they may be most efficiently obtained, combine or assemble them in whatever location may be the most cost-effective, and then distribute them to wherever appropriate demand conditions exist, almost without regard to national boundaries. We see examples throughout the world of the decline in the segmentation of product and factor markets by individual nations as power evolves from nation-states to higher, supra-national units. This occurs in regional trade agreements such as the European Union (EU), where increasing degrees of power are shifting from the individual member nation-states to the pan-European level, as well as in broader international agreements such as the World Trade Organisation (WTO).

This diminution of national power, and its transfer to supra-national or global levels, has profound implications for small businesses and entrepreneurial firms. Primarily, smaller firms now have access to worldwide markets, which most could only have dreamed of a decade ago—as long as they can gain access to the requisite resources.

Reynolds (1997) noted that the recent expansion of markets has not been associated with an expanded role for larger firms. Instead, smaller firms are filling niche roles (Buckley, 1997). Later sections of this article will discuss how smaller firms may use collaborative arrangements—especially with larger firms—to springboard themselves into this new, largely borderless world.

The upward evolution of national powers to higher levels also means that firms everywhere now face global competition, without the domestic-market protection formerly afforded by national governments. Even if a small firm prefers not to enter international markets, it must achieve world-scale efficiencies in order to remain competitive and viable in today's open markets. New avenues by which SMEs may achieve these new efficiencies are discussed and illustrated below.

The integration of product and factor markets implies further that any firm operating outside of its domestic environment—or even one seeking to obtain world-scale efficiencies without leaving its domestic market—will increasingly need to interface with suppliers and customers in other national cultures. The firm can no longer operate solely within its domestic environment, nor can it de-centralise its activities into discreet national profit centres, in which managers often need be sensitive to a single local economy or culture. Therefore, managers of large and small firms alike will need intercultural awareness and skills as never before.

The trend towards localisation of powers

While economic power and sovereignty are clearly seen evolving from national to supra-national levels, we are simultaneously witnessing another important, albeit less obvious, diminution of the traditional powers of nations-states in the opposite direction: from nation-states to local or regional levels. This is especially true in the realm of political and cultural sovereignty.

This trend towards the fragmentation or devolution of national powers is most dramatically evident in the abrupt disintegration of the Soviet Union and the former Yugoslav federation. However, devolution of national powers—albeit on a more gradual and rational basis—is seen elsewhere as well, most obviously in Western Europe:

1. In the United Kingdom, significant new legislative and cultural powers are being decentralised to Scotland and Wales.
2. In Spain, the linguistic and cultural assertiveness of regions such as Catalonia, the Basque Region, and Galicia are becoming far more pronounced than before.
3. Despite the unification of East and West Germany, much greater local autonomy is devolving to the individual German *lender*, or states.

4. Even in France—long considered a bastion of centralised power in the nation-state—a new, semi-autonomous status has been granted to Corsica; and there is a notable resurgence of regional languages and culture, such as Languedoc or Provencal in the south, and Breton in the west.
5. In Canada, the Province of Quebec is enjoying greater cultural and political autonomy than ever before.

It is our belief that local and regional cultural distinctions are becoming more pronounced in the globalised economy, rather than less so. While the consolidation of economic power at increasingly high, supra-national levels may enable internationally oriented firms to achieve new productive efficiencies, the growing devolution of cultural and political sovereignty to local and regional jurisdictions means that large firms may need to rely increasingly on smaller, localised firms to achieve the cultural sensitivities they need for local adaptation, thus providing new niche opportunities for SMEs.

Demise of the firm as the primary microeconomic player

The profound change occurring at the microeconomic level is the demise of the company as the primary unit of competition. Management has long viewed the company as a "black box," a self-contained unit with clearly defined parameters, within which the various management functions take place. Emphasis has been on *internalising* value-added functions, to bring them more fully within the control of the firm's management, and on building walls around the firm to help secure the retention of its internal proprietary advantages from competitors. In the new paradigm, however, firms—large and small alike—are often incapable of acquiring and retaining control of the full range of value-added functions on their own. Increasingly, we see firms forming collaborative alliances with other firms—even with potential or actual competitors in the same industry.

Traditional internationalisation models

Traditional approaches to internationalisation focused on a uni-polar and hierarchic distribution of power and control. Internalisation Theory (Buckley and Casson, 1976; Rugman, 1979, 1981; Teece, 1985; Morck and Yeung, 1991, 1992) taught us that, by investing in its own foreign subsidiaries, a firm could expand operations, while maintaining control at head office. Likewise, the Eclectic Paradigm (Dunning, 1973, 1977, 1980, 1988) focused on ownership-specific advantages and location-specific advantages that a firm can enjoy, while maintaining centralised control.

A uni-polar scenario is implicit, as well, in the Stage Models of incremental internationalisation (Johanson and Wiedersheim-Paul, 1975; Bilkey and Tesar, 1977; Johanson and Vahlne, 1977, 1990; Bilkey, 1978; Newbould et al., 1978; Cavusgil, 1980, 1984; Cavusgil and Nevin, 1981; Buckley, et al., 1988; Bartlett and Ghoshal,

1989; Leonidou and Katsikeas, 1996). Internationalisation could be achieved without giving up power and control; the internationalising firm could maintain its uni-polar distribution of power and control, albeit at a heavy capital cost. Internationalisation, under this model was expensive because ownership and uni-polar (centralised) decision-making led to huge, integrated factory complexes. Iron ore entered a plant from one end, and automobiles drove out the other. Nowadays, even Ford has decentralised operations into a multi-polar structure. The factory where 100,000 employees used to produce 1,200 cars a day, is down to 3,000 employees making 800 cars a day, and this brings us to a new paradigm of international business through networks.

Network models

An alternate to the uni-polar paradigm of internationalisation assumes a multi-polar distribution of power and control. Rather than focusing on the internationalisation of an individual centralised firm with a uni-polar distribution of power and control, we can focus on a multi-polar network of firms. Power and control are divided among independent firms that cooperate voluntarily for increased efficiency and profit. Networks result in the demise of the stand-alone firm (with a hierarchic distribution of power and control) as the principal unit of business competition. Literature pertaining to this networking perspective includes Acs and Dana (2001); Axelsson and Easton (1992); Bodur and Madsen (1993); Brüderl and Preisendörfer (1998); Chetty and Blackenburg-Holm (2000); Coviello and Munro (1997); Dana (2001); Etemad et al., (2001); Fontes and Coombs (1997); Gomes-Casseres (1996); Gynawali and Madhavan (2001); and Holmlund and Kock (1998). As well, Stabell and Fjeldstad (1998) discuss reciprocal interdependence.

Examples of this move towards global alliances among large firms abound, from a variety of industries. In the airline industry, for example, Northwest and KLM used to be true competitors. Each tried to take away market share from the other; each used to advertise to encourage consumers to *select one over the other*. Marketing by one firm actually hurt the other firm: it was a zero sum game with a limited pie. Today, the former rivals engage in symbiotic marketing. By acting together, the two firms increase the attractiveness of flying *either* airline. In other words, it is no longer a zero sum game. We are no longer dealing with two isolated uni-polar firms, but with a multi-polar network—in this case an integrated interline product. People who otherwise would not fly decide to fly, thanks to the new convenience. In other words, symbiotic management yields an enlarged pie. It is possible, therefore, to play a non-zero sum game (Webster, 1992; Jarillo, 1993; Casti and Karlqvist, 1995; Zineldin, 1998). Leading alliances in the airline sector include the Star Alliance (14 airlines) and Oneworld (8 airlines).

Similar alliances among major firms in other industries abound. Examples include:

1. An alliance among IBM (USA), Toshiba (Japan), and Siemens (Germany) in electronics;

2. Another alliance in electronics among ATT (USA), Philips (Netherlands), and Olivetti (Italy);
3. An automotive alliance among Ford (USA), Mazda (Japan), Jaguar (UK), and Volvo (Sweden);
4. Another automotive alliance among GM (USA), Toyota (Japan), Daewoo (South Korea), and Saab (Sweden);
5. A network of alliances between Millennium Pharmaceuticals (USA) and nearly 700 partners. For a discussion of alliances in this industry, see Pangarkar and Klein (1998).

Even academic institutions have become networked. As competition has been increasing, for the recruitment of professors and students, schools such as E M Lyon and HEC Montreal have created partnerships. Perhaps most notable is the AEA Alliance, known as The Cross-Regional Business School. Its founding members are E M Lyon (France), HEC Montreal (Canada), Warwick Business School (UK), Universidad de Belgrano (Argentina), and Lingnan University College—ZSU (China).

The new paradigm of multi-polar competition

Relationships of one form or another have always been at the core of competitiveness. Increasingly, however, firms are finding that networks of relationships need not necessarily be "internalised" or controlled by direct ownership and internal hierarchies to be effective. What we are witnessing today is a shift in paradigm from traditional forms of collaboration, in which the locus of control lies in formal control through ownership and internal hierarchy, to newer forms of collaboration in which mutual control emanates from interdependence and mutuality of benefit. This represents a significant departure from the past tradition. In the newly emerging competitive paradigm, the unit of competition is no longer the individual firm; but rather, networks of firms collaborating interdependently for higher mutual benefit than their respective independent operations can yield. In this network-centred system, SMEs can specialise on a set of capabilities, competencies, knowledge, and skills much needed by the network, in order to generate higher benefits both to themselves and to their network partners than any of them could by operating independently. Each member of such networks—often regardless of size—would specialise on a different part of the value chain, which may be located in different parts of the world.

The alliance imperative for large firms

A rich literature has been developed on collaboration among large firms. Among the most prominent contributions are Doz and Hamel (1997), Forrest (1992), Gomes-Casseres (1994), Kanter (1994), Parkhe (1997), Stafford (1994), and the three-volume series edited by Beamish and Killing (1997).

There are several reasons why alliances are becoming not just a convenience, but also an imperative for large firms competing in the global arena:

1. *High fixed-cost threshold.* Formerly, companies could expand or contract freely by adjusting their variable costs—especially their cost of labour. However, the relative cost of labour to total value has diminished dramatically in many industries: labour now accounts for only 12–15% of the cost of producing electronic goods, for example; and the portion of labour to the total cost of a Japanese car has been reduced to only 10%. Increasingly, a minimum threshold of large fixed costs must be incurred if a company is to become a serious player on the world scene. These include major investments in plant and equipment, R&D, brand-name development, distribution systems, etc. Developing a new car model today costs $3–5 billion; a new aircraft some $7–10 billion. The magnitude of these costs and risks is often beyond the ability of large multinationals to absorb; alliances can share the costs and risks.

2. *Rapid product-life-cycle.* The increasingly rapid dispersion of technology requires swift access to major markets—especially those of the Triad (North America, Europe, and Japan)—before a firm loses its proprietary advantage. Yet, few if any of even the largest firms can achieve instant market presence in all the triad areas on their own. The urgent need for speed to markets dictates reliance on others.

3. *Need for related technologies.* Complex systems today often require the fusing of technologies across industry lines. IBM, for example, uses Lotus for software, Microsoft for operating systems, and Intel for chips. Similarly, technologies from the computer, telecommunications, and entertainment industries are fusing across industry lines. Access to related technologies increasingly requires collaborative linkages with other firms.

4. *Global standards.* Increasingly, rival technologies vie for adaptation as the world standard. An early example was the rivalry for a worldwide VCR standard among Matsushita, Philips, and Sony, each with its own format. Although it originally lagged behind Sony and Philips, Matsushita was able to achieve enormous cost economies—and consequently to get its VHS format accepted as the world standard—largely through collaborative arrangements with other firms (including the U.S. subsidiary of Philips!). A current example is the struggle to establish a worldwide standard technology for high-definition television (HDTV). By allying with other firms, even competitors, a firm may enhance the likelihood of establishing sufficient market presence to become the accepted world standard.

The alliance imperative for small firms

For small firms, perhaps even more than for large ones, partnering with other firms through various forms of collaborative arrangements is becoming imperative:

1. SMEs often lack the resources for gradual, "stages" progression into the international arena over time; particularly within a time frame needed to exploit increasingly short-lived proprietary advantages.

2. SMEs need to achieve world-scale efficiencies even if they are not entering world markets, to withstand new competition from abroad.

As a consequence of these new imperatives, small firms are benefiting increasingly from mutual interaction with other small firms. This is documented by Bartels (2000); Chetty and Blackenburg-Holm (2000); Coviello and Munro (1995, 1997); Holmlund and Kock (1998); Perrow (1992); Sadler and Chetty (2000); Welsh et al. (2000).

A typology of networks

To facilitate the illustrative discussion that follows, we suggest a typology of networking:

• *Horizontal networks*, which transform competitors into allies
• *Vertical networks*, integrating buyers and suppliers
• *Trans-industry networks*, which relate or connect otherwise unrelated value chains.

In the following section we shall discuss the experience of a small firm as it entered into these different types of networking arrangements.

Changing strategies in response to changing economic variables

We have noted a trend towards larger units both at the macroeconomic level and at the microeconomic level. Both the state and the firm have yielded control, in exchange for the advantages inherent in being a part of a larger entity. Simultaneously, at both the macro and micro levels, there is a trend towards greater specialisation and local expertise. Governments feel increasing pressure to delegate political and cultural powers to local jurisdictions, while firms benefit from increased focus and specialisation in their business activities.

In this global environment, the firm faces unprecedented opportunities and complexities. On the one hand, networks allow a firm to compensate for its deficiencies in size and factor endowments by linking existing resources in networks that also allow for an acceleration of growth and international activities, without the heavy capital expenditures that were required in former times. As well, outsourcing allows for delegated management. A paradox, however, is that while networking gives rise to opportunities for delegating management, this is only efficient when an appropriate management framework is in place. This translates into increased managerial complexity, in order to benefit from less complex management. Thus, resource complementarity is a competitive resource, but only when managed appropriately.

Why is network management so complex? Simply because there are more alternatives. Under a uni-polar structure, a firm could employ a single, integrated international strategy. In networks, differentiated strategies may be needed for dissimilar situations:

• Dealing with a small firm in the same network
• Dealing with a large firm in the same network
• Dealing with a small firm in a different network
• Dealing with a large firm in a different network
• Dealing with a different network, and perhaps joining it.

We shall now illustrate these new opportunities and constraints, by focusing on a family business that successfully transformed itself, in response to the changing environmental factors discussed above. We shall begin with a background to the firm—Sicoph S.A.—and then discuss how the company once operated in a compartmentalised uni-polar environment. We will then proceed to illustrate how the firm readjusted its structure and policies to benefit from the advantages of multi-polar collaboration: what we call symbiotic management. A network orientation caused a complete restructuring of the firm's financing, marketing, and strategic posture.

The uni-polar operation of a family business

The origins of Sicoph go back to the early 20th century, when its predecessor was a centralised trading operation, with no production facilities. The enterprise was completely based on arbitrage. If there was a drought in Nation X and a surplus in Nation Y, the entrepreneur—Leone—would transfer produce and merchandise from Y to X. Leone was an owner-manager, and his competitive advantage was his knowledge of prices and markets. He understood where and when to buy what, and where and when to sell. At the time, search costs were high, and information was valuable. Born in 1885, fluent in several languages, and well-travelled, Leone was a popular socialite and philanthropist, he knew many people, he had countless contacts and his knowledge was a great asset. World War II, however, threatened all of Europe.

During the war, Leone relocated his family business to Cairo—away from the wartime activities. Much business was done with the Allied Forces in Egypt, which needed to feed and supply their men. Leone would source sheep in Libya and have them walked to Egypt. He consulted with his brothers Raphaelo and Josebe and it was suggested that if the family could raise some food locally, it would save them importing it. Leone's eldest son subsequently established a chicken farm. The problem now was where to get chicken feed, in the middle of a war. Importing the grain was a problem because of exchange controls. To import feed, the entrepreneurs were required to export at least the equivalent of what was imported, in order to obtain hard currency. Hence, they exported Egyptian cotton, cloth, and fruit, and were able to obtain plenty of chicken feed. Leone also became distributor for

Packard automobiles, in Egypt; however, the war disrupted a shipment of cars, and these arrived only after the war.

In time, Leone's sons took over the family firm. One of them had gone to school at Victoria College with King Farouk, and the family developed good relations with the palace. This was good for business, until Farouk was forced to abdicate, and Alberto, the elder of Leone's sons, was forced to leave Egypt on short notice. He followed Farouk to Italy and set up a branch of the family business. When he subsequently expanded to India, Switzerland, Spain, and Canada, internationalisation of his enterprise was based on a traditional, uni-polar and hierarchic distribution of power and control. However, the heavy capital expenditures involved in owning overseas operations limited the firm's internationalisation. Larger firms could set up, own and operate production facilities in many nations; smaller enterprises were restricted to activities in fewer nations.

Alberto's brother Clemente remained in Egypt where he prospered in business until 1956, when he was imprisoned for being a British sympathiser during the Sinai Campaign. Although his firm and assets were nationalised without compensation, his entrepreneurial spirit was not extinguished. Instead, he became a key player in the development of a market among the detainees. He traded Red Cross food rations, and cultivated relationships with sellers as well as with buyers. Prices fluctuated with supply and demand inside the prison. Clemente began to store supplies of food, and this allowed prices to stabilise. When he was released and exiled, in 1957, he went to Paris and launched Sicoph. He kept in touch with others who had served as prisoners of war with him, and this helped him develop business networks later on. Soon, he expanded to Hong Kong, where sourcing was less costly than in Europe. As was the case with his father's firm and with his older brother's business, internationalisation was based on a uni-polar and hierarchic distribution of power and control.

Sicoph became involved in the production and international marketing of cameras, chairs, sporting goods, furniture, and shoes. Yet, in the context of the uni-polar structure, in a nation-state that was the primary economic actor, the strategic options for Sicoph were very limited. A company spokesman told the authors:

> Given these external constraints, it was very easy for us to have a single, standard expansion strategy, which was applicable in almost any situation. The prevailing belief was that ownership was an absolute necessity, in order to have control. In Romania, where ownership was a complex matter, we entered a joint venture.

Internationalisation was gradual, in line with the Stage theories, as growth was limited by financial constraints. Soon, this would change, as networks would allow expansion without additional investment. Outsourcing would result in delegated management, and accelerated growth would be possible through resource complementarity.

INTERNATIONAL ENTREPRENEURSHIP STRATEGY 145

Towards multi-polar networks

Sicoph's policy shift from internationalisation through direct ownership, towards decentralised alliances, was summarised succinctly by a senior manager:

> In response to the changes taking place in the international business environment, our strategy at the firm level had to adapt accordingly. We could no longer use our generic "one solution fits all" strategy. We needed one strategy for horizontal networks, another for vertical networks, and we had to consider trans-industry networks. In the past we had to own everything in order to control it. The new environment allowed us to achieve more effective control by not owning. In Romania, for example, we withdrew from the joint venture and subcontracted to the same factory. Suddenly, the production per hour increased and sick days were reduced. The quality of the product increased and we could sell it as a premium brand, which we couldn't do before. This was very unexpected for us, because the traditional theory said that if you owned, you knew what was happening. Yet, we became more profitable when our former workers were given greater incentives.

This quote corresponds to a passage in McMillan (2002): "The best way to motivate creative people is to give them a stake...This means using a decentralised system." (p. 157)

The firm thus moved away from direct ownership as the means of internationalisation. The ownership structure changed, as preference shifted from a corporate strategy involving FDI, to one of networking. The new path to internationalisation was, in the words of a Sicoph manager:

> ...to link up with firms who needed us as much as we needed them. The fact that they depended on us was the guarantee that they would work properly. The strength of any one of us was limited to the weakest link among all of us. This was a very powerful motivating factor, which increased quality and reduced the number of factory seconds that were sent back by the stores...

Commenting further on the company's response to the new competitive paradigm:

> We used to own five companies to operate in five geographic regions, on the assumption that geography (nation-states) was the way of segmenting markets. Then we realised that it was better to have five independently owned firms with each one having a specialised niche, with no geographic limits. Rather, each of the five serviced the world market for a specific good.

Sicoph had previously distributed cameras, chairs, sporting goods, furniture, and shoes across France. A sister company, Wicotrade, was responsible for the distribution of cameras, chairs, sporting goods, furniture, and shoes across the

United States. Another sister company, Omnidiffusion, had a similar mandate for Canada; while still another, Diana Diffusion, focused on China. In other words, the family business was structured and defined largely by the boundaries of nation-states. Within a few years, this changed dramatically. Each of what had been five nationally focused subsidiaries began to focus instead on producing a single product line for the world market, in collaboration with the other four. As well, the ownership structure changed as each subsidiary became locally owned.

As the nation-state lost importance and the individual firm lost relative power, Sicoph dropped its lines of cameras, sporting goods, furniture, and shoes. It decided to focus on chairs, for the global market, and it engaged in symbiotic management in order to network with the other four firms. The company prospered: multi-polar, symbiotic management within a network proved to be more efficient than had been operations under a uni-polar model. Horizontal networks linked the resources and competencies of firms, which might otherwise have been competitors. Vertical networks integrated buyers and suppliers, and trans-industry networks brought together otherwise unrelated value chains. As firms found themselves serving the European Economic Community, and later the EU, rather than France, it became increasingly interesting to appear large. How could small firms appear like large players in the larger playing field? By working together and bidding together, for deals that none could win alone. Rather than compete with its German equivalent, Sicoph could network with like firms; together, they could produce sufficient quantities to win large contracts. A Sicoph executive explained:

> We started out very misguided, because of the texts we used in our MBA class. These led us to believe that we could run our small firms with the same strategies we had learned in the business case studies of large corporations. But soon, we realised that by operating alone, we could never deliver the massive quantities required by the big buyers such as Macy's and Bloomingdale's. Only in networks could we succeed.

In other words, **horizontal networks** transformed competitors into allies, and symbiotic management resulted in a win–win situation. Horizontal networks allowed the realisation of formerly unattainable economies of scale; bulk purchasing reduced costs; and network members gained market power, as well as access to otherwise expensive technology.

Likewise, the firm entered **vertical networks** resulting in integration with retailers (buyers) and suppliers. The vertical networks facilitated market research, and provided better access to raw materials.

As well, when a Sicoph representative went to visit a client, he also represented deBotton, producers of unrelated goods that were distributed by the same retailers. Such **trans-industry networks** saved costs, provided a more complete product line, and resulted in a better market presence when selling to large buyers.

Symbiotic management, in networks, thus allowed Sicoph to optimise competitive advantage by linking its resources with those of others. At the firm level, differences in factor endowments were compensated through network participation. Sicoph executives met with another 100 small firms in Melbourne, Florida in the summer of 1983, leading to the creation of private label sporting goods for what came to be the Athletic Dealers Association.

The production function within Sicoph's system was dramatically restructured, phasing out the formerly used concept of national-market compartmentalisation. Instead, the firm focused on product specialisation. Expansion strategy was redesigned such that entry into new markets was no longer dependent upon ownership. Paradoxically, the new strategy of symbiotic management, with its multi-polar control structure, provided more effective control than had been the case with ownership. Marketing in networks significantly reduced selling costs. Even finance was restructured to benefit from banking networks. Simultaneously, Sicoph benefited from new technologies. Transaction costs were lowered via the Internet, which reduced the cost of acquiring information. Previously local or regional markets became global. One executive summarised the shift in Sicoph's management strategy as follows:

> We coped with increased managerial complexity by delegating to network participants. This was more efficient than burdening ourselves with elaborate management structures. It was important to maintain a spirit of entrepreneurship.

Conclusions

The strategic alternatives facing small firms have changed, and businesses must recognise that spatial constraints, based on the geography of nation-states, are no longer significant barriers to internationalisation. This article has explained how the demise of nation-states and individual firms has led to international multi-polar business networks. We have discussed collaborative imperatives as they relate to small and medium enterprises, and we have provided a summary of ideas about networks and value chains.

It used to be sufficient to think of individual value chains. As these were either horizontal or vertical, this could be conceptualised along two dimensions. Nowadays, trans-integration causes the collapse of specialised elements of a value chain, resulting in larger units. This is due to several factors, including economies of scale and comparative as well as absolute cost advantage. The result is a systems unit, as opposed to a simple value chain.

These sea-changes in the global business environment have far-reaching implications for business managers, public-policy formulators, and researchers alike. Changes at the macroeconomic level will necessitate strategic changes at the microeconomic level. While differences in resource endowments can be compensated by symbiotic marketing (Etemad et al., 2001), and network membership (Chen, 1996), networking also increases managerial complexity (Dyer et al., 2001; Pangarkar and

Klein, 2001). To cope with increased managerial complexity, firms will need multi-prong strategies to handle the different sets of scenarios introduced above:

- Symbiotic management with an ally in the same network
- Competing with a rival in a different network
- Dealing with a different network, and perhaps joining it.

Implications for managers

The essence of the emerging paradigm is that preferential treatment, when reciprocated, reduces transaction costs and provides the key to survival and long-term profitability. Gone are the days when everybody could expect equal treatment and equal pricing; it is important that managers take note of this.

The economic environment facing organisations is becoming increasingly dynamic and complex, transcending traditional geographic and political boundaries. Consequently, organisations, including SMEs, must face the reality that they must now compete on a global stage, regardless of where they are based. For some entrepreneurs and small-business managers, this reality may be a daunting one, because traditionally organisations have focused on uni-polar management, in which resources and control were retained largely within the individual company. SMEs are no longer faced with insurmountable barriers to internationalisation, perpetuated by larger and more-established firms. Business organisations—both large and small—are moving towards a multi-polar distribution of power and control, focused on the development of networks. While this provides new opportunities for SME managers, it also adds new complexity to their tasks. The "old and the proven" methods may no longer work, as the conventional economics of competition, mainly based on the models of the firm-type economy, is largely incapable of capturing the newly emerging paradigm of global competition based on relationships, customisation, and collaborative alliances.

Entrepreneurs and small-business managers will need dramatically different strategies to compete successfully in the multi-polar world economy. They will need world-class efficiency in order to survive, and for many the means to achieving that efficiency is by symbiotic networks. Above all, they must reorient themselves and their firms from their traditional models of competition of the firm-type economy, based on centralised control and stand-alone competition, towards competing by collaborating. Just as a focus on the product gave way to a focus on the market, the emerging paradigm involves a focus on symbiotic management within networks.

New skills will be needed to manage relationships and networks—with suppliers, with customers, and with other firms. Entrepreneurs will need to develop ways to identify network-based opportunities for developing the capabilities and acquiring the specialised resources needed to compete in today's global marketplace, and to understand their own strategic value in the context of networks as an interdependent, as opposed to an independent entity.

INTERNATIONAL ENTREPRENEURSHIP STRATEGY 149

Implications for public policy

With the accelerating transfer of powers from nation-states to both larger and smaller units, the nature of public policy-making and regulation has changed. Increasingly, relevant powers and control are evolving from the national level to both supra-national and local/regional levels. Public-policy leaders will need to decide on the optimal degree of governmental policy and regulation, as well as the appropriate level at which to locate those powers, in order to provide the most suitable environment conducive to internationalisation without excessive regulation, which may hinder growth.

This new environment also calls for increased cooperation among the different levels of government, if they are to create an environment that will foster entrepreneurship—an environment in which entrepreneurs will easily identify networks and participate in them.

Implications for future research

Given the above discussion, we suggest that future research on entrepreneurship and international business should reflect the context of networks rather than focusing solely on the firm or the individual entrepreneur. Specifically, we would like to encourage the following:

- Clarification of the domain of international entrepreneurship, relevant theories and constructs
- More research on the nature and variation of public support for entrepreneur initiatives at various levels of government
- Research reflecting the context of networks, rather than focusing solely on the firm or the individual entrepreneur.

References

Acs, Zoltan J. and Leo Paul Dana, "Contrasting Two Models of Wealth Redistribution", *Small Business Economics 16*(2), 63–74, (March, 2001).

Axelsson, Bjorn and Geoff Easton (eds), *Industrial Networks: A New View of Reality*. London: Routledge, 1992.

Bartels, Frank L., "International Competition and Global Cooperation", In Leo Paul Dana (ed.), *Global Marketing Cooperation and Networks*, pp. 85–98. Binghamton, NY: International Business Press, 2000.

Bartlett, Christopher A. and Sumatra Ghoshal, *Managing Across Borders: The Transnational Solution*. Boston: Harvard Business School Press, 1989.

Beamish, Paul W. and J. Peter Killing (eds), *Cooperative Strategies: European Perspectives/Asian Pacific Perspectives/North American Perspectives*. San Francisco: The New Lexington Press, 1997.

Bilkey, Warren J., "An Attempted Integration of the Literature on the Export Behavior of Firms", *Journal of International Business Studies 9*(1), 33–46, (1978).

Bilkey, Warren J. and George Tesar, "The Export Behavior of Smaller Sized Wisconsin Manufacturing Firms", *Journal of International Business Studies 8*(1), 93–98, (Spring/Summer, 1977).

Bodur, Muzaffer and Tage Koed Madsen, "Danish Foreign Direct Investments in Turkey", *European Business Review 93*(5), 28–43, (1993).

Brüderl, Josef and Peter Preisendörfer, "Network Support and the Success of Newly Founded Businesses", *Small Business Economics 10*(3), 213–225, (1998).

Buckley, Peter J., "International Technology Transfer by Small and Medium-Sized Enterprises", *Small Business Economics 9*, 67–78, (1997).

Buckley, Peter J. and Mark Casson, *The Future of the Multinational Enterprise*. London: Macmillan, 1976.

Buckley, Peter J., Gerald D. Newbould, and Jane C. Thurwell, *Foreign Direct Investment by Smaller UK Firms*. London: Macmillan, 1988.

Casti, John L. and Anders Karlqvist (eds), *Cooperation and Conflict in General Evolutionary Process*. New York: Wiley, 1995.

Cavusgil, S. Tamer, "On the Internationalisation Process of Firms", *European Research 8*, 273–281, (1980).

Cavusgil, S. Tamer, "Differences among Exporting Firms Based on Their Degree of Internationalisation", *Journal of Business Research 12*(2), 195–208, (1984).

Cavusgil, S. Tamer and John R. Nevin, "International Determinants of Export Marketing Behavior", *Journal of Marketing Research 28*, 114–119, (1981).

Chen, Ming-Jer, "Competitor Analysis and Interfirm Rivalry: Toward a Theoretical Integration", *Academy of Management Review 2*(1), 100–134, (1996).

Chetty, Sylvie and Desirée Blackenburg-Holm, "Internationalisation of Small to Medium-sized Manufacturing Firms: A Network Approach", *International Business Review 9*, 77–93, (2000).

Coviello, Nicole E. and Hugh J. Munro, "Growing the Entrepreneurial Firm: Networking for International Market Development", *European Journal of Marketing 29*(7), 49–61, (1995).

Coviello, Nicole E. and Hugh J. Munro, "Network Relationships and the Internationalisation Process of Small Software Firms", *International Business Review 6*(2), 1–26, (1997).

Dana, Leo Paul, "Networks, Internationalization and Policy", *Small Business Economics 16*(2), 57–62, (March, 2001).

Doz, Yves and Gary Hamel, "The Use of Alliances in Implementing Technology Strategies", In Michael L. Tushman and Philip Anderson (eds), *Managing Strategic Innovation and Change*. Oxford: Oxford University Press, 1997.

Dunning, John H., "The Determinants of International Production", *Oxford Economic Papers*, pp. 289–336, November, 1973.

Dunning, John H., "Trade, Location of Economic Activity and MNE: A Search for an Eclectic Approach", *The International Allocation of Economic Activity: Proceedings of A Nobel Symposium Held at Stockholm* pp. 395–418. London: Macmillan, 1977.

Dunning, John H., "Toward an Eclectic Theory of International Production: Empirical Tests", *Journal of International Business Studies 11*(1), 9–31, (1980).

Dunning, John H., "The Eclectic Paradigm of International Production: A Restatement and Some Possible Extensions", *Journal of International Business Studies 19*, 1–31, (Spring, 1988).

Dyer, Jeffrey, Prashant Kale, and Harbir Singh, "How to Make Strategic Alliances Work", *MIT Sloan Management Review 42*(4), 37–43, (Summer, 2001).

Etemad, Hamid, Richard W. Wright, and Leo Paul Dana, "Symbiotic International Business Networks: Collaboration Between Small and Large Firms", *Thunderbird International Business Review 43*(4), 481–499, (2001).

Fontes, Margarita and Rod Coombs, "The Coincidence of Technology and Market Objectives in the Internationalisation of New Technology-Based Firms", *International Small Business Journal 15*(4), 14–35, (1997).

Forrest, Janet E., "Management Aspects of Strategic Partnering", *Journal of General Management 17*(4), 25–40, (1992).

Gomes-Casseres, Benjamin, "Group Versus Group: How Alliance Networks Compete", *Harvard Business Review 72*, 62–74, (July–August, 1994).

INTERNATIONAL ENTREPRENEURSHIP STRATEGY 151

Gomes-Casseres, Benjamin, *The Alliance Revolution: The New Shape of Business Rivalry*. Cambridge, MA: Harvard University Press, 1996.

Gynawali, Devi R. and Ravindranath Madhavan, "Network Structure and Competitive Dynamics: A Structural Embeddedness Perspective", *Academy of Management Review 26*(3), 431–445, (July, 2001).

Holmlund, Maria and Soren Kock, "Relationships and the Internationalisation of Finnish Small and Medium-sized Companies", *International Small Business Journal 16*(4), 46–63, (1998).

Jarillo, Carlos J., *Strategic Networks—Creating the Borderless Organization*. Oxford: Butterworth-Heineman, 1993.

Johanson, Jan and Jan-Erik Vahlne, "The Internationalization Process of the Firm—A Model of Knowledge Development and Increasing Foreign Market Commitments", *Journal of International Business Studies 8*(1), 23–32, (Spring/Summer, 1977).

Johanson, Jan and Jan-Erik Vahlne, "The Mechanism of Internationalisation", *International Marketing Review 7*(4), 11–24, (1990).

Johanson, Jan and Finn Wiedersheim-Paul, "The Internationalisation of the Firm: Four Swedish Cases", *Journal of International Management Studies 12*(3), 305–322, (October, 1975).

Kanter, Rosabeth Moss, "Collaborative Advantage: The Art of Alliances", *Harvard Business Review 72*, 96–108, (July–August, 1994).

Leonidou, Leonidas C. and Constantine S. Katsikeas, "The Export Development Process", *Journal of International Business Studies 27*(3), 517–551, (1996).

McMillan, John, *Reinventing the Bazaar: A Natural History of Markets*. New York & London: W. W. Norton & Company, 2002.

Morck, Randal and Bernard Yeung, "Why Investors Value Multinationality", *Journal of Business 64*(2), 165–187, (1991).

Morck, Randal and Bernard Yeung, "Internalization: An Event Study Test", *Journal of International Economics 33*, 41–56, (1992).

Newbould, Gerald D., Peter J. Buckley, and Jane C. Thurwell, *Going International—The Enterprise of Smaller Companies Overseas*. New York: John Wiley and Sons, 1978.

Pangarkar, Nitin and Saul Klein, "Bandwagon Pressures and Interfirm Alliances in the Global Pharmaceutical Industry", *Journal of International Marketing 6*(2), 54–73, (1998).

Pangarkar, Nitin and Saul Klein, "The Impacts of Alliance Purpose and Partner Similarity on Alliance Governance", *British Journal of Management 12*, 341–353, (2001).

Parkhe, Arvind, "Strategic Alliance Structuring: A Game Theoretic and Transaction Cost Examination of Inter-firm Cooperation", *Academy of Management Journal, 36*(4), 794–829, (1997).

Perrow, Charles, "Small Firm Networks", In Nitin Nohria and Robert G. Eccles (eds), *Networks and Organizations: Structure, Form, and Action*, pp. 445–470. Boston: Harvard Business School Press, 1992.

Reynolds, Paul D., "New and Small Firms in Expanding Markets", *Small Business Economics 9*(1), 79–84, (1997).

Rugman, Alan M., *International Diversification and the Multinational Enterprise*. Farborough: Lexington, 1979.

Rugman, Alan M., *Inside the Multinationals: The Economics of Internal Market*. New York: Columbia University Press, 1981.

Sadler, Aaron and Sylvie Chetty, "The Impact of Networks on New Zealand", In Leo Paul Dana (ed.), *Global Marketing Co-Operation and Networks*, pp. 37–58. Binghamton, New York: International Business Press, 2000.

Stabell, Charles and Øystein Fjeldstad, "Configuring Value for Competitive Advantage: On Chains, Shops and Networks", *Strategic Management Journal 19*, 413–437, (1998).

Stafford, Edwin R., "Using Co-operative Strategies to Make Alliances Work", *Long-Range Planning 27*(3), 64–74, (1994).

Teece, David J., "Multinational Enterprise, Internal Governance and Economic Organization", *American Economic Review 75*, 233–238, (1985).

Webster, Frederick E., "The Changing Role of Marketing in the Corporation", *Journal of Marketing 56*, 1–17, (October 1992).

Welsh, Denice, Lawrence Welsh, Ian Wilkinson, and Louise Young, "An Export Grouping Scheme", In Leo Paul Dana (ed.), *Global Marketing Cooperation and Networks*, pp. 59–84. Binghamton, New York: International Business Press, 2000.

Zineldin, Mosad Amin, "Toward an Ecological Collaborative Relationship Management: A "Co-opetive" Perspective", *European Journal of Marketing 32*(11/12), 1138–1164, (1998).

[8]

International Entrepreneurship: The Current Status of the Field and Future Research Agenda

Shaker A. Zahra, Gerard George

With the globalization of the world economy, interest in international entrepreneurship has increased rapidly over the past decade (Brush 1993, 1995; Hitt and Bartkus, 1997; Hisrich, et al., 1996). One of the most important features of today's global economy is the growing role of young entrepreneurial new ventures (Almeida and Bloodgood, 1996; Bell, 1995; Clark and Mallory, 1997; Fujita, 1995; Haug, 1991). Through the 1990s, researchers' attention has centered on exploring the motivations for, the pattern of, and the pace of internationalization by new ventures (i.e., firms eight years old or younger). Invoking multiple theoretical perspectives, some researchers suggest that new ventures frequently become active players in the global economy soon after the birth of these firms (e.g., Oviatt and McDougall, 1999; Zahra, Matherne, and Carleton, 2000b). More recently, however, researchers have focused on examining the entrepreneurial activities of established companies (i.e., firms older than eight years), aiming to uncover the key patterns of innovative activities associated with successful internationalization (e.g., Zahra and Garvis, 2000). By doing so, researchers have sought to explain how international entrepreneurship may lead to superior financial performance among established firms.

Recent attempts to develop a well-grounded framework to understand the nature and effect of international entrepreneurship have concentrated mainly on the application of various theoretical perspectives to explain this phenomenon by refuting the applicability of traditional frameworks (e.g., McDougall, Shane, and Oviatt, 1994; Oviatt and McDougall, 1994). While insightful and informative, past research in this emerging area has followed different theoretical and methodological traditions, raising questions about its overall value added. This research has also lacked a unified framework that connects the antecedents, types, and outcomes of entrepreneurial activities pursued by new ventures and established companies (McDougall and Oviatt, 2000; Oviatt and McDougall, 1999). These shortcomings suggest a need to pause

256   Shaker A. Zahra, Gerard George

and consider the current status and cumulative contributions of research into international entrepreneurship and to discuss ways to enhance future contributions.

In this chapter, we seek to achieve four objectives. First, we analyze the concept of international entrepreneurship and its theoretical domain. We believe that the ambiguity of the international entrepreneurship term has led to confusion in past research and caused researchers to overlook important issues. Our discussion distinguishes between international entrepreneurship activities of new ventures and established companies. Second, we review past empirical work on international entrepreneurship and analyze its theoretical foundations and then arrive at a synthesis of the key factors believed to influence international entrepreneurship. Third, we offer an integrative framework that connects the antecedents, types, and outcomes of international entrepreneurship. This framework recognizes the importance of contextual variables in determining the value some companies derive from pursuing international entrepreneurship. Finally, we outline ways to improve future international entrepreneurship scholarship, hoping to increase its rigor and impact while making it accessible and relevant to the managers of new ventures and well-established companies.

Prior international entrepreneurship scholars have observed the close theoretical link between entrepreneurship and international business (IB) research (Oviatt and McDougall, 1994; McDougall and Oviatt, 2000). One of the most interesting revelations from reading published international entrepreneurship research is the extent to which scholars have made use of existing and emerging strategy theories and frameworks. In many ways, international entrepreneurship research has mirrored published strategy research, while also weaving together IB and entrepreneurship explanations of complex organizational phenomena. We believe this integration offers some important opportunities to develop more realistic and comprehensive frameworks of international entrepreneurship dimensions, antecedents, and effects. Therefore, throughout this chapter we highlight areas of convergence and divergence among international entrepreneurship and strategy scholars. We also discuss ways in which international entrepreneurship researchers can better employ strategy theories.

In the first section of this chapter, we present an overview of early research in international entrepreneurship, explain the growth of interest in this important phenomenon, and highlight key transition points in this research. We then review and critique studies that suggest that international entrepreneurship focuses on young firms. Attention will center on "born global" new ventures, recognizing the merits and shortcomings of this focus. Equally important, we also consider international entrepreneurship in established companies and explore the importance of studying these firms and the distinguishing characteristics of their international entrepreneurship. To move the field forward, we propose a comprehensive definition of international entrepreneurship and make some key distinctions between our definition and those definitions available in extant literature.

In the second section of the chapter, we analyze the contributions and cumulative value added of past international entrepreneurship research. We examine empirical and conceptual contributions, highlighting their theoretical foundations, data collection methods, and major findings. The discussion aims to distill what we know about international entrepreneurship and identify areas that need further research. We pay special attention to the challenges that researchers face in conducting research in international entrepreneurship of new ventures or established companies. Here, we categorize and then analyze the key findings of these studies into organizational, environmental, and strategic factors influencing international entrepreneurship. By doing so, we synthesize past research in a way that we hope will document and better model the relationships between international entrepreneurship and firm performance. The discussion also highlights several areas where strategy and entrepreneurship researchers converge and diverge.

In the third section of this chapter, we present a framework that connects its antecedents, types, and outcomes. Antecedents encompass the firm (e.g., top management team characteristics and firm resources). Types of international entrepreneurship activities refer to the extent, speed, and scope of a firm's international operations. International entrepreneurship outcomes include financial and non-financial (e.g., learning) gains that new ventures and established companies seek from internationalization (Barkema and Vermeulen, 1998). Factors that might affect the payoff from international entrepreneurship (e.g., strategic and environmental factors) are also considered. The proposed model makes use of theories from IB (Dunning, 1988; Craig and Douglas, 1996; Hymer, 1976), global strategy (Hitt, Hoskisson, and Ireland, 1994; Hitt et al., 1995; Hitt, Hoskisson, and Kim, 1997), strategic management (Grant, 1991, 1996, 1998), and entrepreneurship (Katz and Gartner, 1988; Kirzner, 1973). This model highlights the necessity of integrating these views as we seek to better understand the nature and implications of international entrepreneurship.

In the concluding section of this chapter, we discuss ways to improve future international entrepreneurship research by enhancing both its rigor and contribution. The discussion covers theory building and empirical issues, highlighting the potential gains scholars can make by capitalizing on innovative methods applied in the strategic management and IB disciplines. We also identify some emerging issues that deserve greater attention in future international entrepreneurship research.

Definition and Domain of International Entrepreneurship

Recently, researchers have drawn on IB and entrepreneurship theories to define and study international entrepreneurship. Originating in the entrepreneurship literature, a stream of research suggests that some new ventures are "born global" and therefore differ significantly from businesses that become international in scope over time as they accumulate resources or competencies (Oviatt and McDougall, 1994, 1999). Researchers, however, have noted that this phenomenon is not new and has existed in other countries, such as Sweden and Switzerland, and is a function of their resources and the size of their home markets (e.g., Bloodgood, Sapienza, and Almeida, 1996). Indeed, the IB literature provides multiple established theories that explain global expansion through market entry and the creation of new or joint ventures in other countries. Examples are the life cycle (Vernon, 1979) and internationalization (Johanson and Vahlne, 1977) theories. Though some argue that these theories are not applicable due to the unique context of "born global" organizations (Oviatt and McDougall, 1994; McDougall, Shane, and Oviatt, 1994), such conclusions appear to overlook

258   Shaker A. Zahra, Gerard George

venturing by established firms. Therefore, we believe the larger research issue concerns the incongruence in the definition and scope of international entrepreneurship. This section of the chapter, therefore, defines the concept and domain of international entrepreneurship.

To date, the bulk of international entrepreneurship research has focused on studying the internationalization of new ventures. These past efforts have been limited in their scope, concentrating on international new ventures as an independent entrepreneurial act by an individual. This limited focus has several drawbacks. This focus ignores the fact that entrepreneurial activities are an ongoing process that unfolds over time. These activities reflect the creativity of various members of a new venture's top management team. Members of these teams usually draw upon their innate abilities, skills, and talents as well their experience. Another limitation of prior research is precluding the notion of corporate entrepreneurship or venturing by established firms, especially in international markets. Companies of different age and size often engage in entrepreneurial activities as they venture into international markets (Zahra and Garvis, 2000) and these firms should be included in the study of international entrepreneurship. Similarly, the study of entrepreneurship in multinational firms has received considerable attention in recent IB research (e.g., Bartlett and Ghoshal, 2000; Birkinshaw, 1997), and therefore could provide additional insights into the domain, antecedents, and consequences of international entrepreneurship (Barnevik, 1991; Zahra and Garvis, 2000).

Table 12.1 presents an overview of the evolution of research into international entrepreneurship. The first known reference dates back to Morrow's (1988) discussions of the age of the international entrepreneur. Morrow suggested that advances in technology, coupled with increased cultural awareness, have made once-remote markets accessible to companies, whether new ventures or established companies. McDougall's (1989) study of new ventures' international sales was one of the first empirical efforts in this emerging area. This study has provided rich insights into differences between these firms and those ventures that did not go international.

In the early 1990s, McDougall and Oviatt (and their students) developed a series of case studies that clearly showed that some young ventures have gone international early in their life cycles. These case analyses clarified some of the approaches new ventures have followed in going international. Oviatt and McDougall (1994) followed this effort with an influential paper that defined international entrepreneurship, following the study of "born global" new ventures. This definition was narrower in scope than those offered in the literature. Zahra (1993), for example, suggested that the study of international entrepreneurship should encompass both new firms and established companies. A report by an entrepreneurship panel (Giamartino, McDougall, and Bird, 1993) called for a broader definition of international entrepreneurship. Zahra and Schulte (1994) also observed a need to go beyond the "born international" criterion highlighted in the early work of McDougall and Oviatt.

Wright and Ricks (1994) noted the growing importance of international entrepreneurship as an emerging research issue in IB. These authors also suggested that international entrepreneurship is a firm-level activity that crosses national borders and focuses on the relationship between businesses and the international environments in which they operate. This definition helped to shift attention away from using the age of the

Table 12.1 A chronicle of international entrepreneurship definitions

- McDougall (1989) states:

   "international entrepreneurship is defined in this study as the development of international new ventures or start-ups that, from their inception, engage in international business, thus viewing their operating domain as international from the initial stages of the firm's operation."

- Zahra (1993) defines international entrepreneurship as "the study of the nature and consequences of a firm's risk-taking behavior as it ventures into international markets."

- Giamartino, McDougall, and Bird (1993), heading an entrepreneurship-division-wide panel, suggested that the domain of international entrepreneurship be expanded.

- Oviatt and McDougall (1994) state:

   ". . . a business organization that, from inception, seeks to derive significant competitive advantage from the use of resources and sale of outputs in multiple countries."

- Wright and Ricks (1994) highlighted the growing importance of international entrepreneurship as an emerging research theme. They suggested that international entrepreneurship is a firm-level activity that crosses national borders and focuses on the relationship between businesses and the international environments in which they operate.

- McDougall and Oviatt (1996) state:

   "new and innovative activities that have the goal of value creation and growth in business organization across national borders."

- McDougall and Oviatt (2000) state:

   "A combination of innovative, proactive, and risk-seeking behavior that crosses or is compared across national borders and is intended to create value in business organizations." They note that firm size and age are defining characteristics here. But they exclude nonprofit and governmental agencies.

---

firm or timing of internationalization as the sole criterion to define international entrepreneurship. This definition also included young new ventures *and* established companies as being worthy of study. Wright and Ricks' definition, moreover, highlighted the context in which entrepreneurial activities occur, within new ventures or established corporations. This important insight further helped to set the stage for connecting the antecedents, types, and outcomes of international entrepreneurship. A firm's business environment plays an important role in spurring certain types of entrepreneurial activities (Zahra, 1991, 1993) and determining the payoff from these activities (Zahra and Covin, 1995). Finally, an advantage of the Wright and Ricks (1994) definition was the inclusion of comparative analyses of entrepreneurial activities within the domain of international entrepreneurship. There is much to be gained from conducting comparative analyses of international entrepreneurship in new ventures and established companies (McDougall and Oviatt, 2000; Wright and Ricks, 1994; Zahra and Schulte, 1994). These analyses can improve our understanding of the role of national

260   Shaker A. Zahra, Gerard George

cultures, national institutional environments, and centers (clusters) of innovations in promoting and shaping international entrepreneurship activities. These analyses can also improve theory development efforts by highlighting the role of contextual variables on relationships of interest.

Recently, Oviatt and McDougall (1999) offered a more inclusive list of topics that fall under the umbrella of international entrepreneurship. These topics included, among others, corporate entrepreneurship research. This research agenda reflected an important change in Oviatt and McDougall's view of international entrepreneurship; it recognized the importance of international entrepreneurship in established firms. McDougall and Oviatt (2000), moreover, suggested a broader definition of the entrepreneurship phenomenon; the study of established companies, and the recognition of comparative (cross-national) analysis. As table 12.1 indicates, McDougall and Oviatt's recent definition appears to accept Miller's (1983) definition of entrepreneurship as an organizational-level phenomenon that focuses on innovation, risk taking, and proactiveness. This definition has been widely used in the literature (Zahra, Jennings, and Kuratko, 1999). This focus links international entrepreneurship research to other research already under way in the field of entrepreneurship. It also makes it easier to follow what firms actually do, rather than attempting to decipher the intent of the individual entrepreneurs.

The inclusion of established companies also corrects an oversight in the entrepreneurship field; namely, the presumption that well-established companies are not innovative and refuse to take risks. Many highly regarded well-established companies work hard to foster innovation, support venturing, and encourage risk taking. To ignore these firms automatically precludes an important and vital part of the US and other economies. International entrepreneurship researchers, therefore, have several important opportunities as they study established companies. We outline some of these opportunities later in the chapter.

Despite the progress made toward defining international entrepreneurship, we remain concerned that the domain of this phenomenon remains vague. Lists that attempt to canvass and define the topics covered within international entrepreneurship also remain broad, raising questions about the unique research questions international entrepreneurship scholars should examine. For example, McDougall and Oviatt (2000) list the following topics as belonging within the domain of international entrepreneurship: cooperative alliances, corporate entrepreneurship, economic development activities, entrepreneur characteristics and motivations, exporting and other market entry modes, new ventures and IPOs, transitioning economies, and venture financing. While we applaud the desire to be inclusive, many of these issues have been the focus of considerable research by entrepreneurship, IB, and strategy scholars. This suggests the question: *What makes international entrepreneurship a distinct area of scholarly inquiry?*

We believe that what makes international entrepreneurship a unique and, indeed, worthwhile topic of research is the interplay between entrepreneurship and internationalization processes. Specifically, the innovativeness and risk taking that firms undertake as they expand (or contract) their international operations is what makes international entrepreneurship an interesting research area. Those insights and acts that bring new perspectives and strategies on how, what, when, and why to internationalize a business activity give meaning to the international entrepreneurship phenomenon. For instance, an e-commerce venture that goes international instantly at birth is an interesting organizational form that deserves examination. This can be studied using the theoretical lens from organizational theory, sociology, strategy, entrepreneurship, or IB. The innovativeness by which the firm identifies a market opportunity, defines (configures) its value chain, selects areas to be internationalized, and identifies unique ways to reach potential customers in cyberspace is what makes this an international entrepreneurship-type study. Similarly, we can find examples of established firms that are innovative, make proactive choices, and take risks to enter international markets (Zahra and Garvis, 2000).

Focusing on the innovativeness and entrepreneurial nature of a firm's internationalization has several advantages. It compels us to think about the processes by which entrepreneurial firms and their managers go about justifying their existence. These firms exist for many reasons, one of which is to offer a new way of doing things. As readily acknowledged in the strategy literature, this new way can create value through efficiency, speed, uniqueness, and/or customization. New ventures continue to exist due to the inability of other firms to copy or undo the advantages of these firms. Entrepreneurial firms know that their advantages lie in continuous innovation. The ability to sustain this entrepreneurial spirit is what makes these organizations viable. Rivals, large or small, do not easily duplicate this entrepreneurial capability. Thus, it makes sense to focus on this entrepreneurial capacity as the theoretical engine in studying international entrepreneurship. New ventures that reach the global market quickly after their birth might be driven by a set of internal and external forces to do so. What matters is *how* these firms succeed in the global market, a variable that requires innovativeness, risk taking and entrepreneurship. As the global strategy literature suggests, some of these arguments apply equally well to established companies (Bartlett and Ghoshal, 2000). This focus is consistent also with the strategy literature, where companies that excel in their industries are believed to exhibit a great deal of creativity and innovativeness in leveraging their core competencies. These companies stretch and leverage their capabilities to achieve superior value creation for their customers and other stakeholders (Hamel and Prahalad, 1994).

Focusing on innovativeness as a characteristic of international entrepreneurship has additional advantages. Innovativeness connects the concept of international entrepreneurship to ongoing research in the broader field of entrepreneurship such as corporate entrepreneurship (Burgelman and Sayles, 1986; Zahra et al., 1999); research into entrepreneurial orientation (Lumpkin and Dess 1996); and comparative literature that suggests certain cultures are being more innovative or entrepreneurial (Mitchell et al., 2000; Shane, 1993; Steensma et al., 2000).

The above discussion leads us to define international entrepreneurship as *"the process of creatively discovering and exploiting opportunities that lie outside a firm's domestic markets in the pursuit of competitive advantage"*. This definition builds on recent writings in the field of entrepreneurship that highlight the importance of opportunity recognition, discovery, and exploitation as a distinguishing characteristic of entrepreneurship (Shane and Venkataraman, 2000; Zahra and Dess, 2001). Further, the term "creatively," included in our definition, reinforces the need for innovativeness in the way a firm discovers and/or exploits opportunities, as discussed above. The definition also recognizes the fact that opportunities are sometimes discovered by some firms but are exploited by others. This is why we borrow the term competitive advantage from the strategic management literature (Barney, 1991; Collis, 1995). Having a competitive advantage can enable new ventures to create wealth to their owners by expanding internationally. Firms that internationalize their operations in innovative and creative ways stand to achieve significant gains that go beyond superior financial performance. Also, this definition is more inclusive than other definitions because it does not center on the size or age of the firm that pursues internationalization, consistent with McDougall and Oviatt (2000). Next, we review past research on international entrepreneurship literature.

Conceptual and Empirical Treatment of International Entrepreneurship: A Review

In this section, we review the conceptual and empirical studies with international entrepreneurship as their central premise of investigation. Several observations emerge from reviewing the international entrepreneurship research. First, past research has substantially benefited from the application of multiple theoretical foci. These theoretical perspectives include: the resource-based view (Autio et al., 1997; Bloodgood et al., 1996); transaction cost theory (Steensma et al., 2000; Zacharakis, 1997); organizational learning (Autio et al., 2000; Zahra, Ireland, and Hitt, 2000a); and product life cycle theory (Roberts and Senturia, 1996). However, McDougall et al. (1994) suggest that traditional IB theories may not be applicable to "born global" ventures. According to these authors, each of the traditional theories has several assumptions about the nature of the market or the sources of competitive advantages to be derived within certain market structures. McDougall et al. contend that many of these assumptions are not relevant in today's global markets or do not match the characteristics of "born international" new ventures. Similarly, we believe that the acceptance of a narrow definition of the international entrepreneurship domain is likely to have restricted the use of certain theoretical frameworks. Conversely, the expanded definition we have just offered above provides a broader range of issues where theoretical foci can be applied to future studies of international entrepreneurship.

Second, the development of international entrepreneurship has relied to a large extent on samples based in the US (Bloodgood et al., 1996; McDougall, 1989; McDougall and Oviatt, 1996; Zahra et al., 2000a, b; Zahra and Garvis, 2000). However, there are some studies that draw on non-US firms. For example, Autio et al. (2000, 1997) and Holmlund and Kock (1998) analyzed ventures in Finland, Coviello and Munro (1995) studied firms from New Zealand, and Fontes and Coombs (1997) studied Portuguese firms. Unfortunately, these studies and those that use US data have tended to evolve independent of each other. Therefore, there is little congruence and overlap in theory building that would account for the potential differences in international entrepreneurship across countries. A promising development is recent work using multi-country data to compare cross-cultural effects on venture creation and alliance formation (Mitchell et al., 2000; Steensma et al., 2000).

Third, past studies appear to draw thematic conclusions based on case studies or small samples. For example, Autio et al. (2000) suggest learning advantages of newness using a sample of 57 privately held Finnish firms. Bloodgood et al. (1996) examined the antecedents and outcomes of the internationalization of 61 ventures. Similarly, McDougall and Oviatt (1996) draw conclusions on performance implications of internationalization using a sample of 62 firms. Other articles rely on case studies (e.g., Tiessen and Merrilees, 1999). Also, most studies concentrated on high-technology samples, thereby limiting the ability to generalize to samples of low technology or traditional industries (Burgel and Murray, 1998; Fontes and Coombs, 1997; Karagozoglu and Lindell, 1997; Reuber and Fischer, 1997; Zahra et al., 2000a, b). Only a few studies have examined service industries (e.g., Mößlang 1995). To summarize, while we commend prior authors for developing and establishing the domain of a new area of scholarly inquiry, there is a need to develop a stronger theoretical rationale and empirical testing with larger and more representative samples.

Fourth, the lack of longitudinal design is a major weakness of prior international entrepreneurship research. The dominance of cross-sectional research designs in past research has resulted in non-cumulative and inconsistent findings. Even though conducting longitudinal research is a time-consuming and challenging process (Davidsson and Wiklund, 2000), it can improve our understanding of the relationships examined in international entrepreneurship research (Sexton, Pricer, and Nenide, 2000). Such research designs can be especially helpful in identifying the potential causal links among variables of interest.

Limitations aside, the studies just reviewed have helped expand the domain of international entrepreneurship. These studies have tested international entrepreneurship as a multidimensional construct. These dimensions are further explored below. Also, several key relationships such as the factors that determine internationalization or its outcomes have been addressed. We categorize these key issues as organizational factors, environmental factors, and strategic factors. To set the stage for the discussion, the next section of this chapter analyzes the various dimensions of international entrepreneurship explored in prior research.

Dimensions of international entrepreneurship

Prior researchers focused on three key dimensions of international entrepreneurship. In table 12.2, we present these dimensions and identify the studies that examined them. As table 12.2 shows, the majority of prior studies examined the extent (or degree) of a new venture's sales internationalization. Typically, the extent of internationalization was measured by the percent of a firm's sales generated from foreign markets. Some studies also examined the speed by which a new venture internationalized their operations. In these studies, speed was defined as the length of time that elapsed between the year the venture was created and the year of its first foreign sales. Table 12.2 also shows that some studies examined the scope of a new venture's sales internationalization, measured by the number of countries (other than country of origin) in which the new venture generated sales. Finally, two studies investigated the regional scope of a new venture's sales internationalization.

One of the most striking features of past international entrepreneurship research is the fact that it has focused almost exclusively on indicators of internationalization of

Table 12.2   Dimensions of international entrepreneurship

Extent/degree of internationalization	Speed	Scope	
		Countries	Regions
• McDougall (1989)	• Reuber and Fischer (1997)	• Zahra et al. (2000a)	• Reuber and Fischer (1997)
• McDougall et al. (1994)	• Zahra et al. (2000b)	• Roberts and Senturia (1996)	• Roberts and Senturia (1996)
• Brush (1995)	• Roberts and Senturia (1996)	• Burgel and Murray (1998)	
• Bloodgood et al. (1996)	• Fontes and Coombs (1997)		
• McDougall and Oviatt (1996)	• Lindqvist (1997)		
• Karagozoglu and Lindell (1997)	• Burgel and Murray (1998)		
• Reuber and Fischer (1997)			
• Burgel and Murray (1998)			
• Zahra et al. (2000a)			
• Zahra et al. (2000b)			

the firm's operations, both in scope (e.g., regions) and scale (i.e., level of sales derived from international operations). A glaring deficiency in past research is ignoring the internationalization of a firm's value chain or inputs into the production process. As acknowledged by strategy (Porter, 1986) and global strategy (Bartlett and Ghoshal, 2000) researchers, these variables can significantly influence the nature and magnitude of a firm's competitive advantage. International entrepreneurship researchers have also overlooked one of the key areas that can give young and established firms enduring competitive advantages that set them apart from their rivals: the ability to recognize opportunities and pursue them creatively (Kirzner, 1973).

Organizational factors influencing international entrepreneurship

One area that has received some attention in prior studies is the effect of firm-related variables on international entrepreneurship. Researchers examined three sets of variables: top management team (TMT) characteristics, firm resources, and firm-specific variables. These variables have been widely discussed in strategy and entrepreneurship research. Table 12.3a summarizes the key findings from prior research on the effect of the top management team and resources on international entrepreneurship. Table 12.3b presents the results for the effect of firm variables on international entrepreneurship.

Strategy researchers have long maintained that the characteristics of the firm's top management team can spell the difference between its success and failure. These characteristics significantly affect firms' strategic choices (Finkelstein and Hambrick, 1996), such as internationalization (Carpenter and Frederickson, 2001; Calof and Beamish, 1994). In table 12.3a, we note the importance of TMT characteristics such as foreign work experience, foreign education, background, and vision as they relate to internationalization. Exposure to international markets or market practices significantly influences the firm's drive to internationalize. These findings are corroborated through case analyses (Oviatt and McDougall, 1995) and empirical studies (Bloodgood et al., 1996; Burgel and Murray, 1998). This is important because senior managers' international experience is positively related to some indicators of firm performance (Carpenter, Sanders, and Gregersen, 2001; Daily, Certo, and Dalton, 2000).

Strategy researchers have invoked the resource-based theory as a key basis for explaining the various strategic choices companies make (Barney, 1991). Our review also highlights the importance of firm resources as a factor influencing international entrepreneurship (table 12.3a). Particular attention has been given to how the firm's unique assets such as product innovativeness (Burgel and Murray, 1998) influence the internationalization process (Zahra et al., 2000a). Also, intangible assets such as reputation and networks can significantly influence the speed and degree of internationalization (Zahra et al., 2000b). The proposition that unique organizational assets and knowledge bases can influence international entrepreneurship also is supported by case analyses (Oviatt and McDougall, 1995). In turn, international expansion enhances the firm's learning and gives it access to new knowledge bases, as found in the study by Zahra et al. (2000a).

Researchers also have examined the effect of several organizational factors on a firm's international entrepreneurship. Specifically, researchers have examined the effects of

Table 12.3a Influence of organizational factors on international entrepreneurship (TMT and resources)

Variable	Dimension	Findings
Top Management Team	Foreign work experience	• Case analyses showed that new ventures led by managers with foreign work experience were able to quickly internationalize their operations and do so successfully (Oviatt and McDougall, 1995; McDougall et al., 1996). • Found a positive and significant association between managers' foreign work experience and degree of new venture's internationalization (Bloodgood et al., 1996; Burgel and Murray, 1998). • A higher percentage of managers of companies that internationalized worked for a foreign company at home (Burgel and Murray, 1998).
	Education abroad	• Found a positive (not significant) relationship between managers receiving education outside the USA and new ventures' international expansion (Bloodgood et al., 1996) • A higher percentage of managers of companies that internationalized received education abroad than those of startups that did not internationalize (Burgel and Murray, 1998).
	Background	• Firms with principal founders drawn from managerial parental backgrounds were significantly more likely to export than firms with other types of founders (Westhead et al., 1998).
	Global vision	• Case analyses suggested that new ventures led by managers with global visions were able to internationalize quickly and successfully (Oviatt and McDougall, 1995).
Resources	Unique assets	• Case analyses suggested that new ventures with unique intangible assets were able to internationalize quickly and successfully (Oviatt and McDougall, 1995). • Companies that internationalized their operations had products that required significantly less customization and maintenance than those that did not (Burgel and Murray 1998). There were no differences between the two groups in the amount of installation or training required to use their products. • Startup companies that did not internationalize were more likely to describe their products as being less innovative (Burgel and Murray, 1998).
	R&D spending	• Positively (not significant) related to internationalization status, speed, or degree (Zahra et al., 2000b). • Startups that internationalized their operations had higher R&D-to-sales ratio (Burgel and Murray, 1998). • Startups that internationalized their operations had higher ratio of employees who worked 50% or more of their time on new product development as percent of sales than those that did not (Burgel and Murray, 1998).

Network	• Case analyses suggested that new ventures with extensive networks were able to internationalize quickly and successfully (Oviatt and McDougall, 1995). • Technological networks are positively and significantly associated with status, speed, and degree of internationalization, and this effect is higher for new firms with high R&D spending (Zahra et al., 2000b). • There were no significant differences between startups that internationalized and those that did not with regard to access to venture or angel capital (Burgel and Murray, 1998). • Firms that had received industry grants were significantly more likely to export (Westhead et al., 1998).
Reputation	• A reputation for technological superiority is positively and significantly associated with status, speed, and degree of internationalization. This effect is higher for status and degree of internationalization of new firms with high R&D spending (Zahra et al., 2000b). Interaction of reputation and R&D is not significant in the case of speed.

Table 12.3b Influence of organizational factors on international entrepreneurship (firm-related variables)

Variable	Findings
Size	• Venture size is positively associated with degree of internationalization (Bloodgood et al., 1996).
	• Venture size (time 1) was negatively (not significant) associated with relative market share in time 2 (McDougall and Oviatt, 1996).
	• Venture size was positively (not significant) associated with internationalization status, speed, or degree (Zahra et al., 2000b).
	• Company size is negatively associated (not significant) with degree of internationalization (Reuber and Fischer, 1997).
	• High-tech startups that internationalized were significantly larger in sales and employment than firms that did not internationalize (Burgel and Murray 1998).
	• There was no significant difference in employment of exporters vs. non-exporters (Westhead et al., 1998).
Age	• Age was negatively (not significant) associated with ROI in time 2 (McDougall and Oviatt, 1996).
	• Age is positively associated with degree of internationalization in one equation but negative (not significant) in another (Reuber and Fischer, 1997).
	• Startups that internationalized were significantly older than firms that did not internationalize (Burgel and Murray, 1998).
	• Venture age was positively (not significant) associated with internationalization status or degree (Zahra et al., 2000b). Speed of internationalization was not explored in the analysis.
	• There were no significant differences in age between exporters and non-exporters (Westhead et al., 1998).
Location	• There was no significant difference between firms that exported and those that did not in rural vs. urban location (Westhead et al., 1998).
	• National culture influences the formation of technology alliances by entrepreneurial firms (Steensma et al., 2000).
Origin	• Corporate origin was negatively and significantly associated with status. Corporate origin was negatively (not significant) associated with degree and speed of internationalization (Zahra et al., 2000b).
Growth orientation	• Firm growth orientation was positively associated with average absolute annual international sales growth (Autio et al., 1997).

Environmental scanning	• Average amount of environmental scanning was positively and significantly associated with international collaborative relationships which, in turn, was positively and significantly associated with average absolute annual international sales growth (Autio et al., 1997). • Analyses indicated that limited global information-gathering capabilities limited companies' internationalization (Karagozoglu and Lindell, 1997).
Financial strength	• ROE was positively (but not significant) with internationalization status, positive and marginally significant (p<10) with speed and degree of sales internationalization (Zahra et al., 2000b). • Leverage was positively (not significant) associated with degree of internationalization (Bloodgood et al., 1996).

270   Shaker A. Zahra, Gerard George

age and size, speculating that experience and resources (firm size as proxy) intensify international entrepreneurship. As table 12.3b shows, research findings did not support theoretical explanations. A similar conclusion emerged from prior studies on the effect of location, which was believed to give companies unique knowledge and resources that can intensify internationalization. Here too, empirical findings did not support theoretical explanations.

As table 12.3b indicates, researchers have also examined venture origin, defined as whether the firm was established by a corporation or an independent entrepreneur. For example, Zahra et al. (2000b) found that ventures created by established firms were less likely to internationalize their sales. A corporate venture status was not significantly associated with the degree or speed of sales internationalization. Future international entrepreneurship researchers are likely to gain a great deal of insight from examining the effect of intangible assets and resources typically associated with venture origin on different dimensions of internationalization. Some strategy research has already uncovered significant differences between independent and corporate ventures in their resource bases (Shrader and Simon, 1997) and competitive strategies, especially with respect to technological choices (Zahra, 1996). Whether or not these differences manifest themselves in the extent or speed of new ventures' internationalization remains unknown. Also, it is not clear if there are differences among independently owned (private) firms vs. publicly owned and managed companies in internationalization or the gains achieved from this important but complex activity.

Growth orientation   Managers' motivation to achieve growth can influence a firm's international entrepreneurship activities. One study that tested this proposition found that firms that had a high growth orientation were likely to internationalize their operations (Autio et al., 1997). This finding highlighted the importance of managerial attitudes in shaping the strategic direction of their enterprises (Finkelstein and Hambrick, 1996), especially in terms of global expansion. However, the dearth of empirical studies that document the types of attitudes that are conducive to globalization and the direction of the relationship between these attitudes and success in international expansion remains a gap in this emerging research stream.

Environmental scanning   Information about the industry and/or potential foreign markets can spur international entrepreneurship. Evidence indicates that the exposure and ability to gather information from foreign markets is positively associated with internationalization (Autio et al., 1997; Karagozoglu and Lindell, 1997). These findings are consistent with strategic management research that highlights the importance of environmental analysis for the effective selection of the strategies companies pursue (Hambrick 1981; Miles and Snow, 1978). Still, much can be gained from conducting more analyses that examine the various systems and processes by which companies gather information about opportunities in their international markets and how they interpret this information as they craft the strategies they pursue.

Financial strength   Table 12.3b suggests that some researchers have begun to examine the effect of a firm's financial status on its internationalization. This research is guided by a belief that successful past organizational performance creates the slack resources needed to support international expansion. Two aspects of a new venture's financial status were considered in prior studies: past ROE and debt leverage. Zahra et al. (2000b) concluded that past ROE was not significantly associated with the status of internationalization (internationalized vs. not). Past ROE was positively but marginally associated with the speed and degree of sales internationalization. In terms of financial leverage, Bloodgood et al. (1996) reported a non-significant association with the degree of internationalization, raising a question about the potential contribution of past performance to new ventures' internationalization. Perhaps the results are unique to the samples examined to date. Alternatively, financial performance may not play a key role in explaining the internationalization of new ventures' sales. That is, regardless of their financial position, some new ventures expand internationally to achieve a variety of strategic goals. Given that only a few studies have been conducted on this issue to date, however, it would be premature to drop indicators of past financial performance from future studies of international entrepreneurship.

In summary, consistent with long-established tradition in the strategic management field, past empirical research has attempted to gauge the influence of several organizational variables on international entrepreneurship. Some key organizational variables are TMT characteristics, firm resources, and firm-level variables such as size, age, location, origin, growth orientation, environmental scanning, and financial strength. However, as the list of variables examined would suggest, a coherent theoretical framework that explains the potential influence of these variables on internationalization is lacking. Table 12.3b also shows that many of these studies do not provide statistically significant support for these relationships. It is possible that external environmental factors play a more significant role in international entrepreneurship and may serve to lessen the effects of organizational factors on international entrepreneurship. Therefore, we now examine research that links a firm's external environment to its international entrepreneurial activities.

Influence of the external environment on international entrepreneurship

Strategic management and entrepreneurship researchers have long acknowledged the importance of the external environment on a firm's various strategic choices (Boyd, Dess, and Rasheed, 1993; Zahra and Bogner, 2000). Consequently, researchers have explored the effect of a firm's external environment on different aspects of international entrepreneurship. Past empirical studies that have investigated these issues appear in table 12.4. These results suggest that new ventures that internationalize their operations early in their life cycles compete in industries that are perceived as being different in their attributes from those where new ventures do not internationalize as quickly or as broadly. Table 12.4 also shows that the characteristics of a new venture's major industry may determine the gains to be made from internationalization (Roberts and Senturia, 1996; Zahra, Neubaum, and Huse, 1996). That is, the characteristics of the industry may significantly moderate the relationship between international entrepreneurship and the financial gains from these activities, as found by Zahra and Garvis (2000).

One has to be cautious in interpreting prior results on the effect of the environment on international entrepreneurship and a firm's future gains from international

Table 12.4 Influence of the external environment on international entrepreneurship

Variables	Findings
Intensity of domestic competition	• No differences between international and purely domestic new venture; sign is positive (McDougall, 1989). • Domestic market saturation was mentioned by only 26% of responding firms as a motivation for internationalization (Karagozoglu and Lindell, 1998).
Limited domestic growth	• Case studies showed the limited growth of domestic markets was a major reason for the rapid internationalization of high-technology new ventures (Coviello and Munro, 1995). • Insufficiency of domestic sales to achieve competitive levels of R&D was key motivation to internationalization, as mentioned by 35% of responding companies (Karagozoglu and Lindell, 1998).
Intensity of international competition	• International new ventures competed in industries that exhibited significantly higher levels of international competition (McDougall, 1989). • Case studies showed that intensity of global competition in the industry was one important factor in explaining the rapid internationalization of high-technology new firms (Coviello and Munro, 1995).
Restrictive government policies	• International new ventures competed in industries that exhibited significantly higher levels of governmental protection and regulations (McDougall, 1989).
Institutional environment	• Institutional environments significantly influence international entrepreneurship (Mitchell et al., 2000). • Institutional structures in emerging economies facilitate entrepreneurship through effective governance mechanisms (George and Prabhu, 2000).
Economies of scale	• No differences between international and purely domestic new venture; sign is positive (McDougall, 1989).
Retaliation by industry incumbents	• No differences between international and purely domestic new venture; sign is positive (McDougall, 1989).
Industry gross profits	• Is negatively and significantly associated with degree of internationalization (Bloodgood et al., 1996).
Industry sales growth	• Positively (not significant) associated with degree of internationalization (Bloodgood et al., 1996).
Type of Industry	• Service firms tended to internationalize less than manufacturing firms (Burgel and Murray, 1998; Westhead et al., 1998).

entrepreneurship. Only a limited number of studies have explored this issue to date, as becomes evident from reviewing table 12.4. Prior studies have also focused primarily on high-technology industries, probably because these industries have experienced the highest rates of growth in the formation of new ventures. Low technology, both in manufacturing and service industries, has not received as much interest in international entrepreneurship research, raising the possibility that past findings do not generalize equally well to all economic sectors.

Researchers also have failed to examine the specific attributes of the environment on international entrepreneurship variables. This is evident in those studies that collected data from single industries in an effort to control for industry variability. This measurement strategy overlooks the possibility that managers within the same industry may view their environments quite differently, which would lead to significant differences in international entrepreneurship. The same variables may also have different implications for internationalization and the gains to be achieved from this strategy at different points in time in the life of a given industry. Also, different segments of the same industry also may experience significant forces of competition, leading to significant differences in international entrepreneurship patterns and outcomes. Finally, researchers have been inconsistent in measuring industry attributes (whether objective or perceived), making it difficult to compare findings across studies and discern clear patterns in prior results. Other researchers have expressed a similar concern about strategic management research (Boyd et al., 1993) and suggested controlling for industry variables (Dess, Ireland, and Hitt, 1990). We believe that international entrepreneurship researchers would benefit significantly from using these recommendations in designing future empirical studies.

The above observations urge greater caution in interpreting prior research results on the relationships between the characteristics of a firm's business environment and international entrepreneurship. These studies also call attention to the need for greater and better theoretically grounded research. One issue that has escaped attention to date is the configuration of international entrepreneurship activities across business environments. Past researchers have examined individual international entrepreneurship dimensions while ignoring the overall configurations of these activities and their implications for a company's performance. Past research ignores the possibility that the payoff from international entrepreneurship might be determined by the trade-offs or synergies that might exist among these activities.

Influence of strategic factors on international entrepreneurship

International entrepreneurship researchers also have examined the effect of a company's competitive strategies on international entrepreneurship. Therefore, in table 12.5, we summarize the key strategy variables used in prior research and their influence on a firm's international entrepreneurship. Table 12.5 suggests that these variables cover generic strategies, functional strategies, and entry strategy. Below we discuss each of these variables in turn.

Generic strategies Researchers propose that a firm's competitive strategy can spur its international entrepreneurship. Consequently, prior studies have attempted to relate

Table 12.5 Influence of strategic factors on international entrepreneurship

Variables	Findings
Generic strategy	
• Low cost	• Case analyses suggested that product differentiation was important for rapid internationalization (Oviatt and McDougall, 1995).
• Differentiation	• Product differentiation is positively associated with degree of internationalization (Bloodgood et al., 1996).
	• Unique product is important for internationalization (Fontes and Coombs, 1997).
	• R&D spending positively and significantly associated with international collaborative relationships which were positively and significantly associated with absolute annual international sales growth (Autio et al., 1997).
	• Product quality is conducive to internationalization that is achieved through networks (Holmlund and Kock, 1998).
Functional strategy	• International new ventures emphasized a distribution and marketing strategy less than domestic ventures (McDougall, 1989).
• Production	• Firms that had the majority of their customers located in the same country as those measured six years earlier were significantly less likely to export (Westhead et al., 1998).
• Distribution	• Product attributes may have important implications for the pace of new ventures' internationalization (Roberts and Senturia, 1996).
• Marketing	• Production competence was conducive to internationalization (Holmlund and Kock, 1996).
	• A negative sign (marginally significant) between marketing differentiation and degree of internationalization (Bloodgood et al., 1996).
Entry strategy	• International new ventures emphasized grand entry scale significantly more than domestic ventures (McDougall, 1989).
	• Firms that targeted niche markets composed of advanced clients were prepared to internationalize (Fontes and Coombs, 1997).
	• Technology alliances by entrepreneurial firms affected by national culture (Steensma et al., 2000).

low-cost strategy and differentiation strategy to internationalization. Past studies found that unique products and product differentiation were positively related to internationalization (Bloodgood et al., 1996; Fontes and Coombs, 1997), thereby highlighting the importance of intangible factors in explaining international entrepreneurship. These findings are consistent with the resource-based theory of the firm, indicating that unique resources can intensify and expedite a firm's international expansion. Also, Autio et al. (1997) emphasized the importance of R&D spending and international collaborative relationships, which were conducive to internationalization. Zahra et al. (2000b) noted that such relationships could give new ventures the knowledge and resources that can expedite international expansion.

Functional strategies Researchers also emphasized production, distribution, and marketing functions and their relationships with international entrepreneurship. Roberts and Senturia (1996) underscored the importance of product attributes such as uniqueness and customization, while Holmlund and Kock (1998) highlighted the importance of production competence for international entrepreneurship. However, McDougall (1989) and Bloodgood et al. (1996) found that international new ventures de-emphasize a distribution and marketing strategy.

Entry strategy International new ventures have also been profiled for their entry strategy. McDougall (1989) found that international new ventures have emphasized a large-scale entry strategy significantly more than small ventures. Fontes and Coombs (1997) related the composition of their clientele with internationalization in a niche market. Also, Beamish (1999) theorized that different types of alliances are an appropriate mode of entry choices for international entrepreneurship. Still, more empirical work is needed in this area, especially with regard to entrepreneurial firms.

To date, only a handful of studies have connected competitive strategy variables to international entrepreneurship. The selection of the variables, however, does not appear to follow established theories, even though comprehensive reviews of these theories are easily accessible (Carroll, 1993; Teece et al., 1997; Williamson, 1999). Most prior studies have not linked entry strategies to non-financial gains to be achieved through internationalization such as knowledge and learning. The paucity of prior empirical studies and lack of theoretical grounding also suggest a need to further explore these relationships within an integrated and coherent framework. We broadly categorized past studies into generic, functional, and entry strategies. Clearly, opportunities for future scholarly inquiry abound.

Toward an Integrated Model of International Entrepreneurship

In this section, we propose a model of international entrepreneurship that is consistent with our previously stated definition and review of the literature. As already noted, past research shows a need to develop an integrative framework that can serve as a foundation for future theory building and testing of international entrepreneurship. Figure 12.1 presents a proposed integrative framework.

The model includes three sets of factors that we believe to influence international

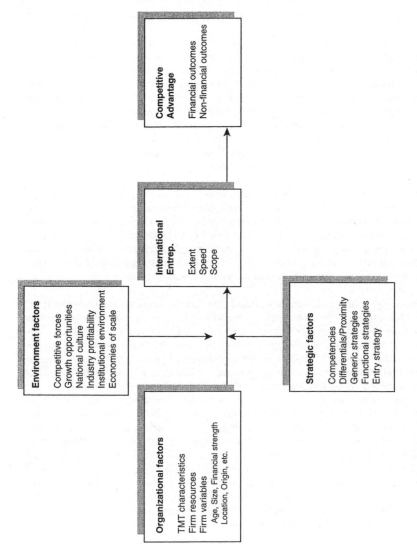

Figure 12.1   An integrated model of international entrepreneurship

entrepreneurship. It indicates that organizational factors significantly influence a firm's drive to internationalize and therefore are modeled as antecedents of international entrepreneurship, which supports the research summarized in tables 12.3a and 12.3b. These organizational factors include the TMT, firm resources, and firm-related variables (such as age, size, financial strength, location, and origin). Given the formative stage of this stream of research, our list of organizational variables is meant to be representative rather than exhaustive. As research on international entrepreneurship grows, scholars are likely to identify additional organizational variables that significantly determine a firm's drive to internationalize.

Consistent with previous work, figure 12.1 suggests that international entrepreneurship is multidimensional. Figure 12.1 highlights three dimensions of international entrepreneurship: extent, speed, and scope (table 12.2). These three dimensions reveal different facets of international entrepreneurship. Extent would imply the dependence of the firm on international revenues or the number of new markets that a firm has entered. Speed signifies the rate at which the firm enters new markets. Scope could be geographic scope wherein we can possibly consider the economic regions as the unit of analysis or product scope, where we consider the breadth of the product mix that has been effectively internationalized. These dimensions are by no means exhaustive but they provide an adequate launching point for future work.

Next, we list strategic and environmental factors as potential moderators of the relationship between organizational factors and international entrepreneurship dimensions. The strategy literature suggests that a firm's general and task environments significantly influence the motivation or the rate of internationalization (Hitt, Hoskisson, and Kim, 1997). Within the strategic set, we include two variables that were not present in our synthesis of past research. First, we believe that firm competencies are likely to be moderators. Firms that have particular competencies, say in production, can effectively or quickly transfer such capabilities to international markets. These companies, therefore, stand to achieve greater gains from their international expansion. Next, we use the term "differentials" or "proximity" to suggest the amount of difference between the home market and emerging opportunities. These differentials could be, for example, in market practices. For example, distribution systems differ greatly between countries and therefore influence certain dimensions of international entrepreneurship. Other differentials could be in national culture, customer profiles, and habits, among others. The other variables, including generic, functional, and entry strategies listed as potential moderators, have been discussed in the review section (table 12.5).

Though one could argue that environmental factors and strategic factors overlap, we make the distinction in the interest of parsimony and clarity. Environmental factors included in the proposed model are competitive forces (number of competitors, bargaining power, etc.), growth opportunities (rate of market growth, countries with open markets, etc.), regulatory environment, industry profitability, institutional environment, and economies of scale (table 12.4). These factors will act as moderators and determine the strength of the relationship between organizational variables and international entrepreneurship dimensions discussed above. Organizational variables (e.g. senior management's international experience) might affect international entrepreneurship quite differently in different levels of environmental uncertainty (Carpenter and Frederickson, 2001). Research from strategic management highlights the

278   Shaker A. Zahra, Gerard George

contingent nature of these relationships (Finkelstein and Hambrick, 1996). In particular, the strategic choice approach suggests that certain organizational characteristics may promote (or inhibit) international entrepreneurship activities in different business environments. Thus, a moderating relationship is appropriate when considering the effects of strategic and environmental factors on international entrepreneurship.

Finally, we suggest a set of outcomes from international entrepreneurship. These include outcomes such as financial and non-financial performance indicators. Past empirical research in international entrepreneurship has provided inconclusive results regarding the link between international entrepreneurship and performance. For example, Bloodgood et al. (1996) found a positive and marginally significant relationship between international entrepreneurship and firm income. Whereas Zahra and Garvis (2000) found no relationship between international entrepreneurship and return on assets, McDougall and Oviatt (1996) reported a non-significant relationship. Consequently, future studies would benefit by relating international entrepreneurship to multiple indicators of a company's financial performance. Moreover, few past studies have related international entrepreneurship to non-financial performance. Oviatt and McDougall (1995) connected international entrepreneurship to market share, while Zahra et al. (2000a) related international entrepreneurship to technological learning and acquisition of new knowledge. The importance of non-financial outcomes of international entrepreneurship suggests a need to apply multiple measures to further improve future research in this area.

Future Research in International Entrepreneurship

Our review and analysis suggest that there are tremendous opportunities for research in international entrepreneurship. More recent work in this area has helped provide visibility and underscore the importance of this emerging research stream. Our definition, however, expands the domain of international entrepreneurship to include both new and corporate ventures. By doing so, we hope to expand the boundaries of and domain of the international entrepreneurship phenomenon, providing greater opportunities for discovery and integration. Also, we hope international entrepreneurship scholars draw from the entrepreneurship, strategic management, and IB literatures, thereby enhancing the theoretical rigor and significance of their research. In this section, we outline three areas that may position international entrepreneurship as a prominent and productive research stream: the international entrepreneurship process, the context of international entrepreneurship, and post-internationalization agenda. Below we discuss these issues in turn.

The international entrepreneurship process

The fundamental questions in this area are: "*How, why, and when do entrepreneurial firms discover and exploit opportunities outside their home country?*" These questions raise several interesting secondary research issues. The first issue includes those factors that may influence the firm's desire to search for opportunities beyond its domestic market. Some of these factors have been introduced in our proposed model (figure

12.1). These factors may include TMT characteristics such as ability, exposure, and composition, among others. Managers' creativity and insights may also contribute to this process. Also, factors such as unused or slack firm resources that could be more effectively utilized in alternate market environments. Similarly, financial strength allows the firm the requisite latitude to take calculated risks to expand its market opportunities.

A second research issue involves the characteristics of internationalized firms. We illustrate with the issue of firm size and age. Though past research predominantly considers age as a significant factor in internationalization, it does not necessarily illustrate how age matters in the international entrepreneurship process. To remedy this situation, we suggest going beyond the use of age and size as control variables to address more creative research issues. These issues may include conducting research that determines if small new ventures adopt different strategies than larger corporate ventures. If so, the next step would be to uncover the reasons behind these differences, using traditional theoretical frameworks such as transaction cost economics or resource-based view, to suggest the constraints, benefits, and different configurations adopted by these ventures in the international entrepreneurship process.

Researchers studying new ventures should also recognize that major changes occur in firms' resource and skill base even during the early years of their life cycles. As aptly illustrated by Bantel (1998), for example, startup and adolescent new ventures might adopt different strategies. Presently, it is not clear if and how these differences extend to international entrepreneurship. Future researchers, therefore, would benefit from taking these key organizational transitions as they examine new ventures' international entrepreneurship activities.

A third future research issue centers on the dimensions of international entrepreneurship. We suggest a need to examine the three dimensions of international entrepreneurship: extent, speed, and scope. Though few studies have sought to link firm characteristics to international entrepreneurship dimensions, considerably more work is required in this area. Future research may attempt to better understand the theoretical underpinning of differential relationships between top management, resources, and firm characteristics and international entrepreneurship dimensions. For example, researchers could examine firm-level conditions under which international entrepreneurship is speedier or more geographically dispersed using, say, resource dependence or product life cycle arguments. Future empirical studies along these lines would greatly enhance our understanding of international entrepreneurship processes.

We have proposed a definition of international entrepreneurship as a process of creatively identifying and exploiting opportunities in markets that lie outside the firm's domestic operations. This definition raises additional research questions that center on the sources of creativity associated with opportunity recognition in international markets. These sources may include managerial insights, experience, connections and contacts, network relationships, and informal and formal industry analyses. Sources also include the types of information sources firms use to spot these opportunities, and the approaches companies use to exploit opportunities in international markets. Are these processes shaped by industry conditions? What role does national culture play in this regard (Kogut and Singh, 1988)? How and when are these processes institutionalized? What types of organizational learning occur in and through these processes? How does this learning influence the future entrepreneurial activities of the firm? These and similar questions serve to highlight the range of theoretical and empirical issues that can (and perhaps should) be investigated in future international entrepreneurship research.

The context of international entrepreneurship

The fundamental question here is: "*What contextual factors influence the internationalization of entrepreneurial firms?*" By context of internationalization, we mean those conditions that make internationalization more attractive or lucrative than solely domestic operations. It is critical for future research to account for the context within which international entrepreneurship occurs. We list several environmental and strategic variables within our integrative framework that may guide future work in international entrepreneurship (figure 12.1).

A key research issue concerns the major environmental factors affecting international entrepreneurship. There are other significant factors that merit attention in international entrepreneurship, including industry characteristics, country institutional and regulatory environments, among others (figure 12.1). This area is virtually unexplored because of the number of combinations of factors that can help explain international entrepreneurship. For example, the role of institutions in fostering entrepreneurship and internationalization of these ventures has not been investigated. Recent theoretical work suggests that certain types of institutions provide opportunities for firms to develop their networks and attract international partnerships for expansion (George and Prabhu, 2000). Unexplored areas also include industry characteristics and internationalization processes since many past studies have used small samples.

A second important research issue involves strategic variables that influence international entrepreneurship. Figure 12.1 indicates that firm competencies, strategic differentials, generic, functional, and entry strategies influence international entrepreneurship. How competencies moderate the relationship between organizational factors (such as firm resources) and international entrepreneurship dimensions (such as scope) is an interesting question to explore. Similarly, strategic differentials between home market practices and foreign markets are likely to moderate the relationship between firm resources and the speed of internationalization. Research that explores these issues could develop strong theoretical arguments based on the cognition or industrial-organization literatures.

Post-internationalization processes and outcomes

The fundamental question in this area is "*What happens after internationalization?*" The importance of this area and its overlap with strategy literature is derived primarily on the basis of firm performance. Yet, to date, there are few studies that have explored the relationship between international entrepreneurship and performance, with inconclusive and contradictory results. Our proposed definition of international entrepreneurship suggests that entrepreneurial firms enter international markets in the pursuit of opportunities that lead to competitive advantage that position them to create wealth.

Future research should explore the links between international entrepreneurship and competitive advantage or financial and non-financial performance outcomes.

Similarly, we know little about what these firms do after they enter new markets and how they remain entrepreneurial in their approach. Figure 12.1 suggests a direct link between dimensions of international entrepreneurship and performance, implying a certain set of combinations in which international entrepreneurship may be related to performance. For example, first mover advantages (Mascarenhas, 1997) would suggest that international entrepreneurship speed would be related to competitive advantage while extent of internationalization may be related to non-financial outcomes such as organizational learning or multiple locations of value chain components to reduce transaction costs. Future research can help improve our understanding of these interesting but complex issues.

An area that demands research attention is the type of competitive advantages new ventures vs. established firms gain as they go international. These firms may pursue different goals and utilize different approaches in internationalizing their operations. If this is true, new ventures and established companies might gain very different types of advantages in their global markets. These advantages have implications for firm survival and effective performance. Research into such potential differences would be helpful.

Researchers have begun to examine the effect of international entrepreneurship variables on the non-financial measures of firm performance. Given the few studies completed to date, we do not know the extent to which international entrepreneurship contributes to organizational learning. In particular, we do not know if international entrepreneurship affects a firm's social (Sohn, 1994), technological (Zahra et al., 2000a), or other types of learning (Leonard-Barton, 1995). A noteworthy issue to explore in future studies is whether international entrepreneurship enables established companies to overcome myopia of learning (Levinthal and March, 1993). A related question that requires research attention is whether new ventures have a learning advantage over established companies in international entrepreneurship activities, as has been argued recently in the literature (Autio et al., 2000). The effect of entry strategies on different types of learning is another issue that deserves further attention.

Entrepreneurship (Autio et al., 1997; Larson, 1991; Lipparini and Sobrero, 1994), strategy (Gulati, 1998; Jarrilo, 1988; Keil, Autio, and Robertson, 1997), and IB (Welch and Welch, 1996) have highlighted the importance of networks for successful organizational performance. Some past work has recognized the important role of networks for international entrepreneurship (Autio et al., 1997; Zahra et al., 2000b). Future research should explore the link between networks and international entrepreneurship and how this link affects the speed, scope, and extent of internationalization. Given the diversity of networks that might prevail in an industry, it is especially important to connect the types of resources and information that exist and international entrepreneurship (Hara and Kanai, 1994). Of interest is the effect of networks on a firm's reputation and how this reputation allows the firm to pursue international entrepreneurship opportunities. Reputation is an important strategic asset (Fombrun, 1994; Hall, 1993), especially for young entrepreneurial companies (Bell and McNamara, 1991). A favorable reputation, connection to powerful and established networks, and other invisible assets can profoundly influence the ways companies proceed to position themselves (Itami and Roehl, 1987), especially in foreign markets.

Finally, we need to stress the importance of methodology in future empirical research. As noted earlier, our review indicates a sample bias in many studies. Past studies sampled high-technology firms with little emphasis on traditional industries, or had small sample sizes that may not be entirely representative of the industry. A primary reason is the scarcity of good data. By expanding the domain and providing a framework, we, however, encourage future researchers to include multiple data sources and address issues of sample representativeness. For instance, researchers can access industry- and country-level data from established secondary data sources. Future studies could also be improved by using surveys by partnering with research colleagues in different countries. Such data collection methods would permit drawing generalizable and well-supported conclusions that can improve managerial practice in multiple countries. Second, further work may explore internationalization and successes using longitudinal data and therefore address issues of causality and temporal stability (Sexton et al., 2000). Longitudinal studies of international entrepreneurship processes are especially lacking. Longitudinal studies also allow us to better explain the significance of the results and the relationship between international entrepreneurship variables and future company performance, if any.

In summary, we have highlighted multiple avenues for future scholarly work. We suggest three broad overlapping areas for future research; namely, the process, context, and post-internationalization outcomes of international entrepreneurship. We have also offered examples of how such research would benefit and expand the knowledge that we presently have about international entrepreneurship. Past work has helped us develop a model that we used to suggest specific directions for future research (figure 12.1). We believe that there are numerous opportunities available for further inquiry into international entrepreneurship and hope that scholars will systematically address these issues.

Conclusion

International entrepreneurship is a growing and important research stream, one that offers great opportunities for scholars to employ and integrate theories from multiple disciplines and draw on established theoretical frameworks. Changes in the competitive environment and the interdependence of the global economy make internationalization attractive to entrepreneurial firms. Yet, little is known about the process, context, and outcomes of such internationalization. As our review makes clear, there are several opportunities to conduct meaningful research that both can enrich the development of theory and have significant implications for practicing managers.

In this chapter, we have sought to achieve four objectives. First, we have attempted to expand the definition and domain of international entrepreneurship. Second, we have reviewed past research to identify and consolidate factors that may affect international entrepreneurship. Third, we have advanced an integrative framework that links factors affecting international entrepreneurship and their outcomes. Finally, we also have provided specific directions and suggestions for the future scholarly pursuit of international entrepreneurship. We hope that this chapter and our proposed framework of international entrepreneurship will increase future research in this young but interesting area of the literature.

Notes

The authors gratefully acknowledge the support of the Kauffman Center for Entrepreneurial Leadership as well as the comments of the SMS-Kauffman conference participants. The constructive comments of the editors, especially Michael Hitt, have also improved this chapter significantly. We have received many helpful suggestions from seminar participants in Helsinki University of Technology, Jonkoping International Business School, and Norwegian School of Management.

References

Almeida, J. G. and Bloodgood, J. M. 1996. Internationalization of new ventures: Implications of the value chain. *Frontiers of entrepreneurship research* [electronic edition].

Autio, E., Sapienza, H. J., and Almeida, J. G. 2000. Effects of age at entry, knowledge intensity, and imitability on international growth. *Academy of Management Journal*, 43(5): 909–24.

Autio, E., Yli-Renko, H., and Salonen, A. 1997. International growth of young technology-based firms: A resource-based network model. *Journal of Enterprising Culture*, 5(1): 57–73.

Bantel, K. A. 1998. Technology-based "adolescent" firm configurations: Strategy identification, context, and performance. *Journal of Business Venturing*, 13: 205–30.

Barkema, H. G. and Vermeulen, F. 1998. International expansion through start-up or acquisition: A learning perspective. *Academy of Management Journal*, 41: 7–26.

Barney, J. B. 1991. Firm resources and sustained competitive advantage. *Journal of Management*, 17(1): 9–120.

Bartlett, C. A. and Ghoshal, S. 2000. *Transnational management*. 3rd edn. New York: McGraw Hill.

Beamish, P. 1999. The role of alliances in international entrepreneurship. In R. Wright (ed.), *Research in global strategic management*, 7: 43–61.

Bell, C. and McNamara, J. 1991. *High-tech ventures: The guide for entrepreneurial success*. Reading, MA: Addison-Wesley.

Bell, J. 1995. The internationalization of small computer software firms: A further challenge to stage theories. *European Journal of Marketing*, 29(8): 60–75.

Birkinshaw, J. 1997. Entrepreneurship in multinational corporations: The characteristics of subsidiary initiatives. *Strategic Management Journal*, 18: 207–29.

Bloodgood, J. M., Sapienza, H. J. and Almeida, J. G. 1996. The internationalization of new high-potential US ventures: Antecedents and outcomes. *Entrepreneurship Theory and Practice*, 20(4): 61–76.

Boyd, B. K., Dess, G. G., and Rasheed, A. M. A. 1993. Divergence between archival and perceptual measures of the environment: Causes and consequences. *Academy of Management Review*, 18: 204–26.

Brush, C. G. 1993. Factors motivating small companies to internationalize: The effect of firm age. *Entrepreneurship Theory and Practice*, 17(3): 83–4.

Brush, C. G. 1995. International entrepreneurship: The effect of firm age on motives for internationalization. In Stuart Bruchey (ed.), *Garland studies in entrepreneurship*. New York: Garland.

284   Shaker A. Zahra, Gerard George

Burgel, O. and Murray, G. C. 1998. The international activities of British start-up companies in high-technology industries: Differences between internationalisers and non-internationalisers. In P. D. Reynolds, W. D. Byrave, N. M. Carter, S. Manigart, C. M. Mason, G. Meyer and K. Shaver (eds), *Frontiers of entrepreneurship research*. Babson Park, MA: Babson College, 447–63.

Burgelman, R. A. and Sayles, L. R. 1986. *Inside corporate innovation: Strategy, structure, and managerial skills*. New York: Free Press.

Calof, J. and Beamish, P. 1994. The right attitude for international success. *Business Quarterly*, Autumn, 105–10.

Carpenter, M. A. and Fredrickson, J. W. 2001. Top management teams, global strategic posture, and the moderating role of uncertainty. *Academy of Management Journal*, in press.

Carpenter, M. A., Sanders, W., and Gregersen, H. 2001. Bundling human capital with organizational context: The impact of international assignment experience on multinational firm performance and CEO pay. *Academy of Management Journal*, in press.

Carroll, G. R. 1993. A sociological view on why firms differ. *Strategic Management Journal*, 14: 237–50.

Clark, T. and Mallory, G. 1997. The impact of strategic choice on the internationalisation of the firm. In George Chryssochoidis, Carla Millar, and Jeremy Clegg (eds), *Internationalisation strategies*. New York: St. Martin's Press, 193–206.

Collis, D. J. and Montgomery, C. A. 1995. Competing on resources: Strategy in the 1990s. *Harvard Business Review*, 73(4): 118–28.

Coviello, N. E. and Munro, H. J. 1995. Growing the entrepreneurial firm: Networking for international market development. *European Journal of Marketing*, 29(7): 49–61.

Craig, C. S. and Douglas, S. P. 1996. Developing strategies for global markets: An evolutionary perspective. *Columbia Journal of World Business*, 31(1): 70–81.

Daily, C. M., Certo, S. T., and Dalton, D. R. (2000). International experience in the executive suite: The path to prosperity? *Strategic Management Journal*, 21: 515–23.

Davidsson, P. and Wiklund, J. 2000. Conceptual and empirical challenges in the study of firm growth. In D. Sexton and H. Landstrom (eds), *Handbook of entrepreneurship*. Oxford, UK: Blackwell.

Dess, G. G., Ireland, D., and Hitt, M. (1990). Industry effects and strategic management research. *Journal of Management*, 16: 7–27.

Dunning, J. H. 1988. The eclectic paradigm of international production: A restatement and some possible extensions. *Journal of International Business Studies*, 19(1): 1–31.

Finkelstein, S. and Hambrick, D. C. 1996. *Strategic leadership: Top executives and their effects on organizations*. Minneapolis, MN: West Publishing.

Fombrun, C. 1994. *Reputation: Realizing value from the corporate image*. Boston: Harvard Business School Press.

Fontes, M. and Coombs, R. 1997. The coincidence of technology and market objectives in the internationalisation of new technology-based firms. *International Small Business Journal*, 15(4): 14–35.

Fujita, M. 1995. Small and medium-sized transnational corporations: Salient features *Small Business Economics*, 7: 251–71.

George, G. and Prabhu, G. 2000. Developmental financial institutions as catalysts of entrepreneurship in emerging economies, *Academy of Management Review*, 25(3): 620–30.

Giamartino, G. A., McDougall, P. P., and Bird, B. J. 1993. International entrepreneurship: The state of the field. *Entrepreneurship Theory and Practice*, 18(1): 37.

Grant, R. M. 1991. The resource-based theory of competitive advantage: Implications for strategy formulation. *California Management Review*, 33(3): 114–35.

Grant, R. M. 1996. Prospering in dynamically-competitive environments: Organizational capability as knowledge integration. *Organization Science,* 7: 375–87.

Grant, R. M. 1998. *Contemporary Strategy Analysis,* 3rd edn. Malden, MA: Blackwell.

Gulati, R. 1998. Alliances and networks. *Strategic Management Journal,* 19 (special issue): 293–317.

Hall, R. 1993. A framework linking intangible resources and capabilities to sustainable competitive advantage. *Strategic Management Journal,* 14(8): 607–18.

Hambrick, D. C. 1981. Strategic awareness within top management teams. *Strategic Management Journal,* 2 (3): 263–79.

Hamel, G. and Prahalad, C. K. 1994. *Competing for the future.* Boston: Harvard Business School Press.

Hara, G. and Kanai, T. 1994. Entrepreneurial networks across oceans to promote international strategic alliances for small businesses. *Journal of Business Venturing,* 9(6): 489–507.

Haug, P. 1991. Survey evidence on the international operations of high tech firms. *Management International Review,* 31(1): 63–77.

Hisrich, R., Honig-Haftel, S., McDougall, P., and Oviatt, B. 1996. International entrepreneurship: Past, present and future. *Entrepreneurship Theory and Practice,* 20(4): 5.

Hitt, M. A. and Bartkus B. 1997. International entrepreneurship. In J. Katz (ed.), *Advances in entrepreneurship, firm emergence and growth,* Greenwich, CT: JAI Press, 3: 7–30.

Hitt, M. A., Hoskisson, R. E., and Ireland, R. D. 1994. A mid-range theory of the interactive effects of international and product diversification on innovation and performance. *Journal of Management,* 20(2): 297–326.

Hitt, M. A., Hoskisson, R. E., and Kim, H. 1997. International diversification: Effects on innovation and firm performance in product-diversified firms. *Academy of Management Journal,* 40: 767–98.

Hitt, M. A., Tyler, B. B., Hardee, C., and Park, D. 1995. Understanding strategic intent in the global marketplace. *Academy of Management Executive,* 9(2): 12–19.

Holmlund, M. and Kock, S. 1998. Relationships and the internationalisation of Finnish small and medium-sized companies. *International Small Business Journal,* 16(4): 46–63.

Hymer, S. H. 1976. *The international operations of national firms: A study of foreign direct investment.* Cambridge, MA: MIT Press.

Itami, H. and Roehl, T. W. 1987. *Mobilizing invisible assets.* Cambridge, MA: Harvard University Press.

Jarillo, J. C. 1988. On strategic networks. *Strategic Management Journal,* 9(1): 31–41.

Johanson, J. and Vahlne, J.-E. 1977. The internationalization process of the firm - A model of knowledge development and increasing foreign market commitments. *Journal of International Business Studies,* 8(1): 23–32.

Karagozoglu, N. and Lindell, M. 1998. Internationalization of small and medium-sized technology-based firms: An exploratory study. *Journal of Small Business Management,* 36(1): 44–59.

Katz, J. and Gartner, W. 1988. Properties of emerging organizations. *Academy of Management Review,* 13(3): 429–41.

Keil, T., Autio, E. and Robertson, P. 1997. Embeddedness, power, control and innovation in the telecommunications sector. *Technology Analysis and Strategic Management,* 9(3): 299–316.

Kirzner, I. 1973. *Competition and entrepreneurship.* Chicago, IL: University of Chicago Press.

Kogut, B. and Singh, H. 1988. The effect of national culture on the choice of entry mode. *Journal of International Business Studies,* 19: 411–32.

Larson, A. 1991. Partner networks: Leveraging external ties to improve entrepreneurial performance. *Journal of Business Venturing,* 6(3): 173–88.

Leonard-Barton, D. 1995. *Wellsprings of Knowledge.* Boston: Harvard Business School Press.

Levinthal, D. A. and March, J. G. 1993. The myopia of learning. *Strategic Management Journal*, 14 (special issue): 95–112.

Lindqvist, M. 1991. Infant multinationals: The internationalization of young, technology-based Swedish firms. Unpublished doctoral dissertation, Stockholm School of Economics, Stockholm.

Lipparini, A. and Sobrero, M. 1994. The glue and the pieces: Entrepreneurship and innovation in small-firm networks. *Journal of Business Venturing*, 9(2): 125–40.

Lumpkin, G. and Dess, G. 1996. Clarifying the entrepreneurial orientation construct and linking it to performance. *Academy of Management Review*, 21(1): 135–72

Mascarenhas, B. 1997. The order and size of entry into international markets. *Journal of Business Venturing*, 12(4): 287–99.

McDougall, P. P. 1989. International versus domestic entrepreneurship: new venture strategic behavior and industry structure. *Journal of Business Venturing*, 4: 387–400.

McDougall, P. P. and Oviatt, B. M. 1996. New venture internationalization, strategic change, and performance: A follow-up study. *Journal of Business Venturing*, 11(1): 23–40

McDougall, P. P. and Oviatt, B. M. 2000. International entrepreneurship: The intersection of two paths. Guest Editor's Introduction, *Academy of Management Journal*, 43(5): 902–8.

McDougall, P. P., Shane, S., and Oviatt, B. M. 1994. Explaining the formation of international new ventures: The limits of theories from international business research. *Journal of Business Venturing*, 9(6): 469–87.

Miles, R. E. and Snow, C. C. 1978. *Organizational strategy, structure, and process*. New York: McGraw-Hill.

Miller, D. 1983. The correlates of entrepreneurship in three types of firms. *Management Science*, 29: 770–91.

Mitchell, R. K., Smith, B., Seawright, K., and Morse, E. A. 2000. Cross-cultural cognitions and venture creation decision. *Academy of Management Journal*, 43(5): 974–93.

Morrow, J. F. 1988. International entrepreneurship: A new growth opportunity. *New Management*, 3(5): 59–61.

Mößlang, A. 1995. Internationalization of service companies. *Management International Review*, 37(4): 387–404.

Oviatt, B. M. and McDougall, P. P. 1994. Toward a theory of international new ventures. *Journal of International Business Studies*, 25(1): 45–64.

Oviatt, B. M. and McDougall, P. P. 1995. Global start-ups: Entrepreneurs on a worldwide stage. *Academy of Management Executive*, 9(2): 30–43.

Oviatt, B. M. and McDougall, P. P. 1999. A framework for understanding accelerated international entrepreneurship. In R. Wright (ed.), *Research in global strategic management*, 7: 23–42.

Porter, M. E. 1986. Competition in global industries: A conceptual framework. In M. E. Porter (ed.), *Competition in global industries*. Boston: Harvard Business School Press, 15–60.

Reuber, A. R. and Fischer, E. 1997. The influence of the management team's international experience on the internationalization behaviors of SMEs. *Journal of International Business Studies*, 28(4): 807–25.

Roberts, E. B., and Senturia, T. A. 1996. Globalizing the emerging high-technology company. *Industrial Marketing Management*, 25(6): 491–506.

Sexton, D., Pricer, R., and Nenide, B. 2000. Measuring performance in high growth firms. Presented at the Babson-Kauffman conference, Babson Park, MA.

Shane, S. 1993. Cultural influences on national rates of innovation. *Journal of Business Venturing*, 8: 59–73.

Shane, S. and Venkataraman, S. 2000. The promise of entrepreneurship as a field of research. *Academy of Management Review*, 25(1): 217–26.

Shrader, R. and Simon, M. 1997. Corporate versus independent new ventures: Resource, strategy, and performance differences. *Journal of Business Venturing*, 12: 47–66.

Sohn, J. H. D. 1994. Social knowledge as a control system: A proposition and evidence from the Japanese FDI behavior. *Journal of International Business Studies*, 25: 295–324.

Steensma, K., Marino, L., Weaver, M., and Dickson, P. 2000. The influence of national culture in the formation of technology alliances by entrepreneurial firms. *Academy of Management Journal*, 43(5): 951–73.

Taylor, W. 1991. The logic of global business: An interview with ABB's Percy Barnevik. *Harvard Business Review*, 69(2): 91–105.

Teece, D. J., Pisano, G., and Shuen, A. 1997. Dynamic capabilities and strategic management. *Strategic Management Journal*, 18: 509–33.

Tiessen, J. H. and Merrilees, B. 1999. An entrepreneurial model of SME internationalization: Evidence from six cases. In R. Wright (ed.), *Research in Global Strategic Management*, 7: 131–57.

Vernon, R. 1979. The product cycle hypothesis in a new international environment, *Oxford Bulletin of Economics and Statistics*, 4, 255–67

Welch, D. E. and Welch, L. S. 1996. The internationalization process and networks: A strategic management perspective. *Journal of International Marketing*, 4(3): 11–28.

Westhead, P., Wright, M. and Ucbasaran, D. 1998. The internationalization of new and small firms. In P. D. Reynolds, W. D. Byrave, N. M. Carter, S. Manigart, C. M. Mason, G. D. Meyer and K. G. Shaver (eds), *Frontiers of entrepreneurship research 1998*. Babson Park, MA: Babson College, 464–77.

Williamson, O. E. 1999. Strategy research: Governance and competence perspectives. *Strategic Management Journal*, 20(12): 1087–8.

Wright, R. W. and Ricks, D. A. 1994. Trends in international business research: Twenty-five years later. *Journal of International Business Studies*, 25(4): 687–701.

Zacharakis, A. L. 1997. Entrepreneurial entry into foreign markets: A transaction cost perspective. *Entrepreneurship Theory and Practice*, 21: 23–40.

Zahra, S. 1991. Predictors and financial outcomes of corporate entrepreneurship: An exploratory study. *Journal of Business Venturing*, 6: 259–86.

Zahra, S. A. 1993. Conceptual model of entrepreneurship as firm behavior: A critique and extension. *Entrepreneurship Theory and Practice*, 14(4): 5–21.

Zahra, S. 1996. Technology strategy and performance. A study of corporate-sponsored and independent biotechnology ventures. *Journal of Business Venturing*, 11(4): 289–321.

Zahra, S. and Bogner, W. 2000. Technology strategy and software new venture performance: The moderating effect of the competitive environment. *Journal of Business Venturing*, 15(2): 135–73.

Zahra, S. and Covin, J. G. 1995. Contextual influences on the corporate entrepreneurship-performance relationship. A longitudinal analysis. *Journal of Business Venturing*, 10: 43–58.

Zahra, S. and Dess, G. 2001. Defining entrepreneurship as a scholarly field. *Academy of Management Review*, in press. (Dialogue)

Zahra, S. and Garvis, S. 2000. International corporate entrepreneurship and company performance: The moderating effect of international environmental hostility. *Journal of Business Venturing*, in press.

Zahra, S. A., Ireland, D. R., and Hitt, M. A. 2000a. International expansion by new venture firms: International diversity, mode of market entry, technological learning and performance. *Academy of Management Journal*, 43(5): 925–50.

Zahra, S. A., Jennings, D. F., and Kuratko, D. 1999. Guest Editors' Introduction: Corporate entrepreneurship in a global economy. *Entrepreneurship Theory and Practice*, 24(1): 5–8.

Zahra, S., Matherne, B. and Carleton, J. 2000b. Leveraging technological resources for com-

288   Shaker A. Zahra, Gerard George

petitive advantage: The case of Software New Ventures. Proceedings of the 2nd Annual McGill University Conference on Globalization, in press.

Zahra, S., Neubaum, D. and Huse, M. 1996. The effect of the environment on the firm's export intensity. *Entrepreneurship: Theory and Practice*, 1997, 22(1): 25–46.

Zahra, S., Nielsen, A. and Bogner, W. 1999. Corporate entrepreneurship, knowledge and competence development. *Entrepreneurship Theory and Practice*, 23(3): 169–89.

Zahra, S. and Schulte, W. 1994. International entrepreneurship: Beyond folklore and myth. *International Journal of Commerce and Management*, 4(1/2): 85–95.

Part II
New Ventures

[9]

The International Market Entry Choices of Start-Up Companies in High-Technology Industries

For a young, resource-constrained, technology-based start-up embarking on international sales, the choice of entry mode is a strategic decision of major importance. Yet within the emerging research stream of international entrepreneurship, curiously little attention has been devoted to the empirical analysis of foreign market entry forms. The authors address this important issue by analyzing the determinants of 398 export decisions taken from a U.K. survey of 246 technology-based start-ups with international activities. The findings show that the entry mode decision is necessarily a trade-off between the resources available and the support requirements of the customer. Issues of the innovativeness of the technology and the historic channel experience of the firm in its domestic market are particularly strong determinants of mode choice. The authors suggest that an organizational capability perspective on these firms' behavior offers a better explanation of their entry decisions than either transaction cost or stage theory.

ABSTRACT

During the past decade, the phenomenon of globalization has received considerable attention and has shaped both the discourse and the actions of managers, policymakers, and academics. Research on the topic is rooted primarily in sociology, cultural studies, political science, and economics. A common denominator is the definition of globalization as a process in which the constraints of geography on social, cultural, political, and economic arrangements recede (Waters 1995). One manifestation of a globalizing world is the emergence of entrepreneurial start-ups that have an international outlook from inception. Some of these firms even carry out different activities along their value chains in different countries and thereby blur the national identity of the firm. The international activities of these exceptional young firms—labeled "infant multinationals" (Lindqvist 1991), "born globals" (Knight and Cavusgil 1996; McKinsey & Company 1993), and "international new ventures" (Oviatt and McDougall 1994)—have received an increasing amount of attention from researchers over the past couple of years. Yet relatively little attention has been devoted to the empirical analysis of foreign entry modes. Most studies provide descriptive information on the chosen entry modes, but with the exception of Lindqvist (1991), Bell (1995), and Shrader, Oviatt, and Mc-Dougall (1997), few researchers have attempted to explain

Oliver Burgel and Gordon C. Murray

Submitted December 1998
Revised June 1999

© *Journal of International Marketing*
Vol 8, No 2, 2000, pp 33–62
ISSN 1069-031X

33

the choice of entry modes. This omission is even more surprising given that it is widely acknowledged that the initial foreign entry behavior of a young firm can be of major importance in its future economic success.

PREVIOUS RESEARCH IN INTERNATIONAL ENTREPRENEURSHIP

Empirical studies in international entrepreneurship have been both exploratory and, less frequently, explanatory in nature. Whereas some have had an explicit focus on international business theories, others have focused more on general performance issues. Qualitative studies have described product characteristics (Jolly, Alahuhta, and Jeannet 1992; Murray 1996; Roberts and Senturia 1996), market entry forms (Jolly, Alahuhta, and Jeannet 1992; McDougall, Shane, and Oviatt 1994; Roberts and Senturia 1996), and characteristics of founders and key employees (Boter and Holmquist 1996; McDougall, Shane, and Oviatt 1994; Murray 1996; Roberts and Senturia 1996). Quantitative studies we surveyed have analyzed structural characteristics of the firms, including age, size, and technology intensity (Lindell and Karagozoglou 1997; Lindqvist 1991), market entry forms (Bell 1995; Lindqvist 1991; Shrader, Oviatt, and McDougall 1997), geographic spread of foreign sales (Bell 1995; Shrader, Oviatt, and McDougall 1997), the relation between strategic orientation and growth/profitability (Bloodgood, Sapienza, and Almeida 1996; McDougall and Oviatt 1996; Shrader, Oviatt, and McDougall 1997), characteristics of founders and key employees (Bloodgood, Sapienza, and Almeida 1996), and the role of risk in internationalization decisions (Shrader, Oviatt, and McDougall 1997).

Three empirical studies that investigate entry modes in more detail stand out. Lindqvist (1991) reports that the preferred entry modes of the Swedish firms in her sample were direct exporting and foreign sales through intermediaries such as agents and distributors. However, she does not investigate the determinants that influence the choice of entry modes. Instead, she explores the propensity to use sales subsidiaries. Here, she finds no or weak relationships between entry mode choices and product characteristics, research and development (R&D) intensity, or market size. Lindqvist's findings suggest that internationalization could be understood as "jumping a threshold"; that is, when the firms have decided to operate internationally, their choice of entry modes is not influenced by structural characteristics, such as size and R&D intensity. In Bell's (1995) study of the international operations of Irish, Finnish, and Norwegian software firms, 70% of all sales transactions were carried out through either direct exports or agents and distributors. Few firms engaged in foreign direct investment, and when this did occur, they were preoccupied with setting up marketing and sales subsidiaries. Firms that commercialized highly customized products almost exclusively relied on direct exporting, whereas firms

Oliver Burgel and Gordon C. Murray

that sold standard, off-the-shelf products were more likely to use sales intermediaries. Shrader, Oviatt, and McDougall (1997) argue that different entry modes represent different degrees of resource commitment and therefore risk for the firm. They argue that firms actively manage their risk in international operations by balancing entry mode risk, country risk, and risk from overdependence of foreign markets. Their empirical findings on U.S. firms that high-risk countries were entered using low-risk/low-commitment market entry modes and vice versa support their theoretical argument.

Two theoretical articles analyze the structural aspects of international activities in more detail. Oviatt and McDougall (1994) examine international new ventures (INVs), a type of firm that "from inception, seeks to derive significant competitive advantage from the use of resources and the sale of outputs in multiple countries" (Oviatt and McDougall 1994, p. 49). They argue that sustainable INVs must have an innovative organizational structure—for example, assuming a controlling position in a network or using hybrid arrangements involving subcontractors and intermediate sellers. More directly related to the choice of entry mode, Zacharakis's (1997) contribution explicitly deals with the choice of export agents and distributors to enter international markets. Zacharakis only considers the use of intermediaries, because he claims that direct exporting is not an appropriate choice for start-ups. Given the wealth of studies on exporting (for a recent review, see Leonidou and Katsikeas 1996) and internationalization processes (Johanson and Vahlne 1990) that indicate that direct exporting is actually a widespread entry mode of small firms, we believe that Zacharakis's perspective is too constrained to capture the full scope of decisions that managers of a new venture will face.

These contributions represent important first steps in explaining the entry decisions of internationally operating start-ups. These studies have several common elements. The firms investigated predominantly operate in high-technology industries. In addition, the majority of the studies have an explicit focus on young firms. Findings from quantitative surveys agree that the preferred entry modes of technology-based start-ups are characterized by relatively low resource commitment and are directed toward commercialization rather than foreign production. However, they also report that technology-based start-ups have a tendency to enter several foreign markets within a short time span. Most articles based on a case study methodology include firms that made bold commitments to international operations during their early years. Rapid and sometimes resource-intensive market entries into different countries were described. Some extreme cases were international from inception and performed different activities along their value chains in different countries (McDougall, Shane, and Oviatt 1994). Together, these findings contrast previous research that examines the international activities of more traditional small and medium-sized enterprises (Bamberger and Evers 1994; Leonidou and Katsikeas 1996). However, they also leave questions about the determinants of the choice of a particular entry mode largely unaddressed. Acknowledging the dearth of empirical studies in this area, Oviatt and McDougall (1997) conclude that there is a need for further work to analyze the prevalence and determinants of international entrepreneurship.

RESEARCH OBJECTIVE AND HYPOTHESES

The purpose of this study was to use a large data set to determine what modes of foreign market entry our respondent firms chose and what were the primary reasons for their elected choices. The modeled entry decision was simplified to the choice of selling abroad either by direct exporting or through the use of distributors. Our reasons for this choice are both pragmatic and theoretically justified. First, we receive empirical support from previous studies, which report that exporting and the use of intermediaries are in reality the two predominant alternatives employed by entrepreneurial high-technology firms (Bell 1995; Lindqvist 1991). In short, our model mirrors what small firms actually do.

Second, the choice between direct exporting and the use of distributors is of utmost managerial relevance for technology entrepreneurs. With the singular exception of the U.S. economy, the finite market opportunities in many countries may not justify the development expenditures for certain highly specialized niche technologies unless international expansion is considered from inception. Technology-based start-ups therefore face a dangerous dilemma. On the one hand, they may be forced to venture abroad to help amortize their initial development expenditures and generate sufficient revenues to finance ongoing development activities. On the other hand, because many technology-based start-ups experience negative cash flows during their early years, they may lack the necessary human and financial resources required for the effective commercialization of their products on their own. Given these resource constraints, identifying end customers and providing pre- and after-sales support services may be handled better by a local partner. The downside of this arrangement is that revenues must be shared between the start-up and the distributor. Additional costs can be incurred by the start-up because of the need to provide technical training and the creation of incentives and monitoring mechanisms. Early on, technology entrepreneurs therefore must make complex and highly strategic trade-offs, because the choice of the foreign sales mode may have profound implications for both costs and revenue generation.

Third, the main theoretical frameworks in the field of international business that analyze entry modes come to different conclusions when they are applied to firms that at the same time are young (or inexperienced) and operate in high-technology sectors. Process models (Johanson and Vahlne 1977, 1990) consider commitment to internationalization a function of experiential knowledge of foreign markets. Accordingly, a start-up company would be expected to gain initial experience through reactive exporting before proactively venturing into foreign markets. The choice between direct exporting and the use of more complex and proactive entry modes thus depends on firm experience and foreign market knowledge. Despite having received empirical support, process models and the subsequently developed "stage models of internationalization" (e.g., Cavusgil 1980) are frequently criticized for being too deterministic and for failing to take firm-specific factors other than experience into account (Andersen 1993).

A rival approach, the transaction cost economics (TCE) approach, has been influential, as it provides a decision rule with regard to individual entry decisions. Firms are expected to choose the governance or entry mode that minimizes the costs of carrying out particular transactions. In its application, TCE is concerned with comparing different institutional arrangements for carrying out economic activity (Williamson 1985). As the choice between direct exporting and involving foreign distributors is essentially a choice between an internal arrangement and an arrangement involving an external third party, the tools of TCE are applicable to model the decision. Yet the TCE approach assumes a capacity for discretionary resource deployment. For example, the commercialization of a product incorporating advanced technology may require a high degree of asset specificity. If this asset specificity leads to high costs of involving a distributor, a firm is expected to switch from direct exporting to a sales subsidiary when its foreign sales to a particular country exceed a certain level. However, this option may not reflect the reality of resource constraint start-ups. They may rather be inclined, or obliged, to establish collaborative relationships with intermediaries to get access to assets, resources, and capabilities they do not own. Cooperation may not be a choice but an imperative for the young firm. The widespread use of collaborative strategies in technology-intensive industries has triggered the development of the organizational capability (OC) perspective. Its proponents argue that OC, compared with TCE, represents a superior approach for the analysis of collaborative governance arrangements (Madhok 1997). To date, we do not know of any study that has applied the OC perspective to the internationalization of smaller, entrepreneurial firms.

Start-Up Companies in High-Technology Industries

The key elements of these three competing internationalization theories (stage, TCE, and OC) can be isolated as separate and independent sets of variables in our decision model. Accordingly, they are incorporated in our hypothesis construction. The employment of an integrated multivariate approach should provide further evidence whether or not these sets of variables explain the choice of entry modes made by high-tech start-ups. Following established research practice, we have chosen the entry decision and not the firm as the unit of analysis. Similar to many other researchers, we argue that entry decisions are a function of firm-specific factors, product-specific factors, and target country–specific factors (Cavusgil, Zou, and Naidu 1993; Erramilli and Rao 1993). Essentially, the choice between direct exporting and sales through distributors is a choice between an internalized transaction or an externalized transaction involving intermediaries. We find ourselves within the established tradition of researchers that have conceptualized entry modes choices as binary (see, e.g., Barkema and Vermeulen 1998; Davidson and McFetridge 1985; Erramilli and Rao 1993; Kogut and Singh 1988). Accordingly, we develop a set of hypotheses to test which variables account for the choice between direct exporting and exporting through distributors as the two predominant modes of foreign market entry for technology-based start-ups.

Hypotheses

This discussion of our research objective leads to the generation of seven related or closely associated hypotheses pertaining to those factors that most instrumentally influence the choice of channel mode used in entering first foreign markets. As has already been stressed, the choice for the young firm of either going alone (direct exporting) or allying with a partner (using a distributor) is of pivotal strategic importance given the risk/reward implications of this decision. Direct exporting gives the firm autonomy and control but denies it the assets (including networks) and experience of the distributor. Alternatively, to contract with a distributor raises the sensitive issues of sharing profit margins. The latter is likely to be influenced by the distribution of bargaining power within the manufacturer–distributor relationship (Zacharakis 1997). From the local distributor's perspective, the smaller the foreign manufacturer and the lower the potential sales volume, the less profitable the medium-term relationship is. Below a certain projected sales volume, the decision to provide the service will not be bilateral but will, in practice, be solely that of the distributor. Aligning the objectives of the two parties has been studied widely in a domestic context (e.g., Anderson and Narus 1990; Heide and John 1994). Yet in a foreign country, the task of monitoring a distributor is likely to be even more difficult for a small entrepreneurial firm. Therefore, selling through an established distributor relationship is likely to require higher up-front investment than exporting. In the particular case of technology-based start-ups, the availability of resources is probably an even more crucial predictor of subsequent firm actions (Oakey, Rothwell, and Cooper 1988). Accordingly, we argue that this route to foreign markets will be employed by start-ups commanding greater resources.

H_1: Firms that sell into foreign markets through inter-mediaries are larger than firms that export directly to end customers.

A related hypothesis pertains to the international experience of the firm. The internationalization process perspective argues that firms increase their commitment to international sales over time as their experiential knowledge of foreign markets increases (Johanson and Vahlne 1977, 1990). According to this logic, firms that are more experienced in international sales are expected to use more resource-intensive entry modes. This view also posits that, over time, firms that start international sales with low-commitment entry modes switch to entry modes that require a higher degree of commitment as a result of better knowledge of foreign markets. Formalizing a distribution agreement frequently involves legal and other administrative costs. The distributor's staff must be trained in selling the product, installing it, and providing subsequent maintenance or upgrades. Therefore, we believe that the use of distributors represents a more committed entry mode that is used by more experienced firms.

H_2: Firms that sell into foreign markets through inter-mediaries are more experienced in international operations than firms that export directly to end customers.

It is, however, not necessary that experience in international operations has to be gained by the firm as organizational entity. A young firm initiating its first market entries cannot be expected to have direct experiential knowledge of international operations embodied in its processes and routines.[1] In the case of start-ups, the founders' international experience can be a substitute for organizational experience. If key managers in the young firm have previous experience in foreign markets, it may initiate cross-border activities using more complex entry modes. Accordingly, the international experience of senior managers has in the past been used to predict the scale and scope of international activities of start-up firms (Bloodgood, Sapienza, and Almeida 1996; Reuber and Fischer 1997).

H_3: Managers of firms that sell into foreign markets through intermediaries will be more likely to have international experience than managers of firms that export directly.

The experience of the firm is also a key variable in research contributions that apply the OC perspective to the choice of entry modes (Aulakh and Kotabe 1997; Madhok 1997). Theorists of OC argue that present outcomes are strongly influenced by past experiences and routines that have become embedded in the organization (Madhok 1997). If a firm uses a particular sales channel in its domestic market, it may be expected to replicate this familiar practice (i.e., negotiating contracts, incentivizing, and motivating intermediaries) in foreign markets. Thus, the higher costs or risks of arranging more complex foreign sales modes can arguably be reduced through leveraging experiences gained earlier in a domestic market.[2]

H_4: Firms will sell into foreign markets through intermediaries rather than export directly if they already use distributors for their domestic sales.

The OC perspective argues that a firm's value-creating activities are a function of its resource and capability base (Madhok 1997; Teece, Pisano, and Shuen 1997). Madhok distinguishes between activities in which the focus is capability development and activities in which the focus is the exploitation of an existing advantage. In the case of start-ups—given our focus on sales modes—we argue that the objective of their international sales is to exploit fully the commercial value of their technological competency to ensure their survival. Madhok also introduces the notions of "ownership effect" and "locational effect." The former is represented by the ratio of embedded-to-generic firm-specific know-how, whereas the latter is defined as the ratio of embedded-to-generic market-specific knowledge (Madhok 1997). According to Madhok, a firm will carry out a transaction itself (internalization) if there is a high potential for the erosion in the value of the firm's know-how stemming from the ownership effect. In contrast, a firm will have a preference for collaboration if there is a high potential for the erosion in the value of the firm's know-how from the locational effect. In summary, collaborative arrangements will be preferred in countries where the idiosyncratic ways of doing business erode the value of firm-specific know-how. Conversely, a firm is less likely to involve third parties if firm-specific know-how is inimitable or immobile, which thereby makes the sharing of routines with intermediaries difficult (Hill, Hwang, and Kim 1990; Madhok 1997). This suggests that a firm will have a higher propensity to avoid the use of intermediaries if its technology is advanced or if the firm is unfamiliar with potential users in its target market. Given the importance of tacit knowledge for such products, market-based support infrastructures may not be effective or available (Meldrum 1995). Therefore, effective commercialization may only be possible by internalization of the sales process. Idiosyncratic ways of doing business abroad may therefore represent a lesser barrier than in the case of more established technologies, especially if the product is sold to industrialized countries. Collaborations are expected to occur more frequently when the technology is more mature and established, a proposition that has received some validity in prior research on international technology transfers (Davidson and McFetridge 1985).

H₅: The products of firms that sell into foreign markets through intermediaries are technologically more mature than those of firms that export directly.

Previous research on internationalization has found that product characteristics affect the way firms manage their international activities (Cavusgil and Zou 1994; Cavusgil, Zou, and Naidu 1993). Product characteristics have also been found to influence the chosen entry modes in the case of young technology-based firms (Lindqvist 1991). The importance of client-specific customization as a barrier to internationalization has been reported in studies that examine product characteristics of international start-ups (Lindell and Karagozoglou 1997; Murray 1996; Roberts and Senturia 1996). The transformation from offering customized technology solutions to offering standardized or "shrink-wrapped" products in which the technology is embedded is associated with an increasing market orientation of the firm (Roberts 1991). Companies whose products are tailor made for particular customers have been found to be more likely to sell directly without involving intermediaries (Bell 1995). Furthermore, it is more probable that the technological skills required to tailor a particular product to the needs of a customer reside within the company that developed the product rather than with the distributor in a target country.

H₆: The products of firms that sell into foreign markets through intermediaries require less client-specific customization than those of firms that export directly.

The tools of TCE have also been widely used to analyze the determinants of entry mode choices. In essence, TCE is concerned with finding the most efficient institutional or contractual arrangement for economic transactions (Hennart 1989). Instead of following the methods used by researchers who measure transaction costs indirectly by defining situations in which asset specificity and uncertainty are supposedly high (see, e.g., Anderson and Gatignon 1986; Hennart 1990), we follow the approach of Klein, Frazier, and Roth (1990) and attempt to measure the costs involved in the selling process of high-technology goods directly. During the sales process for high-technology goods, the vendor may be required to spend considerable time advising and educating the potential customer on the key features and relative merits of the product. After the sale, more complex products may require installation by trained staff, regular after-sales service, and periodic upgrades (Cavusgil and Zou 1994; Hutt and Speh 1992). To carry out these tasks, the sales and technical staff of the vendor will require particular skills. In the case of exporting, these skills are normally resident within the manufacturer. Selling a product through an intermediary, however, requires those skills also to be already present within, or transferable to, the distributor. The producer may therefore need to provide regular training to the staff of the intermediary to transfer the necessary skills and routines and effectively support the product. High up-front investments into these specific assets reduce the subsequent bargaining power and margins of the party that incurs these costs. Zacharakis (1997) argues that a small entrepreneurial firm is more likely to be obliged to reduce the distributor's set-up costs through the provision of training or other transfers than a large established multinational. Furthermore, a distributor may not be motivated to push a complex product that requires substantial presale consulting and installation efforts. Therefore, products and services that incur substantial costs during the sales process should make it more difficult to align the interests of the start-up and a potential distributor. However, selling a technologically advanced product is likely to require an effective support infrastructure (Meldrum 1995). Using distributors that can exploit economies of scale and scope not available to the young firm may be the only way to provide the necessary infrastructure to service foreign customers. Furthermore, the costs of learning how to perform the relatively standardized tasks of installation, end-user training, and maintenance are likely to be relatively low when the distributor already has a portfolio of related products in place. Therefore, we hypothesize that in international markets, distributors represent the preferred vehicle for start-ups to ensure effective customer support for products whose commercialization is resource intensive.

H_7: The pre- and after-sales transaction costs of products sold into foreign markets through intermediaries are higher than the costs of products of firms that export directly.

Control Variables

We include R&D intensity as a control variable. It has in the past been used as a proxy variable in studies that have applied the framework of transaction costs to international market entry choices (Davidson and McFetridge 1985) to operationalize asset specificity and information asymmetries in exchange relations. We argue that there are two problems with this measure. First, it constitutes an input variable and may not necessarily have an impact on the asset specificity required to commercialize the output of the firm. High R&D

Oliver Burgel and Gordon C. Murray

expenditures may not give rise to asset specificity or information asymmetries per se. Indeed, higher R&D investment may even allow a reduction in transaction costs by designing out complexity for the customer. Second, it is usually measured at firm level, not at product level, because it is difficult to obtain R&D intensity (R&D expenditure divided by sales) on a product group basis. Although high R&D expenditures and the need to amortize them quickly probably have an impact on the decision to internationalize, we do not believe that this variable has an impact on the entry modes chosen. Therefore, we argue that the dimensions are better represented by measuring transaction costs directly and by measuring the maturity of the technology. Because of its widespread use in empirical studies, however, we include R&D intensity as a control variable to detect any firm-level effects it might have on the choice of entry mode. We do not present any hypotheses regarding the target country, but include it as a control variable as well. We follow the approaches of Erramilli and Rao (1993), Shrader, Oviatt, and McDougall (1997), and Barkema and Vermeulen (1998) and include the additional variables country risk, absolute size of the target country, and gross domestic product (GDP) per capita. We also include further dummy variables to control for any industry-specific effects that may affect the chosen sales mode.

To summarize, similar to other researchers before us (e.g., Cavusgil, Zou, and Naidu 1993), we attempt to explain the international entry modes using firm-specific variables, product-specific variables, and variables specific to the environment in which the firms operate. Firm size and experience in international activities can be seen as operationalizations of the internationalization process model. Experience with the domestic sales mode and the innovativeness of the technology can be seen as operationalizations of the OC perspectives, whereas product characteristics are proxies for the transaction cost perspective.

METHOD

For the purpose of this study, we define a high-tech start-up as a legally independent company that is not older than ten years and that operates in one or more high-technology sectors. An operationalizable definition of high-technology sectors in the United Kingdom has been established by Butchart (1987), who provides a definition of high-tech industries based on the two ratios of R&D expenses to sales and employees working in R&D to total employees. Employing this definition, we identified 33 high-technology industries as having above average expenditures for R&D (for a list of included industries, see Appendix A). Using a database obtained from Dun and Bradstreet, we identified firms operating in those industries that had at least three employees in 1997 and had been founded between 1987 and 1996.

We acknowledge that this method cannot consider high-tech firms in industries that are not included by Butchart's definition. Yet as opposed to targeting low-technology sectors in the search for high-technology start-ups, we expected the proposed approach to result in an increased likelihood of obtaining responses from firms that fulfil the specified eligibility criteria. In total, we identified a gross sample of 7788 U.K. firms. We subsequently screened all identified company records to exclude those firms whose business activities suggested they were not carrying out any R&D activities (e.g., retailers, wholesalers, assemblers). As a result, we retained 3590 firms as eligible for inclusion in the research sample.[3] We then chose 2000 firms using a random sampling process stratified by size class and service/manufacturing.

On the basis of a review of the specialized literature, we developed a four-page questionnaire. We carried out four pilot case studies to test whether the questions in the survey instrument appeared relevant, easy to understand, and unambiguous to the target respondents. As a result, we modified the questionnaire to take into account the expressed concerns. We posted an introductory letter and questionnaire followed by three reminders, if appropriate, to the managing directors of these 2000 firms. Managing directors have been used in past studies to collect data on the overall performance of entrepreneurial firms and have been identified as reliable sources of information (Brush and Vanderwerf 1992). A total of 134 envelopes came back unopened from companies that could no longer be located at their addresses in the database. Nine companies wrote back saying they were in the process of receivership. Sixty-one firms contacted us, indicating that they did not wish to participate in the survey. Altogether, 466 firms returned the completed questionnaires, which resulted in a response rate of 24%. After consistency checks to confirm that each firm fulfilled all the criteria for eligibility (i.e., firms needed to be less than ten years old and independently owned firms), 362 (19%) firms could be retained in the data set. We performed t-tests using the original Dun and Bradstreet data to check for nonresponse bias. We did not detect any statistically significant differences using information on sales, sales change (in relation to the previous financial year), number of employees, and credit rating. The latter measure reflects the credit worthiness of the firm as attributed by credit rating analysts and is therefore of particular interest when judging the firm's overall performance status. The absence of significant differences suggests that the firms in our sample do not differ from the nonrespondents.

Operationalization of Variables

In specifying the entry modes, we followed the definitions of Root (1994), Klein, Frazier, and Roth (1990), and Aulakh and Kotabe (1997). Accordingly, we asked respondents to specify whether the chosen mode of their international activities was direct exporting, the use of an agent or sales representative selling on a commission basis, the use of a distributor, a sales joint venture, a wholly owned sales subsidiary, or licensing. We asked firms to make similar statements regarding their domestic sales mode. We measured size using two variables: sales during the last financial year and number of employees. Because of the high correlation of these two variables ($r = .74$, $p > .0001$), we constructed a single measure out of the standardized scores. We decided against using the share of nondomestic revenues as a measure of experience (Aulakh and Kotabe 1997). In principle, we accept the reasoning behind that choice; that is, firms that score high on that measure have an understanding of foreign operations. However, we argue that in the case of a sample composed of start-ups, it is impossible to distinguish between cause and effect; that is, the share of nondomestic revenues could at the same time be a function of the entry modes used. Therefore, we measure international experience as the number of years the firm has already been engaged in international operations before entering a particular market. To operationalize the international experience of the firms' senior managers, we include dummy variables for whether the founders had lived abroad or had worked for internationally operating companies before starting their present business (Bloodgood, Sapienza, and Almeida 1996). The innovativeness of the technology employed was measured using a four-item scale (see Appendix B). Respondents were asked whether their products are best classified as incorporating tested combinations of existing technology, new combinations of existing technology, novel technology developed externally, or novel technology developed specifically for this product by the company. We measured the extent to which a product requires client-specific customization and the transaction costs incurred during the sales process using five-point Likert scales (see Appendix B). The four items measuring transaction costs were then combined into a single scale (alpha .73). Dummy variables were included to specify whether or not the firm belonged to a particular industry. We divided the firms into the five industry categories: software, information technology (IT) and communications hardware, engineering, biomedical technology, and electronics (see Appendix A). We obtained country risk ratings from the publication *Institutional Investor* (see also Shrader, Oviatt, and McDougall 1997). Because of the high correlation between country risk data and GDP per capita data ($r = .93$, $p > .0001$), we only included risk in our analysis. Appendix C shows a correlation table of our variables.

Of the 362 firms that participated in the survey, we subsequently only retained firms with international activities. Altogether, 246 (68%) firms were engaged in international sales. Table 1 describes these respondent firms. On average, they were six years old, started with 5 employees, and had grown to 22 employees by the time of the survey. Eight per-

RESULTS

International Entrepreneurship

Table 1.
Descriptive Statistics

Variable	Mean	Standard Deviation	Minimum	Maximum	Median
Age	5.8	2.6	0	10	6
Sales, first year*	274	508	0	6900	124
Sales, last year*	1215	1722	50	16100	650
Employees, first year	4.4	6.5	1	50	3
Employees, last year	20.0	24.2	1	180	12
R&D intensity (% of sales)	16.7	22.0	0	150	8
R&D intensity (% of employees)	30.7	23.0	0	1.00	25

*Sales in thousands of English pounds

cent of the firms indicated that they did not carry out any R&D activities. The indicators for both R&D share and percentage of employees working on product development suggest that the remaining 92% of sampled firms operate in technology-intensive and/or knowledge-intensive areas and spend, on average, the equivalent of 15% of their annual sales revenue on R&D.

Table 2 gives an overview of the international activities of the start-ups in our total sample. On average, these firms generated 38% of their total turnover from international sales (median 30%) through operations in ten countries (median 6). A third of these firms (34%) generated more than 50% of their revenues from nondomestic sales. A total of 28% of all born international firms generated international revenues within their first year of formation. This latter group now generates, on average, 46% of its revenues from foreign sales. Roughly half the sample firms (46%) had entered their first foreign market by the end of their second year. However, foreign direct investment in internationally dispersed assets played a minor role among the firms in our sample. Only 11 companies had established either a joint venture or a wholly owned subsidiary to manufacture their products abroad.

Table 2.
International Activities
of Sample Firms

Variable	Mean	Standard Deviation	Minimum	Maximum	Median
International sales (% of total firms)	67.9	46.7			
Share of nondomestic revenue (%)	38.4	31.7	1	100	30
Number of countries entered	10.0	11.9	1	90	6
Years before first international sales	2.2	2.1	0	10	2

Oliver Burgel and Gordon C. Murray

Because our chosen unit of analysis is the market entry decision, we asked respondents to provide us with information on their three most important foreign markets, defined by their contribution to the total sales of the firm's best-selling product. This resulted in a data set of 547 market entry decisions (see Table 3). Ten cases were excluded from the analysis, because respondents either could not provide country level sales or indicated that they operated using entry modes that were difficult to classify.[4]

Of the 547 market entry decisions in our sample, the preferred current entry mode used by the firms was distributors (42%) followed by direct exporting (36%) and use of sales agents (11%). Market entry modes that required some form of direct investment were not extensively used by the firms in our sample. A total of 27 entries (5%) were carried out using the joint venture form, and 15 entries (3%) were through wholly owned subsidiaries. The generation of international sales revenues through licensing equally had a marginal role (9, 2%). In comparison with the first entry modes used by these firms, it appears that aggregate changes of entry modes over time reflect a tendency to use arrangements that represent a higher commitment to international sales. Of the 121 observed changes, 95 (79%) represented a move toward increasing commitment to foreign sales. These descriptive findings provide further evidence for the validity of our choice to compare direct exporting and exporting through distributors as the main strategic options for the majority of high-tech start-ups.

Table 4 gives an overview of the geographic spread of the international firms in our sample. The most important markets for British high-tech start-ups are found in Western European countries, followed by North American and East Asian countries. When individual countries are examined, however, the most frequently entered export market is the United States, with 96 entries, followed by France (68) and Germany (64).

Entry Modes

Geographic Spread of Entries

Entry Mode	First Entry	%	Current Entry	%
Exporting	241	44	199	36
Agents	68	12	60	11
Distributors	198	36	227	42
Sales joint venture	12	2	27	5
Wholly owned sales subsidiary	7	1	15	3
Licensing	11	2	9	2
Missing/other	10	2	10	2
Total	547	100	547	100

Table 3.
First and Current Entry Modes

Notes The table shows the first and current entry modes used in the most important foreign markets for the company's best-selling product

Table 4.
Geographic Focus of
International Activities

Unit of Analysis	Entries		Firms	
Entry Mode	Current Entries	%	First Country Entered	%
European Union/European Free Trade Association	307	56	138	57
United States and Canada	106	19	56	22
East Asia (Japan, Hong Kong, Singapore, Korea, Taiwan)	37	7	14	6
Australia and New Zealand	25	5	6	2
Emerging markets, Europe	12	2	2	1
South America	3	1	3	1
Middle East	22	4	11	5
Emerging markets, Asia	13	2	4	2
Other	21	4	10	4
Total	547	100	244	100

For the first market entered—which may not be the firms'
largest market—a similar picture emerges. Although the majority of firms (138, 57%) had their first international sales in
Western Europe, the most popular country of first entry was
the United States (52, 21%). It is noteworthy that 43% of first
entries were made to countries that do not belong to the European Union/European Free Trade Association. When the
second, third, fourth, and fifth market entries are examined, a
similar pattern is evident (not shown here). These results
lend broad support to the findings of Lindqvist (1991) and
Bell (1995). Although a narrow majority of firms chose geographically close countries for their first international sales,
an important minority of firms entered spatially distant markets first.

The descriptive results suggest that there is some support
for the theoretical claims of process models when the aggregate sample is considered; that is, firms' entry modes
changed over time to reflect an increase of commitment to
foreign markets, and most firms first sell into relatively close
markets. However, several individual firms deviate from this
pattern. That the single most important target country, both
for first entry and for absolute numbers of market entries, is
the United States suggests that entry mode choices are also
driven by more compelling strategic reasons than psychic
distance alone. The economic size of the target market or the
recognition of significant, country-specific opportunities
may be more persuasive factors. We next present the results
of the regressions and investigate to what extent the chosen
firm-specific, product-specific, and country-specific factors
influenced the foreign entry decision.

Oliver Burgel and Gordon C. Murray

To test the hypotheses stated previously, we estimated three probit models with the entry mode (1 = distributor, 0 = direct export) as the dependent variable. These two entry modes capture 78% of the observed entry modes in our sample. Still, we excluded 28 cases because of missing information on one or more independent variables. We report the marginal parameter coefficients of the model to compare the magnitude of the effects of the different variables. We estimated our principal model including all cases available for analysis (Model 1). We base our discussion of the hypotheses primarily on the results of this first model.

The overall solution is statistically significant at $p > .0001$. Among the 398 entry mode choices for which all variables were complete, 213 (55%) firms chose distributors and 174 (45%) firms chose to export directly. The classification ratio of more than 70% therefore suggests that the predictive ability of the estimated model represents a substantial improvement over the 55% maximum chance criterion (equivalent to assuming that all firms are distributors). In all three models, the measure of size is positively related to the use of distributors, and the effects are highly significant in a statistical sense. However, when the marginal effects are examined, the real impact of size on entry mode is very small. Nonetheless, H_1 can be accepted. The international experience of the firm at the time of the market entry is not significantly related to the choice of a particular sales mode in any of the three models. H_2 therefore cannot be accepted. H_3 also must be rejected. Living experience abroad and previous work for an internationally operating company are both negatively related to the use of intermediaries. However, only living experience abroad is statistically significant. H_4 was supported. Firms that used distributors domestically also had a higher propensity to use intermediaries for their international sales. A comparison of the marginal effects also shows that this variable has the strongest effect of all the variables included in the model. H_5, following the organizational capability perspective, states that the products of firms that export directly incorporated newer technologies than the products of firms that entered foreign markets through intermediaries. This hypothesis must be rejected. Compared with the base case of a product incorporating tested combinations of existing technology, more advanced technology tends to be sold through intermediaries. However, the coefficients indicate that this is a curvilinear relationship, as the probability to sell through an intermediary is highest for products that had the second highest score of technological novelty. H_6 is supported by the model. Products that require extensive customization are more likely to be sold internationally without the use of intermediaries. H_7 cannot be accepted. The measures used to operationalize the costs of commercialization turned out to have a statistically insignificant impact on the decision to involve intermediaries in the sales process.

Regression Analysis

Among the control variables, only one industry effect turned out to be significant. All other things being equal, firms in biotechnology and medical technology rely much more on intermediaries to sell their products abroad compared with the base case of the electronics industry. Effects for software, engineering, and IT hardware were not significantly different from the base case. Research and development intensity was used as a control variable and resulted in a significant, albeit weak, effect. Accordingly, firms that have higher R&D expenditures have a lower propensity to sell through distributors. However, as the size of the marginal effect in Table 5 indicates, firm differences of at least one order of magnitude must be present to have a substantial impact. Finally, among the country variables, only the absolute market size appears to have a significant impact on the entry mode decision. The size of a national market thus seems to be positively related to the propensity to use distributors. The estimates for country risk did not have a statistically significant effect within the model.

To examine the validity of our findings, we tested two additional models. Over time, some sample firms had changed the modes of market entry employed. Thus, the current entry mode could be a result of dynamic learning effects rather than of actual differences in firm or product characteristics. Model 2 therefore only includes those entry modes that have not been subject to changes over time. We make a further modification in Model 3, in which only those entry modes that represent at least 10% of the total turnover of the firm were included. Our results could be biased by the presence of reactive, unsolicited foreign sales that are not a result of firm-specific factors or managerial action. Choosing a relatively high threshold of 10% should lead to the exclusion of the majority of these cases. The estimation of both Model 2 and Model 3 confirmed the results of our main model. Models 2 and 3 equally represent statistically significant solutions, and their respective classification ratios of 70.60 and 71.04 compare favorably with chance criteria of 50% (Model 2) and 51% (Model 3). Furthermore, as Table 5 shows, the effects of our explanatory variables in the three models are strikingly consistent. The only differences were marginal changes of statistical significance for management's foreign living experience in Model 3 and the insignificance of one of the technology dummy variables in Models 2 and 3. The latter, however, does not contradict the results of Model 1, because newer technologies remain more likely to be sold through intermediaries compared with the base case.

DISCUSSION

From the previous analysis, a couple of results merit further consideration. First, we were surprised by the very incidence of international activities among the firms in our sample. A majority of start-ups (68%) engaged in international sales. On average, these technology-based young firms sold 38% of their turnover in foreign countries, and 33% of the firms generated more turnover from international than domestic sales. Respondents typically sold into ten countries at the time of the survey and had initiated international activities two

Variable	Model 1	Model 2	Model 3	
Firm size	.095	.119	.08	Table 5.
	(.008)***	(.002)***	(.037)**	Estimation Results of the
Management—living experience abroad	– 106	–.129	–.105	Probit Models
	(.081)*	(.058)*	(.140)	
Management—previous work experience in internationally operating firm	–.020	–.017	–.091	
	(.734)	(.801)	(.199)	
Firm experience in international sales before market entry (in years)	–.004	.006	–.224	
	(.780)	(.680)	(.231)	
Domestic sales mode	.368	.457	.343	
	(.000)***	(.000)***	(.000)***	
Products based on new combinations of tested technology	.162	.128	.118	
	(.069)*	(.188)	(.272)	
Products based on novel technology developed outside	319	346	.258	
	(.001)***	(.002)***	(.043)**	
Products based on novel technology developed in-house	.204	.179	.188	
	(.021)**	(.062)*	(.073)*	
Degree of customization	–.068	–.053	–.057	
	(.001)**	(.017)**	(.016)**	
Cost of sales	.001	–.009	041	
	(.976)	(.800)	(.307)	
Industry. software	–.084	–.061	.010	
	(.424)	(.591)	(.929)	
Industry: IT hardware	.070	.060	.112	
	(.435)	(.553)	(.284)	
Industry· engineering	.122	.141	.157	
	(.179)	(.173)	(.145)	
Industry: biotechnology/medical technology	.429	.460	.469	
	(.000)***	(.000)***	(.000)***	
R&D expenditures	–.003	–.002	–.003	
	(030)**	(.142)	(.080)*	
Target country: absolute market size	–.005	–.033	–.005	
	(.006)***	(.078)*	(.010)***	
Target country: country risk	.001	.001	.001	
	(.643)	(.538)	(.730)	
Number of observations	398	339	297	
Log-likelihood	–219.26	–185.52	–167.71	
χ² (d f.)	109 98	98.90	76.22	
Prob > χ²	.0000	.0000	0000	
Pseudo R²	20	.21	.19	
Classification ratio	70 60	73.16	71.04	

*10% significance level
**5% significance level
***1% significance level.
Notes base case = an electronics company selling products that incorporate tested technology

Start-Up Companies in High-Technology Industries

years after formation. Second, given the importance of international activities, we looked at the target countries and entry modes used. The majority of firms chose countries in Western Europe for their first market entry. However, the most frequently targeted country is the United States (19% of all entries). A sizeable proportion of firms (42%) entered more distant non-European markets first. Strategic considerations and the exploitation of new opportunities rather than psychic/economic distance are more likely to account for these entry decisions.

According to the sample average, these young firms elected to choose entry modes that were not resource intensive. But among these low-resource entry modes, the use of intermediaries was currently more prevalent than direct exporting. Arguably, selling through distributors represents a more complex and advanced managerial arrangement because of the requirement to attract, train, incentivize, and monitor a third-party agent. We therefore expected, all other things being equal, the use of foreign intermediaries to be more prevalent among more experienced and larger firms. As hypothesized, we found a positive effect of firm size on the propensity to sell through intermediaries. However, an analysis of the marginal effect reveals that—similar to the statistically significant but weak effect of R&D intensity—the real impact of that variable is quite small. Firm differences of at least one order of magnitude must be present to have a substantial impact on the choice of entry mode. The influence of experience on mode choice turned out to be contrary to our hypotheses. Direct firm experience did not have a significant impact on the commitment of the chosen entry mode. However, as intensive experience with foreign operations cannot realistically be expected among young firms initiating their first foreign sales, we also tested for management's international experience, a substitute for direct company experience. This variable had a significant impact on the choice of entry mode, albeit not in the hypothesized direction. This result suggests that managers who have lived abroad are more likely to sell internationally without the assistance of intermediaries. A possible interpretation of this finding is that internationally experienced managers do not need to rely on the superior market knowledge or commercial network of a local distributor to commercialize their products abroad. Their tenure abroad means that they already have their own personal networks and can evaluate them in comparison with the services offered by a distributor. We conclude from these findings that experiential knowledge, the key variable in the internationalization process theory (Andersen 1997), is of limited value to explain the entry mode choices of the high-tech start-ups in our sample. This echoes the findings of other researchers (see, e.g., Bell 1995). In addition, our findings could provide further evidence for those researchers that argued that different entry modes do not so much represent distinct levels of commitment determined by past experience but rather represent distinct managerial choices determined by product- and firm-specific considerations (Andersen 1993; Leonidou and Katsikeas 1996).

In the case of start-ups, the choice of foreign entry modes may therefore represent a compromise between the limited resources of the start-up and the support requirements demanded by the customers of its products. As hypothesized, our results indicate that a high degree of required customization leads to the exclusion of intermediaries during the sales process. Products that require a high level of client-specific adaptation are more likely to be sold directly by the manufacturer. We argue that this is the case because the expertise and tacit knowledge required to configure a product according to customers' detailed specifications are more likely to reside with the manufacturer than with the intermediary. We further hypothesized that start-ups whose products require extensive pre- and after-sales support will be more likely to sell through distributors. However, this hypothesis could not be supported, because the level of required support did not affect the choice of entry mode significantly.

We suggest the following interpretation of this result. The effects of the customization (H_6) and after-sales support (H_7) variables are somewhat related, which is also manifest in the significant positive correlation between the two.[5] From the distributor's point of view, they both incorporate the notion of having to acquire or invest in certain skills to guarantee the effective commercialization of a client manufacturer's product. Such a commitment is attractive to the distributor only if a large volume of sales is a reasonably guaranteed consequence of this investment. All other things being equal, customization and after-sales support should act as a barrier to the interest or involvement of intermediaries in the sales process. However, from the point of view of a firm that wants to serve large or remote foreign markets, the use of a local distributor may be the only practicable way of providing the necessary customer-focused infrastructure for installation, maintenance, upgrading, and/or training of end users. We tried to decompose this dilemma and argue that highly customized products are more likely to be exported by manufacturers directly because of their singular familiarity with their core technology. The costs of acquiring these specialized technological skills may be prohibitive and economically irrational for a distributor. However, in certain cases in which the distributor already has a portfolio of related products and technologies in place, the relative costs of both learning and subsequently operationalizing the standard and routinized tasks of installation, end-user training, and maintenance are likely to be much lower because of both scale and scope effects. Therefore, in these circumstances, selling a volume product or product family whose commercialization requires high levels of support through intermediaries might be less problematic. That the two variables have different effects in the regression (significantly negative in the case of customization versus insignificantly positive for sales support) is therefore an interesting result in itself and goes a certain way to support our reasoning. It suggests that customization represents a barrier to involving intermediaries, whereas the attendant cost of sales support can be managed and may even be a source of attractive profit for the distributor given sufficient trading volume to ensure scale effects.

The newness of the technology incorporated had a significant impact on the choice of the entry mode, albeit in the opposite direction to the one we hypothesized. Compared with the base case of mature and tested technologies, transactions involving products that incorporated more innovative technology (and therefore embodied a higher degree of tacit knowledge according to the theorists of OC) had a higher chance of being dealt with through collaborative arrangements than being exported. Although this indicates that the international market entry forms are influenced by product-specific factors, the effects observed directly contradict the theoretical prescriptions and findings on technology transfer modes of larger firms (Davidson and McFetridge 1985). However, they corroborate the recent findings of Robertson and Gatignon (1998), who report that firms that experienced higher technology uncertainties were more likely to engage in alliances.

Our strongest predictor of the chosen foreign entry mode was the existing, domestic sales mode of the firm.[6] The effect of this variable can be explained in two ways. First, it is a proxy for different strategic and structural influence factors that affect sales channel choice irrespectively of the context. This variable therefore partly accounts for unobservable effects whose determination was not among the objectives of the study. Second, the explanatory effect of this variable is arguably due to the presence of embedded routines and experiences with the domestic sales mode. This finding therefore supports theoretical propositions that stress the importance of firm-specific routines and the path dependence of organizational outcomes (Madhok 1997). However, further research should necessarily use a more refined measure to determine to what extent foreign entry decisions are a result of path dependency or company marketing strategy.

MANAGERIAL IMPLICATIONS

The results of this research confirm what the high-tech entrepreneurial manager already knows, namely, that the early decision of an appropriate mode of exporting is not a trivial activity. On the contrary, it is an activity of the most profound strategic import and has long-term implications. In an ideal world, it is likely that any firm would prefer to be in charge of its destiny and would chose a direct export mode of operation or build up a wholly owned subsidiary. Yet the latter is usually outside the reach of a young start-up company. Exporting, in contrast, is not always an appropriate choice. If there are serious questions regarding the firms' ability to provide user support in distant markets, the firm may have little choice but to choose a more established and recognized distributor. In making this choice, the firm is, in effect, subcontracting a part of its growth strategy to an agent. For the distributor, the young firm is only one of several clients. In addition, the firm's bargaining power may be small in comparison with bigger, higher-volume, and longer committed clients of the distributor. As a result, a situation with high conflict potential emerges. To the distributor, providing a service to this type of immature firm represents a series of necessary but highly speculative, specialist investments or sunk costs. The distributor's choice of accepting the innovative products of an unknown start-up will therefore depend on the projected sales volume. As a result, young firms that cannot meet their distributors' expectations will be left with no other choice than to sell directly.

Our research has identified several practical implications for the managers of technology-based start-ups. We isolate three findings that we believe professional managers might find helpful. First, those young firms wishing to use distributors in foreign markets can benefit from using collaborative relationships in their domestic market first. Learning effects in managing relationships with intermediaries may be more easily gained in the domestic market and at less cost. In certain circumstances, this learning may also be less risky given, for example, easier communication and/or negligible psychic distance. Even for born global firms, market-based experimentation in the domestic market may still have these advantages.

Second, firms that sell a highly customized product should be prepared to commit appropriate resources to their presales and after-sales service strategy given their reliance on direct exports. In giving this advice, we are aware that our research findings show that firms appear to choose a mode of foreign market entry irrespective of the resource implications of the commercialization process. Similarly, our findings also show that the size or resource endowment of individual firms has a weak, albeit statistically significant, effect on the choice of mode of market entry. In short, it does not appear that resource constraints prevent firms from choosing between the two discussed entry modes. Instead, managers should be aware that the choice is more likely to be influenced by the degree of customization of the product.

Third, it appears that in getting a new, technologically advanced product into the market, start-ups with a necessarily limited record of achievement should seriously consider collaboration to exploit the track record or reputation of an established intermediary. The much-quoted concept of "liability of newness" posits that young firms face disadvantages, because stable relations with clients are not yet established (Brüderl and Schüssler 1990; Stinchcombe 1965). In cross-border business relationships, this may amplify into what we call the "liability of alienness." The reluctance of customers to rely on small, untested, and foreign suppliers is particularly important in the sensitive field of medical technology, as is evidenced in our results. However, this antipathy to uncertainty by customers can be extended to all users of mission-critical technologies provided by young and unproven third-party suppliers. In such circumstances, and particularly when there are costly implications for product failure or nonperformance, an exclusive dependence on a young company provider is not an acceptable proposition for any established corporate user. The use of a trusted distributor, or more accurately a value-added reseller, and its existing sales force is frequently the only effective way for a young high-tech company to present products to mainstream customers early in its development. Distributors may also be essential for supplying widely dispersed customers in a continental-scale market such as the United States or in markets where there are major cultural disparities between provider and user, such as China.

LIMITATIONS

Our study is not without limitations. First, we focus on only two distinct entry modes in our analysis, because licensing and entry modes requiring direct capital investments were of only marginal importance in our sample. Further research on those technology start-ups that engage in a wider spectrum of entry modes could reveal whether the effects identified by our research can account for differences between the involvement of intermediaries and the completely internalized entry decisions when firms set up foreign subsidiaries. Second, for the moment, our study cannot reveal any performance implications of the choice of different entry modes. Despite the availability of data on firm growth, we cannot presently distinguish between cause and effect for the majority of firms in our sample; that is, either the growth could be a result of the chosen entry mode, or vice versa. However, we plan to contact the participants of our study again in the future to investigate long-term performance implications of different market entry strategies. Finally, our sample is drawn exclusively from high-tech start-ups in the United Kingdom. Further research should therefore address whether similar findings can be reported from other countries and other industry sectors characterized by the presence of internationally operating entrepreneurial start-ups.

Industry	NACE Classifications
Software	7220, 7260
IT and communications hardware	3001, 3002, 3220, 3230
Engineering	3320, 3330, 3340
Life sciences and medical technology	2441, 2442, 3310
Other (mainly electronics, components)	3110, 3120, 3210, 3530, 2416, 2417

Notes The NACE classification system is the European Union equivalent of the standard industrial classification code system.

**APPENDIX A
INDUSTRY SECTORS
INCLUDED IN THE STUDY**

**APPENDIX B
OPERATIONALIZATION
OF VARIABLES**

1. Innovativeness of Technology

How would you best describe the innovativeness of your product or service?

☐ It incorporates "tried and tested" combinations of existing technology.

☐ It incorporates new combinations of existing technology.

☐ It incorporates novel technology that has been developed elsewhere.

☐ It incorporates novel technology that had to be developed specifically for this product by your company.

2. Customization

Please describe the extent to which your product or service requires

	low		substantial			does not apply
Individual client customization	☐	☐	☐	☐	☐	☐

3. Transaction Cost Intensity

Please describe key characteristics of the product/service, particularly the extent to which it requires

	low		substantial			does not apply
Technical consultation prior to sales	☐	☐	☐	☐	☐	☐
Complex or time-consuming installation	☐	☐	☐	☐	☐	☐
Regular maintenance and/or upgrades	☐	☐	☐	☐	☐	☐
Specialized training required for front line and sales personnel	☐	☐	☐	☐	☐	☐

APPENDIX 3
CORRELATION TABLE

	distri	size	exp_abr	exp_mult	exp_int	dis_dom	rd_sh	tec_2	tec_3	tec_4	custom	cost
distri	1.0000											
size	.0567	1.0000										
exp_abr	-.0795	.0201	1.0000									
exp_mult	.0295	-.0390	.1802*	1.0000								
exp_int	.0164	.0842	-.0147	.0904*	1.0000							
dis_dom	.2893*	-.0318	-.1262*	.1157*	-.0037	1.0000						
rd_sh	-.1010*	.0797	.0418	.0077	-.0827	-.0837	1.0000					
tec_2	.0732	-.0869*	.0095	-.0232	-.0904*	.1850*	-.0689	1.0000				
tec_3	.0108	.0680	.0041	.0481	.0487	-.1242*	.1407*	-.2449*	1.0000			
tec_4	-.0297	-.0702	.0684	-.0710	.0375	-.1103*	.1279*	-.5418*	-.3213*	1.0000		
custom	-.2262*	-.0335	.0297	.0071	-.0167	-.1706*	-.0843*	-.0303	.0284	-.0951*	1.0000	
cost	.0103	.1584*	.0176	.0347	.1447*	-.0433	.0853*	-.0707	.1711*	.1145*	.3004*	1.0000

* Significant at p > 05.

distri = dummy (1 = foreign sales through distributors, 0 = direct exporting)
size = size of the firm.
exp_abr = living experience abroad (1 = yes, 0 = no).
exp_mult = work experience in internationally operating firm (1 = yes, 0 = no).
exp_int = international experience of firm (year of analyzed entry decision – year of first foreign sales).
dis_dom = domestic sales through dealers/distributors (1 = yes, 0 = no)
rd_sh = R&D expenditure relative to total sales.
tec_2 = new combinations of existing technology (1 = yes, 0 = no)
tec_3 = product incorporates novel technology developed externally (1 = yes, 0 = no)
tec_4 = product incorporates novel technology developed internally (1 = yes, 0 = no).
custom = extent to which product requires client-specific customization (1=little, 5=substantial).
cost = pre- and after-sales requirements during the commercialization (1=little, 5=substantial).

NOTES

1. As Oviatt and McDougall (1994) point out, this may not be a disadvantage. For international new ventures, organizational routines that make no difference whether sales are domestic or international can be a source of future competitive advantage.

2. Furthermore, this variable enables us to capture different effects that affect the sales channel choice irrespectively of the setting. It is not our objective in this study to determine those factors, as we are primarily interested in the implications of doing business in a foreign environment. We do, however, include this variable as a proxy to avoid a possible bias in our results.

Oliver Burgel and Gordon C. Murray

3. The chosen service NACE codes (telecommunications services and software) allow for only a crude classification of relatively new industries, such as software. Accordingly, retail outlets for software and computer hardware are frequently classified as NACE 72.20. The sharp reduction of the number of eligible firms can be attributed mainly to the removal of these firms from the database.

4. Respondents did, for example, indicate sales modes such as the formation of export cooperatives and global distribution deals with multinationals. In the latter case, the sales transaction has been carried out between the U.K. subsidiary of the multinational and the start-up, whose international activities mainly consisted of setting up technical support offices abroad. Because of their heterogeneity, these entry modes are excluded from the analysis.

5. We are grateful to one of the reviewers, whose comments helped clarify this point.

6. We have also estimated our models excluding this variable. This did not lead to any directional changes of the effects of the independent variables. Furthermore, there were no changes of significance, and the magnitude of effects in relation to each other remained fairly similar. Results are available from the authors on request.

ACKNOWLEDGMENTS

The authors thank the Anglo-German Foundation for the Study of Industrial Society, Apax Partners & Co. Ventures Ltd., and the Innovation Unit of the Department of Trade and Industry for their generous financial support. The authors are also indebted to Dun and Bradstreet UK Ltd. for providing the database from which the sample is drawn. The authors acknowledge the valuable contributions of Andreas Fier and Georg Licht from the Center for European Economic Research in Mannheim, Germany, and Robin Wensley from Warwick Business School. The views expressed in this article are solely those of the authors, as is the responsibility for any errors of fact or omission. A previous version of this article was presented at the International Conference on Globalization and Emerging Businesses in Montreal, August 1998.

REFERENCES

Agarwal, Sanjeev and Sridhar Ramaswami (1992), "Choice of Foreign Market Entry Mode: Impact of Ownership, Location and Internalization Factors," *Journal of International Business Studies*, 23 (1), 1–27.

Andersen, Otto (1993), "On the Internationalization Process of Firms: A Critical Analysis," *Journal of International Business Studies*, 24 (2), 209–31.

——— (1997), "Internationalization and Market Entry Mode: A Review of Theories and Conceptual Frameworks," *Management International Review*, 37 (Special Issue 2), 27–42.

Anderson, Erin and Hubert A. Gatignon (1986), "Modes of Foreign Market Entry: A Transaction Cost Analysis and Propositions," *Journal of International Business Studies*, 17 (3), 1–26.

Anderson, James C. and James A. Narus (1990), "A Model of Distributor Firm and Manufacturer Firm Working Partnerships," *Journal of Marketing*, 54 (1), 42–58.

Aulakh, Preet S. and Masaaki Kotabe (1997), "Antecedents and Performance Implications of Channel Integration in Foreign Markets," *Journal of International Business Studies*, 27 (1), 145–75.

Bamberger, Ingolf and Michael Evers (1994), "Internationalization Behavior of Small and Medium-Sized Enterprises—Empirical Results," in *Product/Market Strategies of Small and Medium-sized Enterprises*, Ingolf Bamberger, ed. Aldershot: Ashgate Publishing, 310–63.

Barkema, Harry G. and Freek Vermeulen (1998), "International Ex-

THE AUTHORS

Oliver Burgel *is a research fellow at the Foundation for Entrepreneurial Management at London Business School.*

Gordon Murray *is associate professor of entrepreneurial management at London Business School.*

pansion Through Start-Up or Acquisition: A Learning Perspective," *Academy of Management Journal*, 41 (1), 7–26.

Bell, Jim (1995), "The Internationalization of Small Computer Software Firms—A Further Challenge to Stage Theories," *European Journal of Marketing*, 29 (8), 60–75.

Bloodgood, James M., Harry J. Sapienza, and James G. Almeida (1996), "The Internationalization of New High-Potential U.S. Ventures: Antecedents and Outcomes," *Entrepreneurship Theory & Practice*, 20 (4), 61–76.

Boter, Håkan and Carin Holmquist (1996), "Industry Characteristics and Internationalization Processes in Small Firms," *Journal of Business Venturing*, 11, 471–87.

Brüderl, Josef and Rudolf Schüssler (1990), "Organizational Mortality: The Liabilities of Newness and Adolescence," *Administrative Science Quarterly*, 35 (3), 530–47.

Brush, Candida G. and Pieter A. Vanderwerf (1992), "A Comparison of Methods and Sources for Obtaining Estimates of New Venture Performance," *Journal of Business Venturing*, 7 (2), 157–70.

Butchart R. (1987), "A New UK Definition of High-Technology Industries," *Economic Trends*, 400, 82–88.

Cavusgil, S.T. (1980), "On the Internationalization Process of the Firm," *European Research*, 8 (6), 273–81.

——— and Shaoming Zou (1994), "Marketing Strategy-Performance Relationship: An Investigation of the Empirical Links in Export Markets," *Journal of Marketing*, 58 (January), 1–21.

——— Shaoming Zou, and G.M. Naidu (1993), "Product and Promotion Adaptation in Export Ventures: An Empirical Investigation," *Journal of International Business Studies*, 24 (3), 479–506.

Davidson, W.H. and D.G. McFetridge (1985), "Key Characteristics in the Choice of International Technology Transfer Mode," *Journal of International Business Studies*, 16 (Summer), 5–21.

Erramilli, M.K. and C.P. Rao (1993), "Service Firms' International Entry-Mode Choice: A Modified Transaction Cost Analysis Approach," *Journal of Marketing*, 57 (July), 19–38.

Gemünden, Hans G. (1991), "Success Factors of Export Marketing: A Meta-Analytic Critique of the Empirical Studies," in *New Perspectives on International Marketing*, Stanley J. Paliwoda, ed. London: Routledge, 33–62.

Heide, Jan B. and George John (1994), "Interorganizational Governance in Marketing Channels," *Journal of Marketing*, 56 (April), 32–44.

Hennart, Jean F. (1989), "Can the 'New Forms of Investment' Substitute for the 'Old Forms'?" *Journal of International Business Studies*, 20 (2), 211–34.

——— (1990), "A Transaction Cost Theory of Equity Joint Ventures," *Strategic Management Journal*, 9 (4), 361–74.

Hill, Charles W.L., Peter Hwang, and W.C. Kim (1990), "An Eclectic Theory of the Choice of International Entry Mode," *Strategic Management Journal*, 11 (2), 117–28.

Hutt, Michael D. and Thomas W. Speh (1992), *Business Marketing Management*. Orlando, FL: The Dryden Press.

Johanson, Jan and Jan-Erik Vahlne (1977), "The Internationalization Process of the Firm—A Model of Knowledge Development and Increasing Foreign Market Commitment," *Journal of International Business Studies*, 4 (1), 20–29.

—— and —— (1990), "The Mechanism of Internationalization," *International Marketing Review*, 7 (4), 11–24.

Jolly, V.K., Matti Alahuhta, and Jean-Pierre Jeannet (1992), "Challenging the Incumbent: How High-Technology Start-Ups Compete Globally," *Journal of Strategic Change*, 1, 71–82.

Klein, Saul, Gary L. Frazier, and Victor J. Roth (1990), "A Transaction Cost Analysis Model of Channel Integration in International Markets," *Journal of Marketing Research*, 27 (May), 196–208.

Knight, Gary A. and S.T. Cavusgil (1996), "The Born Global Firm: A Challenge to Traditional Internationalization Theory," *Advances in International Marketing*, 8, 11–26.

Kogut, Bruce and Harbir Singh (1988), "The Effect of National Culture on the Choice of Entry Mode," *Journal of International Business Studies*, 19 (3), 411–32.

Leonidou, Leonidas C. and Constanine S. Katsikeas (1996), "The Export Development Process: An Integrative Review of Empirical Models," *Journal of International Business Studies*, 27 (3), 517–51.

Lindell, Martin and Necmi Karagozoglu (1997), "Global Strategies of US and Scandinavian R&D Intensive Small- and Medium-Sized Companies," *European Management Journal*, 15 (1), 92–100.

Lindqvist, Maria (1991), "Infant Multinationals: The Internationalization of Young, Technology-Based Swedish Firms," doctoral dissertation, Stockholm School of Economics, Institute of International Business.

Madhok, Anoop (1997), "Cost, Value and Foreign Market Entry Mode: The Transaction and the Firm," *Strategic Management Journal*, 18 (1), 39–61.

McDougall, Patricia P. and Benjamin Oviatt (1996), "New Venture Internationalization, Strategic Change and Performance: A Follow-Up Study," *Journal of Business Venturing*, 11 (1), 23–40.

——, Scott Shane, and Benjamin Oviatt (1994), "Explaining the Formation of International New Ventures: The Limits of International Business Research," *Journal of Business Venturing*, 9 (November), 469–87.

McKinsey & Company (1993), *Emerging Exporters: Australia's High Value-Added Manufacturing Exporters*. Melbourne: Australian Manufacturing Council.

Meldrum, M.J. (1995), "Marketing High-Tech Products: The Emerging Themes," *European Journal of Marketing*, 29 (10), 45–58.

Murray, Gordon C. (1996), "A Synthesis of Six Exploratory, European Case Studies of Successfully-Exited, Venture Capital Financed, New Technology Based Firms," *Entrepreneurship Theory and Practice*, 20 (4), 44–60.

Oakey, Ray, Roy Rothwell, and Sarah Cooper (1988), *The Management of Innovation in High-Technology Small Firms*. London: Pinter Publishers.

Start-Up Companies in High-Technology Industries

Oviatt, Benjamin, and Patricia P. McDougall (1994), "Toward a Theory of International New Ventures," *Journal of International Business Studies*, 25 (1), 45–64.

—— and —— (1997), "Challenges for Internationalization Process Theory: The Case of International New Ventures," *Management International Review*, 37 (Special Issue 2), 85–99.

Reuber, A.R. and Eileen Fisher (1997), "The Influence of the Management Team's International Experience on the Internationalization Behavior of SMEs," *Journal of International Business Studies*, 28 (4), 807–825.

Roberts, Edward B. (1991), *Entrepreneurs in High Technology.* New York: Oxford University Press.

—— and Todd A. Senturia (1996), "Globalizing the Emerging High-Technology Company," *Industrial Marketing Management*, 25 (6), 491–506.

Robertson, Thomas S. and Hubert A. Gatignon (1998), "Technology Development Mode: A Transaction Cost Conceptualization," *Strategic Management Journal*, 19 (6), 515–31.

Root, Franklin R. (1994), *Entry Strategies for International Markets.* New York: Lexington Books.

Shrader, Rodney C., Benjamin M. Oviatt, and Patricia P. McDougall (1997), "Overcoming Foreign Market Risks: The Case Of New Ventures," paper presented at the Annual Academy of Management Conference, Boston (August).

Stinchcombe, Arthur (1965), "Social Structure and Organizations," in *Handbook of Organizations*, James G. March, ed. Chicago: Rand McNally, 153–93.

Teece, David J., Gary Pisano, and Amy Shuen (1997), "Dynamic Capabilities and Strategic Management," *Strategic Management Journal*, 18 (7), 509–533.

Waters, Malcolm (1995), *Globalization.* London: Routledge.

Williamson, Oliver E. (1985), *The Economic Institutions of Capitalism.* New York: The Free Press.

Zacharakis, Andrew L. (1997), "Entrepreneurial Entry into Foreign Markets: A Transaction Cost Perspective," *Entrepreneurship Theory & Practice*, 21 (Spring), 23–39.

[10]

Journal of International Business Studies (2004) 35, 124–141
© 2004 Palgrave Macmillan Ltd   All rights reserved 0047-2506 $25 00
www.jibs.net

Innovation, organizational capabilities, and the born-global firm

Gary A Knight[1] and
S Tamar Cavusgil[2]

[1]College of Business, Florida State University,
Tallahassee, FL, USA; [2]Eli Broad Graduate School
of Business, Michigan State University, East
Lansing, USA

Correspondence:
Dr GA Knight, College of Business, Florida
State University, Tallahassee, FL 32306-
1110, USA.
Tel: +1 850 644 1140
Fax: +1 850 644 4098
E-mail: gknight@cob.fsu.edu

Abstract
We investigate born-global firms as early adopters of internationalization – that is, companies that expand into foreign markets and exhibit international business prowess and superior performance, from or near their founding. Our explication highlights the critical role of innovative culture, as well as knowledge and capabilities, in this unique breed of international, entrepreneurial firm. Case studies are analyzed to better understand the early internationalization phenomenon and reveal key orientations and strategies that engender international success among these innovative firms. Case findings are then validated in a survey-based study. Despite the scarce resources typical of young firms, our findings reveal that born-global firms leverage a distinctive mix of orientations and strategies that allow them to succeed in diverse international markets. Findings have important implications for the internationalization of contemporary firms.
Journal of International Business Studies (2004) 35, 124–141.
doi:10.1057/palgrave.jibs.8400071

Keywords: early adopters of internationalization; innovation and capabilities; born-global firms

Innovation, knowledge, and capabilities have been central themes of research on the strategy and performance of the firm. Companies that operate internationally from an early stage in their development – early adopters of internationalization or 'born-global firms' – are emerging in substantial numbers worldwide. Despite the scarce financial, human, and tangible resources that characterize most new businesses, these early internationalizing firms leverage innovativeness, knowledge, and capabilities to achieve considerable foreign market success early in their evolution. Sometimes referred to as *international new ventures* or *global start-ups*, they have come of age during the current era of globalization and advanced technologies. Consistent with other scholars (e.g., Autio *et al.*, 2000; Knight and Cavusgil, 1996; Oviatt and McDougall, 1994; Rennie, 1993), we define *born globals* as business organizations that, from or near their founding, seek superior international business performance from the application of knowledge-based resources to the sale of outputs in multiple countries.

The distinguishing feature of these firms is that their origins are international, as demonstrated by management's global focus and the commitment of specific resources to international activities. In contrast to the traditional pattern of firms that operate in the

Received: 19 November 2002
Revised: 19 October 2003
Accepted: 19 November 2003
Online publication date: 8 January 2004

domestic market for many years and gradually evolve into international trade (e.g., Johanson and Vahlne, 1977), these early adopters of internationalization begin with a global view of their markets, and develop the capabilities needed to achieve their international goals at or near the firm's founding. We focus on the phenomenon of early internationalization and the capabilities that born globals leverage for achieving superior performance in international markets.

Reports on the widespread emergence of born globals in numerous nations (e.g., Moen and Servais, 2002; Nikkei Sangyoo Shimbun, 1995; Rennie, 1993) indicate that it is an important phenomenon. These businesses first emerged in countries with small domestic markets, but are now appearing in markedly large numbers throughout the world. The phenomenon appears to be relatively universal, with researchers noting its occurrence in virtually all major trading countries (e.g., Nikkei Sangyoo Shimbun, 1995; OECD, 1997; Simon, 1996). Despite the scarce financial, human, and tangible resources that characterize most new businesses, born globals progress to internationalization relatively rapidly – the period from domestic establishment to initial foreign market entry is often 3 years or less (Autio *et al.*, 2000; McDougall and Oviatt, 2000; OECD, 1997; Rennie, 1993). The smaller size typical of young firms appears to confer a sort of flexibility that provides key benefits for succeeding in foreign markets.

In the external international business environment, early adoption of internationalization is likely driven by two key trends that have substantially reduced the transactions costs of foreign market expansion. The first is the globalization of markets, which involves countless firms in international sourcing, production, and marketing as well as cross-border alliances for product development and distribution. Globalization is associated with increasing homogenization of buyer preferences around the world, which has made international business easier by simplifying product development and positioning in foreign markets. The second trend is technological advances in information and communications technologies, production methods, transportation, and international logistics, which are reducing business transactions costs and facilitating extraordinary growth in international trade. Widespread diffusion of e-mail, the Internet, and related technologies has made internationalization a more viable and cost-effective option.

Although these trends facilitate early internationalization, by themselves they are insufficient to explain intriguing processes at work in the firm's internal environment. Despite their current and projected impact, there has been little research that attempts to explain why born globals internationalize early. More significantly, there has been almost no empirical research that examines the factors that drive the superior international performance of these young, highly entrepreneurial firms. In addition, there has been very little empirical research aimed at uncovering the actual bundles of capabilities that characterize truly innovative firms, as well as the causal link between the possession of particular types of knowledge, organizational routines, and superior performance (Lewin and Massini, 2003; Massini *et al.*, 2003).

Accordingly, a substantive investigation in this area is overdue. The study reported here explores the role of innovative culture and organizational capabilities in the early adoption of internationalization and subsequent international performance in the born-global firm. We intend to make several contributions. First, we investigate the phenomenon of early internationalization among a unique breed of international organization. Second, we highlight the importance of several key organizational capabilities that engender international success in born globals – research that has implications not only for these firms but also for internationalizing smaller firms in general. Third, and more specifically, we examine the critical linkages among entrepreneurial orientation, marketing orientation, and other key organizational capabilities in born-global international success. In the process, we extend the innovation literature by linking innovation to the phenomenon of early adoption of internationalization.

In the next section, we offer a conceptual framework that provides the rationale for the emergence of early adopters of internationalization in the current era. We then summarize the research methods used in this study. Specifically, we conduct a series of exploratory case studies on born-global firms, which lead to a set of hypotheses. We then assess these hypotheses in a confirmatory, survey-based study. Finally, we report on empirical findings, providing an overview and substantive discussion.

Conceptual foundations

The ability to internationalize early and succeed in foreign markets is a function of the internal capabilities of the firm (Autio *et al.*, 2000; McDougall *et al.*, 1994; Zahra *et al.*, 2000). The importance of internal capabilities is rooted in evolutionary economics (Nelson and Winter, 1982), wherein innovation processes are explicitly described. The evolutionary economics view implies that the superior ability of certain firms to sustain *innovation* and, as a result, create new *knowledge* leads to the development of organizational *capabilities*, consisting of critical *competences* and embedded *routines*. These firm resources in turn lead to superior performance, particularly in highly competitive or challenging environments (Nelson and Winter, 1982).

Innovation results from two major sources: (1) internal R&D that draws on the firm's accumulated knowledge, and (2) imitation of the innovations of other firms (Lewin and Massini, 2003; Massini *et al.*, 2003; Nelson and Winter, 1982). In addition to introducing new goods and methods of production, R&D also supports the opening of new markets and reinvention of the firm's operations to serve those markets optimally (Nelson and Winter, 1982; Schumpeter, 1934). Innovation is particularly the domain of entrepreneurs, whose function is:

to reform or revolutionize the pattern of production by exploiting an invention or, more generally, an untried technological possibility for producing a new commodity or producing an old one in a new way, by opening up... a new outlet for products

and so forth (Schumpeter, 1942: 132). Firms' innovative culture, combined with appropriate accumulated knowledge stocks, engenders the development or improvement of products and new methods for doing business (Dosi, 1988; Nelson and Winter, 1982). Internationalization, or new entry into markets overseas, is an innovative act (Casson, 2000; Schumpeter, 1939; Simmonds and Smith, 1968), and born-global firms are particularly innovative in this regard.

The resource-based view (RBV) (e.g., Grant, 1996a; Penrose, 1959; Rumelt, 1984; Teece and Pisano, 1994; Wernerfelt, 1984) helps to explain how, in the context of an innovative culture, knowledge and resultant organizational capabilities are developed and leveraged by enterprising firms. Differential endowment of resources is an important determinant of organizational capabilities and performance (Barney, 1991; Grant, 1996a; Teece and Pisano, 1994; Wernerfelt, 1984). Foundational resources are particularly important in turbulent

business environments because they are a more stable basis for strategy formulation (Grant, 1996a; Prahalad and Hamel, 1990). Knowledge is the most important resource, and the integration of individuals' specialized knowledge is the essence of organizational capabilities (Conner and Prahalad, 1996; Dierickx and Cool, 1989; Grant, 1996a; Leonard-Barton, 1992; Nelson and Winter, 1982; Solow, 1957).

In international business, knowledge provides particular advantages that facilitate foreign market entry and operations (e.g., Kogut and Zander, 1993). Knowledge is used here to refer to the capacity of the firm to apprehend and use relationships among informational factors to achieve intended ends (Autio *et al.*, 2000). Gross output and overall organizational performance are directly traceable to increases in stocks of organizational knowledge (Nelson and Winter, 1982; Solow, 1957). The integration of specialist knowledge hinges on the nature and quality of the firm's organizational routines, which involve continuous conversion of, especially, *tacit* knowledge (Polanyi, 1966) into business activities that create value for customers. Tacit knowledge is embedded in individuals and cannot be expressed explicitly or codified in written form (Nonaka, 1994).

In this regard, the most important knowledge resources are unique, inimitable, and immobile, reflecting the distinctive pathways of each individual firm (Dierickx and Cool, 1989; Grant, 1991, 1996a). Uniqueness facilitates profitable pricing that minimizes the need to consider competitors' offerings, inimitability helps ensure that profits will not be competed away, and immobility reduces the threat that proprietary knowledge will be disseminated to rival firms (Nelson and Winter, 1982; Teece and Pisano, 1994). Ultimately, the firm *accumulates* firm-specific knowledge internally (Barney, 1991; Dierickx and Cool, 1989; Teece *et al.*, 1997). Organizational knowledge derived from multiple individual sources is greater than the sum of its parts, and becomes a key strategic asset (Nelson and Winter, 1982). It is reinforced in all the activities of the firm and becomes increasingly embedded in its routines (Autio *et al.*, 2000).

The idiosyncratic knowledge base acquired by following unique pathways gives rise to organizational capabilities (Dierickx and Cool, 1989; Nelson and Winter, 1982; Nonaka, 1994; Teece *et al.*, 1997). Organizational capabilities reflect the ability of the firm to perform repeatedly, or 'replicate', productive tasks that relate to the firm's capacity to create value through effecting the transformation of inputs into outputs (Nelson and Winter, 1982; Teece and Pisano, 1994). Capabilities emerge via the integration of specialist knowledge across a number of individuals, and are associated with the development of organizational competences and routines (Grant, 1991; Teece and Pisano, 1994). Competences are those knowledge-intensive, performance-enhancing business activities in which the firm is particularly skilled (Teece et al., 1997). Routines consist of regular and consistently practiced patterns of individual and business behaviors that institutionalize individual or organizational knowledge about the firm's ongoing, rent-generating activities (Dosi, 1988; Nelson and Winter, 1982; Teece and Pisano, 1994). Routinization of organizational activities embeds capabilities into organizational memory, engendering a unique configuration of firm resources.

Organizational capabilities are the main source of the firm's performance advantages (e.g., Grant, 1991). Capabilities have two major aspects: (1) the shifting character of the business environment; and (2) strategic management in appropriately adapting, integrating, and re-configuring knowledge-based capabilities toward the changing environment. Ideally, capabilities are 'dynamic', reflecting the ability of managers to renew the firm's competences so as to achieve congruence with the changing business environment (Teece et al., 1997). Replication of organizational capabilities involves transferring or re-deploying capabilities from one organizational or business environmental setting to another, so as to extend the firm's performance into new markets, new product categories, and new ways of doing business (Nelson and Winter, 1982; Teece et al., 1997).

Organizational capabilities and the born-global firm

Innovating firms develop their own unique knowledge and resultant capabilities that engender organizational performance. New product-market development in young, innovative firms is fluid and dynamic, with ongoing market expansion and redefinition resulting in frequent competitive improvements to the firm's offerings and routines (Utterback and Abernathy, 1975). Whereas larger, long-established firms usually experience substantial bureaucratization that hinders their innovative activities, smaller or younger firms are more flexible, less bureaucratic, and generally enjoy internal conditions that encourage innovativeness

(e.g., Lewin and Massini, 2003; Penrose, 1959; Schumpeter, 1942).

Lewin and Massini (2003) point to various empirical studies on the effects of firm size and age on innovation. The studies conclude that there is a positive relationship between firm size and R&D activities, but innovation capabilities appear to be less than proportional to size, and therefore R&D productivity declines with size, and also therefore with age. The flexibility of young and agile firms enhances the ability to transform product and process innovations into business activities that support superior business performance (Lewin and Massini, 2003).

We conjecture that young firms with a strong innovation culture and a proclivity to pursue international markets tend to internationalize earlier than internationally oriented young firms that lack an innovation culture. This same innovation culture also should facilitate the acquisition of knowledge, leading to capabilities that drive organizational performance. Our research suggests that born globals are inherently entrepreneurial and innovative firms that possess these types of characteristics. These businesses display a specific pattern of knowledge and capabilities that engenders early internationalization and sustainable, superior performance in foreign markets.

The youth of these firms is interlinked with entrepreneurial and innovative approaches to doing business. Being young, born globals tend to lack substantial financial and human resources, as well as plant, equipment, and other physical resources. It is these *tangible* resources that older firms typically have relied upon to drive their performance in foreign markets. In contrast, born globals leverage a collection of fundamental *intangible* knowledge-based capabilities in the cultivation of foreign markets early in their evolution.

Superior performance is an outcome of the firm's entrepreneurial and managerial knowledge (Autio et al., 2000; Penrose, 1959). Knowledge about international markets and operations, as well as the efficiency with which such knowledge is acquired, is a critical determinant of superior international performance in entrepreneurial firms (Autio et al., 2000). Lewin and Massini (2003) contend that firms with superior innovation and knowledge-creation processes have more sophisticated, more highly developed and elaborated knowledge-creation routines and learning regimes. Consistent with innovation scholars (e.g., Lewin and Massini, 2003; Nelson and Winter, 1982), we conjecture that born globals undertake R&D projects that lead to entering new foreign markets, *or* they observe other early adopters of internationalization entering foreign markets and imitate such behaviors accordingly.

Capabilities-based resources are especially important to born globals, typically poor in tangible resources, because they deal with diverse environments across numerous foreign markets (Luo, 2000). Possession of such capabilities helps firms to attenuate their liabilities of foreignness and newness (Oviatt and McDougall, 1994). Foreignness reflects the unfamiliarity and strangeness that firms experience in foreign markets. Newness refers both to the state of being a young or new firm and to the entering of new markets – both characteristics of born-global firms. The ability to consistently replicate the firm's capabilities across numerous and varied markets produces value for born globals by supporting, especially, international expansion (Teece *et al.*, 1997).

Organizational routines and administrative heritage

A key dimension of born-global firms is that they appear to lack the deeply rooted administrative heritage (Collis, 1991; Miller and Friesen, 1984) of long-established businesses. Well-established firms typically must unlearn routines rooted in domestic operations before new, internationally oriented routines can be learned. Unlearning embedded routines becomes more difficult as firms get older, because new knowledge that leads to new routines tends to conflict with existing operations and management's embedded mental models (Autio *et al.*, 2000; Barkema and Vermeulen, 1998). Well-established firms have systematized routines that are costly to change and limit the ability of the firm to innovate (Utterback and Abernathy, 1975). The older firm's previous investments and its repertoire of organizational routines constrain its future behavior (Leonard-Barton, 1992; Teece and Pisano, 1994). Bounded rationality and embedded 'hierarchies' (Grant, 1991) of routines inhibit the ability of well-established firms to adopt new technological solutions, leading to an emphasis on developing knowledge and routines closely related to or adjoining their existing knowledge and routines, but which may be sub-optimal in light of evolving or varying environmental circumstances.

In contrast, from their earliest days, the innovative culture of born-global firms gives rise to specific capabilities suitable for success in foreign

markets. Their entrepreneurial orientation is associated with an innovative and proactive approach to internationalization. Organizational learning theory suggests that the development of new knowledge occurs best under conditions in which there are little or no existing organizational routines to unlearn (Autio *et al.*, 2000; Cohen and Levinthal, 1990). This implies that young firms may be better equipped to acquire the requisite knowledge about international business. Escalating internationalization facilitates further learning opportunities that benefit their performance because of the range of unique environments and competitive situations to which these firms are exposed. Thus early internationalization may confer substantial benefits in terms of knowledge acquisition about international markets and how to succeed there. In the next section, we describe the specific capabilities that drive the international performance of born-global firms.

Delineation of key capabilities and linkages

As the widespread emergence of born globals is relatively recent, little empirical work has been attempted on this topic. Accordingly, a two-phase research design was adopted that began with qualitative interviews to develop a broader understanding of these organizations and to uncover key constructs and linkages. In the second phase, we conducted survey-based research on a large sample of born-global firms to validate findings from the qualitative phase. In-depth interviews were conducted with 33 professionals. These included senior managers at 24 early internationalizing firms, six scholars who have investigated born globals, and three international trade experts who are key observers of global business trends. Most of the interviewed firms were founded after 1985, were selling half or more of their total sales abroad, and had ventured abroad within 3 years of founding. The interviews typically lasted about 45 min and were analyzed and organized according to patterns of consistent themes of firm culture, strategy, and performance. In all, 18 of the businesses marketed various industrial products, and the remaining six sold consumer goods. The average firm had $52 million in annual sales and 296 employees. The capabilities and associated relationships that emerged from these interviews are discussed below.

In general, the qualitative phase of the study revealed that born globals are likely to be formed by entrepreneurs who pursue foreign ventures with a strong marketing orientation. They tend to leverage

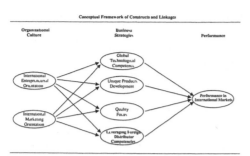

Figure 1   Conceptual framework of constructs and linkages.

technological prowess, relatively unique products, and a strong quality focus to sell their offerings via independent distributors in markets worldwide. Among operational attributes, entrepreneurial culture, marketing skills, superior and distinctively positioned products, and leveraging strong distributors, all emerged as important capabilities for born globals to position themselves in foreign markets.

Figure 1 highlights the specific constructs and relationships that emerged from the qualitative research. Ultimately, the interviewed firms were seeking superior *performance in international markets*, which is defined as the extent to which financial and other goals are achieved as a function of business strategies. Performance comprises expectations about the achievement of these objectives in addition to more conventional economic goals, such as profitability, sales growth, market share, and general international success. Each firm's unique base of resource-derived capabilities drives its international performance. The performance antecedents and associated linkages proposed in Figure 1 are elaborated next.

Organizational culture

Within the framework of evolutionary economics, specific ways of doing business emerge from the core capabilities founded on the knowledge and skills embodied in organizational employees, and codified and structured into a base of tacit information and routines. Innovative firms devise particular types of knowledge and capabilities that become embedded in the organization's culture. In our case studies, the great majority of interviewed managers at born-global firms spoke about the importance of being internationally oriented as well as entrepreneurial and innovative in the pursuit of foreign

markets. They also emphasized the importance of developing and applying a strong marketing prowess abroad. Based on these findings, we conceive that the most important organizational culture attributes in born-global firms are what we term international entrepreneurial orientation and international marketing orientation.

Having an *international entrepreneurial orientation* implies that these firms make the leap into international markets because of unique entrepreneurial competences and outlook (e.g., Autio *et al.*, 2000; McDougall *et al.*, 1994). The interviewed born globals seem to possess a distinctive entrepreneurial orientation that, when combined with other resources and capabilities such as strong marketing skills, allows them to see and exploit opportunities in foreign markets. International entrepreneurial orientation reflects the firm's overall innovativeness and proactiveness in the pursuit of international markets. It is associated with innovativeness, managerial vision, and proactive competitive posture (Covin and Slevin, 1989; Dess *et al.*, 1997; Lumpkin and Dess, 1996; Miller and Friesen, 1984). These activities are consistent with what Lumpkin and Dess (1996) term 'new entry,' the 'central idea underlying the concept of entrepreneurship' (p 136). For born globals, it implies the entering of new (that is, international) markets with new or established goods. A posture that is innovative, visionary, and proactive may be necessary amongst a class of firms that, in the face of relatively limited resources, takes the initiative to pursue new opportunities in complex markets, typically fraught with uncertainty and risk.

Dess *et al.* (1997) point to a substantial literature that emphasizes the inherent value in entrepreneurial behavior and a linkage between this behavior and desired organizational outcomes. Possession of an entrepreneurial orientation gives rise to certain 'processes, practices, and decision-making activities' associated with successful entry into new markets (Lumpkin and Dess, 1996). Whereas unbridled risk seeking may engender inferior performance, having an entrepreneurial orientation in diverse foreign environments tends to support the realization of key strategic initiatives that augment international success. Accordingly, international entrepreneurial orientation should be instrumental to the development and enactment of key organizational routines in born-global firms.

The critical role of marketing prowess overseas was also strongly emphasized by virtually all interviewees in the case studies. We conceptualize this as *international marketing orientation*, which refers to a managerial mindset that emphasizes the creation of value, via key marketing elements, for foreign customers (Cavusgil and Zou, 1994). Market orientation, marketing competence, and other marketing-related activities engender superior organizational performance (e.g., Albaum and Peterson, 1984; Cavusgil *et al.*, 1993; McKee *et al.*, 1992; Slater and Narver, 1992). Within their markets, marketing-oriented firms seek to offer products and services whose value buyers perceive to exceed the expected value of alternative offerings. The urge to continuously provide superior buyer value and attain superior performance drives the firm to create and maintain a business culture that fosters the requisite business behaviors. Globalization is facilitating the emergence of customers who are better organized, have more information, and are generally more demanding. A heightened focus on the customer is driven by a more competitive international marketplace, rapid changes in technology that have shortened product life cycles, and the mediocre financial performance of many firms. A marketing orientation provides the foundation from which the firm interacts with diverse foreign markets. Managers with this orientation create specific marketing-related strategies aimed at overcoming these challenges and maximizing performance.

Business strategies

The RBV suggests a holistic view of the firm, in which the coordinated deployment of resources and capabilities provides the foundation for creating, producing, and marketing products (Young *et al.*, 2000). Along these lines, the case studies suggest that born globals are highly innovative firms whose possession of the foundational capabilities of international entrepreneurial orientation and international marketing orientation engender the development of a specific collection of organizational strategies. The most important business strategies employed by born-global firms that emerged in our investigation are global technological competence, unique products development, quality focus, and leveraging of foreign distributor competences. These are described next.

Most interviewed firms exhibited strong technological capabilities in their respective product or industry categories. *Global technological competence* refers to the firm's technological ability relative to cohort firms in its industry. It facilitates the creation of superior products and the improvement

of existing products, as well as greater effectiveness and efficiency in production processes. Advances in production technologies facilitate low-cost, small-scale manufacturing that enable smaller-scale firms to efficiently serve the specialized needs of market niches worldwide. Moreover, global technological leaders tend to leverage information and communications technologies to interact more efficiently with channel members and customers, and to obtain various other benefits (Clark, 1987; Zahra *et al.*, 2000).

Emphasis on developing new technologies is a natural routine for innovative, entrepreneurial firms (Nelson and Winter, 1982; Schumpeter, 1934). Entrepreneurship derives from 'the capacity of small firms to leverage resources and transform existing markets through innovation' (Steensma *et al.*, 2000: 951). This basic innovativeness gives rise to new ideas and creative processes, reflecting a willingness to depart from existing technologies (Lumpkin and Dess, 1996). Entrepreneurial firms continually seek to create products and operating methods that improve organizational performance (e.g., Lumpkin and Dess, 1996; Miller and Friesen, 1984; Mintzberg, 1973; Zahra *et al.*, 2000). Overall, innovation is a critical entrepreneurial process for firm performance in competitive international markets (e.g., Kotabe, 1990; Miller and Friesen, 1984; Steensma *et al.*, 2000; Zahra *et al.*, 2000).

International marketing orientation can also foster global technological competence. Firms leverage technology to innovate in the creation and improvement of products, as well as the adaptation of products for foreign markets. Information and communication technologies facilitate learning about customers and competitors, efficient channel interaction, and other benefits. Overall, as with most companies, technology facilitates the marketing process in born-global firms. The above discussion leads to our first hypothesis, which, consistent with Figure 1, relates international entrepreneurial and marketing orientations to global technological competence:

H1: In the born-global firm, global technological competence is a function of (a) international entrepreneurial orientation and (b) international marketing orientation.

In addition to technology, the interviewed firms also emphasized having relatively unique products. The ability to develop unique products derives from the innovative and knowledge-intensive capabilities of these firms. *Unique products development* reflects the creation of distinctive products, and is akin to differentiation strategy, which involves creating customer loyalty by uniquely meeting a particular need. Marketing scholars have long recognized the inherent value in providing unique offerings, so as to differentiate the firm from rivals (e.g., Cavusgil *et al.*, 1993; Smith, 1956). *A priori*, valuable unique products should allow resource-constrained firms to readily enter foreign markets and may be particularly appropriate to born-global firms, which tend to operate in niche markets and hold relatively specialized resources. The approach is typically associated with innovative product features, excellent customer service, or patented know-how – all factors that distinguish the firm from its competitors (Miles and Snow, 1978; Miller and Friesen, 1984; Porter, 1980).

Knowledge developed within innovative processes provides the capabilities needed for new technology development, and is perhaps the key resource that born globals use to develop unique products and overcome the indigenous advantages enjoyed by local firms (Oviatt and McDougall, 1994). To the extent that the knowledge used to develop a unique product is tacit or imperfectly imitable (Barney, 1991; Grant, 1996b; Autio *et al.*, 2000), individual firms are able to keep such knowledge proprietary. The knowledge intensity of young, entrepreneurial firms is positively related to their growth in international sales (Autio *et al.*, 2000; Zahra *et al.*, 2000). Knowledge and the firm's technological competence should also facilitate the development of unique products. Knowledge that fosters unique products development also allows born globals to serve specific markets well, giving rise to increased market share and sales growth. Offering unique products, at least to the extent that buyers' special needs are served and direct competitive rivalries are minimized, supports superior international performance.

Generally, internationally entrepreneurial firms proactively seek success in foreign markets. However, owing to their youth and relatively smaller size, born globals minimize direct competition with larger or more established rivals. Born globals that aggressively pursue international success develop differentiated offerings and target them at niche markets overseas. This approach is appropriate for maximizing share and other performance goals in a competitive international marketplace typically dominated by larger, resource-endowed firms. Moreover, differentiation strategy and the creation of unique products are marketing-based strategies.

Smaller, resource-constrained firms that are strongly marketing-oriented will be more inclined to undertake strategies that differentiate their offerings from those of rivals, thereby facilitating superior performance. These ideas are evidence of the next hypothesis:

H2: In the born-global firm, unique products development is a function of (a) international entrepreneurial orientation and (b) international marketing orientation.

Virtually all of the executives interviewed emphasized the importance of superior quality in the products that they developed. Born globals appear to leverage their innovativeness and knowledge base to develop offerings of relatively superior quality. *Quality focus* reflects efforts to develop products that meet or exceed customer expectations with respect to features and performance. It represents a broad-based concept that potentially encompasses the full range of the firm's value-adding activities (Aaker and Jacobson, 1994; McGuinness *et al.*, 1991; Mohr-Jackson, 1998). Consumers favor superior quality products, and are willing to pay higher prices for them. Producers and consumers in globalizing environments may be more inclined to benchmark their quality standards against those of foreign-based firms. The new awareness resulting from such comparisons pressures companies to improve (McGuinness *et al.*, 1991). Moreover, emphasis on quality entails innovative processes and provides a means to differentiate goods from those of competitors (Porter, 1980). Quality has been linked to improved performance in domestic (e.g., Aaker and Jacobson, 1994; Buzzell and Gale, 1987; Mohr-Jackson, 1998) and international markets (e.g., McGuinness *et al.*, 1991; Szymanski *et al.*, 1993). To the extent that superior quality reduces rework and service costs while enhancing value, market share and profits can rise, and thus it is likely to be associated with superior performance in born globals (Buzzell and Gale, 1987; Deming, 1982; Szymanski *et al.*, 1993).

Entrepreneurial orientation gives rise to innovative processes and practices intended to maximize organizational success in new markets (Lumpkin and Dess, 1996). Having an international entrepreneurial orientation engenders the development of key strategies, of which our research reveals quality focus is a key component. As an important marketing strategy, firms with a strong international marketing orientation are also likely to promote a quality focus. Providing valuable, quality-enhanced offerings is one of the approaches closely associated with strong marketing capabilities (e.g., Szymanski *et al.*, 1993). Accordingly:

H3: In the born-global firm, quality focus is a function of (a) international entrepreneurial orientation and (b) international marketing orientation.

Internationalizing firms must choose appropriate entry modes. Compared with traditional multinational enterprises, young resource-poor firms tend to favor exporting as their primary entry mode. Exporting offers a high degree of international business flexibility – the ability to change systems and approaches quickly and cost-effectively – a critical consideration in evolving foreign markets (Buckley and Casson, 1998). Indeed, all of the interviewed firms were exporters and tended to rely on independent intermediaries to distribute their products abroad. Foreign export intermediaries typically possess strong market knowledge and particular competences, and perform valuable functions in foreign markets (Peng and York, 2001; Rosson and Ford, 1982).

Although born globals possess various superior capabilities on their own, they must rely to some extent on the capabilities of facilitators in foreign markets to deal with the range of complexities found there. *Leveraging foreign distributor competences* refers to the tendency of born globals to rely on foreign independent distributors and those distributors' specific competences to maximize performance outcomes associated with downstream business activities abroad. The uncertainty, risk, and unique challenges present in foreign markets can be overcome by leveraging the localized market knowledge and competences of foreign intermediaries (Bowersox and Cooper, 1992; Rosson and Ford, 1982).

The flexibility afforded through judicious use of foreign distributors enables entrepreneurial firms to respond rapidly to evolving customer needs, competitor actions, and shifting environmental contingencies. Entrepreneurial firms are given to active exploration of new business opportunities in foreign markets, and the use of competent local intermediaries facilitates this task. Aggressive top managers eager for international success will tend to leverage competent foreign distributors. Strongly marketing-oriented firms will also tend to seek competent foreign intermediaries because, in international markets, strong distribution capabilities facilitate superior promotion, customer relation-

ship management, and other downstream marketing activities. Siguaw *et al.* (1998) found that marketing-oriented attitudes in suppliers are associated with the presence of such attitudes in distributors. In general, the more skillful international marketing is emphasized, the greater the importance that is accorded to the foreign distribution channel (Cavusgil *et al.*, 1993; Mortanges and Vossen, 1999). Accordingly, we hypothesize that:

H4: In the born-global firm, leveraging foreign distributor competences is a function of (a) international entrepreneurial orientation and (b) international marketing orientation.

As elaborated earlier and in Figure 1, the above knowledge- and capabilities-based business strategies are expected to engender superior international performance in born-global firms. To summarize, global technological competence is a critical source of new products and business methods, and has the potential to foster information technology and e-commerce proficiency, all of which can positively influence born-global international performance (e.g., Kotabe, 1990; Zahra *et al.*, 2000). Unique product development yields differentiation strategy benefits (e.g., Porter, 1980; Smith, 1956), which can allow born globals to serve niche markets more capably and minimize harmful interaction with competitors, giving rise to increased sales and other performance gains. Quality focus implies a system of firm resources specifically devoted to creating superior offerings, prompting enhanced customer satisfaction and differentiation benefits, leading to increased customer loyalty and improved performance (e.g., Buzzell and Gale, 1987; Deming, 1982). Leveraging foreign distributor competences is markedly critical to born-global international success because, to the extent that these firms emphasize external market-based entry modes, skillful foreign intermediaries can perform a range of downstream marketing and other activities that enhance international performance. (e.g., Rosson and Ford, 1982; Bowersox and Cooper, 1992). The above reasoning leads to the final hypothesis:

H5: In the born-global firm, superior performance in international markets is primarily a function of (a) global technological competence, (b) unique products development; (c) quality focus, and (d) leveraging foreign distributor competences.

Lastly, it should be noted that foreign distributor competences are likely to drive, and be supported by, the firm's quality focus. This is because quality products are easier for foreign distributors to sell, and foreign distributors can also enhance product quality by providing superior after-sales service, intensive distribution, and so forth. Similarly, to the extent that foreign distributors seek to differentiate themselves and/or focus on target markets, these tasks also can be facilitated when handling relatively unique goods. The hypotheses described above are tested next, by means of a mail survey study.

Method

To provide empirical support for the conceptual framework proposed above, we conducted a cross-industry field survey to collect primary data. The survey instrument was developed in several stages, following appropriate procedures (e.g., Fowler, 1988; Gerbing and Anderson, 1988; Joreskog *et al.*, 2000; Nunnally, 1978) and based on insights gained from the interviews and available literature. The literature was searched to obtain information on the key constructs and scales appropriate for measuring them. Seven-point Likert scales were used to minimize executive response time and effort (Fowler, 1988).

For all constructs except international entrepreneurial orientation and international marketing orientation, the identified unit of analysis was the firm's main export venture to its primary export market. The unit of analysis for the organizational culture constructs was the general firm level. Exporting was emphasized because case studies and other research (e.g., OECD, 1997) suggest it is the most common entry mode of born-global firms. Information on the measurement scales is provided in the Appendix. The scale for international entrepreneurial orientation was based on the scale devised by Khandwalla (1977) and Covin and Slevin (1989). A version of it was used most recently by Steensma *et al.* (2000). The international marketing orientation scale was created for the study based on research by McKee *et al.* (1992). It asks subjects about their skillfulness in marketing management, product adaptation, pricing, advertising, distribution, and other marketing functions, relative to competitors. The global technological competence scale was created for the study and asks subjects about their position relative to competitors with respect to technology, technological innovativeness, and so forth. The scale for unique products

development was derived from research by several scholars (e.g., Miller, 1988; Porter, 1980; Roth and Morrison, 1992). It asks respondents about the relative uniqueness of the firm's main export product, its design, technology, and performance. The quality focus scale is based primarily on the work of Buzzell and Gale (1987) and asks subjects about product quality as well as the extent to which the product meets or exceeds customer expectations with respect to performance and customer service. The scale for leveraging foreign distributor competences was developed for the study, but based partially on McKee *et al.* (1992). It asks about the extent to which respondent expectations have been satisfied with respect to distributor performance of various marketing-related functions, logistical arrangements, after-sales service, and related activities. Lastly, the scale for performance in international markets was obtained from Cavusgil and Zou (1994).

Once a draft questionnaire was completed, it was circulated among four international business scholars, who provided commentary that led to further refinement of the instrument. Next, a pilot study was conducted among 82 small exporting firms to refine the questionnaire. Firms were identified primarily via two databases: *Directory of United States Exporters* (*Journal of Commerce*) and *CorpTech Directory of Technology Companies*. The final questionnaire was targeted to a random sample of 900 manufacturing firms across the United States, founded in 1980 or later, and exporting at least 25% of total production. The 25% cut-off, although somewhat arbitrary, was established in light of the exploratory goals of the research and the attendant need to study exemplary firms. It is more restrictive than the criteria, ranging from 5 to 10%, used in previous studies on early adopters of internationalization (Zahra *et al.*, 2000). Except for these criteria, the surveyed businesses were selected at random from the above commercial databases.

Following a three-wave mailing, 203 usable surveys were returned, reflecting a response rate of about 23%. To assess non-response bias we compared key variables in surveys from a sample of the earliest responding to those of a sample of the latest responding firms (Armstrong and Overton, 1977). In a second test, we compared randomly chosen samples of responding and non-responding firms. Compared variables included number of employees, founding year, total sales, product category, return on investment, sales growth, and market share in main export market. No significant differences ($P<0.05$) were found in these tests and thus non-response bias is not expected to significantly affect study results. Following data collection, measures were subjected to a purification process to verify reliability and validity (Gerbing and Anderson, 1988; Joreskog and Sorbom, 1997; Joreskog *et al.*, 2000).

Initially, exploratory factor analysis was conducted to identify and eliminate potentially troublesome items. Confirmatory factor analysis (CFA) was then conducted in LISREL8 (Joreskog and Sorbom, 1997; Joreskog *et al.*, 2000) to estimate a single measurement model representing relations among all constructs and associated items. The model achieved adequate fit with CFI=0.92, NNFI=0.91, DELTA2=0.92, RNI=0.92, and RMSEA=0.046 (Gerbing and Anderson, 1992; Joreskog and Sorbom, 1997; Joreskog *et al.*, 2000). A second CFA model was estimated, using data from a separate sample of general exporting firms ($n=134$) collected for another study, using the same scales. Results for this model also were satisfactory (CFI=0.90, NNFI=0.89, DELTA2=0.90, RNI=0.90, and RMSEA=0.14). All standardized coefficient loadings in this model were significant at $P<0.01$.

Composite reliability was calculated using the procedures outlined by Fornell and Larcker (1981). The specific formula is

$$CR_\eta = \frac{\left(\Sigma\lambda_{\gamma_i}\right)^2}{\left(\Sigma\lambda_{\gamma_i}\right)^2 + \Sigma\varepsilon_i} \quad (1)$$

where CR_η is the composite reliability for scale η, λ_{γ_i} is the standardized loading for scale item γ_i, and ε_i is the measurement error for scale item γ_i. In the main study, the CR_η values ranged from 0.72 to 0.92, exceeding acceptable standards for exploratory research (Fornell and Larcker, 1981; Nunnally, 1978). In the LISREL measurement model on the main data, all standardized coefficients were sig-

nificant at $P<0.01$, confirming convergent validity. Composite reliability values and standardized coefficient loadings for all construct items from CFA analyses on the main data set are reported in the Appendix. Table 1 presents information on construct means, standard deviations, and Pearson's correlation coefficients among the constructs. LISREL modification indices revealed no substantive cross-loadings of questionnaire items intended to measure specific constructs. We also compared all possible pairs of construct measures (21 in all) by constraining and freeing the associated phi coefficients (ϕ) (Fornell and Larker, 1981). The change in $\chi^2_{(1)}$ in these tests ranged from 54 to 343, greatly exceeding the critical value 3.84 in each case. These tests confirmed the discriminant validity of all construct measures. In all, the study scales were found to be reliable and valid.

Data analysis

Respondent firms represent a range of industries that manufacture various products, such as wastewater treatment systems, medical devices, alarm systems, coiled steel tubing, computer software, textile printing blankets, and oil field surfactants. The average firm had 190 employees and generated $32 million in total sales. On average, foreign customers accounted for 41% of total sales, with firms targeting some 20 countries at the median. The median firm began selling internationally within 2 years of founding.

Table 2 portrays results of the tests to assess hypotheses on born-global firms. The data were analyzed in LISREL8, using path analysis. Results provide strong evidence that global technological competence is significantly ($P<0.01$) a function of international entrepreneurial orientation, partially supporting hypothesis H1. However, the posited relationship between international marketing

Table 1 Construct means, standard deviations, and Pearson's correlation coefficients

Construct	Mean	Standard deviation	(1)	(2)	(3)	(4)	(5)	(6)	(7)
(1) International entrepreneurial orientation	5 13	0.98	1.00						
(2) International marketing orientation	4.64	0.84	0.36	1.00					
(3) Global Technological Competence	5.12	1.02	0.33	0.23	1.00				
(4) Unique products development	4.84	0.98	0.27	0.30	0.44	1.00			
(5) Quality focus	5.75	0.70	0.36	0.44	0.19	0.31	1.00		
(6) Leveraging foreign distributor competences	4.32	0.88	0.19	0.29	0.16	0.17	0.29	1.00	
(7) Performance in international markets	4.58	0.96	0.32	0.49	0.36	0.35	0.44	0.32	1.00

Note: All coefficients greater than 0.18 and 0.15 are significant at $P<0.01$ and <0.05, respectively.

Table 2 Results of analyses on hypothesized relationships

Hypothesized relationships	Standardized coefficient	Assessment
H1 In the born-global firm, global technological competence is a function of:		
(a) international entrepreneurial orientation	0.28	S
(b) international marketing orientation	0.13	NS
H2 In the born-global firm, unique products development is a function of:		
(a) international entrepreneurial orientation	0.19	S
(b) international marketing orientation	0.24	S
H3 In the born-global firm, quality focus is a function of:		
(a) international entrepreneurial orientation	0.23	S
(b) international marketing orientation	0.35	S
H4 In the born-global firm, leveraging foreign distributor competences is a function of:		
(a) international entrepreneurial orientation	0.10	NS
(b) international marketing orientation	0.26	S
H5 In the born-global firm, performance in international markets is a function of:		
(a) global technological competence	0.21	S
(b) unique products development	0.14	S
(c) quality focus	0.30	S
(d) leveraging foreign distributor competences	0.18	S

Notes: All standardized coefficients greater than 0.18 and 0.13 are significant at $P < 0.01$ and < 0.05 respectively
S=supported; NS=not significant.

orientation and global technological competence was not significant. Findings also suggest that unique products development and quality focus are both significantly ($P < 0.01$) driven by international entrepreneurial orientation and international marketing orientation, supporting H2 and H3. In addition, although results suggest that leveraging foreign distributor competences is a significant ($P < 0.01$) function of international marketing orientation, partially supporting H4, the linkage posited between international entrepreneurial orientation and leveraging foreign distributor competences in H4 was not significant. Findings also provide evidence that global technological competence, unique products development, quality focus, and leveraging foreign distributor competences are all significant ($P < 0.05$) drivers of performance in international markets in born-global firms, supporting H5. Finally, as suggested earlier, Table 1 indicates that global technological competence is correlated with unique products development, and leveraging foreign distributor competences is correlated with both unique products development and quality focus. In all, results of the survey-based study generally confirm the case studies and support the critical importance of

organizational capabilities, as applied here to born-global firms.

Discussion

Cast in an evolutionary economics (Nelson and Winter, 1982) framework, our findings imply that the strongly innovative nature of born-global firms supports these businesses in developing particular types of knowledge, which drives the development of organizational capabilities that support early internationalization and superior performance in diverse international markets. Innovative activities in these firms support the opening of new markets and reinvention of the firm's operations to serve those markets optimally. Our findings also revealed and confirmed the importance of specific key organizational capabilities that engender international success in born globals. These findings have implications as well for internationalizing smaller firms in general. Born globals are young businesses characterized by a particular pattern of innovativeness that gives rise to early internationalization. Thus our investigation also contributes to the innovation literature by linking innovation to the phenomenon of early adoption of internationalization.

The resource-based perspective emphasizes that the firm's foundational resources are particularly important in diverse business environments because they provide a stable basis for strategy development. Knowledge possessed by born globals appears to be a critical resource in this process. Managers in young, internationally oriented firms should develop knowledge that is both relatively unique and inimitable, in order to maximize its utility for superior international performance. Knowledge generates appropriate organizational capabilities that become embedded into the firm's cultures via ongoing replication of routines, producing a unique configuration of resources.

Young and small firms normally endure a scarcity of financial, human, and tangible resources that results in a reduced set of competitive options. Historically, substantial international business activities were beyond the reach of such firms. However, relatively recent advances in information, communications, production, and logistics technologies, as well as the emergence of other useful infrastructures and conditions associated with the globalization phenomenon, have given rise to a business environment in which young, smaller firms can participate actively in global markets. Although born globals undoubtedly existed in the past, especially in nations with small domestic markets, contemporary scholars and practitioners are witnessing the widespread emergence of countless such businesses throughout the world.

Despite this, there are perhaps millions of other young and smaller firms that are not international, appear to have little or no international aspirations, and continue to operate strictly within their own domestic markets. It is likely, therefore, that emergent globalization and high technology trends, while necessary, are insufficient to account for the widespread emergence of born globals. In light of the theoretical and empirical results presented here, it appears that, in addition to the presence of facilitating environmental factors, firms must possess specific knowledge-based *internal* organizational capabilities that support both early internationalization and subsequent success in foreign markets. We have highlighted these capabilities and confirmed their explanatory value in born globals. Moreover, we underscore the role of youth and smaller size, which confer a degree of flexibility and agility that appears to help these businesses succeed abroad. This flexibility is characteristic of young firms that lack the adminis-

trative heritage of large, older competitors. The absence of a firmly embedded infrastructure and managerial mindset facilitates early and rapid internationalization.

At the organizational culture level, international entrepreneurial orientation reflects an innovation-focused managerial mindset that appears to lead born globals to pursue a collection of strategies aimed at maximizing international performance. Our findings imply that international entrepreneurial orientation may be especially important to these firms because it appears to drive them to develop high-quality goods that are distinctive and technologically advanced, and which are associated, in turn, with born-global international success.

Like international entrepreneurial orientation, international marketing orientation is also particularly relevant to born globals and appears to engender specific innovation-based strategies that in turn drive superior international performance. This arises within a multi-country context that imposes numerous uncontrollable and often unique challenges on born-global managers. Their international marketing orientation facilitates knowledge of customers, product development and adaptation, as well as meticulous manipulation of key marketing tactical elements to target foreign customers with quality, differentiated goods.

Limited resources imply that born globals must succeed in foreign markets earlier, and with superior efficiency and effectiveness. International performance and the ultimate survival of the firm appear to hinge on well-conceived manipulation of strategic variables. International entrepreneurial and marketing orientations are particularly important to born globals because, owing to limited traditional resources, they cannot afford to make the mistakes that have afflicted the internationalization of other firms.

At the strategy level, global technological competence, unique products development, quality focus, and leveraging foreign distributor competences all appear to be significant drivers of superior performance overseas. Leveraging quality and technological excellence helps born globals to develop offerings that appeal to niche markets around the world. The finding is consistent with research in Australia (Rennie, 1993), which found that early exporters thrive by leveraging proprietary technologies and high-quality goods. The combined, significant roles of global technological competence, unique products development, and quality focus provide further evidence that organizational activities related to innovation, R&D, knowledge development, and capabilities leveraging play important roles in positioning born globals for international success. These are all critical activities in the development or positioning of the firm's product offerings. Having relatively unique products can also allow born globals to achieve a sort of 'monopolistic advantage' (Hymer, 1976) that further supports international success. The literature specifies numerous approaches for achieving international business success, but innovative processes that drive the development of superior, unique products appear particularly important to born-global success.

Strong relationships that born globals develop with competent foreign distributors also help pave the way for superior performance abroad. Descriptive measures reveal that the randomly chosen born globals in our study are targeting their goods to a median of 20 countries worldwide. Given the limited traditional resources of these young firms, and the tendency of many to internationalize via exporting, leveraging strong foreign distributors is a key strategy. Foreign distributors provide local advantages related not only to downstream international business activities, but also to gathering market intelligence, forging links with key foreign contacts, deepening relations within extant markets, and cultivating new buyer segments.

Conclusion

Among the firms examined here, youth and lack of experience, as well as paucity of financial, human, and tangible resources, are no longer major impediments to the large-scale internationalization and global success of the firm. Companies that possess the characteristics and capabilities described in this study can and do internationalize early, and succeed in international markets. Managers at born globals begin with a global vision, and devise a collection of capabilities at the strategy and organizational-culture levels of the firm that give rise to early adoption of internationalization and success in a broad range of foreign markets. Born globals acquire a substantial, fundamental base of international experience and knowledge that traditional MNEs typically have taken longer to acquire. In this sense, born globals pose an important new challenge to traditional views on the internationalization of the firm.

During the past couple of decades, the volume of global business activity has increased dramatically, and is associated with the emergence of mechanisms and infrastructures that are facilitating the internationalization of countless smaller, entrepreneurial firms. The trend has been hastened by the development of technologies that allow companies to internationalize and conduct global business much more efficiently than ever before. Electronic interconnectedness in particular is driving the emergence of a borderless global economy. Information technology and the Internet are liberating forces, permanently altering the landscape of international trade. Absent the burden of administrative heritage, younger, smaller firms are playing a much greater role in international trade than ever before.

Accordingly, the traditional view of the large multinational corporation as the dominant international form might well be evolving. Born globals are emerging in substantial numbers worldwide, and likely reflect an emergent paradigm, with the potential to become a leading species in the ecosystem of international trade. In this sense, the born-global phenomenon is heartening because it implies the emergence of an international exchange system in which any firm, regardless of age, experience, and tangible resources, can be an active international business participant. Although large global corporations and the negative aspects of globalization often dominate reports in the popular press with respect to the emergent world order, the increasing role of born globals implies a more optimistic view. In relative terms, born globals might be seen to herald a more diverse international business system in which any firm can succeed internationally. Future research should aim at deepening our understanding of early adopters of internationalization, which represent a widespread, ongoing trend.

Acknowledgements
We thank Tomas Hult, Peter Liesch, Tage Madsen, Benjamin Oviatt, two *JIBS* reviewers, and Arie Lewin, *JIBS* Editor-in-Chief, for their insightful and constructive suggestions in developing this manuscript. Financial support from the Center for International Business Education and Research, Michigan State University, in the completion of this research is gratefully acknowledged.

References

Aaker, D. and Jacobson, R. (1994) 'The financial information content of perceived quality', *Journal of Marketing Research* 31(2): 191–201.

Albaum, G. and Peterson, R.A. (1984) 'Empirical research in international marketing: 1976–82', *Journal of International Business Studies* 15(Spring/Summer): 161–173.

Armstrong, J.S. and Overton, T.S. (1977) 'Estimating non-response bias in mail surveys', *Journal of Marketing Research* 14(3): 396–402.

Autio, E., Sapienza, H. and Almeida, J. (2000) 'Effects of age at entry, knowledge intensity, and imitability on international growth', *Academy of Management Journal* 43(5): 909–924.

Barkema, H. and Vermeulen, F. (1998) 'International expansion through start-up or acquisition: a learning perspective', *Academy of Management Journal* 41(1): 7–26.

Barney, J. (1991) 'Firm resources and sustained competitive advantage', *Journal of Management* 17(1): 99–120.

Bowersox, D. and Cooper, M.B. (1992) *Strategic Marketing Channel Management*, McGraw-Hill: New York.

Buckley, P.J. and Casson, M.C. (1998) 'Models of the multinational enterprise', *Journal of International Business Studies* 29(1): 21–44.

Buzzell, R. and Gale, B. (1987) *The PIMS Principles: Linking Strategy to Performance*, The Free Press: New York.

Casson, M. (2000) *Economics of International Business*, Edward Elgar: Cheltenham.

Cavusgil, S.T. and Zou, S. (1994) 'Marketing strategy–performance relationship: an investigation of the empirical link in export market ventures', *Journal of Marketing* 58(1): 1–21.

Cavusgil, S.T., Zou, S. and Naidu, G.M. (1993) 'Product and promotion adaptation in export ventures: an empirical investigation', *Journal of International Business Studies* 24(3): 479–506.

Clark, K. (1987) 'Investment in New Technology and Competitive Advantage', in D. Teece (ed.) *The Competitive Challenge: Strategies for Industrial Innovation and Renewal*, Ballinger: Cambridge, MA. pp. 59–81

Cohen, W. and Levinthal, D. (1990) 'Absorptive capacity: a new perspective on learning and innovation', *Administrative Science Quarterly* 35(1): 128–152.

Collis, D. (1991) 'A resource-based analysis of global competition', *Strategic Management Journal* 12(Summer, Special Issue): 49–68.

Conner, K. and Prahalad, C.K. (1996) 'A resource-based theory of the firm: knowledge versus opportunism', *Organization Science* 7(5): 477–501.

Covin, J. and Slevin, D. (1989) 'Strategic management of small firms in hostile and benign environments', *Strategic Management Journal* 10(1): 75–87.

Daniels, J and Radebaugh, L. (1998) *International Business: Environments and Operations*, 8th edn. Addison-Wesley: Reading, MA.

Deming, W.E. (1982) *Quality, Productivity, and Competitive Position*, MIT Center for Advanced Engineering Study: Boston, MA.

Dess, G., Lumpkin, G. and Covin, J. (1997) 'Entrepreneurial strategy making and firm performance: tests of contingency and configurational models', *Strategic Management Journal* 18(1): 2–23.

Dierickx, I. and Cool, K. (1989) 'Asset stock accumulation and sustainability of competitive advantage', *Management Science* 35(12): 1504–1510.

Dosi, G. (1988) 'Sources, procedures, and microeconomic effects of innovation', *Journal of Economic Literature* 26(3): 1120–1171.

Fornell, C. and Larcker, D.F. (1981) 'Evaluating structural equation models with unobservable variables and measurement errors', *Journal of Marketing Research* 18(1): 39–50.

Fowler, F. (1988) *Survey Research Methods*, Sage: Newbury Park, CA.

Gerbing, D. and Anderson, J. (1988) 'An updated paradigm for scale development incorporating unidimensionality and its assessment', *Journal of Marketing Research* 25(2): 186–192.

Gerbing, D. and Anderson, J. (1992) 'Monte Carlo evaluations of goodness-of-fit indices for structural equation models', *Sociological Methods and Research* 21(November): 132–160.

Grant, R.M. (1991) 'The resource-based theory of competitive advantage: implications for strategy formulation', *California Management Review* 33(3): 114–135.

Grant, R.M. (1996a) 'Prospering in dynamically competitive environments: organizational capability as knowledge integration', *Organization Science* 7(4): 375–387.

Grant, R.M. (1996b) 'Toward a knowledge-based theory of the Firm', *Strategic Management Journal* 17(December): 109–122.

Hymer, S. (1976) *The International Operations of National Firms*, MIT Press: Cambridge, MA.

Johanson, J. and Vahlne, J. (1977) 'The internationalization process of the firm: a model of knowledge development and increasing foreign commitments', *Journal of International Business Studies* 8(1): 23–32.

Joreskog, K. and Sorbom, D. (1997) *LISREL 8: A Guide to the Program and Applications*, SPSS Inc.: Chicago, IL.

Joreskog, K., Dag, S., Stephen, D.T. and Mathilda, D.T. (2000) *LISREL 8: New Statistical Features*, Scientific Software International: Lincolnwood, IL.

Khandwalla, P. (1977) *The Design of Organizations*, Harcourt Brace Jovanovich: New York.

Knight, G.A. and Cavusgil, S.T. (1996) 'The Born Global Firm: A Challenge to Traditional Internationalization Theory', in S.T. Cavusgil and T. Madsen (eds.) *Advances in International Marketing*, Vol. 8 JAI Press: Greenwich, CT. pp. 11–26.

Kogut, B. and Zander, U. (1993) 'Knowledge of the firm and the evolutionary theory of the multinational corporation', *Journal of International Business Studies* 24(4): 625–645.

Kotabe, M. (1990) 'Corporate product policy and innovative behavior of European and Japanese multinationals: an empirical investigation', *Journal of Marketing* 54(2): 19–33.

Leonard-Barton, D. (1992) 'Core capabilities and core rigidities: a paradox in managing new product development', *Strategic Management Journal* 13: 111–126.

Lewin, A.Y. and Massini, S. (2003) 'Knowledge Creation and Organizational Capabilities of Innovating and Imitating Firms', in H. Tsoukas and N. Mylonopoulos (eds.) *Organizations as Knowledge Systems*, Palgrave: Basingstoke.

Lumpkin, G.T. and Dess, D. (1996) 'Clarifying the entrepreneurial orientation construct and linking it to performance', *Academy of Management Review* 21(1): 135–172.

Luo, Y. (2000) 'Dynamic capabilities in international expansion', *Journal of World Business* 35(4): 355–378.

Massini, S., Lewin, A.Y. and Greve, H.E. (2003) 'Innovators and imitators: organizational reference groups and adoption of organizational routines', (unpublished manuscript).

McDougall, P. and Oviatt, B. (2000) 'International entrepreneurship: the intersection of two research paths', *Academy of Management Journal* 43(5): 902–906.

McDougall, P., Shane, S. and Oviatt, B. (1994) 'Explaining the formation of international new ventures: the limits of theories from international business research', *Journal of Business Venturing* 9(6): 469–487.

McGuinness, N., Campbell, N. and Leontiades, J. (1991) 'Selling machinery to China: Chinese perceptions of strategies and relationships', *Journal of International Business Studies* 22(2): 187–207.

McKee, D., Jeffery, C., Rajan Varadarajan P. and Michael, M. (1992) 'Success-producer and failure-preventer marketing skills: a social learning theory interpretation', *Journal of the Academy of Marketing Science* 20(1): 17–26.

Miles, R.E. and Snow, C.C. (1978) *Organizational Strategy, Structure, and Process*, McGraw-Hill: New York.

Miller, D. (1988) 'Relating Porter's business strategies to environment and structure: analysis and performance implications', *Academy of Management Journal* 31(2): 280–308.

Miller, D. and Friesen, P.H. (1984) *Organizations: A Quantum View*, Prentice Hall: Englewood Cliffs, NJ.

Mintzberg, H. (1973) *The Nature of Managerial Work*, Harper & Row: New York.

Moen, O. and Servais, P. (2002) 'Born global or gradual global? Examining the export behavior of small and medium-sized enterprises', *Journal of International Marketing* 10(3): 49–72.

Mohr-Jackson, I. (1998) 'Conceptualizing total quality orientation', *European Journal of Marketing* 32(1/2): 13–22.

Mortanges, C.P. and Vossen, J. (1999) 'Mechanisms to control the marketing activities of foreign distributors', *International Business Review* 8(1): 75–97.

Nelson, R. and Winter, S. (1982) *An Evolutionary Theory of Economic Change*, Belknap Press: Cambridge, MA.

Nikkei Sangyoo Shimbun (1995) *Benchaa Shin Sedai (New Generation Ventures)*, Nihon Keizai Shimbun: Tokyo.

Nonaka, I. (1994) 'A dynamic theory of organizational knowledge creation', *Organization Science* 5(1): 14–37.

Nunnally, J.C. (1978) *Psychometric Theory*, McGraw-Hill: New York.

OECD (1997) *Globalization and Small and Medium Enterprises (SMEs)*, Organization for Economic Cooperation and Development: Paris.

Oviatt, B. and McDougall, P. (1994) 'Toward a theory of international new ventures', *Journal of International Business Studies* 25(1): 45–64.

Peng, M. and York, A. (2001) 'Behind intermediary performance in export trade: transactions, agents, and resources', *Journal of International Business Studies* 32(2): 327–346.

Penrose, E. (1959) *The Theory of the Growth of the Firm*, Basil Blackwell: London.

Polanyi, M. (1966) *The Tacit Dimension*, Routledge & Kegan Paul: London.

Porter, M.E. (1980) *Competitive Strategy*, The Free Press: New York.

Prahalad, C.K. and Hamel, G. (1990) 'The core competence of the corporation', *Harvard Business Review* 68(3): 79–91.

Rennie, M. (1993) 'Born global', *McKinsey Quarterly* (4): 45–52.

Rosson, P. and Ford, I.D. (1982) 'Manufacturer–overseas distributor relations and export performance', *Journal of International Business Studies* 13(2): 57–72.

Roth, K. and Morrison, A. (1992) 'Business-level competitive strategy: a contingency link to internationalization', *Journal of Management* 18(3): 473–487.

Rumelt, R.P. (1984) 'Towards a Strategic Theory of the Firm', in R.B. Lamb (ed.) *Competitive Strategic Management*, Prentice Hall: Englewood Cliffs, NJ. pp. 131–145.

Schumpeter, J. (1934) *The Theory of Economic Development*, Cambridge University Press: Cambridge.

Schumpeter, J. (1939) *Business Cycles*, Vol. 1 McGraw-Hill: New York.

Schumpeter, J. (1942) *Capitalism, Socialism, and Democracy*, Harper & Brothers Publishers: New York.

Siguaw, J., Simpson, P. and Baker, T. (1998) 'Effects of supplier market orientation on distributor market orientation and the channel relationship: the distributor perspective', *Journal of Marketing* 62(3): 99–111.

Simmonds, K. and Smith, H. (1968) 'The first export order: a marketing innovation', *British Journal of Marketing* 2(Summer): 93–100.

Simon, H. (1996) *Hidden Champions: Lessons from 500 of the World's Best Unknown Companies*, Harvard Business School Press: Boston.

Slater, S. and Narver, J. (1992) *Superior Customer Value and Business Performance: The Strong Evidence for a Market-Driven Culture*, Marketing Science Institute: Cambridge, MA, pp. 92–125.

Smith, W. (1956) 'Product differentiation and market segmentation as alternative marketing strategies', *Journal of Marketing* 21(July): 3–8.

Solow, R.M. (1957) 'Technical change and the aggregate production function', *The Review of Economics and Statistics* 39(February): 312–320.

Steensma, H.K., Marino, L., Weaver, K.M. and Dickson, P. (2000) 'The influence of national culture on the formation of technology alliances by entrepreneurial firms', *Academy of Management Journal* 43(5): 951–973.

Szymanski, D., Bharadwaj, S. and Varadarajan, P.R. (1993) 'Standardization versus adaptation of international marketing strategy: an empirical investigation', *Journal of Marketing* 57(4): 1–17.

Teece, D. and Pisano, G. (1994) 'The dynamic capabilities of firms: an introduction', *Industrial and Corporate Change* 3(3): 537–556.

Teece, D., Pisano, G. and Shuen, A. (1997) 'Dynamic capabilities and strategic management', *Strategic Management Journal* 18(7): 509–533.

Utterback, J.M. and Abernathy, W.J. (1975) 'A dynamic model of process and product innovation', *Omega* 3(6): 639–656.

Wernerfelt, B. (1984) 'A resource-based view of the firm', *Strategic Management Journal* 5(2): 171–180.

Young, S., Bell, J. and Crick, D. (2000) 'The Resource-based Perspective and Small Firm Internationalization: An Exploratory Approach', in C. Millar, R. Grant and C. Choi (eds.) *International Business: Emerging Issues and Emerging Markets*, St Martin's Press: New York.

Zahra, S., Ireland, R. and Hitt, M. (2000) 'International expansion by new venture firms: international diversity, mode of market entry, technological learning, and performance', *Academy of Management Journal* 43(5): 925–950.

Appendix: Measurement scales

Construct (composite reliability, CR_n)

Item (standardized coefficient loading from CFA analyses in LISREL8)

(Source)

International entrepreneurial orientation ($CR_n=0.80$)

Top management tends to see the world, instead of just the USA, as our firm's marketplace (0.92)

The prevailing organizational culture at our firm (management's collective value system) is conducive to active exploration of new business opportunities *abroad* (0.89)

Management continuously communicates its mission to succeed in international markets to firm employees (0.95)

Management develops human and other resources for achieving our goals in *international* markets (0.89)

Our top management is experienced in international business (0.73)

Over the past 5 years, our firm has marketed very many products in *foreign* markets*

In *international* markets, our top managers have a proclivity for high-risk projects (with chances for high returns)*

※

When confronted with *international* decision-making situations, we typically adopt a cautious, 'wait-and-see' posture in order to minimize the chance of making costly mistakes[#][*]

Management communicates information throughout the firm with respect to about our successful and unsuccessful customer experiences abroad[*]

Management believes that, owing to the nature of the *international* business environment, it is best to explore it gradually via conservative, incremental steps[#][*]

Top management is willing to go to great lengths to make our products succeed in foreign markets[*]

Vision and drive of top management are important in our decision to enter foreign markets[*]

(Covin and Slevin, 1989; Khandwalla, 1977; Miller and Friesen, 1984)

International marketing oirientation ($CR_n=0.85$)

(In international markets, own firm rating relative to main competitors; 1=much worse than main competitors; 7=much better than main competitors)

Knowledge of customers and competitors (0.80)

Marketing planning process (0.82)

Development or adaptation of the product (0.68)

Effectiveness of pricing (0.62)

Advertising effectiveness (0.70)

Effectiveness of distribution (0.77)

Image of your firm (0.88)

Locations of sales outlets[*]

Ability to work well with distributors[*]

Ability to respond quickly to developing opportunities[*]

Skill to target and segment individual markets[*]

Ability to use marketing tools (product design, pricing, advertising, etc.) to differentiate this product (0.81)

Control and evaluation of marketing activities (0.80)

(Adapted from McKee *et al.*, 1992)

Global technological competence ($CR_n=0.72$)

Our firm is at the leading technological edge of our industry in this market (0.75)

We invented a lot of the technology imbedded in this product (0.94)

Compared with local competitors, we're often first to introduce product innovations or new operating approaches (0.91)

We are recognized in our main export market for products that are technologically superior[*]

Our firm is highly regarded for its technical expertise among our channel members in this market[*]

In the design and manufacture of this product, we employ some of the most skilled specialists in the industry[*]

Unique products development ($CR_n=0.78$)

Our primary export product caters to a specialized need that is difficult for our competitors to match (0.88)

In our industry, this product represents a new, innovative approach to addressing the customer's basic need (0.85)

Compared with our main competitors' offerings, this product is unique with respect to design (0.81)

Compared with our main competitors' offerings, this product is unique with respect to technology (0.97)

Compared with our main competitors' offerings, this product is unique with respect to performance (0.75)

(Miller, 1988; Porter, 1980; Roth and Morrison, 1992)

Quality focus ($CR_n=0.72$)

Emphasizing quality customer service is important to our firm's strategy in this market (0.46)

Emphasizing product quality is important to our firm's strategy in this market (0.41)

For us, success in this market is driven by truly satisfying the needs of our customers there (0.59)

The performance of this product truly meets the expectations of customers in this market (0.53)

The service and support provided with this product truly meet the expectations of customers in this market (0.79)

(Buzzell and Gale, 1987)

Leveraging foreign distributor competences ($CR_n=0.92$)

(Extent to which foreign distributor meets expectations with respect to the following; 1=falls very short of expectations; 7=meets expectations very well)

Setting local prices (0.78)

Local selling (0.93)

Local advertising (0.98)

After-sales service (0.89)

Collecting local market information (0.72)

Liaison with local government (0.79)

Cultivating *new* business/expansion (0.81)

Product modification (if any)[*]

Arranging international shipping*
Arranging local shipping*
Local public relations*
Customer technical support/training*
Translation of sales literature, usage instructions, or labels*
(Adapted from McKee *et al.*, 1992; Daniels and Radebaugh, 1998)

Performance in international markets ($CR_\eta=0.86$)
(1=very unsatisfied; 7=very satisfied)
Relative to *prior expectations*, how satisfied have you been *over past 3 years* with product's performance regarding:

Market share in this market (0.87)
Sales growth in this market (0.85)
Pre-tax profitability in this market (0.97)

Compared with your *main competitor(s), sales growth* of this product in its main export market has been: substantially lower 1 2 3 4 5 6 7 substantially higher (0.78)
On a scale from 1 to 10, how would you rate the success of this product in its main export-market over the past 3 years? unsuccessful 1.10 successful (0.92)
Gaining new knowledge/technology in this market*
Compared with your *domestic business*, the *total return on your investment* (ROI) of this product in its main export market has been. . . substantially lower 1 2 3 4 5 6 7 substantially higher*
(Adapted from Cavusgil and Zou, 1994)

Notes
Except as noted, a seven-point ordinal scale was used where 1=not at all and 7=to an extreme extent.

All standardized coefficient loadings are significant at $P<0.01$.
*Indicates item that was dropped in the scale purification process.
#Indicates reverse-polarity item.

About the authors
Gary A Knight is Associate Professor of Marketing and Director of International Business Programs at Florida State University (FSU). His research focuses on international entrepreneurship, international marketing strategy, and internationalization in the SME. He is the author of more than 60 refereed conference and journal articles. He has lectured in numerous countries worldwide, and launched FSU's international business programs in London, Paris, Tokyo, and Valencia, Spain. He received his Ph.D. at Michigan State University.

S Tamer Cavusgil is University Distinguished Faculty and The John W Byington Endowed Chair in Global Marketing at Michigan State University. Professor Cavusgil specializes in international marketing strategy, early internationalization, and export trade policy. He is the author of several books and over 100 refereed articles. Doing Business in Emerging Markets (Sage Publications, 2002) is his most recent contribution. Cavusgil is the Associate Editor-in Chief, Journal of International Business Studies, and Editor of Elsevier book series, Advances in International Marketing. He also serves on the editorial review boards of over a dozen professional publications.

Accepted by Arie Lewin, Editor in Chief, 19 November 2003 This paper has been with the author for one revision

[11]

Strategic Management Journal
Strat. Mgmt. J., **22** 565–586 (2001)
DOI: 10.1002/smj.184

THE INTERNATIONALIZATION AND PERFORMANCE OF SMEs

JANE W. LU[1,2]* and PAUL W. BEAMISH[1]
[1]*Richard Ivey School of Business, University of Western Ontario, London, Ontario, Canada*
[2]*Faculty of Business Administration, National University of Singapore, Singapore*

We discuss and explore the effects of internationalization, an entrepreneurial strategy employed by small and medium-sized enterprises (SMEs), on firm performance. Using concepts derived from the international business and entrepreneurship literatures, we develop four hypotheses that relate the extent of foreign direct investment (FDI) and exporting activity, and the relative use of alliances, to the corporate performance of internationalizing SMEs. Using a sample of 164 Japanese SMEs to test these hypotheses, we find that the positive impact of internationalization on performance extends primarily from the extent of a firm's FDI activity. We also find evidence consistent with the perspective that firms face a liability of foreignness. When firms first begin FDI activity, profitability declines, but greater levels of FDI are associated with higher performance. Exporting moderates the relationship FDI has with performance, as pursuing a strategy of high exporting concurrent with high FDI is less profitable than one that involves lower levels of exports when FDI levels are high. Finally, we find that alliances with partners with local knowledge can be an effective strategy to overcome the deficiencies SMEs face in resources and capabilities, when they expand into international markets. Copyright © 2001 John Wiley & Sons, Ltd.

Growth by international diversification is an important strategic option for both small and large firms. During recent years, a significant development within the broad internationalization trend has been the increasingly active role played by small and medium-sized enterprises (SMEs) in international markets (Oviatt and McDougall, 1994, 1999). The internationalization of SMEs can be expected to gain further momentum because the world economy is becoming increasingly integrated with continued declines in government-imposed barriers and continued advances in technology.

The prominence of the internationalization phenomenon has captured the interest of researchers in strategic management, international business and entrepreneurship. For researchers in the strategy and international business areas, international diversification is a traditional domain, though the focus has been on large, well-established firms (McDougall and Oviatt, 1996). For entrepreneurship researchers, SMEs have been a primary focus, while entering new geographic markets has essentially been regarded as an act of entrepreneurship (Burgelman, 1983; Lumpkin and Dess, 1996; Barringer and Greening, 1998). Numerous studies in these literatures have looked at the antecedents and the process of internationalization of SMEs (e.g., Special Issues in *Entrepreneurship Theory and Practice*, 1996 and *Academy of Management Journal*, 2000; Preece, Miles, and Baetz, 1999; Wolff and Pett, 2000). Yet, to date, little is known about the

Key words: entrepreneurship; internationalization; exporting; foreign direct investment; international alliances
*Correspondence to: Jane W. Lu, Department of Business Policy, Faculty of Business Administration, National University of Singapore, 15 Law Link, FBA 1-02-29, Singapore 117591

566   *J. W. Lu and P. W. Beamish*

effects of internationalization on SMEs' performance (Covin and Slevin, 1991; McDougall and
Oviatt, 1996; Coviello and McAuley, 1999). We
contend more attention should be devoted to
exploring whether and how value is created in
the internationalization of SMEs. This is because
managers are ultimately concerned with whether
such entrepreneurial strategies can lead to higher
performance and how their firms can become
more competitive when expanding geographically.
We address these issues by exploring the performance implications of various internationalization strategies used by SMEs.

SMEs tend to move into foreign markets as
exporters and/or as foreign investors (Reynolds,
1997). Exporting and foreign direct investment
(FDI) are also common strategies used in the
international activities of large, multinational
firms. While previous literature has focused on
the identification of the determinants of one or
the other of these internationalization strategies,
little consideration has been given to the shared
impact these two internationalization activities
have on firm performance, particularly for SMEs.
In the analyses reported in this paper, we consider
the joint effect of exporting and FDI strategies
on firm performance in the context of SMEs.
This research provides a useful complement to
previous studies that have utilized samples of
large firms by showing that newly internationalizing SMEs face liabilities of foreignness
that translate into lower corporate performance at
low levels of FDI activity. However, our research
shows that these liabilities can be overcome, as
higher levels of FDI are positively related to
performance. Further, our analyses demonstrate
that a key strategy for overcoming the resource
limitations that frequently constrain an SME's
expansion is the use of alliances with firms that
have local knowledge. Finally, our study shows
that exporting has a negative moderating effect
on the relationship between FDI and performance,
which points to the importance of the configuration of internationalization strategies.

We base these inferences on our analysis of
longitudinal data comprising 164 Japanese SMEs'
internationalization activities spanning the 1986–
97 period. The use of a Japanese sample extends
the empirical scope of both the internationalization and entrepreneurship literatures.
Further, as explained later in the Sample Characteristics section in which we used multiple criteria

to examine the entrepreneurial character of our
sample, the Japanese empirical setting helps to
ensure that the internationalization strategies we
observe are indeed entrepreneurial activities.

INTERNATIONAL EXPANSION AND ENTREPRENEURSHIP

Geographic expansion is one of the most
important paths for firm growth. It is a particularly important growth strategy for SMEs whose
business scope has been geographically confined
(Barringer and Greening, 1998). By broadening
customer bases through entering into new markets, firms are able to achieve a larger volume
of production, and grow. Further, there are differences in market conditions across different geographic areas. By leveraging resources in different
markets, firms are in a position to capitalize on
market imperfections and achieve higher returns
on their resources. Sooner or later, in the pursuit
of growth and/or higher return to resources, SMEs
will adopt a geographic expansion strategy to
pursue new opportunities to leverage core competences across a broader range of markets
(Zahra, Ireland, and Hitt, 2000).

While expanding into new geographic markets
presents an important opportunity for growth and
value creation, the implementation of such a strategy involves many unique challenges in addition
to the common ones associated with the domestic
growth of SMEs. Many of the challenges are
typical of the difficulties associated with the liabilities of foreignness (Hymer, 1976) and newness
(Stinchcombe, 1965), if the target markets are
dissimilar to the original markets, and if new
subsidiaries are established. In the former liability, significant differences between markets
mean that the knowledge and capabilities that an
SME has developed by operating in its original
markets, are often not suited to operations in the
new market. New knowledge and capabilities
need to be acquired or developed to successfully
enter the new markets. In the latter liability, a
new subsidiary faces many of the same challenges
as a start-up. It needs to build business relationships with stakeholders, the subsidiary needs to
establish its legitimacy, and it must recruit and
train new employees to staff new operations
(Barringer and Greening, 1998). These challenges
are compounded when first entering an inter-

national market because differences between host and home markets, along political, economic, legal and cultural dimensions, require an internationalizing firm to change many of its ways of doing business that were developed in a domestic context (McDougall and Oviatt, 1996).

Aside from having to develop new resources and capabilities on foreign entry, an internationalizing firm faces heightened political risks as well as the operational risks stemming from the foreignness of the new environment (Delios and Henisz, 2000). The higher levels of risk an SME faces when entering a foreign market, relative to domestic expansion, reinforces the entrepreneurial characteristics of the internationalization strategy. Taken together, these characteristics reinforce the idea that internationalization is an act of entrepreneurship because it is a strategy in search of opportunities for firm growth and wealth by expanding into new markets (Lumpkin and Dess, 1996; Zahra, Kuratko and Jennings, 1999). Further, it is a strategy that requires a fundamental departure from existing practices (Damanpour, 1991; Birkinshaw, 1997) and an act that entails high levels of risk (Miller, 1983). This is particularly the case for SMEs, which are characterized by limited resources, and whose small size magnifies the downside implications of an expansion activity.

The entrepreneurial features of the internationalization of SMEs have captured the interest of entrepreneurship researchers who traditionally study start-ups that have a domestic business scope. The rapidly growing interest in the internationalization of SMEs has led to substantial research on the phenomenon. While the field of international entrepreneurship is still in its infancy (Hisrich *et al.*, 1996; Brazeal and Herbert, 1999), two distinct streams have already emerged (McDougall and Oviatt, 2000). One stream focuses on international new ventures: start-ups that are international from inception. The other stream, to which this study belongs, looks at the internationalization of established, yet small firms. In the former stream, researchers have looked at both the antecedents and outcomes of internationalization (e.g., Autio, Sapienza, and Almeida, 2000; Zahra *et al.*, 2000). In the latter stream, however, previous studies tended to focus on various aspects of SME export activities in terms of the antecedents and the process (behaviors and

strategies) of exporting, and export performance (for reviews, see Dichtl *et al.*, 1984; Miesenbock, 1988; Shoham, 1998). More recently, researchers have extended investigation beyond exporting to include more broadly the processes and patterns of internationalization (for a review, see Coviello and McAuley, 1999). However, few studies have addressed the performance implications of internationalization even though this is of central concern to entrepreneurs (Covin and Slevin, 1991; McDougall and Oviatt, 1996; Coviello and McAuley, 1999). This is primarily due to the difficulties in obtaining detailed information on SMEs' foreign investments and firm performance. Archival data about many SMEs is simply not publicly available.

While studies on the performance implications of internationalization strategies have been sparse in the entrepreneurship literature, studies in international business and strategic management literatures have long explored the performance implications of international diversification strategies. Numerous researchers have argued and empirically observed that higher levels of international diversification lead to higher firm performance (e.g., Daniels and Bracker, 1989; Grant, 1987; Kim, Hwang and Burgers, 1993; Tallman and Li, 1996), up to a point, after which performance begins to decline with increasing internationalization (Geringer, Beamish, and daCosta, 1989; Hitt, Hoskisson, and Kim, 1997). Consistent with the traditional foci of strategy and international business research, the empirical findings were based on studies of large, well-internationalized firms (McDougall and Oviatt, 1996; Dana, Etemad, and Wright, 1999). It has been well argued and documented that smaller businesses 'are not smaller versions of big business' (Shuman and Seeger, 1986: 8). Rather, they differ fundamentally from larger firms in ownership, resources, organizational structures and processes, as well as management systems (Smith *et al.*, 1988; Carrier, 1994). These differences could very well have an impact on the outcome of an SME's internationalization, which is a notion we examine in this study.

This study attempts to address the aforementioned gaps in the entrepreneurship and international literatures. To that end, we focus on the question of 'whether and how value is created in the internationalization of SMEs.' To address this question, we directly test the performance impli-

568   *J. W. Lu and P. W. Beamish*

cations of four international diversification strategies of SMEs. Internationalization is a multidimensional construct (Sullivan, 1994; Ramaswamy, Kroeck, and Renforth, 1996; Nehrt and Phene, 1998).

Two of the most prominent avenues of internationalization are exporting and FDI and we explore both the individual impacts of exporting and FDI activities as well as the joint effects of these two strategies. A second important feature of our investigation is that we not only look at the benefits but also consider the costs in the internationalization of SMEs as they stem from the intrinsic differences between SMEs and larger firms, particularly the costs that stem from the financial and managerial resource constraints that SMEs face (Jarillo, 1989; Oviatt and McDougall, 1994). While highlighting these costs or constraints, using insights from entrepreneurship researchers, we try to identify means by which these can be overcome or minimized through network relationships that help alleviate resource constraints (Larson, 1991; Deeds and Hill, 1996; Weaver and Dickson, 1998). In the array of network options, strategic alliances have gained increasing popularity with internationalizing entrepreneurial firms (Beamish, 1999). Hence, we explore how SMEs can overcome constraints to internationalization by investigating the impact of alliances on the internationalization and performance of internationalizing SMEs.

HYPOTHESIS DEVELOPMENT

Exporting

Exporting has been traditionally regarded as the first step to entering international markets, serving as a platform for future international expansions (Kogut and Chang, 1996). This strategy is particularly applicable to the internationalization of SMEs because SMEs frequently lack the resources, financial or otherwise, for FDI (Dalli, 1995; Zahra, Neubaum, and Huse, 1997). Exporting provides SMEs with fast access to foreign markets, with little capital investment required, but the opportunity to gain valuable international experience. (Root, 1994; Zahra *et al.*, 1997; Sullivan and Bauerschmidt, 1990; Erminio and Rugman, 1996). While many studies have explored the performance effects of exporting strategies, there has been little consistency in

conceptual and operational definitions of export performance (Shoham, 1998) which limits the conclusiveness of the findings from this literature (Aaby and Slater, 1989).

Conceptually, several economic benefits can be gained by exporting. The most obvious are gains related to scale and scope economies (Kogut, 1985; Grant, Jammine, and Thomas, 1988) as achieved from larger volumes of sales and production made possible by revenue growth in the geographic extension of markets. In addition, a presence in multiple, diverse international markets can lead to advantages related to increases in market power (Kim *et al.*, 1993) and gains from the diversification of revenues (Ramaswamy, 1992a). The potential economic benefits from exporting, together with the stepping-stone effect for future international expansion (Erminio and Rugman, 1996), suggest that the extent of exporting should be positively related to an SME's financial performance.

Hypothesis 1: An SME's performance is positively related to its level of exporting activities.

Foreign direct investment

Internalization theorists argue that multinational firms can gain economic benefits from the exploitation of various assets across a large number of international markets either by exporting or FDI (Buckley and Casson, 1976). While exporting is an internationalization mode that involves less risk in terms of capital investment, when a firm's assets are proprietary (such as brand equity, trademarks, or patents) exporting can expose a firm to greater risks in terms of distributor opportunism or asset appropriation and devaluation. When faced with this risk, FDI becomes an attractive means of internationalization, because it enables firms to minimize transaction-related risks through internalizing markets for proprietary asset exchange (Hennart, 1982; Rugman, 1982).

Aside from the benefits gained from the internalization of proprietary asset exchange across international borders, FDI in diversified locations enables a firm to leverage various location-based advantages (Kogut, 1985), such as a competitively priced labor force, to have access to critical resources (Deeds and Hill, 1998) and to develop new knowledge and capabilities that enhance its international competitiveness (Shan and Song, 1997). The potential to promote organizational learning in diverse international markets has been argued to be a key benefit of international expansion (Porter, 1990; Zahra et al., 2000).

While FDI holds these potential benefits, it requires a greater level of resource commitment in foreign countries than exporting and is more difficult to reverse. It is also less flexible than exporting in coping with investment hazards such as political instability and fluctuating market conditions in host countries. At the same time, there are different costs associated with international diversification at different levels of internationalization. At the beginning of internationalization, an entrepreneur is subject to the 'liability of foreignness' (Hymer, 1976) which stems from doing business outside the firm's home country (Buckley and Casson, 1976; Dunning, 1973). This liability means that the global entrepreneur may incur higher costs than local (host country) competitors. While this initial disadvantage might diminish with greater levels of experience in host country markets, a second disadvantage, which is related to increasing transaction and coordination costs (Tallman and Li, 1996), can be encountered at very high levels of internationalization. As a firm increases its commitment to international markets by establishing more foreign subsidiaries, the number of internal transactions increases and governance costs can reach a point where they outweigh any potential benefits, which in turn translates into lower financial performance (Tallman and Li, 1996; Hitt et al., 1997). The same logic applies to international expansion into many dissimilar markets. The costs of managing locational diversity, along political, cultural and idiosyncratic market dimensions, can eventually erode profit margins when high levels of internationalization are achieved (Geringer et al., 1989; Ramaswamy, 1992b).

This pattern of cost and benefits suggests that given a full range of FDIs, there is a sideways 'S' shaped relationship between the degree of FDI and firm performance. At the very beginning of internationalization, performance might decline as SMEs are subject to the liability of foreignness and may have to pay some 'tuition' in terms of profits for their mistakes in their initial expansion into international markets. Performance will increase as ownership advantages are exploited in a greater international spread and as new capabilities are developed in international markets (Tallman and Li, 1996; Hitt et al., 1997). However, performance will eventually fall off as governance costs and coordination costs surpass the benefits from internationalization. At this point, the higher rents attributable to internationalization will be offset by rapidly increasing governance and coordination costs, and firm performance will be depressed, although the falling-off point could be delayed as managers learn how to better manage a worldwide operation (Hitt et al., 1997).

Prior research on internationalization and performance has generally focused on large, internationally diversified firms and emphasized the downward effect on performance exerted by increasing governance and coordination costs at high levels of internationalization (Geringer et al., 1989; Hitt et al., 1997). Using well-internationalized firms as samples, these studies have shown a threshold to international diversification, that is, an inverted U curve relationship (the latter half of the sideways 'S') between internationalization and firm performance. We argue that the notion of a threshold of international diversification in these studies is much more of a concern for larger firms than for internationalizing SMEs. We contend that for SMEs, the liability of foreignness is the primary concern when first entering international markets via FDI. Given such liabilities, SMEs may not realize immediately the potential benefits from FDI. However, these liabilities can be reduced through experience accumulation. As firms gain experience via FDI, new FDIs can contribute positively to higher firm performance. We hypothesize such an effect; that is, a U curve relationship (the first half of the sideways 'S') between FDI and performance.

Hypothesis 2: The relationship between the level of FDI and an SME's performance is nonlinear, with the slope negative at low levels of FDI but positive at higher levels of FDI.

Alliances

As discussed in the previous section, the potential benefits from investment expansion into international markets are appealing. However, SMEs may not have the full range of resources and capabilities to successfully undertake FDI and realize these benefits. By definition, entrepreneurial firms are confronted with limited resources and capabilities (Jarillo, 1989; Beamish, 1999). SMEs face internal shortages of information, capital, management time and experience, while externally, SMEs face constraints arising from their vulnerability to environmental changes (Buckley, 1989). Such intrinsic deficiencies in resources and capabilities impose constraints on the internationalization of SMEs (Zacharakis, 1997). These constraints inflate the liabilities of foreignness (Hymer, 1976) and of newness (Stinchcombe, 1965) and make internationalization a daunting challenge to SMEs.

Alliances have been suggested as one important means of overcoming resource and capability deficiencies and enhancing the likelihood of success for internationalizing firms (Jarillo, 1989; Zacharakis, 1997; Beamish, 1999). Prior research on alliances points to several benefits including the minimization of transaction costs, increased market power, shared risks and better access to key resources such as capital and information (Kogut, 1988; Mowery, Oxley, and Silverman, 1996; Gulati, Nohria, and Zaheer, 2000). For SMEs, foremost among these benefits is access to the partner's resources, or 'network resources' (Gulati, 1998).

Alliance partners can help SMEs overcome shortages of capital, equipment and other tangible assets through resource sharing between the two or more separate firms engaged in the alliance. More importantly, alliance partners represent an important source of host country knowledge to SMEs. SMEs can acquire host country knowledge and develop new organizational capabilities internally through incremental experience accumulation in new geographic regions (Johanson and Vahlne, 1977). However, this learning-by-doing process takes time and can result in mistakes (Dierickx and Cool, 1989) that are disproportionately more expensive to an SME than a large firm (Beamish, 1999; Eisenhardt and Schoonhoven, 1990; Erramilli and De Souza, 1993). By accessing alliance partners' knowledge base, an SME can expedite its learning process and minimize mistakes. Hence, entering into alliances and having access to alliance partners' resources offers a potentially efficient way to overcome deficiencies in an SME's resource and capabilities.

However, alliances are not risk-free and face problems in successful implementation (Kogut, 1989; Hamel, 1991; Deeds and Hill, 1998). Compared with wholly-owned entries, alliances have complexities arising from the cooperation and coordination of two or more partners (Inkpen and Beamish, 1997). There are such potential problems as goal conflicts, lack of trust and understanding, cultural differences, and disputes over the division of control. Any of these can lead to instability or even failure. While the need for additional resources frequently necessitates the formation of alliances (Deeds and Hill, 1996; Weaver and Dickson, 1998), the difficulties with alliance management mean that the formation of an alliance itself is no guarantee to an SME's successful entry into international markets. A real issue facing an SME entering into an alliance is to find the right partner (Zacharakis, 1997; Park and Kim, 1997; Baum, Calabrese, and Silverman, 2000).

An SME has three basic partner choices: it can partner with firms from the host country, with firms from the home country, or with firms from a third country (Makino and Delios, 1996). All three kinds of alliances could help an SME overcome shortages in financial capital and tangible resources. However, when it comes to providing a source of host country knowledge, these partner choices differ substantially (Makino and Beamish, 1998). A local partner represents a primary source of local knowledge. A local partner tends to have more detailed knowledge about various aspects of the host country environment, as compared to the other partner options. A local firm is familiar with the needs and tastes of the local consumers, it has information about local competitors and has the local contacts that can provide the focal firm with timely information. In sum, an alliance with a local partner can alleviate an SMEs' local knowledge deficiencies and this strategy has been found to be an effective means of entering new host countries (Beamish and Banks, 1987; Makino and Delios, 1996).

In contrast, an alliance with firms from the home country, or with firms from a third country, holds fewer local knowledge benefits. If the partners have not made investments in the target markets, they provide little benefit to SMEs seeking to overcome deficiencies in host country knowledge. As foreign investors themselves, partners from the home country or from a third country usually do not have full access to local resources that could provide their participants with a continuous flow of information and other benefits. Therefore, alliances with partners from the home country, or with partners from a third country are not as likely to alleviate the SME's local knowledge deficiencies as are alliances with local firms. Given the potential risks and costs of alliances and the low marginal benefits, alliances with home country firms or third country firms might have a negative impact on an SME's performance. As our data source did not provide information to identify third country partners, hypotheses were developed only for local partners and home country partners, even though the rationale for home country partners holds for third country partners.

Hypothesis 3a: An SME's performance is positively related to its level of alliances with local partners formed in the process of internationalization.

Hypothesis 3b: An SME's performance is negatively related to its level of alliances with only home country partners formed in the process of internationalization.

Interaction effects of export and foreign direct investment

As discussed earlier, both exporting and FDI have the potential to contribute to higher firm performance. At the same time, each strategy requires substantially different organizational structures and management capabilities (Roth, 1992; Ramaswamy, 1995). Exporting activities, for example, usually require the centralization of decision-making to balance the needs of different markets and to achieve maximum operating efficiency. In contrast, foreign subsidiaries are located in a variety of sites outside the home country. A dispersed set of subsidiaries across disparate geographic areas can require the decentralization of decision-making to adapt to the peculiarities of the location. Differences, such as these, in the organization of exporting and FDI (Beamish et al., 1999) make it difficult to coordinate the activities of the export unit and disparate foreign subsidiaries. Given the additional concern of the constraints on management time and experience in SMEs, the coordination costs of

these two international expansion activities can readily become excessive and reduce the potential benefits from either of these two internationalization modes.

Moreover, export units and foreign subsidiaries have different mandates, with the export unit having sales in overseas markets as its primary goal and foreign subsidiaries having more complicated objectives such as market-seeking and/or resource-seeking. In the pursuit of their own mandates, these are potential conflicts and risks of cannibalization exist when firms both export to and establish local market oriented foreign direct investment in the same host country. The conflicts and cannibalization between export units and foreign subsidiaries could erode profit margins.

At a micro-level, the management of exporting and foreign subsidiaries requires different management skills. In exporting, sales skills are among the most important management skills needed. In foreign subsidiaries, a more diverse set of skills is required. Given both these macro- and micro-level concerns, it is plausible that a firm that has a high export intensity while making extended FDI activities will face a significant stretch in management resources. For the larger firms, it might not be too great a challenge because these firms have more abundant management resources and extensive international experience which help develop management capabilities in managing complexities (Hitt et al., 1997). For SMEs who have limited management resources and international experience, the complexity of managing these two international expansion activities can stretch management capabilities to the extent that it could depress overall performance.

Hypothesis 4: Exporting activities will exert a negative moderating effect on the relationship between FDI and performance.

DATA AND METHODOLOGY

Sample and data sources

There is no generally accepted definition of a small and medium-sized firm (an SME). The most widely used one in the entrepreneurship literature is the definition provided by the American Small Business Administration (SBA). The SBA defines

572   *J. W. Lu and P. W. Beamish*

SMEs as stand-alone enterprises with fewer than 500 employees (Baird, Lyles, and Orris, 1994; Hodgetts and Kuratko, 1998; Beamish 1999; Wolff and Pett, 2000). Following the SBA's definition of an SME, we limited our sample to all Japanese firms listed on the first and second sections of the Tokyo stock exchange in 1999, that had fewer than 500 employees.

For this sample, we collected corporate-level accounting and performance information from the Nikkei NEEDS tapes, an electronic data base that provides information on the corporate performance, and other financial indicators, of Japanese firms listed on the first and second sections of the Tokyo stock exchange. Where required, additional parent company information was gathered from various editions of the *Japan Company Handbook*. As we required FDI information for our analyses, we matched the list of Japanese SMEs to the list of parent firms in the 1999 edition of *Kaigai Shinshutsu Kigyou Souran-Kuni Betsu* (Japanese Overseas Investments—by Country). This directory of Japanese foreign investment is published annually by Toyo Keizai Inc. Its coverage is close to the population of overseas subsidiaries of major listed and non-listed Japanese firms. Because the data are compiled annually, it is possible to develop a longitudinal profile of an SME's internationalization process. For this study, we used the 1986, 1989, 1992, 1994, 1997, and 1999 editions of *Kaigai Shinshutsu Kigyou Souran* to construct a 12-year (1986–97) panel of data. We used the 1999 edition to ensure we had the most complete information on FDI in 1996 and 1997. For first and second section firms not listed in *Kaigai Shinshutsu Kigyou Souran* we confirmed that they had no FDIs by searching annual reports and industry reports.

The 164 Japanese SMEs that comprised our sample represented 7.5 percent of all firms listed on the Tokyo stock exchange. These 164 Japanese SMEs were engaged in 19 different industries, as defined by the Nikkei NEEDS tapes. The average number of employees in our sample is 321 with the smallest firm having 58 employees and the largest 499. All firms had export activities, and 95 had made FDIs. For the firms with FDI activities, half had made two investments or less in two or fewer host countries. These figures show that our sample captures SMEs that are in various phases of the early stage of the internationalization process.

Sample characteristics

In previous research, several criteria have been used to identify entrepreneurial firms. These criteria can be classified into three categories: firm demographics such as size, age and ownership, firm performance such as growth rate, and firm behavior such as risk-taking (Stevenson and Jarillo, 1990). In constructing the sample for our study, we attempted to satisfy the criteria of entrepreneurial firms in each category, but as McDougall and Oviatt (2000) advocate, we emphasize the latter two defining criteria.

For the first category, we used the criterion of firm size, in which smaller firms are typically thought of as entrepreneurial firms. Using the SBA definition, we restricted our sample to small and medium-sized enterprises. In the second category, we used the criterion of firm growth. Entrepreneurial firms are typically characterized as having higher growth rates than non-entrepreneurial firms (Stevenson and Jarillo, 1990). We make this assessment by comparing overall sales growth rates as well as growth in international markets via exporting and FDI. The comparison on growth rates in sales and exporting was made between the 164 firms in our sample and the remaining 1248 Tokyo stock exchange firms that operated in the same industries as our sample firms. For FDI, our analysis was limited to the firms that had made FDIs (95 sample firms and 1228 other firms, see Table 1). As it is difficult to compare and interpret growth rates of the two groups (sample for the study and the reference group) by 19 industries along three dimensions (using four measures), we calculated overall growth rates for the two groups after verification that the industrial distribution of our sample was qualitatively similar to the inter-industry distribution of the firms in the reference group. The overall annual growth rates are summarized in Table 1.

For overall growth, the firms in the sample expanded sales at mean rate of 5.74 percent which was 8.3 percent higher than the 5.30 percent for all other firms. For international activities, the growth rate of sample firms was much higher on both the export and FDI dimensions. The difference was greatest for exports where the growth rate of the sample firms was 3.5 times that of all other firms. For FDI growth, the rate of expansion in terms of the number of subsidi-

Internationalization and Performance of SMEs 573

Table 1. Sample characteristics: growth rates

Firm characteristic	Annual growth rate (%)		Comparison
	Sample	All other firms	
Overall sales	5.74	5.30	+8.3%
Export	22.73	6.61	+343.8%
FDI (subsidiaries)	12.06	8.32	+145.0%
FDI (host countries)	8.99	6.06	+148.3%

aries, or number of host countries, was approximately 1.5 times greater.

This comparison of growth rates shows that the SMEs in our sample were expanding at a rate slightly higher than all other firms in domestic markets, but at a considerably greater rate in international markets. This latter aspect, fast growth in international markets, relates to the third category for identifying entrepreneurial firms, and is consistent with the approach taken by Autio *et al.* (2000). This category bases the identification of entrepreneurial firms on the nature of activities a firm undertakes. In earlier discussion, we have stressed that internationalization is an entrepreneurial activity, particularly for SMEs. The comparatively high growth rates of the sample firms, in an area which involves greater risks and entails more resource constraints, highlights the entrepreneurial character of our sample.

The entrepreneurial character of our sample firms' growth is further reinforced by the Japanese context. As Ronen and Shenkar (1985) identified, there are culturally isolated countries such as Japan and Korea, which do not have any close cultural counterparts, such as the United States has with Canada, or Portugal with Spain. This means that when a firm in a culturally isolated country, such as Japan, goes international it faces a much greater hurdle because, wherever it goes outside of home country, it must conduct business in a culturally, socially or linguistically very different context. This feature of the study is important because the more different the setting into which the firm is expanding, the more entrepreneurial the nature of the expansion, particularly for SMEs that have limited resources but want to 'create or seize an opportunity regardless of the resources possessed' (Timmons, 1994: 7).

Variables

Our models analyze the annual performance of SMEs over the 1986–97 period. To conduct the analysis, we created a record for each firm in each year of the 12-year period. Parent firm profitability is the dependent variable for all models. The main independent variables are the levels of exports, FDI activities and alliance activities. We also developed a number of control variables to account for other factors known to affect corporate performance.

Dependent variables

We measured the performance of Japanese firms using two accounting-based measures, return on assets (ROA) and return on sales (ROS) (Tallman and Li, 1996; Hitt *et al.*, 1997). We obtained both measures from the Nikkei NEEDS tapes for each year in the 1986–97 period. These two variables were highly correlated ($r = 0.873$) and generated similar findings. As we report a large number of specifications, we confine the information in the tables to the results for ROA.

Exporting activities

We measured the level of exporting activities through export intensity, the percent of parent firm sales that were derived from export revenues. This variable was derived from annual export and revenue information found in the Nikkei NEEDS tapes.

Foreign investment activities

We developed two measures to gauge the magnitude of FDI activities, both of which were counts. The first count was the number of FDIs in which

574   *J. W. Lu and P. W. Beamish*

the parent firm had a 10 percent or greater equity share. The second count was the number of countries in which the firm had FDIs. Ramaswamy (1995) and Delios and Beamish (1999) used these two counts, which provide a reasonable indicator of the extent of FDI activities. These measures were derived from information reported in Toyo Keizai (1999, 1997, 1994, 1992, 1989 editions) for the 1986–97 period. These two measures are highly correlated (see the Appendix, $r = 0.952$); hence, we entered these two measures separately in parallel sets of models.

Alliance activities

We developed two measures to capture the level of international alliance activities. We based these measures on the identity of the equity joint venture partners (Japanese or local partners). We focus on equity joint ventures in the international market because of the data availability and because this is the form where the stakes are highest for the international entrepreneur (Beamish, 1999). We could not identify third-country partners, because our data source, Toyo Keizai did not provide information on the nationality of non-Japanese partners making it difficult to distinguish local partners from third-country partners. Prior research has found that the vast majority of non-Japanese partners are local firms (Makino, 1995), hence we coded all non-Japanese partners as local partners.

The first set of measures we developed gauges the use of equity joint ventures with Japanese partners (without the participation of local partners). We first counted the number of Japanese–Japanese (J-J) equity joint ventures and the number of host countries in which the firm had J-J equity joint ventures. The counts were then divided by the total number of subsidiaries to derive J-J equity joint venture intensities by subsidiaries and by host countries. The second set of measures gauges the use of equity joint ventures with local partners (J-L) and was computed in a similar way as that for the J-J equity joint ventures. Both sets of measures were computed annually for the 1986–97 period. The measures by subsidiaries and by host countries for both J-J and J-L joint ventures are highly correlated (see the Appendix) and we entered these separately in the models.

Control variables

We included two measures to account for the proprietary content of an SME's assets. The first gauged the level of propriety content in technological assets (R&D as percent of sales), and the second in marketing assets (advertising as percent of sales). We next calculated two control variables for the characteristics of the SMEs. These were the size of the SME (log of total number of employees) and product diversification of the SME (a Herfindahl measure). The first three variables were derived from the NEEDS tapes on an annual basis for the 1986–97 period. The Herfindahl measure was computed from information in the *Japan Company Handbook* for 1996 and the value was assigned to observations from 1986–97. Further, we included U.S.–yen exchange rates from the International Financial Statistics Yearbook to control for the exchange rate impact on the profitability of FDI. We used a U.S. dollar–yen exchange rate because the U.S. dollar is a frequently used reference point for exchange rates. Also, in Asia, where many of the Japanese subsidiaries were located, the U.S. dollar is used for business transactions because of its greater stability relative to local currencies. Our final control was a set of industry dummies based on 2-digit industry codes.

Modeling procedure

Because our theoretical argument posited that the internationalization of SMEs would, over time, drive changes in corporate performance, we lagged the effects of our independent variables. We explored 1-, 2-, and 3-year lags and found the results to be robust across the different lags. As a 1-year lag provides the least reduction in our data (it permits us to model events across 11 separate 1-year time periods), we report the results for models with a 1-year lag. Our sample using the 1-year lag comprises 164 cross-sections and an 11-year time series, or 1804 observations.

In modeling this sample, we assume that each observation of our dependent variable is generated by an underlying process described by:

$$Y_{f,t} = \alpha + \beta' W_{f,t-1} + \varepsilon_{f,t}$$

where W is a vector of explanatory variables, f denotes firm, and t denotes the time period. As we pooled our cross-sectional and time series data to take advantage of the greater degrees of freedom offered by pooling, and to capture both the dynamic information of time series and the variation due to cross-sections, we needed to be concerned about autocorrelation and heteroscedasticity (Bergh and Holbein, 1997). To correct for the presence of autocorrelation and heteroscedasticity, we entered the exchange rate for each different year to absorb the time-related variance in the least square regressions. In addition, we verified our regression coefficient estimates with the Fuller and Battese method by TSCSREG procedure in SAS, a General Linear Square Model in which corrections are made to account for the presence of autocorrelation and heteroscedasticity (Kmenta, 1986). In comparing estimates across the two methods, there was no change in the sign of estimated coefficients, although significance levels did vary in some instances. However, the changes in the significance levels did not change the hypothesis test results. As the TSCSREG procedure does not generate results on some key model statistics such as F-statistics and R^2, we report the results from the OLS estimations.

RESULTS

The Appendix presents the descriptive statistics and correlation for the study's variables. Except for the multiple measures for one variable (such as the two measures of FDI, by subsidiary and by host country, $r = 0.952$), the magnitude of the correlation and the results of regression diagnostics (e.g., VIF statistics) suggested that multicollinearity was not a serious problem.

We tested the four hypotheses using two sets of 10 regressions: one for the full sample of 164 Japanese SMEs (95 with FDIs and 69 without FDIs) and the other with a subsample of 95 Japanese SMEs with FDIs. The results of these regressions are displayed in Tables 2 and 3. All models were significant and each had reasonable explanatory power. Further, the results for the full and subsamples were consistent, but the effects for the internationalization strategy variables were more prominent in the subsample of SMEs with FDIs. While we discuss the results with reference to the models in Table 2, the discussion could be applied to the models in Table 3, with no changes except where noted.

The first model in Table 2 is the baseline model which only includes the five control terms plus the set of industry dummies. As expected, R&D intensity was positively related to firm performance ($p < 0.01$), while product diversification had a negative relationship ($p < 0.01$) to firm performance. Firm size was negatively related to performance at the 0.01 level, while advertising intensity was not significant. The latter result was also observed for a sample of larger Japanese firms (Delios and Beamish, 1999). Finally, the exchange rate (yen per U.S. dollar) had a positive relationship ($p < 0.01$) indicating that firm performance was higher when the yen was weaker. These results were consistent across all models, and we focus the rest of our discussion on the tests of our hypotheses.

Model 2 in Tables 2 and 3 tested Hypothesis 1, which predicts that exporting is positively related to firm performance. Contrary to the prediction in Hypothesis 1, the exporting measure had a negative ($p < 0.05$) relationship to firm performance. Models 3 and 4 test Hypothesis 2, which predicted a nonlinear (U-curve) relationship between the level of FDI activity and firm performance. In Model 3, the negative sign on the number of FDIs term ($p < 0.05$) and the positive sign on its squared term ($p < 0.10$) provide support for this hypothesis. For the number of countries measure, a similar result is observed, although the squared term is not significant. However, we note that in subsequent models, and subsamples (e.g., the models in Table 3), the number of country terms behave as predicted. Taken together, these findings suggest a U curve relationship between the level of FDI activity and SME performance; that is, firm performance declines with initial FDI activity but improves with a greater extent of FDI.

Hypotheses 3a and 3b make predictions about the effect of alliances on firm performance. Joint ventures with local firms are predicted to have a positive effect on firm performance (Hypothesis 3a), while joint ventures with other Japanese firms are predicted to have a negative effect on performance. Models 5 and 6 use two measures of JV partner intensity (respectively, by host country and by subsidiary) to test Hypothesis 3a. The positive signs ($p < 0.01$) on both measures provide support for Hypothesis 3a, indicating that forming joint ventures with local firms improved the performance of internationalizing SMEs.

576 J. W. Lu and P. W. Beamish

Table 2. Regressions of return on assets (ROA) on export, FDI and JV: 164 Japanese SMEs, 1986–96[a,b]

Independent variables	Model 1	Model 2	Model 3	Model 4	Model 5	Model 6	Model 7	Model 8	Model 9	Model 10
1. Intercept	0.080*** (2.464)	0.085*** (2.614)	0.086*** (2.653)	0.085*** (2.627)	0.085*** (2.631)	0.086*** (2.655)	0.076** (2.355)	0.079** (2.444)	0.086*** (2.642)	0.085*** (2.640)
2. R&D intensity	0.742*** (6.409)	0.832*** (7.101)	0.875*** (7.377)	0.869*** (7.301)	0.891*** (7.528)	0.882*** (7.418)	0.849*** (6.225)	0.863*** (7.285)	0.884*** (7.458)	0.867*** (7.302)
3. Advertising intensity	0.105 (0.886)	0.082 (0.693)	0.092 (0.775)	0.078 (0.657)	0.090 (0.760)	0.052 (0.442)	0.118 (1.006)	0.104 (0.880)	0.084 (0.708)	0.070 (0.589)
4. Number of employees (log)	-0.019*** (-3.883)	-0.019*** (-3.891)	-0.017*** (-3.624)	-0.017*** (-3.533)	-0.018*** (-3.720)	-0.018*** (-3.651)	-0.017*** (-3.625)	-0.017*** (-3.520)	-0.017*** (-3.609)	-0.017*** (-3.536)
5. Product diversity	-0.037*** (-2.451)	-0.043*** (-2.844)	-0.041*** (-2.743)	-0.041*** (-2.742)	-0.041*** (-2.734)	-0.041** (-2.748)	-0.037** (-2.477)	-0.038** (-2.538)	-0.042*** (-2.786)	-0.043*** (-2.873)
6. Exchange rate	0.001*** (6.412)	0.001*** (6.524)	0.001*** (6.049)	0.001*** (5.987)	0.001*** (6.251)	0.001*** (6.141)	0.001*** (6.539)	0.001*** (6.275)	0.001*** (6.031)	0.001*** (5.957)
7. Export intensity		-0.056*** (-4.192)	-0.051*** (-3.657)	-0.048*** (-3.430)	-0.050*** (-3.634)	-0.045*** (-3.279)	-0.045*** (-3.241)	-0.046*** (-3.343)	-0.032* (-1.893)	-0.016 (-0.887)
8. Number of foreign investments			-0.005** (-2.469)		-0.007** (-3.338)		-0.001 (-0.271)		-0.001** (-2.615)	
9. Number of foreign investments (squared)			0.001* (1.850)		0.001** (2.562)		0.001 (0.556)		0.001*** (2.604)	
10. Number of countries invested in				-0.007** (-2.361)		-0.009*** (-3.001)		-0.027 (-0.921)		-0.007** (-2.297)
11. Number of countries invested in (squared)				0.001 (1.254)		0.001* (1.741)		0.001 (0.539)		0.001** (2.317)
12. JV (local partner) intensity (by subsidiary)					0.072*** (3.310)					
13. JV (local partner) intensity (by host country)						0.045** (2.935)				
14. JV (Japanese partner) intensity (by subsidiary)							-0.072*** (-5.966)			
15. JV (Japanese partner) intensity (by host country)								-0.043*** (-4.282)		
16. Export intensity * Number of foreign investments									-0.006** (-2.021)	
17. Export intensity * Number of countries invested in										-0.014*** (-3.008)
Model indices										
R^2	0.079	0.088	0.091	0.092	0.097	0.096	0.109	0.101	0.093	0.096
Adjusted R^2	0.067	0.075	0.078	0.079	0.083	0.082	0.095	0.087	0.079	0.083
F-statistic	6.614***	7.129***	6.848***	6.910***	7.037***	7.002***	8.041***	7.398***	6.757***	7.020***

[a] Dummy variables for industry are included in the models, but not shown in the table.
[b] Upper number in a cell is a parameter estimate, numbers in the parentheses are t-statistics; ***$p < 0.01$; **$p < 0.05$; *$p < 0.10$ (all two-tailed tests).

Table 3. Regressions of return on assets (ROA) on export, FDI and JV: 95 Japanese SMEs, 1986–96[a,b]

Independent variables	Model 1	Model 2	Model 3	Model 4	Model 5	Model 6	Model 7	Model 8	Model 9	Model 10
1. Intercept	0.141*** (3.078)	0.172*** (3.724)	0.193*** (4.174)	0.198*** (4.295)	0.189*** (4.108)	0.195*** (4.244)	0.171*** (3.797)	0.171*** (3.760)	0.183*** (3.952)	0.186*** (4.030)
2. R&D intensity	0.657*** (4.550)	0.709*** (4.927)	0.784*** (5.421)	0.785*** (5.427)	0.805*** (5.581)	0.794*** (5.515)	0.702*** (4.982)	0.722*** (5.080)	0.801*** (5.542)	0.784*** (5.450)
3. Advertising intensity	-0.235 (-1.203)	-0.308 (-1.582)	-0.256 (-1.320)	-0.312* (-1.617)	-0.257 (-1.331)	-0.376 (-1.948)	-0.240 (-1.259)	-0.256 (-1.329)	-0.275 (-1.418)	-0.324* (-1.685)
4. Number of employees (log)	-0.024*** (-3.443)	-0.027*** (-3.909)	-0.026*** (-3.775)	-0.025*** (-3.619)	-0.026*** (-3.859)	-0.025** (-3.683)	-0.027*** (-4.005)	-0.026*** (-3.917)	-0.024** (-3.540)	-0.023** (-3.345)
5. Product diversity	-0.040* (-1.813)	-0.054** (-2.436)	-0.057** (-2.580)	-0.060*** (-2.685)	-0.057** (-2.556)	-0.059** (-2.667)	-0.047** (-2.164)	-0.048** (-2.186)	-0.057** (-2.566)	-0.061*** (-2.751)
6. Exchange rate	0.001*** (3.912)	0.001*** (3.591)	0.001*** (3.004)	0.001*** (2.733)	0.001*** (3.274)	0.001*** (2.970)	0.001*** (4.072)	0.001*** (3.987)	0.001*** (3.009)	0.001*** (2.757)
7. Export intensity		-0.068*** (-4.173)	-0.065*** (-3.910)	-0.062*** (-3.715)	-0.064*** (-3.853)	-0.059*** (-3.563)	-0.058*** (-3.593)	-0.064*** (-3.921)	-0.035* (-1.643)	-0.014 (-0.613)
8. Number of foreign investments			-0.009*** (-3.664)		-0.011*** (-4.330)	-0.017*** (-4.649)	-0.081*** (-6.634)		-0.010** (-3.785)	
9. Number of foreign investments (squared)			0.001*** (3.136)		0.001*** (3.721)	0.002*** (3.500)	-0.021 (-0.727)		0.001** (3.861)	
10. Number of countries invested in				-0.016*** (-4.200)				-0.055*** (-5.253)		-0.015*** (-4.029)
11. Number of countries invested in (squared)				0.001*** (3.123)				-0.022 (-0.723)		0.002*** (4.047)
12. JV (local partner) intensity (by subsidiary)					0.075*** (3.216)					
13. JV (local partner) intensity (by host country)						0.050*** (3.023)				
14. JV (Japanese partner) intensity (by subsidiary)							-0.030* (-1.827)			
15. JV (Japanese partner) intensity (by host country)								-0.310* (-1.850)		
16. Export intensity * Number of foreign investments									-0.001*** (-3.861)	
17. Export intensity * Number of countries invested in										-0.017*** (-3.204)
Model indices										
R^2	0.079	0.094	0.106	0.111	0.115	0.119	0.132	0.118	0.111	0.120
Adjusted R^2	0.059	0.074	0.084	0.089	0.092	0.096	0.111	0.97	0.088	0.097
F-statistic	3.965***	4.611***	4.831***	5.091***	5.086***	5.285***	6.438***	5.683***	4.873***	5.334***

[a]Dummy variables for industry are included in the models, but not shown in the table.
[b]Upper number in a cell is a parameter estimate, numbers in the parentheses are t-statistics; *** $p < 0.01$; ** $p < 0.05$; * $p < 0.10$ (all two-tailed tests)

578   *J. W. Lu and P. W. Beamish*

Meanwhile, the results for Models 7 and 8 show that joint venture activity with other Japanese firms has a negative impact ($p < 0.10$) on firm performance. These results demonstrate the importance of alliance partner selection and suggest that local partners provide more value to SMEs than partners from the home country.

Models 9 and 10 in Tables 2 and 3 tested Hypothesis 4, which predicted that the extent of exporting activity will exert a negative moderating effect on the relationship between FDI and firm performance. We tested this hypothesis using two interactions constructed between exporting and the two measures of FDI activity. To guard against the observance of a significant interaction result that is spurious, we tested whether the overall change in the model's explanatory power was significant, compared to the baseline model, after the inclusion of the interaction term. For Model 9, the relevant baseline was Model 3, and for Model 10 it was Model 4. In all cases, the improvement in model fit (change in R^2) was significant at $p < 0.01$. As expected, given the improvement in the model, the interaction term was significant ($p < 0.05$ or less) and negatively signed in all instances. The negative sign indicates that a high export intensity exerted a negative influence on the performance impact of FDI activities. We discuss this effect in more detail in the next section.

DISCUSSION

Our main objective in this paper was to examine the effects of an international aspect of an entrepreneurial strategy, namely the relationship between an SME's internationalization strategy and its performance. To that end, we explored the relationships that exporting, FDI and alliances had on firm performance for a sample of internationalizing small and medium-sized Japanese firms.

Notably, we found that exporting and FDI had different impacts on firm performance. Exporting had a negative and linear relationship with performance, whereas FDI had a nonlinear relationship with performance, that is, low levels of FDI were associated with decreasing performance, but greater levels of FDI with higher performance. Before concluding that exporting is detrimental to firm performance, the interpretation of the negative impact of exporting on SME perform-

ance needs to be considered in relation to the time period for this study. Over the 1986–96 period, the Japanese yen experienced a general trend towards appreciation, which was substantive in its aggregate impact. As a result of this yen appreciation (or endaka), exports from Japan became less competitive in international markets. The higher costs associated with exporting from Japan represented a significant barrier to the financial success of Japanese exports, particularly for products that were manufactured almost exclusively in Japan. To test the impact of exchange rate fluctuations on the relationship between export and firm performance, we interacted exchange rate with export intensity in the 1986–97 period (which was the period for this study) and the 1964–96 period, which covers a broader period of yen appreciation and Japanese firm's internationalization.

The results of this analysis are reported in Table 4. The first model in Table 4 is the baseline model (the same as Model 2 in Table 2) which included only the main effects of exchange rate and exporting. The second model shows the addition of the interaction term to the baseline model. Reflecting the nonsignificance of the first interaction model in Table 4, was the nonsignificant improvement in model fit over the baseline model. The nonsignificance of the interaction is not surprising when we consider the comparatively small variance in yen values (from 239 per U.S. dollar to 169) during this 11-year period. Over a longer time span in which the strength of the yen increased markedly, from 360 in 1964 to 169 in 1996, the interaction effect is significant (Model 4 in Table 4) both at a model and individual coefficient level. The positive sign on the interaction term indicates that when the yen was weaker, a higher export intensity contributed positively to firm performance. As the models in Tables 2 and 3 test the main effects of export intensity during a period of a relatively strong yen, these models capture the latter half of the exporting, exchange rate and performance relation- ships. That is, during the time of a relatively strong yen (1986–96, as compared to the previous two decades), the intensity of export activities had a negative relationship with performance.

As has been reported in the popular and academic press, the response of many Japanese firms to this endaka, and the declining export competitiveness and performance shown in the two mod-

Strat Mgmt J, **22** 565–586 (2001)

Table 4. Regressions of return on assets (ROA) on export: 164 Japanese SMEs[a,b]

Independent variables	Model 1	Model 2	Model 3	Model 4
1. Intercept	0.0849***	0.0644*	0.137***	0.148***
	(2.614)	(1.868)	(11.029)	(11.811)
2. R&D intensity	0.832***	0.847***	0.687***	0.681***
	(7.101)	(7.210)	(10.956)	(10.888)
3. Advertising intensity	0.082	0.090	−0.114**	−0.130**
	(0.693)	(0.756)	(−1.918)	(−2.194)
4. Number of employees	−0.019***	−0.018**	−0.018***	−0.018***
(log)	(−3.891)	(−3.733)	(−8.941)	(−8.954)
5. Product diversity	−0.043***	−0.043**	−0.028***	−0.029***
	(−2.844)	(−2.856)	(−4.171)	(−4.903)
6. Exchange rate	0.001***	0.001***	0.001***	0.001***
	(6.524)	(6.289)	(10.063)	(4.903)
7. Export Intensity	−0.056**	0.065	−0.016**	−0.098***
	(−4.192)	(0.930)	(−2.379)	(−6.105)
8. Exchange rate *		−0.001		0.001***
Export intensity		(−1.059)		(5.621)
Model indices				
R^2	0.088	0.089	0.086	0.091
Adjusted R^2	0.075	0.077	0.082	0.087
F-statistic	7.129***	6.977***	21.050***	21.586***
Length of time series	11	11	33	33

[a]Dummy variables for industry are included in the models, but not shown in the table.
[b]Upper number in a cell is a parameter estimate, numbers in the parentheses are t-statistics, ***$p < 0.01$; **$p < 0.05$; *$p < 0.10$ (all two-tailed tests)

els in Table 4, has been to shift manufacturing activities to offshore locations. Our sample captured firms in the process of this shift in manufacturing orientation and strategy. The negative relationship between export and firm performance demonstrates the motivation behind the shift to offshore production.

Interestingly, this negative relationship between exporting and performance has not been confined to SMEs in Japan. One expectation might be that large firms would be better able to cope with endaka by re-structuring their manufacturing and exporting activities to take advantage of lower cost production locations. SMEs did not have such an option because they did not have the international capabilities or facilities to implement such comprehensive strategies, and the only way to maintain export markets was to lower the prices of export goods in yen terms. Consequently, export margins diminished. While this logic suggests that larger firms may have been less exposed to the negative effects of endaka, in fact, Delios and Beamish (2000) and Geringer, Tallman, and Olsen (2000) reported similar export–performance relationships for the large

Japanese MNCs studied in their research. Supporting the endaka explanation of export–performance is Geringer et al.'s (2000) observation that exporting activities contributed positively to Japanese MNCs corporate performance in the 1977–86 period, but not in the 1986–93 period.

While we found exporting to have a linear relationship with performance, FDI had nonlinear effects. To facilitate interpretation of the nonlinear effects we constructed a plot based upon the results of Model 6 in Table 3. Figure 1 illustrates the nonlinear relationship between the number of FDIs and firm performance. This curve shows an initially negative relationship which becomes positive as the number of FDIs increases. The shape of the line is a flattened U or a saucer-shaped curve. As shown in Figure 1, at the initial stages of FDI (from one FDI country to five FDI countries) there is a negative impact on performance with a more than 2 percent reduction in ROA when the number of FDI countries reaches five (as compared to zero FDI countries). Beyond this point, a greater extent of FDI contributes to higher performance at an accelerating rate. The findings of a saucer-shaped curve

580   *J. W. Lu and P. W. Beamish*

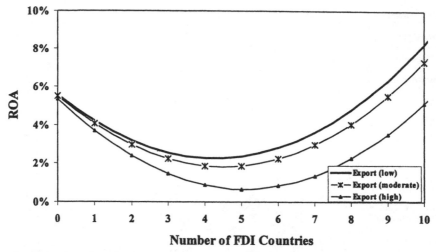

Figure 1. Moderating effect of export intensity on the relationship between number of FDI countries and ROA

relationship between FDI and performance seem to contradict the inverted U curve found by Beamish and da Costa (1984) and Hitt *et al.* (1997). However, when the differences in the characteristics of the samples (their focus on large well-internationalized firms and our focus on internationalizing SMEs) are taken into consideration, our findings of a saucer-shaped curve actually complements their findings of an inverted U curve. Taken together, the findings are consistent with our contention that a sideways 'S' curve represents the relationship between internationalization and performance. The initial decline in performance during early stages of FDI are in line with the notion of the liability of foreignness (Hymer, 1976). The results also illustrate the magnitude of the challenges SMEs face when going international.

While the challenges can be formidable, our results suggest they are not insurmountable. One strategy that can be used to counter the challenges is to use alliances in the internationalization process. Our conceptual arguments and empirical results suggest that while alliances have the potential to help overcome the difficulties that SMEs encounter when entering foreign markets, they involve risks if not planned and implemented properly. The contrasting performance implications of alliances with Japanese partners and alliances with local partners is consistent with the

findings of Makino and Beamish (1998). In the context of internationalization, local knowledge is of crucial importance to SMEs who usually have a domestic focus. Partnering with local firms (J-L alliances) provides SMEs with a direct source of local knowledge in addition to other location-specific resources (Makino and Delios, 1996). In contrast, same-country partners (J-J alliances) may or may not possess local knowledge about specific locations and hence present a less direct and reliable source of local knowledge to SMEs.

We tested this interpretation by looking at the moderating effects of the local knowledge base of the alliance partners from the home country. We gauged the local knowledge base of each alliance partner by its number of subsidiaries and the number of host countries. We then calculated the average number of subsidiaries and the average number of host countries of its alliance partners for each Japanese SME engaged in alliances. We tested the moderating effect in the subsample of 95 firms with FDI activities. The specifications in both samples yielded similar results and we report the results in the subsample of 95 firms with FDI activities, since in the larger sample, 69 firms had zero FDIs and zero alliances. As shown in Table 5, the local knowledge base of alliance partners had a significant and positive impact on the J-J alliance intensity and firm performance. Further investigation of the local

Internationalization and Performance of SMEs 581

Table 5. Regressions of return on assets (ROA) on JV: 95 Japanese SMEs, 1986–96[a,b]

Independent variables	Model 1	Model 2	Model 3	Model 4
1. Intercept	0.180***	0 193***	0.191***	0.201***
	(3.946)	(4.228)	(4.162)	(4.399)
2. R&D intensity	0.748***	0.732***	0.782***	0.765***
	(5.245)	(5.161)	(5.447)	(5.363)
3. Advertising intensity	−0.226	−0.307*	−0.264	−0.330*
	(−1.173)	(−1.593)	(−1.374)	(−1.720)
4. Number of employees	−0.026***	−0.028***	−0.025***	−0.027***
(log)	(−3.903)	(−4.182)	(−3.706)	(−4.060)
5. Product diversity	−0.049**	−0.045**	−0.053**	−0.046**
	(−2.248)	(−2.037)	(−2.410)	(−2.106)
6. Exchange rate	0 001***	0.001***	0.001***	0.001***
	(3.591)	(3 475)	(3.061)	(3.155)
7. Export intensity	−0.060***	−0.067***	−0.061***	−0.067***
	(−3.656)	(−4.058)	(−3.683)	(−4.044)
8. Number of foreign	−0.005*	−0.005*		
investments	(−1.874)	(−1.841)		
9. Number of foreign	0.001**	0.001		
investments (squared)	(2.041)	(1.550)		
10. Number of countries			−0.012***	−0.010***
invested in			(−3.091)	(−2.688)
11. Number of countries			0.001***	0.001**
invested in (squared)			(2.577)	(2.056)
12. JV (Japanese partner)	−0.076***	−0.091***		
intensity (subsidiary)	(−5.876)	(−6.674)		
13. JV (Japanese partner)			−0.047***	−0.070***
intensity (host country)			(−4.208)	(−5.564)
14. Japanese partners'	0.001	−0.001		
FDI (subsidiary)	(0.092)	(−0.811)		
15. Japanese partners'			−0.001	−0.001
FDI (host country)			(−0.102)	(−1.303)
16. JV (Japanese partner) intensity *		0.001***		
Japanese partners' FDI		(3.379)		
(subsidiary)				
17. JV (Japanese partner) intensity *				0.003***
Japanese partners' FDI (host country)				(3.823)
Model indices				
R^2	0.135	0.145	0.127	0.139
Adjusted R^2	0.112	0.121	0.103	0.115
F-statistic	5.896***	6.151***	5.455***	5.852***

[a]Dummy variables for industry are included in the models, but not shown in the table.
[b]Upper number in a cell is a parameter estimate, numbers in the parentheses are t-statistics; ***$p < 0 01$; **$p < 0 05$; *$p < 0.10$ (all two-tailed tests)

knowledge base of the same-country partners (J-J alliances) showed that when partnering with same-country partners with local knowledge, firm performance is higher as compared to J-J alliances with partners without local knowledge. Our findings reinforce the importance of alliance partner selection. Different alliance partners possess different resources and SMEs should form alliances with partners who can provide the SMEs with the crucial resources needed in international expansion.

Finally, we found that the configuration of exporting and FDI had an impact on firm performance; that is, a high export intensity coupled with a greater extent of FDI resulted in lower performance. Referring back to Figure 1, we can see that as the extent of FDI increases, a higher export intensity depresses performance, reducing the net improvement in performance from the FDIs at high levels of FDI. The trend continues at higher levels of FDIs. It should also be noted

582   *J. W. Lu and P. W. Beamish*

that despite the decline in ROA at the initial stage of FDIs, the overall trends in Figure 1 illustrate growth in ROA, suggesting that firms are more profitable with increased levels of FDIs, regardless of whether export intensity is high or low. This general pattern is important, because it reveals the intrinsic value associated with higher levels of internationalization irrespective of the forms of internationalization. It is also consistent with the findings of Delios and Beamish (1999) who demonstrated that there is intrinsic value in the expansion of geographic scope beyond that found in the exploitation of firm-specific proprietary assets. One implication of our results is that SMEs should not be discouraged by initial setbacks in the internationalization process. Rather, managers in SMEs should focus on learning from early experiences and finding effective ways to overcome the disadvantages encountered when initially operating in foreign lands. Eventually, as our results suggest, if knowledge is gained about foreign markets, the intrinsic benefits associated with internationalization will eventually outweigh the costs and the net performance impact will be positive.

Limitations

While the empirical results are interesting, caution should be exerted when generalizing the findings beyond the scope of this study. First, the results were derived from a sample of Japanese SMEs. While the Japanese setting reinforced the entrepreneurial features of the internationalization activities undertaken by these firms, it raises the concern that the findings might be country-specific. Studies with comparative samples of firms from other countries should be used to test and extend the generalizability of our findings. Further, our sample consisted of publicly listed firms. Future research could investigate the performance implications of the internationalization efforts of private and smaller-sized firms to complement the picture of the relationship between internationalization and performance for the full range of firm sizes.

CONCLUSION AND CONTRIBUTIONS

Although this study has limitations, it makes important contributions to the entrepreneurship

and internationalization literatures and it provides useful insights for practitioners. First, to the best of our knowledge, it is the first time that the performance implications of four internationalization strategies have been studied separately and simultaneously using concepts derived from the internationalization and entrepreneurship literatures. The prominent differences in the impact of exporting and FDI on firm performance provide strong support for our argument that FDI is potentially a more competitive way than exporting for operating in international markets. However, initial investment forays into international markets may entail a high cost to a newly internationalizing firm. The implication is that SMEs should not curtail internationalization activities at the export stage, nor be deterred by the potentially high costs in initializing FDI, but explore opportunities to make FDIs so as to benefit from the latent value associated with such investments.

Second, our findings of the saucer-shaped relationship between FDI and SME performance complements the findings of an inverted U curve by Beamish and daCosta (1984), and Hitt *et al.* (1997). Considering the differences in samples, it completes a sideways 'S' curve conception of the relationship between internationalization and performance. In the initial stages of internationalization, performance declines as the firm deals with the liability of foreignness. However, performance then improves as new knowledge and capabilities are developed, as competitiveness is enhanced and as market opportunities are captured by the firm's investment activities in international markets. Eventually, performance declines as the costs associated with the complexity stemming from managing many subsidiaries and in dissimilar markets increases beyond the intrinsic benefits of internationalization.

Third, the saucer-shaped relationship between FDI and SME performance also provides support for the notion of liability of foreignness (Hymer, 1976). Given their limited resources and capabilities, SMEs are more susceptible to the liability of foreignness than large firms. Our results suggest one effective strategy for managing this aspect of internationalization, namely forming alliances with local partners who can help overcome deficiency in host country knowledge.

Finally, this study reveals the importance of the configuration of activities in the context of internationalization. The configuration effects on SME performance demonstrate that the impact of one internationalization mode is not in isolation from the other. The employment of both high export levels and relatively extensive FDI activities might escalate coordination costs that reduce internationalization benefits from either mode. While these costs do not reverse the long-term positive relationship between internationalization and SME performance, our findings show the differential effects of varying exporting and FDI configurations and illustrate the importance of the configuration strategy to the overall success of a firm's internationalization.

ACKNOWLEDGEMENTS

This research was supported in part by a Social Sciences and Humanities Research Council of Canada Grant (# 411-98-0393), and by the Asian Management Institute at the University of Western Ontario. The authors wish to acknowledge the useful suggestions received from Andrew Delios, Mike Hitt, and Duane Ireland and, the reviewers and participants in 'Creating a New Mindset: Integrating Strategy and Entrepreneurship Perspectives Conference.'

REFERENCES

Aaby N, Slater SF. 1989. Management influences on export performance: a review of the empirical literature 1978–88. *International Marketing Review* 6(4): 7–26.

Autio E, Sapienza HJ, Almeida JG. 2000. Effects of age at entry, knowledge intensity, and imitability on international growth. *Academy of Management Journal* 43(5): 909–924.

Baird IS, Lyles MA, Orris JB. 1994. The choice of international strategies by small businesses. *Journal of Small Business Management* 32(1): 48–60.

Barringer BR, Greening DW. 1998. Small business growth through geographic expansion: a comparative case study. *Journal of Business Venturing* 13: 467–492.

Baum JAC, Calabrese T, Silverman BS. 2000. Don't go it alone: alliance network composition and startups' performance in Canadian Biotechnology. *Strategic Management Journal* 21(3): 267–294.

Beamish PW. 1999. The role of alliances in international entrepreneurship. In *Research in Global Strategic Management*, Vol. 7: Wright R (ed). JAI Press: Stanford, CT; 43–61.

Beamish PW, Banks JC. 1987. Equity joint ventures and the theory of the multinational enterprise. *Journal of International Business Studies* 18(2): 1–16.

Beamish PW, daCosta RC. 1984. Factors affecting the comparative performance of multinational enterprises. Proceedings, European International Business Association Conference, Rotterdam.

Beamish PW, Karavis L, Goerzen A, Lane C. 1999. The relationship between organizational structure and export performance. *Management International Review* 39(1): 37–54.

Bergh DD, Holbein GF. 1997. Assessment and redirection of longitudinal analysis: demonstration with a study of the diversification and divestiture relationship. *Strategic Management Journal* 18(7): 557–571.

Birkinshaw J. 1997. Entrepreneurship in multinational corporations: the characteristics of subsidiary initiatives. *Strategic Management Journal* 18(3): 207–229.

Brazeal DV, Herbert TT. 1999. The genesis of entrepreneurship. *Entrepreneurship Theory and Practice* 23(3): 29–45.

Buckley PJ. 1989. Foreign direct investment by small- and medium-sized enterprises: the theoretical background. *Small Business Economics* 1: 89–100.

Buckley PJ, Casson MC. 1976. *The Future of Multinational Enterprise*. Macmillan: Basingstoke, UK.

Burgelman RA. 1983. A process model of internal corporate venturing in the diversified major firm. *Administrative Science Quarterly* 28(2): 223–244.

Carrier C. 1994. Intrapreneurship in large firms and SMEs: a comparative study. *International Small Business Journal* 12(3): 54–61.

Coviello NE, McAuley A. 1999. Internationalization and the smaller firm: a review of contemporary empirical research. *Management International Review* 39(3): 223–256.

Covin JG, Slevin DP. 1991. A conceptual model of entrepreneurship as firm behavior. *Entrepreneurship Theory and Practice* 16: 7–24.

Dalli D. 1995. The organization of exporting activities: relationships between internal and external arrangements. *Journal of Business Research* 34(2): 107–115.

Damanpour F. 1991. Organizational innovation: a meta-analysis of effects of determinants and moderators. *Academy of Management Journal* 34(3): 555–590.

Dana LP, Etemad H, Wright RW. 1999. The impact of globalization on SMEs. *Global Focus* 11(4): 93–105.

Daniels JD, Bracker J. 1989. Profit performance: do foreign operations make a difference? *Management International Review* 29(1): 46–56.

Deeds DL, Hill CWL. 1996. Strategic alliances and the rate of new product development: an empirical study of entrepreneurial biotechnology firms. *Journal of Business Venturing* 11(1): 41–56.

Deeds DL, Hill CWL. 1998. An examination of opportunistic action within research alliances: evidence from the biotechnology industry. *Journal of Business Venturing* 11(1): 41–56.

Delios A, Beamish PW. 1999. Geographic scope, product diversification and the corporate performance of Japanese firms. *Strategic Management Journal* 20(8): 711–727.

584   *J. W. Lu and P. W. Beamish*

Delios A, Beamish PW. 2000. Multinationality and performance in Japanese firms. In *Asian Business*, Tse D, Lau CM, Law K, Wong CS (eds). Prentice-Hall: Englewood Cliffs, NJ; 61–78.

Delios A, Henisz WJ. 2000. Japanese firms investment strategies in emerging economies. *Academy of Management Journal* **43**(3): 305–323.

Dichtl E, Leibold M, Koglmayr H-G, Muller S. 1984. The export decision of small and medium-sized firms: a review. *Management International Review* **24**(2): 49–60.

Dierickx I, Cool K. 1989. Asset stock accumulation and sustainability of competitive advantage. *Management Science* **35**(12): 1504–1510.

Dunning JH. 1973. Determinants of international production *Oxford Economic Papers* **25**: 289–335.

Eisenhardt KM, Schoonhoven CB. 1990. Organizational growth: linking founding team, strategy, environment, and growth among U.S. semiconductor ventures. *Administrative Science Quarterly* **35**: 504–529.

Erminio F, Rugman AM. 1996. A test of internalization theory and internationalization theory: the Upjohn Company. *Management International Review* **36**(3): 199–215.

Erramilli MK, De Souza DED. 1993. Venturing into foreign markets: the case of the small service firm. *Entrepreneurship Theory and Practice* **17**(4): 29–45.

Geringer JM, Beamish PW, daCosta RC. 1989. Diversification strategy and internationalization: implications for MNC performance. *Strategic Management Journal* **10**(2): 109–119.

Geringer JM, Tallman S, Olsen DM. 2000. Product and international diversification among Japanese multinational firms. *Strategic Management Journal* **21**(1): 51–80.

Grant RM. 1987. Multinationality and performance among British manufacturing companies. *Journal of International Business Studies* **18**(1): 79–89.

Grant RM, Jammine AP, Thomas H. 1988. Diversity, diversification and profitability among British manufacturing companies, 1972–1984. *Academy of Management Journal* **31**: 771–801.

Gulati R. 1998. Alliances and networks. *Strategic Management Journal* **19**(4): 293–317.

Gulati R, Nohria N, Zaheer A. 2000. Strategic networks. *Strategic Management Journal* **21**(3): 203–215.

Hamel G. 1991. Competition for competence and inter-partner learning within international strategic alliances. *Strategic Management Journal* Summer Special Issue **12**: 83–103.

Hennart J-F. 1982. *A Theory of Multinational Enterprise*. University of Michigan Press: Ann Arbor, MI.

Hisrich RD, Honig-Haftel S, McDougall PP, Oviatt BM. 1996. International entrepreneurship: past, present, and future. *Entrepreneurship Theory and Practice* **20**(4): 5–11.

Hitt MA, Hoskisson RE, Kim H. 1997. International diversification: effects on innovation and firm performance in product-diversified firms. *Academy of Management Journal* **40**: 767–798.

Hodgetts RM, Kuratko DR. 1998. *Effective Small Business Management*, 6th edn. Dryden: Fort Worth, TX.

Hymer SH. 1976. *A Study of Direct Foreign Investment*. MIT Press: Cambridge, MA.

Inkpen AC, Beamish PW. 1997. Knowledge, bargaining power, and the instability of international joint ventures. *Academy of Management Review* **22**(1): 177–202.

Jarillo JC. 1989. Entrepreneurship and growth. the strategic use of external resources. *Journal of Business Venturing* **4**: 133–147.

Johanson J, Vahlne JE. 1977. The internationalization process of the firm: a model of knowledge development and increasing foreign market commitments. *Journal of International Business Studies* **8**(1): 23–32.

Kim WC, Hwang P, Burgers WP. 1993. Multinationals' diversification and the risk–return trade-off. *Strategic Management Journal* **14**(6): 257–286.

Kmenta J. 1986. *Elements of Econometrics*. Macmillan: New York.

Kogut B. 1985. Designing global strategies: profiting from operational flexibility. *Sloan Management Review* **26**: 27–38.

Kogut B. 1988. Joint ventures: theoretical and empirical perspectives. *Strategic Management Journal* **9**(4): 319–332.

Kogut B. 1989. The stability of joint ventures: reciprocity and competitive rivalry. *Journal of Industrial Economics* **38**: 183–198.

Kogut B, Chang SJ. 1996. Platform investments and volatile exchange rates: direct investment in the U.S. by Japanese electronic companies. *Review of Economics and Statistics* **78**(2): 221–232.

Larson A. 1991. Partner networks: leveraging external ties to improve entrepreneurial performance. *Journal of Business Venturing* **6**(3): 173–189.

Lumpkin GT, Dess GD. 1996. Clarifying the entrepreneurial orientation construct and linking it to performance. *Academy of Management Review* **21**(1): 135–172.

Makino S. 1995. Joint venture ownership structure and performance: Japanese joint ventures in Asia. Ph.D. dissertation. University of Western Ontario: London, Ontario.

Makino S, Beamish PW. 1998. Performance and survival of joint ventures with non-conventional ownership structures. *Journal of International Business Studies* **29**(4): 797–818.

Makino S, Delios A. 1996. Local knowledge transfer and performance: implications for alliance formation in Asia. *Journal of International Business Studies* **27**(5): 905–928.

McDougall PP, Oviatt BM. 1996. New venture internationalization, strategic change, and performance: a follow-up study. *Journal of Business Venturing* **11**(1): 23–40.

McDougall PP, Oviatt BM. 2000. International entrepreneurship: the intersection of two research paths. *Academy of Management Journal* **43**(5): 902–908.

Miesenbock KJ. 1988. Small business and exporting: a literature review *International Small Business Journal* **6**(2): 42–61.

Miller D. 1983. The correlates of entrepreneurship in

three types of firms. *Management Science* **29**: 770–791.

Mowery DC, Oxley JE, Silverman BS. 1996. Strategic alliances and interfirm knowledge transfer. *Strategic Management Journal*, Winter Special Issue **17**: 77–92.

Nehrt C, Phene A. 1998. An investigation of inconsistent findings on international diversification. Mimeo, Quinnipiac College.

Oviatt BM, McDougall PP. 1994. Toward a theory of international new ventures. *Journal of International Business Studies* **25**(1): 45–61.

Oviatt BM, McDougall PP. 1999. A framework for understanding accelerated international entrepreneurship. In *Research in Global Strategic Management*, Vol. 7, Wright R (ed). JAI Press: Stamford, CT; 23–40.

Park SH, Kim D. 1997. Market valuation of joint ventures: joint venture characteristics and wealth gains. *Journal of Business Venturing* **12**: 83–108.

Porter ME. 1990. *The Competitive Advantage of Nations*. Free Press: New York.

Preece SB, Miles G, Baetz MC. 1999. Explaining the international intensity and global diversity of early-stage technology-based firms. *Journal of Business Venturing* **14**: 259–281.

Ramaswamy K. 1992a. Multinationality and performance: a synthesis and redirection. *Advances in International Comparative Management* **7**: 241–267.

Ramaswamy K. 1992b. Multinationality and performance: an empirical examination of the moderating effect of configuration. *AIB Best Paper Proceedings* 142–146.

Ramaswamy K. 1995. Multinationality, configuration, and performance: a study of MNCs in the U.S. drug and pharmaceutical industry. *Journal of International Management* **1**: 231–253.

Ramaswamy K, Kroeck KG, Renforth W. 1996. Measuring the degree of internationalization of a firm: a comment. *Journal of International Business Studies* **27**(1): 167–177.

Reynolds PD. 1997. New and small firms in expanding markets. *Small Business Economics* **9**(1): 79–84.

Ronen S, Shenkar O. 1985. Clustering countries on attitudinal dimensions: a review and synthesis. *Academy of Management Review* **10**(3): 435–454.

Root F. 1994. *Entry Strategies for International Markets*, 2nd edn. Lexington Books: Lexington, MA.

Roth K. 1992. International configuration and coordination archetypes for medium-sized firms in global industries. *Journal of International Business Studies* **23**(3): 533–549.

Rugman AM. 1982. *New Theories of the Multinational Enterprise*. St Martin's Press: New York.

Shan W, Song J. 1997. Foreign direct investment and the sourcing of technological advantage: evidence from the biotechnology industry. *Journal of International Business Studies* **28**(2): 267–284.

Shoham A. 1998. Export performance: a conceptualization and empirical assessment. *Journal of International Marketing* **6**(3): 59–81.

Shuman JC, Seeger JA. 1986. The theory and practice of strategic management in smaller rapid growth companies. *American Journal of Small Business* **11**(1): 7–18.

Smith KG, Gannon MJ, Grimm C, Mitchell TR. 1988. Decision-making in smaller entrepreneurial and larger professionally managed firms. *Journal of Business Venturing* **3**: 223–232.

Stevenson HH, Jarillo JC. 1990. A paradigm of entrepreneurship: entrepreneurial management. *Strategic Management Journal*, Summer Special Issue **11**: 17–27.

Stinchcombe AL. 1965. Social structure and organizations. In *Handbook of Organizations*, March J (ed). Rand McNally: Chicago, IL; 142–193.

Sullivan D. 1994. Measuring the degree of internationalization of a firm. *Journal of International Business Studies* **25**(2): 325–342.

Sullivan D, Bauerschmidt A. 1990. Incremental internationalization: a test of Johanson and Vahlne's thesis. *Management International Review* **30**(1): 19–30.

Tallman S, Li JT. 1996. Effects of international diversity and product diversity on the performance of multinational firms. *Academy of Management Journal* **39**: 179–196.

Timmons J. 1994. *New Venture Creation*, 4th edn. Irwin: Burr Ridge, IL.

Weaver KM, Dickson PH. 1998. Outcome quality of small- to medium-sized enterprise-based alliances: the role of perceived partner behaviors. *Journal of Business Venturing* **13**(6): 505–522.

Wolff AJ, Pett TL. 2000. Internationalization of small firms: an examination of export competitive patterns, firm size, and export performance. *Journal of Small Business Management* **38**(2): 34–47.

Zacharakis AL. 1997. Entrepreneurial entry into foreign markets: a transaction cost perspective. *Entrepreneurship Theory and Practice* **21**(3): 23–39.

Zahra SA, Ireland RD, Hitt MA. 2000. International expansion by new venture firms: international diversity, mode of market entry, technological learning and performance. *Academy of Management Journal* **43**(5): 925–950.

Zahra SA, Kuratko DF, Jennings DF. 1999. Guest editorial: entrepreneurship and the acquisition of dynamic organizational capabilities. *Entrepreneurship Theory and Practice* **23**(3): 5–10.

Zahra SA, Neubaum DO, Huse M. 1997. The effect of the environment on export performance among telecommunications new ventures. *Entrepreneurship Theory and Practice* **22**(1): 25–46.

Appendix: Descriptive statistics and correlations

Variables	Mean	S.D.	2	3	4	5	6	7	8	9	10	11	12	13	14	15
1. ROA	0.036	0.090	0.130	0.016	-0.127	-0.042	0.139	-0.085	-0.093	-0.114	0.030	0.024	-0.157	-0.130	0.002	-0.003
2. R&D intensity (percent sales)	0.014	0.022		-0.101	-0.025	0.034	-0.035	0.192	0.066	0.062	0.017	-0.006	0.015	0.017	-0.075	-0.084
3. Advertising intensity (percent sales)	0.024	0.021			0.090	0.009	-0.061	-0.142	-0.045	-0.084	0.007	0.063	-0.029	-0.023	0.113	0.113
4. Number of employees	321.189	121.317				0.105	0.015	0.014	0.080	0.113	0.064	0.092	0.035	0.056	0.021	0.031
5. Product diversification (Herfindahl)	0.577	0.158					0.000	-0.102	-0.004	0.002	0.023	0.033	0.063	0.070	0.055	0.039
6. Exchange rate (yen per U.S. dollar)	127.425	20.921						0.013	-0.142	-0.135	-0.102	-0.092	0.002	-0.004	0.000	0.000
7. Export intensity (percent sales)	0.128	0.177							0.317	0.329	0.078	0.036	0.185	0.154	-0.026	-0.031
8. Number of subsidiaries	1.243	2.352								0.952	0.226	0.268	0.358	0.388	0.111	0.130
9. Number of host countries	0.968	1.605									0.219	0.207	0.370	0.368	0.074	0.096
10. JV (local partner) intensity (subsidiaries)	0.024	0.100										0.914	0.086	0.154	0.046	0.052
11. JV (local partner) intensity (host countries)	0.034	0.140											0.141	0.269	0.096	0.104
12. JV (Japanese partner) intensity (subsidiaries)	0.079	0.210												0.950	0.004	0.010
13. JV (Japanese partner) intensity (host countries)	0.093	0.240													0.064	0.070
14. Japanese partners' FDI (subsidiaries)	38.660	116.448														0.981
15. Japanese partners' FDI (host countries)	4.792	12.956														

Notes 1 All descriptive statistics reported for non-transformed values.
2. Pearson correlations > 0.060 or < -0.060 significant at the 0.01 level (two-tailed test)

[12]

EXPLAINING THE FORMATION
OF INTERNATIONAL
NEW VENTURES: THE LIMITS
OF THEORIES FROM
INTERNATIONAL BUSINESS
RESEARCH*

PATRICIA PHILLIPS McDOUGALL
Georgia Institute of Technology

SCOTT SHANE
Georgia Institute of Technology

BENJAMIN M. OVIATT
Georgia State University

EXECUTIVE SUMMARY

International new ventures (INVs) represent a growing and important type of start-up. An INV is defined as a business organization that, from inception, seeks to derive significant competitive advantage from the use of resources and the sale of outputs in multiple countries (Oviatt and McDougall 1994). Their increasing prevalence and important role in international competition indicates a need for greater understanding of these new ventures (Oviatt and McDougall 1994).

Logitech, as described in a case study by Alahuhta (1990), is a vivid example of an INV. Its founders were from two different countries and had a global vision for the company from its inception. The venture, which produces peripheral devices for personal computers, established headquarters in both Switzerland and the U.S. Manufacturing and R&D were split between the U.S. and Switzerland, and then quickly spread to Taiwan and Ireland. The venture's first commercial contract was with a Japanese company.

Using 24 case studies of INVs, we found that their formation process is not explained by existing theories from the field of international business. Specifically, neither monopolistic advantage theory,

Address correspondence to Professor Patricia Phillips McDougall, Strategic Management Group, Ivan Allen College of Management, Policy and International Affairs, Georgia Institute of Technology, Atlanta, GA 30332-0520.

The authors gratefully acknowledge financial support for this research from the Society of International Business Fellows (SIBF), based in Atlanta, Georgia, and from the Bernard B. & Eugenia Ramsey Chair of Private Enterprise at Georgia State University.

* An earlier version of this paper was presented at the 1994 Babson Entrepreneurship Conference.

470   P.P. MCDOUGALL ET AL.

product cycle theory, stage theory of internationalization, oligopolistic reaction theory, nor internalization theory can explain the formation process of INVs. These theories fail because they assume that firms become international long after they have been formed, and they therefore highlight large, mature firms. They also focus too much on the firm level and largely ignore the individual and small group level of analysis (i.e., the entrepreneur and his or her network of business alliances).

We propose that an explanation for the formation process of INVs must answer three questions: (1) who are the founders of INVs? (2) why do these entrepreneurs choose to compete internationally rather than just in their home countries? and (3) what form do their international business activities take?

Who are the founders of INVs? We argue that founders of INVs are individuals who see opportunities from establishing ventures that operate across national borders. They are "alert" to the possibilities of combining resources from different national markets because of the competencies (networks, knowledge, and background) that they have developed from their earlier activities. Following the logic of the resource-based view of the firm, we argue that the possession of these competencies is not matched by other entrepreneurs. Only the entrepreneur possessing these competencies is able to combine a particular set of resources across national borders and form a given INV.

Why do these entrepreneurs choose to compete internationally rather than just in their home countries? The founders of INVs recognize they must create international business competencies from the time of venture formation. Otherwise, the venture may become path-dependent on the development of domestic competencies and the entrepreneur will find it difficult to change strategic direction when international expansion eventually becomes necessary. As the founder of one INV explained, "The advantage of starting internationally is that you establish an international spirit from the very beginning" (Mamis 1989:38).

What form do their international business activities take? Founders of INVs prefer to use hybrid structures (i.e., strategic alliances and networks) for their international activities as a way to overcome the usual poverty of resources at the time of start-up.

This study has important implications for the practice of management. In financing decisions relating to INVs, venture capitalists and other venture financiers should look for entrepreneurs who have a global vision, international business competence, and an established international network. When entrepreneurs start INVs they should create hybrid structures to preserve scarce resources. Finally, given the path-dependence of competence development, founders of new ventures should consider whether establishing a domestic new venture with plans to later internationalize will be as successful a strategy as establishing a new venture that is international from inception.

INTRODUCTION

International new ventures (INVs)—firms that are international from the time of their formation—are growing in significance. This article shows that the generally accepted theories of international business fail to explain their existence. Indeed, the theories fail even to ask vital questions about INVs.

An INV *is a business organization that, from inception, seeks to derive significant competitive advantage from the use of resources and the sale of outputs in multiple countries* (Oviatt and McDougall 1994). A number of international entrepreneurship researchers (Jolly, Alahuhta, and Jeannet 1992; Oviatt et al. 1994; Ray 1989) have begun to focus attention on INVs, and the popular business press has reported that such firms represent a new and growing phenomenon (Brokaw 1990; *The Economist* 1992, 1993; Gupta 1989; Mamis 1989).

An example is Logitech, a manufacturer of mouse devices and other computer peripherals. As described by Alahuhta (1990), Logitech's founders (one of whom was Swiss and the other two Italian) had the strategic vision to make the new venture a global company from its inception. The venture established dual headquarters at start-up: its administration was also split between the U.S. and Switzerland, and then quickly spread to both Taiwan and Ireland. Logitech's first commercial contract was with a Japanese company.

Whereas small numbers of INVs have actually existed for centuries, their increasing prevalence and importance in international markets indicate a need for greater understanding of these ventures (Oviatt and McDougall forthcoming). Our own attempts to understand them essentially followed the order of the major sections of this article. First, we compiled case studies of INVs and compared them with case studies of INVs written by other scholars in several countries. All these studies were exploratory attempts to discover common patterns in real-world situations rather than attempts at hypothesis testing. Such exploration is a commonly used technique to gain an initial understanding about a little-known issue (Quinn 1992).

In the second section, we analyze five generally accepted theories from international business. Since Steven Hymer wrote his pathbreaking thesis in 1960,[1] the field of international business has sought to understand why firms engage in international operations. Numerous theories have been developed, all of which seek to answer three crucial questions, first proposed by Hymer (1976) and subsequently reiterated by nearly all theorists (and textbook writers) on international business (Caves 1982; Vernon 1966; Johanson and Vahlne 1977; Knickerbocker 1973; Hennart 1982; Rugman 1981; Buckley and Casson 1976). The first question is, which firms engage in international business? Second, why do these firms choose to compete internationally rather than just in their home countries? Third, what structural form do these activities take?

The five generally accepted theories from international business which we examine in the second section—monopolistic advantage theory (Hymer 1976; Caves 1982), product cycle theory (Vernon 1966), stage theory of internationalization (Johanson and Vahlne 1977, 1990), oligopolistic reaction theory (Knickerbocker 1973) and internalization theory (Hennart 1982; Rugman 1981; Buckley and Casson 1976)—all fail to explain the formation process of INVs. The analysis presented in this article will show that they fail because they all focus on firm-level analysis of large, mature firms, rather than on individual and small group analysis of the entrepreneur and his or her social network of business alliances. In addition, the theories wrongly assume that firms become international long after formation.

To avoid these failures, the third section of the article shifts the level of analysis and combines concepts from the entrepreneurship and strategic management literatures to recast Hymer's three vital questions. First, who are the founders of INVs? Second, why do these entrepreneurs choose to compete internationally rather than just in their home countries? Third, what form do their international business activities take?

COMPILING CASE STUDIES

We examined 24 case studies of INVs. Because no directories or publicly available resources are available for identifying INVs (Brush 1992), we used business press articles and an iterative networking process to locate them. This process allowed us to identify 12 INVs that had been described in academic journals or meetings. Another 12 cases were compiled by two of this study's authors. Following the recommendations of Eisenhardt (1989), the selection of cases was not random, rather; "extreme examples" were selected. As Eisenhardt (1989:537)

---

[1] Although Steven Hymer's thesis was completed in 1960, and was widely read and accepted by international business scholars prior to publication, it was not actually published until 1976, two years after his untimely death.

472   P.P. MCDOUGALL ET AL.

notes, "random selection is neither necessary nor even preferable" when one is extending theory. Table 1 identifies the 24 case studies, along with each study's reference, the location of the venture's headquarters, its product or service, and the key issue in the study.

Three points are evident from the table. First, INVs are present in at least ten countries throughout Europe, North America, South America, Asia, the Middle East and the South Pacific. Thus, it is not a local phenomenon. Second, many of the firms appear to have formed in recent years, suggesting it may be a relatively new phenomenon. Third, although the ventures are primarily high-tech businesses, the presence of services and even aquaculture indicates that INVs emerge in a variety of industries.

For the 12 case studies developed by the authors, the method of investigation involved analysis of three sources of evidence: (1) documents, such as business plans, financial statements, letters, faxes, and minutes of meetings; (2) physical artifacts, such as the firm's products; and (3) personal interviews.

Semi-structured personal interviews, which were recorded and later transcribed, were conducted with either the founder or founding team of ten of the ventures. In the other two ventures, personal interviews were conducted with the chief financial officers, both of whom had joined the venture soon after it began operations. The researchers were also able to interview an additional key manager, a board member, or an investor in several of the ventures. There were follow-up personal interviews (sometimes more than one) in four cases and additional telephone interviews in all cases. In addition, there were personal interviews with three venture capitalists (one in Silicon Valley, one in New York, and one in Munich) who had been involved in financing such ventures.

The remaining sections of the article use many specific examples from this database to explore the generally accepted international theories and the questions we believe are vital to improved understanding of INVs. Major arguments are supported by multiple examples. Most of those examples are from our own case studies, because they are our richest source of data. It should be noted that although the case studies written by others did not contain all the data necessary to address each of the three crucial questions about the formation of INVs, we found no contradictions of our findings in any of those case studies.

GENERALLY ACCEPTED THEORIES FROM INTERNATIONAL BUSINESS

A core argument of this article is that the formation process of INVs cannot be explained by generally accepted theories from the field of international business. To show that the behavior of INVs is at odds with the predictions of existing theory, we discuss each of the five theories in turn. We begin with monopolistic advantage theory.

Monopolistic Advantage Theory

Monopolistic advantage theory holds that multinational enterprises[2] (MNEs) exist because a firm has unique sources of superiority over foreign firms in their own markets (Hymer 1976). The advantages belong to the MNE and cannot be acquired by other firms.

---

[2] We borrow Casson's (1982:36) definition of a multinational enterprise (MNE), "An MNE is any firm which owns outputs of goods or services originating in more than one country.... In particular it includes firms which merely operate foreign sales subsidiaries, since these subsidiaries produce market-making services and so qualify as foreign locations of production, within the terms of the definition. Note also that the MNE does not need to be a foreign direct investor, since all resources (except possibly inventories) in the foreign location can be hired rather than owned outright."

TABLE 1 Case Studies of International New Ventures

Reference and Venture Name	Headquarters	Product/Service	Key Issues
Coviello and Munro (1992)			
Cowan Bowman Associates	New Zealand	Computer software	Linkages with partners
Datacom Software Research	New Zealand	Computer software	influenced the
Fact International Ltd.	New Zealand	Computer software	internationalization process.
MANA Systems Ltd.	New Zealand	Computer software	
Jolly, Alahuhta, and Jeannet (1992)			
Conner Peripherals Inc.	United States	Computer disk drives	Features of their global
LASA Industries, Inc.	United States and and Europe	Prototyping systems for ASICs	strategy: global vision, industry redefinition, success
Logitech SA	Switzerland	PC desk-top aids	in lead markets, volume built
Technophone Ltd.	United Kingdom	Hand-portable telephones	quickly, selective foreign investments, early product breadth, and tight organizational structure.
McDougall and Oviatt (1991)			
Crytologics International	United States	Data compression and metering device	Forces driving global start-ups: resource needs,
International Investment Group	United States	Business consulting	financing, market scale,
Momenta Corporation	United States	Pen-based computer	competitor reactions, needs
Techmar Jones International Industries	United States	Water treatment systems	for technological standards, and domestic inertia.
McDougall and Oviatt (1992)			
Ecofluid Ltd.	Czechoslovakia	Waste treatment technology	Patterns of success: global vision, internationally
EEsof, GmbH.	Germany	Computer software	experienced managers,
IXI Ltd.	United Kingdom	Computer software	international networks,
OASiS Group PLC	United Kingdom	Business consulting	preemptive technology or
Oxford Instruments	United Kingdom	High field magnets	marketing, unique intangible
SPEA, Software AG	Germany	PC graphics controllers	assets, linked product extension, and tight
Technomed International, SA	France	Medical equipment	organizational coordination.
Oviatt et al. (1994)			
Heartware International Corporation	United States	Medical equipment	With strategic alliances, even the smallest new ventures can be international. However, failure is a risk.
Ray (1989)			
Camarao Brasiliensis Ltda.	Brazil	Shrimp aquaculture	Internationally oriented
Femcare International	United Kingdom	Female sterilization device	founders can enable a new venture to leapfrog the
Sci-Tex	Israel	Electro-optical systems	normally expected stages of internationalization.
Singatronics	Singapore	Medical equipment	

One type of monopolistic advantage is superior ability. Hymer (1976) argued that MNEs have superior knowledge, found in the form of superior manufacturing processes, brand names, differentiated products, organizational talents, or patented technology. Monopolistic advantage theory holds that once a firm has developed this superior knowledge, it can exploit

474   P.P. MCDOUGALL ET AL.

this advantage overseas at virtually no additional cost over that of exploiting that advantage in the home market (Caves 1971). Because local entrepreneurs have to pay the full cost of developing this knowledge, they are unable to compete with the foreign firm despite their advantage in local market knowledge, and foreign investment takes place (Caves 1982).

The difficulty in explaining the formation process of INVs through monopolistic advantage theory lies in its assumptions regarding the rationality of foreign investment. The theory is based in economic literature that assumes complete rationality and that all firms with the same monopolistic advantage will act identically. Therefore, the theory depicts internationalization as simply an optimization of costs and revenues across international borders.

Entrepreneurship theory, however, recognizes that these assumptions are unusual and that entrepreneurs are people who "are alert" to potentially profitable resource combinations when others are not (Barreto 1989:9). This means that two individuals, both possessing the same monopolistic advantage, may not both choose to engage in international entrepreneurial activity. Monopolistic advantage theory cannot explain why entrepreneurs perceive the opportunity of using their monopolistic advantage to internationalize from inception, whereas other people do not.

In addition, the tradition of monopolistic advantage theorists has been to argue that a firm will engage in foreign investment *after* some monopolistic advantage has been developed and exploited in the home country (e.g., Buckley and Casson 1976). By extending its mature operations to foreign countries, the advantaged MNE can exploit the *already developed asset* at a low marginal cost. However, that argument does not explain the establishment of INVs, because these firms often make foreign investments *before* the knowledge that provides for the monopolistic advantage has been developed and exploited in the home country market.

One example of this phenomenon is Technomed International, S.A., a medical equipment venture founded in France in December 1985. Its initial product, the Sonolith (then under development), was a machine that used lithotripsy to destroy kidney and gall stones with ultrasonic pulses and without surgery. Just nine months after establishing the parent company, and before the product even had FDA approval, Technomed established a U.S. subsidiary. Although eventual plans were for it to handle sales and after-sales support and to ensure regulatory approval of products, the subsidiary initially concentrated primarily on obtaining regulatory approval. Because Technomed International established its overseas subsidiary before its product had been approved for sale in the U.S. market, it is difficult to view this foreign investment as an extension of an existing monopolistic advantage.

Thus, although one of the purposes of monopolistic advantage theory is to explain why firms choose to compete internationally rather than just in their home markets, our analysis shows that it provides an inappropriate explanation for INVs.

Product Cycle Theory

The product cycle theory argues that MNEs exist because of the cycle of product development. According to this model, firms make direct foreign investments to protect markets that they originally served through exporting, only after products mature and competition becomes cost-based. Foreign investment in low-cost-of-production countries allows the foreign investor to compete with local entrepreneurs who enjoy low production costs and who seek to make inroads into the export market (Vernon 1966). Although Vernon (1979) himself has argued that the predictive power of the product cycle theory has waned, it is still said to apply to "small firms or others that have not established substantial foreign operations" (Garland, Farmer, and Taylor 1990:11).

However, the product cycle theory does not explain the purchase of foreign assets by the founders of INVs for two reasons. First, many INVs engage in foreign investment to sell products for which competition has not yet become standardized and cost-based. For example, Logitech and LASA made the decision to engage in foreign investment while their products were still in what Vernon (1966) calls the "new product stage." Therefore, the foreign investment occurred when product cycle theory would argue that foreign markets would be served by exporting.

Second, the entrepreneurs founding INVs sometimes purchase foreign assets prior to exporting to foreign markets (Jolly et al. 1992). In the cases of Logitech and LASA, foreign markets are served by production from foreign investment sites even though local competitors have not yet driven down the cost of production to a point at which the products are standardized and competition is based on price (Vernon 1966). Product cycle theory would argue that exporting from the country of firm origin would be the preferred mechanism for serving foreign markets until such cost shifts had occurred. Therefore, product cycle theory does not appear to explain the direct foreign investment decisions of INVs.

One of the purposes of the product cycle theory is to answer Hymer's (1976) question concerning why firms choose international rather than exclusively home-market operations. However, our analysis shows that product cycle theory, like monopolistic advantage theory, provides an inappropriate explanation for INVs.

Stage Theory of Internationalization

The stage theory of internationalization argues that firms progress in a relatively orderly manner from local firms with ad hoc exporting to full-fledged MNEs as they become more experienced in international business. Under this model, companies begin to export because they receive unsolicited requests from foreigners to sell their products overseas (Aharoni 1966; Bilkey and Tesar 1977). As the demand for their products increases overseas, they progress to the development of an international division that exports in an organized manner (Stopford and Wells 1972). Exporting increases knowledge about the foreign markets, language, and culture of the customers, and it reduces uncertainty about foreign investment (Johanson and Vahlne 1977). Eventually, this added knowledge increases the probability of success in foreign investment (Newbould, Buckley, and Thurwell 1978) and leads companies to become MNEs.

Yet a growing number of empirical studies appear to contradict the stage theory of internationalization. For example, Welch and Loustarinen (1988) discussed reports of small English firms, Australian start-ups, and established Swedish firms that skipped important stages and were involved with unexpected speed in direct foreign investments. Ganitsky (1989) investigated a sample of 18 Israeli "innate exporters" that served foreign markets from inception. Brush (1992) found that 13% of her nationwide sample of internationalized, small U.S. manufacturers were firms that had internationalized during their first year of operation.

Sullivan and Bauerschmidt (1990) found no differences in perceived barriers and incentives to firm internationalization among the managers of 62 Swedish, Finnish, Austrian, and German forest product firms in varying stages of internationalization, even though managers of firms in varying stages of international activity should have knowledge and beliefs that vary according to those stages. Although Sullivan and Bauerschmidt (1990:27) were "reluctant to reject this intuitively logical view of internationalization," the mounting challenges to the theory are impressive.

Johanson and Vahlne (1990) have attempted to deflect criticism of stage theory by stressing that it applies best to the earliest periods of firm internationalization. However, our evidence suggests that the stage theory of internationalization does not explain the formation process of INVs very well. None of the 24 INVs shown earlier in Table 1 followed the incremental stages of internationalization. The oldest case study in our sample, Oxford Instruments, which was founded in 1959, derived more than 50% of its revenues from international markets during its first year of operation. Oxford Instruments manufactured high-field magnets for laboratories that were conducting research in low temperature physics. In explaining his company's early internationalization, founder Sir Martin Wood stated, "[with] about 90% of our market abroad we 'thought international' from day one" (Wood 1992).

Similarly, SPEA Software AG, which manufactures graphic boards for computers, was also an early internationalizer. As Bernd Holzhauer, the President and CFO of SPEA Software AG stated, "To be successful, you have to be a global player right from the first day . . .. You have to go international or the international companies come to you, so you are fighting in your own market" (Holzhauer 1992). Therefore, he stressed international activity from firm formation and did not wait for unsolicited requests from foreign customers to internationalize.

Technomed International also had a proactive internationalization strategy. Jean-Francois Fevrier, vice president of finance and administration for Technomed International, explained why. "In the medical high-technology products industry, if we are not international we cannot survive and grow. We cannot rely on only one market, and we must be international from day one. In the United States a company might be able to make it, but a French company could not because the local market is too small" (Fevrier 1992).

In summary, the stage theory of internationalization, like the others already considered, has failed to provide an appropriate explanation for why INVs compete internationally rather than just in home markets.

Oligopolistic Reaction Theory

The oligopolistic reaction theory, as postulated by Knickerbocker (1973), holds that firms become multinational to match the actions of other members of an oligopoly. The core concept of this theory is that firms imitate one another's actions to reduce the risk of being different. If firms internationalize at the same time as their competitors, they are equally advantaged when the internationalization decision proves to be beneficial and equally disadvantaged when it proves to be detrimental. By imitating competitors, the risk associated with the decision to internationalize is reduced.

The oligopolistic advantage theory does not explain investment in INVs for two reasons. First, many times the INV is the first firm in an industry to invest internationally. And, as many observers have pointed out, oligopolistic reaction cannot explain the initial decision to invest abroad.

Many of the INVs we studied were the first in their industries to internationalize. For example, the founder of IXI did not consider its desktop windowing computer software for UNIX operating systems to be in competition with any software competitor. Rather, its founder and chairman, Ray Anderson, identified a need in the market and founded his INV to serve that need. He conceived the idea for the software product in late 1987. As Anderson explained, "UNIX computers were becoming a big thing but nobody was concerned about making them easy to use. There was a big gap, and more and more of the big companies like NCR, IBM, and Apollo were starting to realize that they are going into UNIX but it wasn't easy to use . . .. IXI started up because these people wanted this software. They couldn't get it from anywhere, so I started IXI to deliver it" (Anderson 1992). Clearly, Anderson did not see IXI as part of an oligopoly; in fact, he did not even view his venture as having a competitor at the time he founded the company and began to market the software in the United States.

The second reason oligopolistic advantage theory fails is that oligopolists match the behavior of other firms to reduce the uncertainty of being different from their competitors only if they see the other firm as a competitor and feel that the competitor's action is truly a threat. Many INVs are formed by entrepreneurs that feel they are too small to immediately compete directly with established players in an industry. Many of these entrepreneurs formed INVs to avoid direct competition with established firms, rather than to imitate them (Jolly et al. 1992).

Thus, we have shown that oligopolistic reaction theory provides inappropriate answers for INVs to at least two of Hymer's crucial questions. First, in answer to the question of which firms engage in international business, the theory predicts that industry groups go international together. However, oligopolistic reaction theory does not even address why an INV would initiate internationalization. Second, in answer to the question of why INVs choose international rather than domestic operations, the theory cannot explain why INVs take the seemingly riskier path.

Internalization Theory

Internalization theory holds that MNEs exist because market imperfections create the opportunity for firms to earn higher economic rents by internalizing the transfer of factor goods and services across national boundaries within a single firm than they can by arm's-length transactions between firms (Hennart 1982; Buckley and Casson 1976; Magee 1977). In other words, when international markets are likely to fail, firms form to govern economic transactions by ownership of operations in multiple countries. Internalization theory holds that the decision to engage in international transactions should reduce costs. As Buckley writes, "The internalization approach to modern theory of the MNE rests on two general axioms: (1) firms choose the least cost location for each activity they perform, and (2) firms grow by internalizing markets up to the point where the benefits of further internalization are outweighed by the costs" (Buckley 1988: 181–182). We argue that internalization theory fails to explain INVs if INVs act in ways counter to these axioms.

We found that in some of the INVs, the entrepreneur does not always "choose the lowest cost location for each activity the firm performs" (Buckley 1988: 181–182). IXI's establishment of a U.S. subsidiary was not driven by cost reduction. Rather, as IXI's chairman Ray Anderson explained, "[the company] has to be over there to find out what the customers want" (Anderson 1992). In fact, he felt that because IXI had a U.S. subsidiary it actually spent more on selling its product. He explained, "Because IXI has a U.S. subsidiary, it costs more to travel in the U.S. We can't use air passes, but must buy full-price tickets. So with a subsidiary, it actually costs us more to do business in the U.S." (Anderson 1992). Anderson went on to explain that travel was one of the company's major costs. The special air passes for travel within the U.S., which he and his employees were allowed to purchase as U.K. nationals, were so much less expensive than what a U.S. traveler paid that the increased travel costs had a substantial impact on overall cost structure. Anderson further indicated that as the American office had grown, lots of other cost advantages of doing business in the U.K. had disappeared.

478   P.P. MCDOUGALL ET AL.

Similarly, cost considerations were not the primary driver of location decisions for Logitech. In order to compete successfully in the computer industry, its founders felt the company had to operate in Silicon Valley in order to be aware of technology trends and changes in customer requirements (Alahuhta 1990). This was the driving factor in their decision to establish manufacturing and marketing operations in Silicon Valley, and later in Taiwan. The Silicon Valley facility served Hewlett-Packard and AT&T, and the Taiwan facility served Apple, which had a production unit in Singapore.

There is evidence that firms do not choose the structure of their international business activities on the basis of "internalizing markets up to the point where the benefits of further internalization are outweighed by the costs" (Buckley 1988: 181–182). Most INVs favor a hybrid structure to govern transactions and make extensive use of their business and personal networks, even when they have proprietary knowledge that they risk losing by employing that business structure.

All four of the New Zealand software companies listed in Table 1 relied heavily on strategic alliances in competing internationally, even though software is one of the most difficult products to protect from expropriation by opportunistic partners. Their reasoning was that they had insufficient funding to use governance structures that provided greater control. One of these firms, MANA Systems Ltd., formed a strategic alliance with Fujitsu Australia Ltd. to market its software in Australia; whereas in Japan, MANA Systems formed a strategic alliance with Computer Engineering and Consulting Ltd. to market its product. MANA Systems also formed a strategic alliance with Fujitsu Japan for developing systems software for the worldwide market. MANA Systems' managing director, Robert Barnes, described the alliances as necessary to ensure survival of the venture (Coviello 1991a). Fact International Ltd.'s strategic alliances were also described by its management team as being critical to its very survival (Coviello, 1991b).

Like the other four theories considered here, internalization theory fails to provide an appropriate explanation for why INVs are international. Clearly, cost reduction is not the key. Moreover, the focus of internalization theory on firm-level analysis rather than on entrepreneurs and their social networks makes it unable to answer Hymer's (1976) question about the structural form of international activities in INVs.

EXPLANATION FOR INTERNATIONAL NEW VENTURES

The five theories discussed in the preceding sections all fail to explain the formation process of INVs. These theories fail because of the perspective from which they were developed. As noted in our introduction and borne out by our analysis, they all focus on firm-level analysis of large, mature firms, rather than on the analysis of entrepreneurs and their social networks of business alliances. In addition, the theories wrongly assume that firms become international long after formation.

Having shown that generally accepted theory does not explain how INVs form, it is incumbent upon us to try to provide an explanation. We propose that such an explanation must answer three questions about the internationalization of firms that are roughly analogous to Hymer's (1960) original questions, but at a different level of analysis. First, who are the founders of INVs? Second, why do these entrepreneurs choose to compete internationally rather than just in their home countries? Third, what form do their international business activities take?

Who Are the Founders of INVs?

Multi-country markets may be served by either multiple local entrepreneurs, or by an international entrepreneur who establishes an INV to serve them. An explanation for the latter case requires a combination of Kirzner's (1973) economic theory of entrepreneurship and the "resource-based" view of the firm (Barney 1990). Following Kirzner (1985), we argue that markets are not in equilibrium as neoclassical economics suggest. "At any given date a market economy is likely to be less than fully coordinated with respect to information currently possessed" (Kirzner 1985: 157–158). This lack of complete information makes entrepreneurship possible.

Entrepreneurs are people who "are alert" to information about potentially profitable resource combinations when others are not (Barreto 1989:9). The entrepreneur uses this superior information to create profit-making opportunities before others perceive them. Kaish and Gilad (1991: 48) demonstrated empirically that "not everyone looking at the same market data will come to the same conclusion about the possibility of profit. Successful entrepreneurs are those individuals who are capable of foreseeing disequilibrium profit opportunities *when they come across them.*"

Research has shown that this alertness to new business opportunity is influenced by previous experience (Casson 1982; Ronstadt 1988) because that experience provides a framework for processing information. For example, entrepreneurs usually found firms producing the same goods and services as those produced by their previous employers, and tend to target the same customers as their previous employers (Cooper and Dunkelberg 1986; Aldrich 1990). They are also more likely to have traveled overseas and to be educated (Birley and Norburn 1987). Our research also showed that the founders of INVs were often immigrants and had family and personal contacts overseas.

We argue that founders of INVs are more alert to the possibilities of combining resources from different national markets because of the competencies that they have developed from their earlier activities. Following the logic of the resource-based view of the firm, we argue that these entrepreneurs possess an unusual constellation of competencies. Only the entrepreneur possessing these competencies is able to combine a particular set of resources across national borders and form a given INV. For example, the founders of International Investment Group (IIG), a business consulting firm, considered what they refer to as their "proprietary network" to be their key competitive advantage. Their worldwide network comprised highly successful individuals, most of whom were retired. Primarily, these individuals had a personal, as opposed to business, relationship with one of the founders. The network members identified opportunities for the venture, offered business advice, assisted in negotiations, and sometimes lent their names and reputations to business deals. No compensation was paid to these individuals unless a transaction actually occurred. IIG, like most new ventures, had very limited funds. Only through this type of arrangement could this small venture achieve a worldwide presence. Their founders believed they had been able to tap into this critical resource of business knowledge and wisdom only because of their personal relationships with these individuals.

Gerald Seery discovered the technology for his venture while on a European business trip. During a business call on a client, Seery learned of recently developed cardiac medical equipment at a medical center in Holland. When his company decided not to pursue the technology, Seery purchased the technology and founded Heartware International Corporation. The venture was headquartered in the United States, with production in Holland. The first sales of the product were in Europe and South America.

480   P.P. MCDOUGALL ET AL.

Ray Anderson conceived the idea for his software while he was employed by a U.K. company that had operations in the U.S. and Canada. It was through his business interactions in the U.S. that Anderson identified the product need that led him to found IXI.

When Musa Marto took early retirement from IBM, he planned to consult for medium-sized and large corporations on becoming global. Struck by the lack of global vision among American CEOs, Marto decided instead to establish his own multinational company. Marto had no product idea he wanted to take to market; rather, he planned to build a company leveraging his international business knowledge and network. Mr. Marto stated in an interview that he considered his international business experience to be his key competence. After researching a number of previously domestic industries, he eventually secured the international rights to a water treatment product. Marto headquartered his venture, Techmar Jones International Industries, Inc., in Atlanta, Georgia, but all revenues were earned from operations overseas.

Twin brothers, Svatopluk and Vladimir Machrle, founded Ecofluid soon after the Velvet Revolution that led to the collapse of the communist regime in Czechoslovakia. Prior to the revolution, the brothers had been employed by academic institutions and had obtained a number of patents for the treatment and purification of water. Under the communist government in Czechoslovakia, all patents were owned by the state. However, both brothers had developed strong international networks. One had studied at the Massachusetts Institute of Technology in the U.S., and one had been educated in France. As academics, they had been allowed to travel to further develop their research. After the collapse of the communist regime, the brothers were able to acquire the patents they had previously earned. They then leveraged their network for access to markets, capital, employees, and other resources.

Access to superior international networks for funding has also been a factor driving the entrepreneur to compete internationally instead of just locally. The firm Momenta was able to obtain funding from the U.S., Singapore, Taiwan, and Europe primarily because of the business networks of its four founders. Its founders, who were from Iran, Tanzania, Cuba, and the U.S., each had extensive international connections. Momenta's founder and president, Kamran Elahian, had previously founded two highly successful high-tech companies, C.A.E. Systems, Inc. and Cirrus Logic, Inc. Through these companies, Elahian had developed a strong business network in the Far East.

Peter Sprague, founder of Crypotologics International, established an INV because his personal network, created as chairman of both National Semiconductor and Astin Martin, established his close relations with both European and U.S. private investors. He is also a former board member of LASA and was involved in its formation. Sprague believed that his relationship with foreign investors led him to focus on foreign opportunities more than he may otherwise have done, and more than other entrepreneurs do. He explained, "If your financing comes from abroad, they [the investors] are going to want you to move more rapidly into their own markets . . . .. If 20% of your company is owned by a Frenchman, then you begin to think about going to France a lot quicker than you would if 20% of your company is owned by a guy from Peoria" (Sprague 1990).

Why Do These Entrepreneurs Choose to Compete Internationally Rather Than Just in Their Home Countries?

We draw on the resource-based view of the firm to explain why entrepreneurs chose to make their ventures international from inception. Inertia permeates organizations, and forces promoting inertia include organizational routines (Dosi, Teece, and Winter 1990; Teece,

Pisano, and Shuen 1990; Quinn 1980; Collis 1991), structural impediments to change (Hannan and Freeman 1984; Tushman and Romanelli 1985), demands of stakeholders (Hannan and Freeman 1984; Dimaggio and Powell 1983), perceptual biases of managers (Bower 1970; Milliken and Lant 1991), the location of power in organizations (Pettigrew 1987; Pfeffer 1981; Staw 1981), and market stickiness to reorganizing economic relationships (Yao 1988; Mahoney and Pandian 1992: 370).

Collis (1991) extended those concepts to the international arena when he noted that the existing physical assets held by firms, the power and influence of decision-makers, and the firm's culture and history ensure that decisions about international business activities are path-dependent.

> ... most investments are essentially incremental decisions, and firms only periodically reoptimize their system configuration. Once a plant is built, for example, its location is fixed, and as it will, within broad bounds continue to operate, it will affect the location of subsequent facilities even if, *tabula rasa,* it is incorrectly located (Collis 1991: 53).

Collis' (1991) empirical work confirmed that the foreign investment decisions of companies are influenced by unique competencies developed over their histories. Research has also shown that organizational routines and capacities that create competitive advantages in the domestic arena are not the same as those that create competitive advantages in the international arena (Ghoshal 1987).

For domestic firms wishing to enter international markets, inertia becomes a problem because it inhibits change to routines appropriate to international environments. International entrepreneurs, however, seem to recognize this, and therefore they try to avoid domestic path-dependence by establishing ventures, which, at their inception, have routines for managing multicultural workforces, for coordinating resources located in different nations, and for targeting customers in multiple geographic locations simultaneously. In its simplest terms, the founders of INVs believe that ventures will not develop international competencies except by practicing international business.

One example of this attitude was expressed by Technomed International's founder, Gerard Hascoet, whose philosophy of doing business was to establish a geocentric company from the very beginning. He chose the name Technomed because it could be understood in any language, with the exception of Japanese (McFarland 1991). Hascoet did not see Technomed International as a French company, but as a world company: "The advantage of starting internationally is that you establish an international spirit from the very beginning" (Mamis 1989: 38).

Technomed's international spirit was reflected at its Lyon, France headquarters and by its multilingual staff. The flags of the countries in which the company had offices were flown at the entrance of its French headquarters, and all conference areas carried miniature versions of the flags as centerpieces (McFarland 1991). Although it is very uncharacteristic of French companies to use the English language within the company, Technomed International conducted meetings and business in English from its inception. Annual reports were published in English. A large television monitor in the lobby of its headquarters presented information to visitors about the company, all in English. As previously noted, French-based Technomed International established a U.S. subsidiary before it had FDA approval for its lithotripsy machine. This allowed the venture to better scan its foreign environment and observe its foreign competitors.

Momenta's founder and president, Kamran Elahian, considered the establishment of a multinational work force as a key international competence. Discussing how Momenta's

482   P.P. MCDOUGALL ET AL.

hiring practices enabled Momenta to instill a global spirit within the organization, Elahian explained, "[We] hire either people who are foreign immigrants who have done work in their own cultures and have come here to work, or Americans who have lived in different foreign cultures and have learned how to have sympathy for it . . . If you hire all domestic people who were born and raised here and have not traveled around the world, then it becomes very difficult obviously . . . If you walk around within the company, you see lots of foreign faces. It's like the United Nations" (Elahian 1991). In addition, by hiring individuals from many nations Momenta could create from inception a multi-cultured workforce which would later be useful in marketing its product and servicing its customers in those countries.

Fred Nazem, a New York venture capitalist who had invested in Momenta and several other technology-based INVs, considered early internationalization to be critical. He noted in an interview with the authors that there was a need for the type of technology ventures in which his company invested to be world competitors. He felt strongly that the product must be world-class, not just good enough for the U.S. To correctly recognize the market, the venture was required to get into the international market at a very early stage of the design process. The larger and more established a domestic venture becomes, the more difficult it is to make the adjustment to world market requirements. Using a metaphor, he explained, "It's like a rowboat and the Queen Mary. You cannot turn the Queen Mary as fast as you can a rowboat. It takes you a while because your drag ratio is large" (Nazem 1990). If efficient policies and procedures are established for a domestic market over several years, employees will naturally resist the disruptive changes required to successfully address overseas markets. In addition, if the business has been successful, it will be larger and, therefore, slower to change even if employees are willing.

What Form Do Their International Business Activities Take?

We now turn to an explanation of why founders of INVs seek the form of international business activities that they do. Here again we draw on the logic of the resource-based view of the firm and add to it research on entrepreneurship. At the time that INVs make the decision to establish a structure for their international activities, they tend to have different resource endowments and historical legacies than do established firms which choose to internationalize. Key differences between established firms and start-ups lie in the amount of resources that the firms have relative to the internal demands for resources and in the way the founders go about gathering resources.

The process of founding a firm demands sufficient resources within a short period of time to avoid negative cash flows leading to firm failure. Because start-up activities demand relatively large amounts of resources, new ventures often have few resources left over for other activities. This means that entrepreneurs are unlikely to make expensive investments in the ownership of assets when alternative governance structures are possible. Thus, start-ups tend to internalize a smaller percentage of the resources essential to their survival than do mature organizations (Cooper and Dunkelberg 1986), and entrepreneurs must rely on hybrid structures for controlling many vital assets (Vesper 1990; Oviatt and McDougall, 1994).

One of the limitations of hybrid structures is that founders of new ventures face a threat of opportunism from their partners that could lead to venture failure (Larson 1992). However, if founders of these firms rely on members of their close personal networks as partners in these hybrid structures, they can often avoid these problems of opportunism. Founders depend on trust developed through repeated interaction over time to diminish opportunistic behavior in hybrid partners (Aldrich and Zimmer 1986; Larson 1992). Repeated interaction over time inhibits opportunism because it makes the one-time gain from a single opportunistic action quite low in comparison to the damage done to one's long-term reputation (Larson 1992).

The actions of the INV founders we studied were consistent with the logic described above. For example, the founder of Techmar Jones International Industries indicated that because of very limited funds he built his entire company using strategic alliances.

Similarly, limited funding forced Heartware International to rely on a strategic alliance with the University of Maastricht in The Netherlands for R&D and for production of its electrophysiology equipment, which is sold to hospitals. Its founder, who had a marketing background and no formal technical experience, expressed a clear preference for internalizing R&D to both ready the product for the American market and to make continual upgrades. The founder had even identified and held discussions with the technical person he wished to hire for this function. However, because he had only been able to secure limited funding, he concluded that the venture did not have the resources to employ this individual and internalize the R&D function.

In contrast, ventures such as Momenta and Technomed International, which had significant capital investments, relied much less on strategic alliances. It appears that INVs that engage more in ownership of international operations, rather than in hybrid structures, tend to be ones for which resources are relatively more available. Under these circumstances, it becomes possible for the firm to make a cost–benefit analysis of the value of the internalization decision. However, under conditions of resource poverty, the case common to most start-ups, the internalization of transactions is limited.

CONCLUSIONS

In this article we show that firms exist that are international from formation. The international business activities of these firms appear to be at odds with the predictions of generally accepted theories from international business. The cases we investigated appear to follow a pattern of international activity that takes the following form: first, the founders of INVs are individuals who see opportunities for earning high returns for establishing businesses that operate across national borders. These entrepreneurs see opportunities that others do not see because of the competencies (networks, knowledge, and background) that are unique to them. Second, the founders of these firms engage in international business from the time of firm formation so as to create international business competencies and to avoid path-dependence on domestic competencies that the firm may not be able to shift out of due to inertial forces. Third, the founders of INVs tend to use hybrid governance structures for their international activities to preserve resources during the cash-draining formation process.

One of the limitations of theory development from case studies is that one may be developing specific explanations for narrow phenomena that cannot be generalized to a higher level (Eisenhardt 1989). We accept the criticism that our explanation of the formation process of INVs may explain the behavior of a much smaller subset of firms than is usually the focus of the more general theories from international business. Indeed, we do not claim to provide any general explanation of international business, but are seeking to explain only the behavior of INVs. Nevertheless, we argue that such micro explanations are necessary because the behavior of INVs are at odds with the predictions of existing theories from international business.

This article has important implications for research, teaching, and the practice of management. Researchers need to develop a richer explanation for INVs that goes beyond the concepts expressed here and by Oviatt and McDougall (1994). For example, a detailed

484   P.P. MCDOUGALL ET AL.

comparison of the networks of INVs and domestic new ventures should offer valuable insights. We have demonstrated that existing theories from international business are inadequate to the task because they focus on the wrong questions and the wrong level of analysis.

From the pedagogical standpoint, this study suggests that teaching only the existing theories of the international operations of firms to students seeking to become international entrepreneurs may provide them with an incomplete, and perhaps misleading, guide for establishing INVs. Teachers of entrepreneurship may need to design separate international entrepreneurship classes that augment traditional international business courses.

This study also has three implications for the practice of management. First, for venture capitalists and other venture financiers, the three questions are relevant in the financing decision of INVs. Venture capitalists should seek entrepreneurs who have a global vision, international business competence, and an established international network. Second, when entrepreneurs start INVs they should create hybrid structures to preserve scarce resources. Third, in light of the path-dependence of competence development, new venture founders should consider whether establishing a domestic new venture with plans to later internationalize will be as successful a strategy as establishing a new venture that is international from inception.

This research followed the direction of Eisenhardt (1989), who showed how to build theory using a theoretical sampling process where cases are identified that contradict the predictions of existing theory. We have described examples of the phenomenon of INVs that behave in ways counter to the predictions of existing theories from international business. Thus, although our conclusions are tentative, the topic appears worthy of further investigation.

The next step in the process of understanding the formation process of INVs would be to show that the predictive accuracy of our explanation of the behavior of these firms is greater than the predictive accuracy of existing theories. This statement can only be made after large-sample empirical studies have been conducted to compare the predictive validity of different explanations.

The primary objective of this article was to provoke a discussion of the limitations of existing theories from the field of international business in explaining what the business press and many investors see as an increasingly important subset of international businesses. It is our hope that this article will stimulate other scholars to undertake research on INVs.

REFERENCES

Aharoni, Y. 1966. *The Foreign Investment Decision Process.* Boston, MA: Harvard University, Division of Research, Graduate School of Business Administration.

Aldrich, H.E. 1990. Using an ecological perspective to study organizational founding rates. *Entrepreneurship Theory and Practice* 14(3):7–24.

Aldrich, H., and Zimmer, C. 1986. Entrepreneurship through social networks. In D.L. Sexton and R.W. Smilor, eds., *The Art and Science of Entrepreneurship.* Cambridge, MA: Ballinger.

Alahuhta, M. 1990. Global growth strategies for high technology challengers. *ACTA Polytechnica Scandinavia.* Electrical Engineering Series No. 66. Helsinki: Doctoral dissertation.

Anderson, R. June 23, 1992. Personal interview.

Barney, J. 1990. Firm resources and the theory of competitive strategy. *Journal of Management* Call for papers.

Barreto, H. 1989. *The Entrepreneur in Microeconomic Theory.* London: Routledge.

Birley, S., and Norburn, D. 1987. Owners and managers: the Venture 100 vs the Fortune 500. *Journal of Business Venturing* 2(4):351–363.

Bilkey, W.J., and Tesar, G. 1977. The export behavior of smaller sized Wisconsin manufacturing firms. *Journal of International Business Studies* 3(Spring/Summer):93–98.

Bower, J. 1970. *Managing the Resource Allocation Process.* Boston, MA: Harvard Business School Press.

Brokaw, L. 1990. Foreign affairs. *Inc.* November:92–104.

Brush, C.G. 1992. Factors motivating small companies to internationalize: the effect of firm age. Boston, MA: Doctoral dissertation, Boston University.

Buckley, P. 1988. The limits of explanation: testing the internalization theory of the multinational enterprise. *Journal of International Business Studies* 19(2):181–194.

Buckley, P.J., and Casson, M. 1976. *The Future of the Multinational Enterprise.* New York: Holmes & Meier.

Casson, M. 1982. Transaction costs and the theory of the multinational enterprise. In A.M. Rugman, ed., *New Theories of the Multinational Enterprise.* New York: St. Martin's Press.

Caves, R.E. 1971. International corporations: the industrial economics of foreign investment. *Economica* 38(February):1–27.

Caves, R.E. 1982. *Multinational Enterprise and Economic Analysis.* Cambridge, MA: Cambridge University Press.

Collis, D.J. 1991. A resource-based analysis of global competition: the case of the bearings industry. *Strategic Management Journal* 12(Special Issue, Summer):49–68.

Cooper, A.C., and Dunkelberg, W.C. 1986. Entrepreneurship and paths to business ownership. *Strategic Management Journal* 7:53–68.

Coviello, N. 1991a. MANA Systems Ltd.—Evolution of international operations. Unpublished case, New Zealand: University of Auckland.

Coviello, N. 1991b. Fact International Ltd.: the evolution of a firm. Unpublished case, New Zealand: University of Auckland.

Coviello, N., and Munro, H. 1992. Internationalizing the entrepreneurial technology-intensive firm: growth through linkage development. Paper presented at the Babson Entrepreneurship Research Conference, INSEAD, France.

DiMaggio, P.J., and Powell, W.W. 1983. The iron cage revisited: institutional isomorphism and collective rationality in organizational fields. *American Sociological Review* 48(April):147–160.

Dosi, G., Teece, D., and Winter, S. 1990. Toward a theory of corporate coherence. Mimeo.

The Economist. 1992. Go west, young firm. May 9:88–89.

The Economist. 1993. America's little fellows surge ahead. July 3:59–60.

Eisenhardt, K.M. 1989. Building theories from case study research. *Academy of Management Review* 14(4):532–550.

Elahian, K. May 17, 1991. Personal interview.

Fevrier, J.-F. July 6, 1992. Personal interview.

Ganitsky, J. 1989. Strategies for innate and adoptive exporters: lessons from Israel's case. *International Marketing Review* 6(5):50–65.

Garland, J., Farmer, R.N., and Taylor, M. 1990. *International Dimensions of Business Policy and Strategy.* 2nd edition. Boston, MA: P.W.S. Kent.

Ghoshal, S. 1987. Global strategy: an organizing framework. *Strategic Management Journal* 8:425–440.

Gupta, U. 1989. Small firms aren't waiting to grow up to go global. *The Wall Street Journal.* December 5:B2.

Hannan, M.T., and Freeman, J. 1984. Structural inertia and organizational change. *American Sociological Review* 49:149–164.

Hennart, J.-F. 1982. *A Theory of the Multinational Enterprise.* Ann Arbor, MI: The University of Michigan Press.

Holzhauer, B. May 19, 1992. Personal interview.

486   P.P. MCDOUGALL ET AL.

Hymer, S.H. 1976. The international operations of national firms: a study of direct foreign investment. Doctoral dissertation, MIT. Subsequently published by Cambridge, MA: MIT Press.

Johanson, J., and Vahlne, J.E. 1977. The internationalization process of the firm—A model of knowledge development and increasing foreign market commitment. *Journal of International Business Studies* 4:20–29.

Johanson, J., and Vahlne, J.E. 1990. The mechanism of internationalization. *International Marketing Review* 7(4):11–24.

Jolly, V.K., Alahuhta, M., and Jeannet, J.-P. 1992. Challenging the incumbents: how high technology start-ups compete globally. *Journal of Strategic Change* 1:71–82.

Kaish, S., and Gilad, B. 1991. Characteristics of opportunities search of entrepreneurs verses executives: sources, interests, general alertness. *Journal of Business Venturing* 6(1):45–61.

Kirzner, I. 1973. *Competition and Entrepreneurship.* Chicago, IL: University of Chicago Press.

Kirzner, I. 1985. *Discovery and the Capitalist Process.* Chicago, IL: University of Chicago Press.

Knickerbocker, F.T. 1973. *Oligopolistic Reaction and the Multinational Enterprise.* Cambridge, MA: Harvard University Press.

Larson, A. 1992. Network dyads in entrepreneurial settings: a study of the governance of exchange relationships. *Administrative Science Quarterly* 37:76–104.

Magee, S.P. 1977. Information and the multinational corporation: an appropriability theory of foreign direct investment. In J.N. Baghwati, ed., *The New International Economic Order.* Cambridge, MA: MIT Press.

Mahoney, J., and Pandian, J. 1992. The resource based view within the conversation of strategic management. *Strategic Management Journal* 13:363–380.

Mamis, R.A. 1989. Global start-up. *Inc.* (August):38–47.

McDougall, P.P., and Oviatt, B.M. 1991. Global start-ups: new ventures without geographic limits. *The Entrepreneurship Forum* (Winter):1–5.

McDougall, P.P., and Oviatt, B.M. 1992. United States and European global start-ups. Atlanta, GA: Unpublished report to the Society of International Business Fellows.

McFarland, S. 1991. Insight and intensity shine in Lyon. *Byline: A Bimonthly Newsletter Covering Medical Electronics* (February):1,4.

Milliken, F.J., and Lant, T.K. 1991. The effect of an organization's recent performance history on strategic persistence and change: the role of managerial interpretations. In J. Dutton, A. Huff, and P. Shrivastava, eds., *Advances in Strategic Management.* Greenwich, CT: JAI Press 7:125–152.

Nazem, F. July 24, 1990. Personal interview.

Newbould, G.D., Buckley, P.J., and Thurwell, J.C. 1978. *Going International: The Experience of Smaller Companies Overseas.* New York: Wiley.

Oviatt, B.M., and McDougall, P.P. 1994. Toward a theory of international new ventures. *Journal of International Business Studies.* 25(1):45–64.

Oviatt, B.M., McDougall, P.P., Simon, M., and Shrader, R. 1994. Heartware International Corporation: a medical equipment company "born international" (Part A). *Entrepreneurship Theory and Practice.* 18(2):111–128.

Pettigrew, A.M. 1987. Context and action in the transformation of the firm. *Journal of Management Studies* 24(6):649–670.

Pfeffer, J. 1981. *Power in Organizations.* Cambridge, MA: Ballinger.

Quinn, James. 1980. *Strategies for Change: Logical Incrementalism.* Homewood, IL: R.D. Irwin.

Quinn, J.B. 1992. *Intelligent Enterprise.* New York: The Free Press.

Ray, D.M. 1989. Entrepreneurial companies "born" international: four case studies. Presented at Babson Entrepreneurship Research Conference on Entrepreneurship, St. Louis, IL.

Ronstadt, R.C. 1988. The corridor principle. *Journal of Business Venturing* 3(1):31–40.

Rugman, A.M. 1981. *Inside the Multinationals: The Economics of Internal Markets.* New York: Columbia University Press.

Sprague, P.J. July 24, 1990. Personal interview.

Staw, B. 1981. The escalation of commitment to a course of action. *Academy of Management Review* 6:577–587.

Stopford, J.M., and Wells, L.T. 1972. *Managing the Multinational Enterprise.* New York: Basic Books.

Sullivan, D., and Bauerschmidt, A. 1990. Incremental internationalization: a test of Johanson and Vahlne's thesis. *Management International Review* 30(1):19–30.

Teece, D.J., Pisano, G., and Shuen, A. 1990. Firm capabilities, resources and the concept of strategy. Consortium on Competitiveness and Cooperation Working paper, no. 90-8.

Tushman, M.L., and Romanelli, E. 1985. Organizational evolution: a metamorphosis model of convergence and reorientation. In L.L. Cummings and B.M. Staw, eds., *Research in Organizational Behavior* Greenwich, CT: JAI Press, 7:171–222.

Vernon, R. 1966. International investment and international trade in the product cycle. *Quarterly Journal of Economics* 80:190–207.

Vernon, R. 1979. The product cycle hypothesis in a new international environment. *Oxford Bulletin of Economics and Statistics* Special Issue, 41(4):255–267.

Vesper, K.H. 1990. *New Venture Strategies.* Revised edition, Englewood Cliffs, NJ: Prentice Hall.

Welch, L.S., and Loustarinen, R. 1988. Internationalization: evolution of a concept. *Journal of General Management* 14(2):34–55.

Wood, M. June 24, 1992. Personal interview.

Yao, D. 1988. Beyond the reach of the invisible hand: and profitability. *Strategic Management Journal* 9:59–79.

[13]

Born Global or Gradual Global? Examining the Export Behavior of Small and Medium-Sized Enterprises

Over the past decade, several studies have questioned the stage models of the internationalization process. Many of these studies concentrate on the exporting versus nonexporting factor, identifying an increasing number of firms that are active in international markets shortly after establishment. Limited empirical evidence exists as to whether this actuality indicates simply a reduced time factor in the preexport phase or an important change in the export behavior of firms. Using small and medium-sized exporting firms from Norway, Denmark, and France, the authors focus on the concept of gradual development. The results suggest that export intensity, distribution, market selection, and global orientation are not influenced by the firm's year of establishment or first year of exporting activity. One-third of the firms sampled reported that the time period between establishment and export commencement was less than two years. In terms of export intensity, these firms outperform those that waited several years before exporting. The results indicate that the future export involvement of a firm is, to a large extent, influenced by its behavior shortly after establishment. The results further indicate that the development of resources in support of international market competitiveness may be regarded as the key issue and that the basic resources and competencies of the firm are determined during the establishment phase. The authors review how the management challenges differ depending on the type of firm (age and export involvement) in question.

ABSTRACT

In many studies, the international involvement of a firm has been described as a gradual development process (Bilkey and Tesar 1977; Cavusgil 1980; Johanson and Vahlne 1977). According to Johanson and Vahlne (1990, p. 11), internationalization is "a process in which the enterprise gradually increases its international involvement. This process evolves in the interplay between the development of knowledge about foreign markets and operations on one hand and increasing commitment of resources to foreign markets on the other." On the basis of a review of the literature dating from the first presentation of the Uppsala internationalization model, Johanson and Vahlne (1990) conclude that their original model had strong theoretical and empirical support. Aaby and Slater (1989) present an extensive literature review, stating that the existence of a gradual development

Øystein Moen and Per Servais

Submitted October 2000
Revised November 2001

© *Journal of International Marketing*
Vol 10, No 3, 2002, pp 49–72
ISSN 1069-031X

process is one of the few solid conclusions in international marketing research. In his assessment of the stage models, Andersen (1993, p. 227) notes that both the Uppsala internationalization model and the innovation-related internationalization model have "general acceptance in the literature."

However, in the past decade, studies have focused on what have been termed "international new ventures" (McDougall, Shane, and Oviatt 1994), "born globals" (Knight 1997; Knight and Cavusgil 1996; Madsen and Servais 1997), "instant internationals" (Preece, Miles, and Baetz 1999), or "global startups" (Oviatt and McDougall 1994). These studies focus on firms that are heavily involved in exporting from the time they are established. Such firms are found in large numbers in several countries, including the United States, Australia, Norway, France, Denmark, and Canada. In-depth discussions of the major driving forces that enhance the establishment of these firms have been presented by Madsen and Servais (1997), as well as Knight and Cavusgil (1996). The empirical results and theoretical reasoning in many of these studies question the concept of a gradual internationalization process through various stages. As expressed by Knight and Cavusgil (1996, p. 17), "the Born Global phenomenon presents an important new challenge to traditional internationalization theory." McDougall, Shane, and Oviatt (1994, p. 476) conclude that the stage theory "has failed to provide an appropriate explanation for why International New Ventures compete internationally rather than just in home markets."

This new stream of studies that has emerged over the past decade questions one of the established "truths" of international marketing research. Building on a three-country empirical investigation, the aim of our study is to examine a key element of the stage models—the existence of a gradual development. To examine this issue, we present a more detailed description of the stage models. Furthermore, we include some critical studies and empirical results that question the stage models, and we give special attention to studies that focus on what have been described as "born global" firms.

THE INTERNATIONALIZATION PROCESS MODELS

Andersen (1993) distinguishes between the Uppsala internationalization model and the innovation-related internationalization model, stating, however, that these two approaches are closely related. In the innovation-related models, internationalization is considered an innovation of the firm. Management's learning is important (Bilkey and Tesar 1977); the slow nature of the learning process is due to management's aversion to risk taking and a lack of knowledge. Different development stages have been presented. An example is Cavusgil's (1980) model, which differentiates among domestic marketing, preexport stage, experimental involvement, active involvement, and committed involvement. Bilkey and Tesar

(1977) and Czinkota (1982) have presented other classifications of the stages.

The Uppsala model focuses on acquisition, integration, the use of knowledge about foreign markets, and an increasing commitment and resource allocation to the markets, including the state and change aspects. The state aspects include knowledge about foreign markets and the resources allocated to those markets, and the change aspects include the decisions made about the commitment of resources and the activities performed in these markets. A primary rationale is that the firm will commit itself through incremental steps to gradually build experience and reduce the risk involved in exporting. The process is described as evolutionary and cyclical: The firm's behavior is influenced more by internal and environmental conditions than by a deliberate development of strategies. According to Johanson and Vahlne (1990), the process model explains two patterns. The first is the type of engagement. Johanson and Vahlne (1990, p. 13) describe it thus: "at the start no regular export activities are performed in the market, then export takes place via independent representatives, later through a sales' subsidiary, and eventually manufacturing may follow." The second pattern Johanson and Vahlne explain is the successive choice of more *psychically* distant markets. However, the authors also indicate that other manifestations of the process model may exist. Their arguments implicitly assert that a time-dependent increase in the export intensity of the firm could be expected—as the firm first builds its national activities and then gradually increases export involvement. According to the model, the aspects determining the incremental nature of the process are related to two factors: lack of market knowledge and uncertainty associated with the decision process.

Johanson and Vahlne (1990) include references for a great deal of the literature that focuses on the internationalization process of the firm. They find that many studies fundamentally support the stage model. Some studies mentioned take a more negative view; however, Johanson and Vahlne (1990, p. 14), when examining the literature, conclude that "overall, the model has gained strong support in studies of a wide spectrum of countries and situations. The empirical research confirms that commitment and experience are important factors explaining international business behavior."

Criticism of the Process Models

Some criticism of the stage models has been presented. Turnbull (1987) illustrates that many U.K. exporters do not follow a stage development in their international activities. Hedlund and Kverneland (1985) study Swedish firms in Japan, concluding that their behavior is not in accordance with the Uppsala model. They suggest that because of the internationalization of markets, market knowledge has increased and uncertainty has then decreased, which makes the basic mechanisms of the Uppsala model less important than they had been in the past. In a comment on Hedlund and Kverneland's study, Johanson and Vahlne (1990) state that their results are consistent with the process model, indicating a misfit between the discussion and the empirical results in Hedlund and Kverneland's (1985) article. In a nationwide study of small U.S. manufacturers, Brush (1992) finds that 13% of the sample commenced international activities during the first year of operation. In an Australian study, Rennie (1993) identifies several firms whose management views the world as its marketplace right from the birth of the company. Knight and Cavusgil (1996) even show that studies from the late 1970s have documented examples of internationalization patterns similar to those of born globals in different countries.

One development during the past decade is that much of the criticism directed at the stage models focuses on newly established high-involvement exporters. Because the studies focusing on these firms are especially important in the discussion of the process models, we provide a more detailed presentation next.

The Concept of Born Globals

The interest in born globals started early in the 1990s, and an increasing number of publications focused on this issue throughout the decade. One of the first attempts to summarize the literature was presented by Oviatt and McDougall (1994, p. 47), who conclude, "collectively, these case studies indicate that international new ventures are an important phenomenon. They have identified the formation of international new ventures in more than ten countries in all parts of the world, suggesting that global forces may be promoting their development."

Oviatt and McDougall (1994, p. 49) focus on newly created firms and define an international new venture as "a business organization that, from inception, seeks to derive significant competitive advantage from the use of resources from and the sale of outputs in multiple countries." This definition is in accordance with that of Knight (1997, p. 1), who defines a born global company as "a company which, from or near its founding, seeks to derive a substantial proportion of its revenue from the sale of its products in international markets." Other terms describing the same phenomenon have been used, including "instant internationals" and "global start-ups."

In their study of 24 born globals, McDougall, Shane, and Oviatt (1994) conclude that the stage models fail to provide an appropriate explanation of why such firms operate in international markets rather than just in their home markets. Regarding the governance structure of activities, McDougall, Shane, and Oviatt claim that there are key differences between established firms and start-up firms because of the amount and source of resources. The latter type of firms will have only few resources left for expensive investments in distribution channels, for example; therefore, in comparison with established firms, the entrepreneur must rely more on hybrid structures for controlling sales and marketing activities (e.g., close personal relationships, joint ventures).

This is in accordance with Bell's (1995) findings in his study of small computer software firms, in which he finds that existing internationalization models do not adequately reflect the underlying factors of the internationalization processes in these firms. He finds that the process is strongly influenced by domestic and foreign client patronage, the targeting of niche markets, and industry-specific consideration rather than the psychic distance to export markets. He also finds little support for the notion that firms progress systematically from exporting to other market entry modes, even though he finds an increasing commitment to exporting among the responding firms. Finally, not all firms establish themselves with domestic sales before starting foreign sales. According to Bell (1995), this could be due to the entrepreneurs' prior experiences or to entrepreneurs' tendency to initiate exports when searching for suppliers abroad.

In contrast to Oviatt and McDougall (1994), Rennie (1993) focuses on already established firms, especially small and medium-sized enterprises. In a study conducted for the Australian Manufacturing Council that covers 310 firms, Rennie splits the emerging exporters into two categories. The first one consists of more traditional, domestic-based firms, accounting for approximately 75% of the total sample. Firms in this category typically build a strong domestic base before exporting. On average, they have been in business 27 years when they first export, and they reap 15%–20% of sales in foreign markets. The second category is born globals; they export 75% of their total sales, starting after less than 2 years of operation. They generally produce leading-edge technology products for significant international niche markets, such as scientific instruments or machine tools. Rennie (1993) describes them as competing on quality and value created through innovative technology and product design. The mainstream born global of this study is close to its customers, flexible, and able to adapt its products to the rapidly changing needs and wants.

The latter findings are somewhat in contrast to those of Jolly, Alahuhta, and Jeannet (1992), who conclude that high-technology start-ups must choose a business area with homogeneous customers and minimal adaptation in the marketing mix. The argument is that these small firms cannot take a multidomestic approach as large firms can, simply because

Born Global or Gradual Global?   **53**

they do not have the sufficient scale in their operations worldwide. They are vulnerable because they are dependent on a single product, which they must commercialize in lead markets first, no matter where such markets are situated geographically. The reason is that such markets are the keys to broad and rapid market access, which is important because the fixed costs of these firms are relatively high. Because this is the key factor influencing the choice of the initial market, the importance of psychic distance in the market selection criterion is reduced. Often, these firms govern their sales and marketing activities through a specialized network in which they seek partners that complement their own competence; this is necessary because of the firms' limited resources.

Recent research carried out in the Nordic countries by Lindmark and colleagues (1994) also demonstrates the existence of born globals. Based on a study of 328 exporters from Finland, Norway, Sweden, and Denmark, the research concludes that the firms' domestic markets no longer seem to be as important a "learning place" as previous studies have demonstrated. From Canada, Preece, Miles, and Baetz (1999) report a tendency toward an increasing number of instant internationals. In a longitudinal study (1985–93) of 948 newly established firms in Denmark, Christensen and Jacobsen (1996) report that a rising number of these firms began exporting within their first years of existence. The authors conclude (p. 7) that different firms have different routes to internationalization "based on differences in established contacts and knowledge acquired prior to the initiated new business." Market knowledge; the personal network of the entrepreneur; international contacts; and experience transmitted from former occupations, relations, and education are examples of such international skills obtained before the birth of the firm.

Also from Scandinavia, Moen (2002) finds that the export intensity of the newly established Norwegian exporters is often remarkably high. In his study, the average export share of exporting firms established after 1990 is 65%, and more than 50% of newly established exporters have an export share higher than 25%.

Madsen and Servais (1997) discuss the factors giving rise to born globals and conclude that this group of firms should be expected to grow in number and importance throughout the years to come. Developments in information technology, new and flexible production technology, the increased importance of niche marketing, the number of students gaining international experience, and the reduction of trade barriers are all examples of the factors contributing to the increasing number of born globals. In-depth discussion of these factors is provided by Knight (1997), Knight and Cavusgil (1996), and Madsen and Servais (1997).

One possible explanation is that because many industries are "globalized," the uncertainty described in the Uppsala and innovation-related models is less important than before. Hedlund and Kverneland (1985) have expressed this view. It follows that globalization on the industrial level may be one of the reasons for the change found in the export behavior of small and medium-sized firms over the past decade.

Both the Uppsala model and the innovation-related internationalization model describe a gradual development pattern, based on lack of knowledge and uncertainty (Andersen 1993). Most of the studies focusing on the born globals phenomenon concentrate on whether the firms are exporting versus nonexporting, supplying empirical evidence related to a more rapid start-up of international activities (a short time after establishment) in many firms. However, few of the studies investigate the development stages after export involvement. Therefore, two scenarios must be considered: First, it is possible that the factors described as giving rise to the born globals are those that most significantly reduce the time from firm establishment to initial export involvement. If this is the case, a stage development may still exist related to operational forms, for example. In situations such as this, in which the stage models may still be valid, what we have observed could be characterized as a change in the time factor related to the initial (pre-export) stages. The contrasting second scenario would be that several factors have rendered the stage models inadequate in explaining the export behavior of firms. In keeping with this hypothesis, we expect firms to choose the distribution form most suitable in their industry, choose the most attractive markets regardless of psychic distance, and have a strong international orientation right from establishment.

If there is indeed a gradual development process, the articles that present the original Uppsala model suggest that this development would be reflected in the firm's distribution method and would be evident from an examination of the psychic distance of a firm's export markets (Johanson and Vahlne 1977, 1990). Implicitly, it should also be expected that the global orientation of managers would increase during the process. In addition, it might be expected that both the number of countries exported to and the export intensity would be different for firms in different development phases. The firms that have operated in international markets for a longer period of time would be expected to serve more markets and achieve a higher percentage of sales outside their home markets. Also, the innovation-related models append expectations that firms will export to an increasing number of countries, gradually expand operations to more psychologically distant markets, and develop their international orientation and commitment—as well as increase export intensity, as expected from the stage development model (Bilkey and Tesar 1977).

THE HYPOTHESES

Born Global or Gradual Global?   **55**

On the basis of the widely accepted nature of the process view of internationalization, we expect that

H_1: There is a gradual development in the type of distribution used.

H_2: There is a gradual development in the distance to the markets served.

H_3: There is a gradual development in the number of markets served.

H_4: There is a gradual development toward stronger global orientation.

H_5: There is a gradual development in the export intensity of the firm.

This study does not focus on the preexport phase or foreign direct investments. The issue addressed is the identification of manifestations of a gradual development among small and medium-sized exporting firms. This includes an analysis of how a firm's first year of exporting, year of establishment, and time period between establishment and export activity commencement are related to distribution forms, export intensity, number of export markets, management's international orientation, and export market selection. If we find no difference when comparing the manifestations implicitly or explicitly described in the stage models with time-related factors such as a firm's year of establishment or first year of exporting, the indication will be that we need to develop better theories to explain the export behavior of firms.

METHODOLOGY

Most international marketing research builds on samples from one nation. This inhibits the researcher's ability to generalize the results. In this study, we include data from three European countries: Norway, France, and Denmark. In total, this study builds on returned questionnaires from 677 firms. Both Norway and Denmark are small countries in the northern part of Europe. An important difference between the two countries is that popular elections in Norway have twice resulted in a majority vote in opposition to joining the European Union. Both Denmark and France are members of the European Union. France is different from the two other countries in terms of both language and culture and has a population approximately ten times larger than either Norway or Denmark. In Norway and France, the main section of the questionnaire is a translation of a questionnaire that was previously used in the United States (Knight 1997). The Danish survey covers most of the issues addressed in the other samples, though the questions are expressed somewhat differently. It should be noted that the Danish data do not include the various aspects of global orientation, nor do they include the question about the number of markets served.

In Norway and France, questionnaires were addressed to top managers in small and medium-sized exporting firms (less

Øystein Moen and Per Servais

than 250 employees), which were classified as producers. In Denmark, firms within the range of 10–499 employees were targeted. In Norway and France, company classification and address lists were obtained from Kompass Norway and Kompass France databases, and the database CD-Direct was used in Denmark. In Norway, the response rate was 23%, yielding 335 usable returns. In France, 70 usable responses generated a response rate of 5%, and the Danish response from 272 firms yielded a response rate of 48%. Overall, the advantages of having a three-nation survey sample were considered more important than the limited response rate in France and the questionnaire design differences.

All industrial sectors were included in all three national samples. Table 1 gives some key information about the included firms from each nation. As indicated in Table 1, the Danish firms are the largest (in terms of employees and total sales) and oldest and have the highest export involvement; the French firms are smaller and younger and have less export involvement than the firms from both Norway and Denmark.

To test the hypotheses, we included questions regarding the year of establishment, first year of exporting, number of employees, annual total sales, export share, number of countries exported to, and which markets were most important. Focusing on distribution, we asked managers to select which distribution concept they used for the most important products in the most important export market. In Norway and France, the alternatives included direct sales, usage of agents or distributors, sales offices, and joint ventures. The answers revealed that few of these small firms were involved in joint ventures (less than 10 of 405 firms), so joint ventures were subsequently excluded from the analysis. Because some of

MEASUREMENT

	Norway (n = 335)	France (n = 70)	Denmark (n = 272)
Annual Total Sales (1000 Euro)			
Mean	8.008	5.392	16.282
Median	4.142	2.366	9.254
Number of Employees			
Mean	49	33	84
Median	26	18	39
Year of Establishment			
Mean	1960	1970	1955
Median	1970	1981	1966
First year of Exporting			
Mean	1976	1985	1973
Median	1985	1990	1977
Export Share			
Mean	40.8	30.9	48.6
Median	34.3	22.0	50.0

Table 1.
Firm Descriptives

the firms combined more than one method, often direct sales in cooperation with their agents, the summary percentage may be higher than 100. In Denmark, the classification included two groups: direct sales to end users and sales through intermediaries (agents or distributors).

The concept of psychic distance has been important in the development of the stage models, the expectation being that firms start exporting to countries regarded as "close," later expanding to more distant nations. Stöttinger and Schlegelmilch (1998) investigate both geographic and psychic distance. Both their results and previous studies (Holzmüller and Kasper 1991) show inconsistent results, with great variations in the correlation between these measures. We therefore decided to use both geographic and psychic distance in the study. Focusing on the most important export market of the firm, we classified the market on a 1 to 4 scale regarding the psychic and geographic distance. We based the classification into groups according to psychic distance on Hofstede's (1980) cultural dimensions. This means that each group is classified differently depending on the country of origin—Norway, France, or Denmark.

In both the Norwegian and French studies, several dimensions of global orientation were included. These were based on the original questionnaire presented by Knight (1997), in which he provides a detailed description of the theoretical base and the testing of these constructs in a U.S. setting. Table 2 presents the coefficient alphas in the Norwegian and French samples regarding the various aspects of global orientation. As Table 2 illustrates, 10 of the 12 alpha scores are higher than .60, indicating satisfactory measure validity.

Classification of the Firms

We classified the firms using three dimensions: year of establishment, first year of exporting, and time period from establishment until export commencement. For the year of establishment, the firms were divided into three groups, established before 1975 (old firms), between 1976 and 1989, and after 1989 (new firms). The division between firms established before versus after 1975 is based on Sengenberger, Loveman, and Piore's (1990) results. The shift in importance of small and medium-sized firms in the mid-1970s is well documented in their Organisation for Economic Co-operation and Development report. Using numbers from several nations (including, among others, the United Kingdom, the United States, Germany, and France), Sengenberger, Loveman, and Piore find both a growing number and an increasing importance of small firms after 1975. The division between 1989 and 1990 is founded on the studies that describe the emergence of born globals, which report that many of the main driving forces for the establishment of these firms are evident beginning in the late 1980s. Furthermore, we

International Orientation	Alpha (Norway)	Alpha (France)
International commitment (adequacy of financial investments, sufficiency of human resources)	.62	.56
International vision (world as marketplace, communicates mission to succeed in export markets, focused on developing resources)	.78	.81
International proactiveness (culture for exploring opportunities, boldness in decision making, conservativeness in international environment)	.61	.54
International customer orientation (understanding needs, success by satisfying needs, after-sales service)	.68	.71
International responsiveness (communicates customers experiences, responds quickly, discusses strengths and weaknesses, understand how to create value)	.74	.66
International marketing competence (knowledge of customers, product adaptations, effective pricing, effective advertising, effective distribution, ability to use marketing tools for differentiation)	.76	.80

Table 2.
Description of the Indexes: Cronbach's Alphas for the Norwegian (n = 335) and French (n = 70) Samples

used the same year markers as previously to classify the firms according to their first year of exporting and divide them into groups. On the basis of this classification, some of the firms may be old according to year of establishment but new as exporters according to their first year of exporting. The third classification addresses the time between establishment and the first year of exporting, grouping the firms as born globals (those that began exporting within less than two years after establishment), average-time exporters (three to ten years), and late starters (more than ten years). Table 3 presents the number of firms in each group and classification.

Two observations must be made on the basis of Table 3. First, a large number of firms (ranging between 30.7 and 38.8%) in all three nations began exporting within two years of their establishment. As many as one of three firms from these nations began exporting less than two years after establishment. Second, the French sample includes a larger number of firms established late that began exporting within the past decade than do the Norwegian and Danish samples.

We performed the analysis using a one-way analysis of variance in SPSS 9.0. It should be noted that we decided to mark statistically significant differences even though they were in the opposite direction of the hypothesis. The first issue addressed was the relationship among firm age, first year exporting, and time from establishment until export, with a focus on the export involvement of the firm (export intensity measured as the percentage of sales in international markets).

RESULTS

Born Global or Gradual Global?   **59**

According to the stage models, we expected that old firms and firms that had exported for a long time would have a higher export involvement than younger firms and firms that had been exporting for a shorter period of time. The results are displayed in Table 4.

The first issue was the influence of a firm's year of establishment on export intensity. As reported in Table 4, no significant differences were found in the samples from Norway and Denmark, but the youngest firms in the French sample had a significantly higher export share than did older firms. Examining the first year of exporting, the results in both Norway and Denmark showed that the firms that began exporting before 1975 had a higher export share than firms that began exporting later. In France, no such effect was found. It is possible to interpret this as part of a gradual process. How-

Table 3.
Number of Firms in Each Classification Group

	Norway (n = 335)	France (n = 70)	Denmark (n = 272)
Year of Establishment			
1800–1975	57.1%	37.1%	67.4%
1976–89	27.3%	47.0%	24.0%
1990–98	15.7%	15.8%	8.6%
First Year of Exporting			
1800–1975	34.5%	11.9%	46.6%
1976–89	35.1%	37.3%	36.7%
1990–98	30.4%	50.7%	16.7%
Time Before Export (Years)			
0–2	38.8%	34.3%	30.7%
3–10	23.3%	22.4%	21.1%
11–100	37.9%	43.3%	48.2%

Table 4.
Firm Classification Versus Export Intensity

	Norway (n = 335)	France (n = 70)	Denmark (n = 272)
Year of Establishment			
1800–1975	38.1	20.9	49.0
1976–89	45.6	29.5	48.3
1990–98	43.8	58.9	44.7
F-value	1.84	11.056**	.188
First Year of Exporting			
1800–1975	48.4	15.3	54.8
1976–89	41.6	37.1	47.7
1990–98	32.7	30.1	33.6
F-value	6.242*	2.065	7.562*
Time Before Export (Years)			
0–2	54.3	48.9	58.7
3–10	37.3	26.5	49.2
11–100	30.5	20.2	40.6
F-value	18.787**	10.223**	7.752*

$*p < 01$
$**p < 001$

Øystein Moen and Per Servais

ever, closer examination of the data reveals that the significance of the first year of exporting in Norway and Denmark is
due to several old firms that began exporting late, achieving
limited export sales. If the old firms (established before 1975)
are excluded from the analysis of the first year of exporting,
no significant differences occur.

In all countries, there was a strong indication that the time
between firm establishment and the first year of exporting is
an important indicator of later export intensity. The difference in export share between born globals and late starters
was 24%, 28%, and 18% in Norway, France, and Denmark,
respectively. It may be that the old firms had established considerable sales in their home markets so that the use of export
share would result in an underestimation of their export involvement. Therefore, we also performed the analysis using
export sales as the dependent variable. The same results were
found. There was no difference in export sales based on year
of establishment in Norway and Denmark, and there were
higher sales in the newly established French firms. Significantly higher export sales were found in the firms that began
exporting early in Norway and Denmark because of the low
export sales of the same older firms that began exporting late.
Furthermore, the time between establishment and exporting
differentiated the groups significantly: The born globals had
the highest export sales.

In conclusion, the key element in understanding export involvement on the basis of these results is the time between
establishment and the first year of exporting. Old firms trying
to export several decades after they are established seem to
be "losers" in terms of export intensity and export sales.

The second issue is the differences in global orientation
among the managers in the different groups of firms. According to the stage models, older firms and firms that have exported for a long time are expected to score higher with
regard to their managers' global orientation than are newer
firms. The results from the Norwegian sample are provided
in Table 5. High scores indicate a strong global orientation.

Examining the firm's year of establishment, we found no significant differences in global orientation. Regarding the first
year of exporting, the oldest firms scored higher on proactiveness than firms that began exporting later. Again, in-
depth investigation showed that old firms that began
exporting many years after establishment were the main reason for this difference. Considering the time between establishment and export activity commencement revealed a
significance in terms of international vision, proactiveness,
and responsiveness. More precisely, the firms that began exporting shortly after their establishment had the highest

Born Global or Gradual Global?   **61**

	Commitment	Vision	Proactiveness	Customer Orientation	Responsiveness	Marketing Competence
Table 5. **Year of**						
Firm Classification **Establishment**						
Versus Global Orientation 1800–1975	4.06	4.86	4.21	5.17	4.67	4.19
(Norway, n = 335) 1976–89	4.02	5.04	4.39	5.42	4.91	4.33
1990–98	3.83	5.26	4.38	5.21	4.89	4.23
F-value	.640	1.812	.824	2.014	1.966	.865
First Year **of Exporting**						
1800–1975	4.13	5.11	4.52	5.29	4.81	4.26
1976–89	4.06	4.88	4.20	5.30	4.84	4.23
1990–98	3.88	4.86	4.12	5.10	4.69	4.21
F-value	1.09	1.22	3.49*	1.40	.65	.10
Time Before **Export (Years)**						
0–2	3.94	5.21	4.58	5.31	4.98	4.28
3–10	4.07	5.20	4.29	5.41	4.81	4.29
11–100	4.06	4.64	4.00	5.10	4.57	4.16
F-value	.359	6.843**	7.483**	2.444	4.893**	.997

$*p < 05$
$**p < 01$

scores for these three global orientation dimensions. Table 6 gives the results for the French firms.

Examining the mean values, we find the same tendency as in the Norwegian sample; however, these values are not statistically significant. Only one significant difference was identified, signifying a higher score for international proactiveness among the newly established firms. These results from the Norwegian and French samples do not support a time-dependent development toward increased global orientation; the Danish questionnaire did not include these measures.

Table 7 presents the results pertaining to the use of the different distribution methods included. As explained previously, the percentage may be higher than 100, as some firms use more than one distribution method within the same market—for example, agents combined with direct sales efforts.

All the questions pertain to the most important product in the most important market for the respondent firm. The results are similar for all three nations: There are no significant differences among the groups of firms. Therefore, there is no indication of a time-dependent (gradual) development in distribution forms. As noted in the "Methodology" section, joint ventures were not included, because few firms partook in them—though the inclusion of joint ventures would not have altered the conclusion.

Øystein Moen and Per Servais

	Commitment	Vision	Proactiveness	Customer Orientation	Marketing Responsiveness	Competence
Year of Establishment						
1800–1975	4.30	4.24	3.31	5.15	4.78	4.62
1976–89	3.83	4.95	3.87	5.04	5.15	4.90
1990–98	4.50	5.42	4.51	5.91	4.98	5.09
F-value	1.501	2.614	4.209*	2.017	.915	.708
First Year of Exporting						
1800–1975	3.94	4.14	3.58	4.71	4.90	4.57
1976–89	4.38	5.36	4.03	5.56	5.16	5.02
1990–98	4.00	4.48	3.60	5.21	4.83	4.82
F-value	.722	3.018	1.607	.703	.610	1.599
Time Before Export (Years)						
0–2	4.41	5.21	4.17	5.58	5.02	4.94
3–10	3.97	4.66	3.71	5.39	5.25	5.22
11–100	4.00	4.48	3.42	4.98	4.76	4.63
F-value	.814	1.436	2.320	1.773	1.134	1.742

*$p < 05$

Table 6.
Firm Classification Versus Global Orientation (France, n = 70)

	Norway (n = 335)			France (n = 70)			Denmark (n = 272)	
	Direct Sales	Agent or Distributor	Sales Office	Direct Sales	Agent or Distributor	Sales Office	Direct to End Users	Through Intermediaries
Year of Establishment								
1800–1975	52.7	54.4	15.3	61.5	62.2	15.4	43 2	48.5
1976–89	48.3	51.7	20.7	78.8	60.6	12.1	56.1	53.4
1990–98	60.0	48 0	14.2	63.6	62.3	18.2	38.5	47 2
F-value	.873	.341	.741	1.114	015	.139	1.371	.357
First Year of Exporting								
1800–1975	53.6	50.9	15.5	75.0	74.2	12.5	49.5	48.3
1976–89	52.7	55.4	17.9	72.0	64.0	20.0	52.6	53.0
1990–98	54.6	47.4	17.5	60.5	55.9	8.8	58.7	41.6
F-value	873	712	.478	031	.627	.548	619	1.125
Time Before Export (Years)								
0–2	53 8	53 9	16.8	73.9	69.6	13.0	48.0	54.1
3–10	50.6	47 7	19 4	73 3	53 3	20.0	62 6	43.8
11–100	54 5	52.9	16.5	68.9	58.6	10 3	56 4	45 4
F-value	.129	.333	.138	087	.559	.385	1.531	1.284

Table 7.
Firm Classification Versus Distribution

The next issue addressed is the differences among the groups of firms in terms of the geographic and psychic market coverage. Table 8 presents the results. An examination of the results reveals no significant relationship between a firm's year of establishment or the first year of exporting and the geographic or psychic distance to the most important market. This result is consistent for all three national samples. In the samples from both Norway and France, it was found that

Born Global or Gradual Global?

Table 8.
Classification of Firms
Versus Export Markets

	Norway (n = 335)			France (n = 70)			Denmark (n = 272)	
	Geographic Distance	Cultural Distance	Number of Countries	Geographic Distance	Cultural Distance	Number of Countries	Geographic Distance	Cultural Distance
Year of Establishment								
1800–1975	2.05	1.91	11.5	1.46	1.92	15.5	1.44	1 88
1976–89	2.23	1 98	11.5	1.80	2.20	12.3	1.33	1.83
1990–98	2.22	1.96	8.2	1.71	1.92	9.6	1 27	2.00
F-value	.857	.153	1.542	.661	.728	.853	1 450	455
First Year of Exporting								
1800–1975	2 24	2.03	14 5	1 43	1.86	26.3	1.47	1 95
1976–89	2.10	1 93	10.6	1.69	2.26	16.3	1 32	1 77
1990–98	2 02	1.84	7.3	1.63	1.91	8.12	1.26	1.84
F-value	.947	.996	8.980***	.166	1.135	7.933**	1.114	1.615
Time Before Export (Years)								
0–2	2.35	2.16	13.1	1.60	2.05	13.0	1.43	2.01
3–10	2 08	1.82	11.7	1 94	2.29	11.5	1.21	1.76
11–100	1 96	1.81	8.8	1.46	1.89	13.9	1 44	1 80
F-value	3.533*	4 158*	3.481*	1.213	.847	.152	1.089	2.349

*$p < 05$
**$p < 01$.
***$p < .001$

firms that had been exporting for the longest period of time exported to more nations than did firms that began exporting later. In Denmark, the questionnaire did not include the question about the number of countries to which a firm exports. In Norway, the firms that began exporting soon after establishment exported to the most distant markets in terms of psychic and geographic distance, and these firms were found to export to a greater number of countries. No such differences were found in the samples from France and Denmark.

DISCUSSION

Table 9 summarizes the results presented in the study. It should be noted that with regard to global orientation, one weak significant relationship was found that was contrary to the hypotheses (year of establishment in France), but another relation supported the hypotheses (first year of exporting in Norway). Because 22 of 24 relations are nonsignificant and the other two are in different directions, a conclusion of no differences is recorded in Table 9 for the interaction of global orientation with year of establishment and first year of exporting. Table 9 indicates whether the stage models are supported or whether the results indicate that the most important differences are linked to the short time period from establishment to exporting ("BG supported"). This notation is also used when the most recently established or new exporters significantly differ from older firms and exporters, contrary to the stage models' expectations.

We expected to find gradual development in international activity with regard to export intensity, distribution, distance to markets served, number of countries, and global orientation.

Øystein Moen and Per Servais

	Norway	France	Denmark
Export Intensity			
Year of establishment	—	BG supported	—
First year of exporting	—ᵃ	—	—ᵃ
Time before export	BG supported	BG supported	BG supported
Global Orientation			
Year of establishment	—	—	n.i.
First year of exporting	—	—	n.i.
Time before export	BG supported	—	n.i.
Distribution			
Year of establishment	—	—	—
First year of exporting	—	—	—
Time before export	—	—	—
Export Markets (Distance)			
Year of establishment	—	—	—
First year of exporting	—	—	—
Time before export	BG supported	—	—
Export Markets (Number)			
Year of establishment	—	—	n.i.
First year of exporting	Stage model supported	Stage model supported	n.i.
Time before export	BG supported	—	n.i.

Table 9.
Summary of Results

ᵃComment in text
Notes BG = influence of year of establishment/born global behavior, — = no significant relation, n.i = not included in this national survey.

Examining the emerging pattern, we found no relationship between the firms' year of foundation and export intensity, global orientation, distribution, psychic or geographic market distance, or the number of markets served. These results were consistent in all three countries included in this study. The first year of exporting had no significant influence on global orientation, distribution, or distance to export markets. Higher export intensity was found among the old exporting firms. As discussed in the "Results" section, this is because some of the older firms began exporting late, which effectively lowered the average representation of firms that began exporting later. One result in accordance with the stage models did occur: Firms that had exported for a long period of time exported to a larger number of countries than did newly established exporting firms.

The third classification of firms was based on the time between establishment and the first export involvement. Considerable differences were identified. Firms that began exporting within two years of establishment had a significantly higher export share than did the other firms in all three nations. In the Norwegian sample, managers in firms that began exporting soon after establishment were found to have a stronger global orientation in terms of vision, proactiveness, and responsiveness than did managers in firms that had more time between establishment and export activity commencement. Also, these firms had a greater degree of export activity in the more geographically and psychically distant markets

Born Global or Gradual Global?

and exported to a greater number of markets. These relationships were not found in the sample from France. It should be noted that time-dependent development in the distribution type did not emerge. In total, these results indicate that a firm's export involvement is influenced by the period of time between establishment and the commencement of exporting, and this time period is more important than the firm's year of establishment or first year of exporting.

These results are not consistent with the premises of the stage models. However, Johanson and Vahlne (1990) define three situations in which the process would not necessarily occur in small steps: focusing resources, environmental stability, and experience from similar markets. In these authors' view, firms having considerable resources, operating in stable environments, or having experience from similar markets would have the opportunity to leapfrog several stages. There is no reason to expect that the firms included in this study would suit these conditions. The median for the number of employees is 39, 26, and 18 in Denmark, Norway, and France, respectively. Consequently, it is not likely that considerable resources are an explanation why they do not behave as expected in the process model. Many of these small exporters use leading-edge technology; in such settings, the environment may be expected to undergo rapid changes. Furthermore, it is not likely that experience from similar markets should be more widespread among the firms in these three samples than in other exporting firms. This means that the exceptions presented by Johanson and Vahlne (1990) do not seem to explain the results observed.

IMPLICATIONS

The results presented in this study have several important implications for public policy, management, and further research.

Implications for Public Policy

In most European countries, government considers it important to stimulate and increase exports. This is because of balance of payment considerations, employment, and economic growth. Because most firms in many nations are small, stimulating and developing the export involvement of these small firms has received considerable attention. This has driven the establishment of export promotion or export development programs. The Norwegian Export Council, founded by the trade department, has worked with a small and medium-sized enterprise export program throughout the 1990s, which involves a large number of firms. An examination of the content and focus of this program shows that the focus is small and medium-sized established (old) firms, not newly established firms. On the basis of the results of our study, the Norwegian small and medium-sized enterprise export program is targeting a group of firms with limited export potential—old firms with no or little export experience. It seems that the most no-

Øystein Moen and Per Servais

table export potential is found among old firms with strong export involvement, and many newly established exporting firms also show promise. In both Norway and Denmark, this study is part of activities sponsored by the national research foundations. As a part of these projects, information related to the results is distributed and presented in various manners. This study's most important contribution to public policy may be the development of knowledge regarding the importance of export activity by newly established firms, which underlines the need for the inclusion of this group of firms in the developing public programs. Implicitly, these results also suggest that the establishment of new firms with international marketing potential is important for the export development in a nation, suggesting a need for coordination between public export development and business start-up programs.

At the firm level, managers are facing different situations depending on the type of firm in which they work. Managers in old firms with strong international involvement should take note that they are increasingly competing against newly established, highly specialized, and aggressive firms. The managers of the old exporting firms should be especially focused on preserving their firms' competitiveness, because Moen's (1999) results suggest that many firms gradually lose their technological competitiveness as they grow older and larger. Furthermore, it seems that many old firms are more reluctant than younger firms to use new marketing tools, such as information and communication technology (Knight 1997). To develop competitiveness consistently and to avoid acting too conservatively in terms of using new technology are therefore some of the most important tasks for managers in these firms.

Implications for Managers

The challenges for the managers of older firms with limited export involvement are different and are likely to be even more difficult. It seems that many of these firms are unable to compete successfully in international markets. This may be due to a lack of competitive products, the firm's competencies, and an unwillingness to commit resources to the export venture. The managers in these firms should heed three important points: First, they need to examine the firm's international competitiveness, not least regarding the products offered and the technology used. Developing the competitive advantages needed for export success should be a critical management responsibility. Second, the firm should target selected market segments to focus its resources. Third, management commitment is important, especially in developing the international orientation of employees. If the implications of our results are taken to the extreme, old nonexporting firms trying to engage in international markets may find that setting up a special export project away from the basic organization may be necessary in order to develop a successful export venture independent of the existing organization's orientation and culture. A new firm with little or no export activities should be aware that it may be more and more difficult to manage an export venture the longer the firm operates with only limited export sales.

New firms with high international ambitions need access to external funding for their export ventures, which implies that access to capital from different sources may be more important for them than for any other group of firms. Moen (2000) shows that a consistent niche focus strategy has a significant, positive impact on the export performance of small firms. For small firms with limited resources, targeting homogeneous market segments with standardized products, as recommended by Jolly, Alahuhta, and Jeannet (1992), will be advantageous in that it reduces the resources needed. For small exporting software firms, Alajoutsijarvi, Mannerma, and Tikkanen (2000, p. 157) state that a critical endeavor is "to identify actions which reduced the uncertainty and risks perceived by foreign customers." For many small firms, development of close relations to established firms in their targeted markets will be advantageous for reasons of market access and the reduction of customer uncertainty.

For all firms, the necessity of having a global orientation when they develop new products should be stressed. Li (1999), focusing on U.S. software firms, finds that the interface is strong among marketing, new product research and development processes, and new product performance in international markets. The results presented in our study underscore the importance of firms having a global orientation, particularly when firms in the establishment phase are developing their first product generation.

Implications for Research

The results presented in this study have important implications for research. It should be noted that all firms included in this study were small and medium sized. It is possible that these firms established the type of distribution most often used within their industrial sector when they began exporting. Consequently, agents in several markets may be able to handle considerable sales growth, which makes it unnecessary for the firm to change the type of distribution used. A distribution development according to the stage models would occur only if the firm had grown much larger, reaching a size not included in this study. Following this argument, most small and medium-sized firms do not develop into larger firms, which implies that the stage models have limited validity for these firms. The situation may be different for large firms, as is illustrated by the case studies that form the basis for the development of the Uppsala model that Johanson and Vahlne (1977) present. Overseas production and manufacturing may still be expected to occur primarily among larger firms with prior international engagement and experience; this implies that some gradual development still exists.

Another of this study's implications involves the necessity for further empirical studies of the international involvement of firms and the development of better models and theories to explain the real behavior of the firms. The need for such model development has been discussed by Knight and Cavusgil (1996) and McDougall, Shane, and Oviatt (1994). Furthermore, most empirical studies in the field of international marketing treat firms as one homogeneous group, as described by Zou and Stan (1998). There may be different key performance factors for the newly established, highly involved exporters than for the larger, older, highly involved exporters and old firms with limited export sales. Another important issue for research is the investigation of whether one general theory is able to explain the export behavior of firms. It is possible that firms operating in their home market for a long time before entering international markets may follow a behavioral pattern in congruence with the stage models, but new or modified theories should be applied to newly established exporting firms.

Some of the main findings of this study are as follows:

1. In Norway, France, and Denmark, 38.8%, 34.3%, and 30.7% of the exporting firms commenced their export activities within two years of establishment. This means that there are large numbers of newly established exporting firms.
2. Three of four of these firms that began exporting within two years of establishment had an export share higher than 25%.
3. The time period between a firm's establishment and first year of exporting seems to be important. It seems that the future export involvement of the firm is influenced to a large extent by its behavior shortly after establishment.
4. The empirical results question the concept of a general, gradual international process occurring in various stages among the firms included in the study.
5. It may be that firms' development of resources in order to be competitive in international markets is the key issue and that the basic resources and competencies of a firm are determined within the establishment phase.
6. For managers, the challenges differ depending on the degree of international involvement and the age of the firm.

CONCLUSIONS

However different the Uppsala and the innovation-related internationalization models are, both describe a gradual development pattern of the internationalization process. Several studies have questioned these models, criticizing their limited ability to explain the phenomena of newly established firms with strong international involvement (Aspelund and Moen 2001; Oviatt and McDougall 1994). This study includes both newly established and older small and medium-sized exporting firms from Norway, France, and Denmark. It does not include the preexport phase or the development of operation type (foreign direct investment), but the results indicate that the phenomenon of a gradual development among small and medium-sized exporting firms may be questioned.

The stage models have had a considerable impact on the field of international marketing for nearly three decades. Perhaps the reason for the strength and acceptance of this stage perspective is that several of these studies were well written and easy to understand and provided the opportunity for marketers to structure teaching and research in a manner that has been welcomed. It has been easy to find examples of individual firms that fit this gradual development model. Although firms that follow this incremental development pattern may still exist, the normal pattern may be different in the new millennium. It is possible that a new situation now exists in which firms either will be established with the products, competencies, orientation, and resources to successfully compete in international markets or will be established primarily with a home-market focus. For firms that are not established with a strong international focus, it may be difficult to develop later into high-involvement exporters, as Moen (2002) argues. It is possible, however, that these firms that do not start exporting shortly after establishment will develop more in line with the stage models of internationalization. To understand what might be an important change in the export behavior of small and medium-sized firms, further research is recommended to investigate the development of the international activities of both newly established and older firms.

REFERENCES

Aaby, Nils-Erik and S.F. Slater (1989), "Management Influences on Export Performance: A Review of the Empirical Literature 1978–1988," *International Marketing Review*, 6 (4), 7–26.

Alajoutsijarvi, Kimmo, K. Mannermaa, and H. Tikkanen (2000), "Customer Relationships and the Small Software Firm: A Framework for Understanding Challenges Faced in Marketing," *Information & Management*, 37 (3), 153–59.

Andersen, Otto (1993), "On the Internationalization Process of Firms: A Critical Analysis," *Journal of International Business Studies*, 24 (Second Quarter), 209–31.

Aspelund, Arild and Ø. Moen (2001), "A Generation Perspective on Small Firms Internationalization—from Traditional Exporters and Flexible Specialists to Born Globals," in *Advances in International Marketing: Reassessing the Internationalization of the Firm*, Vol. 11, C.A. Axinn and P. Matthyssens, eds. Oxford, UK: JAI Press, 197–226.

Bell, Jim (1995), "The Internationalization of Small Computer Software Firms: A Further Challenge to 'Stage' Theories," *European Journal of Marketing*, 29 (8), 60–75.

Bilkey, Warren J. and G. Tesar (1977), "The Export Behaviour of Smaller-Sized Wisconsin Manufacturing Firms," *Journal of International Business Studies*, 8 (Spring/Summer), 93–98.

Brush, Candida G. (1992), "Factors Motivating Small Companies to Internationalize: The Effect of Firm Age," doctoral dissertation, School of Management, Boston University.

Cavusgil, S. Tamer (1980), "On the Internationalization Process of Firms," *European Research*, 8 (November), 273–81.

Christensen, P.R. and L. Jacobsen (1996), "The Role of Export in New Business Formation," paper presented at RENT X Conference on Entrepreneurship and SMEs, Brussels, Belgium (November).

Czinkota, Michael R. (1982), *Export Development Strategies: U.S. Promotion Policy*. New York: Praeger.

Hedlund, Gunnar and Å. Kverneland (1985), "Are Strategies for Foreign Market Entry Changing? The Case of Swedish Investment in Japan," *International Studies of Management and Organization*, 15 (2), 41–59.

Hofstede, Geert H. (1980), *Culture's Consequences: International Differences in Work Related Values*. Beverly Hills, CA: Sage Publications.

Holzmüller, H.H. and H. Kasper (1991), "On a Theory of Export Performance: Personal and Organizational Determinants of Export Trade Activities Observed in Small and Medium-Sized Firms," *Management International Review*, 31 (Special Issue), 45–70.

——— and B. Stöttinger (1996), "Structural Modeling of Success Factors in Exporting: Cross-Validation and Further Development of an Export Performance Model," *Journal of International Marketing*, 4 (2), 29–55.

Johanson, Jan and J.-E. Vahlne (1977), "The Internationalization Process of the Firm: A Model of Knowledge Development and Increasing Foreign Market Commitments," *Journal of International Business Studies*, 8 (Spring/Summer), 23–32.

——— and ——— (1990), "The Mechanism of Internationalization," *International Marketing Review*, 7 (4), 11–24.

Jolly, Vijay K., M. Alahuhta, and J.-P. Jeannet (1992), "Challenging the Incumbents: How High Technology Start-Ups Compete Globally," *Journal of Strategic Change*, 1 (April), 71–82.

Knight, Gary A. (1997), "Emerging Paradigm for International Marketing: The Born Global Firm," doctoral dissertation, Department of Marketing and Supply Chain Management, Michigan State University.

——— and S. Tamer Cavusgil (1996), "The Born Global Firm: A Challenge to Traditional Internationalization Theory," in *Advances in International Marketing*, Vol. 8, S. Tamer Cavusgil, ed. Greenwich, CT: JAI Press, 11–26.

Li, Tiger (1999), "The Effect of Marketing–R&D Interface on New Product Export Performance: A Contingency Analysis," *Journal of International Marketing*, 7 (1), 10–33.

Lindmark, L., P.R. Christensen, H. Eskelinen, B. Forsström, O.J. Sørensen, and E. Vatn (1994), *Småföretagens internationalisering—en jämförende studie*. Stockholm, Sweden: Nord REFO.

THE AUTHORS

Øystein Moen is an associate professor, Department of Industrial Economics and Technology Management, Norwegian University of Science and Technology.

Per Servais is an associate professor, Department of Marketing, University of Southern Denmark.

Madsen, Tage K. and P. Servais (1997), "The Internationalization of Born Globals: An Evolutionary Process?" *International Business Review*, 6 (6), 561–83.

McDougall, Patricia P. and B.M. Oviatt (1996), "New Venture Internationalization, Strategic Change, and Performance: A Follow-Up Study," *Journal of Business Venturing*, 11 (1), 23–40.

——, S. Shane, and B.M. Oviatt (1994), "Explaining the Formation of International New Ventures: The Limits of Theories from International Business Research," *Journal of Business Venturing*, 9 (6), 469–87.

Moen, Øystein (1999), "The Relationship Between Firm Size, Competitive Advantages and Export Performance Revisited," *International Small Business Journal*, 18 (1), 53–71.

—— (2000), "SMEs and International Marketing: Investigating the Differences in Export Strategy Between Firms of Different Size," *Journal of Global Marketing*, 13 (4), 7–28.

—— (2002), "The Born Globals: A New Generation of Small European Exporters," *International Marketing Review*, (forthcoming).

Oviatt, Benjamin M. and P.P. McDougall (1994), "Toward a Theory of International New Ventures," *Journal of International Business Studies*, 25 (1), 45–64.

Preece, Stephen B., G. Miles, and M.C. Baetz (1999), "Explaining the International Intensity and Global Diversity of Early-Stage Technology-Based Firms," *Journal of Business Venturing*, 14 (3), 259–81.

Rennie, Michael W. (1993), "Global Competitiveness: Born Global," *The McKinsey Quarterly*, 4, 45–52.

Sengenberger, W., G. Loveman, and M. Piore (1990), *The Reemergence of Small Enterprises: Industrial Restructuring in Industrial Countries*. Geneva, Switzerland: International Institute for Labor Studies.

Stöttinger, Barbara and Bodo B. Schlegelmilch (1998), "Explaining Export Development Through Psychic Distance: Enlightening or Elusive?" *International Business Review*, 15 (5), 357–72.

Turnbull, Peter W. (1987), "A Challenge to the Stages Theory of the Internationalization Process," in *Managing Export Entry and Expansion*, Philip J. Rosson and Stan D. Reid, eds. New York: Praeger, 21–40.

Zou, Shaoming and S. Stan (1998), "The Determinants of Export Performance: A Review of the Empirical Literature Between 1987 and 1997," *International Marketing Review*, 15 (5), 333–56.

[14]

© *Academy of Management Journal*
2000, Vol 43, No 6, 1227–1247

HOW NEW VENTURES EXPLOIT TRADE-OFFS AMONG INTERNATIONAL RISK FACTORS: LESSONS FOR THE ACCELERATED INTERNATIONIZATION OF THE 21st CENTURY

RODNEY C. SHRADER
University of Illinois at Chicago

BENJAMIN M. OVIATT
Georgia State University

PATRICIA PHILLIPS McDOUGALL
Indiana University

The Organisation for Economic Co-operation and Development predicts that the internationalization of businesses will accelerate in the 21st century. Our study examined how the risks of accelerated internationalization may be managed in 212 foreign market entries by 87 new ventures based in the United States. Findings suggested that ventures managed strategic international risks by exploiting simultaneous trade-offs among foreign revenue exposure, country risk, and entry mode commitment in each country.

A recent study of small and medium-sized firms in 26 developed and developing countries makes the case that an era of accelerated firm internationalization has begun and will make its effects felt even more in the 21st century (Organisation for Economic Co-operation and Development [OECD], 1997). "Accelerated internationalization" refers to the phenomenon of firms engaging in international business activities earlier in their organizational life cycles than they have historically. According to the OECD study, more than a quarter of the world's small manufacturing firms already derive greater than 10 percent of their revenues from foreign sources, and at least one-third of them are predicted to do so by the year 2005. One to two percent of small manufacturing firms are estimated to be international at inception. Although that percentage may seem small now, it represents at least

30,000 to 40,000 firms worldwide. As the new millennium begins, the number of young firms experiencing rapid internationalization appears to be increasing, yet understanding of them is rudimentary.

Most international management theory focuses on large, established, multinational corporations (Oviatt & McDougall, 1994). Existing internationalization theory highlights slow and incremental foreign market commitment because such behavior has been frequently observed and because internationalization seems so risky for small firms and new ventures (Johanson & Vahlne, 1990). International business is considered inherently risky because it may involve loss of profits and/or assets as a result of changes in political, legal, economic, and social factors in foreign markets where firms compete (Cosset & Roy, 1991; Ghoshal, 1987; Roth, 1992). However, there is little theory about managing international risk for firms experiencing the accelerated internationalization that has become apparent in recent years. Since it is predicted that the phenomenon will be increasingly prevalent in the new millennium (OECD, 1997), theory development and testing would appear to be valuable for both academics and entrepreneurs.

Many issues surrounding accelerated internationalization are worthy of investigation, but the research question we focus on here is, How do firms already experiencing the risks of relatively small size and newness also successfully manage

This research was funded in part by the Ewing Marion Kauffman Foundation. The dissertation, "Influences on and Performance Implications of Internationalization by Publicly Owned U.S. New Ventures: A Risk Taking Perspective," completed at Georgia State University by Rodney C. Shrader, which is the foundation for this article, won the 1997 Heizer Award for the best dissertation in new venture creation. An early version of the article was presented at the 1997 Academy of Management meeting in Boston and won the 1997 Michael H. Mescon Award for the best empirical paper presented in the Entrepreneurship Division.

the additional strategic risks of entering foreign markets so early in their existence? Fortunately, Miller's (1992) discussion of integrated international risk management suggests a theoretical approach to answering that question. Miller argued that multiple international risks can be managed by trading off one risk against another to keep overall firm risk lower than it would be without such trade-offs. Three of the most important international risk factors discussed in the literature are (1) foreign location (Dunning, 1998), (2) type of commitment to that foreign location, as evidenced by the modes of entry chosen (Ghemawat, 1991; Root, 1987), and (3) the proportion of revenue exposure a firm has in that location (Miller, 1992). To test whether such trade-offs actually occur, we focused on a sample of successful U.S.-based new ventures that internationalized within a few years of founding.[1] Our empirical results showed that there was indeed significant evidence of trade-offs among those three types of strategic international risks.

Our findings are important because the dominant theories on the management of international risks emphasize other approaches. Established corporations are said to manage risks by coordinating resource flows among large, multinational networks of subsidiaries (Ghoshal, 1987; Kogut, 1989). Smaller firms that are new to the international arena are believed to manage the risks by cautious and slow-paced foreign entries (Johanson & Vahlne, 1990). Our research provides the first empirical demonstration that firms experiencing accelerated internationalization and lacking large networks of foreign subsidiaries may manage international risks by trading foreign location, entry mode commitment, and foreign revenue exposure off against each other in each country they enter. The work reported here responds directly to Miller's (1992) call for research that explicitly recognizes trade-offs among various international uncertainties. Furthermore, our observations are consistent with some managers' beliefs that firm risks can be influenced by managers' actions (Shapira, 1995) but are inconsistent with some scholars' claims that such beliefs, particularly among entrepreneurs, most of-

ten represent wishful thinking and self-deception (Busenitz & Barney, 1997; Shapira, 1995). We conclude that at least some leading-edge entrepreneurs appear able to manage the risks of the accelerated internationalization that may characterize business organizations in the 21st century, and they do so through a process of making simultaneous trade-offs among various international risks.

THEORY AND HYPOTHESES

Accelerated Internationalization

Toward the end of the 1980s, the popular business press noted that some businesses were internationalizing at a younger age and a smaller size than were usually expected (Gupta, 1989; Mamis, 1989). This media interest continued into the early 1990s (Brokaw, 1990; *Economist*, 1992, 1993) with speculations about a new trend. Additional evidence was provided by a McKinsey study of new ventures in Australia that uncovered surprisingly aggressive international activities (McKinsey & Co., 1993). The United Nations surveyed small transnational corporations around the world and found falling barriers to small firm internationalization and an increasing number of small firms that bypassed the traditional, incremental, pattern of internationalizing (United Nations Conference on Trade and Development [UNCTAD], 1993). Collectively, this evidence indicated that just prior to the late 1980s, a noticeable number of ventures began to sell outputs across national borders earlier in their existence than was typical of similar ventures in prior decades and earlier than was described in the most influential internationalization theories (Johanson & Vahlne, 1977, 1990).

Academics also began to notice that significant numbers of new ventures, especially in high-technology industries, were international (McDougall, 1989). Internationalization was said to provide such firms with an important opportunity for growth (Brush, 1992) that, due to their usual relative poverty of resources, often occurred through interorganizational alliances (Coviello & Munro, 1997). A theoretical framework for understanding their existence has appeared (Oviatt & McDougall, 1994). Yet the incongruence between received international business theory, according to which international evolution is slow, and the accelerated internationalization of new ventures has suggested the importance of further research (Knight & Cavusgil, 1996; McDougall, Shane, & Oviatt, 1994).

At the same time, some scholars believe that the rapid internationalization of new and small ventures is either an unimportant anomaly or a world-

---

[1] The research reported here involved no test for differences in performance; rather we asked whether certain hypothesized but previously untested international risk management actions existed among new ventures. Scholars who research new ventures have typically adopted either six years (e.g., Carter, Stearns, Reynolds, & Miller, 1994) or eight years (e.g., Biggadike, 1979) from founding as the cutoff point for classifying a firm as a new venture. We adopted the more conservative convention of six years.

wide expansion of the Japanese *keiretsu* model (Dunning, 1993; Johanson & Vahlne, 1990). In the latter model, small firms operate as thoroughly dependent suppliers to large, established, multinational corporations. Thus, internationalization of the small firm is driven completely by the larger firm, making the international role of small or new ventures much less interesting. Undoubtedly, such a model explains many situations, but not all.

Some published case summaries describe independent and successful new ventures that were international from inception (Jolly, Alahuhta, & Jeannet, 1992; Oviatt & McDougall, 1995). Empirical work on larger samples has shown that clear product differentiation and internationally experienced directors and managers are associated with the early internationalization of independent new ventures (Bloodgood, Sapienza, & Almeida, 1996; Reuber & Fischer, 1997). Among early-stage technology-based firms, the proportions of revenues derived from foreign sources are significantly dependent on managers' positive attitudes toward internationalization (Preece, Miles, & Baetz, 1999). And, in recent years, internationalization appears to have become a requirement for participation in some high-technology industries for even the smallest and newest firms (Burrill & Almassy, 1993).

Throughout this article, we make the assumption, which is supported by the evidence provided above, that accelerated internationalization is an established fact in many parts of the world. Nevertheless, as a new millennium during which accelerated internationalization will be increasingly encountered begins, a better understanding of it would appear to be important for both researchers and practitioners. As we noted earlier, a variety of questions about accelerated internationalization emerge, but our current interest is in explaining how firms experiencing it handle the considerable strategic risks of internationalization in addition to the risks of newness and relatively small size that they already face.

Risk Management in the International Arena

Scholars have debated whether the concept of internationalization has a single dimension or several separate dimensions (Ramaswamy, Kroeck, & Renforth, 1996; Sullivan, 1994, 1996). Miller (1992) showed that it is most accurate to view internationalization, and the risks inherent in managing it, as having multiple dimensions that are distinct but simultaneously determined. This is the view we adopt and apply here to the accelerating internationalization of new ventures. Indeed,

our research is one of the few published empirical applications of Miller's concept of integrated risk management in international business. This concept highlights the fact that trade-offs are required among the multiple dimensions of international risk.

Miller (1992) explained that when a firm enters a foreign country, the risks it faces may be managed by two broad kinds of firm actions: financial and strategic. Handling the former involves (1) the purchase of insurance to protect against property, casualty, and liability losses due to foreign operations and (2) the buying and selling of financial instruments, such as forward contracts, futures, swaps, and options, to lock in fixed prices and to protect against foreign exchange risk. However, such financial mechanisms require the existence of markets for insurance and for financial instruments, both of which fail when information is lacking and the probable effects of uncertainties are not estimable. Thus, as Miller emphasized, insurance and hedging mechanisms are never complete, and all firms engaged in international business must use strategic actions to manage some of their risks. Financial actions are well described in sources such as Smith, Smithson, and Wilford (1990). Thus, we focus on strategic actions for managing international risk.

Miller (1992) described five types of strategic actions that are possible responses to international risks. One is *imitation*. It is commonly observed that firms competing in the same industry enter the same countries (UNCTAD, 1997). Such actions are sometimes motivated by a desire to protect market share but may also be a reaction to uncertainty about the best course of action (DiMaggio & Powell, 1983). That is, copying the actions of another company whose behavior is judged appropriate grants legitimacy to the imitator. Whatever the motivation, such behavior tends to create oligopolistic competition among multinational corporations (Dunning, 1993). However, observations of new ventures suggest that, although imitation may occur, it is not a predominant way of handling the risks of accelerated internationalization (McDougall et al., 1994; Oviatt & McDougall, 1995). The "deep niche" strategies often used by new ventures in the international arena (Kohn, 1997), whereby firms deploy unusual products or services to focus on a narrow sliver of a market, mean that their forte is uniqueness, not imitative oligopolistic competition (Almeida & Kogut, 1997).

The other four types of strategic actions for managing international risks are avoidance, flexibility, cooperation, and control. All are important for accelerated internationalization among new ventures.

Risk *avoidance* occurs when the decision makers of a firm believe that operating in a particular geographic area is unacceptably uncertain. The firm may refuse to enter a country or exit a country it has already entered (Bonaccorsi, 1992). Such decisions, along with decisions to enter certain attractive countries, determine the foreign locations a firm enters.

In the international environment, the essence of the *flexibility* strategy is decreasing the cost of internal organizational adaptation to changing international circumstances. Flexibility in terms of design, manufacturing, workforce size, employee skills, and cost structure provides a firm with the capability of responding rapidly and effectively when prices, demand, or technological standards change (Miller, 1992). Flexibility of these types may be an important competitive advantage of new ventures over established firms in the international marketplace (UNCTAD, 1993), and the desire to have such flexibility may help determine which countries a new venture enters and which modes of entry are used. That is, countries and entry modes, such as foreign direct investment, that require greater commitment undoubtedly limit firm flexibility and increase the risk of losing revenues, profits, and assets. In the rapidly changing environment of the new millennium, flexibility of action will be a requirement for successful competition by firms experiencing accelerated internationalization (OECD, 1997).

With the strategic response of *cooperation*, ventures enter into agreements with other parties to reduce uncertainty in exchange for giving up unilateral control. Cooperative arrangements, such as alliances and joint ventures in foreign countries, are common means of reducing the risks of entering an unfamiliar country (Dunning, 1995). Some of the literature on international new ventures highlights alliances as a means of influencing or controlling vital resources without owning them, although a significant number of new ventures and small business do internationalize without the use of cooperative alliances (cf. Coviello & Munro, 1997; OECD, 1997; Oviatt & McDougall, 1994; Preece et al., 1999; UNCTAD, 1993). Ventures that do not use alliances may sense risk in losing unilateral control (Kim & Hwang, 1992). However, sometimes foreign entry through cooperative action is forced upon a firm by foreign laws mandating some arrangement such as a joint venture with a host country business. Whether forced, chosen, or avoided, the decision about cooperation directly affects the mode of entry employed by a firm. For example, the use of direct exporting or of direct investment in a foreign wholly-owned asset is obviously a decision not to use

cooperation as a means of managing foreign risks. Furthermore, firms may prefer certain modes of cooperation over others. For example, a firm interested in maintaining relatively tight control over its technology may choose to enter a foreign country through a joint venture rather than through a long-term sourcing agreement, both of which are cooperative modes of entry.

The final strategic method of international risk management identified by Miller (1992) is *control*. It involves direct attempts to influence the behavior of others, especially other firms. Miller (1992) highlighted a wide range of possibilities, including vertical and horizontal integration, moves designed to gain market share, and political action. New ventures tend not to vertically integrate, and their relatively weak organizational legitimacy and, often, smallness when compared to established multinational corporations and indigenous firms in foreign countries limit their ability to influence local politics. Nonetheless, other means of control are available, although their effects are a matter of debate.

Typically, experienced managers believe they can apply their skills to influence the amounts of risk to which their firms are exposed (March & Shapira, 1987). However, scholars of classical decision theory have asserted that such beliefs represent self-deception, wishful thinking, hubris, or some combination of these conditions. These scholars depict managers as often behaving illogically in the face of business risk (Shapira, 1995). Entrepreneurs who start new companies may be among the most likely business people to hold biases about risk, else few businesses would be started when the chances of failure are so high. Indeed, entrepreneurs have been shown to exhibit more overconfidence and more errors in judging risks than regular managers (Busenitz & Barney, 1997). At the same time, it must be recognized that experienced entrepreneurs can, in fact, significantly influence some aspects of risk. They can gather additional information about foreign markets when it is lacking. If they have uniquely desirable products, they may be able to press host country distribution channels and suppliers to adjust their operations to meet new customer demands. They can actively work to change customer behavior through advertising, thereby increasing revenues and gaining market share. In summary, even entrepreneurs of new ventures entering foreign countries are able to influence, if not control, international risks.

It is useful at this point to summarize, from the prior paragraphs, the primary implications of Miller's (1992) five strategic methods for managing the international risks of foreign market entry. Avoidance of certain high-risk countries and the need for flexibility of operations help influence which foreign locations are chosen for entry. The choice of entry mode is influenced by the flexibility needed and by a venture's openness to cooperation with other organizations. The percentage of a firm's total revenue derived from any single country may be influenced by its strategies of control. Thus, our empirical research on how new ventures manage international risks focused on: (1) the risks of the foreign location entered (Dunning, 1998), (2) the mode of entry, and therefore the degree of resource commitment, to that location (Ghemawat, 1991; Root, 1987), and (3) the proportion of firm revenue that is exposed to the risks of being derived from a specific foreign location (Miller, 1992). The frequency with which these three decisions are considered in the literature indicate that they are among the most important decisions a firm can make about foreign entry (Dunning, 1993). Each has important implications for international risk. The more a firm relies on a foreign market for revenues, the more it can be exposed to international risk there. Countries vary in characteristics that directly affect the risk of doing business. Entry modes vary in the complexity and commitment of resources they involve, and, therefore, in risk (Agarwal & Ramaswami, 1992; Hill, Hwang, & Kim, 1990; Kim & Hwang, 1992; Root, 1987). None of these factors is completely controlled by organizational decision makers, but each can be greatly influenced by them.

Trade-Offs in Managing the Risks of Accelerated Internationalization

Miller (1992) highlighted the fact that the risks of firm internationalization can be represented neither on a single dimension nor on multiple independent dimensions, but instead must be seen as multiple, interdependent concepts. His distinctive insight was the fact that the management of interdependent risks often involves trade-offs. Applying the idea to the present case, we view managers as exploiting trade-offs among the risks of the country entered, the mode of entry used, and the proportion of total firm revenue exposed to the risks of operating in that country. For example, firms entering high-risk countries may elect not to depend on them for a large proportion of revenue and may employ entry modes that require only minor commitments of resources, such as exporting. Thus, these relationships are very likely to be simultaneously and endogenously determined.

Despite the fact that the reasoning described above seems logical and is perhaps in use, we are aware of no previous empirical test following Mill-

er's (1992) theory of interdependent international risk trade-offs. The literature on multinational management currently emphasizes dependence on a large multicountry network of subsidiaries to manage international risks (Bartlett & Ghoshal, 1998; Ghoshal, 1987; Kogut, 1989) or dependence on a long-term and incremental commitment of resources to guide initial foreign entries, which are usually perceived as especially risky (Johanson & Vahlne, 1990). Thus, although Miller's theory of risk trade-offs may be applicable to foreign market entry by any firm, it seems especially relevant for young firms experiencing accelerated internationalization because few of the latter will have a large multicountry network available and because the incremental internationalization so universal until recent years will be irrelevant for an increasing number of firms in the 21st century.

Therefore, we hypothesize:

Hypothesis 1. For new ventures entering a specific foreign country, the degrees of foreign market revenue exposure, host country risk, and entry mode commitment are simultaneously determined.

Hypothesis 2. For new ventures entering a specific foreign country, the degrees of foreign market revenue exposure, host country risk, and entry mode commitment are traded off against each other. That is, when the level of one increases, the levels of one or both of the others decrease.

Number of Countries Entered

The previous section of this article described ways that new ventures can influence the overall amount of international risk to which they are exposed by exploiting trade-offs among various risk factors in *each* country they enter. However, it is important to note that some new ventures experiencing accelerated internationalization in the new millennium may also use geographic diversification in order to maintain flexibility and manage the overall level of international risk to which they are exposed (Miller, 1992). Shifting resources among various country subsidiaries in response to changes in relative prices and knowledge has been shown in theory (Ghoshal, 1987), in case studies (Bartlett & Ghoshal, 1998), and in large-sample empirical studies (Rangan, 1998) to be an important way of managing risk in large multinational corporations. Indeed, Kogut (1989) noted that the operational flexibility afforded by geographic diversification is the foundation for long-term competitive advantage in large multinational corporations. Our focus on managing the risks of accelerated internationalization, however, directed our attention to international entry among relatively young firms, which usually enter only a few countries (Preece et al., 1999; Tang & Tikoo, 1999).

Perhaps the breadth of a venture's foreign entry strategy, as represented by the number of countries it enters, influences the manner in which the international risk trade-offs are managed for each country. However, a priori, the decision about how many countries a firm enters is unlikely to be endogenously determined by the risks of each specific country entry. As far as we know, these relationships have not been formally explored. Still, some logic seems intuitive.

First, as a venture enters more countries, it seems likely that the proportion of its revenue exposure in any single country will decrease. In the extreme, this negative relationship is mathematically determined. Yet when only a portion of total revenues comes from foreign sources (as will be shown later to be true in our sample), entry into additional countries does not necessarily reduce the percentage of sales revenue from any single foreign country.

Second, the relationship between foreign country risk and the number of countries entered is less clear, but it seems likely to be positive. A venture may adopt a policy of not entering countries that exceed a certain risk level. Thus, the number of countries entered and foreign country risk would have no relationship. However, as the number of countries entered rises, the venture gains experience in handling foreign market risk and may be willing to enter countries with greater political and economic risks (Johanson & Vahlne, 1977, 1990). At some point, a traditional portfolio diversification effect occurs (Copeland & Weston, 1983). That is, assuming the risk of a poor outcome in each country is sufficiently independent from the comparable risk in other countries and the risk-return relationship is positive, then outcomes may be countercyclical, and overall nonsystematic risk (in the sense described in the capital asset pricing model) may be reduced. At some point, a multicountry network effect may also occur. As more countries are entered, new ventures begin to obtain the capabilities of established multinational corporations for transferring mobile resources among countries to manage risk (Ghoshal, 1987; Kogut, 1989). Of course, neither the portfolio diversification effect nor the multicountry network effect may emerge until the number of countries entered rises to some significant plateau, the level of which is an empirical question.

Third, the a priori relationship between the number of countries entered and entry mode commitment is more difficult to determine. The number of countries entered by a firm may have no systematic relationship with entry mode. Rather, the modes employed may be particular to the laws and social conditions of each country. Recent empirical evidence indicates that, for those reasons, even small firms are increasingly using a variety of entry modes simultaneously (OECD, 1997). Alternatively, as a new venture attempts to enter more countries, it is likely to use entry modes that conserve and put at risk fewer of its resources. Entry into several countries at a young age may be a sign that a new venture is mainly an exporter, able to enter many countries quickly with as little commitment of resources as possible. We believe that is the stronger logic, and that a negative relationship will exist between the number of countries entered and entry mode commitment.

Thus, we hypothesize:

Hypothesis 3. For new ventures, the degree of foreign market revenue exposure in a specific country will be negatively related to the number of countries entered.

Hypothesis 4. For new ventures, the degree of host country risk will be positively related to the number of countries entered.

Hypothesis 5. For new ventures, the degree of entry mode commitment will be negatively related to the number of countries entered.

Other Influences on New Venture Internationalization

Research has revealed many other influences on the degree of foreign market revenue exposure, the level of host country risk, and the level of entry mode commitment employed. Previous research and theory on risk, international business, and entrepreneurship made it clear that multiple levels of influence needed to be accounted for in this research. Thus, we identified top management teams, firm-level conditions and strategies, and industry conditions as potentially important influences that could impact the international risk trade-offs in ways beyond those already hypothesized (Baird & Thomas, 1985; McDougall et al., 1994; Miller, 1992). Because the influences discussed below have already been the subject of much research, they were not the focus of the research reported here and were therefore introduced as controls in an effort to eliminate alternative explanations for the hypothesized relationships discussed earlier.

Top management team. By definition, new ventures do not have much organizational experience. A new venture has mainly the experience of its

2000   *Shrader, Oviatt, and McDougall*   1233

management team and the skills its members bring with them to the new organization. It is believed that the prior experience of managers can compensate for lack of organizational experience (Cooper & Dunkelberg, 1986). Therefore, when managers possess prior experience that is particularly relevant to pursuing foreign markets, it may allow new ventures to accelerate their internationalization. Thus, higher levels of foreign revenue exposure early in a firm's life cycle, entry into higher-risk countries, and greater entry mode commitments are observed. The types of experiences most relevant for the accelerated internationalization of new ventures include *international experience, technical experience, marketing experience, and new venture experience. Top management team size* may also be important. A paragraph on each of these elements follows:

Prior work experience in international business is arguably the most beneficial type of experience for new venture managers seeking to manage international risks. Such experience provides managers with knowledge of foreign markets as well as knowledge of international business (Brush, 1992; Johanson & Vahlne, 1977, 1990; Knight & Cavusgil, 1996; McDougall et al., 1994). As a result, this experience can reduce the ambiguity and complexity of pursuing foreign markets. Thus, internationally experienced managers may be better equipped to deal with and more comfortable accepting international risks. Furthermore, managers with international experience may have international social networks that can compensate for an organization's lack of established networks (Coviello & Munro, 1997; Jolly et al., 1992; McDougall et al., 1994; Oviatt & McDougall, 1994, 1995) and thereby help a new venture overcome international risks.

According to stage theory and monopolistic advantage theory, firms develop and hone basic business skills in their domestic markets prior to entering foreign markets (Aharoni, 1966; Hymer, 1976; Johanson & Vahlne, 1977, 1990). Entrepreneurs struggling to develop basic business skills have less time and energy to focus on the management of international risks. This notion is supported by research indicating that lack of technical experience and lack of marketing experience are two of the greatest obstacles to internationalization by young and small firms (Brush, 1992; Jolly et al., 1992). Thus, ventures whose managers have significant technical and marketing experience are likely to be able to adapt existing skills to serve diverse and higher-risk markets much more readily than ventures struggling to develop those skills initially.

Prior experience with new ventures may also provide basic business skills and confidence that can lead new venture managers to more skillfully manage international risks. Perhaps more than any other type of experience, new venture experience can help compensate for the liabilities of newness. Experienced entrepreneurs are more efficient at decision making (Cooper, 1970), which may be particularly important when a complex international business problem requires a rapid response. That is, entrepreneurs with prior new venture experience may be able to dispense more quickly with start-up problems, permitting them to spend more time and energy focusing on the management of international risks.

Given the importance of management experience, it appears likely that larger management teams will have broader experience than smaller teams. In addition, larger teams are likely to be tied into more external networks, which are particularly important for young firms that internationalize (Coviello & Munro, 1997). Furthermore, increasing foreign market revenue exposure and increasingly complex entry modes require more people and greater specialization among top managers (OECD, 1997). For these reasons, we included management team size as a control variable.

Firm-level conditions and strategies. Firm strategies will also impact a firm's willingness to accept and manage international risks. Specific elements of strategy that are most relevant to the context of internationalization include *growth objectives, differentiation, strategic focus, low-cost emphasis, size, and age at international entry.* A paragraph on each of these elements follows:

Scholars of organizational risk taking argue that risk cannot be adequately understood apart from expected return. Organizations take greater risks when they have higher aspirations (Bromiley, 1991; Fiegenbaum & Thomas, 1986; Singh, 1986). Thus, higher performance objectives may lead a firm to assume greater international risk. For new ventures, performance objectives are most frequently stated in terms of sales growth (e.g., Cooper, Gimeno-Gascon, & Woo, 1994; Eisenhardt & Schoonhoven, 1990; Feeser & Willard, 1990).

According to monopolistic advantage theory, firms can overcome some international risks if they have a particular advantage that differentiates them from indigenous competitors. This is the ownership advantage in Dunning's (1993) eclectic theory. In addition, small firms have traditionally been advised to pursue differentiation as a means of competing against larger, established firms (Porter, 1985). Research indicates that young and small firms entering international markets differentiate themselves by relying on product innovation (Brush, 1992; Jolly et al., 1992; McDougall, 1989;

McDougall et al., 1994; Oviatt & McDougall, 1994, 1995), higher relative product quality (Kaynak, Ghuari, & Olofsson-Bredenlow, 1987), or increased emphasis on service (Quinn, 1992). In summary, the greater a firm's ability to differentiate itself from an indigenous foreign competitor, the more likely it is to derive strong sales from a foreign market.

The more firms focus on narrowly defined niches, the more likely it is that their domestic markets will be inadequate for their sales objectives, and the more likely they will be to enter foreign markets or to depend on them more (Bryan, Fraser, Oppenheim, & Rall, 1999). Case studies suggest that the ability to identify market niches that are multinational or global is critical for new ventures seeking to internationalize (Coviello & Munro, 1997; Jolly et al., 1992). Furthermore, if the target foreign markets are similar to their domestic markets, it is less complex (and less risky) to enter those foreign markets because market knowledge is transferable from one market to another (Hedlund & Kverneland, 1985).

Likewise, firms with limited product lines encounter less complexity when targeting foreign markets than firms attempting to introduce full product lines. Moreover, simple resource limitations may dictate that new ventures pursuing accelerated internationalization in multiple markets have more limited product offerings. Not surprisingly, case research indicates that new ventures enter foreign markets with extremely limited product lines (Jolly et al., 1992; Oviatt et al., 1994). Firms serving niche markets with limited product lines may be able to leverage their deep domestic market and product knowledge to serve similar niches in other countries with relatively little increased uncertainty.

According to theories of international business, cost concerns are central to internationalization decisions (e.g., Buckley & Casson, 1976; Vernon, 1966). Firms that compete on the basis of cost frequently enter foreign countries, even risky ones, to achieve economies of scale, to lower production costs, and to prolong product life cycles and thereby increase sales. Such a strategy may also lead to more committed operating modes that allow greater cost control. We believe these same arguments apply to new ventures competing on the basis of low cost.

The influence of firm size on internationalization has been the subject of much research in the international business literature and has been linked to propensity to export, the specific countries exported to, and entry mode (Agarwal & Ramaswamy, 1992). Larger firms often have greater resources with which to pursue more aggressive internationalization and the slack resources necessary to absorb the increased risks associated with internationalization.

Organizational learning is a foundation of the Uppsala theory of internationalization (Johanson & Vahlne, 1990, 1977). Although learning about foreign markets would of necessity be compressed among ventures experiencing accelerated internationalization, given the steep learning curves firms have in their early years, it was necessary to control for the age of each venture at the time it first internationalized. When compared to another venture of the same age, a venture that first internationalized at a younger age would be more likely than a venture that internationalized later to have high foreign market exposure, to enter riskier countries, and to use more complex entry modes, given accumulation of international experience within the organization.

Industry conditions. According to theories such as oligopolistic reaction theory (Knickerbocker, 1973) and product cycle theory (Vernon, 1966), industry conditions determine firms' international activities. Among oligopolies, firms increase foreign revenues, enter specific countries, or use particular operating modes in response to competitor moves (Knickerbocker, 1973). The nature of competition in some industries requires that most firms, even the smallest and youngest, engage in international business (Burill & Almassy, 1993). Case evidence has led researchers to conclude that industry conditions play a major role in the internationalization of new ventures (Coviello & Munro, 1997; Jolly et al., 1992; McDougall et al., 1994; Oviatt & McDougall, 1994, 1995). For new ventures, the industry conditions with the greatest influence include the *degree of global integration* (Jolly et al., 1992; Oviatt & McDougall, 1994, 1995), the *speed of technological change* (Coviello & Munro, 1997; Jolly et al., 1992; Oviatt & McDougall, 1994, 1995), *domestic competitive intensity* (Coviello & Munro, 1997; Oviatt & McDougall, 1994, 1995) and the *rate of industry growth* (OECD, 1997).

When many firms within an industry coordinate their activities and their competitive strategies across a variety of countries, the industry is said to be globally integrated (Kobrin, 1991). New ventures seeking to enter such industries find opportunities that are unavoidably international and global in nature (Jolly et al., 1992; Oviatt & McDougall, 1994, 1995).

In industries where technological change is rapid, short product cycles may naturally lead to increased internationalization (Vernon, 1966). New venture researchers have found that ventures in such industries will internationalize in order to recoup high R&D costs (Jolly et al., 1992; Oviatt & McDougall, 1994, 1995) or in order to take advantage of rapidly closing windows of opportunity (Ray, 1989). In knowledge-based, rapidly advancing, technologically intensive industries, firms may use more committed operating modes, such as those requiring equity investments in foreign countries, in order to reduce the risks of knowledge appropriation by predatory partners.

Some firms may enter foreign markets or depend on foreign markets more in order to escape domestic competition. For new ventures seeking growth within highly competitive industries, foreign markets may be their best option (Coviello & Munro, 1997).

International business theorists have long argued that industry growth influences firm internationalization (Hymer, 1976; Vernon, 1966). A frequent argument is that firms seek growth in international markets when growth in their home markets stagnates or declines (Dunning, 1993). In contrast, however, some scholars studying accelerated internationalization have argued that firms internationalize in order to aggressively take advantage of rapid industry growth (Ray, 1989). Given either case, it would be necessary to control for industry growth.

METHODS

Sample

To test the hypotheses, we collected data for firms that met the following five conditions: (1) they were new ventures—that is, they were six years old or younger, (2) they were founded between 1983 and 1988, (3) they had made initial public offerings (IPOs) of stock within six years of founding, (4) they were headquartered in the United States, and (5) they reported international sales in their sixth year after founding. Each of these criteria was important for reasons explained below.

We focused on new ventures because, when firms go international early (within six years of founding)—as they are predicted to do with greater frequency in the 21st century (OECD, 1997)—they represent the clearest examples of accelerated internationalization and the most obvious violation of the conventionally expected incremental move into foreign markets (Johanson & Vahlne, 1990). Six years old or younger is a conventional operational definition of new venture (Brush, 1992; Robinson & McDougall, 1998) because the first six years appear to be a crucial period in which survival is determined for the majority of companies (U.S. Small Business Administration, 1992).

The mid 1980s was a period of significant economic growth and, therefore, many new ventures were formed and available to study. The period also provided the earliest opportunity to gather a large sample of ventures experiencing accelerated internationalization. That is, the initial reports of accelerated internationalization came from just after that time (Brokaw, 1990; Gupta, 1989; Mamis, 1989). Some scholars have argued that the spread of advanced digital and communication technology was the principal enabler of this phenomenon (Oviatt & McDougall, 1999). An advantage of using that time period was that sampling over multiple years provided an adequate sample size and helped avoid potential biases introduced by sampling from only one year (McBain & Krause, 1989).

We made extensive use of detailed and consistent IPO prospectuses and other archival data. Much of that data guides investor decisions, and firms publish it in a standardized format with the understanding that significant penalties may be incurred for providing inaccurate information. Thus, many researchers consider these documents to be valid and reliable sources (Kunkel, 1991; McGee & Dowling, 1994; Robinson & McDougall, 1998). The use of such public sources also enabled us to include a cross section of industries in the sample.

Using data about new ventures near the time of their IPOs also offered the additional important benefit that we had a sample of successful firms. An IPO is an indicator that a venture has achieved at least sufficient success on all fronts to attract some number of investors. Importantly, successful firms are the ones most likely to exhibit the thoughtful and theoretically desirable international trade-offs that we hypothesized. Since no prior study that we are aware of has shown that these trade-offs actually occur, we believe that our focus on successful firms was appropriate. However, since our sampling method did restrict the range of firm performance to relatively successful new ventures, future researchers should investigate the degree to which trade-offs among international risks are associated with firm performance.

Using only U.S. firms ensured that the dimensions of internationalization were not subject to variations in national laws, regulations, and customs in several home countries. Although such differences may be valuable to understand, we believed these influences were best controlled in this initial test of the hypothesized relationships.

It was, of course, essential to identify specific ventures that had made foreign entries early in their existence. Although accelerated internationalization is becoming more prevalent, not all ventures internationalize quickly, and it was important to eliminate those firms that had not clearly internationalized. Of the 214 new ventures that met the first four conditions for inclusion in our sample, 127 ventures had to be eliminated because they had not reported international sales by their sixth year of operations. To identify individual firms for the sample, we compiled a comprehensive list of companies that went public within six years of founding from the *Investment Dealer's Digest*. Information from various volumes of *Moody's OTC Industrial Manual, Moody's Industrial Manual*, and *Moody's OTC Unlisted Manual* was later used to screen the sample. Investment funds, holding companies, firms incorporated more than six years prior to their IPOs, firms established for the sake of acquiring established firms, and firms headquartered outside the United States were excluded. We then telephoned the remaining companies to verify their founding dates, and those more than six years old at the time of their IPOs were deleted. Following this sampling procedure yielded 214 new ventures. International sales data from COMPUSTAT PC+ was then used to determine which firms had entered foreign markets.

The sampling technique outlined above resulted in a sample of 87 U.S. firms founded between 1983 and 1988, each of which had both made an IPO and entered foreign markets within its first six years of existence. Thus, about 41 percent of the most obviously successful new ventures in the United States were experiencing accelerated internationalization as early as the 1980s. They made 212 foreign market entries in countries throughout the world and used a variety of entry modes. Because our interest was in how firms manage the risks associated with entering specific foreign markets, the unit of analysis was the individual foreign market entry. Therefore, the effective sample size for analyses was 212.

Measures

Internationalization variables. Foreign sales data were collected for the sixth year of each individual firm's operation. That allowed us to capture a snapshot of the level of foreign market involvement each firm was able to achieve while still a new venture. Data on foreign sales, specific countries entered, and entry modes were collected from the firms' sixth-year annual reports. When a venture's annual report was not detailed enough, we interviewed its chief financial officer by phone to complete this information.

Foreign market revenue exposure was calculated as sales in a given foreign country ex-

pressed as a percentage of a firm's total sales. *Country risk* for each country was the average of risk ratings published in *Euromoney, Institutional Investor*, and the *Wall Street Journal* ($\alpha = .96$). These publications present annual ratings of countries based on composite measures of both political and economic risk. The entry modes used by the ventures in our research were exporting, licensing, foreign sales office, joint venture, and solely owned foreign production subsidiary (none of the firms in our sample used franchising). These entry modes vary on a variety of dimensions, such as profit potential, control over outcomes in the foreign location, and resource commitments required. For ventures, like the firms in our sample, that are small relative to most multinational corporations, it is the resource commitment required that generally governs the entry mode decision because of their disadvantage in terms of resources and organizational slack (Root, 1987). Generally, exporting requires the fewest resources and is, therefore, the mode often used for a firm's initial foreign entry. Licensing is somewhat riskier because a firm's special knowledge is being shared. A foreign sales office may entail yet greater commitment of resources and, therefore, greater risk, stemming from the purchase or lease of an office in a foreign location and hiring, training, and managing representatives in that location. The final two entry modes, joint venture and solely owned production subsidiary, are riskier because they require equity investments in some immobile resources. Because partners split the investment, joint ventures may risk fewer resources, depending, of course, on the relative sizes of the joint venture and the subsidiary. Several scholars have depicted the increasing level of resource risk in approximately the order just described (Agarwal & Ramaswami, 1991; Hill, Hwang, & Kim, 1990; Kim & Hwang, 1992; Root, 1987). Although it is a simplification, this sequence does permit a rank ordering of the international risk involved in entry modes (Kim & Hwang, 1992). Therefore, we used a five-level variable (exporting, licensing, sales office, joint venture, and solely owned production subsidiary) to indicate *entry mode commitment* risk in a given foreign market. In the order listed, each mode represents increased complexity, increased commitment of resources and, therefore, increased market and political risk (Baird & Thomas, 1985; Ghemawat, 1991; Hill, Hwang, & Kim, 1990; Root, 1987). The firm-level variable, *number of countries entered*, was a count of the number of foreign markets in which each firm operated in its sixth year.

Control variables. Data about the top management teams were collected from the firms' IPO prospectuses. The top management team was defined as the group of managers described in a prospectus as composing a firm's management team. Given the public nature of this disclosure, we felt that this list would include the managers with the most power to influence strategic decision making. *International, technical,* and *marketing experience* were calculated as the average number of years of work experience each top management team had in each area, as reported by the prospectus. *New venture experience* was calculated as the average number of prior new ventures started by the top managers, as reported by the prospectus. *Top management team size* was measured by counting the number of managers described in each prospectus as comprising the firm's management team.[2]

Following precedents within the entrepreneurship literature (e.g., Kunkel, 1991; McGee & Dowling, 1994), we based measures of individual strategy elements on a content analysis of IPO prospectuses. Because content analysis depends on the subjective evaluation of researchers, we took four steps to help establish the validity and reliability of the strategy data. First, all measures were theoretically derived and were based on precedents within the literature. Second, a detailed coding sheet was used to ensure consistent data were collected from each prospectus. Third, a pilot study with multiple raters was used to fine-tune the coding sheets and to train the raters. Fourth, two raters independently coded all strategy data, and inter-rater reliabilities were evaluated using Cronbach's alpha. Details on how each variable was measured are discussed below.

Innovation was measured on a three-point scale signifying whether the firms marketed proven products, products representing modest improvements over existing products, or radically new products ($\alpha = .78$). Using a five-point Likert scale, raters were instructed to indicate the degree to which they agreed that a firm emphasized *growth, quality, service,* and *low cost* ($\alpha = .81, .81, .79,$ and

.90, respectively). A dichotomous variable indicated whether or not a firm targeted only one market segment ($\alpha = .73$). *Product line breadth* was measured using a scale with four levels to indicate whether the firm's offerings could best be described as a single product, a limited product line, an intermediate product line, or a full product line ($\alpha = .84$).

Overall firm sales was each firm's total sales in its sixth year of operation. Data were collected from COMPUSTAT PC+. We measured *firm age at international entry* by subtracting the year a firm was founded from the year it made its first entry into a foreign market. The date of each firm's founding and first foreign market entry were gathered from annual reports and IPO prospectuses.

Identifications of the industries in which firms participated were based on the primary Standard Industrial Classification (SIC) codes reported by COMPUSTAT PC+. All but two of the firms reported sales in only one SIC code, and those two ventures reported at least 75 percent of their sales in their primary SIC codes. We measured *global integration* as the ratio of intrafirm cross-border trade to total international trade within each industry (Kobrin, 1991). Data were obtained from the *U.S. Direct Investment Abroad: 1989 Benchmark Survey Data* (U.S. Bureau of Economic Analysis, 1989). We measured *technological change* by counting the average number of patents issued in each SIC code during the first five years of the venture's existence, using data from *Patenting Trends in the United States: 1963–1994* (U.S. Patent Office, 1995). We calculated *competitive intensity* by first listing the eight firms holding the largest market shares in a venture's SIC during each of the first five years of the venture's existence. Then the number of different firms appearing in those lists was added, and that sum was multiplied by the average market share change that occurred among the firms that remained on the lists during the entire five years. The variable combined a measure of the swings in market share change with a measure of change in the set of dominant firms in the industry (see Sharfman & Dean, 1991). Market share data were gathered from various volumes of *Ward's Directory of U.S. Private and Public Firms. Industry growth* was calculated with aggregated sales data for all the publicly owned firms in each venture's four-digit SIC code during the first five years of the venture's existence. Aggregate sales data were collected from COMPUSTAT PC+.

---

[2] The control variables described in this section were included for theoretical reasons. However, since data were collected over a range of years, we also conducted analyses using control variables indicating the founding date of each firm, the year of its IPO, the year it internationalized, whether the firm went public before or after the 1987 stock market crash, and its age at IPO. None of these variables had any impact on the results shown in the tables and are, therefore, not presented.

Analyses

To test the study's hypotheses, we used three-stage least squares (3SLS) regression analysis to simultaneously estimate a system of three equations containing foreign market revenue exposure, country risk, and entry mode commitment as endogenous variables. This procedure was appropriate given that Hypothesis 1 states that decisions about each of the endogenous variables are made simultaneously and that managers trade levels of one risk dimension against levels of the others (Johnston, 1972). Prior to using 3SLS regression, we used three separate ordinary least squares (OLS) regressions to help determine which exogenous variables should be omitted for mathematical purposes in the 3SLS analysis.[3] In addition, OLS regression provided useful information regarding the variance explained by each separate equation.

RESULTS

We begin with a general description of the international new ventures in our sample. On average, they had 334 employees and $66 million in revenue by their sixth year. The majority (61) had their IPO in their fifth or sixth year after founding. They were headquartered in 20 states of the United States. California was home to 37 of the 87 ventures (42.5%). With 11 ventures (12.6%), Massachusetts had the next largest group. Four additional states, Florida, Minnesota, New Jersey, and Texas, were each home to at least 3 international new ventures in the sample.

As might be expected from their geographic distribution, our sample was overwhelmingly composed of high-technology firms, as Table 1 reveals. According to the National Science Foundation's classification of industries, 88.5 percent of our international new ventures competed in high-technology arenas. Computer and communications equipment and related products dominated the list.

Tables 2 and 3 demonstrate the ventures were, in fact, experiencing accelerated internationalization.

---

[3] Each simultaneously estimated equation must be mathematically identified. The number of exogenous variables excluded from each equation must be at least as great as the number of endogenous variables in the model, less one (Johnston, 1972). Thus, for mathematical purposes it was necessary in this analysis to omit two exogenous variables from each equation. Because there was no strong theoretical reason to omit any variables, those that were deleted were the least significant exogenous variables and were therefore the least important empirically in the OLS regressions.

TABLE 1
Sample of International New Ventures by Industry[a]

High-technology industries	
Pharmaceutical preparations	4
Industrial machinery	2
Computers & peripherals	22
Communications equipment	9
Electronic components	11
Measurement devices	3
Medical instruments	9
Photocopy equipment	2
Computer software	8
Computer & data processing services	3
Health care	1
Research & testing services	3
Subtotal	77
Low-technology industries	
Oil & gas extraction	1
Construction	1
Food & kindred products	1
Electrical supplies	2
Transportation equipment	1
Sporting goods	2
Wholesale trade	1
Motion pictures/entertainment	1
Subtotal	10
Total	87

[a] Industries were classified according to the U.S. National Science Foundation system.

On average, these young firms derived one-third of their revenues from foreign sources by their sixth year of existence, and 16 ventures (18.4%) derived more than half their revenues from outside the United States. Nearly 29 percent of the ventures entered four countries. Moreover, they were not just exporting; 60 percent of the foreign entries employed licensing, establishment of a sales office, formation of a joint venture, or full ownership of a foreign production subsidiary. The complete lack of franchising and the relatively few cases of licensing (7.1 percent of all entries) and joint ventures (4.7 percent) in our sample suggest that these ventures possessed sufficient ownership advantages, in the sense of the eclectic theory (Dunning, 1993), to usually enable them to conduct foreign operations without partners, perhaps to protect their technologies from appropriation. As expected, low-risk developed countries were more frequently entered. Japan and Germany topped the list of countries entered, perhaps reflecting the prevalence of high-tech firms in the sample. In summary, it was a sample of young and largely technology-based firms experiencing accelerated, rather than incremental, internationalization during the mid 1980s.

Table 4 presents descriptive statistics for the

TABLE 2
Patterns of Internationalization in the Sample

Variable	Number of Ventures
International sales as a percentage of total sales	
Less than 5%	4
5–10	5
11–20	23
21–30	15
31–40	17
41–50	7
51–60	1
61–70	6
71–80	3
81–90	2
91–100	4
Mean	.33
s.d.	.24
Number of countries entered[a]	
1	27
2	20
3	15
4	25
Total entries	212

[a] Six new ventures entered more than 4 foreign countries, with three entering more than 50. However, nearly all (85 percent or more in every case) the sales of the six firms were concentrated in 4 or fewer countries. Sales to other nearby and similar markets appeared to be idiosyncratic and relatively unimportant in terms of dollar values. Therefore, to simplify data handling, we used the locations of foreign sales offices for these six firms as proxies for the countries entered. All analyses reported here were also conducted excluding these six ventures, and results were unchanged.

variables used in this study. Our average sampled venture made its first foreign entry only 4.1 years after founding, further confirming that our sample was indeed experiencing accelerated internationalization. The means indicated that the top management teams of the ventures in our sample were of moderate size (6.1 people, on average), had little international business experience (0.64 years, on average, for each team member), little experience starting previous ventures (0.85 prior ventures, on average, for each team member), moderate technical experience (2.90 years, on average, for each team member), and moderate marketing experience (2.03 years, on average, for each team member). The ventures emphasized growth (the mean rating was 4.09 out of a possible 5.0), innovation (2.09 out of 3.0), and quality (4.18 out of 5.0). On the average, they had entered nearly 3 (2.91) foreign countries by their sixth year after founding and depended on each country entered for 14 percent of their revenues. Neither the pattern of correlations nor the collinearity diagnostics indicated any problems with multicollinearity.

Table 5 shows the results for the OLS regression analyses. When examined independently, the three equations were all significant in explaining foreign market revenue exposure ($p < .001$), country risk ($p < .01$), and entry mode commitment ($p < .001$), and they explained from 9 to 30 percent of the variance in the dependent variables (adjusted R^2s were .30, .09, and .13, respectively).[4]

Hypothesis Tests

Table 6 presents the 3SLS regression results, which were employed to test the study's hypotheses. Most were supported.

Hypothesis 1: Simultaneously determined internationalization dimensions. The weighted system R^2 (squared multiple correlation coefficient) for the simultaneous solution (.38) was higher than any R^2 or adjusted R^2 for the three separate OLS solutions, indicating that the simultaneous solution provided a better fit to the data than the OLS solution. Furthermore, most of the variables that were significant in the individual OLS equations had a higher level of significance in the 3SLS solution, further indicating that the simultaneous solution was a better fit for the data. Thus, Hypothesis 1, which states that foreign market revenue exposure in a specific country, host country risk, and entry mode commitment are simultaneously determined, was supported.

Hypothesis 2: Trade-offs among international risks. The results reported in Table 6 also provide support for Hypothesis 2, which states that venture entrepreneurs will exploit the possibilities for trade-offs among foreign market revenue exposure, country risk, and entry mode commitment. There was a highly significant negative relationship between country risk and both foreign market revenue exposure and entry mode in each equation ($p < .001$ in all cases). Thus, ventures experiencing accelerated internationalization that entered higher-

---

[4] In addition to finding the OLS results reported in Table 4, we tested OLS models for each dependent variable using only the control variables and then examined whether a significant amount of additional variance was explained when international variables were included. Results indicated that models predicting foreign revenue exposure and entry mode using only the control variables were significant ($F = 3.25$, $p < .001$, and $F = 2.41$, $p < .001$, respectively). The model predicting country risk was not significant. However, introducing the international variables (as reported in Table 4) significantly improved the explanatory power of each equation ($F = 13.79$, $p < .001$, $F = 4.74$, $p < .01$, and $F = 27.74$, $p < .001$, respectively).

TABLE 3
Entry Mode Frequency

Host Country[a]	Exports	Licensing	Sales Office	Joint Venture	Production Subsidiary	Total
Japan	23	4	9	4	3	43
Germany	18	3	12	1	7	41
Netherlands	1	1	3		1	6
Canada	6	3	11	1	5	26
United Kingdom	5		13	1	11	30
France	4		5		4	13
Belgium		1	2		1	4
Singapore	2		2	1	1	6
Taiwan	2	1	1			4
Sweden					1	1
Italy	2		3	1		6
Spain	2					2
Australia	6	1	1		1	9
Hong Kong	1					1
Korea			1			1
Malaysia					2	2
United Arab Emirates	1					1
Czech Republic	1					1
Israel	2				1	3
Mexico	3					3
Russia	2					2
Colombia				1		1
Brazil	4					4
Philippines					1	1
Poland		1				1
Totals	85	15	63	10	39	212

[a] Host countries are arranged with the lowest-risk countries at the top of the table and the highest-risk countries at the bottom. Risk ratings were the average of risk ratings published in *Euromoney, Institutional Investor,* and the *Wall Street Journal.*

risk countries relied on those countries for lower percentages of their total sales and chose less committed entry modes. Conversely, firms with high foreign revenue exposure in a specific country or using high entry mode commitment entered less risky countries.

Foreign market revenue exposure and entry mode were moderately positively related ($p < .1$). As with more established multinational corporations, one would expect a positive relationship because a firm's most important foreign markets are often served with more committed entry modes (Dunning, 1993).

Hypotheses 3, 4, and 5: Number of countries entered. Table 6 also shows that the number of foreign markets entered by a firm is significantly and negatively related to both foreign market revenue exposure and entry mode commitment. Thus, both Hypotheses 3 and 5 were supported. However, support for Hypothesis 4 was not found. Instead, results indicated that the number of countries entered by these ventures was not significantly related to the level of host country risk. A positive relationship had been hypothesized, but it depended upon enough countries being entered to

create a portfolio diversification effect or a capability for transferring assets among a network of country subsidiaries. Perhaps our sample of new ventures experiencing accelerated internationalization had not entered enough countries for either effect to be significant.

Control Variables

The large number of significant control variables in the simultaneous solution presented in Table 6 indicate how important it was to employ the array of controls that we did for top management teams, firm strategy, firm size, firm age at international entry, and industry conditions. Although technical experience was not significant in any of the equations, all other types of top management experience (international, marketing, and prior new venture) were positively associated with riskier and more committed international operations. Such a combination of experience undoubtedly gives managers the skills and confidence to accelerate the internationalization of their firms. Management team size was positively related to entry mode commitment, which is consistent with the findings of others that

TABLE 4
Means, Standard Deviations, and Correlations[a]

Variable	Mean	s.d.	1	2	3	4	5	6	7	8	9	10	11	12	13	14	15	16	17	18	19	20	21
1. International experience	0.64	1.60																					
2. Technical experience	2.90	2.40	.24																				
3. Marketing experience	2.03	1.86	.48	.35																			
4. New venture experience	0.85	1.03	-.04	.14	.17																		
5. Top management team size	6.14	4.20	.31	.58	.56	.21																	
6. Growth	4.09	0.87	-.06	.27	.23	.09	.12																
7. Innovation	2.09	0.54	.16	.35	-.14	-.05	.23	.55															
8. Quality	4.18	0.92	.33	.14	.25	.05	.21	.24	.17														
9. Service	3.37	1.32	-.08	-.04	.39	.06	.29	.19	-.02	.29													
10. Niche marketing	0.57	0.50	.14	-.01	.00	-.06	-.01	-.07	-.10	.05	.08												
11. Product line breadth	2.01	0.88	-.06	-.00	.01	-.02	.04	.07	-.04	-.11	.11	-.16											
12. Low cost	3.07	1.19	-.03	-.02	.02	.11	.00	-.28	-.25	-.05	-.12	-.03	-.09										
13. Overall sales	66M	47M	-.04	-.07	.22	.31	.23	.12	-.04	.07	.08	-.06	.12	.27									
14. Age at international entry	4.10	1.60	.03	.12	.15	-.09	.24	.22	.11	.05	.26	-.04	.00	-.14	-.17								
15. Global integration	0.34	0.10	.28	.44	.28	.07	.24	.40	.50	.28	.06	-.16	-.02	-.09	.08	.05							
16. Technical change	4,560.00	3,720.00	.21	.21	.24	.04	.09	.23	.25	.29	.15	.01	-.01	.07	.01	.08	.48						
17. Competitive intensity	0.70	1.69	-.04	-.17	.01	.03	-.05	-.12	-.18	-.14	-.02	.01	.01	.01	-.04	.00	-.15	.11					
18. Industry growth	0.04	0.11	-.07	.25	-.11	.03	.00	.04	.07	-.21	-.24	.08	.00	-.07	.01	.04	.09	-.18	-.08				
19. Number of countries entered	2.91	1.19	.16	.07	.20	.05	.20	.09	-.00	.33	.41	.08	-.03	-.05	.20	.02	.19	.13	-.19	-.13			
20. Foreign revenue exposure	0.14	0.17	-.01	.04	.17	.09	-.10	-.01	.09	.16	-.19	.13	-.20	.14	-.03	-.08	-.08	-.11	.07	.13	-.38		
21. Country risk	15.62	11.44	.02	.04	.05	.15	-.04	-.07	-.13	.01	.01	.11	-.01	.12	.03	-.19	-.14	.01	.01	-.14	.10	-.13	
22. Entry mode commitment	2.54	1.50	.16	.09	.21	.14	.28	.10	.01	.01	.15	-.08	.08	.01	.17	.06	.04	-.09	-.05	-.00	-.05	.03	-.10

[a] Correlations with absolute values greater than .13 were significant at $p < .05$. M = millions of dollars. SAS collinearity diagnostics indicated no multicollinearity (all tolerances > .54)

TABLE 5
Ordinary Least Squares Regression Results[a]

Independent Variables	Foreign Revenue Exposure	Country Risk	Entry Mode Commitment
Intercept	.01	.10	.11
Controls for top management team			
International experience	25***	.14	.36**
Technical experience	.03	.03	−.06
Marketing experience	.34**	.17	.21
New venture experience	.15*	.19**	.11
Management team size	.10	.08	.23[†]
Controls for firm and strategy			
Growth objective	.17*	.10	.16[†]
Innovation	.09	−.03	−.03
Quality	−.17**	−.08	−.10
Service	.16*	.09	.27**
Niche marketing	.16**	.08	−.01
Product line breadth	−.25***	−.07	− 06
Low cost	.32***	.25**	.10[†]
Overall firm sales	−.03	.08	.15
Firm age at international entry	−.05	−.18*	.03
Controls for industry conditions			
Global integration	.01	−.18*	.02
Technical change	−.09	−.01	−.12
Competitive intensity	−.08	−.02	−.18*
Industry growth	.07	.04	−.14
International variables			
Number of countries entered	−.39***	.02	−.31**
Foreign revenue exposure		−.24**	.07
Country risk	−.19**		−.18*
Entry mode commitment	.04	−.11	
F	5.31***	2.02**	2.56***
R^2	.37	.18	.25
Adjusted R^2	.30	.09	.13

[a] Coefficients are standardized.
[†] $p < .10$
* $p < .05$
** $p < .01$
*** $p < .001$

TABLE 6
Three-Stage Least Squares Regression Results

Independent Variables	Foreign Revenue Exposure	Country Risk	Entry Mode Commitment
Intercept	.01	10	.13
Controls for top management team			
International experience	.26***	.19*	.35***
Technical experience	.04	−.03	−.09
Marketing experience	.36***	.25*	.30**
New venture experience	.19**	.25**	.12
Management team size	12	.14	.34**
Controls for firm and strategy			
Growth objective	.24**	.18*	.24*
Innovation	.09	−.15[†]	
Quality	−.24**	−.16[†]	−.23*
Service	.20**	.15[†]	.31***
Niche marketing	.18*	10[†]	
Product line breadth	−.26***	−.12[†]	−.11
Low cost	35***	.30***	.12[†]
Overall firm sales		.05	.11
Firm age at international entry	−.07	−.19*	− 11
Controls for industry conditions			
Global integration		−.24*	−.02
Technical change	−.08[†]		−.17*
Competitive intensity	−.17		−.34*
Industry growth	.07	.05	−.15*
International variables			
Number of countries entered	−.43***	−.09	−.28***
Foreign revenue exposure		−.45***	.15[†]
Country risk	−.35***		−.22***
Entry mode commitment	.12	−.22***	
Weighted system R^2		.38	

[a] Coefficients are standardized. Two exogenous variables were excluded from each equation to meet the conditions for identity. The least significant variables in each OLS solution were selected for exclusion.
[†] $p < .10$
* $p < .05$
** $p < .01$
*** $p < 001$

the increasing complexity of entry modes requires more people and greater specialization among top managers (OECD, 1997).

Table 6 shows that firm strategies were especially important influences on the degree of foreign market revenue exposure. Innovative ventures with high growth objectives serving niche markets with focused, low-cost, product lines and supportive service derived more of their revenues from foreign markets and entered riskier countries. Such firms obviously have ownership advantages that permit successful accelerated internationalization (Dunning, 1993). Having high growth objectives along with a need to provide strong service at a low cost encourages more committed foreign entry modes, such as joint venture and wholly owned subsidiary. Contrary to expectations, emphasis on quality was

negatively related to all three internationalization variables. It would appear that firms emphasizing quality as a competitive weapon were more likely to emphasize production and sales within the United States and other more sophisticated (and less risky) markets. As might be expected, the younger firms were when they made their first foreign entry, the more often they entered less risky, more developed countries. Firm size (total sales) was not related to any of the international variables.

Table 6 also shows that global integration in an industry, rapid technical change, strongly competitive industry conditions, and industry growth were associated with lower foreign market risks in our sample. Perhaps our finding that ventures in globally integrated industries operate in lower-risk countries simply reflects the fact that the global integration of trade occurs primarily among developed countries. High-risk countries participate less in advanced globally integrated industries. Our new ventures in industries experiencing the most intense competition and the most rapid technological change depended less on foreign markets and used less-committed entry modes. Most (88%) of the firms in our sample were in high-technology industries. Perhaps, in the presence of extremely competitive technological change, U.S. ventures focus on the U.S. market rather than risk some loss of control in foreign markets.

DISCUSSION

Drawing data from a broad sample of successful United States–based new ventures, this study showed that 41 percent were experiencing accelerated internationalization as early as the 1980s. That is, the 87 international new ventures in our sample sold outputs in foreign markets within six years of their founding, a period during which many firms have yet to fully establish themselves domestically (U.S. Small Business Administration, 1992). Our percentage of international firms is consistent with McDougall's (1989) finding, drawn from a different sampling frame, that in certain high-technology industries 52 percent of new ventures were experiencing accelerated internationalization.

Overview

To our knowledge, this study provides the first empirical demonstration of how the risks of internationalization may be managed by such emerging new ventures. The results provide some interesting new insights. First, in established multinational corporations, flexibility that enables moving knowledge and assets among a diversified set of countries has been highlighted as an advantage and a way of managing risk (Bartlett & Ghoshal, 1998; Ghoshal, 1987; Kogut, 1989). In contrast, our study has shown that new ventures experiencing accelerated internationalization in a single foreign country can manage risks by simultaneously determining trade-offs among three risk factors: the economic and political riskiness of the country entered, the degree of commitment to the foreign location (indicated by the entry mode employed), and the percentage of foreign revenue exposure in that country. Analyzing our data as a simultaneous partially endogenous system was shown to yield the best-fitting model. Thus, selling outputs in a risky country was accompanied by employing an operating mode that committed fewer resources and

depending on that country for a relatively small proportion of total revenues. Apparently making further efforts to conserve precious resources and manage risk, U.S. venture entrepreneurs who decided to enter a number of countries maintained lower dependence on any single foreign country for sales and used entry modes that committed few resources. This demonstration that international risks can be successfully managed on a smaller (that is, less than global or regional) scale is important for new venture entrepreneurs to know about because they normally do not have the resources to gain advantage through vast geographic diversification.

Another important insight has to do with management theory. Many decision theory scholars remain puzzled about why managers seem to take unreasonable risks (Shapira, 1995). Yet many managers believe they have more influence on organizational outcomes than scholars give them credit for (March & Shapira, 1987). A new venture, constrained by relatively small size and lacking the legitimacy of an established organization, would be seen by many as taking excessive risks if it internationalized early in its existence. Furthermore, scholars have shown that entrepreneurs who start businesses are among the kinds of managers most likely to make errors in judging risk (Busenitz & Barney, 1997). Thus, our empirical demonstration that some complex international risks can, in fact, be managed by entrepreneurial managers may be enlightening for both entrepreneurship scholars and decision theorists. Although there is no doubt that some managers take unwarranted risks, perhaps some scholarly attention might shift toward seeking a further understanding of how managers successfully manage organizational risk after decisions are made.

Insights about internationalization theory also emerge from our results. Johanson and Vahlne (1977, 1990) formulated the best-established theory of the internationalization process, the Uppsala theory, to explain the incremental internationalization that was prevalent prior to 1980. The study reported here shows that by the mid-1980s, many new ventures were aggressively and successfully internationalizing early in their existence, prior to thoroughly establishing themselves domestically. Incremental internationalization is still widespread, but a theory of accelerated internationalization is needed for the 21st century.

The results reported here suggest that such a theory may adapt some parts of the Uppsala theory, according to which tacit foreign market knowledge derived from experience encourages firms to increase foreign market commitments (Johanson & Vahlne, 1977). Although the theory is unclear about whose experience is important, it clearly states that tacit foreign market knowledge will be embedded in an organizational decision-making system that is influenced by the inertia of organizational routines and by political maneuvering. In new ventures, nascent systems, fewer routines, and less politics should make the experience most important to decision making the entrepreneurial team's personal experience (Oviatt & McDougall, 1997). In the current research, we showed that the team's international, marketing, and prior new venture experience significantly influenced degree of foreign market revenue exposure and commitment. Thus, for a theory of accelerated internationalization, the locus of relevant foreign market knowledge may be more the entrepreneur or entrepreneurial team than the organizational decision-making system.

Anderson (1993) noted that the Uppsala theory does not actually explain how foreign market knowledge is translated into foreign market commitments. Among new ventures experiencing accelerated internationalization, perhaps it is an entrepreneur's personal knowledge of foreign markets that enables the successful management of risk trade-offs in each country entered. Our research has shown that such trade-offs exist and that those trade-offs may be an important dimension of a theory of accelerated internationalization.

Small firms tend to internationalize by combining advanced technologies with deep-niche strategies to gain advantages sufficient to overcome the costs of doing business abroad (Kohn, 1997). That description also applies to our new ventures, because 88 percent of them competed in high-technology industries. In addition, aggressive growth objectives and highly focused business strategies were associated with a larger percentage of foreign revenues and greater foreign commitments. These findings suggest that possession of advanced technology and its rapid application in technological spaces not occupied by established firms (Almeida & Kogut, 1997) may be vital for new ventures entering the international arena. In summary, our research indicates that international entrepreneurial experience, trade-offs among strategic international risk factors, and a foundation in advanced technology may be important elements in a theory of accelerated internationalization.

Limitations and Suggestions for Future Research

The empirical research report here, like all other such research, has limitations. A sample of public new ventures was appropriate for this study, but such firms are clearly a distinct group of unusually high-potential firms with greater resources than the average new venture. Therefore, although it was interesting to find international risk trade-offs in our sample, it remains to be seen whether such trade-offs more generally occur among new ventures in less favorable circumstances. In fact, the possibility remains that some, perhaps many, firms perform poorly despite employing the theoretically desirable international risk trade-offs demonstrated by this research. Thus, it is appropriate for future research to explore the relationship between Miller's (1992) theory and firm performance in a sample where the range of performance is less restricted.

Another special characteristic of our sample was the predominance of high-technology firms. To explore the generalizability of our findings, it would be valuable to test whether international risk trade-offs are present in other types of industries.

Perhaps the economic and political situation in some countries is so risky that trade-offs among international uncertainties are ineffective at influencing overall venture risk. In other words, there may be boundary conditions restricting what trade-offs are effective. Research to explore such boundary conditions would be appropriate.

New ventures typically have relatively simple structures, simple strategies, limited product diversification, and limited geographic diversification when compared with larger, established, multinational corporations. Such characteristics probably made it easier to observe the relationships we hypothesized. Yet it should be recognized that Miller's (1992) concepts may also be in use among established multinational corporations. Although their greater complexity will make the hypotheses more difficult to test with such firms, in future research the foreign market entries and risk management techniques of large, established multinationals should be investigated country-by-country. In addition, because this study focused only on U.S. firms, we do not know whether similar results would be found for firms headquartered in other countries. In summary, additional research is warranted to assess the generalizability of our findings.

Most of this study focused on entry into foreign countries. Future study should also include consideration of exits (Bonaccorsi, 1992). Exiting a country may be a powerful method of influencing international risk. In addition, studies that seek an understanding of the relationship between foreign inputs and outputs may help provide a more comprehensive understanding of how international risks are managed.

Finally, given the nature of this study, the arm's-length approach to data collection was appropriate.

The data were collected from secondary sources. Although this approach has definite advantages, including availability of reliable data, elimination of nonresponse bias, and reduction of single-source bias, it inherently reduces the richness of data. In the future, research should employ survey and case study methodologies to further refine the findings presented here.

REFERENCES

Agarwal, S., & Ramaswami, S. 1992. Choice of foreign market entry mode: Impact of ownership, location and internalization factors. *Journal of International Business Studies*, 23: 1–27.

Aharoni, Y. 1966. *The foreign investment decision process*. Boston: Harvard University, Division of Research, Graduate School of Business Administration.

Almeida, P., & Kogut, B. 1997. The exploration of technological diversity and the geographic location of innovation. *Small Business Economics*, 9(1): 21–31.

Andersen, O. 1993. On the internationalization process of firms: A critical analysis. *Journal of International Business Studies*, 24: 209–231.

Baird, I. S., & Thomas, H. 1985. Toward a contingency model of strategic risk taking. *Academy of Management Review*, 10: 230–243.

Bartlett, C. A., & Ghoshal, S. 1998. *Managing across borders: The transnational solution* (2nd ed.) Boston: Harvard Business School Press.

Biggadike, E. R. 1979. *Corporate diversification: Entry, strategy, and performance*. Cambridge, MA: Harvard University Press.

Bloodgood, J. M., Sapienza, H. J., & Almeida, J. G. 1996. The internationalization of new high-potential U.S. new ventures: Antecedents and outcomes. *Entrepreneurship Theory and Practice*, 20: 61–76.

Bonaccorsi, A. 1992. On the relationship between firm size and export intensity. *Journal of International Business Studies*, 23: 605–635.

Brokaw, L. 1990. Foreign affairs. *Inc.*, November: 92–104.

Bromiley, P. 1991. Testing a causal model of corporate risk taking and performance. *Academy of Management Journal*, 34: 37–59.

Brush, C. G. 1992. *Factors motivating small companies to internationalize: The effect of firm age*. Unpublished doctoral dissertation, Boston University.

Bryan, L., Fraser, J., Oppenheim, J., & Rall, W. 1999. *Race for the world*. Boston: Harvard Business School Press.

Buckley, P. J., & Casson, M. 1976. *The future of the multinational enterprise*. New York: Holmes & Meier.

Burrill, G. S., & Almassy, S. E. 1993. *Electronics '93: The new global reality (Ernst & Young's 4th annual report on the electronics industry)*. San Francisco: Ernst & Young.

Busenitz, L. W., & Barney, J. B. 1997. Differences between entrepreneurs and managers in large organizations: Biases and heuristics in strategic decision-making. *Journal of Business Venturing*, 12: 9–30.

Carter, N. M., Stearns, T. M., Reynolds, P. D., & Miller, B. A. 1994. New venture strategies: Theory development with an empirical base. *Strategic Management Journal*, 15: 21–41.

Cooper, A. C. 1970. Entrepreneurial environment. *Industrial Research*, 12: 75.

Cooper, A. C., & Dunkelberg, W. C. 1986. Entrepreneurship and the initial size of firms. *Strategic Management Journal*, 7: 53–68.

Cooper, A. C., Gimeno-Gascon, F. J., & Woo, C. Y. 1994. Initial human and financial capital as predictors of venture performance. *Journal of Business Venturing*, 9: 371–395.

Copeland, T. E., & Weston, J. F. 1983. *Financial theory and corporate policy*. Reading, MA: Addison-Wesley.

Cosset, J., & Roy, J. 1991. The determinants of country risk ratings. *Journal of International Business Studies*, 22: 135–142.

Coviello, N. E., & Munro, H. J. 1997. Network relationships and the internationalisation process of small software firms. *International Business Review*, 6: 361–386.

DiMaggio, P. J., & Powell, W. W., 1983. The iron cage revisited: Institutional isomorphism and collective rationality in organizational fields. *American Sociological Review*, 48: 147–160.

Dunning, J. H. 1993. *Multinational enterprises and the global economy*. Wokingham, England: Addison-Wesley.

Dunning, J. H. 1995. Reappraising the eclectic paradigm in an age of alliance capitalism. *Journal of International Business Studies*, 26: 461–491.

Dunning, J. H. 1998. Location and the multinational enterprise: A neglected factor? *Journal of International Business Studies*, 29: 45–66.

Economist. 1992. Go west, young firm. May 9: 88–89.

Economist. 1993. America's little fellows surge ahead. July 3: 59–60.

Eisenhardt, K. M. & Schoonhoven, C. B. 1990. Organizational growth: Linking founding team strategy, environment, and growth among U.S. semiconductor ventures. *Administrative Science Quarterly*, 35: 504–529.

Feeser, H. R., & Willard, G. E. 1990. Founding strategy and performance. *Strategic Management Journal*, 11: 87–98.

Fiegenbaum, A., & Thomas, H. 1986. Dynamic and risk

measurement perspectives on Bowman's risk-return paradox for strategic management: An empirical study. *Strategic Management Journal*, 7: 395–407.

Ghemawat, P. 1991. *Commitment: The dynamic of strategy*. New York: Free Press.

Ghoshal, S. 1987. Global strategy: An organizing framework. *Strategic Management Journal*, 8: 425–440.

Gupta, U., 1989. Small firms aren't waiting to grow up to go global. *Wall Street Journal*, December 5: B2.

Hedlund, G., & Kverneland A. 1985. Are strategies for foreign markets changing? The case of Swedish investment in Japan. *International Studies of Management and Organization*, 15(2): 41–59.

Hill, C. W. L., Hwang, P., & Kim, W. C. 1990. An eclectic theory of the choice of international entry mode. *Strategic Management Journal*, 11: 117–128.

Hymer, S. H. 1976. *The international operations of national firms: A study of direct foreign investment*. Cambridge, MA: MIT Press.

Johanson, J., & Vahlne, J.-E. 1977. The internationalization process of the firm: A model of knowledge development and increasing foreign market commitment. *Journal of International Business Studies*, 4: 20–29.

Johanson, J., & Vahlne, J.-E. 1990. The mechanism of internationalization. *International Marketing Review*, 7(4): 11–24.

Johnston, J. 1972. *Econometric methods*. New York: McGraw-Hill.

Jolly, V. K., Alahuhta, M., & Jeannet, J.-P. 1992. Challenging the incumbents: How high-technology start-ups compete globally. *Journal of Strategic Change*, 1: 71–82.

Kaynak, E., Ghuari, P. N., & Olofsson-Bredenlow, T. 1987. Export behavior of small Swedish firms. *Journal of Small Business Management*. 25(2): 26–32.

Kim, W. C., & Hwang, P. 1992. Global strategy and multinationals' entry mode choice. *Journal of International Business Studies*, 23: 29–53.

Knickerbocker, F. T. 1973. *Oligopolistic reaction and the multinational enterprise*. Cambridge, MA: Harvard University Press.

Knight, G. G., & Cavusgil, S. T. 1996. The born global firm: A challenge to traditional internationalization theory. In T. K. Madsen (Ed.), *Advances in international marketing*, vol. 8: 11–26. Greenwich, CT: JAI.

Kobrin, S. J. 1991. An empirical analysis of the determinants of global integration. *Strategic Management Journal*, 12: 17–31.

Kogut, B. 1989. A note on global strategies. *Strategic Management Journal*, 10: 383–389.

Kohn, T. O. 1997. Small firms as international players. *Small Business Economics*, 9(1): 45–51.

Kunkel, S. W. 1991. *The impact of strategy and industry structure on new venture performance*. Unpublished doctoral dissertation, University of Georgia, Athens.

Mamis, R. A. 1989. Global start-up. *Inc.*, August: 38–47.

March, J. G., & Shapira, Z. 1987. Managerial perspectives on risk and risk taking. *Management Science*, 33: 1404–1418.

McBain, M. L., & Krause, D. S. 1989. Going public: The impact of insiders' holdings on the price of initial public offerings. *Journal of Business Venturing*, 4: 419–428.

McDougall, P. P. 1989. International versus domestic entrepreneurship: New venture strategic behavior and industry structure. *Journal of Business Venturing*, 4: 387–399.

McDougall, P. P., Shane, S., & Oviatt, B. M. 1994. Explaining the formation of international new ventures: The limits of theories from international business research. *Journal of Business Venturing*, 9: 469–487.

McGee, J. E., & Dowling, M. J. 1994. Using R&D cooperative arrangements to leverage managerial experience: A study of technology-intensive new ventures. *Journal of Business Venturing*, 9: 33–48.

McKinsey & Company. 1993. *Emerging exports: Australia's high value-added manufacturing exporters*. Melbourne: Australian Manufacturing Council.

Miller, K. D. 1992. A framework for integrated risk management in international business. *Journal of International Business Studies*, 23: 311–331.

Organisation for Economic Co-operation and Development (OECD). 1997. *Globalisation and small and medium enterprises*. Paris: OECD.

Oviatt, B. M., & McDougall, P. P. 1994. Toward a theory of international new ventures. *Journal of International Business Studies*, 25: 45–64.

Oviatt, B. M., & McDougall, P. P. 1995. Global start-ups: Entrepreneurs on a worldwide stage. *Academy of Management Executive*, 9(2): 30–44.

Oviatt, B. M., & McDougall, P. P. 1997. Challenges for internationalization process theory: The case of international new ventures. *Management International Review*, 37(2): 85–99.

Oviatt, B. M., & McDougall, P. P. 1999. A framework for understanding accelerated international entrepreneurship. In R. Wright (Ed.), *Research in global strategic management*: 23–40. Stamford, CT: JAI Press.

Porter, M. E. 1985. *Competitive advantage: Creating and sustaining superior performance*. New York: Free Press.

Preece, S. B., Miles, G., & Baetz, M. C. 1999. Explaining the international intensity and global diversity of early-stage technology-based firms. *Journal of Business Venturing*, 14: 259–281.

Quinn, J. B. 1992. *Intelligent enterprise.* New York: Free Press.

Ramaswamy, K., Kroeck, K. G., & Renforth, W. 1996. Measuring the degree of internationalization of a firm: A comment. *Journal of International Business Studies,* 27: 167–177.

Rangan, S. 1998. Do multinationals operate flexibly? Theory and evidence. *Journal of International Business Studies,* 29: 217–237.

Ray, D. M. 1989. *Entrepreneurial companies "born" international: Four case studies.* Paper presented at Babson Entrepreneurship Research Conference on Entrepreneurship, St. Louis, MO.

Reuber, A. R., & Fischer, E. 1997. The influence of the management team's international experience on the internationalization behaviors of SMEs. *Journal of International Business Studies,* 28: 807–825.

Robinson, K. C., & McDougall, P. P. 1998. The impact of alternative operationalizations of industry structural elements on measures of performance for entrepreneurial manufacturing ventures. *Strategic Management Journal,* 19: 1079–1100.

Root, F. R. 1987. *Entry strategy for international markets.* Lexington, MA: Heath.

Roth, K. 1992. Implementing international strategy at the business unit level: The role of managerial decision-making characteristics. *Journal of Management,* 18: 769–789.

Shapira, Z. 1995. *Risk taking: A managerial perspective.* New York: Russell Sage Foundation.

Sharfman, M. P., & Dean, J. W. Jr. 1991. Conceptualizing and measuring the organizational environment: A multidimensional approach. *Journal of Management,* 17: 681–700.

Singh, J. V. 1986. Performance, slack, and risk taking in organizational decision making. *Academy of Management Journal,* 29: 562–585.

Smith, C. W., Jr., Smithson, C. W., & Wilford, D. S. 1990. *Managing financial risk.* New York: Harper & Row.

Sullivan, D. 1994. Measuring the degree of internationalization of a firm. *Journal of International Business Studies,* 25: 325–342.

Sullivan, D. 1996. Measuring the degree of internation-

alization of a firm: A reply. *Journal of International Business Studies,* 27: 179–192.

Tang, C. Y., & Tikoo, S. 1999. Operational flexibility and market valuation of earnings. *Strategic Management Journal,* 20: 749–761.

United Nations Conference on Trade and Development (UNCTAD). 1993. *Small and medium-sized transnational corporations.* New York: UNCTAD.

United Nations Conference on Trade and Development (UNCTAD). 1997. *World investment report, 1997.* New York: UNCTAD.

U.S. Bureau of Economic Analysis. 1989. *U. S. direct investment abroad: 1989 benchmark survey data.* Washington, DC: Department of Commerce.

U.S. Patent Office. 1995. *Patenting trends in the United States, 1963–1994.* Washington, DC: Department of Commerce.

U.S. Small Business Administration. 1992. *The state of small business.* Washington, DC: U.S. Government Printing Office.

Vernon, R. 1966. International investment and international trade in the product cycle. *Quarterly Journal of Economics,* 80: 190–207.

Rodney C. Shrader is an assistant professor of managerial studies at the University of Illinois at Chicago. He received his Ph.D. from Georgia State University. His primary research interests are the internationalization of new ventures and the internationalization of electronic commerce.

Benjamin M. Oviatt is an associate professor of management and the director of the Herman J. Russell, Sr., International Center for Entrepreneurship at Georgia State University. He received his Ph.D. from the University of South Carolina. His research interests focus on understanding the accelerated internationalization of organizations.

Patricia Phillips McDougall is a professor in and the chair of the Management Department at Indiana University. She is also a senior fellow in the Johnson Center for Entrepreneurship and Innovation. She received her Ph.D. from the University of South Carolina. Her current research interests focus on international entrepreneurship and new ventures.

Part III
Knowledge and Learning

[15]

ELSEVIER

Journal of Business Venturing 17 (2002) 99–122

JOURNAL
of BUSINESS
VENTURING

Home base and knowledge management in international ventures

Walter Kuemmerle*

Graduate School of Business Administration, Harvard University, Soldier's Field, Boston, MA 02163, USA

Received 1 October 1998; received in revised form 1 January 2000; accepted 1 February 2000

Abstract

This paper examines the scope and sequence of international activities carried out by nascent international ventures. Building on earlier research about foreign direct investment (FDI) and knowledge management in international firms and on the analysis of six international ventures the paper develops a number of propositions. We suggest that international ventures are conceived as 'international' because cross-border activities increase the chances of venture survival and growth. We also suggest that, in the early stages of international ventures, cross-border activities that augment the venture's knowledge base are more prevalent than cross-border activities that exploit the venture's knowledge base. Finally, the paper points out research trajectories for more detailed studies of knowledge management in international ventures. © 2001 Elsevier Science Inc. All rights reserved.

Keywords: International entrepreneurship; Typology of international ventures; Knowledge management

1. Executive summary

The international dimension of entrepreneurship is becoming increasingly important for scholars and practitioners. A growing number of entrepreneurs start ventures by simultaneously establishing operations in several countries in order to increase the likelihood of venture success. Furthermore, an increasing number of ventures carry out some type of economic activity in foreign countries at an earlier point in the venture's life than comparable ventures did in the past. While a number of studies have

* Tel.: +1-617-495-6353; fax: +1-617-496-4066.
E-mail address: wkuemmerle@hbs.edu (W. Kuemmerle).

0883-9026/02/$ – see front matter © 2001 Elsevier Science Inc. All rights reserved.
PII: S 0 8 8 3 - 9 0 2 6 (0 0) 0 0 0 5 4 - 9

examined the phenomenon of international entrepreneurship, further theory development is needed, particularly with regard to the nature and evolution of international ventures as well as with regard to traits of the entrepreneurs involved. This paper develops a number of testable propositions on evolution of and knowledge management in international ventures.

The efficient management of knowledge flows across national borders is relevant for firm success especially in nascent firms that operate under considerable resource constraints. This paper builds on earlier research about knowledge management in established multinational companies. Specifically, the paper applies a framework for knowledge management to the phenomenon of international ventures. Using this framework, this paper first refines an existing definition of international entrepreneurship to better reflect divergent activities carried out by international ventures. Second, using this framework the paper analyzes the scope and sequence of international activity of six ventures as well as the motivation of entrepreneurs to conduct such activity. Third, building on this analysis, the paper develops a number of testable propositions regarding the probability of occurrence and evolution of international ventures.

The framework for knowledge management developed in earlier research suggests that firms venture abroad for two distinctive reasons, either in order to use extant firm-specific knowledge, primarily for manufacturing and sales activities, or in order to increase the firm's stock of knowledge, primarily through research and development activities. The former type of activity can be labeled home base-exploiting (HBE) while the latter can be labeled home base-augmenting (HBA). The paper suggests that ventures are international in nature if they carry out either or both types of activities from their inception.

The empirical part of the paper analyzes six cases in detail. The analysis draws on published case studies as well as on a detailed follow-up investigation of the entrepreneurs and other constituencies involved in the six ventures. Since the cases are published, the analysis can be largely replicated. The analysis focuses on four aspects of international ventures: prior international exposure of the entrepreneurs, industry specific-conditions, location-specific conditions, and sequencing of international activities.

The analysis suggests four groups of propositions. First, prior international exposure of entrepreneurs can act as a trigger for the founding of an international venture. Second, the international orientation of a venture is determined by industry-specific requirements at the time of venture creation. Third, international ventures are generally managed from one central location that can be called 'home base.' This location acts as a knowledge flow coordinator. Fourth, international ventures generally focus first on HBA activities. These activities tend to increase the venture's profits in the home-country. Only at a later stage in the venture's evolution are HBA activities complemented by HBE efforts. The latter type of international activity is generally more resource-intensive and requires a sizable stream of revenues from activities in the home base country as well as a comprehensive stock of product and process knowledge.

The proposition that ventures generally carry out HBA activities prior to carrying out HBE activities is in line with findings by a number of researchers who have studied the nature of international activities of larger firms. On the other hand, the way in which ventures manage knowledge differs from established firms. International ventures tend to

W. Kuemmerle / Journal of Business Venturing 17 (2002) 99–122 101

use fewer established routines for the exploitation and augmentation of the firm's stock of knowledge. Furthermore, the entrepreneur, rather than a dedicated organization within the firm, assumes a key role as a knowledge flow coordinator.

2. Introduction

Entrepreneurs distinguish themselves from the general public by a higher level of alertness to business opportunities and by a stronger willingness to pursue them without regard to the resources they control at inception stage of an entrepreneurial venture (Stevenson and Jarillo, 1990; Venkataraman, 1997). Furthermore, entrepreneurs distinguish themselves through their ability to accumulate and manage knowledge as well as through their ability to mobilize resources in order to achieve an ex-ante specified business goal.

The management of knowledge and the mobilization of resources are particularly challenging in cross-national settings where different cultures, corporate governance systems, time zones, and languages are involved. At the same time, the potential rewards from cross-national ventures tend to be commensurate with the managerial challenges (Boter and Holmquist, 1996; McDougall and Oviatt, 1996).

Recently, international entrepreneurship has received an increasing level of attention in the academic literature (McDougall, 1989; McDougall et al., 1994; Oviatt and McDougall, 1994; Wright and Ricks, 1994; Brush, 1995; Kuemmerle, 1995), but the academic domain of international entrepreneurship is still in its early stages. At the same time, practice evolves rapidly and an increasing number of entrepreneurs start their businesses in a manner that involves economic cross-border transactions from the venture's inception. An even larger number of entrepreneurs start their business in one country only, but rely heavily on cross-border knowledge that they accumulated prior to starting the business.

This paper develops theory by building on prior research on knowledge management in established multinational companies. Specifically, we develop a number of testable propositions about the drivers, scope, and sequence of activities that international ventures carry out outside of their home countries.

We first present a framework for knowledge management in international settings developed in earlier research. Using this framework, we develop a definition of international entrepreneurship. We then use case study research methodology to analyze the scope and sequence of international activity of six ventures that were created over the last 20 years. We then develop four groups of propositions (profiles of entrepreneurs, business strategy requirements, home base location, HBA/HBE activities). Finally, the paper points out limitations of this research and suggests a future research agenda.

3. Prior research on entrepreneurs crossing borders

One way of categorizing international entrepreneurship research is to distinguish that which studies entrepreneurs in different countries from that which studies entrepreneurs who cross borders as an integral part of their entrepreneurial activity. Both streams of research are represented in the literature. The first stream provides valuable insights through comparative analysis (Adams and Hall, 1993; Birley and MacMillan, 1995; McGrath et al., 1995).

The second stream of research provides insights on how and why entrepreneurs engage in cross-border business early in the life cycle of a venture. Moreover, this stream examines to what degree an early international presence increases the likelihood of success for an international venture. McDougall's definition of international entrepreneurship falls within this second stream of research:

> International entrepreneurship is defined as the development of international new ventures or start-ups that, from their inception, engage in international business, thus viewing their operating domain as international from the initial stages of the firm's operation (McDougall, 1989).[1]

In this paper, we build on McDougall's definition of international entrepreneurship rather than a definition related to comparative research on entrepreneurs. Our objective is not to examine entrepreneurship comparatively across countries but to study how multinationality from inception is related to a venture's growth.

McDougall et al. (1994), after a careful examination of five theories of international business, concluded that international entrepreneurship is not fully explained by any one theory. They argue that the creation of international ventures is triggered primarily by the founders' ability to see market opportunities in a cross-national context. Founders developed this ability through activities earlier in their career (McDougall et al., 1994; Oviatt and McDougall, 1995). Prior international activities lead to capabilities including language skills, skills in accessing national networks of contacts, and skills in forming ties with foreign companies.

An important difference between theories of multinational enterprise and a theory of international ventures seems to be the unit of analysis. Theories of multinational enterprise argue that some enterprises are multinational because of certain firm-specific capabilities and routines that they possess and cultivate over time (Kogut, 1984; Doz and Prahalad, 1991; Leonard-Barton, 1995; Caves, 1996). The resource-based view of the firm has described and analyzed the nature of these routines extensively (Mahoney and Pandian, 1992; Teece et al., 1997). Theories of international entrepreneurship, on the other hand, argue that some firms start out internationally because of certain entrepreneur-specific capabilities (Bloodgood and Sapienza, 1995; Knight and Cavusgil, 1996; McDougall and Oviatt, 1996). When the entrepreneur creates the enterprise, there are no routines in place, but the entrepreneur has vision and a network of contacts that he or she is going to build up further. Over time, the entrepreneur seeks to exploit this network in order to mobilize resources and build an organization. Thus, a study of international ventures has to be concerned with individual

---

[1] In her empirical study, McDougall defines ventures as international if their export share exceeds 5% of sales. Also, a venture is defined as 'new' by McDougall if it is less than 8 years old. In the empirical part of this paper, international ventures are defined more narrowly. Only ventures that carried out activities at dedicated *sites* abroad (rather than ventures that just exported) were included. Also, this paper only examines ventures that started activities abroad within *1 year* after founding.

W. Kuemmerle / Journal of Business Venturing 17 (2002) 99–122 103

learning by the entrepreneur as well as with organizational learning of the emerging entrepreneurial firm.

Besides studies that compare entrepreneurship in different countries and studies that examine the creation of international ventures, a few studies have examined the relationship between performance and internationalization. These studies have found some evidence for a higher performance of international ventures (Tyebjee, 1990; McDougall and Oviatt, 1996), although McDougall finds that a higher degree of internationalization is associated with a higher market share but not with a higher return on investment. An important issue for international ventures is the geographic organization and sequence of international activities. The following section examines some findings from prior research on cross-border expansion of multinational firms and relates these findings to international ventures.

4. Knowledge flows in international ventures

The increasing incidence of international entrepreneurship warrants an investigation into different features of international ventures (Rennie, 1993; Barrett, 1995; Levine, 1997). Rennie, for example, in a study of 294 Australian firms found two types of firms. Traditional firms carried out their first exports after 27 years of existence on average and their mean export ratio in 1992 was 20% of sales. 'Born global' firms, on the other hand, carried out their first exports after 2 years of existence and their mean 1992 export ratio was 76%. One key feature of international entrepreneurship is cross-border knowledge management (Knight and Cavusgil, 1996). We argue that gaining access to knowledge in other nations and appropriate processing of knowledge from other nations and cultures are important issues in the creation and evolution of an international venture. Furthermore, we argue that most ventures are built from one, rather than several, home bases. Our argument builds on results from an extensive research project about knowledge management in established multinational firms (Kuemmerle, 1999a,b).

Before the creation of the venture, the future entrepreneur crosses borders and learns about different national business environments. Often, the idea for an international venture is conceived during or immediately after exposure to a foreign environment. Over time, the entrepreneur collects more information and, if the opportunity seems sufficiently large, starts a company. For example, in the case of Heartware International, a medical device company, a well-traveled manager discovered a new electrophysiology product that was developed at a hospital in the Netherlands. About 1 year later, the manager started his own company in the US (Oviatt et al., 1993).

During the detail planning stage for a new venture, the entrepreneur evaluates the informational and resource requirements of the nascent firm. Based on the assessment of these requirements, the entrepreneur further expands her network of relationships with capital providers, potential customers, and suppliers. The pursuit of opportunities without full control over the resources required is a tricky task. Knowledge about how things can get done quickly at critical points in time has been a major factor in the success of most ventures studied by Hart et al. (1995), who shows that this factor is more critical than access to capital alone.

104   *W. Kuemmerle / Journal of Business Venturing 17 (2002) 99–122*

At some point in the process of venture creation, the entrepreneur must make a decision regarding the location of the venture's home base. The home base is the location where strategic decisions are made, where resources are allocated, and where knowledge is managed (Porter, 1990; Kuemmerle, 1999a). For most ventures, the decision about the location of the home base is a decision between different locations at the regional or micro-regional level. Thus, for Hewlett-Packard, it was never a real question that the company would get started anywhere but in close proximity to Stanford University, because the company drew most of its technical knowledge base from Stanford. The actual location turned out to be the garage of one of the founders. And Hewlett-Packard has kept its home base in Silicon Valley. Microsoft started out in Albuquerque, NM, in 1975, close to the company that manufactured the computer for which Microsoft was writing software. In 1979, the company relocated to Seattle, WA, primarily because the opportunities for knowledge management were better there. In Seattle, Microsoft had access to a larger pool of graduates in computer sciences. At the same time, Seattle was Bill Gates' hometown and it was here that he could tap into a dense network of business contacts beyond the software community.

For international ventures the decision about where to locate the firm's home base can be much more tricky, particularly if several countries are considered of nearly equal importance for the firm's success. Also, if the firm is co-founded by a number of entrepreneurs with different countries of residence, the question of where to locate the home base can be difficult and put a strain on the interpersonal relationships of both founders and early-stage employees.

After the formal creation of a venture the entrepreneur has to strike the right balance between using the venture's existing network of contacts and augmenting the network further in order to access the knowledge required for the firm's growth. It is generally critical that the entrepreneur carries out both activities at the same time. On the one hand, she has to convert product ideas and service ideas into revenues in order to generate cash flows; on the other hand, she has to invest in order to enhance the firm's capabilities. The above-mentioned study on knowledge management in multinational companies found that large firms carry out foreign direct investment (FDI) for two reasons: they invest either to augment the firm's knowledge base or to exploit the firm's knowledge base. The first motive can be called *HBA* investments, while the second motive can be called *HBE*. This distinction was developed and empirically validated in earlier research (Kuemmerle, 1997a, 1999a).

In HBA efforts, the firm seeks the opportunity to benefit from a specific local environment by absorbing knowledge available from that environment, through investments in R&D sites, and manufacturing and marketing sites. For multinational companies, such HBA investments are a relatively recent phenomenon compared to HBE investments (Kuemmerle, 1999b).

In HBE efforts, the firm seeks to benefit from its *existing* knowledge and product base; the firm invests abroad in order to exploit its existing stock of knowledge in a better way. Most FDI into manufacturing is carried out because of HBE reasons (Hymer, 1976; Vernon, 1979). We argue that the framework of HBA and HBE activities can be applied to international entrepreneurial ventures in a way that explains the international character of creation and

W. Kuemmerle / Journal of Business Venturing 17 (2002) 99–122 105

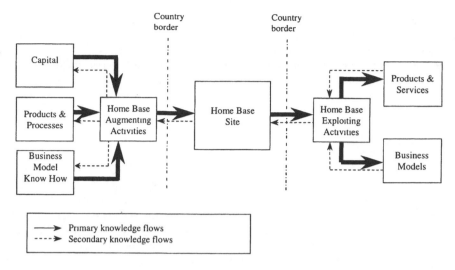

Fig. 1. A framework for knowledge management in international ventures.

growth of these ventures. Entrepreneurs cross-borders both to augment and to exploit their home base very early in the life cycle of the venture. Fig. 1 shows the application of the HBA and HBE framework to international ventures. Building on McDougall's definition we now define international entrepreneurship as:

> The development of international new ventures or start-ups that, from their inception, engage in either home-base-augmenting (HBA) or home-base-exploiting (HBE) activities or both, thus viewing their operating domain as international from the initial stages of the firm's operation.

This extension of McDougall's definition emphasizes the distinctive character of cross-border activities. HBA activities consist primarily of those that provide insights about new products, markets, and business models. Such activities can be conducted either from a dedicated site in the foreign country or from a temporary location in the foreign country. HBA activities include, but are not limited to, R&D activities and strategic alliances that are formed to gain access to product and process technology. HBE activities consist primarily of manufacturing and marketing operations abroad. These include sales offices, market-specific product development, manufacturing facilities, and facilities that provide engineering support for contract manufacturers. HBE activities are generally conducted from a dedicated site (or office) in the foreign country (Porter, 1990; Kuemmerle, 1997a).[2]

---

[2] Many international ventures, particularly in manufacturing industries, start their HBE activities through exports. Frequently, however, these ventures establish dedicated sales and marketing offices in the most important foreign market(s) soon after they start exporting. Often, manufacturing facilities are also established in these countries around the same time. Furthermore, international ventures in service industries (such Internet Securities or African Communications group) need dedicated facilities and local employees to deliver their services from the point in time at which they start cross-border activities.

106   *W. Kuemmerle / Journal of Business Venturing 17 (2002) 99–122*

Based on this extended definition of international entrepreneurship we can now develop propositions about the scope and sequencing of international activities. Our research questions are: What are the drivers of international entrepreneurship? What are the characteristics of the home base in an international entrepreneurial venture? Which activities (HBA or HBE) do international entrepreneurial ventures carry out abroad? If both types of activities are carried out, which activity comes first?

5. Six international ventures

The analysis in this section is based on six cases and seeks to generate propositions that can be tested with large-scale data sets (Eisenhardt, 1989). Analysis and proposition development are segmented into five topics: (1) profiles of entrepreneurs, (2) business strategy requirements, (3) role of the home base, (4) HBA activities, (5) HBE activities. Case selection was driven by a number of criteria, including variance across home countries and industries as well as variance in the date of venture creation. We also checked whether it was possible to interview entrepreneurs and venture investors. Finally, we also sought to ensure that our results would be at least partially replicable by other researchers.

We decided to use case studies that had been published by Harvard Business School as the starting point for our analysis for two reasons. First, since these case studies have been published, others can at least partially replicate our analysis. Second, we were able to contact the entrepreneurs and investors to carry out detailed and structured follow-up interviews. In these interviews, we focused on understanding the drivers for the international character of the ventures in greater detail. Furthermore, in the interviews we investigated whether international activities were HBA or HBE. During the interviews, we also obtained a detailed update on the venture's development since the case study had been compiled.

The case studies were selected as follows: First, we screened the Harvard Business School database of case studies for international entrepreneurial ventures that carried out international activities at the venture's inception or within 1 year after the founding. We identified 14 case studies that fit our definition of international entrepreneurial ventures. Next, we excluded case studies older than 20 years and those that did not provide extensive information about the entrepreneur's personal background and motivation. Finally, we excluded those case studies where the entrepreneur could not be contacted or where the case author had disguised case data. This left us with six case studies (Stevenson, 1983, 1994; Sahlman, 1995; McGahan, 1996; Applegate, 1997; Kuemmerle, 1997b). Fig. 2 gives an overview of these six ventures. In this paper, we analyze all six case studies with the objective of replicating findings across different geographies and stages of venture evolution (Yin, 1989). All of the ventures were still in existence by 1999, but some of them (Michael Bregman and DDI) had expanded their business to other product and service lines.

Classified in order of their date of establishment, all six ventures are in the media, communication, and service industries. The strong representation of these industries in our sample is indicative of the international entrepreneurship opportunities in these industries. Four out of six ventures are active in emerging markets and teams of two entrepreneurs

W. Kuemmerle / Journal of Business Venturing 17 (2002) 99–122 107

Venture name	Internet Securities	African Communications Group	Richina	Telewizja Wisla	DDI	Michael Bregman
Business	Provider of data on emerging markets via Internet	Wireless pay phone and paging systems in Tanzania & other emerging market countries	Magazine publishing in China	Supra-regional television station in Poland	Long-distance telephone service in Japan	"Mmmuffin" stores and French bakeries in North-America
Date of venture creation	1994	1993	1993	1991	1984	1979
Founder(s)	Gary & George Mueller	Monique Maddy & Come Lague	Richard Yan	Wojtek Szczerba & Claire Hurley	Kazuo Inamori Sacho Semmoto	Michael Bregman
Amount of initial funding (1st/2nd/3rd stage)	$1.2m/$5m	$0.6million / $2million / $13.8million		$200,000/$2million/ $2million	$80million	$450,000
Current employment level	160	70	>150	192	2830	NA
Ownership status	Privately held	Privately held	privately held	acquired by Central European Media Enterprises (in 1997)	public (IPO in 1993)	privately held

Fig. 2. Overview of six international ventures.

founded four out of six firms. Four ventures are still privately held; a strategic buyer acquired one, and one went public.

Interviews with entrepreneurs and other parties lasted for at least 2 h each and for up to 12 h cumulatively for each interviewee. We also sought additional information from investors and from the authors of the case studies (one of the case studies was written by the author of this paper). In four of the six firms, we also interviewed other parties such as customers or suppliers. Two of the cases, DDI and Michael Bregman, are several years old (1983 and 1994). While we carried out extensive interviews with the entrepreneurs and other parties for both cases, we were somewhat concerned about the interviewees' ability to recall events accurately. Therefore, we relied more heavily on the published cases and secondary sources (including case writer notes) generated at the time the cases were written. Fig. 3 gives an overview of the field study effort.

We used within-case-analysis as well as cross-pattern search (Eisenhardt, 1989) to analyze the data. Data and interview notes were coded independently by the author and a senior researcher for each firm along a number of dimensions, including the nature of international activities, international presence, and home base. Inter-rater-reliability was very high ($\kappa = 0.76$; range: $0.67 – 1:00$).[3] Wherever differences were recorded, we went back to the firm to seek clarification. Eleven tabular devices were used for data analysis (Miles and Huberman, 1984). Results of the analysis are summarized in Figs. 4 and 5. Data analysis led to the shaping of propositions that we consider relevant for further study of international entrepreneurship.

5.1. Profiles of entrepreneurs

An analysis of the entrepreneurs' training and professional experience prior to starting their ventures revealed that all of them had had considerable previous international exposure. Five out of ten had studied in at least two different countries. Seven out of ten held an MBA degree and had been exposed to international business issues as part of their curricula. Nine out of ten entrepreneurs had work experience in at least two countries prior to starting their venture. The one who had not worked outside the US (George Mueller of Internet Securities) was responsible primarily for the technical part of the venture, which consisted of creating and maintaining a database and a complex Web site. While George Mueller was based in the US, his brother, Gary Mueller, set up offices in 14 emerging markets countries.

All entrepreneurs were influenced by their international experience when they planned and started their ventures. This evidence supports McDougall et al.'s (1994) and Bloodgood and Sapienza's (1995) observations. This evidence is also in line with the general literature on prior experience and its impact on enterprise development (Cohen and Levinthal, 1990, 1994). In four cases (Internet Securities, Richina, African Communications Group, and Telewizja Wisla (TVW)), the entrepreneurs conceived the idea of the ventures they eventually started while they were abroad on prior jobs. In the remaining two cases, Mmmuffin, and

---

[3] Statistical analysis was carried out using Stata 6.0. A κ of $0.61 – 0.80$ is considered 'substantial.' A $\kappa > 0.81$ is considered 'almost perfect' (Landis and Koch, 1977).

W. Kuemmerle / Journal of Business Venturing 17 (2002) 99–122

Venture name	Internet Securities	African Communications Group	Richina	Telewizja Wisla	DDI	Michael Bregman
Interview with entrepreneur(s) (# of interviews)	Yes (1)	Yes (2)	Yes (3)	Yes (>5)	Yes (2)	Yes (2)
Interview with investor(s) (# of interviews)	Yes (2)	Yes (1)	Yes (3)	Yes (2)	Yes (1)	NA
Interview with others	Yes (customers)	No	Yes (customers, government)	Yes (suppliers, customer, competitor)	Yes (competitors)	No
Analysis of industry documents and secondary sources (beyond case study)	Yes	Yes	Yes	Yes	Yes	Yes
Interview with case writer	Yes	Yes	Yes	Yes	Yes	Yes

Fig. 3. Overview of data collection.

Venture name	Internet Securities	African Communications Group	Richina	Telewizja Wisla	DDI	Michael Bregman
Entrepreneur's current residence/original residence	Entrepreneur 1: US/US; Entrepreneur 2: US/US	Entrepreneur 1: US/Europe/ Tanzania, Angola, Indonesia; Entrepreneur 2: US/Canada	China/China	Entrepreneur 1: US/US; Entrepreneur 2: Poland/Poland	Entrepreneur 1: Japan/Japan; Entrepreneur 2: Japan/Japan	Canada/Canada
Entrepreneur's education	Entrepreneur 1: MBA, Fulbright scholar in Germany; Entrepreneur 2: BS in engineering	Entrepreneur 1: MBA; Entrepreneur 2: MBA	MBA	Entrepreneur 1: MBA; Entrepreneur 2: MBA	Entrepreneur 1: Ph.D. (engineering); Entrepreneur 2: Ph.D. (engineering)	MBA
Entrepreneur's international work experience (major countries only)	Entrepreneur 1: yes (in Eastern Europe); Entrepreneur 2: no (US only)	Entrepreneur 1: yes (Africa, Asia, Europe, US); Entrepreneur 2: yes (Canada, US)	yes (China, US, New Zealand)	Entrepreneur 1: yes (US, UK, Poland); Entrepreneur 2: yes (Poland, UK)	Entrepreneur 1: yes (Japan, US, Canada); Entrepreneur 2: yes (Japan, US)	yes (Canada, US)
Business model	Subscription-model; providing emerging markets data primarily for corporate customers	Card-operated pay phones and paging operations	Publishing of magazines with foreign content	Operation of TV station covering 33% of Poland	Operation of long-distance telephone service (100% coverage of Japan)	Chain of French bakeries and muffin shops
Important managerial challenges (in order of priority)	1. Speedy establishment of presence in all emerging markets 2. Building up subscriber base	1. Raising capital 2. Dealing with bureaucracy in Tanzania 3. Selecting equipment 4. Speedy market entry (1st mover challenge)	1. Raising capital 2. Dealing with bureaucracy in China 3. Transferring editorial content from the US to China	1. Raising capital 2. Finding strategic partner for television content	1. Selecting technology 2. Convincing real estate owners to provide transmission space 3. Fast market penetration	1. Improving pilot stores 2. Raising capital 3. Selecting roll-out model (franchising vs. owned stores)

Fig. 4. Profiles of entrepreneurs and overview of business strategy requirements.

Venture name	Internet Securities	African Communications Group	Richina	Telewizja Wisla	DDI	Michael Bregman
Home base	Initially: Pittsburgh, PA and London, UK After 18 months: Boston (new headquarters)	Cambridge, Massachusetts, US	Beijing, China	Krakow, Poland	Tokyo, Japan	Toronto, Canada
International presence	Offices in major cities in 14 countries	Operations in Dar es Salaam, Tanzania; since 1997 also in Accre, Ghana	Office in New York City	Offices in London, UK and Newton, Massachusetts, US	Office in New York City	Frequent trips to US (Chicago, New York City, Boston)
Home-base-augmenting activities	Sourcing of emerging markets information via offices in 14 countries	Providing knowledge about emerging countries' phone markets to potential strategic partners (e.g. Motorola)	Raising capital, sourcing of magazine deals	Raising capital, sourcing of management know how and media content from strategic partners	Sourcing of long distance technology. Forming deals with strategic partners	Sourcing of product ideas
Home-base-exploiting activities	Sales offices in 2 countries. Future vision: 14 home-base-augmenting offices will also perform home-base-exploiting function	Knowledge-transfer from US to Tanzania (wireless communications technologies, management of wireless pay-phone service)			Exploration of partnerships for international long-distance telephone service	Exploration of franchising opportunities in the US

Fig. 5. HBA and HBE activities of six international ventures.

112   *W. Kuemmerle / Journal of Business Venturing 17 (2002) 99–122*

DDI, the entrepreneurs made use of their prior international exposure when searching for, developing, and executing their business ideas. This finding is in line with Bloodgood and Sapienza (1995) who finds that the degree of internationalization of ventures is positively correlated with prior work experience of the venture's top management abroad.

Gary Mueller of Internet Securities, for example, spent a number of years in Germany as a Fulbright scholar and was there when the Berlin Wall fell. At that time, he decided that he definitely wanted to be involved in the transformation of emerging economic markets. He subsequently spent a number of years as a privatization consultant in Eastern Europe. During this period, he developed the idea for an emerging markets news service. His brother, who majored in computer engineering, was pivotal in the decision to distribute information via the Web, which, in 1992, was an emerging technology.

Richard Yan of Richina is a Chinese citizen. He went to New Zealand at age 17 for his undergraduate education; he subsequently worked in the financial industry in New Zealand, got an MBA degree, and then worked as a buyout specialist in New York City for 4 years. His responsibility was to finance Taiwanese companies' expansion throughout Asia. During his time on Wall Street, Yan continually thought about how to start a business in China that would capitalize on China's qualified but low-cost workforce, as well as on expanding domestic demand and on the large number of Chinese nationals living overseas. Yan's vision was to raise an investment fund that would invest in start-up companies in that country. In late 1992, when he felt that the political situation in China had stabilized sufficiently, he quit his job and quickly raised $52.5 million. One of the lead investors in the fund had excellent contacts in the publishing industry. The first enterprise Yan set up was a publishing company that aimed at becoming the leading publisher of magazines with foreign content in China. Yan also envisioned that the publishing company would eventually venture into other countries with large Chinese-speaking populations. Although the fund raised by Yan was subsequently invested in additional business opportunities in China, Yan spent most of his time starting the publishing venture.

Wojtek Szczerba, the founder of TVW, had moved to London in 1984 because he was frustrated with work conditions in the media industry in his native Poland. When political changes took place in Poland in 1991, Szczerba began actively thinking about starting a television station, although the pursuit of this opportunity seemed beyond his financial means. Also, the Polish government was slow in enacting legislation that would allow independent operators to own commercial television stations. However, when in September 1993 the government finally invited applications for TV licenses, Szczerba was prepared. He had teamed up with Claire Hurley, a former investment banker with media experience. Ten applicants submitted applications for licenses. TVW submitted an innovative supra-regional license application. The concept was appealing and TVW, together with only one other applicant, received a license covering more than a local area. Szczerba also envisioned to export the supra-regional TV station concept to other East European countries.

Monique Maddy, the co-founder of African Communications Group, got acquainted with her industry of choice while working for the United Nations Development Program in Geneva on a project called 'Telecommunications Strategies for Africa.' During her tenure at the UN, Monique realized that the culture of a large bureaucratic organization did not suit her well. She subsequently attended business school and, between her first

W. Kuemmerle / Journal of Business Venturing 17 (2002) 99–122

and second year, worked as a summer associate at 20th Century Fox on media projects. After graduation, she went to Tanzania where she hoped to find a business opportunity. Monique stated, "I was basically willing to pursue any idea in Africa that was media or communications industry related and that seemed promising." While in Tanzania, Monique was approached by a local businessman who operated 10 payphones and was looking for capital to expand. "That's when I got interested in payphones. By chance, I hooked up with a former business school classmate, Come Lague, who was vacationing in Africa. Together we analyzed the business opportunity in detail and decided to raise money. By the time we had raised $600,000 in capital, the local businessman was not interested in a cooperation any more. By that time we had invested so much time and we had figured out a number of interesting details about the operation of payphones that nobody else knew. Also, we had established contacts to manufacturers and capital providers in the US. So we went ahead with the venture on our own."

In 1977, Michael Bregman worked for a Canadian supermarket chain on corporate development of unbranded products. The concept of no-name products had been pioneered in the US, and Bregman was involved in transferring know-how about unbranded products from the US to Canada. The idea for a muffin shop chain occurred to him not because of his exposure to US chain stores but because his father was in the bakery business. However, once the idea was conceived, Bregman leveraged his skills in transferring know-how from the US to Canada. His decision about whether and how to franchise stores was driven by his own analysis of franchising operations in the US.

The creation of DDI happened in anticipation of the falling monopoly for long-distance telephone service in Japan. The venture was funded primarily by Kyocera and Sony. DDI was one of three new entrants. The two other entrants used the rights-of-way for long-distance cabling of either highways or railways. Since DDI as a late entrant did not have any 'real estate' to install its lines, few industry experts gave the firm a chance — yet it emerged as the leading competitor. The founders were Dr. Inamori and Dr. Semmoto. Many gave credit to the organizational leadership of Dr. Inamori, who had also founded Kyocera, and to the technical and strategic vision of Dr. Semmoto, a former NTT employee. Dr. Semmoto had a detailed understanding of telecommunications technology and had also spent considerable time studying the dynamics of telecommunications deregulation in the US while he was still at NTT. From its inception, DDI envisioned making extensive use of telecommunications technology developed in the US in order to overcome its competitive disadvantage of having no 'real estate.' At its creation, DDI also envisioned the creation of partnerships with foreign telephone companies for international telephone services. DDI won the battle against the two other entrants because it made a virtue out of necessity: microwave technology that had been developed in the US and that DDI initially employed because it had no 'real estate' to install lines, in fact, turned out to be less costly than line-based technologies.

The examination of these profiles of entrepreneurs leads to the first proposition.

Proposition 1: International entrepreneurship activity is positively correlated with the entrepreneur's exposure to foreign environments, primarily in a professional or academic context, prior to starting an international venture.

5.2. Business strategy requirements

Common to all six ventures was the requirement of rapid growth; slow growth would have entailed a loss of significant first-mover advantages. In the case of all six ventures, the requirement for rapid growth entailed activity in several countries very early in the ventures' life. Internet Securities wanted to become the dominant provider of emerging markets information. There were approximately 3000 firms providing on-line financial information in the US in 1994, but none provided extensive coverage of emerging markets and none were using the Web as uncompromisingly as Internet Securities planned to do. In order to achieve high growth and an optimal return on its massive investment in a Web-platform and in order to sign up many blue-chip subscribers early, the company needed to cover at least all major East European emerging markets countries from the start. This enabled the firm to position itself as an emerging markets expert on one world region from the start. In 1995, African Communications Group faced competition from 20 payphone operators, including the national Tanzanian Telephone, which had been issued licenses in Tanzania. Rapid market penetration in Tanzania was a necessary condition for success. In order to achieve this objective, the firm needed access to superior technology that existed particularly at two payphone manufacturers in the US. Also, the entrepreneurs needed to interact closely with initial and potential future investors. At the same time, the entrepreneurs needed to be on the ground in Tanzania.

Richina wanted to become the leading publisher of computer magazines in China. Rapid growth was required in a market that had just been opened to numerous competitors. For this purpose, Richina needed access to magazine content of high quality. This input was available in New York City. Richina needed a site in the US not just to negotiate content deals but also to build up its own expertise about technology trends and the quality of magazine content.

TVW started out against at least one new competitor and three incumbent national TV stations while the Polish TV advertising market was up for grabs. Judging from the example of other countries that had recently allowed privately owned stations to compete, it was probable that only one or two competitors would succeed in garnering sufficient advertising market share. In order to succeed TVW needed access to superior programming from the start, which in turn required a large amount of capital. In order to attract both capital and programming, the company needed a presence in either the US or the UK.

DDI began as an underdog against one incumbent firm and two other new entrants. DDI was the only competitor without rights-of-way. Therefore, DDI had to understand microwave technologies in detail and early in the life cycle of these technologies. It turned out that these technologies were available in the US, in France and the UK. And Michael Bregman established his first French Bakery after having studied Au Bon Pain, the US-based chain, and other US competitors in great detail through frequent study trips to the US. These trips occurred before and during the incorporation of his firm.

Our analysis suggests that international activities have strongly contributed to speedy growth of the ventures we studied. As Fig. 4 shows, the most pressing management challenges varied across ventures. Some needed to raise capital, others needed access to

W. Kuemmerle / Journal of Business Venturing 17 (2002) 99–122   115

cutting-edge technology, a third group needed primarily operations know-how, and Internet Securities needed to develop a strong presence in emerging markets fast. But all ventures accommodated these requirements via HBA and/or HBE activities.

This study did not systematically analyze ventures that could have carried out international activities but chose not to do so. Thus, we do not have a control group against which to measure performance of the ventures we studied. However, evidence from interviews with the entrepreneurs, investors, customers, suppliers, and competitors suggests that the six ventures studied here achieved faster growth and eventually had a higher level of profitability than competitors because of international activities.

The examination of business strategy requirements for the six ventures leads to the following proposition.

Proposition 2: International entrepreneurship activity is initiated in order to achieve more rapid venture growth than could be achieved through entrepreneurship activity confined to one country.

5.3. Role of home base

A home base is the location where top management resides, where knowledge is created, where flows are coordinated, and where resource allocation decisions are made. For all six ventures, the location of the home base was not entirely obvious by the time the venture was started. The entrepreneurs had choices. All six ventures required a complex coordination of inputs and outputs that were available or sought in different locations. The eventual location choice in terms of both country and city within a country was generally also the location characterized by the lowest overall coordination and input/output costs. Fig. 5 summarizes the analysis of HBA and HBE activities.

In the case of Richina, it turned out that Beijing was the optimal location. Although Richina relied heavily on capital, operational advice, and magazine content from New York City, the entrepreneur felt that setting a symbolic location priority in China was important. A home base in China made it easier to deal with bureaucrats and to monitor employees. Capital and magazine content could be obtained from New York City through a subsidiary. Within China, Beijing provided closest proximity to publishing authorities and to potential sources of news information.

In the case of African Communications Group, Cambridge, MA, turned out to be the best home base location. First, the firm had long-term plans to enter several national pay phone markets in Africa; a close affiliation with a particular country might have reduced the chances of obtaining licenses in other African countries. Second, the venture's success depended heavily on sourcing the right technology. Making the right technology choices required close proximity to telecommunication suppliers. Furthermore, being located in Boston had a positive effect on African Communications Group's technological competence as perceived by foreign business partners. Third, the firm's early financiers were located in the Boston area. As the venture required considerable additional capital before achieving profitability, it was important for the entrepreneurs to stay in close touch with current and potential future sources of funding. Finally, both founding entrepreneurs had attended university in Cambridge, MA, and moving away from the area would be costly.

The home base history of Internet Securities is particularly interesting. The firm started out with a dual home base. Gary Mueller developed news offices in Eastern Europe from London in 1994. He reasoned that London was a good beachhead into Eastern Europe and also was the site of many potential customers for Internet Securities news services. George Mueller, who was in charge of the firm's distribution technology, had graduated from Carnegie-Mellon University in Pittsburgh and hired a number of classmates to work with him. The company also established a small sales office in New York City to cover customers there. Over the next 26 months, the company established 14 offices in 14 countries. Each office had to communicate with both home bases, Pittsburgh and London. Over time, three-way communication between London, Pittsburgh, and the 14 offices became very difficult; in particular, the communication between R&D, operations, and sales suffered. In 1995, an experienced operations manager was hired who pushed for one unified home base. Since the company now had firmly established its sales offices in Eastern Europe and was focusing on establishing new offices in South America and Asia, it was decided that the home base should be in the US. Boston was chosen as a location, because it combined the virtues of a large pool of technology workers with close proximity to customers, i.e., the financial and corporate communities in Boston and New York City. The Pittsburgh office was closed, and London assumed a pure sales function. Moving the home base was costly, however. A number of key employees on the technical side did not want to move from Pittsburgh and proved difficult to replace.

The analysis of all six ventures suggests that firms tend to start from or converge upon a single home base. This finding coincides with earlier research on the characteristics of the home base in multinational companies (Porter, 1990; Kuemmerle, 1997a). However, our findings also suggest that entrepreneurs who start international ventures have a choice regarding the location of their home base. International exposure prior to starting a venture widens the entrepreneur's perspective, not only as far as business ideas are concerned but also regarding alternative home base locations. Third, entrepreneurs tend to choose the location that represents the lowest overall cost. Entrepreneurs specifically consider the cost of transferring information from critical sources to the venture and vice versa in their decision. Cambridge, for example, might not be the optimal long-term home base for African Communications Group, but for the critical first years, the entrepreneurs felt that proximity to technology providers and investors was sufficiently important to justify this home base location. Fourth, our findings for Internet Securities show that a home base can be moved, but only at a cost. Fifth, as a firm's network of sites expands and especially as the firm creates one or more HBA sites, managers and workers at the home base need to shift the focus of their activities from knowledge creation to knowledge flow coordination among sites. Finally, our findings suggest that although international entrepreneurial ventures are not constrained by existing routines in the same way as established companies are constrained, international ventures are constrained by the entrepreneur's inertia. The entrepreneur's location prior to starting the venture is one inertial element. In a sense, the core rigidities (Leonard-Barton, 1992) of an entrepreneurial venture at the stage of its inception are concentrated primarily in one person, the entrepreneur.

W. Kuemmerle / Journal of Business Venturing 17 (2002) 99–122   117

The analysis of the nature of home base locations leads to the following propositions.

Proposition 3a: International entrepreneurship activity is conducted from one home base as opposed to multiple home bases.

Proposition 3b: One of the principal roles of the home base is that of coordination of information flows. This is increasingly the case as international activities expand.

5.4. HBA activities

All six ventures engaged in HBA activities early in the venture's life. The entrepreneurs considered these to be very important for the survival and growth of their ventures. In every case except Bregman, HBA activities were carried out from dedicated office locations in the foreign country. Michael Bregman made frequent trips from his home base in Canada to the US, primarily because the financial condition of his venture did not permit the immediate establishment of an HBA site in the US.

HBA activities varied across ventures. In all ventures, the entrepreneur was keen on sourcing knowledge that was more easily accessible through a direct presence in the foreign country rather than through intermediaries, such as consultants. HBA facilities were considered particularly important for capturing tacit knowledge. This finding is in line with previously reported findings about the challenges of accessing knowledge (Kedia and Bhagat, 1988; Nonaka and Takeuchi, 1995; Mowery et al., 1996). While the nature of the targeted knowledge varied, all entrepreneurs used HBA activities as a response to some of the most important managerial challenges their ventures faced.

African Communications Group performed equipment tests at its location in Tanzania. These activities augmented the firm's knowledge base in Cambridge, where test results were analyzed and summarized for suppliers. The augmented knowledge base, in turn, made African Communications Group a more interesting customer for US and Canadian equipment suppliers that wanted to learn more about emerging technical requirements for telecommunications equipment in Africa and other emerging market countries.[4]

A key requirement for successful HBA activities is a receptive home base. If the home base is not receptive, knowledge-sourcing efforts will be futile. TVW was co-founded in Krakow by a Polish and a US entrepreneur. An HBA office in Newton, MA, was set up in order to raise capital, preferably from a strategic investor who could provide management know-how and media content. Since no foreign investor could be attracted for early stage investing, the founders invited two Polish firms to invest, in exchange for a majority of the shares. The entrepreneurs hoped to find a strategic foreign investor for the next stage. Claire Hurley, working out of the Newton office, successfully approached the Walt Disney Company. When TVW was close to a deal with Disney, the Polish majority owners objected and the deal fell

---

[4] In September 1998, African Communications Group (later renamed as Adesemi Communications Group) was present in Tanzania and Ghana and was close to entering two additional countries, one in Africa and one in Asia.

through. During the negotiations with Disney, the Polish majority owners, who had very little experience with basic market economy principles, did not realize how badly the firm needed foreign knowledge and capital. Only when the entrepreneur succeeded in educating the Polish majority owners regarding the need for cash and additional know how could a new strategic investor be attracted.

In the case of DDI, an HBA site in the US proved crucial, not only for short-term technology sourcing when DDI started its long-distance service in 1984, but also for long-term technology monitoring. Through its US presence, DDI was able to track the evolution of telecommunications inventions. This led to an alliance with Motorola in the Iridium project (which is developing advanced mobile communication technology) and with Lockheed and Raytheon in a project focused on satellite communications.

5.5. HBE activities

As one would expect, the prevalence of HBE activities depended on demand for the product or service in foreign countries and on the relative advantage of rapid international sales growth for future competition. In the ventures studied here, HBE activities were carried out at a later stage in the venture's life than HBA activities. In the case of Internet Securities, the time lag between HBA and HBE activities was about 4 months, for DDI and Michael Bregman it was somewhat less than 2 years. Only four out of six ventures engaged in HBE activities (see Fig. 5).

At Internet Securities, the entrepreneurs were keenly aware of the high fixed costs of gathering information in emerging markets and of the extremely low marginal costs of distributing the firm's products to additional subscribers via the Internet. Virtually on the first day of the venture's existence, the company set up a sales office in London. A sales office in New York City followed 4 months later. After 1 year, Internet Securities had over 500 institutional customers, including JP Morgan, Merrill Lynch, and KPMG.

At TVW and Richina, on the other hand, there was no demand for the firms' products overseas. Both firms hoped to eventually exploit their know-how in other countries. TVW planned to create TV stations in other Eastern European markets; Richina planned sales in countries with large Chinese populations. In the short term, however, revenue growth depended exclusively on successful penetration of the Chinese home base market. Thus, HBE activities were pushed into a distant secondary role.

For firms that carry out both HBA and HBE activities the question arises whether and under which conditions both activities should be carried out at the same location. The co-location of activities is efficient if the benefits of shared overhead outweigh the costs of increased distance from the optimal location for each activity. In the case of Internet Securities, 14 HBA sites were established in emerging markets within a period of 2 years; these sites were principally sourcing local information about emerging markets economies and firms. Over time, however, a number of firms in emerging markets prospered and became potential customers. About 1 year after establishing an HBA site, Internet Securities started HBE efforts at the same sites that had been established with an HBA mission. This effort consisted of local marketing, pricing, and

W. Kuemmerle / Journal of Business Venturing 17 (2002) 99–122 119

sales. It was prima facie efficient to co-locate both types of activity because major sources of information and customers were available at the same location. However, the entrepreneurs soon discovered that management requirements for both types of activities differed strongly. HBA activities required 'keen listeners' with a high absorptive capacity and a good understanding of what type of knowledge was useful for the venture. HBE activities, for their part, were driven by aggressive sales managers who had a detailed understanding of the firm's capabilities and of demand characteristics in the local market. Because of the difficulties encountered in juggling these two management requirements, the entrepreneurs eventually decided to operate both activities as entirely separate organizational units within each site.

The management of DDI also realized the challenges of co-location of HBA and HBE activities in the US and soon opted for separate locations, New Jersey and New York City, for both types of activities.

The analysis of HBA and HBE activities and the sequencing of these activities leads to the following propositions.

Proposition 4a: In most international ventures there is a need to carry out HBA or HBE activities in foreign locations. Most ventures eventually carry out both types of activities.

Proposition 4b: HBA activities and HBE activities are characterized by differing input requirements and therefore different location needs. The two types of activities are generally not co-located. If co-location occurs, the two types of activities are operated by separate organizational groups.[5]

Proposition 4c: In most international ventures the need for HBA activities arises before the need for HBE activities arises. Thus, international ventures generally carry out HBA activities before they carry out HBE ones.

6. Conclusion

In this paper, we analyzed the drivers and sequence of cross-border activities in international ventures by using a knowledge-management framework developed in earlier research on established multinational firms. The framework distinguishes two types of cross-border knowledge flows: knowledge flows that augment the venture's home base and knowledge flows that exploit this home base. We have argued that the knowledge-management framework can be used to develop a new definition of international entrepreneurship: International entrepreneurship is defined as the development of international new ventures or start-ups that, from their inception, engage in either HBA or HBE

---

[5] While this paper only examined ventures with dedicated HBE sites or no HBE activity at all, evidence from other cases we studied suggests that Proposition 4b applies equally well to exporters and ventures with foreign direct investment. In the case of exporting firms, the exporting function generally does not interact directly and intensively with any HBA function. Rather, the link between both functions is managed by senior management.

activities or both, thus viewing their operating domain as international from the initial stages of the firm's operation. When applying the framework to the six cases of international ventures, we found that propositions about the international *evolution* of these ventures can be developed. We suggest that the international *character* of ventures can be explained by the need for rapid growth and by the entrepreneur's prior exposure to international settings. Our propositions further suggest that all ventures start from or converge to one home base. The home base plays the role of an initial knowledge creator but subsequently assumes more and more the role of a knowledge flow coordinator. Finally, we suggest that during the early stages of an international venture HBA activities are more prevalent than HBE activities and that both types of activities are generally carried out in different locations or at least by different organizational units within the venture. The propositions developed in this paper can be tested with larger samples of international ventures.

Our analysis has a number of limitations. First, we examined only international ventures. Our finding that prior international experience predisposes an entrepreneur to starting an international venture would be strengthened if one found a similar result in a random sample of national and international ventures. Second, our sample of six ventures is biased towards media/communications and service industries. It seems that service and media/communications industries offer particularly good opportunities for entrepreneurs. Nevertheless, it might be interesting to test to what degree the knowledge-management framework applies to international manufacturing ventures.

Future research should focus on a number of questions. First, the propositions developed in this paper can be tested with a larger data set on international ventures. Second, a more fine-grained analysis of knowledge flows in international (as opposed to national) ventures seems promising. Some questions that need to be answered are: What determines the quality of cross-border intra-firm knowledge flows? How does the quality of these knowledge flows influence the performance of international ventures? How much complexity does the international dimension add to the management of a venture?

Third, and on a more general level, the study of international entrepreneurship has great potential to influence the field of entrepreneurship research as a whole and to increase the interest of other disciplines in the phenomenon of entrepreneurship. This paper has argued that international ventures engage in distinctive and focused cross-border activities to achieve higher growth rates than similar ventures could achieve in a domestic setting. An increasing number of international ventures are likely to join the ranks of the largest and most profitable companies in the world. Unlike Toyota or WalMart who operated domestically for many years before venturing abroad, some of these firms will become worldwide household names long before they have reached growth limits in their original home base country. This phenomenon of rapid international growth from the start raises important questions: How can these international high-growth firms ensure organizational stability? How should their resource allocation processes be designed? When should management shift its attention from HBA to HBE activities? These questions will be of high interest to organization science scholars as well as business strategy scholars, who will build on important and ongoing work by entrepreneurship scholars.

Acknowledgments

I am indebted to two anonymous referees, Howard H. Stevenson, Benjamin M. Oviatt, and Alan MacCormack for suggestions. Also, I am grateful to seminar participants at the 1998 Academy of International Business Meeting and at the Harvard Business School for comments. Support for this work by the Division of Research, Harvard Business School, is gratefully acknowledged.

References

Adams, G., Hall, G., 1993. Influences on the growth of SMEs: an international comparison. Entrepreneurship Reg Dev 5, 73–84.

Applegate, L.M., 1997. Internet Securities, Inc.: building an organization in Internet time (N2-398-007). Harvard Business School Press, Boston.

Barrett, A., 1995. It's a small (business) world. Bus Week, 96 (4/17/95).

Birley, S., MacMillan, I.C. (Eds.), 1995. International entrepreneurship. Routledge, London.

Bloodgood, Sapienza, 1995. The internationalization of new high potential ventures: antecedents and outcomes. Entrepreneurship Theory Pract 20, 61–76 (Summer).

Boter, H., Holmquist, C., 1996. Industry characteristics and internationalization process in small firms. J Bus Venturing 11, 471–487.

Brush, C.G., 1995. International entreprenership. Garland Publishing, New York.

Caves, R.E., 1996. Multinational enterprise and economic analysis. Cambridge Univ. Press, Cambridge.

Cohen, W., Levinthal, D., 1990. Absorptive capacity: a new perspective on learning and innovation. Adm Sci Q 35, 128–152.

Cohen, W.M., Levinthal, D.A., 1994. Fortune favors the prepared firm. Manage Sci 40 (2), 227–252.

Doz, Y.L., Prahalad, C.K., 1991. Managing DMNCs: a search for a new paradigm. Strategic Manage J 12, 145–164.

Eisenhardt, K.M., 1989. Building theories from case study research. Acad Manage Rev 14 (4).

Hart, M.M., Stevenson, H.H., Dial, J., 1995. Entrepreneurship: a definition revisited. In: Bygrave, W.D., Bird, B.J., Birley, S., Churchill, N.C., Hay, M., Keeley, R.H., Wetzel, W.E. (Eds.), Frontiers of entrepreneurship research. Babson College, Wellesley.

Hymer, S.H., 1976. The international operations of multinational firms: a study of foreign direct investment. MIT Press, Boston.

Kedia, B.L., Bhagat, R.S., 1988. Cultural constraints on transfer of technology across nations: implications for research in international and comparative management. Acad Manage Rev 13 (4), 559–571.

Knight, Cavusgil, 1996. The born global firm: a challenge to traditional internationalization theory. Adv Int Mark 8, 11–26.

Kogut, B., 1984. Normative observations on the international value-added chain and strategic groups. J Int Bus Stud 151–167 (Fall).

Kuemmerle, W., 1995. Analyzing foreign direct investment in research and development — an entrepreneurial perspective. In: MacMillan, I.C., Birley, S. (Eds.), International entrepreneurship. Routledge, London.

Kuemmerle, W., 1997a. Building effective R&D capabilities abroad. Harv Bus Rev 61–70 (March/April).

Kuemmerle, W., 1997b. Telewizja Wisla (2-898-033). Harvard Business School Press, Boston.

Kuemmerle, W., 1999a. The drivers of foreign direct investment into research and development. J Int Bus Stud 30 (1), 1–24.

Kuemmerle, W., 1999b. Foreign direct investment in industrial research in the pharmaceutical and electronics industries — results from a survey of multinational firms. Res Policy 28 (2–3), 179–193.

Landis, J.R., Koch, G.G., 1977. The measurement of observer agreement for categorical data. Biometrics 33, 159–174.

Leonard-Barton, D., 1992. Core capabilities and core rigidities: a paradox in managing new product development. Strategic Manage J 13, 111–125 (Special issue).

Leonard-Barton, D., 1995. Wellsprings of knowledge: building and sustaining the sources of innovation. Harvard Business School Press, Boston.

Levine, D.S., 1997. Little big shots. World Trade 10 (1), 42–44.

Mahoney, J., Pandian, J., 1992. The resource-based view within the conversation of strategic management. Strategic Manage J 13, 363–380.

McDougall, P.P., 1989. International versus domestic entrepreneurship: new venture strategic behavior and industry structure. J Bus Venturing 4, 387–400.

McDougall, P.P., Oviatt, B.M., 1996. New venture internationalization, strategic change and performance: a follow-up study. J Bus Venturing 11, 23–40.

McDougall, P.P., Shane, S., Oviatt, B.M., 1994. Explaining the formation of international ventures: the limits of theories from international business research. J Bus Venturing 9, 469–487.

McGahan, A., 1996. African Communications Group (9-796-128). Harvard Business School Press, Boston.

McGrath, R.G., MacMillan, I.C., Venkataraman, S., 1995. Global dimensions of new competencies: creating a review and research agenda. In: Birley, S., Macmillan, I.C. (Eds.), International entrepreneurship. Routledge, London.

Miles, M., Huberman, A.M., 1984. Qualitative data analysis. Sage Publications, Beverly Hills, CA.

Mowery, D.C., Oxley, J.E., Silverman, B.S., 1996. Strategic alliances and interfirm knowledge transfer. Strategic Manage J 17, 77–91 (Winter).

Nonaka, I., Takeuchi, H., 1995. The knowledge-creating company: how Japanese companies create the dynamics of innovation. Oxford Univ. Press, New York, NY.

Oviatt, B.M., McDougall, P.P., 1994. Toward a theory of international ventures. J Int Bus Stud, 45–64.

Oviatt, B.M., McDougall, P.P., 1995. Global start-ups: entrepreneurs on a worldwide stage. Acad Manage Exec 9 (2), 30–44.

Oviatt, B.M., McDougall, P.P., Simon, M., Shrade, R.C., 1993. Heartware international (A&B). Entrepreneurship Theory Pract, 111–139 (Winter).

Porter, M.E., 1990. The competitive advantage of nations. The Free Press, New York.

Rennie, 1993. Born global. McKinsey Q , (4), 45–52.

Sahlman, W.A., 1995. Richina Capital Partners Limited. Harvard Business School Press, Boston.

Stevenson, H.H., 1983. Michael Bregman (9-383-107). Harvard Business School Press, Boston.

Stevenson, H.H., 1994. DDI Corporation: 1994 (9-394-187). Harvard Business School Press, Boston.

Stevenson, H.H., Jarillo, J.C., 1990. A paradigm of entrepreneurship: entrepreneurial management. Strategic Manage J 11, 17–27.

Teece, D.J., Pisano, G., Shuen, A., 1997. Dynamic capabilities and strategic management. Strategic Manage J 18 (7), 509–533.

Tyebjee, T.M., 1990. The internationalization of high tech ventures. In: Churchill, N.C., Bygrave, W.D., Hornaday, J.A., Muzyka, D.F., Vesper, K.H., Wetzel, W.E. Jr. (Eds.), Frontiers of entrepreneurship research. Babson College, Wellesley.

Venkataraman, S., 1997. The distinctive domain of entrepreneurship. Adv Entrepreneurship, Firm Emergence Growth 3, 119–138.

Vernon, R., 1979. The product cycle hypothesis in a new international environment. Oxford Bull Econ Stat 41, 255–267 (November).

Wright, R.W., Ricks, D.A., 1994. Trends in international business research: twenty-five years later. J Int Bus Stud, 687–701.

Yin, R.K., 1989. Case study research: design and methods. Sage Publication, Newbury Park, CA.

[16]

ELSEVIER

Available online at www.sciencedirect.com

SCIENCE @ DIRECT·

Journal of Business Venturing 20 (2005) 437–457

JOURNAL
of BUSINESS
VENTURING

Antecedents of international and domestic learning effort

Harry J. Sapienza[a,*], Dirk De Clercq[b], William R. Sandberg[c]

[a]*Carlson School of Management, University of Minnesota, 3-312 321, 19th Avenue South,
Minneapolis, MN 55455, USA*
[b]*Vlerick Leuven Gent Management School and Ghent University, 9000 Ghent, Belgium*
[c]*Moore School of Business, University of South Carolina, Columbia, SC 29208, USA*

Received 30 March 2002; received in revised form 25 March 2004; accepted 25 March 2004

Abstract

We examine the antecedents of international and domestic learning effort in independent firms. We combine learning theory and the "attention-based" view to examine how firms' degree of internationalization, the age at international entry, and entrepreneurial orientation are associated with the extent to which they engage in foreign and domestic learning activities. In particular, our study shows that early entry in foreign markets and an entrepreneurial orientation are positively related to a culture that promotes learning effort in international and domestic markets. On the other hand, whereas a firm's degree of internationalization does not have a significant association with international learning effort, the degree of internationalization is negatively related to domestic learning effort. We discuss the implications of our study for theory, practice, and future research.
© 2004 Elsevier Inc. All rights reserved.

Keywords: Internationalization; Entrepreneurial orientation; Learning

1. Executive summary

Where do internationalized firms devote their learning effort? The attention-based view of the firm argues that the answer depends on how they direct attention and efforts across activities (Ocasio, 1997). Learning theory (Cohen and Levinthal, 1990) suggests that firms

---

* Corresponding author. Tel.: +1-612-624-2442; fax: +1-612-626-1316.
E-mail address· hsapienza@csom.umn.edu (H.J. Sapienza).

0883-9026/$ – see front matter © 2004 Elsevier Inc. All rights reserved.
doi:10.1016/j.jbusvent.2004.03.001

learn more when they exert significant effort in processing new external knowledge. As such, we suggest that learning theory complements the attention-based view by revealing how much effort firms might devote to different external knowledge.

Consistent with these views, we examine the relationship between a firm's efforts to learn from its home and foreign market(s) and its foreign presence, foreign "identity," and competitive orientation. More specifically, we examine how the firm's degree of internation-alization, age at first international entry, and entrepreneurial orientation are related to the attention it devotes to learning activities in international and domestic markets. Whereas we focus primarily on factors that explain why firms exert more or less effort to learn about foreign markets (i.e., "international learning effort"), we also consider the implications of such factors on the extent to which firms undertake learning activities in domestic markets (i.e., "domestic learning effort").

Our sample of independent, owner-managed Belgian firms afforded a high likelihood for firms to have engaged in international activity. At the same time we could expect important variation in the timing and degree of internationalization among the firms as earlier studies in small, European countries have shown that many such firms see cross-border operations as necessary while others avoid, postpone, or minimize them.

Regression analyses show that (1) the degree of internationalization is negatively related to domestic learning effort but not related to international learning effort; (2) the earlier a firm engages in international activity, the greater its international and domestic learning efforts; and (3) entrepreneurial orientation is positively related to the intensity of learning effort undertaken in international and domestic markets.

One contribution of this study is its examination of how the firm's existing international operations, age at foreign entry, and entrepreneurial orientation are associated with its development of learning capacities. Prior research has examined how "born global" firms enter foreign markets based on their entrepreneurial skills and capacities (e.g., Oviatt and McDougall, 1997).

We find that degree of internationalization is (mildly) positively associated with interna-tional learning effort but (significantly) negatively related to domestic learning effort. These results suggest that a firm's strategic attention is directed by the scope of its cross-border operations. Our finding that earlier entry into foreign markets is related to greater interna-tional *and* domestic learning effort suggests that early internationalization may create a company-wide learning culture: that is, international operations likely involve the whole organization rather than only the unit(s) dedicated to international activities. Furthermore, the positive relationship between entrepreneurial orientation and both types of learning effort indicates that a proactive, experimental market stance may promote learning-by-doing through the intense assimilation of information regarding domestic *and* international markets. Overall, then, our study suggests that if learning is essential to success, firms may be well advised to adopt an entrepreneurial orientation and to enter foreign markets earlier rather than later. This prescription should be tempered by the recognition that early entry may also increase risk. In addition, because high levels of internationalization may retard domestic learning effort, internationalizing firms should remain mindful of domestic learning to maintain their overall competitive posture.

H.J. Sapienza et al. / Journal of Business Venturing 20 (2005) 437–457 439

2. Introduction

In the increasingly knowledge-based global economy, firms seek proactively to internationalize earlier in their existence and more rapidly than in the past (Autio et al., 2000). Some ventures are even "born global." For many ventures, internationalization is not just an afterthought, but an essential gambit. However, internationalization inevitably alters the focus of a firm's strategic attention (Ocasio, 1997). For firms that have internationalized, the important questions are no longer, "why should we internationalize?" or "when should we internationalize?" but rather "how much effort should be put in the international marketplace?" and "how should our domestic activities evolve to accommodate our multicountry status?"

With the development of the knowledge-based economy, what a firm learns and how it develops its learning capacity become increasingly critical (Grant, 1996; Zahra and George, 2002). We adopt the attention-based view and learning theory as a framework for theory and hypotheses regarding where internationalized firms devote their learning effort. The attention-based view of the firm argues that firm behavior depends on how its decision makers direct their attention across activities (Ocasio, 1997). More specifically, it holds that the focus of attention and effort depends upon what resources have been accumulated, what type of identity and relationships have been developed, and what rules are embedded within the organization. Thus, the current disposition of international assets, the firm's international "identity," and its orientation toward competing should all be critical to where a firm directs its effort. Learning theory (Autio et al., 2000; Cohen and Levinthal, 1990; Zahra and George, 2002) holds that firms learn best when new knowledge is related to prior knowledge and when they devote intense effort to processing new external knowledge. As such, learning theory complements the attention-based view by revealing how much effort firms might devote to different external knowledge.

Much recent literature has argued that learning and knowledge creation are the most important strategic activities of the firm (Grant, 1996; Spender, 1996). Learning's importance stems from the centrality of knowledge to the firm, in that the firm may be understood "as a knowledge-creating entity" (Nonaka et al., 2000). In other words, a firm can be conceived as a means to acquire, assimilate and exploit knowledge to achieve commercial ends (Cohen and Levinthal, 1990); therefore, knowledge and the capability to create and use it "are the most important source of a firm's sustainable competitive advantage" (Nonaka et al., 2000, p. 1). Important to new knowledge creation is the *effort* undertaken to identify and gather knowledge (Cohen and Levinthal, 1990; Spender, 1996). If firms are to renew themselves via the renewal of their knowledge bases and their capacities to learn, they must expend requisite effort to obtain and assimilate new external knowledge (Zahra and George, 2002). For firms that compete not only domestically but also in one or more foreign markets, a critical question is how to allocate learning effort between domestic and foreign markets. Zahra et al. (2000) claim that the ability to acquire and integrate foreign and domestic knowledge is critical to a multicountry firm's development and performance. Therefore, we focus in this study on factors that drive such effort.

Consistent with attention- and learning-based views, we focus on the relationship of a firm's effort to learn from its home market and its foreign market(s) to its foreign presence, the extent of its foreign "identity," and its orientation toward competing. We assume that international learning effort and domestic learning effort are systematically related. That is, firms may be more or less "learning active," a condition that would result in some positive covariance of international and domestic learning effort. At the same time, the framework we develop suggests that domestic and international learning effort may at times be driven in different directions. As suggested in the above discussion, the extent of a firm's current international presence should affect its allocation of learning effort. We also suggest that the extent of a firm's international "identity" will affect its attention. Some researchers (e.g., Autio et al., 2000; Brush, 1992; Sapienza et al., 2000) have argued that the age at which a firm internationalizes affects the extent to which it sees itself primarily as a single-country or a truly "inter- or multinational" firm. Therefore, a firm's age at foreign entry can be seen as a proxy for its identity. Finally, the firm's entrepreneurial orientation (i.e., its proactivity, innovation, and risk-taking [Miller, 1983]) establishes its rules and norms for expending effort toward knowledge development and renewal.

To study these issues, it was important to choose a market in which most firms would be operating in multiple countries. Earlier studies have indicated that multicountry operation is commonplace in smaller European countries, even among independent, owner-managed firms (Autio et al., 2000; Eriksson et al., 1997). We selected Belgium as the research site.

3. Theoretical framework and hypotheses

Learning theory suggests that organizations learn when their routines, systems, and policies assimilate individuals' activities and experiences (Grant, 1996). A premise of our research is that the greater a firm's attention to developing new knowledge and to exploiting existing knowledge, the greater its learning. This premise is consistent with prior theory which holds that the amount of information learned and the ease of its retrieval depend upon the intensity of effort in its acquisition (Cohen and Levinthal, 1990), and with the notion that a firm's behavior can be envisioned as the pattern of effort and attention devoted to specific activities (Ocasio, 1997). Learning is path dependent: what a firm attends to and learns in one period helps define its feasible set in the next (Cohen and Levinthal, 1990). Therefore, firms' success depends significantly on their early choices and on the focus and level of their attention and effort (Autio et al., 2000). We therefore conceive of the extent to which firms devote attention to learning in international as well as domestic markets as a critical outcome variable, and we focus on the question of how several factors affect this "learning effort."

Ocasio (1997) argued that a firm's behavior depends on existing resources, relationships and rules, and the manner in which these factors focus its strategic effort or attention. We apply Ocasio's framework to firms' development and renewal of their domestic and foreign market knowledge. Learning is critical to the survival and growth of firms competing across borders (Johanson and Vahlne, 1991; Zahra et al., 2000), but prior to the 1980s research into internationalization related only indirectly to learning's role. Instead, it focused on identifying how external factors (e.g., extending the product life cycle, securing needed resources and low-cost factors of production) affected the timing and mode of internationalization (Kogut,

H.J. Sapienza et al. / Journal of Business Venturing 20 (2005) 437–457 441

1989). In the 1980s research emphasized the benefits of transferring knowledge between domestic and foreign markets and of coordinating effort across a network of locations (Bartlett and Ghoshal, 1989; Kogut, 1989). Firms may learn directly from foreign market experience and indirectly via observation of foreign firms or from interactions with foreign partners, and may transfer learning's benefits between foreign and domestic markets (Hamel, 1991; Johanson and Vahlne, 1991). Thus, scholars increasingly recognize learning's importance as a means to an end (such as extending the product life cycle) or for its own regenerative properties (Zahra et al., 2000).

Researchers have widely addressed the factors that drive internationalization but rarely examined the effects of internationalization itself on firms' behavior (Zahra et al., 2000). Thus, the timing of internationalizing has been studied (e.g., Brush, 1992; Eriksson et al., 1997; Johanson and Vahlne, 1991), yet few have investigated the *subsequent* effects of timing and extensiveness on firms' behavior in international and domestic markets (Autio et al., 2000). For instance, whereas new venture internationalization theory (McDougall and Oviatt, 2000; Oviatt and McDougall, 1997) argues that "born global" firms enter foreign markets on the basis of their unique knowledge and skills, we examined the reciprocal effect: how the firm's scope of international activities ("degree of internationalization") and the timing of its first international activities ("age at international entry") relate to the intensity of the firm's learning activities.

Consistent with Eriksson et al. (1997) and Johanson and Vahlne, (1991, 2003), we consider not only the "state" of a firm's international presence but also the firm's propensity to "change" that status. Describing internationalization as a continual interplay between current commitments of the firm's resources and decisions to alter those commitments, Johanson and Vahlne (1991, 2003) posited that commitments to foreign markets mount as experience diminishes uncertainty about foreign competition. We posit that a firm's entrepreneurial orientation (Miller, 1983) influences the pace of accumulation. Classically risk-averse firms will follow the slow, incremental process described in Johanson and Vahlne's (1991) early formulations, whereas proactive, risk-taking firms will move rapidly to acquire and assimilate as much new external knowledge as possible. In attention-based terminology, such firms could be said to have developed rules and norms that favor innovation, proactiveness, and risk-taking.

In summary, prior research is not explicit about the correlates of international and domestic learning effort, activities at the core of performance (Grant, 1996). The effect of the internationalization process itself on learning has received scant examination. Ocasio's (1997) attention-based view suggests, however, that the antecedents of a firm's allocation of learning effort reside in the resources, identity, and rules it has built. Autio et al. (2000) argued that a firm's international identity and learning are shaped by when in its life cycle it becomes international and how rapidly it grows into this identity. Although supporting the notion that a firm's current extent of internationalization is important to its ongoing effort, Johanson and Vahlne's (1991, 2003) model stops short of explaining why firms with the same level of resource commitment to international activities might proceed at different rates. We suggest below that in addition to current commitment, the timing of initial foreign entry and current entrepreneurial orientation are also important correlates of effort. Thus, we seek to develop a simple model of domestic and international learning effort that will extend thinking on firm learning and internationalization.

442   *H.J. Sapienza et al. / Journal of Business Venturing 20 (2005) 437–457*

3.1. Degree of internationalization and learning effort

Ocasio (1997) argued that a firm's resources affect its behavior through their effects on its capacity to perform activities in a given area. A firm's degree of internationalization represents its allocation of physical and human resources to foreign versus domestic activities; as such, it is a multidimensional construct (Sullivan, 1994). To a greater extent than *years* of foreign operation, *degree* of internationalization measures a firm's commitment to activities outside its domestic market. Furthermore, although internationalization is often operationalized as percentage of foreign sales, it also implies investment in assets, people, and activities (Sullivan, 1994).

Degree of internationalization is likely associated with a firm's attention to exploring and exploiting opportunities in foreign markets because it shapes what resources the firm acquires, the rules of operations it adopts, and the relationships it develops. Eriksson et al. (1997) found that as degree of internationalization increases, perceived risks of further commitment to foreign markets diminishes. Johanson and Vahlne (1991) argued that the reduction of perceived risks would lead to broader, more intense devotion to new markets outside the firm's borders.

Learning theory suggests that more intense and repetitive processing leads to greater knowledge acquisition. As a firm devotes more resources to and obtains more sales from foreign markets, the intensity of its learning effort in these contexts may also increase (Ocasio, 1997). For example, Zahra et al. (2000) found that diversity of foreign market presence enhances technology-based firms' ability to learn in international markets. In our setting, the implication is that firms' increase of their sources of foreign revenue, number of employees devoted to foreign activities, and scope of foreign operations, will be associated with greater foreign learning effort. Thus, we hypothesize:

Hypothesis 1a: The degree of internationalization is positively related to international learning effort.

Because degree of internationalization reflects not just the magnitude of a firm's foreign presence but also the importance of such presence relative to domestic activities, the issue arises as to internationalization's relationship to firms' learning effort in domestic markets. Is there a trade-off in a firm's devotion of effort to foreign versus domestic learning activity when that firm is in many countries, or does international learning effort reinforce its domestic counterpart? Our earlier arguments suggest that the *capacity to learn* in domestic markets may increase with internationalization: broader and deeper experiences in varied markets may well raise a firm's overall learning capacity (Cohen and Levinthal, 1990; Zahra et al., 2000). However, the relative incentive to learn in the domestic market may diminish as the firm becomes more internationalized. As firms increase their international presence, the returns to learning effort increase outside their domestic market and decrease at home. Compare, for example, a firm that conducts 90% of its business abroad to one of similar size that conducts only 15% of its business abroad. The latter has greater incentive to focus its effort in the domestic market.

H.J. Sapienza et al. / Journal of Business Venturing 20 (2005) 437–457 443

The degree of internationalization represents the weighted scope of a firm's operations. As such, we expect that learning effort may be focused accordingly. Implicit in earlier arguments is the idea that learning gained in one arena may be reallocated elsewhere (Kogut, 1989). However, learning derived from foreign markets may not have as full or immediate an impact in the domestic market as it does in its original markets. Consequently, with rising internationalization, a firm is likely to shift its attention to foreign markets in order to reap fully the benefits of further expansion. If, as Johanson and Vahlne (1991) have argued, a firm's internationalization follows a pattern of movement to ever more geographically and culturally distant locales, the *benefits* of domestic learning effort will diminish correspondingly as the firm becomes more internationalized. For example, a German food processor that has developed networks of high-quality suppliers for its plants in France and Poland may expend less effort learning what will satisfy German suppliers than would a food processor that relies almost exclusively on domestic suppliers.

In summary, although increased internationalization may be associated with an enhanced learning capacity, it also draws attention from the home market as the prospective returns to learning increase elsewhere. Furthermore, as the typical pattern is for internationalization to move over time to ever more remote markets, the payoff to effort at home becomes less attractive. Thus, we hypothesize:

Hypothesis 1b: The degree of internationalization is negatively related to domestic learning effort.

3.2. Age at international entry and learning effort

Prior research has suggested that firms develop their nature, mindset, and identity early in their existence (Autio et al., 2000; Boeker, 1989; Sapienza et al., 2000). Therefore, a firm that embarks early on international operations is more likely to see itself from the outset as "inter- or multinational" (Brush, 1992) and will recognize early on the benefits of learning effort in foreign markets. In other words, operating internationally from an early age will likely have path-dependent effects on its attention and what it accumulates (Ocasio, 1997).

Prior research has found empirical support for an effect of age at first entry on learning outcomes and on identity. For instance, Autio et al. (2000) found that starting international activity early on increased the firm's international growth; they attributed this phenomenon to more effective learning in international markets. They argued that early internationalizers see foreign markets as less "foreign." Consistent with this view, Brush (1992) showed that the earlier firms internationalized, the more they identified themselves as international firms. Johanson and Vahlne (1991, 2003) argued that the earlier a firm's experience with foreign markets, the less risk it perceives in such markets. In short, early entry into foreign markets reduces the fear of expending effort in learning about foreign markets.

Furthermore, when the firm internationalizes early on, relationships with domestic partners likely are the primary source of its business contacts (Autio et al., 2000). The attention-based view suggests that the firm's existing relationships are important drivers of its behavior (Ocasio, 1997). That is, the firm's current engagement vis à vis others may give rise to future activities that are commensurate with those relationships. Therefore, we argue that early international-izers are less constrained by existing domestic relationships, and more likely to develop knowledge through relationships that have been built internationally. Thus, we hypothesize:

Hypothesis 2a: The firm's age at international entry is negatively related to its international learning effort.

Although we hypothesized that early internationalization increases international learning effort, its effects on domestic learning effort and attention are less clear. Autio et al. (2000) argued that early internationalization helps to instill a *learning culture* in an organization that should benefit domestic as well as foreign effort; they labeled the overall benefits as "learning advantages of newness" that help some new firms overcome liabilities of foreignness and newness in entering foreign markets. While it is possible that early foreign entry may help establish a general learning culture in a firm, the logic of Hypothesis 2a suggests that very young firms that venture beyond their own borders will identify less strongly with their domestic markets than will firms that operated solely in one market for a longer time. Managers of late entrants to international competition are likely to have built habits and routines that affix great attention to the domestic market (Ocasio, 1997). Furthermore, learning theory suggests that prolonged focusing of attention in a restricted domain creates competency traps that are difficult to overcome (Cohen and Levinthal, 1990; Levinthal and March, 1993). For example, a Spanish chemical company that has focused on complying with domestic environmental standards may be less capable of adjusting to Scandinavia's stricter standards.

In brief, when a firm initiates involvement in international activities early on, it is more likely to develop routines aimed at international rather than domestic markets. Conversely, the domestic learning routines of firms that internationalize late will be deeply embedded. Therefore, we hypothesize:

Hypothesis 2b: The firm's age at international entry is positively related to its domestic learning effort.

3.3. Entrepreneurial orientation and learning effort

In the attention-based view, a firm's rules or norms are critical to its ongoing effort. Thus, we expect a firm's entrepreneurial orientation to affect its learning effort in both foreign and domestic markets. Furthermore, as entrepreneurial orientation represents the rules and norms by which a firm makes decisions, its "organizing principles," it is likely to be associated consistently with domestic and learning effort. The three behaviors signifying entrepreneurial orientation around which there is growing consensus are innovation, proactivity, and risk taking (McDougall and Oviatt, 2000; Miller, 1983). Although many entrepreneurship theorists have touted the benefits of an entrepreneurial orientation, few have empirically tested its effects (Lumpkin and Dess, 1996).

Firms that enter foreign markets are exposed to high uncertainty emanating from both their lack of knowledge and the increased complexity of operating in multiple, dissimilar markets

(Eriksson et al., 1997; Johanson and Vahlne, 1991). Learning in a foreign market involves identifying and understanding a country's different requirements (e.g., product standards, industry norms, customer needs) as well as the tendencies and capabilities of local competitors (Eriksson et al., 1997; Zaheer and Mosakowski, 1997). The extent to which a firm engages in learning effort in new markets is likely to be related to its entrepreneurial orientation. For instance, the firm's propensity to search proactively for new business partners is reflected in its orientation (Lumpkin and Dess, 1996). Firms proactive in seeking foreign suppliers, customers, and alliance partners will more likely exchange knowledge intensively with their foreign partners to benefit from these relationships.

Zaheer and Mosakowski (1997) suggested that first-mover advantages may be available to innovative firms entering foreign markets so long as they rapidly learn in the new settings. Their study suggested that a rationale for learning effort abroad is that it makes more likely the successful adoption of new technological developments in foreign markets. As their "liability of foreignness" concept suggests, however, such learning effort risks running afoul of local customs and laws, miscalculating local trends and preferences, and paying higher prices for access to channels and supplies. We contend that the more entrepreneurially oriented the firm, the more likely it will go beyond mere exporting or licensing to learn about and engage in the day-to-day activities of the foreign market. Without risk taking, knowledge acquisition in foreign domains may be extremely limited. Eriksson et al. (1997) maintained that critical foreign knowledge is gained only through bold foreign operations. "Timid" firms may not make the learning effort.

It is important to note that whereas entrepreneurial firms may learn far more through their aggressive behavior, they may also make more mistakes than their less entrepreneurial counterparts. In other words, performance may vary greatly across highly entrepreneurial firms, as some experiments fail miserably while others succeed. Nonetheless, we argue that an entrepreneurial orientation should typically be associated with greater effort devoted to learning about foreign markets as firms probe for new opportunities. Thus, we hypothesize:

Hypothesis 3a: A firm's entrepreneurial orientation is positively related to its international learning effort.

As implied above, entrepreneurial orientation is also likely to be positively associated with effort devoted to learning in the *domestic* market. Identifying, acquiring, and assimilating knowledge may not be as risky in domestic markets as in foreign markets, but an entrepreneurial orientation implies proactive opportunity seeking in these markets as well. Learning in the domestic market requires special effort to ensure periodic review and challenge of all assumptions. By definition, entrepreneurial firms need no provocation to seek new ways to do things. In short, learning effort in domestic markets should also be higher when the firm has the bias for action that characterizes an entrepreneurial orientation. Thus, we hypothesize:

Hypothesis 3b: A firm's entrepreneurial orientation is positively related to its domestic learning effort.

4. Methodology

Our sample was drawn from a database maintained by the Entrepreneurial Center at the Vlerick Leuven Gent Management School in Belgium that includes owner-managed, independent firms (i.e. not units of other companies). Firms in the sample compete in the measuring equipment, construction, transportation, chemical, nonfinancial services, food, textile, computer peripherals, and other industries. We pretested our questionnaire with academics experienced in knowledge-based and international research, then revised potentially confusing items.

We used previously validated measures (e.g., degree of internationalization, entrepreneurial orientation) wherever possible to help ensure their validity. Where prior scales did not exist (e.g., learning effort), we constructed measures based on suggestions in the literature (see Appendix A for detailed items). The questionnaire was addressed to each firm's CEO because firms' top executives have relevant information about their internationalization (McDougall, 1989); our sample of owner–managers presumably were especially well informed and influential in the strategic direction of their companies. We collected the data via two mailings of our questionnaire to 500 firms randomly selected from the database. In the spring of 2000, we received 59 responses; in the summer, we received 33 responses to the second mailing. We retained for further analyses only firms that had fewer than 1,000 employees. As a result, the final sample consisted of 90 respondents, which represents a response rate of 18%. Because late respondents may share characteristics with nonrespondents, we compared early and late respondents on the variables under study (Churchill, 1991). We found no statistically significant differences between early and late respondents. Thus, we have no evidence to suggest response bias.

Because there are no precise proxies for many of the variables in our study, we relied on the self-reported assessments of each firm's CEO. Such an approach raises the possibility that the relationships among variables result from common-method variance (Wagner and Crampton, 1993). We reduced that possibility by employing previously validated measures where possible (Spector, 1987). In addition, we conducted Harman's one-factor test on all variables included in the study (except for the industry variable), as suggested by Podsakoff and Organ (1986). Substantial common-method variance would result in few factors accounting for most variance in the variables. Factor analysis resulted in multiple factors with eigenvalues greater than 1, with the first factor accounting for only 24% of the total variance. This indicates that common-method variance did not cause the relationships among the variables in our sample (Podsakoff and Organ, 1986). Finally, our inclusion of multiple items to measure learning effort, degree of internationalization, and entrepreneurial orientation promoted content validity.

4.1. Dependent variables

4.1.1. International learning effort
Consistent with prior research (Eriksson et al., 1997; Yu, 1990), we measured learning effort in foreign markets via items asking to what extent the firm engages in effort to *exploit* (1)

general international procedures and systems (Items 1 and 2 in Appendix A) and (2) specific factors in its most significant foreign market (items 5–8). Combining these items resulted in an international exploitation scale (α=.74). Parallel items focused on effort to *explore* general international procedures and systems (Items 3–4) and specific factors in the most significant market (items 9–12); the combined items had an α of .80. Factor analysis indicated that the subscales could be combined into a single international learning effort scale (α=.85). On a scale from 1 to 5, responses ranged from 1 to 4.5 with a mean of 2.83. To examine convergent validity, we conducted a confirmatory factor analysis. All items but one had a factor loading higher than .35 thereby demonstrating good convergent validity (Sharma, 1996).

4.1.2. Domestic learning effort

For the sake of comparability, we measured domestic learning effort in a manner consistent with international learning effort. We employed similar activities to assess domestic exploitation (items 1–6 in Appendix A) and exploration (Items 7–12) as in the international setting, attaining α values of .83 and .85 respectively. Again, factor analysis indicated that the two subscales could be productively combined into a single domestic learning effort scale (α=.92). On a scale from one to five, responses ranged from 1 to 4.75 with a mean of 3.11. Confirmatory factor analysis revealed that all 12 items had factor loadings higher than .35, demonstrating good convergent validity (Sharma, 1996).

One could argue that international learning effort and domestic learning effort are two dimensions of the same construct; that is, they reflect the common idea of how much attention the firm devotes to learning activities overall. However, it is important to note that we did not conceive of "learning effort" as an inherent organizational characteristic, but rather as activity. In other words, whereas it may be true that many firms score either high or low on both dimensions, conceptually it is feasible that some firms score differently on the two dimensions. To check for discriminant validity between international and domestic learning effort, we undertook a confirmatory factor analysis with the two correlated factors. We found that the variance the two factors have in common with each other (.22) is substantially lower than the total variance each of the factors has in common with its respective items (.34 for international learning effort and .48 for domestic learning effort). This finding suggests good discriminant validity between the constructs of international and domestic learning effort (Sharma, 1996).

4.2. Independent variables

4.2.1. Degree of internationalization

Appropriate measurement of a firm's internationalization has been subject to discussion (e.g., Fischer and Reuber, 1997; Ramaswamy et al., 1996; Sullivan, 1994). Based on Fischer and Reuber (1997), we measured the degree of internationalization through a multidimensional approach (Sullivan, 1994) that included subfactors to address some limitations to typical measures of internationalization (Ramaswamy et al., 1996): (1) foreign sales as a percentage of total sales, a single-item measure of a firm's degree of internationalization; (2) the percentage of employees who spend a significant part of their time on international activities; and (3) the geographic scope of foreign sales, as measured by Fischer and Reuber

448   *H.J. Sapienza et al. / Journal of Business Venturing 20 (2005) 437–457*

(1997); for this last dimension we calculated a single, weighted score for each respondent by counting the areas (out of 12 countries or groups of countries) in which the firm realized foreign sales. Weights assigned to the categories represented their geographic and cultural distance from the firm's domestic market: a weight of "one" was assigned to the five countries bordering Belgium (including the United Kingdom), "two" to other countries within the European Union, "three" to other European countries and North America, and "four" to other countries. Because scales differed across the three internationalization dimensions, we standardized and then averaged the items. Cronbach's α for this measure was .82.

4.2.2. Age at international entry

The age at international entry was determined by subtracting the founding year from the year of first realized revenues outside the domestic market. We used realized foreign sales as the sole criterion to obtain an unambiguous date for each firm. Other researchers have indicated that foreign sales is the most widely used measure of foreign activity (Autio et al., 2000). The average age at first internationalization was 16 years.

4.2.3. Entrepreneurial orientation

We used the scale validated by Miller (1983) to gauge entrepreneurial orientation; the seven items capture the firm's innovation, risk taking, and proactivity. This measure had a Cronbach's α of .65. Although a confirmatory factor analysis of the seven items demonstrated good convergent validity, the α for entrepreneurial orientation (.65) is lower than the cutoff value of .70 suggested by Nunnally (1978). The reason for this relatively low reliability may be that the construct's dimensions do not always covary and may vary independently in a given case (Lumpkin and Dess, 1996; Ramaswamy et al., 1996). However, we chose to use a composite measure consistent with Miller's (1983) original measure. In other words, we argue that a fundamental set of behaviors may underlie entrepreneurial processes (Covin and Slevin, 1989; Miller, 1983).

4.3. Control variables

4.3.1. Years of international experience

We added international experience as a control variable because a firm's international experience may affect its learning effort in foreign markets (Eriksson et al., 1997; Johanson and Vahlne, 1991). For instance, firms with great international experience may be less motivated to expend effort in international learning activities. On the other hand, firms possessing significant international experience may want to leverage that experience by further increasing their learning effort abroad. Furthermore, by simultaneously examining years of experience and age at international entry, we were able to examine the effects of age at first internationalization *beyond* the effects of experience.

4.3.2. Firm size

We included number of employees as a control variable because large firms may have more resources to devote to learning activities. Firm size averaged 87 for the sample.

Table 1
Means, standard deviation, ranges, coefficient α, and correlations of the variables

	1	2	3	4	5	6	7
(1) Degree of internationalization							
(2) Age at international entry	− .065						
(3) Entrepreneurial orientation	.035	.109					
(4) International experience	.290**	.048	− .151				
(5) Firm size	.397**	.170	− .053	.446**			
(6) International learning effort	.274**	− .216*	.392**	.105	.087		
(7) Domestic learning effort	− .105	− .148	.323**	.037	.036	.524**	
Mean	− .02	15.82	3.21	15.91	87.48	2.83	3.11
Standard deviation	0.84	24.35	0.59	16.02	164.60	0.68	0.81
Minimum	− 0.99	0.00	1.71	0.00	1.00	1.00	1.00
Maximum	2.07	127.00	5.00	66.00	1000	4.50	4.75
α	.82	n/a	.65	n/a	n/a	.85	.92

For firm size, the natural logarithm is used in correlations, but actual values are reported in descriptive statistics. *$P \le .05$, **$P \le .01$; two-tailed tests ($N=76$).

4.3.3. Industry

We also controlled for industry sector because firms in more knowledge-intensive industries may be more inclined to exert learning effort. We assigned the responding firms to seven categories corresponding to SIC divisions (agriculture, construction, manufacturing, transportation, wholesale trade, retail trade, and service). We coded the categories with dummy variables, with agriculture serving as the base case in regression analyses.

As can be seen from Table 1, the correlations among the independent variables and control variables are generally modest. However, we checked for multicollinearity in the two regression models shown in Table 2 and found no threat to interpretation.

5. Results

As mentioned earlier, an analysis of the bivariate correlation coefficients showed a positive relationship between international learning effort and domestic learning effort (Table 1; $r=.52$; $P<.001$); this suggests that learning activities regarding international and domestic issues tend to move in concert. All hypotheses were tested using multiple regression analysis. The first column in Table 2 summarizes the results for Hypotheses 1a to 3a which pertain to the association of independent variables with a firm's international learning effort. We included only the 76 firms that already had undertaken international activity to examine international learning effort. Although a positive correlation exists between the degree of internationalization and international learning effort (Table 1), Hypothesis 1a does not receive support: degree of internationalization is not related to international learning effort when controlling for all other variables. However, Hypothesis 2a is supported: age at international entry is negatively related to international learning effort at $P<.05$. Finally, Hypothesis 3a is also supported: entrepreneurial orientation is positively related to international learning effort at $P<.01$.

Table 2
Regression tests

Dependent variables →	International learning effort	Domestic learning effort
H1a and b: degree of internationalization	.136	− .269*
H2a and b: age at first internationalization	− .225*	− .252*
H3a and b: entrepreneurial orientation	.382**	.384**
International experience	.055	.082
Firm size (log of number of employees)	.041	.149
Construction (SIC division C)[a]	.278[+]	.014
Manufacturing (SIC division D)[a]	.733[+]	.429
Transportation (SIC division E)[a]	.215	.207
Wholesale trade (SIC division F)[a]	.218	.224
Retail trade (SIC division G)[a]	.359	.261
Service (SIC division I)[a]	.304	.231
Adjusted R^2	.246	.120
F value	3.225**	2.101*
Degrees of freedom	(11; 64)	(11; 78)

Coefficients are standardized beta weights.
  *$P \leq .05$, two-tailed tests.
  **$P \leq .01$, two-tailed tests.
  [a] The base industry is agriculture, forestry and fishing (SIC division A).
  [+] $P \leq .10$, two-tailed tests.

The second column in Table 2 summarizes the results for Hypotheses 1b to 3b, which pertain to the independent variables and domestic learning effort. For this analysis we included all 90 firms in the sample. First, Hypothesis 1b is supported: degree of internationalization is negatively related to domestic learning effort ($P < .05$). Hypothesis 2b is not supported: age at international entry is significantly related to domestic learning effort ($P < .05$), but opposite the direction hypothesized. That is, we found that early internationalization increases rather than decreases domestic learning effort. Finally, Hypothesis 3b receives support: entrepreneurial orientation is positively related to domestic learning effort ($P < .01$).

The regression analyses also showed that the control variables "years of internationalization" and "firm size" are not significantly related to either international or domestic learning effort. However, firms in the construction and manufacturing sector are found to exert somewhat higher international learning effort than firms in other industry sectors.

6. Discussion

We combined learning theory (Grant, 1996) and the attention-based view (Ocasio, 1997) to understand the antecedents of international and domestic learning effort. Specifically, we examined how degree of internationalization, age at international entry, and the entrepreneurial orientation of the firm are related to the intensity of effort undertaken in international and domestic markets. Our selection of a set of firms in a small European country (Belgium) enhanced the likelihood that the firms would engage in significant cross-border activity;

indeed, 84% of the firms had international activities. We found that (1) the degree of internationalization is negatively related to domestic learning effort but only marginally positively related to international learning effort, (2) the younger a firm is when it first engages in international activities, the greater its subsequent international and domestic learning effort, and (3) entrepreneurial orientation is positively related to both international and domestic learning effort.

Although it is easy for firms to become caught up in the enthusiasm over international markets, we intended to examine the implications of firms' internationalization on strategic attention in international *and* domestic markets. Our results regarding the degree of internationalization suggest that the scope of cross-border operations is related to organizational learning effort in domestic markets such that greater internationalization is associated with less domestic learning effort. This result may suggest that domestic competitive strategy is affected by the scope of international operations. The lack of a relationship between degree of internationalization and international learning effort is the more surprising result. One explanation is the possibility that internationalization requires significant learning effort that is relatively invariant to the degree of internationalization. Alternatively, it is possible that increments beyond some low level of internationalization do not add much to learning effort. Another possibility is that some aspects of internationalization are more related to learning effort than others. Additional analyses shed some light on these interpretations. Contrary to the first two explanations, we find that the correlation between the degree of internationalization and international learning effort is not significantly greater at lower levels of internationalization. We do find that geographic scope is more strongly related to international learning effort than are percentage of foreign sales and employee time dedicated to foreign activities; however, the three relationships do not differ enough to warrant definitive conclusions. The most likely explanation for the lack of a relationship between degree of internationalization and international learning effort is that the variance that degree of internationalization shares with years of international experience causes the former's insignificance in the regression equations. Table 1 indicates a strong bivariate relationship between degree of internationalization and international experience ($r=.29$; $P<.01$), supporting this view.

Overall then, our results suggest that greater involvement in international markets is associated with *less* domestic learning effort and with perhaps marginally greater international learning effort. This relationship may represent a conscious trade-off; it is also possible that the trade-off is not conscious but is the unintended consequence of shifting resources from domestic to international effort. The potential consequences of such a shift are a fertile area for study.

Our finding that earlier initiation of international activity foretells greater learning effort is consistent with the idea that early venturing into new environments may embed in firms a propensity for experimentation. This interpretation is consistent with Autio et al. (2000), who argued that early internationalizers might be able to learn more rapidly in new foreign settings than those who internationalize at an older age. We extended their work by showing that such effects apply not only to international but also to domestic learning. More startling, perhaps, is the apparent persistence of those effects well into the firm's life. This result may also suggest that organizational learning accumulates rather than depreciates over time (Argote, 1996), in line with Boeker's (1989) contention that a firm's early actions enduringly affect its character and propensities. Whereas the high-tech firms in Autio et al.'s (2000) sample were early internationalizers, the average age at first internationalization for our firms was 16 years, and our firms were not primarily high tech. Yet our results suggest, as did theirs, that the earlier a firm ventures abroad, the more fully that step embeds in the firm an identity conducive to learning (Ocasio, 1997). One possibility is that early internationalizers avoid subsequent "lock-out" from new knowledge (Cohen and Levinthal, 1990) as their learning culture allows more effective assimilation of international knowledge than other firms can attain. Zahra et al. (2000) argued that a firm inculcates important learning skills throughout its organization by operating in diverse markets. The earlier that this process begins, the stronger the firm's learning culture should become and the more it will learn about both foreign and domestic markets. Consistent with Zahra et al. (2000), our results regarding domestic learning effort suggest that early international operation affects the whole organization rather than being restricted to its unit(s) dedicated to international activities.

In short, we find that early venturing into foreign markets is associated with a greater learning culture. Firms that survive early internationalization are likely not only to put greater effort into learning in foreign markets, but also to see greater opportunities for productive learning at home (Shane and Venkataraman, 2000). Consistent with behavioral and learning theory, Autio et al. (2000) pointed out that because learning and organizational mindset are path dependent, how organizations solve their early problems will have a compounded effect over time on how they handle problems. Our results are consistent with their argument that early internationalizing allows firms to learn more rapidly and thereby to grow *both* in foreign markets and domestically.

Our results regarding entrepreneurial orientation suggest that a proactive, experimental market stance involves active learning at home and abroad. Lumpkin and Dess (1996) proposed that an entrepreneurial orientation will lead to better organizational performance but did not explain how this takes place. Our study proposed that the effects of entrepreneurial orientation are realized through its association with learning effort. By definition, an entrepreneurial orientation involves innovation and risk-taking (Lumpkin and Dess, 1996). We suggest that an entrepreneurial orientation promotes a learning-by-doing dynamic whereby firms *must* assimilate more information—whether regarding domestic or international markets (or both)—to survive the additional requirements of this strategic posture. If successful, such increased attention may lead to increased dynamic capabilities (Zahra et al., 2000). Greater competence in the use of information may help decision makers to overcome the fear of failure and reluctance to change (Aldrich, 1979; Hannan and Freeman, 1989). However, proactivity is not a panacea; increased risk-taking may threaten survival or profitability (Shaver et al., 1997).

6.1. Contributions of this study

We used the attention-based view and learning theory to develop theory and hypotheses in terms of where internationalized firms devote their learning effort. The attention-based view of

H.J. Sapienza et al. / Journal of Business Venturing 20 (2005) 437–457   453

the firm argues that firm behavior depends on how attention and efforts are directed across activities (Ocasio, 1997). Learning theory (Cohen and Levinthal, 1990; Zahra and George, 2002) suggests that firms learn more when they exert significant effort in processing new external knowledge. As such, learning theory complements the attention-based view by revealing how much effort firms might devote to different external knowledge. Consistent with the two views, we examined the relationship between a firm's effort to learn from its markets, both home and foreign, and its foreign presence, foreign "identity," and orientation toward competing.

Another contribution was to extend examinations of the relationship between internationalization itself and organizational learning (Zahra ct al., 2000). Whereas new venture internationalization theory (McDougall and Oviatt, 2000; Oviatt and McDougall, 1997) posits that "born global" firms enter foreign markets on the strength of their superior entrepreneurial skills, capacities, and vision, we looked at the reciprocal effects of this phenomenon. That is, we examined how venturing into foreign territory at an early age and expanding international scope may develop the firm's learning capacities. Our study also brought entrepreneurial orientation into the explanation of internationalization. To an often-abstract discourse on "entrepreneurial" approaches to internationalizing firms, we add a learning theory logic and empirical support.

Furthermore, this study sheds light on whether firms sacrifice the pursuit of domestic opportunity in pursuing other markets. In short, our results suggest that international and domestic learning are generally complementary. The one exception we observed was that increased internationalization might come at the expense of learning effort in the domestic market. Furthermore, our results also indicate that learning firms do not tend to trade off exploration for exploitation; indeed, supplementary analyses showcd that the two forms of learning effort appear to work in concert in whatever realm the firm emphasizes.

In terms of managerial practice and public policy, our study helps to clarify the factors that promote or inhibit organizational learning among independent companies when their domestic economy offers insufficient opportunities for growth. Our results suggest that firms can undertake significant effort to learn about international markets regardless of their years of international experience. Moreover, our results suggest that if learning is essential to success, the firm may be well advised to adopt an entrepreneurial orientation and enter foreign markets early rather than risk falling behind competitively. The fact that high levels of internationalization retard domestic learning effort is potentially important. Reduced attention to learning in the domestic market could impair effectiveness, a possibility salient both for individual firms and for government policy.

6.2. Limitations and future directions

Our study is subject to several limitations that typify behavioral research and suggest caution in interpreting its results. First, our sample consisted only of surviving firms. The learning effort of failed companies and of companies that abandoned international involvement would add substantially to the richness of the research, especially if firm performance were to be added to the research model. Second, the cross-sectional design of the study cannot guarantee the direction of causality among variables. Although our argumentation and discussion often implied causal ordering, we recognize the uncertainty attending such claims. Some relationships may be susceptible to reverse causality. For instance, higher levels of international learning effort may induce further entrepreneurial initiatives in foreign markets. Nonetheless, the central hypotheses were based on solid theory, and it may be difficult to imagine, e.g., that international learning effort drives the age of international entry rather than the reverse. Even so, future research should focus on collecting data over time to clarify these relationships.

The lack of public data on key constructs required that we rely on self-reported data for many variables. We took several precautions to guard against various forms of bias yet could not eliminate the possibility that bias affected our data. Although some of the constructs under consideration are perhaps best measured via questionnaires, outside proxies would increase confidence in the external validity of our measures. This study's focus on one country, Belgium, may call into question its applicability to other domains. We find no reason, however, to believe that the theoretical foundation for our hypotheses should obtain more fully in Belgium than elsewhere. Furthermore, restricting our study to one relatively homogenous country removed many market variables as potential sources of "noise" that could cause nonsignificant results.

Several interesting paths exist for further investigation. We posited that an entrepreneurial orientation, through its effects on a firm's effort to learn, *creates* advantage. It is possible, though, that this orientation is a product of the firm's history, fostered by past successes and the advantages they established. We know little about factors that impede firms that otherwise might have pursued international opportunities; identification of the causes of their inertia or fear could clarify the antecedents of learning. Finally, much remains to be discovered about the conversion of knowledge to competitive advantage and what factors might inhibit it.

We set out to examine how a firm's degree of internationalization, its age at foreign entry, and its devotion to entrepreneurial action are associated with its effort to learn. We treated internationalization as an independent variable and also added entrepreneurial orientation as a possible determinant of learning effort. We found evidence for the importance of both features in understanding the level of organizational learning effort and hope that others will be stimulated to examine these issues further.

7. Uncited references

McEvily and Zaheer, 1999
Sapienza et al., 2000

Acknowledgements

We thank Erkko Autio, Jim Bloodgood, Ken G. Smith, and Sri Zaheer for comments on early drafts of this manuscript.

H.J. Sapienza et al. / Journal of Business Venturing 20 (2005) 437–457 455

Appendix A.

International learning effort. Please indicate the extent to which your firm undertakes significant effort in:

1. Exploiting current internal procedures regarding your international activities.
2. Exploiting current reward systems regarding your international activities.
3. Developing new internal procedures regarding your international activities.
4. Developing new reward systems regarding your international activities.

For the most important foreign market, please indicate the extent to which the firm undertakes significant effort in:

1. Exploiting current knowledge regarding local competitors.
2. Exploiting current knowledge regarding local cooperative agreements in your industry.
3. Exploiting current knowledge regarding local laws that affect your business.
4. Exploiting current knowledge regarding local business norms in your industry.
5. Developing new knowledge regarding local competitors.
6. Developing new knowledge regarding local cooperative agreements in your industry.
7. Developing new knowledge regarding local laws that affect your business.
8. Developing new knowledge regarding local business norms in your industry.

Domestic learning effort. Please indicate the extent to which your firm undertakes significant effort in:

1. Exploiting current internal procedures for managing the domestic market.
2. Exploiting current reward systems regarding your domestic activities.
3. Exploiting current knowledge regarding domestic competitors.
4. Exploiting current knowledge regarding domestic cooperative agreements in your industry.
5. Exploiting current knowledge regarding domestic laws that affect your business.
6. Exploiting current knowledge regarding domestic business norms in your industry.
7. Developing new internal procedures for managing the domestic market.
8. Developing new reward systems regarding your domestic activities.
9. Developing new knowledge regarding domestic competitors.
10. Developing new knowledge regarding domestic cooperative agreements in your industry.
11. Developing new knowledge regarding domestic laws that affect your business.
12. Developing new knowledge regarding domestic business norms in your industry.

Degree of internationalization. Please give the following information regarding your international activities in 1999:

1. Total revenues _____; Revenues outside Belgium _____.
2. Percentage of employees who spent significant time in activities pertaining to international markets: _____%.

3. Which of the following (groups of) countries belong to your international markets (Netherlands, Luxembourg, France, Germany, UK, other EU countries, other countries outside the EU, North America, South America, Asia, Africa, Australia)? Please circle all those that are appropriate.

Entrepreneurial orientation. Please indicate the extent to which the following characterizes your firm's activities:

1. Our firm spends more time on long-term R&D (3+ years) than on short-term R&D.
2. Our firm is usually among the first to introduce new products in the industry.
3. Our firm rewards taking calculated risks.
4. Our firm shows a great deal of tolerance for high-risk projects.
5. Our firm uses only "tried and true" procedures, systems, or methods.
6. Our firm challenges, rather than responds to its major competitors.
7. Our firm takes bold, wide-ranging strategic actions rather than minor changes in tactics.

References

Aldrich, H., 1979. Organizations and Environments. Prentice Hall, Englewood Cliffs.

Argote, L., 1996. Organizational learning curves: persistence, transfer and turnover. Int. J. Technol. Manag. 11 (7,8), 759–769.

Autio, E., Sapienza, H.J., Almeida, J.G., 2000. Effects of age at entry, knowledge intensity, and imitability on international growth. Acad. Manage. J. 43 (5), 909–924.

Bartlett, C.A., Ghoshal, S., 1989. Managing Across Borders: The Transnational Solution. Harvard Business School Press, Boston.

Boeker, W., 1989. Strategic change: the effects of founding and history. Acad. Manage. J. 32, 489–515.

Brush, C.G., 1992. Factors motivating small firms to internationalize: the effect of firm age. Unpublished doctoral dissertation. Boston University.

Churchill, G.A., 1991. Marketing Research: Methodological Foundations. Dryden Press, Chicago.

Cohen, W.M., Levinthal, D.A., 1990. Absorptive capacity: a new perspective on learning and innovation. Adm. Sci. Q. 35, 128–152.

Covin, J.G., Slevin, D.P., 1989. Strategic management of small firms in hostile and benign environments. Strateg. Manage. J. 10, 75–87.

Eriksson, K., Johanson, J., Majkgård, A., Sharma, D.D., 1997. Experiential knowledge and cost in the internationalization process. J. Int. Bus. Stud. 28, 337–360.

Fischer, E., Reuber, A., 1997. The influence of the management team's international experience on the internationalization behaviors of SMEs. J. Int. Bus. Stud. 28, 807–825.

Grant, R., 1996. Prospering in dynamically-competitive environments: organizational capability as knowledge integration. Organ. Sci. 7, 375–387.

Hamel, G., 1991. Competition for competence and inter-partner learning within international strategic alliances. Strateg. Manage. J. 12, 83–103.

Hannan, M.T., Freeman, J., 1989. Structural inertia and organizational change. Am. Sociol. Rev. 49, 149–164.

Johanson, J., Vahlne, J.E., 1991. The mechanism of internationalization. Int. Mark. Rev. 7 (4), 11–24.

Johanson, J., Vahlne, J.E., 2003. Business relationship learning and commitment in the internationalization process. Int. J. Entrep. 1 (1), 83–101.

Kogut, B., 1989. A note on global strategies. Strateg. Manage. J. 10, 383–389.

Levinthal, D.A., March, J.G., 1993. The myopia of learning. Strateg. Manage. J. 14, 95–112.

Lumpkin, G.T., Dess, G.G., 1996. Clarifying the entrepreneurial orientation construct and linking it to performance. Acad. Manage. Rev. 21 (1), 135–172.

McDougall, P., 1989. International versus domestic entrepreneurship: New venture strategy behavior and industry structure. J. Bus. Venturing 4 (6), 387–400.

McDougall, P.P., Oviatt, B.M., 2000. International entrepreneurship: the intersection of two paths. Acad. Manage. J. 43, 902–906.

Miller, D., 1983. The correlates of entrepreneurship in three types of firms. Manage. Sci. 29, 770–791.

Nonaka, I., Toyama, R., Nagata, A., 2000. A firm as a knowledge-creating entity: a new perspective on the theory of the firm. Ind. Corp. Change 9, 1–20.

Nunnally, J.C., 1978. Psychometric Theory, 2nd ed. McGraw-Hill, New York.

Ocasio, W., 1997. Towards an attention-based view of the firm. Strateg. Manage. J. 18, 187–206.

Oviatt, B.M., McDougall, P.P., 1997. Challenges for internationalization process theory: the case of international new ventures. Manag. Int. Rev. 37 (special issue 2), 85–99.

Podsakoff, P.M., Organ, D.W., 1986. Self-reports in organization research: problems and prospects. J. Manage. 12 (4), 532–544.

Ramaswamy, K., Kroeck, K., Renforth, W., 1996. Measuring the degree of internationalization of a firm: a comment. J. Int. Bus. Stud. 27 (1), 167–177.

Sapienza, H.J., Autio, E., Zahra, S., (2000). Liabilities and advantages of newness: toward a knowledge-based theory of new firm internationalization. Paper presented at the Kauffman Foundation Symposium on Strategy and Entrepreneurship, Kansas City.

Shane, S., Venkataraman, S., 2000. The promise of entrepreneurship as a field of research. Acad. Manage. Rev. 25 (1), 217–226.

Sharma, S., 1996. Applied Multivariate Techniques. John Wiley and Sons, New York.

Shaver, J.M., Mitchell, W., Yeung, B., 1997. The effect of own-firm and other-firm experience on foreign direct investment survival in the United States, 1987–92. Strateg. Manage. J. 18, 811–824.

Spector, P.E., 1987. Method variance as an artifact in self-reported affect and perceptions at work: myth or significant problem? J. Appl. Psychol. 73 (3), 423–443.

Spender, J.-C., 1996. Making knowledge the basis of a dynamic theory of the firm. Strateg. Manage. J. 17, 45–62.

Sullivan, D., 1994. Measuring the degree of internationalization of a firm. J. Int. Bus. Stud. 25 (2), 325–342.

Wagner, J.A., Crampton, S.M., 1993. Percept–percept inflation in micro organizational research: an investigation of prevalence and effect. In: Moore, D. (Ed.), Academy of Management Best Paper Proceedings, pp. 310–314.

Yu, C.-M.J., 1990. The experience effect and foreign direct investment. Weltwirtsch. Arch. 126 (3), 561–580.

Zaheer, S., Mosakowski, E., 1997. The dynamics of the liability of foreignness: a global study of survival in financial services. Strateg. Manage. J. 18, 439–464.

Zahra, S.A., George, G., 2002. Absorptive capacity: a review, reconceptualization, and extension. Acad. Manage. Rev. 27 (2), 185–203.

Zahra, S.A., Ireland, R.D., Hitt, M.A., 2000. International expansion by new venture firms: international diversity, mode of market entry, technological learning, and performance. Acad. Manage. J. 43 (5), 925–950.

[17]

© *Academy of Management Journal*
2000, Vol 43, No 5, 925–950

INTERNATIONAL EXPANSION BY NEW VENTURE FIRMS: INTERNATIONAL DIVERSITY, MODE OF MARKET ENTRY, TECHNOLOGICAL LEARNING, AND PERFORMANCE

SHAKER A. ZAHRA
Georgia State University

R. DUANE IRELAND
University of Richmond

MICHAEL A. HITT
Arizona State University

An increasing number of new venture firms are internationalizing their business operations early in their life cycles. Previous explanations of this trend have focused on the importance of technological knowledge, skills, and resources for new ventures' international expansion. However, little is known about how these firms use the technological learning gained through internationalization. This study examined the effects of international expansion, as measured by international diversity and mode of market entry, on a firm's technological learning and the effects of this learning on the firm's financial performance.

New venture firms, defined here as companies six years old or younger (Brush, 1995), are moving into international markets early in their life cycles (Oviatt & McDougall, 1994, 1997). Previous research has examined the antecedents (e.g., Oviatt & McDougall, 1997), processes (Oviatt & McDougall, 1995), and performance effects of new ventures' international operations (Bloodgood, Sapienza, & Almeida, 1996; McDougall & Oviatt, 1996). Prior studies have shown that a combination of institutional factors (for instance, regulations), industry factors (such as competitive forces), and organizational factors fuel international expansion by new venture firms (Brush & Vanderwerf, 1992). Such expansion allows new ventures to achieve growth and positive returns by capitalizing on their unique resources and capabilities. It also facilitates learning, thereby allowing new ventures to both create and exploit knowledge.

The importance of organizational learning for a company's survival and effective performance has been emphasized in the literature (Barkema & Ver-

We acknowledge with appreciation the financial support of Georgia State University's Institute of International Business, Beebe Institute, and Ramsey Chair for Free Enterprise. The research assistance of Betul Bullat, Selen Uzunai, Gaogao Wang, and Asli Yildir in data collection is gratefully acknowledged. The helpful comments of the guest editors and three anonymous reviewers are also acknowledged with gratitude.

meulen, 1998; Bartlett & Ghoshal, 1987a, 1987b; Hitt, Hoskisson, & Ireland, 1994; Huber, 1991). Even when it has a technologically superior product, a new venture firm must learn other skills to position its product successfully and develop the competencies that are necessary for superior performance (McGrath, MacMillan, & Venkataraman, 1995). International expansion can promote organizational, especially technological, learning (Barkema & Vermeulen, 1998; Ghoshal, 1987), facilitating the development of skills and competencies that help the firm achieve a competitive advantage (Dodgson, 1993).

Although research on the international activities of new venture firms exists, gaps remain. Currently, there is limited (but useful) research on new ventures' technological learning through international operations. This research, based largely on case studies, suggests that new ventures gain knowledge as they diversify further into international markets. However, little is known about the amount of technological learning that occurs as new venture firms diversify internationally. Similarly, the effect on the firms' technological learning of their modes of entry into international markets has not been examined systematically.

Knowledge creation through technological learning in international markets can be challenging. Technological learning is a multifaceted, and sometimes chaotic, process yielding knowledge that is often fragmented and unfocused. New ventures must manage this process with the intent of integrating the technological learning that has occurred in their international operations (Bartlett & Ghoshal, 1987b; Ghoshal, 1987). Integration is the process by which managers determine what has been learned, evaluate its potential importance, and explore ways in which the new knowledge can be used. Theory suggests that new ventures undertaking such integration achieve greater, deeper, and speedier technological learning from their international operations than those that fail to do so (Grant, 1996a). Thus, knowledge integration moderates the relationship between international expansion and technological learning.

This study makes three contributions. First, we examine the effects of international diversity and international mode of entry on technological learning by new venture firms, a critical relationship suggested by several authors (cf. Bloodgood et al., 1996). Even though the relationship between knowledge creation and performance in international markets has been suggested (e.g., Brown & Garten, 1995; Caves, 1982), little is known about how international diversity and mode of entry affect technological learning in new venture firms. Second, we examine the effect of knowledge integration (such as the development of organizational routines) on the relationship between international expansion activities and technological learning. The need to understand the effect of knowledge integration on the development and exploitation of a competitive advantage by promoting organizational learning has been highlighted in the literature (Leonard-Barton, 1992, 1995; Nonaka & Takeuchi, 1995). Third, we document the effect of technological learning on new venture performance. Technological learning can provide a major foundation for the organizational routines that reinforce existing core competencies or facilitate building new ones (Lei, Hitt, & Bettis, 1996; Teece, Pisano, & Shuen, 1997), processes that can lead to higher new venture performance.

In the presentation of our conceptual model, theory, and hypotheses, we highlight the effects of new venture firms' international expansion activities (that is, international diversity and mode of entry) on their technological learning and the implications of knowledge integration for technological learning *gained* through international expansion.

THEORY AND HYPOTHESES

International expansion positively influences new ventures' survival, profitability, and growth (Oviatt & McDougall, 1997). By entering international markets, new ventures acquire knowledge that can be used to build additional value-creating skills (Barkema & Vermeulen, 1998; Ghoshal, 1987). New ventures competing in international markets, for instance, draw from multiple knowledge bases in their research and development, manufacturing, and marketing operations to learn new skills that augment current capabilities.

Firms need to harvest and exploit their knowledge to create competitive advantages (Grant, 1996b). Indeed, the ability to manage and cultivate knowledge differentiates success from failure (Nonaka & Takeuchi, 1995). Effective learning is cumulative in nature (Helfat, 1994). Thus, internalizing learning from international operations is important for building a venture's competencies and achieving high performance (Ghoshal, 1987). The development of new technological knowledge is important for success in international markets (Bartlett & Ghoshal, 1987b). This knowledge influences a venture's ability to adapt its products to local market conditions (Afuah, 1998), capitalize on market dynamism through rapid new product developments (McCann, 1991), and identify emerging technological changes that can influence firm performance.

Figure 1 presents the study's model. As shown in the model, a new venture's international expansion promotes technological learning, which in turn enhances performance. Building on prior work, this study focuses on two key aspects of international expansion: international diversity (as indicated by geographic scope and the technological and cultural diversity of the countries in a firm's portfolio) *and* the mode of entry into international markets. International diversity and mode of entry are expected to influence the breadth, depth, and speed of a venture's technological learning. *Breadth* denotes the multiple areas in which a venture learns new technological skills (Teece, Rumelt, Dosi, & Winter, 1994). *Depth* refers to a venture's mastery of new knowledge, evidenced by an ability to draw new conclusions and find new links among diverse knowledge bases (Huber, 1991). *Speed* of technological learning describes how rapidly the venture acquires new insights and skills (Dodgson, 1993; Hitt, Keats, & DeMarie, 1998).

Figure 1 also suggests that technological learning is influenced by a venture's ability to integrate the knowledge it gains through international expansion. Technological learning can be serendipitous and unfocused (Dodgson, 1991a, 1993) and, thus, it should be integrated into the company's operations (Bartlett & Ghoshal, 1987b). Therefore, knowledge integration moderates the relationship between international expansion activities and technological

FIGURE 1
Conceptual Model[a]

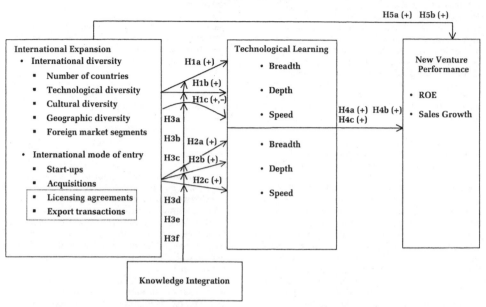

[a] Dotted lines indicate no relationship was hypothesized.

learning. In light of past research, we also expected a positive relationship between international expansion and performance. International expansion not only affects performance through technological learning, but also can have a direct effect on performance, by allowing a firm to take advantage of substantial opportunities in international markets (Hitt, Hoskisson, & Kim, 1997). Finally, technological knowledge is expected to enhance new venture performance.

International Diversity and Technological Learning

International diversity denotes a firm's increased reliance on foreign markets as a means of growth and financial performance improvement. It refers to the scope of a firm's foreign operations (Tallman & Li, 1996). International diversity has five components: (1) the number of countries in which a firm has foreign business operations (Tallman & Li, 1996), (2) the technological diversity of the collection of foreign markets entered (Kidd & Teramoto, 1995), (3) the number of diverse social cultures of the countries in which the

firm operates (Hofstede, 1980), (4) the geographic diversity of the foreign markets (Sambharya, 1995), and (5) the number of foreign market segments targeted by the firm (Morrison & Roth, 1992). Diversity therefore reflects the significant cultural and technological variations across the countries, markets, and segments in which a new venture undertakes foreign operations.

Ghoshal (1987) suggested that learning is an important goal for firms pursuing international diversity. Learning derived from national differences and economies of scale and/or scope can be a source of competitive advantage. The diversity of a venture's international business environment enhances its knowledge stock through learning based on interactions with local knowledge bases and exposure to different systems of innovation. The venture's access to "soft" resources (such as interorganizational relationships) also promotes learning and innovation. International diversity provides exposure to new and diverse ideas from multiple market and cultural perspectives (Hitt et al., 1997). A venture's quest for scope economies also induces learning through sharing the knowledge used to differentiate a product or by pooling the knowledge developed in different markets. Countries vary in their cultures (Hofstede, 1980, 1993), technological development (Kogut & Singh, 1988), natural resource endowments and skills, innovativeness, and the organization of industries, markets, and distribution channels (Porter, 1990), each of which affects technological learning.

These arguments suggest that international diversity affects technological learning (Johanson & Vahlne, 1977; Welch & Welch, 1996), as demonstrated by the acquisition of new technological skills (Craig & Douglas, 1996; Kodama, 1995; Regnier, 1993). This is important because, increasingly, new ventures compete in several countries (Shrader, 1996). Variations in competitive, scientific, technological, and regulatory environments can, therefore, influence new ventures' technological learning (Nakata & Sivakumar, 1996). Consequently, new ventures competing in several countries, with operations in different international regions and targeting multiple market segments, are expected to differ from ventures competing in markets located in only one country or focusing on a single foreign market segment in breadth, depth, and speed of their technological learning.

Breadth. A venture that expands internationally by entering markets in several foreign countries is more likely to experience different cultures (Hofstede, 1980) and institutional systems than one that focuses on a single or a few countries (Hitt, Dacin, Tyler, & Park, 1997). Exposure to diverse environments facilitates system openness and promotes technological learning (Kim, 1997). International diversity also fosters involvement in established networks of manufacturers and other technology providers, which in turn increases technological learning. As the geographic dispersion and/or cultural diversity of the countries served by a new venture increases, the breadth of its technological learning is expected to increase. International diversity helps firms accumulate both universal and tacit technical knowledge (Lei et al., 1996). Regional differences also magnify the importance of the venture's social learning (Sohn, 1994). This learning emerges from understanding and using cultural values in designing and marketing the firm's products and process technologies. As a firm enters distant markets (that is, markets or segments that differ substantially from its home base), its ability to learn expands (Teece et al., 1994). These arguments suggest:

Hypothesis 1a. There is a positive relationship between a new venture firm's international diversity and the breadth of its technological learning.

Depth. International diversity also influences the depth of a new venture's technological learning. Although learning many concepts or skills can be complex, developing a deep understanding of them is more challenging (Bohn, 1994). The different business settings that are associated with separate countries facilitate deeper technological learning by new venture firms (Makino & Delios, 1996). Exposure to, and direct involvement with, businesses and customers in multiple countries is an important means of "learning by doing" (Dodgson, 1991a), which promotes deeper technological learning (Ganesh, Kumar, & Subramaniam, 1997). Learning by doing helps firms redefine organizational heuristics (Lei et al., 1996). Diverse ideas and capabilities encountered in international business operations produce combinative knowledge (Zander & Kogut, 1995). This knowledge leads to the development of dynamic routines that promote complex problem solving (Lei et al., 1996). This evidence suggests:

Hypothesis 1b. There is a positive relationship between a new venture firm's international diversity and the depth of its technological learning.

Speed. Although beneficial to the breadth and depth of technological learning, international diversity has both positive and negative effects on the speed of learning. International diversity can enhance the speed of learning as a firm experiences multiple cultures and markets (Ghoshal, 1987). Early exposure to international markets speeds learning, but continued expansion into more international markets can result in information overload owing to increased transaction costs and cultural diversity. Information overload reduces the speed of technological learning (Hitt et al., 1997; Huber, 1991). As the number of countries and market segments in a firm's portfolio increase, the venture's ability to process and internalize all of the potential information from its international activities is tested. The diversity of information gained, therefore, may require managers to sift through large amounts of data to identify patterns or cues. Much of the technological knowledge gained is likely to be tacit in nature (Makino & Delios, 1996), further slowing the identification, interpretation, and articulation of the resulting technological insights. This evidence suggests:

Hypothesis 1c. There is a curvilinear relationship between a new venture firm's international diversity and the speed of technological learning, with the slope positive at lower and moderate levels of international diversity and negative at higher levels.

Mode of International Entry and Technological Learning

Internationalization stage theories (Johanson & Vahlne, 1977; Stopford & Wells, 1972) suggest an evolutionary pattern in a firm's international expansion. Usually depicted along a continuum, the choices include exporting, licensing, alliances, and start-ups (Andersen, 1993). However, some new ventures forgo some of these stages and undertake "high-control" transactions (like acquisitions) that require close interactions with multiple international market stakeholders (Oviatt & McDougall, 1994).

International business transactions differ in their risks and payoffs and the experience gained from them (Ghoshal, 1987; Hill, Hwang, & Kim, 1990). In contrast to the high-control transactions characteristic of foreign direct investment (FDI), some low-control transactions (for instance, exporting, licensing) require few interactions with markets, suppliers, and customers. The deep stakeholder involvement associated with high-control transactions exposes a firm to unique knowledge bases and experiences (Kim, 1997). Thus, the extent to which a new venture emphasizes direct and deep involvement modes of entry into international markets affects its ability to acquire new technological skills (Afuah, 1998).

High-control international entry modes may increase the breadth, depth, and speed of technological learning. These modes typically require closeness to a market and its customers, thus increasing the venture's exposure to different information sources. Interactions with alliance partners, for example, provide important insights into other firms' research-in-progress and products being developed for commercialization. Partners' design of products to meet local expectations can also be observed. If a new venture uses FDI, it may gain insights into the product attributes that are the most critical in local markets. Interactions with local suppliers also provide information about the market, customers, and competition (Dodgson, 1991a, 1991b). Additionally, the firm can study possible substitute products to further improve its product offerings. These activities increase a firm's exposure to multiple and varied sources of technological information and serve as a catalyst to technological learning (Leonard-Barton, 1995). These arguments suggest:

Hypothesis 2a. There is a positive relationship between a new venture firm's use of high-control modes of international market entry and the breadth of its technological learning.

A new venture firm using high-control entry modes in international markets is likely to experience more radical learning than those using modes requiring less involvement. High-control entry modes usually promote the firm's experiential learning through close observation of other companies' strategic moves. They also promote learning by doing. New knowledge has a tacit component that can be gained only by doing (Dodgson, 1993). Tacit knowledge cannot be communicated precisely using words, numbers, or pictures and is difficult to codify (Helfat, 1994). Tacit knowledge is the cornerstone of dynamic capabilities that are used to build competitive advantages (Teece et al., 1997). High-control entry modes create the potential for higher-intensity successes and failures. Important insights can be gained from successes and failures in international operations. The use of high-control modes of entry therefore facilitates in-depth technological learning. These arguments suggest:

Hypothesis 2b. There is a positive relationship between a new venture firm's use of high-control modes of international market entry and the depth of its technological learning.

High-control modes of international entry can also increase the speed of a firm's technological learning. One of the advantages of new ventures is their closeness to markets and to customers' needs. Closeness to the market and its customers is conducive to rapid learning (Brown, 1994; Day, 1994; Kim, 1997). By using high-control entry modes that ensure closeness to customers in international markets, a new venture increases the speed of its learning. The venture can thus gather market and competitive data quickly, analyze trends, and rapidly obtain feedback from its customers, suppliers, and other key stakeholders in foreign markets. Immediate feedback promotes learning and expedites the upgrading of existing products, planning new product developments, and/or targeting new market segments. This evidence suggests:

Hypothesis 2c. There is a positive relationship between a new venture's use of high-control modes of international market entry and the speed of its technological learning.

The Moderating Effect of Knowledge Integration

For technological learning to yield an advantage, it must be captured, interpreted, and deployed effectively (Grant, 1991, 1996b, 1997). Hamel and Prahalad (1994) referred to this process as integration; a firm recognizes what it has learned and decides how to use it. Knowledge integration makes the information and skills gained from international expansion activities an integral component of the routines that guide the firm's future strategic actions (Teece et al., 1987).

The acquisition of technological learning does not translate automatically into strong competitive market positions or high performance (McGrath et al., 1995). Some of this knowledge is tacit, making it difficult to use unless it is integrated into the firm's operations. Technological learning is also fragmented throughout new venture firms, making new knowledge difficult to identify and use. Managers and employees are often unaware of the amount or importance of what they have learned from their firm's international expansion activities. Integration enables the firm to internalize what it has learned in its international operations. It also permits the firm to capitalize on local knowledge that exists in different parts of its operations. Finally, learning is not always a sequential process (Nonaka, 1994), and managerial attention might be distracted as the firm continues to expand internationally. Integration helps managers to develop shared learning and accumulate knowledge over time (Lei et al., 1996; Teece et al., 1994).

Knowledge can be integrated formally or informally (Grant, 1996). Following the literature (Bartlett & Ghoshal, 1987b; Ghoshal, 1987), in this study we emphasized formal integration, defined as the process by which managers inventory, synthesize, and use the knowledge they have gained from their firm's international expansion. *Inventory* refers to managers' systematic attempts to determine what has been learned and to evaluate its importance. *Synthesis* denotes managers' efforts to understand what has been learned and to articulate this knowledge (Nonaka & Takeuchi, 1995). *Use* refers to management's efforts to devise ways to competitively exploit the knowledge; this requires diffusion of the knowledge throughout the organization (Ghoshal, 1987).

New ventures can excel at knowledge integration and establish a competitive advantage relative to their well-established rivals. New ventures usually have organic structures that permit speedy and effective flow of knowledge and its subsequent use in new product development activities. These structures encourage the exchange of information and experiences, which promotes learning by managers and employees.

Top-level managers are also actively involved in the ventures' international operations, which gives them firsthand access to the new knowledge being created as the firm expands and enters new mar-

kets. This involvement provides opportunities for learning by doing and synthesizing what has been learned. Consequently, this involvement can be crucial in establishing knowledge integration as a firm-level competence that differentiates the firm from its competitors.

As indicated in Figure 1, knowledge integration is expected to moderate the relationship between international diversity and the breadth of a new venture's technological learning. Integration makes possible the combination of different insights and skills learned from a firm's different markets and national systems of innovation (Grant, 1998). New ventures that engage in knowledge integration, therefore, are more likely to recognize the importance of cultivating the diverse technological skills, capabilities, and systems that exist in their different foreign markets into their operations. Thus, knowledge integration facilitates combining new and different technological skills with existing ones, thereby broadening the firm's technological skill set. Additionally, for new ventures that undertake formal knowledge integration, international diversity is more conducive to broader technological learning.

Knowledge integration also compels managers to consider the skills learned from their diverse international markets and how they can be used to overcome deficiencies in their company's knowledge base. This process of self-examination provides managers with major insights into the deficits of their firm's skill base and competencies (Bohn, 1994; Dodgson, 1993). As managers explore ways to overcome these deficits by cultivating the knowledge that resides in their company's foreign markets, the depth of the new venture's technological learning increases. Managers are likely to share what they have learned with others in the firm, thereby increasing the depth of technological learning (Huber, 1991). Therefore, we conclude that new ventures undertaking formal knowledge integration and international diversity achieve deeper technological learning.

Integration also encourages managers to recognize and rapidly internalize the technological knowledge gained from their firm's international diversity. Knowledge integration promotes communication and discussions among managers (Grant, 1996), thereby promoting the quick recognition, inventory, synthesis, and use of the knowledge gained from the firm's diverse international markets (Stewart, 1998). Consequently, in new ventures that engage in formal knowledge integration, international diversity is more conducive to speedier technological learning.

As indicated in Figure 1, knowledge integration

is also expected to moderate the relationship between the international modes of entry and technological learning. Knowledge integration is an organizational rather than a subunit capability (Grant,
1996, 1998; Leonard-Barton, 1995). A company
gains this capability by experimenting with different approaches (Senge, 1990). Experimentation
promotes learning by doing (Huber, 1991), which is
important for new ventures. Most new ventures
have limited prior international experience. As
they expand internationally using high-control entry modes, these ventures have to invest a great deal
of effort toward building their supply and distribution channels. This process requires understanding
and evaluating the skills and capabilities of potential suppliers and distributors, which can broaden
the new venture's learning. The decision to use
high-control entry modes also necessitates analysis
of potential rivals and their skills. This analysis can
also broaden the firm's exposure to different technological skills.

High-control entry modes (such as FDI) require a
stronger commitment to and involvement in foreign markets, thereby providing greater access to
the bases of knowledge that exist in these markets.
The significant involvement in the markets exposes
the firm to and promotes its acquisition of different
types of knowledge (Ghoshal, 1987). When this
knowledge is formally integrated, the firm also develops deeper understanding of the various foreign
markets in which it competes. The rapid dissemination and sharing of information resulting from
formal knowledge integration processes increases
the speed of technological learning gained from
using high-control modes of entry. These arguments suggest:

*Hypothesis 3a. The interaction of international
diversity and knowledge integration is positively related to the breadth of technological
learning.*

*Hypothesis 3b. The interaction of international
diversity and knowledge integration is positively related to the depth of technological
learning.*

*Hypothesis 3c. The interaction of international
diversity and knowledge integration is positively related to the speed of technological
learning.*

*Hypothesis 3d. The interaction of high-control
modes of international market entry and
knowledge integration is positively related to
the breadth of technological learning.*

*Hypothesis 3e. The interaction of high-control
modes of international market entry and
knowledge integration is positively related to
the depth of technological learning.*

*Hypothesis 3f. The interaction of high-control
modes of international market entry and
knowledge integration is positively related to
the speed of technological learning.*

Technological Learning and Performance

As noted in Figure 1, greater breadth, depth, and
speed of technological learning is expected to enhance a new venture's performance. Without technological learning, the firm's skills become out-
dated, its products obsolete, and its future
uncertain. Technological learning provides a base
of knowledge upon which innovations can be developed (Leonard-Barton, 1995). International
trade theories suggest that companies need to offer
superior products to overcome the liability of foreignness and to achieve competitive advantage
(Caves, 1982). The success of international new
ventures is explained by their ability to leverage the
knowledge gained from foreign operations (McDougall, Shane, & Oviatt, 1994).

The breadth of technological learning is useful in
designing new products and upgrading existing
ones (Afuah, 1998; Zahra, 1996). The depth of technological learning improves a firm's ability to redesign its products for ease of use, offer customized
applications, or radically change product definitions (Usunier, 1996). These actions help the firm
target new markets and earn higher profits
(McCann, 1991). Finally, the speed of technological
learning improves the venture's performance by
compressing the product development cycle, enabling the firm to gain the benefits associated with
being among the first to the market (Dodgson,
1993). This discussion suggests:

*Hypothesis 4a. The breadth of technological
learning in international markets is positively
related to new venture performance.*

*Hypothesis 4b. The depth of technological
learning in international markets is positively
related to new venture performance.*

*Hypothesis 4c. The speed of technological
learning in international markets is positively
related to new venture performance.*

**International Diversity, Mode of Entry, and
Performance**

There is evidence that new ventures with international operations usually outperform those that

are without them (McDougall & Oviatt, 1996). Feeser and Willard (1990) found that higher-growth new ventures gained more revenue from international markets than ventures with lower levels of growth. Likewise, Bloodgood and colleagues (1996) reported a positive association between the intensity of a venture's internationalization and its operating income. The results reported herein extend prior work by examining the specific links between international diversity, international mode of entry, and new venture performance.

Figure 1 suggests a direct link between international expansion and performance, which is consistent with established theory (Hitt et al., 1994) and recent evidence (Hitt et al., 1997). International expansion provides new market opportunities in which a firm can sell its product innovations. As the firm enters more countries, it can leverage its skills and products over a broader array of markets (Kim, Hwang, & Burgers, 1993), thereby increasing growth and profitability (Geringer, Beamish, & daCosta, 1989). A broad international market scope also stabilizes the firm's earnings (Caves, 1982) and increases the chances of survival (Hitt et al., 1994). International expansion connects the firm with important constituencies in diverse markets, allowing it to obtain key resources economically. International diversity allows the new venture to enter and profit from beneficial networks (Hitt & Bartkus, 1997). Networks also provide marketing, technological, cultural, and competitive information that increases a firm's chances of survival (Mohrman & Von Glinow, 1990). Although Hitt, Hoskisson, and Kim (1997) found a curvilinear relationship between international diversity and performance, new ventures are unlikely to have increased their international diversity to the point of decreasing returns. Furthermore, Hitt and his colleagues (1997) discovered that product diversity moderated this relationship; new venture firms are, however, unlikely to offer diversified product lines (Zahra, 1996). All modes of entry, if implemented effectively, should have positive effects on firm performance. Therefore, this evidence suggests:

Hypothesis 5a. International expansion (as measured by international diversity and modes of market entry) is positively related to new venture profitability.

Hypothesis 5b. International expansion (as measured by international diversity and modes of market entry) is positively related to new venture sales growth.

METHODS

Sample

It is difficult to obtain data on the international activities, technological learning, and other organizational practices of new ventures. Thus, this study used a combination of a two-wave mail survey, archival data, and phone and e-mail contacts with companies and trade associations to reduce source bias and obtain reliable and valid data.

The difficulty of identifying international new ventures has been noted (cf. Oviatt & McDougall, 1997). To develop a representative sample, we employed four criteria. First, to increase the findings' generalizability, we selected new ventures from multiple high-technology industries. These industries are important for U.S. global competitiveness, job creation, and innovativeness (Datar, Jordan, Kekre, Rajiv, & Srinivasan, 1997). The complexity of these industries' products and their dynamic environments also increased their attractiveness for this study. We used the U.S. Department of Commerce classifications (Brown & Garten, 1994, 1995) to select 12 industries: biotechnology, computer software, factory automation, telecommunication, environmental technologies, medical and surgical equipment, pharmaceuticals, specialty chemicals, aerospace, test measurements, advanced materials, and semiconductors. Finally, secondary data for several variables were also available, making it possible to cross-validate the results. This, too, encouraged us to study these industries.

A second sample selection criterion was company age. Even though different age ranges have been used in the literature, there is a growing consensus that firms 6 years and younger are new ventures (Brush, 1995; Brush & Vanderwerf, 1992; Shrader, 1996). Previously, researchers have used different cutoff points, such as 12 (Covin, Slevin, & Covin, 1990) and 8 years (McDougall, 1989; Zahra, 1996). However, Bantel (1998) argued that by the age of 5, many start-up firms that have failed to build strong market positions have become extinct. Older companies (up to the age of 12) have survived the liability of newness but have not yet "reached the mature stage where they resemble established firms" (Bantel, 1998: 207). Given this evidence, the need to control for changes in the firm's environments, and the desire to be consistent with the literature, we used only firms 6 years of age or younger in this study.

The third criterion concerned a new venture's ownership. We included both independent (private) and corporate new ventures because both compete directly in several markets (Bell & McNamara, 1991; McDougall, Deane, & D'Souza,

1992; Zahra, 1996). Privately owned ventures are established and managed by individual entrepreneurs. Corporate ventures are created and managed by established companies, subsidiaries, or business units of established companies (Shrader & Simon, 1997). Units that have been acquired, spun-off, or divested by established companies were not considered because these transactions significantly alter the relationship between the parent corporation and their new ventures, making it difficult to discern the transfer of resources from the corporation to its ventures. We excluded joint ventures because partners usually share responsibility for their operations, decision making, and resource provisions.

Finally, using the above criteria, we compiled a list of companies with international operations. An international new venture has been defined as one that has obtained at least 10 percent of its sales from foreign markets (McDougall, 1989), a criterion used in research on established companies (e.g., Hitt et al., 1997; Tallman & Li, 1996). However, this figure is high for young ventures that are early in their internationalization. The 10 percent figure might also restrict the range of international sales, making it difficult to determine the effects of varying degrees of internationalization on technological learning. To capture a broader spectrum of international business operations among new ventures, we used a minimum of 5 percent of sales from foreign markets.

Different secondary sources were used to develop a mailing list. As noted in the Appendix, the components of these lists were obtained from computerized searches (including visits to companies' Internet home pages), trade and business publications, and contacts with the U.S. Department of Commerce and national trade associations. Because of the lack of information about companies and their international operations, several difficulties surfaced during this process. For example, as Porter (1980) noted, young industries are often populated by hundreds of young and unknown companies. Therefore, to develop our list, we reviewed articles included in trade publications, scanned announcements of new products, and read ads for new products to identify potential companies. We then reviewed additional secondary sources, such as lists of companies from trade associations. Still, identifying firms with international operations proved to be exceedingly difficult because the necessary information was not available for all firms. Consequently, we identified articles that mentioned international operations by new ventures and cross-validated this information to ensure that each company met the 5 percent threshold. Also, we contacted several knowledgeable U.S. Department of Commerce employees who followed specific industry sectors. These analysts provided information on the companies they tracked and connected us with people in trade associations who knew their respective industries. Through this iterative process, we identified 1,417 companies. Before mailing the final questionnaires, however, we contacted 73 companies about which we had questions to verify their active involvement in international markets. Of these, 29 indicated that they did not have significant international operations and thus were eliminated, reducing the target population to 1,388.

Two mailings were completed in 1993. Of the questionnaires mailed, 34 were returned as undeliverable, reducing the sample to 1,354. The two mailings resulted in 321 completed questionnaires (a 23.8 percent response rate). This rate compares favorably with those reported in past surveys of new ventures (e.g., Chandler & Hanks, 1993; McDougall, 1989). Responding firms averaged 3.4 years (s.d. = 1.1) of age, 71.9 (s.d. = 59.3) full-time employees, and 17.3 (s.d. = 11.5) percent of their sales from international operations. Respondents included CEOs and presidents (68%), vice presidents for international operations (19%), and senior vice presidents (13%). These managers/executives were among the most informed about their companies' international operations, innovation, and learning.

We tested for response bias by examining the differences between respondents to the first and second mailings. A t-test showed no significant differences between the two groups based on age, size, or sales growth. A chi-square test, moreover, showed no significant association between respondent status (first versus second mailing) and a firm's location, industry type, or ownership. We conducted the same analyses (using the chi-square and t-tests) for responding and nonresponding companies. These results, too, were insignificant, suggesting that responding firms represented the population from which they were drawn.

To ensure the reliability and validity of the data, we pretested the survey by seeking comments from five new venture firm managers (representing three industries) and two venture capitalists. These individuals, who had a combined high-technology industry experience of 21 years, closely reviewed and critiqued the survey and offered several suggestions for improving its wording, design, and administration. A revised copy of the survey was then sent to 50 venture managers in high-technology companies (representing 10 of the study's 12 industries), located in a southeastern metropolitan area. One mailing yielded complete responses from 17 companies. Managers were asked to comment on the survey questions and suggest other items. Information from the 17 pretest surveys was used to improve the survey instrument's wording, organization, and presentation.

We also attempted to ensure reliable and valid data by using multiple and different data sources and cross-validating them to ensure accuracy. Further, as reported below, when we relied on data supplied by managers, we tested for interrater agreement, as has been done in previous studies (e.g., Hitt, Hoskisson, Johnson, & Moesel, 1996; McDougall, 1989). This test required sending a copy of the questionnaire to a second executive in each responding venture ($n = 321$). When possible, managers responsible for international operations were targeted; otherwise, senior executives responsible for strategic planning or marketing were targeted. Completed responses from a second executive were received from 103 of the 321 responding companies. These data were used to determine interrater agreement. Where possible, we also validated survey-based measures through secondary data, again following previous research (Covin et al., 1990; Hitt et al., 1996). Finally, where appropriate, we calculated Cronbach's coefficient alpha to ensure internal consistency.

Measures

The following measures were constructed for the study's independent, dependent, and control variables:

International diversity. Five indicators were used to measure international diversity. Using the secondary sources presented in the Appendix to obtain a proxy of the geographic diversity of a firm's international operations, we counted the number of countries in which the venture sold its products (Tallman & Li, 1996). These data were validated by cross-checking. Information was available from at least two secondary sources for 59 companies, and the simple correlations between the figures in the two sources were high ($r = .81$, $p < .01$). Also, the survey asked managers to provide data on the number of foreign countries to which their companies' products were exported. This number also correlated strongly with the number of countries gathered from secondary sources ($r = .86$, $n = 259$, $p < .001$). Finally, managers were asked, "In how many countries (other than the US) are this company's products sold?" Responses to this question were strongly correlated with data collected from secondary figures ($r = .91$, $n = 301$, $p < .001$). These analyses supported the validity of the secondary data on the number of countries.

The *technological diversity* of international markets was believed to influence a venture's technological learning (Kidd & Teramoto, 1995). According to Kogut and Singh (1988), a key indicator of a country's technological advancement is R&D expenditures. Sources of data for this variable are reported in the Appendix. International publications also included detailed time series of data for different regions and countries, affording an opportunity to cross-check the information. Cross-checking publications of reputable organizations such as the United Nations Educational, Scientific, and Cultural Organization (UNESCO), the National Science Foundation, and the Organisation for Economic Cooperation and Development (OECD) further enhanced confidence in the data's quality. Still, we correlated the data gathered from at least two sources on R&D spending by different countries; the correlation was high ($r = .91$, $n = 163$, $p < .001$). Average country R&D spending, computed as a percentage of gross domestic product (GDP), was used as an indicator of the technological vitality of a venture's international markets. This average was calculated by dividing the total of R&D ratios across the countries the new venture had entered by the number of these countries.

The *cultural diversity* of countries was measured using Hofstede's (1980) classification of national cultures; 11 country groups were indicated. We counted the number of cultural groups in a venture's markets. Thus, a firm that entered the Japanese, Mexican, and South African markets had a score of 3, because each of these countries fell into a separate cultural group in Hofstede's classification.

The *geographic diversity* of foreign revenue was calculated using an entropy measure that was developed from data provided by managers regarding the percentage of their companies' international revenues earned from operations outside the United States, in Canada, Europe, Asia, Australia, Latin America, or Africa. The Appendix explains this measure. Using this information, we developed a geographic diversity *(GD)* index that was calculated with the formula $GD = \Sigma S_{ij}$, where S_{ij} was the percentage of a venture's sales in a given market, summed across the six regions noted above.[1] We

---

[1] We also calculated an entropy-type measure of international diversity *(ID)* using the same data and the formula $ID = \Sigma_i [P_i \cdot \ln (1/P_i)]$, where P_i is the proportion of a firm's sales in a given market i and $\ln (1/P_i)$ is the weight given to each market, defined by the natural logarithm of the inverse of its sales. Prior researchers have used similar formulas to measure the related construct of

used secondary data from 103 firms to validate this measure. The correlation between the two was high and statistically significant ($r = .74$, $n = 103$, $p < .001$); the Appendix presents the sources of these data. Interrater agreement between the responses provided by two managers on the entropy measure was also high ($r = .71$, $n = 98$, $p < .001$).

Finally, we measured the number of *foreign market segments* using data provided by managers. Buzzell and Gale (1987) indicated that companies differ in their definitions of served markets, a factor that favored the use of survey data. For each country in which a firm's products were sold, managers provided the number of different market segments their firms targeted, using the measure presented in the Appendix. We then divided the total number of segments by the number of countries a firm entered and used the average in the analyses. The study's measure was strongly correlated to managers' responses to the item "This company targets many foreign market segments" (5 = strongly agree, 1 = strongly disagree; $r = .73$, $n = 307$, $p < .001$). Interrater agreement between the responses provided by two company managers was also significant ($r = .72$, $n = 97$, $p < .001$). Secondary data for 71 new ventures' market segments were also highly correlated with the survey measure ($r = .61$, $n = 71$, $p < .001$). Secondary data came from newspaper and trade publication articles, press releases, and companies' Internet home pages. We searched for phrases such as "foreign customer groups," "foreign market segments" and "end users," which previous work has used to indicate the narrowness or breadth of companies' markets (Buzzell & Gale, 1987).

Mode of international market entry. International market entry mode was measured with data on firms' international export agreements, licensing agreements, joint ventures, acquisitions, and start-ups, or greenfield investments (cf. Anand & Singh, 1997; Arora & Gambardella, 1997; Mitchell & Singh, 1996; Pennings & Harianto, 1992) collected from Lexis-Nexis, one of the most reputable research data bases. Data are from a large number of specialized trade publications, newspapers, magazines, and company press releases. The large number of sources and the details provided on each episode increase confidence in the data used to develop the measures. However, databases such as Lexis-Nexis typically give more attention to the

strategic actions of large, established, well-known companies and may not capture all the international business announcements made by small, young new ventures. Thus, the results reported here are conservative.

The search process yielded 641 announcements of international activities covering 693 transactions. Of these transactions, 273 were related to *exporting* (39.5 percent), 191 to *licensing* (27.6 percent), 23 to *acquisitions* (3.3 percent), and 206 to *start-ups* (29.7 percent). We used the number of announcements of international transactions within each of the five entry modes as the study's measures.

To validate measures derived from secondary sources, we asked managers to indicate the percentage of their firm's revenues earned from foreign activities by allocating 100 points among exports, licensing, joint ventures, and subsidiary operations. The simple correlations between these figures and the number of announcements of international business transactions averaged .83 ($n = 307$, $p < .001$).

Technological learning. Technological learning was measured with multiple survey items. The studies by Olk and Young (1997), Simonin (1997), and Zander and Kogut (1995) used survey-based measures of learning. Given that our sample consisted of young firms, we thought that traditional measures might obscure the *breadth*, *depth*, and *speed* of learning. Moreover, we were able to locate secondary data (on such features as cycle time) to measure technological learning for only a handful of new ventures. Thus, we asked managers about their firms' technological learning, an approach suggested by five new venture managers and two venture capitalists. The interrater agreement on the study's three measures was strong and statistically significant ($p < .001$): breadth ($n = 98$, $r = .72$), depth ($n = 95$, $r = .65$), and speed ($n = 98$, $r = .71$). The measures also had acceptable Cronbach alphas: breadth, .78; depth, .71; and speed, .72. The Appendix presents the measures, which were based on several sources (Dodgson, 1991a, 1991b; Huber, 1991; Nonaka & Takeuchi, 1995; Senge, 1990).

Knowledge integration. Again following previous research (Bartlett & Ghoshal 1987a, 1987b; Ghoshal, 1987; Grant, 1991, 1996a, 1996b, 1997; Hamel & Prahalad, 1994; Nonaka, 1991, 1994) we developed seven items to measure *knowledge integration.* Using a five-point scale (5 = widely used, 1 = never used), we asked managers to indicate the extent to which their ventures used each of seven activities to capture, interpret, synthesize, and integrate what they had learned from their interna-

---

international diversification (e.g., Hitt et al., 1997; Sambharya, 1995). The correlation between *GD* and *ID* was high ($r = .83$, $p < .001$). Therefore, we present the results based on the geographic diversity measure.

tional operations. The items focused on the use of regular formal reports and memos that summarize learning, information-sharing sessions, face-to-face discussions by cross-functional teams, use of experts and consultants to synthesize learning, formal analysis of failing international projects, formal analysis of successful projects, and formal discussions of the best ways to use what has been learned in designing new products (or upgrading existing ones). When these items were factor-analyzed (with a varimax orthogonal rotation), one factor explaining 64.8 percent of the variance emerged. The sum total of managers' responses to the seven items was averaged and used as the measure of knowledge integration ($\alpha = .67$). Interrater agreement between the two responding managers was statistically significant ($r = .62$, $n = 94$, $p < .001$).

New venture performance. The importance of profitability and growth as key outcomes of new venture international operations (McDougall & Oviatt, 1996; Oviatt & McDougall, 1994) and technological learning (Bartlett & Ghoshal, 1987a, 1987b) has been noted. Three issues required attention in measuring new venture performance. The first was the length of the lag effect of the study's variables on performance. Most prior studies have not used lagged performance in their analyses, and the few that have used one- or two-year lags (e.g., Tallman & Li, 1996; Sambharya, 1995). Here, data were collected for, and averaged over, the period 1995–96. Thus, the performance data represented a time period of two to three years after the data on the independent variables were collected. Given the youth of the sample's ventures, a two-year time frame was believed to capture some of the effects of international expansion and technological learning. Also, averaging data over two years controlled for unusual events in the firms' markets. Although a longer time lag (four or five years) might have been desirable, it would have introduced considerable noise into the performance data. Ramanujam and Varadarajan (1989) argued that diversification activities are likely to change drastically over time, necessitating adjustments for macroeconomic conditions, industry structures, and firm strategy variables.

A second issue was the timing of the new venture firm performance measures as a consequence of internationalization. This study follows the literature in measuring performance two years *after* collection of data on the other variables (Hitt et al., 1997; Tallman & Li, 1996; Sambharya, 1995) rather than at the time of the initial international transactions (identifying the initial transactions would have been very difficult). Further, this study focuses on linking a new venture's international operations to its overall performance to discern a general pattern of relationships among the variables. This approach has the advantage of gauging the firm's commitment to international expansion rather than capturing temporary benefits accruing from individual transactions.

The final issue was the selection of performance criteria. This is an issue on which there is considerable debate (Brush, 1995; Brush & Vanderwerf, 1992; Shrader, 1996). Two performance measures were selected: *sales growth* and *return on equity (ROE)*. Sales growth is widely considered a key indicator of new ventures' performance (Bloodgood et al., 1996; Brush, 1995; Chandler & Hanks, 1993). ROE has also been used widely as well (cf. Chandler & Hanks, 1993; Zahra, 1996). Although both measures have been criticized (Brush & Vanderwerf, 1992), they are used extensively to evaluate new venture performance by trade publications, industry experts, and venture capitalists. Sales growth and ROE may be more volatile than other measures, such as market share. Unfortunately, data on market share were not available from secondary sources. Moreover, market share data have serious limitations because the definitions of market and industry boundaries are often unclear, especially in young industries such as those examined in this research (Grant, 1998; Porter, 1980).

Data for the sales growth and ROE variables were gathered from these secondary sources for the years shown in parentheses: *Business Week* (1995–98), the *100 Best Small Companies* (1995–97), COMPUSTAT PC+ (1994–97), *Electronics Business* (1995–98), *Fortune* (1995–98), *Hoover's Handbook of Emerging Companies* (1995–98), *Hoover's Guide to Computer Companies* (1995–98), *Inc.* (1995–98), *International Business* (1995–98), American Electronics Association (AEA) directories (1993–97), and *Software Magazine* (1995–98). Most of these publications reported the sales growth and ROE measures as percentages. Further, these figures were reported without an explanation of their calculation. Therefore, we took several steps to validate the sales growth and ROE measures.

First, we contacted most of the trade publications listed above to obtain the formulas used to calculate sales growth and ROE. In every case, ROE was measured by dividing net profits by equity. Sales growth was measured as the difference between sales in two consecutive years divided by sales one year earlier, with the quotient multiplied by 100. Our phone calls to trade publications indicated that they sometimes obtained the percentage of increase or decrease in sales from company informants; these informants were unwilling to share absolute sales data. Second, to further ensure reliable data, we validated the sales growth and ROE data using the secondary references mentioned above. The correlations were high for both variables (ROE, r = .83, n = 91, p < .001; sales growth, r = .74, n = 82, p < .001).[2] Data on ROE and sales growth were available for 243 and 229 ventures, respectively.

To address the volatility of sales growth and ROE figures, we explored two options. First, for each measure, we subtracted the overall sample mean from a firm's sales growth and ROE figures. Next, we reran the analyses after subtracting the industry-specific average (determined at the two- or four-digit Standard Industrial Classification [SIC] code level) from a firm's scores. We performed these analyses controlling for past performance by entering past sales growth and ROE figures, as reported later. The results were similar; therefore, the results reported herein reflect industry-specific adjustments in sales growth and ROE.

Control variables. This study also included controls for several variables that might affect the hypothesized relationships, including company age, company size, major industry type, venture ownership, length of international business experience, and prior new venture performance.

Company age was measured by the number of years a venture had been in existence. Age may influence a venture's technological learning (Dodgson, 1993), international business activities (Brush & Vanderwerf, 1992), and the profitability of foreign operations. Also, sales growth is age-sensitive (Chandler & Hanks, 1993). The Appendix provides information on the secondary sources used to collect information about company age. However, some secondary sources may include reorganization and mergers as a basis for firm age. Such transactions can influence the resources a firm has for internationalization. To validate the study's measures, we asked managers to report their companies' ages as of 1993. There was agreement between

secondary and survey data in 91.3 percent of the cases, leaving contradictory information on 28 responding companies. In these 28 instances, we examined the responses provided by the second manager and reconciled 7 cases. We contacted each of the remaining 21 cases by phone, e-mail, or fax and asked for the year the company was established. These actions resolved 17 of the 21 cases. The remaining 4 cases were excluded from further consideration.

Company size was measured by the natural logarithm of a firm's full-time employees. Company size may affect ability to learn (Simonin, 1997), internationally diversify operations (Erramilli & D'Souza, 1993), select an entry mode (Brush, 1995), and survive in international markets (Li, 1995). Information for this variable was gathered through the survey and validated using the secondary references listed in the Appendix under company age. The simple correlation between the information obtained from the survey and secondary references was strong (r = .93, n = 281, p < .001).

Major industry type was measured at the two- or four-digit SIC code level. The industries varied in their technological opportunities and ability to induce learning (Li, 1995), globalization (Brown & Garten, 1995), and profitability (Brown & Garten, 1994). The survey asked managers to provide the name of the company's major industry (defined in the survey as the one from which the company generated most of its sales) and, where possible, its two- or four-digit SIC code. We collected information for this variable from the secondary references listed in the Appendix under company age. There was strong agreement between the information obtained from secondary sources and data provided by executives (r = .98, n = 306).

The study also controlled for venture *ownership* because differences between independent and corporate new ventures in their strategic choices and technological strategies have been reported (Zahra, 1996). Ownership may also affect ventures' international operations and the resources available to them. We asked "How would you classify this company's current ownership?" (independently owned private company, unit of a corporation, or other). We coded these responses as a dichotomous variable, with 0 for independent firms and 1 for corporate units. There was strong agreement between secondary and survey data on this variable (r = .95, n = 291).

We controlled for the length of *international experience* because companies with more international business experience might have gained more resources and skills, which would affect their performance. We asked managers, "In what year were

---

[2] We also attempted to measure new venture performance using data on market share (or on changes in this share). Secondary data on market shares were available for only 86 companies, precluding testing the study's hypotheses using this generally more stable measure. Further, there were strong correlations between market share data and sales growth (r = .83, n = 81, p < .001) and ROE (r = .71, n = 63, p < .001). During the summer of 1998, we used phone calls and faxes to collect data to validate the results and obtain information on market shares from companies. This process yielded information on the market shares of 91 companies. The market share figures obtained from companies were correlated with ROE (r = .67, n = 85, p < .001) and sales growth (r = .79, n = 81, p < .001).

TABLE 1
Means, Standard Deviations, and Correlations[a]

Variable	Range	Mean	s.d.	1	2	3	4	5	6	7	8	9	10	11	12	13	14	15	16	17	18	19	20
1 Number of countries	1–8	2.17	1.06																				
2 Technological diversity	0.23–4.17	1.51	1.43	21																			
3 Cultural diversity	1–5	2.09	1.60	25	09																		
4 Geographic diversity	.05–.73	0.21	0.23	31	−.11	.03																	
5 Foreign market segments	1–5	2.07	1.58	19	15	08	.19																
6 Start-ups	0–3	0.29	0.31	03	11	04	09	13															
7 Acquisitions	0–3	0.19	0.23	09	20	18	−03	07	26														
8 Licensing	1–7	1.03	0.81	12	17	08	−09	22	19	25													
9 Exporting	1–10	1.17	0.97	20	08	16	14	17	22	21	07												
10 Breadth	1.12–4.31	2.97	1.63	19	23	19	20	28	24	15	−15	26											
11 Depth	1.51–4.27	2.71	1.31	−09	19	16	−09	23	28	21	−04	−05	.19										
12 Speed	1.23–4.81	3.05	1.76	−08	20	−06	−10	−14	19	26	−06	−15	−.13	−23									
13 Knowledge integration	1.00–4.06	2.74	1.18	05	03	11	09	07	11	10	05	08	.09	12	09								
14 Company age	2–6	3.41	1.12	13	05	07	08	13	19	13	07	05	03	−06	−05	08							
15 Company size	0.11–3.61	.85	1.45	07	01	04	14	12	15	06	05	13	11	−09	−13	.13	10						
16 Ownership	0–1	0.18	0.23	15	−09	11	12	06	23	11	−02	08	−12	−05	−09	−09	15	17					
17 Prior ROE	−16.7–23.1	6.17	9.44	27	11	14	12	14	17	21	19	17	.09	08	07	05	29	24	.19				
18 Prior sales growth	−27.5–34.7	13.10	17.91	31	09	25	14	16	12	13	04	07	02	29	19	08	23	29	37	.31			
19 International experience	1–5	2.30	2.50	17	11	−09	06	11	15	24	19	09	.13	04	15	07	03	18	17	.19	25		
20 ROE	−10.1–26.2	8.12	11.37	23	18	−14	03	−21	23	−08	25	18	08	22	29	07	17	11	−08	.25	.21	21	28
21 Sales growth	−9.0–42.1	15.09	17.08	27	29	19	07	−.10	29	−13	19	23	25	31	10	11	09	13	14	.33	19	.31	36

[a] Values of *n* vary, for an *n* of 180 or higher, a simple correlation has to be at least .15 to be significant at $p < .05$

your company's products sold outside the USA for the first time?" Responses to this question were validated by collecting data from the multiple sources listed in the Appendix under geographic diversity and the number of countries. The correlation between the survey and secondary sources was strong ($r = .79$, $n = 83$, $p < .001$). We subtracted the year a firm was established from the year its products were first sold overseas; this figure was then entered into the analyses.

We also controlled for prior performance because it can affect the speed, extent, and mode of a firm's internationalization. Therefore, we included *prior ROE* and *prior sales growth* figures in the analyses. Information was gathered from the survey. Interrater agreement on these two variables was significant (ROE, $r = .76$, $n = 99$, $p < .001$; sales growth; $r = .79$, $n = 101$, $p < .001$). We also validated the information gathered through surveys by collecting data from secondary sources (using the references described earlier). The correlations between the two sources were high (ROE, $r = .81$, $n = 284$, $p < .001$; sales growth, $r = .84$, $n = 273$, $p < .001$).

ANALYSIS AND RESULTS

Table 1 presents ranges, means, standard deviations, and correlations. The magnitude of the correlations and the results of regression diagnostics (Hair, Anderson, Tatham, & Black, 1996) suggested that multicollinearity was not a serious problem.

Before conducting tests of the hypotheses, we adjusted all the study's variables except the dichotomous ownership measure for interindustry effects. Adjustments were made by subtracting an industry's mean score, calculated with either the secondary or the survey data, from a firm's score, as in prior research (Dess, Ireland, & Hitt, 1990; Sousa De Vasconcellos E Sá & Hambrick, 1989; Zahra, 1996).

Hypotheses 1a–1c and 2a–2c concern the associations between international diversity, modes of international market entry, and technological learning. Hypotheses 3a through 3f focus on the moderating effect of knowledge integration on the relationships covered in the first two sets of hypotheses. These three sets of hypotheses were tested jointly using moderated regression analyses. Following Cohen (1968), we regressed each dimension of technological learning on international diversity (five measures), entry mode (four measures), and the knowledge integration measure after first introducing the control variables. The results from this step (the base model) appear in the columns marked 1 in Table 2. Next, we introduced nine interaction terms into the analysis, as reported

in the columns marked 2, in Table 2, which present the full model.

As shown in Table 2, the equation for the breadth of technological learning was statistically significant. Consistent with Hypothesis 1a, four of the five international diversity measures were significant predictors of breadth of technological learning: number of countries, technological diversity, cultural diversity, and number of foreign market segments. Also, and consistent with Hypothesis 2a, acquisitions and exports were positively associated with the breadth of a new venture's technological learning.

The equation for the depth of technological learning was also statistically significant. Consistent with Hypothesis 1b, the technological and cultural diversity of foreign markets and the number of foreign segments were positively associated with the depth of technological learning. Both start-ups and foreign acquisitions were also positively related to the depth of technological learning, supporting Hypothesis 2b.

The equation for the speed of technological learning was statistically significant. Technological diversity was positively associated with speed. However, the number of foreign countries entered had a negative effect on speed. None of the other measures of international diversity was related to speed of technological learning. To test for the curvilinear relationship posited in Hypothesis 1c, we reran the analyses reported in Table 2 after adding squared terms for each of the five measures of international diversity. The curvilinear relationship was supported for both the number of foreign countries and segments, but not for technological, cultural, or geographic diversity. Thus, the results provided marginal and mixed support for Hypothesis 1c.

The results in Table 2 show that, consistent with Hypotheses 2a–2c, start-ups and acquisitions had positive effects, but licensing and exports were insignificant predictors of the speed of technological learning.

The results regarding the moderating effect of knowledge integration (third set of hypotheses) on the international diversity and mode of international entry on technological learning are presented in the columns marked 2 in Table 2. The equation for the breadth of technological learning was statistically significant. When the results for the full model (step 2) were examined, the multiple squared correlation coefficient (R^2) increased to .37, and the change in the R^2 between the base and full models was also statistically significant, providing support for a moderating effect. Consistent with Hypothesis 3a, the interactions of knowledge

TABLE 2
Results of Regression Analyses: Effects of Internationalization on Technological Learning

Variable	Breadth		Depth		Speed	
	1	2	1	2	1	2
Control						
Constant	1 08	1.41†	1 67*	1.96*	0.53	0 87
Firm age	0.13	0.12	0.03	0.01	0.05	−0.02
Firm size	0 07	0.10	−0.09	−0.05	−0.16†	−0.15†
Ownership	−0.04	−0 03	0.08	0 04	−0.07	−0.03
International experience	0 10	0 09	0.23*	0.20*	0 29*	0.20*
Prior ROE	0.23*	0.26*	0.05	0 04	0.06	0.11
Prior sales growth	0.19*	0.14†	0.16†	0.15†	0.09	0.07
International diversity						
Number of countries	0.26*	0.31*	−0.07	−0.10	−0.19*	−0.24*
Technological diversity	0.36*	0 32*	0.24*	0 29*	0 26*	0 21*
Cultural diversity	0.44**	0.47**	0.27*	0.29*	−0.06	−0.09
Geographic diversity	0.08	0 09	−0.09	−0 04	−0.07	−0.01
Foreign segments	0 26*	0 35**	0.27*	0.38**	−0 08	−0.11
Mode of entry						
Start-ups	0 04	0.09	0 21*	0.24*	0.20*	0.28*
Acquisitions	0 28*	0 39*	0.22*	0.31*	0.20*	0.29*
Licensing	−0.04	−0.02	−0.04	−0 08	−0 02	−0.09
Exporting	0.22*	0.23*	−0.03	−0.01	−0.03	−0.08
Knowledge integration	0.07	0.09	0.07	0.03	0.09	0 13
Interactions						
Knowledge integration × number of countries		0 25*		−0.01		0.06
Knowledge integration × technological diversity		0.41**		0.27*		0.28*
Knowledge integration × cultural diversity		0.48**		0.34**		−0 05
Knowledge integration × geographic diversity		0 05		−0 09		−0.13
Knowledge integration × foreign segments		0 24*		0.49**		0.09
Knowledge integration × start-ups		0.11		0.20*		0.35**
Knowledge integration × acquisitions		0.48**		0.29*		0.25*
Knowledge integration × licensing		−0.05		−0.07		−0.09
Knowledge integration × exporting		0 14†		−0.05		−0.02
Adjusted R^2	.27	.37	25	.31	.22	.29
F	4 80***	9 04***	3 39***	8 04***	2 93***	6.81***
df	16, 284	25, 275	16, 281	25, 272	16, 291	25, 282
ΔR^2		10		06		07
$F(\Delta R^2)$		4.65***		2.67**		3 11***

† $p < 10$
* $p < 05$
** $p < .01$
*** $p < 001$

integration with the following variables were statistically significant: number of countries, technological diversity, cultural diversity, and number of foreign segments. Consistent with Hypothesis 3d, the interaction of knowledge integration and acquisitions was statistically significant. The interaction of knowledge integration with exports was marginally statistically significant.

Consistent with Hypothesis 3b, the full model for depth of learning was statistically significant. The R^2 increased to .31, and the change in the R^2 between the base and full models was statistically significant, providing support for a moderating effect. Consistent with Hypothesis 3b, the interactions of knowledge integration with the following variables were statistically significant: technological diversity, cultural diversity, and number of foreign segments. Consistent with Hypothesis 3e, the interactions of knowledge integration with acquisitions and start-ups were statistically significant.

The full model for the speed of technological learning was also statistically significant. The R^2 increased to .29, and the change in R^2 between the base and full models was also statistically significant, again supporting moderation. The interactions of knowledge integration with technological diversity were also positive and statistically significant, providing support for Hypothesis 3e. Also, the interactions of start-ups and acquisitions with knowledge integration were statistically significant, supporting Hypothesis 3f.

To test the effect of technological learning on new venture performance, we regressed ROE and sales growth separately on technological learning after first introducing the study's control variables. The results appear in Table 3.

The model for ROE was statistically significant, with an R^2 of .20. Further, the breadth, depth, and speed of technological learning were positive and significant predictors of ROE. Table 3 also shows that the model for sales growth was statistically significant, with an R^2 of .18. The breadth and speed of technological learning were positive predictors of sales growth. The depth of technological learning was not significant in the sales growth model, however. Overall, the results provided strong support for Hypotheses 4a and 4c and partial support for 4b.

The final set of hypotheses predict that international diversity and modes of entry are positively related to a new venture firm's ROE (Hypothesis 5a) and sales growth (Hypothesis 5b). We considered several analytical techniques to test these hypotheses. For example, we examined use of structural equations models (SEM) and path analysis. However, these techniques were ruled out because of potential problems with the degrees of freedom and multicollinearity concerns. Also, the treatment of interaction terms in SEM is controversial. For these reasons, multiple regression analysis was used. Results appear in Table 4.

As shown, the predictors explained 24 percent of a venture's ROE and 27 percent of its sales growth. Two of the five measures of international diversity were positively related to ROE: the number of foreign countries entered and the cultural diversity of these countries. These results provide support for Hypothesis 5a. Licensing and exports were positive predictors of ROE, supporting Hypothesis 5a. However, contrary to expectations, the number of foreign segments was negatively related to ROE. These results provided strong, but not complete, support for Hypothesis 5a.

TABLE 3
Results of Regression Analysis of the Moderating Effect of Knowledge Integration

Variable	ROE	Sales Growth
Control		
Constant	2 01*	2 27*
Firm age	0.14†	0.05
Firm size	0.08	0.07
Ownership	−0 03	−0.09
International experience	0 18*	0.16†
Prior ROE	0.24*	0.11
Prior sales growth	0.19*	0.31**
Technological learning		
Breadth	0 21*	0.23**
Depth	0 37**	0.09
Speed	0 43**	0.37**
Adjusted R^2	20	.18
F	4.47***	2.91**
df	9, 187	9, 172

† $p < 10$
* $p < 05$
** $p < 01$
*** $p < .001$

TABLE 4
Effect of Internationalization on New Venture Performance

Variable	ROE	Sales Growth
Control		
Constant	1.41	2.21*
Firm age	0.17†	0.25*
Firm size	0.09	0.11
Ownership	−0.04	−0.07
International experience	0.21*	0.22*
Prior ROE	0.45**	0.20*
Prior sales growth	0.23*	0.39**
International diversity		
Number of foreign countries	0.27*	0 22*
Technological diversity	−0.04	0 25*
Cultural diversity	0 22*	0 39**
Geographic diversity	0.08	0.16†
Foreign segments	−0 14†	0.05
Modes of entry		
Start-ups	−0.03	−0.07
Acquisition	−0 07	0.21*
Licensing agreements	0.25*	0.34**
Export agreements	0 29*	0 49**
Adjusted R^2	24	27
F	4.27***	4.09***
df	15, 181	15, 166

† $p < 10$
* $p < 05$
** $p < .01$
*** $p < 001$

The results in Table 4 show that the number of foreign countries a new venture entered and their technological and cultural diversity were positively related to sales growth. Geographic diversity of revenue was also positively associated with sales growth. Licensing, acquisitions, and exports were also positively associated with sales growth. These results are consistent with Hypothesis 5b.

DISCUSSION

Increasingly, new ventures are entering international markets early in their life cycles. The results show a strong relationship between international diversity and mode of market entry and the breadth, depth, and speed of a new venture firm's technological learning, especially when the firm undertakes formal knowledge integration. In turn, the breadth, depth, and speed of technological learning are related to new venture firm performance. International diversity and mode of international entry are also positively related to new venture performance. Table 5 is an overall summary of the study's results, which are discussed in more detail below.

Evaluation of Results

Hypotheses 1a–1c. Innovation is important for effective firm performance in competitive global markets (e.g., Franko, 1989; Hitt et al., 1998). An important criterion for the development of innovation is the possession of adequate knowledge.

Thus, firms must build knowledge to develop and use innovation effectively. Organizational learning enables a firm to develop new knowledge. One means by which firms learn is to move into new foreign markets in which they are exposed to and then assimilate different types of knowledge. Thus, the higher the diversity of foreign markets entered, the greater the opportunity for organizational learning. As Table 5 shows, the results provide strong but not universal support for this hypothesis.

For most firms, moving into new international markets produces an exposure to the greatest diversity of knowledge. This may be particularly true for smaller and younger new venture firms. The results strongly support these arguments. Indeed, as new venture firms move into a broader set of and more diverse international markets, they increase the potential for greater breadth and depth of technological learning. However, greater diversity of markets can reduce the speed of technological learning. The results partially supported the hypothesized curvilinear relationship between international diversity and learning speed. In particular, they indicate that the effect of diversity on the speed of technological learning can be negative. New ventures that diversify internationally, therefore, may have to trade speed off against the breadth and depth of technological learning. Learning can be quite important, and the knowledge gained may partially transfer from one market to another, thereby enriching the value of the learning that occurs. Learning from one market with cultural values similar to those of another market may allow some knowledge to be ap-

TABLE 5
Summary of the Predictions and Results

Independent Variable	Hypothesis	Predicted Sign	Dependent Variable	Overall Results
International diversity	H1a	+	Breadth	Strong support
	H1b	+	Depth	Partial support
	H1c	Inverted ∪	Speed	Marginal and mixed support
Mode of entry	H2a	+	Breadth	Strong support
	H2b	+	Depth	Strong support
	H2c	+	Speed	Strong support
Knowledge integration	H3a	+	Breadth	Partial support
× international diversity	H3b	+	Depth	Partial support
	H3c	+	Speed	Mixed support
Knowledge integration × mode	H3d	+	Breadth	Partial support
of entry	H3e	+	Depth	Strong support
	H3f	+	Speed	Strong support
Technological learning				
Breadth	H4a	+	New venture performance	Strong support
Depth	H4b	+	New venture performance	Partial support
Speed	H4c	+	New venture performance	Strong support
International diversity	H5a	+	ROE	Partial support
Mode of entry	H5a	+	ROE	Strong support
International diversity	H5b	+	Sales growth	Strong support
Mode of entry	H5b	+	Sales growth	Strong support

plied in the newer market. Thus, new technical knowledge acquired in Canada may also be at least partially useful in the United States and the United Kingdom. Younger entrepreneurial firms are generally more effective at developing and exploiting innovation, particularly radical innovation (Afuah, 1998). Therefore, if new ventures can increase the breadth, depth, and speed of their technological learning, they can create and market innovation more quickly, thereby gaining competitive advantage, even over larger, more resource-endowed firms.

Hypotheses 2a–2c. As Table 5 shows, the results provide strong support for these predictions. Indeed, one of this study's contributions is its documentation of the potential effect of different modes of international market entry on the breadth, depth, and speed of technological learning. Previously, it has been suggested that firms establish start-ups to transfer knowledge to their subsidiaries and use acquisitions to gain access to new knowledge (Hennart & Park, 1994). Although our data do not allow us to corroborate the motives for choosing a particular mode of international entry, the results show that start-ups and foreign acquisitions may have different effects on separate dimensions of technological learning for new venture firms.

The results show a positive association between the use of acquisitions and the breadth of technological learning. Acquisitions give a firm access to different knowledge bases (Hennart & Park, 1994). There was no relationship between start-ups and breadth of learning, perhaps because some time may elapse before a new venture gains knowledge from creating these units. The results also show that the use of high-control modes of entry in the forms of acquisitions and start-ups is positively associated with the depth of technological learning. Thus, these transactions deepen a firm's technological knowledge. Start-ups are likely to serve a dual role by transferring knowledge from and to parent firms.

Foreign start-ups and acquisitions enhance the speed of technological learning. In contrast, lower-control modes of entry have a negative effect on speed. These results extend the literature by showing that new ventures can benefit from using higher-control entry modes through increasing the speed with which they acquire new technological knowledge.

Hypotheses 3a–3f. The results also suggest that knowledge integration increases the breadth and depth of the technological learning new ventures gain from international diversity. Broad and deep technological learning can provide a competitive advantage (Kodama, 1995). Table 5 shows support

for the moderating effect of knowledge integration. Integration is useful in enhancing technological learning when the technological diversity of foreign markets is high.

The results also show that knowledge integration plays a more important role with the modes of entry. Knowledge integration, in conjunction with acquisitions, positively affects the breadth of technological learning. Additionally, the depth and speed of technological learning derived from foreign start-ups and acquisitions are higher with greater formal knowledge integration. Thus, for new firms, knowledge integration can be an important organizational competence.

Hypotheses 4a–4b. The literature suggests that technological learning can enhance a company's performance (Dodgson, 1991, 1993). As Table 5 suggests, the results support this proposition, showing that technological learning is positively associated with new venture performance. New ventures that achieve technological learning gain important knowledge that can be used to design and offer a greater variety of innovative products (breadth of knowledge), to offer highly differentiated, high-quality products (depth of knowledge), and to move products to market faster (speed of developing and using knowledge), and therefore these ventures should achieve higher financial performance. In the current environment, in which short product life cycles result in pressure for faster development-to-market cycles, the emphasis is on speed. In fact, some authors have argued that true competitive advantage is not derived from size or from having more resources, but from being able to move faster than competitors (Hitt et al., 1998). Thus, increasing the breadth, depth, and speed of technological learning is important for the success of new venture firms.

Hypotheses 5a–5b. Table 5 shows that the results also support previous work suggesting that international expansion can have a positive effect on a firm's performance (Ghoshal, 1987; Hitt et al., 1997; Leontiades, 1986; Prahalad & Doz, 1987). Hitt and his coauthors (1997) presented arguments for and found an inverted U-shaped curvilinear relationship between international diversification and performance. Early movement into international markets generally creates positive returns, but continued international diversification may eventually produce negative returns. These researchers suggested that negative returns were caused by the increased transaction costs and the challenges of managing a geographically dispersed organization operating in multiple and diverse markets. Although several of the dimensions of international diversity examined in this study showed a positive effect on performance indicators, the number of foreign segments had a negative effect on ROE. Technological diversity and cultural diversity had no relationship with ROE. Also, acquisitions and start-ups had no relationship with ROE. Acquisitions, however, had a positive and significant association with sales growth. This pattern of findings suggests that some dimensions of international diversity have positive effects on performance, and others have negative or no effects. Alternatively, four of the five measures of international diversity and three of the four modes of entry had positive effects on sales growth. Obviously, there are more costs, both financial and managerial, related to FDI than to licensing and exporting. This difference might be reflected in the lack of relationships observed between acquisitions and start-ups and ROE. The lack of a relationship between start-ups and sales growth highlights the possibility that a start-up business has to work diligently to establish distribution channels and position its products before it can generate significant sales. Acquisitions, on the other hand, may result in almost immediate sales growth.

The lack of relationships observed between FDI indicators and ROE serves as a reminder for new ventures to patiently invest to build global operations. New ventures usually have limited resources, and managers need to seriously consider the attractiveness of FDI transactions and balance their effects on short-term performance with the learning to be gained from these operations. If firms experience broad and deep learning from these transactions, their long-term performance may improve. As argued earlier, FDI provides greater opportunities for learning because of the intensity of involvement in the new markets. However, it takes greater time for this learning to develop and to affect performance. Thus, the effect of FDI on firm performance is mediated by the amount of learning created and internalized within start-up and acquired businesses. Conversely, licensing and export transactions provide fewer opportunities for learning but, in the shorter term, have higher potential for direct effects on performance. Thus, FDI is likely to have greater longer-term effects on new venture firm performance.

Finally, the results show that international diversity is positively associated with ROE, whereas the number of foreign segments in which a firm operates has a negative effect on ROE. Given the youth of the companies examined in this research, the negative relationship between the number of segments and ROE is understandable. Managing and serving these segments can tax the resources of the firm, thereby reducing its short-term performance.

However, because targeting a large number of foreign segments is sometimes a precursor to international diversity, a negative relationship between diversity and ROE may be evident earlier than a negative association between international diversity and venture performance.

This research makes several contributions to scholars' knowledge. First, there has been little empirical research on the effects on the performance of new venture firms of international diversity and modes of entry. Thus, this study adds to knowledge not only of international diversity and entry modes and their effects on performance and learning, but also to knowledge about different types of organizations, in particular new venture firms. Perhaps, more importantly, we have provided specific data on the learning that occurred, in this case technological learning, whereas in much prior research, organizational learning has been assumed and left unmeasured (e.g., Hitt et al., 1997). Our research showed that international diversity and high-control entry modes indeed increase technological learning. In turn, technological learning, or new knowledge created, has a positive effect on firm performance, as measured by ROE and sales growth. Our research also suggests that international diversity and mode of entry have a positive, direct effect on firm performance, in addition to their more indirect effect of increasing technological learning.

Managerial Implications

The results of this study should encourage managers to articulate, identify, and capture the technological learning achieved by their new ventures. This learning can play a pivotal role in differentiating a new venture firm's products, achieving speedy market introductions, and gaining a competitive advantage. The results also show that international diversity and modes of entry provide an important means of increasing a new venture firm's learning of technological skills and exploiting this knowledge in its operations. Thus, managers must develop and nurture skills that ensure effective integration of learning as their firms expand internationally. However, managers cannot assume that learning will occur automatically or that it will lead to improved performance.

The results also emphasize the importance of international business operations for successful new venture performance. These operations are largely associated with more growth and profitability. These findings should encourage managers to explore when, where, and how to best internationalize their firms' business operations. Managerial attitudes and preferences are at the core of a venture's internationalization activities.

Future Research Directions

The results of this study suggest several avenues for future research on the internationalization of new ventures. One important avenue is to converge on the definition of a new venture. As noted previously, researchers have used different firm ages to classify new ventures. We used six years of age, a choice consistent with some past work (e.g., Brush & Vanderwerf, 1992; Shrader, 1996). Definition in terms of age is important because over time, ventures may develop the expertise needed to more successfully enter international markets and to learn new technological skills from those operations. Furthermore, internationalization can be a lengthy process. Future researchers, therefore, should explore the effects of different and perhaps longer time frames on the nature and strength of the relationships among the variables examined in this study. Also valuable would be research to determine the appropriate time lags between international diversity and learning and between learning and higher performance.

New ventures might seek to achieve different strategic goals through international expansion. Future researchers, therefore, should explore additional performance measures to establish the link between international expansion and performance. In particular, the use of market share could help to validate the current results and provide additional insights into the effects of international diversity and modes of entry on new venture performance.

This study has focused on the benefits of international diversity among new ventures. However, international diversity can tax a firm's resources, structure, and management team. It can also complicate the communication process within the organization and the relationships the new venture establishes with other companies. Thus, future research should explore the costs of international diversity in new ventures.

There is also a need to document the effects of international diversity on different types of organizational learning (marketing, competitive, and social) and link them to new venture performance. The field could benefit from research documenting the approaches companies use to capture and exploit the knowledge gained from their learning activities. The development and testing of a framework linking learning, competence development, strategic choices, and performance (McGrath et al., 1995) could yield valuable insights. Such a framework would be useful for examining the effects of technological learning on a new venture firm's future international expansion. The evolution of organizational capabilities may serve as a catalyst to additional expansion in existing or new international markets. These capabilities may also shape the new venture firm's future choice of entry modes and the types of markets it chooses to enter.

A fertile area for future research is how new ventures learn. One cannot and should not assume that new companies learn in the same way as established companies. We need to understand better the antecedents and the process of learning by new ventures. The quality of a venture's founders (Huber, 1991), information-processing capacity, and environment likely have important implications for learning and the value that can be achieved from it. Future research is needed to examine if differences in learning among new ventures are determined by the background and prior international experience of their founders and managers and/or by the characteristics of the markets entered. Future studies should also clarify the moderating effect of a firm's managers' international experience on the relationship between international diversity and technological learning. Prior exposure to foreign cultures and markets might alert managers to the potential new knowledge that can be gained from international diversity, a factor that can affect the speed, depth, and breadth of the firm's future technological learning.

Additionally, there is a need for research into the international business activities of new ventures in low-technology industries. The structural characteristics of these industries (for instance, slow technological change) can affect the need for and speed of internationalization and, as a consequence, the benefits the firms gain from international operations. The amount and value of technological learning from international operations might also be more limited in low- than in high-technology industries. These intuitively appealing variations, however, require systematic analysis and validation using either comparative studies (low vs. high technology) or analyses of different low-technology sectors.

Comparative studies of the approaches used by new ventures and established companies for knowledge integration are also needed. Little is known about the nature of these approaches or the effects of organizational structures and management systems on knowledge integration. Future researchers should also explore differences between established companies' and new ventures' international diversity and modes of entry and their effects on learning and performance. Comparative studies along these lines could enrich understanding of potential sources of competitive advantage for new ventures and established firms.

In conclusion, our research shows the value and importance of international diversity and modes of entry for new venture firms. Furthermore, it has shown the more specific effects of international expansion on technological learning, long assumed to be an important characteristic of newer and more established firms. Finally, both international expansion and technological learning have largely positive effects on the performance of new venture firms. Thus, these findings have important implications for the theory and practice of managing new venture firms.

REFERENCES

Afuah, A. 1998. *Innovation management: Strategies, implementation, and profits.* New York: Oxford University Press.

Anand, J., & Singh, H. 1997. Asset redeployment, acquisitions and corporate strategy in declining industries. *Strategic Management Journal,* 18(special issue): 99–118.

Andersen, O. 1993. On the internationalization process of firms: A critical analysis. *Journal of International Business Studies,* 24: 209–231.

Arora, A., & Gambardella, A. 1997. Domestic markets and international competitiveness: Generic and product-specific competencies in the engineering sector. *Strategic Management Journal,* 18(special issue): 53–74.

Bantel, K. A. 1998. Technology-based "adolescent" firm configurations: Strategy identification, context, and performance. *Journal of Business Venturing,* 13: 205–230.

Barkema, H. G., & Vermeulen, F. 1998. International expansion through start-up or acquisition: A learning perspective. *Academy of Management Journal,* 41: 7–26.

Bartlett, C. A., & Ghoshal, S. 1987a. Managing across borders: New organizational responses. *Sloan Management Review,* 28(4): 7–17.

Bartlett, C. A., & Ghoshal, S 1987b. Managing across borders: New strategic responses. *Sloan Management Review,* 28(5): 45–53.

Bell, C. G., & McNamara, J. E. 1991. *High-tech ventures: The guide for entrepreneurial success.* Reading, MA: Addison-Wesley.

Bloodgood, J. M., Sapienza, H. J., & Almeida, J. G. 1996. The internationalization of new high-potential U.S. ventures: Antecedents and outcomes. *Entrepreneurship Theory and Practice,* 20(4): 61–76.

Bohn, R. E. 1994. Measuring and managing technological knowledge. *Sloan Management Review,* 36(1): 61–73.

Brown, R. H. 1994. *Competing to win in a global economy.* Washington, DC: U.S. Department of Commerce.

Brown, R. H., & Garten, J. E. 1994. *U.S. industrial outlook: An almanac of industry, technology and services* (35th ed.). Austin, TX: Reference Press.

Brown, R. H., & Garten, J. E. 1995. *U.S. global trade outlook: 1995–2000.* Washington, DC: U.S. Department of Commerce.

Brush, C. G. 1995. *International entrepreneurship: The effects of firm age on motives of internationalization.* New York: Garland.

Brush, C. G., & Vanderwerf, P. A. 1992. A comparison of methods and sources for obtaining estimates of new venture performance. *Journal of Business Venturing,* 7: 157–170.

Buzzell, R. D., & Gale, B. T. 1987. *The PIMS principles: Linking strategy to performance.* New York: Free Press.

Campbell, D. T., & Stanley, J. C. 1963. *Experimental and quasi-experimental designs for research.* Chicago: Rand McNally.

Caves, R. E. 1982. *Multinational enterprise and economic analysis.* Cambridge, England: Cambridge University Press.

Chandler, G. N., & Hanks, S. H. 1993. Measuring the performance of emerging businesses: A validation study. *Journal of Business Venturing,* 8: 391–408.

Cohen, J. 1968. Multiple regression as a general data-analytic system. *Psychological Bulletin,* 70: 426–443.

Covin, J. G., Slevin, D. P., & Covin, T. J. 1990. Content and performance of growth-seeking strategies: A comparison of small firms in high- and low-technology industries. *Journal of Business Venturing,* 5: 391–412.

Craig, C. S., & Douglas, S. P. 1996. Developing strategies for global markets: An evolutionary perspective. *Columbia Journal of World Business,* 31(1): 70–81.

Datar, S., Jordan, C., Kekre, S., Rajiv, S., & Srinivasan, K. 1997. New product development structures and time-to-market. *Management Science,* 43: 452–464.

Day, D. L. 1994. Raising radicals: Different processes for championing innovative corporate ventures. *Organizational Science,* 5: 148–172.

Dess, G. G., Ireland, R. D., & Hitt, M. A. 1990. Industry effects and strategic management research. *Journal of Management,* 16: 7–27.

Dodgson, M. 1991a. Technology learning, technology strategy and competitive pressures. *British Journal of Management,* 2: 133–149.

Dodgson, M. 1991b. *The management of technological*

learning: Lessons from a biotechnology company. New York: de Gruyter.

Dodgson, M. 1993. *Technological collaboration in industry: Strategy, policy, and internalization in innovation.* London: Routledge.

Erramilli, M. K., & D'Souza, D. E. 1993. Venturing into foreign markets: The case of the small service firm. *Entrepreneurship Theory and Practice,* 17(3): 29–41.

Feeser, H. R., & Willard, G. E. 1990. Founding strategy and performance. *Strategic Management Journal,* 11: 87–98.

Franko, L. G. 1989. Global corporate competition: Who's winning, who's losing and the R&D factor as one reason why. *Strategic Management Journal,* 10: 449–474.

Ganesh, J., Kumar, V., & Subramaniam, V. 1997. Learning effect in multinational diffusion of consumer durables: An exploratory investigation. *Journal of the Academy of Marketing Science,* 25: 214–228.

Geringer, J. M., Beamish, P. W., & daCosta, R. C. 1989. Diversification strategy and internationalization: Implications for MNE performance. *Strategic Management Journal,* 10: 109–119.

Ghoshal, S. 1987. Global strategy: An organizing framework. *Strategic Management Journal,* 8: 425–440.

Grant, R. M. 1997. The knowledge-based view of the firm: Implications for management practice. *Long Range Planning,* 30: 450–454.

Grant, R. M. 1998. *Contemporary strategy analysis* (3rd ed.). Cambridge, MA: Blackwell Business.

Grant, R. M. 1991. The resource-based theory of competitive advantage: Implications for strategy formulation. *California Management Review,* 33(3): 114–135.

Grant, R. M. 1996a. Toward a knowledge-based theory of the firm. *Strategic Management Journal,* 17: 109–122

Grant, R. M. 1996b. Prospering in dynamically-competitive environments: Organizational capability as knowledge integration. *Organization Science,* 7: 375–387.

Hair, J. F., Jr., Anderson, R. E., Tatham, R. L., & Black, W. C. 1996. *Multivariate data analysis* (3rd ed.). New York: Macmillan.

Hamel, G., & Prahalad, C. K. 1994. *Competing for the future.* Boston: Harvard Business School Press.

Helfat, C. E. 1994. Firm-specificity in corporate applied R&D. *Organization Science,* 5: 173–183.

Hennart, J-F., & Park, Y-R. 1994. Location, governance, and strategic determinants of Japanese manufacturing investment in the United States. *Strategic Management Journal,* 15: 419–436.

Hill, C. W. L., Hwang, P., & Kim, W. C. 1990. An eclectic theory of the choice of international entry mode. *Strategic Management Journal,* 11: 117–128.

Hitt, M. A., & Bartkus, B. 1997. International entrepreneurship. In J. A. Katz & R. H. Brockhaus (Eds.), *Advances in entrepreneurship, firm emergence and growth:* 7–30. Greenwich, CT: JAI Press.

Hitt, M. A., Dacin, M. T., Tyler, B. B., & Park, D. 1997. Understanding the differences in Korean and U.S. executives' strategic orientations. *Strategic Management Journal,* 18: 159–167.

Hitt, M. A., Hoskisson, R. E., & Ireland, R. D. 1994. A mid-range theory of the interactive effects of international and product diversification on innovation and performance. *Journal of Management,* 20: 297–326.

Hitt, M. A., Hoskisson, R. E., Johnson, R. A., & Moesel, D. D. 1996. The market for corporate control and firm innovation. *Academy of Management Journal,* 39: 1084–1119.

Hitt, M. A., Hoskisson, R. E., & Kim, H. 1997. International diversification: Effects on innovation and firm performance in product-diversified firms. *Academy of Management Journal,* 40: 767–798.

Hitt, M. A., Keats, B. W., & DeMarie, S. 1998. Navigating in the new competitive landscape: Building strategic flexibility and competitive advantage in the 21st century. *Academy of Management Executive,* 12(4): 22–42.

Hofstede, G. 1980. *Culture's consequences: International differences in work-related values.* Beverly Hills, CA: Sage.

Hofstede, G. 1993. Cultural constraints in management theories. *Academy of Management Executive,* 7(1): 81–94.

Huber, G. P. 1991. Organizational learning: An examination of the contributing processes and the literatures. *Organization Science,* 2: 88–115.

Johanson, J., & Vahlne, J-E. 1977. The internationalization process of the firm—A model of knowledge development and increasing foreign market commitments. *Journal of International Business Studies,* 8(1): 23–32.

Kidd, J. B., & Teramoto, Y. 1995. The learning organization: The case of the Japanese RHQs in Europe. *Management International Review,* 35(2, special issue): 39–56.

Kim, L. 1997. *Imitation to innovation: The dynamics of Korea's technological learning.* Boston: Harvard Business School Press.

Kim, W. C., Hwang, P., & Burgers, W. P. 1993. Multinationals' diversification and the risk-return trade-off. *Strategic Management Journal,* 14: 275–286.

Kodama, F. 1995. *Emerging patterns of innovation: Sources of Japan's technological edge.* Boston: Harvard Business School Press.

Kogut. B., & Singh, H. 1988. The effect of national culture on the choice of entry mode. *Journal of International Business Studies,* 19: 411–432.

Lei, D., Hitt, M. A., & Bettis, R. 1996. Dynamic core competences through meta-learning and strategic context. *Journal of Management,* 22: 549–569.

Leonard-Barton, D. 1992. The factory as a learning laboratory. *Sloan Management Review,* 34(1): 23–38.

Leonard-Barton, D. 1995. *Wellsprings of knowledge.* Boston: Harvard Business School Press.

Leontiades, J. C. 1986. Going global—Global strategies versus national strategies. *Long Range Planning,* 19: 96–104.

Li, J. T. 1995. Foreign entry and survival: The effects of strategic choices on performance in international markets. *Strategic Management Journal,* 16: 333–351.

Makino, S., & Delios, A. 1996. Local knowledge transfer and performance: Implications for alliance formation in Asia. *Journal of International Business Studies,* 27: 905–927.

McCann, J. E. 1991. Patterns of growth, competitive technology, and financial strategies in young ventures. *Journal of Business Venturing,* 6: 189–208.

McDougall, P. P. 1989. International versus domestic entrepreneurship: New venture strategic behavior and industry structure. *Journal of Business Venturing,* 4: 387–399.

McDougall, P. P., Deane, R. H., & D'Souza, D. 1992. Manufacturing strategy and business origin of new venture firms in the computer and communications equipment industries. *Product and Operations Management,* 1: 53–69.

McDougall, P. P., & Oviatt, B. M. 1996. New venture internationalization, strategic change, and performance: A follow-up study. *Journal of Business Venturing,* 11: 23–40.

McDougall, P. P., Shane, S., & Oviatt, B. M. 1994. Explaining the formation of international new ventures: The limits of theories from international business research. *Journal of Business Venturing,* 9: 469–487.

McGrath, R. G., MacMillan, I. C., & Venkataraman, S. 1995. Defining and developing competence: A strategic process paradigm. *Strategic Management Journal,* 16: 251–275.

Mitchell, W., & Singh, K. 1996. Survival of businesses using collaborative relationships to commercialize complex goods. *Strategic Management Journal,* 17: 169–195.

Mohrman, S. A., & Von Glinow, M. A. 1990. High technology organizations: Context, organization and people. *Journal of Engineering and Technology Management,* 6: 261–280.

Morrison, A. J., & Roth, K. 1992. A taxonomy of business-level strategies in global industries. *Strategic Management Journal,* 13: 399–417.

Nakata, C., & Sivakumar, K. 1996. National culture and new product development: An integrative review. *Journal of Marketing,* 60: 61–72.

Nonaka, I. 1991. The knowledge-creating company. *Harvard Business Review,* 69(6): 96–104.

Nonaka, I. 1994. A dynamic theory of organizational knowledge creation. *Organization Science,* 5: 14–37.

Nonaka, I., & Takeuchi, H. 1995. *The knowledge-creating company: How Japanese companies create the dynamics of innovation.* New York: Oxford University Press.

Olk, P., & Young, C. 1997. Why members stay in or leave an R&D consortium: Performance and conditions of membership as determinants of continuity. *Strategic Management Journal,* 18: 855–877.

Oviatt, B. M., & McDougall, P. P. 1994. Toward a theory of international new ventures. *Journal of International Business Studies,* 25: 45–64.

Oviatt, B. M., & McDougall, P. P. 1995. Global start-ups: Entrepreneurs on a worldwide stage. *Academy of Management Executive,* 9(2): 30–43.

Oviatt, B. M., & McDougall, P. P. 1997. Challenges for internationalization process theory: The case of international new ventures. *Management International Review,* 37(special issue): 85–99.

Pennings, J. M., & Harianto, F. 1992. Technological networking and innovation implementation. *Organization Science,* 3: 356–382.

Porter, M. E. 1980. *Competitive strategy.* New York: Free Press.

Porter, M. E. 1990. *The competitive advantage of nations.* New York: Free Press.

Prahalad, C. K., & Doz, Y. L. 1987. *The multinational mission: Balancing local demands and global vision.* New York: Free Press.

Ramanujam, V., & Varadarajan, P. 1989. Research on corporate diversification: A synthesis. *Strategic Management Journal,* 10: 523–552.

Regnier, P. 1993. The dynamics of small and medium-sized enterprises in Korea and other Asian NIEs. *Small Business Economics,* 5: 23–36.

Sambharya, R. 1995. The combined effect of international diversification and product diversification strategies on the performance of US-based multinational corporations. *Management International Review,* 35: 197–218.

Senge, P. M. 1990. *The fifth discipline: The art and practice of the learning organization.* London: Doubleday Currency.

Shrader, R. 1996. *Influences on and performance implications of internationalization by publicly owned U.S. new ventures: A risk taking perspec-*

tive. Doctoral dissertation, Georgia State University, Atlanta.

Shrader, R. C., & Simon, M. 1997. Corporate versus independent new ventures: Resources, strategy and performance differences. *Journal of Business Venturing,* 12: 47–66.

Simonin, B. L. 1997. The importance of collaborative know-how: An empirical test of the learning organization. *Academy of Management Journal,* 10: 1150–1174.

Sohn, J. H. D. 1994. Social knowledge as a control system: A proposition and evidence from the Japanese FDI behavior. *Journal of International Business Studies,* 25: 295–324.

Sousa de Vasconcellos E Sá, J. A., & Hambrick, D. C. 1989. Key success factors: Test of a general theory in the mature industrial-product sector. *Strategic Management Journal,* 10: 367–382.

Stewart, T. 1998. Is this job really necessary? *Fortune,* January 12: 154–155.

Stopford, J. M., & Wells, L. T. 1972. *Managing the multinational enterprise.* New York: Basic Books.

Tallman, S., & Li, J. 1996. Effects of international diversity and product diversity on the performance of multinational firms. *Academy of Management Journal,* 39: 179–196.

Teece, D. J., Pisano, G., & Shuen, A. 1997. Dynamic capabilities and strategic management. *Strategic Management Journal,* 18: 509–533.

Teece, D. J., Rumelt, R., Dosi, G., & Winter, S. 1994. Understanding corporate coherence: Theory and evidence. *Journal of Economic Behavior and Organization,* 23: 1–30.

Usunier, J-C. 1996. *Marketing across cultures.* London: Prentice-Hall.

Welch, D. E., & Welch, L. S. 1996. The internationalization process and networks: A strategic management perspective. *Journal of International Marketing,* 4(3): 11–28.

Zahra, S. A. 1996. Technology strategy and new venture performance: A study of corporate-sponsored and independent biotechnology ventures. *Journal of Business Venturing,* 11: 289–321.

Zander, U., & Kogut, B. 1995. Knowledge and the speed of the transfer and imitation of organizational capabilities: An empirical test. *Organization Science,* 6: 76–92.

APPENDIX

This Appendix presents the secondary sources used to select the companies in the sample and gather the secondary data used to measure the study's variables.

Sources of Data

Company names. Companies to be surveyed were identified from a list of 100 industrial and service companies (*Black Enterprise,* June 1993); 100 Best Small Companies (*Business Week,* 1993); COMPUSTAT (1993); the Global 100 List (*Electronics Business,* 1991–93); the 100 Fastest-Growing Companies (*Fortune,* 1993); *Hoover's Guide to Computer Companies* (1992); the 100 Fastest-Growing Public Companies (*Inc.,* May 1993); the 100 Fastest-Growing International Companies (*International Business,* December 1992); the *American Electronics Association Directory* (1993); the Top 100 Independent Software Vendors (*Software Magazine,* 1993); and America's Top 50 Women Business Owners (*Working Women,* May 1993).

Number of countries. We gathered secondary data for this variable from the list of 100 industrial and service companies (*Black Enterprise,* June 1993), 100 Best Small Companies (*Business Week,* 1993–94); COMPUSTAT PC+ (1993–94); the Global 100 list (*Electronics Business,* 1991–93); 100 Fastest-Growing Companies (*Fortune,* 1993–94); *Hoover's Guide to Computer Companies* (1993–94); 100 Fastest-Growing Public Companies (*Inc.,* May 1993); the *American Electronics Association Directory* (1993); Top 100 Independent Software Vendors (*Software Magazine,* 1993); and America's Top 50 Women Business Owners (*Working Women,* May 1993). We also visited companies' Internet home pages (n = 33), where available.

Technological diversity. Data for this variable were obtained from a 1997 OECD report on industrial competitiveness; Web pages of the National Science and Technology Board (1997); Web pages of the American Institute for Physics (1997); *National Patterns of R&D Resources* (1996); National Science Foundation, NSF 96-333 (Arlington, VA), Table C-17 for 1993; OECD electronic reports (Figures 3.1a & 3.1b), 1981–95 *(http://sahar.fsw.denuniv.nl/cwts/nofarmes/sum_text.html);* Facts & Stats on-line: Canadian Research Expenditures (1963–93); the Japanese Mission to the European Union's Web pages (1980–95); Malaysian science and technology indicators' Web page (1992–94); science and technology indicators for the APEC Economies' Web pages (1997); R&D activities [Japanese] Web pages (1989–95); the Science Coalition's Web pages: Trends in R&D–European Union (1997); UNESCO: Selected Science and Technology Indicators, statistics on education, for South America (1990–95); and the *U S. Statistical Abstracts* (1988–95).

Geographic diversity (GD). Data used in validating this measure came from multiple secondary sources that included these: *Hoover's Handbook of Emerging Companies* (1993–96); *Hoover's Guide to Computer Companies* (1993–95); and companies' Internet home pages (n = 29). Combined, these lists provided data on 71 companies. Newspaper and trade publication articles (obtained through Lexis-Nexis) provided information for 32 companies.

Company age and size. This information was collected from the list of 100 industrial and service companies (*Black Enterprise,* June 1993); the 100 Best Small Companies (*Business Week,* 1993–94); COM-

PUSTAT PC+ (1993–94); Global 100 List (*Electronics Business*, 1991–93); 100 Fastest-Growing Companies (*Fortune*, 1993–94); *Hoover's Guide to Computer Companies* (1993–94); 100 Fastest-Growing Public Companies (*Inc.*, May 1993); *American Electronics Association Directory* (1993); Top 100 Independent Software Vendors (*Software Magazine*, 1993); and America's Top 50 Women Business Owners (*Working Women*, May 1993).

Timing of international market entry. Validation data for this variable were gathered for a subset of 83 ventures from *Hoover's Handbook of Emerging Companies* (1993–96); *Hoover's Guide to Computer Companies* (1993–95); companies' Internet home pages; and newspaper and trade publication articles (obtained through Lexis-Nexis).

Technological learning. Three measures were developed with survey data, as follows: (1) *Breadth* was measured by managers' responses to 19 items that were extracted from the literature, as noted in the text. Instructions read as follows: "In the course of their international operations companies sometimes learn different things or gain new insights. Listed below are several items that pertain to a company's technology (defined as know-how), research and development, and technological innovation activities. Please read each statement carefully and then indicate the extent your company has gained knowledge and new insights, or learned skills or capabilities from its international business operations in each of the areas listed below. A score of 5 would mean that you believe your company has learned many different and varied skills in a given area. A score of 1 would mean that your company has learned only a few (or a limited number of) skills in a particular area. If an item does not apply to your company's situation, please circle 'not applicable.'"

The items used in this measure were developed to cover a broad range of a new venture firm's technological activities. They were: (1) designing new products (processes), (2) prototyping new products (processes), (3) pretesting new products (processes), (4) timing new product (process) introductions, (5) sequencing new product (process) introductions, (6) customizing products for local markets, (7) manufacturing, (8) sourcing technology, (9) integrating technologies acquired from other companies with your own technologies, (10) organizing the R&D function, (11) staffing the R&D function, (12) determining R&D spending levels, (13) funding new technology, (14) managing the R&D process, (15) coordinating R&D with other organizational units (functions), (16) identifying emerging technologies, (17) forecasting technological trends, (18) transferring technologies across international borders, and (19) protecting your technological trade secrets. Managers' responses were averaged, and the resulting score was used as the study's measure.

To validate the breadth index, we used responses to three semantic differential scales. Managers described the learning their firms had gained from their international operations using these items: narrow vs. broad (=5), specialized vs. general (=5), and limited vs. wide-ranging (=5). Average responses to the three items were significantly correlated with the study's measure ($r = .63$, $p < .001$). According to Campbell and Stanley (1963), the convergent validity of a scale can be established by correlating two measures that purport to gauge the same construct. The .63 correlation therefore indicates that the two measures gauge the same construct, though imperfectly. However, this is a strong correlation.

(2) *Depth* was measured as the average rating on the same 19 items listed under breadth. Managers were asked: "Please indicate how well your company has learned or mastered new skills in each of the areas listed below. As you evaluate these items, please bear in mind that we are interested in the depth or quality of learning your firm has attained because of its international operations. A score of 5, therefore, would mean that you believe your company has thoroughly and completely mastered new skills in the area(s) listed. A score of 1, however, would mean that your company has been exposed to these skills at a elementary or basic level but has not mastered these skills yet. If an item does not apply to your company's situation, please circle 'not applicable.'" Three semantic differential scale items were used for validation. Managers were asked to describe the learning their firm had achieved in international operations as basic vs. advanced (=5), simple vs. complex (=5), and shallow vs. deep (=5). The average on the three items was then correlated with the study's measure ($r = .71$, $p < .001$).

(3) *Speed* was also measured with the 19 items. Managers were asked: "After reading each statement carefully, please indicate your opinion as to how fast your company was in learning and mastering new skills in the areas listed below. If an item does not apply to your company's situation, please circle 'not applicable.'" Two semantic differential scales were used for validation: learning in international markets as slow vs. fast (=5) and sluggish vs. rapid (=5). The average of the two items was then correlated with the study's measure ($r = .61$, $p < .001$).

Shaker A. Zahra is a professor of strategic management at the J. Mack Robinson College of Business, Georgia State University. His research focuses on entrepreneurship in high-technology ventures, internationalization, and strategy making in global high-technology industries.

R. Duane Ireland holds the W. David Robbins Chair in Business Policy and is a professor of management systems in the E. Claiborne Robins School of Business, University of Richmond. His current research interests include strategic decision making processes, the acquisition, integration, and application of knowledge through strategic alliances, innovation, corporate governance, factors influencing the gathering of competitive intelligence, and the formulation and implementation of strategies in high-growth entrepreneurial ventures.

Michael A. Hitt holds the Weatherup/Overby Chair in Executive Leadership at Arizona State University. He received his Ph.D. from the University of Colorado. His current research interests include international strategies, partner selection in international strategic alliances, the importance of knowledge and human capital for competitive advantage, strategic entrepreneurship, and the effects of corporate governance on firm resources and outcomes.

Part IV
Top Management Teams

[18]

Strategic Management Journal

Strat Mgmt J. **24** 803–820 (2003)

Published online 16 June 2003 in Wiley InterScience (www interscience wiley com). DOI. 10 1002/smj 338

TESTING A MODEL OF REASONED RISK-TAKING: GOVERNANCE, THE EXPERIENCE OF PRINCIPALS AND AGENTS, AND GLOBAL STRATEGY IN HIGH-TECHNOLOGY IPO FIRMS

MASON A. CARPENTER,[1]* TIMOTHY G. POLLOCK[2] and MYLEEN M. LEARY[3]

[1] *School of Business, University of Wisconsin, Madison, Wisconsin, U.S.A.*
[2] *Robert H. Smith School of Business, University of Maryland, College Park, Maryland, U.S.A.*
[3] *Orfalea College of Business, California Polytechnic State University, San Luis Obispo, California, U.S.A.*

Research on the governance of risky ventures, like the initial public offerings (IPOs) of high-technology firms, has focused primarily on the relationship between governance mechanisms and firm performance. While such an emphasis is clearly important, it does little to shed light on potential relationships between governance and the strategies pursued by risky firms, nor does it take into account the complementary role of key stakeholders in affecting those strategies. To partially remedy this deficit we integrate agency and behavioral perspectives to develop a theory of 'reasoned risk-taking,' whereby the nature of risks undertaken is a consequence of the interaction of governance mechanisms and stakeholder characteristics We demonstrate our theory by predicting when corporate governance should be associated with strategic risk-seeking beyond a firm's technical core—as seen in the degree to which it has expanded internationally. Surprisingly, even though venture capitalists (VC) are risk specialists, we find that technology-based IPO firms are less likely (i.e., a negative relationship) to have extensive global sales when they are backed by a VC. In support of our reasoned risk-taking theoretical framework, we find that VCs are indeed risk-seeking when VC backing is complemented by the international experience of their board appointees, top management team (TMT) members, or both. IPO firms with significant insider ownership are similarly global risk-seekers, and those effects are strongest with an internationally seasoned board and TMT at the helm. Copyright © 2003 John Wiley & Sons, Ltd.

For many strategy and organizations researchers, young high-technology firms are the embodiment of risk. These firms are typically viewed as risky since they have limited histories of operation and profitability, their technology and product cycles are of relatively short duration, they are tasked with quickly establishing defensible market positions in highly competitive industry segments, and the segments themselves are emerging and hence ill defined. For these reasons it is perhaps not surprising that, prior to going public, the management teams of many young technology firms focus their strategies on enhancing their technological capabilities and advantages within the familiar confines of domestic markets, and only much later embark on the more complex strategy of developing an

Key words: corporate governance; top management teams; international strategy; international entrepreneurship

*Correspondence to Mason A Carpenter. School of Business, University of Wisconsin, Grainger Hall, 975 University Avenue, Madison, WI 53706-1323, U S A

Received 22 June 2001
Final revision received 29 January 2003

804   *M. A. Carpenter, T. G. Pollock and M. M. Leary*

extensive international presence (Johanson and Vahlne, 1977; Kuemmerle, 2001).

The focus of such firms on domestic markets poses a strategic dilemma, since most of their larger established brethren are clearly global in scope. Indeed, Porter (1986), Franko (1989), Mitchell, Shaver, and Yeung (1992), and many others have noted that an industry's technological intensity is a prime indicator of the degree to which its constituents *should* be global, and that in turn creates institutional expectations that having a commanding international presence will be a key driver of competitive advantage and long-term survival. In addition, recent research on new ventures has suggested that pursuing an international strategy early in an organization's life can enhance legitimacy, technological learning, sales growth, and performance (Autio, Sapienza, and Almeida, 2000; Lu and Beamish, 2001; Zahra, Ireland, and Hitt, 2000). However, internationalization can have adverse effects on firm performance and survival if inadequately planned or poorly implemented (Mitchell *et al.*, 1992; Hitt, Hoskisson, and Kim, 1997). It is against the backdrop of this dilemma that we suggest the domestic focus of technology IPO firms may be a consequence of the classic agency problem where their top managers have an aversion to particular risks—that is, international expansion may be perceived by many top management teams (TMTs) as simply too risky when added on top of the risks arising from the firm's technical core. And yet, such avoidance of international risk may prevent the firm from gaining the legitimacy needed to acquire the resources necessary to sustain firm growth (Zimmerman and Zeitz, 2002), and eventually undermine an otherwise sound business strategy.

From an agency perspective, managers are generally viewed as being risk averse (Jensen and Meckling, 1976). Owners, on the other hand, may be considered risk neutral, because they can diversify away particular risks by holding shares in a variety of firms (Wiseman and Gomez-Mejia, 1998). Owners will accept more risk-taking behavior by a firm to the extent that such risks are accompanied by commensurate potential increases in return on their investments. To the extent that the agents' risk aversion exceeds the owners' willingness to accept greater risks in order to maximize shareholder value, a potential agency problem exists. In this sense, 'agency theory ... [is characterized] by its emphasis on the risk attitudes

of principals and agents' (Barney and Hesterly, 1996: 124). In the view of agency theory, it is then the role of corporate governance mechanisms like influential stockholders, outside board members, and ownership structure to encourage risk-taking by managers (Beatty and Zajac, 1994) and enhance shareholder value. However, the results of agency studies linking governance to market performance and other strategic outcomes have been inconsistent and inconclusive (Murphy, 1999; Tosi *et al.*, 2000). This may be due in part to the narrow scope of past studies which have neglected the characteristics of investors, board members, and executives. Indeed, most agency-based research has assumed that these different groups of actors are relatively homogeneous in terms of their experience.

Another limitation of agency theory is that it has traditionally been silent with regard to the specific types of risks managers will be encouraged to take, and thus effectively treats all types of risky behavior equivalently. In contrast, upper echelons research has focused specifically on the characteristics of different actors and groups that will lead corporate leaders to pursue strategies of varying risk (see Finkelstein and Hambrick, 1996, for a full review of this literature). Based on the assumption that executive experiences influence strategic choices, this area of research argues that observable top management team (TMT) demographic characteristics will be reflected in organizational outcomes. For example, recent upper echelons studies have explored how international experience gained by the TMT and its board of directors may impact a firm's degree of internationalization (e.g., Bloodgood, Sapienza, and Almeida, 1996; Carpenter, Sanders, and Gregersen, 2001; Sanders and Carpenter, 1998). However, research in this vein has failed to consider whether or not there are governance mechanisms in place that promote or discourage this particular type of risk-taking. We develop the notion that risks are not equivalent, either in the amount of actual risk being taken or as perceived by TMT and board members. Indeed, our theory predicts how the experience of upper echelon members may significantly affect their perceptions regarding the riskiness of particular activities, and therefore their firms' consequent strategic behavior.

An important opportunity thus exists to show how the background characteristics and experience of particular actors may interact with important organizational governance mechanisms, and in so doing help us better understand the role of individual risk perceptions in agency-based governance remedies. While there have been recent theoretical developments in this area (e.g., Wiseman and Gomez-Mejia, 1998), there has been little supporting empirical research (see articles by Gedajlovic and Shapiro, 2002, and Pollock, Fischer, and Wade, 2002, as recent exceptions). In addition, the focus of such theory development and research has been in the context of executive compensation, and has typically not explored how governance structures and risk perceptions impact the types of strategies management decides to pursue. For these reasons, in this study we contend that governance (i.e., stock ownership by venture capitalists and top executives) may partially explain how a number of young technology firms overcome international risk aversion, as demonstrated by extensive international sales at the time of their initial public offering (IPO). We then draw on behavioral theories to introduce the concept of 'reasoned risk-taking,' and show how the international experience of the board of directors and members of the top management team interact with agency-prescribed governance mechanisms to further explain such international activity, both at the time of IPO and subsequently. As a result, our research provides a novel contribution to emerging literature linking governance and corporate strategy, particularly the corporate strategy of firm internationalization.

THEORY DEVELOPMENT

Research context

While we believe that our theory of reasoned risk-taking may be relevant to a variety of national and industry contexts, U.S. high-technology IPO firms are especially attractive given their lofty profile, inherent high risk, and the participation of a unique risk-taking specialist known as the venture capitalist (VC). The market for initial public offerings in the United States has become well established (449 IPOs in 1999 valued at U.S. \$64 billion, 605 in 2000 valued at U.S. \$165 billion, 79 in 2001 valued at U.S. \$56 billion, and 46 in the first half of 2002 valued at U.S. \$15 billion (Hoover's *IPO Central*)), and provides a unique but important context for the study of agency theory and the roles of key investors, boards, and executive stock ownership in corporate governance (Beatty and Zajac,

1994). Risk is inherent in IPO technology companies since many of them are relatively young, small, and have yet to make a profit. Consequently, the initial resource endowments of such firms are inordinately concentrated in the experience and social capital of their top managers and board of directors (Deshpande, 2001).

The risky yet specialized and capital-intensive nature of technology firms also increases the likelihood that firm governance will include a particular type of investor—the VC. These financial intermediaries specialize in raising capital from a variety of institutional and wealthy private investors to invest in high-risk, but high-potential companies. VCs are usually looking for firms that are likely to grow rapidly and to generate annual returns in excess of 40 percent (Bagley and Dauchy, 1999). Moreover, unlike most other intermediaries, VCs also actively mold the company and its strategy through participation in strategic decision-making, placement of directors on the board, recruitment of key executives, determination of ownership structure, and mobilization of other valuable resources via their networks of contacts (Bygrave and Timmons, 1992; Van den Berghe and Levrau, 2002). Therefore, U.S. high-technology IPOs provide an ideal context for examining potential relationships among corporate governance, executive experience, and risk-taking.

Perceptions of risk

Risk is a multidimensional concept, and such dimensionality has important behavioral implications for strategic risk-taking (Sitkin and Pablo, 1992; Wiseman and Gomez-Mejia, 1998). Indeed, risk is never absolute in that one firm may view a certain strategic action as highly risky, while another views it as less risky (Wiseman, Gomez-Mejia, and Fugate, 2000). Wiseman et al. (2000: 321) suggest that, 'a decision maker's consideration of risk is colored by individual (that is, subjective) assessments of the decision context in addition to whatever objective information may be available.' Such differences in perspective stem in part from differing levels of experience with the action in question. The greater a manager's experience and past success in dealing with a particular action, the less uncertainty that manager will have regarding the likely outcome of taking the action, and the more reasonable the risk will seem (Sitkin and Pablo, 1992; Wiseman and

806   *M. A. Carpenter, T. G. Pollock and M. M. Leary*

Gomez-Mejia, 1998). This is because these differing levels of experience can affect expectations regarding the magnitude and the probability of loss associated with taking a particular risk (Wiseman *et al.*, 2000). Perceptions can be driven by the expectation that particular experiences will lead to a decrease in the actual risk being faced (i.e., the probabilities of success and failure are actually changed through superior selection of risks or execution of the strategy; March and Shapira, 1987; Shapira, 1995), and/or by the fact that experience reduces uncertainty regarding the actual probabilities of success and failure (Sitkin and Pablo, 1992).

In this study we will focus on the degree to which a high-technology IPO firm is willing to accept one particular risk, the risk associated with international sales (i.e., the risks inherent in maintaining and increasing a high-tech IPO firm's international presence). Pursuing an international strategy adds another layer of risk to the significant amounts of risk new high-tech ventures already face. For instance, in the global medical equipment industry, Mitchell and colleagues found that 'attempting to become an international medical player is risky' (Mitchell *et al.*, 1992: 419) and concluded that, even when potentially desirable, international expansion could have negative effects on both domestic operations and overall firm survival. Based on a series of supplemental case studies, Mitchell *et al.* (1992) further observed that internationalization success was a consequence of both focused management and learning from international experience. More recently, Sanders and Carpenter (1998) noted that internationalization was risky for U.S. firms because it both fragments managerial attention and creates agency problems by limiting the ability of boards to directly monitor executives' actions. However, most established high-tech firms are highly global, which in turn is likely to create intense institutional pressures for new entrants to be global as well. Therefore, if there are indeed differences (real or perceived) between domestic and international business risks, and assuming the principals involved in high-tech ventures perceive the potential benefits associated with pursing an international strategy early in a firm's development to be worth the risks (Autio *et al.*, 2000; Mitchell *et al.*, 1992; Zahra *et al.*, 2000), then we suggest that varying bases of international experience and governance practices will be associated with the pursuit of international strategies by high-tech IPO firms.

Venture capitalists, TMT stock ownership, and international sales

Before exploring how experience may moderate the impact of governance mechanisms on internationalization, we first develop some baseline hypotheses regarding the relationship between governance mechanisms and the pursuit of international strategies. Looking initially at two particular governance mechanisms, we predict that VC backing and stock ownership by members of the top management team will be associated with greater risk-taking by management teams of technology IPO firms—as demonstrated by the global presence of their firms at the time of their IPO—than they would take absent such governance mechanisms. Since being a technology company already constitutes a relatively high degree of risk, risk-averse managers may perceive the addition of a global strategy as too much risk during the initial stages of development, especially if they also expect to be taking on the additional risks associated with conducting an IPO at some point in the near future.

As an agency remedy, the presence of a VC could encourage management to take on such added risk, in addition to the practical benefit of providing the funding requisite to international expansion. Indeed, from an agency theory perspective, VCs are a very powerful governance mechanism since they are (1) risk-*seeking*, (2) actively participate in and monitor management and strategy setting, and (3) have a significant amount of experience in risk-*taking*. They are, in fact, risk-taking specialists. Moreover, VC directors in high-technology firms 'play an active role in human resources, monitoring and control, mergers and acquisitions, reporting systems, etc.' (Van den Berghe and Levrau, 2002: 133). VCs also bring a large network of contacts that can further reduce the perceived and actual risk accompanying global operations—both for themselves and the managers of the funded IPO technology firm, thus making the risks associated with internationalization appear more reasonable. Therefore, we predict that:

Hypothesis 1a: There will be a positive relationship between venture capitalist backing and firm internationalization in high-technology IPO firms.

As noted above, internationalization is problematic for shareholders since it typically makes direct monitoring of management more difficult (Roth and O'Donnell, 1996; Sanders and Carpenter, 1998). One generally accepted remedy to such an agency problem is stock ownership by members of the top management team (Jensen and Meckling, 1976; Murphy, 1999; Tosi *et al.*, 1999). Direct stock ownership aligns the interests of agents and principals by offering contractual rewards to management for increases in shareholder wealth (Murphy, 1999). Stock ownership has also been found to be more effective at aligning management interests with those of shareholders than other executive compensation tools, such as stock options (Murphy, 1999; Pollock *et al.*, 2002; Tosi *et al.*, 1999). In the case of firms competing in global industries, like the high-technology IPO firms studied here, TMT stock ownership may serve two important purposes by (1) serving as a more efficient substitute for direct board monitoring and (2) increasing managerial risk-taking as demonstrated by firm internationalization. This latter contention is also supported by the finding that large firm globalization is associated with long-term forms of executive pay, including stock ownership (Sanders and Carpenter, 1998). It is therefore hypothesized that:

Hypothesis 1b: There will be a positive relationship between top management team stock ownership and firm internationalization in high-technology IPO firms.

Experience, risk, and governance effects

Up to this point we have argued that VC backing and TMT stock ownership will be associated with IPO firm risk-taking—in the form of international sales at the time of the initial public offering. Agency theory suggests that governance mechanisms can encourage managerial risk-taking; however, it does not shed much light on the nature of the risks that they will take. Such an oversight may not be problematic if risks are viewed equivalently, and if all risks have the same chances of resulting in good firm performance. However, there is evidence that international risk, particularly for firms in global industries, is positively associated with firm performance and survival (Kim, Hwang, and Burgers, 1989; Mitchell *et al.*, 1992). Therefore, for institutional reasons internationalization may

be of interest to investors in high-technology IPO firms.

A related matter concerns agency theory's assumption that risk preferences, or a manager's propensity to engage in risky behaviors, vary little across managers and contexts (Wiseman *et al.*, 2000). Substantial research exists (see Wiseman *et al.*, 2000, for a review) suggesting that individuals exhibit a variety of risk preferences. One factor that has received relatively little attention in the agency literature is the role executive experience may play as a partial determinant of risk preference. The role of experience in helping investors and executives make assessments among risky alternative actions is what we refer to as 'reasoned risk-taking.' Sitkin and Pablo described this as 'problem domain familiarity,' whereby 'decision makers learn through their experience, and lessons learned are reflected in both their standardized response to routine stimuli, and in their responses to new stimuli' (Sitkin and Pablo, 1992: 22–23). Similarly, Wiseman and Gomez-Mejia analogized this phenomenon to 'framing,' and suggested that 'executives' choices of risk also may be influenced by their prior [experience with] selecting risky alternatives' (Wiseman and Gomez-Mejia, 1998; 134). As mentioned previously, experience can reduce the magnitude of potential loss and/or the probability of loss through improving performance in executing the activity, and by improving the selection process, whereby the actor identifies those risky actions within a set of potential actions that have the greatest probability for success (March and Shapira, 1987; Shapira, 1995). Experience can also make an activity appear more reasonable by reducing an individual's subjective perceptions of the risks involved with an activity, even if it does not have a concomitant effect on the actual risks (Sitkin and Pablo, 1992).

Based on the assumptions that investors are risk neutral, but tolerant of taking reasonable risks, and that agents are risk averse, agency theory prescribes governance remedies that provide for the monitoring of management actions and the alignment of managers' and investors' risk preferences through stock ownership. However, if an executive's (i.e., board or top management team member) particular work experience allows him or her to better understand and justify taking actions that are otherwise deemed too risky absent such experience (i.e., makes them seem more reasonable), then particular governance

Strat Mgmt J, **24**, 803–820 (2003)

remedies may in fact be more effective, as demonstrated by strengthened relationships between governance and organizational outcomes. In the context of the particular decision being examined here, prior experience with international markets, either through prior work experience or education (Bloodgood et al., 1996; Sanders and Carpenter, 1998), can impact the perceived riskiness of internationalization. Perhaps, for this reason, Van den Berghe and Levrau suggested that 'due to international experience, the VC can judge the success or failure of similar scenarios' (Van den Berghe and Levrau, 2002: 131) and, consequently, 'keep the venture from making professional mistakes' (Van den Berghe and Levrau, 2002: 131). Looking first at the governance mechanism of VC backing in the context of high-technology IPO firms, we therefore offer the reasoned risk-taking hypothesis that:

Hypothesis 2a: The positive relationship between venture capitalist backing and firm internationalization will be stronger when the venture capitalist is represented by a board member with international experience.

Paralleling the logic of Hypothesis 2a, we further suggest that the relationship between TMT member stock ownership and firm internationalization will be enhanced when the top executives comprising the TMT also have international experience. Specifically, even though stock ownership should make top managers seek risk, in line with investors' interests, such ownership does not necessarily mean that they will push the firm to undertake international risks. High-technology IPO firms have many growth avenues to consider, and all of them can be classified as relatively risky. However, with international experience, the top management team may consider internationalization to be a more viable avenue for expansion, particularly for firms in global industries. Therefore, we predict that:

Hypothesis 2b: The positive relationship between top management team member stock ownership and firm internationalization will be stronger when members of the TMT have international experience.

It is also possible that outside board member international experience can act as a substitute for TMT

international experience, whereby stock ownership provides the financial incentive but the board serves as a motivator and monitor of internationalization by virtue of its relevant experience. Similarly, a top management team that does not have international experience may be hesitant to pursue an aggressive global strategy absent a trusted and experienced sounding board like that provided by outside directors. Finally, as a practical matter, an internationally experienced board may help an otherwise inexperienced team to sell an internationalization strategy to their venture capitalist backers and other key stakeholders. In summary then:

Hypothesis 2c: The positive relationship between top management team member stock ownership and firm internationalization will be stronger when outside board members have international experience.

Our fourth hypothesis in this set summarizes the argument that the relationship between international experience and firm internationalization will be strongest when both outside directors and TMT members possess international experience. Previous research has explored the main effects of board member and TMT experience on new firm internationalization (Bloodgood et al., 1996), but did not examine the potential for interaction effects between these two sources of experience. The prior hypotheses suggested that the agency remedies of VC backing and executive stock ownership would be most effective when coupled with the perceptions of the reasonableness of the risk entailed, based on requisite experience. Our hypothesis extends the reasoned risk-taking perspective to suggest that the effects of director and executive experience are actually interdependent. Indeed, research concerning the influence of executives' backgrounds on organizational outcomes suggests that the impact of their background needs to be considered in its sociopolitical context (Hambrick and Mason, 1984; Jackson, 1992). For instance, Jackson (1992) observed that a particular executive's experience is most likely to affect outcomes when it is possessed by at least one other key decision-maker. According to this view, common experiences (i.e., international, functional, industry) often provide a shared basis for communication, build mutual trust, and ultimately enable the evaluation and choice of strategic actions (O'Reilly, Synder, and Boothe, 1993; Rousseau and Parks, 1993).

In the case of high-technology IPO firms, key TMT decisions about internationalization would need to be validated by outside members of the board. When those board members also have international experience, the TMT may be better able to communicate, build consensus, and implement global strategic imperatives (Doz and Prahalad, 1981; Bartlett and Ghoshal, 1992). Indeed, such shared international orientation may contribute to 'the cognitive processes that balance competing country, business, and functional concerns' (Murtha, Lenway, and Bagozzi, 1998: 97). Greater international experience among top management team and board members also typically provides the TMT with a greater awareness of international opportunities and the credibility with the board and other stakeholders regarding those opportunities, thereby providing management with more degrees of freedom in managing the complexities of global multimarket competition (Salancik and Meindl, 1984; Prahalad and Doz, 1987; Bartlett and Ghoshal, 1989). Thus, the shared understanding, cohesiveness, and monitoring capabilities that accompany such common experiences among directors and top managers can further enable TMTs to translate their strategic intentions into highly global new ventures. Therefore, we propose to test the multiplicative effects of international experience through the following hypothesis:

Hypothesis 2d: The positive association between firm internationalization and international experience will be stronger when such experience is possessed by both board outsiders and members of the top management team than when they do not both possess it.

Subsequent firm internationalization

Our final two hypotheses are offered to test the notion that firms which are able to combine international experience and executive stock ownership should be the most aggressive in pursuing a stronger international presence—as revealed by greater international sales 1 year following the initial public offering.[1] As a reminder, the

prior hypotheses sought to establish relationships between governance, experience, and firm internationalization at the time of IPO. Mitchell *et al.* (1992) reported that firms in global industries were best able to achieve superior market share and longer-term survival when they had strong international sales. While about half of the firms in our sample had some degree of internationalization at the time they went public, most of them expressed a strong global strategic intent (see methods).

However, through the integration of agency and behavioral decision-making perspectives, we contend that the internationalization of risky firms, while perhaps desirable or even intended, will be most likely when both executive incentives and risk perceptions are aligned. One way such alignment takes place is for TMT members to be both shareholders and have international experience, as summarized in the following hypothesis:

Hypothesis 3a: Top management team member stock ownership will have stronger effects on subsequent firm internationalization when members of the TMT have international experience.

Absent TMT international experience, as with Hypothesis 2c, executive stock ownership may also lead to further internationalization when nonexecutive board directors have such experience. In this latter view, board member international experience is not simply a substitute for TMT member experience. Indeed, it may serve two additional roles by allowing the board (1) to be more adamant in encouraging international risk-taking by the TMT and, (2) to more effectively monitor such risk-taking. We therefore hypothesize that:

Hypothesis 3b: Top management team member stock ownership will have stronger effects on subsequent firm internationalization when outside board members have international experience.

RESEARCH METHOD

Sample

We study the hypothesized relationships in the context of all firms less than 10 years of age at the time of IPO that had gone public in the electrical and electronic equipment industry (SIC 36)

---

[1] We do not develop hypotheses regarding the effects of VC participation post IPO because VCs tend to reduce their active participation in company activities once the IPO has occurred, and often liquidate some or all of their holdings in the company

from January of 1990 through December of 1999. The electrical and electronic equipment industry was selected for this study because (1) it is portrayed by Porter (1986) and others as a global industry, (2) among S&P large and mid-cap firms this sector had the highest degree of globalization (i.e., Compustat showed nearly every SIC 36 large mid-cap firm reported foreign activity and foreign sales averaged 49% for those firms), (3) firms varied significantly in their degree of globalization at the time of IPO, and (4) using one segment allows us to control for industry effects. Drawing on the SEC's Edgar database and Disclosure's IPO database, 256 U.S. companies in the target industry were identified as conducting IPOs between January of 1990 and December of 1999. Firms that were greater than 10 years old, reverse leveraged buyouts (LBOs), spin-offs of existing public companies, and companies that were formed solely for purposes of conducting the IPO (i.e., immediately following a combination of assets) were eliminated from our sample. As a result of these selection criteria, 159 firms were eliminated, leaving a final sample of 97 firms. For tests of Hypotheses 3a and 3b (using lagged internationalization variables), mergers, acquisitions, and closings further reduced the sample to 73 firms. The 24 dropped firms were not statistically different from the retained firms on the dimensions of total sales, international sales, or profitability.

We eliminated spin-offs and reverse LBOs because, as former public firms or parts of public firms, they are not truly new ventures and have experience with the public markets that true new ventures do not possess. New firms based on mergers, even if both firms meet our other criteria, were eliminated because the history, structure, and financial performance of the new entity would be confounded by the separate histories of the pre-merger firms. Finally, we chose 10 years as the age cut-off for our sample in order to be consistent with the general age range used in previous research on young firms (i.e., Eisenhardt and Schoonhoven, 1990; Bloodgood *et al.*, 1996; Calof, 1994; Preece, Miles, and Baetz, 1998), and because we wanted to ensure firms had adequate opportunity to establish themselves but could still be considered in the formative period of development. Industries can vary in the amount of time a firm may be considered to be in the early phase of development. For example, although firms in our final sample

ranged in age from 2 to 10 years with an average age of 6 years, the average age for the initial pool of firms was 30 years at the time of IPO. This disparity suggests that, relative to all IPO firms in their industry, our sampled firms are in the initial stages of their life cycle.

Dependent variables

Internationalization was calculated as the ratio of foreign sales to total sales. Estimation of composite, multi-item indicators of global strategy, such as Sullivan's (1994) or Sanders and Carpenter's (1998), produced statistically unreliable measures. Specifically, foreign sales, foreign assets, and the geographic dispersion of same did not load on one factor, nor did they yield a statistically reliable coefficient alpha. Moreover, over half of the sampled firms reported some amount of foreign sales, while less than 10 reported any foreign assets. Young firms, even those in industries with the greatest globalization pressures, typically follow a path whereby international sales are developed first, followed by investment in international assets (Johansen and Vahlne, 1977; Kuemmerle, 2001). Although we retain foreign sales as our primary measure of international strategy, given the obvious relevance of foreign assets to our risk-based arguments, we report and discuss these results in the text as well. For Hypotheses 1a through 2d, the ratio of foreign sales to total sales was calculated for the fiscal year ending prior to the IPO year using data drawn from the offering prospectuses. For Hypotheses 3a and 3b, the ratio was calculated for the first full fiscal year after the IPO. Internationalization at the time of the IPO was also included as a control measure when testing Hypotheses 3a and 3b. The data used to calculate these measures were gathered using COMPUSTAT and firm annual reports.

Independent variables

Hypotheses 1a and 1b test the effects of VC backing and TMT member stock ownership on firm internationalization. Seventy-seven percent of the companies in our sample received venture backing. A dummy variable was coded 1 if the company had received *venture financing* prior to the IPO and 0 otherwise. Consistent with Beatty and Zajac (1994), *ownership by top managers* was operationalized as the log of the percentage of the company owned by the top managers before the IPO. Data for both these measures were collected from the offering prospectuses.[2]

The next two sets of Hypotheses, 2a through 3b, tested whether international experience moderated the theorized agency relationships. All board- and TMT-level data were drawn from the IPO offering prospectuses included in the Edgar and Disclosure databases. As part of the filing requirements for conducting an IPO, companies must separately list all members of the board of directors and all of the key executives of the corporation. To operationalize international experience, the number of board and TMT members with international work experience and international education were calculated. An individual was considered to have international work experience if they reported having a year or more of international work experience in the offering prospectus. To eliminate the possibility of double-counting the international orientation of inside board members, the board international experience and education data reflect the backgrounds of outside board members only. International education was defined as having received a degree from a school domiciled outside the United States. Values could range from zero to the total number of board or TMT members for each of the four categories.

Actual values ranged from 0 to 4 for TMT international work experience, 0 to 5 for TMT international education, and 0 to 3 for both board international work experience and education. Total *board international experience* and *TMT international experience* were then calculated by summing the number of individuals with international work experience and international education for each group. To identify those venture capitalist board appointees who have prior international work or education experience, *venture capitalist board member international experience* was coded 1 if a board member with international experience represented the firm's VC and 0 otherwise. Using a dummy variable to operationalize this measure is reasonable, since there was only one case where a

board contained more than one VC board member who had international experience.

Controls

We have argued that the firms in our sample are under some pressure to be global. However, it is still critical to empirically differentiate those firms that view international expansion as necessary or desirable. While most objective measures of strategy (i.e., entropy-like measures of diversification, entropy and component-type measures of globalization) are good at gauging *what* a firm is doing—its realized strategy—such measures provide no qualitative insight into the international direction management is steering its firm.

To gauge and control for such global intent, we developed a measure that incorporates both actual international risk and management's estimation of the potential consequences of the firm's strategy for international risk and complexity in the future. Its measurement is based on the total number of risk factors listed in the offering prospectus that were unique to international business. Companies going public are required to disclose all factors that could have a material adverse impact on the future prospects and operating performance of the company in their offering prospectus (Husick and Arrington, 1998). We identified and coded five factors that were unique to firms pursuing global strategies: foreign currency fluctuations, changes in foreign economies, risks associated with foreign suppliers, foreign competition risks, and changes in governmental tariffs. *Global strategic intent* was operationalized as the number of such international factors per firm divided by five.

Firm size and *firm age* have been argued to affect the relationship between executive characteristics and organizational outcomes (Miller and Toulouse, 1986; Miller, 1991). Therefore, size and age were included as control variables. Firm size was operationalized as the total number of employees in the year prior to the IPO. Firm age was measured as the number of years between founding and the IPO. *Firm accounting performance* has also been suggested as being related to a firm's degree of globalization (Geringer, Beamish, and daCosta, 1989; Kim *et al.*, 1989; Hitt *et al.*, 1997). A firm's accounting performance was operationalized as the firm's net income before interest and taxes in the year prior to the IPO. These measures were also obtained from firms' offering prospectuses.

---

[2] The value of an executive's stock options might also be expected to impact the executive's willingness to engage in riskier behaviors Unlike actively traded public companies, there are no clear-cut methods for valuing stock options Therefore, following Beatty and Zajac (1994), we used dummy coding to capture the presence of options (1 = use of options) Since this variable was not significant in any of the models, and didn't change the variance explained or the significance of any results, we omitted it from the analyses reported in the tables

Prior research has suggested that board and TMT size may be related to internationalization (Sanders and Carpenter, 1998), and we controlled for the effects of both. *Board size* was defined as all individuals listed as board members in the offering prospectus. *TMT size* was defined as all individuals identified as key executives of the corporation in the offering prospectus. The average board size was 6.01 and ranged from 2 to 12 board members. The average TMT size in our sample was 6.4 and ranged from 2 to 12 executives.

In addition to the governance mechanisms identified above, the ratio of nonexecutive directors (outside directors) to board size is also important (Sanders and Carpenter, 1998). Greater numbers of outsiders on the board is expected to result in greater representation of shareholders' interests. The number of outside board members was defined as the number of board members who were not current or former employees of the organization, or family members of current or former employees. This definition is consistent with the notion of independent, or unaffiliated, directors (Finkle, 1998). The *outsider ratio* was then calculated by dividing the number of outside directors by board size. To otherwise show their independent effects, our control models for Hypotheses 1a through 2c also account for the main effects of *board international experience, TMT international experience*, and *venture capitalist board member international experience*.

Finally, nine dummy codes were used to control for *year* effects because the characteristics and number of IPOs varies by year, and any one year may otherwise have unobserved effects. The excluded year was 1990.

RESULTS

Descriptive statistics and intercorrelations are presented in Table 1. Firm internationalization averaged 0.26 (out of 1.0) and ranged from 0 to 0.79, with 60 percent of the firms showing some foreign sales at the time of their initial public offering. When firms had foreign sales, those sales averaged approximately 60 percent of the firms' total sales. Among the 10 firms reporting foreign assets, these averaged less than 3 percent of total assets, perhaps consistent with the view that new firms may place greater reliance on foreign sales as the first step towards internationalization (Johanson and Vahlne,

1977). Firm age was not correlated with foreign sales at the time of the IPO, but it was significantly correlated with internationalization during the post-IPO period. Firm size was negatively correlated with foreign sales at the time of the IPO, but was not significantly correlated with post-IPO internationalization. Foreign sales at time of IPO is positively correlated with global strategic intent, but the correlation is only 0.29, suggesting that firms anticipate greater international risks if their proposed strategies are successful. This is further borne out by the much higher correlation between strategic intent and relative foreign sales 1 year later ($r = 0.40$).

Table 2 presents the standardized regression coefficients for each of the models testing Hypotheses 1a–b and 2a–d. Model 1 in Table 2 presents the control model predicting internationalization at the time of the IPO. Model 2 tests Hypothesis 1a, that VC backing would be positively associated with internationalization. Contrary to the hypothesis, VC backing has a *negative* and significant relationship with internationalization. This significant negative effect persists in all of the models. Model 3 supports Hypothesis 1b, which suggested TMT ownership would be positively associated with internationalization.

Model 4 tests Hypothesis 2a, that the positive effect of VC backing on internationalization would be stronger when the VC is represented by a board member with international experience. Consistent with this hypothesis, the standardized coefficient for the interaction term is positive, significant, and larger than the main effect term for VC backing, which is still negative and significant. Thus, the otherwise negative effect of VC backing on internationalization is reversed if the VC also has international experience. Hypotheses 2b and 2c suggested that the effect of TMT ownership on internationalization would be stronger if the TMT and the outside members of the board, respectively, had international experience. Neither of these hypotheses is supported in Model 5. The results in Model 6 support Hypothesis 2d, that the association between international experience and internationalization will be strongest when both the TMT and the outside board members (including the VC-appointed board members) possess international experience. All of the significant findings also result in statistically significant improvements in the variance explained by the models.

Table 1. Descriptive statistics

Variable name	Mean	S.D.	1	2	3	4	5	6	7	8	9	10	11	12	13
1 Internationalization prior to IPO	0.26	0.31													
2 Internationalization after IPO	0.41	0.29	0.41												
3 Global strategic intent	0.35	0.28	0.29	0.40											
4 Firm age	6.29	2.22	0.00	-0.15	0.04										
5 Employees	203.93	243.69	-0.40	0.12	0.01	0.23									
6 Net income ($000s)	-319.10	938.00	-0.17	-0.33	-0.23	0.14	0.24								
7 Outsiders	0.68	0.13	0.23	0.03	0.18	0.08	0.25	-0.30							
8 Board size	6.01	1.62	-0.06	-0.11	-0.06	-0.04	-0.01	-0.26	0.20						
9 TMT size	6.50	1.92	-0.02	0.18	0.00	-0.18	0.33	0.04	-0.04	0.06					
10 VC backing	0.79	0.40	-0.19	0.06	0.11	-0.05	0.27	-0.12	0.16	0.09	0.09				
11 TMT ownership prior to IPO	2.35	1.26	0.02	0.07	0.05	-0.04	0.19	0.24	-0.45	-0.11	-0.03	-0.23			
12 VC international experience	0.10	0.30	0.31	0.25	0.13	-0.02	-0.16	-0.46	0.03	0.05	-0.19	0.07	-0.19		
13 TMT international experience	1.20	1.50	0.31	0.31	0.21	-0.15	0.00	-0.11	-0.04	0.15	0.26	0.02	0.04	0.34	
14 Board international experience	0.62	1.17	0.38	0.10	0.30	0.22	-0.15	-0.24	0.17	0.20	-0.13	-0.18	-0.02	0.45	0.26

$n = 97$, correlations greater than $0.15 = p < 0.05$

814   *M. A. Carpenter, T. G. Pollock and M. M. Leary*

Table 2.   OLS regression: standardized coefficients predicting internationalization prior to IPO

	Control Model 1	H1a Model 2	H1b Model 3	H2a Model 4	H2b and 2c Model 5	H2d Model 6
Control variables						
Global strategic intent	0.22**	0.24**	0.22**	0.23**	0.23**	0.23**
Firm age	−0.10	−0.09	−0.09	−0.06	−0.10	−0.12
Employees	0.31*	0.29*	0.29†	0.29†	0.26*	0.28*
Net income	−0.03	−0.03	−0.05	−0.04	−0.05	−0.07
Board size	−0.28*	−0.27*	−0.29*	−0.27**	−0.29**	−0.29**
TMT size	−0.06	−0.05	−0.05	−0.06	−0.06	−0.05
Outsiders	0.32**	0.35**	0.41**	0.36**	0.37**	0.42**
VC int'l experience	0 03	0.08	0.09	−0.39	0 09	
TMT int'l experience	0.21*	0.20*	0.19†	0 18†	0 45*	0.13
Board int'l experience	0.23*	0.18†	0.18†	0.14†	0.17†	0.03
Main theoretical variables						
VC backing		−0.20**	−0.17*	−0.16*	−0 18*	−0.17*
TMT ownership prior to IPO			0.15†	0.11	0.21†	0 15†
Interaction terms						
VC backing × VC int'l experience				0.54*		
TMT ownership prior to IPO × TMT int'l experience					−0.29	
TMT ownership prior to IPO × Board int'l experience					−0.01	
TMT int'l experience × Board int'l experience						0.24*
R^2	0.28**	0.32**	0.33**	0.34**	0.34**	0.36**
Change in R^2		0.04**	0.01†	0.06**	0.00	0.02*

$N = 97$; †$p < 0 10$, *$p < 0 05$; **$p < 0 01$, one-tailed tests for directional hypotheses. All models control for year effects but, to conserve space, these nine dummy variables are omitted from the table

Table 3 presents the analyses testing Hypotheses 3a and 3b. The first regression presents the control model. The results presented in Model 2 support Hypothesis 3a, that the positive association between TMT ownership and internationalization in the year following the IPO will be enhanced by TMT international experience. The addition of the interaction term to this model increases the variance explained by the model by 0.12. Model 3 provides support for Hypothesis 3b, that board international experience will enhance the positive association between TMT ownership and post-IPO internationalization. The effect is significant and in the predicted direction, and the addition of the interaction term significantly improves the variance explained by the model.

DISCUSSION

Following calls for integrative governance research (Wiseman and Gomez-Mejia, 1998), our objective

in this paper was to develop a theory of reasoned risk-taking, and show that agency prescriptions could be better understood when coupled with predictions suggested by behavioral theory. Through our focus on the intersection of governance, the international experience of key stakeholders, and international strategy in the context of high-technology IPO firms, we have presented a pattern of results that largely supports this objective. While agency theory has been of tremendous importance to the field of strategy—suggesting how executive and shareholder risk preferences can be aligned—it does not take into account the fact that assessments of the degree of risk, as well as the appropriateness of particular kinds of risks, may vary based on the nature of individuals' experience. We therefore were able to draw on behavioral theory to (1) identify when risks would be viewed differently by firms, and (2) show that individual director and executive experiences tempered the degree

Reasoned Risk-Taking and Global Strategy in High-Technology IPO Firms 815

Table 3   OLS regression (standardized coefficients) predicting internationalization 1 year after IPO

	Control Model 1	H3a Model 2	H3b Model 3
Control variables			
Global strategic intent	0.40**	0.29**	0.37**
Prior internationalization	0.24*	0 28**	0.26*
Firm age	−0.15	−0.06	−0.16
Employees	0.34*	0.34*	0.37*
Net income	−0.38**	−0 44**	−0.41**
Outsiders	0.01	0.10	−0.00
Board size	−0.15	−0.17†	−0.17†
TMT size	0.07	0.14	0.02
VC backing	−0.02	0.06	−0.02
TMT ownership prior to IPO	0.13	−0.06	0.04*
TMT international experience	0.20*	−0.72**	0 22*
Board international experience	−0.06	−0.10	−0.43†
Interaction terms			
TMT ownership prior to IPO × TMT int'l experience		0.86**	
TMT ownership prior to IPO × Board int'l experience			0.40*
R^2	0.45**	0.57**	0.47**
Change in R^2		0.12**	0.02*

$N = 73$, † $p < 0$ 10, * $p < 0$ 05; ** $p < 0$ 01, one-tailed tests for directional hypotheses All models control for year effects but, to conserve space, these nine variables are omitted from the table

to which particular strategic actions were understood as acceptable risks.

Implications of results

The first set of Hypotheses (1a and 1b) predicted relationships between VC backing, TMT stock ownership, and firm internationalization. Both models were statistically significant and the theorized associations explained greater variance than the control model. It was striking to find the VC effect to be negative—entirely opposite the direction of our prediction (Hypothesis 1a). Indeed, we expected VCs to be associated with global high-technology IPO firms, especially given the economic benefits and concomitant financial investments accruing to internationalized firms in global industries. However, upon reflection the negative VC effect is consistent with our argument suggesting that these actors are *reasoned* risk-takers; that is, absent other critical mitigating factors like international experience, VCs may see early firm internationalization as too risky, and encourage their new ventures to pursue domestic strategies more in line with the firm's experience and understanding.

Our reasoned risk-taking view of corporate governance effects becomes more fully apparent in the

support of Hypotheses 2a, 2d, 3a, and 3b. Specifically, whereas the association between VC backing and firm internationalization is consistently negative, this relationship is positive when VCs are able to place an internationally seasoned director on the board (Hypothesis 2a). High-technology IPO firms also exhibit greater international presence when board international experience is complemented by similar experience among members of the top management team (Hypothesis 2d). Finally, those firms that couple TMT stock ownership with board or executive international experience have a greater ability to grow international sales (Hypotheses 3a and 3b).

Based on the traditional role of VCs in organizational development and growth, as well as the limited life span of the pools of investment funds managed by VCs (typically 10 years), we did not expect VCs to have sustained effects on the strategic decisions of companies during the post-IPO period. Nonetheless, in order to empirically verify this assumption, in analyses reported only here we tested the impact of VC backing, and the interaction of VC backing with VC director international experience, on internationalization in the year following the IPO. Although the relationship between VC backing and internationalization was strong at

816   *M. A. Carpenter, T. G. Pollock and M. M. Leary*

the time of the IPO (Hypotheses 1a and 2a), consistent with our assumption, it dropped out entirely for firm internationalization a year later. At the same time, the effects of aligning stock ownership with executive and board experience on later internationalization are strong and positive, although their effects were not significant prior to the public offering.

Such a dynamic pattern of results is consistent with the notion that VCs are instrumental in creating initial conditions for successful IPOs, but that their direct influence diminishes rapidly thereafter. The results suggest that governance mechanisms may have differential levels of effectiveness based on the organization's stage of development (Beatty and Zajac, 1994), and support the continued need to take the interplay among executive characteristics and governance mechanisms into account when evaluating firm strategy and performance. Also noteworthy is the fact that our results held when foreign sales were used as a measure of international strategy, but vanished entirely when retested using foreign assets in supplementary analyses reported only here—arguably foreign assets are the riskiest facet of firm internationalization. On the one hand, this second pattern of results may simply capture the typical internationalization process whereby firms initially focus on international sales (Johanson and Vahlne, 1977), a perspective reflected by the fact that few of the relatively young firms in our sample reported international assets. On the other hand, even when governance and stakeholder experience do lead IPO technology firms to take on the added risks associated with internationalization, they may choose first to pursue the least risky aspects of a global strategy. This latter view would also be conceptually consistent with the reasoned risk-taking framework developed and supported in our study.

Limitations and future research directions

Like all research, this study has left questions unanswered, which in turn suggests future research opportunities. Five of these questions are particularly important. The first question concerns firm performance. Given the complexity and uncertainty surrounding IPOs and IPO firms, especially highly global ones, it might be surprising that board and TMT characteristics would be able to predict any variance in strategy at all. In contrast, if any of the board and TMT characteristics

noted here can be considered valuable resources (Barney, 1991; Penrose, 1959), then it would be somewhat disappointing if none of them could be translated into greater market or accounting performance. However, in supplementary analyses we were unable to show that governance mechanisms or international experience were reflected in firm performance—no effects of internationalization were found for predicting (1) first-day IPO trading returns, (2) 1-year shareholder returns, (3) 1-year sales growth, and (4) 1-year profit growth. Nor were performance effects detected when governance and international experience were interacted with internationalization.

One partial explanation may be that, since directors and top executives actually comprise a large proportion of a new venture's initial resource stock, they may be able to extract greater returns for themselves at the expense of shareholders and other stakeholders (Carpenter *et al.*, 2001). It is also unclear what merits the correct measure of performance for these fledgling firms, and even whether internationalization is discretionary or obligatory (i.e., a different question from Porter's, 1986, assertion that firms in technology-intensive industries *should* be global). Therefore, it would be important to study how the boards and top executives of global high-tech IPO firms extract returns for themselves in the form of compensation and other remuneration, and/or convert their specialized expertise into firm strategy and performance. Finally, deciding to pursue an international strategy does not mean that the firm necessarily executes the strategy well. The lack of a significant relationship between pursuing an international strategy and financial performance may thus be due to the fact that some firms implement the strategy successfully and others implement it poorly, thereby making it difficult to identify a central tendency in the relationship.

A second question relates to whether or not managers are behaving in the manner proscribed by our theory. Indeed, we did not actually measure VC, director, or top team behaviors, cognitions, or perceptions, but instead inferred them from their characteristics (international experience). Consequently, by following the norms of upper echelons research we have 'black-boxed' important underlying processes and causal mechanisms that may have been pertinent to our arguments. Specifically, we do not know whether international experience allowed particular directors or executives to understand that the risks they were taking were acceptable, or that they were taking risks at all. Nor have we gauged the actual risk preferences of either the board or TMT members studied here, or their motivations for undertaking international risks. Nonetheless, studies of cognitive complexity among executives (Calori, Johnson, and Sarnin, 1994; Murtha *et al.*, 1998), as well as executives' international advice networks (Athanassiou and Nigh, 1999), have found that both of these factors are related to firm globalization. Similarly, Carpenter and Westphal (2001) showed that directors were better able to contribute to international strategy formulation and implementation when they possessed relevant experience, by virtue of their appointments to other firms following similar international strategies. What is still missing, however, is research that establishes a direct link between such factors and certain board and TMT characteristics. Therefore, studies are needed that further illuminate the nature of the relationships between such characteristics and the actual cognitions and behaviors of upper-echelon executives.

A third research question is raised by our sampling of only U.S. high-technology IPOs, and only those in one high-technology industry. This was done to keep the scope of this initial research project within reason, and to focus first on an industry in which our reasoned risk-taking perspective would be most likely to play out in the form of global IPOs. Moreover, we quickly discovered that reliable TMT and board data, like those needed in this study and in other organizations research, are not typically available for non-U.S. firms (even those in Western Europe). A recent study of governance practices in Belgian high-technology new ventures using structured interviews suggests that VCs, outside directors, and management play similar roles to those portrayed here (Van den Berghe and Levrau, 2002). Regardless, the question of whether our findings generalize to new ventures in other industries or other countries has not been addressed. Obviously, tests of our reasoned risk-taking framework with other industries and non-U.S. samples are needed.

The fourth question relates to causality. Indeed, owing largely to the nature of available data, we worded the development of Hypotheses 1a through 2d and tested them in terms of associations and relationships. Although we viewed the relationships among VCs, boards, and top executives to be

recursive, it is entirely possible that some causal chains may, in fact, exist. And while the lagged structure of our data for Hypotheses 3a and 3b allows us to suggest causal relationships between international experience, stock ownership, and subsequent internationalization, we have not established causality; nor have we been able to gauge these firms' global intent beyond the risk factors that they disclosed. For example, it is possible that global new ventures recruit internationally seasoned executives and board members to manage and grow their far-flung operations. If so, it could be that international strategy is a predictor of TMT and board characteristics rather than the reverse. While no social science research can prove causality (Cook and Campbell, 1979), we have established that certain governance mechanisms and executive characteristics preceded internationalization, and have identified and included those control variables most likely to provide alternative explanations for internationalization if omitted. However, it is important to continue delving into the question of whether some governance practices, top management teams, and boards of directors (i.e., those with more international experience) are more likely to lead their firms to expansive global strategic postures than are others.

Finally, the discussion of causality gives rise to a fifth research question—one that concerns the other factors that may influence the effects of TMTs and boards on international strategy implementation and firm performance. Specifically, global firms differ significantly in the degree to which their far-flung operations are actually coordinated and integrated (Roth, 1995). Moreover, research suggests that the level of such interdependence influences the pattern of executive characteristics and governance mechanisms that are ideal for top managers and boards to contribute to firm performance (Michel and Hambrick, 1992; Roth, 1995; Roth and O'Donnell, 1996). In support of this contention, Roth (1995) found that CEOs' backgrounds were predictive of differences in firms' global interdependence and integration. He also noted that certain CEO characteristics helped performance in low-interdependence contexts but hindered it in high-interdependence contexts. Therefore, investigators should do the field research that takes them inside entrepreneurial firms to better understand the roles of governance and top managers in global strategy implementation and firm performance.

Strat Mgmt J, **24** 803–820 (2003)

818   *M. A. Carpenter, T. G. Pollock and M. M. Leary*

CONCLUSION

By developing and testing a theory of reasoned risk-taking, this study addresses an important topic at the intersection of international business, entrepreneurship, and IPOs. The purpose of our research has been to develop novel theory using the interaction between governance and stakeholder characteristics to contextualize executive choice, and then empirically demonstrate how they jointly influence the direction of corporate strategy in the form of firm internationalization. In doing so we believe that this study contributes to the literature on boards of directors, top management teams, and new venture strategies for growth and internationalization. Specifically, it reinforces the critical role of boards and TMTs in shaping new ventures, and suggests the governance conditions that give rise to reasoned risk-taking. Moreover, we have tried to demonstrate how the complexity surrounding globalization and technology IPOs make it particularly germane to the study of boards and TMTs, and that such complexity provides a unique context for assessing the similarities and differences of how board and TMT characteristics are reflected in organizational outcomes. This study is also among the first to provide empirical support for theoretical arguments regarding the importance of individual risk perceptions in understanding the functioning of agency controls (Wiseman and Gomez-Mejia, 1998; Wiseman *et al.*, 2000), and extends discussion of this topic beyond executive compensation to explore its impact on firm strategy. And while our work emphasizes that there are limits to the impact and interpretation of the effects of governance arrangements, boards, and TMT characteristics, it also suggests that such factors can continue to play an important role in organizational research.

ACKNOWLEDGEMENTS

This research was supported by the University of Wisconsin School of Business Research Fund and Center for International Business Education and Research (CIBER). We thank Ray Aldag, Ted Baker, Todd Finkle, Mike Hitt, June-Young Kim, Sharon McDougall, Anne Miner, W. Gerry Sanders, and Don Schwab for their helpful comments on earlier versions of this manuscript.

REFERENCES

Athanassiou N, Nigh D. 1999 The impact of U.S. company internationalization on top management team advice networks: a tacit knowledge perspective. *Strategic Management Journal* **20**(1). 83–92.

Autio E, Sapienza HJ, Almeida JG. 2000. Effects of age of entry, knowledge intensity, and imitability on international growth. *Academy of Management Journal* **43**: 909–924.

Bagley C, Dauchy C. 1999. Venture capital In *The Entrepreneurial Venture*, 2nd edn, Sahlman W, Stevenson H, Roberts M, Bhide A (eds). Harvard Business School Press: Boston, MA; 262–303.

Barney JB. 1991. Firm resources and sustained competitive advantage. *Journal of Management* **17**: 99–120.

Barney JB, Hesterly W. 1996. Organizational economics: understanding the relationship between organizations and economic analysis. In *Handbook of Organization Studies*, Clegg SR, Hardy C, Nord WR (eds). Sage: London; 115–147.

Bartlett C, Ghoshal S. 1989. *Managing Across Borders: The Transnational Solution*. Harvard Business School Press: Boston, MA.

Bartlett C, Ghoshal S. 1992. What is a global manager? *Harvard Business Review* **70**(5): 124–132.

Beatty RP, Zajac EJ. 1994. Managerial incentives, monitoring and risk bearing: a study of executive compensation, ownership, and board structure in initial public offerings. *Administrative Science Quarterly* **39**: 313–335.

Bloodgood JM, Sapienza HJ, Almeida JG. 1996. The internationalization of new high-potential U.S. ventures: antecedents and outcomes. *Entrepreneurship Theory and Practice* **20**: 61–75.

Bygrave WD, Timmons JA. 1992. *Venture Capital at the Crossroads*. Harvard Business School Press: Boston, MA.

Calof JL. 1994. The relationship between firm size and export behavior revisited. *Journal of International Business Studies* **25**: 367–380.

Calori R, Johnson G, Sarnin P. 1994. CEOs' cognitive maps and the scope of the organization. *Strategic Management Journal* **15**(6): 437–458.

Carpenter MA, Sanders WG, Gregersen HB. 2001. Bundling human capital with organizational context: the impact of international assignment experience on multinational firm performance and CEO pay. *Academy of Management Journal* **44**: 493–511.

Carpenter MA, Westphal JD. 2001. The strategic context of external network ties. examining the impact of director appointments on board involvement in strategic decision making. *Academy of Management Journal* **44**: 639–660.

Cook TD, Campbell DT. 1979. *Quasi-Experimentation: Design and Analysis Issues for Field Settings*. Houghton Mifflin: Boston, MA.

Deshpande D. 2001. Entrepreneur in residence. *Red Herring* **95**(1 April): 104.

Doz Y, Prahalad CK. 1981. Headquarters influence and strategic control of MNCs. *Sloan Management Review* Winter: 15–21.

Eisenhardt KM, Schoonhoven CB 1990. Organizational growth: linking founding team, strategy, environment, and growth among U.S. semiconductor ventures, 1978–1988. *Administrative Science Quarterly* **35**: 504–529.

Finkelstein S, Hambrick DC. 1996. *Strategic Leadership* West Publishing: St. Paul, MN.

Finkle TA. 1998. The relationship between boards of directors and initial public offerings in the biotechnology industry. *Entrepreneurship Theory and Practice* **22**. 5–29.

Franko L. 1989. Global corporate competition: who's winning, who's losing, and the R&D factor as one reason why. *Strategic Management Journal* **10**(5): 49–74.

Gedajlovic E, Shapiro D. 2002. Ownership structure and firm profitability in Japan. *Academy of Management Journal* **45**: 565–576.

Geringer J, Beamish P, daCosta R. 1989. Diversification strategy and internationalization: implications for MNE performance. *Strategic Management Journal* **10**(2): 109–119.

Hambrick DC, Mason PA. 1984. Upper echelons: the organization as a reflection of its top managers. *Academy of Management Review* **9**: 193–206.

Hitt M, Hoskisson R, Kim H. 1997. International diversification: effects on innovation and firm performance in product-diversified firms. *Academy of Management Journal* **40**: 767–798.

Husick GC, Arrington JM. 1998. *The Initial Public Offering: A Practical Guide for Executives*. Bowne: New York.

Jackson S. 1992. Consequences of group composition for the interpersonal dynamics of strategic issue processing. In *Advances in Strategic Management*, Shrivastava P, Huff A, Dutton J (eds). JAI Press: Greenwich, CT; 345–382.

Jensen M, Meckling W. 1976. Theory of the firm: managerial behavior, agency costs, and ownership structure. *Journal of Financial Economics* **3**: 305–360.

Johansen J, Vahlne JE. 1977. The internationalization process of the firm: a model of knowledge development and increasing foreign market commitments. *Journal of International Business Studies* **8**: 23–32.

Kim W, Hwang P, Burgers W. 1989. Global diversification strategy and corporate profit performance. *Strategic Management Journal* **10**(1): 45–57.

Kuemmerle W. 2001. Go global—or no? *Harvard Business Review* **79**(6): 37–49.

Lu WJ, Beamish PW. 2001. The internationalization and performance of SMEs. *Strategic Management Journal*, Special Issue **22**(6–7): 565–586.

March JG, Shapira Z. 1987 Managerial perspectives on risk and risk taking. *Management Science* **33**: 1404–1418.

Michel J, Hambrick D. 1992. Diversification posture and top management team characteristics. *Academy of Management Journal* **35**: 9–37.

Miller D. 1991. Stale in the saddle: CEO tenure and the match between organization and the environment. *Management Science* **37**: 34–54.

Miller D, Toulouse J. 1986 Chief executive personality, corporate strategy and structure in small firms. *Management Science* **32**: 1389–1409

Mitchell W, Shaver JM, Yeung B. 1992. Getting there in a global industry: impacts on performance of changing international presence. *Strategic Management Journal* **13**(6): 419–432.

Murphy KJ. 1999. Executive compensation. In *Handbook of Labor Economics*, Vol. 3, Ashenfelter O, Card D (eds). North-Holland: New York.

Murtha T, Lenway S, Bagozzi R 1998. Global mindsets and cognitive shifts in a complex multinational corporation. *Strategic Management Journal* **19**(2): 97–114.

O'Reilly C, Synder R, Boothe J. 1993. Effects of executive team demography on organizational change. In *Organizational Change and Redesign*, Huber G, Glick W (eds). Oxford University Press: New York; 147–175.

Penrose E. 1959 *The Theory of the Growth of the Firm*. Oxford University Press: London.

Pollock TG, Fischer HM, Wade JB. 2002. The role of politics in repricing executive options. *Academy of Management Journal* **45**: 1172–1182.

Porter M. 1986. *Competition in Global Industries*. Harvard Business School Press: Boston, MA.

Prahalad CK, Doz YL. 1987. *The Multinational Mission: Balancing Local Demands and Global Vision*. Free Press: New York.

Preece SB, Miles G, Baetz MC. 1998. Explaining the international intensity and global diversity of early-stage technology-based firms. *Journal of Business Venturing* **14**: 259–281.

Roth K. 1995. Managing international interdependence: CEO characteristics in a resource-based framework. *Academy of Management Journal* **38**: 200–231.

Roth K, O'Donnell S. 1996. Foreign subsidiary compensation strategy: an agency theory perspective. *Academy of Management Journal* **39**: 678–703.

Rousseau D, Parks JM. 1993. The contracts of individuals and organizations. In *Research in Organizational Behavior*, Vol. 15, Cummings LL, Staw BM (eds). JAI Press: Greenwich, CT; 1–43.

Salancik GR, Meindl JR. 1984 Corporate attributions as strategic illusions of management control. *Administrative Science Quarterly* **29**: 238–254.

Sanders WG, Carpenter M. 1998. Internationalization and firm governance: the roles of CEO compensation, top team composition, and board structure. *Academy of Management Journal* **41**: 158–178.

Shapira Z. 1995. *Risk Taking: A Managerial Perspective*. Russell Sage Foundation: New York.

Sitkin S, Pablo A. 1992. Reconceptualizing the determinants of risk behavior. *Academy of Management Review* **17**: 9–38.

Sullivan D. 1994. Measuring the degree of internationalization of a firm. *Journal of International Business Studies* **25**: 325–342.

Tosi HL, Gomez-Mejia LR, Loughry ML, Werner S, Banning K, Katz J, Harris R, Silva P. 1999 Managerial discretion, compensation strategy, and firm performance. In *Research in Personnel and Human*

820   *M. A. Carpenter, T. G. Pollock and M. M. Leary*

Resources Management, Vol. 17, Ferris GR (ed) JAI Press: Greenwich, CT, 163–208.

Tosi HL, Werner S, Katz JP, Gomez-Mejia LR. 2000. How much does performance matter? A meta-analysis of CEO pay studies. *Journal of Management* **26**: 301–339.

Van den Berghe LAA, Levrau A. 2002. The role of venture capitalist as monitor of the company: a corporate governance perspective. *Corporate Governance: An International Review* **10**: 124–135.

Wiseman R, Gomez-Mejia LR. 1998. A behavioral agency model of risk taking. *Academy of Management Review* **23**: 133–153.

Wiseman RM, Gomez-Mejia LR, Fugate M. 2000. Rethinking compensation risk. In *Compensation in Organizations*, Rynes SL, Gerhart B (eds). Josey-Bass: San Francisco, CA; 311–347.

Zahra SA, Ireland RD, Hitt MA. 2000. International expansion by new venture firms: international diversity, mode of market entry, technological learning, and performance. *Academy of Management Journal* **43**: 925–950.

Zimmerman MA, Zeitz GJ. 2002. Beyond survival: achieving new venture growth by building legitimacy. *Academy of Management Review* **27**: 414–431.

[19]

THE INFLUENCE OF THE MANAGEMENT TEAM'S INTERNATIONAL EXPERIENCE ON THE INTERNATIONALIZATION BEHAVIORS OF SMES

A. Rebecca Reuber*
University of Toronto

Eileen Fischer**
York University

Abstract. Why are some small and medium-sized enterprises (SMEs) more successful in selling outside their domestic markets than are other SMEs in the same industry? Although the traditional explanation is that firms can gain valuable knowledge and resources as they become older and larger, small and young firms are not necessarily disadvantaged if they develop other mechanisms to acquire the requisite knowledge and resources. We examine the role of the management team's international experience as such a mechanism, for the internationalization of Canadian software product firms. We show that internationally experienced management teams have a greater propensity to develop foreign strategic partners and to delay less in obtaining foreign sales after start-up, and that these behaviors are associated with a higher degree of internationalization.

Obtaining sales outside their own domestic market is an objective of many small and medium-sized enterprises (SMEs) and their governments (for example, Economic Development Board [1993]; Manley and Martin [1994]; Yamamoto and Igusa [1996]). Despite the purported benefits of inter-nationalization for smaller firms [Beamish, Craig and McLellan 1993], the extant literature holds a relatively negative view of their prospects (e.g., Cavusgil, Bilkey and Tesar [1979]; Cavusgil and Nevin [1981]; Cavusgil and Naor [1987]; Chandler [1986]; Christensen, Rocha and Gertner [1987];

*A. Rebecca Reuber (PhD, MSc., Queen's University) is an Associate Professor at the Joseph L. Rotman School of Management, University of Toronto. Her research interests focus on the internationalization of SMEs and the management of rapid growth start-ups.

**Eileen Fischer (PhD, Queen's University; MASc., University of Waterloo) is an Associate Professor and Associate Dean of Research at the Schulich School of Business, York University. Her research interests focus on the antecedents and consequences of internationalization for SMEs and on the social and situational learning of entrepreneurial behavior.

This research is partially funded by a Strategic Grant from the Social Sciences and Humanities Research Council of Canada. The authors are grateful for the helpful comments and suggestions of four anonymous reviewers, Paul Beamish, Ida Berger and seminar participants at Queen's University and The Australian National University, and for the research assistance of Wendy Bryan, Marion McKenzie and Tricia Sands.

Received: July 1995; Revised: August & October 1996, January, March & May 1997; Accepted: May 1997.

Maleksadeh and Nahavandhi [1985]). It has been argued that, compared with large firms, SMEs are disadvantaged in entering and expanding sales in international markets because they lack the necessary skills and resources. Moreover, young firms are seen as being disadvantaged further because they lack the experience and credibility that a domestic track record provides.

These arguments have recently been challenged. The use of size and age variables as proxies for more meaningful constructs – such as knowledge of foreign markets, general management skill and international selling ability – has been criticized in favour of measuring these other constructs directly [Calof 1994; Cavusgil 1984; Reid 1982, 1983]. The small amount of variance in export behavior explained by firm size [Calof 1994] calls into question the relevance of firm size as a strong determinant. Furthermore, the emergence of firms that are international from start-up [McDougall, Shane and Oviatt 1994; Oviatt and McDougall 1994] and that enter and exit foreign markets in a flexible manner [Bonaccorsi 1992] calls into question the relevance of a domestic track record as a consistent predictor. Although in large firms the availability of slack resources or the efficiencies to be gained by internalizing markets may explain internationalization [Dunning 1980, 1988], in newer and smaller firms (with, typically, a poverty of resources), the skills and knowledge of the top decisionmaker(s) are likely to be more predictive of, and influential on, patterns of internationalization [Miesenbock 1988; Oviatt and McDougall 1994; Reid 1981].

The purpose of this paper is to explore the relationship between management's international experience and the internationalization of SMEs. The empirical findings are based on a sample of Canadian software product firms. We focus on one industry in order to control for industry effects on internationalization (cf. Calof [1994]; Erramilli and D'Souza [1993]). The Canadian software product industry is conducive to the study of the potentially early internationalization of firms because it is dominated by small, new entrepreneurial ventures and there are low barriers to entry. Furthermore, it is an industry in which decisionmakers have a relatively high degree of discretion and therefore can be expected to affect organizational outcomes [Hambrick and Abrahamson 1995]. Finally, the domestic market in Canada, as in many other countries, is too small to support much growth even for small and medium-sized software product firms (cf. Abramson and Lane [1992]), so effective internationalization is an ongoing practical concern.

RELEVANT LITERATURE

International Experience

Studies have already considered the impact of the top manager's exposure to foreign markets on a firm's internationalization behaviors (e.g., Angelmar and Pras [1984]; Brooks and Rosson [1982]; Ganier [1982]; Karafakioglu [1986];

Mayer and Flynn [1973]; Ogram [1982]; Simmonds and Smith [1968]; Simpson and Kujawa [1974]). Characteristics that have been found (though not invariably) to predict propensity for, or success in, exporting include: the extent to which the manager had engaged in foreign travel; the number of languages spoken by the manager; and whether the top decisionmaker was born abroad, lived abroad or worked abroad (cf. Meisenbock [1988]; Reid [1981]). Hambrick and Mason's "upper echelons" perspective on organizational outcomes [Bantel and Jackson 1989; Finkelstein and Hambrick 1990; Hambrick 1994; Hambrick and D'Aveni 1992; Hambrick and Finkelstein 1987; Hambrick and Mason 1984] suggests that this body of research can usefully be extended in two ways: a) by considering the experience of the top management team as a whole, rather than solely the experience of the highest ranking decisionmaker in the firm; and b) by specifying the way in which management experience is related to the firm's internationalization. These extensions are discussed below.

The body of research on the upper echelons of management has raised awareness that management is a shared effort by the dominant coalition in an organization, and that organizational behaviors are shaped collectively, rather than being outcomes influenced by the CEO alone. Although much of the research on top management teams is based on large firms, the correspondence between top management experience and organizational outcomes is expected to be even more pronounced in SMEs, since these businesses reflect the dominant role of the founding team to a greater extent [Chandler and Hanks 1994; Feeser and Willard 1990; Mintzberg 1988].

Directly relevant to our focus on the influence of the top management team on the internationalization of SMEs is recent work by McDougall and her colleagues [McDougall et al. 1994; Oviatt and McDougall 1994] which shows that firms that are international from birth are typically founded by a team of individuals with international experience. Also relevant are the findings of Bloodgood, Sapienza and Almeida [1995] that the international experience of the entire top management team was related to greater internationalization at the time of an IPO. Indeed, Buckley [1993] has argued that the role of teams is likely to become a major plank in internationalization research. Thus, both the upper echelons literature and recent international research support systematic consideration of the role of the management team versus that of the single top decisionmaker in influencing firms to internationalize.

A second extension suggested by an upper echelons perspective is that the influence of top decisionmakers should be modelled as indirect rather than direct. The importance of articulating and studying constructs which mediate between group characteristics and organizational outcomes has been recognized by a number of researchers (e.g., Jackson [1992]; Smith, Kofron and Anderson [1995]; Reuber and Fischer [1995]), who argue that there has been

FIGURE 1
The Mediated Relationships

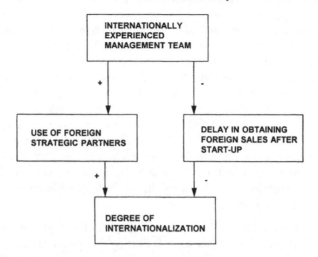

too much emphasis on the direct relationships between group characteristics and organizational performance without specifying and studying the intervening variables. In other words, the experience of the founder or the management team is likely to influence the behaviors of an SME, and these behaviors, in turn, will influence subsequent firm performance.

Internationalization Behaviors

We identify two different behaviors that internationally experienced leaders may influence their firms to engage in, which will increase the degree of internationalization of their firms. These relationships are shown in Figure 1.

The first behavior is the use of foreign strategic partnerships. Eisenhardt and Schoonhoven [1996] show that more experienced top management teams are more likely to form partnerships because they have a better ability to know, attract and engage partners. We expect that decisionmakers with more international experience, in particular, are more likely to have observed first hand the advantages that foreign partnerships may offer, are more likely to have in place a foreign business network, and are more likely to have developed the skills needed to identify and negotiate with firms in a different culture.

Moreover, partnerships formed in order to ease entry into foreign markets are likely to increase the degree of internationalization of the firm. Eisenhardt and Schoonhoven [1996] point out that, in general, when firms are in vulnerable strategic positions, partnerships provide concrete critical resources such as specific skills and financial resources, as well as more abstract resources such as legitimacy and market power. These resources are particularly important when a new or young firm, with a poverty of resources, is attempting to increase foreign sales [Oviatt and McDougall 1994], and, indeed, McDougall et al. [1994] report that owners of ventures that have international sales at start-up relied heavily on foreign partners. In addition, since partnerships can allow new and small ventures to control resources without owning them, there is greater flexibility in disposing of resources that are no longer needed. This is an added advantage, if, as Bonaccorsi [1992] argues, SMEs need to be able to enter *and exit* foreign markets nimbly.

Thus, it is expected that strategic partnerships can be valuable for SMEs with a limited domestic market, such as Canadian software product firms. Furthermore, it is expected that a more internationally experienced top management team will use foreign strategic partnerships to a greater extent, which will promote the internationalization of the firm. This leads to the following hypotheses:

H1a: The international experience of the top management team in Canadian software product SMEs is related to the use of foreign strategic partnerships by the firm; and

H1b: The use of foreign strategic partnerships by Canadian software product SMEs mediates the relationship between the team's international experience and the firm's degree of internationalization.

The second behavior that internationally experienced leaders may influence their firms to engage in, which will increase the degree of internationalization of their firms, is the speed with which foreign sales are first obtained after start-up. Ghoshal [1987] has argued that organizations that internationalize earlier are likely to develop fewer routines and resources which make it difficult for them to move out of domestic markets. Or, as Buckley [1993] notes, firms may become dependent on cultural attributes derived largely from their home countries, and these may be non-transferable, or even have hidden costs in new environments. Supportive of these ideas is a finding by Brush [1993], in a sample of small U.S. manufacturers, that having a longer domestic track record before obtaining foreign sales was not beneficial to levels of foreign sales. Likewise, McDougall et al. [1944] argue that a delay in entering foreign markets can be detrimental, and provide examples of "international from birth" firms which set out to establish international competencies from start-up. They note that becoming international early on is particularly important for knowledge-based firms, such as software product firms, which need to develop international mechanisms to protect their commercial value from expropriation [Oviatt and McDougall 1994].

What is of interest from this perspective is not for how *long* a firm has been selling in foreign markets, but rather, for how long the firm delayed *before* selling in foreign markets. SMEs managed by internationally experienced teams are likely to delay less. Experience with, and knowledge of, foreign markets make it more likely that decisionmakers will consider mechanisms to sell outside the domestic market early on and less likely that they will set up routines based on a purely domestic perspective. This leads to the second and final set of hypotheses:

> H2a: The international experience of the top management teams in Canadian software product firms is negatively related to the delay after start-up in selling to foreign markets; and

> H2b: The delay after start-up in selling to foreign markets by Canadian software product firms mediates the relationship between the team's international experience and the firm's degree of internationalization.

METHODOLOGY

Data relevant to the hypotheses were collected from Canadian software product firms. A questionnaire was developed on the basis of previous research and interviews.[1] Questions were pre-tested with a sample of owner-managers in the targeted industry in order to ensure that they were clear and captured the desired information.

The questionnaires were administered to the firm's founder or to a member of the firm's top management team by trained research assistants. A research assistant contacted the firm by telephone to arrange an interview and sat with the respondent while the questionnaire was being completed. The research assistants were trained to clarify the nature of the questions and to explain their rationale, in order to enhance the completeness and accuracy of the data collected. Data collection took place in the first five months of 1994.

Sample

Firms to be contacted were identified from a directory of Canada's premier software product firms compiled by Industry, Science and Technology Canada. The directory listed 164 firms. To focus on a reasonably homogenous industry and on owner-managed smaller firms, firms were excluded if they: did not derive a majority of their revenue from software products (rather than, for example, hardware or consulting); had more than 200 employees; were not managed by a founding partner; were subsidiaries of other firms; and/or had been purchased by other firms. This left 132 eligible firms.

By the cutoff date of June 1, 1994, 58 firms had provided usable replies, yielding a response rate of 42%. We included a firm in the sample only if the respondent was a founder, in order to ensure that the respondent was with the firm when it made its first foreign sale and was knowledgeable about the back-

TABLE 1
Characteristics of Firms in the Sample (N = 49)

	Mean	SD	Range
Age of firm (yrs)	11.16	5.34	3–24
Number of employees	40.98	39.01	4–180
Foreign sales (%)	53.67	36.23	0–100
Delay in foreign sales (yrs)	5.10	5.69	0–23
Number of foreign partners	2.18	2.52	0–10
Employees spending > 50% time on			
international activities (%)	36.83	39.58	0–100

	% Firms
Total Sales	
$500,000–$999,999	8.5
$1 million–$1,999,999	23.4
$2 million–$4,999,999	34.0
$5 million–$10 million	17.0
Over $10 million	17.0
Geographic scope of sales	
Canada only	12.2
Canada and North America	16.4
Canada, N.Am., outside N.Am.	71.4
Mgmt team has foreign experience	55.1

grounds of all other members of the top management team. This left a sample of 49 cases, representing 37% of the original population in the directory.

Despite the response rate, however, there may be systematic differences in the characteristics of the sample and of the population. To consider whether responding firms differ systematically from nonrespondents, the mean number of employees and the mean annual revenue of responding firms were compared with those of eligible firms. *T*-tests indicate that there are no significant differences in the mean values of these variables for the sample of software product firms and for all eligible firms identified in the directory. However, the firms listed in the directory are not representative of all owner-managed software product firms in Canada, and so we must be cautious in generalizing our results.

The firms in the sample are described in Table 1. The sample exhibits a wide range of internationalization. Ten percent of the firms had no foreign sales at all and 51% had at most one foreign partner. On the other hand, for 20% of the firms, at least 90% of their sales were foreign. Fourteen percent of the sample had foreign sales within the first year of operation, and 51% had foreign sales by their fourth year.

Measures

Degree of Internationalization – DOI$_{SME}$. Discussion has arisen recently concerning the most appropriate way to measure the degree of

814   JOURNAL OF INTERNATIONAL BUSINESS STUDIES, FOURTH QUARTER 1997

internationalization of a firm, the study's dependent variable. Sullivan [1994] argues that, based on the precepts of measurement theory, multiple item measures should be used, rather than, for example, foreign sales as a percentage of total sales (FSTS). To measure degree of internationalization, he constructed DOI_{INTS}, a five-item measure that reflects performance aspects of internationalization (FSTS), structural aspects of internationalization (foreign assets as a percentage of total assets and overseas subsidiaries as a percentage of total subsidiaries) and attitudinal aspects of internationalization (top managers' international experience and the psychic dispersion of international operations).

Ramaswamy, Kroeck and Renforth [1996] recognize that multiple item measures are more reliable than single item measures, but caution that aggregating components can mask the effects of individual components. Moreover, they identify several limitations of the DOI_{INTS} construct, which relate to the individual items used, as well as the process used to combine them into a single measure.

In this study, we take an intermediate position with respect to measuring the degree of internationalization. Following Sullivan [1994], we construct a multiple-item measure, but in doing so, we modified DOI_{INTS} to address some of the limitations identified by Ramaswamy et al. [1996] and to make it more relevant for the SMEs in our sample, as described in the two paragraphs below.

There are three components of DOI_{SME}, our measure of the degree of internationalization of an SME. The first component is FSTS, foreign sales as a percentage of total sales, which is a standard single-item measure of degree of internationalization. The second component is the percentage of the firm's employees that spends over 50% of their time on international activities, to capture the structural aspects of an SME's degree of internationalization in a sample where foreign assets and overseas subsidiaries were likely to be rare. Finally, the third component measures the geographic scope of sales by asking which of three regions, each increasingly distant from the domestic market, the company made sales to: Canada only, North America only, outside North America. We could not include an experience measure as a component of internationalization, as did Sullivan [1994], because experience plays a conceptual role by itself in our hypotheses.

We converted each of the three items to a ratio measure and standardized them, as suggested by Ramaswamy et al. [1996]. We then summed the three z-values to create a single score, DOI_{SME}. DOI_{SME} has a Cronbach's *alpha* of .78, indicating acceptable reliability. Factor analysis indicated that a single unambiguous factor comprises DOI_{SME}, with eigenvalue 2.079 and loadings of .88 (FSTS), .84 (percentage of employees spending over 50% of their time on international activities), and .77 (geographic scope of sales).

International Behaviors – PARTNERS, DELAY. There are two behaviors to measure: the delay after start-up in obtaining foreign sales and the use of foreign strategic partners. The first measure, *DELAY*, is the number of years the firm operated domestically before having any foreign sales.

The second measure, *PARTNERS*, is the number of strategic partners of the firm with a headquarters outside of Canada. It should be noted that there are many types of strategic partners. This measure does not attempt to differentiate among them, but rather to include all parsimoniously.

Our implicit definition of "strategic partnerships" is "relatively enduring interfirm cooperative arrangements, involving flows and linkages that utilize resources and/or governance structures from autonomous organizations, for the joint accomplishment of individual goals linked to the corporate mission of each sponsoring firm" [Parkhe 1991]. Whether a particular relationship is "strategic" or not is decided by the respondent. In the context of this sample, this task is not difficult to do. The firms are extremely small on average, and the respondent is the founder and CEO of the firm, and so is well positioned to identify strategic partnerships.

We needed to find a term to capture such a relationship, and "strategic partnership," "partnership," and "strategic alliance" were all contenders. We chose "strategic partnership" over "partnership" because we wanted to convey explicitly the strategic nature of the relationship to respondents, to exclude mere exchange relationships (cf: Young, Gilbert and McIntyre [1996]). We chose the term "strategic partnership" over "strategic alliance," because, in our initial interviews with top managers in the software product industry (prior to the questionnaire design) we found that the term "partnership" was more widely used among interview subjects.[2]

In preliminary field work and pre-testing of the questionnaire, we found that respondents had no difficulty in using or understanding the term "strategic partnership". During the administration of the final questionnaire, the two research assistants made detailed notes about the questions that arose at each interview, in order to ensure that questions were consistently answered across respondents and the entire team was aware of the answers that had been provided. No questions or comments about strategic partnerships were reported. A follow-up to the original survey was conducted in 1997 with two senior officers from each of twelve firms in the original sample to explore the extent to which respondents tended to define as strategic those partnerships that were relatively enduring relationships and that they considered important to their strategic goals. This survey indicated that the average duration of relationships with firms identified as strategic partners was longer than five years, and that the average strategic importance of the partnerships was scored at higher than a 4 on a scale of 1 to 5 where 1 represents *not at all important* and 5 represents *extremely important*. These results suggest that respondents

816   JOURNAL OF INTERNATIONAL BUSINESS STUDIES, FOURTH QUARTER 1997

do converge across firms in their implicit definitions of strategic partners. They also converge within firms. For over 54% of the thirty-five partnerships identified, the two respondents from the same firm rated the importance of a given partnership identically. For 40%, there was only a one-point difference between the two raters (for example, if one of the firm's respondent's rated the importance as a "4," the other rated the importance as a "5"). In less than 6% (i.e., in two of the thirty-five partnerships) there was a two-point difference in the rating of the partnership.

International Experience – INTEREXP. Given that we wished to build on the prior literature that examined international experience, we used two binary indicators of a team's international experience. The first measure relates directly to previous measures that reflect an individual's exposure to foreign market environments, and asked whether the CEO ever worked outside Canada prior to joining or founding the firm. The second measure of international experience taps into an aspect of international experience not often previously considered, but extremely relevant for SMEs in Canada, because of the small size of the domestic market: experience in selling to foreign markets. The underlying construct here might best be termed "international sales experience". The question asked was whether, before founding or joining this company, any member of the current management team had experience in selling outside Canada.

We used a binary indicator to measure both aspects of international experience since the relationship between management experience and organizational outcomes is unlikely to be linear across time or across individuals [Reuber and Fischer 1995], and the management development literature suggests that exposure to a particular type of experience, regardless of its length, is likely to be consequential (see, for example, McCauley, Ruderman, Ohlott, and Morrow [1994]). The correlation between these variables was, as expected, high (.40, $p=.005$). Thus it seemed appropriate to add them together to form a single measure of the team's international experience, *INTEREXP*.

It should be noted that experience in this study is viewed as a characteristic of the management teams of SMEs, rather than as a characteristic of SMEs themselves. We are interested in the impact of a manager's experience, not a firm's experience. Although experience at these two levels of analysis are inter-related [Reuber and Fischer 1995], our model is based on the former. Thus, our conceptualization and operationalization of international experience is different from studies that focus on a firm's international experience (see, for example, Cavusgil and Zou [1994]; Erramilli [1991]; Johanson and Vahlne [1977]).

Firm Demographics. We measured the age of the firm in years (*FIRMAGE*) and the size of the firm in terms of number of full-time employees (*FIRMSIZE*).

FIGURE 2
Measures of Research Variables

Variable Label	Wording of Measure(s) of Variables
FIRMAGE	When was this company started? (The response was given as a year, which was subtracted from 1994.)
FIRMSIZE	How many full-time employees does this company have now?
PARTNERS	How many of your strategic partners are headquartered outside Canada?
DELAY	What was the year of your first sale outside Canada? (The response was given as a year, which was subtracted from the year of start-up.)
INTEREXP	Before founding or joining this firm: (a) Did you or any member of the current management team have experience selling outside Canada? (no/yes) (b) Did you ever work outside Canada? (no/yes) Sum 0/1 responses in (a) and (b).
DOI	a. What percentage of this year's sales is from Canada? (Subtract from 100 to determine the percentage of foreign sales and convert to a z-score.) b. Today, how many of the full-time employees spend over 50% of their time on international activities? (Express this as a percentage of the total number of employees (FIRMSIZE) and convert to a z-score.) c. What percentage of this year's sales is from each of three different regions: Canada; United States or Mexico; and Outside North America? (Create a variable indicating how many of these regions there are sales in, express this as a percentage of three regions and convert to a z-score.) Sum the z-scores created in steps (a), (b) and (c).

TABLE 2
Zero-Order Correlation Matrix

	FIRMAGE	FIRMSIZE	PARTNERS	DELAY	INTEREXP
2. FIRMSIZE	.194				
3. PARTNERS	−.473***	.121			
4. DELAY	.750***	.010	−.267*		
5. INTEREXP	.092	.439**	.349**	−.373**	
6. DOI$_{SME}$	−.134	.172	.456***	−.504***	.488***

$*p < .05$; $**p < .01$; $***p < .001$

The exact wording of each measure is summarized in Figure 2 and zero-order correlations for these variables are shown in Table 2.

RESULTS

Controlling for the Effect of Firm Size and Age

We have argued that age and size are not themselves the factors that account for degree of internationalization of SMEs, but are instead surrogates for skills and resources that are better measured directly. The correlations reported in Table 2 support this notion, as neither *FIRMAGE* nor *FIRMSIZE* is directly and significantly related to *DOI$_{SME}$* for the firms in our sample. We note, however, that *FIRMAGE* is strongly related to one behavioral variable, *DELAY*, suggesting that older firms delayed longer in obtaining foreign sales. This might reflect the increased globalization of the software industry in recent years, and the decreased propensity of software product firms to evolve from software consulting firms. Further, *FIRMSIZE* is positively and significantly correlated with the measure of the team's international selling experience, *INTEREXP*: larger firms are more likely to have teams with international selling experience. This could be due to the fact that larger firms tend to have larger management teams ($p=.000$) and it takes only one person with prior international selling experience for this variable to be positive.

Despite limited relationships between *FIRMAGE, FIRMSIZE* and the other variables, it was thought prudent to control for these variables to ensure that the results found were not indirectly attributable to age and size. *FIRMAGE* and *FIRMSIZE* are, therefore, included as predictors in each regression equation.

Modelling International Behaviors as Mediators of Experience

Baron and Kenny [1986] specify the process to test for mediation. It requires estimating three regression equations: one regressing the mediator on the independent variable; a second regressing the dependent variable on the independent variable; and a third regressing the dependent variable on both the independent variable and the mediator. Therefore, to test whether the use of foreign strategic partners mediates the relationship between the international experience of the management team and the degree of internationalization of the firm, the following equations were estimated:

$$PARTNERS = \alpha + \beta_1 INTEREXP + \beta_2 FIRMSIZE + \beta_3 FIRMAGE + \mu, \quad (1)$$

$$DOI_{SME} = \alpha + \beta_1 INTEREXP + \beta_2 FIRMSIZE + \beta_3 FIRMAGE + \mu, \quad (2)$$

$$DOI_{SME} = \alpha + \beta_1 INTEREXP + \beta_2 FIRMSIZE + \beta_3 FIRMAGE + \beta_4 PARTNERS + \mu. \quad (3)$$

The same three equations are used to test whether the other international behavior to be investigated – delay in obtaining foreign sales after start-up – mediates the relationship between the international experience of the management team and the degree of internationalization of the firm, except that *DELAY* is substituted for *PARTNERS*. The results of these analyses are shown in Tables 3 and 4.

To establish that a mediational model exists, Baron and Kenny [1986] state that four conditions must hold: the independent variable must affect the mediator in the first equation; the independent variable must affect the dependent variable in the second equation; the mediator must affect the dependent variable in the third equation; and the effect of the independent variable on the dependent variable must be less in the third equation than in the second.

TABLE 3
Results of Tests for Mediation by *PARTNERS*

	Equation 1	Equation 2	Equation 3
Dependent Variables	*PARTNERS*	*DOI$_{SME}$*	*DOI$_{SME}$*
Independent Variables			
INTEREXP	.391*	.542***	.416**
FIRMAGE	.054	−.043	−.061
FIRMSIZE	−.088	−.138	−.109
PARTNERS			.321*
Adjusted R^2	.06	.208	.280
F	2.17	5.20**	5.86***

Note: Standardized regression coefficients are shown.
*$p < .05$; **$p < .01$; ***$p < .001$

TABLE 4
Results of Test for Mediation by *DELAY*

	Equation 1	Equation 2	Equation 3
Dependent Variables	*PARTNERS*	*DOI$_{SME}$*	*DOI$_{SME}$*
Independent Variables			
INTEREXP	−.243*	.542***	.321*
FIRMAGE	.714***	−.043	.479**
FIRMSIZE	.009	−.138	−.097
DELAY			−.744***
Adjusted R^2	.570	.208	.405
F	26.74***	5.20**	9.30***

Note: Standardized regression coefficients are shown.
*$p < .05$; **$p < .01$; ***$p < .001$

The data in Table 3 indicate that, as predicted in H1a, *INTEREXP* does effect *PARTNERS*. In equation 1, predicting *PARTNERS*, the coefficient for *INTEREXP* (but not for *FIRMAGE* nor *FIRMSIZE*) is significant, and the sign is positive. The data in Table 4 indicates that, as predicted in H2a, *INTEREXP* does effect *DELAY* In equation 1, the coefficients for *INTEREXP* and *FIRMAGE* are significant, and the sign for *INTEREXP* is negative as anticipated. In addition to offering support for H1a and H2a, these results suggest that the first condition for mediation of the effect of *INTEREXP* on *DOI$_{SME}$* by both *PARTNERS* and *DELAY* is met.

The results in Tables 3 and 4 also show that *INTEREXP* is a significant predictor of DOI_{SME} (equation 2 in each table). The coefficient for *INTEREXP* in this equation is significant and positive while those for *FIRMAGE* and *FIRMSIZE* are not significant. This result suggests that the second condition for the mediation models is also met.

Equation 3 in both Tables 3 and 4 indicates that the regression coefficients for *PARTNERS* and *DELAY* are significant in their respective models. As expected, the coefficient for *PARTNERS* is positive while that for *DELAY* is negative. Moreover, the coefficients and significance levels for *INTEREXP* in each equation 3 is less than in the corresponding equation 2. These results satisfy the third and fourth conditions for mediation.

Since the four conditions are met, we can conclude that both *PARTNERS* and *DELAY* mediate the effect of *INTEREXP* on DOI_{SME}, which supports H1b and H2b.

DISCUSSION AND CONCLUSIONS

This paper combines and integrates both resource-based and behavior-based explanations of the internationalization of SMEs. Internationally experienced management teams are viewed as a resource that influences SMEs to engage in behaviors leading to a greater degree of internationalization. Consistent with our hypotheses, we show that internationally experienced management makes a difference to SMEs in the Canadian software products industry. Firms with more internationally experienced management teams use more foreign strategic partners and delay less in obtaining foreign sales after start-up, which leads to a greater degree of internationalization.

The paper convincingly demonstrates that a firm's size and age do not in themselves determine the capacity of the firm for internationalization. It supports the research of Bonaccorsi [1992] and Calof [1994], by showing that firm size is not a good predictor of international activity, at least in countries with relatively small domestic markets. It also builds on studies of international new ventures – ventures that are international from start-up [McDougall et al. 1994; Oviatt and McDougall 1994]. Although very few firms in our sample were international from start-up, the use of foreign partners and the presence of international experience in those that obtained foreign sales early is consistent with the characteristics ascribed to international new ventures. Thus, these results suggest that McDougall and Oviatt's theoretical work can be extended to SMEs that internationalize early.

Further research should investigate more specifically what knowledge, skills and abilities are acquired experientially, and what their behavioral consequences are. A promising avenue along these lines is to examine the relationship between top managers' international experience and the formation of geocentric attitudes [Calof and Beamish 1994; Kobrin 1994; Perlmutter

1969]. While Kobrin [1994] reports that multinational corporations do not consider international experience to be a major factor in expatriate selection and that *a firm's* geocentric mind-set is unrelated to the importance it places on international experience, Calof and Beamish [1994] suggest that an *individual's* geocentricity is associated with international experience. An empirical test of the relationship could examine whether such a relationship exists, and, if so, the direction of causality: whether international experiences lead to geocentric attitudes, whether geocentric attitudes lead to more international experiences, or whether experience and attitudes are mutually causal. An advantage of studying centricity in the context of SMEs versus multinationals is that the relationship between individual characteristics and firm characteristics is likely to be more direct [Chandler and Hanks 1994; Feeser and Willard 1990; Mintzberg 1988].

Our findings are based on a sample of SMEs in the Canadian software products industry. The limited domestic market of this industry makes the study a conservative test of the consequences of managerial experience. Even though there is a small domestic market, firms in the industry exhibit a considerable range in foreign sales as a percentage of total sales, the use of foreign strategic partners, and the delay in obtaining foreign sales after start-up. One would expect that in industries with a larger domestic market, where internationalization is more a strategic option than a necessity, the experience of the management team would be even more consequential in differentiating differing degrees of internationalization among SMEs.

However, further research is needed to determine if the results generalize to other industries. There are high capital costs of R&D in the software products industry, and so internationalization may be a preferable growth strategy to product diversification (cf. Bonaccorsi [1992]). Products are relatively abstract in nature and are knowledge-based, which likely favours both partnership formation and speed in obtaining foreign sales. It is expected that these industry-specific characteristics will affect the way in which managerial experience influences not just the degree of SME internationalization, but also the firm behaviors that are associated with internationalization.

Despite this caveat, our findings are consistent both with emerging research on the internationalization of small and young firms and with the model here developed. We believe that research that integrates management experience, expertise and actions is a promising approach to gain a better understanding of the internationalization of SMEs.

NOTES

1. A copy of the full questionnaire is not included due to space constraints, but may be obtained from the authors upon request.

2. We found that different terms are used interchangeably in the research literature. For example, Hagedoorn [1993] uses the terms "strategic alliances" and "strategic technology

partnering" interchangeably, Mohr and Spekman [1994] use the terms "partnerships," "strategic partnerships" and "strategic alliances" interchangeably, Eisenhardt and Schoonhoven [1996] use the terms "strategic alliances" and "strategic technology partnering" interchangeably, and Kotabe and Swan [1995] use the terms "strategic alliances " and "new cooperative organizational forms " interchangeably. Consistent with this practice, we feel that "partnership" or "strategic alliance" *could* have been used instead, but we believe that "strategic partnership" was the best term to elicit the interpretation that we wanted from this sample of software firm CEOs.

REFERENCES

Abramson, Neil R. & Henry W. Lane. 1992. *Key factors affecting the performance of Canadian software companies doing business in the U.S.: A summary report to Industry, Science and Technology Canada.*

Angelmar, R. & B. Pras. 1984. Product acceptance by middlemen in export channels. *American Journal of Small Business,* 3(1): 25–34.

Bantel, Karen A. & Susan E. Jackson. 1989. Top management and innovations in banking: Does the composition of the team make a difference? *Strategic Management Journal,* 10: 107–24.

Baron, Reuben M. & David A. Kenny. 1986. The moderator-mediator variable distinction in social psychological research: Conceptual, strategic and statistical considerations. *Journal of Personality and Social Psychology,* 15(6): 1173–82.

Beamish, Paul W., Ronald Craig & Kerry McLellan. 1993. The performance characteristics of Canadian versus U.K. exporters in small and medium sized firms. *Management International Review,* 33(2): 121–37.

Bloodgood, James M., Harry J. Sapienza & James G. Almeida. 1995. The internationalization of new high potential ventures: Antecedents and outcomes. In *Frontiers of entrepreneurship research,* 533–46. Wellesley, Mass.: Babson College Center for Entrepreneurial Studies.

Bonaccorsi, Andrea. 1992. On the relationship between firm size and export intensity. *Journal of International Business Studies,* 23(4): 605–35.

Brooks, M.R. & Philip J. Rosson. 1982. A study of export behavior of small- and medium-sized manufacturing firms in three Canadian provinces. In M. R. Czinkota & G. Tesar, editors, *Export management: An international context,* 39–54. New York: Praeger Publishers.

Brush, Candida. 1993. International entrepreneurship: Motives and the effect of age at internationalization on performance. In *Frontiers of entrepreneurship research.* Wellesley, Mass.: Babson College Center for Entrepreneurial Studies.

Buckley, Peter. 1993. The role of management in internalisation theory. *Management International Review,* 33(3): 197–207.

Calof, Jonathan L. 1994. The relationship between firm size and export behavior revisited. *Journal of International Business Studies,* 25(2): 367–87.

—— & Paul W. Beamish. 1994. The right attitude for international success. *Business Quarterly,* 59(1): 105–10.

Cavusgil, S. Tamer. 1984. Organizational characteristics associated with export activity. *Journal of Management Studies,* 21(1): 3–22.

——, Warren Bilkey & George Tesar. 1979. A note on the export behavior of firms: Exporter profiles. *Journal of International Business Studies,* 10(1): 91–97.

Cavusgil, S. Tamer & Jacob Naor. 1987. Firm and management characteristics as discriminators for export behavior. *Journal of Business Research,* 15(3): 221–35.

Cavusgil, S. Tamer & John R. Nevin. 1981. Internal determinants of export marketing behavior: An empirical investigation. *Journal of Marketing Research*, 23 (February): 114–19.

Cavusgil, S. Tamer & Shaoming Zou. 1994. Marketing strategy-performance relationship: An investigation of the empirical link in export market ventures. *Journal of Marketing*, 58(1): 1–21.

Chandler, Alfred D. 1986. The evolution of modern global competition. In M. E. Porter, editor, *Competition in global industries*, 405–58. Boston: Harvard Business School Press.

Chandler, Gaylen N. & Stephen Hanks. 1994. Founder competence, the environment and venture performance. *Entrepreneurship, Theory and Practice*, 18(3): 77–89.

Christensen, Carl H., Angela da Rocha & Rosane Kerbel Gertner. 1987. An empirical investigation of the factors influencing exporting success of Brazilian firms. *Journal of International Business Studies*, 18(3): 61– 77.

Dunning, John H. 1980. Toward an eclectic theory of international production: Some empirical tests. *Journal of International Business Studies*, 11(1): 9–31.

———. 1988. The eclectic paradigm of international production: A restatement and some possible extensions. *Journal of International Business Studies*, 19 (1), 1–32.

Economic Development Board. 1993. *Growing with enterprise· A national effort*. Singapore.

Eisenhardt, Kathleen M. & Claudia Bird Schoonhoven. 1996. Resource-based view of strategic alliance formation: Strategic and social effects in entrepreneurial firms. *Organization Science*, 7(2): 136–50.

Erramilli, M. Krishna. 1991. The experience factor in foreign market entry behavior of service firms. *Journal of International Business Studies*, 22(3): 479–501.

——— & Derrick E. D'Souza. 1993. Venturing into foreign markets: The case of the small service firm. *Entrepreneurship Theory and Practice*, 17(4): 29–41.

Feeser, Henry R. & Gary E. Willard. 1990. Founding strategy and performance: A comparison of high and low growth high tech firms. *Strategic Management Journal*, 11(x): 87–98.

Finkelstein, Sydney & Donald C. Hambrick. 1990. Top management team tenure and organizational outcomes: The moderating role of managerial discretion. *Administrative Science Quarterly*, 35(3): 484–503.

Ganier, Gérard. 1982. Comparative export behavior of small Canadian firms in the printing and electrical industries. In M. R. Czinkota & G. Tesar, editors, *Export management: An international context*, 113–31. New York: Praeger.

Ghoshal, Sumantra. 1987. Global strategy: An organizing framework. *Strategic Management Journal*, 8: 425–40.

Hagedoorn, John. 1993. Understanding the rationale of strategic technology partnering: Interorganizational modes of cooperation and sectoral differences. *Strategic Management Journal*, 14: 371–85.

Hambrick, Donald C. 1994. Top management groups: A conceptual integration and reconsideration of the "team" label. *Research in Organizational Behavior*, 16: 171–213.

——— & Eric Abrahamson. 1995. Assessing managerial discretion across industries: A multimethod approach. *Academy of Management Journal*, 38(5): 1427–41.

Hambrick, Donald C. & Richard A. D'Aveni. 1992. Top team deterioration as part of the downward spiral of large corporate bankruptcies. *Management Science*, 38(10): 1445–66.

Hambrick, Donald C. & Sydney Finkelstein. 1987. Managerial discretion: A bridge between polar views of organizations. *Research in Organizational Behavior*, 7: 369–406.

Hambrick, Donald C. & Phyllis A. Mason. 1984. Upper echelons: The organization as a reflection of its top managers. *Academy of Management Research,* 9(2): 193–206.

Jackson, Susan E. 1992. Consequences of group composition for the interpersonal dynamics of strategic issue processing. *Advances in Strategic Management:* 435–62.

Johanson, Jan & Jan-Erik Vahlne. 1977. The internationalization process of the firm: A mode of knowledge development and increasing foreign market commitments. *Journal of International Business Studies,* 8(1): 23–32.

Karafakioglu, M. 1986. Export activities of Turkish manufacturers. *International Marketing Review,* 3(4): 34– 43.

Kobrin, Stephen J. 1994. Is there a relationship between a geocentric mind-set and multinational strategy? *Journal of International Business Studies,* 25 (3): 493–511.

Kotabe, Masaaki & K. Scott Swan. 1995. The role of strategic alliances in high-technology new product development. *Strategic Management Journal,* 16: 621–36.

Maleksadeh, Ali R. & Afsaneh Nahavandi. 1985. Small business exporting. Misconceptions are abundant. *American Journal of Small Business,* 9(4): 7–14.

Manley, John & Paul Martin. 1994. *Growing small businesses.* Ottawa: Government of Canada.

Mayer, Charles & Jay E. Flynn.1973.Canadian small businesses abroad: Opportunities, aids and experiences. *Business Quarterly,* 38: 33–47.

McCauley, Cynthia D., Marian N. Ruderman, Patricia J. Ohlott & Jane E. Morrow. 1994. Assessing the developmental components of managerial jobs. *Journal of Applied Psychology,* 79(4): 544–60.

McDougall, Patricia Phillips, Scott Shane & Benjamin M. Oviatt. 1994. Explaining the formation of international new ventures: The limits of theories from international business research. *Journal of Business Venturing,* 9 (November): 469–87.

Miesenbock, Kurt J. 1988. Small business and exporting: A literature review. *International Small Business Journal,* 6(2): 42–61.

Mintzberg, Henry. 1988. The simple structure. In J.B. Quinn, H. Mintzberg & R.M. James, editors, *The strategy process. Concepts, contexts and cases,* 532–39. Englewood Cliffs, N.J.: Prentice-Hall.

Mohr, Jakki & Robert Spekman. 1994. Characteristics of partnership success: Partnership attributes, communication behavior, and conflict resolution techniques. *Strategic Management Journal,* 15: 135–52.

Ogram, Ernest. W. 1982. Exporters and non-exporters: A profile of small manufacturing firms in Georgia. In M. R. Czinkota & G. Tesar, editors, *Export management· An international context,* 70–84. New York: Praeger.

Oviatt, Benjamin M. & Patricia Phillips McDougall. 1994. Toward a theory of international new ventures. *Journal of International Business Studies,* 25(1): 45–64.

Parkhe, Arvind. 1991. Interfirm diversity, organization learning, and longevity in global strategic alliances. *Journal of International Business Studies,* 22(4): 579–601.

Perlmutter, Howard. 1969. The tortuous evolution of the multinational corporation. *Columbia Journal of World Business,* January-February: 9–18.

Ramaswamy, Kannan, K. Galen Kroeck & William Renforth. 1996. Measuring the degree of internationalization of a firm: A comment. *Journal of International Business Studies,* 26(1): 167–77.

Reid, Stan D. 1981. The decision maker and export entry and expansion. *Journal of International Business Studies,* 12(2). 101–12.

——. 1982. The impact of size on export behavior in small firms. In M. R. Czinkota & G. Tesar, editors, *Export management: An international context,* 18–38. New York: Praeger.

——. 1983. Export research in crisis. In M. R. Czinkota, editor, *Export promotion The public and private sector interaction,* 129–50. New York: Praeger.

Reuber, A. Rebecca & Eileen M Fischer. 1995. Reconceptualizing entrepreneurs' experience. Presented at the Annual Meeting of the Academy of Management, Vancouver, British Columbia.

Simmonds, Kenneth & H. Smith. 1968. The first export order: A marketing innovation. *British Journal of Marketing,* 2: 93–100.

Simpson, Claude L. & Duane Kujawa. 1974. The export decision process: An empirical inquiry. *Journal of International Business Studies,* 5(1): 107–17.

Smith, Ken A., Elizabeth A. Kofron & Melinda Anderson. 1995. Strategy implementation: A missing variable in top management team research. Presented at the Annual Meeting of the Academy of Management, Vancouver, British Columbia.

Sullivan, Daniel. 1994. Measuring the degree of internationalization of a firm. *Journal of International Business Studies,* 25(2): 325–42.

Yamamoto, Kazumi & Kunio Igusa, editors. 1996. *Proceedings of the international seminar on internationalization of SMEs and human resource development in the Asia-Pacific region.* Tokyo, Japan: Institute of Developing Economies.

Young, Joyce A., Faye W. Gilbert & Faye S. McIntyre. 1996. An investigation of relationalism across a range of marketing relationships and alliances. *Journal of Business Research,* 35: 139–51.

Part V
Alliances and Networks

Pergamon

PII: S0969-5931(97)00010-3

International Business Review Vol 6, No 4, pp. 361–386, 1997
© 1997 Elsevier Science Ltd All rights reserved
Printed in Great Britain
0969-5931/97 $17 00 + 0.00

Network Relationships and the Internationalisation Process of Small Software Firms

Nicole Coviello* and Hugh Munro†

Faculty of Management, University of Calgary, 2500 University Dr NW, Calgary, AB, Canada T2N 1N4

†*School of Business and Economics, Wilfrid Laurier University, Waterloo, Ontario, Canada N2L 3C5*

Abstract—This paper examines the influence of network relationships on the internationalisation process of small firms, using multi-site case research on the software industry. The study empirically integrates the traditional models of incremental internationalisation with the network perspective. The findings show that the internationalisation process of small software firms reflects an accelerated version of the stage model perspective, and is driven, facilitated, and inhibited by a set of formal and informal network relationships. These relationships impact foreign market selection and mode of entry, as well as product development and market diversification activities. The paper offers a conceptual framework of the small firm internationalisation process which integrates the "stage" and "network" perspectives, and concludes with a discussion of research and managerial implications. © 1997 Elsevier Science Ltd

Key Words —Internationalisation Process, Networks, Small Firms, Software

Introduction

Historically, research on the internationalisation process has tended to focus on large manufacturing organisations, in spite of the importance of small service and/or knowledge-based firms to most economies. Such firms are of particular interest given they often possess limited capabilities and management resources (Erramilli and D'Souza, 1993; Buckley, 1989; O'Farrell and Hitchins, 1988). However, the success of these firms, particularly those pursuing niche strategies in small domestic markets, may depend on their ability to internationalise their operations (Luostarinen, 1989). If the firm is faced with increasing demand, sophisticated customers, and a volatile competitive market, as well as a product

---

*Dr Nicole Coviello is Associate Professor in the Faculty of Management, University of Calgary, Canada. Her research interests focus on internationalisation issues, networks, entrepreneurial firm growth, and the role of marketing in the current business environment.
*Dr Hugh Munro is Associate Professor of Marketing in the School of Business and Economics, Wilfrid Laurier University, Canada. His research interests encompass international business, strategy development, and new product development, with a current emphasis on the role of networks in entrepreneurial firm growth.

362

International
Business
Review
6,4

that is strategically important or unable to be standardised, successful internationalisation may well require the firm to leverage the skills and resources of other organisations (Hara and Kanai, 1994). This is supported by McDougall *et al.* (1994) and Bell (1995), who highlight the potential impact of network relationships on small firm internationalisation. More specifically, Coviello and Munro (1995) found that the conduct of international marketing activities of small firms was impacted by larger partners in their network. The conclusions of each of these studies call for further research on the role of networks in the internationalisation process of small firms.

The purpose of this research is to further our understanding of how network relationships impact internationalisation patterns and processes. More specifically, this research seeks to understand how network relationships influence the small firm's approach to internationalisation, particularly in terms of foreign market and entry mode selection.

While the primary interest is on small firm processes, the research also focuses on software developers; firms characterised as high technology, knowledge-based, and service-intensive. This sector is similar to those examined by Bell (1995) and Coviello and Munro (1995), and provides an interesting contrast to much of the internationalisation literature which focuses on traditional manufacturing organisations. Examination of high technology firms also allows for a deeper understanding of a global, fast-growing, and pervasive industry which is receiving increased attention in the international business literature (McDougall *et al.*, 1994; Oviatt and McDougall, 1994).

The paper proceeds with a review of the internationalisation process literature, discussed in the context of small firms. This review highlights the need for research in the area, leading to the identification of two research questions. This is then followed by a discussion of the research method and research findings. The paper concludes by offering an empirically-based framework describing the influence of network relationships on the internationalisation process of small software firms, and a discussion of research and managerial implications.

Literature Review

Since Welch and Luostarinen's (Welch and Luostarinen, 1988) comprehensive analysis of the internationalisation concept, a number of useful reviews have assessed and synthesised the general internationalisation process literature (eg Johanson and Vahlne, 1990, 1992; Melin, 1992; Andersen, 1993). Each of these reviews seems to agree that efforts to encapsulate the internationalisation concept in a definitive manner have been inadequate.

If it is accepted that internationalisation is a dynamic concept (Johanson and Vahlne, 1992; Melin, 1992), then the definition of internationalisation offered by Beamish (1990) is perhaps appropriate:

"...the process by which firms both increase their awareness of the direct and indirect influences of international transactions on their future, and establish and conduct transactions with other countries."

This view, like many others, is process-based, and incorporates: (1) the internal dynamics and learning of the firm as it expands internationally, and (2) the "outward" pattern of international investment exemplified by market selection and mode of entry. Beamish's definition also allows for recognition of the fact that firms may begin the internationalisation process through involvement in activities such as foreign sourcing or countertrade, i.e. reflecting an "inward" pattern of internationalisation (Welch and Luostarinen, 1988, 1993; Korhonen *et al.*, 1995).

Efforts to understand the process of internationalisation have been numerous. One area of the extant literature discusses an incremental approach to international market expansion, whereby a series of "stages" of internationalisation reflect the firm's increasing market knowledge and commitment over time. A second area suggests the internationalisation process involves, and is influenced by, the set of connected relationships a firm develops as part of its "network". Both of these perspectives will be discussed in turn, including a review of the small firm research in each area.

Models of Incremental Internationalisation
The notion of a firm expanding to international markets in an incremental, stepwise manner is widely documented in the literature, with Johanson and Vahlne (1977) providing the most commonly cited conceptual and empirical base. Their research on the activities of large Swedish manufacturing firms emphasises managerial learning during the internationalisation process, and shows that a series of "stages" of internationalisation occur in order of increasing commitment and investment in foreign markets. For example, the model offered by Johanson and Vahlne (1977) suggests that initial internationalisation activities are targeted to "psychically close" markets, i.e. markets having similar culture, language, political systems, trade practices, etc. Following initial expansion with low risk, indirect exporting to similar markets, firms improve their foreign market knowledge. Over time and through experience, firms then increase foreign market commitment and expand to more "psychically distant" markets. This in turn enhances market knowledge, leading to further commitment, including equity investment in off-shore manufacturing and sales operations. Overall, the Johanson and Vahlne model illustrates how managerial learning drives internationalisation. At the same time, the model captures manifestations of the process in terms of market selection and the mechanisms used to enter foreign markets.

In addition to the Johanson and Vahlne model, other important research also reports an incremental approach to internationalisation (e.g. Cavusgil, 1984; Czinkota, 1982; Reid, 1981; Bilkey and Tesar, 1977). For example, Cavusgil (1984) empirically identifies five stages (Preinvolvement, Reactive/Opportunistic, Experimental, Active, and Committed Involvement), reflecting differences in the firm's orientation and management attitude to international market expansion. As summarised by Andersen (1993) and Thomas and Araujo (1985), this type of incremental approach is a result of innovation adoption behaviour, whereby the perceptions and beliefs of managers

Network Relationships and the Internationalisation Process

364

influence, and are shaped by, involvement in foreign markets. Like the Johanson and Vahlne model, these studies highlight the role of managerial learning in the internationalisation process.

Models of Incremental Internationalisation and the Small Firm
The general literature discussing incremental internationalisation has led to a number of efforts to validate earlier work across different firm characteristics, including firm size. In a recent review of contemporary empirical research on small firm internationalisation, Coviello and McAuley (1996) identified eight studies which either:

(1) support the traditional view of incremental internationalisation (Hakam *et al.*, 1993; Calof and Viviers, 1995);

(2) confirm a gradual process of internationalisation, but note the prevalence of inward investment preceding outward investment and foreign market entry (Hyvaerinen, 1994);

(3) redefine the traditional perspective by describing different "stages" in the context of firm and market characteristics (Rao and Naidu, 1992);

(4) identify a process of incremental commitment for small firms that may be different to that of larger firms (Lau, 1992);

(5) identify stages of competitive strategy in the small firm internationalisation process, but no linear relationships between these stages and the mechanisms used in internationalisation (Chang and Grub, 1992); or

(6) challenge the traditional view of incremental internationalisation (Lindqvist, 1988; Bell, 1995).

As a result, while some recent small firm findings support the view that firms follow an incremental process of internationalisation in terms of increasing knowledge, commitment, and investment, others do not. This apparent contradiction reflects patterns also found in the large firm literature, where empirical findings both identify and support the incremental approach (see Johanson and Vahlne, 1990; also Luostarinen, 1989; Buckley, 1989), while others challenge it (e.g. Whitelock and Munday, 1993; Millington and Bayliss, 1990; Turnbull, 1987; Sharma and Johanson, 1987).

Each of the studies examined by Coviello and McAuley (1996) provides a contribution in its own right, however the findings of Bell (1995) and Lindqvist (1988) are particularly interesting as they suggest that:

• the pace and pattern of international market growth and choice of entry mode for small firms is influenced by (for example) close relationships with customers (Lindqvist, 1988); and

• interfirm relationships (with clients, suppliers, etc) appear influential in both market selection and mode of entry for small firms (Bell, 1995).

These results are perhaps not surprising, as both Bell (1995) and Lindqvist

(1988) examined high technology industries; industries often characterised by relationships between various organisations for product development and marketing. Also, if the firms examined by Bell (1995) and Lindqvist (1988) consisted of "committed internationalists" (Sullivan and Bauerschmidt, 1990; Bonaccorsi, 1992), or "international new ventures" (McDougall *et al.*, 1994; Oviatt and McDougall, 1994) it might be expected that their international growth patterns would differ from those proposed in the models of incremental internationalisation (McDougall *et al.*, 1994).

The findings of Bell (1995) and Lindqvist (1988) are exploratory in nature and do not examine the influence of network relationships in detail. Nevertheless, their results suggest that while the literature examining incremental internationalisation describes certain patterns related to managerial learning and market entry mechanisms, it may not fully capture the internationalisation process. This is particularly relevant given the foreign market entry process is increasingly recognised to be:

> "...unclear, complex, continuously changing...strategy emerges out of interplay between actors in the foreign market and the firm." (Johanson and Vahlne, 1992)

This *interplay between actors* is manifested in relationships (as identified by Bell, 1995 and Lindqvist, 1988), and has received significant attention in the network literature (e.g. Axelsson and Easton, 1992; Johanson and Vahlne, 1992). This perspective will now be discussed. in the context of the internationalisation process.

Networks and the Internationalisation Process
As defined by Axelsson and Easton (1992), a network involves "sets of two or more connected exchange relationships". Following from this, markets are depicted as systems of social and industrial relationships among, for example, customers, suppliers, competitors, family, and friends. According to the network perspective, the nature of relationships established between various parties will influence strategic decisions, and the network involves resource exchange among its different members (Sharma, 1993). Members of the network value relationships rather than discrete transactions, thus opportunistic behaviour is expected to be controlled and minimised.

In the context of internationalisation, Johanson and Vahlne's (1992) examination of two case studies found foreign market entry to be a gradual process, resulting from interaction between parties, and developing/maintaining relationships over time. This supports Sharma and Johanson (1987), who found that technical consultancy firms operate in networks of connected relationships; relationships which become "bridges to foreign markets", providing firms with the opportunity and motivation to internationalise. Similarly, Johanson and Mattsson (1988) suggest that a firm's success in entering new international markets is more dependent on its position in a

366

International
Business
Review
6,4

network and relationships within current markets, than on market and cultural characteristics.

Overall, the network perspective goes beyond the models of incremental internationalisation by suggesting that a firm's strategy emerges as a pattern of behaviour influenced by a variety of network relationships. As stated by Benito and Welch (1994):

> "...the sometimes erratic character of internationalisation for individual firms appears to be related to the seeming randomness with which opportunities and threats relevant to international activity arise in a company's external environment."

Such opportunities and threats may be presented to the firm by their network relationships. As such, these external contact systems or relationships may drive, facilitate, or inhibit a firm's international market development. Such relationships might also influence the firm's choice of foreign market and entry mode.

Networks and the Small Firm

Much of the small firm network research focuses on general network influences on firm behaviour (e.g. Tjosvold and Weicker, 1993; Dubini and Aldrich, 1991; Larson, 1991; Lorenzoni and Ornati, 1988). As noted previously however, certain studies highlight the potential role of networks in small firm internationalisation (Lindqvist, 1988; McDougall *et al.*, 1994; Bell, 1995).

Other findings also recognise the importance of networks to a small firm (e.g. Hansen *et al.*, 1994; Hara and Kanai, 1994; Coviello and Munro, 1995; Kaufmann, 1995; Korhonen *et al.*, 1995). For example, Korhonen *et al.* (1995) found that over half of Finnish SMEs started their internationalisation process with "inward" foreign operations, largely through the import of physical goods or services. From this, Korhonen *et al.* (1995) conclude that such inward operations allow for international network connections to be established, thus supporting Welch and Luostarinen (1993). Also, Coviello and Munro (1995) found that successful New Zealand-based software firms are actively involved with international networks, and outsource many market development activities to network partners.

Finally, Bonaccorsi's (1992) study of small Italian exporters suggests that "access to external resources" (through for example, buyer–seller relationships) can play an important role in the firm's internationalisation process. This view is also held by Welch (1992), who provides a thorough discussion of the potential use of alliances or cooperative arrangements by small firms in the internationalisation process, concluding that while alliances are "no panacea," they can improve the potential for foreign market penetration by providing access to a network of additional relationships.

Overall, research examining network issues in the context of small firms is increasing. However, none of the above authors identify and examine specific network and relationship influences in any detail, in the context of the internationalisation process. This weakness is particularly evident when considering the causes or drivers of internationalisation, and how the process is manifested in terms of foreign market selection and the mechanisms used for market entry.

Summary and Identification of Research Questions
Empirical research to date shows that the various models of incremental internationalisation provide useful frameworks for analysis of international growth patterns, in terms of a firm's gradual learning and commitment to international markets. Similarly, there is a growing body of literature highlighting the potential influence of network relationships on the internationalisation process. At the same time, while Johanson and Vahlne (1990) suggest that researchers should investigate how internationalisation is related to surrounding processes, and more fully understand the influences on internationalisation strategies, little empirical work has been done in this regard, in the specific context of small firms and networks.

Therefore, the purpose of this research is to empirically examine the internationalisation process of small firms, integrating the incremental or "stage" views of internationalisation with the network perspective. Using the context of the software industry, the research seeks to understand:

(1) how the internationalisation process of small software firms is manifested in their choice of foreign market and mode of entry; and

(2) how network relationships influence the small software firm's choice of foreign market and model of entry.

Method
To most effectively identify and understand detailed international growth patterns and processes, this research used multi-site case study methodology, following the principles of data collection established by Eisenhardt (1989) and Yin (1989). Multiple sources of evidence were used (depth interviews, documents, archival records), and a case study data base was created using four case sites.

The population from which the case sites were selected consists of New Zealand-based software developers. These firms are small by international standards, and have knowledge as a core competency. The industry is active internationally, serving diverse and complex markets from a small domestic base. While the findings of the study are perhaps limited to high technology firms, the choice of a single sector minimises the impact of inter-industry differences (as per Turnbull, 1987; Strandksov, 1986). Further, characteristics of the software industry are similar to other knowledge-based industries competing internationally, and are the same as those examined by Bell (1995) and McDougall *et al.* (1994). Thus, a basis for comparison is provided,

International
Business
Review
6,4

enhancing theory development, and our understanding of the internationalisation patterns and processes of an important business sector.

The case sites were chosen for theoretical rather than statistical reasons, to replicate and extend the emergent theory under examination. Sites were generated based on a number of different characteristics, as suggested by Eisenhardt (1989). For the purposes of this research, the case sites had differing product and market characteristics, and their histories included both success and failure in foreign markets. Individual sample elements were upper-level managers in the company, primarily the Managing Director/Chief Executive, and key informants identified by the Managing Director. These respondents were directly involved in decision-making for internationalisation, and able to provide responses based on personal experience.

Data analysis was designed to identify patterns relevant to international market growth and the influence of network relationships on the case firms. The techniques of pattern-matching and explanation-building developed by Yin (1989) were used. This approach was aided by a variety of analytical tools applied within and across the cases, as suggested by Miles and Huberman (1984). For example, Checklists, Time-Ordered Matrices, and Event Listings were used to identify and chronicle critical events pertaining to growth, product-market and relationship development, and decision-making. As is consistent with qualitative research methods, no attempt was made to operationalise and measure concepts on an a priori basis. Rather, verbatim transcripts were content analysed, then interpreted and coded as a means for labelling dimensions which emerged in the process of data collection. In most instances, direct quotes from case informants were used, as they were believed to best reflect the phenomena under investigation.

Given the historical and longitudinal perspective of the research, all analysis was conducted chronologically as the basic sequence of cause/effect should not be inverted. Further, a major area of the literature base on the internationalisation process focuses on sequential stages, thus chronological analysis was relevant. This approach is also supported by Axelsson and Johanson (1992) and Melin (1992), as appropriate to the study of the internationalisation process and network development. Finally, the processes under examination may be context specific, requiring subjective and interpretive analysis. An inductive approach to the research is therefore warranted, following the relativist view (Hunt, 1991).

Findings and Discussion

To address the research questions developed previously, the international growth patterns of the case firms will be presented, followed by a discussion of the influence of network relationships on the internationalisation process. To begin, the case firm characteristics are briefly summarised.

At time of data collection, each case firm had extensive experience in the international software industry. All four firms were founded between 1978 and 1983, and had experienced significant growth. For example, firm size (at time of data collection) ranged from 25 employees located in one country to 140 employees in four countries. Annual turnover ranged from $2 million to approximately $15 million, and the number of countries served ranged from five to seventeen. The average per annum growth rate for these firms was 83%. Their products ranged from modular applications packages for the financial accounting market, to complex system programming software.

Network
Relationships
and the
International-
isation Process

International Growth Patterns

The international growth patterns of the four case firms are summarised in Fig. 1 (below). This figure captures the internationalisation process in terms of the firm's orientation toward international expansion, the time frame associated with internationalisation, the foreign markets entered, and the modes of entry used.

Three "stages" of international activity are apparent in the case findings. In terms of firm orientation, the small software firms had a largely domestic focus in the initial stage (Year 0–1), but clear intentions to internationalise. The second stage (Year 1–3) is characterised by the small firms becoming actively involved in their first foreign market. Managers also began to seriously evaluate potential market expansion opportunities. Finally, the third stage (beginning at Year 3) is evidenced by each of the four firms showing committed involvement across numerous markets, with international sales dominating their growth.

Interestingly, while certain internationalisation stages are able to be identified, they do not fully match the extant literature. For example, only three stages of evolution are evident, and market expansion was not on a "trial" or "experimental" basis. Rather, the internationalisation process began with management exploring the feasibility of international expansion from the time of firm inception. Thus, Fig. 1 depicts the compressed time frame in which the internationalisation process occurs, with the small software firms commencing operations with a foreign market intention, and being "committed" internationalists within three years. This supports Sullivan and Bauerschmidt (1990) and McDougall *et al.* (1994).

In terms of entry mode, the second stage of Fig. 1 shows that prior to entering their first market, some firms established a product development agreement with a large overseas partner. This in fact occurred for three of the four cases, impacting their future growth patterns in that the agreements provided them with development funding, and led to loose piggy-backing arrangements being established. These relationships quickly evolved to become formal distribution agreements,* in a psychically close market (Australia). While the expansion to close markets supports Johanson and Vahlne (1977) among others, the initial mechanism for internationalisation is different, and the resultant pattern therefore supports Welch and Luostarinen

---

*While one firm attempted direct sales to its first market, it quickly realized it was unable to invest the effort and time required for market development, and due to its limited resource base, established a distributor.

370

Figure 1.
The International Process of
Small Software Firms

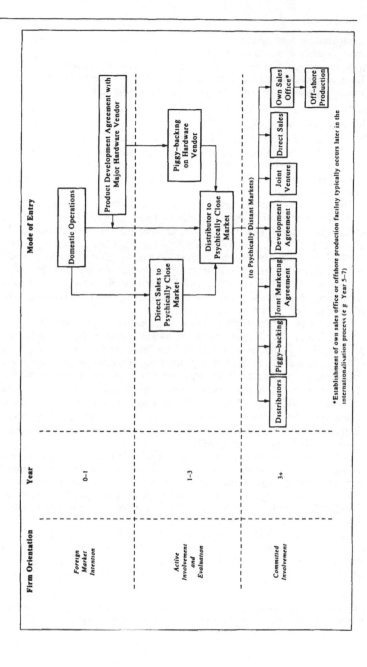

(1993), as well as the findings of Korhonen *et al.* (1995) and Hyvaerinen (1994). Of note, the psychically close market was also physically close, perhaps reflecting the importance of physical proximity for small firms that are geographically distant from potential markets.

The third stage of Fig. 1 highlights that based on their initial experience off-shore, the case firms quickly began to develop more complex relationship structures (cf. Welch and Luostarinen, 1993). They made simultaneous use of multiple entry modes, including distributors, joint marketing and/or development agreements, piggy-backing, and joint ventures. In addition, the markets selected for international expansion in this phase were worldwide and psychically "distant," often reflecting little psychic similarity or physical proximity (e.g. Hong Kong, Spain). These patterns reflect the findings of Bell (1995).

Finally, two firms established a foreign sales office during the internationalisation process, to support sales made through partner subsidiaries or establish regional headquarters in a distant market. This occurred relatively late in the internationalisation process (e.g. Year 5–7), and reflects internalisation of activities in order to better support existing relationships and increase control over marketing activities. Only one firm travelled the length of the internationalisation process as described by Johanson and Vahlne (1977), by attempting to establish an offshore product development facility in the US. As this market was viewed as critical, and management believed their major partner was unable to provide the necessary market access, technology, or capital, a separate organisation was established for introduction of a new product, independent of the partner. The subsidiary was closed within twelve months however, and all software development activities returned to New Zealand.

Overall, if management is expected to show a gradual awareness of, interest in, and involvement with foreign markets, the small software firm behaves differently to those represented by the general models of incremental internationalisation. The case firms began their internationalisation process with the intent to enter foreign markets, and although their first entry was to a psychically and physically close market, other relatively early expansion, was not.

Similarly, if the internationalisation process of small software firms is examined in terms of entry mode, and increased learning and commitment is expected to result in the establishment of host country production, the internationalisation process of small software firms is manifested differently from those patterns generally found in the literature. According to Johanson and Vahlne (1977, 1990) however, such patterns are typical only of firms: (1) with large resources; (2) with experience in other markets with similar conditions; or (3) competing in easily predictable market conditions. None of these parameters fit the small, young, software firm, competing in volatile markets with rapid growth and technological change.

Some of these findings are perhaps to be expected given the target market for these small firms is inevitably beyond New Zealand, and usually, is geographically distant. This, combined with the limited resource base of the

Right margin heading:

Network Relationships and the Internationalisation Process

372

International
Business
Review
6,4

small software firm at early stages of its lifecycle (when internationalisation begins for these firms), would suggest that it would be difficult for such firms to expand international operations on their own. This in fact, was the situation in this research, and thus Oviatt and McDougall (1994), McDougall *et al.* (1994), and Bell (1995) are supported. That is, the small software firms show a pattern of externalising their activities during the internationalisation process, often relying on network relationships for market selection as well as mode of entry. This will now be discussed.

The Influence of Networks on the Internationalisation Process
As seen previously in Fig. 1, the small software firm's internationalisation process is rapid, with the firm using a variety of mechanisms to enter a diverse number of foreign markets in as little as three years. This activity appears to be largely driven by existing network relationships. That is, the rapid and successful growth of the case firms appears to be a result of their involvement in international networks, with major partners often guiding foreign market selection and providing the mechanism for market entry. Thus, network relationships may not only drive internationalisation, but influence the pattern of market investment.

To understand this, critical incident listings were used to describe the pattern of international market development and network relationships in a chronological manner. Table 1 (below) provides a summary of each firm's internationalisation process over time, including information on the sequence of foreign market development, the entry mode used for each market, and how the direct and indirect network relationships influenced each firm's internationalisation process.

Using one firm (FACT) as a representative example from Table 1, it can be seen that FACT's major relationship was with a Japanese multinational (Wang). In this relationship, FACT leveraged the market access provided by Wang, and Wang harnessed FACT's technological capabilities for product development. At a more subtle level, Wang played a significant role in directly or indirectly providing FACT with market development opportunities world-wide. For example, FACT's expansion to Australia was triggered by an informal contact generated indirectly by FACT's product development agreement with Wang.

Following expansion to Australia, FACT pursued the UK market independently of Wang. However, the Wang relationship ultimately impacted FACT's growth patterns in Australia and the UK in that the original distributor relationships in both countries were terminated at the request of Wang, and UK distribution rights were transferred to Wang's subsidiary. Beyond Australia and the UK, Wang offered FACT market access to Hong Kong, Europe, and the Eastern Bloc countries, through Wang's international subsidiaries. Thus, Wang influenced FACT's international market selection and also provided the entry mode.

A different pattern emerges for the US market in that FACT established a

Network
Relationships
and the
International-
isation Process

Foreign Market Entry	CBA	DSR	FACT	MSL
A. Initial Foreign Market Entry	● following successful NZ distribution of product for a US MNC, CBA management was approached by a distributor in Australia (initiated by the US MNC both it and CBA represented) ● Australian distributor signed	● while identifying product and market opportunities, DSR's CEO met a New Zealander managing the Australian subsidiary of a Japanese MNC hardware vendor ● contact led to a joint product development and marketing agreement for Australia	● following establishment of a product development agreement with a Japanese MNC, FACT was approached by a distributor in Australia (referred by a NZ-based industry contact) ● first Australian distributor signed	● sold direct to major customer in Australia
B. Subsequent Market Entries	*All Products* ● Australian distributor grew to include a dealer network across Australia ● Singapore distributor for CBA's own range of products established, initiated by a member of the Australian dealer network ● based on word-of-mouth, CBA was approached by two distributors in the UK, one of which distributed product for the same US MNC represented by CBA in NZ and Australia	*Product 1* ● Australian partner helped established a distributor relationship with the Japanese MNC's US subsidiary ● DSR piggy-backed on Japanese MNC's distribution network to Canada, Europe, and the UK	*All Products* ● interested UK distributor identified and signed ● Australian sales office established ● second Australian distributor signed; initiated through previous business contacts	*Product 1* ● established agent in Australia through personal contact of MSL's CEO; agency agreement terminated after 1 year ● selected a distributor in US (through active search) but distributor declared bankruptcy; MSL on verge of insolvency

Table 1.
Market Selection and Mode of Entry Patterns for the Four Case Firms (Presented Chronologically)

continued overleaf

374

Table 1.
Continued

Foreign Market Entry	CBA	DSR	FACT	MSL
	• one UK firm signed for distribution and product enhancement; informal relationship established with the other firm (the distributor for the US MNC) • Malaysian distributor established, initiated through the family and business contacts of a member of the NZ dealer network.	*Product 2* • initially sold direct to Australia; success led to agreements with five agents and one distributor • Singapore distributor established, initiated through a personal contact of the DSR Product Manager • CEO and management team used industry contacts to identify two Scandinavian hardware manufacturers to act as distributors for Europe • joint marketing and development agreement also established with the two Scandinavian firms	• entered Hong Kong by piggy-backing on Japanese MNC's distributor • used Japanese MNC's contacts to establish US sales office (independent of the Japanese firm) • at Japanese MNC's direction, terminated first Australian distributor relationship, acquired second Australian distributor, and transferred UK distribution rights to Japanese MNC's UK subsidiary • entered Europe through Japanese MNC's German subsidiary, connected to subsidiaries in Holland, Belgium, Austria, and Poland • withdrew from the US	*Product 2* • approached several international hardware vendors for product development support, including a Japanese MNC • contacted by NZ subsidiary of same Japanese firm, to established a product development agreement with the Japanese firm's Australian subsidiary, development agreement evolved to include marketing activities • entered Malaysia and Spain by piggy-backing on sales of the Japanese MNC's Australian subsidiary • same Japanese MNC recommended an independent distributor for Japan; Japanese distributor signed • long-term product development agreement established with original Japanese MNC partner, for world markets

375

Network
Relationships
and the
International-
isation Process

Foreign Market Entry	CBA	DSR	FACT	MSL
		Product 3 • CEO and management team used industry contacts and advice from personal contact at Japanese MNC partner to establish distributors in Singapore, Hong Kong, Canada, and the US *Product 4* • UK distributor established, initiated through DSR's Product Manager and his industry	• Japanese MNC experienced financial difficulties • Japanese distributor established (independent of the Japanese MNC), initiated by one of the distributor's NZ-born employees • Indonesian distributor established, initiated by a major competitor of the initial Japanese MNC partner • reentered US with US venture capital, establishing a US-based marketing operation, independent of initial Japanese MNC partner	

¹ Australian distributor became a joint venture in Year 3, and then a wholly-owned sales subsidiary in Year 7.

Table 1.
Continued

376

International
Business
Review
6,4

local sales office independent of Wang's subsidiary network. Nevertheless, the FACT office relied informally on Wang for market intelligence and support.

Of all the markets served by FACT, only Japan and Indonesia were entered through contacts outside the Wang network. For example, the Japanese relationship was initiated through previously established personal contacts (a New Zealander working for the Japanese firm). Entry to Indonesia resulted from an approach by another well-established hardware vendor: Compaq, a competitor to Wang. Thus, additional sets of network relationships were introduced to FACT.

Overall, FACT's internationalisation process was driven and shaped by a complex set of network relationships, influenced by one large international partner. As commented by the General Manager:

> "...you congregate around a particular honey pot, and in the past it was called Wang. So, we buzz around the Wang pot, and they [potential partners] buzz around, and Wang may put you in contact or you may bump into each other."

In a pattern similar to FACT, the other case firms were also linked to extensive, established international networks at a very early stage of their life cycle. This presented the small software firms with new market opportunities and established organisations as potential partners, thus accelerating and shaping their internationalisation efforts. More specifically, each firm's choice of foreign market and entry mode was clearly influenced by their early partner(s) and resultant network relationships. Through network contacts, all four case firms were well-established offshore within three years of company formation, and actively looking to further their international expansion through development of additional relationships. This supports Johanson and Vahlne's more recent views, recognising the influence of networks and multiple market relationships in the internationalisation process.

Of note, the early partners of these small software firms tended to be large, internationally-established hardware vendors. As stated by FACT's General Manager, small software firms are undercapitalised and created on the efforts and strengths of only two or three people. Thus,

> "...you have to be in some way associated with a hardware partner, or a substantial company."

In the case of MSL, a product development relationship was critical to the company's survival, and the Managing Director believed the only viable option for international growth was to develop a relationship with an overseas partner. As he commented:

> "...if you have got a piece of the jigsaw they want, then you know its going to go very well because you're not fighting to sell your product in isolation."

Therefore, the findings of this study support Welch and Luostarinen (1993) and Korhonen *et al.* (1995) in that the initial product development relationship established with hardware vendors provided the catalyst and resources for international growth. That is, the "inward" relationship facilitated "outward" expansion.

This behaviour also supports the findings of McDougall *et al.* (1994) in that the small software firms externalised certain activities in order to minimise their financial and market risk during international expansion. Thus, network relationships facilitate international growth. However, while network relationships enhanced the internationalisation activities of all four case firms, they also constrained the pursuit of other opportunities. Referring back to the FACT example, market access and international reputation was strongly associated with Wang. Thus, when Wang suffered financial difficulties in the late 1980s, FACT found it necessary to establish separate, independent relationships with parties outside the Wang network.

The case firms also experienced a number of difficulties associated with internationalising through a large firm, primarily related to market and product planning. For example, the Managing Director of MSL noted there was a degree of vagueness in the MSL-Fujitsu relationship:

> "...in some ways we seem to be extremely lucky that we are part of Fujitsu's dream for the future, and they're feeding us a few bits and pieces of what that is [but] we don't actually have a blue-print of what we are going to be doing in five years time...there's just no detail."

These constraints and the associated fears of total dependence* on a major partner contributed to three of the firms developing new products for diversified markets, or establishing separate support/service facilities. For example, DSR's original product was strongly associated with their partner's brand name in international markets, and the initial products for FACT and MSL were developed specifically for their partner's hardware platform. Therefore, DSR began to develop products outside their partner's area of expertise, and FACT and MSL developed software that was compatible with other competitive systems. All three firms also established separate service and support facilities to decrease reliance on their partners for customer contact and support.

The case findings also reveal that as each firm experienced market success, it began to desire greater control in network relationships (i.e. more autonomy in its decision-making with respect to product and relationship development, market selection, and mode of entry). In two of the cases (CBA and FACT), technological and market success allowed the New Zealand-based firm to evolve over time to become the central firm in its network. DSR also increased in strength and negotiating influence within its network. For these three firms,

Network
Relationships
and the
International-
isation Process

---

*"Dependence" was the term used by informants to reflect the percentage of sales attributed to a network partner.

International Entrepreneurship

378

International
Business
Review
6,4

the case findings suggest that managerial learning occurred, whereby market experience and success over time led to increased knowledge about both markets and managing relationships. This in turn led to increased commitment to foreign market development, and further learning. This pattern supports Johanson and Vahlne (1977, 1990).

Finally, as the three firms became more successful in international markets, they caught the attention of major organisations in their industry areas. In late 1990, FACT was acquired by a Canadian multinational outside their formal network, but part of a wider industry network. DSR was acquired in 1991 by a US company connected through product development to their formal network. In 1993, CBA was also acquired by a US firm which was part of CBA's informal industry network, and owned by a New Zealander familiar with the local market. Each of these New Zealand firms had felt increasingly vulnerable to acquisition due to their market success, and in fact, *chose* their new parent through existing network relationships rather than risk a buy-out by existing partners (e.g. FACT and DSR), or firms that were unknown to them (e.g. CBA). For these three firms, it is apparent that the impact of network relationships went beyond the internationalisation process per se, to affect their ownership structure (and perhaps, future internationalisation efforts).

In the case of MSL, the fourth firm, diversification efforts were made to minimise the risk in being associated solely with one large firm, as MSL's growth was limited to that of its partner. Also, the partner restricted MSL's direct access to existing and potential customers. These diversification efforts (into service and support areas) were halted by the partner however, and MSL remained positioned as a "development arm" for the partner's network. This situation continued until 1993, when the "long-term" product development agreement was completed, and the formal relationship between the two parties was terminated, in a decision made by the larger partner. This had a severe effect on MSL, causing it to downsize to half its employee base, and seek alternative product development opportunities and relationships.

Overall, the case findings indicate that the internationalisation decisions and growth patterns of small software firms, particularly with respect to initial and subsequent market selection and mode of entry, are very much shaped by their network of formal and informal relationships. Thus, both Johanson and Vahlne (1992) and Johanson and Mattsson (1988) are supported, as are Benito and Welch (1994) who suggest that network development is one of a number of explanatory factors in the "ability and preparedness of a company to expand it's foreign market servicing commitments". Further, the small firm empirical findings of Lindqvist (1988), Bonaccorsi (1992), Hansen *et al.* (1994), Bell (1995), and Kaufmann (1995) are also supported.

Conclusions

The general purpose of this research was to extend our understanding of the impact of network relationships on the internationalisation patterns and processes of small firms, with particular interest in the influence of network relationships on the small firm's approach to foreign market selection and mode of entry. To achieve this, the international growth patterns of four small software firms were empirically assessed relative to their network relationships. Within the context of knowledge-based, non-manufacturing software developers, the findings suggest that our understanding of the internationalisation process for small firms, at least small software firms, can be enhanced by integrating the models of incremental internationalisation with the network perspective. The specific findings of this study are elaborated on below.

To begin, the internationalisation process of small knowledge-based software firms differs from those typically discussed in the literature in that:

- it is very rapid, with firms becoming established and committed internationalists in as little as three years;

- it is characterised by only three "stages," beginning with foreign market intention, and excluding extensive foreign market trial, experimentation, or evaluation; and

- it is characterised by the small firms making simultaneous use of multiple and different modes of entry; mechanisms which are part of a larger firm's international network.

These findings are perhaps explained by the fact that the case firms were "international new ventures" (cf. Oviatt and McDougall, 1994), competing in a dynamic global market characterised by rapid market change and product obsolescence. Thus, these findings support McDougall *et al.* (1994) and Bell (1995).

Also, the case findings indicate that small software firms show a pattern of externalising their international market development activities through investment in network relationships. This is perhaps not surprising given the nature of the software industry and the need for small, resource-constrained, technically-oriented firms to leverage the complementary capabilities of other organisations (Hara and Kanai, 1994; McDougall *et al.*, 1994; Oviatt and McDougall, 1994). As seen in this study, network relationships can drive market expansion and development activities, including choice of market and entry mode. In addition, they can both facilitate and inhibit product development and market diversification activities.

Overall, this research has shown that we are better able to understand the internationalisation process of small firms by expanding our research focus to integrate the models of incremental internationalisation with the network perspective. Based on these findings, Fig. 1 (describing the basic internationalisation process of the small software firm) is extended to include the role and influence of networks (Fig. 2 below). That is, the internationalisation process of small software firms relative to surrounding network processes is superimposed on the three "stages" of internationalisation previously discussed.

This framework also reflects how the characteristics of the small software firm change as the firm moves through the internationalisation process.

Network
Relationships
and the
Internationalisation Process

380

International
Business
Review
6,4

Figure 2.
Growth Patterns, Network
Influences and Firm
Charactersitics through the
Internationalisation Process
of Small Software Firms

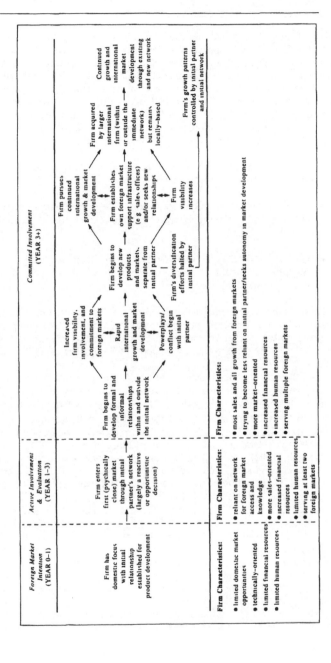

For these firms, the pattern of internationalisation is depicted as evolving in the following manner:

(1) the small firm commences operations with the intent to internationalise;

(2) an initial relationship with a larger firm is developed in the first year of the small firm's lifecycle, often in an opportunistic or reactive manner, and usually for the purposes of product development. This relationship also provides a mode of entry to a psychically close market;

(3) over time, a network of formal and informal contacts is developed, usually facilitated by the small firm's initial relationship. This network provides market knowledge and potential access/mode of entry to markets around the world. Network relationships facilitate international market development and sales growth, with the small firm entering at least two foreign markets in as little as three years;

(4) this growth then leads to increased visibility for the small firm in international markets, as well as an increase in both financial and human resource capabilities. Managerial experience in international markets continues to increase, leading to greater knowledge and confidence in market and relationship decisions;

(5) increased experience with network relationships, combined with strong market performance, leads to the small firm desiring increased autonomy and control over their market development activities. At this point, one of two patterns may emerge:

• the small firm may begin to: (1) diversify from its core product areas, (2) proactively pursue new markets, and/or (3) establish its own sales and marketing offices overseas (all independent from existing network partners). The small firm may also actively pursue the development of new network relationships, or such relationships may emerge from product and market development activities. With the increased market visibility, the small firm may become a prime candidate for acquisition by another organisation, often a larger firm within or peripheral to the small firm's main network (exemplified by the FACT, DSR, and CBA, and consistent with Bell, 1995). This exposes the small firm to additional sets of network relationships and further growth opportunities;

OR

• although the small firm may desired increased autonomy from initial network relationships, the major network partner may have enough control over the small firm (e.g. financial control), to limit its product and market diversification opportunities (as in the case of MSL). Thus, the

Network Relationships and the Internationalisation Process

382

International
Business
Review
6,4

major partner continues to influence the small firm's internationalisation process, and growth is restricted to the initial set of network relationships.

The contribution of this framework is that it presents the internationalisation process in the context of: (1) the stages of internationalisation evident in these small software firms, (2) their network relationships. and (3) their firm characteristics over time. By superimposing the three identified stages of internationalisation onto the pattern of network influence, this framework complements the earlier description of the internationalisation process (Fig. 1), and provides an understanding of how a firm's international growth patterns relate to surrounding network processes.

This integration is of particular importance given the network perspective introduces a "more multilateral element" to the rather unilateral process found in the traditional models of incremental internationalisation (Johanson and Vahlne, 1990). On one hand, the "stages" view suggests an evolution to internationalisation based on cognitive learning and competency development which increases, through experience, over time. That is, more of an internally-driven approach to internationalisation in which firms expand their market scope and entry methods as managers gain confidence and learn from personal experience. On the other hand, the network perspective shows that international market development activities emerge from, and are shaped by, an external web of formal and informal relationships. From this network-driven behaviour, cognitive development also occurs, with learning focused on: (1) the markets entered, (2) the modes of entry used, and (3) the relationships developed during the process of internationalisation. Therefore, both perspectives to internationalisation encompass cognitive processes. Integration of these perspectives brings the internally and externally-driven views together, allowing a richer understanding of both the drivers of internationalisation, and the emergent patterns of international market development activities.

Research Implications
This research was context specific in that it examined the internationalisation patterns and processes of small software firms. Such firms tend to be owned and managed by technical specialists who develop and market software; an offering more intangible than traditional manufactured goods, and requiring significant support and service to add value. At a market level, the ease with which software can be distributed electronically may affect both foreign market selection and mode of entry decisions. This is compounded by the fact that development and marketing agreements between hardware vendors and software developers is an industry norm, thus the industry is characterised by interfirm cooperation. Finally, the small software firms examined in this study are likely to be resource constrained, and serving a small domestic market. This may contribute to (1) outsourcing and leveraging the capabilities of other firms, and (2) managerial motivation to pursue international markets to sustain

383

Network
Relationships
and the
International-
isation Process

firm growth. Each of these factors may influence both the pattern and rate of internationalisation.

Such contextual factors need to be considered when reviewing the results of this study, and it is important to recognise that while theory development specific to high technology firms is possible, the findings may not be generalisable to a wider population. Therefore, it is suggested that future research extend this investigation to other industrial contexts, including small firms which are:

- low technology and knowledge-based;

- low technology and manufacturing-based; or

- high technology and manufacturing-based.

Also, given the small software firms studied in this research may have been influenced by rapid industry growth, the findings of this study should be compared with the internationalisation patterns of newer software firms; firms which began the process of internationalisation in a maturing rather than new industry.

Future research should also incorporate the perspectives of multiple players in the network rather than just that of a single firm. This would yield richer insights into the shift of positions within a network of relationships over time. Network analysis may also be used to more fully examine the impact of specific types of network relationships on foreign market selection, the evolution of power and control in networks, and the specific effect of network relationships on the rate and success of international growth.

In terms of method, the use of case research provides a richness and depth of understanding to the internationalisation process which is not possible with survey data. To enhance the qualitative approach in future, it is suggested that in-depth, longitudinal, "in-process" methods be applied (cf. Benito and Welch, 1994).

Managerial Implications
From a practical viewpoint, the findings of this research suggest that managers of small software firms need a better understanding of the impact of network relationships on their internationalisation activities, and the potential for such relationships to provide entry to foreign markets. Further, managers should be aware of the speed at which internationalisation can occur through network relationships, and that network partners may govern both market selection and mode of entry.

Given the apparent reliance on network relationships for international growth, more attention should be paid to how and with whom relationships are established, and what network management skills are required over time. Related to this, managers must understand the benefits and risks associated with externalising activities to network partners. This is important since

384

International
Business
Review
6,4

managers of small software firms tend to sacrifice some managerial control for market access, potentially weakening their position in a relationship.

Management of established relationships also warrants more attention, particularly when larger partners tend to take control over the activities of smaller firms. Issues related to managing relationships with partners operating in different cultures must also be considered, as well as how best to manage multiple, complex relationship structures. Finally, it is important that managers continue to successfully position their firms such that they have a wide array of relationship options open to them. Their existing networks as well as their ability to establish new network relationships should be managed as a key competitive capability.

Acknowledgements — The authors gratefully acknowledge the constructive comments of Rod Brodie and two anonymous IBR reviewers, on earlier versions of this paper.

References

Andersen, O. (1993) On the internationalisation process of firms: a critical analysis. *Journal of International Business Studies* **24**(2), 209–231.

Axelsson, B. and Easton, G. (Eds.) (1992) *Industrial Networks: A New View of Reality*. Routledge, London.

Axelsson, B. and Johanson, J. (1992) Foreign market entry—the Textbook vs the Network View. In *Industrial Networks: A New View of Reality*, eds. B. Axelsson and G. Easton, pp. 218–234. Routledge, London.

Beamish, P.W. (1990) The internationalisation process for smaller Ontario firms: a research agenda. In *Research in Global Strategic Management — International Business Research for the Twenty-First Century: Canada's New Research Agenda*, ed. A. M. Rugman, pp. 77–92. JAI Press, Greenwich.

Bell, J. (1995) The internationalisation of small computer software firms—a further challenge to "stage" theories. *European Journal of Marketing* **29**(8), 60–75.

Benito, G. R. G. and Welch, L. S. (1994) Foreign market servicing: beyond choice of entry mode. *Journal of International Marketing* **2**(2), 7–27.

Bilkey, W. J. and Tesar, G. (1977) The export behaviour of smaller-sized Wisconsin manufacturing firms. *Journal of International Business Studies* **8**, 93–98.

Bonaccorsi, A. (1992) On the relationship between firm size and export intensity. *Journal of International Business Studies* **4**(4), 605–635.

Buckley, P. J. (1989) Foreign direct investment by small and medium-sized enterprises: the theoretical background. *Small Business Economics* **1**, 89–100.

Calof, J. C. and Viviers, W. (1995) Internationalisation behaviour of small- and medium-sized South African enterprises. *Journal of Small Business Management* **33**(4), 71–79.

Cavusgil, S. T. (1984) Differences among exporting firms based on their degree of internationalization. *Journal of Business Research* **12**, 195–208.

Chang, T. L. and Grub, P. D. (1992) Competitive strategies of Taiwanese PC firms in their internationalisation process. *Journal of Global Marketing* **6**(3), 5–27.

Coviello, N. E. and McAuley, N. A. (1996) Internationalisation processes and the smaller firm: a review of contemporary research. Working Paper, Faculty of Management, University of Calgary.

Coviello, N. E. and Munro, H. J. (1995) Growing the entrepreneurial firm: networking for international market development. *European Journal of Marketing* **29**(7), 49–61.

Czinkota, M. R. (1982) *Export Development Strategies: US Promotion Policies*. Praeger, New York.

Dubini, P. and Aldrich, H. (1991) Personal and extended networks are central to the entrepreneurial process. *Journal of Business Venturing* **6**, 306–313.

Eisenhardt, K. M. (1989) Building theories from case study research. *Academy of Management Review* **14**(4), 532–550.

Erramilli, M. K. and D'Souza, D. E. (1993) Venturing into foreign markets: the case of the small service firm. *Entrepreneurship Theory and Practice*, Summer, 29–41.

Hakam, A. N., Lau, G. T., and Kong, S. B. (1993) The export behaviour of firms in Singapore: an application of the stage of internationalisation model. *Asia Pacific Journal of Marketing and Logistics*, Summer, 1–15.

Hansen, N., Gillespie, K. and Gencturk, E. (1994) SME's and export involvement: market responsiveness, technology, and alliances. *Journal of Global Marketing* **7**(4), 7–27.

Hara, G. and Kanai, T. (1994) Entrepreneurial networks across oceans to promote international strategic alliances for small businesses. *Journal of Business Venturing* **9**, 489–507.

Hunt, S. D. (1991) *Modern Marketing Theory: Critical Issues in the Philosophy of Marketing*. Southwestern Publishing Company, Cinncinnati.

Hyvaerinen, L. (1994) Internationalisation of Finnish SMEs: commitment, internationalisation paths and innovation. In *Internationalisation, Networks, and Strategy*, ed. J. M. Veciana, pp. 76–100. Ashgate Publishing Ltd, Aldershot.

Johanson, J. and Mattsson, L.-G. (1988) Internationalization in industrial systems–a network approach. In *Strategies in Global Competition*, eds N. Hood and J.-E. Vahlne, pp. 287–314. Croom Helm, London.

Johanson, J. and Vahlne, J.-E. (1977) The internationalization process of the firm—a model of knowledge development and increasing foreign market commitment. *Journal of International Business Studies*, Spring/Summer, 23–32.

Johanson, J. and Vahlne, J.-E. (1990) The mechanism of internationalization. *International Marketing Review* **7**(4), 11–24.

Johanson, J. and Vahlne, J.-E. (1992) Management of foreign market entry. *Scandinavian International Business Review* **1**(3), 9–27.

Kaufmann, F. (1995) Internationalization via co-operation: strategies of SME. *International Small Business Journal* **13**(2), 27–33.

Korhonen, H., Luostarinen, R. and Welch, L. (1995) *Internationalisation of SMEs: Inward–Outward Patterns and Government Policy*. Working Paper 7/1995, Department of Marketing/ The Centre for International Management and Commerce, University of Western Sydney, Nepean.

Larson, A. (1991) Partner networks: leveraging external ties to improve entrepreneurial performance. *Journal of Business Venturing* **6**, 173–188.

Lau, H. F. (1992) Internationalisation, internalisation, or a new theory for small, low technology multinational enterprise. *European Journal of Marketing* **26**(10), 17–31.

Lindqvist, M. (1988) *Internationalization of Small Technology-Based Firms: Three Illustrative Case Studies on Swedish Firms*. Stockholm School of Economics Research Paper 88/15.

Lorenzoni, G. and Ornati, O. A. (1988) Constellations of firms and new ventures. *Journal of Business Venturing* **3**, 41–57.

Luostarinen, R. (1989) *Internationalisation of the Firm* (first published 1979). Acta Academiae Oeconomicae Helsingiensis, Series A:30, Helsinki.

McDougall, P. P., Shane, S. and Oviatt, B. M. (1994) Explaining the formation of international new ventures: the limits of theories from international business research. *Journal of Business Venturing* **9**, 469–487.

Melin, L. (1992) Internationalization as a strategy process. *Strategic Management Journal* **13**, 99–118.

Miles, M. B. and Huberman, A. M. (1984) *Qualitative Data Analysis: A Sourcebook of New Methods*. Sage Publications Ltd, Beverly Hills.

Millington, A. I. and Bayliss, B. T. (1990) The process of internationalisation: UK companies in the EC. *Management International Review* **30**(2), 151–161

O'Farrell, P. N. and Hitchins, P. W. N. (1988) Alternative theories of small firm growth: a critical review. *Environment and Planning* **20**, 365–382

Network Relationships and the Internationalisation Process

386

International
Business
Review
6,4

Oviatt, B. M. and McDougall, P. P. (1994) Toward a theory of international new ventures. *Journal of International Business Studies* **25**(1), 45–64.

Rao, T. R. and Naidu, G. M. (1992) Are the stages of internationalisation empirically supportable?. *Journal of Global Marketing* **6**(1-2), 147–170.

Reid, S. D. (1981) The Decision-maker and export entry and expansion. *Journal of International Business Studies*, Fall, 101–112.

Sharma, D. (1993) Introduction: industrial networks in marketing. In *Advances in International Marketing*, eds S. T. Cavusgil and D. Sharma, Vol. 5, pp. 1–9. JAI Press, Greenwich.

Sharma, D. D. and Johanson, J. (1987) Technical consultancy in internationalisation. *International Marketing Review*, Winter, 20–29.

Strandksov, J. (1986) *Toward a New Approach of Studying the Internationalization Process of Firms*. WP 4/1986, Copenhagen School of Economics and Business Administration.

Sullivan, D. and Bauerschmidt, A. (1990) Incremental internationalization: a test of Johanson and Vahlne's thesis. *Management International Review* **30**, 19–30.

Thomas, M. J. and Araujo, L. (1985) Theories of export behaviour: a critical analysis. *European Journal of Marketing* **19**(2), 42–52.

Tjosvold, D. and Weicker, D. (1993) Cooperative and competitive networking by entrepreneurs: a critical incident study. *Journal of Small Business Management* **31**(1), 11–21.

Turnbull, P. W. (1987) A challenge to the stages theory of the internationalization process. In *Managing Export Entry and Expansion*, eds P. J. Rosson and S. D. Reid, pp. 21–40. Praeger, New York.

Welch, L. S. (1992) The use of alliances by small firms in achieving internationalisation. *Scandinavian International Business Review* **1**(2), 21–37.

Welch, L. S. and Luostarinen, R. (1988) Internationalisation: evolution of a concept. *Journal of General Management* **14**(2), 34–55.

Welch, L. S. and Luostarinen, R. (1993) Inward–outward connections in internationalisation. *Journal of International Marketing* **1**(1), 46–58.

Whitelock, J. and Munday, P. (1993) Internationalisation of the firm: two cases in the indusrial explosives industry. *Journal of International Marketing* **1**(4), 19–30.

Yin, R. K. (1989) *Case Study Research: Design and Methods*, Sage Publications Ltd, Beverly Hills.

Received January 1995
Revised February 1996

[21]

Journal of International Entrepreneurship 1, 83–101, 2003
© 2003 Kluwer Academic Publishers. Manufactured in The Netherlands.

Business Relationship Learning and Commitment in the Internationalization Process

JAN JOHANSON
Uppsala University, Mid Sweden University, and Mälardalen University, P.O. Box 513, SE-75120, Uppsala, Sweden

JAN-ERIK VAHLNE*
Göteborg University, P.O. Box 610, SE-40530, Gothenburg, Sweden

Abstract. This paper is based on a case study of an international venture and on the observations reported by a number of researchers that the received models of the internationalization process of the firm do not capture some important phenomena in the modern international business world. As several researchers argue that networks play an important role in the early internationalization the paper outlines a network model of the internationalization process of the firm. It combines the experiential learning–commitment interplay as the driving mechanism from the old internationalization process model with a similar experiential learning–commitment mechanism focusing on business network relationships. In the resulting model we can see firms learning in relationships, which enables them to enter new country markets in which they can develop new relationships which give them a platform for entering other country markets.

Keywords: Internationalization process, relationship, learning, commitment

A need for new models of internationalization

There seems to be a need for models that can capture the early phase of internationalization better than received models. This is an observation, which has been made by a number of researchers and reflects a general agreement among both businessmen and academics that global competition and accelerating technological development now are forcing firms to internationalize more rapidly than some decades ago. The old models of incremental internationalization are no longer valid (Bilkey and Teasar, 1977; Johanson and Vahlne, 1977; Cavusgil, 1980; Davidson, 1980, Luostarinen, 1980; Welch and Luostarinen, 1988). Consequently, there is a need for new models of internationalization, it has been argued in a number of studies. Several, partially connected, streams of research seem to have come to this conclusion. One stream studies international new ventures or born globals (Oviatt and MacDougall, 1994; Madsen and Servais, 1997), another focuses on high technology based firms (Autio et al., 2000) and still another on firms in service industries (Coviello and Munro, 1997; Majkgård and Sharma, 1998), and one, finally, on small business firms (Chetty and Blankenburg Holm, 2000). A common

*Corresponding author: Email: jan-erik.vahlne@handels.gu.se. Tel.: 46317735615

feature of much of this research is that it places attention on networks and network relationships when trying to understand and explain the rapid internationalization of the firms (Oviatt and McDougall, 1994; Bell, 1995; Coviello and Munro, 1997; Chetty and Blankenburg Holm, 2000). In addition, the old models of the internationalization process of the firm have also been criticized more generally in a number of articles (Benito and Gripsrud, 1992; Andersen, 1993; Petersen and Pedersen, 1997; Forsgren, 2002).

However, a number of studies during the last decades have supported ideas and concepts from some of the behavioral models of internationalization. Thus, it seems that experiential learning has become a critical concept in internationalization research (Kogut and Singh, 1988; Erramilli, 1991; Chang, 1995; Barkema et al., 1996; Eriksson et al., 1997; Delios and Beamish, 2000; Luo and Peng, 2001). An interesting finding of some of these studies is that performance is closely related to experiential learning (Li, 1995; Barkema et al., 1996; Luo, 1999).

It seems that we have a situation where old models of internationalization processes are still applied quite fruitfully at the same time as a number of studies have suggested that there is a need for new and network-based models of internationalization. We think that it might be worthwhile to reconcile and even integrate the two approaches. Admittedly, the two types of studies focus on different problems and there are often difficult conceptual problems associated with integrating different models. In this paper, however, we try to take a step toward a common conceptual approach to the two. A strong reason is that we have an interest in both network models and process models (Johanson and Vahlne, 1977, 1990; Johanson and Mattsson, 1988). Another reason is that we believe that experiential learning can have a strong role in an integrated model (Autio et al., 2000). Similarly, Madsen and Servais (1997) found in their study of born globals that they can fruitfully be understood as evolutionary processes with a strong element of learning and Chen's (forthcoming) study of international network building of Taiwanese firms is also an example of an evolutionary process.

The objective of this paper is to outline a business network model of the internationalization process. As a first step we present a case of what could be labelled a born global or an international entrepreneurship. This is meant as an empirical illustration of the problem we are trying to conceptualize. After that the paper specifies some basic features of the internationalization process model. We use the so-called U-model (Uppsala model), which has some advantages in the present context since it does not refer to any particular type of firm (Andersen, 1993; Johanson and Vahlne, 1977). Based on these features and findings from business network research we outline the business network model of the internationalization process. We conclude the paper by discussing some features of the model.

NMCT—Internationalization

Nordic Management of Clinical Trials AB (NMCT) was started in December 1999 by a small group of people, including Professor Lars Sjöström, Sahlgrenska

University Hospital and Göteborg University, Chairman of NMCT, and Marcus Käppi (MK), President. On behalf of pharmaceutical companies, NMCT performs large-scale clinical studies on drugs according to specifications agreed upon with the client. These should be consistent with regulations prescribed by authorities such as the Federal Drug Administration (FDA) in the United States and the corresponding European Agency for the Evaluation of Medical Products (EMEA) in Europe. NMCT has been growing rapidly and the turnover in 2001 was SEK 85 million. The growth has been possible without the use of external capital. This is the story about NMCT's internationalization as told by the President of NMCT, MK.

Professor Sjöström is heading the Department of Body Composition and Metabolism at the Sahlgrenska University Hospital. Professor Sjöström is an international authority on obesity and overweight. Thanks to his reputation and connections, the Department received grants to perform large research projects on risk changes in association with intentional weight loss, the so-called SOS project (Swedish Obese Subjects). Such studies require cooperation with hundreds of health care centres involving thousands of patients. Large numbers of data are generated, transmitted, and analysed. MK was hired to manage the day-to-day operations but came in effect to be also involved in designing ITC-systems for the department in order to speed up and improve the quality of the whole process. One of the lessons learned was that it is important to integrate the two technologies involved—information and medicine. Up to the mid-1990s there was only one customer: the Department itself. But the funding Professor Sjöström generated, permitted constant efforts to be made in improving on the ITC-system and its applications and gradually more and more functions were performed by and via the system in performing empirical research.

In the summer of 1996 discussions started with the Swiss pharmaceutical company Hoffman-La Roche about a large clinical trial on "Xenical in the Prevention of Diabetes in Obese Subjects," called the XENDOS-study. A deal was struck between Roche and Department of Body Composition and Metabolism in July 1997 and the "protocol," the detailed design of the features of the study, was decided upon. The trial was to start in August 1997, and ended in 2002. The fact that the department was asked to run the XENDOS-study was probably due to the track record created through the SOS project. MK was the technical project leader of a team with two more employees and six to seven consultants developing the ITC-system to manage the XENDOS trial. "We were sitting in the basement, working intensively. I made 600 hours overtime September through December and got 'a mousearm'. We had fun!" The trial technologies have been reported (Torgerson et al., 2001) and the results of the study as such have recently been submitted for publication. Some core design principles for the study was that "centralized patient recruitment" and "centralized scheduling of patients and staff" at the collaborating medical departments was to be applied. "The information system was designed to supervise and fine-tune the patient flow to meet the desired inclusion goals." (Torgerson et al., 2001). Also, staff optimization was performed minute-by-minute via the information system. By means of a mass media campaign in 50 Swedish newspapers more than

20,000 applicants were obtained. Of these, 8720 were selected for screening and finally, 3305 patients were included in the study. The screening procedures were accomplished in 4 months' time, which was extremely fast. All in all, some 200,000 events were scheduled in the computer-assisted process and millions of data were stored (Torgerson et al., 2001). The authors claim that thanks to the ITC-system developed, the inclusion rate achieved in a short time frame is "several times faster than ever achieved before in a multicenter clinical trial on obesity" (Torgerson et al., 2001). Initially, some participating medical departments found the scheduling of patients and staff too strict and tayloristic but, as time went by, all participating centers found the scheduling system convenient and labor-saving.

After the process described above MK "suffered from lack of challenges" and thought about leaving the Department. He talked to Professor Sjöström and suggested that they would start a company to commercialize the systems and their applications. As Professor Sjöström was aware of the interest of the Swedish subsidiary of Hoffman-La Roche to have a clinical study performed on Xenical to study potential secondary effects from this drug, he reacted positively on MK's suggestion. Another circumstance for setting up a company was that the Swedish government authorities (as in several other countries) are pushing for the so-called third duty of the universities, that is, in addition to education and research, universities and their employees should try to commercialize ideas created within the academic world. A final circumstance favoring the formation of a company is a special law in Sweden called "The Academic Exemption." This law gives university teachers themselves the exclusive right to their ideas and inventions. These three circumstances in combination made it possible to create NMCT in December 1999. The company has the status of "Knowledge company" at Göteborg University, but the university is not a joint owner.

NMCT was growing rapidly and towards the end of 2001 it had performed several large clinical studies within Prof. Sjöström's area of specialization—obesity and the metabolic syndrome. The NMCT technologies, which can in fact be used in any medical field, have been further refined through some 300 person-years of programming. For instance, NMCT managed to screen 32,000 individuals over 5 weeks at 20 medical departments in one study. In another study, traditional search for rare types of patients had resulted in 11 recruited patients in Sweden over 18 months. At that point, NMCT was asked to help and found 500 eligible patients over 2 months' time. However, a threat for the future was defined during the rapid growing process: Sweden is just too small to find patients enough for a large number of larger, simultaneous studies. Also, as many of the clients NMCT works with are very internationalized, even global in outreach, they are forced to, or find it preferable, to perform clinical studies on many markets. MK foresees that the successful completion of previous studies in Sweden will make it not too difficult to gain contracts with those same clients on foreign markets.

It so happens that the Chairman of NMCT, Professor Lars Sjöström, is intermittently serving as visiting professor at the Pennington Biomedical Research Center (PBRC) at Louisiana State University in the United States. The Center is "a world leading nutrition centre in front line of research into the genetics and treatment of obesity, among other fields." After its start in 1989 thousands of scientific reports have been published and PBRC has performed more than 200 clinical trials in phase 1–4. Professor Sjöström typically spends 3 months every year at Pennington and has excellent relations with its Executive Director. In fact, Professor Sjöström invited the current Executive Director of PBRC to be a member of the steering committee of the SOS project already in 1986 and he still is. Since 1986, the two gentlemen have published numerous papers together in the field of obesity. These circumstances explain why the internationalization of NMCT started in Louisiana, USA. PBRC meets a large number of important criteria, the most important perhaps being that it is a university affiliate. MK regards it as very important to be close to and cooperate with excellent basic and clinical research institutions. "That is how we can stay at the forefront." And Pennington is excellent in the metabolic syndrome area. "We went there for the first time early 2001 to have a discussion, Jan Danielson (board member), Lars (Sjöström) and myself." It turned out that PBRC had an interest in strengthening its for-profit activities. After two or three more negotiation occasions over the next year a deal was struck to the effect that a new company, Pennington Management of Clinical Trials, LLC (PMCT), was started in the summer 2002. PMCT offers a win–win platform: PBRC provides extraordinary knowledge in how to undertake clinical trials in North America and NMCT contributes with knowledge in advanced computer administration of clinical studies. Just as NMCT is a knowledge company at Gothenburg University, PMCT is a knowledge company at Pennington. The knowledge company status at a university has turned out to be a valuable "quality stamp" in the negotiations with the pharmaceutical industry. The ownership of PMCT is distributed so as to give NMCT a majority stake with 80% and the Pennington 20%. The NMCT share is owned by a wholly owned US subsidiary of NMCT, NMCT USA, a Delaware corporation.

> The requirements that must be fulfilled for our systems and methods to function in the US have been thoroughly examined in collaboration with PBRC and the FDA. There are undoubtedly major differences between the USA and Sweden as regards regulation and business culture. But the differences are not so great as to prevent application of our methods to drug trials in the USA. We expect to start our first study in the USA during the fall of 2002 or the spring of 2003. (Annual Report, 2001).

The present R&D Director of NMCT Sweden, Kaj Stenlöf, MD, PhD, will be the president of the U.S. subsidiary. Initially, he will be supported by one Swedish nurse and one Swedish IT-specialist, in order to assist U.S. cooperating clinics to adjust to NMCT's way of conducting the clinical trials. Later, Americans will be employed as required in relation to future business development.

"The immediate reason for examining Poland as the second country in our internationalization process was that two of our international clients wanted to have clinical studies performed in Eastern Europe," says MK. "We started to look at

Poland mid-2001. I have an old friend, Aleksander Ratz, who has served in that country with Volvo Car Corporation and he has been directing the operations of Volvo Truck Corporation on that market. I know him since my own period with Volvo. I make it a point to stay in touch with all the good people I learn to know. Aleksander Ratz has established an excellent contact network in Poland and we can now build on that. And through Aleksander Ratz, we have also learned to know the local representatives of the large pharmaceutical companies." NMCT is now negotiating with one of the largest of these companies about a study to be performed in Eastern Europe. MK has been seeing important people in Poland, such as university rectors and heads of medical departments. He perceives that there will be no problems finding suitable partners. "But this time we are going to set up a subsidiary first as to have the structure in place. After that we will negotiate with potential partners." Aleksander Ratz will be the President of the Polish operations. He will recruit the necessary individuals including doctors and medical heads locally. Marketing and sales will be performed from Sweden as the customers will be the same as those for which NMCT had performed projects in Sweden.

Reflections on NMCT's internationalization

Given our way of explaining internationalization (Johanson and Vahlne, 1977, 1990) it is not so surprising that the case description highlights experiences and relationships. As NMCT at this point in time is a newcomer to foreign markets, the case is relevant concerning observations of entry.

It seems as if existing relationships have an impact even on the choice of markets to enter. In the case of the United States, previous relationships with a local, extremely well-reputed research center made it interesting to form a partnership, as NMCT has a wish, as part of its strategy, to grow not only from scaling up its present operations. It also wants to grow from "local diversification," building on insights from basic and clinical research performed at other universities and not only at the Sahlgrenska University Hospital in Göteborg. Also, NMCT expects to benefit from relationships established with the customers, whom NMCT had already developed relationships with after successful projects in Sweden. They had made it clear they liked to have clinical studies performed in Eastern Europe. Old ties to a trusted Swede with a lot of business experience from Poland, and the large size of its population, made Poland an attractive alternative. In this case scaling up previous operations was a much stronger immediate motivation. Looking for partners to engage in potential "local diversification" was regarded as a second order question.

The issue of entry mode was also partly a result of previous, established relationships. Establishing a jointly owned subsidiary with Pennington was a consequence of a long-term relationship between Professor Sjöstöm and the Pennington Centre and its Executive Director. In the Polish case, MK's decision was to establish the infrastructure before looking for partners as to avoid complicated legal issues. And as relationships to potential customers were already established, there was no need to involve local middlemen or representatives.

It is interesting to note that in neither case does MK worry about problems connected with performing activities on the foreign market. He realizes that indeed the U.S. and Polish regulatory and business environments are different from the Swedish, but that these differences, he expects, will be successfully coped with via the relationships established, for example, PBRC in the United States and the network created by Aleksander Ratz in Poland, respectively.

Finally, psychic distance (Hörnell et al., 1972; Johanson and Vahlne, 1977; Nordström and Vahlne, 1992) originally defined as relevant to national entities is, it seems, more appropriate to relate to organizations and even individuals. The fact that there is a certain psychic distance between Sweden and the United States is not so interesting in this case. Professor Sjöström lives in the United States 3 months a year and has since long established relationship with the Pennington Centre and its Executive Director. In the Polish case, Aleksander Ratz had through living and working in Poland since many years eliminated his psychic distance to Poland and by hiring him to manage the local operations NMCT expects to avoid impact from its psychic distance to this country. It seems as if the concept of psychic distance needs to be reviewed and perhaps include trust in a revised model of internationalization.

The internationalization process of the firm—some basic features

The underlying basic assumption of the literature on international business is that foreign country markets are distinct entities in which operations are performed or not. A related assumption is that country markets, since they are distinct entities require specific modes of operation or forms of organization. Much of the international business literature, consequently, discusses the appropriate entry or governance modes in different country markets. Although foreign market entry and foreign market expansion frequently are analyzed separately it is generally recognized that they are interrelated and in the literature on internationalization they are treated as two different, albeit closely interrelated, aspects of firm internationalization.

According to the U-model internationalization of the firm is a process driven by an interplay between learning about international operations on the one hand and commitments to international business on the other. Lack of knowledge about foreign markets and operations is the main obstacle to internationalization and knowledge can mainly be developed through experience from operations in those markets. Foreign business opportunities and problems are discovered through experiences from foreign markets and operations. Experience gives the firm an ability to see and evaluate business opportunities and thereby to reduce uncertainty associated with commitments to foreign markets. Since knowledge is developed gradually international expansion takes place incrementally.

The U-model was initially conceptualized as an explanation of two empirical findings of the international development of firms, which correspond to the two big issues in international business, foreign market entry and foreign market expansion

(Hörnell et al., 1972; Johanson and Wiedersheim-Paul, 1975). First, it was observed that firms usually go abroad to close and familiar markets to start with and gradually extend foreign operations to more distant and unfamiliar countries. Second, the empirical studies demonstrated that operations in specific country markets are developed gradually too. Together these findings indicated that learning about foreign markets and operations is a critical issue in the internationalization of the firm.

The importance of experience

Only by doing business in a specific country is it possible to learn how customers, intermediaries, competitors, and public authorities act and react in different situations. This subtle understanding of the market can never be replaced by general market information and surveys. This means that it takes time to develop foreign business skills and knowledge and that the skills and the knowledge are associated with the specific situations and contexts in which they are developed.

It is possible to distinguish between market specific experience and operation experience. The former concerns conditions in the specific market and cannot without great difficulties be transferred to other markets, while the latter refers to ways of organizing and developing international business operations and can more easily be transferred from market to market. More generally, operation experience can be seen as internationalization experience, that is, experience about the use of different modes of operations in the international development of the firm (Eriksson et al., 1997). Overall, an important implication of the process view of internationalization is that development, integration, and transfer of knowledge should be regarded as a critical aspect of strategic management of internationalization.

Incremental commitments and commitment decisions

Internationalization is according to the process view a process of increasing commitments to foreign operations. When firms do business abroad and learn from doing business they get something which probably will be of value in the future. By doing business the firm builds market specific assets, but the value of those assets is, to some extent, connected to and dependent on specific contexts. Thus, by doing business in foreign markets the firm also increases its commitment to those markets. This means that a firm doing business internationally always increases its commitment to international business and, in particular, those country markets where it is already operating. An important element in internationalization of the firm is, according to this view, the gradual commitments due to current international business activities (Hadjikhani, 1997). Those commitments are also positively affected by demand-driven foreign market expansion.

Evidently, internationalization of the firm is also associated with distinct steps following from commitment decisions. Such commitment decisions may concern direct investments in manufacturing abroad, agreements with new distributors in foreign markets, cooperative arrangements with other firms, acquisition of firms, etc. Those decisions, or rather actions, are events that stepwise increase the firm's international commitment. They are, to a large extent, influenced by the firm's earlier internationalization, and the consequences of those actions are dependent on the subsequent development processes with regard to development, integration, and utilization of knowledge. The actions provide the firm new experiences and affect the gradual commitments that follow. The process view stresses that internationalization is not only, not even primarily, an outcome of such events but of the current activities performed within the frame of the preceding and the subsequent operation structures.

Through commitment to foreign markets the firm becomes dependent on those markets. It becomes bound to the markets. The greater, the more specific, and the more integrated with other firm activities the activities in those markets are, the stronger is the firm's dependence on them. This implies that the firm establishes foreign market positions, which it has strong reason to defend and develop. This means that there is a reason for the firm to make commitment decisions that defend and develop the firm's positions. Thus there is an interplay between current activity commitments and distinct commitment decisions. For instance, when operating in an expanding market the firm will have reason not only to serve that market to the same extent as earlier but to increase its investments in the market in a way that corresponds to its growing dependence on the sales in that market.

Climbing market barriers in internationalization. Let us now consider a network perspective on firms and business markets assuming that firms are engaged in a set of close business relationships with important customers, suppliers, and other business partners, and that business markets are structured as networks of interconnected business relationships.

Before considering a network perspective on firms and international expansion we shall take a look at the basic assumption of the country market as a specific, bounded entity of received international business theory. According to that view each country market is surrounded by fences corresponding to economic, institutional, and cultural barriers to business. While the economic barriers were stressed in the early international trade theory and international investment theory, institutional and cultural barriers have been more salient in the international business literature during the latest decades. Thus, in the internationalization literature, they are consistently stressed as important obstacles to foreign market entry. The size of those obstacles is usually discussed in terms of psychic distance or cultural distance. Psychic distance usually refers to the obstacles to information flows between countries due to differences in business laws, education levels, business language, etc. (Hörnell et al., 1972). Cultural distance usually refers to differences between countries in terms of four cultural dimensions (Hofstede, 1980;

Kogut and Singh, 1988). Although the two distances are closely related and are initially conceptualized as inter-country-specific distances, psychic distance has in some writings focused on inter-firm distances and has also in some cases been considered as influenced by the experience of the firms involved (Hallén and Wiedersheim-Paul, 1979; Nordström and Vahlne, 1993).

Within the country borders, it is also assumed, the market mechanism operates and specific customers, suppliers, and customers are not relevant. The market is faceless. Entering a country market is according to this view a matter of climbing over the barriers thereby becoming a market insider. There is a qualitative difference between being an insider and an outsider. Consequently, the managerial problems associated with foreign market entry are qualitatively different from those connected with foreign market expansion. Hence, the strong distinction between foreign market entry and foreign market expansion. It is generally assumed that the organization form used in a foreign country is chosen in order to overcome the psychic or cultural distance in an appropriate way.

Towards a business network model of the internationalization process

Since network is a label with many different, more or less specified, meanings we shall clarify our use of the network concept. We define business networks as sets of interconnected business relationships, in which each exchange relation is between business firms conceptualized as collective actors (Anderson et al., 1994). This definition is based on Cook and Emerson's (1978) definition of exchange networks and on empirical studies of business markets mostly within the IMP group tradition (Håkansson, 1982; Ford, 2002). This research demonstrated that close, lasting relationships between firms doing business with each other are considered as critically important by the firms. It takes time and resources to build relationships. According to this research all firms are engaged in a limited set of business relationships with important customer and supplier firms, which, in turn, have relationships with still other firms. Thus, every firm is part of an unbounded business network.

Barriers to relationship building

Within a business network perspective entry problems are not associated with country markets but with specific customer or supplier firms. Instead of foreign market entry and foreign market expansion we have reason to focus on managerial problems associated with establishment and development of relationships with suppliers and customers. Since all relevant business information is channelled through network relationships and each relationship is unique due to the characteristics of the relationship partners and the history of the relationship, the traditional international business issues are, in the pure network case, irrelevant.

BUSINESS RELATIONSHIP LEARNING AND COMMITMENT   93

There is nothing outside the relationships. Internationalization is, in this network world, nothing but a general expansion of the business firm which in no way is affected by country borders. All barriers are associated with relationship establishment and development.

Relationship commitment and learning

Although country borders are no longer relevant, the network model has similar implications for the internationalization process as those discussed above. We can still expect an internationalization process, which is an outcome of an interplay between experiential knowledge development and commitment although neither experiential knowledge nor commitment concerns countries but potential and existing relationship partners. Relationships develop gradually when the firms learn from interaction with each other and commit themselves stronger to the relationship (Anderson and Weitz, 1992; Blankenburg Holm et al., 1999). During this process the relationship partners gradually learn about each other's needs, resources, strategies, and business contexts. This is a time and resource demanding process, which requires that both partners become committed to the relationship. Thus, mutuality is also a basic feature of business relationships. This means also that the relationship partners have a common interest in the future development of the resources. Thus a firm has a common interest with the partners in its business network (Håkansson and Snehota, 1989). As a consequence the relationship partners as well as the wider business network partners have to take each other's interests into consideration when acting. They have a common future.

We can distinguish three types of business network learning (Håkansson and Johanson, 2001; Pahlberg, 2001). First, when firms do business in a customer–supplier relationship—they learn some things which are partner specific such as the partner's way of reacting to certain kinds of action or the roles of different individuals in the partner firm or the willingness and ability of the partner firm to adapt in various ways. They learn about how to coordinate their activities so that their joint productivity is strengthened. They learn about each other in a way that enables them to develop the relationship still more. Such relationship development is also a further commitment to the relationship.

Second, when interacting in a relationship two partner firms learn some skills, which may be transferred to and used in other relationships. Thus, they learn some things which concern skills regarding how to get in touch with new partners and various steps that can be taken in order to develop relationships. It can be seen as relationship development experience. This kind of knowledge is likely to be useful when the firm develops relationships with other customers, in particular, those, which in some way are similar. Similarity may concern partner size, technology, or cultural and institutional setting.

Third, when interacting in a relationship the partner firms learn how to coordinate activities in the relationship with those in another relationship. Such coordination may concern several supplier relationships, for example, just-in-time deliveries. It may also concern coordination between a supplier and a customer relationships in order to speed up the value chain. In this way they develop their network. They connect the relationships to each other.

Fourth, and as a consequence of the three effects of relationship learning mentioned above, the firm learns how to build new business networks and connect them to each other (Chen, forthcoming).

The relationship development experience is likely to be useful also when the firm develops relationships with firms that are connected to strategic relationships, that is, relationships that are regarded as particularly critical. To the firm it is important to defend the strategic relationships, for instance, by developing and strengthening relationships that support and protect the strategic relationships. Typically, this kind of supporting relationships are, in the case of customers, developed with suppliers. Thus, in order to handle the quality demands of an important customer the firm may have to develop a relationship with a certain supplier.

Hence we should expect that international expansion is an outcome first of the firm's development of existing relationships. Second, it will be the result of the firm's establishment of relationships with customer—or supplier—firms that in some important respects are similar to those customers—or suppliers—which they have already successfully developed relationships with. Third, internationalization of the business firm will be a consequence of its development of relationships with customer firms that are connected to those, which they already are working together with. It is nothing in the network model as such that says anything about which countries this will lead to. The internationalization process of the business firm will proceed much in the same way as posited by the general internationalization process literature but country markets are no longer meaningful entities.

Commitments are made to specific business firms whether they are customer firms, supplier firms, intermediary firms, or other cooperating firms. They will also primarily concern gradual development of the relationships in which the firm is already engaged. In a similar way as posited by the internationalization process literature the business firms will develop close interdependencies in relation to the important partners and they will consequently be prepared to defend those relationships by increasing the commitments to those firms with which they already do business. They will also tend to develop other relationships, which can be expected to support the important relationships. Thus they will be engaged in building business network structures surrounding and supporting strategic relationships (Chen and Chen, 1998).

Internationalization versus international network development

The greatest difference between the internationalization view and the network model does not concern the process nature but the empirical observations on which the internationalization process view was based initially. Since country specific barriers do not exist in this network world the network model has nothing to say about which countries firms will enter and expand in. And since the organization of operations in the received view concerns operations in specific countries we have no reason to expect that firms will follow the so-called establishment chain within specific countries. We have reason to expect that firms organize their business primarily in order to develop, support, and coordinate relationships. We have also reason to expect that the organization will develop in response to the development of important relationships, for instance, in order to enhance relationship learning and demonstrating commitment to relationships. But such organizational development will not be related to specific country markets; it will more probably be related to particular strategic relationships and sets of connected network relationships.

We can also expect that commitments may be both continuous as a consequence of current interaction with specific partners and discontinuous following upon commitment decisions of various kinds. For instance, acquisitions may be made in order to secure critical relationships when they are threatened by competitors, or even in order to establish relationships with interesting customers or suppliers (Forsgren, 1989; Anderson et al., 1997). When such acquisitions are made they will lead to discontinuous changes in the business firm's set of critical relationships, which may result in expansions which are not related to the same patterns as those suggested by the internationalization process literature. Nevertheless, the subsequent development will be influenced by current activity commitments following within the framework of the new network relationship structure. Thus by acquiring a company the business firm becomes involved in a set of business relationships and through interaction in those relationships the firm will gradually develop in response to the value of those relationships.

Since relationship building is time and resource demanding we have reason to expect that successful entrepreneurship is based on the entrepreneur's existing network. Her/his experience and earlier commitments will influence where the first market entry will occur. Whether this will be a foreign market entry or not depends on the relationships of the entrepreneur. Foreign market entry or internationalization is not an issue. The important issue will be the subsequent international expansion and network development.

Business experience and networks

The business network model outlined above is just a model with its particular simplifying assumptions, just as the received international business view is based on its specific assumptions. Studies of internationalization have indicated that two different kinds of market-specific experience can be distinguished, business experience and institutional experience (Eriksson et al., 1997). Business experience concerns experience related to the business environment of the firm, which according to the business network view comprises the firms with which it is doing business or is trying to do business with. Institutional experience concerns such factors as language, laws, regulations, and public and semipublic authorities implementing laws and regulations. Thus, institutional experience refers to many of those factors that constitute the psychic distance between countries. The clear distinction between those two kinds of experience means that we have reason to expect that they are developed in different ways and that they have different consequences.

Against that background it seems to be reason to combine the two process model and the network model by assuming that there is one set of direct business-related managerial problems that are relationship-specific and another set of problems that are associated with country-specific institutional and cultural barriers. Thus, we distinguish between relationship-specific psychic distance and country-specific psychic distance.

Network relationship development in internationalization

Considering foreign market entry we can imagine a picture in which there are several paths to foreign market entry. There are patterns of connected network relationships both within country borders and between countries. It is, however, important to recognize that such patterns can never be seen in reality by an actor. The actor, like the observer, can know that they exist but not how the network is structured in the specific case. Each specific relationship is unique and composed of a number of different interdependencies and links, which very much are matters of interpretations and intentions that can never be known but by the exchange partners. Thus, they are invisible to those who are not involved. Still more, the ways in which the relationships are connected are also matters of interpretations and intentions and are impossible to understand from outside. The actors know quite well their own relationships, and they may know some of the relationships that their own partners are engaged in, but further away in the network they can just assume that actors are engaged in business network structures.

The only way of learning about such network structures is to start interacting with one or several of the network actors and thereby provoke them into disclosing how strong and connected their relationships are. This means that foreign country market networks cannot be comprehended by the outsiders, even if they are aware that the networks exist. But this is not a matter of country market insider or outsider; it is a matter of each actor's only knowing about its own specific network context and having only vague ideas about the more distant network patterns, whether this concerns technologies, product markets country markets, or any field, which the actor has no experience of. This is a process of discovering the unknown (Kirzner, 1973; Johanson 2001).

Relationships can be used in climbing over the country market barriers and entering the country market. Moreover, while the received view of internationalization assumes that there is only one way of entering a country market—climbing over the barrier to the country market—the network view assumes that there may be several ports of entry and, consequently, several ways of getting into the country market. The focal firm may try to establish a relationship with a customer firm in a foreign country market. When doing so there are several different firms to approach and since each potential counterpart is unique and may require a specific relationship development process and also can be expected to have its particular consequences, the decision to approach one is an important and difficult decision.

However, establishment and development of a relationship is never a result of unilateral action but of bilateral or even multilateral interaction. Thus, development of a relationship in a foreign market is a complex, uncertain, and time-consuming process which may require considerable commitment on the part of the entering firm (Hohenthal, 2001).

But foreign market entry may as well be the result of initiatives taken by an intermediary, a customer, or a supplier in the foreign market interested in developing a relationship with our focal firm (Ellis, 2000). Evidently, there are differences between firms with respect to their willingness to respond to initiatives taken by other firms, but studies seem to indicate that smaller firms generally are more inclined to be responsive.

Foreign market entries may also follow when a firm's partner demands that the firm accompanies them abroad or otherwise is interested in extending their relationship to encompass business also in foreign markets . This is frequently the case when the firm enjoys close relationships with firms that are internationalizing. In particular, this has been observed in connection with service firms (Majkgård and Sharma, 1998). In this case, the foreign market entries are likely to occur in those countries where the focal firm's customers are operating rather than in countries with large markets or countries on a short psychic or cultural distance. Another consequence of such client or, more generally, partner following is that the firm's internationalization may be quite rapid as suggested by the studies mentioned at the outset of the paper.

While there is a qualitative difference between foreign market entry and foreign market expansion in the earlier internationalization models the network approach to internationalization implies that they concern similar problems. Foreign market expansion is a matter first of developing the firm's relationships in the specific market, second of establishing and developing supporting relationships, third of developing relationships that are similar as, or connected to the focal one. Although all this development may be confined to one country market it may as well cross country borders and lead to entry into other foreign markets. In order to support a strategic relationship the firm may be forced to develop a relationship in another country, thereby entering that country market.

Concluding comments

In this paper we have outlined a network model of the internationalization of the firm. It combines the experiential learning–commitment interplay as the driving mechanism from the old internationalization process model with a similar

International Entrepreneurship

JOHANSON AND VAHLNE

experiential learning–commitment mechanism focusing on business network relationships. Evidently and unfortunately, this increases the complexity of the model but it gives a possibility to retain the old and, as it seems, still useful model while adding some features which seem to correspond to important phenomena in the modern international business world. We try to minimize the resulting complexity by using the same basic mechanism. In the resulting model we can see firms learning in relationships, which enables them to enter new country markets in which they can develop new relationships which give them a platform for entering other country markets.

It follows from what we have said above, that we regard the importance of the world being structured in national entities with different cultures and institutional settings as less than we and others have earlier believed. There could be two reasons for that. One is the process of "globalization" implying countries over time become more similar to each other in terms of culture and institutional settings. It could also be that we, the observers of internationalization, were too much caught in previously existing ways of understanding and explaining internationalization, for example, economists' efforts to explain phenomena such as international trade and the multinational corporation. We believe the latter is the more important of the two explanations to why we were somewhat overemphasizing psychic distance between countries as explanation to the internationalization process. It might be useful to define the concept at the micro level and relate it also to the individual relationship, realizing the distance can change due to experiential learning and trust building.

Similarly, the entry mode issue, which is so important in much writing on internationalization is less important in our analysis. By stressing the significance of close, mutual, and lasting relationships between autonomous actors and the control they have over each other we reduce the importance of ownership control and thereby the whole ownership issue, which has had such a dominating role international business.

A remark perhaps beside the point, but relevant to this very Journal, is the striking similarities between the internationalization and entrepreneurial processes. At least in the more extreme cases they take place under genuine uncertainty. Given some "strategic intention" a lot of the action aims at decreasing that perceived uncertainty. Our introductory case seems to indicate also the entrepreneurial process is about experiential learning and making use of some since before existing relationships.

In fact, we believe that the model has validity far outside international business. Any development requiring that a firm moves into fields in which it has not operated earlier means that it has to handle the experiential learning–commitment mechanism concerning markets and relationships. Zander's (1999) analysis of the evolution of technological capabilities of multinationals demonstrates clearly that the mechanism is at work in technological development.

A final comment, which concerns the managerial implications of the model is that, at the surface it might seem that it is easy to network just as climbing a ladder from relationship to relationship. But this is wrong. The building of business network relationships is a complex and delicate matter, which requires resources and time as well as responsiveness to the interests of the partners. But when business network structures have been built they offer strong opportunities for international expansion.

References

Andersen, O., "On the Internationalization Process of Firms: A Critical Analysis", *Journal of International Business Studies 24*(2), 209–232, (1993).

Anderson, J. C., H. Håkansson, and J. Johanson, "Dyadic Business Relationships Within a Business Network Context", *Journal of Marketing 58*(Oct), 1–15, (1994).

Anderson, U., J. Johanson, and J.-E. Vahlne, "Organic Acquisitions in the Internationalization Process of the Business Firm", *Management International Review 37*(2), 67–84, (1997).

Anderson, E. and B. Weitz, "The Use of Pledges to Build and Sustain Commitment in Distribution Channels", *Journal of Marketing Research 29*, 18–34, (1992).

Autio, E., H. J. Sapienza, and J. G. Almeida, "Effects of Age at Entry, Knowledge Intensity, Imitability on International Growth", *Academy of Management Journal 43*, 909–924, (2000).

Barkema, H. G., J. H. J. Bell and, J. M. Pennings, "Foreign Entry, Cultural Barriers and Learning", *Strategic Management Journal 17*, 151–166, (1996).

Benito, G. and G. Gripsrud, "The Expansion of Foreign Direct Investments: Discrete Rational Location Choices or a Cultural Learning Process", *Journal of International Business Studies 23*, 461–476, (1992).

Bell, J. H. J., "The Internationalisation of Small Computer Software Firms", *European Journal of Marketing 29*(8), 60–75, (1995).

Bilkey, W. and G. Tesar, "The Export Behavior of Smaller Sized Wisconsin Manufacturing Firms", *Journal of International Business Studies 8*, 93–98, (1977).

Blankenburg Holm, D., K. Eriksson, and J. Johanson, "Creating Value Through Mutual Commitment to Business Network Relationships", *Strategic Management Journal 20*, 467–486, (1999).

Cavusgil, S. T., "On the Internationalization Process of Firms", *European Research 8*, 273–281, (1980).

Chang, S. J., "International Expansion Strategy of Japanese Firms: Capability Building Through Sequential Entry", *Academy of Management Journal 38*, 383–407, (1995).

Chen, H. and T.-J. Chen, "Network Linkages and Location Choice in FDI", *Journal of International Business Studies 29*(3), 445–468, (1998).

Chen, T.-J., "Network Resources for Internationalization: The Case of Taiwan's Electronic Firms", *Journal of Management Studies 41*(1), (forthcoming).

Chetty, S. and D. Blankenburg Holm, "Internationalisation of Small to Medium-Sized Manufacturing Firms: An Network Approach", *International Business Review 9*, 77–93, (2000).

Cook, K. S. and R. M. Emerson, "Power, Equity, Commitment in Exchange Networks", *American Sociological Review 43*, 721–738, (1978).

Coviello, N. and H. Munro, "Network Relationships and the Internationalization Process of Small Software Firms", *International Business Review 6*(4), 361–386, (1997).

Davidson, W. H., "The Location of Foreign Direct Investment Activity: Country Characteristics and Experience Effects", *Journal of International Business Studies 11*(2), 9–22, (1980).

Delios, A. and P. W. Beamish, "Ownership Strategy of Japanese Firms: Transactional, Institutional and Experience Influences", *Strategic Management Journal 20*(10), 915–930, (2000).

Ellis, P., "Social Ties and Foreign Market Entry", *Journal of International Business Studies 31*, 443–469, (2000).

Eriksson, K., J. Johanson, A. Majkgård, and D. D. Sharma, "Experiential Knowledge and Cost in the Internationalization Process", *Journal of International Business Studies 28*, 337–360, (1997).

Erramilli, M. K., "The Experience Factor in Foreign Market Entry Behaviour of Service Firms, *Journal of International Business Studies 22*, 479–501, (1991).

Ford, D. (ed.), *Understanding Business Marketing and Purchasing*. London: Thompson Learning, 2002.

Forsgren, M., *Managing the Internationalization Process. The Swedish Case*. London: Routledge, 1989.

Forsgren, M., "The Concept of Learning in the Uppsala Internationalization Process Model: A Critical Review", *International Business Review 11*(3), 257–278, (2002).

Hadjikhani, A., "A Note on the Criticisms Against the Internationalization Process Model", *Management International Review 37*(2), 43–66, (1997).

Hallén, L., J. Johanson, and N. Seyed-Mohamed, "Interfirm Adaptation in Business Relationships", *Journal of Marketing 55*(2), 29–37, (1991).

Hallén, L. and F. Wiedersheim-Paul, "Psychic Distance and Buyer–seller Interaction", *Organisasjon, Marked og Samfund 16*(5), 308–324, (1979).

Hofstede, G., *Culture's Consequences. International Differences in Work-Related Values*. London: Sage Publications, 1980.

Hohenthal, J., *The Creation of International Business Relationships. Experience and Performance in the Internationalization Process of SMEs*. Uppsala: Department of Business Studies, 2001.

Håkansson, H. (ed.), *International Marketing and Purchasing of Industrial Goods*. Chichester: Wiley, 1982.

Håkansson, H. and J. Johanson (eds), *Business Network Learning*. Oxford: Elsevier Science Ltd., 2001.

Håkansson, H. and I. Snehota, "A Business is No Island", *Scandinavian Journal of Management 5*(3), 187–200, (1989).

Hörnell, E., J.-E.Vahlne, and F. Wiedersheim-Paul, *Export och utlandsetableringar* (Exports and foreign establishments). Uppsala: Almqvist & Wiksell, 1972.

Johanson, J. and L.-G. Mattsson, "Internationalisation in Industrial Systems—A Network Approach", In N. Hood and J.-E. Vahlne (eds), *Strategies in Global Competition*. New York: Croom Helm, 1988.

Johanson, J. and J.-E. Vahlne, "The Internationalization Process of the Firm—A Model of Knowledge Development and Increasing Foreign Market Commitment", *Journal of International Business Studies 8*(1), 23–32, (1977).

Johanson, J. and J.-E. Vahlne, "The Mechanism of Internationalisation", *International Marketing Review 7*(4), 11–24, (1990).

Johanson, J. and F. Wiedersheim-Paul, "The Internationalization of the Firm—Four Swedish Cases", *Journal of Management Studies 12*(3), 305–322, (1975).

Johanson, M., *Searching the Known, Discovering the Unknown. The Russian Transition from Plan to Market as Network Change Processes*. Uppsala: Department of Business Studies, 2001.

Kirzner, I. M., *Competition and Entrepreneurship*. Chicago: The University of Chicago Press, 1973.

Kogut, B. and H. Singh, "The Effect of National Cultures on the Choice of Entry Mode", *Journal of International Business Studies 19*(3), 411–432, (1988).

Li, J., "Foreign Entry and Survival: Effects of Strategic Choices on Performance in International Markets", *Strategic Management Journal 16*, 333–352, (1995).

Luo, Y., "Time-Based Experience and International Expansion: The Case of an Emerging Economy", *Journal of Management Studies 36*(4), 504–534, (1999).

Luo, Y. and M. Peng, "Learning to Compete in a Transition Economy: Experience, Environment and Performance", *Journal of International Business Studies 30*(2), 269–295, (1999).

Luostarinen, R., *Internationalization of the Firm*. Helsinki: Helsinki School of Economics, 1980.

Madsen, T. K. and P. Servais, "The Internationalization of Born Globals: An Evolutionary Process? *International Business Review 6*(6), 561–584, (1997).

Majkgård, A. and D. D. Sharma, "Client-Following and Market Seeking Strategies in the Internationalization of Service Firms", *Journal of Business-to-Business Marketing 4*(3), 1–41, (1998).

Nordström, K. A. and J.-E. Vahlne, Is the Globe Shrinking? Psychic Distance and the Establishment of Swedish Sales Subsidiaries During the Last 100 Years, Paper Presented at the Annual Conference of The Trade and Finance Association, Laredo, Texas, 1993.

Pahlberg, C., "Creation and Diffusion of Knowledge in Subsidiary Business Networks", In H. Håkansson and J. Johanson (eds), *Business Network Learning*, pp. 161–181. Oxford: Elsevier Science Ltd., 2001.

Petersen, B. and T. Pedersen, "Twenty Years After—Support ad Critique of the Uppsala Internationalization Model", In I. Björkman and M. Forsgren (eds), *The Nature of the International Firm.* Copenhagen: Copenhagen Business School Press, 1997.

Torgerson, J. S., K. Arlinger, M. Käppi, and L. Sjöström, "Principles for Enhanced Recruitment of Subjects in a Large Clinical Trial: The Xendos Study Experience", *Controlled Clinical Trials 22*, 515–525, (2001).

Welch, L. and R. Luostarinen, "Internationalization—evolution of a concept", *Journal of General Management 14*(2), 34–55, (1988).

Zander, I., "Whereto the Multinational: The Evolution of Technological Capabilities in the Multinational Network", *International Business Review 8*(3), 261–292, (1999).

[22]

ELSEVIER

Journal of Business Venturing 19 (2004) 285–307

JOURNAL of BUSINESS VENTURING

Building a foreign sales base: the roles of capabilities and alliances for entrepreneurial firms

Michael J. Leiblein*, Jeffrey J. Reuer[1]

Fisher College of Business, Ohio State University, Columbus, OH 43210, USA

Received 30 September 1999; received in revised form 31 July 2002; accepted 31 July 2002

Abstract

This study examines how technological capabilities and international collaborative linkages affect entrepreneurial firms' abilities to build a foreign sales base in a highly competitive global industry. The empirical evidence from a sample of North American semiconductor firms indicates that both technological capabilities and international collaboration potentially aid firms' development of foreign sales. Our results also provide initial evidence that the influence of technological capabilities and international alliances differs across entrepreneurial and established firms. The paper argues that these differences are due to the dissimilar strategies and resource characteristics of entrepreneurial and established firms.
© 2003 Published by Elsevier Inc.

Keywords: Foreign sales base; Technological capabilities; Entrepreneurial firms

1. Executive summary

This study considers whether and how entrepreneurial businesses in high-tech industries are able to leverage their internal capabilities and utilize interfirm alliances to build a foreign sales base. Because of heightened competitive pressures, network externalities, and shrinking product life cycles, an entrepreneurial firm's success in a high-tech environment can turn on

---

* Corresponding author. Tel.: +1-614-292-0071; fax: +1-614-292-7062.
E-mail addresses: leiblein_1@cob.osu.edu (M.J. Leiblein), reuer_1@cob.osu.edu (J.J. Reuer).
[1] Tel.: +1-614-292-3045; fax: +614-292-7062.

0883-9026/$ – see front matter © 2003 Published by Elsevier Inc.
doi:10.1016/S0883-9026(03)00031-4

286   *M.J. Leiblein, J.J Reuer / Journal of Business Venturing 19 (2004) 285–307*

its capacity to rapidly develop foreign sales. As a consequence, a surprising number of new ventures, the so-called "born globals," have been able to internationalize rapidly despite resource constraints across the value chain and other administrative challenges that accompany international expansion.

This research draws upon studies in the entrepreneurship, competitive strategy, and international business literatures to examine whether technological capabilities and interfirm alliances positively shape entrepreneurial and established firms' foreign sales. Research in the field of entrepreneurship suggests that the pursuit of international sales by entrepreneurial firms is part of a broader, competitively aggressive posture that emphasizes innovativeness and risk taking. Research in international business and competitive strategy has contended that firms are at a natural disadvantage when expanding into foreign markets. Thus, valuable upstream capabilities that compensate for entrants' lack of familiarity with local market conditions are required to penetrate foreign markets. Finally, research on alliances has long contended that building foreign sales is one of the key rationales for collaborating with other firms. However, there is little empirical evidence on the outcomes of alliances in general or on entrepreneurial firms' abilities to use alliances as vehicles for foreign sales development in particular.

Beyond examining the direct effects of firms' specific capabilities and strategies, this study considers factors that may strengthen or attenuate their effects on foreign sales. Recent studies in entrepreneurship have drawn attention to the need to better understand the mechanisms through which entrepreneurial firms expand internationally, and the competitive strategy literature has also emphasized the need to examine how entrepreneurial and established firms differ in their resource profiles, competitive behaviors, and resulting performance outcomes. In response, this paper considers how the consequences of internal technological capabilities and external alliances potentially vary across entrepreneurial and other firms.

The study utilizes a sample of 101 North American semiconductor firms. A series of analyses examine the relationship among these firms' technological capabilities, international alliances in the form of nonequity and equity collaborative arrangements, and their foreign sales across five separate indicators of venture status. The evidence indicates that both technological capabilities and international alliances are strongly correlated with subsequent foreign sales. Moreover, the influence of technological capabilities remains significant after accounting for heterogeneity in a firm's resources and the configuration of its international operations. In contrast, the effects of alliances tend to vanish once one begins to address firm heterogeneity. The findings suggest that the effectiveness of international alliances hinges upon factors associated with the nature of the venture as well as the type of alliance under consideration.

For entrepreneurs in high-tech industries seeking to build a foreign sales base, the results underscore the importance of developing upstream technological capabilities. Although popular arguments tend to attach a variety of benefits to interfirm alliances, our results caution against such general conclusions absent a careful consideration of a firm's underlying capabilities. Thus, the evidence points to the need for entrepreneurs to consider carefully the balance between the risks and benefits of particular types of alliances as well as alternative mechanisms for organizing the firm's international expansion.

M.J. Leiblein, J.J. Reuer / Journal of Business Venturing 19 (2004) 285–307   287

2. Introduction

The latter part of the twentieth century witnessed not only the globalization of many industries, but also the internationalization of an increasing number of entrepreneurial firms. Prior work has begun to document the internationalization of new ventures (e.g., Oviatt and McDougall, 1994; McDougall and Oviatt, 1996), but the specific means by which these firms internationalize remain unclear. The process of globalization is a difficult undertaking for firms that lack intangibles or have limited slack resources (Zacharakis, 1997), and the administrative challenges that arise from international expansion can be particularly acute for entrepreneurial firms (e.g., Fujita, 1995). Thus, despite opportunities for firms to obtain benefits such as rapid growth and future options (for a review, see Caves, 1996), it is unclear which resource and strategy configurations are most likely to enhance entrepreneurial firms' foreign sales.

In this paper, we analyze the impact of technological capabilities and alliances on the foreign sales of entrepreneurial firms. In so doing, we respond to recent calls for research on the primary firm-level factors that influence the internationalization of new ventures (e.g., Oviatt and McDougall, 1999) and on the different strategies employed by entrepreneurial and established firms (e.g., McDougall et al., 1994; Chen and Hambrick, 1995; Dean et al., 1998). Following Covin and Slevin (1989, 1990), we describe entrepreneurial firms in terms of their inclination to take on business related risks, to favor change and innovation, and to assume an aggressive competitive posture vis-à-vis their competitors. Given the context of our study in a high technology industry, we further portray entrepreneurial firms are those that face severe resource constraints arising from factors such as the possession of few tangible assets and large capital requirements.

Faced with the challenges of overcoming foreign market entry barriers, entrepreneurial firms have frequently attempted to leverage their intangible upstream capabilities by engaging in strategic alliances as a means of obtaining complementary downstream assets. The international business literature has identified a host of outcomes to alliances, which suggest that they will facilitate international expansion (e.g., Sarkar et al., 2001). Among them are the following: overcoming various resource constraints and other hurdles to international expansion (e.g., Contractor and Lorange, 1988; Hara and Kanai, 1994); acquiring country-, partner-, or task-specific knowledge (e.g., Khanna et al., 1998); improving the firm's strategic positioning (e.g., Harrigan, 1988); and achieving flexibility in uncertain environments (Kogut, 1991; Larson, 1991).

This paper addresses the apparent contradiction between traditional process theories of internationalization (e.g., Johanson and Vahlne, 1977) and the emerging literature on "born globals" (e.g., McDougall et al., 1994; Oviatt and McDougall, 1997) by exploring how differences in the capabilities possessed by entrepreneurial and established firms influence the relationship among upstream technological capabilities, international alliances, and foreign sales. The analysis is carried out in the semiconductor industry. Prior work has noted that technical progress is frequently driven by innovations created by entrepreneurial start ups in the Silicon Valley and elsewhere (e.g., Eisenhardt and Schoonhoven, 1996). Casual evidence suggests that these firms have been quite successful. For instance, small entrepreneurial firms were among the fastest growing competitors in the industry during the mid-1990s (Integrated

Circuit Engineering, 1995–1996). Moreover, with nearly two thirds of the worldwide semiconductor demand residing outside the United States (ICE, 1995–1996) and heightened competitive pressures stemming from factors such as shrinking product life cycles and the need to bring together geographically dispersed design and production skills, international expansion is a competitive priority for new ventures and established incumbents alike. Because firms in this industry exhibit substantial heterogeneity in terms of technological capabilities, alliance usage patterns, and other important characteristics (e.g., firm size and age, ownership, founder status, etc.), the industry presents an attractive research context in which to analyze how entrepreneurial firms can uniquely use their technological capabilities and alliances to realize their growth aspirations.

The following section provides background theoretical material and develops hypotheses on the determinants of foreign sales development. This section is followed by a discussion of the research methods, and we then present findings on the internationalization efforts of a sample of 101 North American semiconductor firms. The empirical evidence reveals that firms' technological capabilities and the formation of collaborative linkages are jointly associated with greater foreign sales. The results also indicate that entrepreneurial firms in the semiconductor industry have distinct technological capabilities and alliance usage patterns as compared to their counterparts. Further, the effects of technological capabilities and interfirm collaboration differ across these classes of competitors. The paper concludes with a discussion of the implications of these findings and directions for future research.

3. Theory and hypotheses

3.1. Firm capabilities

Although prior research has drawn attention to international new ventures by bringing together literature on entrepreneurship, and international business (e.g., Oviatt and McDougall, 1994; McDougall and Oviatt, 1996), little empirical work has examined whether and how a new venture's specific resources and strategic choices influence its internationalization. For instance, while prior research has described entrepreneurial firms in terms of aggressive strategic postures, innovativeness, and risk taking (e.g., Covin and Slevin, 1990), these or other more specific characteristics have not been linked to subsequent international performance. While entrepreneurial ventures produce more innovations per employee than large firms (e.g., Acs and Audretsch, 1988), they are also likely to face growth challenges due to resource constraints. In the international context, these resource constraints extend beyond financial constraints to include administrative resource constraints arising from a lack of familiarity with local market conditions and customs in host countries.[2] This

---

[2] Zaheer (1995, p. 343) traces the liability of foreignness to the following four sources: (1) spatial costs due to factors such as transportation and coordination costs, (2) firm-specific costs due to unfamiliarity with the local environment, (3) host country-specific costs due to economic nationalism or a foreign firms' lack of legitimacy, and (4) home country-specific costs due to export restrictions.

"liability of foreignness" (e.g., Hymer. 1976; Zaheer and Mosakowski, 1997) implies that entrepreneurial firms must possess compensating advantages in order to compete viably in unfamiliar markets abroad.

The compensating advantages necessary to succeed in foreign markets can take many forms but are often described and analyzed in terms of intangible resources (e.g., Morck and Yeung, 1992). The general proposition that firms' capabilities affect the likelihood of successful expansion clearly cuts across other theoretical perspectives. For instance, Penrose's (1995) theory of firm growth highlights the importance of underutilized resources in prompting corporate expansion. Related research on the resource-based view of the firm (Wernerfelt, 1984; Barney, 1986; Dierickx and Cool, 1989) points to firm capabilities as fundamental to the firm's success in competing in domestic or international markets. Based on the predictions of these literatures, we expect that firms' capabilities will have an important bearing on their ability to penetrate foreign markets.

While the possession of valuable distinctive capabilities is likely to enhance a firm's ability to compete in foreign markets, the theoretical literature has yet to identify a priori the specific capabilities that most likely to lead to successful internationalization. Since the value of any capability is dependent upon the drivers of performance in that specific context, the degree to which any single capability will retain its value across different geographic markets is likely to be industry specific. The empirical analysis in this paper therefore focuses on a capability that is clearly linked to performance in the semiconductor industry. Specifically, we focus on a key measure of product performance, processing speed, which is tightly linked to the firm's technological capabilities. Products incorporating more advanced technologies can read, process, and output data more quickly than products using less sophisticated technologies. Further, more advanced technologies typically increase production yield and reduce costs (Gruber, 1994). Given the intense price- and product performance-based competition in this industry, firms with more advanced technological capabilities will likely enjoy greater success in building a foreign sales base. We therefore wish to test whether the following prediction holds for entrepreneurial firms and others:

H1: The firm's technological capability will positively influence its subsequent foreign sales base.

3.2. International alliances

An entrepreneurial firm can also use alliances to develop its foreign sales base. By entering into strategic alliances, it can at once exploit its innovativeness as well as access financial resources and partners' complementary resources in order to expand into international markets at a smaller size than possible without the support of its partners. The international business and strategy literatures have long held that cross-border alliances can be helpful to access foreign markets (Stopford and Wells, 1972; Contractor and Lorange, 1988) and to enhance sales growth in general (e.g., Hagedoorn and Schakenraad, 1994; Powell et al., 1996). Despite this conceptual attention, comparatively little research has empirically investigated the specific benefits that firms obtain, or fail to derive, from engaging in interfirm collaboration.[3] Indeed, as "lists" of partnering motives have lengthened, the question remains as to whether or not alliances truly deliver upon their various proposed benefits (e.g., Weaver and Dickson, 1998; Reuer and Leiblein, 2000). Moreover, even if alliances yield certain benefits to firms in general, a further question is whether entrepreneurial firms benefit more or less from alliances than established firms (e.g., Preece et al., 1999).

The literature has identified at least two mechanisms through which alliances may enhance organizational growth in general and the development of foreign sales in particular. First, alliances enable firms to acquire complementary assets and local knowledge. For entrepreneurial firms with proactive competitive strategies, this means that firms may be able to enter into a market before rivalry dissipates rents (Mitchell et al., 1994). Second, alliances can be viewed as transitional learning investments that open doors to future expansion opportunities (e.g., Reuer and Koza, 2000). Hagedoorn (1993) catalogues a number of motives for technology partnering that relate to market access and the search for new prospects. Mitchell and Singh (1992) present evidence of firms using preentry alliances as stepping stones to gain information about emerging markets before expanding on a stand-alone basis into new subfields of an industry.

While alliances in general may facilitate foreign sales development, firms use different types of alliances to meet their objectives. For example, Auster (1992) notes that firms tend to engage in international technological linkages in emerging industries, more commitment-intensive joint ventures in growth industries, and other direct investments in more mature industries. Eisenhardt and Schoonhoven (1996) report that semiconductor firms' usage of product development alliances is highest in emerging markets. Although there are many different types of alliances and there is no consensus regarding an appropriate typology, researchers commonly differentiate between nonequity and equity collaborative agreements. Nonequity alliances such as licensing or research agreements are governed solely through the use of a contract, and equity alliances afford greater control and incentive alignment through the introduction of shared ownership and a joint board (e.g., Pisano, 1989).

The fundamental differences between nonequity and equity alliances may lead to different implications for the firm's development of its foreign sales base. For instance, the emphasis on the performance of a sequence of well-defined tasks implied by a contractual nonequity agreement suggests that these types of alliances can be focused on specific objectives such as enhancing foreign sales in a particular country. However, this same focus suggests that

---

[3] Prior research that has considered the performance effects of alliances generally falls into one of several categories. A number of studies have examined the corporate effects of collaboration by investigating parent firms' share price reactions to alliance formation announcements (e.g., Das et al., 1998; Koh and Venkatraman, 1991). This work differs from other alliance studies measuring the current performance of the venture itself (e.g., Chowdhury, 1992; Woodcock et al., 1994). Still, another approach has been to study the effects of alliances on parent firm survival (Singh and Mitchell, 1996). This is in contrast to the more typical application of longitudinal models to study JV longevity and the determinants of venture survival (e.g., Li, 1995; Park and Ungson, 1997). Other research has considered managers' perceived satisfaction with alliances (e.g., Parkhe, 1993). Recent research has begun to narrow performance assessments by focusing on the relationship between alliances and parent firms' innovativeness as proxied by partners' patenting activities (Hagedoorn and Schakenraad, 1994; Mowery et al., 1996; Almeida et al., 1998).

nonequity alliances are less likely to provide access to the full set of supporting resources necessary to coordinate interdependent activities across countries. By contrast, the greater control and incentive alignment provided by equity alliances allow these arrangements to bring together additional value chain activities and to be used for multiple objectives (Hladik, 1985). Based on these considerations, we hypothesize that both nonequity and equity alliances will be associated with greater foreign sales development. To allow for the possibility that the effects of nonequity and equity alliances differ, we propose the following two related hypotheses.

H2a: The stock of a firm's international nonequity alliances will positively influence its subsequent foreign sales base.

H2b: The stock of a firm's international equity alliances will positively influence its subsequent foreign sales base.

3.3. Venture status: entrepreneurial versus established firms

The previous hypotheses consider the impact of technological capabilities and international collaboration for entrepreneurial as well as established firms. However, the effects may well differ across these classes of firms given the underlying differences in their strategic postures and resource profiles (e.g., Hambrick et al., 1982; Woo and Cooper, 1981, 1982). For instance, to the extent that entrepreneurial firms are better able to protect an innovator's property rights, one would expect these ventures to take on greater risk and to engage in a more frequent and more radical innovative behavior. In fact, entrepreneurial firms are more likely to take on change and enter new markets in a proactive manner (e.g., Chen and Hambrick, 1995) to enjoy advantages in areas such as risk-seeking behavior (Woo. 1987) and production flexibility (Fiegenbaum and Karnanai, 1991) and to generate more patents and product innovations (Acs and Audretsch, 1988). By contrast, established firms tend to possess scale, experience, brand name advantages, and greater financial and other slack resources (e.g., Hambrick et al., 1982; Woo and Cooper, 1981).

These resource and competitive differences suggest that the relationships between firm-level capabilities and alliance strategies may differ across entrepreneurial and established firms. For instance, the tendency of new firms to lack slack resources, brand equity, distribution capacity, and developed marketing skills suggests that upstream technological capabilities will be critical for small firms seeking to develop foreign sales. By contrast, more established firms tend to possess a broader repertoire of capabilities across the value chain that can serve as compensating advantages when expanding overseas (e.g., Hitt et al., 1997).

It is also probable that the efficacy of international collaborative relationships will differ across entrepreneurial and established firms (Gomes-Casseres, 1997). For example, entrepreneurial firms are frequently required to make relationship-specific investments in order to gain access to the downstream assets held by their partners. Given the complexity of managing opportunism and other challenges in alliances (e.g., Deeds and Hill, 1999), entrepreneurial firms' lack of administrative skills and supporting resources suggests that they may benefit less from an alliance at the margin (e.g., Niederkofler, 1991). By contrast, established firms' greater legitimacy, experience, slack financial resources, and breadth of skills across the value chain indicate greater capacity to manage a portfolio of international alliances (Hamel and Prahalad, 1994). These considerations lead us to posit the following hypotheses:

H3: The positive influence that technological capability has on the firm's subsequent foreign sales base will be greater for smaller firms than larger firms.

H4a: The positive influence that a firm's stock of international nonequity alliances has on the firm's subsequent foreign sales base will be greater for larger firms than smaller firms.

H4b: The positive influence that a firm's stock of international equity alliances has on the firm's subsequent foreign sales base will be greater for larger firms than smaller firms.

4. Methodology

4.1. Sample

The sample was derived from reports provided by the ICE (1995–1996) and Dataquest consulting firms. The Dataquest reports provided data on the domestic and foreign semiconductor sales reported by 94 North American semiconductor manufacturers. These data were merged with information pertaining to 142 North American semiconductor manufacturers obtained from the 1995 to the 1996 editions of Integrated Circuit Engineering's *Profiles of IC Manufacturers and Suppliers*. Pooling of the two data sources resulted in a final sample of 101 firms. The sample represented over 60% of industry sales. Moreover, the average sales and average number of employees for our sample were statistically similar to industry averages obtained from Ward's Business Directory at the 0.05 level.

4.2. Model specification

The statistical model used to test our first two hypotheses took the following form:

(1) Foreign sales $= \beta_0 + \beta_1$ technological capability

$+ \beta_2$ international nonequity alliances

$+ \beta_3$ international equity alliances $+$ controls $+ \varepsilon$.

While our interest lies in developing a parsimonious model to assess the impact of technological capabilities and international alliances on the firm's foreign sales base, we introduced measures that captured the level of firms' investment in international marketing and international production to control for an organization's ability to gather information on foreign market conditions, to establish local distribution channels, to overcome local content concerns, and to signal commitment to a particular region via wholly owned operations. We

M.J. Leiblein, J.J. Reuer / Journal of Business Venturing 19 (2004) 285–307   293

also account for the differences between entrepreneurial and established firms through the use of five separate measures of venture status. Interaction effects between venture status and technological capability as well as between venture status and the firm's international alliances were introduced to test the remaining hypotheses.

4.3. Measures and data

4.3.1. Foreign sales

We specified a firm's foreign sales as the log of the revenue generated by sales of semiconductor products outside North America in 1996. This measure is attractive in that it provides an absolute measure of the firm's foreign market penetration and is most strongly associated with the scale advantages thought to accompany international expansion. As the measure of absolute foreign sales exhibited significant positive skew, we redefined our measure as the natural logarithm of foreign sales.

4.3.2. Explanatory variables

A number of proxies for venture status have been introduced in the literature, including measures based on firm size, firm age, growth rate, founder presence, ownership structure, independence, growth orientation, innovativeness, risk preferences, and many others (e.g., Autio et al., 2000). The variety of potential proxies influenced our research design in two respects. First, the lack of a single preferred measure of venture status led us to classify the firms in our sample via a measure grounded in industry practice. Second, to address concerns regarding the validity of our industry-specific measure, we repeated our analyses using four alternative proxies commonly used in the literature. The following paragraphs describe each of the five measures of venture status used in our analysis.

The first measure is derived from a classification used by managers and consultants within the semiconductor industry to identify a firm's competitive posture (e.g., Angel, 1994). This measure, venture status small firm, classifies semiconductor firms based on annual revenue, considering firms with total annual revenues less than US$200 million as "small." Many of these firms are younger rapidly growing start ups founded within areas such as the Silicon Valley or the Route 128 corridor. While the vast majority of these firms reports annual revenues substantially below the imposed revenue threshold (i.e., median U.S. and median Worldwide revenue in the sample is below US$25 million and US$33 million, respectively), the US$200 million cutoff value is used to capture all firms that focus their operations tightly around a single innovative product design or technological application. Most of these small-sized firms outsource all of their production needs.[4] In contrast, medium-sized firms such as

---

[4] We performed additional analyses that identified entrepreneurial firms as those in the lowest quartile of our sample in terms of annual worldwide sales. The revenue threshold implied by this criterion was US$39 million. The lowest annual revenue reported was US$1.3 million and the average annual revenue in the quartile was US$9 million. This is comparable to the average annual revenue of US$8.2 million reported in a survey taken in the late 1980s by Covin and Slevin (1989) and the range of US$500,000 to US$29 million reported in a survey of early stage ventures provided by Preece et al. (1999).

Cypress Semiconductor or LSI Logic typically maintain advanced design and fabrication capabilities and enter a limited number of product lines. During the sample time frame, large firms in the industry such as International Business Machines and Texas Instruments designed and manufactured products across a wide range of product–market applications.

Four additional proxies were developed to tie the venture status construct to the existing theory. These four measures are based on the number of employees in the firm, the age of the firm, the presence of the firm founder on the management team, and whether the firm is public or private. The employee-based measure follows a long tradition in the entrepreneurship and public policy literatures and classifies small ventures as those employing 500 or fewer individuals (e.g., Acs and Audretsch, 1988).[5] Similarly, the new venture measure identifies those firms that are relatively free from institutionalized routines, ingrained organizational structures, and large sunk investments that accrue with age. Following prior literature, we identified new ventures as those that are 8 years old or less (e.g., Biggadike. 1979; McDougall and Oviatt, 1996). The founder measure indicates whether the firm founder is a member of the current management team. A global orientation on the part of the founder has been shown to be an important predictor of early internationalization (e.g., McDougall et al., 1994), and prior research has demonstrated that measures based on founder or new venture status are highly correlated with a number of qualitative measures associated with entrepreneurial behavior including risk-taking propensity (Begley, 1995). Finally, the private measure identifies those firms that have yet to undergo an initial public offering (IPO), and therefore provides a measure that distinguishes between the legitimacy and access to external funds that are thought to accompany public firm status.

Following prior empirical research conducted on the semiconductor industry (e.g., Eisenhardt and Schoonhoven, 1996), the measure of technological capability used in this paper is derived from the minimum feature size at which a firm is a capable of manufacturing a product. Feature size represents the line width at which information is etched onto a semiconductor circuit. Smaller line widths result in lower overall production cost and greater product performance. Technological improvements tend to result in quantifiable discrete reductions in feature size. In 1988, state-of-the-art technology enabled firms to produce products with 1.0 micron feature sizes. Since then, newer generations of technology have been introduced that incorporate 0.8, 0.7, 0.5, 0.35, 0.25, and 0.18 micron technology. In order to exploit the relationship between feature size and a given generation of technology, we defined our measure of technological capability to be equal to "one" for firms using first generation 1.0 micron technology, "two" for firms using second generation 0.8 micron technology, and so on. Firms that had not adopted 1.0 micron technology as of 1995 were coded as using generation 0 technology.

The international nonequity and international equity alliance variables measure a firm's stock of active alliances with foreign partners in 1995. The international nonequity alliance measure includes licensing, codevelopment, and production agreements that include a clause-

---

[5] Again, we conducted analyses that identified entrepreneurial firms as those in the lowest quartile of our sample. The threshold in terms of employee count implied by this criterion was 143. The fewest number of employees reported by a firm in our sample was 17.

M.J. Leiblein, J.J. Reuer / Journal of Business Venturing 19 (2004) 285–307   295

providing access to a foreign market. The international equity alliance measure includes agreements in which the focal firm purchases an equity position in a foreign firm or forms an equity joint venture with a foreign partner. The data on collaborative linkages enacted in any given year obtained from the profile's reports were supplemented by announcement searches conducted for each of the firms in our sample using the relevant editions of the DIALOGUE/ Predicasts F&S Index of American corporations and industries, European corporations and industries, and international corporations and industries.

4.3.3. Control variables

We introduced two control variables to account for factors that might affect firms' foreign sales while also being correlated with our theoretical variables. Following research demonstrating the relationship between international experience and foreign sales (e.g., Johanson and Vahlne, 1977), we accounted for firms' existing international marketing and international production investments. These variables are measured by counts of the number of marketing headquarters and number of production sites that the firm maintained in foreign markets in 1995.

5. Results

Table 1 presents descriptive statistics and a correlation matrix for the sampled firms. In 1996, the firms in our sample exhibited between less than 1 year and 50 years of industry experience and between US$1.3 million and US$13.5 billion in worldwide sales. Foreign sales accounted for a significant portion of these revenues, with the average firm deriving US$308 million from foreign sales. The sampled firms are rather heterogeneous in their technological capabilities, with the majority of firms utilizing second, third, fourth, or fifth generation technology. Only two firms in our sample had produced products incorporating sixth generation technology by 1996. Firms' international alliance activity was similarly

Table 1
Descriptive statistics and correlation matrix

Variable	Mean	S.D.	1	2	3	4	5	6
1. Log of foreign sales	3.93	1.92						
2. Venture status small firm	0.62	0.49	− .69***					
3. International marketing experience	1.30	1.21	.54***	− .54***				
4. International production experience	0.37	1.23	.43***	− .30**	.14			
5. Technological capability	2.38	1.87	.47***	− .35***	.34**	.29**		
6. Nonequity alliances	0.27	0.62	.21*	− .16†	.08	.33***	.24**	
7. Equity alliances	0.26	0.72	.36***	− .18†	.13	.47***	.31**	.21*

 * $P < .05$.
 ** $P < .01$.
 *** $P < .001$.
 † $P < .10$.

varied, the primary difference being that 64% of the firms in the sample did not participate in a single international nonequity or equity alliance aimed at developing foreign sales in 1995. As expected, the smallest firms in our sample tend to have less international marketing and production experience, utilize less advanced technology, and form fewer international alliances than medium or large firms.

Table 1 also reports information regarding the relationship between each of the variables included in the analysis. The correlation matrix indicates that our measure for technological capability is strongly and positively related to foreign sales $(P<.001)$. The zero-order correlations between both international nonequity alliance activity and foreign sales $(P<.05)$ and international equity alliance activity and foreign sales $(P<.001)$ are also positive and highly significant. The controls for international marketing and production experience are positively related to foreign sales (both $P<.001$). Many significant relationships also exist among the independent variables. For instance, firms with advanced technological capabilities tend to be active in international nonequity and equity alliances (both $P<.01$). These high-technology firms also tend to invest heavily in foreign marketing and production sites (both $P<.01$). The significant intercorrelation among these variables indicates that multivariate analyses are needed to examine the partial effects of the theoretical variables on the firm's foreign sales base.

For descriptive purposes, Table 2 provides a comparison of the small, medium, and large U.S. semiconductor firms in our sample. The left-hand column lists the variables included in the analyses. Moving from left to right, the first three data columns provide means and standard deviations, as applicable, for each of the small, medium, and large firm subsamples. The last three columns provide t tests or chi-square tests for the equivalence of means across the subsamples for the continuous and indicator variables, respectively. Most significant, the results indicate that small, medium, and large firms do not differ in terms of their foreign sales intensity, which is consistent with the notion of "born globals." Roughly one third of the small firms are not publicly traded, and as expected this proportion is greater for the small than for the medium and large firms (both $P<.05$). Roughly a third of the small firms were less than 8 years old, and none of the largest firms were new ventures $(P<.05)$. No differences were evident in the involvement of founders across the three subsamples.

Table 2 provides striking evidence which indicates that small firms differ dramatically from large firms in terms of international marketing experience, international production experience, technological capabilities, and their use of alliances. The relatively high-standard deviation associated with the technological capabilities of small firms suggests that some small firms have access to quite sophisticated technological capabilities. This is an interesting observation that highlights the fact that not all small firms are innovators—some may serve niche markets that do not require strong technological capabilities and others may simply lack a competitive advantage. Only those firms with advanced capabilities will be able to overcome the liability of foreignness and successfully expand abroad. Although purely descriptive, this information is suggestive of the type of resource heterogeneity that is likely to influence the ability of firms to leverage their technological capabilities and alliances when expanding overseas.

Table 2
Comparison of descriptive statistics across small-, medium-, and large-sized firms[a]

Variable	Small mean (S.D.)	Medium mean (S.D.)	Large mean (S.D.)	Comparison x_{small} to x_{medium}	Comparison x_{medium} to x_{large}	Comparison x_{small} to x_{large}
Foreign sales intensity	0.41 (0.27)	0.47 (0.27)	0.46 (0.14)	$t = -1.01$	$t = 0.11$	$t = -0.94$
U.S. sales ($ million)	32.94 (24.58)	203.00 (136.95)	2,622.7 (2020.2)	$t = -6.64^{***}$	$t = -3.54^{**}$	$t = -3.79^{**}$
Firm tenure	13.41 (8.42)	17.83 (9.97)	30.22 (13.08)	$t = -2.20^{*}$	$t = -3.02^{**}$	$t = -3.75^{**}$
Employees[b]	244 (171.3)	2,152 (1,832.6)	23,348 (17,633.8)	$t = -5.30^{***}$	$t = -3.39^{*}$	$t = -3.71^{**}$
New venture	0.32	0.17	0.00	$\chi^2 = 2.11$	$\chi^2 = 1.78$	$\chi^2 = 3.96^{*}$
Founder	0.13	0.10	0.00	$\chi^2 = 0.10$	$\chi^2 = 1.01$	$\chi^2 = 1.29$
Private	0.35	0.14	0.00	$\chi^2 = 4.37^{*}$	$\chi^2 = 1.39$	$\chi^2 = 4.52^{*}$
International marketing experience	0.79 (0.95)	1.93 (1.19)	2.78 (0.44)	$t = -4.51^{***}$	$t = -3.18^{**}$	$t = -10.45^{***}$
International production experience	0.08 (0.33)	0.31 (1.00)	2.56 (2.92)	$t = -1.21$	$t = -2.47^{*}$	$t = -2.54^{*}$
Technological capability	1.87 (1.72)	2.62 (1.66)	5.11 (0.60)	$t = -1.96^{†}$	$t = -6.78^{***}$	$t = -10.98^{***}$
Nonequity alliances	0.19 (0.50)	0.21 (0.62)	1.00 (0.87)	$t = -0.44$	$t = -3.05^{**}$	$t = -2.74^{*}$
Equity alliances	0.16 (0.48)	0.21 (0.49)	1.11 (1.69)	$t = 0.13$	$t = -1.58$	$t = -1.68$
N	63	29	9			

Data on number of employees were available for 57 small-, 26 medium-, and 8 large-sized firms.

[a] In constructing this table, we have followed industry norms and defined small firms to include those with worldwide sales of less than US$200 million medium-sized firms as those with worldwide sales between US$200 million and US$1 billion and large firms as those with worldwide sales in excess of US$1 billion (Angel, 1994; ICE, 1995–1996).

[b] Fisher's two-tailed exact test of homogeneity were conducted to assess the equivalence of the private, founder, and new venture variables. Two-tailed t tests of significance under the null that the mean difference is zero were conducted to assess the equivalence of the remaining variables.

* $P < .05$.
** $P < .01$.
*** $P < .001$.
† $P < .10$.

5.1. Hypothesis testing

The regression models employed to test our hypotheses are presented in Tables 3 and 4. Table 3 reports results obtained with the annual revenue-based measure of venture status utilized by practitioners within the industry. Table 4 presents four panels that report analyses conducted with measures of venture status based on number of employees, venture age,

298   M.J. Leiblein, J.J. Reuer / Journal of Business Venturing 19 (2004) 285–307

Table 3
Multivariate regression analyses with foreign sales as the dependent variable[a]

Variable	Foreign sales (log of US$ million)							
	Model 0	Model I	Model II	F statistic	Model III	F statistic	Model IV	F statistic
Intercept	4.45***	4.06***	4.00***		4.03***		4.06**	
	(0.35)	(0.38)	(0.44)		(0.38)		(0.38)	
Venture status-small firm	−1.89***	−1.79***	−1.70***	15.80***	−1.66	17.96***	−1.79***	15.76***
	(0.32)	(0.32)	(0.48)		(0.32)		(0.33)	
International production	0.39***	0.25*	0.24†		0.20†		0.25†	
	(0.11)	(0.12)	(0.13)		(0.12)		(0.13)	
International marketing	0.40**	0.33**	0.32**		0.28*		0.33*	
	(0.13)	(0.13)	(0.13)		(0.13)		(0.13)	
Technological capability		0.16*	0.19	2.32†	0.17*		0.16*	
		(0.08)	(0.13)		(0.08)		(0.08)	
International nonequity alliances		0.01	0.01		0.37	1.64	0.01	
		(0.22)	(0.22)		(0.29)		(0.22)	
International equity alliances		0.35†	0.36†		0.35†		0.36	1.54
		(0.20)	(0.20)		(0.20)		(0.25)	
Venture status small firm—technological capability			−0.04					
			(0.16)					
Venture status small firm—international nonequity alliances					−0.77†			
					(0.43)			
Venture status small firm—international equity alliances							−0.01	
							(0.42)	
Model F	43.63***	24.85***	21.10***		22.28***		21.07***	
Adjusted R^2	.57	.61	.61		.63		.61	

[a] $N = 101$. Standard errors appear in parentheses.
* $P < .05$.
** $P < .01$.
*** $P < .001$.
† $P < .10$.

founder status, and private status, respectively. Model 0 in Table 3 provides information regarding the effects due solely to the control variables. In Table 3 and in each panel of Table 4, Model I augments the baseline control model by including the direct effects of technological capability, international nonequity alliances, and international equity alliances. Models II–IV add a series of interaction terms to examine whether the effects of the theoretical variables vary across entrepreneurial and established ventures. Since the t values for the direct effect terms included in an interaction are sensitive to linear transformations of the variables (Cohen, 1978), significance levels are not reported for the direct effects of variables that also appear in interaction terms. F statistics are reported to indicate the overall affect of variables that also appear in interaction terms in the column to the right of each model in Table 3 and at the bottom of Table 4.

Hierarchical tests testing for the joint significance of the three theoretical variables in Model I indicates that these variables explain a significant amount of the variance in foreign sales for all analyses reported in Tables 3 and 4. Moreover, the results involving the influence of the control variables and the direct effects of technological capability and international nonequity alliances on foreign sales are robust across all models. Models II–IV further indicate that the influence of international nonequity alliances vary across small and large firms as determined by annual revenue or employee count as well as across young and old ventures as determined by the new venture status variable.

H1 predicted that a firm's technological capability positively influences its foreign sales base. The results presented in Model I of Table 3 and each of the panels in Table 4 indicate a positive and stable relationship between technological capability and foreign sales across the models with significance levels ranging from very strong ($P < .01$) to strong ($P < .05$). Analyses presented in Model III indicate that the overall influence of technological capabilities on foreign sales remains significant after accounting for potential moderation by firm size. These results provide strong support for H1.

H2a and H2b argued that firms investing in international nonequity and equity alliances are better positioned to develop their foreign sales base. While both international nonequity and international equity alliances exhibited strong zero-order correlations with foreign sales, the multivariate results presented in Tables 3 and 4 indicate that these effects are greatly diminished once these variables are jointly introduced to the model.[6] The coefficient for equity alliances is modestly significant at the .10 level in models employing the revenue and employee count measures of venture status. The coefficient for nonequity alliances fails to reach statistical significance in all models. Thus, there is a tentative support for H2b on the effects of international equity alliances. The lack of support for H2a is consistent with recent evidence presented by Prœce et al. (1999, p. 271) that indicated a nonsignificant relationship between alliance formation and overseas activity in a sample of early stage technology-based firms.

The final set of hypotheses argued that the influence of technological capabilities and alliances varies across entrepreneurial firms and others. H3 stated that the influence of technological capabilities on foreign sales would be greater for entrepreneurial firms than their more established counterparts. To test this hypothesis, we estimated models incorporat-

---

[6] Given the positive correlation between the formation of international equity and nonequity alliances reported in Table 1, we conducted separate analyses that examined the combined effect of all international alliances. The results obtained from these tests indicated that the combined effect of international alliances on foreign sales was significant at the .05 value.

Table 4
Multivariate regression analyses with alternative measures of entrepreneurial status[a]

Variable	Foreign sales (log of US$ million)														
	Employees				New venture[b]			Founder[b]			Private				
	Model I	Model II	Model III	Model IV	Model I	Model II	Model IV	Model I	Model II	Model IV	Model I	Model II	Model III	Model IV
Intercept	3.61***	3.56***	3.58***	3.70***	2.55***	2.53***	2.55***	2.34***	2.24***	2.33***	2.56***	2.43***	2.57***	2.59***
	(0.36)	(0.45)	(0.36)	(0.37)	(0.28)	(0.30)	(0.28)	(0.26)	(0.26)	(0.26)	(0.37)	(0.30)	(0.29)	(0.29)
Venture status	−1.42***	−1.35**	−1.28***	−1.54***	−0.64†	−0.55	−0.86*	−0.32	0.66	−0.44	−0.62†	−0.14	−0.63†	−0.74*
	(0.30)	(0.50)	(0.31)	(0.32)	(0.34)	(0.49)	(0.35)	(0.46)	(0.76)	(0.50)	(0.33)	(0.48)	(0.34)	(0.35)
International production	0.28*	0.27*	0.23†	0.32*	0.38**	0.38**	0.42**	0.39**	0.37**	0.41**	0.39**	0.37**	0.39**	0.41**
	(0.13)	(0.13)	(0.13)	(0.13)	(0.14)	(0.14)	(0.13)	(0.14)	(0.14)	(0.14)	(0.14)	(0.14)	(0.14)	(0.14)
International marketing	0.50***	0.49***	0.44***	0.49***	0.67***	0.67***	0.65***	0.67***	0.67***	0.68***	0.65***	0.62***	0.65***	0.64***
	(0.12)	(0.12)	(0.12)	(0.12)	(0.12)	(0.13)	(0.12)	(0.13)	(0.12)	(0.13)	(0.12)	(0.13)	(0.13)	(0.13)
Technological capability	0.15*	0.17	0.16*	0.13†	0.19*	0.20*	0.21*	0.22*	0.27*	0.23**	0.20*	0.27**	0.20*	0.19*
	(0.08)	(0.13)	(0.08)	(0.08)	(0.08)	(0.10)	(0.09)	(0.08)	(0.09)	(0.08)	(0.09)	(0.10)	(0.09)	(0.09)
International nonequity alliances	0.01	0.01	0.36	0.01	−0.03	−0.04	−0.03	0.03	0.01	0.03	0.01	−0.01	−0.01	0.01
	(0.22)	(0.23)	(0.31)	(0.22)	(0.25)	(0.25)	(0.24)	(0.25)	(0.25)	(0.25)	(0.25)	(0.25)	(0.26)	(0.25)
International equity alliances	0.37†	0.37†	0.36†	0.24	0.33	0.32	0.19	0.34	0.31	0.24	0.30	0.28	0.30	0.23
	(0.21)	(0.21)	(0.21)	(0.24)	(0.23)	(0.23)	(0.23)	(0.23)	(0.23)	(0.27)	(0.22)	(0.23)	(0.23)	(0.23)
Venture status—technological capability		−0.03				−0.05			−0.42†			−0.27		
		(0.16)				(0.20)			(0.25)			(0.19)		

continued overleaf

M.J. Leiblein, J.J. Reuer / Journal of Business Venturing 19 (2004) 285–307   301

	1	2	3	4	5	6	7	8	9	10	11	12	13	14
Venture status* international nonequity alliances			−0.75† (0.45)										0.04 (0.77)	
Venture status—international equity alliances			−0.52 (0.46)			1.91* (0.88)				0.40 (0.56)				1.39 (1.06)
Overall F statistic for venture status	11.06***	12.77***	11.81***		1.79	4.16*			1.55	0.48		2.74†	1.71	2.62†
Overall F statistic for theoretical covariate	1.84	3.27*	2.47†		2.37†	3.39*			4.75**	1.30		3.63*	0.01	1.73
Model F	21.78***	18.48***	19.42***	18.89***	15.73***	13.36***	14.67***	14.74***	13.23***	13.23***	15.71***	13.89***	13.32***	13.82***
R^2	.58	.58	.59	.59	.50	.50	.53	.48	.50	.50	.51	.50	.50	.51

[a] $N=101$. Standard errors appear in parentheses.

[b] There were no observations that set venture status "new venture" or "founder" measures to one and engaged in an international nonequity alliance during the sample frame. Consequently, it was not possible to test models that include an interaction between international nonequity alliance and entrepreneurial status using these measures.

* $P<.05$.
** $P<.01$.
*** $P<.001$.
† $P<.10$.

ing multiplicative terms constructed between the technological capability measure and indicators of venture status. The estimated interaction effects between technological capability and venture status failed to reach significance at the .10 level in the majority of models presented in Tables 3 and 4. The lone exception was Model II in the founder panel of Table 4. However, the effect in this model was modest ($P=.08$) and indicated that the influence of technological capability on foreign sales was lower for ventures that retained their founder than others. Thus, there is no empirical support for H3, indicating that entrepreneurial firms and established firms benefit equally from upstream technological capabilities when expanding abroad.

H4a and H4b suggest that international nonequity and equity alliances will be more beneficial in generating foreign sales for larger firms than for smaller firms. Again, interaction terms are employed to test whether the effect varies with firm size. The t statistics for the interaction terms associated with international nonequity alliances provide modest evidence ($P<.10$) suggesting that foreign sales of smaller ventures, as measured by annual revenue or employee count, are diminished by the presence of nonequity alliances. The t statistics for the interaction terms associated with international equity alliances indicate ($P<.05$) that the foreign sales of younger ventures are enhanced by the presence of equity alliances. While these findings lend no support for H4a and partial support for H4b, they do provide some initial evidence that the effects of investment in international equity alliances differ across entrepreneurial and established firms.

6. Discussion

This study had two broad objectives. The first was to provide an empirical test of received wisdom regarding the influence of firm capabilities and international alliances on foreign sales activity. The second was to respond to recent calls for research that examines differences in the resource profiles and international expansion strategies employed by different classes of ventures (e.g., McDougall et al., 1994; Chen and Hambrick, 1995). In pursuing this second objective, our broader aim was to begin to identify some relevant contingencies that might strengthen or dampen the positive effects of alliances or technological capabilities as discussed in prior research.

This paper addresses the first of these objectives by putting to an empirical test the basic claims that distinctive capabilities and alliances facilitate expansion in general and the development of foreign sales in particular. While prior work has demonstrated that firms possessing intangible assets gain by leveraging these assets into international markets (e.g., Caves, 1996; Morck and Yeung, 1992), comparatively little is known about the specific performance implications of international alliances. This is striking given that it is often asserted that alliances provide a number of benefits to collaborators (e.g., Contractor and Lorange, 1988). We empirically examine the relationship between investment in international nonequity and equity alliances and foreign sales while controlling for the influence of technological capabilities as well as other forms of foreign direct investment.

M.J. Leiblein, J.J. Reuer / Journal of Business Venturing 19 (2004) 285–307   303

The evidence presented in this paper confirms that both internal technological skills and externally forged relationships exhibit strong bivariate relationships with firms' subsequent foreign sales. While the influence of technological capabilities remains significant after controlling for a wide variety of firm-level characteristics, our multivariate analyses indicate that the influence of alliances diminishes in the presence of controls for venture status or other forms of foreign investment. In contrast to arguments suggesting that investment in international alliances will lead to increased foreign sales, this suggests that alliances per se are not strongly related to foreign sales. This finding cautions against attributing certain organizational outcomes to alliances without controlling for related firm characteristics and resources that might be otherwise linked to firms' decisions to invest in alliances. Future research could adopt the individual transaction as the unit of analysis in order to examine firms' individual alliance decisions, their drivers, and their consequences for entrepreneurial firms. Two-stage modeling approaches originally used in labor economics may be implemented to account not only for observed differences in firm- and transaction-level attributes leading firms to use alliances, but also for unobserved factors affecting organizational governance choices (e.g., Heckman, 1976). For instance, recent applications indicate that the relationships between foreign market entry mode and survival as well as between make versus buy choices and technological performance are due to unobserved factors associated with firms' organizational governance choices (e.g., Shaver, 1998; Leiblein et al., 2002).

This paper addresses our second objective by examining how differences in the strategies and resources of entrepreneurial and established ventures influence their abilities to exploit internal capabilities and international alliances when building a foreign sales base. The descriptive information we present shows that numerous differences exist in the resource and capability profiles of the small, medium, and large firms in our sample. While prior work has demonstrated that small firms are often more innovative than their larger competitors (e.g., Acs and Audretsch, 1988), the existence of relatively weak property rights protection in many developing countries suggests that the technological resources leveraged by smaller firms pursuing overseas expansion may be vulnerable to misappropriation (e.g., Acs et al., 1997). Similarly, while strategic alliances are likely to allow small firms and new ventures to overcome many of the entry barriers associated with foreign expansion, they do so by putting the fate of these organizations in the hands of an international partner with its own objectives. Entrepreneurial firms engaged in international collaboration therefore need to be sensitive to potential adverse selection and moral hazard problems when attempting to exchange technological capabilities for market access.

The present findings indicate the relevance of additional research on the explanatory power of the born-global view (McDougall et al., 1994) vis-à-vis perspectives emphasizing an evolutionary process of internationalization (Johanson and Vahlne, 1977). Our results indicate that small, medium, and large semiconductor firms exhibit the same level of foreign sales intensity, yet the evidence also points to the relevance of downstream assets in infrastructure such as foreign marketing and production facilities. Thus, future research might consider the relative importance of these two perspectives in different settings prone to entry by entrepreneurial firms. Rangan and Adner (2001) recently argued, for instance, that even

Internet startups may not be able to spread quickly across the world, as a born global view suggests, due to three important obstacles: potential customers must learn about these firms, users must trust the company to transact on the site, and the firm's offerings must be consistent with customers' preferences and tastes. They suggest that entrepreneurial firms will continue to benefit by succeeding at home prior to expanding abroad in a manner that accommodates local differences.

The scope and limitations of the present analysis point to a number of other areas where additional research may prove valuable. First, work is needed in other industries to test the generalizability of the findings on the roles of firm capabilities and alliances for entrepreneurial firms. For instance, Zahra et al. (2001) examine a broader cross section of new ventures from 12 different industries, and they find that overall sales growth is associated with acquisitions, licensing agreements, and export agreements. Second, since the present paper provides a cross-sectional analysis, future studies with access to primary longitudinal data may test these predictions using a dynamic framework. Third, as our focus is on the foreign sales implications of entrepreneurial firms' technological capabilities and alliances, future studies could examine other performance outcomes associated with these resources and investments. Finally, as alliances increase in number and diversity, research would be valuable on the specific implications of different alliance forms for entrepreneurial firms. Research in these directions can also provide an empirical testing ground for emerging thinking on the theory of the entrepreneurial firm and the specific implications of its changing boundaries.

Acknowledgements

In developing this paper, we have benefited from conversations with Arnie Cooper, Patricia McDougall, Douglas Miller, Dan Muzyka, and Carolyn Woo. We also thank Joe Grenier from Dataquest and Klaus Schuegraf from Integrated Circuit Engineering for their assistance with data collection and commentary on competition between entrepreneurial and established firms within the semiconductor industry. Financial support for this research was provided by the Ohio State University Center for International Business Education and Research (CIBER). All errors remain the responsibility of the authors.

References

Acs, Z., Audretsch, D., 1988. Innovation in large and small firms: an empirical analysis. Am. Econ. Rev. 78 (4), 678–690.

Acs, Z., Morck, R., Shaver, J.M., Yeung, B., 1997. The internationalization of small and medium-sized enterprises: a policy perspective. Small Bus. Econ. 9, 7–20.

Almeida, P., Grant, R., Song, J., 1998. Firms, alliances, and markets in cross border knowledge flow. Georgetown University (working paper).

Angel, D.P., 1994. Restructuring for Innovation: The Remaking of the US Semiconductor Industry. Guilford Press, New York.

Auster, E.R., 1992. The relationship of industry evolution to patterns of technological linkages, joint ventures, and direct investment between the U.S. and Japan. Manage. Sci. 38, 778–792.

Autio, E., Sapienza, H.J., Almeida, J.G., 2001. Effects of age at entry, knowledge intensity, and imitability on international growth. Acad. Manage. J. 43, 909–924.

Barney, J.B., 1986. Strategic factor markets: expectations, luck, and business strategy. Manage. Sci. 32, 1512–1514.

Begley, T., 1995. Using founder status, age of firm, and company growth rate as the basis for distinguishing entrepreneurs from managers of smaller businesses. J. Bus. Venturing 10, 249–263.

Biggadike, R.E., 1979. The risky business of diversification. Harvard Bus. Rev. 57, 103–111.

Caves, R.E., 1996. Multinational Enterprise and Economic Analysis, 2nd ed. Cambridge Univ. Press, New York, NY.

Chen, M.-J., Hambrick, D., 1995. Speed, stealth, and selective attack: how small firms differ from large firms in competitive behavior. Acad. Manage. J. 38 (2), 453–482.

Chowdhury, J., 1992. Performance of international joint ventures and wholly owned foreign subsidiaries: a comparative perspective. Manag. Int. Rev. 32, 115–133.

Cohen, J., 1978. Partialed products are interactions; partialed powers are curve components. Psychol. Bull. 85, 858–866.

Contractor, F.J., Lorange, P., 1988. Why should firms cooperate? The strategy and economics basis for cooperative ventures. In: Contractor, F.J., Lorange, P. (Eds.), Cooperative Strategies in International Business, D.C. Health, pp. 3–30.

Covin, J., Slevin, D., 1989. Strategic management of small firms in hostile and benign environments. Strateg. Manage. J. 10, 75–87.

Covin, J., Slevin, D., 1990. New venture strategic posture, structure, and performance: an industry life cycle analysis. J. Bus. Venturing 5, 123–135.

Das, S., Sen, P., Sengupta, S., 1998. Impact of alliances on firm valuation. Acad. Manage. J. 41, 27–41.

Dean, T.J., Brown, R.L., Bamford, C.E., 1998. Differences in large and small firm responses to environmental context: strategic implications from a comparative analysis of business formations. Strateg. Manage. J. 19 (8), 709–728.

Deeds, D.L., Hill, C.W., 1999. An examination of opportunistic action within research alliances: evidence from the biotechnology industry. J. Bus. Venturing 14 (2), 141–163.

Dierickx, I., Cool, K., 1989. Asset stock accumulation and sustainability of competitive advantage. Manage. Sci. 35, 1504–1514.

Eisenhardt, K.M., Schoonhoven, C.B., 1996. Resource-based view of alliance formation: strategic and social effects in entrepreneurial firms. Organ. Sci. 7, 136–150.

Fiegenbaum, A., Karnanai, A., 1991. Output flexibility: a competitive advantage for small firms. Strateg. Manage. J. 12, 101–114.

Fujita, M., 1995. Small and medium sized transnational corporations: trends and patterns of foreign direct investment. Small Bus. Econ. 7 (3), 183–204.

Gomes-Casseres, B., 1997. Alliance strategies of small firms. Small Bus. Econ. 9, 33–44.

Gruber, H., 1994. Learning and Strategic Product Innovation: Theory and Evidence for the Semiconductor Industry Elsevier, Amsterdam.

Hagedoorn, J., 1993. Understanding the rationale of strategic technology partnering: interorganizational modes of cooperation and sectoral differences. Strateg. Manage. J. 14, 371–385.

Hagedoorn, J., Schakenraad, J., 1994. The effect of strategic technology alliances on company performance. Strateg. Manage. J. 15, 291–309.

Hambrick, D.C., MacMillan, I.C., Day, D.L., 1982. Strategic attributes and performance in the BCG Matrix: a PIMS-based analysis of industrial product businesses. Acad. Manage. J. 25, 510–531.

Hamel, G., Prahalad, C.K., 1994. Competing for the Future. Harvard Business School Press, Boston, MA.

Hara, G., Kanai, T., 1994. Entrepreneurial networks across oceans to promote international strategic alliances for small businesses. J. Bus. Venturing 9, 489–507.

Harrigan, K.R., 1988. Joint ventures and competitive strategy. Strateg. Manage. J. 9, 141–158.

Heckman, J., 1976. The common structure of statistical models of truncation, sample selection, and limited dependent variables and a simple estimator for such models. Ann. Econ. Soc. Meas. 5 (4), 475–492.

Hitt, M.A., Hoskisson, R.E., Kim, H., 1997. International diversification: effects on innovation and firm performance in product-diversified firms. Acad. Manage. J. 40, 767–798.

Hladik, K.J., 1985. International Joint Ventures: An Economic Analysis of U.S.-Foreign Business Partnerships. Lexington Books, Lexington, MA.

Hymer, S.H., 1976. The International Operations of National Firms: A Study of Direct Investment. MIT Press, Cambridge, MA.

Integrated Circuit Engineering, 1995–1996. Profiles Reports: A Survey of Worldwide IC Manufacturers and Suppliers Integrated Circuit Engineering, Scottsdale, AZ.

Johanson, J., Vahlne, J.E., 1977. The internationalization process of a firm: a model of knowledge development and increasing foreign market commitments. J. Int. Bus. Stud. 9, 22–32.

Khanna, T., Gulati, R., Nohria, N., 1998. The dynamics of learning alliances: competition, cooperation, and relative scope. Strateg. Manage. J. 19, 193–210.

Kogut, B., 1991. Joint ventures and the option to acquire and expand. Manage. Sci. 37, 19–33.

Koh, J., Venkatraman, N., 1991. Joint venture formations and stock market reactions: an assessment of the information technology sector. Acad. Manage. J. 34, 869–892.

Larson, A., 1991. Partner networks: leveraging external ties to improve entrepreneurial performance. J. Bus. Venturing 6, 173–188.

Leiblein, M.J., Reuer, J.J., Dalsace, F., 2002. Do make or buy decisions matter? The influence of organizational governance on technological performance. Strateg. Manage. J. 23, 817–833.

Li, J., 1995. Foreign entry and survival: effects of strategic choices on performance in international markets. Strateg. Manage. J. 16, 333–351.

McDougall, P.P., Oviatt, B.M., 1996. New venture internationalization, strategic change, and performance: a follow-up study. J. Bus. Venturing 11 (1), 23–40.

McDougall, P.P., Shane, S., Oviatt, B.M., 1994. Explaining the formation of international new ventures: the limits of theories from international business research. J. Bus. Venturing 9, 469–487.

Mitchell, W., Singh, K., 1992. Incumbents' use of pre-entry alliances before expansion into new technical subfields of an industry. J. Econ. Behav. Organ. 18, 347–372.

Mitchell, W., Shaver, J.M., Yeung, B., 1994. Foreign entrant survival and foreign market share: Canadian companies' experience in United States medical sector markets. Strateg. Manage. J. 15, 555–567.

Morck, R., Yeung, B., 1992. Internalization: an event study test. J. Int. Econ. 33, 41–56.

Mowery, D.C., Oxley, D.E., Silverman, B.S., 1996. Alliances and interfirm knowledge transfer. Strateg. Manage. J. 17, 77–92 (winter special issue).

Niederkofler, M., 1991. The evolution of alliances: opportunities for managerial influence. J. Bus. Venturing 6 (4), 237–257.

Oviatt, B.M., McDougall, P.P., 1994. Toward a theory of international new ventures. J. Int. Bus. Stud. 25 (1), 45–64.

Oviatt, B.M., McDougall, P.P., 1997. Challenges for internationalization process theory: the case of international new ventures. Manag. Int. Rev. 37, 85–99.

Oviatt, B.M., McDougall, P.P., 1999. A framework for understanding accelerated international entrepreneurship. In: Rugman, A.M., Wright, R.W. (Eds.), Research in Global Strategic Management: International Entrepreneurship, Jai Press, Stamford, Ct, pp. 23–40.

Park, S.H., Ungson, G.R., 1997. The effect of national culture, organizational complementarity, and economic motivation on joint venture dissolution. Acad. Manage. J. 40, 279–307.

Parkhe, A., 1993. Alliance structuring: a game theoretic and transaction costs examination of interfirm cooperation. Acad. Manage. J. 36, 794–829.

Penrose, E.T., 1995. The Theory of the Growth of the Firm, 3rd ed. Wiley, New York, NY.

Pisano, G.P., 1989. Using equity participation to support exchange: evidence from the biotechnology industry. J. Law Econ. Organ. 5, 109–126.

Powell, W.W., Koput, K.W., Smith-Doerr, L., 1996. Interorganizational collaboration and the locus of innovation: networks of learning in biotechnology. Adm. Sci. Q. 41, 116–145.

Preece, S.B., Miles, G., Baetz, M.C., 1999. Explaining the international intensity and global diversity of early-stage technology-based firms. J. Bus. Venturing 14 (3), 259–281.

Rangan, S., Adner, R., 2001. Profits and the Internet: seven misconceptions. Sloan Manage. Rev. 42, 44–53.

Reuer, J.J., Koza, M.P., 2000. Asymmetric information and joint venture performance: theory and evidence for domestic and international joint ventures. Strateg. Manage. J. 21, 81–88.

Reuer, J.J., Leiblein, M.J., 2000. Downside risk implications of multinationality and international joint ventures. Acad. Manage. J. 43, 203–214.

Sarkar, M.B., Echambadi, R.A.J., Harrison, J.S., 2001. Alliance entrepreneurship and firm market performance. Strateg. Manage. J. 22, 701–712.

Shaver, J.M., 1998. Accounting for endogeneity when assessing strategy performance: does entry mode choice affect FDI survival? Manage. Sci. 44 (4), 571–585.

Singh, K., Mitchell, W., 1996. Precarious collaboration: business survival after partners shut down or form new partnerships. Strateg. Manage. J. 17, 99–116 (summer special issue).

Stopford, J.M., Wells, L.T., 1972. Managing the Multinational Enterprise. Basic Books, New York, NY.

Weaver, K.M., Dickson, P.H., 1998. Outcome quality of small- to medium-sized enterprise-based alliances: the role of perceived partner behaviors. J. Bus. Venturing 13 (6), 505–522.

Wernerfelt, B., 1984. A resource-based view of the firm. Strateg. Manage. J. 5, 171–180.

Woo, C.Y., 1987. Path analysis of the relationship between market share, business-level conduct and risk. Strateg. Manage. J. 8, 149–168.

Woo, C.Y., Cooper, A.C., 1981. Strategies of effective low share businesses. Strateg. Manage. J. 2, 301–318.

Woo, C.Y., Cooper, A.C., 1982. The surprising case for low market share. Harvard Bus. Rev. 59, 106–113.

Woodcock, C.P., Beamish, P.W., Makino, S., 1994. Ownership-based entry mode strategies and international performance. J. Int. Bus. Stud. 25, 253–273.

Zacharakis, A.L., 1997. Entrepreneurial entry into foreign markets: a transaction cost perspective. Entrep. Theory Pract. 21, 23–39.

Zaheer, S., 1995. Overcoming the liability of foreignness. Acad. Manage. J. 38, 341–365.

Zaheer, S., Mosakowski, E., 1997. The dynamics of the liability of foreignness: a global study of survival in financial services. Strateg. Manage. J. 18, 439–464.

Zahra, S.A., Ireland, R.D., Hitt, M.A., 2001. International expansion by new venture firms: international diversity, mode of market entry, technological learning, and performance. Acad. Manage. J. 43, 925–950.

[23]

Available online at www.sciencedirect.com

SCIENCE ⓓ DIRECT®

JOURNAL of BUSINESS VENTURING

ELSEVIER

Journal of Business Venturing 21 (2006) 461–486

Partnering strategies and performance of SMEs' international joint ventures

Jane W. Lu[a,*], Paul W. Beamish[b,1]

[a]*Lee Kong Chian School of Business, Singapore Management University, 469 Bukit Timah Road, Singapore 259756, Singapore*
[b]*Asian Management Institute, Richard Ivey School of Business, University of Western Ontario, London, ON, Canada N6A 3K7*

Abstract

The international joint venture (IJV) is an important mode in the internationalization of small- and medium-sized enterprises (SMEs). Internationalization in turn is an entrepreneurial behavior in the pursuit of growth. Partnering strategies in the formation of IJVs can have significant effects on the outcome of SMEs' international expansion. In this study, we examine the performance implications of two types of resources contributed by SMEs' IJV partners, host country knowledge and size-based resources. We develop and test three sets of hypotheses about the longevity and financial performance of a sample of 1117 international joint ventures established in 43 countries by 614 Japanese SMEs that have fewer than 500 employees. Our findings indicate that SMEs' IJVs with local partner(s) may be associated with decreases in longevity, especially when SMEs acquire host country knowledge. The host country experience of Japanese partner(s) does not have any direct effects on IJV profitability but reduces the longevity of IJVs. Finally, the size of Japanese partner(s) increases the longevity of IJVs but may have negative effects on IJV profitability when large Japanese partners have low equity ownership in IJVs. Our findings highlight the differential effects that IJV partners' experience-based and size-based resources have on IJV performance. Our findings also demonstrate that the same strategy could have different effects on different dimensions of performance.
© 2005 Elsevier Inc. All rights reserved.

Keywords: Entrepreneurship; Internationalization; Alliances; Performance; Small- and medium-sized enterprises; International joint ventures

* Corresponding author. Tel.: +65 6822 0758; fax: +65 6822 0777.
  E-mail addresses: janelu@smu.edu.sg (J.W. Lu), pbeamish@ivey.uwo.ca (P.W. Beamish).
[1] Tel.: +1 519 661 3237; fax: +1 519 661 3700.

0883-9026/$ - see front matter © 2005 Elsevier Inc. All rights reserved.
doi:10.1016/j.jbusvent.2005.02.002

462 *J.W. Lu, P.W. Beamish / Journal of Business Venturing 21 (2006) 461–486*

1. Executive summary

The international joint venture (IJV), a form of strategic alliance, is an important means of international expansion. A growing number of small- and medium-sized enterprises (SMEs) have employed this mode in their expansion. Despite the increasing popularity of international joint venturing as an internationalization strategy for small and medium enterprises, the effectiveness of this strategy has been under-explored in the entrepreneurship literature. While researchers in the areas of strategy and international business have explored the performance of international joint ventures, they tend to focus on ventures established by large firms. Their findings may not be generalizable to SMEs' international joint ventures, given the significant differences between smaller and larger firms.

SMEs' foreign subsidiaries encounter three liabilities in their international expansion. They face liability of foreignness due to the lack of local knowledge, which can lead to disadvantages in competing with local firms who are familiar with the local environment. They are subject to liability of newness as newly established firms in the local market. As new firms, they face a series of challenges such as financing, staffing, securing relationships with suppliers and buyers, attracting local customers and ultimately establishing their legitimacy. Their third liability is one of smallness. By definition, small and medium enterprises have limited resources and capabilities. Given this characteristic of SME parent firms, their subsidiaries tend to be small in size and vulnerable to environmental change.

Forming international joint ventures and leveraging IJV partners' resources is a potential way to overcome these three liabilities. In this study, we explore how two types of resources, host country knowledge and size-based resources contributed by IJV partners, can help small and medium enterprises and their foreign subsidiaries mitigate one or all three of the liabilities and ultimately influence the performance of SMEs' international joint ventures. Taking into account both economic and social considerations, we develop and test three sets of hypotheses about the longevity and financial performance of a sample of 1117 international joint ventures worldwide established by 614 Japanese small and medium enterprises that have fewer than 500 employees.

We find that the size of Japanese partner(s) was positively related to the longevity of SMEs' international joint ventures, while either the use of local partner or the host country experience of Japanese partner(s) is associated with decreases in IJV longevity. The contrasting effects that experience-based and size-based resources had on IJV longevity point to the importance of considering the characteristics of resources contributed by IJV partners. When establishing international joint ventures, SMEs may want to contribute a diverse set of resources to reduce the obsolescence of the IJV bargain.

Our findings also indicate that the profitability of SMEs' international joint ventures may suffer when the home country partners are of large size and have low equity ownership in the IJVs. The results of our investigations point to the potential bargaining power asymmetry when SMEs form alliances with partners of large size. Our findings suggest that one way for SMEs to minimize the potential downside effect of bargaining power asymmetry is to increase the stake of large partners in the joint ventures to align the goals of both partners.

J.W. Lu, P.W. Beamish / Journal of Business Venturing 21 (2006) 461–486   463

Finally, the contrasting effects of the same partnering strategy on different dimensions of IJV performance suggest that SMEs should be aware of the pros and cons of different partnering strategies for different organizational objectives and make the choice that helps to achieve the most important objective, whether it is longevity, profitability or another objective.

2. Introduction

Sooner or later, many firms choose to expand their geographic scope from domestic to foreign markets. There is an array of modes for entering international markets, such as exporting, licensing, non-equity strategic alliances, joint ventures and wholly owned subsidiaries, each of which has its own advantages and disadvantages (for a review, see Anderson and Gatignon, 1986). As an important means of international expansion, international joint ventures (IJVs) have been implemented with increasing frequency (e.g., Osborn and Hagedoorn, 1997; Hitt et al., 2000; Dhanaraj and Beamish, 2004). Within this general popularity of international joint ventures, a growing number of them involve small and medium enterprises (Zahra et al., 2000). Although there is a mounting body of research on the outcome of international joint ventures, the focus of prior studies tends to be on IJVs established by large firms with little attention to SMEs' IJVs (e.g., Dussauge et al., 2000; Hennart et al., 1998). Given the significant differences between smaller and larger firms, the antecedents and outcomes of IJVs established by SMEs may well differ from those by large firms. Thus there is a need to examine IJV performance in the context of small and medium enterprises.

Within the array of choices made by small and medium enterprises that might affect the performance of their international joint ventures, this study focuses on the choice of IJV partners because partner selection is one of the first and most fundamental choices that a firm makes after deciding to use an IJV as an entry mode (Hitt et al., 1995). We explored the performance implications of SMEs' partnering strategies by bridging concepts and theories drawn from the entrepreneurship, strategy, and international business areas because our research question is at the intersection of these literatures. We discussed the deficiencies in resource endowments in the form of liabilities of foreignness, newness and smallness confronted by SMEs' international joint ventures. We then propose potential partnering strategies to overcome these three liabilities.

In our theorizing of partner selection, we integrate resource-based view theory with institutional theory to balance economic considerations with social considerations (Lu, 2002). We emphasize the resources that an IJV partner brings into the joint venture and how such resources could help alleviate resource deficiencies faced by the SMEs and their foreign subsidiaries in international expansion. We also differentiate partners' experience-based resources such as host country knowledge from size-based resources such as financial resources and reputation. We further highlight how social considerations among IJV partners could influence IJV performance.

We employed both IJV longevity and IJV profitability as performance measures to capture different dimensions of the performance construct. More importantly, we contend that the antecedents of improved IJV profitability might differ from those for IJV longevity. We directly test such a contention by exploring the differential implications of partnering strategies on IJV profitability and IJV longevity. Finally, in our modeling of IJV longevity, we included profitability as a predictor of longevity to explicitly account for the fact that financial performance is often an antecedent of the exit decision. This kind of two-stage modeling of longevity presents advancement to prior studies which examined profitability and longevity as two independent outcomes (Delios and Beamish. 2001).

We implemented our investigation using a sample of 1117 international joint ventures established by 614 Japanese small and medium enterprises across 43 countries. We also conducted semi-structured interviews with 11 Japanese joint ventures in China to explore the mechanisms through which partnering strategies have effects on IJV performance. The SMEs and their largest Japanese partners in our sample differ dramatically in their sizes and resource bases. For example, the SMEs in our sample have an average of 220 employees and less than 2 years of operating experience in the host countries of the IJVs. In contrast, their large Japanese partners have an average of 5398 employees and on average, 84 years of operating experience in the host countries of the IJVs. The dramatic differences exemplify the potential benefits to SMEs by leveraging large firms' resources in their international expansion as well as the potential problems stemming from bargaining power differences in SME–large firm partnership. Such a sample provides an ideal setting for the test of our hypotheses.

Our findings contribute to the entrepreneurship, strategy and international business literatures by demonstrating differential performance implications of the same partnering strategy and the contrasting effects of partners' experience-based and size-based resources. Our theoretical framework also advances the theorizing of IJV performance by integrating resource-based view theory with institutional theory to provide more balanced considerations on IJV performance.

3. Partnering strategies and IJV performance

A joint venture is "an entity that is created when two or more firms pool a portion of their resources to create a separate jointly owned organization" (Barringer and Harrison, 2000). The increasing importance of joint ventures as an internationalization strategy has led to substantial research on the antecedents and outcomes of international joint ventures, especially among strategy and international business researchers. Consistent with the traditional focus of strategy and international business research on large, well-internationalized firms (McDougall and Oviatt, 1996), most of these empirical studies have focused on international joint ventures established by large firms to the exclusion of SMEs' international joint ventures. The empirical findings on the relationships between partnering strategies and IJV performance based on samples of international joint ventures established by large firms do not necessarily apply to IJVs established by small and medium enterprises because it has been well argued and documented that smaller businesses and larger businesses are different species (Shuman and Seeger, 1986).

Resource-based view of the firm emphasizes the importance of firms' resource endowments (Barney, 1991). Compared to large firms, small and medium enterprises have limited financial and managerial resources (Jarillo, 1989; Oviatt and McDougall, 1994).

J.W. Lu, P.W. Beamish / Journal of Business Venturing 21 (2006) 461–486 465

Further, small and medium enterprises are usually owned and managed by founders, whereas large firms are managed by professionals (Shuman and Seeger, 1986). As a result, the decision-making in SMEs is highly centralized (Carrier, 1994). In a sample of 28 mid-Atlantic small and large electronic firms, Smith et al. (1988) identified that entrepreneurs/owners of SMEs are less comprehensive in their decision behavior as compared to large firms' professional managers. They have further demonstrated that such behaviors have a negative impact on SME performance. In a similar vein, we contend that the distinguishing characteristics of SMEs may well have an impact on the performance of their international joint ventures.

Further, most of the studies on IJV performance have tended to focus on IJV longevity (sometimes called survival), perhaps due to the difficulty in obtaining profitability information. Firm performance is a multidimensional construct and a strategy could well have differential effects on different dimensions of firm performance (Delios and Beamish, 2001). IJV longevity and profitability are two notable dimensions of IJV performance, and it is important to understand the differential influence that partnering strategies have on both.

In contrast to the abundance of research on the relationship between partnering strategies and IJV performance in the international business and strategic management literatures, researchers in the entrepreneurship area have paid sparse attention to international joint ventures, especially to the outcome of SMEs' international joint ventures (McDougall and Oviatt, 1996; Coviello and McAuley, 1999). Given the increasing importance of joint venture as an internationalization mode for small and medium enterprises, it is crucial to start to explore if and how partnering strategies influence IJV performance.

International joint ventures are especially important for small and medium enterprises in their internationalization process. By definition, small and medium enterprises have more constraints in resources and capabilities (Jarillo, 1989; Beamish, 1999) as compared to large firms. As a result, SMEs are subject to the liability of smallness (Aldrich and Auster, 1986) which is reflected in SMEs' difficulties in obtaining and securing critical resources such as capital and staff, and their vulnerability to environmental changes (Buckley, 1989). Such disadvantages impose constraints on the expansion of small and medium enterprises either in the domestic market or international markets (Zacharakis, 1997). More importantly, the liability of smallness can be hereditary and can adversely affect the future of SMEs' subsidiaries. As "children" of SME parents, SMEs' subsidiaries tend to be small in size and are subject to the same set of constraints in resources and capabilities that confront the SME parents. For SMEs' overseas subsidiaries, the liability of smallness inflates the liabilities of foreignness (Hymer, 1976) and newness (Stinchcombe, 1965).

Foreign subsidiaries of all firms, large or small, face the latter two liabilities, when the target markets are new to the parent firms and when they are greenfield investments that involve the establishment of new subsidiaries (instead of brownfield investments such as acquisitions) (Lu and Beamish, 2004). The liability of foreignness places foreign subsidiaries in a disadvantageous position in competition with local firms who are familiar with the local environment and have established good local connections. All overseas subsidiaries face this problem, but it can be a more severe problem for small and medium enterprises because they are less experienced in international markets compared to large firms (Lu and Beamish, 2001).

The liability of newness is reflected in the series of operational challenges facing a start-up, such as financing, recruiting, procuring and marketing. More importantly, the liability of newness raises the issue of legitimacy which directly affects the solution to all the above operational challenges. Compared to incumbents, new entrants have to work hard to prove themselves in order to establish relationships with various stakeholders. The legitimizing process can be both expensive and time-consuming, substantially increasing the challenges faced by the new subsidiaries. This process can be more difficult for SMEs' new subsidiaries because they cannot leverage their SME parents' public awareness as can the new subsidiaries by large firms who are more well-known (Eisenhardt and Schoonhoven, 1990).

Taken together, SMEs' foreign subsidiaries face more resource constraints in undertaking international expansion than large firms' foreign subsidiaries. Such resource constraints are manifest in three liabilities which place small and medium enterprises in a disadvantageous position in competition with local firms and with subsidiaries established by larger firms. International joint venture can be an important means for small and medium enterprises to help their foreign subsidiaries overcome these three liabilities by having access to IJV partners' resources.

Resources of particular interest to SMEs in their international expansion are knowledge about the local markets, firm reputation and financial capital. IJV partners' knowledge about the local markets can help reduce the liability of foreignness confronted by SMEs' foreign subsidiaries (Delios and Henisz, 2000). IJV partners' knowledge about the local markets depends on the partners' experience in the local markets. IJV partners' reputation provides endorsement to SMEs' foreign subsidiaries and thus helps mitigate their liabilities of newness (Baum and Oliver, 1991; Stuart et al., 1999). IJV partners' financial capital can alleviate the financial constraints of SMEs' foreign subsidiaries and help reduce their liabilities of smallness (Hitt et al., 2000). IJV partners' reputation and financial capital are closely associated with the size of the partners. We discuss partners' host country knowledge, an experience-based resource, and partners' reputation and financial resources, two size-based resources and their performance implications to SMEs' international joint ventures in the following sections.

3.1. Partners' host country knowledge

As discussed earlier, knowledge about the host countries is a critical resource for the success of SMEs' foreign subsidiaries. It is possible for small and medium enterprises to acquire local knowledge and develop new organizational capabilities internally through incremental experience accumulation in new markets (Johanson and Vahlne, 1977). However, this learning-by-doing process takes time and can result in mistakes (Dierickx and Cool, 1989). Coupled with the vulnerability as a result of their small size, these mistakes can endanger the longevity of both SME's foreign subsidiaries and their SME parents (Beamish, 1999). By accessing an IJV partners' local knowledge base, an SME's foreign subsidiary can expedite its learning process and minimize mistakes.

A local (host country) partner represents a primary source of local knowledge as compared to home country partners (Yan and Gray, 1994). A local partner tends to have more detailed knowledge about various aspects of the host country environment, as compared to the other partner options. A local firm is familiar with the needs and tastes of the local consumers. It has information about local competitors. It also has local networks that can provide its international joint venture(s) with timely information on the changes in the local environment. In sum, an IJV with a local partner can provide an immediate alleviation of SMEs' local knowledge deficiencies and help overcome its liability of foreignness (Hymer, 1976). The reduction in the disadvantages as compared to local firms should help improve a foreign subsidiary's competitive position in the local market and contribute to improved profitability (Beamish and Banks, 1987; Makino and Delios, 1996).

Prior research has found evidence that there is a positive relationship between the use of a local partner and the performance of international joint ventures (Beamish, 1985; Blodgett, 1992; Makino and Delios, 1996). Although the setting of prior studies employed samples of large firms, we expect the same relationship to exist in a sample of IJVs established by small and medium enterprises because SMEs usually have less international experience and are subject to more severe local knowledge deficiencies when they expand across borders. For example, one of the managers of a Japanese SME joint venture in China said that: "(They) used their relationship with governments to make sure that our business license was issued in time. (They) recruited capable local staff, handled all import and export procedures, helped market the products through their distribution channels. Without local partners, we could not have achieved what we did." Consistent with the findings of our field work and prior studies, we hypothesize:

Hypothesis 1a. The use of local partner(s) is positively associated with the profitability of SMEs' IJVs.

While a local partner can contribute to superior IJV performance through the reduction in the liability of foreignness, its value can depreciate over the life cycle of the international joint venture. As foreign partners accumulate experience in the local environment, they become less dependent on local partners for local knowledge and may even find that the role of local partner is redundant (Makino and Delios, 1996). As the dependence on a local partner's local knowledge decreases, a foreign partner's bargaining power over the local partner increases. The change in the balance of the bargaining power between local and foreign partners can lead to IJV instability or even IJV dissolution (Inkpen and Beamish, 1997). Given this potentially larger instability of international joint ventures with local partners, we expect that IJVs with local partners can have higher exit rates than IJVs between home country partners.

Hypothesis 1b. The use of local partner(s) is negatively associated with the longevity of SMEs' IJVs.

Given SMEs' accumulation of host country knowledge as the major underlying reason for this instability, we also expect SMEs' host country knowledge to strengthen the negative relationship between the use of local partners and the longevity of their international joint ventures.

Hypothesis 1c. SMEs' host country knowledge strengthens the negative effects that the use of local partner(s) has on the longevity of SMEs' IJVs.

Another source of host country knowledge is home country partners. Although home country partners are not "born local" in the same way as local firms are, they can nonetheless have good knowledge about the local environment through their operation in IJVs' host countries. In this experiential process, foreign firms develop general knowledge about the political, social, economic and cultural aspects of the investment locations and specific knowledge about local business practices and local networks (Johanson and Vahlne, 1977). This experience-based local knowledge from home country partners could be as effective as the local knowledge from local partners in helping SMEs' international joint ventures to alleviate their liability of foreignness. The change in the source of local knowledge (from local partner to home country partners) should not change the positive effects of local knowledge on IJV performance. The reduction in the disadvantages in competition with local firms and other experienced foreign subsidiaries should confer competitive advantages to SMEs' international joint ventures and lead to higher profitability.

Hypothesis 2a. The host country experience of home country partner(s) is positively associated with the profitability of SMEs' IJVs.

On the other hand, an international joint venture can be considered as a vehicle for investing firms for learning what the other partner knows (Hamel, 1991; Parkhe, 1991). As long as this learning goal is not satisfied, JV partners have a need for each other, and the incentive to work together and keep the international joint venture in operation. From this perspective, the more a partner has to learn from its international joint venture partner, the longer it takes to acquire the knowledge, the slower the change in bargaining power due to the acquisition of knowledge, and the more stable an international joint venture. As such, the absence of experience in IJVs' host country presents more incentives for learning from the other partner in the joint operation of the IJV. The strong learning incentive should promote IJV longevity.

Hypothesis 2b. The host country experience of home country partner(s) is negatively associated with the longevity of SMEs' IJVs.

2.2. Partner size

The size of the partnering firms is another important consideration, especially for small and medium enterprises. In addition to the liability of foreignness which could be overcome through partnering with a local partner and/or home country partner with local experience, SMEs' international joint ventures are subject to liabilities of smallness and newness. Given the resource constraints of their SME parents, SME subsidiaries tend to be smaller in size, as compared to subsidiaries established by large firms. Being small, they do not have as many resources to withstand mistakes or losses and are vulnerable to environmental selection. The liability of smallness is reflected in problems of raising capital, recruiting and retaining staff, and handling the administrative costs of compliance

J.W. Lu, P.W. Beamish / Journal of Business Venturing 21 (2006) 461–486   469

with government regulations (Aldrich and Auster, 1986). The liability of smallness has been found to be closely and positively related to organizational mortality rates (Freeman et al., 1983; Singh et al., 1986).

As with all new ventures, international joint ventures face a liability of newness (Stinchcombe, 1965) which is rooted in the uncertainty about the viability of a new venture. Compared to international joint ventures established by large firms, SMEs' international joint ventures are likely to be newer to the local community because small and medium enterprises have lower levels of public awareness than large firms. This enhanced newness of SMEs' subsidiaries makes it more difficult to have access to local resources and more time-consuming to develop local business networks in investment sites.

Partnering with large firms could help alleviate these two liabilities. There are a number of contributions that large firms can bring to SMEs' foreign subsidiaries. Two of the most critical are resources and reputation. By definition, large firms are more resource-rich than small and medium enterprises. Partnering with large firms can alleviate SMEs' resource constraints in the establishment of their foreign subsidiaries. With the resource backup from large firms, SMEs' foreign subsidiaries could achieve full operation and growth faster than otherwise would be possible with the resource constraints of SMEs. As the international joint ventures grow, they accumulate greater managerial and financial resources themselves and become less vulnerable. The situation is likely to enhance IJV longevity.

In addition, partnering with large firms also allows small and medium enterprises to leverage the reputations of large firms to quickly establish the legitimacy of their international joint ventures in host countries. Institutional theory emphasizes institutional environments which include cognitive and sociological elements, such as shared norms, standards, and expectations (DiMaggio and Powell, 1991; Scott, 1995). This institutional environment is an underlying driving force behind organizational activities because of an organization's desire for legitimacy (Martinez and Dacin, 1999). Large size tends to legitimate organizations, to the extent that large size is interpreted by external stakeholders as an outcome of an organization's prior success (Baum and Oliver, 1991). Business connections with large firms, either in the form of one-term business transactions or long-term partnership, are likely to enhance the legitimacy of smaller firms (Barringer and Harrison, 2000). In a similar vein, with large firms as a partner in the international joint venture, SMEs' international joint ventures can shorten the time it takes to establish legitimacy in the relevant industries and host countries. With the establishment of their legitimacy and enhanced visibility and image, it would be easier for SMEs' international joint ventures to obtain financial and human resources in local markets and develop local networks with suppliers and buyers (Stuart et al., 1999). Prior research has demonstrated that inter-organizational endorsement helps new organizations to acquire legitimacy which in turn reduces their mortality rate (Baum and Oliver, 1991).

In addition to the above direct and indirect contributions to IJV longevity, large partners have resources and incentives to keep their subsidiaries operating. With "deep pockets", large firms can better sustain losses from some of their subsidiaries. Large firms may also have a longer-term view towards foreign investments, allowing them to keep their subsidiaries operating a bit longer to assess their viability. Further, social considerations may also permit large firms to maintain their subsidiaries, even if they are incurring losses. From an institutional perspective, large firms tend to attract disproportionate attention from the public. Large firms are arguably more concerned than small and medium enterprises about the downside effect on their reputation associated with the dissolution of their international joint ventures. To maintain favorable public image, large firms may hesitate to terminate unprofitable subsidiaries. All factors, from either economic or social perspectives, point to an increase in the longevity of international joint ventures with large partners.

Hypothesis 3a. The size of home country partner(s) is positively associated with the longevity of SMEs' IJVs.

Even with the various benefits associated with partnering with large firms, it has been well documented that partnering with large firms can be detrimental to small and medium enterprises. There is a general concern with the compatibility between the management systems and styles of larger versus smaller firms in the joint management of their foreign subsidiaries (Park and Ungson, 1997). A more fundamental concern from the perspective of small and medium enterprises is the differences in bargaining power stemming from the significant differences in firm sizes (Alvarez and Barney, 2001). The dependence of SMEs' international joint ventures on large partners for resources and legitimacy gives the large partners bargaining power over the SME parents and places them in a position to potentially exploit the international joint ventures or alliances for their own economic gains. Large firms have sometimes appeared to form predatory alliances with SMEs. For example, in Alvarez and Barney's study of 218 alliances between large and entrepreneurial firms in American high-technology industries, almost 80% of entrepreneurial firms experienced exploitation from large partners in their alliances (Alvarez and Barney, 2001).

From an institutional perspective, profitability is less visible than survival because it is difficult for the public to obtain financial information on unlisted firms or on particular subsidiaries. Therefore, in terms of their public image, large firms are more concerned about the survival (rather than profitability) of their subsidiaries. As such, the social considerations around the survival of SMEs' IJVs do not apply to the same extent when considering their profitability.

The exploitation of large partners can take the form of withdrawing or not contributing the crucial resources to alliances with SMEs (Alvarez and Barney, 2001). More often, large firms make unreasonable demands or impose unfair contractual or non-contractual terms in business transactions on alliances with SMEs (Osborn and Baughn, 1990). In our field work, a joint venture established by a Japanese SME in the shipping industry complained that its larger partner, a sogo shosha, expected the joint venture to give priority to the shipment of all the subsidiaries established by the sogo shosha. In addition, there were expectations about higher service standard at lower prices for the sogo shosha's shipments. This arrangement limited the joint venture's choices of customers and the preferential pricing cut into its profit margins. The vulnerability of SMEs to exploitation and the subsequent acceptance of unfair terms could hurt the profitability of their international joint ventures.

J.W. Lu, P.W. Beamish / Journal of Business Venturing 21 (2006) 461–486 471

Hypothesis 3b. The size of home country partner(s) is negatively associated with the profitability of SMEs' IJVs.

Although large firms are in a position to exploit SME partners in their joint ventures, the extent that exploitation by large partners happens depends on the level of equity ownership of large partners in the IJVs. It has long been argued that a firm's level of equity ownership in a venture is reflective of its commitment to the investment (Anderson and Gatignon, 1986). To some extent, equity positions are like "hostages" or "collaterals" which can help mitigate opportunism in joint ventures (Beamish, 1985; Mjoen and Tallman, 1997; Dhanaraj and Beamish, 2004). These findings in the IJV literature on the role of equity position in IJVs are consistent with those from our field work: the exploitative situation described by SME partners usually appears when the large partner takes a small stake in the joint venture. Therefore, we expect that as large partners' equity levels in IJVs increase, there is less incentive for them to exploit the IJVs and their smaller partners. Therefore, we hypothesize:

Hypothesis 3c. The equity ownership of home country partner(s) weakens the negative effects that the size of home country partner(s) has on the profitability of SMEs' IJVs.

The contrasting effects of two resources, experienced-based resources and size-based resources, contributed by IJV partners, on the profitability and longevity of SMEs' IJVs are reflective of the differences in the development of these two resources. SMEs can have access to and leverage larger partners' size-related resources such as financial resources and reputation. But they cannot possess such resources in the joint operation of IJVs and become comparable in size to their larger partners, at least not in the near future. In contrast, experience is easier to develop. In the joint establishment and operation of joint ventures, SMEs can learn local knowledge from their partners and from their own experience in the local environment. As SMEs accumulate their own host country knowledge, their JV partners may become redundant at least in terms of host country knowledge. As such, IJV partners' local knowledge contributes to IJV profitability but may hamper IJV longevity given the diminishing value of JV partners' host country knowledge as SMEs acquire it themselves. In contrast, IJV partners' size-based resources are not a potentially destabilizing factor because SMEs cannot really acquire their partners' size-related resources and are more likely to be dependent on such resources for a long period of time. However, SMEs' dependency on larger firms' size-related resources may depress IJV profitability because larger firms are in a position to take advantage of this dependency and impose unfavorable terms on SMEs in the design and management of their JVs.

4. Methodology

4.1. Sample and data sources

For the implementation of our investigation, we collected data on Japanese small and medium enterprises and their international joint ventures worldwide. We used two

472   *J.W. Lu, P.W. Beamish / Journal of Business Venturing 21 (2006) 461–486*

sources for the corporate-level information on Japanese small and medium enterprises. For listed small and medium enterprises, the main source of Japanese parent company information is the *Nikkei NEEDS* tapes, an electronic database compiled by Nihon Keizai Shinbun-sha, one of the largest compilers and publishers of statistical and corporate information in Japan. This database provides financial information on all Japanese firms listed on the Tokyo stock exchange. The *Nikkei NEEDS* tapes report detailed firm-level information compiled from the firm's balance sheet, income statement and includes other supplementary data (e.g., number of employees). Annual information can be traced since 1964 from this database. For this study, we used information up to the 2000 edition which provided information on more than 3000 publicly listed Japanese firms. Where required, additional parent company information was gathered from the *Analysts' Guide*, a publication by Daiwa Institute of Research, the *GlobalVantage* database and various editions of the *Japan Company Handbook*, all of which have a coverage of parent firms similar to that in the *Nikkei NEEDS* tapes. For unlisted small and medium enterprises, we consulted three editions (1996, 1998 and 2000) of Japanese private firm directory. Each directory provided 3-year information on Japanese unlisted firms in terms of products, number of employees, sales and profits, etc.

The source of information for the foreign direct investment of Japanese firms was *Kaigai Shinshutsu Kigyou Souran, Kuni-Betsu*. This source is published annually by Toyo Keizai Inc., a large Japanese compiler and publisher of business-level, statistical and economic information. The data reported in *Kaigai Shinshutsu Kigyou Souran* was based on responses to questionnaires sent to all firms listed on Japanese stock exchanges, as well as to major unlisted firms. Researchers at Toyo Keizai used press releases, annual reports and telephone interviews to supplement the questionnaire data and to increase the comprehensiveness of the information reported in *Kaigai Shinshutsu Kigyou Souran*. The coverage of *Kaigai Shinshutsu Kigyou Souran* is close to the population of foreign subsidiaries for Japanese firms that responded to the survey (Beamish et al., 1997). In terms of the data in *Kaigai Shinshutsu Kigyou Souran*, it provides information on the date of establishment, the entry mode, the equity position and identity of the subsidiary's parents. It also reports the subsidiary's industry, its equity capital, sales, and total employment, the identity of joint venture partners, local and expatriate employment levels and subsidiary performance. For this study, we coded all the information about foreign subsidiaries established by Japanese SMEs' from the 1986, 1989, 1992, 1994, 1997, 1999 and 2001 editions.

Consistent with other studies on small- and medium-sized firms in the entrepreneurship literature (Baird et al., 1994; Beamish, 1999; Wolff and Pett, 2000; Lu and Beamish, 2001), this study employs the definition of small and medium enterprises provided by the American Small Business Administration (SBA): stand-alone enterprises with fewer than 500 employees. Further, in line with prior studies on joint ventures (e.g., Hennart et al.. 1998; Delios and Beamish, 1999), we include a firm as a parent of the international joint venture if it has more than 5% and less than 95% equity ownership in the investment. Combining these two criteria, we included an international joint venture in the sample if at least one of its parents is an SME who has a minimum of 5% and maximum of 95% equity of the investment.

4.2. Variables

4.2.1. Dependent variables

Given that performance is a complex multidimensional construct, previous researchers (Venkatraman and Ramanujam. 1986) have argued convincingly that studies should include multiple, disparate performance measures. In this study, we used two measures, longevity and profitability, to capture the different dimensions of IJV performance.

We identified exiting subsidiaries by comparing preceding editions of *Kaigai Shinshutsu Kigyou Souran* with later editions. The earliest edition we used was 1986 and the latest edition was 2001. Exits were coded as one, and surviving international joint ventures were coded as zero. The duration of the international joint venture, to its time of exit or to the year 2001, was computed by the number of years from foundation to exit, or to 2001. We backtracked the exact exit year by consulting consecutive editions of *Kaigai Shinshutsu Kigyou Souran* from 1986 to 2001. The exit year was the year that the joint venture was de-listed in the database. Although one could not equate exit completely with failure, one could expect that an IJV would remain in operation as long as it represented the most appropriate organization mode (Inkpen and Beamish. 1997). Empirical evidence from prior studies also suggests that longevity correlates positively with financial and satisfaction measures of performance (Geringer and Hébert. 1991).

The measure of JV profitability was based on a managerial assessment of profitability. Performance was measured by asking the top Japanese manager in each subsidiary to specify performance for the unit on a three-point scale, representing "Loss", "Break-even" and "Gain". This study uses this performance measure because the validity of similar perceptual measures of performance is well supported in the academic literature. For example, perceptual performance measures have been shown to be highly correlated with objective, accounting-based measures (Geringer and Hébert, 1991). Further, prior studies on the performance of Japanese subsidiaries have verified and confirmed the validity and reliability of this measure in Japanese empirical settings (Isobe et al., 2000: Delios and Beamish, 2001).

4.2.2. Independent variables

4.2.2.1. Local partner.
Our data source, *Kaigai Shinshutsu Kigyou Souran*, indicated there were 705 non-Japanese partners. We checked the identity of each of these 705 non-Japanese partners and found that 21 of them were third country partners and the rest were local partners. The proportion of third country partners is consistent with that reported by Makino and Beamish (1998). We deleted the 21 IJVs with third country partners as our theoretical framework focuses on the use of host country partners and home country partners. We coded the use of local partners (with or without the participation of Japanese partners) as one.

4.2.2.2. Japanese partners' host country experience.
We computed Japanese partners' host country experience as the host country experience of the Japanese partner who had the most experience prior to the focal entry in the same host country of the SMEs' international joint ventures. Host country experience is the number of years in which a

firm operated a subsidiary in a particular host country. This measure was computed from information reported in various editions of *Kaigai Shinshutsu Kigyou Souran*. We focused on the Japanese partner with the most host country experience because SMEs should potentially have access to the maximum (rather than the average) resources of their Japanese partners.

4.2.2.3. Japanese partners' firm size.   For the same reason as the focus on the Japanese partners with the most host country experience, we defined Japanese partners' firm size as the number of employees of the largest Japanese partners. This measure was derived from the *Nikkei Needs* database.

4.2.2.4. Japanese partners' equity ownership level.   We computed Japanese partners' equity ownership level as the percent equity ownership by the largest Japanese partner. This measure was obtained from various editions of *Kaigai Shinshutsu Kigyou Souran*.

4.2.2.5. Control variables.   We included three measures to account for major factors at the international joint venture level that could affect IJV performance. They are JV size (measured as total number of employees), SME-IJV product relatedness (coded one if SMEs and their IJVs are in the same product category as defined by 2-digit SIC codes) and JV location (measured as cultural distance between home country and host countries). The cultural distance measure was computed from Hofstede (1980) measures using the methodology outlined in Kogut and Singh (1988).

We next calculated three measures (corresponding to those for Japanese partners as independent variables) to control for factors at the focal SME parent level. We computed the host country experience of the SME parent prior to the focal entry. We computed the size of the SME as the number of employees. We then computed percent equity ownership by SMEs. In addition, we controlled for the ownership type of the SMEs as we have both private and listed firms in our sample. We coded one when an SME is a publicly listed firm. Our final control was a set of industry dummies based on 2-digit industry codes. For the profitability model, we added an extra control variable of subsidiary age defined as the number of years that an IJV operates in a host country. For the longevity model, we added profitability as the extra control variable as profitability is an important consideration in the decision to keep or terminate an IJV.

After matching the parent information with information on foreign direct investments and deleting cases with missing values, we obtained a sample comprising 1117 international joint ventures established by 614 Japanese small and medium enterprises in 43 countries worldwide. 27% of the IJVs in our sample had more than two partners and the maximum number of partners in one international joint venture in our sample is six. For hypotheses regarding home country partners, the sample size was reduced to 631 international joint ventures and further to 522 international joint ventures because of missing information on firm size of some of the partners.

We employed ordered logit analysis to examine the hypotheses about IJV profitability. Ordered logit models are the appropriate procedure when the dependent variable has ordinal properties but is not ratio scaled (Amemiya, 1981). For the test of the hypotheses related to IJV longevity, we used Cox's proportional hazard model

Table 1
Descriptive statistics and correlations

Variable and definition	1117 IJVs		522 IJVs		1	2	3	4	5	6	7	8	9	10	11	12	13	14	15	16
	Mean	S.D.	Mean	S.D.																
1. IJV Exit	0.18	0.39	0.13	0.34		-0.15	-0.03	0.06	-0.09	-0.07	0.08	0.00	0.01	0.05	0.01	0.03	0.00	-0.02	0.06	-0.02
2. Profitability	2.39	0.78	2.36	0.81	-0.06		0.21	-0.02	0.02	-0.04	-0.09	0.00	-0.08	0.01	0.05	0.03	0.07	-0.01	-0.08	0.04
3. IJV age	10.20	7.42	10.60	7.59	0.00	0.18		0.10	-0.09	-0.06	0.02	-0.14	-0.12	0.06	-0.01	0.06	-0.24	0.03	-0.19	0.11
4. IJV size	160	524	185	698	0.03	0.03	0.09		-0.03	-0.05	-0.04	-0.02	-0.02	-0.07	0.10	-0.01	0.04	-0.08	-0.04	0.33
5. IJV location (culture distance)	2.93	0.77	2.97	0.76	-0.02	0.01	-0.12	-0.02		0.09	-0.01	0.05	-0.02	-0.09	-0.07	-0.13	-0.01	0.03	-0.09	-0.05
6. SMEs' equity ownership in IJVs	44.94	23.76	38.30	24.75	-0.02	-0.03	-0.06	-0.06	0.01		0.16	0.13	-0.08	0.15	-0.38	0.03	-0.02	-0.39	0.07	-0.05
7. SMEs' type (listed)	0.19	0.40	0.17	0.37	0.07	-0.08	-0.02	-0.03	-0.02	0.12		0.13	-0.01	0.37	-0.04	0.00	-0.01	-0.08	0.08	0.02
8. SME-IJV relatedness	0.30	0.46	0.21	0.41	0.00	0.03	-0.14	-0.02	0.10	0.10	0.11		0.16	0.14	-0.01	-0.06	0.07	-0.12	0.03	0.01
9. SMEs' host country experience	1.79	6.21	1.54	5.72	0.01	0.00	-0.13	-0.03	-0.02	0.13	0.00	0.11		-0.11	-0.07	-0.08	-0.01	0.09	0.03	-0.07
10. SMEs' size	236	145	220	141	0.05	-0.02	-0.03	-0.08	-0.08		0.38	0.14	-0.11		0.05	0.08	0.09	-0.14	0.08	0.03
11. Local partner	0.62	0.49	0.49	0.50	0.04	0.06	-0.02	0.05	-0.07	-0.21	-0.01	0.04	-0.05	0.07		0.14	0.09	-0.38	-0.14	0.08
12. Japanese partners' type (listed)			0.66	0.48													0.20	-0.14	0.08	0.15
13. Japanese partners—IJV relatedness			0.67	0.47														-0.16	0.20	0.28
14. Japanese partners' equity ownership in IJVs			32.21	22.55															-0.11	-0.13
15. Japanese partners' host country experience			84	257																0.15
16. Japanese partners' size			5398	6966																

(1) All descriptive statistics reported for non-transformed values

(2) Numbers in upper part of correlation matrix for IJVs with Japanese partners. Numbers in lower part of correlation matrix for all IJVs

(3) Significant at the 0.05 level (two-tailed test) when Pearson correlations >0.086 or < -0.086 for upper part of correlation matrix and >0.058 or < -0.058 for lower part of correlation matrix.

476   J.W. Lu, P.W. Beamish / Journal of Business Venturing 21 (2006) 461–486

Table 2
Regression on Performance of Japanese SMEs' IJVs[a,b]

| Variable | Exit=1 | | | | | 3=Profit; 2=Break-even; 1=Loss | | | | |
| | All IJVs (N=1117, 206 exits) | | | IJVs with Japanese partners (N=522, 70 exits) | | All IJVs (N=1117) | | IJVs with Japanese partners (N=522) | | |
	Model 1	Model 2	Model 3	Model 4	Model 5	Model 6	Model 7	Model 8	Model 9	Model 10
1. Loss	2.27*** (0.40)	2.42*** (0.44)	2.44*** (0.44)	4.58*** (1.30)	4.58*** (1.31)					
2. Break-even	1.22 (0.22)	1.23 (0.22)	1.25 (0.23)	1.18 (0.43)	1.16 (0.43)					
3. IJV age[c]						0.78*** (0.10)	0.79*** (0.10)	0.99*** (0.16)	1.05*** (0.17)	1.06*** (0.17)
4. IJV size[c]	1.07 (0.07)	1.07 (0.07)	1.08 (0.07)	0.95 (0.09)	0.95 (0.09)	−0.01 (0.05)	−0.01 (0.05)	0.07 (0.07)	0.07 (0.07)	0.07 (0.07)
5. IJV location	1.16+ (0.10)	1.17+ (0.10)	1.17+ (0.10)	0.94 (0.14)	0.90 (0.14)	0.09 (0.08)	0.10 (0.08)	0.17 (0.13)	0.17 (0.13)	0.17 (0.13)
6. SMEs' equity ownership in IJVs	1.00 (0.01)	1.00 (0.01)	1.00 (0.01)	0.99 (0.01)	0.99 (0.01)	−0.01 (0.01)	−0.01 (0.01)	−0.01 (0.01)	−0.01 (0.01)	−0.01 (0.01)
7. SMEs' type (listed)	1.14 (0.21)	1.16 (0.22)	1.16 (0.22)	1.29 (0.41)	1.53 (0.49)	−0.44** (0.16)	−0.43** (0.16)	−0.53* (0.25)	−0.53* (0.26)	−0.55* (0.26)
8. SME-IJV relatedness (2-digit SIC codes)	1.26 (0.21)	1.19 (0.20)	1.20 (0.20)	1.52 (0.52)	1.54 (0.52)	0.34* (0.14)	0.32* (0.14)	0.32 (0.24)	0.34 (0.24)	0.37 (0.24)
9. SMEs' host country experience[c]	1.22* (0.11)	1.25* (0.11)	0.98 (0.16)	1.10 (0.20)	1.04 (0.19)	0.05 (0.07)	0.05 (0.07)	−0.04 (0.11)	−0.05 (0.11)	−0.02 (0.12)

J.W. Lu, P.W. Beamish / Journal of Business Venturing 21 (2006) 461–486   477

10. SMEs' size[c]	1.19* (0.10)	1.19* (0.10)	1.20* (0.10)	1.17 (0.16)	1.02 (0.15)	0.08 (0.07)	0.07 (0.07)	0.14 (0.11)	0.14 (0.11)	0.14 (0.11)
11. Local partner		1.50* (0.25)	1.32 (0.23)	1.05 (0.35)	1.06 (0.35)		0.21+ (0.13)	0.27 (0.26)	0.28 (0.26)	0.30 (0.26)
12. Japanese partners' equity ownership in IJVs				1.00 (0.01)	1.00 (0.01)			0.01 (0.01)	0.01 (0.01)	-0.08* (0.03)
13. Japanese partners' type (listed)				0.94 (0.28)	1.12 (0.37)			-0.15 (0.20)	-0.11 (0.21)	-0.11 (0.21)
14. Japanese partners—IJV relatedness (2-digit SIC codes)				2.06* (0.60)	2.36** (0.77)			0.64** (0.21)	0.68** (0.23)	0.72** (0.24)
15. Japanese partners' host country experience[c]					1.24** (0.10)				0.05 (0.06)	0.05 (0.06)
16. Japanese partners' size[c]					0.67** (0.09)				-0.12 (0.10)	-0.43** (0.16)
17. SMEs' host country experience[c] × Local partner			1.45* (0.27)							
18. Japanese partners' equity ownership in IJVs × Japanese partners' size[c]										0.02** (0.01)
Log-likelihood	-1173.07	-1169.87	-1167.76	-333.05	326.78	-1044.12	-1042.75	-475.69	-474.85	-471.33
Model chi-square	57.09**	63.47**	67.70**	48.51**	61.06**	84.07*	86.81*	68.30*	69.99**	77.03**
Incremental chi-square		6.38*	4.23*	4.23*	12.55**		2.74+	2.74+	1.69	7.04**

***p<0.001; **p<0.01; *p<0.05; +p<0.10; all two-tailed tests.

[a] Fixed effects for 2-digit SIC industries of entry were included in the models, but are not reported in the table.

[b] Cell entries are unstandardized coefficient estimates. Numbers in parantheses are standard errors.

[c] Logarithmic transformation.

(Cox and Oakes, 1984). This model estimates the influence of explanatory variables (or covariates) on the hazard of exit without specifying a parametric form for the precise time to failure. Instead, it ranks ventures in terms of the sequence of exit and maximizes the partial likelihood that the ith venture should exit conditional on the characteristics of the other ventures at risk at the time of exit. By incorporating the age distribution directly into the estimation, Cox regression procedure corrects the problems of censored data and aging effects on IJV dissolution and brings the exit rate closer to failure rate.

5. Results

Table 1 presents the descriptive statistics and a correlation matrix for the study's variables. As shown in Table 1, there were significant firm-specific differences between SMEs and their largest Japanese partners. For example, the average number of employees was 220 for the SMEs and 5398 for their largest Japanese partners. In addition, the majority of the SME parents was private (83%), had limited operating experience (<2 years) in their IJVs' host countries and in IJVs' industries (21% are related). In contrast, most of their largest Japanese partners were listed firms (66%) and had much more operating experience (>84 years) in the IJVs' host countries and in IJVs' industries (67% are related). These firm-specific differences by size are consistent with our discussions on the differences between SMEs and large firms.

The descriptive statistics also shows that the average exit rate was 0.18 and the average profitability was 2.39 in our full sample of SMEs' joint ventures. To put the performance of SMEs' joint ventures in perspective, we compared the performance of the SMEs' joint ventures with their wholly owned subsidiaries. We identified 1102 wholly owned subsidiaries established by Japanese small- and medium-sized companies. These wholly owned subsidiaries had an exit rate of 0.24 and an average profitability of 2.30. The significantly higher profitability ($p < 0.05$) and longevity ($p < 0.01$) of SMEs' joint ventures suggest that joint venture is an effective organization form for SMEs' foreign expansion.

We tested our three hypotheses using two sets of five regressions: one for profitability and the other for longevity. The results of these regressions are displayed in Table 2. All models were significant. For the interpretation of the results, a hazard ratio lower than one suggests an increase in the longevity of international joint ventures for Models 1–5 while a positive sign indicates an improvement in IJV profitability for Models 6–10.

Models 1 and 6 are the base-line models which only includes all the control variables and the set of industry dummies. In Model 1, the base-line model for longevity, IJV's financial losses increased its likelihood of exit, as did SMEs' firm size (measured as number of employees) and SMEs' experience in the IJVs' host country. In Model 6, the base-line model for profitability, IJV age had a significant positive effect on performance as expected. At the same time, IJV profitability benefits from the product relatedness between SMEs and their IJVs (2-digit SIC codes) but suffers when the SME is a listed firm.

J.W. Lu, P.W. Beamish / Journal of Business Venturing 21 (2006) 461–486   479

Models 2 and 7 tested Hypotheses 1a and 1b which predict that the use of a local partner is positively related to IJV profitability but negatively related to IJV longevity. Consistent with the prediction in Hypothesis 1a, the use of a local partner had a positive relationship to IJV profitability. However, this positive effect is only significant at the level of $p < 0.10$. At the same time, the use of local partner had a negative and significant influence on the longevity of international joint ventures. Hypothesis 1b is supported.

Hypothesis 1c explores the underlying reason for the relationship identified in Hypothesis 1b and identifies SMEs' host country knowledge as a contributing factor to the negative role of local partner in IJV longevity. Model 3 tested this hypothesis by entering the interaction term between SMEs' host country knowledge and the use of local partner. The change in the chi-square suggests that the inclusion of this interaction term significantly improves the model fit. As predicted in Hypothesis 1c, the coefficient estimation of this interaction term is significant and has a value greater than one, suggesting that SMEs' accumulation of host country knowledge strengthens the negative effects of a local partner on IJV longevity.

Hypotheses 2a, 2b, 3a and 3b make predictions about the resource contributions of home country partners. Models 5 and 9 tested these hypotheses by entering Japanese partners' firm size and host country knowledge while including the same set of control variables for the international joint ventures and for the SMEs. Models 4 and 8 are the base-line models for Models 5 and 9, respectively. In Model 5, Japanese partner's host country experience significantly increases the exit rate of international joint ventures, supporting Hypothesis 2b. Japanese partner size has significant and positive impact on the longevity of international joint ventures, as predicted by Hypothesis 3a. In Model 9, the coefficients for both Japanese partners' firm size and host country experience signed as predicted in Hypotheses 2a and 3b. However, they are not statistically significant, providing little support for Hypothesis 2a and 3b.

Finally, Model 10 tested Hypothesis 3c which specifies that Japanese partners' size has a negative effect on SMEs' IJVs when Japanese partners have low equity positions in the IJVs. As shown in the incremental chi-square statistics, the inclusion of the interaction term between the levels of Japanese partners' equity ownership and Japanese partners' size significantly improved the model fit. Japanese partners' size is significant and signed negative, while the interaction term is significant and signed positive, indicating the negative effects of Japanese partners' size on the profitability of SMEs' IJVs are reduced as the levels of these Japanese partners' equity ownership go up. Hypothesis 3c is strongly supported.

6. Discussion

In this paper, we attempted to examine the effectiveness of international joint venture, an important internationalization strategy for small and medium enterprises. To that end, we explored the differential effects that two types of resources contributed by IJV partners, experience-based and firm size-based resources, had on two dimensions of IJV performance, profitability and longevity, in a sample of international joint ventures established by small- and medium-sized Japanese firms. Table 3 summarizes the hypotheses and the results of the empirical tests.

Table 3
Summary of hypotheses and results

Variables		Hypothesized relationship to IJV performance		Model	Results
H1a	Use of local partner	(+)	Profitability	7	(+)
H1b	Use of local partner	(−)	Longevity	2	(−)
H1c	Use of local partner x Japanese SMEs' experience in IJV's host country	(−)	Longevity	3	(−)
H2a	Japanese partners' experience in IJV's host country	(+)	Profitability	9	Not significant
H2b	Japanese partners' experience in IJV's host country	(−)	Longevity	5	(−)
H3a	Japanese partner size	(+)	Longevity	5	(+)
H3b	Japanese partner size	(−)	Profitability	9	Not significant
H3c	Japanese partner size × Japanese partners' equity ownership in IJVs	(+)	Profitability	10	(+)

We found that the use of a local partner had positive impacts on the profitability of SMEs' IJVs. Although the significance level of this positive effect is only significant at $p < 0.10$ level, it provides some support to our Hypothesis 1a. Our findings are consistent with that of prior large-firm studies (e.g., Makino and Delios, 1996; Makino and Beamish, 1998). Our results further confirm the finding of positive impact that the use of local partner has on the corporate performance of small and medium enterprises (Lu and Beamish, 2001). Japanese partners' host country knowledge also had positive effects on IJV profitability. However, such positive effects were not significant. The differences in the effects of host country knowledge between local partners and Japanese partners suggest that while both local partners and home country partners are viable sources of local knowledge, for small and medium enterprises, local partners seem to be a more effective choice than home country partners for access to local knowledge. The positive effects that a local partner has on an IJV's profitability highlight the importance of local knowledge and the fact that a local partner presents a primary source of local knowledge.

In contrast to its weak, yet consistently positive effects on IJV profitability, host country knowledge, either from local partners or Japanese partners, was found to have a strong negative effect on an IJV's longevity. We further tested the seemingly contradictory effects of local partners and found that SMEs' host country knowledge accumulation contributed to the negative relationship between the use of local partners and IJV longevity. Consistent with the findings in prior studies (Makino and Beamish, 1998), our results support the argument that partner bargaining power is a contributing factor to IJV instability (Inkpen and Beamish, 1997). Our findings also illustrate the instability of many international joint ventures. One way to reduce this instability is for the partners to contribute a diverse and continuing set of resources and knowledge, rather than the one-time contribution of host country knowledge, to their international joint ventures. In this way, the dependency between partners is enhanced, the partner bargaining power is less likely to change dramatically, and the IJVs will become more stable.

J.W. Lu, P.W. Beamish / Journal of Business Venturing 21 (2006) 461–486 481

Further, we explored whether and how partners' size-related resources had an impact on the performance of SMEs' IJVs. We found that Japanese partners' size had a negative effect on the profitability of SMEs' IJVs. However, such negative effect is not significant. In contrast, Japanese partners' size had a significant and positive effect on the longevity of SMEs' IJVs. We further found that Japanese partners' size negatively affects the profitability SMEs' IJVs when Japanese partners assumed low equity ownership of the IJVs. Our findings indicate that given the dependency of the small and medium enterprises on their larger partners' size-based resources, larger firms are in a position to leverage their strong bargaining position and exploit the small and medium enterprises and their international joint ventures. One way to reduce larger partners' incentives of exploitation is to increase their equity ownership in the IJVs. The positive effect of large partners on the longevity of SMEs' IJVs indicates the importance of access to resources and the endorsement effect gained from partnering with large partners. More importantly, it shows that the more difficult it is to replicate the partners' resources, the more stable the IJVs. Compared to host country knowledge, an experience-based resource, size-based resources such as financial resources and reputation are often path-dependent and hence take much longer time to develop. SMEs can acquire much more easily their partners' host country knowledge than their size-related resources. Therefore, the contribution of size-related resources leads to IJV longevity while the contribution of host country knowledge increases the exit rates of IJVs. The contrasting effects of host country knowledge and size-related resources on IJV longevity suggest the importance of considering the characteristics of resources that partners contribute to IJVs in the studies of IJV longevity.

Taken together, our findings reveal the differing effects that the same strategy could have on different dimensions of firm performance. It also confirms that firm performance is a multidimensional construct and researchers should treat different dimensions separately in their assessment of firm performance.

Before drawing any conclusions from this study, it should be noted that this study has its limitations. The most notable one is the fact that our empirical results were derived from a sample of Japanese small and medium enterprises and hence the concern that the findings might be country-specific. For example, Japanese culture emphasizes collectivism (Hofstede. 1980). This could be an underlying reason for the observation of an extensive use of partners from home country in our study. This pattern may not hold for firms from a different country such as U.S. which emphasizes individualism. Therefore, it is important for future studies to use samples of firms from other countries such as U.S. to test and extend the generalizability of our findings.

Another limitation of the study is the assumption that IJV termination is an indicator of IJV failure. Although this is a traditional assumption in many empirical studies on IJVs over the last three decades, recent studies have shown that IJVs can also terminate because of the fulfillment of one or more partners' strategic objectives (Reuer and Zollo, 2000). It would be useful to investigate the outcomes of IJV termination in future studies to have a direct measure of IJV success or failure.

Further, this study focused on equity joint ventures. Internationalizing SMEs can use alternative modes such as non-equity strategic alliance. Future study could extend the framework in this study to the context of non-equity strategic alliance and examine whether this study's results are generalizable in non-equity strategic alliances. In a similar way, future studies could examine the generalizability of our model in IJVs established by larger firms. A more meaningful way to extend this study is to compare equity joint ventures and non-equity strategic alliances or compare joint ventures established by SMEs and by larger firms to determine how they differ in different contexts.

In addition, there are other aspects of partnering strategies to be investigated. For example, with two or more partners, IJVs involve a high level of management complexity which could become overwhelming over time and lead to IJV failure (Makino and Beamish, 1998). Trust between IJV partners also plays an important role in determining the outcome of IJVs (Lane et al., 2001). An integration of a wider spectrum of finer-grained partner characteristics will provide a more complete picture of the relationship between partnering strategies and the performance of SMEs' IJVs.

Finally, it would be ideal to examine the characteristics of all partners, both local partners and home country partners. It would be particularly interesting to de-compartmentalize the concept of local knowledge and study whether all aspects of local knowledge, such as age, industry experience and IJV experience, are relevant to IJVs. It would also be useful to investigate whether the variance in the quality and quantity of these aspects of local knowledge would have an impact on IJV performance. For our study, the investment location of our sample was spread across 43 countries and it would be impractical to collect data on local partners. Hence, the examination of the characteristics of partners was limited to those from home country. But de-compartmentalization of the concept of local knowledge could be an important direction for future studies on IJVs.

7. Conclusions

Our study has made several contributions to the entrepreneurship, strategy and internationalization literatures. First, we introduced institutional theory to complement the economic approach in the traditional IJV literature. We believe that our theoretical framework provides a more balanced view than prior studies because of the integration of social and economic considerations. Second, we differentiated between experience-based and size-based resources contributed by IJV partners and theorized their differential effects on IJV performance. This finer-grained classification of resources points to the importance of examining the nature of resources and its subsequent sustainability, an area that has received sparse attention in the literature.

Third, we directly examined the relative effectiveness of these two resources contributed by IJV partners, host country knowledge and size-based resources, on two dimensions of IJV performance, IJV profitability and IJV longevity. We find that the host country knowledge from local partners are more effective than that from home country partners to the improvements in IJV profitability at least in our sample of international joint ventures established by Japanese small and medium enterprises. The implication is that local partner presents a primary source of local knowledge and that small and medium enterprises should explore opportunities to seek partnership with local firms in their internationalization to benefit from immediate local access associated with such a partnering strategy.

Fourth, this study reveals the important role that large firms could play in the alleviation of the liabilities of newness and smallness faced by SMEs' international joint ventures. Partnering with large partners could be a viable strategy for SMEs' international joint ventures in the pursuit of longevity. However, small and medium enterprises should be aware of the higher bargaining power of large firms and the possible negative implications of this strategy for IJV profitability when seeking alliances with large firms in their international expansion.

Fifth, the contrasting effects that host country knowledge and size-based resources had on IJV longevity presents an advancement to the partner bargaining power argument by Inkpen and Beamish (1997) who only considered local knowledge, bargaining power and instability of IJVs. Our findings point to the importance of considering the characteristics of resources contributed by IJV partners. To promote IJV longevity, SMEs could contribute a diverse and continuing set of resources to reduce the obsolescence of the IJV bargain.

Finally, the different effects of the same strategy, such as the use of local partner, on different dimensions of IJV performance highlight the differential outcomes from the same strategy. When forming alliances, small and medium enterprises should be aware of the pros and cons of different partnering strategies for different organizational objectives and make the choice that helps to achieve the most important objective.

Acknowledgments

This research was supported by a research grant from the National University of Singapore (#R-313-000-045-112), by a Social Sciences and Humanities Research Council of Canada Grant (#410-2001-0143), and by the Asian Management Institute at the University of Western Ontario. The authors are grateful to the helpful comments received from Duane Ireland and two anonymous reviewers.

References

Aldrich, H.E., Auster, E.R., 1986. Even dwarfs started small: liabilities of age and size and their strategic implications. In: Cummings, L.L., Staw, B.M. (Eds.), Research in Organizational Behavior, vol. 8. JAI Press, Greenwich, CT, pp. 165–198.

Alvarez, S.A., Barney, J.B., 2001. How entrepreneurial firms can benefit from alliances with large partners. Academy of Management Executive 15 (1), 139–148.

Amemiya, T., 1981. Qualitative response models: a survey. Journal of Economic Literature 19, 1483–1536.

Anderson, E., Gatignon, H., 1986. Modes of entry: a transaction cost analysis and propositions. Journal of International Business Studies 17 (3), 1–26.

Baird, I.S., Lyles, M.A., Orris, J.B., 1994. The choice of international strategies by small businesses. Journal of Small Business Management 32 (1), 48–60.

Barney, J.B., 1991. Firm resources and sustained competitive advantage. Journal of Management 17 (1), 99–120.

Barringer, B.R., Harrison, J.S., 2000. Walking a tightrope: creating value through interorganizational relationships. Journal of Management 26 (3), 367–403.

Baum, J.A.C., Oliver, C., 1991. Institutional linkages and organizational morality. Administrative Science Quarterly 36, 187–218.

484   *J.W. Lu, P.W. Beamish / Journal of Business Venturing 21 (2006) 461–486*

Beamish, P.W., 1985. The characteristics of joint ventures in developed and developing countries. Columbia Journal of World Business 20 (3), 13–19.

Beamish, P.W., 1999. The role of alliances in international entrepreneurship. Research in Global Strategic Management, vol. 7. JAI Press, Greenwich, pp. 43–61.

Beamish, P.W., Banks, J.C., 1987. Equity joint ventures and the theory of the multinational enterprise. Journal of International Business Studies 17 (I), 1–16.

Beamish, P.W., Delios, A., Lecraw, D.J., 1997. Japanese Multinationals in the Global Economy. Edward Elgar Publishing Limited, Basingstoke, UK.

Blodgett, L., 1992. Factors in the instability of international joint ventures: an event history analysis. Strategic Management Journal 13, 475–481.

Buckley, P.J., 1989. Foreign direct investment by small- and medium-sized enterprises: the theoretical background. Small Business Economics 1, 89–100.

Carrier, C., 1994. Intrapreneurship in large firms and SMEs: a comparative study. International Small Business Journal 12 (3), 54–61.

Coviello, N.E., McAuley, A., 1999. Internationalization and the smaller firm: a review of contemporary empirical research. Management International Review 39 (3), 223–256.

Cox, D.R., Oakes, D., 1984. Analysis of Survival Data. Chapman and Hall, New York.

Delios, A., Beamish, P.W., 1999. Ownership strategy of Japanese firms: transactional, institutional, and experience influences. Strategic Management Journal 20 (10), 915–933.

Delios, A., Beamish, P.W., 2001. Survival and profitability: the roles of experience and intangible assets in foreign subsidiary performance. Academy of Management Journal 44 (5), 1028–1038.

Delios, A., Henisz, W.J., 2000. Japanese firms' investment strategies in emerging economies. Academy of Management Journal 43 (3), 305–323.

Dhanaraj, C., Beamish, P.W., 2004. Effect of equity ownership on the survival of international joint ventures. Strategic Management Journal 25, 295–305.

Dierickx, I., Cool, K., 1989. Asset stock accumulation and sustainability of competitive advantage. Management Science 35 (12), 1504–1510.

DiMaggio, P., Powell, W., 1991. The New Institutionalism in Organizational Analysis. University of Chicago Press, Chicago.

Dussauge, P., Garrette, B., Mitchell, W., 2000. Learning from competing partners: outcomes and durations of scale and link alliances in Europe, North America and Asia. Strategic Management Journal 21 (2), 99–126.

Eisenhardt, K.M., Schoonhoven, C.B., 1990. Organizational growth: linking founding team, strategy, environment, and growth among U.S. semiconductor ventures. Administrative Science Quarterly 35, 504–529.

Freeman, John., Carroll, Glenn R., Hannan, Michael T., 1983. The liability of newness and age dependence in organizational death rates. American Sociological Review 48, 692–710.

Geringer, J., Hébert, L., 1991. Measuring performance of international joint ventures. Journal of International Business Studies 22, 249–263.

Hamel, G., 1991. Competition for competence and interpartner learning within international strategic alliances. Strategic Management Journal 12, 83–103 (special issue).

Hennart, J.-F., Kim, D.-J., Zeng, M., 1998. The impact of joint venture status on the longevity of Japanese stakes in U.S. manufacturing affiliates. Organization Science 9 (3), 382–395.

Hitt, M.A., Tyler, B.B., Hardee, C., Park, D., 1995. Understanding strategic intent in the global marketplace. Academy of Management Journal 9 (2), 12–19.

Hitt, M.A., Dacin, T.M., Levitas, E., Arregle, J.-L., Borza, A., 2000. Partner selection in emerging and developed market contexts: resource-based and organizational learning perspectives. Academy of Management Journal 43 (3), 449–467.

Hofstede, G., 1980. Culture's Consequences: International Differences in Work-Related Values. Sage, Beverly Hills.

Hymer, S.H., 1976. A Study of Direct Foreign Investment. MIT Press, Cambridge, MA.

Inkpen, A., Beamish, P.W., 1997. Knowledge, bargaining power and international joint venture instability. Academy of Management Review 22 (1), 177–202.

Isobe, T., Makino, S., Montgomery, D.B., 2000. Resource commitment, entry timing, and market performance of foreign direct investments in emerging economies: the case of Japanese international joint venture in China. Academy of Management Journal 43 (3), 468–484.

Jarillo, J.C., 1989. Entrepreneurship and growth: the strategic use of external resources. Journal of Business Venturing 4, 133–147.

Johanson, J., Vahlne, J.E., 1977. The internationalization process of the firm—a model of knowledge development and increasing foreign market commitments. Journal of International Business Studies 8 (1), 23–32.

Kogut, B., Singh, H., 1988. The effects of national culture on the choice of entry mode. Journal of International Business Studies 19 (3), 411–432.

Lane, P., Salk, J., Lyles, M., 2001. Absorptive capacity, learning, and performance in international joint ventures. Strategic Management Journal 22, 1139–1161.

Lu, J.W., 2002. Intra- and inter- organizational imitative behavior: institutional influences on Japanese firms' entry mode choice. Journal of International Business Studies 33 (1), 19–37.

Lu, J.W., Beamish, P.W., 2001. The internationalization and performance of SMEs. Strategic Management Journal 22, 565–586.

Lu, J.W., Beamish, P.W., 2004. International diversification and firm performance: the S-curve hypothesis. Academy of Management Journal 47 (4), 598–609.

Makino, S., Beamish, P.W., 1998. Performance and survival of joint ventures with non-conventional ownership structures. Journal of International Business Studies 29 (4), 797–818.

Makino, S., Delios, A., 1996. Local knowledge transfer and performance: implications for alliance formation in Asia. Journal of International Business Studies 27 (5), 905–927.

Martinez, R.J., Dacin, M.T., 1999. Efficiency motives and normative forces: combining transaction cost and institutional logic. Journal of Management 25, 75–96.

McDougall, P.P., Oviatt, B.M., 1996. New venture internationalization, strategic change, and performance: a follow-up study. Journal of Business Venturing 11 (1), 23–40.

Mjoen, H., Tallman, S., 1997. Control and performance in international joint ventures. Organization Science 8 (3), 257–274.

Osborn, R.N., Baughn, C.C., 1990. Forms of interorganizational governance for multinational alliances. Academy of Management Journal 33, 503–519.

Osborn, R.N., Hagedoorn, J., 1997. The institutionalization and evolutionary dynamics of interorganizational alliances and networks. Academy of Management Journal 40, 261–278.

Oviatt, B.M., McDougall, P.P., 1994. Toward a theory of international new ventures. Journal of International Business Studies 25 (1), 45–61.

Park, S.H., Ungson, G.R., 1997. The effect of national culture, organizational complementarity, and economic motivation on joint venture dissolution. Academy of Management Journal 40 (2), 279–307.

Parkhe, A., 1991. Interfirm diversity, organizational learning, and longevity in global strategic alliances. Journal of International Business Studies 22, 579–601.

Reuer, J., Zollo, M., 2000. Termination outcomes of high-tech alliances. In: Lewin, A., Koza, M. (Eds.), Co-evolution, Strategic Alliances and Firm Adaptation. JAI Press, Greenwich.

Scott, W.R., 1995. Institutions and Organizations. Sage, Thousand Oaks, CA.

Shuman, J.C., Seeger, J.A., 1986. The theory and practice of strategic management in smaller rapid growth companies. American Journal of Small Business 11 (1), 7–18.

Singh, J.V., House, R.J., Tucker, D.J., 1986. Organizational change and organizational mortality. Administrative Science Quarterly 31, 587–611.

Smith, K.G., Gannon, M.J., Grimm, C., Mitchell, T.R., 1988. Decision-making in smaller entrepreneurial and larger professionally managed firms. Journal of Business Venturing 3, 223–232.

Stinchcombe, A.L., 1965. Social structure and organizations. In: March, J. (Ed.), Handbook of Organizations. Rand McNally, Chicago, pp. 142–193.

Stuart, T.E., Hoang, H., Hybels, R.C., 1999. Interorganizational endorsements and the performance of entrepreneurial ventures. Administrative Science Quarterly 44, 315–349.

Venkatraman, N., Ramanujam, V., 1986. Measurement of business performance in strategy research: a comparison of approaches. Academy of Management Review 11 (4), 801–814.

Wolff, A.J., Pett, T.L., 2000. Internationalization of small firms: an examination of export competitive patterns, firm size, and export performance. Journal of Small Business Management 38 (2), 34–47.

Yan, A., Gray, B., 1994. Bargaining power, management control, and performance in United States–China joint ventures: a comparative case study. Academy of Management Journal 37, 1478–1517.

Zacharakis, A.L., 1997. Entrepreneurial entry into foreign markets: a transaction cost perspective. Entrepreneurship Theory and Practice 21 (3), 23–39.

Zahra, S.A., Ireland, R.D., Hitt, M.A., 2000. International expansion by new venture firms: international diversity, mode of market entry, technological learning and performance. Academy of Management Journal 43 (5), 925–950.

Part VI
Venture Capital

[24]

ELSEVIER

Journal of Business Venturing 18 (2003) 233–259

JOURNAL
of BUSINESS
VENTURING

An institutional view of China's venture capital industry Explaining the differences between China and the West

Garry D. Bruton[a,*], David Ahlstrom[b,1]

[a]Department of Management, M.J. Neeley School of Business, Texas Christian University,
TCU Box 298530, Fort Worth, TX 76129, USA
[b]Department of Management, Chinese University of Hong Kong, Shatin, N.T. Hong Kong, China

Received 30 June 2000; received in revised form 30 August 2001; accepted 31 October 2001

Abstract

Institutional theory argues that institutions in general, and culture in particular, shape the actions of firms and individuals in a number of subtle but substantive ways. The theory has been used to explain a number of significant and substantive managerial differences found in different parts of the world. To date, the examination of venture capital outside the US and Europe, however, has been rather limited. Institutional theory also suggests that there would be differences in how venture capital may operate in other parts of the world, such as Asia where the culture is substantially different from the West. Based on interviews with 36 venture capitalists in 24 venture capital firms investing in China, this exploratory research finds that China's institutional environment creates a number of significant differences from the West. The article discusses the impact of these findings on future research on Asian venture capital, theory development, and the activities of venture capital professionals in that region.
© 2002 Published by Elsevier Science Inc.

Keywords: Venture capital; Institutional theory; China; Private equity

1. Executive summary

Venture capital has been widely studied in the US. However, its examination in other settings has been limited. In Asia, the examination of the industry is almost nonexistent,

* Corresponding author. Tel.: +1-817-257-7421.
E-mail addresses: g.bruton@tcu.edu (G.D. Bruton), davidahlstrom@cuhk.edu.hk (D. Ahlstrom).
[1] Tel.: +852-2-609-7748.

0883-9026/02/$ – see front matter © 2002 Published by Elsevier Science Inc.
doi:10.1016/S0883-9026(02)00079-4

234   *G.D. Bruton, D. Ahlstrom / Journal of Business Venturing 18 (2003) 233–259*

despite the fact that the industry raised new investable capital of over US$7.4 billion in 1998 alone. It cannot be assumed, however, that Western practices are universal around the world.

China is one of the world's fastest growing economies and is home to approximately one-quarter of the world's population. Based on three dozen interviews within venture capital firms active in China, this article examines that nation's venture capital industry. It establishes from this information a basic understanding of how institutions within the country shape the venture capital industry.

It is clear from the information developed that both the challenges encountered by venture capitalists and the nature of the investment framework employed in China differs markedly from that of the West. For example, the screens employed to initially evaluate ventures are different than in the West. The need to fund ventures within reasonable physical distance to accurately monitor those firms and the avoidance of firms without proven or checkable financials are among two differences from of the US. Similarly, since the ability to accurately obtain full information on a firm is so constrained, due diligence commonly focuses on the entrepreneur's background and their contracts even more so than in the West. Once the deal is funded there will also be fewer value-added activities provided by the venture capitalist than would occur with funded firms in the US. Chinese culture promotes resistance to such activities since they are viewed as more intrusive than would be seen in most Western settings. Additionally, the nature of the monitoring function by venture capitalists is far different in China than it is in the US. There is a need in China for much more direct monitoring of funded firms. Overall, it is clear from the evidence presented that the institutional environment in China, and possibly Asia in general, is different enough to make the practice of venture capital different from that of the West. Thus, venture capitalists from the West must be careful to ensure they understand these institutional differences when participating in the market.

2. Introduction

Institutional theory holds that the beliefs, goals, and actions of individuals and groups are strongly influenced by various environmental institutions (Scott, 1987, 1995), and that their role in doing this is subtle but pervasive (Boisot and Child, 1996; Child et al., 2000; Clarke. 1991). However, to date, research from the West has only started to account for the role that different institutional environments play in transition economies, such as China's, (Boyacillier and Adler, 1991; Shenkar and Von Glinow. 1994) and how these differences can help create different organizational and commercial systems (Peng, 2000; Peng and Heath. 1996). This paucity of examination on institutions in transition economies is particularly true of entrepreneurial domains (Giamartino et al., 1993).

China's institutional environment is quite different from the West (Boisot and Child. 1996; Peng, 2000; Peng and Heath. 1996). The nation's socialist tradition and strong culture together create a distinct social and commercial milieu (Boisot and Child, 1988; Child, 1994; Scarborough, 1998). For example, private firms in China still have limited discretion to acquire and allocate resources and conduct operations (Peng, 2001). Additionally, firms must

G.D. Bruton, D. Ahlstrom / Journal of Business Venturing 18 (2003) 233–259 235

often engage in some transactions where personnel connections matter more than firm capabilities (Boisot and Child, 1996; Peng, 2000; Xin and Pearce, 1996). Also, few managers in China have much experience in competing in a market-based economy (Björkman and Lu, 1999). Corporate governance and property rights are typically spotty, and fund allocation, even by private firms in China, must often observe political and other nonmarket motivations (Clarke, 1991; Peng, 2001; Peng and Heath, 1996; Tam, 1999). Thus, for researchers in entrepreneurship, China's institutional environment provides a compelling context to examine and refine our understanding of how institutions may impact firms (Boisot and Child, 1996; Peng et al., 2001), and in turn create differences in entrepreneurial efforts from those of the West (Peng, 2000, 2001).

Venture capital plays a crucial role in the West in the development and growth of entrepreneurial firms (Patricof, 1989). However, the venture capital industry in much of Asia remains largely unexplored (except for Japan, e.g., Hurry et al., 1992; Ray and Turpin, 1993), in spite of the venture capital industry in Asia (excluding Japan) raising over US$6 billion of new capital in 1998 alone (*Guide to Venture Capital in Asia*, 2000).[2] It should not be assumed that the Asian venture capital industry is equivalent to the US industry (Ahlstrom et al., 2000; Boisot and Child, 1996; Chow and Fung, 2000). Institutional factors in China may be creating a venture capital industry with its own idiosyncratic characteristics (Bruton et al., 1999).

The research employing institutional theory in China has tended to emphasize the constraining nature of institutions (e.g. Boisot and Child, 1988; Peng and Heath, 1996). Yet institutions not only specify limits, they also create frameworks that enable certain action (Garud and Jain, 1996; Peng, 2000) and minimize transaction costs (Standifird and Marshall, 2000). To illustrate, China is widely recognized as having a turbulent environment, often hostile to business (Peng, 1997; Steinfeld, 1998). The prevailing attitude of China's government views private ownership as acceptable only to the extent it remains an appendage of public ownership (Tan, 1999). While these institutions prescribe limits on the actions venture capitalists can undertake, they also can establish an enabling framework that helps the venture capitalists and their funded firms to be successful in China when that framework is understood and utilized (cf. Peng, 2001). Therefore, both the enabling and constraining functions of institutions will be examined here (Garud and Jain, 1996).

To investigate how the venture capital industry functions in China's environment, this article begins with a brief examination of institutional theory and its application in China. It then reviews the background of the venture capital industry in China. Next, based on interviews with venture capitalists active in China and three funded firms, the article identifies a framework by which venture capital operates in China and how this compares and contrasts with that of the West. Specifically, four key aspects of venture capital in China will be examined: the selection process for prospective funded firms, structuring of relationships and

---

[2] Venture capital is typically associated with earlier stage ventures in the West while private equity is typically seen as a more inclusive term that would also include activities that involve more mature firms such as buyouts. The industry in Asia is much younger and smaller than in the West.

236   *G.D. Bruton, D. Ahlstrom / Journal of Business Venturing 18 (2003) 233–259*

monitoring the firm, value-added activities provided to the funded firm, and exit. A discussion of implications of these findings for theory development, future research, and practice then follows.

2.1. Institutional theory

Institutions can strongly influence the goals, and beliefs of individuals, groups, and organizations (North, 1990; Scott, 1995). There is support in the West for the belief that institutions have such an impact on the goal formation and processes of venture capital firms (Wright et al., 1992; Bruno and Tyebjee. 1986; Suchman, 1995). The belief is that such institutions have led to strong uniformity in venture capitalists behaviors (Fried and Hisrich, 1995). For example, prior research has found many similarities between US and European venture capital industries (Sapienza et al., 1996). It has even been argued by others that venture capitalists have a similar worldwide model of funding, particularly for latter stage ventures (Jeng and Wells. 2000).

It remains to be seen how institutions actually impact the actions of venture capitalists in different parts of the world, particularly in Asia. The conclusion reached by Jeng and Wells (2000) was based on data where New Zealand served as the only Asian representative in the sample, while the rest of the data was European or North American.[3] Asia in general, and China in particular, has an environment that is substantially different from the US or Europe (Boisot and Child. 1988. 1996; Peng, 2000). This has led some to the alternative belief that venture capitalists will adjust to the local institutional environment making a number of changes in the process and creating a different model of venture capital in the process (Bruton et al., 1999).

Before employing the theory as the basis to evaluate the Chinese venture capital industry it is first necessary to be clear about the nature of such institutions. The two broad approaches to analyzing institutions are sociological and economic, which can be complimentary to each other (Hirsch and Lounsbury. 1997; Scott, 1992). Sociologists primarily focus on legitimacy-building and role-shaping actions of institutions (Suchman, 1995), examining in particular widely shared beliefs that shape the way people in a society think and behave, arguing that behaviors are institutionalizable across a wide range of actions. Such beliefs and actions can arise out of shared cultural and political systems (Scott, 1992; Zucker, 1987). Organizational life and commercial conventions persist due to the taken-for-granted nature of institutions and their self-sustaining ability (DiMaggio and Powell, 1991).

Drawing on neoclassical economics, North (1990) argues that the institutional framework of a society provides a formal rule framework regulating economic activities. For economic institutionalists, the relevant framework is a set of political, social, and legal ground rules that fixes a basis for production, exchange, and distribution in a system or society (North, 1990; Roy. 1997). Such institutions tend to shape a system by structuring political, social, and especially economic incentives involved in exchange. Once institutions

---

[3] New Zealand is culturally much closer to the UK and the US than to China (Backman, 1999).

G.D. Bruton, D. Ahlstrom / Journal of Business Venturing 18 (2003) 233–259 237

are established, they create constraints that are locally rational in an economic sense, but collectively may be suboptimal (DiMaggio and Powell, 1991; Powell, 1991; Zucker, 1986). These limits to the set of choices of individuals and organizations provide, however, a predictable and understood structure; one that has an instrumental if not always an economically efficient basis (Roy, 1997).

Building on DiMaggio and Powell (1983, 1991), North (1990), and Selznick (1957), Scott (1995) more finely categorized these formal and informal institutions into normative, regulatory, and cognitive groupings. The most formal are the regulatory institutions representing standards provided by laws and other sanctions. Normative institutions are less formal or codified and define the roles or actions that are expected of individuals. Normative institutions are often manifest through accepted authority systems such as accounting or medical professional societies. Finally, cognitive institutions represent the most informal, taken-for-granted rules, and beliefs that are established among individuals through social interactions among various participants. A principal means by which cognitive, and less formal normative institutions propagate and influence a society is through a community's culture (Jepperson, 1991). Although this organizing scheme of institutions is not without controversy (e.g., Hirsch and Lounsbury, 1997), it has been widely used and has proved helpful for analytical purposes.

Prior research on institutions in China has typically emphasized their constraining nature, such as how various types of institutions regulate economic exchanges (Xin and Pearce, 1996), limit business activity (Boisot and Child, 1988, 1996), or reduce uncertainty by lowering transaction costs (Standifird and Marshall, 2000). Less commonly examined is the institution's ability to enable action (Garud and Jain, 1996; Peng, 2000). To illustrate, grammar prescribes limits on how sentences may be constructed. Yet, the common grammatical rules enable consistent, accurate communication and the construction of new conceptual terms. Similarly, technological standards such as the common Windows platform create a number of constraints for developers but Windows also enables more rapid advances by creating a standard allowing the sharing of work and information among developers and users (e.g. Majumdar and Venkataraman, 1998). Thus, institutions need not be viewed solely in terms of their constraining nature, they also enable actions that create opportunities for those who understand and use them.

Some literature on venture capital in the West (e.g. Fried and Hisrich, 1994; Suchman, 1995) has shown that institutions present in the West play a significant role in shaping the values and actions of venture capitalists. Before large-scale empirical examinations of China's or the broader Asian venture capital industry can occur, exploratory efforts should establish an understanding of how the institutional environment in China influences the industry in the region. This research will establish a baseline of understanding of the venture capital industry in China upon which future research can build.

2.2. Background of venture capital in China

With about 25% of the world's population and one of the world's fastest growing economies, China's attractive market has seen a rapid inflow of foreign capital, mostly as

238　　　*G.D. Bruton, D. Ahlstrom / Journal of Business Venturing 18 (2003) 233–259*

international joint ventures. However, venture capital now represents another important source of capital inflow; China, including Hong Kong, has the second largest amount of private capital under management in Asia,[4] which comprises about one-third of all capital under management in Asia (*Guide to Venture Capital in Asia*, 2000).[5] The gateway for these funds into China historically has been Hong Kong, where the second largest number of private equity firms in Asia are located.

During the 1980s, a few pioneering private equity professionals entered the China market (for example, Jardine Fleming, Sung Hung Kai and Co., and the American International Group). However, the pace of economic reforms did not encourage significant numbers of firms to enter the market until 1992. The principal vehicles for private equity entry initially were China Direct Investment Funds (CDIFs). These funds were typically listed on the Dublin, London, or Hong Kong stock exchanges in order to attract money from institutional investors. The stock exchanges recognized these funds as investment companies and thus restricted their investments. For example, the London Stock Exchange (the most common listing for CDIFs) required that such funds invest only as a minority investor, taking less than 49% of stock of the target investee firm. Typical additional listing regulations required that CDIFs not play a significant role in management of the firm, or place more than 20% of the fund in any one investment. The investment funds were largely invested in government-owned state or township/village enterprises (TVEs) throughout China, not in the businesses of individual entrepreneurs. The TVEs are owned and operated by local governmental units and have been among the fastest growing industrial segments in China (Bruton et al., 2000). The CDIFs were not usually industry focused, rather they provided mezzanine financing for firms in a wide variety of industries.

The strategic plan of most CDIFs was to build relationships with large state enterprises, and then have those organizations help source good investment opportunities. For example, Sino-Chem is a large state firm whose charge includes building external import–export relationships for the chemical industry in China. A Western CDIF would bring both money and managerial expertise to the table. Sino-Chem would locate deals and provide the *guanxi* or connections to government officials necessary for business success in China (Xin and Pearce, 1996). Thus, firms like Sino-Chem would ideally be able to provide a CDIF access to the best chemical-related funding opportunities in China. Once a CDIF decided to fund the venture, it would create a joint venture between itself, the funded firm, and the large state entity that sourced the deal. The difficulty with the strategic plan for CDIFs was that large state entities like Sino-Chem often kept the very best deals for themselves and only sourced lower quality deals to the CDIFs.

Much of the venture capital active in China today is still organized as CDIFs. Nevertheless, most new investment funds raised today are not listed as investment funds on stock

---

[4] Private equity refers to equity investment in a firm from private sources rather than public equity sources. Public equities are publicly traded stock. Private equity is raised from high net worth individuals, insurance, or pension funds typically. Private equity professionals are the individuals who manage such funds.

[5] Not all of the capital located in Hong Kong is used to fund businesses in China. Many funds take advantage of the Hong Kong location to not only fund businesses in China but also elsewhere around Asia.

exchanges. Rather they are organized as limited partnerships in a manner similar to US venture capital funds or are units of large international financial institutions. Thus, investments today typically are not made as direct investments in Sino joint ventures where only a minority position would be obtained for the private equity fund. Instead, today most funds first create an offshore corporation for the joint venture with the local Chinese firm. In such an arrangement, the venture capital fund may even take a majority or controlling interest in the corporation. In the US, it would be unusual for venture capital funds to take such a large percentage of mature firms but the need for capital is such that in China this opportunity does exist. The local Chinese partner firm and managers hold the remaining stock.

3. Methodology

3.1. Research design

This study is based on field research conducted from 1998 to 2000 in Greater China.[6] The data were gathered and assembled using 36 interviews within 24 venture capitalist firms in a manner consistent with a grounded theory research design (Glaser and Strauss, 1967; Strauss and Corbin, 1990).[7] In addition, three interviews were held with funded firms. Interviews were used for four reasons: (1) The venture capitalists often prefer face-to-face interviews over questionnaires, particularly in Mainland China. (2) It is often necessary when examining China-related business activities to establish a relationship with respondents in order to receive a response. This connection may come through a referral. Such a requirement encourages the use of interviews. (3) Another very important aspect of interviews is that they are less structured than surveys, allowing for spontaneous discussion of problems and solutions as they arise in the interview and, in turn for follow-up questions on a topic and development of recommendations that have practical value (Frey and Oishi, 1995; Lee, 1999). (4) Finally, as this is a new area of study, the benefit of conducting interviews to develop a theoretical understanding of a new domain is well-established (Eishenhardt, 1989; Daft and Lewin, 1990; Lee, 1999).

Our inquiry framework was initially guided by an understanding of numerous agreed-upon aspects of the Western venture capital industry drawn from a variety of established sources in the domain (e.g. Fried and Hisrich, 1994; Gorman and Shalman, 1989; MacMillian et al., 1988; Sapienza, 1992; Sapienza et al., 1996; Zider, 1998). Four broad topical areas were examined: (1) selection process for firms to be funded, (2) structuring of relationships and monitoring of the funded firm, (3) value-added activities provided to the funded firm, and (4) exit. The interviews and the discussion of the findings follow this topical outline.

---

[6] This includes Mainland China, Hong Kong, and Taiwan.

[7] The grounded theory approach to data gathering and analysis is an iterative process that uses theoretic (similar) case comparisons (Yin. 1994), usually to develop propositions in a new area of theory or a new research site.

3.2. Sample selection

The venture capitalists interviewed were initially identified from the *Guide to Venture Capital in Asia* (1997, 2000). Interviews were largely undertaken in China, primarily in the southern cities of Hong Kong, Shenzhen, Guangzhou, and Shanghai. Additional interviews were conducted in Singapore and Taiwan among venture capitalists with significant investment activity in China. Initially, 22 interviews were conducted among randomly selected venture capitalists with significant operations in China.[8] Suggestions from venture capitalists about other key informants in the China market subsequently increased the sample size to 36 venture capitalists and three funded firms. Most of the venture capitalists had worked in private equity in other parts of the world, with an average time in the industry of 8 years, 6 years being in Asia. We continued adding interviews until the incremental learning derived from the subjects became negligible (Glaser and Strauss, 1967).[9] The average amount of funds under management of our sample was US$70 million per firm. Venture capitalists in both large and small funds were queried to obtain as wide a perspective as possible on the nature of the Chinese venture capital industry. All of the venture capitalists interviewed were responsible for funding decisions by their firms and were either a partner or a senior manager in the venture capital firms.

3.3. The interviews

On average, interviews lasted just over 1 hour. We asked the venture capitalists to discuss the venture capital industry in China, including information on their funded firms. They then were asked about the selection process for firms to be funded, structuring of relationships and monitoring of the funded firm, value-added activities provided to the funded firm, and exit. During the interviews, insights provided by each interviewee were also compared with the established Western framework of venture capital. The initial framework discussed with the interviewees represented the basic model of venture capital employed in the West. Then at each interview, the model with information supplied in previous interviews was presented to the next interviewee for validation, and the framework updated as necessary. Follow-up questions were also asked via telephone or email. Thus, over the course of the interviews a consistent picture of venture capital in China began to develop. This model of investigation is called replication logic (Eisenhardt, 1989), and is broadly consistent with a grounded theory approach to data gathering and analysis (Glaser and Strauss, 1967; Strauss and Corbin, 1990). Fried and Hisrich (1994) used a similar method in examining venture capital decision making in the US.

The interviews were taped and transcribed. Twenty of the 36 interviewees were native Chinese, as were the three funded firm subjects. Thirty-one interviews were conducted in

---

[8] We define significant operations as placing an emphasis on identifying and funding entrepreneurial firms in China.

[9] Diesing (1971) argued that six cases often provide such a number; however, in this case, it was felt that the greater number would provide greater validity on the results.

G.D. Bruton, D. Ahlstrom / Journal of Business Venturing 18 (2003) 233–259 241

English. For those conducted in Chinese, a native Chinese speaker was present to pose the questions and translate the answers immediately. Interviews in Chinese were translated simultaneously, taped, and subsequently transcribed.[10] This reduces potential error and allows for follow-up questions. To ensure validity of the transcription process the native Chinese speaker also took notes, as did the authors at all interviews, which were later examined to ensure the information from the subsequent transcription was accurate. All interview results were summarized and venture capitalists contacted for validation. If any discrepancies were found in the transcription, the interview subject would be contacted for clarification.

To further validate the research, summary findings were also shared with other leading venture capitalists in Asia that were not part of the sample. Additionally, to corroborate the research findings, information was gathered from other sources such as industry authorities and government officials responsible for investment and/or industrial policy plus three funded firms.[11] In general, there was great consistency in the evidence gathered from all sources on all issues examined and the efforts to validate the results reported by sources outside the sample also corroborated the findings. When disagreement occurred, these are reported and discussed.

4. Results

4.1. Selection of firms to fund

In the West, venture capitalists rely on financial and accounting information contained in the business plan to initially evaluate the proposal and assess the risk of the proposed ventures (Wright et al., 1992; McGrath, 1997). The issue that arises in China is how to assess which firms to fund when there is an unsteady regulatory institutional environment and weak corporate governance (Becker, 2000; Tam, 1999).

4.1.1. Initial screening

Most firms in the West have a screening mechanism for initial evaluation of all new proposals so that the firm can focus its efforts on the most attractive ventures for funding. Venture capitalists in China have a similar screening mechanism, however, they are influenced by the country's regulatory institutional environment.

China's regulations are largely generated and interpreted by local and regional authorities and not the central government (Clarke, 1991; Lubman, 2001; Peng, 2000). Thus, China may be thought of as more like the European Union than a single state—multiple sovereign agents with varying regulatory structures and interests (Li, 1998; Lubman, 2001; Reynolds, 1984) and different laws, regulations, and traditions within and across provinces (Clarke, 1991; Lubman, 2001; Tan, 1999). Indeed, numerous venture capitalists and entrepreneurs interviewed emphasized the importance of understanding the local setting. Thus, in China

---

[10] One of the authors also understands Chinese and took notes, and a second native Chinese speaker (a management professor from Taiwan) was also present at the interviews to double-check translations.

[11] With thanks to an anonymous reviewer for recommending collecting these additional data.

venture capitalists often try to fund firms that are located nearby and seek to build relationships with local authorities in order to be able to understand and manage the local regulatory regime that their funded firms face. Understanding and controlling the risk from regulatory institutions can become unwieldy if the venture capital firm's investments are geographically diverse.

Therefore, most preliminary screens in China focus attention on firms within specific regions. Recalled one venture capitalist from Shanghai:

> In your city you can know the entrepreneur's background. You know where his family and friends are—it makes it tougher for him to skip off on the deal. It is difficult otherwise to really know people and stay in close contact with them. I almost never fund deals more than a couple of hours' drive from my office.

One implication of focusing on a limited region of the country is that industry is less frequently used as a screen than in the West (cf. Fried and Hisrich, 1994). To overcome such regional constraints some venture capitalists maintain lightly staffed, small offices in various large cities to screen and monitor local deals while also spending time building connections with key local officials. These connections are important to getting all types of business activities done in China and can be a valuable asset (Luo, 2000; Wank, 1996; Yeung and Tung, 1996).

A second screen is that very few funds will finance startups, instead requiring potential funded firms to have at least 3 years of financials. Few legal protections (regulatory institutions) in China against outright fraud, imperfect market information, and the rapid nature of change in the market heighten the venture capitalist's risk and encourage such a screen.

4.1.2. Accounting and auditing practices

The initial screening of firms in the West is based on information presented in the business plan including the firm's financials (Wright and Robbie, 1996; McGrath, 1997); in the West, historical financial performance is particularly important for later stage ventures. While venture capital firms in China like to fund firms that have established financials, the regulatory institutions (laws) and normative institutions (professional standards and commercial conventions) can impact the information presented. China's accounting rules significantly deviate from international accounting standards since they are aimed at managing production rather than asset valuation, thus making timely, accurate, or useful information about firms' financial performance difficult to obtain (Broadman, 1999; Peng, 2000). Additionally, the definition of terms can differ in different industries or regions of China (Broadman, 1999). Venture capitalists pointed out that regulations often do not mean what they seem to mean, nor are they widely and evenly enforced (Becker, 2000; Lubman, 2001). Thus, items such as assets and accounts receivable can often be of questionable nature (Backman, 1999; Broadman, 1999; Mann, 1997). As one China centered venture capitalist summarized:

> You might as well leave your European legalistic approach behind because that is not the way it works here. In the U.S., you invest in a company and you do not have to worry about

the tax system, the accountant, the financials reported, and whether they have a board of directors. You make a mistake in China if you go straight into the investment and do not ensure that all of those things are present in a form you can work with. In China you have to worry about all of those things yourself and even then you still have to worry about the investment itself. It is a good bet many entrepreneurs in China will not even know about GAAP [Generally Accepted Accounting Principles] let alone adhere to them.

Therefore, it is common to ask firms of interest to the venture capitalist to produce financial reports in a form that is interpretable and can be verified. This normally requires that an international accounting firm be hired to help with the financials, and go to firms and actually count items.

4.1.3. Due diligence

Once a firm has passed its initial screening, venture capitalists in the West proceed with due diligence, typically including confirmation of the nature and status of the firm's product, production capability, market demand, and status of key relationships with other organizations (Fried and Hisrich, 1994). When venture capitalists first entered China, due diligence for funded projects in China was limited in scope; in part, because the support activities upon which Western venture capitalists rely to conduct such activities were not present (Bruton et al., 1999; Mann, 1997).

While venture capitalists are increasing efforts to conduct Western-type due diligence, the availability and accuracy of information is still problematic. Regulations in China do not require the same level of public information be provided to the government or other regulatory bodies as occurs in the West. A number of cognitive institutions encourage the tight control of information and knowledge in China (Boisot and Child, 1988, 1996). Under the central planning system, bureaucrats and business people control information crucial to understanding the market and local regulatory environment closely, dispensing it carefully in order to obtain favors and other valued items (Boisot and Child, 1988, 1996). As one venture capitalist explained:

It is common to spend three to six months more on due diligence [in China], compared with similar deals in the West. In particular you need to know what sort of connections the entrepreneur has, both with the government and other organizations. These can represent important assets for the firm. The result is that venture capitalists must expect to make greater efforts in China than in the West to help locate and aggregate a greater range of information in conducting due diligence.

4.1.4. Knowing an entrepreneur's background

The initial investment evaluation in the US often centers on the person leading the proposed investment (Bruton et al., 1998; Tyebjee and Bruno, 1984). Legendary venture capitalist Arthur Rock observed: "Nearly every mistake I've made has been in picking the wrong people . . ." (Bygrave and Timmons, 1992, p. 6). This is even truer in China because of limits on validating company information. The ability to obtain information on, and monitor,

244   *G.D. Bruton, D. Ahlstrom / Journal of Business Venturing 18 (2003) 233–259*

entrepreneurs in China is also hindered due to the legal environment (Becker, 2000; Lubman, 2001) and cultural proclivities (cognitive institutions). Chinese culture, in contrast to the West, would not typically find individuals of responsibility sharing information with anyone they do not have relationships, and even then doing so rather sparingly (Goa et al., 1996; Wank, 1996).

To overcome these limitations venture capitalists seek to build personal contacts with relevant individuals who could provide such information. However, as one Singapore venture capitalist active in China noted about their evaluation process:

> Chinese entrepreneurs, like Chinese families, are extremely private. They're most reluctant and awkward in dealing with strangers ... Building up a comfort level that would enable individuals to judge you, and you to judge them is crucial, and takes some time. This means dinners, drinks, meeting the entrepreneurs' friends and classmates ... It takes time to build trust. Knowing the founder, his colleagues and even family is important. You do that as part of the due diligence process, by asking everyone you can about the founder. It takes time, but there is no substitute for this process.

For venture capital firms that are relatively new to the market, locating these individuals and building the necessary relationships can be difficult, time-consuming, and expensive, though thought to be absolutely necessary.

4.2. Structuring of relationships and monitoring the firm

Once the investment decision is made, venture capitalists in the West typically continue to actively monitor their investment (Sapienza and Gupta, 1994; Fiet, 1995; Gorman and Sahlman, 1989), typically through the venture capital's membership on the board of directors (Fried et al., 1998; Sapienza, 1992). However, the original CDIFs commonly did not obtain board seats from their funded firms. Rather, they sought to protect themselves from abuses by having extensive minority protection clauses in the investment agreements. However, it was difficult to anticipate all the potential problems, and the enforcement of the agreements was often problematic (Bruton et al., 1999) due to underdeveloped regulatory institutions like the court system, and commercial code.

Active monitoring is needed for both government and private enterprises that are funded. For example, one venture capital fund financed the expansion of a private firm producing high-quality paper products. After a short time, the owner/manager of the funded firm did not believe that he was earning enough from the venture. He then set up a competing paper products firm right next door to his existing company, selling the same product line with the same name as the funded venture, but at a lower quality (Bruton et al., 1999). Such activities clearly violated both his contract and the norms of business practice, but the venture capital firm found it difficult to secure a judgment against this individual. This does not mean that the venture capitalists should not carefully draft term sheets and legal agreements and attempt to clearly list the roles and requirements of all parties. Rather, it points to the need in China to maintain even greater vigilance than in the West in monitoring funded firms to ensure that the

G.D. Bruton, D. Ahlstrom / Journal of Business Venturing 18 (2003) 233–259 245

firm is performing as desired, and to act quickly if the funded firm is in violation of the agreement. Several venture capitalists pointed out that this requires regular visits to funded firms, often unannounced, to see how things are going, to look over inventory, and to speak to employees and customers.

4.2.1. Differing goals and the monitoring process

In the US, venture capitalists commonly assume they share the goals of growth and profit maximization with the funded firm's management. However, when monitoring their investment in China, venture capitalists need to recognize their goals for the firm may be fundamentally different from those of the entrepreneur or Chinese government departments with influence over the firm (Peng, 2001).

Chinese firms (publicly or privately owned) are often encouraged by the state to maximize employment and production based largely on institutional forces that push employment maximization. With over 1 billion people, China is concerned that as the state sector shrinks, massive numbers of unemployed will create social instability (Steinfeld, 1998). One China venture capitalist recalled a funded venture (a township enterprise) that suddenly and unexpectedly ended up with an extra 150 workers from an unrelated business on its payroll. The local government quietly had moved those individuals, laid off from another organization, to the funded venture. Without careful oversight, firms can end up with extra employees and overproduction of goods that will result in unsaleable inventory, often at the urging of a local government body seeking to maximize employment.

4.2.2. Board membership

In the West, venture capitalists typically are on of the board of directors of the funded firm and through this role monitor the firm (Fried and Hisrich, 1992, 1995; Fried et al., 1998; Sapienza, 1992; Rosenstein, 1988). Members of a syndication of venture capitalists who fund a firm will typically have one of their number serve as a member of the board to monitor the firm for the entire syndication. They also monitor the firm by requiring formal financial reports at least quarterly, and place contractual restrictions on managerial actions.

In China, venture capitalists increasingly require a board seat for the funded firms. Though the power and information provided to board members is less than in the US, firms in China still operate with little effective corporate governance, information can often be withheld from the board, and the influence of outside directors remains weak (Tam, 1999). In addition, the market for corporate control is virtually nonexistent (Peng et al., 1999). In part, this reflects the fact that in the Chinese regulatory environment a board of directors is not required for a firm. When a firm does have a board most members will be nominated not by commercially oriented owners or their representatives, but by the Party or government bodies (Broadman, 1999). These groups may hold no equity in the firms they are governing so the board members end up safeguarding the state's interest rather than that of shareholders (Tam, 1999).

Thus, it is more important to remain close to their invested firms to obtain the desired information and ensure its accuracy than to depend on a board seat for it. Such close connections between the funded firm and venture capitalist are consistent with the nature of communication between other parties in a Chinese culture. In this cultural setting there are clear insiders and outsiders. The communication between insiders is the focus of most firms with flow of information to outsiders restricted and filtered (Goa et al., 1996). This normally applies to the venture capitalist if viewed as an outsider. The cognitive institutions create an interesting difference from the US: venture capitalists do not have instant credibility with funded firms, but must build that credibility over time. Reflecting on this, one venture capitalist noted:

> The paradox is that although the owners often do not want us [venture capitalists] on the board, I find that my colleagues and I must often get more involved with operational details in our funded ventures in China than we would in similar deals in the West ... It takes work to get to know the top management team well enough to build that credibility and work with them.

Until that occurs, the monitoring effort and costs will be substantially higher than in the West, and advice will only reluctantly be heeded.[12] But also, once that relationship is established the venture capitalists may become more involved in daily operational details than in the West.

4.2.3. Nature of monitoring

Monitoring of funded firms in the West is critical, typically requiring frequent interaction with the firm. As indicated above, when monitoring a funded firm in China, venture capitalists must be even more diligent. In the West, venture capitalists typically require audited annual and quarterly financial data generated internally by the firm. But in China, once the venture capitalist arranges for the firm to report data in a meaningful way, the benefit of internally produced data can be limited. Commented one venture capitalist from a major bank in the region:

> You can ask for any [accounting and financial] numbers that you want, but you have to take the extra time to count everything. Sales are often not what is reported, inventories can be understated. In one company the inventories turned out not to be there altogether. You have to go into the firm yourself regularly and find out what is going on.

It was noted previously that part of the initial screen for ventures is to invest in those that are close to the venture capitalist to help maintain close contact with the funded venture. For example, a Shanghai-based venture capitalist added:

> I try to fund deals close to my office [in Shanghai], certainly no more than a half-day's drive away. In this way, I can monitor the investment very closely. Strange things have happened in the past, assets can disappear. One of my portfolio firms vanished completely

---

[12] This is not to imply that all entrepreneurs in the West readily heed venture capitalists' advice.

... the founder loaded everything from computers to coffee pots into a company car and vanished into the inland of China.

Thus, monitoring funded firms in China requires extensive personal attention. Formal mechanisms, board membership, or protection clauses in a contract will usually not suffice. One Hong Kong venture capitalist experienced in China noted, "if you have to go to court, you have lost already." Also, the venture capitalist cannot assume any information of value will be provided outside of the official channel approved by the organization head. Enforcement of judgments is also problematic (Lubman, 2001). Therefore, building and maintaining relationships, and locating close to the venture is paramount to monitor the funded firm.

4.3. Value added to funded firm

One of the strengths of venture capital in the West is the value added to the firm by the venture capitalist (Bygrave, 1987; Zider, 1998). Providing value added to the firm through advice is also increasingly the case in China's venture capital industry. However, this is a recent change—initial investors in China tended to be China experts or internationally known individuals rather than private equity experts. For example, one of the first venture capital funds that targeted China investments was raised by Henry Kissinger (Bruton et al., 1999). As such, initial private equity investors tended to be passive financial investors.

4.3.1. Nature of input to managers

The value added to firms in the West comes through multiple activities including providing strategic and operating advice to the firm, connecting the firm with buyers and suppliers, and serving as a sounding board for the CEO (Fried and Hisrich, 1995; MacMillan et al., 1988). However, in China the nature of advice provided to Chinese managers frequently is different than in the West, as the level of managerial sophistication in funded ventures in China is often low. For example, the local management of a funded, successful beer company was looking to sell out to another company. The price they were contemplating was based solely on the firm's assets. They gave no value to the established product name, distribution system, established cash flows, or customer contracts. The venture capitalist had to take time to educate the senior managers on how to value their firm. Commented one venture capital based in Hong Kong with extensive dealings in China:

> You may have to get involved at a very basic level with some of your funded firms. For example you might find that they are still doing manual ledger entries and building up a mountain of receipts in the process. They may not know much about accounting packages, certainly don't take it for granted that anyone in the firm will know much about GAAP [Generally Accepted Accounting Principles from the U.S.]. Cash flow can be a constant problem, even if they are making money, its not as easy as in the West to find people who can manage firm accounts as well as arrange short-term financing. You should be prepared to help them with these problems.

Thus, expect a greater time involvement in China to help with fundamental things such as accounting formats, valuation, and understanding cash flow.

4.3.2. Approach to providing advice

In the US, advice provided to CEOs of funded firms is often very direct and may occur in regular interactions (Fried and Hisrich, 1995). However, in China the venture capitalist must deal appropriately with the rather formidable cognitive institution known as *minzi*—face or respect. Its relative greater importance in a Chinese-based culture is widely recognized (Bond, 1988). Venture capitalists can advise managers but in a manner allowing the manager to maintain face. Rather than giving an ultimatum, for example, several venture capitalists suggested that ideas are often best put forth as suggestions or even posed as questions. The setting where suggestions are provided is important as well—not in front of a manager's subordinates, for example. In both cases, the manager can remain "in charge" and take credit for the changes if they prove successful.

4.3.3. Guanxi

In the US, relationships between venture capitalists and their relevant networks of investors, entrepreneurs, and other venture capitalists are important (Bartlett, 1995), but in China even more important. The concept of *guanxi* summarizes these interconnections and is widely recognized as playing a central role in business in China (Standifird and Marshall, 2000). *Guanxi* is a resource that can be traded on when needed, though it can also represent a liability if a favor is owed (Tsang, 1998; Wank, 1996); thus, it can be viewed as both an account receivable and a debt owed (Tsang, 1998). Having *guanxi* with key individuals both inside and outside the firm can help venture capitalists provide value to the funded firm. But building such connections takes time and requires the venture capital firm to provide benefits to such parties as they seek to establish the relationship.

At *guanxi*'s root lies unwritten social rules (cognitive institutions), far more pervasive than economic or legal controls (regulatory institutions) in China. Unlike Americans and Europeans, the Chinese do not rely so heavily on laws, regulations, and contracts (regulatory institutions). As one Hong Kong-based venture capitalist commented, "a signed contract simply provides a green light to more negotiations when it becomes convenient." With such ambiguities the norm, a venture capitalist cannot rely on carefully worded agreements and China's legal system to help solve difficulties. Rather, building on the importance of relationships in Chinese culture, venture capitalists should focus on cognitive institutions for controls over the funded firm. For example, in a Confucius-based belief system, relatives and educators are considered to be more significant than government officials in their ability to influence others. Thus, while such individuals may have no official capacity in a firm's function, a well-informed venture capitalist can build relationships with them and have greater influence over the funded firm than can be negotiated in the contract (Lieberthal and Oksenberg, 1988; Lubman, 2001).

Although *guanxi* is certainly important, early entrants into the China market made the mistake of thinking *guanxi* with several top officials of the central government was all their firms needed (Mann, 1997). But the range of individuals with whom *guanxi* must be built and

G.D. Bruton, D. Ahlstrom / Journal of Business Venturing 18 (2003) 233–259 249

maintained is typically much broader (Luo, 2000). Commented another Hong Kong-based venture capitalist:

> The laws in numerous areas are still in flux. For example, tax laws are quite ambiguous and open to paradoxical interpretations. One of our dotcom investments was compelled to pay taxes in China due to some arcane rules about offshore partner firms, although it earned no profits. Connections with someone important at the tax bureau as well as knowing a good tax lawyer are quite helpful in avoiding these sorts of surprises the government can spring on firms suddenly.

The centrality of *guanxi* results in the venture capitalist needing not only to have his own *guanxi* to help firms, but also the ability to judge the value of the *guanxi* capital of firms they might fund or the managers they might hire. To build such connections, a venture capitalist may be able to not only hire such individuals to help funded firms but should also ensure that the funded firm has identified and hired key individuals (He, 1997). Venture capitalists also mentioned that they often must aid the search for professional managers for their funded firms. This is not unlike what they often have to do in the West, but in China, the venture capitalist must be sure to consider not only managers' professional skills but also the *guanxi* they possess (Pohndorf, 1997).

4.4. Exiting the investment

In the West, most venture capital firms are organized as limited partnerships with a limited life (Sahlman, 1988). Thus, the goal is to ultimately exit their investments through IPO before the venture capital partnership is terminated. Most private equity investors in China also initially expected to exit through IPOs. Presumably, the firms would be listed on either the Hong Kong Stock Exchange or, in more recent years, the stock exchanges within China (Shanghai or Shenzhen). Exiting has proven problematic, however, even for successful ventures. A host of laws on securities markets, disclosure, and accounting standards are not yet in place (Peng, 2000). The selection of which firms may list on the stock exchange in China remains principally a state decision. The central government's position is that venture-capital-backed firms already have strong financial resources and therefore should not need the capital that a stock offering would provide. The funds that can be raised through a stock listing should be directed instead toward state enterprises that are in desperate need of restructuring. Consequently, many firms utilizing internationally sourced capital are not considered for listing locally and may have to look to either strategic buyers or a listing on a foreign exchange such as the NASDAQ.

The only major exit strategies readily available are to locate a strategic buyer, have the firm itself buy back the stock, or obtain a rare overseas listing, the latter two of which are typically difficult and subject to much regulation. Thus, strategic buyers represent the most likely exit mechanism, whereby a buyer, typically a Western firm, would acquire the funded Chinese firm. One venture capital firm reported it was able to exit an investment in China by selling their interest in a paper plant to a major Western firm. This firm supplied the local Chinese company some inputs including machinery and certain raw materials such as some chemical-related items. By investing in this Chinese company, the Western firm was able to sell more inputs upstream while also gaining entry into the Chinese market. However, finding such an ideal strategic partner to help exit an investment can be difficult, and laws regarding transfer of assets can be particularly restrictive and hard to interpret. Also, such strategic partners would typically want a majority stake in the venture. Thus, the venture capital firm will not only need to sell its portion of the stock, but typically convince the Chinese firm to sell part of their share as well, and become a minority owner in the venture—difficult for most Chinese business owners to accept. When exiting via a sale to a strategic partner, the multiple paid on the firm's revenue stream will result in a return significantly lower than that traditionally associated with an IPO.

One result of these exit difficulties is that many venture capital firms have discovered that when they do exit, their returns have not been as high as expected. Private equity firms in China typically target a 20–30% return but the actual returns for many funds have been much lower (e.g., *Asia Pacific Private Equity Bulletin*, 1998). Shanghai and Shenzhen both announced plans for NASDAQ-type markets for smaller firms, Hong Kong's Growth Enterprise Market recently opened, and similar markets exist in Singapore and Taiwan. Given time, these new markets may alleviate the exit problem to some degree. Nevertheless, exit through an IPO is far from straightforward. Numerous rules exist about working with offshore partners, and transferring capital overseas (Peng et al., 1999). Exit mechanisms do exist in China, but the options are more constrained and fraught with greater complexity than in the West.[13]

5. Discussion

This exploratory analysis presents the institutional environment in a transition Asian economy can impact venture capital. It demonstrates that the institutional environment in China yields several significant differences in the actions of venture capitalists compared with those in the West. Table 1 summarizes these differences and associated institutional mechanisms.

Given that the distribution of information is far more restricted in China, the ability to visit with the venture capitalists' funded firms was limited.[14] However, it is important to note that the funded firms that were interviewed verified the findings presented in Table 1, particularly in terms of interaction between the funded firm and the venture capitalist. Additionally, they confirmed the nature of venture capitalists input to the funded firm. One funded firm stated:

> We welcomed the help of the venture capitalist in several areas. We did not know much about accounting and budgeting when we started. We didn't even have any accounting

---

[13] There are recent indications that China will further liberalize equity market rules in 2002, upon entry into the WTO. This may improve the prospects for the local IPO market, which currently is very weak.

[14] In China, there is no equivalent of the *San Jose Mercury News* to list all of the new venture deals.

G.D. Bruton, D. Ahlstrom / Journal of Business Venturing 18 (2003) 233–259   251

Table 1
Institutional forces influencing venture capital actions in China

Venture capital action	Institutional influence	Different approach in China
Selecting firms to fund	Regulatory and normative institutions	The absence of strong regulatory and normative institutions makes it more likely venture capital firms will fund firms near to their offices. Accounting information is less reliable so other means such as a relationship with the entrepreneur or others that know the entrepreneur is crucial.
Structuring of relationships and monitoring funded firms	Cognitive and regulatory institutions	Cannot assume that profit motive is paramount for funded firm founders. The government may also have a strong influence on firm goals. Corporate governance is in its infancy in China. Board membership a far weaker means of monitoring firm than in much of the West. The legal system is nascent and enforcement of judgments is very problematic. This means that having the proper connections and monitoring the firm's activities closely as a substitute for regulatory controls is very important.
Value-added activities provided to firm	Cognitive institutions	The issue of *minzi* (face) makes value-added activities provided to firm more problematic. Advice must be provided diplomatically. *Guanxi* (relationships) with a variety of individuals in the firm's locality is important in a manner not found to same degree in West.
Exit	Regulatory institutions	Exit opportunities through IPO are still very limited. Purchase of firm by strategic buyer is more likely, though market for corporate control is in nascent stage.

software, and things were quite disorganized. The venture capitalists involved helped us with these operational problems so we could focus on our technology.

The funded firms felt that venture capitalists were quite helpful in finding managers with *guanxi* with government agencies in China. They also generally agreed that exit was a problem for the venture capitalists.

One interesting observation made by the funded firms regarded certain similarities and differences between venture capitalists and foreign partners in joint ventures. For example, in terms of the advice given, managers in funded firms with experience in this area felt both venture capitalists and joint venture partners tried to provide Chinese firms with help on operations. However, venture capitalists were generally considered more willing than were foreign joint venture partners to aid the Chinese firms. Perhaps this is because joint ventures do not typically expect to exit the joint venture in a few years with a high rate of return. Venture capitalists, in contrast, need to push for growth in order to package the firm for a public offering or sale to strategic buyers. The foreign joint venture partner also may need to protect their technological knowledge from the Chinese partner so may not transfer certain technology or know-how (cf. Child and Faukner, 1998), whereas the venture capital firm generally does not have this concern.

Venture capitalists were also thought to be better able, or more willing, to connect the Chinese firms to key overseas alliance partners than were joint venture partners. Venture capitalists commonly have existing strong business connections in various regions around the Pacific Rim. These relationships are often very helpful to the Chinese firms. For example, a founder of an e-commerce firm in China observed:

> The venture capitalists have found us alliance partners in both strategic and operational areas. They helped us to work with a firm in India that could do some Web programming for us—some of the best programmers of that type are in India. The venture capitalists also found a strategic partner in the States that has gotten us connected with e-commerce sites there and elsewhere. The venture capital firm has such an extensive network of funded firms, they are able to structure firms together in a virtual team very quickly.

There were other similarities between the joint ventures and venture capitals. Principally, both serve to increase the legitimacy of the Chinese firm. The presence of an international partner served to indicate to regulators and competitors that the Chinese firm is of a certain quality. Thus, although there are some differences between joint venture, and venture capital due to the differing time horizons, goals, and different constraints on alliances and technology transfer, there are also similarities. Venture capitalists can, however, learn from the now extensive experience of joint ventures in China in terms of finding reliable partners, building *guanxi* relations, and monitoring the investment (e.g. Child and Faukner, 1998; Child and Yan, 1999; Hoon-Halbauer, 1999; Mann, 1997; Walsh and Wang, 1999).

5.1. Future research

The research has many implications for future research, theory development, and the practice of venture capital. The evidence here is that operationally venture capital in China is substantially different than in the West. Future research should not only expand the examination of China but also other Asian venture capital markets. Asia's venture capital industry is undergoing rapid expansion. Some of the same differences found in China would be expected in other Asian markets. However, future research will be needed to establish if these differences are uniform across Asia.

Greater information is needed on topics such as the nature of the investment process across Asia. As demonstrated here, cognitive institutions embodied in China's traditions and commercial conventions, as well as normative institutions (such as accounting standards and corporate governance), and the lack of regulatory institutions (laws and regulations) impact venture capitalists in China. These conditions are not unique to China but exist in varying degrees throughout much of Asia (Backman, 1999). For example, accounting standards, corporate governance, and transparency remain a problem throughout the region (Lubman, 2001; Tam, 1999). How venture capitalists deal effectively with these issues, particularly during firm selection, and in the monitoring of funded firms needs to be established.

As noted in discussing the nature of screening of ventures for potential funding, personal relationships are very important. However, exact details on deal origination remain quite opaque. The processes of finding potential transactions and educating a potential target company about why raising money from the venture capital industry need greater exploration. Similarly, the exact nature of the funding made to the ventures, including the nature of subordinated debt, and other ancillary investment instruments remain poorly understood and need greater exploration.

The cognitive institutions carried by China's high context culture in particular, influence how venture capitalists in China can interact with their portfolio firms. Throughout East Asia, Chinese business people dominate business in areas such as Singapore, Thailand, Indonesia, Taiwan, and Malaysia (Backman, 1999). Thus, the cultural proclivities seen here should not be unique to China but likely exert some similar influence on venture capital funding across the East Asian region. For example, the importance of *guanxi* impacts how due diligence is conducted in China. Does it have a similar role in areas of Asia outside of China? Similarly, differences in monitoring the funded firm, value added by venture capitalists, and interactions with management are ripe for additional investigation throughout the Asian venture capital industry.

Regulatory institutions were also seen as playing a role in China and could be expected to produce a variety of differences across Asian venture capital firms. For example, the role of governance, such as board membership, is different in China than in the West (Tam, 1999). Similarly, these regulatory institutions also impacted the ability of venture capitalists to exit funded firms. Each country in Asia has somewhat different regulatory institutions. How these various differences impact the venture capital industry in China and elsewhere around Asia should be explored in the future.

Another important issue concerned the need to monitor outcomes from the venture capital process; that is, to what extent are approaches drawn from Western expertise associated with greater performance? As noted, early evidence suggests that the Chinese venture capital market (and the Asian market in general) is not performing as well as those in the West with returns in China often in the single digits. Can this low rate of return be attributed to macroeconomic factors or differences in the frameworks of venture capital employed? Do the venture capital firms that follow a model more similar to that in the West typically perform better than those that more closely follow the Asian model? Thus, gaining greater perspective on venture capital aspects that have universal application and those that are context-dependent merit closer examination (cf. Child et al., 2000).

The relationships among various parties in China are very important in determining success of the venture. However, the interviews of the venture capitalist emphasized that these interrelationships may play an even more important role than previously thought. A number of the venture capitalists not only sought to connect existing firms with suppliers, buyers, and other key parties, they also acted as intermediaries building a new venture. The venture capitalists see a wide variety of business plans and ideas. They frequently like a given business idea but not the management or some aspect of the given business. The venture capitalists in these cases would then act to pull all of the key parties of a new venture together that would conduct the given activity. Thus, venture capitalists functioned as catalysts spearheading the formation of a venture. Future research should continue to explore this given topic further.

The research opportunities opened here are not limited to China. Research is also needed to examine both the development of the operation of venture capital firms in China over time and compare them to the development of similar firms in developing countries such as India or the transition economies of Southeast Asia and Eastern Europe.

5.2. Theory development

In terms of implications for theory, this study offers us insights about institutional forces operating in an emerging venture capital market. As our data suggest, institutional forces in China create a different context from the Western model of venture capital that needs to be accounted for. Institutions are often thought of in terms of their constraining effects on individuals and organizations in their decisions and choice sets (DiMaggio and Powell, 1983, 1991; North, 1990), but they also can enable (Garud and Jain, 1996; Peng, 2000). There are a set of institutions that help to provide the means for venture capitalists to function in such a challenging commercial setting (cf. Peng, 2000).

Successful venture capitalists in China have found ways to recognize the key institutions at work in different levels of society and how to use them. For example, in some cases an institution such as *guanxi* can hinder the due diligence process since it is difficult to extract information from those with whom the venture capitalist has no established relationship. Yet *guanxi* can also prove helpful in sourcing deals, monitoring the firm, giving the firm assistance, and successfully exiting the venture if the venture capitalist has the right relationships or can hire someone with those relationships. Institutional forces act to prescribe (often-unwritten) guidelines to the function of the system that must be understood both by venture capital practitioners and researchers. This is especially true of communication, information gathering, and its interpretation. Thus, future theory development and examinations based on institutional theory should recognize and employ this constraining and enabling duality of institutions.

5.3. Practice

The research also has clear contribution for practice. As noted, the venture capital funds in Asia are rapidly expanding. Many of these funds are not only funds raised in Asia but also come from the West. The overall growth of venture capital in the West has produced an abundance of resources resulting in large amounts of money chasing a limited number of good deals in the US and Europe. Thus, Westerners increasingly look to the less-crowded and fast-growing Asian market for opportunities, resulting in many new venture capital funds entering China in particular and Asia in general. The evidence presented here is that they cannot expect to unilaterally move their operations from the US or Europe and be successful. There are elements of the venture capital industry that are similar. How those elements are implemented, however, can differ significantly. Venture capitalist firms should seek to build their experience in the region to understand those differences over time to increase the opportunity for success as the China market continues its rapid and consistent expansion.

6. Conclusion

Investing by venture capitalists in China is no simple task. Understanding the local China environment is crucial to success in this market, as is a keen understanding of the venture capital industry in general. Until recently, fund managers often argued that their financial success would be based on China's large market and the resulting ability to skim the best deals off the top. However, now a large pool of venture capitalists have been active in the China market for at least 5 years and, in general, their current performance makes clear that the environment in China is complex and success will not come easily. One recent significant change has been the process of selecting and monitoring the investee firm. Increasingly, investors acknowledge that while China is unique, they must broadly employ steps similar to those used in the West on issues such as due diligence, qualified for China's different institutional environment.

Venture capital investors in the West bring far more to the table than just money. Their advice and connections and global perspective are all important to their funded firms' success. Although Chinese business owners have been reluctant to allow venture capitalists to participate in financial and strategic decisions, they now increasingly recognize and accept that investors will not be passive providers of money. The most sophisticated of the Chinese firms actively seek out a broader array of input from the smorgasbord offered by their venture capital investors. The venture capitalists also increasingly recognize that they must employ the full range of these skills if they are to be successful. The use of these skills does not mean that the venture capitalist can ignore the institutional differences that persist in China. On the contrary, the institutional environment is so different that skills honed in the West must be combined with knowledge acquired in China such that actions can be adjusted accordingly. Thus, the future will likely produce a framework with greater similarities to the Western model but one in which Chinese cultural and commercial characteristics are still prevalent and influence things like who gets hired, how assets are assessed, and the amount of time required to complete the due diligence process. Convergence on a model of venture capital as in the US is by no means assured. The evolving approach to venture capital funding in China acknowledges the local institutional environment and attempts to manage it and use it where possible.

256   *G.D. Bruton, D. Ahlstrom / Journal of Business Venturing 18 (2003) 233–259*

Economic reforms of former Chinese leader Deng Xiaoping in the late 1970s have steadily improved the investment climate, and Premier Zhu has taken steps to make China more inviting to outside investors. Following the 1989 crackdown on the student democracy movement in Tiananmen Square, the government made an informal pact with its people: Do not interfere with our politics, and we will not stop you from conducting business. Venture capitalists interviewed pointed out that while the environment for venture capital and startup firms is certainly friendlier than it was in the past, the overall Chinese economy still needs development that creates opportunity for venture capitalists (cf. Peng, 2000, 2001). The increasing openness of state-owned enterprises to foreign investments and the increasing desire of the government to privatize these businesses will only create additional opportunities for venture capitalist professionals in the future. Additionally, as institutional investors seek to diversify their investments, an obvious move is to include China in their portfolio. Western venture capitalists must be well prepared and well versed in the nuances of the Chinese environment, and adjust to that context if they hope to maximize their chances of success in this intriguing and complex market.

Acknowledgements

The authors would like to thank Vance Fried for the comments on an earlier version of this article.

The work in this article was substantially supported by a grant from the RGC Research Grant Direct Allocation Scheme (Project No. 2070212, 2000–2001) of The Chinese University of Hong Kong, the Hong Kong Special Administrative Region.

References

Ahlstrom, D., Bruton, G.D., Chan, E.S., 2000. Venture capital in China: ground-level challenges for high technology investing. J. Private Equity 3, 45–54.
Asia Pacific Private Equity Bulletin, 1998. Great expectations. Asia Pac. Private Equity Bull., 1–4 (June).
Backman, M., 1999. Asian Eclipse: Exposing the Dark Side of Business in Asia. Wiley, Singapore.
Bartlett, J.W., 1995. Equity Finance: Venture Capital, Buyouts, Restructurings and Reorganizations, second ed. Wiley, New York.
Becker, J., 2000. The Chinese. John Murray, London.
Björkman, I., Lu, Y., 1999. The management of human resources in Chinese–Western joint ventures. J. World Bus., 306–324 (Fall).
Boisot, M.H., Child, J., 1988. The iron law of fiefs: bureaucratic failure and the problem of governance in the Chinese economic reforms. Adm. Sci. Q. 33, 507–527.
Boisot, M.H., Child, J., 1996. From fiefs to clans and network capitalism: explaining China's emerging economic order. Adm. Sci. Q. 41, 600–628.
Bond, M.H. (Ed.), 1988. The Cross-Cultural Challenge to Social Psychology. Sage Publications, Newbury Park, CA.
Boyacillier, N., Adler, N., 1991. The parochial dinosaur: organizational science in a global context. Acad. Manage. Rev. 16, 262–290.
Broadman, H.G., 1999. The Chinese state as corporate shareholder. Finance Dev. 36 (3), 52–55.

G.D. Bruton, D. Ahlstrom / Journal of Business Venturing 18 (2003) 233–259 257

Bruno, A.V., Tyebjee, T.T., 1986. The destinies of rejected venture capital deals. Sloan Manage. Rev. 27 (2), 43–53.

Bruton, G., Fried, V., Hisrich, R.D., 1998. Venture capitalist and CEO dismissal. Entrepreneurship Theory Pract. 21 (3), 41–54.

Bruton, G.D., Dattani, M., Fung, M., Chow, C., Ahlstrom, D., 1999. Private equity in China: differences and similarities with the Western Model. J. Private Equity 1, 7–13 (Winter).

Bruton, G.D., Lan, H., Yuan, L., 2000. China's township and village enterprises: Kelon's competitive edge. Acad. Manage. Exec. 14 (1), 19–30.

Bygrave, W.D., 1987. Syndication investment by venture capital firms: a network perspective. J. Bus. Venturing 2, 139–154.

Bygrave, W., Timmons, J., 1992. Venture Capital at the Crossroads. Harvard Business School Press, Boston.

Child, J., 1994. Management in China During the Age of Reform. Cambridge Univ. Press, Cambridge.

Child, J., Faulkner, D., 1998. Strategies of Co-Operation. Oxford Univ. Press, New York.

Child, J., Yan, Y., 1999. Investment and control in international joint ventures: the case of China. J. World Bus. 34, 3–15.

Child, J., Faulkner, D., Pitkethley, R., 2000. Foreign direct investment in the UK 1985–1994: the impact on domestic management practice. J. Manage. Stud. 37 (1), 141–168 (January).

Chow, K.W.C., Fung, M.K.Y., 2000. Small businesses and liquidity constraints in financing business investment: evidence from Shanghai's manufacturing sector. J. Bus. Venturing 15, 363–383.

Clarke, D.C., 1991. What's law got to do with it? Legal institutions and economic reform in China. Pac. Basin Law J. 10 (1), 1–76.

Daft, R.L., Lewin, A.Y., 1990. Can organization studies begin to break out of the normal science straightjacket? Organ. Sci. 1, 1–11.

Diesing, P., 1971. Patterns of Discovery in the Social Sciences. Adline Atherton, New York.

DiMaggio, P.J., Powell, W.W., 1983. The iron cage revisited: institutional isomorphism and collective rationality in organizational fields. Am. Sociol. Rev. 48, 147–160.

DiMaggio, P.J., Powell, W.W., 1991. Introduction. In: Powell, W.W., DiMaggio, P.J. (Eds.), The New Institutionalism in Organizational Analysis, pp. 1–38.

Eisenhardt, K.M., 1989. Building theory from case study research. Acad. Manage. Rev. 14, 532–550.

Fiet, J.O., 1995. Reliance upon informants in the venture capital industry. J. Bus. Venturing 10 (3), 195–223.

Frey, T., Oishi, 1995. How to Conduct Interviews by Telephone and in Person. Sage Publications, Thousand Oaks, CA.

Fried, V., Hisrich, R., 1992. Venture capital and the investor. Manage. Res. News 4, 28–40.

Fried, V., Hisrich, R., 1994. Towards a model of venture capital investment decision making, financial management. Financ. Manage. 23 (3), 28–37.

Fried, V.H., Hisrich, R.D., 1995. The venture capitalist: a relationship investor. Calif. Manage. Rev. 37 (2), 101–113.

Fried, V.H., Bruton, G.D., Hisrich, R.D., 1998. Strategy and board of directors in venture capital backed firms. J. Bus. Venturing 13, 493–503.

Garud, R., Jain, S., 1996. The embeddedness of technological systems. Adv. Strategic Manage. 13, 389–408.

Giamartino, G.A., McDougall, P.P., Bird, B.J., 1993. International entrepreneurship: the state of the field. Entrepreneurship Theory Pract. 18, 37–42.

Glaser, B., Strauss, A., 1967. The Discovery of Grounded Theory. Aldine de Gruyter, New York.

Goa, G., Ting-Toomey, S., Gudykunst, W., 1996. Chinese communication processes. In: Bond, M. (Ed.), The Handbook of Chinese Psychology, pp. 135–158.

Gorman, M., Sahlman, W.A., 1989. What do venture capitalists do? J. Bus. Venturing 4, 231–248.

Guide to Venture Capital in Asia, 1997–1998. Guide to Venture Capital in Asia. Asian Venture Capital Association, Hong Kong.

Guide to Venture Capital in Asia, 2000. Guide to Venture Capital in Asia. Asian Venture Capital Association, Hong Kong.

He, Q., 1997. Zhongguo de Xianjing (The Primary Capital Accumulation in Contemporary China). Mirror Books, Hong Kong.

Hirsch, P.M., Lounsbury, M., 1997. Ending the family quarrel: toward a reconciliation of "old" and "new" institutionalisms. Am. Behav. Sci. 40, 406–418.

Hoon-Halbauer, S.K., 1999. Managing relationships within Sino–foreign joint ventures. J. World Bus. 34, 344–371.

Hurry, D., Miller, A.T., Bowman, E.H., 1992. Calls on high-technology: Japanese exploration of venture capital investments in the United States. Strategic Manage. J. 13 (2), 85–101.

Jeng, L.A., Wells, P.C., 2000. The determinants of venture capital funding: evidence across countries. J. Corp. Finance 6 (3), 241–289.

Jepperson, R., 1991. Institutions, institutional effects, and institutionalism. In: Powell, W.W., DiMaggio, P.J. (Eds.), The New Institutionalism in Organizational Analysis, pp. 143–163.

Lee, T.W., 1999. Using Qualitative Methods in Organizational Research. Sage Publications, Thousand Oaks, CA.

Li, L.C., 1998. Central–provincial relations: beyond compliance analysis. In: Cheng, J.Y.S. (Ed.), China Review, pp. 157–186.

Lieberthal, K., Oksenberg, M., 1988. Policy Making in China: Leaders, Structures, and Processes. Princeton Univ. Press, Princeton, NJ.

Lubman, S.B., 2001. Bird in a Cage. Stanford Univ. Press, Stanford, CA.

Luo, Y., 2000. *Guanxi* and Business. World Scientific Press, Singapore.

MacMillian, I.C., Kulow, D.M., Khoylian, R., 1988. Venture capitalist involvement in their investments: extent and performance. J. Bus. Venturing 4, 4–47.

Majumdar, S.K., Venkataraman, S., 1998. Network effects and the adoption of new technology: evidence from the U.S. telecommunications industry. Strategic Manage. J. 19, 1045–1062.

Mann, J., 1997. Beijing Jeep: The Short, Unhappy Romance of American Business in China, second ed. Simon & Schuster, New York.

McGrath, R.G., 1997. A real options logic for initiating technology positioning investments. Acad. Manage. Rev. 22, 974–996.

North, D., 1990. Institutions, Institutional Change and Economic Performance. Cambridge Univ. Press, Cambridge.

Patricof, A., 1989. The internationalization of venture capital. J. Bus. Venturing 4 (4), 227–230.

Peng, M.W., 1997. Firm growth in transitional economies: three longitudinal cases from China, 1989–96. Organ. Stud. 18 (3), 385–413.

Peng, M.W., 2000. Business Strategies in Transition Economies. Sage Publications, Thousand Oaks, CA.

Peng, M.W., 2001. How do entrepreneurs create wealth in transition economies? Acad. Manage. Exec. 15 (1), 95–112.

Peng, M.W., Heath, P.S., 1996. The growth of the firm in planned economies in transition. Acad. Manage. Rev. 21 (2), 437–492.

Peng, M.W., Luo, Y., Sun, L., 1999. Firm growth via mergers and acquisitions in China. In: Kelley, L., Luo, Y. (Eds.), China 2000: Emerging Business Issues, pp. 73–100.

Peng, M.W., Lu, Y., Shenkar, O., Wang, D.Y.L., 2001. Treasures in the China house: a review of management and organizational research on Greater China. J. Bus. Res. 52 (2), 95–110.

Pohndorf, D.R., 1997. The fine art of making a success of Asian equity funds. Global Finance, 42–46 (April).

Powell, W.W., 1991. Expanding the scope of institutional analysis. In: Powell, W.W., DiMaggio, P.J. (Eds.), The New Institutionalism in Organizational Analysis. University of Chicago Press, Chicago, pp. 183–203.

Ray, D.M., Turpin, D.V., 1993. Venture capital in Japan. Int. Small Bus. J. 11 (4), 39–56 (July–September).

Reynolds, B., 1984. China in the international economy. In: Harding, H. (Ed.), China's Foreign Relations in the 1980's. Yale Univ. Press, New Haven, pp. 71–106.

Rosenstein, J., 1988. The board and strategy: venture capital and high technology. J. Bus. Venturing 3, 159–170.

Roy, W.G., 1997. Socializing Capital: The Rise of the Large Industrial Corporation in America. Princeton Univ. Press, Princeton, NJ.

Sahlman, W.A., 1988. Aspects of financial contracting in venture capital. J. Appl. Corp. Finance 1, 23–36 (Summer).

Sapienza, H., 1992. When do venture capitalists add value? J. Bus. Venturing 7, 9–27.

Sapienza, H., Gupta, A.K., 1994. Impact of agency risks and task uncertainty on venture capitalist–CEO interactions. Acad. Manage. J. 37, 1618–1632.

Sapienza, H., Manigart, S., Vermeir, W., 1996. Venture capitalist governance and value added in four countries. J. Bus. Venturing 11, 439–469.

Scarborough, J., 1998. Comparing Chinese and Western cultural roots: why "East is East and . . .". Bus. Horizons 41 (6), 15–24.

Scott, W.R., 1987. The adolescence of institutional theory. Adm. Sci. Q. 32, 493–511.

Scott, W.R., 1992. Organizations: Rational, Natural and Open Systems, third ed. Prentice-Hall, Englewood Cliffs, NJ.

Scott, W.R., 1995. Institutions and Organizations. Sage Publications, Thousand Oaks, CA.

Selznick, P., 1957. Leadership in Administration. Harper and Row, New York.

Shenkar, O., Von Glinow, M.A., 1994. Paradoxes of organizational theory and research: using the case of China to illustrate national contingency. Manage. Sci. 40, 56–71.

Standifird, S.S., Marshall, R.S., 2000. The transaction cost advantage of *guanxi*-based business practices. J. World Bus. 35, 21–42.

Steinfeld, E.S., 1998. Forging Reform in China: The Fate of State-Owned Industry. Cambridge Univ. Press, Cambridge.

Strauss, A., Corbin, J., 1990. Basics of Qualitative Research: Grounded Theory Procedures and Techniques. Sage Publications, Newbury Park, CA.

Suchman, M.C., 1995. Localism and globalism in institutional analysis: the emergence of contractual norms in venture finance. In: Scott, W.R., Christensen, S. (Eds.), The Institutional Construction of Organizations, pp. 39–66.

Tam, O.K., 1999. The Development of Corporate Governance in China. Edward Elgar, Cheltenham, UK.

Tan, J., 1999. The growth of entrepreneurial firms in transitional economy: the case of a Chinese entrepreneur. J. Manage. Inq., 83–89 (March).

Tsang, E.W.K., 1998. Can *guanxi* be a source of sustained competitive advantage for doing business in China? Acad. Manage. Exec. 12 (2), 64–73.

Tyebjee, T.T., Bruno, A.V., 1984. A model of venture capital investment activity. Manage. Sci. 30, 1051–1066.

Walsh, J., Wang, E.P., 1999. Same bed, different dreams: working relationships in Sino–American joint ventures. J. World Bus. 34, 69–93.

Wank, D.L., 1996. The institutional process of market clientelism: *guanxi* and private business in a South China city. China Q. 147, 820–838.

Wright, M., Robbie, K., 1996. The investor-led buy-out: a new strategic option. Long Range Plan. 29 (5), 691–702.

Wright, M., Thompson, S., Robbie, K., 1992. Venture capital and management-led leveraged buy-outs: a European perspective. J. Bus. Venturing 7 (1), 47–71.

Xin, K.R., Pearce, J.L., 1996. *Guanxi*: connections as substitutes for formal institutional support. Acad. Manage. J. 39, 1641–1658.

Yeung, I.Y.M., Tung, R.L., 1996. Achieving business success in Confucian societies: the importance of *guanxi* (connections). Organ. Dyn., 54–65 (Autumn).

Yin, R.K., 1994. Case study research: design and methods. Sage Publications, Thousand Oaks, CA.

Zider, B., 1998. How venture capital works. Harv. Bus. Rev. 76, 131–139.

Zucker, L., 1986. Production of trust: institutional sources of economic structure, 1840–1920. Research in Organizational Behavior, vol. 8, pp. 53–111.

Zucker, L., 1987. Institutional theories of organizations. Annu. Rev. Sociol. 13, 443–464.

[25]

Journal of International Entrepreneurship 2, 305–326, 2004
© 2004 Kluwer Academic Publishers. Manufactured in The Netherlands.

Venture Capital Investors, Capital Markets, Valuation and Information: US, Europe and Asia

MIKE WRIGHT
ANDY LOCKETT   andy.lockett@nottingham.ac.uk
SARIKA PRUTHI
Centre for Management Buy-out Research, Nottingham University Business School,
Jubilee Campus, Nottingham NG8 1BB

SOPHIE MANIGART   sophie.manigart@vlerick.be
Vlerick Leuven Gent Management School and Ghent University, Belgium

HARRY SAPIENZA   HSapienza@csom.umn.edu
Carlson School of Management 3-365, University of Minnesota, 321 19th Avenue, South,
Minneapolis, MN 55455

PHILIPPE DESBRIERES
Universite de Bourgogne, Dijon

ULRICH HOMMEL
European Business School, Frankfurt

Abstract. This paper uses a large multi-country sample of venture capital firms to compare the approaches to investee valuation and sources of information used by venture capital investors in English, French and German legal systems as well as geographical regions. Different legal systems are significantly associated with the valuation mechanism used. In particular, compared to English-based Common Law systems, VC firms operating in a Germanic legal system are significantly more likely to use DCF based measures and significantly less likely to use PE comparators. This latter result is also the case for VC firms operating in a French legal system who are also significantly more likely to adopt historic cost valuation methods. VC firms in Europe and Asia are significantly less likely than US VC firms to make use of liquidation value methods but significantly more likely to use PE comparators. European firms are significantly less likely to adopt DCF methods compared to US VC firms. VC firms operating under a Germanic legal system are less likely to utilise information from the financial press but significantly more likely to use interviews with entrepreneurs. VC firms operating under a French legal system are more likely to utilise interviews with company personnel as well as sales and marketing information. VC firms in Europe and Asia are significantly more likely than US VC firms to use financial press. VC firms in Asia are significantly less likely to make use of interviews with entrepreneurs or business plan data. VC firms in Europe are significantly more likely to utilise sales and marketing information.

Keywords: venture capital, valuation, information, Europe, emerging markets

Introduction

International entrepreneurship is receiving growing attention (McDougall and Oviatt, 2000). Much of this work has focused on the behavior of entrepreneurial firms in terms of either their cross-border activities or comparisons between firms in different countries. A key influence on entrepreneurial firm behavior concerns their access to venture finance. To date research into international comparisons of the operation of venture capital firms remains limited (Wright et al., 2002). Early studies examined the general factors influencing the growth of different venture capital (Ooghe et al., 1991; Manigart, 1994) and related management buy-out markets (Wright et al., 1992). Other early studies considered the different broad strategy formulations adopted by venture capital firms in the US and Europe (Roure et al., 1992).

More recently, there is increasing recognition of the impact of differences in institutional, legal and cultural environments on the conduct of financial markets in different countries (La Porta et al., 1997, 1998). These factors may also impact the specific development of venture capital markets (Black and Gilson, 1998; Jeng and Wells, 2000). This raises questions about the need to understand the operation of venture capitalists in different countries. While there may be some degree of commonality of venture capitalists' functions across countries (Sapienza et al., 1996), differences in institutional factors concerning regulation, normative rules of behavior and culture (North, 1990; Scott, 1995) may affect business practices internationally (Bruton et al., 2004).

The increasing international spread of venture capital and private equity as firms seek to invest outside their domestic markets (Allen and Song, 2002) brings these problems into sharp focus. Anecdotal evidence suggests that venture capital firms entering international markets may under-estimate differences both with their home market and between apparently similar countries (see e.g. Wright and Kitamura, 2003 in respect of private equity entrants into the Japanese buyout market). Appreciation of this heterogeneity is important for both researchers and practitioners. Venture capital firms seeking to enter different countries within a particular region may experience problems in generating target returns if they fail to take adequate account of the different modus operandi of individual markets. While there may be differences between countries, these differences may be driven by broader institutional characteristics relating to the state of development of the capital, the underlying legal regime (e.g. English versus French versus Germanic origin legal regimes) or broader geographic factors (e.g. Europe; Asia) (Bruton et al., 2004). Ultimately, these factors may influence the financing of the global development of entrepreneurship.

Key issues for venture capital firms' returns concern the methods used to value investments and the information used to arrive at valuations. Valuations are particularly subjective in venture capital investments where the business typically has less of a track record than an established publicly listed company. The valuation placed on a business at the time of investment can have a dramatic effect on the ability of the venture capital firm to meet its target rate of return. These issues are crucial in domestic markets but may assume greater significance in different capital market environments where the level and nature of information may be at some variance to the domestic market. There is little research comparing venture capitalists' approaches to valuation and sources of information in different institutional environments.

This paper provides an initial exploratory attempt to address gaps in previous research by examining the role of the capital market, valuation methods and information sources used in the process of deciding to make a venture capital investment in differing institutional environments and venture capital market contexts. Specifically we address two research questions. RQ1: To what extent do valuation methods vary across institutional environments? RQ2: To what extent do information sources vary across institutional environments?

In addressing these questions, our focus is on the overall behavior of venture capital firms operating within particular markets. We present evidence based on surveys conducted in nine different countries. These countries cover a range of different legal systems. We include countries from the English law based contexts that include long-established venture capital markets (the US and UK), more recently developed venture capital markets (Hong Kong and Singapore) and a developing venture capital market (India). Also we include a Germanic law (bank) based environment with a developing venture capital market (Germany), a French law-based (network) environment (France, Netherlands and Belgium). We examine differences between these institutional and geographical contexts since we anticipate that influences in behavior will relate to the structural differences between these contexts.

The paper begins by outlining how venture capital markets differ in relation to their structural and institutional differences. Next, we develop the argument that a venture capital firm's behavior, in relation to valuation methods and sources of information used, will vary according to its institutional environment. The third section provides an outline of the representative surveys of venture capital firms in the nine countries in the study. This is followed by an analysis of the findings. In the final section, some conclusions are drawn and implications for researchers and practitioners discussed.

Structural and institutional differences

In this section we argue that venture capital markets throughout the world are heterogeneous in terms of their structure and the different institutions upon which they are based. In particular, there are structural differences in terms of their stage of development and allocation of funds across different investment stages. However, we argue that it is the institutions that underpin these markets that have a greater influence on the behavior of venture capital firms. We expand below.

Structural differences

There are notable differences between the venture capital markets examined here, particularly with respect to their level of development and the relative importance of different investment stages. Table 1 shows some important characteristics of the venture capital industries in each of the countries studied here. The data in the table refer to the total investment by VC firms based in each country. The US market is by far the largest market, followed by the UK, France and Germany. Hong Kong is of a similar size to the combined Dutch and Belgian markets. The Indian market is the smallest.

Table 1. Venture capital in the study countries ($m).

	US	UK	Hong Kong	Singapore	India	Germany	France	Netherlands	Belgium
Investments ($m)									
1999	54,994	11,367	1,735	1,060	384	3,400	3,034	1,841	725
2000	106,391	12,048	2,426	1,281	830	5,133	5,711	2,063	608
Portfolio ($m)									
1999	134,500	27,720	7,187	2,830	802	8,500	12,496	4,921	1,933
2000		35,840	8,919	3,627	1,550	12,359	17,073	6,416	2,326
CAGR 1993–2000 (%)	29		24	27	47	20	20	22	15
VC/GDP in 2000 (%)	1.07	0.86	1.48	1.39	0.17	0.23	0.38	0.48	0.23
CAGR VC/GDP 1993–2000 (%)	24		20	18	38	17	17	18	11
Stage (2000)									
Seed/start-up	22	12	26	30	49	35	22	19	47
Expansion	58	34	35	44	42	45	36	55	46
Buy-out	18	53	30	12	4	18	38	19	6
Other late		1	9	14	5	2	4	7	1

*US stage figures relate to 2001.

At the beginning of the 1990s, the US market was highly developed. In Europe, the UK, Dutch, Belgian and French markets were more established at the beginning of the 1990s while the German market was less developed and remained so at the end of the decade. The venture capital markets in Hong Kong, and Singapore emerged only from the 1980s, with that in India being more recent still (Verma, 1997). The three Asian markets displayed somewhat faster growth rates than in the European countries. However, there are notable differences within regions, especially with respect to the greater growth of the Indian market in Asia. These figures are consistent with Allen and Song's (2002) findings that venture capital in both Europe and Asia grew rapidly in the 1990s.

The markets also vary considerably in relation to countries' GDP in 2000. The annual investments made by venture capital firms in the US in 2000 was 1.07% but this is exceeded by Hong Kong and Singapore with 1.48 and 1.39%, respectively. The European venture capital markets amount to considerably smaller shares of GDP, especially in Germany at 0.23%. These differences between the European countries and US, UK, Hong Kong and Singapore is in line with expectations given the reduced emphasis on capital markets in the former (La Porta et al., 1997; Black and Gilson, 1998). The much newer Indian venture capital market amounts to only 0.17% of GDP.

Early and expansion stage investments dominate the US market in terms of amounts invested (Table 1). Allen and Song (2002) in comparing Asian and European venture capital markets find that in Asia there was more investment in early stage projects while in Europe there was more investment in late stage projects. However, there are notable variations between countries even within these regions. As Table 1 indicates, in Europe early and expansion stage investments are important in Germany and Belgium. The UK and French market have stronger emphases on buyout stage investments than the other countries. Among the three Asian countries examined here, Hong Kong also reports a relatively high share for buyout stage investments while India has the highest early stage share. Expansion-stage investments constitute the most popular area of investment in Hong Kong and Singapore.

Institutional differences

Venture capitalists' valuation approaches, and the information they use in making such valuations, may be influenced by their institutional environments. Institutional theory identifies the effects of norms, culture and regulations on behavior (Scott, 1995). The existence of behavioral norms would suggest a certain degree of commonality of behavior by venture capital firms between countries, while cultural and regulatory differences would suggest differences between countries. One of the key aspects of different regulatory environments is the framework influencing the regulation of financial reporting. Differences in such frameworks have been identified as important in differentiating between markets (Wright et al., 1992). In this paper we focus on a country's legal system as an important influence on the behavior of firms in a country's venture capital market (Jeng and Wells, 2000; Bruton et al., 2004).

A key difference between different venture capital environments has been the legal system of the country (Allen and Song, 2002). The major legal systems of the world are derived from either English law, French Law or German law (LaPorta, 1997). La Porta et al. (1997) show that the legal protection for minority shareholders matters for the size and extent of the country's capital markets. This finding is explained by the fact that a good legal environment protects potential financiers' interests and hence increases their willingness to provide funds in exchange for equity. English-based common-law countries have the strongest legal protection of shareholders, while investor protection is weaker in German civil-law countries, and still weaker in French civil-law countries.

The US, UK, Hong Kong, India and Singapore have been categorised as having the same English-based common law legal origin (La Porta et al., 1997). However, even within English-based systems there is considerable variety of development of stock markets, the US having greater ratios of external capital/GNP, IPOs/population, listed companies/population than is the case in India, with the corresponding figures for UK, Hong Kong and Singapore being even higher (La Porta et al., 1997, 1998). Black and Gilson (1998) argue that a well-developed stock market, providing exit routes, is critical to the existence of a vibrant venture capital market. Jeng and Wells (2000) note that the level of IPOs is especially important for later stage but not early stage venture capital. In the US, the developed nature of the main stock market and the introduction of NASDAQ with less stringent requirements provide opportunities for the realization of venture capital investments. Further, a developed takeover market provides further venture capital realization options. In contrast, the Indian stock market is relatively underdeveloped with little scope for expansion in a regime dominated by state-directed credit.

Black and Gilson (1998) also note that stock markets elsewhere in Europe outside the UK are under-developed as are venture capital markets. With respect to the European markets, studied here, all except the Netherlands have lower external capital/GDP ratios than any of the English-common law-based markets. Secondary tier stock markets have been introduced such as the Second Marche in France the Neuer Markt in Germany but with limited success.

Bruton et al. (2004) argue that the nature of a country's legal environment and, related to this, the development of its capital markets, not only influences the development of its venture capital industry, but also the behavior of its VC firms. Apart from the existence of laws, the enforcement of those laws is an important issue for financial investors. Local cultures affect how different regulations are implemented (Kostova, 1997). Legal enforcement is probably highest in the US, intermediary in Europe and erratic to non-existent in certain parts of Asia (Bruton et al., 2003). It is expected that law enforcement will impact the way VC firms behave.

Besides regulatory institutions, particular countries may be characterised by different cognitive or cultural institutions (Scott, 1995) that may affect how VC firms behave. For example, the strength and importance of social and business networks may impact the VC deal selection process (Bruton et al., 2004). Hence, we might expect that countries with different legal systems are not necessarily homogeneous across geographical contexts.

VC INVESTORS, CAPITAL MARKETS, VALUATION AND INFORMATION   311

In the following sections we develop propositions relating to the behavior of venture capital firms across different institutional environments in terms of their valuation methods and sources of information used in valuation.

Valuation and information in venture capital investment

Valuation approaches

A number of approaches to the valuation of enterprises are available. The limitations of using balance sheet based asset measures, especially historic cost asset values, to value enterprises are well-recognised in standard finance texts. However, in the absence of strong capital markets, historic cost measures may be viewed as more tangible valuation measures. Shareholder protection is lower in French and German legal systems (La Porta et al., 1998, 2000), making assets-in-place somewhat more important than in English legal systems as a form of protection for investors. Further, Sapienza et al. (1996) also note that executives in Continental European venture capital firms are more financially oriented than US venture capital firm managers. In bank-based systems, many VC firms may be owned by banks, with VC executives having a background in banking (Ooghe et al., 1991). Given the importance of collateral in bank lending, such executives may be more likely to pay attention to the asset backing of investees. Hence:

> *P1a:* Asset based valuation methods are likely to be significantly more important in countries with French and German legal systems than countries with an English legal system.

Where there is a high risk of failure, the expected liquidation value of assets may be an important consideration in valuing potential investees. These valuations may be more feasible in market-based systems, which tend to be associated with active takeover markets, especially for forced asset disposals (Shleifer and Vishny, 1992). The US has notably the most developed acquisitions market among the countries studied here while this is less true of Europe and Asia. Hence, although relatively little importance is expected to be placed on asset based valuation methods in general:

> *P1b:* Liquidation value asset based methods are likely to be significantly less important in countries in Europe and Asia than in the US.

Theoretically, discounted cash flow (DCF) valuation methods are superior to asset-based approaches. However, countries with less developed capital markets are less likely to utilise valuation techniques consistent with standard corporate finance theory (e.g. DCF, dividend yield) developed in an advanced capital market context. Hence, we expect that DCF will be less important for VCs in countries with French or German legal systems. Moreover, a lot of VCs are subsidiaries of banks in the bank-centered German financial system. Former bank managers may not be trained to use prospective-looking valuation methods. Further, Hellman et al. (2004) have shown that bank-owned

VC firms pursue other goals than independent VC firms: cross-selling bank products to their portfolio companies seems to be important for them. These features make us expect that prospective-looking DCF methods will be less important for VCs operating in French and German legal systems. Hence:

> *P1c:* DCF based methods are likely to be significantly more important in countries with English legal systems than countries with French and German legal systems.

Capital markets may provide comparator valuations with publicly available information in terms of sector price/earnings ratios. This market-based valuation method is not only relevant for valuation purposes at the time of investment, but it also provides an indication of potential values when going public. P/E and other comparator valuation methods are, however, only relevant when there are enough comparable quoted companies. Given that P/E ratios differ widely across different stock markets, it is important to have access to a wide range of quoted companies on the relevant stock market in order to be able to produce a meaningful P/E ratio. This is only feasible in countries with well-developed stock markets, i.e. in English legal system countries (La Porta et al., 1997, 1998). P/E and other comparator valuation methods are less informative and valuable in countries with few public companies. Hence:

> *P1d:* Price earnings comparator valuation methods are likely to be significantly less important in countries with German and French legal systems than countries with an English legal system.

Sources of information

Unlike publicly listed corporations, venture capital investments are characterised by considerable private information (Wright and Robbie, 1998). The relative importance of information from financial sources versus information from entrepreneurs and information from alternative market sources may vary between countries according to the relative importance of the capital market.

The US has developed a system focused on understanding entrepreneurs and their potential contribution to value creation, which may be especially important given the emphasis in that country on early stage investments. In network-based countries, greater emphasis may be placed on information relating to the entrepreneur than in a market-based system (Manigart et al., 2000; Bruton et al., 2004). Networks between business people are generally seen as stronger in much of Europe compared to the US since the need to be part of a social network is viewed as vital (Wells and Grieco, 1993). Asia is generally recognised as having different cognitive institutions than the United States and Europe (Orru et al., 1997; Peng, 2000). Asian culture also emphasises the importance of networks (Boisot and Child, 1996; Bruton et al., 1999); this may even be much stronger than in Europe (Tsang and Walls, 1998). Claessens et al. (2000) have emphasised the importance of social and particularly family networks in East Asian

VC INVESTORS, CAPITAL MARKETS, VALUATION AND INFORMATION   313

businesses. Bruton et al. (2002) note that in Singapore, for example, connections and relationships with potential clients are likely to be far more important than in the West. In Singapore, applications from individuals who "walk in the door" are therefore less likely to receive funding than in the West. Network relationships are important for bank lending in Southeast Asian countries in the absence of more reliable alternative mechanisms (Rajan and Zingalis, 1998). As the venture capital industry is less regulated and established than the banking industry in Asia, this suggests that relationships and other similar institutions could be even more important in this sector (Bruton et al., 2002). Allen and Song (2002) note that implicit relationships may provide a good substitute for explicit contracts in environments of relatively low contractual enforcement, which may be more problematical in Asia. While members of a network may obtain reliable information (Fiet, 1995), venture capital firms face the potential problem of being outsiders prior to a relationship being established. A common cultural problem in Hong Kong, for example, is the dominance of boards of directors by extended family members, which inhibits venture funds' access to information and subsequent investment decisions. As such, VC firms in Asia may be expected to place less credence on information about the business supplied by the entrepreneur. Hence:

> *P2a:* Venture capital firms in German and French legal system countries are likely to place significantly more emphasis on information provided by the entrepreneur than are venture capital firms in countries with an English legal system.

> *P2b:* Venture capital firms in Asian countries are likely to place significantly less emphasis on information provided by the entrepreneur than are venture capital firms in the US.

The problems in trusting information provided by entrepreneurs may extend to information in the business plans prepared by entrepreneurs. In the US, for example, there is some evidence that the business plans do provide useful financial information. In the US, VCs have legal rights protecting their investment against agency problems relating to the entrepreneur (Bruton et al., 2000). This may be more problematical in an environment of weak legal systems and weaknesses in the enforcement of legal systems. Owners may be asked to give warranties regarding the veracity of information in countries in Europe and Asia. But it may be naïve simply to rely on warranties in environments where the enforceability of contracts may be difficult and where recourse to the courts may have adverse implications for reputation (Ahlstrom and Bruton, 2004). In China, for example, reporting regulations may not be enforced such that reported fixed assets and accounts receivable may be unreliable (Bruton and Ahlstrom, 2003). Accounting standards in the French and German legal system countries studied here score only slightly less highly than those with an English system except for India (La Porta et al., 1997). In this context of relatively strong financial reporting systems, European venture capital firms are likely to emphasise accounting and financial data equally highly as their US colleagues. Hence:

P2c: Venture capital firms in Asia are likely to place significantly less emphasis on accounting and financial data in the business plan as a source of information than venture capital firms in the US.

Venture capital firms may seek to verify the situation in potential investees by placing greater emphasis on other sources of information in an attempt to obtain independent information (Fried and Hisrich, 1994). Less market oriented systems may also be associated with a lower willingness to disclose non-mandatory information. Hence, the financial press in German and French legal system environments may provide less useful information for venture capital firms. The market risks in India, as measured by the risks associated with undertaking contracts, are markedly higher than in Hong Kong or Singapore which are in turn higher than in the US (La Porta et al., 1998). Therefore, venture capital firms in Asia may rely more on independent verification such as through financial press and trade journals. Hence:

P2d: Venture capital firms in German and French legal system environments are likely to place significantly less emphasis on information from attempts at verification from other sources than are venture capital firms in English legal systems.

P2e: Venture capital firms in Europe and Asia are likely to place significantly more emphasis on information gained from attempts at verification from other sources than are venture capital firms in the US.

Methodology

The questionnaire administered to respondents was developed based on a previous questionnaires used in the UK which had been pre-tested with UK venture capitalists, advisors and academics (Wright and Robbie, 1996). An organization-wide response was sought in all cases, with the covering letter to senior investment managers specifically asking respondents to report institutions' perceptions rather than individual approaches; the UK study had suggested that the issues examined here were in any case generally driven by organization-wide policies.

For the UK, the questionnaires were sent to the full members of the British Venture Capital Association in early 1994. The questionnaires were translated into French and Dutch, in order to be used in France, Belgium and the Netherlands. They were sent to the full members of the 'Association Française des Investisseurs en Capital Risque', the Belgian Venturing Association, the 'Nederlandse Vereniging voor Participatiemaatschapppijen' and to the French, Dutch and Belgian members of the European Venture Capital Association in late 1995—early 1996 and to members of the German BVK in 2001. In total, we received 203 responses, giving a response rate for Europe of 38.7%. The responses from these countries consist of a relatively larger number of independent venture capital firms compared to the VC industry in the respective countries. The stage distribution of the investments in the sample under study is, moreover, more heavily weighted towards acquisition/buy-out investments, compared to population statistics. The fact that the venture capital firms in our sample report less early stage investments than found in the EVCA statistics can be explained by the fact that EVCA statistics report the stage distribution of new investments in 1995, whereas our sample reports the stage distribution of the current investment portfolio. This might thus include investments venture capital firms entered at the early stage of development, but which have matured and are now reported as an expansion/development investment.

The US survey was carried out in late 1996. The US questionnaire was sent to a random sample of 299 US venture capitalists listed in Pratt's Guide to Venture Capital Sources. Follow-up reminders were sent after two months. A total of 73 completed and usable replies were received, representing a response rate of 24%. No significant differences were identified between respondents and non-respondents in terms of type of venture capitalist and amount of capital under management.

Multicountry studies are fraught with potential problems relating to the capture of data from respondents. It is recognised that in some environments, there may be resistance or logistical problems relating to particular approaches. Hence, for example, Hitt et al. (2000) note in their study of foreign partner selection in developed and emerging markets that there was some resistance to mail questionnaires in some of their sample countries and that they therefore used face to face interviews in order to obtain acceptable responses rates. We adopt this approach as we were concerned that in the Asian countries in our study, mail questionnaires could be problematical where there is a strong tradition of business secrecy. In India, Hong Kong and Singapore, therefore, attempts were made to conduct face-to-face or telephone interviews where possible in order to maximise the response rate. Personal interviews were also expected to help with comprehension and in the event respondents had no problems comprehending the questionnaire. The same survey instrument was administered as in the US and European countries.

The India survey was conducted during summer 1999. In Singapore and Hong Kong, the study was conducted in summer 2000. We contacted members of the venture capital associations in each country. We received a total of 81 responses, giving are response rate for Asia of 47.4%.

Ideally, it would be appropriate to collect data simultaneously. However, when the study commenced, several of the markets were quite under-developed and it would not have been possible to conduct surveys there. The different actual real time periods during which data were collected may serve to capture markets at closer points in their development stage. In more developed markets such as the US and UK, methods may be more likely to be stable so it is less important to conduct surveys simultaneously. This issue is more important for developing markets, where we have achieved a closer degree of simultaneity.

Results and analysis

Initial background analysis is provided of the similarities and differences between venture capital firms operating in each of the countries using Kruskal-Wallis tests. As a non-parametric test this is more conservative than parametric tests. The data were demeaned on a firm by firm basis in order to address potential problems arising from systematic differences in the use of scales. Multivariate tests were carried out using OLS regression.

Univariate analysis

Valuation methods (see Table 2): Significant differences were identified between legal systems and geographical areas in respect of several valuation methods. Asset based valuation methods were generally the least important valuation methods. We find significant differences between the legal systems (Panel A) in respect of the use of historic cost book values, with this being relatively important in countries with a French legal system. Elsewhere the scores are generally low in Europe, the US and Asia. The DCF method is significantly more important in Germanic countries, followed by English legal system countries. There is widespread use of comparator rule of thumb approximations, with greatest importance attached to price/earnings multiples in English legal system countries. With respect to geographic region (Panel B), historic cost asset methods are significantly more important in Continental Europe than elsewhere. There was no significant difference between regions in the use of DCF techniques but price-earnings multiples were most important in Asian countries followed by US and UK, ahead of Continental Europe.

Sources of information (see Table 3): Business plan data are rated highly in all markets, but there was no significant difference in the importance of this information source between legal system (Panel A). Significantly more emphasis is placed on information from entrepreneurs in Germanic legal system countries, ahead of France, with English legal systems expressing least importance. The financial press is relatively less important generally, but significantly greater emphasis is placed on it in English legal system countries. With respect to geographic area, significantly less emphasis is placed on information from entrepreneurs in Asia, with greatest importance attached to the entrepreneur in Europe, followed by US and UK. Greatest importance is attached to the information in the business plan in Europe, followed by the US and UK, with Asia having lowest importance. Relatively more importance is attached to information from the financial press in Asia, followed by the US and UK ahead of Europe.

Multivariate analysis

Multivariate analysis was conducted to examine the effects of the state of development of external capital markets, the nature of the legal system and other institutional differences with the US as measured by Europe and Asia dummy variables. Combining individual countries in this manner also reduces potential problems arising from small samples in individual countries. Categorization of countries into different legal systems was based on La Porta et al. (1997, 1998). The regressions also controlled for the

Table 2. Methods used in valuing potential investments.

	Legal system	N	Mean	Std. dev.	Chi square
	Panel A: By legal system				
Historic cost book value	English	213	−.9154	.8856	47.88***
	German	47	−.9333	.6781	
	French	70	.2243	1.2005	
	Total	330	−.6762	1.0445	
Liquidation value of asset (forced sale)	English	213	−.9379	.9163	.67
	German	47	−1.0184	.9010	
	French	70	−1.0186	.8254	
	Total	330	−.9665	.8938	
Discounted future cash flow	English	214	.3697	1.0227	19.43***
	German	49	.9721	1.0611	
	French	70	−7.5714E-02	1.3393	
	Total	333	.3647	1.1410	
P/E basis	English	212	.8105	.8265	8.18*
	German	47	.6199	.9283	
	French	70	.4957	.9338	
	Total	329	.7163	.8724	
	Panel B: By geographic region				
	Region	N	Mean	Std. dev.	Chi square
Historic cost book value	US and UK	137	−.9119	.8762	24.28***
	Cont Europe	117	−.2407	1.1681	
	Asia	76	−.9217	.9081	
	Total	330	−.6762	1.0445	
Liquidation value of asset (forced sale)	US and UK	138	−.8430	.9675	3.35
	Cont Europe	117	−1.0185	.8528	
	Asia	75	−1.1127	.7904	
	Total	330	−.9665	.8938	
Discounted future cash flow	US and UK	138	.2874	1.0455	1.42
	Cont Europe	119	.3557	1.3323	
	Asia	76	.5191	.9689	
	Total	333	.3647	1.1410	
P/E basis	US and UK	138	.7729	.8787	9.14**
	Cont Europe	117	.5456	.9296	
	Asia	74	.8804	.7194	
	Total	329	.7163	.8724	

All tests are Kruskal-Wallis tests. Significance levels: *** $p < .001$; ** $p < .010$; * $p < .050$; # $p < .100$.
Note: Scale measures what valuation methods are applied ruing the valuation process to value potential investments. Different methods were rated on a scale of: 5 = Almost always, 3 = Sometimes, 1 = Never. Data has then been de-meaned for all venture capital companies—on an individual company basis.

potential effects of investment stage, ownership type of venture capital firm (whether the firm was independent or captive) and years of experience in the venture capital market as these were seen in Table 1 to vary between countries. We also controlled for the state of development of the capital market based on La Porta et al. (1997).

318   WRIGHT ET AL.

Table 3.   Sources of information in preparing valuations.

	Legal system	N	Mean	Std. dev.	Chi square
	Panel A : By legal system				
Financial press	English	219	−.7152	1.0824	11.86**
	German	53	−1.0539	.6872	
	French	68	−1.1570	.7691	
	Total	340	−.8564	.9899	
Interviews with	English	218	.3503	.8750	23.89***
entrepreneurs	German	53	.9272	.4688	
	French	70	.5230	.7505	
	Total	341	.4754	.8240	
	Total	341	−1.1419	.8831	
Business plan data	English	207	.5514	.8083	3.40
	German	52	.6731	.6661	
	French	68	.7652	.6183	
	Total	327	.6152	.7541	
	Panel B: By geographic region				
	Region	N	Mean	Std. dev.	Chi square
Financial press	US and UK	139	−.8395	1.1844	23.93***
	Cont Europe	121	−1.1119	.7332	
	Asia	80	−.4992	.8415	
	Total	340	−.8564	.9899	
Interviews with	US and UK	138	.5167	.9273	38.35***
entrepreneurs	Cont Europe	123	.6972	.6728	
	Asia	80	6.328E-02	.6929	
	Total	341	.4754	.8240	
Business plan data	US and UK	127	.6935	.8603	18.34***
	Cont Europe	120	.7253	.6384	
	Asia	80	.3258	.6628	
	Total	327	.6152	.7541	

All tests are Kruskal-Wallis tests. Significance levels: *** $p < .001$; ** $p < .010$; * $p < .050$; # $p < .100$.
Scale measures the importance of different sources of information in preparing valuations. Different sources of information were rated on a scale of: 5 = Essential, 3 = Moderately important, 1 = Irrelevant. Data has then been de-meaned for all venture capital companies—on an individual company basis.

Valuation Methods (see Table 4): Years of experience in the venture capital industry, ownership type of VC, number of investment executives and whether the firm is involved in MBOs/MBIs generally have no significant impact on the importance placed on particular valuation methods, except for a weakly signficant positive association of the age variable with the PE method. Early stage investments were weakly significantly positively associated with use of liquidation value and weakly significantly associated with use of the DCF valuation method, while early stage investments were significantly negatively associated with historic cost values of assets.

Different legal systems are significantly associated with the valuation mechanism used. VC firms operating in a French legal system are significantly more likely to adopt historic cost valuation methods, thus providing limited support for Proposition P1a.

Table 4. Methods used in valuing potential investments.

	Asset value Beta (S.E.)	Liquidation asset value Beta (S.E.)	DCF Beta (S.E.)	P/E Beta (S.E.)
German legal system	−.052	.318	1.311	−.756
	(.317)	(.283)	(.365)***	(.290)***
French legal system	1.028	.367	.121	−.855
	(.259)***	(.231)	(.300)	(.237)***
Europe	.266	−.686	−.629	.789
	(.216)	(.192)***	(.250)*	(.196)***
Asia	.095	−.724	−.185	.605
	(.210)	(.188)***	(.243)	(.193)**
External capital per GNP	.100	.272	.337	−.395
	(.281)	(.253)	(.326)	(.261)
Early stage	−.066	.202	−.247	−.015
	(.120)	(.106) #	(.139)#	(.109)
MBO/MBI	.002	−.005	.007	.014
	(.010)	(.009)	(.011)	(.009)
Independent	−1.35	.002	.053	.070
	(.118)	(.105)	(.136)	(.107)
Age	.000	−.004	−.005	.010
	(.007)	(.006)	(.008)	(.006)#
Investment executives	−.001	.003	−.002	−.001
	(.000)	(.003)	(.005)	(.004)
Constant	−1.032	−.723	.586	.561
	(.271)***	(.241)**	(.313) #	(.247)*
N	287	287	290	286
R^2	.214	.107	.116	.097
Adj R^2	.185	.075	.084	.064
F Stat	7.535***	3.335***	3.657***	2.963***

Sources of information measured on a 1–5 likert scale. Data has then been de-meaned for all venture capital companies—on an individual company basis.
Legal system dummies coded - 1 = Yes, 0 = No.
Regional dummies coded 1 = Yes, 0 = No.
Stage involvement dummies coded 1 = Involved in stage, 0 Not involved in stage.
Independent dummy coded as 1 = Independent (in some way), 0 = Fully dependent.
Age is the number of years since the start of the firm.
Investment executives is the number of executives employed in a country.
Significance levels: # < .1; * < .05; ** < .01; *** < .001.

VC firms in Europe and Asia are significantly less likely than US VC firms to make use of liquidation value methods, thus providing support for Proposition P1b. Compared to English-based Common Law systems, VC firms operating in Germanic and French legal systems are significantly less likely to use PE comparators (supporting Proposition P1d).

Sources of information (see Table 5): The number of years of experience in the venture capital industry and whether the firm is involved in MBOs/MBIs have no significant impact on the importance placed on particular sources of information. VC firms operating

Table 5. Sources of information.

	Interviews with entrepreneurs Beta (S.E.)	Business plan data Beta (S.E.)	Financial press Beta (S.E.)
German	.779	−.047	−.494
legal system	(.247)**	(.239)	(.291) #
French	.276	.126	−.692
legal system	(.204)	(.197)	(.241)**
Europe	−.241	−.030	.704
	(.175)	(.174)	(.205)***
Asia	−.387	−.452	.574
	(.168)*	(.167)**	(.196)**
External capital	.049	.030	.175
per GNP Early	(.215)	(.208)	(.254)
stage	.003	.043	−.119
	(.098)	(.095)	(.115)
MBO/MBI	.008	.000	−.004
	(.008)	(.008)	(.009)
Independent	.114	−.076	−.144
	(.095)	(.092)	(.112)
Age	.010	.000	.005
	(.005)#	(.005)	(.006)
Investment	−.005	.003	−.002
executives	(.003)	(.003)	(.004)
Constant	.342	.698	−1.240
	(.214)	(.211)***	(.229)***
N	299	290	299
R^2	.150	.071	.145
Adj R^2	.121	.038	.115
F Stat	5.108***	2.153*	4.885***

Sources of information measured on a 1–5 likert scale. Data has then been de-meaned for all venture capital companies.
Legal system dummies coded—1 = Yes, 0 = No.
Regional dummies coded 1 = Yes, 0 = No.
Stage involvement dummies coded 1 = Involved in stage, 0 Not involved in stage.
Independent dummy coded as 1 = Independent (in some way), 0 = Fully dependent.
Age is the number of years since the start of the firm.
Investment executives is the number of executives employed in a country.
Significance levels: # < .1; * < .05; ** < .01; *** < .001.

under a Germanic legal system are significantly more likely to use interviews with entrepreneurs but this is not the case for VC firms operating under a French legal system. There is thus mixed support for Proposition P2a. VC firms in Asia are significantly less likely to make use of interviews with entrepreneurs or business plan data, providing support for Propositions P2b and P2c. VC firms operating in a German or French legal systems are significantly less likely to place emphasis on the financial press. This provides limited support for Proposition P2d. VC firms in Europe and Asia are significantly more likely than US VC firms to use financial press, thus providing some support for Proposition P2e.

Discussion and conclusions

This paper has presented an exploratory analysis of the valuation methods and information sources used by venture capital firms in different institutional environments. The findings presented here add to the limited data on the internationalization activity of venture capitalists. Hall and Tu (2003) suggest that the willingness of venture capital firms to invest overseas is positively related to the size of venture capital firm and the investment stage of their investees and negatively to the age of the venture capital firm and not related to the type of firm ownership. In contrast, our study explores venture capital firm behavior and adds to the emerging debate regarding the influence of different institutional contexts on firm behavior. The findings of the study present novel insights that are pertinent to the growing internationalisation of venture capital. We have identified significant differences in the valuation methods adopted by venture capital firms in countries with different institutional contexts as well as the sources of information they use. The findings are summarised in Table 6. Overall, a key theme is that it appears that the legal system, and its implication for capital markets, may be more important in explaining the source of information used than it is for the valuation methods used.

However, cultural factors are found to play an important role in the relative importance that is placed on information provided by entrepreneurs and in the business plan, and in the extent to which alternative external sources are sought. This suggests that information sources are not so easily passed from one context to another. The actual sources of information that venture capital firms may trust vary both between and within legal systems and geographic regions. These findings indicate that apparently similar systems and markets may in fact be heterogeneous. Further analysis might usefully explore the rationale for such differences. In this paper, partly because of relatively small sample si7s in some countries, we have focused on geographical regions. It might be fruitful for future research to examine individual countries in more depth, although such analysis may need to await the further development of individual capital markets.

Table 6. Summary of hypotheses and results.

Hypothesis	Prediction	Result
	Valuation methods	
P1a (Asset valuation)	French, German > English	Limited support
P1b (Liquidation asset)	Europe, Asia < US	Supported
P1c (DCF)	English > French, German	Not supported
P1d (PE Comparator)	French, German < English	Supported
	Information sources	
P2a. (Entrepreneur)	French, German > English	Mixed support
P2b. (Entrepreneur)	Asia < US	Supported
P2c. (Business plan)	Asia < US	Supported
P2d (Other information—financial press)	French, German < English	Supported
P2e. (Other information—financial press)	Europe, Asia > US	Supported

In relation to the control variables examined in this study, it is interesting that neither the stage focus, nor the affiliation of the venture capitalist (i.e. independent or not) were significantly related to the valuation methods or sources of information used. This is interesting in the light of earlier research from the UK that did identify differences between both information usage as well as valuation method and the affiliation of the venture capital firm (Wright and Robbie, 1996). While venture capitalists may seek to address information and valuation problems by investing in later stage transactions with more established businesses, this does not appear to be the case across different institutional environments. These findings suggest that regulatory and cultural institutional factors may be more important than the focus of investment attention and ownership of the venture capital firm. The state of development of a country's external capital market was also not significantly related to the valuation methods or sources of information used.

Institutional contexts may not necessarily be static, especially in emerging markets (Hoskisson et al., 2000; Peng, 2003). The recent emergence of venture capital and private equity markets in contexts where they have long been dormant is itself a reflection of changing institutional factors (Wright et al., 1992, 2003, 2004). Longitudinal studies would help in identifying the links between institutional developments and changes in venture capital firm behavior. A feature of such developments may be that institutional differences become less important over time and that agency and other factors may become more important. However, differences between institutional environments are likely to persist such that there may be a need to develop research that considers the interaction of institutional and agency perspectives. Hoskisson et al. (2000) speculated in their examination of strategy in emerging markets that institutional factors would become less important over time. It is clear, however, that institutional differences may take longer to reduce than might be anticipated. Moreover, the pace at which institutions change may also be different. There is, therefore, a need for researchers to continue to develop an institutional perspective on the venture capital industry.

This paper has a number of limitations and hence the findings need to be considered tentative. These limitations also suggest areas for further research. First, the surveys were conducted at different points in time. This may lead to potential issues of comparability if institutional environments change over time. However, offsetting this issue the different points of real time do provide for some reduction in the gap between the stage of development of each market. Second, the study has been based on quantitative survey data. More fine-grained analysis concerning the process by which venture capital firms search for information and undertake valuation might usefully be undertaken with the use of detailed case study approaches. Third, the study has relied on attitudinal data. More detailed analysis might also be carried out using archival data on valuation and information sources. However, obtaining such data is highly sensitive, especially across different country contexts. Again, this may be an area where detailed cross-country case comparisons may be more feasible. Fourth, our analysis is very much cross-sectional. To the extent that venture capital markets are dynamic, there is a need of future research to consider the impact of learning and the diffusion of practices across markets in different institutional environments. For example, to what extent do valuation methods become more sophisticated over the development of a particular market and hence to what extent does convergence of practice occur? Fifth, the study has limited itself to considering only aspects of the venture capital process relating to valuation and sources of information for valuation. Other important aspects of the venture capital life cycle may be important to consider in cross-country contexts. For example, different approaches to monitoring and exiting investments may be appropriate in different contexts (Bruton et al., 2004). The relative importance of contracts versus relationships may differ between institutional contexts depending on the strength of importance of the legal framework and the importance of social networks. The feasibility of different exit routes may vary between legal systems most obviously with respect to the availability of stock markets. However, sales to strategic partners are typically the most common form of exit, yet a number of issues are raised about this option in different contexts. Not only do acquisitions markets vary in terms of their stage of development but there may be different attitudes with respect to the sale of majority versus minority stakes, there may be different regulations regarding sales to foreigners, etc. Cumming and Fleming (2003) show for the Asia-Pacific region that a high legality index is associated with a greater likelihood of exit through IPO or trade sale but that a high legality index is neither necessary nor sufficient for the development of a successful venture capital market. Further research might usefully examine these issues in different institutional contexts.

For practitioners, the findings of the study highlight the need for venture capital firms entering new markets to examine carefully within-regional differences. These differences are important for the success of venture capital firm entry into foreign markets and the avoidance of exit in the face of failure. While it may be relatively straightforward for venture capital firms to use standard valuation methods, a major issue relates to the informational inputs into those techniques. This in turn raises implications for the recruitment and training of venture capital executives, especially in developing markets. In terms of recruitment there may need to be particular emphasis on hiring executives who are experienced in obtaining deal specific information in a particular local context, which is likely to involve them having highly developed networks. Evidence on these recruitment practices is patchy, but a study of German venture capitalists suggests that greatest emphasis is placed in the temporary transfer of executives from the head offices of foreign entrants, followed by the recruitment of experienced foreign nationals and the recruitment of foreign nationals to head up foreign operations (Hommel and Wright, 2004). Evidence from India also indicates a high level of local national representation among executives even in foreign venture capital firms (Wright et al., 2002). Firms in India were also found to recruit mainly executives who were already trained. If these executives are mainly trained in US methods (Bruton and Ahlstrom, 2003), these may not easily carry over into different institutional contexts, especially with respect to the gathering of information. While venture capital firms may implement firm-wide policies regarding various aspects of their investment behavior, these observations suggest the need to allow local offices a significant measure of discretion in their screening and valuation of businesses. Evidence from Germany indicates that greatest discretion to local offices is given with respect to screening, followed by monitoring and, somewhat less to valuation methods (Hommel and Wright, 2004). Further research might usefully examine whether different institutional contexts influence local recruitment and discretion.

Overall, these observations also suggest that venture capitalists entering new markets in legal and geographical contexts with which they are less familiar, may need to take a longer perspective to become familiar with local information sources and networks, otherwise they may run serious risks of investing on the basis of very inadequate information. The authors have obtained extensive anecdotal evidence from venture capitalists new to foreign markets of being presented with business plans 'thick with dust'. A key test is to find independent reliable sources of information to avoid the problems in investing in such cases. Finally, our study also has implications for policy makers internationally. Efforts to develop and enforce harmonization of regulatory environments may play an important indirect role in spreading good reporting practices that can assist the internationalisation of venture capital both in terms of improving the information available to venture capitalists when they screen and value businesses as consider here, as well as subsequent monitoring of performance. A further issue affecting the availability of information concerns the implications of the general state of development of entrepreneurship and importance of social networks in a particular country. While there is some debate about measuring entrepreneurship in different countries, it appears that its extent does vary considerably internationally (Reynolds et al., 2000). Similarly, the importance and nature of social networks also varies between countries and regions (Claessens et al., 2000). Weak legal systems or legal systems that do not promote disclosure relating to private firms present problems for venture capital firms access to information in environments where perception of entrepreneurs is low and entry to social networks is difficult.

Acknowledgments

Thanks to the editor and two anonymous for comments on an earlier version.

References

Allen, F. and Song, Wei-ling, 2002, *Venture Capital and Corporate Governance. Wharton Financial Institutions Center. Wharton School*, University of Pennsylvania, WP 03-05.

Aylward, A., 1998, 'Trends in Venture Capital Financing in Developing Countries', *IFC Discussion Paper No. 36*, Washington, DC: World Bank.

Black, B. and S. Gilson, 1998, 'Venture Capital and the Structure of Capital Markets: Banks versus Stock Markets', *Journal of Financial Economics* **47**, 243–277.

Boisot, M. and J. Child, 1996, 'From Fiefs to Clans and Network Capitalism: Explaining China's Emerging Economic Order', *Administrative Science Quarterly* **41**, 600–628.

Bruton, G. and D. Ahlstrom, 2003, 'An Institutional View of China's Venture Capital Industry: Explaining the Differences Between China and the West', *Journal of Business Venturing* **18**, 233–259.

Bruton, G., D. Ahlstrom, and K. Singh, 2002, 'The Impact of the Institutional Environment on the Venture Capital Industry in Singapore', *Venture Capital* **4**, 197–218.

Bruton, G.D., D. Ahlstrom, and J.C.C. Wan, 2003, 'Turnaround in Southeast Asian firms: Evidence from Ethnic Chinese Communities', *Strategic Management Journal* 24, 519–540.

Bruton, G., M. Dattani, M. Fung, C. Chow, and D. Ahlstrom, 1999, 'Private Equity in China: Differences and Similarities with the Western Model', *Journal of Private Equity* 2 (winter), 7–13.

Bruton, G., V. Fried, and S. Manigart, 2004, 'Institutional Influences on the Worldwide Expansion of Venture Capital', *Entrepreneurship Theory and Practice*, forthcoming.

Claessens, S., S. Djankov, and L. Lang, 2000, 'The Separation of Ownership and Control in East Asian Corporations', *Journal of Financial Economics* 58(1/2), 81–112.

Cumming, D. and G. Fleming, 2003, *The Impact of Legality on Private Equity Markets: Evidence from the Asia-Pacific*, EFMA Conference, Glasgow.

Fiet, J.O., 1995, 'Reliance Upon Informants in the Venture Capital Industry', *Journal of Business Venturing* 10, 195–223.

Fried, V. and R. Hisrich, 1994, 'Towards a Model of Venture Capital Investment Decision Making', *Financial Management* 23 (3), 28–37.

Hall, G. and C. Tu, 2003, 'Venture Capitalists and the Decision to Invest Overseas', *Venture Capital* 5 (2), 181–190.

Hellmann, T., 1998, 'The Allocation of Control Rights in Venture Capital Contracts', *Rand Journal of Economics* 29 (1), 57–76.

Hellman, T., L. Lindsey, and M. Puri, 2004, 'Building Relationships Early: Banks in Venture Capital', NBER Working Paper No. 10535.

Hitt, M., M.T. Dacin, E. Levitas, J.-L. Arregle, and A. Borza, 2000, 'Partner Selection in Emerging and Developed Market Contexts: Resource Based and Organizational Learning Perspectives', *Academy of Management Journal* 43 (3), 449–467.

Hommel, U. and M. Wright, 2004, 'The 3rd Deloitte Survey of Venture Capital and Private Equity in Germany', CMBOR/EBS/Deloitte, Frankfurt.

Hoskisson, R., L. Eden, C.-M. Lau, and M. Wright, 2000, 'Strategy in Emerging Markets', *Academy of Management Journal* 43 (3), 249–267.

Jeng, L. and P. Wells, 2000, 'The Determinants of Venture Capital Funding: Evidence Across Countries', *Journal of Corporate Finance* 6, 241–289.

Khanna, T. and K. Palepu, 2000, 'Is Group Affiliation Profitable in Emerging Markets? An Analysis of Diversified Indian Business Groups', *Journal of Finance* 55 (2), 867–891.

La Porta, R., F. Lopez-De-Silanes, A. Shleifer, and R. Vishny, 1997, 'Legal Determinants of External Finance', *Journal of Finance* 52 (3), 1131–1150.

La Porta, R., F. Lopez-De-Silanes, A. Shleifer, and R. Vishny, 1998, 'Law and Finance', *Journal of Political Economy* 106, 1113–1155.

Manigart, S., 1994, 'The Founding Rates of Venture Capital Firms in Three European Countries (1970–1990)', *Journal of Business Venturing* 9 (6), 525–541.

Manigart, S., M. Wright, K. Robbie, P. Desbrières, and K. De Waele, 1997, 'Venture Capitalists' Appraisal of Investment Projects: An Empirical European Study', *Entrepreneurship Theory and Practice* 21 (4), 29–43.

Manigart, S., K. De Waele, M. Wright, K. Robbie, P. Desbrières, H. Sapienza, and A. Beekman, 2000, 'Venture Capitalists, Investment Appraisal and Accounting Information: A Comparative Study of the USA, UK, France, Belgium and Holland', *European Financial Management* 6 (3), 389–404.

McDougall, P.P. and B.M. Oviatt, 2000, 'International Entrepreneurship: The Intersection of two Research Paths', *Academy of Management Journal* 43, 902–908.

North, D. 1990. *Institutions, Institutional Change and Economic Performance*, Cambridge: Cambridge University Press.

Ooghe, H., S. Manigart, and Y. Fassin, 1991, 'Growth Patterns of the European Venture Capital Industry', *Journal of Business Venturing* 6 (6), 381–404.

Orru, M., N. Biggart, and G. Hamilton, 1991, 'Organizational Isomorphism in East Asia', in W. Powell and P. DiMaggio (eds.), *The New Institutionalism in Organizational Analysis*, Chicago: University of Chicago Press, pp. 361–389.

Pindyck, R.S. and K.A. Dixit, 1995, 'The Options Approach to Venture Capital Investment', *Harvard Business Review* **73** (3), 105–116.

Rajan, R.G. and L. Zingalis, 1998, 'Which Capitalism? Lessons from the East Asian Crisis', *Journal of Applied Corporate Finance* **11**, 40–48.

Rah, J., K. Jung, and J. Lee, 1994, 'Validation of the Venture Evaluation Model in Korea', *Journal of Business Venturing* **9**, 509–524.

Ramachandran, K. and S. Ramnarayan, 1993, 'Entrepreneurial Orientation and Networking: Some Indian Evidence', *Journal of Business Venturing* **8**, 513–524.

Rao, S.L., 1998, 'Protect and Perish, Compete and Grow', *The Chartered Accountant*, March.

Ray, D., 1991, 'Venture Capital and Entrepreneurial Developments in Singapore', *International Small Business Journal* **10** (1), 11–26.

Ray, D. and D. Turpin, 1993, 'Venture Capital in Japan', *International Small Business Journal* **11** (4), 39–56.

Reynolds, P., M. Hay, W. Bygrave, S. Camp, and E. Autio, 2000, *Global Entrepreneurship Monitor: 2000 Executive Report*. Babson College and London Business School, London.

Roure, J.B., R. Keeley, and T. Keller, 1992, 'Venture Capital Strategies in Europe and the U.S. Adapting to the 1990's', in N.C. Churchill et al. (eds.), *Frontiers of Entrepreneurship Research*, Babson Park, MA: Babson College, pp. 345–359.

Sagari, S.B. and G. Guidotti, 1992, 'Venture Capital: Lessons from the Developed World for the Developing Markets', *IFC Discussion Paper Number 13*, The World Bank, Washington, DC, pp. 1–50.

Sapienza, H., S. Manigart, and W. Vermeir, 1996, 'Venture Capitalist Governance and Value Added in Four Countries', *Journal of Business Venturing* **11** (6), 439–469.

Scott, W.R., 1995, *Institutions and Organizations*, Thousand Oaks, CA: Sage Publications.

Shleifer, A. and R.W. Vishny, 1992, 'Liquidation Values and Debt Capacity: A Market Equilibrium Approach', *Journal of Finance* **47** (4), 1343–1367.

Verma, J.C., 1997, *Venture Capital Financing in India*, London: Sage.

Virmani, B. and S. Guptan, 1991, *Indian Management*, New Delhi: Vision Books.

Wright, M., S. Pruthi, and A. Lockett, 2002, 'Internationalization of Western Venture Capitalists into Emerging Markets: Risk Assessment and Information in India', *Small Business Economics* **19** (1), 13–29.

Wright, M., S. Thompson, and K. Robbie, 1992, 'Venture Capital and Management-led Buy-outs: A European perspective', *Journal of Business Venturing* **7** (1), 47–71.

Wright, M. and K. Robbie, 1996, 'Venture Capitalists, Unquoted Equity Investment Appraisal and the Role of Accounting Information', *Accounting and Business Research* **26** (2), 153–170.

Wright, M. and K. Robbie, 1998, 'Venture Capital and Private Equity: A Review and Synthesis', *Journal of Business Finance and Accounting* **25** (5/6), 521–570.

Wright, M., M. Kitamura, and R. Hoskisson, 2003, 'Management Buyouts and Restructuring Japanese Corporations', *Long Range Planning* **36** (4), 355–374.

Wright, M., J. Kissane, and A. Burrows, 2004, 'Private Equity and the EU Accession Countries of Central and Eastern Europe', *Journal of Private Equity* **7** (3), 32–46.

Zutshi, R., W. Tan, D. Allampalli, and P. Gibbons, 1999, 'Singapore Venture Capitalists Investment Evaluation Criteria: A Re-examination', *Small Business Economics* **13**, 9–26.

Part VII
Country Comparisons

[26]

Journal of International Business Studies (2005) 36, 492–504
© 2005 Academy of International Business All rights reserved 0047-2506 $30 00
www.jibs.net

PERSPECTIVE

A framework for comparing entrepreneurship processes across nations

Ted Baker[1], Eric Gedajlovic[1] and Michael Lubatkin[2]

[1]University of Connecticut School of Business, Storrs, CT, USA; [2]University of Connecticut School of Business and EM Lyon, Storrs, CT, USA

Correspondence:
T Baker, University of Connecticut School of Business, 2100 Hillside Road, Storrs, CT 06269, USA
Tel: +1 860 408 1567;
Fax: +1 860 408 1567;
E-mail: baker.ted@comcast.net

Abstract
Shane and Venkataraman's Discovery, Evaluation and Exploitation entrepreneurship framework ignores issues central to comparative international entrepreneurship (IE) because of unnecessarily under-socialized assumptions regarding entrepreneurial opportunities and the individuals who discover them. To better promote comparative IE research, we develop a *Comparative Discovery, Evaluation and Exploitation* framework (CDEE), which takes as a starting point that individuals motivated by diverse goals enact market opportunities in a variety of social settings. Building on this characterization, the paper explores how and why processes of opportunity discovery, evaluation and exploitation vary across and within nations, as well as the implications of these differences.
Journal of International Business Studies (2005) 36, 492–504.
doi:10.1057/palgrave.jibs.8400153

Keywords: entrepreneurship; comparative; stratification

Received: 20 May 2003
Revised: 17 December 2004
Accepted: 24 January 2005
Online publication date: 2 June 2005

Introduction

The study of international entrepreneurship (IE) lies at the intersection of the fields of entrepreneurship and international business (IB) (McDougall and Oviatt, 2000). Like entrepreneurship, IE pertains to the discovery, evaluation and exploitation of market opportunities. Like IB, IE comprises two related, but distinct, streams of research: an *internationalization* stream, in which focus is placed on how, why, when and where firms internationalize their operations; and a *comparative* stream that examines how and why business processes differ across national contexts, as well as the implications of these differences. As such, IE's conceptual domain can be defined as the study of processes related to the discovery, evaluation and exploitation of market opportunities that take place across national boundaries, as well as cross-national comparisons of these three entrepreneurial processes.

The emergence of IE as a distinct field of study is relatively recent. An important milestone was Oviatt and McDougall's (1994) paper that questioned whether research in IB was sufficient to understand the internationalization processes of entrepreneurial firms. Their paper, which recently was awarded the 2004 JIBS Decade Award for its influence on IB, pointed the way for others to clarify these processes (e.g., Barkema and Vermeulen, 1998; Autio et al., 2000; Zahra and George, 2002). The comparative IE stream, however, has not developed at a similar pace. Indeed, while research has shown that large cross-national variations exist in the amounts and types of entrepreneurial activity (Ageev *et al.*, 1995; Smallbone *et al.*, 1999; Reynolds *et al.*, 2003), the body of comparative IE research provides limited theoretical insights regarding the entrepreneurial processes that underlie these cross-national variations. We try to address this gap by examining *how* and *why* entrepreneurial processes of opportunity discovery, evaluation and exploitation vary across nations, and then we discuss some implications of these cross-national variations.

To do so, we build upon Shane and Venkataraman's (S&V) (2000) Discovery, Evaluation and Exploitation (DEE) framework, which extends the work of Austrian economists such as Schumpeter (1934), Hayek (1945) and Kirzner (2000). S&V's framework has gained prominence in the field of entrepreneurship, largely because it provides a mechanism for integrating various schools of thought in the entrepreneurship literature, while identifying a distinct domain for entrepreneurship research. We will argue that their framework relies on simplifying assumptions that limit its usefulness as a framework for comparative IE research. In its place, we propose a modified version, which we call the *Comparative Discovery, Evaluation and Exploitation* framework, or CDEE (Figure 1), and is designed to be more relevant to scholars of comparative IE. Of great significance to the comparative stream of IE, but notably absent from the DEE portrayal, is a consideration of social-level environmental antecedents of entrepreneurship, as well as the consequences of such activity (Zahra and Dess, 2001). The CDEE's core assumption is that a

nation's social context (i.e., its institutional and cultural structures) strongly influences the character of opportunities and the individuals who discover, evaluate and exploit them.

To better understand cross-national variation in each entrepreneurial process (i.e., discovery, evaluation and exploitation), we develop the CDEE framework in three stages, each of which adopts a different theoretical lens. First, we employ stratification theory from sociology to argue that who discovers what opportunities in a particular nation is neither random nor solely a function of individual differences. Instead, fundamental aspects of the 'who' and 'what' elements associated with 'discovery' are explained by examining how a nation divides and stratifies its labor. Second, we draw on IO economic theory related to rent appropriation and opportunity costs to explain the role played by a nation's institutional and cultural structures in determining how entrepreneurial opportunities are 'evaluated'. Third, we use theory from organizational ecology and economic geography to describe how the amount and specificity of resources and supporting institutional infrastructure influences how and where favorably evaluated opportunities are 'exploited'.

In concluding the paper, we note that by accounting for national differences in each of the three entrepreneurial processes, the CDEE framework offers a foundation for theory-based explanations as to why entrepreneurial processes in different nations evolve differently and generate different outcomes for entrepreneurs and the economies in which they are embedded. Our

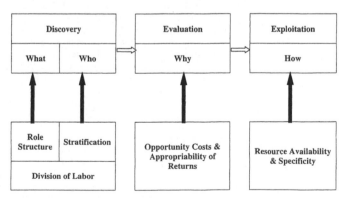

Figure 1 Cross-national context and the entrepreneurial process.

paper opens with the argument that DEE's characterizations of entrepreneurial opportunities, and the individuals who discover them, are based on simplifying assumptions that hold constant meaningful variation that is central to the study of comparative entrepreneurship.

IE and the conceptualization of individuals and opportunities

The focus of each of the three stages of S&V's (2000) DEE framework is on opportunities, and entrepreneurship is portrayed as the nexus of enterprising individuals and valuable opportunities (Venkataraman, 1997; Eckhardt and Shane, 2003). This focus begs two questions: what exactly are these opportunities, and who are the individuals that discover them? According to S&V, opportunities are objective phenomena that exist whether or not anyone discovers them. Following Kirzner (1973), S&V portray the discovery of entrepreneurial opportunities as a form of arbitrage, and define them as 'those situations in which new goods, services, raw materials and organizing methods can be introduced and sold at greater than their cost of production (Kirzner 2000, 220)'. Following Kirzner (1997), the DEE framework accounts only for those profit opportunities related to new means–end relationships, while excluding opportunities related to optimizing existing means–end frameworks. Finally, S&V constrain the concept of opportunities to include only those pursued for the purpose of financial profit. In this section, we argue that the DEE characterizations of the individuals who discover opportunities, and the opportunities themselves, are both too restrictive and under-socialized to account for the range of entrepreneurial activities found within and across nations.

Like many other microeconomic-based theories (e.g., agency theory and transaction cost economics), the DEE framework is based on very narrow '*Homo economicus*' assumptions about rationality. That is, it assumes that all individuals are driven by the single-minded desire to maximize very narrowly defined self-interests, and thus are only minimally influenced by social relationships and context. We reason that the DEE's characterization of the individuals who discover entrepreneurial opportunities falls short of advancing comparative IE scholarship because it does not accommodate fundamental differences in tastes and preferences of the individuals who discover opportunities. It is ironic, and unnecessarily limiting, that the DEE framework, which places such a strong emphasis on

'individual differences', leaves so little room for the expression of those differences in what motivates people.

Psychologists and behavioral economists such as Kahneman and Tversky (1979) note that human motives may be economic as well as non-economic (e.g., to improve the quality of life in a community): some for instant gratification and others for delayed gratification; some other-regarding and others self-regarding. As Cyert and March (1963, 9) put it: 'Entrepreneurs, like anyone else, have a host of personal motives'. Such differences in what motivates entrepreneurial activity have been found within and across nations. Scheinberg and MacMillan (1988) found 38 distinct motives for entrepreneurship that reduced to six distinct dimensions, only one of which was related to financial results or wealth. Similarly, research about entrepreneurs of family enterprises find that some are driven by 'parental altruism' geared to providing family members with secure employment, perquisites and privileges that they would otherwise not receive (Schulze *et al.*, 2003), whereas others may be driven by the need to preserve familial wealth (Carney and Gedajlovic, 2002b). Overall, the DEE, by virtue of its stark behavioral assumptions, holds constant the range of individual motivations central to the comparative study of entrepreneurship.

We also reason that the DEE's conceptualization of entrepreneurial opportunities as a purely objective phenomenon is under-socialized and, as a consequence, inappropriate as a basis for comparative IE scholarship. Such a conceptualization obscures the fact that differences in an individual's tastes and preferences are themselves embedded in, and influenced by, the national context in which people perceive opportunities (Lubatkin *et al.*, forthcoming). These contexts can vary by important institutional (Whitley, 1999; Khanna and Palepu, 2000) and cultural dimensions (Busenitz *et al.*, 2000). They also vary by resource endowments, norms (Hamilton and Biggart, 1988; Porter, 1990) and path-dependent trajectories (Carney and Gedajlovic, 2002a). In addition, while the DEE framework considers only opportunities related to new means–end relationships to be entrepreneurial, wide-ranging cross-national differences and significant imperfections in factor and product markets (Vernon, 1966; Hymer, 1976) mean that what is 'new' in one context is often well established in another. In other words, distinctions between existing and new means–end relationships must take cross-national social context into account.

To conclude, we argue that to advance the comparative stream of IE research, a cross-nationally valid conceptualization of individuals and entrepreneurial opportunities is required. From the perspective of comparative entrepreneurship, opportunities are not simply arbitrage opportunities seized upon by utility maximizers with a singular focus on economic profit. Rather, individuals are influenced by social circumstance and express a broad range of idiosyncratic motives as they enact entrepreneurial opportunities. By drawing attention to – rather than holding constant – differences in human motivations and national contexts, we base the CDEE framework on the view that entrepreneurial opportunities – and not just their discovery – are inescapably subjective and context dependent.

Who discovers what opportunities: the role of the division of labor

Given the broader view of entrepreneurial opportunities outlined above, the question still remains: 'Why do some people, and not others, discover them?' S&V (2000) answer this question by drawing on the work of Hayek (1945) and Kirzner (1973) and identify information asymmetries and individual cognitive differences as two broad categories of factors influencing the probability that a particular opportunity will be discovered by a particular subset of the population. But why do some people belong to that privileged subset, and how do they get there? Absent from S&V's (2000) explanation is a consideration of the social causes and consequences of the information asymmetries and cognitive differences they describe. This gap is especially significant in the field of comparative entrepreneurship, because its focus is how and why entrepreneurial activity differs across national contexts. In this section, we address this gap using insights from the sociological theory of stratification to identify and describe national social processes that affect *who* discovers *what* opportunities.

Both economists (Smith, 1776) and sociologists (Durkheim, 1949; Weber, 1978) have long used the phrase 'division of labor' to refer to the manner in which the specialized productive roles of individuals are distributed in a national marketplace, as well as the processes by which individuals are prepared and selected for their roles. How a nation's labor is divided and stratified depends on the nation's institutional heritage and the overall state and development of its economy (Kuznets, 1955;

Nielsen and Alderson, 1995). At the broadest level, nations differ in the percentage of their workforce employed in agricultural, extraction, manufacturing and service sectors. They also differ in terms of how global forces of competition affect the degree to which their workforce is specialized within a particular sector (Wallerstein, 1974; Scott, 1996). Nations vary in how they sort individuals into roles, including the provision of education to prepare individuals for specific roles; the formalization of occupational closure through informal mechanisms and through licensing, apprenticeship and union requirements; the intersection of economic and kinship roles; the relative importance of ascription and achievement in filling particular roles; and the ease with which people move from one role to another (Lenski, 1966; Kalleberg and Berg, 1987; Grusky, 1994). Another important aspect of social stratification is the differential access to particular occupations provided to members of different social groups. Such unequal access or 'occupational segregation' is very common and varies considerably between nations (Smith, 2002).

Each of these differences may have important implications for a nation's economic development and the individuals who discover opportunities. Broadly, as a consequence of social stratification, individuals are embedded in the division of labor through systematic processes that result in members of different social categories having unequal access to the roles that shape entrepreneurial discovery. We reason that differential placement and experience within a nation's division of labor may account for much of the variance in opportunity discovery. Such a division of labor embeds individuals in different roles and experiences, and shapes what Shane (2000) terms 'knowledge corridors' – processes that direct an individual's attention and funnel information to them. In this manner, stratification processes increase the likelihood that structurally advantaged individuals will discover entrepreneurial opportunities, sometimes through searching for them, and sometimes without engaging in active search, but rather by virtue of being in the right place at the right time with the right stock of knowledge and network contacts (Kirzner, 2000; Baker *et al.*, 2003).

Research in cognition and problem-solving offers additional evidence, suggesting that stratification processes influence the likelihood that a particular individual will discover a particular opportunity. In this regard, an individual's placement in a division of labor functions like the task settings that stimulate the development of expertise and what Dearborn and Simon (1958) call 'selective perceptions'. With repeated exposure to the complementary flows of information within a division of labor, individuals develop specialized expertise related to their role, which they tend to impose on any new information that is funneled their way. Moreover, their social networks promote sensemaking, including the processes through which individuals learn and develop a sense of identity, and the mental frameworks that they use to guide their future actions and interpretations (Weick, 1995). This allows them to become more adept at processing new information (Chase and Simon, 1973), asking perceptive questions and knowing what information is relevant and how to interpret it (Newell and Simon, 1972).

In general, a social stratification perspective suggests that the more excluded the members of a group are from a nation's most attractive economic roles, the less likely they are to discover the kind of entrepreneurial opportunities that contribute to that nation's economic growth and vitality. Paradoxically, however, such exclusion may actually promote discovery by compelling individuals from marginal or disadvantaged groups to search for alternatives not considered by more structurally privileged individuals. Such search can lead to the discovery of new means–end relationships. As a consequence, the very groups that are denied access to a nation's privileged schools, networks, occupations and knowledge corridors may turn out to be an important discovery force in that nation. Examples of such groups include the ethnic Chinese in Indonesia and Malaysia, the Lebanese in Jamaica and Trinidad, and ethnic Indians in Fiji and Guyana (McVey, 1992; Davis *et al.*, 2001).

In summary, we reason that complex social stratification processes related to a nation's division of labor shape the matching of enterprising individuals with the stocks of information and knowledge through which they might discover and make sense of opportunities. From the perspective of market efficiency, these processes create substantial labor market imperfections (Melkas and Anker, 1997; Kunovich and Hodson, 2002) and affect *who* discovers *what* entrepreneurial opportunities. At a more general level, we posit that theories of social stratification can provide a grounded explanation of currently unexplained variation in entrepreneurial behaviors both within and between nations.

The whys of evaluation: appropriability and opportunity cost

Why do people view some discovered opportunities favorably and reject others? How do individuals decide whether or not to pursue the entrepreneurial opportunities they discover? S&V (2000) contend that characteristics of the opportunity and individual differences jointly determine how favorably a particular discovery is evaluated. Absent from their discussion is a consideration of the social processes underlying how individuals evaluate opportunities. For example, an important 'individual difference' cited by S&V (2000) is the potential entrepreneur's opportunity cost assessment – the weighing of the value of the opportunity against the value of alternatives that would be forgone to pursue that opportunity. In developing the evaluation section of the CDEE framework, we argue that opportunity costs are invariably context dependent, and that national structures shape both the range of options available to an entrepreneur and the types of costs and benefits considered by them. Similarly, building on research from IO economics regarding appropriability, we describe how a nation's infrastructure and institutions strongly influence the potential value from an opportunity that may be captured by an individual.

Opportunity costs and national context

Although research in entrepreneurship indicates that individuals are more likely to evaluate an opportunity positively if they face low opportunity costs (Amit *et al.*, 1995; Shane and Venkataraman, 2000), the comparative IE literature has not yet focused much attention on how institutional and cultural factors influence how potential entrepreneurs evaluate these costs. In our view, a consideration of such processes should play a central role in the study of comparative entrepreneurship because opportunity costs represent key reference points that entrepreneurs consider in evaluating whether to pursue entrepreneurial opportunities, and because they are likely to vary significantly across nations. We argue that national culture and institutions influence a potential entrepreneur's opportunity cost estimations in two broad ways.

First, as described above in the opportunity discovery section, nations differ in the range and distribution of opportunities available to potential entrepreneurs. This occurs because of stratification processes, and also because nations vary widely in their capacity to support different types of economic activity (Porter, 1990), as well as in the varieties of market and institutional voids (Khanna and Palepu, 1997) that may present (or limit) opportunities to potential entrepreneurs. A broad variety of national institutional and cultural factors may influence an entrepreneur's range of alternatives. For example, the recent increased availability of wage employment in some areas of China has corresponded to decreasing relative returns to entrepreneurship (Walder, 2002). In some national settings, potential entrepreneurs may be able to choose from several attractive options. In other countries, due, for instance, to the absence of opportunities for paid employment and a limited (or nonexistent) social safety net, pursuing an entrepreneurial venture will be the only viable option. In its survey, GEM (2000) found that such 'necessity' entrepreneurship accounts for 27% of new business creation across all countries studied, but is much more common in poorer countries. For instance, rates of necessity entrepreneurship in China, Brazil, Argentina and Uganda were found to be at least five times higher than that observed in Belgium, France, The Netherlands, Sweden and Denmark (Reynolds et al., 2003, 39). These statistics point to the importance of national context in shaping the opportunity set, and consequently the opportunity cost evaluations of potential entrepreneurs.

Second, institutional and cultural factors also affect the discoverers' evaluation of the cost of abandoning their current situation in favor of an alternative one. In national contexts such as the US, where health insurance is tied to employment, the costs associated with losing such coverage may be high relative to the value of the discovered opportunity (Baker and Aldrich, 1996). In national contexts such as Japan, where loyalty and long employment tenure to a single organization are highly valued, the personal cost may be high to those individuals who exit their place of employment in order to pursue an entrepreneurial opportunity, particularly if their new venture fails. For example, researchers have found that enterprising Japanese individuals who tried and failed at an entrepreneurial venture faced diminished career prospects, diminished social status and personal shame (Okano, 1994; Begley and Tan, 2001). In other social contexts such as Silicon Valley, some forms of failure can add luster to an entrepreneur's status (Lewis, 1998; Bronson, 1999), and thus lessen the opportunity cost of abandoning one's current work.

Appropriability and national context
Teece (1986) used the term 'appropriability regime' to refer to aspects of a commercial environment that govern the ability of a party to profit from an activity. The IO literature suggests that appropriability does not itself affect the expected value of an opportunity (Milgrom and Roberts, 1992), but instead determines the portion of the expected benefit from the opportunity that can be captured by the individual who discovered it.

In this subsection, we argue that it is not the value of the opportunity, per se, that is most relevant to an individual's opportunity evaluation, but rather the appropriable benefits – the portion of the value of an opportunity that a potential entrepreneur expects to be able to capture for their own purposes. From the perspective of comparative entrepreneurship, nations differ markedly in aspects of their commercial environments that determine appropriable benefits. For example, the efficiency of basic supporting infrastructures, such as a country's transportation and telecommunication networks and available sources of energy, are factors that matter when evaluating whether the benefits from an entrepreneurial opportunity are appropriable, because inefficiencies in these areas dissipate the potential value that can be appropriated by an entrepreneur.

In addition, a country's legal, financial, fiscal and education systems, which Khanna and Palepu (1997) term 'soft infrastructure', also strongly influence how much value from an opportunity is appropriable. In terms of legal systems, matters such as degree of protection for property rights, patent protection and the legal rights afforded labor, creditors and customers are factors that vary widely across nations (La Porta et al., 1998) and which play an important role in evaluating the attractiveness of an opportunity to an entrepreneur. Financial systems influence the evaluation process most directly through the cost and availability of capital. In contexts where market inefficiencies raise the cost of acquiring financing, benefits appropriable by entrepreneurs are diminished (Claessens et al., 1999). In national contexts where capital is unavailable, the benefits from a good business opportunity may not be appropriable at all (Carney and Gedajlovic, 2002a).

Tax and fiscal policies also vary widely across nations and affect appropriable benefits in various ways. Taxes on profits diminish appropriable benefits directly. Many fiscal policies such as government subsidies, tax breaks and depreciation rules influence the effective cost of the basic factors of production (i.e., land, labor, capital). A country's education system may, in effect, subsidize training costs by influencing the availability and supply of some skilled workers. More subtly, through the role it plays in socializing a nation's population, the education system influences attitudes and beliefs regarding work and consumption (Whitley, 1999), as well as social norms pertaining to the role played by governments in directing the economy and how the value-added from economic activity should be divided (DeJong, 1995).

In summary, we have proposed a theory-based answer to questions about why some discovered opportunities are viewed favorably in some nations while others are not. We did so by drawing on concepts from IO economics about opportunity costs and appropriability. We have argued that opportunity costs and appropriability are subjective reference points that entrepreneurs rely on when evaluating opportunities. Further, we have described how the institutional and cultural features of a nation influence these reference points by affecting the amounts and type of benefits that an entrepreneur can expect to appropriate from a discovered opportunity, the range of options available to individuals and the costs of abandoning current circumstances to pursue opportunities. These factors are central to comparative entrepreneurship and to our CDEE framework, because they influence how vigorously an entrepreneurial opportunity will be pursued in a given national context, or even whether it will be pursued at all.

How and where of opportunity exploitation: resource availability and specificity

What happens after someone has discovered an opportunity and decided it is worth pursuing? How and where are resources acquired and mobilized in pursuit of that opportunity? From a comparative entrepreneurship perspective, we describe how the amount and types of resources available to an entrepreneur are important factors influencing *how* and from *where* favorably evaluated opportunities are pursued by entrepreneurs. Using ecological theory and drawing on research from the field of economic geography, we develop this basic idea to build insights regarding the exploitation element of the CDEE framework.

A basic tenet of theories of organizational ecology (Aldrich and Pfeffer, 1976; Hannan and Freeman, 1977), widely accepted in the organizational sciences (Stinchcombe, 1965; Aldrich, 1999), is that

organizations strongly reflect the environmental conditions that support them. Within- and between-nation differences in institutional support and available resources create very different founding conditions for entrepreneurial ventures (Porter, 1990; Whitley, 1999). These differences influence the types of organization that are developed to exploit favorable opportunities, as well as their location.

Regarding location, economic geographers suggest that nations contain multiple local ecologies that differ in variety and amount of resources that may be mobilized in pursuit of entrepreneurial opportunities (Scott, 1996). In the remainder of this section, we describe how such local differences shape modes of entrepreneurial opportunity exploitation. We focus on three representative types of ecology: regional agglomerations, broadly developed niches (BDNs) and less developed niches (LDNs).

Regional agglomerations

Regional agglomerations (e.g., Marshall, 1920; Scott, 1996) exist when complementary businesses, labor markets and resource providers cluster geographically. Examples include Silicon Valley and the 'Third Italy' (Bianchi, 1992). Agglomerations provide easy access to specialized sources of risk capital, physical infrastructure and skilled labor (Harrison, 1994; Saxenian, 1994). They encourage the creation of new firms by providing easier access to resources, and also by providing a context where start-ups more easily acquire legitimacy as a taken-for-granted solution to problems of collective action (Suchman, 1995).

Consequently, we reason that being located in an agglomeration improves the likelihood that individuals who discover good entrepreneurial opportunities will achieve success through *de novo* start-ups. For example, the proximity of firms with complementary resources and robust specialized strategic factor markets present firms within agglomerations with viable governance alternatives to vertical integration by allowing them to gain access to required resources without the costs of direct ownership (Miles and Snow, 1986; Saxenian, 1994). Such an ability to control important resources can influence organizational scale and scope requirements, reduce growth constraints and facilitate the early internationalization of entrepreneurial ventures (McDougall and Oviatt, 2003).

As Pouder and St John (1996) note, however, agglomerations can also represent an institutional 'blind spot' owing to their highly specialized nature. Good opportunities that do not fit the specialization will find resources to be relatively scarce. For instance, an entrepreneur seeking to finance a motion picture is likely to meet with more success in Southern California than in Silicon Valley, whereas the reverse is likely to be true of an entrepreneur wishing to exploit an opportunity related to computer software or telephony. In addition, the specialized terms on which resources are made available within agglomerations (Humphrey and Schmitz, 1996) may affect not only which opportunities are pursued but also the form of organization created to exploit them. For instance, in high technology agglomerations such as Silicon Valley, relatively plentiful venture capital facilitates the exploitation of high-risk/return opportunities. However, such venture capital financing requires the construction of organizations oriented toward generating large returns quickly (Gompers, 1995; Pollock *et al.*, 2004) and founding entrepreneurs ceding significant control to investors favoring a quick sale either through an IPO or to an established firm (Lerner, 1995; Hellmann, 1998). Entrepreneurs whose goals include building a business remaining under family control may find little fit between their goals and the terms under which such capital is available (Sahlman, 1988).

Broadly developed niches

What we call BDNs describe ecologies that lack the specialized and complementary resources and institutions of agglomerations, but nonetheless provide entrepreneurs with good generic infrastructure, such as transportation and telecommunication networks and reliable energy supplies. BDNs also offer effective supporting institutions such as banks, universities and legal systems that provide enforcement mechanisms for commercial transactions. Entrepreneurs may find it easier to exploit a broader range of entrepreneurial opportunities in BDNs than in more specialized agglomerations.

However, because entrepreneurs operating in BDNs cannot rely on the presence of specialized and complementary infrastructure, we reason that they may need to develop specialized assets internally. For instance, the absence of specialized local labor markets requires firms to hire and train workers for many complex professional and technical tasks. Similarly, the absence of reliable distribution networks may require that firms integrate vertically and develop such a capacity internally. The upshot of such challenges is that

firms designed to exploit opportunities from BDNs will often need to be of greater scale and complexity than agglomeration-based firms. Consequently, BDN firms may take longer to gain commercial success and be slower to internationalize. On the other hand, such requirements may eventually reward entrepreneurial patience. Although time-consuming and expensive, the need to develop specialized systems and processes internally can create valuable social capital (Nahapiet and Ghoshal, 1998) that is central to theories of resource-based competitive advantage (Dierickx and Cool, 1989; Barney, 1991; Peteraf, 1993).

Less developed niches

Many entrepreneurs in developing and emerging economies face ecologies that provide neither specialized resources and institutional support nor good general-purpose financial, educational, political or legal infrastructure (George and Prabhu, 2000). In these LDNs, entrepreneurs may play a vital role in addressing basic social needs (e.g., clean water, new farming techniques, jobs), but are burdened by a lack of environmental munificence. As a consequence, many entrepreneurial firms in LDNs are quite local in scale and scope (Carney, 1998).

One indigenous entrepreneurial response to problems associated with inadequate local resources and infrastructure has been the formation of family business groups (FBGs). FBGs are networks of many (usually small-scale) businesses that are linked together through kinship ties (Redding, 1990). Such networks have emerged and become a dominant form of business enterprise in many developing and emerging markets in Asia and Latin America (Claessens *et al.*, 1999). Research suggests that the form and function of FBGs owe much to the ecological niche in which they are founded (Carney and Gedajlovic, 2002a). In a series of papers, Khanna and his colleagues (e.g., Khanna and Palepu, 1997; Ghemewat and Khanna, 1998; Khanna and Rivkin, 2001) provide evidence suggesting that FBGs represent a common entrepreneurial response to 'institutional voids'. In this regard, FBGs provide an interstitial or gap-filling function that supports economic activity that would not otherwise be possible. For example, FBGs have been described as 'havens' where property rights are respected (Khanna and Palepu, 1997, 47) because of their ability to surmount deficiencies in legal and political systems by developing the ability to make extensive use of relational contracts (Fukuyama, 1995). Similarly, the absence of reliable suppliers and distribution networks in LDNs has led FBGs to pursue aggressive vertical integration strategies (Khanna and Palepu, 1999).

From an economic development standpoint, the emergence of FBGs as a means of exploiting favorable opportunities in LDNs can promote growth and wealth that helps create niches more closely resembling BDNs. For example, the remarkable success of the Hong Kong, Taiwan and Singapore economies over the past 30 years is largely attributable to FBGs (Weidenbaum and Hughest, 1996). On the other hand, research suggests that the unwieldy conglomerate form adopted by FBGs often under-performs more focused businesses in competitive markets (Rumelt, 1982; Jensen, 1989). Additionally, other research suggests that kinship-based businesses, such as FBGs, may suffer from financial and human resource constraints relative to public companies (Gedajlovic *et al.*, 2004; Zahra and Filatotchev, 2004). While their strong kinship-based governance may facilitate new business formation, it can inhibit later growth, which may depend on moving away from what Hite and Hesterly (2001) called 'identity-based' networks and toward more instrumental transactions and ties (Rowley *et al.*, 2000).

Summary
We describe how entrepreneurs face ecologies that differ widely in terms of the amounts and types of resources and institutional support available. We argue that the characteristics of organizations (i.e., scale, scope, capabilities) constructed by entrepreneurs to exploit opportunities are strongly influenced by such differences. To simplify our discussion, we focus on three common and representative types of ecology – agglomerations, BDNs and LDNs – but other types and hybrids undoubtedly exist.

Discussion and conclusions
At the outset of the paper, we noted that IE's conceptual domain can be defined as the study of processes related to the discovery, evaluation and exploitation of market opportunities that take place across national boundaries, as well as cross-national comparisons of these three entrepreneurial processes. To advance the comparative IE stream, we propose and develop a CDEE framework that builds on S&V's (2000) Austrian-economic-inspired DEE framework. We argue that the DEE framework offers an unsuitable basis for promoting comparative IE

research because it strongly de-emphasizes the role of social processes in creating and shaping the nexus of opportunities and individuals, while also ignoring, or holding constant, social and cultural phenomena that are central to comparative entrepreneurship research.

In contrast to the DEE assumption that individual entrepreneurs have singular goals and are minimally affected by their social circumstances, we propose that entrepreneurial behavior is motivated by a diverse set of motives and is strongly influenced by the social context in which that behavior is embedded. Our characterization of entrepreneurial opportunities also differs substantially from DEE assumptions. Whereas S&V (2000) portray entrepreneurial opportunities as fundamentally objective phenomena, the CDEE takes as a starting point the notion that opportunities have an irreducible subjective aspect because individuals enact opportunities in a manner that is strongly influenced by their social circumstances and expresses a broad range of goals. We believe that our assumptions are more realistic, and form a better basis for exploring how and why the entrepreneurial processes of opportunity discovery, evaluation and exploitation vary across and within nations, as well as the implications of these differences.

Building on these assumptions regarding individuals and opportunities, we describe how the CDEE can promote theory-based answers to a number of interesting comparative entrepreneurship research questions: What are the social processes in a nation affecting 'who' discovers 'what' opportunities? Why are some discovered opportunities viewed favorably while others are not? What happens after someone has discovered an opportunity and evaluated it as being worth pursuing? How do nations differ in the ways that they permit entrepreneurs to acquire and mobilize resources in pursuit of an opportunity? Although discovery, evaluation and exploitation are not entirely independent, they represent distinct processes. We therefore draw on different theoretical perspectives for each, using research in social stratification to explore cross-national variations in how individuals are matched with the opportunities they discover; I/O economics to frame cross-national differences in opportunity evaluation; and organizational ecology and economic geography to explain how and from where opportunities are exploited.

Entrepreneurship begins with opportunity discovery. One implication of our analysis is that patterned social circumstances play an important role in determining the resources an entrepreneur brings to bear on opportunity discovery. We reason that a framework for comparative IE research that pivots entirely on the notion of opportunities begs the fundamental question, 'What are the patterns of inequality of opportunity within and between nations that shape the nature and extent of entrepreneurial activity?' Aside from a few notable exceptions focusing on ethnic and gender differences (e.g., Aldrich and Waldinger, 1990; Brush, 1992), and some work on post-Soviet transition economies (e.g., Smallbone and Welter, 2001), the entrepreneurship literature is largely silent on this question. We hope that the development of the CDEE framework will provide the impetus for more research examining how these patterned cross-national variations affect entrepreneurial processes and outcomes. Indeed, given the increasing salience of differences between the 'haves' and the 'have-nots', both within and between societies, such research appears especially salient for IE theory and practice in general, and specifically for the comparative IE stream.

The process of evaluating an opportunity may range from a successful technology entrepreneur's musings about which project will be most satisfying (financially or otherwise) to an impoverished farmer's anxious decision about what course of action will provide more reliable support for her family. Indeed, studies such as the GEM surveys suggest that high levels of entrepreneurship can be integral to a healthy social and economic context or, alternatively, a sign that people will exploit even the tiniest opportunity if it is the only chance they see. It is also not clear that opportunity evaluation typically takes the form of a coldly rational and thorough weighing and evaluation of alternatives. We argue, nonetheless, that opportunity costs and appropriability are typically important subjective reference points for entrepreneurs, and that they exhibit important cross-national differences. Our arguments are consistent with existing research findings, but very little research has investigated entrepreneurial opportunity evaluation. The CDEE highlights the importance of additional and comparative research on entrepreneurial opportunity evaluation.

Would-be entrepreneurs face extreme cross-national differences in exploitation environments, and we provide only an outline of how these differences are likely to matter. In some national settings a single ecology prevails, whereas in other countries multiple ecologies are present. For instance, Bangalore represents a robust agglomeration, whereas most of India resembles an archetypal LDN. Similarly, in China, pockets of BDNs, such as the Shenzhin and Xiamen Special Enterprise Zones, exist alongside the LDNs that still dominate the economic landscape. Such differences suggest that comparative IE research must account for both within- and across-nation variance in order to account for how and where enterprising individuals exploit entrepreneurial opportunities. Such a comparative approach may be especially useful in developing and testing context-sensitive, contingency-based theories regarding issues central to IE, such as why particular organizational forms are selected over others, why some opportunities are exploited by the creation of new firms while others are sold to existing firms, and why some entrepreneurial ventures are born global while others remain local. Such comparative research can also address important questions about the contingent strengths and weaknesses of different modes of organizing entrepreneurial ventures, both cross-nationally and over time.

In this paper, we focus on the influence of social context on the ability of individuals to discover, evaluate and exploit entrepreneurial opportunities, and on what they perceive to be these opportunities. In doing so, we downplay the role that entrepreneurial human agents can have on their environments. Said differently, we limit the scope of our discussion about the CDEE to that of a one-way direction of influence, going from a nation's social context to each of the entrepreneurial processes. Clearly, the system is more dynamic, open and reciprocal: that is, just as a nation's social context influences an entrepreneur's behaviors, so too do such behaviors influence the social contexts by filling institutional gaps and by addressing unmet needs (Pfeffer and Salancik, 1978; Carney and Gedajlovic, 2002a).

In conclusion, we note that the study of comparative entrepreneurship requires that researchers bring social context into the foreground. The 'nexus' of enterprising individuals and entrepreneurial opportunities is strongly shaped, and sometimes dominated, by social structures and processes. In developing the CDEE framework, we limit our focus to a few salient cross-national contextual factors that exemplify the importance of social differences. We acknowledge, however, that other institutional factors will also have systematic effects on the shape and extent of entrepreneurship. Comparative cross-national scholarship (e.g., the GEM surveys) provides a preliminary, but strong, indication that broad arrays of formal and informal institutions differentially influence entrepreneurial processes and outcomes.

A number of scholars (McDougall and Oviatt, 2000; Zahra and George, 2002) have suggested that entrepreneurship belongs closer to the core of the IB research agenda. Through developing the CDEE framework, we try to pave the way towards that objective. Of course, frameworks are by nature difficult to falsify because of the many context-dependent processes embedded within them. It remains for future work to generate and test a wide variety of specific theory-based hypotheses. We believe that the CDEE framework can accommodate and help integrate the multiplicity of perspectives and empirical contexts that should characterize work in comparative entrepreneurship.

Acknowledgements

We like to thank the three anonymous reviewers and Special Departmental Editor Professor Patricia P McDougall for their help in substantially improving our paper.

References

Ageev, A.J., Gratchev, M.V. and Hisrich, R.D. (1995) 'Entrepreneurship in the Soviet Union and Post-Socialist Russia', *Small Business Economics* 7: 365–376.

Aldrich, H.E. (1999) *Organizations Evolving*, Sage: London.

Aldrich, H.E. and Pfeffer, J. (1976) 'Environments of organizations', *Annual Review of Sociology* 2: 79–105.

Aldrich, H.E. and Waldinger, R. (1990) 'Ethnicity and entrepreneurship', *Annual Review of Sociology* 16: 111–135.

Amit, R., Muller, E. and Cockburn, I. (1995) 'Opportunity costs and entrepreneurial activity', *Journal of Business Venturing* 10: 95–106.

Autio, E., Sapienza, H.J. and Almeida, J.G. (2000) 'Effects of age at entry, knowledge intensity, and imitability on international growth', *Academy of Management Journal* 43(5): 909–1014.

Baker, T. and Aldrich, H.E. (1996) 'Prometheus Stretches: Building Identity and Knowledge in Multiemployer Careers', in M.B. Arthur and D.M. Rousseau (eds.) *The Boundaryless Career: A New Employment Principle for a New Organizational Era*, Oxford University Press: New York, pp: 132–149.

Baker, T., Miner, A. and Eesley, D. (2003) 'Improvising firms: bricolage, account giving and improvisational competencies in the founding process', *Research Policy* 32: 255–276.

Barkema, H.G. and Vermeulen, F. (1998) 'International expansion through start-up or acquisition: a learning perspective', *Academy of Management Journal* 41: 7–26.

Barney, J.B. (1991) 'Firm resources and sustained competitive advantage', *Journal of Management* 17: 99–120.

Begley, T.M. and Tan, W.L. (2001) 'The socio-cultural environment for entrepreneurship: a comparison between East Asian and Anglo-Saxon countries', *Journal of International Business Studies* 32(3): 537–553.

Bianchi, P (1992) 'Levels of Policy and the Nature of Post-Fordist Competition', in M. Storper and A.J. Scott (eds.) *Pathways to Industrialization and Regional Development*, Routledge: London, pp: 303–315.

Bronson, P. (1999) *The Nudist on the Late Shift* (1st edn), Random House: New York.

Brush, C.G. (1992) 'Research on women business owners: past trends, a new perspective, and future directions', *Entrepreneurship Theory and Practice* 16(4). 5–30.

Busenitz, L.W., Gomez, C. and Spencer, J.W. (2000) 'Country institutional profiles: unlocking entrepreneurial phenomena', *Academy of Management Journal* 43(5): 994–1003.

Carney, M. (1998) 'A management capacity constraint? Barriers to the development of the overseas Chinese family business', *Asia-Pacific Journal of Management* 15: 137–162.

Carney, M. and Gedajlovic, E. (2002a) 'The co-evolution of institutional environments and organizational strategies: the rise of family business groups in The ASEAN Region', *Organization Studies* 23(1): 1–29.

Carney, M. and Gedajlovic, E. (2002b) 'The coupling of ownership and control and the allocation of financial resources: evidence from Hong Kong', *Journal of Management Studies* 39(1): 123–146.

Chase, W.G. and Simon, H.A. (1973) 'The Mind's Eye in Chess', in W.G. Chase (ed.) *Visual Information Processing*, Academic Press: New York, pp: 215–281.

Claessens, S., Djankov, S., Fan, J. and Lang, L. (1999) *Expropriation of Minority Shareholders: Evidence from East Asia*, World Bank Working Paper.

Cyert, R.M. and March, J.G. (1963) *A Behavioral Theory of the Firm*, Prentice-Hall: Englewood Cliffs, NJ.

Davis, K., Trebilcock, M.J. and Heys, B. (2001) 'Ethnically homogenous commercial elites in developing countries', *Law and Policy in International Business* 32: 331–361.

Dearborn, D.C. and Simon, H.A. (1958) 'Selective perception: a note on the departmental identification of executives', *Sociometry* 21: 140–144.

DeJong, H.W. (1995) 'European capitalism: between freedom and social justice', *Review of Industrial Organization* 10: 399–419.

Dierickx, I. and Cool, K. (1989) 'Asset stock accumulation and sustainability of competitive advantage', *Management Science* 35: 1504–1514.

Durkheim, E. (1949) *The Division of Labor in Society*, Free Press: Glencoe, IL.

Eckhardt, J.T. and Shane, S.A. (2003) 'Opportunities and entrepreneurship', *Journal of Management* 29(3): 333–349.

Fukuyama, F. (1995) *Trust: The Social Virtues and the Creation of Prosperity*, Free Press: New York.

Gedajlovic, E., Lubatkin, M.H. and Schulze, W.S. (2004) 'Crossing the threshold from founder management to professional management: a governance perspective', *Journal of Management Studies* 41(5): 899–912.

GEM (2000) *Executive Report: Global Entrepreneurship Monitor*, Kauffman Foundation for Entrepreneurial Leadership: Kansas City, MO.

George, G. and Prabhu, G.N. (2000) 'Developmental financial institutions as catalysts of entrepreneurship in emerging economies', *Academy of Management Review* 25(3): 620–629.

Ghemawat, P. and Khanna, T. (1998) 'The nature of diversified business groups: a research design and two case studies', *Journal of Industrial Economics* 46: 35–61.

Gompers, P.A (1995) 'Optimal investment, monitoring, and the staging of venture capital', *Journal of Finance* 50(5): 1461–1489.

Grusky, D.B. (1994) 'The Contours of Social Stratification', in D.B. Grusky (ed.) *Class, Race and Gender: Social Stratification in Sociological Perspective*, Westview Press: San Francisco, pp: 3–35.

Hamilton, G.G. and Biggart, N.W. (1988) 'Market, culture and authority: a comparative analysis of management in the far east', *American Journal of Sociology* 94: S52–S94.

Hannan, M.T. and Freeman, J H. (1977) 'The population ecology of organizations', *American Journal of Sociology* 82: 929–984.

Harrison, B. (1994) *Lean and Mean: The Changing Landscape of Corporate Power in the Age of Flexibility*, Basic Books: New York.

Hayek, F. (1945) 'The use of knowledge in society', *American Economic Review* 35: 519–530.

Hellmann, T. (1998) 'The allocation of control rights in venture capital contracts', *Rand Journal of Economics* 29(1): 57–76.

Hite, J.M. and Hesterly, W.S (2001) 'The evolution of firm networks: from emergence to early growth of the firm', *Strategic Management Journal* 22: 275–286.

Humphrey, J. and Schmitz, H. (1996) 'The triple C approach to local industrial policy', *World Development* 24(12). 1859–1877.

Hymer, S.H. (1976) *The International Operation of National Firms: A Study of Direct Foreign Investment*, MIT Press· Cambridge, MA.

Jensen, M.C. (1989) 'The eclipse of the public corporation', *Harvard Business Review* 67: 61–74.

Kahneman, D. and Tversky, A. (1979) 'Prospect theory: an analysis of decision under risk', *Econometrica* 47: 263–290.

Kalleberg, A.L. and Berg, I. (1987) *Work and Industry: Structures, Markets, and Processes*, Plenum Press: New York.

Khanna, T. and Palepu, K. (1997) 'Why focused strategies may be wrong for emerging markets', *Harvard Business Review* 75(4)· 41–49.

Khanna, T. and Palepu, K. (1999) 'Policy shocks, market intermediaries, and corporate strategy: the evolution of business groups in Chile and India', *Journal of Economics and Management Strategy* 8(2): 271–310.

Khanna, T. and Palepu, K. (2000) 'The future of business groups in emerging markets: long-run evidence from Chile', *Academy of Management Journal* 43(3): 268–285.

Khanna, T. and Rivkin, J.W. (2001) 'Estimating the performance effects of business groups in emerging markets', *Strategic Management Journal* 22(1): 45–74.

Kirzner, I.M. (1973) *Competition and Entrepreneurship*, University of Chicago Press: Chicago.

Kirzner, I.M. (1997) 'Entrepreneurial discovery and the competitive market process: an Austrian approach', *Journal of Economic Literature* 35: 65–80.

Kirzner, I.M. (2000) *The Driving Force of the Market. Essays in Austrian Economics*, Routledge: London.

Kunovich, R.M. and Hodson, R. (2002) 'Ethnic diversity, segregation, and inequality: a structural model of ethnic prejudice in Bosnia and Croatia', *Sociological Quarterly* 43(2): 185–212.

Kuznets, S.S. (1955) 'Economic growth and income inequality', *American Economic Review* 45(1): 1–28

La Porta, R., Lopez-de-Silanes, F., Shleifer, A. and Vishny, R.W (1998) 'Law and finance', *Journal of Political Economy* 106(6). 1113–1155.

Lenski, G.E. (1966) *Power and Privilege. A Theory of Social Stratification*, McGraw-Hill: New York.

Lerner, J. (1995) 'Venture capital and the oversight of private firms', *Journal of Finance* 50(1): 301–318.

Lewis, M. (1998) 'Losers: the cult of failure in silicon valley', *Slate Magazine* Online http://slate.msn.com/id/2712/ (accessed 29 January 2004).

Lubatkin, M., Lane, P., Collin, S. and Very, P. An embeddedness framing of governance and opportunism: towards a cross-nationally accommodating theory of agency', *Journal of Organizational Behavior*, (forthcoming).

Marshall, A. (1920) *Principles of Economics*, (8th edn) Macmillan: London.

McDougall, P.P. and Oviatt, B.M. (2000) 'International entrepreneurship: the intersection of two research paths', *Academy of Management Journal* 43(5): 902–906.

McDougall, P.P. and Oviatt, B.M. (2003) 'Some fundamental issues in international entrepreneurship', [www document] http://www.usasbe.org/knowledge/whitepapers.   (accessed June 2004).

McVey, R. (1992) 'The Materialization of the Southeast Asian Entrepreneur', in R. McVey (ed.) *Southeast Asian Capitalism*, Cornell University Press: New York, pp: 7–33.

Melkas, H. and Anker, R. (1997) 'Occupational segregation by sex in Nordic countries: an empirical investigation', *International Labour Review* 136(3): 341–363.

Miles, R.E. and Snow, C.C (1986) 'Network organizations: new concepts for new forms', *California Management Review* 28: 62–73.

Milgrom, P. and Roberts, J. (1992) *Economics, Organization, and Management*, Prentice-Hall: Englewood Cliffs, NJ.

Nahapiet, J. and Ghoshal, S. (1998) 'Social capital, intellectual capital, and the organizational advantage', *Academy of Management Review* 23(2): 242–266.

Newell, A. and Simon, H.A. (1972) *Human Problem Solving*, Prentice-Hall: Englewood Cliffs, NJ.

Nielsen, F. and Alderson, A.S. (1995) 'Income inequality, development, and dualism: results from an unbalanced cross-national panel', *American Sociological Review* 60(5): 674–701.

Okano, K.I. (1994) 'Shame and social phobia: a transcultural viewpoint', *Bulletin of the Menninger Clinic* 58(3): 325–338.

Oviatt, B.M. and McDougall, P.P. (1994) 'Toward a theory of international new ventures', *Journal of International Business Studies* 25(1): 45–64.

Peteraf, M.A. (1993) 'The cornerstones of competitive advantage: a resource-based view', *Strategic Management Journal* 14: 179–191.

Pfeffer, J. and Salancik, G. (1978) *The External Control of Organizations,*, Harper & Row: New York.

Pollock, T.G., Porac, J.G. and Wade, J.B. (2004) 'Constructing deal networks: brokers as network architects in the US IPO market and other examples', *Academy of Management Review* 29: S0–72.

Porter, M.E. (1990) *The Competitive Advantage of Nations*, The Free Press: New York.

Pouder, R. and St John, C.H. (1996) 'Hot spots and blind spots: geographical clusters of firms and innovation', *Academy of Management Review* 21(4): 1192–1225.

Redding, S.G. (1990) *The Spirit of Chinese Capitalism*, DeGruyter: New York.

Reynolds, P.D., Bygrave, W.D. and Autio, E. (2003) *GEM 2003 Executive Report*, Babson College: Babson Park, MA.

Rowley, T., Behrens, D. and Krackhardt, D. (2000) 'Redundant governance structures: an analysis of structural and relational embeddedness in the steel and semiconductor industries', *Strategic Management Journal* 21(3): 369–386.

Rumelt, R.P. (1982) 'Diversification strategy and profitability', *Strategic Management Journal* 3: 359–369.

Sahlman, W.A. (1988) 'Aspects of financial contracting in venture capital', *Journal of Applied Corporate Finance* 1(2). 23–36.

Saxenian, A. (1994) *Regional Advantage: Culture and Competition in Silicon Valley and Route 128*, Harvard University Press: Cambridge, MA.

Scheinberg, S. and MacMillan, I.C. (1988) 'An 11 country study of motivations to start a business', Paper Presented at the Eighth Annual Babson College Entrepreneurship Research Conference, Calgary, Alberta.

Schulze, W., Lubatkin, M. and Dino, R. (2003) 'Toward a theory of agency and altruism in family firms', *Journal of Business Venturing* 18: 473–490.

Schumpeter, J.A. (1934) *The Theory of Economic Development: An Inquiry into Profits, Capital, Interest, and the Business Cycle*, Harvard University Press: Cambridge, MA.

Scott, A.J. (1996) 'Regional motors of the global economy', *Futures* 28(5): 391–411.

Shane, S. (2000) 'Prior knowledge and the discovery of entrepreneurial opportunities', *Organization Science* 11(4): 448–469.

Shane, S. and Venkataraman, S. (2000) 'The promise of entrepreneurship as a field of research', *Academy of Management Review* 25(1): 217–226.

Smallbone, D. and Welter, F. (2001) 'The distinctiveness of entrepreneurship in transition economies', *Small Business Economics* 16: 249–262.

Smallbone, D., Welter, F., Isakova, N., Klochko, Y., Aculai, E. and Slonimski, A. (1999) *Identifying the Support Needs of Small Enterprises in Ukraine, Belarus and Moldova to Develop an Agenda for Policy at the National and Regional Levels*, Centre for Enterprise and Economic Development Research, Middlesex University: UK.

Smith, A. (1994 [1776]) *The Wealth of Nations*, The Modern Library: New York.

Smith, R.A. (2002) 'Race, gender, and authority in the workplace: theory and research', *Annual Review of Sociology* 28: 509–542.

Stinchcombe, A.L. (1965) 'Social structure and organizations', in J.G. March (ed.) *Handbook of Organizations*, Rand McNally: Chicago, pp: 142–193.

Suchman, M.C. (1995) 'Managing legitimacy: strategic and institutional approaches', *Academy of Management Review* 20: 571–610.

Teece, D.J. (1986) 'Profiting from technological innovation: implications for integration, collaboration, licensing and public policy', *Research Policy* 15(6): 285–305.

Venkataraman, S. (1997) 'The distinctive domain of entrepreneurship research', in J. Katz and R. Brockhaus (eds.) *Advances in Entrepreneurship, Firm Emergence and Growth*, JAI Press: Greenwich, CT, Vol. 3. pp: 119–138.

Vernon, R. (1966) 'International investment and international trade in the product cycle', *Quarterly Journal of Economics* 80: 190–207.

Walder, A.G. (2002) 'Markets and income inequality in rural China: political advantage in an expanding economy', *American Sociological Review* 67(2): 231–253.

Wallerstein, I.M. (1974) *The Modern World-System*, Academic Press: New York.

Weber, M. (1978) *Economy and Society*, University of California Press: Los Angeles, CA.

Weick, K.E. (1995) *Sensemaking in Organizations*, Sage: Thousand Oaks, CA.

Weidenbaum, M. and Hughest, S. (1996) *The Bamboo Network: How Expatriate Chinese Entrepreneurs Are Creating a New Economic Superpower in Asia*, Free Press: New York.

Whitley, R.D. (1999) *Divergent Capitalisms: The Social Structuring and Change of Business Systems*, Oxford University Press: Oxford.

Zahra, S. and Dess, G.D. (2001) 'Entrepreneurship as a field of research: encouraging dialogue and debate', *Academy of Management Review* 26(1): 8–10.

Zahra, S. and Filatotchev, I. (2004) 'Governance of the entrepreneurial threshold firm: a knowledge-based perspective', *Journal of Management Studies* 41(5): 885–897.

Zahra, S. and George, G. (2002) 'International entrepreneurship: the current status of the field and future research agenda', in M.A. Hitt, R.D. Ireland, D.L. Sexton and S.M. Camp (eds.) *Strategic Entrepreneurship: Creating an Integrated Mindset*, Blackwell Publishers: Oxford, pp: 255–258.

About the authors

Ted Baker teaches Management and Entrepreneurship at the University of Connecticut. His current research focuses on entrepreneurship in resource-constrained environments and on improvization and bricolage as forms of entrepreneurial behavior, especially in technology-intensive start-ups. Recent and forthcoming papers appear in *Administrative Science Quarterly*, *Journal of Business Venturing* and *Research Policy*.

Eric Gedajlovic is an Associate Professor in the Management Department at the University of Connecticut. His research pertaining to the influence of corporate governance on venture creation, capability development and organizational performance has appeared in the *Academy of Management Journal*, *Strategic Management Journal*, *Journal of Management Studies* and *Organization Studies*.

Michael Lubatkin is the Wolff Family Chaired Professor of Strategic Entrepreneurship at the University of Connecticut. He specializes in corporate diversification issues as they pertain to problems of core competence transfer and risk management between divisions and across national borders, and in corporate governance issues as they pertain to family and entrepreneurial firms. One of 34 management professors inducted into the Academy of Management's Journals' 'Hall of Fame', and past elected Chair President of the BPS Division of AOM (1997), his research has been honored with three international awards (1983, 1992, 2001) and three US-based awards (1990, 1990, 1997). He regularly teaches in the MBA programs at EM Lyon (France) and Ben Gurion University (Israel).

Accepted by Patricia P. McDougall, Special Departmental Editor, 24 January 2005. This paper has been with the author for two revisions.

[27]

ELSEVIER

Journal of Business Venturing 18 (2003) 261–281

JOURNAL
of BUSINESS
VENTURING

Ethics and entrepreneurs
An international comparative study

Branko Bucar[a,b], Miroslav Glas[b], Robert D. Hisrich[c,*]

[a]*Case Western Reserve University, Cleveland, OH, USA*
[b]*University of Ljubljana, Ljubljana, Slovenia*
[c]*Weatherhead School of Management, Case Western Reserve University, 10900 Euclid Avenue,
513 Enterprise Hall, Cleveland, OH 44106-7235, USA*

Received 1 June 2000; received in revised form 1 April 2001; accepted 1 May 2001

Abstract

In this study, we develop a conceptual framework for the examination of cross-cultural differences in ethical attitudes of business people based on the assumptions of integrative social contract theory (ISCT). ISCT reveals the relevant cultural and economic norms that are predictive of the level of the ethical attitudes among societies and at the same time points out the more subtle impact of social institutions on ethical attitudes of different groups within a society. The evidence supports the use of integrative theoretical approaches within the field of business ethics.
© 2002 Elsevier Science Inc. All rights reserved.

Keywords: Business ethics; American, Russian and Slovenian businesspeople; Integrative social contract theory

1. Executive summary

Societies with higher levels of business ethics tend to be characterized by greater certainty of actions and lower costs of regulation and policing. In order to fully understand this concept, it is important to study the ethical attitudes and standards of businesspeople in different countries. A deterioration in business ethics has increased the difficulties in

---

* Corresponding author. Tel.: +1-216-368-5354; fax: +1-216-368-4785.
E-mail address: rdh7@po.cwru.edu (R.D. Hisrich).

0883-9026/02/$ – see front matter © 2002 Elsevier Science Inc. All rights reserved.
doi:10.1016/S0883-9026(01)00083-0

conducting business in some formerly centrally controlled economies. Using social contract theory and stakeholder theory as the framework, the differences in ethical attitudes of entrepreneurs and managers were examined; surveys using the same measuring instrument were carried out in Slovenia, Russia, and the US.

The findings confirm many hypotheses based on the literature, but there are some interesting differences between knowing what is right or wrong and the actual behavior resulting from reactions to different scenarios. Social contract theory posits that countries with institutions of higher quality will have more efficient economic interaction. The comparison of some key societal institutions (law, educational system, and government) and of the quality of economic interactions led to a hypothesis that the US would rank the highest in ethical attitudes, followed by Slovenia, and then Russia. The hypothesis was confirmed, with Slovenian businesspeople exhibiting a surprisingly high level of business ethics (sometimes even higher than American standards), and in some cases, Russian entrepreneurs exhibiting a rather discouraging low level of ethical attitudes.

A comparison between entrepreneurs and managers in Slovenia and the US was based on the assumptions of stakeholder theory. Due to a different type and degree of financial risks assumed by entrepreneurs compared to managers, it is hypothesized that entrepreneurs are more sensitive to the ethical aspects of decision making. The hypothesis was not confirmed in Slovenia, where a large proportion of entrepreneurs originated from previous managerial positions.

2. Introduction

During the 1990s, discussion of negative aspects of corruption and some aspects of unethical business behavior has become a worldwide phenomenon. International organizations find that financial aid is often subjected to ethically questionable practices and behavior. These unethical practices have frustrated donor countries since there is evidence that more ethical societies tend to be somewhat more economically efficient.

The increased costs of conducting business in countries with low ethical standards are evident to businesses involved in international markets. Yet, apart from anecdotal evidence, there is a lack of empirical verification based on comparative research. This study presents some findings from a survey conducted in three different countries, the US, Russia, and Slovenia, based on the theoretical expectations of social contract theory.

3. International perspective

Social contract theory is based on the concept of a social contract between society and an artificial entity in which the entity is deemed legitimate by serving the interests of society in certain specified ways (Hasnas, 1998). The origins of the theory can be traced to the political social contract theories of philosophers such as Thomas Hobbes, John Locke, and Jean-Jacques Rousseau. Locke (1632–1704) argued that "a citizen's obligation to obey the law

B. Bucar et al. / Journal of Business Venturing 18 (2003) 261–281   263

can be grounded only in that citizen's personal consent to the authority of the law" (Simmons, 1992, p. 919). Contemporary adaptations of social contract theory maintain that a group of rational people will establish a mutually beneficial principle of justice as the foundation for regulating all rights, duties, power, and wealth (Rawls, 1971). Dunfee et al. (1999) suggested that three elements are common to most social contract theories: (1) consent of the individual, (2) agreement among the moral agents, and (3) a device or mechanism by which an agreement is obtained.

The normative social contract theory of business ethics builds on similar fundamental elements to derive social responsibilities of businesses. Donaldson (1982) suggested a comparison of a society without productive organizations with a society with productive organizations to understand the benefits, which form the basis of the social contract between a society and productive organizations. The social contract theory presumes "an implicit contract between the members of society and businesses in which the members of society grant businesses the right to exist in return for certain specified benefits" (Hasnas, 1998, p. 29). A central tenet of the theory is that the benefits should at least outweigh the detriments of the existence of productive organizations.

Donaldson (1982) argued that "society" is a vague term and that "it might represent the aggregate of individuals who make up society or something over and above the sum of those individuals" (p. 43). Donaldson resolved the issue by stipulating that the social contract is between productive organizations and individual members of society. On the other hand, Rousseau and Schalk's (2000) notion of societies is as national level institutions. Members of society construct higher level institutions, such as law, government, educational systems, and others, to formalize social activities. The institutions are shaped by local influences and are therefore different across nations. The differences in political, economic, and social institutions are reflected in the social contract, which specifies (or quite often implies) the acceptable modes of behavior within a given nation.

Society utilizes various mechanisms to specify the terms of the social contract. Axelrod (1986) suggested a wide variety of mechanisms that are important in the generation of norms: law, internalization, dominance, deterrence, membership, social proof, and reputation. Among these, law plays a key role in legitimating the terms of social contracts (Rousseau and Schalk, 2000). While national legal systems introduce obligations regarding the behavior of social actors, societies differ greatly in the degree of freedom they support. Additionally, there is a discrepancy between the people's belief and the reality of law, leaving vast gray areas in which other mechanisms shape social interaction. A study by Forbes and Jones (1986) is a good example of misperceptions by the general public, where an overwhelming number of respondents in Nebraska believed that the termination of employees at will is not legal, although the state law supports it.

The operation of other norm support mechanisms depends on the nature of existing institutions in society. Collectivistic societies may have institutions that enhance the operation of mechanisms like membership, social proof, and reputation, while individualistic societies may be governed by dominance and internalization. Under the mechanism of dominance, more powerful groups define the dominant behavioral norms in a society, whereas the mechanism of deterrence builds norms through discouraging particular actions or behavior (see examples in Axelrod, 1986; Donaldson and Dunfee, 1999). These mechanisms, supported by various institutions, establish different standards of acceptable behavior across different societies. On the other hand, there are some universally accepted norms that have an equalizing effect on the standards of social behavior. Gouldner (1960) defined reciprocity as "a generalized moral norm, which defines certain actions and obligations as repayments of benefits received" (p. 171). The norm of reciprocity is just one example of the universal norms or hypernorms as defined by Donaldson and Dunfee (1999).

The nature of ethical behavior in economic systems helps determine the quality and efficiency of economic interactions (Donaldson and Dunfee, 1999). For example, in the case of the mutual fund industry in Russia in 1990s, economic systems that do not have sufficient institutions to provide legal protection against fraud will have difficulty developing activities that require some level of trustworthiness. Economic systems with institutions of higher quality and efficiency will have higher quality and more efficient economic interaction.

Donaldson and Dunfee (1999) argue that local economic communities possess moral free space in which they build institutions of certain quality, which determine ethical attitudes and behaviors, which in turn determine the quality of economic interactions. This view can be contrasted with the work of La Porta et al. (1999), who have established a direct link between the quality of institutions and the quality of economic interactions in the context of corporate governance. However, authors recognize that legal, judicial, and political systems to a certain extent still allow the expropriation of profits by company insiders (i.e. managers) and recognize the possibility of existence of other mechanisms through which outside investors can protect themselves. Others, such as Hirschmann (1982) and Maitland (1997), present historical views in which economic interaction is seen as having a civilizing effect on individuals, thus implying that the quality of economic interactions is the cause of ethical behavior. However, both authors also offer alternative explanations, which confirm the views of Donaldson and Dunfee (1999). Hirschmann (1982) writes about American sociologists in the early twentieth century who attribute a key role in social cohesion to the ability of various social groups to make norms and rules effective. They do not see the rules of ethical conduct as rising out of the market itself. Maitland (1997) sees the role of markets somewhat differently. He suggests that the market rewards and reinforces certain virtues, by which the market "strengthens its own foundations and reproduces a moral culture that is functional to its own needs" (p. 28). In this argument, the author implies the preexistence of certain traits or virtues that lead to economic interaction of superior quality based on mutual interest among members of society, which in turn reinforces these virtues. This reciprocal relationship is not in contradiction with our hypothesis but rather introduces additional complexities that should be considered in future research.

In order to develop a framework concerning ethical attitudes in US, Russia, and Slovenia, recent developments in some key institutions in society (legal codes, educational systems, and government and its stability) in these countries are examined and their economic efficiency compared (see also Table 1 for the summary of basic quantitative indicators). Recent studies about ethics are also reviewed. An examination of the differences in legal codes, educational systems, and government stability in US, Russia, and Slovenia revealed several interesting facts. First, the US legal system is based on centuries-

B. Bucar et al. / Journal of Business Venturing 18 (2003) 261–281   265

Table 1
Comparison of institutional and economic indicators for the US, Slovenia, and Russia

	US	Slovenia	Russia
1. Enrolment ratio for secondary education (in 1998; %)	97	91	87
2. Enrolment ratio in tertiary education (in 1998; %)	81	36	43
3. Change in (2) compared to 1991 (in percentage points)	same	+8	−7
4. Gross national product per capita (US$ in 1998)	30,000	10,000	2300
5. Average annual growth of GNP (in 1991–1998; %)	2.5	2	−6.5
6. Telephone mainlines (per 1000 people)	661	375	197
7. Personal computers (per 1000 people)	459	251	41

old Anglo Saxon legal principles and has not undergone any radical changes recently. In Russia and Slovenia, on the other hand, private companies were allowed to operate only in the last decade and legal systems in the area of business activity are still being developed. One important difference between these two countries is that Russian companies were owned by the state, whereas companies in Slovenia were owned by employees—a situation somewhat closer to private ownership. Second, several UNESCO indicators of the educational system were examined. The enrolment rates for secondary education are high for all three countries in the observed period (US 97%, Russia 87%, and Slovenia 91%). The enrolment ratio in tertiary (postsecondary or college level) education is the highest in US (81%), followed by Russia (43%, a decrease from 50% in 1991), and then Slovenia (36%, an increase from 28% in 1991). The data showed some negative tendencies in the educational level obtained in Russia and some positive trends in Slovenia. The third institution examined was the stability of the political system. The US can be characterized as a stable and mature democracy. Slovenia is a young democratic country with the Council of Ministers nominated by the Prime Minister and elected by the National Assembly. It has seen some turmoil, especially through rather frequent changes of ministers in the government, reflecting the need to form a coalition government. Russia has struggled in its efforts to build a democratic political system, where reform efforts have resulted in contradictory political regulations and practices.

The comparison of economic efficiency was based on the indicators of economic development. The US is the most developed of the three countries with GNP per capita of US$30,000, followed by Slovenia with $10,000, and Russia $2300. The long-term trends show a similar picture. The average annual growth of GNP in the period 1991–1998 in the US was 2.5%, 2% in Slovenia, and −6.5% in Russia. Two other indicators of economic development are telephone mainlines per 1000 people and personal computers per 1000 people with the following values: US (661 and 459), Slovenia (375 and 251), and Russia (197 and 41) in 1998.

Finally, recent articles about ethics in the US, Slovenia, and Russia were examined. Discussion about ethics has quite a long tradition in the US. Hisrich (1999) describes the formation of America as demonstrating a society reconciling both personal values and socioeconomic responsibility. Vogel (1992) described key differences of business ethics in the US compared to other developed economies. In the US, ethics is focused more on the individual and is more legalistic and rule oriented, with economic behavior more regulated by law. In Slovenia, business ethics was never a priority in Slovene business curricula, and during the 1980s, ethical dilemmas primarily attracted philosophers. Ivanjko (1996) identified the informal character of control mechanisms during the socialist period as the reason why researchers avoided this issue. The absolute political power of the Communist Party with the informal control mechanisms such as threat of political persecution and nepotism prevented social scientists from questioning or studying any ethical practices. During the transition period, ethical issues started to occupy a more prominent place in the public discussion. Glas (1997) cited several reasons for this, including the destruction of the former moral and value system, the existence of poorly protected social ownership that opened an area for wild privatization, slow legal changes that provided for gray zones for circumventing rules, harsh economic recession, a decreasing standard of living, and a liberal, highly permissive environment. The academic discussion opened up (Pleskovič, 1994; Ivanjko et al., 1996) but conceptual disputes predominated, with only some anecdotal evidence of the attitudes and ethical views of different social groups. For Russia, the continuing problems of poor business ethics and the interplay of politics, business, and the mafia have become a paradigm for the period following Perestroika. Neimanis (1997) explored highly publicized unethical business practices in the former Soviet Union and looked at some more covert ethical problems like nonfulfillment of contracts, the lack of manners, and pernicious envy that justifies any action taken against the successful.

Looking at the quality of institutions in the three surveyed countries (antecedents of ethical behavior) and at the quality of economic interactions (consequences of ethical behavior), it is expected that the US would rank the highest in ethical attitudes, followed by Slovenia, and then Russia. This inference posits two questions. First, how large and consistent are the differences between these three countries. Second, do these differences really follow the same pattern for different aspects of ethical choices?

Hypothesis 1: Based on the quality of institutions and efficiency of economic interactions, ethical attitudes will be the highest in US, followed by Slovenia, and then Russia.

4. Entrepreneurs and managers

We also wanted to explore the differences in ethical attitudes between entrepreneurs and managers. The social contract theory provides only a limited foundation to explain potential differences between these two groups of actors. Traditional social contract theory operates on a macro level, where it defines a hypothetical agreement among rational members of a community. To a large extent, managers and entrepreneurs would have to perform under a very similar influence of social institutions. The main differences may originate from their differential relations towards other stakeholders in the business activity. Entrepreneurs form social contracts with employees and the general public, while managers have a contract with business owners and higher level managers in addition to all the contracts that define

B. Bucar et al. / Journal of Business Venturing 18 (2003) 261–281   267

responsibilities of entrepreneurs. These potential differential relations among business stakeholders are better explained by stakeholder theory.

Donaldson and Dunfee (1999) developed an ISCT, combining the macro and micro forms of social contract, where micro contracts represent the actual agreements within industries or associations. ISCT is complementary to stakeholder theory or rather serves as the normative foundation for the stakeholder theory, because "relevant sociopolitical communities are a primary source of guidance concerning the stakeholder obligations of organizations formed or operating within their boundaries" (Donaldson and Dunfee, 1999, p. 248).

It is important to understand the defining characteristics of business managers and entrepreneurs. In their review of 10 previous studies of personality characteristics, Ginsberg and Buchholtz (1989) found that these studies characterize an entrepreneur as someone who is a founder, owner, and manager of a business and who creates a new and different venture. While entrepreneurs assume financial, psychic, and social risks and receive the resulting rewards of monetary and personal satisfaction and independence (Hisrich and Peters, 1998), managers have the power to allocate the resources but are not taking the same risks. Specifically, financial risks assumed by managers are not of the same type and degree as the ones assumed by entrepreneurs. Entrepreneurs, more often than managers, obtain loans that are secured by their personal property and risk loosing a large part of their personal wealth. Managers, on the other hand, usually only assume limited liability for the operations of the firm. A similar distinction was made by Baumol (1993) who defined the manager "as the individual who oversees the ongoing efficiency of continuing processes" (p. 3) and the entrepreneur as someone whose job is "to locate new ideas and to put them into effect" (p. 4). At the same time, Baumol (1993) cautioned that entrepreneurship should not be taken as a synonym for virtuousness. He made a clear distinction between value creating and unproductive, rent-seeking entrepreneurial activities.

At the core of stakeholder theory is the idea that a business usually interacts with five stakeholder groups: shareholders, customers, employees, suppliers, and the community at large. Hasnas (1998) identified two principles of stakeholder management: the principle of corporate legitimacy and the stakeholder fiduciary principle. The principle of corporate legitimacy states that the company should be managed for the benefit of its stakeholders. The stakeholder fiduciary principle states that management must act both in the interest of the stakeholders as their agent and in the interest of the corporation to ensure the survival of the firm, safeguarding the long-term stakes of each group. The stakeholder fiduciary principle is similar to the main relationships of agency theory.

Hill and Jones (1992) developed the stakeholder-agency theory where managers can be seen as the agents of other stakeholders. They noted that stakeholders differ among themselves with respect to (a) the importance of their stake in the firm and (b) their power vis-à-vis the managers. In most large corporations, few, if any, of the stockholders own significant enough shares of the company to be able to directly influence the operations of the company. The managers are governed by the boards of directors and indirectly by the stockholders who can always sell the stock of the company when not satisfied with its operations. This influence is inherently imperfect since boards of directors are often elected from candidates proposed by top management, and stockholders will often hold their stocks even in cases of unethical managerial behavior as long as the stock meets certain investment criteria. Jackall (1988) made the argument that ethical views of managers are affected by a complex interaction between the manager's personal value system and that of upper management, frequently resulting in a manager's ethical decisions being influenced by considerations other than their personal value systems. The theoretical articulation of this phenomenon of separating personal values from business decisions is known as the Separation Thesis (Freeman, 2000).

Entrepreneurs, on the other hand, usually do not face the issue of the separation of ownership and control. Often, entrepreneurs are the founders and majority (or at least significant) owners of their companies. Unethical behavior in their own company would present an internal contradiction. The ethics of entrepreneurs should rely more on their individual or personal views. As owner-managers, entrepreneurs could employ their personal values to a much greater extent than managers within large businesses (Humphreys et al., 1993), since they are not constrained by the structure of bureaucratic corporate organizations. A very interesting paper by Sarasvathy et al. (1998) provides empirical support for our hypothesis that entrepreneurs will exhibit higher ethical standards than managers (although their research was conducted with only eight subjects). The authors found that entrepreneurs bring personal values into their business decisions and assume greater personal responsibility for the outcomes.

Recent studies used different research approaches to study this ethical phenomenon. Two studies focused on the distinction between small and large companies. Longenecker et al. (1989) used 16 vignettes in a survey of 2290 respondents. The authors found statistically significant differences on 12 vignettes. Small business respondents expressed more stringent ethical views on the issues of faulty investment advice, favoritism, acquiescing in dangerous design flaws, misleading financial reports, misleading advertising, and defending the healthfulness of smoking cigarettes. Yet, this same group indicated a significantly more permissive stance in situations involving financial benefits derived at the expense of others, discrimination against women, computer program copying, tax avoidance, and insider information. Dunfee et al. (1991) in a survey of 62 respondents in firms with up to 1000 employees found significant differences in ethical behaviors of managers from large and small companies. Managers of larger companies were more accessible for briberies but quicker to introduce formal inquiries on sexual harassment. Managers of smaller firms were more likely to use insider trading but, on the other hand, were more likely to punish whistle-blowers and refuse a job offer from a competitor. Other studies have suggested that not only the size of the company but also other variables should be included in a detailed study of ethical behavior, such as individual characteristics of employees, specific features of the industry, and country-specific environment (Smith and Oakley, 1994; Vehovec, 2000). Smith and Oakley (1994) found that business owners are influenced significantly by the community in which their firms operate, with nonurban owners adhering to stricter ethical values than their urban counterparts. Vehovec (2000) showed that businesspeople in Croatia have clear ethical attitudes in the area of personal responsibilities, but these attitudes weakened in relation to an employer due to opportunistic behavior. Lower ethical standards were explained by the slow development of informal institutions in this transitional economy.

The contradictory results of these studies merit additional investigation in this area. Since country-specific institutions may confound the results and blur the differences between entrepreneurs and managers, the US and Slovenia were analyzed separately. This analysis was not possible for the Russian sample, because it included only entrepreneurs. The following hypothesis was tested.

Hypothesis 2: A greater percentage of entrepreneurs than managers will exhibit ethical attitudes in business.

5. Methodology

The survey instrument used needed to be the same and developed from a literature review, with the objective, as put in Hisrich (1999), to be capable of being replicated in different cultures and economic environments. After extensive tests of the initial pool of 56 questions and 44 business scenarios used in previous research, the resulting instrument contained four sections: 32 questions with a binary response modified from Akaah and Lund (1994); 12 vignettes having a multidimensional scale modeled after Reidenbach and Robin (1990); seven scenarios using a seven-point Likert scale; and comprehensive demographic information. The vignettes were intended to measure ethical judgments (Reidenbach and Robin, 1990), which are the basis of ethical attitudes (or intentions; Hunt and Vitell, 1986). The section with 32 questions was designed to measure ethical attitudes, while the section with seven scenarios was designed to measure projected behaviors (which are a function of an individual's attitudes and situational constraints; Hunt and Vitell, 1986). The use of scenario techniques is well established in ethics research for testing behavioral science models (Hunt and Vitell, 1986). The questionnaire was pretested with a group of entrepreneurs and managers, and mailing lists were sampled according to the following criteria. For entrepreneurs, the individual had to be the founder and majority owner of a business. For managers, the individual had to be in top or middle management in a large organization without ownership stake.

In the US, mailing lists were obtained from Council of Smaller Enterprises of the Cleveland Growth Association (COSE), Enterprise Development (EDI, an incubator), and the Executive Management Development Program of the Weatherhead School of Management at Case Western Reserve University, Cleveland. Questionnaires ($N=1243$) were sent to entrepreneurs and managers, of which 40 were returned as nondeliverable. The response rate of the mail survey was 22% for entrepreneurs and 28% for managers. In Slovenia, the business directories from the Chamber of Economy and the Chamber of Crafts were used. A sample of 887 businesses was randomly selected from two subsamples. There was a separate subsample of entrepreneurs (520) and a subsample of managers in medium and large companies (367). The 166 returned questionnaires, a response rate of 19% (16% for entrepreneurs and 22% for managers), was good for research in Slovenia, considering the topic and the length of the questionnaire. In Russia, a list of 200 entrepreneurs associated with the Academy of the National Economy was obtained. The entrepreneurs were from various regions in Russia–Siberia, Urals, and the Central Region, including Moscow and St.

Petersburg. Due to anonymity being guaranteed and the fact that the academy is well known for its high-quality academic programs, 159 responses were obtained, an extremely high (80%) response rate. Since we were not able to obtain mailing lists of Russian managers, we only included the sample of entrepreneurs in this study to provide for some interesting cross-cultural comparisons.

6. Findings

The findings will be discussed in terms of sample composition and the ethical codes and attitudes of entrepreneurs and managers. The discussion will focus primarily on two issues: (1) the differences in the ethical attitudes of entrepreneurs in different countries and (2) the differences in the ethical attitudes between entrepreneurs and managers. A third issue, the stability of changes in the ethical attitudes over time could also be explored, since a survey using basically the same questionnaire was conducted in Slovenia during 1996. However, the size of the subsample—only 42 entrepreneurs and 99 managers—is problematic in making reasonable conclusions. An initial analysis revealed a remarkable stability of results, supporting the notion of doing a follow-up survey in 2 years.

6.1. Sample composition

While sample size differs among the countries, they provide sufficient data for comparative analysis as a basis for appropriate conclusions. Although the sample in Slovenia is a little smaller, it is well balanced between entrepreneurs and managers and is in line with previous results. The male/female percentages in all three countries indicate lower percentages of women in each of the samples (see Table 2). This structure for Slovenia does not represent the actual share of women entrepreneurs—it is roughly 24% for incorporated businesses and even less for sole proprietors (Glas and Petrin, 1998). A similar situation occurred in Russia. While the share of women entrepreneurs in the US sample is closer to the actual figures for the US, it still is a little smaller (Brush, 1997).

The age of the entrepreneurs is similar for Slovenia and the US, while the Russian entrepreneurs are relatively young. This difference reflects the characteristics of the former economic systems. In Slovenia, the self-management system was quite liberal and crafts constituted a fairly strong private sector. In Slovenia, establishing small private businesses was a possible career choice during the socialist period and there are many experienced entrepreneurs from that time. In Russia, the socialist system was in existence for a longer period of time with much less economic freedom. This helps explain why a new generation with higher educational status quickly grasped the option of establishing a private business.

The difference in the educational levels is worth mentioning when comparing the entrepreneurs and managers on one side and the country differences between Slovenia and the US. American entrepreneurs exceed even Slovene managers in terms of their education and share of college graduates. The educational levels of entrepreneurs in Slovenia and the US are quite similar to the educational levels of the general populations in the respective

B. Bucar et al. / Journal of Business Venturing 18 (2003) 261–281   271

Table 2
Sample characteristics (in %; except for sample respondents which are in absolute numbers)

Characteristics		Slovenia		US		Russia
		Entrepreneurs	Managers	Entrepreneurs	Managers	Entrepreneurs
Sample	Respondents	84	82	165	128	159
Sex	Male	62	82	77	68	55
	Female	38	18	22	29	35
	No answer	–	–	1	3	10
Age	– 30 years	14	2	7	23	35
	30–39 years	29	20	28	33	29
	40–49 years	42	48	37	31	25
	50–59 years	10	24	20	12	–
	60 and more	4	4	8	–	3
	No answer	2	2	1	2	9
Education	Less than secondary	5	–	–	–	–
	Secondary	46	10	9	3	1
	Some college	26	18	27	4	40
	University	20	51	29	21	10
	MBA, PhD	2	21	34	72	35
	No answer	–	–	1	–	14
Company size	Small[a]	87	16	77	24	55
	Medium	13	53	19	15	28
	Large	–	32	2	60	7
	No answer	–	–	2	1	9
Income level	up to 20,000	99	86	7	3	77
	20,000–39,999	–	1	14	16	11
	40,000 and more	1	13	79	81	2
	No answer	–	–	–	–	10

[a] The company size. For Slovenia: small, up to 50 employees; medium, 51–250 and large, over 250 employees. For the US and Russia: small, up to 99 employees; medium, 100–999 and large, over 1000 employees.

countries, while managers in both countries and entrepreneurs in Russia have higher than average educational levels. The size structure is related to the size of the domestic market. Thus, the majority of entrepreneurs from Slovenia have run small businesses, and entrepreneurs from US and Russia more often manage larger enterprises.

While other demographic data were collected, care needs to be taken in interpreting the comparisons because of significant difference in levels of development. Considering income levels, the two groups differ significantly. In the US, significantly more entrepreneurs (47%) were in the upper income brackets, with US$100,000 and over income level, whereas only 25% of managers were at this level. In Slovenia, managers had significantly higher incomes. In Russia, in spite of its poor average income, entrepreneurs were doing surprisingly well in terms of income.

Business-oriented characteristics of the entrepreneurs and managers also differed to a certain degree. In the US, more entrepreneurs worked in consumer services, mining and extraction, and retail/wholesale trade and more managers were in banking, investment, and insurance. In Slovenia, entrepreneurs were largely in services (49%), with only 25% in manufacturing and 14% in trade. About 49% of Slovenian managers were in manufacturing, 33% in services, and 10% in trade.

6.2. Ethical attitudes

The ethical codes and attitudes of the entrepreneurs and managers were explored from several perspectives. First, 18 questions explored what the respondents consider as ethical (right) or unethical (wrong). For different aspects of behavior, they had only a binary response—the behavior is either right or wrong. The questions were classified into groups according to the content and/or ethical principle that should be used to evaluate the decision. The questions mostly focused on the unauthorized use of company's resources, the relationship within the organization, and views about the environment (see Table 3).

On the misappropriation of resources, respondents condemned the use of company supplies (physical resources) for private use, while the evaluation of the misuse of services or time was less stringent. Most critical of such behavior were Slovenians (entrepreneurs and managers equally), followed by Americans (managers being less sensitive). Russians expressed a significantly lower level of responsibility.

While overstating expenses was considered unethical, Americans were more permissive of smaller amounts of overstatement. Russians, again, were least sensitive and a smaller percentage of them (19%) did not consider this as unethical perhaps because they believed it was merely cheating the government.

On the issue of gifts and bribes, Americans indicated the highest level of refusal, while at least giving gifts was considered as unethical by less than 50% of Russian entrepreneurs. While accepting gifts is considered highly unethical, giving gifts is more acceptable as a way of doing business in some societies.

Breaking internal rules, in terms of falsifying reports to appropriate some undeserved rewards, was considered unethical (not so much in Russia), while avoiding to report violations of law was strongly condemned by Americans. Slovenians did not differentiate between company policy and law. However, respondents from all three countries were not very eager to report violators; they might feel that this is the job of supervisors or inspectors. Respondents were strongly against passing blame to innocent persons or claiming ownership for other people's efforts in all three countries. Even Russians showed a surprisingly high percentage, agreeing with this view.

However, in some business practices, the answers differed widely: insider trading was considered unethical by Americans (tradition of stock exchange operations) but highly acceptable for Russians. The lower score level of feeling for Slovenian managers probably reflects the privatization scheme that turned most managers into a kind of "insider" through taking a minor share in the internal sale of the company's shares. The survey in 1996 found almost the same result for Slovenia (92.5:73.2%). Respondents were generally against the disclosure of company secrets to outsiders. Slovenians were also against hiring competitor's employees to obtain the competitor's trade secrets. Russians would have no problems in using this approach. Slovenian and American managers were more apt to use such a practice than entrepreneurs.

B. Bucar et al. / Journal of Business Venturing 18 (2003) 261–281   273

Table 3
The share of respondents evaluating certain type of behavior as unethical, wrong behavior (in %)

It is ethical for "someone" to	Slovenia		US		Russia
	Entrepreneurs	Managers	Entrepreneurs	Managers	Entrepreneurs
Use of resources					
Remove company supplies for personal use	97.6	98.8	93.3	85.9	84.6
Use company services for personal use	90.5	90.2	81.5	71.8	61.4
Use company time for noncompany benefits or for personal business	91.7	95.1	80.7	70.4	72.3
Overstate expense accounts by more than 10% of the correct amount	97.6	98.8	98.8	94.5	81.1
Overstate expense accounts by less than 10% of the correct amount	97.6	97.6	92.7	86.6	81.6
Gifts and bribes					
Give gifts/favors in exchange for preferential treatment	81.0	75.0	84.8	88.3	49.7
Accept gifts/favors in exchange for preferential treatment	88.1	88.9	92.7	89.0	67.5
Extra time use					
Take extra personal time (lunch hour, breaks, early departure)	91.7	92.6	80.0	56.8	69.8
Take longer than necessary to do a job	72.8	75.0	90.8	77.8	76.7
Breaking rules/policies/laws					
Authorize subordinates to violate company policy	96.4	98.8	95.1	85.7	65.8
Fail to report a coworker's violation of company policy	82.1	88.8	73.2	64.5	43.7
Falsify internal time/quality/quantity reports	100.0	98.8	98.2	92.1	86.2
Fail to report a coworker's violation of law	83.3	84.0	87.0	79.8	66.9
Internal relations					
Pass blame for errors to an innocent coworker	100.0	100.0	98.8	96.1	87.4
Claim credit for a peer's work	96.4	98.8	98.2	96.1	86.8
Other issues					
Purchase shares upon hearing/seeing privileged company information	83.1	70.7	88.9	89.1	46.2
Hire competitor's employees in order to learn competitor's trade secrets	91.6	82.7	73.9	63.2	44.3
Divulge confidential information to parties external to the firm	100.0	98.8	95.8	91.3	89.9

274 B Bucar et al. / Journal of Business Venturing 18 (2003) 261–281

Table 4
Affirmative responses of entrepreneurs and managers about ethics and business (in %)

	Slovenia		US		Russia
	Entrepreneurs	Managers	Entrepreneurs	Managers	Entrepreneurs
Business and government					
Free enterprise is the best form of an economic system	81.0	76.3	94.4	94.4	75.5
The government has too many laws regulating business	83.3	65.4	79.0	59.5	60.1
The government has too many laws governing my life	80.7	51.3	73.8	56.7	59.7
Business and ethics					
Having a prescribed "code of ethics" assist in decision making	78.3	82.9	73.5	70.9	62.7
Personal ethics are sacrificed to the goals of business	60.7	40.2	52.1	70.6	64.6
Doing business					
Most businesses truly do not care about individual customers/consumers	41.0	19.5	30.2	25.8	50.3
Most businesses generally try to deal with me in a fair way, and thus, I try to deal in a fair way with them	95.2	92.7	93.3	87.3	67.3
If you deal honestly with a person he/she will deal honestly with you	60.2	67.9	67.7	65.9	50.0
I never purchase anything from a door-to-door salesperson	48.8	53.8	39.3	55.1	68.6
Most salespeople cannot be trusted; they will say whatever is needed to make a sale	67.5	43.9	27.6	42.5	67.6
Executives of large corporations are typically more honest than the executives of small business enterprises	13.4	24.1	7.0	10.4	25.8
People and ethics					
Man is basically good	71.4	74.4	88.8	91.2	66.0
The average person is more ethical than myself	20.3	10.7	3.9	6.8	38.3
If something is illegal, then it is ethically wrong to do it	53.0	30.0	52.5	38.7	51.9

6.3. Ethics and business values

Entrepreneurs and managers were also asked about their concepts and beliefs in doing business with other companies and to evaluate the degree of government interference with business. These questions were again classified into groups of statements with responses categorized in Table 4.

Americans generally believed in the free enterprise system. While there were more entrepreneurs than managers in Slovenia believing in this system, the difference was not statistically significant. The difference was significant in 1996, when 90% of entrepreneurs and only 64% of managers liked this system. As expected, Russians were less enthusiastic.

Slovenian entrepreneurs felt the country had too many laws governing business as well as their personal lives. Significantly more entrepreneurs than managers felt this way as the latter group was better able to separate the company from their personal life. The same opinion was shared by Americans. Russians, surprisingly, in spite of complaints about the bureaucracy and the administrative barriers confronting businesses, do not blame the government for excessive legislation.

Slovenians believed in the usefulness of a code of ethics although it was not a traditional practice for Slovenian companies to have such codes. This is in line with the European tradition of being inclined to develop strict internal regulations rather than follow more general codes.

Considering the issue of whether personal ethics should be sacrificed to the goals of business, the hypothesized rank order of countries occurred for entrepreneurs. Americans were the most against this, followed by Slovenians, and then Russians. However, a large number of American managers felt they had to follow this practice.

The mistrust of the ethical behavior of other businesses/businesspeople revealed a diverse picture. Americans felt most strongly that businesses cared for their customers. The belief in fair treatment by most businesses was strong in Slovenia and the US but weak in Russia. However, there is a puzzling distinction—businesses should be trusted for their fair treatment but not individual people. Americans trusted salespeople more than Slovenians and Russians did, although in the US, entrepreneurs had more trust while managers had more trust in Slovenia. The ranking of purchasing from door-to-door salespersons followed this same pattern (see Table 4).

Trust is a very important issue in business particularly with the increased number of small businesses where the sheer number of business partners compared to limited human and financial resources in small businesses makes it difficult to trade without a basic trust. The belief in the goodness of people is far stronger among Americans and is probably one of the psychological barriers in former Eastern European countries. Without trust it is difficult to build entrepreneurial teams and obtain outside private equity capital; these difficulties are hindering the growth of the economy.

Respondents do not consider themselves as less ethical than the average person, but a kind of self-criticism is strongest in Russia. This is an interesting finding because it runs against the general notion in the field of business ethics that individuals tend to believe that they are more ethical than their peers. In Russia, there is a feeling that doing business demands a relaxation of ethical attitudes. Neimanis (1997) suggests a few reasons for such an attitude of Russian businesspeople. First, ethical considerations in business were subordinated to plan fulfillment during the Soviet command economy and no such unethical behavior was dictated in personal relationships. Second, the absence of personal responsibility in the Communist Party, where each decision required dozens of approvals, did not promote ethical behavior. Finally, the transition from managed collectivism to a system driven by individual initiative was slow to introduce new official rules for conducting business, therefore leaving vast gray areas in which many unethical practices were not sanctioned. Russia is followed by Slovenians in this aspect, while American businesspeople consider themselves no different than others.

6.4. Ethics and business scenarios

The third section of the questionnaire contained 12 vignettes short scenarios, describing certain questionable actions of different businesses or businesspersons. The respondents had to evaluate these actions along the following four dimensions using a five-point scale:

- *just or unjust*: regarding the existing laws, regulations, and ethical values;
- *fair or unfair*: using the fairness and honesty as a pure principle for judgment;
- *right or wrong*: regarding the prevailing ethical values from the point of view of the duty-based ethical principle;
- *good or bad*: using the utility-based approach, with the focus on the ultimate result for the company and other stakeholders.

This section was the most difficult for respondents particularly in understanding the differences between the four dimensions. Some respondents chose to answer the question on only one of the four dimensions; some simply allocated the same point value on each of the four dimensions. Some respondents simply skipped this section of the questionnaire. However, the majority correctly considered the "fair–unfair" dimension as a "pure" ethical assessment, while the "good–bad" dimension was considered as a matter of practical consequences for the business. It is also possible that these four dimensions were not understood in the same way in all three countries due to differences in language and a different cultural meaning. Because these dimensions were not explained in a great detail to respondents, it is quite likely that they were not interpreted in the same way even within the same country.

Despite the unreliable and mostly statistically insignificant findings, the few significant ones that follow previously described patterns of ethical attitudes will be discussed. One of the scenarios having a valid response rate is *The seller sells the more expensive product to the customer, although he knows that a cheaper one would better suit the needs of the particular customer*. Russians display the lowest level of ethical responsiveness on all four dimensions. However, the comparison of Slovenians and Americans reveals an interesting feature. The comparison of entrepreneurs with managers shows entrepreneurs as being ethically more sensitive than managers on all four dimensions in both countries. However, Slovenians were very critical on the dimension of "fairness" or "honesty," but they fell below the American level on the "pragmatic" dimension of good/bad. Perhaps, Slovenians know what is ethically right/wrong (fair or just) and they clearly condemn such behavior. However, when they make their business decisions, they bend under economic and profit pressures and accept less honest behavior for the sake of better financial results for the business.

This may reflect the fact that the transition phase is still operating on in Slovenia. In the current situation, it is still more profitable for businesses to exploit market opportunities and there still is a gap in the knowledge of customers about the true quality of products. The competition is still not strong enough to remedy this kind of behavior and minimize the gap in consumer information. The market does not punish sellers for not caring enough for the well-being of customers. In the US, the hypercompetitive market and more adequate market information do not allow for this lack of customer focus.

The same results occurred on many of the other vignettes such as the internal bank auditor destroying the evidence on illegal loans, the car dealer taking a small bribe from the customer to arrange for a sizeable discount on the new car, a bicycle company paying a large fee to a foreign businessman for opening the foreign market, a company shifting a cleaning process producing a lot of dust to the night shift, a subcontractor selling truck axles falling short of prescribed quality standard, and falsified results of a marketing research presented to the company board.

The fourth section contained seven scenarios asking the respondents the likelihood of adopting an unethical behavior in a particular circumstance. Overall, when considering the likely behavior facing real-life scenarios, Americans displayed the highest level of business

Table 5
Mean values of answers to scenarios (1 = *likely*, 7 = *unlikely*)

Scenario	Russia/ entrepreneurs	Slovenia/ managers	Slovenia/ entrepreneurs	US/ managers	US/ entrepreneurs	F
1. Guarantee shipment that you cannot deliver on time	2.82	3.63	3.95	4.72	4.93	38.8***
2. Conceal your supervisor's wrong expense report	3.03	4.65	4.46	4.66	4.88	27.0***
3. Obtain a copy of secret competitor's new product feature	2.34	2.69	3.21	4.33	4.10	29.9***
4. Reveal the unethical actions of the plant manager to top management	3.13	2.06	2.52	2.35	2.07	10.9***
5. Buy ergonomically designed tools to avoid muscle injuries	2.89	2.21	2.36	2.39	2.29	6.0***
6. Offer the retraining option to the displaced employees	2.85	2.25	2.69	2.78	2.39	3.6***
7. Look inside your competitors' written proposals	2.89	3.02	3.38	5.20	5.42	57.0***

* Significant at .10 level or better.
** Significant at .05 level or better.
*** Significant at .01 level or better.

ethics, while Slovenians lagged behind, followed by the Russians. The exact differences did vary among the scenarios (see Table 5).

One of the scenarios used in the questionnaire is commonly used in research on business ethics: *You could conclude a large order providing you promise the delivery in 2 weeks. However, it is beyond your current capability and 1-week delay is necessary, which will not really damage your customer. How likely it is that you will give the (unrealistic) promise to get the order?*

Ethical behavior would be honesty in dealing with customers and dealing in good faith in negotiations. Therefore, an ethical response would be admitting the need for an additional week for delivery in obtaining the order. Some interesting things are revealed: the country ranking follows the previous pattern (US → Slovenia → Russia). Slovenia and Russia have a much larger share of uncertainty as an option, and entrepreneurs are less likely to lie to the client in order to secure the order. Perhaps, entrepreneurs feel more comfortable in trying to persuade the client to agree on the different delivery schedule. While this scenario clearly differentiates between Slovenians and Russians, some other scenarios displayed even larger differences between Slovenians and Americans, with Russians being closer to Slovenian respondents.

7. Conclusions

This research provides a unique comparison of the ethical attitudes of entrepreneurs and managers from three highly different countries. Despite some problems on the use of a US-based instrument in different cultural and economic environments, it provides unique international comparisons.

Slovenian entrepreneurs and managers revealed a surprisingly high level of business ethics in the sense of "knowing what is right/wrong," while the ethical attitudes of Russian entrepreneurs had in some cases a rather discouraging low level, particularly on gifts/bribes, insider trading, ignorance of violations of company policy, or law. American entrepreneurs and managers revealed a high level of ethical attitudes, but there is a sense of pragmatism particularly in some cases such as insider trading and gifts/bribes. These cases are reminiscent of some well-known affairs of the past (Lockheed and Milken) and the awareness of the impropriety of such behavior is still very strong (i.e. the Foreign Corrupt Practices Act). There were only few cases where entrepreneurs and managers differed significantly in their ethical attitudes. This was especially true in Slovenia, where a large proportion of entrepreneurs originated from previous managerial positions. In some cases in the US, where the difference is statistically significant, almost as a rule, managers were less sensitive to the ethical aspect of decision making.

The vignette part of the survey illustrated the relationship between business and some ethical views. Slovenians, and Russians in particular, have a long way to go in building a truly competitive business environment that would also deserve trust from businesspeople. These vignettes mostly evaluated what respondents consider as right/wrong and their perception of the market economy and the role of businesses, managers, and salespeople as important stakeholders in the business activities. The question that remains is if and how these ethical attitudes would transfer into the everyday business practice. Would the respondents stick with these attitudes or would they adapt to economic pressures?

The findings followed a pattern, which was anticipated from the general knowledge about the countries surveyed. Americans were assumed to be the most ethical businesspeople due to a longer tradition of a competitive market economy, where unethical behavior would result in dissatisfied customers and criticism. Slovenians do not face the same type of competition, but due to a more liberal system in the past, they are already somewhat accustomed to the ethical values of a market economy. However, in reality, they are still inclined to use short cuts and capitalize on the limited information of customers and the lack of competition. Russians displayed the highest level of disregard for ethics, reflecting the lack of tradition of market economics and the harsh reality of the country's economic situation where survival might become priority over the ethics.

One of the most interesting findings is the significant dichotomy in Slovenians between people being well aware of what is right/wrong (even higher than Americans) to being less ethical in practice where the everyday economic pressures seem to dominate ethical attitudes and practices. Ethics appears to be something to know and to be used in an ideal world with a strong distinction existing between knowing and doing as is indicated in the few significant differences found in comparing the entrepreneurs and managers.

A comparison of ethical attitudes between entrepreneurs and managers in the two countries is a good example of the relevance of the integrative theoretical approaches within the field of business ethics. The distinction between entrepreneurs and managers is made on a micro level, where attitudes of each group are explored in relation to other organizational stakeholders. However, the international comparison is made on a macro level and requires introduction of various country-specific characteristics. Many relations that are a constant within a certain nation become a variable for international comparisons. Rousseau and House (1994) argued that micro and macro distinction is an oversimplification. Integration of micro and macro theory, or a meso approach, offers numerous benefits such as richer and more diverse interpretation of the meaning and functioning of organizations, deeper understanding of the assumptions of researchers, and investigation of fundamental building blocks of organizations.

The study shows support for ISCT of business ethics. ISCT is particularly important for global business ethics (Donaldson and Dunfee, 1994), because it can help identify authentic ethical norms for different international communities by revealing the relevant existing cultural and economic norms. The hypothesized ranking of countries regarding the ethical attitudes of businesspeople was confirmed. The level of development and stability of social institutions was predictive of the level of ethical attitudes in a society. However, a comparison between entrepreneurs and managers in the US and Slovenia pointed out a more subtle impact of the institution of private ownership on ethical attitudes of businesspeople. While in the US, there are some interesting differences in ethical attitudes between the two groups, we found no such differences in Slovenia. Although the ownership of property is recognized as one of the hypernorms (Donaldson and Dunfee, 1994), there are apparent cultural and historical influences on the functioning of this hypernorm.

One major limitation of this study needs to be pointed out. The questionnaires are self-reported. Therefore, the measures are more perceptual/attitudinal and may or may not be behavioral. Individuals are likely to portray themselves as more ethical than they really are. This is not a major problem for the study as the focus is on relative and not absolute scores. A future study should address the issues of any discrepancies between self-reported ethical attitudes and observed ethical behaviors.

The study also provides some practical implications. It suggests that countries can, at least in the long-term, influence the ethical nature of business behavior by developing formal and informal institutions that are conducive to high ethical standards. As Baumol (1993) has suggested, the key to rational policy relating to entrepreneurship is in the pursuit of means to discourage or prevent entrepreneurial talent from devoting itself to unproductive courses. Societies are normally concerned that their economic systems create wealth and allocate resources efficiently, which may be compromised by unethical behavior. In future research, additional countries should be examined and their cultural differences in understanding and implementing ethical concepts should be studied in more detail to fully understand ethics in a variety of country cultures.

References

Akaah, I.P., Lund, D., 1994. The influence of personal and organizational values on marketing professionals' ethical behavior. J. Bus. Ethics 13, 417–430.

Axelrod, R., 1986. An evolutionary approach to norms. Am. Polit. Sci. Rev. 80 (4), 1095–1111.

Baumol, W.J., 1993. Entrepreneurship, Management and the Structure of Payoffs. MIT Press, Cambridge.

Brush, C., 1997. A Resource Perspective on Women's Entrepreneurship: Research, Relevance, and Recognition. The OECD Conference, Boston.

Donaldson, T., 1982. Corporations and Morality. Prentice-Hall, Englewood Cliffs, NJ.

Donaldson, T., Dunfee, T.W., 1994. Toward a unified conception of business ethics: integrative social contracts theory. Acad. Manage. Rev. 19 (2), 252–284.

Donaldson, T., Dunfee, T.W., 1999. Ties That Bind—A Social Contracts Approach to Business Ethics. Harvard Business School Press, Boston, MA.

Dunfee, T.W., Bowie, N.E., Hennessy, J.E., Nelson, K., Robertson, D.C., 1991. Firm size and attitudes about ethics: some preliminary empirical evidence. In: Harvey, B., van Luijk, H., Corbetta, G. (Eds.), Market Morality and Company Size. Kluwer Academic Publishing, London, UK, pp. 103–117.

Dunfee, T.W., Smith, N.C., Ross Jr., W.T. 1999. Social contracts and marketing ethics. J. Mark. 63, 14–32.

Forbes, F.S., Jones, I.M., 1986. A comparative, attitudinal, and analytical study of dismissals of at-will employees without cause. Labor Law Rev. 37, 157–166.

Freeman, R.E., 2000. Business ethics at the millenium. Bus. Ethics Q. 10 (1), 169–180.

Ginsberg, A., Buchholtz, A., 1989. Are the entrepreneurs a breed apart? A look at the evidence. J. Gen. Manage. 15 (2), 32–40.

Glas, M., 1997. The ethics of business in Slovenia: is it really bad? In: Montanheiro, L., Haigh, B., Morris, D., Fabjancic, Z. (Eds.), Public and Private Sector Partnerships: Learning for Growth. Sheffield Hallam Univ. Press, Sheffield, pp. 101–114.

Glas, M., Petrin, T., 1998. Entrepreneurship: new challenges for Slovene women. Working Paper No. 74. Ljubljana: University of Ljubljana.

Gouldner, A.W., 1960. The norm of reciprocity: a preliminary statement. Am. Sociol. Rev. 25 (2), 161–178.

Hasnas, J., 1998. The normative theories of business ethics: a guide for the perplexed. Bus. Ethics Q. 8 (1), 19–42.

B. Bucar et al. / Journal of Business Venturing 18 (2003) 261–281   281

Hill, C.W.L., Jones, T.M., 1992. Stakeholder-agency theory. J. Manage. Stud. 29, 131–154.

Hirschmann, A., 1982. Rival interpretations of market society: civilizing, destructive, feeble. J. Econ. Lit. 20 (4), 1463–1484.

Hisrich, R.D., 1999. Ethics of business managers vs. entrepreneurs. Working Paper No. 86. Ljubljana: University of Ljubljana.

Hisrich, R.D., Peters, M.P., 1998. Entrepreneurship. McGraw-Hill, Boston, MA.

Humphreys, N., Robin, D.P., Reidenbach, R.E., Moak, D.L., 1993. The ethical decision making process of small business owner-managers and their customers. J. Small Bus. Manage. 31 (3), 9–22.

Hunt, S.D., Vitell, S., 1986. A general theory of marketing ethics. J. Macromarketing, 5–16.

Ivanjko, Š., Bohinc, R., Bratina, B., Kocbek, M., Tavčar, M., Tičar, B., 1996. Ethics of Management. Inštitut za evalvacijo in management v raziskovalni in razvojni dejavnosti, Ljubljana.

Jackall, R., 1988. Moral Mazes: The World of Corporate Managers. New York, NY: Oxford Univ. Press.

La Porta, R., Lopez-de-Silanes, F., Schleifer, A., Vishny, R., 1999. Investor protection: origins, consequences, reform. Working Paper 7428. Cambridge: National Bureau of Economic Research.

Longenecker, J., McKinney, J.A., Moore, C.W., 1989. Ethics in small business. J. Small Bus. Manage. 29 (2), 27–31.

Maitland, I., 1997. Virtuous markets—the market as school of the virtues. Bus. Ethics Q. 7 (1), 17–31.

Neimanis, G.J., 1997. Business ethics in the former Soviet Union: a report. J. Bus. Ethics 16, 357–362.

Pleskovič, B., 1994. The ethics of the period of transition towards a market economy. Slovenia—Values and the Future. ŠOU—Enota za časopisno in založniško dejavnost, Ljubljana.

Rawls, J., 1971. A Theory of Justice. Harvard Univ. Press, Cambridge, MA.

Reidenbach, R.E., Robin, D.P., 1990. Toward the development of a multidimensional scale for improving evaluations of marketing activities. J. Bus. Ethics 7, 639–653.

Rousseau, D.M., House, R.J., 1994. Meso organizational behavior: avoiding three fundamental biases. Trends Organ. Behav. 1, 13–30.

Rousseau, D.M., Schalk, R. (Eds.), 2000. Psychological Contracts in Employment: Cross Cultural Perspectives. Sage, Thousand Oaks, CA.

Sarasvathy, D.K., Simon, H.A., Lave, L., 1998. Perceiving and managing business risks: differences between entrepreneurs and bankers. J. Econ. Behav. Organ. 33, 207–225.

Simmons, A.J., 1992. Obedience to law. In: Becker, L.C., Becker, C.B. (Eds.), Encyclopedia of Ethics. Garland Publishing, New York, pp. 918–921.

Smith, P.L., Oakley III, E.F. 1994. A study of the ethical values of metropolitan and nonmetropolitan small business owners. J. Small Bus. Manage. 32 (4), 17–27.

Vehovec, M., 2000. Uloga neformalnih institucija u tranzicijskoj ekonomiji. Round Table on Institutionalizm, Zagreb.

Vogel, D., 1992. The globalization of business ethics: why America remains distinctive. Calif. Manage. Rev. 35 (1), 30–49.

[28]

° *Academy of Management Journal*
2000, Vol 43, No 5, 994–1003

COUNTRY INSTITUTIONAL PROFILES:
UNLOCKING ENTREPRENEURIAL PHENOMENA

LOWELL W. BUSENITZ
University of Oklahoma

CAROLINA GÓMEZ
Towson University

JENNIFER W. SPENCER
George Washington University

This study introduces and validates a measure of country institutional profile for entrepreneurship consisting of regulatory, cognitive, and normative dimensions. Subscales based on data from six countries show reliability, discriminant validity, and external validity. The instrument provides researchers with a valuable resource for exploring why entrepreneurs in one country may have a competitive advantage over entrepreneurs in other countries and how specific country-level institutional differences contribute differently to levels and types of entrepreneurship.

Entrepreneurship has long been viewed as an engine that drives innovation and promotes economic development (Reynolds, 1997; Schumpeter, 1934). For instance, countries such as Great Britain and the United States industrialized fairly rapidly because entrepreneurial skills were allowed to proliferate (Casson, 1990; Storey, 1994). Entrepreneurship is currently revitalizing some formerly planned economies (Chow & Fung, 1996), and it has facilitated economic growth in many others (Acs, 1992; Aronson, 1991; Oviatt & McDougall, 1994; Storey, 1994). However, scholars have only a limited understanding of why rates of entrepreneurship vary cross-nationally and why certain types of start-ups may be more successful in one country than in another (Aronson, 1991; Rondinelli & Kasarda, 1992). A greater understanding of na-

tional differences will aid entrepreneurship researchers as well as would-be entrepreneurs, potential investors, and government policy makers trying to revitalize their national economies.

It is clear that the definition of entrepreneurship is multidimensional and that different research questions draw attention to different dimensions of the construct. Entrepreneurship research has focused broadly on the development of smaller firms (Acs, 1992; Aronson, 1991) and more narrowly on the founding and success of firms that are introducing new products to the marketplace (Schumpeter, 1934). In both cases it is argued that these firms are the ones that provide the impetus for economic growth (Reynolds, 1997; Rondinelli & Kasarda, 1992).

A basic premise of much international management research has been that firms are embedded in country-specific institutional arrangements. For instance, unique institutional structures guide firms' strategic activities and help determine the nature and amount of innovation that take place within a country's borders (Nelson, 1993). Bartholomew (1997) articulated how national institutional patterns, such as access to research and educational institutions, access to sources of financing, and availability of pools of educated labor, help determine the manner in which an innovation emerges within a country. Differences in national institutions may also bring about different levels of entrepreneurial activity across countries. Casson (1990) argued that an infrastructure that enhances cooperation between a country's entrepreneurs will facilitate problem-solving activities and increase entrepreneurial activity. Others have studied how patent

The authors contributed equally to this work and are listed alphabetically. We gratefully acknowledge Wynne Chin for his invaluable help in data analysis and Dennis P. Bozeman, Robert Keller, Paula Rechner, Craig Russell, and our colleagues at the University of Houston for their many helpful comments. We also extend our thanks to this journal's three anonymous reviewers and to Patricia McDougall for their many insightful comments. International research is never possible without assistance from global partners. Our most sincere thanks to Isabel Gutierrez Calderon, Marilu Ferrara, Mahmoud Ezzamel, Andres Gronlund, Morten Huse, Heinz Klandt, Mark P. Kriger, Hanno Roberts, and Klaus Tragsdorf for assisting us with data collection. Finally, we would like to thank the University of Houston's Office of Sponsored Programs for its financial assistance.

rights (Nelson, 1982), societal norms, and shared cognitive schemas (Busenitz & Lau, 1996) affect the level of entrepreneurship within an economy.

Despite this literature, which points to a diverse set of country-level differences to explain international differences in entrepreneurship, most cross-national empirical research has focused narrowly on the role of culture. Many of these studies have linked Hofstede's (1980) dimensions of culture to countries' entrepreneurial tendencies, with particular interest in the dimension of individualism. However, Acs (1992) concluded that there is a limited correlation between countries' levels of individualism and the strength of small companies, and subsequent research has continued to find inconsistent results (European Network for SME Research, 1996; Mueller & Thomas, 1997). These findings suggest that Hofstede's measures of culture, alone, do not adequately describe cross-country differences in entrepreneurial activity. We believe that cross-national differences in entrepreneurship are best explained by a broader set of institutions that guide and constrain private business behavior in every national economy.

Kostova (1997) introduced the concept of a three-dimensional *country institutional profile* to explain how a country's government policies (constituting a regulatory dimension), widely shared social knowledge (a cognitive dimension), and value systems (a normative dimension) affect domestic business activity. She emphasized that countries' institutional profiles lose meaning when they are generalized across a broad set of issues. Institutional profiles must, instead, be measured with regard to specific domains. Research in cognitive psychology has shown that cognitive and normative categories are domain-specific (Abelson & Black, 1986; Walsh, 1995). Countries' regulations and government policies also tend to affect specific domains differently.

We used Kostova's (1997) approach as our foundation for exploring how and why levels of entrepreneurship vary by country. In this study, we developed and validated a measure of a country institutional profile for the domain of entrepreneurship. Following Kostova's lead, we articulated and measured regulatory, cognitive, and normative dimensions of countries' institutional profiles.

COUNTRY INSTITUTIONAL PROFILES FOR ENTREPRENEURSHIP

By providing a three-dimensional institutional profile, we clarify the distinct roles that the regulatory, cognitive, and normative dimensions play in determining levels of entrepreneurship across countries. Some previous research has muddied the distinctions between these dimensions by categorizing elements of all three as *culture*. Although there undoubtedly are connections among the three dimensions and relationships between elements of each dimension and the construct of culture, we follow Kostova (1997) and Scott (1995) in viewing the regulatory, cognitive, and normative dimensions as conceptually and empirically distinct.

The *regulatory dimension* of the institutional profile consists of laws, regulations, and government policies that provide support for new businesses, reduce the risks for individuals starting a new company, and facilitate entrepreneurs' efforts to acquire resources. Firms can leverage resources that are available through government-sponsored programs and enjoy privileges stemming from government policies that favor entrepreneurs (Rondinelli & Kasarda, 1992). For instance, the U.S. government provides advice and assistance for those starting new businesses and offers grants for new technology development in small enterprises. Several European governments provide small companies with financial assistance for exporting and trade development (Reynolds, 1997). Other government policies encourage individuals to make their own investments by allowing new firms to be legally incorporated with ease, or by protecting investors from the full extent of investment risk.

The *cognitive dimension* consists of the knowledge and skills possessed by the people in a country pertaining to establishing and operating a new business. Within countries, particular issues and knowledge sets become institutionalized, and certain information becomes a part of a shared social knowledge (Busenitz & Barney, 1997; Lau & Woodman, 1995). For instance, in some countries, knowledge about how to found a new business may be widely dispersed (Busenitz & Lau, 1996). In other countries, individuals may lack the knowledge necessary to understand even the most basic steps required to start and manage a new or small business.

The *normative dimension* measures the degree to which a country's residents admire entrepreneurial activity and value creative and innovative thinking. International entrepreneurship researchers have argued that a country's culture, values, beliefs, and norms affect the entrepreneurial orientation of its residents (Busenitz & Lau, 1996; Knight, 1997; Tiessen, 1997).

Although most popular measures of countries' normative environment depend on Hofstede's (1980) dimensions of culture, we concur with Kostova (1997) that it is imperative to develop a measure that is specific to the domain of entrepreneurship. For example, although a country's score on a measure of individualism may hold predictive power in countries where most entrepreneurship comes in the form of new high-technology start-ups, it may be inappropriate in places where most entrepreneurship consists of small, family-owned businesses. We believe that members of societies hold common values about entrepreneurial activities themselves. In some value systems, entrepreneurs are admired for their creativity and initiative (Casson, 1990), but in others they are not.

METHODS

Scale Development

To begin operationally defining the country institutional profile for entrepreneurship, we generated a large pool of items as potential measures for each of the three dimensions (DeVellis, 1991). For the regulatory dimension, ten items were generated that focused on government policies supporting new businesses, government regulations that affected new businesses, and indirect government support for entrepreneurs that came through other public institutions, such as universities. An extremely wide range of governmental institutions affect a country's business environment. However, many of these institutions affect various sectors of the economy differently. For instance, government support for high-technology research and government-sponsored industry consortia primarily benefit entrepreneurial firms within specific sectors. Furthermore, countries vary on the degree to which governments target this assistance toward specific firms and industries (Murtha & Lenway, 1994). The intent of the regulatory dimension here was to measure those institutional arrangements that are likely to affect the domain of entrepreneurship as a whole.

The cognitive items, numbering 11 in all, focused on the public's awareness of successful entrepreneurs and the public's knowledge about how to finance, structure, and manage new businesses. Finally, the normative questions, of which there were 15, focused on society's admiration for individuals who start their own businesses, the belief that innovative and creative thinking is good, and the belief that starting a business is an acceptable and respected career path.

We pretested the survey instrument with 257 U.S. undergraduate students from a large state university in the Southwest. Kaiser's eigenvalues-greater-than-one criterion and the scree plot indicated three to four factors. Both solutions were analyzed, and a three-factor solution obtained with

varimax rotation[1] was subsequently retained and used to identify items that did not load within their intended scale or discriminate clearly (DeVellis, 1991). Problematic items were analyzed one-by-one, and a decision was made to eliminate or rewrite each item. A second pretest with shorter scales was administered to a new sample of 108 undergraduate business students from the same university. Again, both the eigenvalues and the scree plot indicated three to four factors. The three-factor solution using a varimax rotation provided meaningful factors that reflected regulatory, cognitive, and normative dimensions. After we dropped items with loadings below .40 (DeVellis, 1991), Cronbach's alphas for the dimensions were .83, .72, and .69, respectively. The final survey instrument consisted of 17 items: 7 regulatory, 6 cognitive, and 4 normative.

We chose to validate the instrument with university students because using either entrepreneurs or corporate managers would have significantly biased our results, owing to their obvious career preferences. In contrast, business students have not yet chosen definitive career paths, represent a broad cross section of society, and have a deeper knowledge of relevant business issues than the general public. Accordingly, the survey was administered to business students in six countries: Germany, Italy, Norway, Spain, Sweden, and the United States. We selected these countries to ensure variance of both entrepreneurial activity and expected diversity within the three dimensions measured. We translated the survey to German, Italian, and Spanish using back-translation as recommended by Brislin (1980). We collected a total of 636 usable surveys in the six countries.[2] Most respondents (97%) were between 20 and 35 years old. Slightly more than half of the sample's members were men (53%).

We used structural equation modeling to perform a confirmatory factor analysis (CFA) on the country institutional profile measure. Since we are in the early stages of developing this construct, we considered it appropriate to perform a procedure of cross-validation that would allow us to test the fit of the full model against that of an alternative model. According to Bagozzi and Yi (1988), cross-validation procedures have a long history in both econometric and psychometric studies and have been adapted for use in structural equation model-

---

[1] A similar analysis was done using an oblique rotation, and results were largely the same.

[2] The breakdown by country was 112 surveys from Spain, 59 from Norway, 107 from Sweden, 92 from Germany, 100 from Italy, and 166 from the United States.

TABLE 1
Means, Standard Deviations, and Correlations for All Countries[a]

Variable	Mean	s.d.	1	2	3	4	5	6	7	8	9	10	11	12
1. Cognitive, 1	3.95	1 31												
2. Cognitive, 2	4 02	1.29	28											
3. Cognitive, 3	3 82	1 15	.29	52										
4. Cognitive, 4	3.98	1 33	28	.29	.41									
5. Normative, 1	4 96	1.47	17	19	08	15								
6. Normative, 2	5 13	1 48	13	13	17	.25	39							
7 Normative, 3	5.00	1.47	10	13	08	15	49	49						
8 Normative, 4	4 84	1 45	12	10	.07	12	.51	47	70					
9 Regulatory, 1	4.18	1.63	.23	08	13	11	19	12	17	15				
10. Regulatory, 2	3 81	1.37	.11	18	18	15	.22	14	15	28	32			
11 Regulatory, 3	4 34	1 39	09	.10	.13	10	14	05	.13	12	57	.25		
12 Regulatory, 4	4 23	1 28	07	.10	14	13	18	09	16	.19	.45	.38	.54	
13 Regulatory, 5	3 46	1.41	.13	.08	12	10	15	16	.14	13	40	.22	.40	.36

[a] $n = 636$, all correlations greater than 08 are statistically significant at $p < .05$ Correlation tables for each country are available from the authors

ing (Cudeck & Browne, 1983). We began by randomly splitting the total sample of 636 observations into halves. Half of the data sample, called a calibration sample, was used to identify items that did not load strongly[3] on the appropriate factor. The resulting model consisted of four cognitive items, four normative items, and five regulatory items.

We then followed the double cross-validation procedure (Bagozzi & Yi, 1988; Bentler, 1980). We first ran CFA on the calibration sample using both the full model (17 items) and the reduced model (13 items). We then tested the predictive effectiveness of the parameters calculated from the calibration sample on the remaining half of the data, called the validation sample. The reduced model showed a better fit to the validation sample (cross-validation fit index [CVFI] = 0.74), indicating that the reduced model was preferable to the full one (CVFI = 1.49). To verify these results, we performed a second cross-validation in which the second half of the data was used as the calibration sample and the first half was used as the validation sample. This analysis also showed that the reduced model (CVFI = 0.65) was better than the full model (CVFI = 1.62). Furthermore, even when the number of parameters in each model was taken into account, the reduced model continued to have a stronger fit (the first CVFI divided by number of parameters was .010 on the full model versus .008 on the reduced model; the second CVFI divided by the number of parameters was .011 on the full model versus .007 on the reduced model). Conducting the double cross-validation procedure greatly

reduced the likelihood of a respecification that capitalizes on chance (Bagozzi & Yi, 1988).

Scale Validation

The shortened scale, with four cognitive, four normative, and five regulatory items was retained, and a CFA was performed on the 636 responses from all six countries. Table 1 shows the means, standard deviations, and correlations between items for the six countries. In Table 2, the test for the difference in chi-square shows the superiority of a three-factor model over plausible two- and one-factor models. A one-factor model is plausible if the three subscales really reflect "culture" as an overarching construct. A two-factor model is plausible if the cognitive and normative dimensions are closely related, through values and norms both affecting mental schemas.

However, the three-factor model showed the best fit, meeting or exceeding the .90 threshold on a wide range of goodness-of-fit measures (GFI = .95, AGFI = .93, NFI = .91, NNFI = .92, CFI = .94, IFI = .94). No problems were found in residuals or standard errors. The distribution of residuals was symmetrically centered around zero. The average off-diagonal value was .04 and the largest off-diagonal value was .18, which reflected a good fit to the data. All parameter estimates were significant, with appropriate standard errors. Table 2 summarizes results from the CFA. Cronbach's alphas on the resulting scales were .76 for regulatory, .68 for cognitive, .81 for normative, and .78 for the overall country institutional profile.

One objective of this study was to test the equivalency of factor structures across the six countries.

---

[3] A conservative cutoff of .55 was used.

FIGURE 1
Confirmatory Factor Analysis Results

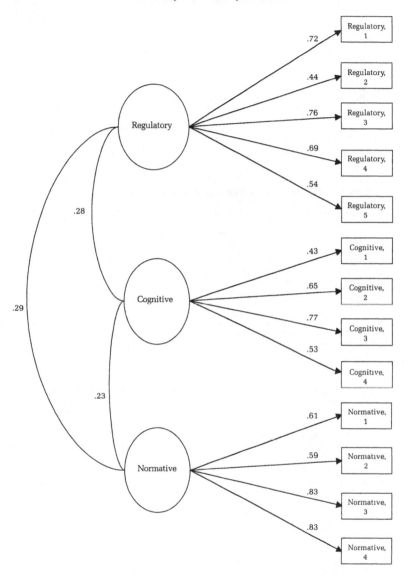

International Entrepreneurship

Busenitz, Gómez, and Spencer

TABLE 2
Summary of Confirmatory Factor Analyses[a]

Model	χ^2 (df)	$\Delta\chi^2$ (Δdf)	CFI	NFI	NNFI	RMSR	RMSEA	GFI	AGFI	IFI
Null	2,295.60 (78)**									
One-factor	1,171 31 (65)**	1,124.29 (13)**	50	.49	.40	.14	.16	.73	.62	.50
Two-factor	576.25 (64)**	595.06 (1)**	.77	.75	.72	10	.11	.86	.80	.77
Three-factor	206.59 (62)**	396.66 (2)**	.94	.91	.92	.05	.06	.95	.93	.94

[a] The chi-square test is a measure of the overall fit of a model to the data; an acceptable model is one in which the analysts fail to reject the null hypothesis. Note that when a sample is large, it is close to impossible to fail to reject the null hypothesis. The comparative fit index (CFI) examines the portion of total variance accounted for by a model and overcomes difficulties associated with sample size; .90 is considered an acceptable level. The normed fit index (NFI), nonnormed fit index (NNFI), and incremental fit index (IFI) are incremental fit indexes that measure the proportionate improvement in fit by comparing the model with a more restricted baseline model; .90 is considered an acceptable level. The root-mean-square residual (RMSR) is a standardized summary statistic for residuals; .05 is considered an acceptable level. The root-mean-square error of approximation (RMSEA) is a test of the null hypothesis of close fit; .05 indicates a very good fit, .05 to .08 indicates a fair to mediocre fit. Goodness of fit (GFI) is a global indication of how well a model fits the data; .90 is considered an acceptable level. The adjusted goodness-of-fit index (AGFI) is adjusted for model parsimony; 90 is considered an acceptable level.

** $p < .01$

TABLE 3
Means, Standard Deviations, Rankings, and Results of Analyses of Variance[a]

Country	Institutional Profile			Regulatory			Cognitive			Normative		
	Rank	Mean	s.d.	Rank	Mean	s.d.	Rank	Mean	s.d.	Rank	Mean	s.d.
United States	1	4.75[G, I, N, Sp, Sw]	0.61	2	4.32[G, I, Sp, Sw]	0.87	1	4.18[G, I, Sw]	0.92	1	5.86[G, I, Sp, N, Sw]	0.94
Sweden	2	4.40[G, I, Sp, US]	0.65	1	4.62[G, I, N, Sp, US]	0.75	4	3.89[US]	0 80	4	4.67[US]	1.02
Norway	3	4.24[G, I, Sp, US]	0.64	3	4.26[G, I, Sp, Sw]	0.77	2	3.96	0.97	6	4.47[US]	1.07
Spain	4	4.04[N, Sw, US]	0.64	4	3 61[N, Sw, US]	0.93	3	3.95	0.80	5	4.66[US]	1.03
Italy	5	3 98[N, Sw, US]	0.78	5	3 55[N, Sw, US]	1.18	5	3.76[US]	0 95	2	4.74[US]	1.14
Germany	5	3.98[N, Sw, US]	0.68	6	3.53[N, Sw, US]	0.96	5	3.76[US]	0.90	2	4.74[US]	1.14
F[b]		28 75***			28.00***			4 17***			32.56***	

[a] Superscripts indicate differences between country means significant at $p < .05$ I = Italy, G = Germany, N = Norway, Sp = Spain, Sw = Sweden, US = United States.

[b] For F-tests, df = 5, 630.

*** $p < .001$

A nonconstrained multisample model provided evidence that every item loaded on the appropriate factor in each country (CFI = .90), supporting the idea that the instrument is appropriate for use in countries outside the United States. To assess a greater degree of model equivalency, we performed a multisample analysis, constraining factor loadings to be the same across all six countries. The CFI for the fully constrained multisample analysis was marginally good at .87. A chi-square difference test, however, showed that the unconstrained model was a better fit ($\Delta\chi^2$ = 127.14, 65 df). The superiority of the unconstrained model led us to reject the hypothesis that all factor loadings were identical across all six countries. Interestingly, factor loadings were not significantly different within culturally homogeneous regions such as the Latin-European culture of Italy and Spain ($\Delta\chi^2$ = 18.70, 13 df) and the Scandinavian culture of Norway and Sweden ($\Delta\chi^2$ = 10.05, 13 df). Because all items

loaded on the appropriate factor in each of the six countries, we compared country rankings using the means of the items within each factor.[4]

External Validity

As is shown in Table 3, analyses of variance (ANOVAs) indicated country differences on scores for the overall profile as well as for the regulatory, cognitive, and normative subscales. Our sample size of six countries did not afford much statistical power. Even so, rank-order correlations provided evidence of convergent and predictive validity.

---

[4] Although this study compared the means of each factor across six countries, variations from the reported means may exist owing to different factor loadings by country.

Convergent validity. We assessed the convergent validity of each of the subscales using archival data on constructs that logically should be related to each dimension of our institutional profile. We compared our regulatory dimension to a survey question contained in a publication of the International Institute for Management Development (IMD, 1994) that asked chief executives and economic leaders to rate their country's fiscal policy on a ten-point scale ranging from "discourages" to "encourages" entrepreneurial activity. A Spearman rank-order correlation between our regulatory dimension and this external measure was positive ($\rho = .77$, $p < .07$).

We compared our cognitive dimension to two external sources. First, in countries in which a large percentage of residents pursue postsecondary education, knowledge about starting new businesses may be more prevalent. Second, entrepreneurs often start businesses in order to commercialize new products and innovations. Therefore, we would expect a relationship between our cognitive dimension and the percentages of a country's residents who pursue higher education and who are trained as scientists. We found that our cognitive dimension was positively associated with the prevalence of both higher education and scientific training, using data from both the IMD (1994) and UNESCO (United Nations Educational, Scientific, and Cultural Organization, 1995) ($\rho = .99$, $p < .01$ and $\rho = .52$, $p < .29$, respectively).

We compared our normative dimension to Hofstede's (1980) ranking of countries based on the degree of individualism in their cultures. Previous research has linked individualism and an entrepreneurial orientation (Mueller & Thomas, 1997). Our normative dimension correlated with this external measure positively ($\rho = .64$, $p < .17$). In sum, these comparisons indicate respectable correspondence between our measures of the regulatory, cognitive, and normative dimensions and relevant variables from independent sources.

Predictive validity. It was noted earlier that entrepreneurship can be defined and measured in different ways. Therefore, we considered two distinct measures of each country's level of entrepreneurship. The first reflects the percentage of companies within the country's electronics and advanced manufacturing sectors[5] that are small (0–19 employees) (European Commission, 1996).

The second reflects the percentage of the domestic companies on each country's stock exchange that were newly listed.[6]

Interestingly, our multiple dimensions of the institutional profile parallel the two different measures of entrepreneurship. Once again, owing to the very small sample size, the correlations only approach significance. Countries' rankings on the normative dimension relate to the ratio of small companies to total companies within their electronics and advanced manufacturing sectors ($\rho = .72$, $p < .17$). It appears that in countries where entrepreneurs are admired, people are more likely to attempt to start or manage entrepreneurial businesses. In contrast, the rankings of countries on the cognitive and regulatory dimensions relate to their rankings on the percentage of publicly traded companies that were newly listed ($\rho = .63$, $p < .18$ and $\rho = .81$, $p < .05$, respectively). It appears that it is the cognitive and regulatory environments that provide the skills and support necessary for firms to become successful enough to make initial public offerings. Hence, although the normative environment encourages people to become entrepreneurs, it takes a strong cognitive and regulatory environment for firms to obtain the resources and legitimacy necessary to obtain external investors.

DISCUSSION

In this study, we developed and empirically validated a survey instrument for measuring the institutional profile of entrepreneurship across six countries. The study makes three important contributions to the international entrepreneurship literature. First, although a country's culture may well affect its business systems, we concur with Kostova (1997) that the breadth of the concept of culture has led to overgeneralization in terms of both conceptual arguments and empirical results. A country institutional profile can serve as a viable alternative for exploring broad country differences. In this study, we developed such a measure for entrepreneurship and validated three distinct dimensions against external measures. This institutional approach moves beyond previous research to provide a more complete profile of country differences with respect to entrepreneurial activities.

Second, the study highlights the usefulness of understanding the distinctions among the dimensions of a country's institutional profile. Table 3 shows that countries' scores are rarely consistent across all three

---

[5] We believe that firms in these sectors are the most innovative. Note that data were only available for the European countries.

[6] We averaged the 1996 and 1997 percentages to take into account the cyclical nature of new firm listings.

dimensions. For example, Italy occupies the lowest rank on the cognitive dimension and the second-lowest rank on the regulatory dimension yet scores second-highest on the normative dimension. In the future, policy makers could assess their own country's scores on each dimension and devise strategies for improving their domestic institutional environments for entrepreneurship.

Third, given that the three dimensions of the institutional profile appear to relate to different aspects of entrepreneurship across countries, the institutional profile provides the opportunity to evaluate the source of each country's strengths and weaknesses more precisely. The scales may help researchers understand why some countries tend to maintain an advantage in new business development within a particular industry (Storey, 1994) or with a specific organizational form. For example, small family businesses may enjoy a great deal of success in countries with a certain profile, but technology firms devising strategies for moving toward initial public offerings may succeed in countries with a different profile. An understanding of a country's institutional profile may help globally focused entrepreneurs start firms that have international missions from their inception (Oviatt & McDougall, 1994), by identifying obstacles they may need to overcome before they expand into new countries (Rondinelli & Kasarda, 1992). In future inquiry, researchers should probe whether country profiles motivate particular forms of cooperation (Casson, 1990), modes of entry, or types of organizational structures.

Our instrument was conceived as a broad measure of countries' institutional profiles. Nevertheless, future researchers might use single dimensions of our instrument to enrich more targeted studies of specific determinants of entrepreneurship across countries. For example, scholars attempting to thoroughly understand countries' regulatory environments for entrepreneurship might couple the regulatory dimension of this instrument with other, more specific, regulatory measures, such as fiscal policies toward entrepreneurs, bankruptcy laws, and national policies toward innovation.

The modest fit obtained in the multisample analysis and the evidence for inequality among factor loadings across countries reflects the difficulty inherent in developing etic measures. Future research should clarify which scales (such as country institutional profiles) need to be generalizable across countries and what level of equivalency across samples is required to conclude that a scale is etic. In addition, future larger-scale studies might adjust the means comparisons on the basis of variations in the factor structure by country. Potential further development of the country profiles for en-

trepreneurship should be performed as future researchers apply the instrument to other countries.

Although this study focused on industrialized Western countries with relatively small differences on each of the three dimensions, we believe future research should apply the profile to other countries. The restricted range of variation here, although providing a conservative test, likely made it more difficult to expose interesting relationships between the three dimensions and other variables.

In sum, the scales developed in this study can improve both the empirical and theoretical rigor of international entrepreneurship research. The scales underlying our country institutional profile have good reliability, strong discriminant validity, adequate cross-cultural validity, and reasonable external validity. This institutional profile should provide a useful tool with which researchers can explore a variety of issues regarding cross-national differences in entrepreneurship.

REFERENCES

Abelson, R., & Black, J. 1986. Introduction. In J. Galambos, R. Abelson, & J. Black (Eds.), *Knowledge structures:* 1–18. Hillsdale, NJ: Erlbaum.

Acs, Z. J. 1992. Small business economics: A global perspective. *Challenge*, 35(6): 38–44.

Aronson, R. L. 1991. *Self-employment: A labor market perspective.* Ithaca, NY: ILR Press.

Bagozzi, R. P., & Yi, Y. 1988. On the evaluation of structural equation models. *Journal of the Academy of Marketing Science*, 16(1): 74–94.

Bartholomew, S. 1997. National systems of biotechnology innovation: Complex interdependence in the global system. *Journal of International Business Studies*, 28: 241–266.

Bentler, P. M. 1980. *Causal models in marketing.* New York: Wiley.

Brislin, R. W. 1980. Translation and content analysis of oral and written materials. In H. C. Triandis & J. W. Berry (Eds.), *Handbook of cross-cultural psychology:* 389–444. Boston· Allyn & Bacon.

Busenitz, L. W , & Barney, J. B. 1997. Biases and heuristics in strategic decision making: Differences between entrepreneurs and managers in large organizations. *Journal of Business Venturing*, 12: 9–30.

Busenitz, L. W., & Lau, C. M. 1996. A cross-cultural cognitive model of new venture creation. *Entrepreneurship Theory and Practice*, 20(4): 25–39.

Casson, M. 1990. *Enterprise and competitiveness.* New York: Oxford University Press.

Chow, C. K. W., & Fung, M. K. Y. 1996. Firm dynamics and industrialization in the Chinese economy in transition: Implications for small business policy. *Journal of Business Venturing*, 11: 489–505.

Cudeck, R. & Browne, M. W. 1983. Cross-validation of covariance structures. *Multivariate Behavioral Research*, 20: 147–167.

DeVellis, R. F. 1991. *Scale development: Theory and applications.* Newbury Park, CA: Sage.

European Network for SME Research (ENSR). 1996. *The European observatory for SMEs* (4th annual report). Zoetermeer, The Netherlands: ENSR.

European Commission. 1996. *Enterprises in Europe* (4th report). Luxembourg: Office for Official Publications of the European Communities.

Hofstede, G. 1980. *Culture's consequences: International differences in work-related values.* Beverly Hills, CA: Sage.

International Institute for Management Development (IMD). 1994. *The world competitiveness report* (14th ed.). Geneva: World Economic Forum.

Knight, G. A. 1997. Cross-cultural reliability and validity of a scale to measure firm entrepreneurial orientation. *Journal of Business Venturing*, 12: 213–225.

Kostova, T. 1997. Country institutional profiles: Concept and measurement. *Academy of Management Best Paper Proceedings*: 180–189.

Lau, C. M., & Woodman, R. W. 1995. Understanding organizational change: A schematic perspective. *Academy of Management Journal*, 38: 537–554.

Mueller, S. L., & Thomas, A. S. 1997. *National culture and entrepreneurial orientation: A nine-country study.* Paper presented at the annual meeting of the Academy of Management, Boston.

Murtha, T. P., & Lenway, S. A. 1994. Country capabilities and the strategic state: How national political institutions affect multinational corporations' strategies. *Strategic Management Journal*, 15(summer special issue): 113–129.

Nelson, R. R. 1982. *Government and technical progress: A cross-industry analysis.* New York: Pergamon.

Nelson, R. R. 1993. A retrospective. In R. Nelson (Ed.), *National innovation systems:* 505–524. New York: Oxford University Press.

Oviatt, B., & McDougall, P. P. 1994. Toward a theory of international new ventures. *Journal of International Business Studies*, 25: 45–64.

Reynolds, P. D. 1997. New and small firms in expanding markets. *Small Business Economics*, 9: 79–84.

Rondinelli, D. A., & Kasarda, J. D. 1992. Foreign trade potential, small enterprise development and job creation in developing countries. *Small Business Economics*, 4: 253–265.

Schumpeter, J. A. 1934. *The theory of economic development.* Cambridge, MA: Harvard University Press.

Scott, R. 1995. *Institutions and organizations.* Thousand Oaks, CA: Sage.

Storey, D. J. 1994. *Understanding the small business sector.* London: Routledge.

Tiessen, J. H. 1997. Individualism, collectivism, and entrepreneurship: A framework for international comparative research. *Journal of Business Venturing*, 12: 367–384.

United Nations Educational, Scientific, and Cultural Organization. (UNESCO). 1995. *Selected statistics on education.* New York: UNESCO.

Walsh, J. 1995. Managerial and organizational cognition: Notes from a trip down memory lane. *Organization Science*, 6: 280–321.

APPENDIX

Country Institutional Profiles

Respondents were given the following instructions: "Think of the country in which you live and tell us the extent to which you agree with the following statements" (1 = strongly disagree, 2 = disagree, 3 = disagree somewhat, 4 = neutral, 5 = agree somewhat, 6 = agree, and 7 = strongly agree). The name of the variable used in analyses is in parentheses after the appropriate item.

Regulatory Dimension
1. Government organizations in this country assist individuals with starting their own business. (regulatory, 1)
2. The government sets aside government contracts for new and small businesses. (regulatory, 2)
3. Local and national governments have special support available for individuals who want to start a new business. (regulatory, 3)
4. The government sponsors organizations that help new businesses develop. (regulatory, 4)
5. Even after failing in an earlier business, the government assists entrepreneurs in starting again. (regulatory, 5)

Cognitive Dimension
6. Individuals know how to legally protect a new business. (cognitive, 1)
7. Those who start new businesses know how to deal with much risk. (cognitive, 2)
8. Those who start new businesses know how to manage risk. (cognitive, 3)
9. Most people know where to find information about markets for their products. (cognitive, 4)

Normative Dimension
10. Turning new ideas into businesses is an admired career path in this country. (normative, 1)
11. In this country, innovative and creative thinking is viewed as the route to success. (normative, 2)
12. Entrepreneurs are admired in this country. (normative, 3)
13. People in this country tend to greatly admire those who start their own business. (normative, 4)

Lowell W. Busenitz is currently an associate professor of management in the Price College of Business at the University of Oklahoma He received his Ph D from Texas A&M University His research interests include strategic decision making, international entrepreneurship, and venture capitalist/entrepreneur relationships.

Carolina Gómez received her Ph D. from the University of North Carolina at Chapel Hill and is currently an assistant professor of management at Towson University.

Her current research focuses on cross-cultural organizational behavior and the application of institutional theory to the management of multinational enterprises.

Jennifer W. Spencer received her Ph.D. from the University of Minnesota and is currently an assistant professor of international business at George Washington University. Her current research interests include firms' innovation strategies in emerging industries and cross-national differences in firms' institutional environments.

[29]

CULTURE AND ENTREPRENEURIAL POTENTIAL: A NINE COUNTRY STUDY OF LOCUS OF CONTROL AND INNOVATIVENESS

STEPHEN L. MUELLER
Florida International University, Miami, FL

ANISYA S. THOMAS
Florida International University, and Stockholm School of Economics, Stockholm, Sweden

EXECUTIVE SUMMARY

Entrepreneurship research has identified a number of personal characteristics believed to be instrumental in motivating entrepreneurial behavior. Two frequently cited personal traits associated with entrepreneurial potential are internal locus of control and innovativeness. Internal locus of control has been one of the most studied psychological traits in entrepreneurship research, while innovative activity is explicit in Schumpeter's description of the entrepreneur. Entrepreneurial traits have been studied extensively in the United States. However, cross-cultural studies and studies in non-U.S. contexts are rare and in most cases limited to comparisons between one or two countries or cultures. Thus the question is raised: do entrepreneurial traits vary systematically across cultures and if so, why?

Culture, as the underlying system of values peculiar to a specific group or society, shapes the development of certain personality traits and motivates individuals in a society to engage in behaviors that may not be evident in other societies. Hofstede's (1980) extensive culture study, leading to the development of four culture dimensions, provide a clear articulation of differences between countries in values, beliefs,

Address correspondence to Professor Stephen L. Mueller, Assistant Professor, Florida International University, College of Business Administration. Department of Management and International Business, Miami, FL 33199; Phone: (305) 348-4219; Fax: (305) 348-3278; E-Mail: Muellers@fiu.edu

An earlier version of this paper was presented at the National Academy of Management Meeting in Boston on August 12, 1997. The authors gratefully acknowledge the contributions of Professor Jan Luytjes who was instrumental in initiating the cross-national collaborative team that gathered the data used in the project. We are also grateful to our collaborators in the various countries whose effort and cooperation were essential to the completion of this study.

Journal of Business Venturing **16**, 51–75
0883-9026/01/$–see front matter
PII S0883-9026(99)00039-7

52 S.L. MUELLER AND A.S. THOMAS

and work roles. Although Hofstede did not specify the relationship between culture and entrepreneurial activity per se, his culture dimensions are useful in identifying key aspects of culture related to the potential for entrepreneurial behavior.

In this paper we offer several hypotheses about the relationship between two of Hofstede's culture dimensions and psychological traits associated with entrepreneurial potential. We expect that an internal locus of control orientation is more prevalent in individualistic cultures than in collectivistic cultures. Likewise, we expect that an innovative orientation is more prevalent in low uncertainty avoidance cultures than in high uncertainty avoidance cultures. However, since neither internal locus of control nor innovativeness alone is sufficient to explain entrepreneurial motivation, we also hypothesize that individuals with both an internal locus of control and innovative orientation should appear more frequently in highly individualistic and low uncertainty cultures.

These hypotheses were tested on a sample of over 1,800 responses to a survey of third- and fourth-year students at universities in nine countries. Eighteen items in the survey instrument were used to construct scales for innovativeness and locus of control. Items for the innovativeness scale were adapted from the Jackson Personality Inventory while items used for the locus of control scale were adapted from Rotter's I-E scale.

The results of this exploratory study support the proposition that some cultures are more conducive for entrepreneurship than others. In individualistic cultures we found an increased likelihood of an internal locus of control orientation. There was also support for the hypothesis that an entrepreneurial orientation, defined as internal locus of control combined with innovativeness, is more likely in individualistic, low uncertainty avoidance cultures than in collectivistic, high uncertainty avoidance cultures.

Culture, it appears, may condition potential for entrepreneurship, generating differences across national and regional boundaries. One tentative conclusion is that a "supportive" national culture will, ceteris paribus, increase the entrepreneurial potential of a country. This suggests that in addition to support from political, social, and business leaders, there needs to be a supportive culture to cultivate the mind and character of the potential entrepreneur. To be motivated to act, potential entrepreneurs must perceive themselves as capable and psychologically equipped to face the challenges of a global, competitive marketplace. Business education can play an important role in this regard by providing not only the technical tools (i.e. accounting, marketing, finance, etc.), but by also helping to reorient individuals toward self reliance, independent action, creativity, and flexible thinking.

This study examines only two entrepreneurial traits (innovativeness and internal locus of control) and only one of the many contextual factors (culture) which may explain differences among countries in the rate of new venture formation. Future research should expand this investigation to include other traits associated with entrepreneurial behavior as well as the effect of other contextual factors such as education system, political economy, and stage of economic development.   © 2000 Elsevier Science Inc.

INTRODUCTION

With diminished political and economic barriers between countries and the globalization of business activities, the process of new venture formation has become an increasingly relevant and interesting area for research. The renewed interest in entrepreneurship by government policy makers and business leaders worldwide has been prompted by several factors. In advanced industrialized countries, particularly the United States, increased entrepreneurial activity is seen as a means to revitalize stagnating industries and provide new jobs to compensate for employment problems created by corporate restructuring and downsizing (Birley 1986; Birch 1979). Furthermore, entrepreneurship, touted by economists in the Schumpeterian tradition for over a century, has been rediscovered as a potential catalyst for technological progress (Schumpeter 1934; Hagen 1962; Kilby 1971; Baumol 1986). Today, entrepreneurial ventures are often seen as incubators for product and market innovation (Reynolds 1987).

In less developed countries, the encouragement of entrepreneurial activities is recommended as a way to stimulate economic growth (Harper 1991). Consequently, national incentive and education programs designed to stimulate new venture development have been instituted by the governments of a large number of Asian and Latin American countries as well as in the transition economies of Central and Eastern Europe (Audretsch 1991; Gibb 1993).

Despite the apparent universal appeal of entrepreneurship as a prescription for economic growth and development, many questions about new venture formation in non-U.S. contexts remain unanswered. For example, there is a question as to whether many of the human motivation and performance theories underlying the entrepreneurship field, developed primarily by North American researchers in a North American context, are generalizable to countries with distinctly different cultural, social, and economic climates (Adler 1991; Boyacigiller and Adler 1991; Thomas, Shenkar, and Clarke 1994). Such questions can only be answered through cross-cultural, cross-contextual research. However, with a few exceptions (Shane 1992, 1993; McGrath, MacMillan, and Scheinberg 1992; Huisman 1985; Baum et al. 1993), international comparative studies of entrepreneurship are rare, hampered by barriers such as difficulty in gaining access to entrepreneurs in other countries, high expense, and lack of reliable secondary data.

In spite of these limitations, entrepreneurship research has been instrumental in clarifying and articulating many of the key contextual factors necessary to encourage entrepreneurial activity (Pennings 1980; Bruno and Tyebjee 1982). However, a separate but equally important question has not been addressed: At a national or regional level, is there an adequate supply of prospective entrepreneurs? That is, are there sufficient numbers of individuals with the requisite personal attitudes, aptitudes, values, perceptions, and ambitions to exploit opportunities and initiate business ventures? If not, then programs designed to encourage entrepreneurial activity within a given country or region may fall short of achieving the desired results.

In this paper, we investigate the relationship between national culture and two personal characteristics commonly associated with entrepreneurial potential: internal locus of control and innovativeness. Building on both cross-cultural management and entrepreneurship research, we develop and test hypotheses linking national culture to entrepreneurial traits using an international sample of nine countries. The results of this study provide the basis for assessing cross-national differences in potential for entrepreneurial activity. Implications for future cross-cultural research in entrepreneurship are also discussed.

MOTIVATING NEW VENTURE FORMATION

The connection between entrepreneurs and new venture formation is well established. Many authoritative definitions of *entrepreneur* actually include some reference to venture or enterprise creation. For example, Bygrave and Hofer (1991) define an entrepreneur as ". . . someone who perceives an opportunity and creates an organization to pursue it" (Bygrave and Hofer 1991, p. 14). In formulating national policy recommendations, Vesper defines entrepreneurship as "the creation of new independent businesses" (Vesper 1983, p. 1).

Although theoretical models of the new venture creation process differ in the assumptions and variables they encompass, they include common elements as well. Shapero (1975) for example, sees the prospective entrepreneur's readiness to act as deter-

54 S.L. MUELLER AND A.S. THOMAS

mined jointly by prior experience and the perception of current opportunities. According to Shapero, general readiness becomes a predisposition to initiate a venture when the individual experiences a precipitating event such as a layoff. However, this predisposition turns to action only when the individual perceives a suitable opportunity and can assemble the financial and other required resources from a supportive environment (Shapero 1975; Shapero and Sokol 1982; Krueger 1993; Martin 1984). Gartner (1985) defines the creation of a new venture as an interaction among four dimensions: personal characteristics of the entrepreneur (individual), competitive entry strategies (organization), push and pull factors (environment), and the actions taken by the entrepreneur to bring the enterprise into existence (process). Shapero and Sokol (1982) describe the entrepreneurial venture formation process as a life path change in which situational factors such as negative displacement (e.g., job termination), along with a positive pull from a partner, mentor, or customer, combined with a perception that entrepreneurship is both desirable and feasible, leads to the initiation of a new venture.

These and other venture creation process frameworks (e.g., Moore 1986; Krueger and Brazeal 1994), implicitly or explicitly suggest that the rate of new venture formation is contingent upon not only the economic, social, and political climate which facilitates and supports entrepreneurial activity, but also the availability of individuals predisposed to initiate new ventures.

Entrepreneurial Potential

In describing entrepreneurs, Joseph Schumpeter noted that these were the individuals who attempted to ". . . reform or revolutionize the pattern of production by exploiting an invention . . . or untried technical possibility for producing a new commodity or producing an old one in a new way . . . [This] requires aptitudes that are present in only a small fraction of the population . . ." (Schumpeter 1934, p. 132).

Schumpeter's observation suggests that in addition to an entrepreneurial climate, the creation of new ventures and entrepreneurial activity depends upon the availability of prospective entrepreneurs, i.e. individuals possessing personality traits combined with personal circumstances which are likely to lead them to forming a new venture.

Motivations for becoming an entrepreneur have generally been categorized as either push/pull situational factors or personal characteristics. Research has shown that new venture initiation often occurs as a result of situational pushes or pulls that include frustration with present life-style, childhood, family environment, education, age, work history, role models, and support networks (Hisrich 1990; Martin 1984; Moore 1986; Krueger 1993; Scheinberg and MacMillan 1988). Some individuals are *pushed* into entrepreneurship by negative factors such as dissatisfaction with existing employment, loss of employment, and career setbacks. A number of empirical studies support this view and characterize entrepreneurs as misfits, rejects from society, or displaced individuals (Brockhaus 1980; Shapero 1975; Kets de Vries 1977; Gilad and Levine 1986). Alternatively, individuals may be *pulled* into entrepreneurship by positive factors such as early training and exposure to business which encourages the search for business opportunities (Krueger 1993; Mancuso 1973; Gilad and Levine 1986; Scheinberg and MacMillan 1988).

In addition to push and pull factors, personal characteristics (sometimes referred to as *personality traits*) also play a role in new venture initiation. Beginning with McClelland (1961), there has been a stream of entrepreneurship research which focuses on the personal characteristics of the *actor* instead of the *act* of new venture creation. McClelland (1961) asserted that qualities associated with a high need for achievement, namely preferences for challenge, acceptance of personal responsibility for outcomes, and innovativeness, are defining characteristics of successful initiators of new businesses. McClelland's work spurred a number of entrepreneurial *traits* studies to identify those characteristics which not only motivate individuals to initiate new ventures, but also contribute to venture success (Dunkelberg and Cooper 1982; Hornaday and Aboud 1971; Timmons 1978). Despite recent criticism of the traits approach (e.g., Brockhaus and Horwitz 1986; Carsrud, Olm, and Eddy 1986; Gartner 1988), there is a continued interest in determining what motivates some individuals to initiate a venture while others do not (Carland, Hoy, Boulton, and Carland 1984; Carland, Hoy, and Carland 1988; McClelland 1987; Solomon and Winslow 1988; Winslow and Solomon 1989). Furthermore, a number of recent empirical studies suggest that entrepreneurs can be distinguished from the general population on the basis of motivation (Spangler 1992; Johnson 1990), values (McGrath et al. 1992), and attitudes (Robinson, Stimpson, Huefner, and Hunt 1991).

Several theorists have argued that some personal characteristics or traits define the entrepreneur and are instrumental in motivating entrepreneurial behavior. Hisrich, in summarizing research on entrepreneurial behavior, notes that the entrepreneur is someone who demonstrates initiative and creative thinking, is able to organize social and economic mechanisms to turn resources and situations to practical account, and accepts risk and failure (Hisrich 1990). McClelland offers a similar set of defining traits to explain entrepreneurial behavior. These traits are high need for achievement, moderate risk-taking propensity, preference for energetic and/or novel activity, and assuming personal responsibility for successes or failure (McClelland 1961). Begley and Boyd found that entrepreneurs (founders) scored significantly higher than small business managers (non-founders) in need for achievement, risk-taking propensity, and tolerance of ambiguity (Begley and Boyd 1987). Brockhaus reviewed a number of trait studies and identified three consistent attributes associated with entrepreneurial behavior: need for achievement, internal locus of control, and a risk-taking propensity (Brockhaus 1982). In this paper we examine two frequently cited personal traits associated with entrepreneurial potential, namely internal locus of control and innovativeness.

Internal Locus of Control

Although the search for the Heffalump (Kilby 1971) continues with no consensus on a clear, universally acceptable definition of the entrepreneur (Perry 1990), there is at least some general agreement that the entrepreneur, however defined, is a self-motivated individual who takes the initiative to start and build an enterprise relying primarily on self rather than others to formulate and implement his or her goals. Personal attributes such as independence, need for control, self reliance, confidence, initiative, and resourcefulness have been frequently cited as closely associated with entrepreneurial values and behavior (McClelland 1987; Hornaday and Aboud 1971; Solomon and Winslow 1988; Timmons 1978).

In psychology research, there is a long tradition of research related to perceived control and its effects on human behavior in various situations (Strickland 1989). Rotter (1966) made a significant contribution to this tradition with the development of a "locus of control" construct. According to Rotter, an individual perceives the outcome of an

56 S.L. MUELLER AND A.S. THOMAS

event as being either within or beyond his or her personal control and understanding. An "internal" believes that one has influence over outcomes through ability, effort, or skills. On the other hand, "externals" believe that forces outside the control of the individual determine outcomes (Rotter 1966).

Rotter's locus of control construct and later adaptations and refinements of his original I-E scale (Levenson 1974) have been widely used in studies related to organizational and managerial issues (Durant and Nord 1976; Kets de Vries 1977; Spector 1982; Jennings 1983). Not surprisingly, internal locus of control has also been one of the most studied psychological traits in entrepreneurship research (Perry 1990). An association between entrepreneurial behavior and an internal locus of control orientation has strong face validity. Entrepreneurs by most definitions are initiators, taking responsibility for their own welfare and not dependent on others (McClelland 1961). Furthermore, if one does not believe that the outcome of a business venture will be influenced by personal effort, then that individual is unlikely to risk exposure to the high penalties of failure. Since perception of both risk and ability to affect results are crucial to the new venture formation decision, it follows that prospective entrepreneurs are more likely to have an internal locus of control origination than an external one (Brockhaus 1982; Brockhaus and Horowitz 1986).

The identification of internal locus of control as a possible entrepreneurial trait spurred numerous empirical studies. Early studies during the 1970s showed generally positive findings (Jennings 1983). For example, Borland found in a sample of 375 business-school students that those students who expected to start a company someday had a stronger belief in internal control (Borland 1974). Brockhaus found that business students with entrepreneurial intentions tended to have an higher internal locus of control than those who did not have such intentions (Brockhaus 1975). Shapero administered Rotter's I-E questionnaire to 134 Texan and Italian entrepreneurs and found that they scored significantly more internal than other groups tested (Shapero 1975). In a similar study, Pandey and Tewary (1979) found entrepreneurs to score higher on internal locus of control measures.

Investigation of the locus of control construct and entrepreneurs continued into the 1980s with mixed results (Ahmed 1985; Begley and Boyd 1987; Brockhaus 1980; Cromie and Johns 1983; Venkatapathy 1984). In most of these studies, locus of control was assessed with Rotter's (1966) I-E scale. One possible explanation for inconclusive results is that as more recent locus of control researchers have shown (e.g., Collins 1974; Levenson 1974; Lefcourt 1981; Paulhus 1983), the original Rotter measure is multidimensional and not all of its dimensions appear to be equally plausible predictors of entrepreneurial behavior (Shaver and Scott 1991; Gatewood, Shaver, and Gartner 1995). More recent empirical studies using multidimensional measures of locus of control, however, generally support the claim that entrepreneurs are more internal than non-entrepreneurs. For example, Bonnett and Furnham (1991) used a three-dimensional (internal, external, and chance) economic locus of control scale and found a group of student entrepreneurs to be more internal than a control group. Similarly, Levin and Leginsky (1990) used Levenson's (1974) IPC scale and found that entrepreneurial social workers tended to exhibit a greater internal locus of control than the general population.

An internal locus of control orientation can also been viewed as a prerequisite for action. Shapero (1982) and Krueger (1993) proposed that *propensity to act*, a disposition to act upon one's decisions, is an essential element of the new venture initiation process. They argue that an individual who perceives an entrepreneurial opportunity to be both desirable and feasible may not actually initiate a new venture unless the individual is predisposed psychologically to actually act upon his or her decision (Shapero 1975; Krueger 1993; Krueger and Brazeal 1994). Furthermore, according to Shapero, the propensity to act on an opportunity depends on one's perception of control (Shapero 1975). Thus conceptually at least, an internal locus of control orientation (ILOC) increases the likelihood that a potential entrepreneur will take action to carry out his/her plans.

Innovativeness

Innovation is the "... process that turns an invention ... into a marketable product" (Gabor 1970). Innovation is therefore more than invention; it also involves the commercialization of ideas, implementation, and the modification of existing products, systems and resources (Bird 1989, p. 39).

Innovative activity is explicit in Schumpeter's description of the entrepreneur. Schumpeter (1934) defined the role of the entrepreneur as a catalyst of change, seeing the entrepreneur as "... an idea man and a man of action ... instrumental in discovering new opportunities" (Schumpeter 1965). Drucker further elaborated the innovator role of the entrepreneur and described innovation as "the specific tool of entrepreneurs ... [and] ... the means by which they exploit change ..." (Drucker 1985). In differentiating the entrepreneur from the small business owner, Carland, Hoy, Boulton, and Carland (1984) argue that innovative strategic practices are necessary for new ventures to be profitable and grow. In making this distinction, they define the entrepreneur as "... an individual who establishes and manages a business for the principal purposes of profit and growth ... [and] ... is characterized principally by innovative behavior ..." (Carland et al. 1984, p. 358).

Assigning the role of innovator to the entrepreneur implies that successful entrepreneurs adopt and implement competitive strategies such as introducing new products and services, new methods of production, opening new markets or sources of supply, or even reorganizing an entire industry (Bird 1989; Carland et al. 1984). However, prior to implementation, the potential entrepreneur must be able to effectively formulate such strategies suggesting the possession of personal characteristics which reflect creativity and innovativeness.

There appears to be strong empirical evidence to support the claim that entrepreneurs, particularly those successful at growing an enterprise, are more innovative than non-entrepreneurs. For example, research by Sexton and Bowman-Upton (1986) shows that entrepreneurship students tend to be more innovative than other business administration students. Carland, Carland, Hoy, and Boulton (1988) found that entrepreneurs who establish and manage a business for the principal purposes of profit and growth have a higher preference for innovation than other small business owners. Carland and Carland (1991) found that both male and female entrepreneurs have significantly higher levels of innovative preference than their managerial counterparts. Buttner and Gryskiewicz (1993) found entrepreneurs scored higher on Kirton's adaption-innovation scale (Kirton 1976) than general managers of large organizations. Also using Kirton's adaption-innovation scale, Goldsmith and Kerr (1991) found that entrepreneurship students were more innovative than other business students. Smith and Miner (1985) found that founders of fast-growing firms scored significantly higher in personal innovation than individuals holding managerial positions. Tuunanen and Hyrsky (1997) found that in both Finnish and American samples of business owners, those who report their primary objectives to be profit and growth scored higher on Jackson's innovativeness measure than did those reporting family income as their primary goal. Furthermore, for the American sample at least, founders scored higher than non-founders. (Tuunanen and Hyrsky 1997).

Other studies have shown that innovation is a primary motive to start a business. For example, Shane, Kolvereid, and Westhead (1991) report that the opportunity to innovative and be in the forefront of new technology was frequently given as a reason for starting a business. The opportunity to innovate is also frequently cited in international studies as a motive for starting an enterprise (Scheinberg and MacMillan 1988; Blaise, Toulouse, and Clement 1990).

It is apparent from these and other studies that entrepreneurial traits, particularly locus of control, have been studied extensively in the United States. However, cross-cultural studies of entrepreneurial traits and studies in non-U.S. contexts are rare and in most cases limited to comparisons between one or two countries or cultures (e.g., McGrath, MacMillan, and Scheinberg 1992; Tuunanen 1997; Koiranen, Hyrsky, and Tuunanen 1997; Tuunanen and Hyrsky 1997). In the cases of locus of control and innovativeness, to our knowledge there have been no comprehensive investigations to determine whether these particular traits vary across a wide spectrum of cultures. The question remains: do entrepreneurial traits vary systematically across cultures and if so why? Furthermore, if differences across culture do exist, what are the new venture formation implications? In the following section we examine the role of culture in the development of entrepreneurial values and formulate hypotheses relating national culture to the prevalence of individuals with internal locus of control and innovative orientations.

CULTURE AND ENTREPRENEURIAL TRAITS

Barnouw (1979) defines culture as ". . . the configuration of . . . stereotyped patterns of *learned behavior* which are handed down from one generation to the next through the means of language and imitation . . ." (p. 5). Kroeber and Parson's (1958, p. 583) earlier cross-disciplinary definition of culture included ". . . patterns of *values*, ideas, and other symbolic-meaningful systems as factors in the shaping of *human behavior* . . ." Hofstede (1980) refers to culture as "the collective programming of the mind which distinguishes the members of one human group from another . . . [and] includes systems of *values*" (p. 25).

Values and norms are powerful forces for controlling and directing human behavior. Erez and Earley (1993) note that culture shapes the cognitive schema which ascribe meaning and values to motivational variables and guide choices, commitments, and standards of behavior. Further, since values are typically determined early in life (Hofstede 1980; Barnouw 1979), they tend to be "programmed" into individuals resulting in behavior patterns which are consistent with the cultural context and endure over time (Hofstede 1980).

Thus culture, as the underlying system of values peculiar to a specific group or society, shapes the development of certain personality traits and motivates individuals in a society to engage in behaviors that may not be as prevalent in other societies. Entrepreneurial activity (i.e., new venture creation) may be one of these behaviors which varies across countries due to differences in cultural values and beliefs. Clearly many factors underlying entrepreneurial behavior are common across cultures (e.g., economic incentives can motivate action in all cultures). However, since culture reinforces certain personal characteristics and penalizes others, we would expect some cultures to be more closely aligned with an entrepreneurial orientation than others. Huisman (1985) for example noted wide variance in entrepreneurial activity across cultures and concluded that cultural values influence entrepreneurial behavior. McGrath et al. (1992) reached a similar conclusion in a 10-country study of entrepreneurs and non-entrepreneurs. They found that entrepreneurs differed significantly from their career professional counterpart in culture-based values and beliefs such as "Success is owning your own company," "Rewards should be based on merit," and "Equality is everyone's right." (McGrath et al. 1992, p. 126).

Dimensions of Culture

Using the results of his 40-country study of 88,000 employees and managers of a single U.S. multinational (IBM), Geert Hofstede (1980) constructed four distinct dimensions of culture as an underlying framework to identify and explain differences in cultural patterns observed across countries. Hofstede's power distance, uncertainty avoidance, individualism and masculinity dimensions define a specific set of values which describe some aspect of culture and human activities. Although Hofstede did not specify the relationship between culture and entrepreneurial activity per se, his culture dimensions are useful in identifying the key elements of culture related to entrepreneurial orientation.

In the following sections, we examine two of Hofstede's culture dimensions, individualism and uncertainty avoidance, and offer hypotheses linking these dimensions to the prevalence of individuals exhibiting innovativeness and internal locus of control orientations.

Individualism

Individualism pertains to societies in which social ties and commitments are loose. Everyone is expected to look after himself or herself and the immediate family. *Collectivism*, at the opposite pole from individualism, pertains to societies in which people from birth onwards are integrated into strong, cohesive ingroups which throughout a lifetime continue to protect them in exchange for unquestioning loyalty (Hofstede 1991, p. 51).

In individualistic cultures, social identity is based on individual contribution. Basic social values emphasize personal initiative and achievement. Autonomy, variety, pleasure, and personal financial security take precedent over group loyalty. As a result, in highly individualistic countries, there is greater employment mobility since individuals are expected to look after their own interests (Hofstede 1980, p. 235).

In collectivistic cultures, people are born into extended families or clans which protect them in exchange for loyalty. Social identity is based on group membership. There is greater emphasis on belonging vis-à-vis personal initiative. Thus individual initiative is not highly valued and deviance in opinion or behavior is typically punished. In collectivistic cultures, group decisions are considered to be superior to individual decisions. (Hofstede 1980, p. 235).

As noted earlier, entrepreneurs are frequently characterized as exhibiting an *internal locus of control*. As "internals," entrepreneurs believe in their own abilities to achieve and give little credence to external forces such as destiny, luck, or powerful others (Rotter 1966). In highly individualistic countries (e.g., United States, United

60   S.L. MUELLER AND A S. THOMAS

Kingdom, Australia), individual freedom of action and independence are highly valued. Therefore, entrepreneurs who exhibit high levels of self-confidence, self-reliance, and bravado are admired and encouraged.

In a recent study, Busenitz and Barney (1997) showed that entrepreneurs' decision-making styles differ from that of managers in a large organizations in how they perceive risk. Specifically they found that entrepreneurs tend to be more overconfident than managers in making decisions in situations where information is limited or there is a high degree of outcome uncertainty (Busenitz and Barney 1997). Such findings support the notion that entrepreneurs tend to discount risk in business situations and perceive themselves as "in-control" of their ventures. Since individualistic cultures are more supportive of individual action and more tolerant of independent action than are collectivistic cultures, we would expect that an internal locus of control orientation would be less prevalent in collectivistic cultures than in individualistic cultures.

A review of cross-cultural studies of locus of control suggests a considerable amount of empirical support for expecting differences in the prevalence of internals (and hence potential entrepreneurs) across cultures. For example, using Rotter's I-E scale, Parsons and Scheider (1974) found that U.S. students were significantly more internal than Japanese students. Reitz and Groff (1974) found U.S. workers to be more internal than Mexican workers on Rotter's leadership/success subscale and more internal than Japanese and Thai workers on the respect, politics, and luck/fate subscales.

Several studies using the IPC scales (Levenson 1974) also found significant differences in locus of control orientation between some of the more collectivistic cultures and the United States. Cole and Cole (1974) for example, found U.S. male business students to have a higher internal IPC score than Mexican male business students. Mahler (1974) found that Japanese university students were less internal than U.S. university students. In a rare study comparing entrepreneurs across cultures, Kaufmann, Welsh, and Bushmarin (1995) found that Russian entrepreneurs scored significantly lower on the internal IPC scale than did U.S. entrepreneurs sampled in an earlier study by Rupke (1978).

The formation of successful new ventures clearly requires initiative on the part of the founder or the founding team. Whether founded by an individual or small team, the business initiators must be independent, self-reliant, and self-confident. Individualistic cultures tend to reinforce and reward independent action and initiative; collectivistic cultures reward these actions less. Thus,

> *H1:* An internal locus of control orientation is more prevalent in individualistic cultures than in collectivistic cultures.

Uncertainty Avoidance

Hofstede defines *uncertainty avoidance* as ". . . the extent to which the members of a culture feel threatened by uncertain or unknown situations" (Hofstede 1991, p. 113). According to Hofstede, strategies for coping with uncertainty are rooted in culture and reinforced through basic institutions such as family, school, and state (Hofstede 1980). In low uncertainty avoidance cultures, members are expected to cope with uncertainty as best they can. In high uncertainty avoidance cultures, structures are established which minimize the level of uncertainty faced by individual members.

In low uncertainty avoidance cultures, the inherent uncertainty of life is more easily accepted and each day is taken as it comes. It is believed that conflict and competition can be controlled within the rules of "fair play" and used constructively. Social deviants are not perceived as threatening, hence there is a greater tolerance for creative or novel behavior. In low uncertainty avoidance cultures, there is more willingness to take risks, and achievement is often recognized in terms of pioneering effort (Hofstede 1980, p. 184).

In high uncertainty avoidance cultures on the other hand, it is believed that conflict and competition unleashes destructive aggression and should be avoided. Deviant persons and ideas are considered dangerous; hence a lack of tolerance for anyone or anything that is perceived as "different." In high uncertainty avoidance cultures, younger people, prone to antiestablishment attitudes and behavior, are regarded with suspicion. There is more concern with security in life, and achievement is defined in terms of security. Hofstede also found that in high uncertainty avoidance societies, there is a greater fear of failure, a lower willingness to take risks, lower levels of ambition, and lower tolerance for ambiguity (Hofstede 1980, p. 184).

As noted earlier, innovativeness has long been associated with entrepreneurial behavior and even regarded by some as a defining element of the entrepreneurial role (Schumpeter 1934; Carland, et. al 1984). Creativity and innovativeness have also been linked to a high tolerance for ambiguity, another common characteristic of entrepreneurs (Schere 1982; Begley and Boyd 1987). Entrepreneurs also tend to have an optimistic bias and evaluate uncertain situations as more favorable than the facts justify (McClelland 1987). The tendency to discount external constraints is also considered to be a key attribute of creative individuals (Whiting 1988). Since creative and entrepreneurial behavior is by definition *deviant* in a social context, some researchers even go so far as to suggest that successful entrepreneurs may be mildly sociopathic (Winslow and Solomon 1989).

Since low uncertainty avoidance cultures are more accepting of non-traditional behaviors, it follows that entrepreneurs in these contexts enjoy greater freedom and legitimacy than their counterparts in high uncertainty avoidance cultures where the "deviance" of entrepreneurs would be viewed with suspicion. In support of this contention, Tuunanen et al. (1997) found that U.S. entrepreneurs had somewhat higher preferences for innovation than their counterparts in Finland, a country with a relatively high uncertainty avoidance culture compared to the United States (Hofstede 1980). In a cross-national study of innovation rates, Shane (1992) found that in terms of the number of trademarks granted to nationals of 33 different countries, per capita rate of innovation was lower in uncertainty avoiding countries compared to uncertainty accepting countries.

> *H2:* An innovative orientation is more prevalent in low uncertainty avoidance cultures than in high uncertainty avoidance cultures.

Entrepreneurial Orientation and Culture

No single trait or characteristic defines the entrepreneur, nor does it allow one to predict entrepreneurial behavior. It is a configuration of traits that separates the potential entrepreneur from those who are not predisposed or motivated to engage in new venture formation. Neither internal locus of control or innovativeness alone is sufficient to explain entrepreneurial motivation nor to define what we call an *entrepreneurial orienta-*

62   S.L. MUELLER AND A.S. THOMAS

tion: a predisposition which is likely to lead to behavior associated with entrepreneurial activity.[1]

Given the theoretical and empirical support as outlined above, we would expect that an entrepreneurial orientation should include as a minimum, both internal locus of control and innovativeness. Entrepreneurial orientation implies an individual who is self-reliant, self confident, with strong determination and perseverance to initiate and grow an enterprise. Thus, individuals with both an internal locus of control and innovative orientation should appear more frequently in highly individualistic cultures which support the strongly independent and persevering element of entrepreneurial behavior and at the same time support creativity and innovative problem-solving to deal with an uncertain and ambiguous world. As an extension of H1 and H2, we expect that countries which are both low in uncertainty avoidance and highly individualistic would yield the greatest number of individuals with an entrepreneurial orientation.

> *H3:* An entrepreneurial orientation (i.e., internal locus of control combined with innovativeness) is more prevalent in individualistic, low uncertainty avoidance cultures than in collectivistic, high uncertainty avoidance cultures.

METHODS

Survey Administration

The sample used for this study was drawn from a large data set containing responses to a survey of third- and fourth-year students at 25 universities in 15 countries. The instrument administered to the students surveyed their attitudes and perceptions about free-markets, competition, and the contribution of entrepreneurs to economic development. It also contained items designed to measure locus of control and innovative orientations. Respondents were additionally instructed to provide specific biographical background information so they could be categorized by age, gender, and national origin.

The instrument was pre-tested on approximately 400 undergraduate business students at an American university. As a result of this pre-test, several of the questions were modified to reduce or eliminate ambiguity. Subsequently, during 1996 the questionnaire was distributed to students studying business, economics, or engineering in a variety of different universities worldwide. Questionnaires were administered in a classroom setting by local professors who agreed to participate in the project and administer the surveys in exchange for access to the data set.

University students were selected as subjects for this study for several reasons. Today's university students, we believe, represent a significant share of the pool of potential entrepreneurs in both the developed and developing countries. As the demands of technology and global competition increases, the need for university-trained entrepreneurs will becomes more evident, and success in business will increasingly be dependent

---

[1] The term *entrepreneurial orientation* has been used by other researchers in the context of firm behavior. For example, Covin and Slevin (1989) referred to entrepreneurial orientation as a strategic posture of the firm. Covin and Slevin (1988) also used the term to refer to a top management team's decision-making style. In later work (e.g. Covin and Slevin 1991), these authors abandoned the term *entrepreneurial orientation* in favor of "entrepreneurial posture." More recently, Lumpkin and Dess (1996) used the term as a construct representing the extent to which a firm's strategic profile contains autonomy, innovativeness, risk taking, proactiveness, and competitive aggressiveness. We use the term *entrepreneurial orientation* as a label for a set of personal traits associated with entrepreneurial potential. Our use of the term should not to be confused with a firm-level attribute as found in Covin and Slevin or Lumpkin and Dess.

upon the founder's education and training. Furthermore, sampling only students in business, economics, and engineering enhances cross-national comparability by effectively controlling for important variables such as literacy, work experience, age, and education. Finally, as a matter of practicality, student subjects are generally convenient, accessible, and through the support of administering professors, it was possible to maintain control over the testing environment.

Translation

In the United States, Canada, Ireland, and at schools in European countries where the students' command of English was highly proficient, the survey was administered in English. In the case of the Latin American countries, the survey instrument was first translated into Spanish by a bilingual native Spanish speaker and then backtranslated into English by a bilingual native English speaker. For European countries where translations were required, (i.e., Croatia, the Czech Republic, Slovenia, Germany), the instrument was translated by bilingual professors at the local institutions where the instrument was administered.

Measures

The survey instrument was composed of 62 items. Respondents were asked to indicate the extent to which they agreed or disagreed with each item by choosing one of five responses: (A) strongly agree, (B) agree, (C) neither agree or disagree, (D) disagree, or (E) strongly disagree.

Of the 62 items, 18 were used to construct scales for innovativeness (10 items) and locus of control (8 items). Items for the innovativeness scale were adapted from the Jackson Personality Inventory (Jackson 1994) while items used for the locus of control scale were adapted from Rotter's I-E scale (Rotter 1966). Both scales were subjected to reliability testing using data collected in this nine-country study. Reliability test results indicate that Cronbach's alpha scores were in an acceptable range for both scales with minimal variance across country samples. For example, alpha scores ranged from 0.82 (Canada) to 0.66 (China) for the innovativeness scale and from 0.81 (Canada) to 0.53 (Slovenia) for the internal locus of control scale. Both scales were also determined to be unidimensional based on results obtained from principal component analysis.

Innovativeness

The Jackson Personality Inventory Manual (JPI), which defines innovativeness as a tendency to be creative in thought and action, was used to capture this construct as innovation, creativity, and initiative have been consistently identified as one of the enduring characteristics of entrepreneurs. (McClelland 1987; Fernald and Solomon 1987; Hornaday and Aboud 1971; Timmons 1978).

Adjectives on the instrument used to describe entrepreneurs which highly correlate with innovativeness include imaginative, inventive, enterprising, original, resourceful, and farsighted (Jackson 1994). A high score on the JPI innovativeness scale indicates a preference for novel solutions to problems and an appreciation for original ideas. For this study, 8 items were adapted from the JPI innovativeness scale. Typical of these are

64 S.L. MUELLER AND A.S. THOMAS

statements such as "I often surprise people with my novel ideas" and "I like to experiment with various ways of doing the same thing."

Locus of Control

A modified Rotter I-E Scale was used in this study to measure internal locus of control (Rotter 1966). This scale is designed to measure the respondent's perceived ability to influence events in his or her own life. Internal persons believe that fate and fortune is within their own personal control. In contrast, external persons believe that their lives are controlled by external forces such as destiny, luck, or powerful others (Begley and Boyd 1987). Ten items were adapted for this purpose. Typical of these are statements such as "My life is determined by my own actions" and "When I get what I want, it is usually because I worked hard for it."

To minimize the effect of response bias in which some respondents tend to give more extreme responses than others, innovativeness and locus of control scores were converted from a numeric to a binary score (high or low). Scores ranged from a maximum of 40 to a minimum of 8 for innovativeness and a maximum of 60 to a minimum of 10 for internal locus of control. A frequency distribution of scores for both measures was used to determine a suitable breakpoint value which separated the upper 50 percentile from the lower 50 percentile. In this manner, each respondent's score was converted from a numeric score to a high/low value.

Entrepreneurial Orientation

For analysis purposes, innovativeness and internal locus of control were treated as two essential elements of an entrepreneurial predisposition. Thus individuals with an entrepreneurial orientation (EO) are defined as those who are at the same time innovative and have an internal locus of control orientation. In operationalizing this EO construct, if a respondent were categorized as HIGH innovativeness and HIGH internal locus of control, then that respondent would also be designated as HIGH entrepreneurial orientation. If however, the respondent was categorized as LOW innovativeness, LOW internal locus of control, or both, then that respondent would be categorized as LOW entrepreneurial orientation. Using this scheme, 378 of the 1,790 respondents (21%) were categorized as HIGH EO, and 1,412 (79%) were categorized as LOW EO.

Culture

Student respondents were asked a series of background questions to determine their nationality. If a student indicated that he or she was not a native or a long time resident of the country in which their university was located, then that response was eliminated from the data set. The remaining responses were then coded by nationality (i.e., Canada, Ireland, United States, etc.) based on the university's location.

Of the 15 countries surveyed, only nine were in the Hofstede 1980 study thereby limiting the culture analysis to the United States, Croatia and Slovenia (former Yugoslavia), Canada, Ireland, Belgium, Germany, Singapore, and China (PRC). Each of these countries was scored using Hofstede's cultural indices denoted as "UAI" (uncertainty avoidance) and "IDV" (individualism). Hofstede did not obtain culture data for the PRC directly but did score both Taiwan and Hong Kong. Based on the results of a study

CULTURE AND ENTREPRENEURIAL POTENTIAL **65**

TABLE 1 Descriptive Statistics and Correlations[a]

Variables	Means	Standard Deviations	1	2	3	4	5
1. Gender[b]	0.53	0.5					
2. Individualism[c]	54.25	30.75	0.0991***				
3. Uncertainty Avoidance[d]	56.11	22.83	0.0641**	−0 4601***			
4. Innovativeness[e]	0.41	0.49	0.1287***	0.0576+	0.0272		
5. Locus of Control[f]	0.41	0.49	0.0367	0.2451***	−0.0946***	0.2011+**	
6. Entrepreneurial Orientation[g]	0.22	0.41	0.0993***	0.1645***	−0.0414	0.6299***	0.6318***

[a] N = 1790, [b] Male = 1, Female = 0; [c] Hofstede 1980, [d] Hofstede 1980, [e] High Innovativeness = 1, Low Innovativeness = 0; [f] Internal LOC = 1, External LOC = 0; [g] Innovativeness x Locus of Control, *** $p < 0.001$, ** $p < 0.01$, * $p < 0.05$

by McGrath, MacMillan, Yang and Tsai (1992) in which they concluded that 50 years of ideological pressure had little effect on the basic collectivist values and attitudes among mainland Chinese, we used Hofstede's Taiwan and Kong Hong data to provide an estimate of culture dimension scores for the Peoples Republic of China.

RESULTS

Table 1 provides descriptive statistics and zero order correlations for each of the variables. Gender is modeled as a dichotomous variable with "1" representing male and "0" representing female. As shown in Table 1, the mean value for gender is 0.53 indicating 53% of the sample is male and 47% of the sample is female. Innovativeness and locus of control are also dichotomous variables with "1" representing high innovativeness and internal locus of control and "0" representing low innovativeness and external locus of control respectively. Entrepreneurial orientation is a constructed dichotomous variable which equals "1" when both innovativeness and locus of control are "1" and "0" when either innovativeness or locus of control is "0." As the mean values in Table 1 indicate, 41% of the sample have an innovative orientation, 41% have an internal locus of control orientation, and 22% have both. This relatively low occurrence of an *entrepreneurial orientation* (i.e., high innovativeness plus ILOC) in our sample is consistent with the expectation that entrepreneurial potential is a relatively rare characteristic.

Multivariate logistic regression analysis was used to test the three hypotheses as to the effect of culture on the likelihood of (1) an internal locus of control orientation, (2) an innovative orientation, or (3) a combined ILOC/innovative orientation defined as *entrepreneurial orientation*. Using the SAS LOGISTIC procedure (SAS Institute 1989), maximum likelihood estimates for each independent variable included in the model are generated and various measures of model fit such as the -2 log likelihood statistic are reported. Logistic regression is similar to least-squares regression except it is most appropriately used when the dependent variable is binary, i.e., 1 or 0, yes or no, high or low.

The results of the logistic regression analysis are summarized as Table 2. Gender was included as a control variable in all regression models tested.

Results of regression analysis provide support for Hypothesis 1 and Hypothesis 3, but not for Hypothesis 2. While controlling for gender, the sign of the coefficient for the individualism-collectivism dimension of culture is positive and significant at the 0.99 confidence level supporting the claim that an innovative orientation is more likely in

66 S.L. MUELLER AND A.S. THOMAS

TABLE 2 Logistic Regression Analysis: Effects of Culture and Gender on Locus on Control and Innovativeness

	H1 Internal Locus of Control	H2 Innovativeness	H3 Entrepreneural Orientation (Innovativeness + Internal LOC)		
Intercept	1.3265***	0.8363***	1.3283***	2.3972***	2.1718***
	(0.1172)	(0.1482)	(0.1745)	(0.1558)	(0.1280)
Gender	0.0710	0.5787***	0.6041***	0.5231***	0.5503***
(Male = 1, Female = 0)	(0.0959)	(0.0984)	(0.1200)	(0.1210)	(0.1209)
Individualism	0.0166***		0.0131***		
	(0.0016)		(0.0020)		
Uncertainty Avoidance		0.0017		−0.0055*	
		(0.0022)		(0.0026)	
Entrepreneur Supportive					0.0002***
(Low UA × IDV)					(0.0000)

Std. Errors in Parentheses: ***p < 0 001; **p < 0 01, *p < 0 05

individualistic cultures and less likely in collectivistic cultures (Hypothesis 1). However, although the sign of the coefficient for uncertainty avoidance was is the predicted direction for Hypothesis 2 (i.e., negative), this result is not statistically significant indicating no difference in the likelihood of an innovative orientation between low and high uncertainty avoidance cultures. The effect of gender on innovativeness was, however, significant indicating that an innovative orientation is more likely among males in the sample than females. On the other hand, there was no significant difference between males and females in the likelihood of an internal locus of control orientation.

Hypothesis 3, which predicts that an entrepreneurial orientation (internal locus of control combined with innovativeness) is more likely in low uncertainty avoidance and individualistic cultures, was tested using three different regression models. First, the effect of individualism on the likelihood of entrepreneurial orientation was tested alone. Similarly, the effect of uncertainty avoidance on the likelihood of entrepreneurial orientation was tested. In the third model, a combined uncertainty avoidance/individualism culture scale was constructed by computing the product of a country's uncertainty avoidance score and individualism score. Because of its hypothesized relationship with entrepreneurial potential, this combined culture scale is label as "entrepreneurship supportive." All three regression models tested provide support for Hypothesis 3. As shown in Table 1, the likelihood of an entrepreneurial orientation is (a) greater in individualistic cultures, (b) greater in low uncertainty avoidance cultures, and (c) greatest in cultures which are at the same time low uncertainty avoidance and highly individualistic.

DISCUSSION

The results of this exploratory study support the proposition that some cultures are more conducive for entrepreneurship than others. As hypothesized, individualism was found to increase the likelihood of an internal locus of control orientation supporting the argument that individualistic cultures foster strong entrepreneurial values that promote self-reliance and independent action while collectivistic cultures do not. Furthermore there was support for the hypothesis that an entrepreneurial orientation, defined as internal locus of control combined with innovativeness, is more likely in individualistic, low uncertainty avoidance cultures than in collectivistic, high uncertainty avoidance cultures.

However, contrary to Hypothesis 2, an innovativeness orientation is by itself no more likely in a low uncertainty avoidance culture than in a high uncertainty avoidance culture.

The lack of support for Hypothesis 2, suggesting that prevalence of innovativeness may not be associated with any particular culture or country, is an interesting finding and requires closer examination. Our data show that innovativeness (measured using the Jackson Personality Inventory scale) is equally likely in low uncertainty avoidance cultures (e.g., Anglo-American) as in high uncertainty avoidance cultures (e.g., Asian). The explanation for this finding may lie in how innovative orientation is measured.

Although we found that an entrepreneurial orientation varies in frequency across cultures, we suspect that the propensity to think creatively, which is what the JPI scale measures, may in fact be a universal trait and not shaped by culture. This is to say that creativity and creative thinkers are equally prevalent in a variety of cultural contexts. However, innovativeness, as it relates specifically to the new venture creation process and the problems that entrepreneurs must solve, may be another matter.

As other researchers have demonstrated, entrepreneurs differ from non-entrepreneurs in their decision-making *styles*. Buttner and Gryskiewicz (1993), for example, found that entrepreneurs have a more innovative problem-solving style than their managerial counterparts in larger U.S. organizations. Similarly, Goldsmith and Kerr (1991) found that entrepreneurship students used a more innovative problem-solving style than general business students. Both studies used the Kirton Adaption-Innovation Inventory instrument to measure stylistic differences in problem solving and decision making with "adaption" at one end of a continuum and "innovation" at the other (Kirton 1976). According to Kirton, adaptors try to do things "better" through incremental improvement while innovators try to do things "differently" by changing the way things are (Kirton 1976). What we suspect is that decision-making and problem-solving styles vary in frequency across cultures rather than creative thinking per se. If that is the case, then we would expect to find adaptive styles to be more prevalent in high uncertainty avoidance cultures (e.g., Japan) and innovative styles to be more prevalent in low uncertainty avoidance cultures (e.g., the United States).

Despite the inconclusive results on innovativeness, the overall positive findings of this study (i.e. support for Hypothesis 1 and Hypothesis 3) suggest that culture is an important variable in determining entrepreneurial potential at the national or regional level. Culture, it appears, may condition potential for entrepreneurship, generating differences across national and regional boundaries. As we have demonstrated, some cultures, particularly cultures which are low uncertainty avoidance and individualistic appear to be more supportive of entrepreneurs than are other cultural configurations. One tentative conclusion is that a "supportive" culture increases, ceteris paribus, the entrepreneurial potential of a country.

Krueger and Brazeal (1994) noted that support from political, social, and business leaders is critical to the encouragement of entrepreneurial activity. This support is typically provided in the form of incentive programs or inducements to encourage the founding of new enterprises. But our research suggests that it is equally important that there be a supportive culture to cultivate the mind and character of the potential entrepreneur. To be motivated to act, potential entrepreneurs must perceive themselves as capable and psychologically equipped to face the challenges of a global, competitive marketplace.

Traits such as internal locus of control and innovativeness are not necessarily immutable. As entrepreneurship educators are found of saying "entrepreneurs are made, not

68 S.L. MUELLER AND A.S. THOMAS

born." This statement implies that entrepreneurship can be taught and an individual's self-perception and potential for entrepreneurship can be enhanced. For example, Krueger and Brazeal (1994) note that research suggests we can train individuals to behave more autonomously. Such training would be aimed at enhancing a student's perceived self-efficacy at specific tasks or competencies critical to launching and maintaining a successful venture.

Clearly business education can play an important role in this regard by providing not only the technical tools of business (accounting, marketing, finance, etc.), but also helping students develop the necessary skills for self-management and coping with adversity and uncertainty (Krueger and Brazeal 1994).

Entrepreneurial Traits Research

The use of personal characteristics such as locus of control and innovativeness in entrepreneurship studies has been questioned (Gartner 1988). Much of the criticism of the *traits* approach to the study of entrepreneurship is based on the implied assumption that traits are acquired at birth or an early age. The use of the term "personality" in many traits studies also implies that such characteristics are immutable and unaffected by experience or circumstance. However, characteristics such as locus of control and innovativeness are not necessarily imprinted at birth or an early age and may be acquired at a later time due to experiences in the work place, education, exposure to role models, parents, and social setting (culture) which shape values and beliefs.

Criticism of the entrepreneurial traits research is also based on a lack of significant empirical findings to support the claim that entrepreneurs are psychologically "different" from the general population. The application of certain psychometric tests which measure need for achievement and risk-taking propensity for example, have generally failed to discriminate between entrepreneurs and professional business managers (Brockhaus 1982; Gartner 1985). However, this failure to confirm empirically the psychological differences between practicing entrepreneurs and non-entrepreneurs may be misleading. Clearly not all those predisposed actually become entrepreneurs. Other factors such as push/pull and the environment also affect the probability that one will initiate a venture. It is therefore reasonable to expect that a significant portion of the non-entrepreneur population possess entrepreneurial tendencies as well. In other words, having entrepreneurial values, attitudes, and perceptions is simply a precondition for entrepreneurial behavior and not to be confused with the act itself (McClelland 1961). In this study the concern is with potential entrepreneurs, not practicing entrepreneurs. Therefore it was appropriate to investigate those characteristics, whether learned or innate, for which there is a theoretical basis for predicting an increase in the likelihood of venture initiation.

Entrepreneurial Potential and New Venture Creation

The bulk of entrepreneurship research and theorizing about factors which stimulate new venture creation would seem to suggest that all that is needed is a supportive infrastructure or economic incentives to provide the motivation to initiate new ventures. However, as we have argued, an adequate pool of entrepreneurially oriented individuals must also be available. Since the culture of a country influences the values, attitudes, and beliefs of its people, we can expect variety in the distribution of individuals with entrepreneurial potential across cultural contexts. Extending this logic leads to the proposition that the greater the frequency of the entrepreneurial orientation among the population of a country, the greater the stock of potential entrepreneurs, and hence (ceteris paribus) the higher the rate of new venture formation.

Study Limitations

As noted, the study sample consists exclusively of third- and fourth-year university students. This sampling approach has the advantage of forcing homogeneity of respondents across countries and thereby eliminating the need to control for critical demographic variables such as age, education, and experience. However, at the same time we recognize the possibility that a lack of uniformity in the demographic composition of student bodies across countries might be a source of sample bias.

This study is also limited by the number and type of countries selected. Although every attempt was made to sample a wide range of countries based on region, countries were not selected with a goal to achieve maximum variance across cultural dimensions. As a result, it was not possible to account for the independent effect of each culture dimension. In recognizing this limitation, we are in the process of collecting data from additional countries (e.g., Mexico, Australia, Italy, South Africa, and Turkey).

In retrospect we recognize that the choice of measures for innovativeness and control orientation may be another limitation of this pilot study. In future studies, we plan to incorporate alternative measures of innovativeness (e.g., Kirton 1973) and control (e.g., Burger 1985; Palhus 1983).

Future International Entrepreneurship Research

This study advances entrepreneurship research by demonstrating that certain characteristics associated with entrepreneurial potential are more prevalent in some cultures and less prevalent in others. These findings highlight the need for the development of entrepreneurial profiles which recognize both commonality and differences across cultures. Empirically this means a call for finer grained studies and inductive research in different contexts to determine the traits profiles of potential entrepreneurs in different cultures. Such efforts should provide a baseline profile from which deviations can be assessed and the impact of culture on entrepreneurship more thoroughly examined.

The observed differences between males and females in this study also highlights the need for a more thorough examination of gender effects across a variety of cultural, economic, and political context. Although innovativeness is more frequently observed among the males in this sample, there were no significant differences among men and women in locus of control orientation. This finding of differences between men and women in the likelihood of an entrepreneurial orientation suggests systematic gender differences in motives leading to new venture initiation (Birley 1989; Bowen and Hisrich 1986; Fischer, Reuber, and Dyke 1993). Given that the rate of new business start-ups by women is increasing rapidly in many countries and most of the literature on entrepreneurship was derived by studying male entrepreneurs, the theoretical foundation of the field needs to be expanded to include the issue of gender in an international context. One approach would be to explore the interaction effect of gender and culture on the likelihood of an entrepreneurial orientation. The research question would be: Are the

70 S.L. MUELLER AND A.S. THOMAS

observed differences between men and women as our study reports the same across cultures or is the entrepreneurship "gap" greater in some cultures than in others? If so, what is the theoretical basis for such differences?

This study examined only two entrepreneurial traits (innovativeness and internal locus of control) and only one of the many contextual factors (culture) which may help to explain differences among countries in the rate of new venture formation. Future research should expand this avenue of research to include other traits associated with entrepreneurial behavior and macro level factors including education system, political economy, and stage of economic development. Ultimately, consensus among these various perspectives will provide a more complete theoretical framework for explaining entrepreneurial behavior within and across varying political and socioeconomic contexts.

In this study we were able to overcome the barrier of access, a significant hurdle to international entrepreneurship research, by soliciting the cooperation of colleagues from 25 universities in 15 countries during the data collection phase of the project. As a result, there is now in place a valuable network of entrepreneurship researchers to investigate the new venture creation process in the developing economies of Latin American, Asia, and Eastern Europe.

REFERENCES

Adler, N.J. 1991. *International dimensions of organizational behavior, Second ed.* Boston: Kent Publishing.

Ahmed, S.U. 1985. nAch, risk-taking propensity, locus of control and entrepreneurship. *Personality and Individual Differences* 6(6):781–782.

Audretsch, D.B. 1991. The role of small business in restructuring Eastern Europe. *5th Workshop for Research in Entrepreneurship.* Vaxjo, Sweden.

Barnouw, V. 1979. *Culture and personality.* Homewood, IL: The Dorsey Press.

Baum, J.R., Olian, J.D., Erez, M., Schnell, E.R., Smith, K.G., Sims, H.P. Scully, J.S., and Smith, K.A. 1993. Nationality and work role interactions: A cultural contrast of Israeli and U.S. entrepreneurs' versus managers' needs. *Journal of Business Venturing* 8:499–512.

Baumol, W.J. 1986. Entrepreneurship and a century of growth. *Journal of Business Venturing* 1:141–145.

Begley, T.M. and Boyd, D.P. 1987. Psychological characteristics associated with performance in entrepreneurial firms and smaller businesses. *Journal of Business Venturing* 2:79–93.

Birch, D.L. 1979. *The job generation process.* Cambridge, MA: M.I.T. Program on Neighborhood and Regional Change.

Bird, B. 1989. *Entrepreneurial behavior.* Glenview, IL: Scott Foresman.

Birley, S. 1986. The role of new firms: Births, deaths and job generation. *Strategic Management Journal* 7:361–376.

Birley, S. 1989. Female entrepreneurs: Are they really any different? *Journal of Small Business Management* 27:32–37.

Blaise. R., Toulouse, J., and Clement, B. 1990. International comparisons of entrepreneurial motivation based on personal equation, hierarchial analysis, and other statistical methods. In R. Gomulka. and W. Ward, eds., *Proceedings of the 39th World Conference of Small Business.* Washington, D.C.: International Council.

Bonnett, C. and Furnham, A. 1991. Who wants to be an entrepreneur? A study of adolescents interested in a Young Enterprise scheme. *Journal of Economic Psychology* 12(3):465–478.

Borland, C.M. 1974. Locus of control, need for achievement and entrepreneurship. *Unpublished Dissertation.* University of Texas.

Bowen, D. and Hisrich, R. 1986. The female entrepreneur: A career development perspective, *Academy of Management Review* 11(2):393–407.

Boyacigiller, N.A. and Adler, N.J. 1991. The parochial dinosaur: Organizational science in a global context. *Academy of Management Review* 16:262–290.

Brockhaus, R.H. 1975. I-E locus of control scores as predictors of entrepreneurial intentions. *Proceedings of the Academy of Management,* 1975, pp. 433–435.

Brockhaus, R.H. 1980. The effect of job dissatisfaction on the decision to start a business. *Journal of Small Business Management* 18(1):37–43.

Brockhaus, R.H. 1982. The psychology of the entrepreneur. In C.A. Kent, D.L. Sexton, and K.H. Vesper, eds., *Encyclopedia of entrepreneurship.* Englewood Cliffs, NJ: Prentice Hall.

Brockhaus, R.H. and Horwitz, P.S. 1986. The psychology of the entrepreneur. In D.L. Sexton and R.W. Smilor, eds., *The art and science of entrepreneurship.* Cambridge, MA: Ballinger.

Bruno, A.V. and Tyebjee, T.T. 1982. The environment for entrepreneurship. In C.A. Kent, D.L. Sexton, and K.H. Vesper, eds., *Encyclopedia of entrepreneurship.* Englewood Cliffs, NJ: Prentice-Hall.

Burger, J. 1985. Desire for control and achievement-related behaviors. *Journal of Personality and Social Psychology* 48:1520–1533.

Busenitz, L.W. and Barney, J.B. 1997. Differences between entrepreneurs and managers in large organizations: Biases and heuristics in strategic decision-making. *Journal of Business Venturing* 12:9–30.

Buttner, E.H. and Gryskiewicz, N. 1993. Entrepreneurs' problem-solving styles: An empirical study using the Kirton adaption/innovation theory. *Journal of Small Business Management* 31(1):22–31.

Bygrave, W.D. and Hofer, C.W. 1991. Theorizing about entrepreneurship. *Entrepreneurship Theory and Practice* 16(2):13–21.

Carland, J.C. and Carland, J.W. 1991. An empirical investigation into the distinctions between male and female entrepreneurs and managers. *International Small Business Journal* 9(3):62–72.

Carland, J.W., Carland, J.C., Hoy, F., and Boulton, W.R. 1988. Distinctions between entrepreneurial and small business ventures. *International Journal of Management* 5(1):98–103.

Carland, J.W., Hoy, F., Boulton, W.R., and Carland, J.C. 1984. Differentiating entrepreneurs from small business owners: A conceptualization. *Academy of Management Review* 9(2): 354–359.

Carland, J.W., Hoy, F., and Carland, J.C. 1988. "Who is an entrepreneur?" is a question worth asking. *American Journal of Small Business* 12(4):33–39.

Carsrud, A.L., Olm, K.W., and Eddy, G.G. 1986. Entrepreneurship: Research in quest of a paradigm. In D.L. Sexton and R.W. Smilor, eds., *The art and science of entrepreneurship.* Cambridge, MA: Ballinger.

Cole, D. and Cole, S. 1974. Locus of control and cultural conformity: On going against the norm. *Personality and Social Psychology Bulletin* 1:351–353.

Collins, 1974. Four components of the Rotter internal-external scale: Belief in a difficult world, a just world, a predictable world, and a politically responsive world. *Journal of Personality and Social Psychology* 29(3):381–391.

Cromie, S. and Johns, S. 1983. Irish entrepreneurs: Some personal characteristics. *Journal of Occupational Behavior* 4:317–324.

Covin, J.G. and Slevin, D.P. 1988. The influence of organization structure on the utility of an entrepreneurial top management style. *Journal of Management Studies* 25:217–234.

Covin, J.G. and Slevin, D.P. 1989. Strategic management of small firms in hostile and benign environments. *Strategic Management Journal* 10:75–87.

Covin, J.G. and Slevin, D.P. 1991. A conceptual model of entrepreneurship as firm behavior. *Entrepreneurship Theory and Practice* 16(1):7–25.

72 S.L. MUELLER AND A.S. THOMAS

Drucker, P. 1985. *Innovation and entrepreneurship: Practice and principles.* New York: Harper and Row.

Dunkelberg, W.C. and Cooper, A.C. 1982. Entrepreneurial typologies. In K.H. Vesper, ed., *Frontiers of entrepreneurship research.* Wellesley, MA: Babson College.

Durant, D.E. and Nord, W.R. 1976. Perceived leader behavior as a function of personality, characteristics of supervisors and subordinates. *Academy of Management Journal* 19:427–438.

Erez, M. and Earley, P.C. 1993. *Culture, self-identity, and work.* New York: Oxford University Press.

Fernald, L.W. and Solomon, G.T. 1987. Value profiles of male and female entrepreneurs. *Journal of Creative Behavior* 21:235–1247.

Fischer, E.M., Reuber, A.R. and Dyke L.S. 1993. A theoretical overview and extension of research on sex, gender, and entrepreneurship, *Journal of Business Venturing* 8:151–168.

Gabor, D. 1970. *Innovations: Scientific, technical and social.* Oxford: The University Press.

Gartner, W.B. (1985). A conceptual framework for describing the phenomenon of new venture creation. *Academy of Management Review* 10(4):696–706.

Gartner, W.B. 1988. "Who is an entrepreneur?" is the wrong question. *American Journal of Small Business* 12(4):11–32.

Gatewood, E.J., Shaver, K.G., and Gartner, W.B. 1995. A longitudinal study of cognitive factors influencing start-up behaviors and success at venture creation. *Journal of Business Venturing* 10:371–391.

Gibb, A. 1993. Small business development in Central and Eastern Europe—Opportunity for a rethink? *Journal of Business Venturing* 8:461–486.

Gilad, B. and Levine, P. 1986. A behavioral model of entrepreneurial supply. *Journal of Small Business Management* 24(4):44–53.

Goldsmith, R.E. and Kerr, J.R. 1991. Entrepreneurship and adaption-innovation theory. *Technovation* 11(6):373–382.

Hagen, E.E. 1962. *On the theory of social change: How economic growth begins.* Homewood, IL: Dorsey Press.

Harper, M. 1991. The role of enterprise in poor countries. *Entrepreneurship Theory and Practice* 15(4):7–11.

Hisrich, R.D. 1990. Entrepreneurship/intrapreneurship. *American Psychologist* 45(2):209–222.

Hofstede, G. 1980. *Culture's consequences: International differences in work-related values.* Beverly Hills, CA: Sage Publications.

Hofstede, G. 1991. *Cultures and organizations: Software of the mind.* London: McGraw Hill.

Hornaday, J.A. and Aboud, J. 1971. Characteristics of successful entrepreneurs. *Personnel Psychology* 24:141–153.

Huisman, D. 1985. Entrepreneurship: Economic and cultural influences on the entrepreneurial climate. *European Research* 13(4):10–17.

Jackson, D.N. 1994. *Jackson Personality Inventory—Revised Manual.* Port Heron, MI: Sigma Assessment Systems, Inc.

Jennings, D.F. and Zeithaml, C.P. 1983. Locus of control: A review and directions for entrepreneurial research. In *Proceedings of the National Academy of Management*, 1983, pp. 417–421.

Johnson, B.R. 1990. Toward a multidimensional model of entrepreneurship: The case of achievement motivation and the entrepreneur. *Entrepreneurship Theory and Practice* 14:39–54.

Kaufmann, P.J., Welsh, D.H.B., and Bushmarin, N.V. 1995. Locus of control and entrepreneurship in the Russian Republic. *Entrepreneurship, Theory and Practice* 20(1):43–56.

Kets de Vries, M.F.R. 1977. The entrepreneurial personality: A person at the crossroads. *Journal of Management Studies* 14(1):34–57.

Kilby, P. 1971. Hunting the Heffalump. In P. Kilby, ed., *Entrepreneurship and economic development.* New York: Free Press.

Kirton, M.J. 1976. Adaptors and innovators: A description and measure. *Journal of Applied Psychology* 61:759–762.

Koiranen, M., Hyrsky, K. and Tuunanen, M. 1997. Risk taking propensity of US and Finnish SME's: Findings on similarities and differences. *Paper presented at the 2nd International Risk Conference*, Stockholm, Sweden, June 1997.

Kroeber, A.L. and Parsons, T. 1958. The concepts of culture and of social system. *American Sociological Review* 23:582–583.

Krueger, N. 1993. The impact of prior entrepreneurial exposure on perceptions of new venture feasibility and desirability. *Entrepreneurship Theory and Practice* 18(1):5–21.

Krueger, N.F. and Brazeal, D.V. 1994. Entrepreneurial potential and potential entrepreneurs. *Entrepreneurship, Theory and Practice* 18(3):91–104.

Lefcourt, H. M. 1981. *Research with the locus of control construct.* New York: Academic Press.

Levenson, H. 1974. Activism and powerful others: Distinctions within the concept of internal-external control. *Journal of Personality Assessment* 38(4):377–383.

Levin, R. and Leginsky, P. 1990. The independent social worker as entrepreneur. *Journal of Independent Social Work* 5(1):22–31.

Lumpkin, G.T. and Dess, G.G. 1996. Clarifying the entrepreneurial orientation construct and linking it to performance. *Academy of Management Review* 21(1):135–172.

Mahler, I. 1974. A comparative study of locus of control. *Psychologia* 17(3):135–139.

Mancuso, J.R. 1973. *Fun and guts: The entrepreneur's philosophy.* Reading, MA: Addison-Wesley.

Markus, H.R. and Kitayama, S. 1991. Culture and the self: Implications for cognition, emotion, and motivation. *Psychological Review* 98(2):224–253.

Martin, M.J.C. 1984. *Managing technological innovation and entrepreneurship.* Reston, VA: Prentice-Hall.

McClelland, D.C. 1961. *The achieving society.* Princeton, NJ: Van Nostrand Reinhold.

McClelland, D.C. 1987. Characteristics of successful entrepreneurs. *Journal of Creative Behavior* 21:219–233.

McGrath, R.G., MacMillan, I.C., and Scheinberg, S. 1992. Elitists, risk-takers, and rugged individualists? An exploratory analysis of cultural differences between entrepreneurs and non-entrepreneurs. *Journal of Business Venturing* 7:115–135.

McGrath, R.G., MacMillan, I.C., Yang, E.A., and Tsai, W. 1992. Does culture endure, or is it malleable? Issues for entrepreneurial economic development. *Journal of Business Venturing* 7:441–458

Moore, C.F. 1986. Understanding entrepreneurial behavior: A definition and model. *Proceeding of the National Academy of Management*, pp. 66–70.

Pandey, J. and Tewary, N.B. 1979. Locus of control and achievement values of entrepreneurs. *Journal of Occupational Psychology* 50:107–111.

Parsons, O.A. and Schneider, J.M. 1974. Locus of control in unversity students from Eastern and Western societies. *Journal of Consulting and Clinical Psychology* 42(3):456–461.

Paulhus, D. 1983. Sphere-specific measures of perceived control. *Journal of Personality and Social Psychology* 44(6):1253–1265.

Pennings, J.M. 1980. Environmental influences on the creation process. In J.R. Kimberly and R. Miles, eds., *The organization life cycle.* San Francisco: Jossey Bass.

Perry, C. 1990. After further sightings of the Heffalump. *Journal of Managerial Psychology* 5(2):22–31.

Reitz, H.J. and Groff, G.K. 1974. Economic development and belief in locus of control among factory workers in four countries. *Journal of Cross-Cultural Psychology* 5(3):344–355.

Reynolds, P.D. 1987. New firm's societal contribution versus survival potential. *Journal of Business Venturing* 2:231–246.

Robinson, P.B., Stimpson, D.V., Huefner, J.C., and Hunt, H.K. 1991. An attitude approach to the prediction of entrepreneurship. *Entrepreneurship, Theory and Practice* 15(4):13–31.

74 S.L. MUELLER AND A.S. THOMAS

Rotter, J.B. 1966. Generalized expectancies for internal versus external control of reinforcement. *Psychological Monographs: General and Applied* 80, Whole No. 609.

Rupke, R.H. 1978. Entrepreneurial potential and assessments. *Unpublished doctoral dissertation*, Pepperdine University.

SAS Institute Inc. 1989. *SAS/STAT User's Guide, Version 6, Fourth Edition, Volume 1.* Cary, NC: SAS Institute Inc.

Scheinberg, S. and MacMillan, I. 1988. An eleven country study of the motivations to start a business. In B. Kirchhoff, W. Long, W. McMullan, K.H. Vesper, and W. Wetzel, eds., *Frontiers of entrepreneurship research.* Wellesley, MA: Babson College.

Schere, J.L. 1982. Tolerance of ambiguity as a discriminating variable between entrepreneurs and managers. *Proceedings of the National Academy of Management*, pp. 404–408.

Schumpeter, J.A. 1934. *The theory of economic development.* Cambridge, MA: Harvard Press.

Sexton, D.L. and Bowman-Upton, N.B. 1986. Validation of personality index: Comparative psychological characteristics analysis of female entrepreneurs, managers, entrepreneurship students and business students. In R. Ronstadt, J. Hornaday, R. Peterson, and K. Vesper, eds., *Frontiers of entrepreneurship research.* Wellesley, MA: Babson College.

Shane, S.A. 1992. Why do some society invent more than others? *Journal of Business Venturing* 7:29–46.

Shane, S.A. 1993. Cultural influences on national rates of innovation. *Journal of Business Venturing* 8:59–73.

Shane, S.A., Kolvereid, L., and Westhead, P. 1991. An exploratory examination of the reasons leading to new firm formation across country and gender. *Journal of Business Venturing* 6:431–446.

Shapero, A. 1975. The displaced, uncomfortable entrepreneur. *Psychology Today* 9(6):83–88.

Shapero, A. and Sokol, L. 1982. The social dimensions of entrepreneurship. In C.A Kent, D.L. Sexton, and K.H. Vesper, eds., *Encyclopedia of Entrepreneurship.* Englewood Cliffs, NJ: Prentice-Hall.

Shaver, K.G. and Scott, L.R. 1991. Person, process, choice: The psychology of new venture creation. *Entrepreneurship, Theory and Practice* 16(2):23–45.

Smith, N.R. and Miner, J.B. 1985. Motivational considerations in the success of technologically innovative entrepreneurs: Extended sample findings. In J. Hornaday, E. Shile, J. Timmons, and K. Vesper, eds., *Frontiers of entrepreneurship research.* Wellesley, MA: Babson College.

Solomon, G.T. and Winslow, E.K. 1988. Toward a descriptive profile of the entrepreneur. *Journal of Creative Behavior* 22:162–171.

Spangler, W.D. 1992. The validity of questionnaire and TAT measures of achievement: Two meta-analyses. *Psychological Bulletin* 112:140–154.

Spector, P.E. 1982. Behavior in organizations as a function of employee locus of control. *Psychological Bulletin* 91:482–495.

Stevenson, L.A. 1986. Against all odds: The entrepreneurship of women. *American Journal of Small Business* 24(4):30–36.

Strickland, B.R. 1989. Internal-external control expectancies. *American Psychologist* 44(1):1–12.

Thomas, A.S., Shenkar, O., and Clarke, L.D. 1994. The globalization of our mental maps: Evaluating the geographic scope of JIBS coverage. *Journal of International Business Studies* 25(4):675–686.

Timmons, J.A. 1978. Characteristics and role demands of entrepreneurship. *American Journal of Small Business* 3:5–17.

Tuunanen, M. and Hyrsky, K. 1997. Innovation preferences among Finnish and U.S. entrepreneurs. *Academy of Entrepreneurship Journal* 3(1):1–11.

Venkatapathy, R. 1984. Locus of control among entrepreneurs: A review. *Psychological Studies* 29(1):97–100.

Vesper, K.H. 1983. *Entrepreneurship and national policy.* Chicago, IL: Heller Institute for Small Business Policy Papers.

Whiting, B.G. 1988. Creativity and entrepreneurship: How do they relate? *Journal of Creative Behavior* 22(3):178–183.

Winslow, E.K. and Solomon, G.T. 1989. Further development of a descriptive profile of entrepreneurs. *Journal of Creative Behavior* 23:149–161.

APPENDIX

Survey Items Related to Locus of Control and Innovativeness

Respondents were to indicate the extent to which they agree or disagree with the following statements. Five structured choices were offered: Strongly Agree, Agree, Neither Agree nor Disagree, Disagree, Strongly Disagree.

Ten items comprise the locus of control scale (adapted from Rotter 1966):

1. My success depends on whether I am lucky enough to be in the right place at the right time.
2. To a great extent my life is controlled by accidental happenings.
3. When I get what I want, it is usually because I am lucky.
4. My life is determined by my own actions.
5. When I get what I want, it is usually because I worked hard for it.
6. It is not wise for me to plan too far ahead, because things turn out to be a matter of bad fortune.
7. Whether or not I am successful in life depends mostly on my ability.
8. I feel that what happens in my life is mostly determined by people in powerful positions.
9. I feel in control of my life.
10. Success in business is mostly a matter of luck.

Eight items comprise the innovativeness scale (adapted from Jackson Personality Inventory 1994):

1. I often surprise people with my novel ideas.
2. People often ask me for help in creative activities.
3. I obtain more satisfaction from mastering a skill than coming up with a new idea.
4. I prefer work that requires original thinking.
5. I usually continue doing a new job in exactly the way it was taught to me.
6. I like a job which demands skill and practice rather than inventiveness.
7. I am not a very creative person.
8. I like to experiment with various ways of doing the same thing.

Part VIII
Economic Growth

[30]

Small Business Economics (2005) 24 323–334
DOI 10 1007/s11187-005-1998-4

Entrepreneurship, Agglomeration and Technological Change

Zoltán J. Ács
Attila Varga

ABSTRACT. A growing body of literature suggests that variations across countries, in entrepreneurial activity and the spatial structure of economies could potentially be the source of different efficiencies in knowledge spillovers, and ultimately in economic growth. We develop an empirical model that endogenizes both entrepreneurial activity and agglomeration effects on knowledge spillovers within a Romerian framework. The model is tested using the GEM cross-national data to measure the level of entrepreneurship in each particular economy. We find that after controlling for the stock of knowledge and research and development expenditures, both entrepreneurial activity and agglomeration have a positive and statistically significant effect on technological change in the European Union.

KEY WORDS: agglomeration, economic geography, economic growth; entrepreneurship, knowledge spillovers, technological change

JEL CLASSIFICATION: O3, R1, J24, M13

1. Introduction

The story of the entrepreneurial process is one of the entrepreneur recognizing and acting on unexploited opportunity. Opportunity frequently

Final version accepted on February 9, 2005

Zoltán J. Ács
Max-Plank-Institute for Research into Economic Systems
Jena
Germany
and Merrick School of Business
University of Baltimore
Baltimore, MD 21201, USA
E-mail· zacs@ubalt,edu

Attila Varga
Center for Research in Economic Policy (CREP)
and Department of Economics
Faculty of Business and Economics
University of Pécs
Pécs, Rákóczi 80, H-7622, Hungary
E-mail vargaa@ktk.pte.hu

exists in a crowded space of knowledge creating institutions, networks and venture capitalists. This 'Silicon Valley' story has been told in the context of other high technology agglomerations including Seattle, WA, Austin, TX, Boston, MA, and Washington, D.C. It also has its international counter parts in Bangalore, India, London, UK and Baden-Würtenberg, Germany. While this suggests that entrepreneurship and agglomerations play an important role in economic growth this has not been worked out theoretically (Bresnahan, Gambardella and Saxenian, 2001).

The seminal contribution of Romer (1986, 1990) to the literature on economic growth was to endogenize technological change within an economy in a general equilibrium model with well-specified market forms, selfish agents, perfect foresight and clearing markets. This provided a more realistic explanation of economic growth than the neoclassical theory that focuses on the role of investment in physical capital, increases in the supply of labor, and an exogenous change in technology. According to Romer (1996, 204):

> New growth theory started on the technology-as-public good path and worried about where technology came from, but it soon backed up and reconsidered the initial split that economists make in the physical world. New growth theorists now start by dividing the world into two fundamentally different types of productive inputs that can be called "ideas" and "things". Ideas are nonrival goods that could be stored in a bit string. Things are rival goods with mass (or energy). With ideas and things, one can explain how economic growth works. Nonrival ideas can be used to rearrange things, for example, when one follows a recipe that transforms noxious olives into tasty and healthful olive oil. Economic growth arises from the discovery of new recipes and the transformation of things from low to high value configurations.

The above view leads to insights that do not follow from the neoclassical model. It emphasizes

324   *Zoltán J. Ács and Attila Varga*

that ideas are goods that are produced and distributed just as other goods are. If economic growth arises from the creation of new recipes to rearrange things, might not entrepreneurship and geography play some role in this transformation? However, the theory offers no insight into what role, if any, entrepreneurship and agglomeration might play in economic growth. In other words, it does not answer the question, "What is the role of entrepreneurship and agglomeration in technological change?"

An answer to this question can be pursued through the lens of the new economic geography and the modern theory of entrepreneurship. The distinguishing characteristic of the new economic geography is that it studies the economy within a framework that integrates space into general equilibrium theory (Fujita, et al., 1999; Krugman, 1991). One aspect of economic geography is the agglomeration of knowledge. Over the past decade, the new economic geography literature has tried to explain the development, and the economic role of geographic structures, and one of the important questions is related to the role of agglomeration in technological change and ultimately in macroeconomic growth (Fujita and Thisse, 2002).

The recent literature on entrepreneurship has shifted the emphasis in entrepreneurship from cultural and psychological traits to the discovery and exploitation of new knowledge by profit-seeking agents (Shane and Venkataraman, 2000). If entrepreneurs play an important role in the exploitation of technological opportunity the impact of entrepreneurship on growth becomes an important research question (Carree and Thurik, 2003). This relationship is especially important at the spatial level (Acs and Armington, 2004).

Both the relationship between geography and technological change, and between entrepreneurship and technological change, is interesting because these lines of research may prove fruitful in better explaining economic growth through knowledge spillovers. However, both approaches have severe limitations. For example, while there have been several attempts to model new growth theory with endogenously generated spatial structures this work is still in its infancy, until the very recent attempts by Fujita and Thisse (2002) and Baldwin et al. (2003). The purpose of this paper is to develop an empirical framework that endogenizes both entrepreneurial activity and agglomeration effects on knowledge spillovers. We present the first empirical test of the impact of entrepreneurial activity and agglomeration effects on the spillover of new knowledge, based on the Romerian (1990) model of endogenous technological change, as modified by Jones (1995). The model allows us to directly test the relationship between technological change and knowledge creation, conditioned by entrepreneurship and agglomeration effects, while controlling for knowledge spillovers.

We use a new and novel data set from the Global Entrepreneurship Monitor (GEM) project to test the effects of entrepreneurship on knowledge spillovers, and an index is created to measure the effect of agglomeration on knowledge spillovers in the European Union. Section 2 examines the relationship between agglomeration, knowledge spillovers and economic growth and the relationship between entrepreneurship, knowledge spillovers and economic growth. Section 3 extends the basic Romer framework, develops the empirical specification and presents the data, Section 4 has the results and the final section presents the conclusions. We find significant empirical support for the Romer model, where the coefficient on the stock of knowledge is significant but less then one. We also find support for the hypothesis that both agglomeration effects and entrepreneurship facilitate the knowledge spillover mechanism of new knowledge in economic growth.

2. Entrepreneurship and agglomeration

Technological change is the most important factor in long-run macroeconomic growth (Solow 1957). In new growth theory the technological element of the growth process is directly modeled within the economic system as a result of profit motivated choices of economic agents. Recently published findings in entrepreneurship, the geography of innovation and the new economic geography suggest that the extent to which a country is 'entrepreneurial' and its economic system is 'agglomerated' could be a factor that explains technological change. In this section we outline these literatures from an economic growth perspective.

2.1. *Entrepreneurship and technological change*

The origins of the discussion about the existence of opportunity can be traced to Joseph Schumpeter (1934). Schumpeter believed that the existence of opportunity required the introduction of new knowledge not just differentiated access to existing knowledge (Kirzner, 1973). One source of new knowledge came from changes in technology. These technological opportunities are innovative and break away from existing knowledge.

Opportunity therefore comes in part from the research and development (R&D) process that takes place in society. Technological change is an important source of entrepreneurial opportunity because it makes it possible for people to allocate resources in different and potentially more productive ways (Casson, 1995).

However, as was pointed out by Arrow (1974) the link between knowledge and economic knowledge is not well understood. The central problem is a gap in our understanding between technological change and the market that come into existence based on that innovation – this gap in our understanding is filled by the concept of entrepreneurial opportunity. An entrepreneurial opportunity consists of a set of ideas, beliefs and actions that enable the creation of future goods and services in the absence of current markets for them.

If technological opportunity is in part created by the production of new knowledge how is this opportunity discovered? One way in which people discover technological opportunity is through knowledge spillovers. Entrepreneurial discovery is in fact a process of knowledge spillover where knowledge is a non-rival good. Once entrepreneurs discover new opportunities, which are only partially excludable, they have the chance to exploit the opportunity. While most R&D is carried out in large firms and universities it does not mean that the same individuals that discover the opportunity will carry out the exploitation. In fact, because knowledge spills over, one person may discover an opportunity and another may exploit it.

The uncertainty inherent in new economic knowledge, combined with asymmetries between the agent possessing that knowledge and the decision making of the incumbent organization with respect to its expected value potentially leads to a gap between the valuations of the knowledge. This initial condition of not just uncertainty but greater degree of uncertainty vis-à-vis incumbent enterprises in the industry is captured in the theory of firm selection and industry evolution proposed by Jovanovic (1982). An implication of the theory of firm selection is that new firms may begin at a small scale of output, and then if merited by subsequent performance expand. What emerges from the new evolutionary theories and empirical evidence on the role of new firms is that markets are in motion, with a lot of new firms entering the industry and lots of firms leaving (Audretsch, 1995). The empirical evidence supports such an evolutionary view of entrepreneurship (Caves, 1998; Sutton, 1997).

The empirical evidence also supports the argument that technological change is a source of entrepreneurial opportunity. The evidence is indirect since we cannot measure the existence of opportunity. Acs and Audretsch (1989) found that young entrepreneurial firms play a key role in generating technological innovations, at least in some industries. Blau (1987) examined self-employment rates in the United States over a two-decade period and found that an increase in the rate of technological change led to an increase in the self-employment rate, Shane (1996) looked at the number of organizations per capita from 1899 to 1988 found that the rate of technological change, measured as the annual number of new patents issued, had a positive effect on the number of organizations per capita in the economy in the subsequent year.

While the relationship between technological change and opportunity cannot be measured directly, several authors have tried to measure the relationship between entrepreneurship and employment growth. Acs and Armington (2004) found that differences in the level of entrepreneurial activity, and the extent of human capital are positively associated with variation in growth rates. Holtz-Eakin and Kao (2003) using a rich panel of state-level data to quantify the relationship between productivity growth and entrepreneurship found that the effect of new firm formation on productivity is quite persistent.

These results are consistent with Audretsch and Keilbach (2004) who estimate a production function model for German regions based on start-up data from the 1990s. The empirical evidence suggests that entrepreneurship plays an important role in the discovery and exploitation of technological opportunity through knowledge spillovers, lead to higher economic growth.

Theories of entrepreneurship and economic growth are still relatively new even though the entrepreneurship literature does recognize that R&D is an important source of technological opportunity. The process by which knowledge spills over from the firm producing it for use by a third-party firm is exogenous in the model proposed by Romer (1990). The emphasis was on the influence of knowledge spillovers on technological change without specifying *why* and *how* new knowledge spills over. Yet, the critical issue in modeling knowledge-based growth rests on the spillover of knowledge. This was to some extent remedied by the neo-Schumpeterian models of endogenous growth (Aghion and Howitt, 1992, Cheng and Dinopoulos, 1992, Schmitz, 1989, Segerstrom,1991, Segerstrom, et al.,1990). However, these neo-Schumpeterian models design entrepreneurship as an R&D race where a fraction of R&D will turn into successful innovations.

While this implies a step forward, the essence of the Schumpeterian entrepreneur is missed. The innovation process stretches far beyond R&D races that predominantly involve large incumbent firms and concern quality improvements of existing goods. As pointed out by Schumpeter (1947) "the inventor produces ideas, the entrepreneur 'gets things done' ... an idea or scientific principle is not, by itself, of any importance for economic practice." Indeed, the Schumpeterian entrepreneur, by and large, remains absent in those models (Acs et al., 2004).

2.2. *Agglomeration and technological change*

As long as the knowledge necessary for technological change is codified (i.e., it can be studied in written forms either in professional journals and books or in patent documentations) the access to it is essentially not constrained by spatial distance: among other means libraries or the Internet can facilitate the flow of that knowledge to the interested user no matter where the user actually locates.

However, in case knowledge is not codified, because it is not yet completely developed, or it is so practical that it can only be transmitted while knowledge is actually being applied, the flow of knowledge can only be facilitated by personal interactions. Thus, for the transmission of tacit knowledge spatial proximity of knowledge owners and potential users appears to be critical (Polanyi, 1967). For example, several firms move their research facilities to geographic areas where significant amounts of related knowledge has already been accumulated in order to get easier access to that knowledge. Knowledge from other (industrial or academic) research facilities can be channeled via different means, such as, a web of social connections, the local labor market for scientists and engineers or by different types of consultancy relations between universities and private firms.

A large body of literature exists on the spatial extent of knowledge spillovers. At different levels of spatial aggregation (such as states, metropolitan areas, countries) in different countries (e.g. the US, France, Germany, Italy, Austria) and with the application of different econometric methodologies (e.g., various spatial or a-spatial methods) many of these studies conclude that geographical proximity to the knowledge source significantly amplifies spillovers between research and innovating firms. Strong evidence is provided both for the US (Acs et al., 2002; Jaffe et al., 1993; Varga 1998) and for Europe (e.g., Autant-Bernard, 2001, Fischer and Varga, 2003) that knowledge flows are bounded within a relatively narrow geographical range. Although certain industrial differences exists (such as for innovation in the microelectronics, instruments or biotechnology sectors proximity is more significant than for new technology development in the chemicals or the machinery industries) the hypothesis that spatial proximity is an important factor in innovation is strongly supported in the literature.

Varga (2000, 2001) provides empirical evidence that the spillover impact in knowledge production is positively related to the size of the region. Different types of agglomeration effects are at work to explain this phenomenon. Larger regions inhabit more firms connected by richer network linkages and as such the same knowledge generated by research in the area spills over to potentially more applications. Larger regions also offer a wider selection of producer services essential in technological innovation (e.g., information technology, legal, marketing services) contributing to a larger number of new technologies developed from the same knowledge base generated by (public and private) research in the area.

The new economic geography literature provides a general equilibrium framework where spatial economic structure is endogenously determined simultaneously with equilibrium in goods and factor markets (Fujita et al., 1999; Krugman,1991). This is a real breakthrough in economics given that before the appearance of the new economic geography no any school of economics since von Thünen' *Der Isolirte Staat* in the early nineteenth century had been able to build an economic model where the development of spatial structure is treated endogenously within a general equilibrium framework (Samuelson, 1983). The most recent models in the new economic geography incorporate the effects of knowledge spillovers on the formation of spatial economic structure as well as provide the first attempts to explicitly integrate the two 'new' schools of economics: the new growth theory and the new economic geography (Baldwin et al., 2003 Fujita and Thisse 2002). The need for the integration of the two schools is clear if one takes into account that agglomeration facilitates knowledge spillovers (according to the new economic geography) and knowledge spillovers determine per-capita GDP growth (according to the new growth theory) then it is not an unrealistic assumption that spatial economic structure affects macroeconomic growth.

Unfortunately, empirical investigations in the area of agglomeration and technological change are still relatively uncommon in the literature. The very few exceptions include Ciccone and Hall (1996), Ciccone (2002) and Varga and Schalk (2004). The following section presents the empirical modeling framework to integrate entrepreneurship and agglomeration into the explanation of technological change (and implic-

itly into the explanation of macroeconomic growth).

3.The empirical modeling framework

Our framework for empirical investigation is based on the Romer (1990) model of aggregate knowledge production as extended by Jones (1995). One of the most original contributions of Romer (1990) is the separation of economically useful scientific technological knowledge into two parts. The total set of knowledge consists of the subsets of non-rival, partially excludable knowledge elements that can practically be considered as public goods and the rival, excludable elements of knowledge. Codified knowledge published in books, scientific papers or in patent documentations belongs to the first group. This knowledge is non-rival since eventually it can be used by several actors at the same time and many times historically. On the other hand it is only partially excludable since only the right of applying a technology for the production of a particular good can be guaranteed by patenting while the same technology can spill over to further potential economic applications as others can study the patent documentation. Rival, excludable knowledge elements include the personalized (tacit) knowledge including particular experiences, insights developed and owned by the researchers themselves.

Equation (1) presents the manner the two types of knowledge interact in the production of economically useful new technological knowledge.

$$\mathring{A} = \delta H_A \lambda A^\varphi \tag{1}$$

where H_A stands for the number of researchers working on knowledge production in the business sector, A is the total stock of technological knowledge available at a certain point in time whereas $\mathring{A}$ is the change in technological knowledge resulting from private efforts to invest in research and development: δ, λ and φ are parameters. Equation (1) plays a central role in economic growth explanation since on the steady state growth path the rate of per capita GDP growth equals the rate of technological change $(\mathring{A}/A)$.

328   *Zoltán J. Ács and Attila Varga*

Technological change is generated by research and it depends on the number of researchers involved in knowledge creation (H_A). However, their efficiency is directly related to the total stock of already available knowledge (A). Knowledge spillovers are central to the growth process: the higher A, the larger the change in technology produced by the same number of researchers. The same number of researchers with a similar value of A can raise the level of already existing technological knowledge with significant differences depending on the size of the parameters. Consider $\delta > 0$, which is the research productivity parameter. The larger is δ, the more efficient is H_A in producing economically useful new knowledge.

The size of φ reflects the extent to which the total stock of already established knowledge impacts knowledge production. Given that A stands for the level of codified knowledge (available in the academic literature or patent documentation), φ is called the parameter of codified knowledge spillovers. The size of φ reflects the portion of A that spills over and as such its value largely influences the effectiveness of research in generating new technologies. Hence the value of the aggregate codified knowledge spillovers parameter φ should be between 0 and 1.

However, not only codified but also non-codified, tacit knowledge can spill over as detailed in the previous section. The value of λ, in (1) reflects the extent to which tacit knowledge spills over within the research sector. The larger is λ in equation (1), the stronger the impact the same number of researchers plays in technological change. In contrast to φ and δ, which are determined primarily in the research sector and as such their values are exogenous to the economy, λ is endogenous because its value depends on the spatial pattern of economic activities and the level of entrepreneurial activity in the country. The size of λ in equation (1) relates to spatial economic structure in two ways. First, the higher the spatial concentration of research, the higher λ because spatial proximity promotes spillovers to a large extent. Second, as recent empirical studies suggest, the magnitude of localized knowledge spillovers from research is also influenced by agglomeration.

The value to λ is also influenced by the amount of entrepreneurial activity because the value of new economic knowledge is uncertain. While most R&D is carried out in knowledge creating institutions (large firms and universities) it does not mean that the same individuals that discover the opportunity will carry out the exploitation. An implication of the theory of firm selection is that new firms may enter an industry in large numbers to exploit knowledge spillovers. The higher the rate of new firm entry the greater should be the value of λ because of knowledge spillovers.

Based on the literature we assume that these spillovers are influenced largely by agglomeration as well as by the level of entrepreneurial activity in the country.To empirically investigate the extent to which entrepreneurship and agglomeration affect knowledge spillovers we develop an empirical model in which we endogenize the parameter λ in equation (1).

$$\log(NK) = \delta + \lambda \log(H) + \varphi \log(A) + \varepsilon \qquad (2)$$

$$\lambda = (\beta_1 + \beta_2 \log(ENTR) + \beta_3 \log(AGGL)) \qquad (3)$$

where NK. stands for new knowledge (i.e., the change in A), ENTR is entrepreneurship, AGGL is agglomeration, A is the set of publicly available scientific-technological knowledge and ε is stochastic error term, Implementation of (3) into (2) results in the following estimated equation:

$$\begin{aligned} \log(NK) = {} & \delta + \beta_1 \log(H) \\ & + \beta_2 \log(ENTR)\log(H) \\ & + \beta_3 \log(AGGL)\log(H) \\ & + \varphi \log(A) + \varepsilon \end{aligned} \qquad (4)$$

In (4) the estimated values of the parameters β_2 and β_3 measure the extent to which research interacted with entrepreneurship and agglomeration contributes to knowledge creation.

In the estimation of (4) the units of observation are selected industrial sectors in European countries for the year 2001.[1] The selection of countries and sectors is determined by data availability. The number of patent applications operationalizes NK. Although patents are good indicators of new technology creation, they do not measure the economic value of these technologies (Hall et al., 2001). According to Griliches (1979) and Pakes and Griliches (1980, 378) "patents are a flawed measure (of innovative output) particularly since not all new innovations are patented and since patents differ greatly in their economic impact." However, a recent comparative study of direct innovation measures and patent applications evidence that patent applications are good proxy for innovation in econometric models (Acs et al, 2002).

R&D expenditures in Euro measure H. Data accessibility explains this choice to measure H in (1). An earlier comparison of R&D expenditures and employment data conclude that the two measures are highly correlated with each other and the results of regression analyses are not significantly different (Varga, 1998). This makes us confident to apply R&D expenditures in our study.

A is operationalized by the total number of available patents in all the sectors in the country (i.e., the total number of patents granted by inventors of the country in the last 20 years). The source of patent data is the OECD patent database. International patent classification (IPC) classes are assigned to industrial classes (ISIC Rev. 2) by the application of the MERIT concordance table developed by Verspagen, Moergastel and Slabbers (1994), Eurostat provides R&D expenditures data.

AGGL is measured by the agglomeration index that is calculated as the share of employment of city regions where the number of employees exceeds 500,000 in country total employment.[2] Eurostat provides regional employment data. ENTR is empirically measured by the total entrepreneurial activity (TEA) index developed within the framework of the GEM project.

The intent of GEM is to systematically assess two things: the level of start-up activity or the prevalence of nascent firms and the prevalence of new or young firms that have survived the start-up phase. First, start-up activity is measured by the proportion of the adult population (18–64 years of age) in each country that is currently engaged in the process of creating a nascent business. Second the proportion of adults in each country who are involved in operating a business that is less than 42 months old measures the presence of new firms. The distinction between nascent and new firms is made in order to determine the relationship of each to national economic growth. For both measures, the research focus is on entrepreneurial activity in which the individual involved have a direct but not necessarily full, ownership interest in the business. There are numerous ways to measure entrepreneurial activity. One important distinction is between opportunity-based entrepreneurial activity and necessity-based entrepreneurial activity. Opportunity entrepreneurship represents the voluntary nature of participation and necessity reflecting the individual's perception that such actions presented the best option available for employment but not necessarily the preferred option. Opportunity entrepreneurship differs from necessity by sector of industry and with respect to growth aspirations. Opportunity entrepreneurs expect their ventures to produce more high growth firms and provide more new jobs. The 16 European Union countries in 2001 had an average prevalence rate of about 8 percent (Reynolds et al., 2001).

To further explore this question of high potential entrepreneurs the 2002 GEM researchers added several new questions to the GEM protocol in order to isolate those ventures widely believed to have the greatest possibility for having a substantial impact on the economy. These new items were utilized to locate those ventures with potential to create new markets. Two additional criteria were added to further distinguish those new ventures with the potential to make a major contribution to the national economy: (1) the expectation of 20 or more jobs created within five years and (2) the intention to export goods or services. Of the 9615 star-ups and new firms identified in the 37 countries, only 926 met all of these criteria, about 9.6 percent (Reynolds et al., 2002).

4. Empirical results

In empirically estimating equation (4) two issues should get particular attention: multicollinearity (because H appears three times in the equation) and heteroskedasticity (since the expected heterogeneity of the country-industry dataset).

Table I presents empirical estimation results for equation (4). The equation is estimated by OLS. Standard errors are based on the White heteroskedasticity consistent covariance matrix estimator that provides correct estimates of the coefficient covariances in the presence of heteroskedasticity of unknown form (White 1980).

In Model 1 the estimated parameter of $\log(H)$ is highly significant. The logarithm of R&D expenditures explains 75 percent of the variations in the logarithm of patent applications at the country-industry level. The additional effect of $\log(A)$ where A is measured by the aggregate stock of available patents is considerable: it improves regression fit by 24 percent. Both coefficients are highly significant indicating that the original Romer (1990) equation captures well the main factors in technological change.

In Model 2 ENTR is measured by the high potential index. Extending Model 1 by the interaction terms $\log(H)*\log(AGGL)$ and $\log(H)*\log(ENTR)$ improves regression fit only slightly.[3]

The estimated parameter for $\log(H)*\log(ENTR)$ is significant at ($p < 0.05$) while the agglomeration effect is not significant in Model 2. This latter result might be the outcome of a shortcoming of the measurement applied (i.e., the agglomeration index is not sensitive to differences in the relative geographical positions of city regions within a country). Technical constraints could not make it possible for us to improve on this agglomeration measure. However, we also assumed that perhaps the United Kingdom as an outlier observation of AGGL might cause the unexpected result.[4]

To account for this effect in agglomeration a dummy variable (DUMUK) is included in Model 2a. The parameter of DUMUK is marginally significant ($p < 0.10$) whereas the interaction term's parameter becomes significant ($p < 0.05$). This supports the hypothesis that in Model 2a the high potential index enters the estimated equation with a highly significant parameter value ($p < 0.01$). Regression fit increases only slightly as compared to the original Romer equation in

TABLE I

Ols regression results for Log(Patent applications) for selected industries in selected European countries ($N = 63$, 2001)

	Model 1 Romer	Model 2 Extended Romer with TEA high potential	Model 2a Extended Romer with TEA high potential	Model 3 Extended Romer with TEA Opportunity	Model 4 Extended Romer with TEA Necessity	Model 5 Extended Romer with TEA
Constant	$-3\,175^{a}$	$-2\,843^{a}$	$-2\,966^{a}$	$-3\,711^{a}$	-3.506^{a}	-3.513^{a}
	$(0\,346)$	$(0\,360)$	$(0\,368)$	$(0\,467)$	$(0\,468)$	$(0\,482)$
Log (H)	$0\,298^{a}$	$0\,355^{a}$	0.442^{a}	$0\,204^{c}$	$0\,396^{a}$	$0\,257^{c}$
	(0.061)	(0.074)	$(0\,080)$	$(0\,102)$	$(0\,079)$	(0.134)
Log(H) *Log(AGGL)		$0\,024$	$0\,086^{b}$	$0\,112^{b}$	$0\,100^{c}$	$0\,089^{c}$
		$(0\,032)$	$(0\,042)$	$(0\,046)$	$(0\,054)$	$(0\,047)$
Log(H)*Log(ENTR)		$0\,069^{b}$	$0\,079^{a}$	$0\,143^{b}$	$0\,038$	$0\,073$
		$(0\,028)$	$(0\,030)$	$(0\,056)$	$(0\,048)$	$(0\,062)$
Log(A)	$0\,723^{a}$	0.679^{a}	$0\,698^{a}$	$0\,794^{a}$	$0\,775^{a}$	$0\,773^{a}$
	$(0\,063)$	$(0\,055)$	$(0\,056)$	$(0\,072)$	$(0\,077)$	(0.075)
DUMUK			-0.740^{c}	$-0\,852^{b}$	$-0\,716^{c}$	$-0\,711^{c}$
			(0.378)	(0.327)	$(0\,407)$	(0.407)
R^2-adj	0.92	0.93	$0\,93$	$0\,93$	$0\,93$	$0\,93$
F-statistic	357^{a}	189^{a}	160^{a}	162^{a}	145^{a}	147^{a}

Note: TEA high potential index is available only for year 2002, White heteroscedasticity–consistent estimated standard errors are in parentheses
[a] Denotes significance at least at 0.01
[b] Denotes significance at least at 0.05.
[c] Denotes significance at least 0 10; variables are introduced in the main text

Model 1. Estimated parameters of the Romer equation as well as their significance patterns are stable across models 1 to 2 These observations suggest that multicollinearity is not a serious issue in the model.

Table I also shows estimates for the different additional measures of entrepreneurship provided by the GEM project. Model 3 shows results for opportunity entrepreneurship, Model 4 gives the results for necessity entrepreneurship and Model 5 is the output with TEA. While in Model 3 the coefficient for opportunity entrepreneurship is positive and statistically significant, for both Model 4 and Model 5, the interaction term for entrepreneurial activity is not significant. This result is consistent with the fact that necessity entrepreneurship, having to become an entrepreneur because you have no better option, will not lead to technological change, although it may lead to employment growth. The same is true of entrepreneurial activity in general.

The estimated elasticity of technological change with respect to available codified knowledge is less than 1 (0.7) that corresponds to what is suggested by Jones (1995). The estimated research spillover effect in Model 2a is related to high potential entrepreneurship and agglomeration according to the following equation:

$$\lambda = 0.44 + 0.086^*Log(AGGL)$$
$$+ 0.079^*Log(ENTR) \qquad (5)$$

What do these results suggest for entrepreneurship and agglomeration? Table II shows the coefficients for knowledge spillovers for the nine countries with and without the effect of entrepreneurship and agglomeration. As shown in column two agglomeration varies considerably from country to country with a high of 0.59 in the UK to a low of 0.14 in Poland. The TEA high potential index also varies from a low of 0.19 percent in Belgium to a high of 1.52 in Ireland. The elasticity of R&D spillovers with respect to new knowledge is 0.30 (Model 1 in Table I), This number is relatively small with respect to the 0.70 elasticity found for the total stock of knowledge.

One would suspect that entrepreneurship and agglomeration would be able to significantly raise the effect of R&D spillovers from new knowledge. This would especially be true if entrepreneurs played an important role in knowledge spillovers as suggested by the entrepreneurship literature. In Table II, column four shows the value of the coefficient of λ extended by entrepreneurship and agglomeration effects. The coefficient varies between 0.31 and 0.42 and is greater than 0.30 in all the countries in the sample. How should we interpret these results? Compared to what? The only other study we know of that measures the interaction between entrepreneurship and research and development is Michelacci (2003) who found that the value of λ for the United States varied between 0.24 and 0.48 for the post-war period. These findings are broadly consistent with those results. The last column shows the ratio of the extended coefficient divided by the non-extended coefficient. The ratio varies from 1.04 to 1.41.

TABLE II
Country coefficients with and without extension for entrepreneurship and agglomeration

	AGGL	TEA HIGH	Coefficient (Model 2a)	Coefficient (Model 1)	Coefficient ratio
Belgium	0 31	0 64	0 38	0.30	1.28
France	0 34	0 57	0 38	0 30	1.28
Germany	0 18	1 47	0 39	0 30	1 31
Hungary	0 24	0 76	0 38	0 30	1 27
Ireland	0 35	1.52	0 42	0.30	1 40
Italy	0 18	0.71	0 37	0.30	1 23
Poland	0.14	0 19	0 31	0.30	1 04
Spain	0 43	0 64	0 40	0 30	1 33
United Kingdom	0 59	0 99	0 42	0 30	1 41

332   *Zoltán J. Ács and Attila Varga*

These results suggest that increasing research and development expenditures, without increasing entrepreneurial activity, and or agglomeration effects, may not achieve the same result as if it was accompanied by entrepreneurial activity and agglomeration effects (Acs et al., 2004). After taking into account the effect of the stock of knowledge and research and development expenditures, both agglomeration and entrepreneurship have a weak positive effect on technological change. It is unlikely that a substantial high technological entrepreneurial sector will develop in the absence of broad national participation in entrepreneurship. If one wanted to increase technological change in the European Union more agglomeration of economic activity and more entrepreneurship may increase the amount of knowledge spillovers.

5. Conclusion

This paper developed an empirical model that endogenizes both entrepreneurial activity and agglomeration effects on knowledge spillovers within a Romerian framework. We tested a modified model of technological change to ascertain the impact of agglomeration effects and entrepreneurial activity on endogenous technological change. Specifically, we examine the impact of entrepreneurial activity and agglomeration effects on the spillover of new knowledge. The effect of agglomeration on technological change is positive and statistically significant. The effect of entrepreneurship on technological change is positive and highly significant. When the interactive terms are taken into account the regression fit increases only slightly. Consequently we found significant, but not too strong agglomeration and entrepreneurship effects on technological change for selected European countries. These results are broadly consistent with a growing body of literature suggesting that entrepreneurial activity and agglomeration play a positive role in knowledge spillovers and therefore in technological change and economic growth.

We also find that the endogenous growth model developed by Romer (1990) does a good job of modeling economic growth. We found support for Jones (1995) that the spillover effects from codified knowledge are less then one. There

are several caveats that should be kept in mind. First, the GEM data might not be a good measure of either opportunity entrepreneurship in general or high technology entrepreneurship in particular. However, strong co-occurrence among these diverse measures indicated that the indices are reasonable measures of the overall level of different types of entrepreneurial activity. Second, we only have one year of data at the start of a recession. A longer time period may reveal different results. Finally, the inter relationship between agglomeration effects and entrepreneurial activity may be important. However, we did not model this in our paper and is an interesting topic for further research.

Notes

[1] Industrial sectors include Chemistry and Pharmaceuticals, Computers and Office Machines, Electrical Machinery, Electronics, Instruments, Other Machinery, Transportation Vehicles. The following European countries are included; Belgium, Germany, France, Hungary, Ireland, Italy, Poland, Spain and the United Kingdom.

[2] With the exception of Belgium and the UK where the highest level of data aggregation is NUTS 2 for the rest of the countries the agglomeration index is calculated using NUTS 3 level aggregated employment data.

[3] Equation (4) forms the basis of our empirical investigations. This explains why we do not account for the direct effect of either ENTR or AGGL on technological changer.

[4] A closer investigation of the agglomeration index suggests that economic activities exhibit an exceptionally high level of spatial concentration in the UK (relative to the rest of the countries in the sample). While the agglomeration index for the UK is 0 59 the corresponding average value for the rest of the sample countries is 0.27 According to this the UK economy appears to be more than two times concentrated geographically than the rest of Europe. This observation might well be the sign of aggregation bias as the lowest level of data aggregation for the UK is NUTS 2 while for the rest of the countries (with the exception of Belgium) data are aggregated at NUTS 3 level. While this does not seem to distort the value of the index for Belgium (i e, the size of NUTS 2 regions are compatible with the average size of NUTS 3 regions in our sample) it might not be the case for the UK Running separate regressions with and without the UK further supports the presence of regional data aggregation bias: with the exception of the 'agglomeration effect' the UK follow very similar patterns to the rest of Europe: parameter estimates and their significances are similar for log(*H*), log(*A*) and log(*H*)*log (ENTR) This is not repeated for the geography effect: the number of patents in the UK exceeds the rest of the sample

average only slightly as it is 632 in the UK and 478 otherwise while AGGL is more than twice as high in the UK

Acknowledgements

We wish to thank Edward Malecki, participants at the first GEM conference in Berlin, Germany and at the international workshop on "Regions in Action: The Nexus of Innovation, Entrepreneurship and Public Policy" at the Tinbergen Institute in Amsterdam, the Netherlands, two anonymous referees and the editors of this special issue for valuable comments. The usual caveat applies.

References

Acs, Zoltan J , Luc Anselin, and Attila Varga, 2002, 'Patents and Innovation Counts as Measures of Regional Production of New Knowledge', *Research Policy* **31**, 1069–1085.

Acs, Zoltan J. and Catherine Armington, 2004, 'Employment Growth and Entrepreneurial Activity in Cities', *Regional Studies* **38**(8), 911–927.

Acs, Zoltan J. and David B. Audretsch, 2003, *Handbook of Entrepreneurship Research*, Boston: Kluwer Academic Publishers.

Acs, Zoltan J., David B, Audretsch, Pontus Braunerhjelm and Bo Carlsson, 2004, *The Missing Link: The Knowledge Filter and Entrepreneurship in Endogenous Growth*, Discussion Paper, No 4783, December, Center for Economic Policy Research, London, UK.

Aghion, Philip and Peter Howitt, 1992, 'A Model of Growth through Creative Destruction', *Econometrica* **60**, 323–351.

Arrow, Keneth, 1974, 'Limited Knowledge and Economic Analysis', *American Economic Review* **64**(1), 1–10.

Audretsch, David, 1995, *Innovation and Industry Evolution*, Cambridge: The MIT Press

Audretsch, David and Max Keilbach, 2004, 'Entrepreneurship Capital and Economic Performance', *Regional Studies* **38**(8), 949–959.

Autant-Bernard, Corinne, 2001, 'Science and Knowledge Flows. Evidence from the French Case', *Research Policy* **30**, 1069–1078

Baldwin, Richard, Rikard Forslid, Philippe Martin, Gianmarco Ottaviano, and Frederic Robert-Nicoud, 2003, *Economic Geography and Public Policy*, Princeton: Princeton University Press

Blau, David, 1987, 'A Time-series Analysis of Self-employment in the United States', *Journal of Political Economy* **95**, 445–467

Bresnahan, Timothy, Alfonso Gambardella and Annalee Saxenian, 2001, 'Old Economy' Inputs for 'New Economy' Outcomes: Cluster Formation in the New Silicon Valleys', *Industrial and Corporate Change* **10**, 835–860.

Carree, Martin and Roy Thurik, 2003, 'The Impact of Entrepreneurship on Economic *Growth*', *Handbook of Entrepreneurship Research*, Boston Kluwer Academic Publishers.

Casson, Mark, 1995, *Entrepreneurship and Business Culture*, Brookfield: Aldershot, US: Edward Elgar.

Caves, Richard, 1998, 'Industrial Organization and New Findings on the Turnover and Mobility of Firm', *Journal of Economic Literature* **36**, 1947–1982.

Cheng, Leonard K. and Elias Dinopoulos, 1992, 'Schumpeterian Growth and International Business Cycles', *American Economic Review* **82**, 409–414.

Ciccone, Antonio, 2002, 'Agglomeration Effects in Europe', *European Economic Review* **46**, 213–227.

Ciccone, Antonio, and Robert Hall, 1996, 'Productivity and the Density of Economic Activity', *American Economic Review* **86**, 54–70.

Fischer, Manfred and Attila Varga, 2003, 'Spatial Knowledge Spillovers and University Research: Evidence from Austria', *Annals of Regional Science* **37**, 303–322

Fujita, Masahisa and Jacques-François Thisse, 2002, *Economics of Agglomeration Cities, Industrial Location, and Regional Growth*, Cambridge Cambridge University Press.

Fujita, Masahisa, Paul Krugman, and Anthony J. Venables, 1999, *The Spatial Economy*, Cambridge: MIT Press.

Griliches, Zvi, 1979, ' Issues in Assessing the Contribution of R&D to Productivity Growth', *Bell Journal of Economics* **10**, 92–116.

Hall, Bronwyn, Adam Jaffe, Manuel Trajtenberg, 2001, *The NBER Patent Citations Data File. Lessons, Insights and Methodological Tools*, WP 8498, National Bureau of Economic Research.

Holtz-Eakin, Doug and Chihwa Kao, 2003, *Entrepreneurship and Economic Growth: The Proof is in the Productivity*, Center for Policy Research, Syracuse University mineo.

Jaffe, Adam, Manuel Trajtenberg, Rebecca Henderson, 1993, 'Geographic Localization of Knowledge Spillovers as Evidenced by Patent Citations', *Quarterly Journal of Economics* **108**, 577–598

Jones, Charles, 1995, 'R&D Based Models of Economic Growth', *Journal of Political Economy* **103**, 759–84.

Jovanovic, Boyan, 1982, 'Selection and Evolution of Industry', *Econometrica* **50**, 649–670.

Kirzner, Israel M., 1973, *Competition and Entrepreneurship*, Chicago: University of Chicago Press.

Krugman, Paul, 1991, 'Increasing Returns and Economic Geography', *Journal of Political Economy* **99**(3), 483–499

Michelacci, Claudio, 2003, 'Low Returns in R&D due to the Lack of Entrepreneurial Skills', *The Economic Journal* **113**, 207–225.

Pakes, Ariel and Zvi Griliches, 1980, 'Patents and R&D at the Firm Level. A First Report', *Economics Letters* **5**, 377–381.

Polanyi, Michael, 1967, *The Tacit Dimension* New York: Doubleday Anchor

Reynolds, Paul D., S. Michael Camp, William D Bygrave, Erkko Autio, and Michael Hay, 2001, *Global Entrepreneurship Monitor, 2001 Executive Report.*

Reynolds, Paul. D , William D. Bygrave, Erkko Autio, L. W. Cox, Michael Hay, 2002, *Global Entrepreneurship Monitor, 2002 Executive Report.*

Romer, Paul, 1986, 'Increasing Returns and Long-run Growth ', *Journal of Political Economy* **94**, 1002–1037.

Romer, Paul, 1990, 'Endogenous Technological Change', *Journal of Political Economy* **98**, S71–S102.

Romer, Paul, 1996, 'Why, Indeed, in America? Theory, History, and the Origins of Modern Economic Growth', *American Economic Review* **86**, 202–207.

Samuelson, Paul, 1983, 'Thunen at Two Hundred', *Journal of Economic Literature* **21**, 1468–1488.

Schmitz, James, 1989, 'Imitation, Entrepreneurship, and Long-Run Growth', *Journal of Political Economy* **97**, 721–739.

Schumpeter, Joseph, 1934, *The Theory of Economic Development,* Cambridge, MA: Harvard University Press.

Schumpeter, Joseph, 1947, 'The Creative Response in Economic History', *Journal of Economic History* **7**, 149–159.

Segerstrom, Paul, 1991, 'Innovation, Imitation and Economic Growth', *Journal of Political Economy* **99**, 190–207.

Segerstrom, Paul, T. C. A. Anant and Elias Dinopoulos, 1990, 'A Schumpeterian Model of the Product Life Cycle', *American Economic Review* **80**, 1077–1091.

Shane, Scott, 1996, 'Explaining Variation in Rates of Entrepreneurship in the United States 1899–1988', *Journal of Management* **22**, 747–781.

Shane, Scott and Sankaran Venkataraman, 2000, 'The Promise of Entrepreneurship as a Field of Research', *Academy of Management Review* **25**, 217–221.

Solow, Robert, 1957 'Technical Change in an Aggregative Model of Economic Growth', *International Economic Review* **6**, 18–31.

Sutton, John, 1997, 'Gibrat's Legacy', *Journal of Economic Literature* **35**, 40–59.

Varga, Attila, 1998, *University Research and Regional Innovation. A Spatial Econometric Analysis of Academic Technology Transfers, Boston* : Kluwer Academic Publishers.

Varga, Attila, 2000, 'Local Academic Knowledge Spillovers and the Concentration of Economic Activity', *Journal of Regional Science* **40**, 289–309.

Varga, Attila, 2001, 'Universities and Regional Economic Development: Does Agglomeration Matter?', in Johansson Bent, Karlsson Charlie and Stough Roger (eds.), *Theories of Endogenous Regional Growth –Lessons for Regional Policies,* Berlin: Springer, pp. 345–367.

Varga, Attila and Hans J. Schalk, 2004, 'Knowledge Spillovers, Agglomeration and Macroeconomic Growth: An Empirical Approach', *Regional Studies* **38**, 977– 989.

Verspagen, Bart, T. Moergastel and M. Slabbers, 1994, 'MERIT Concordance Table: IPC ISIC (rev. 2)', *MERIT Research Memorandum 2/94/004,* Maastricht Economic Research Institute on Innovation and Technology, University of Limburg.

White, Halbert L., 1980, 'A Heteroskedasticity-Consistent Covariance Matrix and a Direct Test for Heteroskedasticity', *Econometrica* **48**, 817–838.

[31]

Small Business Economics (2005) 24: 311–321
DOI 10.1007/s11187-005-1996-6

The Effect of Entrepreneurial Activity on National Economic Growth

André van Stel
Martin Carree
Roy Thurik

ABSTRACT. Entrepreneurial activity is generally assumed to be an important aspect of the organization of industries most conducive to innovative activity and unrestrained competition This paper investigates whether *total entrepreneurial activity* (TEA) influences GDP growth for a sample of 36 countries. We test whether this influence depends on the level of economic development measured as GDP per capita. Adjustment is made for a range of alternative explanations for achieving economic growth by incorporating the *Growth Competitiveness Index* (GCI). We find that entrepreneurial activity by nascent entrepreneurs and owner/managers of young businesses affects economic growth, but that this effect depends upon the level of per capita income. This suggests that entrepreneurship plays a different role in countries in different stages of economic development.

KEY WORDS: entrepreneural activity, economic growth, economic development, nascent entrepreneurs.

JEL CLASSIFICATION: Ll6, M13, O11, O40.

1. Introduction

There are many factors that influence the speed of economic progress. Such factors may include

Final version accepted on February 9, 2005

André van Stel
Max Planck Institute for Research into Economic Systems
Kahlaische Strasse 10
D-07745 Jena
Germany
Email. stel@mpiew-jena.mpg de

Martin Carree
University of Maastricht

Roy Thurik
Erasmus University Rotterdam
EIM
Max Planck Institute Jena

climate, education, property rights, saving propensity, presence of seaports, etc. The empirical growth literature has suggested a large number of economic and non-economic variables that may influence economic growth (Sala-i-Martin, 1997; Bleaney and Nishiyama, 2002). Entrepreneurship has failed to be included in this list of variables (see e.g. Table I in Bleaney and Nishiyama, 2002). On the one hand, this is surprising since many economists would claim that entrepreneurial activity is vital to economic progress.[1] They will, for example, refer to the demise of communist economies where entrepreneurial activity was almost absent and to contributions by Schumpeter (1934) and (neo-)Austrian economists (like Kirzner, 1973).[2] On the other hand, it is less surprising since the measurement of the factor 'entrepreneurship' is far from easy. Most factors contributing to economic progress can be measured using existing secondary sources for a wide variety of countries. However, aside from self-employment measures, which are questionable measures of entrepreneurial activity, there were no sources up till recently to compare this activity across countries. The *Global Entrepreneurship Monitor* (GEM) has changed this.

There are various ways in which entrepreneurship may affect economic growth. Entrepreneurs may introduce important innovations by entering markets with new products or production processes (Acs and Audretsch, 1990, 2003). Entrepreneurs often play vital roles in the early evolution of industries, examples of such (successful American) entrepreneurs include Andrew Carnegie, Michael Dell, Thomas Edison, Henry Ford, Bill Gates, Ray Kroc and Sam Walton. Entrepreneurs may increase productivity by increasing competition (Geroski, 1989; Nickel, 1996; Nickel et al.,

1997). They may enhance our knowledge of what is technically viable and what consumers prefer by introducing variations of existing products and services in the market. The resulting learning process speeds up the discovery of the dominant design for product–market combinations. Knowledge spillovers play an important role in this process (Audretsch and Feldman, 1996; Audretsch and Stephan, 1996; Audretsch and Keilbach, 2004). Lastly, they may be inclined to work longer hours and more efficiently as their income is strongly linked to their working effort.

In this paper, we empirically investigate the effect of entrepreneurial activity on economic growth at the country level. We use recent and new material provided by the GEM. It contains the *Total Entrepreneurial Activity* (TEA) rate measuring the relative amount of nascent entrepreneurs and business owners of young firms for a range of countries. This variable is (consistently) measured across a variety of countries and appears to be a useful index for measuring the extent of 'entrepreneurship'. An important element in our analysis is to consider whether entrepreneurial activity plays a similar growth-stimulating role in highly developed economies (relatively rich countries) and in less developed economies (relatively poor countries, including both transformation economies and developing countries). Carree and Thurik (1999), for example, indicate that the presence of small firms in manufacturing industries benefits growth for the richest among EU-countries, but not for EU-countries with somewhat lower GDP per capita, like Portugal and Spain. This is in line with the regime shift introduced by Audretsch and Thurik (2001). They argue that there has been a shift from a model of the 'managed economy' towards that of the 'entrepreneurial economy' in highly developed economies.

Our test of the influence of 'entrepreneurship' is based on a statistical analysis of whether TEA influenced GDP growth in the 1999–2003 period for a sample of 36 countries. We test whether this influence depends upon the level of economic development measured as GDP per capita. We also distinguish between the extent of influence of 'entrepreneurship' for three groups of countries, viz. highly developed economies, transition economies and developing countries. Although

the limited number of observations does not allow for many competing explanatory variables, we include the *Growth Competitiveness Index* (GCI) in our model. This variable captures a range of alternative explanations for achieving sustained economic growth. In addition, we incorporate the initial level of economic development to correct for convergence.

The rest of this paper is organized as follows. In Section 2 the relation between entrepreneurial activity and economic growth and its dependence on the stage of economic development are discussed and the TEA and GCI rates are introduced. In Section 3 we present our model and a description of the variables. Section 4 is used for results and Section 5 concludes.

2. Entrepreneurship, competitiveness and growth

There have been efforts to empirically investigate the importance of the impact of entrepreneurship on economic performance, especially at the firm, region or industry level (e.g. Audretsch, 1995; Caves, 1998; Audretsch and Fritsch, 2002).[3] However, contributions at the level of the nation state are limited. Two recent exceptions are studies into the effect of self-employment rates on economic growth figures: Blanchflower (2000) and Carree et al. (2002). Even in these cases it is questionable whether self-employment rates are an adequate measure of entrepreneurial activity. This paper is a first attempt to investigate whether differences in the start-up activity and presence of young firms across countries has an impact on their economic performance.

The last two decades have witnessed both large (conglomerate) companies increasingly concentrating on core competences and experiencing mass lay-offs (especially in traditional manufacturing industries) and high-technology innovative small firms having come to the forefront of technological development in many (new) industries. These developments would suggest the key importance for modern economies of a sound entrepreneurial climate for achieving economic progress. In particular, Audretsch and Thurik (2001) argued that highly developed economies have experienced a shift from the model of the 'managed economy' towards that of the 'entrepreneurial economy'. The model of the 'managed economy' is the political, social and economic response to an economy dictated by the forces of large-scale production, reflecting the predominance of the production factors of capital and (unskilled) labor as the sources of competitive advantage. By contrast, the model of the 'entrepreneurial economy' is the political, social and economic response to an economy dictated not just by the dominance of the production factor of knowledge – which Romer (1990, 1994) and Lucas (1988) identified as replacing the more traditional factors as the source of competitive advantage – but also by a very different, but complementary factor they had overlooked: the presence of entrepreneurial activity to accommodate knowledge spillovers (see Acs and Audretsch, 2003; Audretsch and Keilbach, 2004).

The transition as described by Audretsch and Thurik (2001) can also be described in more 'Schumpeterian' terms.[4] In Schumpeter (1934) the role of the entrepreneur as prime cause of economic development was emphasized. Schumpeter described how the innovating entrepreneur challenges incumbent firms by introducing new inventions that make current technologies and products obsolete. This process of creative destruction is the main characteristic of what has been called the Schumpeter Mark I regime. In Schumpeter (1950) the focus was on innovative activities by large and established firms. Schumpeter described how large firms outperformed their smaller counterparts in the innovation and appropriation process through a strong positive feedback loop from innovation to increased R&D activities. This process of creative accumulation is the main characteristic of what has been called the Schumpeter Mark II regime. The extent to which either of the two Schumpeterian technological regimes prevails in a certain period and industry varies. It may depend upon the nature of knowledge required to innovate, the opportunities of appropriability, the degree of scale (dis)economies, the institutional environment, the importance of absorptive capacity, demand variety, etc. Industries in a Schumpeter Mark II regime are likely to develop a more concentrated market structure in contrast to industries in a Schumpeter Mark I regime where small firms will proliferate. The distinction between the Schumpeter Marks I and II regimes is closely related to that of the 'entrepreneurial' versus 'managed' economy.

These discussions suggest that the role and importance of entrepreneurial ventures may differ from one stage of economic development to another. Theoretical support for this idea was given by Lloyd-Ellis and Bernhardt (2000) who described how an economy goes through various stages of economic development.[5] Therefore, we should be careful when comparing countries in different stages of economic development. For example, high start-up rates in developing countries could be less a sign of economic strength when compared to such rates in highly developed economies. That is, a far smaller percentage of these start-ups in developing countries when compared to rich countries may develop into high-growth companies generating substantial value added. In particular, average human capital levels of entrepreneurs may differ between countries (shopkeepers versus Schumpeterian entrepreneurs). High start-up rates, reported in individual surveys, may be a sign of a substantial 'informal sector' in developing countries, not being a characteristic of an economy in progress. The main argument of this paper is that the impact of 'entrepreneurship' on growth differs for countries at different stages of development. For highly developed countries we expect a positive impact of entrepreneurial activity on subsequent economic performance. For relatively poor countries it is more uncertain what high start-up rates stand for, in terms of an industrial organization conducive to innovation and economic growth.

Countries, even in similar stages of economic development, differ strongly in the rates of entrepreneurial activity. The GEM *Global Executive Reports* show considerable differences between countries like Japan, France, Belgium and Sweden with low entrepreneurial activity and countries like the U.S., Canada, Australia and South Korea with high entrepreneurial activity. Some developing countries like Thailand and India top the list of countries with high entrepreneurial activity. Entrepreneurial activity is correlated with the self-employment rate (see e.g. Table I in Carree et al., 2002 and Table A.I in Audretsch et al., 2002). However, there are exceptions to this rule. Japan, for example, has self-employment rates that are relatively close to those of the U.S.

However, the new entry rate is far smaller in Japan, where there are many (inefficient) small establishments in the retail and wholesale sectors. Carree et al. (2002) showed that countries may not only have too few self-employed, but may also have too many. Italy is given as an example for the latter situation.[6]

If entrepreneurial activity is important for economic progress we should find that countries that are highly ranked on the list in terms of this activity also grow relatively fast. The usual ceteris paribus condition applies here since there are many other factors that may explain economic progress. These include factors like schooling, inflation, investment in fixed assets, climate, institutional quality and property rights. It is important to gain insight in alternative explanations for economic growth *next to* entrepreneurial activity.

In the present section we will discuss our two key variables, the TEA rate capturing elements of 'entrepreneurial energy' and the GCI rate encompassing a range of alternative explanatory variables.

Total entrepreneurial activity

Data on TEA are taken from the GEM Adult Population Survey. This database contains various entrepreneurial measures that are constructed on the basis of surveys of -on average- some 3000 respondents per country (37 countries in 2002). The TEA is defined as that percentage of adult population (18–64 years old) that is either actively involved in starting a new venture or is the owner/manager of a business that is less than 42 months old (Reynolds et al., 2002). In 2002 the TEA rate (per 100 adults) ranged from values above 15 in Chile, Thailand and India, to 10.5 in the United States, to values below four in Russia, Belgium, France, Japan, Croatia and Hong Kong. See Appendix 1. For most countries, TEA rates in 2002 were lower than in 2001 due to a universal decline in economic growth rates in 2002 compared to 2001. The relative rankings between countries though remained quite stable (Reynolds et al., 2002). For the 28 countries that participated in GEM both in 2001 and in 2002, the rank correlation (Spearman's ρ statistic) was 0.8. This indicates that TEA may be seen as a

structural characteristic of an economy. This makes the variable suitable for inclusion in models aiming to explain structural growth such as the model that we estimate in this paper.

Growth competitiveness index

The Growth Competitiveness framework is employed by the World Economic Forum's *Global Competitiveness Report* (GCR). A central objective of the GCR is to assess the capacity of the world's economies to achieve sustained economic growth. In the GCR this is done by analyzing the extent to which individual national economies have the structures, institutions, and policies in place for economic growth over the medium term (McArthur and Sachs, 2002). These features of national economies are summarized in the GCI. The GCR identifies three inter-related mechanisms involved in economic growth: efficient division of labor, capital accumulation (including human capital), and technological advance. Concerning the last-mentioned mechanism, a distinction is made between the creation of new technologies (*technological innovation*) and the adoption of technologies that have been developed abroad (*technology transfer*). In the GCR framework technological innovation is seen as the most important factor for achieving long-term economic growth. In this connection the GCR distinguishes between *core economies* (countries that are technological innovators) and *non-core economies*.[7] The core economies are typically the richest countries. It is argued that economic growth is achieved in different ways in these two types of economies. In core economy countries growth is powered by their capacity to innovate and to win new global markets for their technologically advanced products (technological innovation). High growth rates in non-core economies are often achieved by rapidly absorbing the advanced technologies and capital of the core economies, for example through high levels of foreign direct investment from high-tech multinationals of the core economies (technology transfer). This type of growth process is sometimes also called "catch-up growth".

Besides technology, two other major pillars of growth are identified in the Growth Competitiveness framework: the quality of public institutions and the macro-economic environment. Institutions are crucial for their role in ensuring the protection of property rights, the objective resolution of contract and other legal disputes, and the transparency of government. All these factors are important for achieving an efficient division of labor. Public institutions are also important for establishing the societal stability required to achieve economic growth. The macro-economic environment relates to government monetary and fiscal policies and the stability of financial institutions. It involves such things as budget balance, modest taxation, high rates of national savings and a realistic level of the exchange rate that preserves the competitiveness of the export sector. Again, these factors are important conditions for achieving capital accumulation and an efficient division of labor which in turn influence economic growth.

In the GCR the growth potential of economies is measured by the GCI. This index aims to "measure the capacity of the national economy to achieve sustained economic growth over the medium term, controlling for the current level of economic development" (McArthur and Sachs, 2002). The GCI reflects the three major pillars of economic growth identified in the GCR framework: technology, public institutions, and the macroeconomic environment. It is argued that these factors play different roles at different stages of economic development, and therefore these factors (or sub-indexes) are given different relative weights in constructing the overall GCI index for economies at different stages of development. In particular, for the so-called core economies identified in GCR the technology sub-index is given a higher weight compared to the non-core economies. This is because technology is the main source of competitiveness in modern economies. Likewise, within the technology sub-index, innovation gets a higher relative weight compared to technology transfer in the core economies. Information from 'hard' data sources (international statistics) and information from the GCR Executive Opinion Survey are combined for the construction of the GCI.[8]

The GCI tries to capture factors determining economic growth. In a test regression for 75 countries, McArthur and Sachs (2002) showed that the 2001 GCI indeed has a significantly positive influence on economic growth over the period 1992–2000, while controlling for the catch-up effect as measured by initial income level of countries. This supports the view that the GCI indeed captures important factors that determine the capacity of national economies to grow. However, a disadvantage of this approach is that the GCI is used to explain past growth instead of future growth, resulting in a clear direction of causality problem. In this paper, we try to solve this causality problem.

3. Model and data

In this section we discuss our data and present our model. We make use of the GEM, the GCR, and other sources. Data on four basic variables are used in our model: total entrepreneurial activity, growth of GDP, per capita income, and the growth competitiveness index. The sources and definitions of these variables are listed below.

Total Entrepreneurial Activity (TEA)
Data on total entrepreneurial activity are taken from the GEM Adult Population Survey for 2002.

Growth of GDP (ΔGDP)
GDP growth rates are taken from the IMF World Economic Outlook database of the International Monetary Fund, version September 2003.

Per capita income (GNIC)
Gross national income per capita 2001 is expressed in (thousands of) purchasing power parities per US$, and these data are taken from the 2002 World Development Indicators database of the World Bank.

Growth Competitiveness Index (GCI)
Data on the GCI 2001 are taken from page 32 of *The Global Competitiveness Report 2001–2002*. The variable was described in Section 2.

In this paper, we investigate whether entrepreneurship may be considered a determinant of economic growth, next to technology, public institutions and the macroeconomic environment (which are captured in a combined way by the GCI). As both entrepreneurship and the factors underlying the GCI are assumed to be structural characteristics of an economy, we do not want to explain *short term* economic growth but rather growth in the *medium term*. Therefore we choose average annual growth over a period of five years (1999–2003) as the dependent variable in this study.

We stay close to the model of McArthur and Sachs (2002) who explained national growth rates over the period 1992–2000 by the GCI, and (the log of) initial income level of countries (catch-up effect). We add two new features to this model. *First*, we include the total entrepreneurial activity rate from the GEM as an additional determinant. *Second*, we try to solve the causality problem that arises by measuring growth rates in periods preceding the measurement of the GCI. We are not entirely successful in this respect since our dependent variable is measured over the 1999–2003 period and the GCI was measured in 2001. Furthermore, we include a lagged dependent variable (i.e., lagged growth rates) as an explanatory variable to limit the potential impact of reversed causality.

As mentioned, we assume that the impact of entrepreneurial activity is dependent upon the stage of economic development. TEA rates may reflect different *types* of entrepreneurs in countries with different development levels. There are two ways in which this hypothesis is tested. The first approach is to include an interaction term of the TEA rate and per capita income. The model estimated is as follows (*i* is country index):

$$\Delta GDP_{it} = a + bTEA_{i\,t-1} + cTEA_{i\,t-1} * GNIC_{i\,t-1}$$
$$+ d\log(GNIC_{i,t-1}) + eGCI_{i\,t-1}$$
$$+ f\Delta GDP_{i,t-1} + \varepsilon_{it}. \qquad (1)$$

The hypothesis is then that the value of *c* is positive. Alternatively, the effect of TEA for different groups of countries (rich versus poor; rich versus transformation versus developing) can be distinguished, this means that the interaction term is substituted for (*A* and *B* are groups of countries):

$$\Delta GDP_{it} = a + bTEA_{i\,t-1}^{A} + cTEA_{i\,t-1}^{B}$$
$$+ d\log(GNIC_{i,t-1}) + eGCI_{i\,t-1}$$
$$+ f\Delta GDP_{i,t-1} + \varepsilon_{it}. \qquad (2)$$

When *A* is the group of relatively rich countries (and *B* the group of relatively poor countries), our hypothesis is that the value of *b* is larger than that of *c*.

4. Results

Regression results are presented in Table I. The regressions use data for the 37 countries that participated in GEM 2002, minus Croatia.[9] These regressions use TEA 2002 as entrepreneurship measure. The countries participating in GEM 2002 are listed in Appendix 1. There are five countries that we classify as transition economies, viz. China, Hungary, Poland, Russia and Slovenia. There are seven countries that we classify as developing countries, viz. Argentina, Brazil, Chile, India, Mexico, South Africa and Thailand. Eleven of these twelve countries are classified as (relatively) poor, the exception being Slovenia.[10]

All model specifications in Table I use initial income and lagged growth as control variables. We present results for a model including the growth competitiveness index only (Model 1), a model including the GCI and a linear TEA term (Model 2), a model including GCI, TEA and the interaction term of TEA and per capita income (Equation (1), Model 3), a model including GCI, TEA for the 25 (relatively) rich countries and TEA for the eleven (relatively) poor countries (Equation (2), Model 4) and a model including GCI, TEA for the 24 highly developed countries (the rich countries except Slovenia), TEA for the five transition economies and TEA for the seven developing countries (Model 5).

In each of the models we find a negative effect of initial income (logarithm of GNIC), confirming a catch-up effect, and a positive effect of the GCI. The positive effect of the GCI is not significant, though. When we compare Model 2 to Model 1 we find that the addition of only a linear TEA term decreases the adjusted R^2. The effect is also not significant. The addition of a linear term in combination with the interaction term increases the adjusted R^2 considerably, compared to specifications using GCI only. The interaction term has the expected positive effect and this is significant at the 10% significance level.[11] Hence, the impact of entrepreneurial activity

TABLE I

Estimation results of Equations (1) and (2) over period 1999–2003 (36 observations)[a]

	Model 1	Model 2	Model 3	Model 4	Model 5
Constant	0 011	0 018	0 098	0 105**	0 076
	(0 2)	(0.4)	(1.5)	(2 2)	(1 5)
TEA		−0 058	−0 428		
		(0.5)	(1.6)		
TEA*GNIC			0.021*		
			(1 9)		
TEA rich				0.161*	
				(1 8)	
TEA poor				−0 267*	
				(2 0)	
TEA highly developed					0.188**
					(2.1)
TEA transition					0.080
					(0.5)
TEA developing					−0 183
					(1 4)
log (GNIC)	−0 025	−0.028	−0.060**	−0 052**	−0.041**
	(1 5)	(1 3)	(2 1)	(2 5)	(2 3)
GCI	0 017	0 018	0 021	0 014	0.013
	(0 9)	(0.9)	(1.2)	(1 0)	(0 9)
lag GDP growth	0.013	0.031	0.006	0.003	−0 059
	(0 0)	(0.1)	(0 0)	(0.0)	(0 2)
R^2	0 212	0 224	0.363	0 512	0.543
adjusted R^2	0.138	0.124	0.257	0.430	0.448

[a] Absolute heteroskedasticity-consistent t-values are between brackets TEA is total entrepreneurial activity rate (*Global Entrepreneurship Monitor*), GCI is growth competitiveness index 2001 (*Growth Competitiveness Report*), GNIC is per capita income of 2001. Lagged GDP growth is average annual growth of GDP over the period 1994–1998.
* Significant at 0.10 level
** Significant at 0 05 level.

increases with per capita income. The impact can be written as −0.428 + 0.021 *GNIC*. This expression has value zero for a per capita income level of about 20000 US$. Hence, only beyond this level, increasing levels of entrepreneurial activity benefit economic growth. For comparison, 20 out of the 36 countries in our data set have a 2001 per capita income level that is higher than 20000 US$.[12]

The two models in which the effect of TEA is allowed to be different for two or three groups of countries perform much better than Model 3 in terms of adjusted R^2. The effect of TEA is found to be significantly positive for the relatively rich countries, while it is found to be significantly negative for the relatively poor countries. Model 5 shows that the latter effect is mainly due to the developing countries and not so much the transi-

tion economies.[13] For the highly developed economies the effect of TEA is significant at the 5%-confidence interval. The fact that Models 4 and 5 provide a much better fit than Model 3 suggests that the impact of entrepreneurial activity does not change in a continuous way over the course of economic development, but is different in different stages of development (comprising broad ranges of GDP per capita). However, the results should be interpreted with care given the small number of countries (especially the transition and developing economies). In addition, the analysis has a cross-sectional nature and does not follow countries over the entire range of economic development.

The effect of entrepreneurial activity is significant even after correcting for the GCI. This suggests that the two effects are complementary. The additional positive impact of entrepreneurship in highly developed economies may be caused by various factors. It may indicate that entrepreneurial activity is important in the process of the *commercialization* of new (technological) knowledge. It may also indicate that entrepreneurial activity is important for a healthy development of the business population. Eliasson (1995) showed that the absence of new entrants is expected to have a negative impact on the economic performance of the Swedish economy after about two decades. New firms are important in the introduction of various (non-technological) innovations and they may also serve as a vehicle of increased work effort since the reward for entrepreneurs is likely to be more effort-dependent than for employees. Entrepreneurs may also be more likely than incumbent firms to enter (or even create) new industries. The history of the software- and biotech-industries shows the importance of new firms in the early phases of the industry evolution.

Because our entrepreneurship data are from 2002, and we want to measure the impact on medium term growth, we cannot avoid that the periods for which we measure economic growth and entrepreneurship partly overlap. This makes it difficult to assess the correct direction of causality. Therefore we have estimated various model specifications in which the lengths of the growth periods vary from two to five years. We also varied the most recent year for which we measure growth (2002 or 2003). This is because 2003 is a growth projection instead of a realization. Results of these exercises are presented in an early version of this paper (van Stel et al., 2004). The results imply that the longer the growth period, the less strong is the business cycle effect (effect of lagged growth). For five-year periods the business cycle effect is almost absent and this may indicate that the length of the average business cycle is about five years. Obviously, for shorter periods the effect of the lagged dependent variable is stronger, leaving less room for the other variables to contribute to explained variation in growth rates. However, the general pattern is the same throughout all estimations. There is a positive effect on growth of GCI and an effect of TEA that increases with per capita income. Therefore we feel that our results are quite robust.[14]

5. Discussion

Entrepreneurship fails to be a well documented factor in the empirical growth literature because of difficulties defining and measuring entrepreneurship. The investigation of the impact of entrepreneurial activity on economic growth has been one of the main justifications of the GEM project. In the present paper we have critically analyzed whether the acclaimed impact of the TEA rate on economic growth stands the test of adding competing variables. There is an impact but not a simple linear one of the TEA rate on GDP-growth. We find that the TEA rate has a negative effect for the relatively poor countries, while it has a positive effect for the relatively rich countries. The results show that entrepreneurship matters. However, the effect of entrepreneurial activity on growth is not straightforward and can possibly be interpreted using the distinction between the Schumpeter Mark I versus Mark II regimes or the 'entrepreneurial' versus 'managed' economy.

Most of the 20th century can be described as a period of accumulation. From the Second Industrial Revolution till at least the conglomerate merger wave of the late 1960s the large firm share was on the rise in most industries and the economy as a whole. It was the period of "scale and scope" (Chandler, 1990). It was the era of the hierarchical industrial firm growing progressively larger through exploiting economies of scale and scope in areas like production, distribution, marketing and R&D. The period has the characteristics of the Schumpeter Mark II regime. However, by the end of the 20th century things seemed to have changed (Carree et al., 2002). The results of the present study provide some support for such a regime switch. Even so, the small number of observations and the specificity of the time period under investigation do not allow for too strong conclusions.

One striking result of our study is the negative impact of entrepreneurship on GDP growth for developing countries. The result that poorer countries fail to benefit from entrepreneurial activity does not imply that entrepreneurship should be discouraged in these countries. Instead, it may be an indication that there are not enough larger companies present in these countries. Large firms play an important role in the transformation process from a developing economy to a developed economy. Through exploitation of economies of scale and scope they are able to produce medium-tech products. Many local workers may be employed by the large firms and, by training on the job, these local workers may become more productive compared to if they are running a small store and struggling to survive as an "entrepreneur". Furthermore, in the proximity of large firms, smaller firms may also flourish, as they may act as suppliers for large firms (outsourcing) and may learn a lot from the large companies.

A second possible explanation for the negative effect in poorer countries is that the entrepreneurs have lower human capital levels compared to entrepreneurs in developed countries, as we hypothesized earlier. It is likely that the negative effect reflects the presence of many "marginal" entrepreneurs (shopkeepers) in small crafts who may be more productive as wage-earner in a bigger firm. On the contrary, in developed countries TEA may reflect more innovative entrepreneurs in new sectors (for instance software companies). Of course, the human capital levels of the entrepreneurs cannot be identified from the TEA variable, which hampers interpretation. For poorer countries, even if there are not many large firms and also not many people with high human capital levels, it may still be wise to encourage entrepreneurship if the alternative is unemployment. But perhaps entrepreneurship is not as productive then as in the presence of large firms. Small and large firms often complement each other (Rothwell, 1983; Freeman and Perez, 1988; Nooteboom, 1994). It is suggested that developing countries can benefit considerably from foreign direct investment by MNCs since this also increases the potential economic contribution of local entrepreneurial activity.

Acknowledgement

We are grateful to Rolf Sternberg, Sander Wennekers and two anonymous referees for comments and encouragement.

Appendix 1: Participating countries in GEM

In Table A.I we list the countries that participate in the GEM 2002. There are 37 countries. Croatia is excluded from the regressions because the GCI is not available for this country. The table also contains the values for the TEA index for 2002.

TABLE A.I
Countries participating in GEM 2002, with values for TEA in 2002

1. United States (US)	0.105
2. Russia (RU)	0 025
3 South Africa (ZA)	0 065
4 The Netherlands (NL)	0 046
5 Belgium (BE)	0 030
6. France (FR)	0 032

TABLE A I
Continued

7. Spain (ES)	0.046
8 Hungary (HU)	0 066
9 Italy (IT)	0 059
10 Switzerland (SW)	0.071
11 United Kingdom (UK)	0 054
12 Denmark (DK)	0 065
13 Sweden (SE)	0 040
14 Norway (NO)	0 087
15. Poland (PL)	0.044
16. Germany (DE)	0 052
17. Mexico (MX)	0 124
18 Argentina (AR)	0.142
19 Brazil (BR)	0 135
20 Chile (CL)	0.157
21 Australia (AU)	0 087
22 New Zealand (NZ)	0.140
23 Singapore (SG)	0 059
24. Thailand (TH)	0 189
25 Japan (JP)	0.018
26 Korea (KR)	0 145
27 China (CH)	0 123
28 India (IN)	0.179
29 Canada (CA)	0.088
30 Ireland (IE)	0 091
31 Iceland (IS)	0 113
32 Finland (FI)	0 046
33 Croatia (HR)	0.036
34 Slovenia (SL)	0.046
35 Hong Kong (HK)	0 034
36 Taiwan (TW)	0 043
37. Israel (IL)	0 071

Notes

[1] The recognition of the importance of entrepreneurial activity has been absent for a while in mainstream (theoretical) economics. Baumol (1968) complained that entrepreneurship, being hard to capture into mathematical equations, disappeared from mainstream (neo-classical) economics. Kirzner (1973) observed that the neo-classical model constrained the decision making of the entrepreneur, in terms of product quality and price, technology, within limits wholly alien to the context in which real world entrepreneurs characteristically operate. Also see Barreto (1989) and Kirchhoff (1994, p. 30).

[2] Schumpeter (1950, p. 13): "The function of entrepreneurs is to reform or revolutionize the pattern of production by exploring an invention, or more generally, an untried technological possibility for producing a new commodity or producing an old one in a new way... To undertake such new things is difficult and constitutes a distinct economic function, first because they lie outside of the routine tasks which everybody understands, and secondly, because the environment resists in many ways."

[3] See Carree and Thurik (2003) for a survey of studies of the impact of entrepreneurship on growth at various levels of observation.

[4] Other terms are also possible, like the transition from the fourth to the fifth Kondratiev wave (Freeman and Perez, 1988).

[5] The intertemporal relation between occupational choice and economic development has been dealt with in a series of recent papers (Banerjee and Newman, 1993; Iyigun and Owen, 1999; Lloyd-Ellis and Bernhardt, 2000).

[6] See also Van Stel and Carree (2004) who distinguish between the manufacturing and service sector.

[7] A country is defined to be a core economy if it achieves at least 15 US utility patents per million population. Twenty-four countries met this criterion in 2000.

[8] The Executive Opinion Survey is a survey among firms within countries. The goal of the survey is to capture a broad array of intangible factors that cannot be found in official statistics but that nonetheless may influence the growth potential of countries. For details, see Cornelius and McArthur (2002).

[9] Croatia is excluded because the Growth Competitiveness Index is not available.

[10] The richest of the 11 relatively poor countries is Hungary with a 2001 per capita income of 12570 US $. The poorest of the twenty-five relatively rich countries is Taiwan with a 2001 per capita income of 16761 US $. Hence, there is a clear gap between the two groups of countries in terms of *GNIC* Slovenia has a 2001 per capita income of 18160 US $.

[11] The correlation between TEA and the interaction term TEA*GNIC is only 0.35 suggesting no problems of multicollinearity.

[12] Spain is closest to the critical value with a 2001 per capita income of 20150 US$

[13] Note that our specification in Models 4 and 5 is equivalent to including the variable TEA and slope dummies for rich countries (Model 4) or for transition and highly developed countries (Model 5). We choose to present coefficients and *t*-values in deviation from zero instead of presenting estimation results in deviation from a reference group. Furthermore, we assume a constant in Equation (2) equal for each of the groups of countries. Should the constant be assumed to differ for rich and poor countries, the difference of the effect of entrepreneurial activity between the rich and poor country groups remains significant. However, where the constant is assumed different for the three groups of countries (highly developed, transition, developing), the difference of the effect of entrepreneurial activity between the groups fails to be significant. Likelihood ratio tests reveal that Model 2 (which has a log likelihood value of 96.5) is rejected in favor of a specification assuming the constant to be identical across the three groups of countries (but having different effects of entrepreneurial activity), but also in favor of a specification assuming identical effects of entrepreneurial activity (but having different constants). However, the log likelihood value of the former specification is higher (106.0 versus 105.3). Hence, we have decided to present these results. The evidence for the three groups of countries should however be interpreted with care.

[14] Another test of robustness is to consider the impact on the estimation results of leaving out one country (leaving 35 observations). For Model 3 we find that the *t*-values of the interaction term then range between 0 89 (leaving out Russia) and 2.43 (leaving out Ireland). For Model 5 we then find that the *t*-values of TEA for the highly developed economies range between 1.35 (leaving out Korea) and 3.91 (leaving out New Zealand). The *t*-values of TEA for the developing countries range between −0.74 (leaving out Russia) and −1.87 (leaving out Ireland).

REFERENCES

Acs, Z. J and D. B. Audretsch, 1990, *Innovation and Small Firms*, Cambridge, MA: MIT Press.

Acs, Z. J. and D B. Audretsch, 2003, Innovation and technological change, in: Z. J. Acs and D. B. Audretsch (eds.), *Handbook of Entrepreneurship Research*, Boston: Kluwer Academic Publishers, 55–79.

Audretsch, D. B., 1995, *Innovation and Industry Evolution*, Cambridge, MA· MIT Press.

Audretsch, D B. and M. Feldman, 1996, 'R&D spillovers and the Geography of Innovation and Production', *American Economic Review* **86**, 630–640.

Audretsch, D B. and M. Fritsch, 2002, 'Growth Regimes Over Time and Space', *Regional Studies* **36**, 113–124.

Audretsch, D. B and M Keilbach, 2004, 'Entrepreneurship Capital and Economic Performance', *Regional Studies* **38**, 949–959.

Audretsch, D. B. and P. Stephan, 1996, 'Company-scientist Locational Links The Case of Biotechnology', *American Economic Review* **86**, 641–652.

Audretsch, D B and A. R. Thurik, 2001, 'What is New about the New Economy: Sources of Growth in the Managed and Entrepreneurial Economies', *Industrial and Corporate Change* **10**, 267–315.

Audretsch, D. B., A. R. Thurik, I. Verheul and A. R M. Wennekers (eds.), 2002, *Entrepreneurship Determinants* and Policy in a European – US Comparison, Boston/ Dordrecht Kluwer Academic Publishers.

Banerjee, A. V and A. F. Newman, 1993, 'Occupational Choice and the Process of Development', *Journal of Political Economy* **101**, 274–298.

Barreto, H, 1989, *The Entrepreneur in Microeconomic Theory: Disappearance and Explanation*, London: Routledge

Baumol, W. J, 1968, 'Entrepreneurship in Economic Theory', *American Economic Review Papers and Proceedings* **58**, 64–71.

Blanchflower, D. G., 2000, 'Self-employment in OECD Countries', *Labour Economics* **7**, 471–505

Bleaney, M. and A. Nishiyama, 2002, 'Explaining Growth. A Contest Between Models', *Journal of Economic Growth* **7**, 43–56.

Carree, M, A. van Stel, R. Thurik and S. Wennekers, 2002, 'Economic Development and Business Ownership An Analysis Using Data of 23 OECD Countries in the Period 1976–1996', *Small Business Economics* **19**, 271–290.

Carree, M. A. and A. R. Thurik, 1999, 'Industrial Structure and Economic Growth', in D. B. Audretsch and A. R. Thurik (eds.), *Innovation, Industry Evolution and Employment*, Cambridge Cambridge University Press, pp 86–110.

Carree, M. A. and A. R Thurik, 2003, 'The Impact of Entrepreneurship on Economic Growth', in Z. J. Acs and D. B Audretsch (eds), *Handbook of Entrepreneurship Research*, Boston: Kluwer Academic Publishers, pp. 437–471

Caves, R. E., 1998, Industrial Organization and New Findings on the Turnover and Mobility of Firms', *Journal of Economic Literature* **36**, 1947–1982.

Chandler, A. D. Jr, 1990, *Scale and Scope The Dynamics of Industrial Capitalism*, Cambridge: Harvard University.

Cornelius, P K. and J W McArthur 2002, 'The Executive Opinion Survey', in M E. Porter, J. D Sachs, P. K. Cornelius, J. W. McArthur, K. Schwab (eds.), *The Global Competitiveness Report 2001–2002*, New York: Oxford University Press, pp. 166–177.

Eliasson, G., 1995, 'Economic Growth Through Competitive Selection', paper presented at the 22nd EARIE-conference, Juan les Pins, September 1995

Freeman, C and C. Perez, 1988, 'Structural Crises of Adjustment Business Cycles and Investment Behavior', in G. Dosi, C. Freeman, R. Nelson, G. Silverberg, and L. Soete (eds.), *Technical Change and Economic Theory*, London Pinter Publishers.

Geroski, P A, 1989, 'Entry, Innovation, and Productivity Growth', *Review of Economics and Statistics* **71**, 572–578

Iyigun, M F and A L. Owen, 1999, 'Entrepreneurs, Professionals, and Growth', *Journal of Economic Growth* **4**, 213–232.

Kirchhoff, B A, 1994, *Entrepreneurship and Dynamic Capitalism*, Westport, CT Praeger.

Kirzner, I, 1973, *Competition & Entrepreneurship*, Chicago University of Chicago Press

Lloyd-Ellis, H. and D Bernhardt, 2000, 'Enterprise, Inequality and Economic Development', *Review of Economic Studies* **67**, 147–168.

Lucas, R E, 1988, 'On the Mechanics of Economic Development', *Journal of Monetary Economics* **22**, 3–39.

McArthur, J W. and J. D. Sachs, 2002, 'The Growth Competitiveness Index Measuring Technological Advancement and the Stages of Development', in M. E. Porter, J. D. Sachs, P K Cornelius, J. W. McArthur and K Schwab (eds), *The Global Competitiveness Report 2001–2002*, New York: Oxford University Press, pp 28–51

Nickell, S., P. Nicolitsas and N Dryden, 1997, 'What Makes Firms Perform Well?', *European Economic Review* **41**, 783–796.

Nickell, S. J, 1996, 'Competition and Corporate Performance', *Journal of Political Economy* **104**, 724–746.

Nooteboom, B, 1994, 'Innovation and Diffusion in Small Business: Theory and Empirical Evidence', *Small Business Economics* **6**, 327–347.

Reynolds, P. D, W. D. Bygrave, E. Autio, L. W. Cox and M. Hay, 2002, *Global Entrepreneurship Monitor, 2002 Executive Report*, Wellesley, MA: Babson College.

Romer, P. M., 1990, 'Endogenous Technological Change', *Journal of Political Economy* **98**, 71–101.

Romer, P. M., 1994, 'The Origins of Endogenous Growth', *Journal of Economic Perspectives* **8**, 3–22.

Rothwell, R, 1983, 'Innovation and Firm Size. A Case for Dynamic Complementarity, Or, is Small Really so Beautiful'?, *Journal of General Management* **8**, 5–25

Sala-i-Martin, X., 1997, 'I Just Ran Two Million Regressions', *American Economic Review* **87**, 178–183.

Schumpeter, J. A., 1934, *The Theory of Economic Development*, Cambridge, MA: Harvard University Press.

Schumpeter, J. A, 1950, *Capitalism, Socialism and Democracy*, New York: Harper and Row.

Van Stel, A and M Carree, 2004, 'Business Ownership and Sectoral Growth An Empirical Analysis of 21 OECD Countries', *International Small Business Journal* **22**(4), 389–419

Van Stel, A, M Carree and R Thurik, 2004, 'The Effect of Entrepreneurship on National Economic Growth: An Analysis Using the GEM Database', EIM Scales Paper N200320, Zoetermeer, NL EIM This paper can be downloaded from www eim net.

Name Index